THE HOUGHTON MIFFLIN
DICTIONARY OF
GEOGRAPHY

PLACES AND PEOPLES OF THE WORLD

HOUGHTON MIFFLIN COMPANY

Boston · New York

The maps in this book were created by Mapping Specialists Limited, Madison, Wisconsin.

Library of Congress Cataloging-in-Publication Data
Houghton Mifflin dictionary of geography : places and peoples of the world.
    p.   cm
  Based on the American Heritage dictionary of the English language, 3rd ed.
  ISBN 0-395-86448-8 (cloth)
    1. Geography — Dictionaries.   I. American Heritage Publishing Company.
II. American Heritage dictionary of the English language. III. Title:
Dictionary of geography.
G63.H68   1997
910'.3 — DC21   97-10624
                                                                      CIP

Manufactured in the United States of America

Contents

Staff

Preface

The Houghton Mifflin Dictionary of Geography is intended as a concise and authoritative guide to the places and peoples of the world. As outlined below, its more than 10,000 entries cover a broad range of geographic items in varying degrees of detail, from brief descriptive definitions to longer, more informative country histories of up to 250 words in length. Entries are conveniently arranged in a single alphabetical list, with syllables and pronunciations, variant spellings, former names, and cross-references clearly indicated. In addition to the main body, a 13-page appendix provides common geographic abbreviations, tables of currency and measurement, and lists of significant world features, as well as a full complement of four-color world maps created especially for this volume.

Political geography. The primary emphasis of this Dictionary is on the places people live and the states or governments they have created. All modern countries and major cities, along with numerous historical regions and empires, are accompanied by up-to-date capsule histories, typically including such information as original habitation, outside discovery, key historical events, and the names of important leaders. The entry for **South Africa**, for example, follows that country's development from the original San inhabitants through the coming of Bantu and European settlers and ends with Nelson Mandela's victory in the nation's first multiracial elections in 1994. Similarly, at **Saint Petersburg** the reader can learn that the city was established by Peter the Great in 1703, that it served as Russia's capital from 1712 to 1918, and that its name has come full circle from Saint Petersburg to Petrograd to Leningrad back to Saint Petersburg.

Thousands of other cities, towns, and territories the world over are entered with precise geographic locators and a brief descriptive note, always including any information of particular historical or cultural significance. Cities and towns are generally included according to their populations, with cutoff figures as follows: for the United States and Canada, 15,000; for Europe (not including western Russia), 50,000; for Central America, South America, and Australia, 100,000; for Asia (except China), 250,000; and for China, 300,000. U.S. population figures are taken from the 1990 census, and world populations come from the 1994 Demographic Yearbook published by the United Nations. Places of special interest or significance, such as **Salisbury**, England, and **Cripple Creek**, Colorado, are entered regardless of population.

Physical geography. The Dictionary also includes comprehensive coverage of the world's principal mountains, deserts, bodies of water, and other physical features. Statistical information, such as length of rivers and highest elevations of ranges and peaks, is included where appropriate, as is any relevant geological or historical information. Thus the reader can learn that today's **Sahara** desert was a region of extensive shallow lakes during the Ice Age and that **Aconcagua**, the highest peak in the western hemisphere, was first scaled in 1897. Other entries, such as **delta, fumarole,** and **plate tectonics,** define the essential vocabulary of geology and geography.

Rivers and mountains are selected for entry primarily according to length and height. All U.S. rivers of over 100 miles are entered; the cutoff figure for Canadian and European rivers is 200 miles (with exceptions for important rivers of shorter length) and for the rest of the world, 500 miles. Similarly, the cutoff figures for mountains are: U.S., 10,000 feet; Canada, 15,000 feet; elsewhere, 20,000 feet. Mountains that constitute the highest peak in a particular range are generally entered regardless of height.

World peoples and languages. A unique feature of this Dictionary is its inclusion of entries for the major peoples and languages of the world. It is our belief that issues of nationality, ethnicity, and linguistic tradition are intimately linked to geography, and that readers who turn to this volume for information about countries and territories will also have an interest in the peoples who inhabit them. Beginning with the entry for **Mexico,** for example, the reader can go on to consult **Aztec, Nahuatl,** and **Uto-Aztecan** to discover that the founders of the great Aztec empire conquered by Cortés in 1521 are linguistically related to the Utes, the Hopis, and the Shoshones of today's western United States. Following another series of entries related to the Indian subcontinent reveals that the **Singhalese** language spoken by the majority population of Sri Lanka is of Indo-European stock and came to the island from northern India, whereas the **Dravidian** language of the smaller **Tamil** population is native to that region and predates the Indo-European languages.

Pronunciation Key

A list of pronunciation symbols used in this Dictionary is given below in the column headed **HMDG.** The column headed **Examples** contains words that illustrate how the HMDG symbols are pronounced, with the letters that correspond to the HMDG symbols shown in boldface. The column headed **IPA** gives the equivalent transcription symbols from the International Phonetic Alphabet. Under the column headed **Foreign,** note that the IPA shows nasality with a tilde over the vowel whereas the HMDG uses N to reflect that the preceding vowel is nasalized.

Examples	HMDG	IPA
p**a**t	ă	æ
p**a**y	ā	e
c**are**	âr	ɛr, er
f**a**ther	ä	ɑː, ɑ
bi**b**	b	b
chur**ch**	ch	tʃ
dee**d**, mill**ed**	d	d
p**e**t	ĕ	ɛ
b**ee**	ē	i
fi**fe**, **ph**ase, rou**gh**	f	f
ga**g**	g	g
hat	h	h
which	hw	hw, ʍ
p**i**t	ĭ	ɪ
p**ie**, b**y**	ī	aɪ
p**ier**	îr	ɪr, ir
ju**dge**	j	dʒ
kick, **c**at, pi**que**	k	k
lid, need**le**	l	l
mu**m**	m	m
no, sudd**en**	n	n
thi**ng**	ng	ŋ
p**o**t	ŏ	ɑ
t**oe**	ō	o
c**augh**t, p**aw**, f**or**, h**or**rid, h**oar**se	ô	ɔ
n**oi**se	oi	ɔɪ
t**oo**k	ŏŏ	ʊ
b**oo**t	ōō	u
out	ou	aʊ

Examples	HMDG	IPA
po**p**	p	p
roa**r**	r	ɹ
sau**ce**	s	s
ship, di**sh**	sh	ʃ
tigh**t**, stopp**ed**	t	t
thin	th	θ
this	*th*	ð
cu**t**	ŭ	ʌ
urge, t**er**m, f**ir**m, w**or**d, h**ear**d	ûr	ɝ, ɜr
val**v**e	v	v
with	w	w
yes	y	j
zebra, x**y**lem	z	z
vi**si**on, plea**s**ure, gara**g**e	zh	ʒ
about, it**e**m, **e**d**i**ble, gall**o**p, circ**u**s	ə	ə
butt**er**	ər	ɚ

Foreign	HMDG	IPA
French f**eu** *German* sch**ö**n	œ	ø
French **oeu**f, v**eu**ve *German* zw**ö**lf		œ
French t**u** *German* **ü**ber	ü	y
German i**ch** *German* a**ch** *Scottish* lo**ch**	KH	ç / x
French b**on**	N (bôN)	ɔ̃ (bɔ̃)

A

Aa·chen (ä′kən, ä′ĸнən) also **Aix-la-Cha·pelle** (āks′lä-shə-pĕl′, ĕks′-). A city of western Germany near the Belgian and Dutch borders. Charlemagne may have been born here in 742; he later made the city his northern capital. ◉ Pop. 246,671.

Aa·land Islands (ä′lənd, ō′länd′). See **Ahvenanmaa.**

Aal·borg (ôl′bôrg′). See **Ålborg.**

Aa·len (ä′lən). A city of south-central Germany east of Stuttgart. It was a free imperial city from 1360 to 1803. ◉ Pop. 62,861.

Aalst (älst) also **A·lost** (ä-lôst′). A city of west-central Belgium west-northwest of Brussels. It was the capital of Austrian Flanders in the 18th century. ◉ Pop. 78,068.

Aa·re (är′ə) or **Aar** (är). A river of central and northern Switzerland rising in the Bernese Alps and flowing about 295 km (183 mi) to join the Rhine River at the Swiss–German border.

Aar·hus (ôr′ho͞os′). See **Århus.**

A·ba (ä′bə). A city of southeast Nigeria northeast of Port Harcourt. It is an important market and transportation center. ◉ Pop. 210,700.

A·ba·co and Cays (ăb′ə-kō′; kēz, kāz). An island group, the northernmost of the Bahamas, in the Atlantic Ocean east of southern Florida.

Ab·a·dan (ä′bə-dän′, ăb′ə-dän′). A city of southwest Iran on **Abadan Island** in the delta of the Shatt al Arab at the head of the Persian Gulf. The city's oil installations were heavily damaged in 1980 during the war with Iraq. ◉ Pop. 296,081.

A·ba·jo Peak (ä′bə-hō′). A mountain, 3,490.7 m (11,445 ft) high, in the **Abajo Mountains** of southeast Utah near the Colorado border.

A·ba·kan (ä′bə-kän′). A city of south-central Russia east-southeast of Novosibirsk. It is a commercial center on the Yenisey River and the Siberian Railroad. ◉ Pop. 157,593.

Abakan River. A river of south-central Russia rising in the western Sayan Mountains and flowing about 563 km (350 mi) northeast to the Yenisey River.

A·ba·ya (ə-bī′ə), **Lake.** A lake of southwest Ethiopia in the Great Rift Valley south-southwest of Addis Ababa. It was discovered in 1896 and has several inhabited islands.

Ab·e·na·ki (ä′bə-nä′kē, ăb′ə-năk′ē) or **Ab·na·ki** (äb-nä′kē, ăb-). **1.** *pl.* **Abenaki** or **-kis** or **Abnaki** or **-kis.** A member of any of various Native American peoples formerly inhabiting northern New England and southeast Canada, with present-day populations in Maine and southern Quebec. **2.** A member of a confederacy of Abenaki and other peoples formed in the mid-18th century in opposition to the Iroquois confederacy and the English colonists. **3.** Either or both of the two Eastern Algonquian languages of the Abenaki peoples. Also called *Wabanaki.*

A·be·o·ku·ta (ăb′ē-ō-ko͞o′tə). A city of southwest Nigeria north of Lagos. It is a trade center in an agricultural region. ◉ Pop. 301,000.

Ab·er·deen (ăb′ər-dēn′). **1.** A city of northeast Scotland on the North Sea at the mouth of the Dee River. It is known as "the Granite City" because stone from local quarries is used in many of its buildings. ◉ Pop. 218,220. **2.** A town of northeast Maryland east-northeast of Baltimore. Aberdeen Proving Ground, a major research, development, and testing installation, is nearby. ◉ Pop. 13,087. **3.** A city of northeast South Dakota northeast of Pierre. It is a trade center in a wheat and livestock region. ◉ Pop. 24,927. **4.** A city of western Washington west-southwest of Tacoma. Located on Grays Harbor, it has lumbering, fishing, and shipping industries. ◉ Pop. 16,565.

Ab·i·djan (ăb′ĭ-jän′). The largest city of Ivory Coast, in the southern part of the country on an enclosed lagoon of the Gulf of Guinea. It was the capital until 1983, when Yamoussoukro was designated as the new official capital. Abidjan remains the de facto administrative center. ◉ Pop. 1,929,079.

Ab·i·lene (ăb′ə-lēn′). **1.** A city of central Kansas west of Topeka. Dwight D. Eisenhower lived in Abilene during his youth; the Eisenhower Center includes his family homestead, a museum and library, and his grave. ◉ Pop. 6,242. **2.** A city of west-central Texas west-southwest of Fort Worth. Founded in 1881 with the coming of the railroad, the city first prospered as a shipping center for cattle. ◉ Pop. 106,654.

Ab·i·tib·i Lake (ăb′ĭ-tĭb′ē). A lake of eastern Ontario and southwest Quebec, Canada. It is the source of the **Abitibi River,** which flows about 370 km (230 mi) west and north to an arm of James Bay in northeast Ontario.

Ab·na·ki (äb-nä′kē, ăb-). Variant of **Abenaki.**

A·bra·ham (ā′brə-hăm′), **Plains of.** A field adjoining the upper part of Quebec City, Canada. In 1759 the British under Gen. James Wolfe defeated the French under Gen. Louis Montcalm in a decisive battle of the French and Indian Wars. The victory led to British supremacy in Canada.

A·bruz·zi (ä-bro͞ot′sē, ə-bro͞ot′-) also **A·bruz·zi e Mo·li·se** (ā mô-lē′zē). A region of central Italy bordering on the Adriatic Sea. Mostly mountainous, it includes Mount Corno, the highest peak of the Apennines.

Ab·sa·ro·ka Range (ăb-sär′ə-kə). A section of the Rocky Mountains in northwest Wyoming and southern Montana. It rises to 4,007.7 m (13,140 ft) at Franks Peak.

Ab·sa·ro·ke (ăb-sär′ə-kə). See **Crow**[1].

A·bu Dha·bi (ä′boo dä′bē). A sheikdom and city of eastern Arabia on the Persian Gulf. The city is the capital of the federated United Arab Emirates. With enormous oil revenues, the sheikdom has one of the highest per capita incomes in the world. ● Pop. 242,975.

A·bu·ja (ä-boo′jä). The capital of Nigeria, in the central part of the country. Although the capital was officially moved from Lagos to Abuja in 1991, the city is largely undeveloped, and many government offices remain in Lagos.

A·bu·kir or **A·bu Qir** (ä′boo-kîr′, ăb′oo-). A village of northern Egypt in the Nile River delta on the **Bay of Abukir**. Adm. Horatio Nelson's victory over a French fleet off Abukir in 1798 restored British prestige in the Mediterranean and ended French hopes of establishing a stronghold in the Middle East.

A·bu Sim·bel (ä′boo sĭm′bəl, -bĕl). A village of southern Egypt on the Nile River. It is the site of massive rock temples dating from c. 1250 B.C. that were raised (1964–1966) to avoid flooding from the Aswan High Dam.

A·by·dos (ə-bī′dŏs). **1.** An ancient town of Asia Minor on the Asiatic coast of the Hellespont in modern-day Turkey. It was the scene of the legendary tale of Hero and Leander. **2.** An ancient city of southern Egypt on the Nile River northwest of Thebes. One of the oldest Egyptian cities, it was a religious center for the worship of Osiris and a burial site for the kings of the earliest dynasties.

Ab·ys·sin·i·a (ăb′ĭ-sĭn′ē-ə). See **Ethiopia**. —**Ab′·ys·sin′i·an** adj. & n.

A·ca·di·a (ə-kā′dē-ə). A region and former French colony of eastern Canada, chiefly in Nova Scotia but also including New Brunswick, Prince Edward Island, Cape Breton Island, and the coastal area from the St. Lawrence River south into Maine. During the French and Indian War (1755–1763) many Acadians migrated or were deported by the British to southern territories, including Louisiana, where their descendants came to be known as Cajuns.

A·ca·di·an (ə-kā′dē-ən). **1.** Of or relating to Acadia or its people, language, or culture. **2. a.** One of the early French settlers of Acadia. **b.** A descendant of these settlers, especially a Cajun. **3.** A dialect of French spoken by the Acadians.

Ac·a·pul·co (ăk′ə-poōl′kō, ä′kä-poōl′kô) also **Ac·a·pul·co de Juá·rez** (də hwär′ĕs, -ĕz, wär′).

A city of southern Mexico on the Pacific Ocean. It is a popular resort with a fine natural harbor surrounded by cliffs and promontories. ● Pop. 301,902.

Ac·cad (ăk′ăd′, ä′käd′). See **Akkad**.

Ac·cra (ăk′rə, ə-krä′). The capital and largest city of Ghana, in the southeast part of the country on the Gulf of Guinea. Originally the capital of an ancient Ga kingdom, it became an important economic center after the completion in 1923 of a railroad to the mining and agricultural hinterland. ● Pop. 859,640.

Ac·cring·ton (ăk′rĭng-tən). A borough of northwest England north of Manchester. It is the center of a textile-processing area. ● Pop. 36,459.

A·cel·da·ma (ə-sĕl′də-mə). In the New Testament, a potter's field near Jerusalem purchased by the priests as a burial ground for strangers with the reward that Judas had received for betraying Jesus and had later returned to them.

A·chae·a (ə-kē′ə) also **A·cha·ia** (ə-kī′ə, ə-kā′-ə). An ancient region of southern Greece occupying the northern part of the Peloponnesus on the Gulf of Corinth. The cities of the region banded together in the early third century B.C. to form the Achaean League, which defeated Sparta but was eventually beaten by the Romans, who annexed Achaea in 146 B.C. and later gave the name to a province that included all of Greece south of Thessaly.

A·chae·an (ə-kē′ən) also **A·cha·ian** (ə-kā′ən, ə-kī′-). **1.** A native or inhabitant of Achaea. **2.** One of a Hellenic people believed to have inhabited the Peloponnesus and to have created the Mycenaean civilization. **3.** A Greek, especially of the Mycenaean era. —**A·chae′an** adj.

Ach·ill (ăk′ĭl). A mountainous and barren island off the northwest coast of Ireland. At its western end is **Achill Head**.

A·cho·ma·wi (ə-chō′mə-wē′). **1.** pl. **Achomawi** or **-wis**. A member of a Native American people inhabiting northeast California. Also called *Pit River*. **2.** The Hokan language of the Achomawis.

a·clin·ic line (ā-klĭn′ĭk). See **magnetic equator**.

A·co·ma[1] (ăk′ə-mə, -mô′, ä′kə-). **1.** pl. **Acoma** or **-mas**. A member of a Pueblo people, the founders and inhabitants of Acoma. **2.** The Keresan language of the Acomas.

A·co·ma[2] (ăk′ə-mə, -mô′, ä′kə-). A pueblo of west-central New Mexico west of Albuquerque. Founded c. 1100–1250, it is regarded as the oldest continuously inhabited community in the United States. ● Pop. 975.

A·con·ca·gua (ăk′ən-kä′gwə, ä′kən-). A mountain, 7,025.4 m (23,034 ft) high, in the Andes of western Argentina near the Chilean border. The highest peak of the Western Hemisphere, it was first scaled in 1897.

A·ço·res (ä-sôr′ĕsh). See **Azores**.

A·cre (ä′krə, ä′kər) also **Ak·ko** (ä-kō′, ä′kō). A port of northern Israel on the Bay of Haifa. During the Crusades it changed hands many times between Christians and Moslems. Acre was ceded to the Arabs in the United Nations partition of Palestine in 1948 but was captured by Israel shortly thereafter. ● Pop. 37,700.

Ac·ti·um (ăk′shē-əm, -tē-). A promontory and ancient town of western Greece. In 31 B.C. it was the site of Octavian's victory over Mark Antony and Cleopatra. The battle established Octavian (later Augustus) as the ruler of Rome.

Ac·ton (ăk′tən). A town of northeast Massachusetts, a residential and manufacturing suburb of Boston. ● Pop. 17,872.

A·da (ā′də). A city of south-central Oklahoma southeast of Oklahoma City. It is the center of a horse-breeding area. ● Pop. 15,820.

A·dak (ā′dăk′). An island of western Alaska in the central Aleutian Islands. It was an important military base during World War II.

A·da·ma·wa Massif (ăd′ə-mä′wə). An extensive plateau of west-central Africa in north-central Cameroon and eastern Nigeria.

Ad·ams (ăd′əmz), **Mount**. A peak, 3,753.6 m (12,307 ft) high, in the Cascade Range of southwest Washington.

Ad·am's Bridge (ăd′əmz) also **Ra·ma's Bridge** (rä′məz). A chain of shoals extending about 29 km (18 mi) between India and Sri Lanka. According to Hindu legend, the bridge was built to transport Rama, hero of the *Ramayana*, to the island to rescue his wife from the demon king Ravana.

Adam's Peak. A mountain, 2,244.8 m (7,360 ft) high, in south-central Sri Lanka. It is a sacred place of pilgrimage for Buddhists, Hindus, and Moslems.

A·da·na (ä′də-nə, ə-dä′nə). A city of southern Turkey on the Seyhan River near the Mediterranean Sea. Probably founded by the Hittites, it was colonized by the Romans in 66 B.C. ● Pop. 1,047,300.

Ad·dis Ab·a·ba (ăd′ĭs ăb′ə-bə, ä′dĭs ä′bə-bä′). The capital and largest city of Ethiopia, in the center of the country on a plateau more than 2,440 m (8,000 ft) above sea level. Captured by the Italians in 1936 and made the capital of Italian East Africa, it was retaken by the Allies in 1941 and returned to Ethiopian sovereignty. ● Pop. 2,316,400.

Ad·di·son (ăd′ĭ-sən). A village of northeast Illinois, a residential and industrial suburb of Chicago. Population 32,058.

Ad·e·laide (ăd′l-ād′). A city of southern Australia northwest of Melbourne. A port of entry at the mouth of the Torrens River, it was founded in 1836. ● Pop. 1,071,100.

A·dé·lie Coast also **A·dé·lie Land** (ə-dā′lē). A region of Antarctica near George V Coast, under French sovereignty since 1938.

A·den (äd′n, ād′n). **1**. A former British colony and protectorate of southern Arabia, part of Southern Yemen (now Yemen) since 1967. **2**. The largest city of Yemen, in the southern part of the country on the Gulf of Aden. It has been one of the chief ports of southern Arabia since ancient times and became a major trading and refueling station after the opening of the Suez Canal in 1869. Aden was the capital of Southern Yemen from 1967 until 1990. Metropolitan area population, 400,783.

Aden, Gulf of. An arm of the Arabian Sea lying between Yemen on the Arabian Peninsula and Somalia in eastern Africa. It is connected with the Red Sea by the Bab el Mandeb.

A·di·ge (ä′dĭ-jā′, ä′dē-jĕ′). A river of northeast Italy rising in the Alps and flowing about 410 km (255 mi) generally south then east to the Adriatic Sea at the Gulf of Venice.

Ad·i·ron·dack Mountains (ăd′ə-rŏn′dăk′). A group of mountains in northeast New York between the St. Lawrence River valley in the north and the Mohawk River valley in the south. The range is part of the Appalachian system and rises to 1,629.9 m (5,344 ft). Lakes, forests, and numerous winter sports resorts, including Lake Placid, site of the 1932 and 1984 Winter Olympics, attract many tourists.

Ad·mi·ral·ty Inlet (ăd′mər-əl-tē). An arm of the Pacific Ocean in northwest Washington. It is the northernmost part of Puget Sound and lies between Whidbey Island and the mainland.

Admiralty Island. A mountainous, heavily forested island of southeast Alaska in the Alexander Archipelago southwest of Juneau.

Admiralty Islands. A group of volcanic islands of the southwest Pacific Ocean in the Bismarck Archipelago. Discovered by the Dutch in 1616, the islands are now part of Papua New Guinea.

Admiralty Range. A mountain group of Antarctica on the northern coast of Victoria Land northwest of Ross Sea. The range was discovered by Sir James Ross on his 1841 expedition.

A·do (ä′dō). A city of southwest Nigeria northeast of Lagos. It was once the capital of a Yoruba state that was probably founded in the 15th century. ● Pop. 213,000.

A·dour (ə-dōōr′). A river of southwest France rising in the Pyrenees and flowing about 338 km (210 mi) north then west to the Bay of Biscay near Biarritz.

A·do·wa (ä′də-wə, ăd′ə-). See **Adwa**.

A·dri·an (ā′drē-ən). A city of southeast Michigan southwest of Detroit. It is a trade center in a fertile farming region. ◉ Pop. 22,097.

A·dri·a·no·ple (ā′drē-ə-nō′pəl). See **Edirne.**

A·dri·at·ic Sea (ā′drē-ăt′ĭk). An arm of the Mediterranean Sea between Italy and the Balkan Peninsula. It extends from the Gulf of Venice southward to the Strait of Otranto, which links it to the Ionian Sea.

Ad·wa (äd′wə, ăd′-) also **A·du·wa** or **A·do·wa** (ä′də-wə, ăd′ə-). A town of northern Ethiopia south of Asmara, Eritrea. Emperor Menelik II decisively defeated the Italians here in 1896 to secure recognition of Ethiopia's independence. ◉ Pop. 21,107.

Ad·zhar·i·a (ə-jär′ē-ə) or **Ad·zhar·i·stan** (ə-jär′ĭ-stän′, ŭj′ə-ryĭ-stän′). An autonomous republic of southwest Georgia bordering on the Black Sea and Turkey. Colonized by the Greeks in the fourth and fifth centuries B.C., the region was ruled by the Romans and the Turks before its acquisition by Russia in 1878. — **Ad·zhar′** (ə-jär′) *n.* — **Ad·zhar′i·an** *adj. & n.*

Ae·ga·de·an Isles (ē-gā′dē′ən) also **Ae·ga·tes** (-tēz). See **Egadi Islands.**

Ae·ge·an (ĭ-jē′ən). Of or relating to the Bronze Age civilization that flourished in the Aegean area, as at Crete.

Aegean Sea. An arm of the Mediterranean Sea off southeast Europe between Greece and Turkey. The numerous **Aegean Islands** dotting the sea include the Cyclades, the Dodecanese, and the Sporades. Most of the islands belong to Greece.

Ae·gi·na (ĭ-jī′nə). An island off southeast Greece in the Saronic Gulf of the Aegean Sea near Athens. It was a prosperous maritime city-state in the fifth century B.C. but declined after its defeat by Athens and the expulsion of its population. The first Greek coins were struck here.

Ae·gos·pot·a·mi (ē′gəs-pŏt′ə-mī′) or **Ae·gos·pot·a·mos** (-mŏs′). A small river and ancient town of southern Thrace in present-day western Turkey. The culminating battle of the Peloponnesian War, in which Lysander and the Spartans destroyed the Athenian fleet, took place at the mouth of the river in 405 B.C.

Ae·o·li·a (ē-ō′lē-ə). See **Aeolis.**

Ae·o·li·an (ē-ō′lē-ən). 1. Of or relating to Aeolis or its people or culture. 2. One of a Hellenic people of central Greece that occupied Aeolis and Lesbos around 1100 B.C. 3. See **Aeolic.**

Aeolian Islands. See **Lipari Islands.**

Ae·ol·ic (ē-ŏl′ĭk). A group of dialects of ancient Greek that were spoken by the Aeolians. Also called *Aeolian.*

Ae·o·lis (ē′ə-lĭs) or **Ae·o·li·a** (ē-ō′lē-ə). An ancient region of the western coast of Asia Minor in present-day Turkey. It was made up of a group of cities founded by the Aeolians around 1100 B.C.

Aet·na (ĕt′nə), **Mount.** See Mount **Etna.**

Ae·to·li·a (ē-tō′lē-ə, -tōl′yə). An ancient region of central Greece north of the Gulfs of Corinth and Calydon (Patras). Aetolia was briefly significant in Greek history after the formation in 290 B.C. of the Aetolian League, a military confederation that was defeated by the Achaeans later in the third century. — **Ae·to′li·an** *adj. & n.*

A·fars and Is·sas (ə-färs′; ī′səs). See **Djibouti** (sense 1).

Aff·ton (ăf′tən). A city of eastern Missouri, a suburb of St. Louis. ◉ Pop. 21,106.

Af·ghan (ăf′găn′, -gən). 1. Of or relating to Afghanistan or its people, language, or culture. 2. A native or inhabitant of Afghanistan. 3. See **Pashto.**

Af·ghan·i·stan (ăf-găn′ĭ-stän′). *abbr.* **Afg.** A landlocked country of southwest Asia east of Iran and west of Pakistan. Since ancient times the region has been crisscrossed by invaders, including Persians, Macedonians, Arabs, Turks, and Mongols. Afghan tribes united in the 18th century under a single leadership, and warfare with Britain in the 19th century culminated in 1919 with a fully independent state. Economic and political crises during the 1970's led to an invasion by the Soviet Union in 1979. Guerrilla resistance forced the withdrawal of Soviet troops in 1989. An interim government, formed in 1992, failed to unite rebel factions. Kabul is the capital and the largest city. ◉ Pop. 18,879,000.

A·fog·nak Island (ə-fôg′năk′, -fŏg-). An island of Alaska in the western Gulf of Alaska north of Kodiak.

Af·ri·ca (ăf′rĭ-kə). *abbr.* **Afr.** The second-largest continent, lying south of Europe between the Atlantic and Indian oceans. The hottest continent, Africa has vast mineral resources, many of which are still undeveloped.

Af·ri·can (ăf′rĭ-kən). *abbr.* **Afr.** 1. Of or relating to Africa or its peoples, languages, or cultures. **2.** A native or inhabitant of Africa. **3.** A person of African descent.

Af·ri·can-A·mer·i·can or **African American** (ăf′rĭ-kən-ə-mĕr′ĭkən). **1.** Of or relating to Americans of African ancestry or to their history or culture; Afro-American. **2.** An American of African ancestry.

Af·ri·kaans (ăf′rĭ-käns′, -känz′). **1.** A language that developed from 17th-century Dutch and is one of the official languages of South Africa. Also called *Taal*. **2.** Of or relating to Afrikaans or Afrikaners.

Af·ri·ka·ner (ăf′rĭ-kä′nər). An Afrikaans-speaking South African of European ancestry, especially one descended from 17th-century Dutch settlers.

Af·ro-A·mer·i·can (ăf′rō-ə-mĕr′ĭ-kən). **1.** Of or relating to Americans of African ancestry; African-American. **2.** An American of African ancestry.

Af·ro-A·si·at·ic (ăf′rō-ā′zhē-ăt′ĭk, -shē-, -zē-). A large family of languages spoken in northern Africa and southwest Asia, comprising the Semitic, Chadic, Cushitic, Berber, and ancient Egyptian languages; formerly known as Hamito-Semitic. **— Af′ro-A′si·at′ic** *adj.*

Af·ton (ăf′tən). A river, about 14 km (9 mi) long, in southwest Scotland. It is the "sweet Afton" of Robert Burns's 1789 poem.

A·ga·de (ə-gä′də). See **Akkad** (sense 2).

A·ga·na (ə-gä′nyə, ä-gä′nyä). The capital of Guam, on the western coast of the island. It was almost completely destroyed in World War II. ⊛ Pop. 1,139.

Ag·as·siz (ăg′ə-sē), **Lake.** A glacial lake of the Pleistocene epoch (about 11,000 to 2 million years ago) extending over present-day northwest Minnesota, northeast North Dakota, southern Manitoba, and southwest Ontario.

Ag·a·wam (ăg′ə-wŏm). A town of southwest Massachusetts on the Connecticut River near Springfield. It was settled in 1635. ⊛ Pop. 27,323.

Ag·e·nais (ä′zhə-nā′) or **Ag·e·nois** (-nwä′). A historical region of southwest France. Ruled by England at various times during the Hundred Years' War, it finally passed to France after 1444.

A·gin·court (ăj′ĭn-kôrt′, -kôrt′). A village of northern France west-northwest of Arras. On October 25, 1415, Henry V of England decisively defeated a much larger French army here. The victory demonstrated the effectiveness of longbow-equipped troops over heavily armored feudal knights.

a·gon·ic line (ā-gŏn′ĭk, ə-gŏn′-). An imaginary line on the earth's surface connecting points where the magnetic declination is zero.

A·gra (ä′grə). A city of north-central India on the Jumna River southeast of New Delhi. It was a Mogul capital in the 16th and 17th centuries and is the site of the Taj Mahal, built by the emperor Shah Jahan after the death of his favorite wife in 1629. ⊛ Pop. 891,790.

A·gri·gen·to (ä′grĭ-jĕn′tō, äg′rĭ-). A city of southwest Sicily, Italy, overlooking the Mediterranean Sea. It was founded c. 580 B.C. by Greek colonists. ⊛ Pop. 51,931.

A·gua·dil·la (ä′gwə-dē′ə, ä′gwä-thē′ä). A town of northwest Puerto Rico on Mona Passage. Christopher Columbus reputedly landed at the site of Aguadilla in 1493. ⊛ Pop. 22,039.

A·gua Fri·a (ä′gwə frē′ə). A river of western Arizona rising east of Prescott and flowing about 193 km (120 mi) generally southward to the Gila River west of Phoenix.

A·guas·ca·lien·tes (ä′gwäs-kä-lyĕn′tĕs). A city of central Mexico northeast of Guadalajara. It was built over an intricate system of tunnels constructed by ancient, still unidentified inhabitants. ⊛ Pop. 293,152.

A·gul·has (ə-gŭl′əs), **Cape.** A rugged headland of South Africa, the southernmost point of Africa. Its meridian, longitude 20° east, marks the division between the Atlantic and Indian oceans.

Ah·len (ä′lən). A city of west-central Germany southeast of Münster. It is a manufacturing center. ⊛ Pop. 52,537.

Ah·ma·da·bad or **Ah·me·da·bad** (ä′mə-də-bäd′). A city of northwest India north of Bombay. Founded in 1412 as the capital of a former Gujarat kingdom, it is a commercial and cultural center with many outstanding mosques, temples, and tombs. ⊛ Pop. 2,876,710.

Ah·vaz or **Ah·waz** (ä-wäz′). A city of southwest Iran north-northeast of Basra, Iraq. Modern Ahvaz was built on extensive ruins of an ancient Persian city. ⊛ Pop. 828,380.

Ah·ve·nan·maa (ä′və-nän-mä′) also **Å·land Islands** or **Aa·land Islands** (ä′lənd, ō′länd′). An archipelago in the Baltic Sea at the entrance to the Gulf of Bothnia between Sweden and Finland. Colonized in the 12th century by Swedes, the islands were ceded to Russia in 1809 and became part of Finland after World War I.

Ah·waz (ä-wäz′). See **Ahvaz.**

Ai·e·a (ī-ā′ə, ī-ā′ä). A city of south-central Oahu, Hawaii, a residential suburb of Honolulu. ⊛ Pop. 8,906.

ai·guille (ā-gwēl′). A sharp, pointed mountain peak.

Ain·tab (īn-tăb′). See **Gaziantep.**

Ai·nu (ī′nōō). **1.** *pl.* **Ainu** or **-nus.** A member of an indigenous people of Japan, now inhabiting parts of Hokkaido, Sakhalin, and the Kuril Islands. **2.** The language of the Ainu.

air shed (âr′ shĕd′). **1.** The air supply of a given region. **2.** The geographic region that shares an air supply.

Aisne (ān). A river of northern France rising in the Argonne Forest and flowing about 266 km (165 mi) northwest and west to the Oise River. Four major World War I battles were fought along its banks, including the final defeat of the Germans by French and American troops in September–October 1918.

ait (āt). *Chiefly British.* A small island.

Aix-en-Pro·vence (āk′sän-prō-väns′, ĕk′-). A city of southeast France north of Marseille. Founded in 123 B.C. by the Romans as a military colony near the site of mineral springs, the city has long been a popular spa and an important cultural center. ● Pop. 123,778.

Aix-la-Cha·pelle (āks′lä-shä-pĕl′, ĕks′-). See **Aachen.**

A·jac·cio (ä-yä′chō). A city of western Corsica, France, on the **Gulf of Ajaccio,** an inlet of the Mediterranean Sea. Ajaccio was the birthplace of Napoleon Bonaparte. ● Pop. 54,089.

A·jan·ta (ə-jŭn′tə). A village of west-central India southwest of Amravati. Nearby caves dating from c. 200 B.C. to A.D. 650 contain remarkable examples of Buddhist art.

A·jax (ā′jăks′). A town of southeast Ontario, Canada, on Lake Erie northeast of Toronto. It is a manufacturing center. ● Pop. 25,475.

Ajax Mountain. A peak, 3,324.5 m (10,900 ft) high, in the Bitterroot Range of the Rocky Mountains on the Montana-Idaho border.

Aj·man (ăj-män′). A sheikdom of eastern Arabia, part of the federation of United Arab Emirates on the Persian Gulf. ● Pop. 3,725.

Aj·mer (ŭj-mîr′). A city of northwest India southwest of Delhi. Founded c. A.D. 145, it was a Mogul military base and is now a trade and manufacturing center. ● Pop. 402,700.

A·jodh·ya (ə-yōd′yə). A village of northern India on the Ghaghara River. It is a joint municipality with Faizabad, near Lucknow. Long associated with Hindu legend, it is a pilgrimage center and one of the seven sites sacred to Hindus.

A·kan (ä′kän′). **1.** A South Central Niger-Congo language spoken in parts of Ghana and the Ivory Coast whose two main varieties are Fante and Twi, including Ashanti. **2.** *pl.* **Akan** or **A·kans.** A member of a people of Ghana and the Ivory Coast, including the Fante and the Twi. — **A′kan′** *adj.*

A·ka·shi (ä-kä′shē). A city of southwest Honshu, Japan, west of Kobe on **Akashi Strait,** the eastern end of the Inland Sea. Akashi is a manufacturing center. ● Pop. 280,795.

A·ki·ta (ä-kē′tə, ä′kĭ-tä′). A city of northwest Honshu, Japan, on the Sea of Japan. It is a major port. ● Pop. 307,862.

Ak·kad also **Ac·cad** (ăk′ăd′, ä′käd′). **1.** An ancient region of Mesopotamia occupying the northern part of Babylonia. It reached the height of its power in the third millennium B.C. **2.** also **A·ga·de** (ə-gä′də). An ancient city of Mesopotamia and capital of the Akkadian empire.

Ak·ka·di·an (ə-kā′dē-ən). **1.** A native or inhabitant of ancient Akkad. **2.** The Semitic language of the Akkadians, spoken from around 3000 B.C. until the first century A.D. In this sense, also called *Assyrian.* — **Ak·ka′di·an** *adj.*

Ak·ko (ä-kō′, ä′kō). See **Acre.**

A·ko·la (ə-kō′lə). A town of west-central India west-southwest of Amravati. It is a market center in a cotton-growing region. ● Pop. 328,034.

Ak·ron (ăk′rən). A city of northeast Ohio south-southeast of Cleveland. Its first rubber factory was established in 1869 by B.F. Goodrich (1841–1888). In the early 20th century Akron was known as "the rubber capital of the world." ● Pop. 223,019.

Ak·sum or **Ax·um** (äk′sōōm′). A town of northern Ethiopia. From the first to the eighth century A.D. it was the capital of an empire that controlled much of northern Ethiopia. According to biblical tradition, the Ark of the Covenant, the chest containing the Ten Commandments written on stone tablets, was brought here from Jerusalem and placed in the Church of Saint Mary of Zion, where the rulers of Ethiopia were crowned.

Ak·tyu·binsk (äk-tyōō′bĭnsk). A city of western Kazakstan northwest of Astrakhan, Russia. Founded in 1869, it is a metallurgical center. ● Pop. 264,000.

Al·a·bam·a¹ (ăl′ə-băm′ə). **1.** *pl.* **Alabama** or **-as.** A member of a tribe of the Creek confederacy formerly inhabiting southern Alabama and now located in eastern Texas. **2.** The Muskogean language of the Alabamas.

Al·a·bam·a² (ăl′ə-băm′ə). *abbr.* **AL, Ala.** A state of the southeast United States. It was admitted as the 22nd state in 1819. Alabama was first explored by the Spanish, and the southern section was claimed by the United States as part of the Louisiana Purchase (1803). Montgomery is the capital and Birmingham the largest city. ● Pop. 4,062,608. — **Al′a·ba′mi·an** (-bā′mē-ən), **Al′a·bam′an** *adj. & n.*

Alabama River. A river formed in central Alabama north of Montgomery by the confluence of the Coosa and Tallapoosa rivers and flowing about 507 km (315 mi) southwest to join the Tombigbee River north of Mobile.

A·lai or **A·lay** (ä′lī′). A mountain range of southwest Kyrgyzstan. A western branch of the Tien Shan, it extends about 322 km (200 mi) west from the Chinese border and rises to 5,880.4 m (19,280 ft).

Al Al·a·mayn (ăl ăl′ə-mān′, ä′lə-). See **El Ala-mein.**

Al·a·me·da (ăl′ə-mē′də). A city of west-central California on an island in San Francisco Bay near Oakland. It is the site of a naval air base. ⊛ Pop. 76,459.

Al·a·mein (ăl′ə-mān′), **El.** See **El Alamein.**

Al·a·mo (ăl′ə-mō′). A chapel built after 1744 as part of a mission in San Antonio, Texas. During the Texas Revolution against Mexican rule some 182 people were besieged here from February 24 to March 6, 1836. All the insurgents, including Davy Crockett and Jim Bowie, were killed.

Al·a·mo·gor·do (ăl′ə-mə-gôr′dō). A city of south-central New Mexico northeast of Las Cruces. The first atomic bomb was exploded in a test on July 16, 1945, at the White Sands Missile Range northwest of the city. ⊛ Pop. 27,596.

Å·land Islands (ä′lənd, ō′länd′). See **Ahvenanmaa.**

A·las·ka (ə-lăs′kə). *abbr.* **AK, Alas.** A state of the United States in extreme northwest North America, separated from the other mainland states by Canada. It was admitted as the 49th state in 1959 and is the largest state of the Union. The territory was purchased from Russia in 1867 for $7,200,000 and was known as Seward's Folly (after Secretary of State William H. Seward, who negotiated the purchase) until gold was discovered in the late 1800's. Juneau is the capital and Anchorage the largest city. ⊛ Pop. 551,947. — **A·las′kan** *adj. & n.*

Alaska, Gulf of. An inlet of the Pacific Ocean between the Alaska Peninsula and Alexander Archipelago.

Alaska Highway. Formerly **Al·can Highway** (ăl′kăn′). A road extending 2,450.5 km (1,523 mi) northwest from Dawson Creek, British Columbia, to Fairbanks, Alaska. Originally built by U.S. troops in 1942 as a supply route for military installations, it was opened to unrestricted traffic in 1947.

Alaska Peninsula. A peninsula of south-central to southwest Alaska. It is a continuation of the Aleutian Range between the Bering Sea and the Pacific Ocean.

Alaska Range. A mountain range of south-central Alaska rising to 6,197.6 m (20,320 ft) at Mount McKinley.

Alaska Standard Time. Standard time in the ninth time zone west of Greenwich, England, reckoned at 135°W and used throughout Alaska except for the western Aleutian Islands. Also called *Alaska Time.*

A·la-Tau (ăl′ə-tou′, ä′lə-). Several mountain ranges of the Tien Shan in eastern Kyrgyzstan and southeast Kazakstan. The highest elevation is about 5,490 m (18,000 ft).

Al·a·va (ăl′ə-və), **Cape.** A cape of northwest Washington State just south of Cape Flattery. It is the westernmost point of the coterminous United States.

A·lay (ä′lī′). See **Alai.**

Al·ba·ce·te (ăl′bə-sā′tē, äl′vä-thĕ′tĕ). A city of southeast Spain west-southwest of Valencia. It was the site of battles between Moors and Christians in 1145 and 1146. ⊛ Pop. 132,448.

Al·ba Iu·lia (äl′bə yōō′lyə). A town of west-central Romania on the Mureşul River. It is on the site of the ancient settlement Apulum, founded by the Romans in the second century A.D. ⊛ Pop. 59,369.

Al·ba Lon·ga (äl′bə lông′gə, lŏng′-). A city of ancient Latium in central Italy southeast of Rome. Founded before 1100 B.C., it is the legendary birthplace of Romulus and Remus.

Al·ba·ni·a (ăl-bā′nē-ə, -bān′yə, ôl-). *abbr.* **Alb.** A country of southeast Europe on the Adriatic Sea. The region was settled in ancient times by Illyrians and Thracians and later came under Roman, Byzantine, and Ottoman rule. Albania declared its independence in 1912 and became a republic in 1925. Italy invaded the country in 1939 and maintained a puppet government until 1944 when communist guerrillas took control. In 1961 Albania broke with the Soviet Union in favor of closer economic ties with China, remaining effectively isolated from western nations for the rest of the cold war. Elections in 1992 transferred power from the Communist Party to a nominally democratic government. Following the collapse of fraudulent investment schemes in which a large number of Albanians lost their savings, a violent civilian uprising broke out in March 1997. Tiranë is the capital and the largest city. ⊛ Pop. 3,414,000.

Al·ba·ni·an (ăl-bā′nē-ən, -băn′yən, ôl-). *abbr.*
Alb. 1. Of or relating to Albania or its people,
language, or culture. **2.** A native or inhabitant
of Albania. **3.** The Indo-European language of
the Albanians.

Al·ba·no (äl-bä′nō). A lake of central Italy
southeast of Rome in an extinct volcanic crater.

Al·ba·ny (ôl′bə-nē). **1.** A city of western California on the eastern shore of San Francisco Bay
northwest of Berkeley. A U.S. Department of
Agriculture research laboratory is here. ⊛ Pop.
16,327. **2.** A city of southwest Georgia on the
Flint River southeast of Columbus. It is an industrial and processing center in a pecan- and
peanut-growing area. ⊛ Pop. 78,122. **3.** The
capital (since 1797) of New York, in the eastern
part of the state on the west bank of the Hudson
River at the head of deep-water navigation. The
early 17th-century Dutch settlement Fort Orange was renamed Albany when the English
took control in 1664. ⊛ Pop. 101,082. **4.** A city
of northwest Oregon on the Willamette River
south of Salem. It is a lumbering and metallurgical center. ⊛ Pop. 29,462.

Albany River. A river rising in western Ontario, Canada, and flowing about 982 km (610
mi) east and northeast to James Bay. It was an
important fur-trading route.

Al·be·marle (ăl′bə-märl′). A city of central
North Carolina in the Piedmont east-northeast
of Charlotte. It is a trade and processing center.
⊛ Pop. 15,110.

Albemarle Sound. A large body of shallow,
generally fresh water in northeast North Carolina. It is separated from the Atlantic Ocean by a
narrow barrier island.

Al·bert (ăl′bərt), **Lake** also **Mo·bu·to Lake** (mō-
bōō′tō) or **Albert Nyan·za** (nī-ăn′zə, nyän′-).
A shallow lake of east-central Africa in the Great
Rift Valley on the border between Uganda and
Zaire. It was discovered in 1864 by Sir Samuel
Baker and named for Prince Albert, Queen Victoria's consort.

Al·ber·ta (ăl-bûr′tə). *abbr.* **AB, Alta.** A province
of western Canada between British Columbia
and Saskatchewan. It joined the confederation in
1905. Wheat and cattle farming were the basis
of the province's economy until the discovery of
oil and natural gas in the early 1960's. Edmonton is the capital and the largest city. ⊛ Pop.
2,237,724. — **Al·ber′tan** *adj. & n.*

Albert Lea (lē). A city of southern Minnesota
near the Iowa border south of Minneapolis. It is
a trade center in a farming area. ⊛ Pop. 18,310.

Albert Nile. Part of the upper Nile River in
northwest Uganda.

Albert Nyan·za (nī-ăn′zə, nyän′-). See Lake
Albert.

Al·bi·on (ăl′bē-ən). England or Great Britain.
Often used poetically.

Ål·borg also **Aal·borg** (ôl′bôrg′). A city of
northern Denmark north-northeast of Århus.
Chartered in 1342, it is a major port. Metropolitan area population, 157,270.

Al·bu·quer·que (ăl′bə-kûr′kē). A city of central New Mexico on the upper Rio Grande
southwest of Santa Fe. Founded in 1706, it is a
noted health resort. ⊛ Pop. 384,736.

Al·ca·lá de He·na·res (ăl′kə-lä′ dä hĕ-när′əs,
äl′kä-lä′ *thĕ* ĕ-nä′rĕs). A town of central Spain
east-northeast of Madrid. Miguel de Cervantes
(1547–1616) and Catherine of Aragon (1485–
1536) were born here. ⊛ Pop. 159,355.

Al·ca·mo (ăl′kə-mō′). A city of northwest Sicily, Italy, southwest of Palermo. The ruins of the
ancient Greek settlement of Segesta are nearby.
⊛ Pop. 42,059.

Al·can Highway (ăl′kăn′). See **Alaska Highway.**

Al·ca·traz (ăl′kə-trăz′). A rocky island of western California in San Francisco Bay. It was a military prison from 1859 to 1933 and a federal
prison until 1963. It is now a tourist attraction.
The island has long been known as "the Rock."

Al·co·ben·das (äl′kô-bĕn′däs). A city of central Spain, a suburb of Madrid. ⊛ Pop. 66,249.

Al·cor·cón (äl′kôr-kôn′). A city of central Spain,
a suburb of Madrid. ⊛ Pop. 139,662.

Al·coy (äl-koi′). A city of southeast Spain north
of Alicante. It is an important manufacturing
center. ⊛ Pop. 67,431.

Al·dab·ra Islands (äl-däb′rə). A group of four
coral islands in the Indian Ocean north of Madagascar. Part of Seychelles since 1976, the islands are known for their giant tortoises and
other unusual flora and fauna.

Al·dan (äl-dän′). A river of southeast Russia rising in the Stanovoy Range and flowing about
2,253 km (1,400 mi) north and east around the
Aldan Plateau then generally northwest to the
Lena River north of Yakutsk.

Al·der·ney (ôl′dər-nē). A British island in the
English Channel. The northernmost of the larger
Channel Islands, it is separated from the French
coast by a swift channel, the **Race of Alderney.**

Al·der·shot (ôl′dər-shŏt′). A municipal borough
of south-central England southwest of London.
It is the site of a large military training center.
⊛ Pop. 80,800.

A·lek·san·drovsk (ăl′ĭk-săn′drəfsk, ə-lĭk-
sän′-). See **Zaporozhe.**

Al·e·man·ni (ăl′ə-măn′ī). A group of Germanic
tribes that settled in Alsace and nearby areas
during the fourth century A.D. and were defeated by the Franks in 496.

Al·e·man·nic (ăl'ə-măn'ĭk). **1.** A group of High German dialects spoken in Alsace, Switzerland, and parts of southern Germany. **2.** The Germanic dialect of the Alemanni. **3.** Of or relating to the Alemannic dialects of High German. **4.** Of or relating to the Alemanni or their language.

Al·en·çon (ăl-äN-sôN'). A town of northwest France on the Sarthe River west-southwest of Paris. Its lacework industry dates to the 17th century. ◉ Pop. 31,608.

A·lep·po (ə-lĕp'ō) also **A·lep** (ə-lĕp'). A city of northwest Syria near the Turkish border. Inhabited perhaps as early as the sixth millennium B.C., Aleppo was a key point on the caravan route across Syria to Baghdad and later a major center of Christianity in the Middle East. ◉ Pop. 1,542,000.

Al·es·san·dri·a (ăl'ĭ-săn'drē-ə, ä'lĕs-sän'-). A city of northwest Italy east-southeast of Turin. It was founded c. 1168 as a stronghold of the Lombard League, an alliance formed by the communes in Lombardy against the Holy Roman Emperor Frederick I, who was attempting to assert his authority in Italy. Alessandria is named for Pope Alexander III, who supported the league. ◉ Pop. 90,475.

A·leut (ə-lo͞ot', ăl'ē-o͞ot'). **1.** pl. **Aleut** or **A·leuts.** A member of a Native American people inhabiting the Aleutian Islands and coastal areas of southwest Alaska. The Aleut are related culturally and linguistically to the Eskimo. **2.** Either or both of the two languages of the Aleuts.

A·leu·tian (ə-lo͞o'shən). **1.** Of or relating to the Aleuts, their language, or their culture. **2.** A native or inhabitant of the Aleutian Islands, especially an Aleut.

Aleutian Islands. A chain of rugged, volcanic islands of southwest Alaska curving about 1,931 km (1,200 mi) west from the Alaska Peninsula and separating the Bering Sea from the Pacific Ocean. The islands were discovered in 1741 by Vitus Bering, a Danish explorer employed by Russia, and remained under Russian control until Alaska was purchased by the United States in 1867. Military bases on the islands have been of vital strategic importance because of their proximity to Russia.

Aleutian Range. A volcanic mountain chain of southwest Alaska extending about 965 km (600 mi) west from Anchorage along the Alaska Peninsula and continuing, partly submerged as the Aleutian Islands, to Attu Island.

Al·ex·an·der I Island (ăl'ĭg-zăn'dər). An island of British Antarctic Territory in Bellingshausen Sea off the coast of the Antarctic Peninsula. Originally thought to be part of the Antarctic landmass, it was proved to be an island by a U.S. exploratory team in 1940.

Alexander Archipelago. A group of more than 1,000 islands off southeast Alaska. The rugged, heavily forested islands are the exposed tops of submerged coastal mountains that rise steeply from the Pacific Ocean.

Al·ex·an·dret·ta (ăl'ĭg-zăn-drĕt'ə). See **Iskenderun.**

Al·ex·an·dri·a (ăl'ĭg-zăn'drē-ə). **1.** A city of northern Egypt on the Mediterranean Sea at the western tip of the Nile Delta. It was founded by Alexander the Great in 332 B.C. and became a repository of Jewish, Arab, and Hellenistic culture famous for its extensive libraries. Its pharos (lighthouse) was one of the Seven Wonders of the World. ◉ Pop. 3,380,000. **2.** A city of central Louisiana on the Red River northwest of Baton Rouge. The original city was destroyed by Union troops in May 1864 during the Civil War. ◉ Pop. 49,188. **3.** An independent city of northern Virginia on the Potomac River opposite Washington, D.C. Primarily a residential suburb of the capital, the city has many historic buildings, including Gadsby's Tavern, built in 1752. George Washington helped lay out the streets in 1749. ◉ Pop. 111,183.

Al·ex·an·dri·an (ăl'ĭg-zăn'drē-ən). **1.** Of or relating to Alexandria, Egypt. **2.** Of, characteristic of, or belonging to a school of Hellenistic literature, science, and philosophy located at Alexandria in the last three centuries B.C.

Al Fay·yam (ăl' fā-o͞om', fī-, ĕl'). A city of northern Egypt on the Nile River south-southwest of Cairo. The surrounding area is rich in archaeological remains. ◉ Pop. 250,000.

Al·föld (ôl'fəld) also **Great Alföld.** An extensive plain of central and eastern Hungary extending into northern Yugoslavia and western Romania. The **Little Alföld** lies in northwest Hungary and southwest Slovakia.

Al·gar·ve (ăl-gär'və). A medieval Moorish kingdom in present-day southern Portugal. It was conquered in 1253 by Alfonso III (1210–1279).

Al·ge·ci·ras (ăl'jĭ-sîr'əs, äl'hĕ-thē'räs). A city of southern Spain on the **Bay of Algeciras** opposite Gibraltar. It is a port and tourist center. ◉ Pop. 101,256.

Al·ge·ri·a (ăl-jîr'ē-ə). abbr. **Alg.** A country of northwest Africa bordering on the Mediterranean Sea. The region was settled c. 2000 B.C. by Berber-speaking people and later formed a part of the Roman, Byzantine, and Ottoman empires. Arab invaders in the seventh and eighth centuries introduced Islam and the Arabic language and culture. France invaded Algeria in 1830 and declared it a French territory in 1848. Algeria gained its independence from France in 1962 after more than seven years of fighting. The strong showing of pro-Islamic candidates in the 1991 elections led to a military takeover of the government and to increased guerrilla opposition. Algiers is the capital and the largest city. ⊕ Pop. 27,325,000. — **Al·ge′ri·an** *adj. & n.*

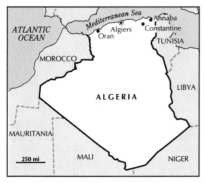

Al·giers (ăl-jîrz′). The capital and largest city of Algeria, in the north on the **Bay of Algiers,** an arm of the Mediterranean Sea. An ancient North African port, Algiers was captured by French forces in 1830 and was later a pivotal center of the struggle for Algerian independence. ⊕ Pop. 1,523,000.

Al·gon·ki·an (ăl-gŏng′kē-ən). Variant of **Algonquian.**

Al·gon·kin (ăl-gŏng′kĭn). Variant of **Algonquin.**

Al·gon·qui·an (ăl-gŏng′kwē-ən, -kē-ən) also **Al·gon·ki·an** (-kē-ən). **1.** A family of North American Indian languages spoken or formerly spoken in an area from Labrador to the Carolinas between the Atlantic coast and the Rocky Mountains. **2.** *pl.* **Algonquian** or **-ans** also **Algonkian** or **-ans.** A member of a people traditionally speaking an Algonquian language. — **Al·gon′qui·an** *adj.*

Al·gon·quin (ăl-gŏng′kwĭn, -kĭn) also **Al·gon·kin** (-kĭn). **1.** *pl.* **Algonquin** or **-quins** also **Algonkin** or **-kins.** A member of any of various Native American peoples inhabiting the Ottawa River valley of Quebec and Ontario. **2.** Any of the varieties of the Ojibwa language spoken by the peoples called Algonquin.

Al·ham·bra¹ (ăl-hăm′brə, äl-äm′brä). A citadel and palace on a hill overlooking Granada, Spain. Built by Moorish kings in the 12th and 13th centuries, the Alhambra is the finest example of Moorish architecture in Spain.

Al·ham·bra² (ăl-hăm′brə). A city of southern California, a residential suburb of Los Angeles. ⊕ Pop. 82,106.

Al Hil·lah (ăl hĭl′ə, ĕl). A city of central Iraq on a branch of the Euphrates River south of Baghdad. It was built c. 1100, largely of material salvaged from the nearby ruins of Babylon. ⊕ Pop. 268,834.

A·li·ák·mon (äl-yäk′môn, ä′lē-äk′-). A river,

about 322 km (200 mi) long, of northern Greece. It is the longest river in the country.

Al·i·can·te (ăl′ĭ-kăn′tē, ä′lē-kän′tĕ). A city of southeast Spain on the Mediterranean Sea south of Valencia. It is a port and tourist center. ⊕ Pop. 267,421.

Al·ice (ăl′ĭs). A city of southern Texas west of Corpus Christi. It is in a cattle-raising area that includes the enormous King Ranch. ⊕ Pop. 19,788.

Alice Springs. A town of Australia located near the center of the country. Tourism and mining are important to its economy. ⊕ Pop. 22,000.

A·li·garh (ăl′ĭ-gär′, ä′lē-gŭr′). A city of north-central India southeast of Delhi. It is noted for its university, established in 1875 as Anglo-Oriental College. ⊕ Pop. 480,520.

Al·i·quip·pa (ăl′ĭ-kwĭp′ə). A borough of western Pennsylvania on the Ohio River northwest of Pittsburgh. It is in a highly industrialized area. ⊕ Pop. 13,374.

Alk·maar (ălk′mär′). A town of northern Netherlands north-northwest of Amsterdam. Chartered in 1254, it has a famous cheese market. ⊕ Pop. 83,892.

Al·la·ha·bad (ăl′ə-hə-băd′, ä′lə-hə-bäd′). A city of north-central India at the junction of the Jumna and Ganges rivers east of Varanasi. It was built on the site of an ancient Indo-Aryan holy city and is still a pilgrimage site for Hindus. ⊕ Pop. 792,858.

Al·le·ghe·ny Mountains (ăl′ĭ-gā′nē) also **Al·le·ghe·nies** (-nēz). A mountain range forming the western part of the Appalachian Mountains. The range extends about 805 km (500 mi) from northern Pennsylvania to southwest Virginia and rises to approximately 1,483 m (4,862 ft) in northeast West Virginia.

Allegheny River. A river rising in north-central Pennsylvania and flowing about 523 km (325 mi) northwest into New York then southwest into Pennsylvania again, where it joins the Monongahela River at Pittsburgh to form the Ohio River.

Al·len Park (ăl′ən). A city of southeast Michigan, a suburb of Detroit. ⊕ Pop. 31,092.

Al·len·ti·ac (ə-lĕn′tē-ăk′). **1.** *pl.* **Allentiac** or **-acs.** A member of a South American Indian people inhabiting west-central Argentina. **2.** The extinct language of the Allentiacs. — **Al·len′ti·ac′** *adj.*

Al·len·town (ăl′ən-toun′). A city of eastern Pennsylvania north-northwest of Philadelphia. Founded in 1762, the city is an industrial and commercial center. ⊕ Pop. 105,090.

Al·li·ance (ə-lī′əns). A city of northeast Ohio southwest of Youngstown. It was settled by Quakers in 1805. ⊕ Pop. 23,376.

Al·lier (ä-lyā′). A river rising in south-central France and flowing about 410 km (255 mi) northward past Vichy to the Loire River.

al·lu·vi·a (ə-lōō′vē-ə). A plural of **alluvium.**

al·lu·vi·al (ə-lōō′vē-əl). Of, relating to, or found in alluvium.

alluvial fan. A fan-shaped accumulation of alluvium deposited at the mouth of a ravine or at the juncture of a tributary stream with the main stream.

al·lu·vi·on (ə-lōō′vē-ən). **1.** See **alluvium. 2.** The flow of water against a shore or bank. **3.** Inundation by water; flood. **4.** *Law.* The increasing of land area along a shore by deposited alluvium or by the recession of water.

al·lu·vi·um (ə-lōō′vē-əm). *pl.* **-vi·ums** or **-vi·a** (-vē-ə). Sediment deposited by flowing water, as in a river bed, flood plain, or delta. Also called *alluvion.*

Al·ma (äl′mə). A city of south-central Quebec, Canada, on the Saguenay River. There are granite quarries in the area. ● Pop. 26,322.

Al·ma-A·ta (äl′mə-ä′tə, əl-mä′ə-tä′). See **Almaty.**

Al Ma·nam·ah (äl′ mə-năm′ə, mă-). See **Manama.**

Al·ma·ty (äl′mə-tē′). Formerly **Al·ma-A·ta** (äl′-mə-ä′tə, əl-mä′ə-tä′). The capital of Kazakstan in the southeast part of the country south of Lake Balkash near the border of Kyrgyzstan. The city was founded in the 1850's as a fort and trading center. ● Pop. 1,176,000.

Al·me·lo (äl′mə-lō′). A city of eastern Netherlands near the German border. It is a manufacturing center. ● Pop. 62,941.

Al·me·rí·a (äl′mə-rē′ə, äl′mĕ-). A city of southeast Spain on the **Gulf of Almería,** an arm of the Mediterranean Sea. Probably founded by Phoenicians, the city is a thriving port. ● Pop. 157,540.

Al·mi·ran·te Brown (äl′mĭ-rän′tĕ, äl′mē-rän′tĕ). A city of eastern Argentina, a suburb of Buenos Aires. It was founded in 1873 by families fleeing a yellow fever epidemic in Buenos Aires. ● Pop. 326,856.

A·lost (ä-lôst′). See **Aalst.**

alp (älp). A high mountain.

Al·phen aan den Rijn (äl′fən än děn rīn′). A city of southwest Netherlands northeast of Rotterdam. It has metalworking industries. ● Pop. 54,560.

Al·phe·us (äl-fē′əs). A river of the Peloponnesus in southern Greece flowing about 113 km (70 mi) to the Ionian Sea.

al·pine (äl′pīn′). **1. Alpine.** Of, relating to, or characteristic of the Alps or their inhabitants. **2.** Of or relating to high mountains.

Alps (älps). A mountain system of south-central Europe, about 805 km (500 mi) long and 161 km (100 mi) wide, curving in an arc from the Riviera on the Mediterranean Sea through northern Italy and southeast France, Switzerland, southern Germany, and Austria and into the extreme northwest part of the Balkan Peninsula. The highest peak is Mont Blanc, 4,810.2 m (15,771 ft), on the French-Italian border.

Al·sace (ăl-săs′, -säs′). A region and former province of eastern France between the Rhine River and the Vosges Mountains. Along with neighboring Lorraine, it was annexed by Germany in 1871 after the Franco-Prussian War and returned to France by the Treaty of Versailles (1919).

Al·sa·tian (ăl-sā′shən). **1.** Of or relating to Alsace or to its inhabitants or culture. **2.** A native or inhabitant of Alsace.

Al·sek (ăl′sĕk′). A river of northwest Canada and southeast Alaska flowing about 418 km (260 mi) to the Pacific Ocean.

Al·sip (ôl′sĭp). A village of northeast Illinois, a suburb of Chicago. ● Pop. 18,227.

Al·ta California (äl′tə) also **Upper California.** The Spanish possessions along the Pacific coast north of the peninsula of Baja California. Early maps of the area often depicted California as an island. When this misconception was corrected in the 18th century, the peninsula came to be called Baja California and the rest of the mainland, Alta California.

Al·ta·de·na (äl′tə-dē′nə). An unincorporated community of southern California at the foot of the San Gabriel Mountains near Pasadena. It is mainly residential. ● Pop. 42,658.

Al·ta·ic (ăl-tā′ĭk). **1.** A language family of Europe and Asia that includes the Turkic, Tungusic, and Mongolian subfamilies. **2.** Of or relating to the Altai Mountains. **3.** Of or relating to Altaic.

Al·tai Mountains or **Al·tay Mountains** (äl′tī′). A mountain system of central Asia, mostly in eastern Kazakstan and south-central Russia but also extending into western Mongolia and northern China. It rises to 4,508.8 m (14,783 ft) at Belukha.

Al·ta·ma·ha (ôl′tə-mə-hô′). A river of southeast Georgia formed by the confluence of the Oconee and Ocmulgee rivers and flowing about 220 km (137 mi) generally east-southeast to **Altamaha Sound,** an inlet of the Atlantic Ocean.

Al·ta·mi·ra (äl′tə-mîr′ə, äl′tä-mē′rä). A group of caverns of northern Spain west-southwest of Santander. The caves contain magnificent specimens of Paleolithic art discovered in 1879.

Al·ta·mont (äl′tə-mŏnt′). An unincorporated community of southern Oregon. It is a suburb of Klamath Falls. ● Pop. 18,591.

Al·ta·monte Springs (ăl′tə-mŏnt′). A city of east-central Florida, a residential suburb of Orlando. ⊛ Pop. 34,879.

Al·ta·mu·ra (äl′tə-mŏŏr′ə, äl′tä-). A city of southeast Italy at the foot of the Apennines south-southwest of Bari. It is a rail junction and processing center. ⊛ Pop. 51,328.

Al·tay Mountains (äl′tī′). See **Altai Mountains.**

Alt·dorf (ält′dôrf). A town of central Switzerland near the southeast tip of the Lake of Lucerne. A statue commemorates the legendary exploits of William Tell, marking the spot where he supposedly shot an apple off his son's head. ⊛ Pop. 8,200.

Al·ten·burg (äl′tən-bûrg′, -bŏŏrk′). A city of east-central Germany south of Leipzig. It was built on the site of early ninth-century Slavic fortifications. ⊛ Pop. 54,999.

al·ti·pla·no (äl′tĭ-plä′nō). *pl.* **-nos.** A high plateau, as in the Andean regions of Bolivia, Peru, and Argentina.

Al·ton (ôl′tən). A city of southwest Illinois on bluffs of the Mississippi River north of St. Louis, Missouri. Lewis and Clark spent the winter of 1803–1804 just south of the site. ⊛ Pop. 32,905.

Al·too·na (ăl-tŏŏ′nə). A city of central Pennsylvania on the eastern slopes of the Allegheny Mountains east of Pittsburgh. It was laid out in 1849 by the Pennsylvania Railroad as a switching point for locomotives used to cross the mountains. ⊛ Pop. 51,881.

Al·tus (ăl′təs). A city of southwest Oklahoma near the Texas border southwest of Oklahoma City. It is a trade center in a farming region. ⊛ Pop. 21,910.

Al U·bay·yid (äl′ ŏŏ-bā′ĭd) also **El O·beid** (ĕl′ ō-bād′). A city of central Sudan southwest of Khartoum. Founded in the 1820's, it is an important transshipment center. ⊛ Pop. 228,096.

Al·um Rock (ăl′əm). An unincorporated community of west-central California, a planned residential suburb of San Jose. ⊛ Pop. 17,471.

Al·vin (ăl′vĭn). A city of southeast Texas south of Houston. It is a trade center for truck and dairy farms. ⊛ Pop. 19,220.

A·ma·ga·sa·ki (ä′mə-gä-sä′kē). A city of southern Honshu, Japan, on Osaka Bay. It is a port, an industrial center, and a suburb of Osaka. ⊛ Pop. 496,313.

Am·a·lek·ite (ăm′ə-lĕk′-īt′, ə-măl′ĭ-kīt′). A member of an ancient nomadic people of Canaan said in the Bible to be descendants of Esau's grandson Amalek.

Am·a·ril·lo (ăm′ə-rĭl′ō, -rĭl′ə). A city of northern Texas in the Panhandle north of Lubbock. The city grew after the coming of the railroad in 1887 and the discovery of gas (1918) and oil (1921). ⊛ Pop. 157,615.

Am·a·zo·ni·a (ăm′ə-zō′nē-ə). The vast basin of the Amazon River in northern South America. It remains largely unpopulated and undeveloped, especially in the interior.

Am·a·zo·ni·an (ăm′ə-zō′nē-ən). Of or relating to the Amazon River or to Amazonia.

Am·a·zon River (ăm′ə-zŏn′, -zən). The second-longest river in the world, flowing about 6,275 km (3,900 mi) from northern Peru across northern Brazil to a wide delta on the Atlantic Ocean. It was probably first explored by the Spanish navigator Vicente Yáñez Pinzón in 1500.

Am·ba·to (äm-bä′tō). A city of central Ecuador in a high Andean valley south of Quito. It is a commercial center and popular tourist site. ⊛ Pop. 100,454.

Am·boi·na (ăm-boi′nə). See **Ambon.**

Am·boi·nese (ăm′boi-nēz′, -nēs′, -ăm′-). Variant of **Ambonese.**

Am·boise (äɴ-bwäz′). A town of west-central France on the Loire River east of Tours. Leonardo da Vinci is said to be buried in the chapel of its Gothic chateau. ⊛ Pop. 10,498.

Am·bon (äm′bôn) also **Am·boi·na** (ăm-boi′nə). An island of eastern Indonesia in the Moluccas near Ceram.

Am·bo·nese (ăm′bə-nēz′, -nēs′, ăm′-) or **Am·boi·nese** (-boi-). **1.** *pl.* **-nese.** A native or inhabitant of Ambon. **2.** The Austronesian language of Ambon.

Am·chit·ka (ăm-chĭt′kə). An island off western Alaska in the Rat Islands of the western Aleutians.

Am·er·a·sian (ăm′ə-rā′zhən, -shən). A person of American and Asian descent, especially one whose mother is Asian and whose father is American. —**Am′er·a′sian** adj.

A·mer·i·ca (ə-mĕr′ĭ-kə). *abbr.* **A., Am., Amer. 1.** The United States. **2.** also **the A·mer·i·cas** (-kəz). The landmasses and islands of North America, South America, Mexico, and Central America included in the Western Hemisphere.

A·mer·i·can (ə-mĕr′ĭ-kən). *abbr.* **A., Amer. 1.** Of or relating to the United States of America or its people, language, or culture. **2.** Of or relating to North or South America, the West Indies, or the Western Hemisphere. **3.** Of or relating to any of the Native American peoples. **4.** A native or inhabitant of America. **5.** A citizen of the United States. —**A·mer′i·can·ness** n.

A·mer·i·ca·na (ä-mĕ′rē-kä′nä). A city of southeast Brazil, a suburb of São Paulo. ⊛ Pop. 153,779.

American English. The English language as used in the United States.

American Falls. A section, 50.9 m (167 ft)

high, of Niagara Falls in western New York north of Buffalo.

American Indian. See **Native American.**

American Samoa. *abbr.* **AS.** An unincorporated territory of the United States in the southern Pacific Ocean northeast of Fiji comprising the eastern islands of the Samoan archipelago. American Samoa has been administered by the United States since 1899. Pago Pago, on Tutuila, the largest island of the group, is the capital. ◉ Pop. 32,279.

American Spanish. The Spanish language as used in the Western Hemisphere.

A·mer·i·cas (ə-mĕr′ĭ-kəz), **the.** See **America** (sense 2).

A·mer·i·cus (ə-mĕr′ĭ-kəs). A city of southwest-central Georgia southeast of Columbus. It is a processing center for the varied resources of the region. ◉ Pop. 16,512.

Am·er·in·di·an (ăm′ə-rĭn′dē-ən) also **Am·er·ind** (ăm′ə-rĭnd′). See **Native American.** — **Am′·er·in′di·an, Am′er·ind′** *adj.* — **Am′er·in′dic** *adj.*

A·mers·foort (ä′mərz-fört′, -fōrt′, ä′mərs-). A city of central Netherlands northeast of Utrecht. The old section of the city has medieval houses. ◉ Pop. 108,520.

Ames (āmz). A city of central Iowa north of Des Moines. Iowa State University of Science and Technology (founded 1858) is here. ◉ Pop. 47,198.

Am·ga (äm-gä′). A river rising in eastern Russia and flowing about 1,287 km (800 mi) generally northeast to the Aldan River east of Yakutsk.

Am·gun (äm-gōōn′). A river of southeast Russia flowing about 788 km (490 mi) northeast to the Amur River.

Am·har·ic (ăm-hăr′ĭk, äm-hä′rĭk). A Semitic language that is the official language of Ethiopia. — **Am·har′ic** *adj.*

Am·herst (ăm′ərst, -hərst). **1.** A town of north-central Nova Scotia, Canada, near the New Brunswick border. It was a thriving Acadian community called Les Planches until it was occupied by the British in the 18th century. ◉ Pop. 9,684. **2.** A town of western Massachusetts northeast of Northampton. Amherst College (established 1821) and a branch of the University of Massachusetts (1863) are here. The poet Emily Dickinson (1830–1886) was born in Amherst and lived in the town her entire life. ◉ Pop. 35,228. **3.** A city of western New York, a suburb of Buffalo. ◉ Pop. 66,100.

Am·i·ens (ăm′ē-ənz, ä-myăn′). A city of northern France on the Somme River north of Paris. Settled in pre-Roman times, it has been a textile center since the Middle Ages. The city's

Gothic cathedral is the largest church in France. ◉ Pop. 131,880.

A·min·di·vi Islands (ä′mĭn-dē′vē). A group of islands in the Arabian Sea off the southwest coast of India, part of the region of Lakshadweep.

A·mish (ä′mĭsh, ăm′ĭsh). **1.** An orthodox Anabaptist sect that separated from the Mennonites in the late 17th century and exists today primarily in southeast Pennsylvania. **2.** Of or relating to this sect or its members.

Am·man (ä-män′, ä′män). The capital and largest city of Jordan, in the north-central part of the country. Occupying a site inhabited since prehistoric times, the city was known as Philadelphia while the Romans and Byzantines controlled it. ◉ Pop. 965,000.

Am·mon·ite (ăm′ə-nīt′). **1.** A member of an ancient Semitic people living east of the Jordan River, mentioned frequently in the Bible. **2.** The Semitic language of the Ammonites. — **Am′·mon·ite′** *adj.*

Am·ne Ma·chin Shan (ăm′nē mə-jĭn′ shän). A range of mountains of west-central China. The highest peak is **Amne Machin** at 7,164.5 m (23,490 ft).

Am·o·rite (ăm′ə-rīt′). A member of one of several ancient Semitic peoples primarily inhabiting Canaan, where they preceded the Israelites, and Babylonia. — **Am′o·rite′** *adj.*

A·moy[1] (ä-moi′). See **Xiamen.**

A·moy[2] (ä-moi′, ə-moi′). The dialect of Chinese spoken in and around the city of Xiamen in Fujian province in southeast China.

Am·ra·va·ti (əm-rä′və-tē, äm-). A town of central India west of Nagpur. It is the site of a Buddhist monument dating from the second century A.D. ◉ Pop. 421,576.

Am·rit·sar (əm-rĭt′sər). A city of northwest India near the Pakistan border. Founded in 1577 by the fourth guru of the Sikhs, Ram Das (1534–1581), it has remained the center of the Sikh faith. In the Amritsar massacre of April 13, 1919, hundreds of Indian nationalists were killed by British-led troops. ◉ Pop. 708,835.

Am·stel·veen (äm′stəl-vān′). A town of western Netherlands, a suburb of Amsterdam. ◉ Pop. 68,518.

Am·ster·dam (ăm′stər-dăm′). **1.** The constitutional capital and largest city of the Netherlands, in the western part of the country on the Ij, an inlet of the Ijsselmeer. Linked to the North Sea by a ship canal, the city has an important stock exchange and is a major center of the diamond-cutting industry. ◉ Pop. 721,976. **2.** A city of east-central New York on the Mohawk River northwest of Albany. Settled in 1783, it was named Amsterdam because many of its early inhabitants were from the Netherlands. • Pop. 20,714.

A·mu Dar·ya (ä′mōō där′yə, ə-mōō′ dŭr-yä′). Formerly **Ox·us** (ŏk′səs). A river of central Asia flowing about 2,574 km (1,600 mi) generally northwest from the Pamir Mountains to the southern Aral Sea. In ancient times it figured significantly in the history of Persia and in the campaigns of Alexander the Great.

A·mund·sen Gulf (ä′mənd-sən, ä′mōōn-). An inlet of the Arctic Ocean in Northwest Territories, Canada, opening on the Beaufort Sea. It was first navigated completely by the Norwegian explorer Roald Amundsen during his 1903–1905 expedition to the region.

Amundsen Sea. An arm of the southern Pacific Ocean off the coast of Marie Byrd Land, Antarctica. It was explored and named by a Norwegian, Nils Larsen, in the late 1920's.

A·mur River (ä-mōōr′) also **Hei·long Jiang** (hā′-lông′ jyäng′). A river of northeast Asia flowing about 2,896 km (1,800 mi) mainly along the border between China and Russia. One of the chief waterways of Asia, it drains into Tatar Strait opposite Sakhalin Island.

A·na·dyr (ä′nə-dîr′). A river of northeast Russia rising in the **Anadyr Plateau** and flowing about 1,118 km (695 mi) south and then east to **Anadyr Bay,** an inlet of the Bering Sea. There are coal and gold deposits near the river's mouth.

An·a·heim (ăn′ə-hīm′). A city of southern California southeast of Los Angeles. It is the site of Disneyland, opened in 1955. • Pop. 266,406.

A·ná·huac (ə-nä′wäk′). An extensive plateau of central Mexico. A heavily populated and highly industrial area that includes Mexico City, it was the center of a pre-Columbian Aztec civilization.

A·ná·po·lis (ä-nä′pōō-lĭs). A city of central Brazil southeast of Brasília. It is a transportation hub. • Pop. 239,047.

A·na·sa·zi (ä′nə-sä′zē). pl. **Anasazi.** A member of a Native American people inhabiting southern Colorado and Utah and northern New Mexico and Arizona from about A.D. 100 and whose descendants are the present-day Pueblo peoples. Anasazi culture includes an early Basket Maker phase and a later Pueblo phase marked by the construction of cliff dwellings and by expert craftsmanship in weaving and pottery.

An·a·to·li·a (ăn′ə-tō′lē-ə, -tōl′yə). The Asian part of Turkey. It is usually considered synonymous with Asia Minor.

An·a·to·li·an (ăn′ə-tō′lē-ən). **1.** Of or relating to Anatolia or its people, language, or culture. **2.** Of or relating to a branch of the Indo-European language family that includes Hittite and other extinct languages of ancient Anatolia. **3.** A native or inhabitant of Anatolia. **4.** The Anatolian languages.

An·chor·age (ăng′kər-ĭj). A city of southern Alaska on Cook Inlet south-southwest of Fairbanks. Founded in 1915 as construction headquarters for the Alaska Railroad, it is the largest city in the state. • Pop. 226,338.

An·co·hu·ma (ăng′kə-hōō′mə, äng′kō-ōō′mä). A mountain, about 6,554 m (21,490 ft) high, of western Bolivia near Lake Titicaca.

An·co·na (ăng-kō′nə, ăn-, än-). A city of central Italy on the Adriatic Sea. It is a leading port and an industrial center. • Pop. 101,179.

An·cy·ra (ăn-sī′rə). See **Ankara.**

An·da·lu·sia (ăn′də-lōō′zhə, -zhē-ə, -shē-ə). A region of southern Spain on the Mediterranean Sea, the Strait of Gibraltar, and the Atlantic Ocean. The area contains magnificent Moorish architecture, including the historic towns of Seville, Granada, and Córdoba. —**An′da·lu′sian** (-zhən, -shən) adj. & n.

An·da·man·ese (ăn′də-mə-nēz′, -nēs′). **1.** also **An·da·man** (ăn′də-mən). pl. **Andamanese** also **Andaman.** A member of an indigenous people of the Andaman Islands. **2.** The language of the Andamanese, of no known linguistic affiliation. —**An′da·man·ese′** adj.

An·da·man Islands (ăn′də-mən). A group of islands in the eastern part of the Bay of Bengal south of Myanmar (Burma). They are separated from the Malay Peninsula by the **Andaman Sea,** an arm of the Bay of Bengal, and are part of the union territory of the Andaman and Nicobar Islands belonging to India.

An·der·lecht (än′dər-lĕkt′, -lĕкнт′). A commune of central Belgium, a suburb of Brussels. The Dutch scholar and theologian Erasmus lived here from 1517 to 1521. • Pop. 92,912.

An·der·son (ăn′dər-sən). **1.** A city of east-central Indiana northeast of Indianapolis. There are numerous prehistoric mounds nearby. • Pop. 59,459. **2.** A city of northwest South Carolina southwest of Greenville near the Georgia border. It is a trade and shipping center in an agricultural region. • Pop. 26,184.

Anderson River. A river of northwestern Northwest Territories, Canada, meandering about 748 km (465 mi) north, west, and north again to Liverpool Bay, an arm of the Arctic Ocean.

An·der·son·ville (ăn′dər-sən-vĭl′). A village of southwest-central Georgia north-northeast of Americus. Its notorious Confederate prison, where more than 12,000 soldiers died during the Civil War, is now a national historic site.

An·des (ăn′dēz). A mountain system of western South America extending more than 8,045 km (5,000 mi) along the Pacific coast from Vene-

zuela to Tierra del Fuego. The Andes rise at many points to more than 6,710 m (22,000 ft).
—**An·de·an** (ăn′dē-ən, ăn-dē′ən) *adj. & n.*

An·di·zhan (ăn′dĭ-zhăn′, än-dĭ-zhän′). A city of eastern Uzbekistan east-southeast of Tashkent. It is an industrial center in a cotton-raising area. ◉ Pop. 275,000.

An·dor·ra (ăn-dôr′ə, -dŏr′ə). *abbr.* **And.** A tiny country of southwest Europe between France and Spain in the eastern Pyrenees. Although it pays nominal yearly homage to its suzerains in France and Spain, it is an independent republic. Andorra la Vella (population, 16,151) is the capital. The country's population is 65,000. —**An·dor′ran** *adj. & n.*

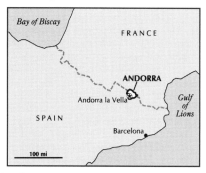

An·do·ver (ăn′dō′vər, -də-). A town of northeast Massachusetts south of Lawrence. Phillips Andover Academy (founded 1778) is here. ◉ Pop. 29,151.

An·dre·a·nof Islands (ăn′drē-ăn′əf, -ôf, än′-drē-ä′nəf). A group of islands of southwest Alaska in the central Aleutian Islands.

An·dri·a (än′drē-ə). A city of southern Italy west-northwest of Bari. The imposing Castel del Monte, built in the 13th century, is nearby. ◉ Pop. 83,319.

An·dros (ăn′drəs). **1.** The largest island of the Bahamas, in the western part of the archipelago. **2.** An island of southeast Greece in the Aegean Sea. The northernmost of the Cyclades, it was colonized by Athens in the fifth century B.C.

An·dros·cog·gin (ăn′drə-skŏg′ĭn). A river of northeast New Hampshire and southwest Maine flowing about 253 km (157 mi) to the Kennebec River near the Maine coast.

A·ne·to (ə-nā′tō, ä-nĕ′-), **Pico de.** A peak, 3,406.2 m (11,168 ft) high, in northeast Spain near the French border. It is the highest elevation in the Pyrenees.

An·ga·ra (än′gə-rä′). A river of central Russia flowing about 1,850 km (1,150 mi) north and west from Lake Baikal to the Yenisey River.

An·garsk (än-gärsk′). A city of south-central

Russia on the Angara River near Irkutsk. It is a manufacturing center. ◉ Pop. 267,910.

An·ge·le·no (ăn′jə-lē′nō). *pl.* **-nos.** A native or inhabitant of Los Angeles.

An·gel Fall or **Falls** (ān′jəl). A waterfall, about 980 m (3,212 ft) high, in southeast Venezuela. It is the highest uninterrupted waterfall in the world.

An·gers (ăn′jərz, äɴ-zhā′). A city of western France east-northeast of Nantes. Of pre-Roman origin, Angers was the historical capital of Anjou. ◉ Pop. 141,354.

An·ge·vin (ăn′jə-vĭn). Of or relating to the historical region and former province of Anjou, France.

Ang·kor (ăng′kôr, -kōr). A major archaeological site in northwest Cambodia and the capital of the Khmer Empire from the 9th to the 15th century. The ruins include two important Hindu temple complexes, Angkor Wat (12th century) and Angkor Thom (13th century). The site has been extensively damaged by warfare.

An·gle (ăng′gəl). A member of a Germanic people that migrated to England from southern Jutland in the 5th century A.D., founded the kingdoms of Northumbria, East Anglia, and Mercia, and together with the Jutes and Saxons formed the Anglo-Saxon peoples.

An·gle·sey or **An·gle·sea** (ăng′gəl-sē). An island of northwest Wales in the Irish Sea. It has druidic ruins, especially dolmens, and is said to have been the last refuge of the druids from the invading Romans.

An·gli·a (ăng′glē-ə). **1.** The Medieval and Late Latin name for England. **2.** See **East Anglia.**

An·gli·an (ăng′glē-ən). **1.** Of or relating to East Anglia or to the Angles. **2.** An Angle. **3.** The Old English dialects of Mercia and Northumbria.

An·glo also **an·glo** (ăng′glō). *pl.* **-glos. 1.** *Informal.* An Anglo-American. **2.** An English-speaking person, especially a white North American who is not of Hispanic or French descent. —**An′glo** *adj.*

An·glo-A·mer·i·can (ăng′glō-ə-mĕr′ĭ-kən). **1.** An American, especially an inhabitant of the United States, whose language and ancestry are English. **2.** Of, relating to, or between England and America, especially the United States. **3.** Of or relating to Anglo-Americans.

An·glo-French (ăng′glō-frĕnch′). **1.** Of, relating to, or between England and France or their peoples; English and French. **2.** See **Anglo-Norman** (sense 2).

An·glo-In·di·an (ăng′glō-ĭn′dē-ən). **1.** Of, relating to, or between England and India. **2.** A person of English and Indian descent. **3.** A per-

son of English birth or ancestry living in India.
4. The variety of English used in India.

An·glo-I·rish (ăng'glō-ī'rĭsh). **1.** A native of England living in Ireland. **2.** A native of Ireland living in England. **3.** A person of mixed Irish and English ancestry. **4.** See **Irish English.**

An·glo-Nor·man (ăng'glō-nôr'mən). **1.** One of the Normans who lived in England after the Norman Conquest of England in 1066 or a descendant of these settlers. **2. a.** The dialect of Old French that was used by the Anglo-Normans. **b.** The form of this dialect used in English law until the 17th century. In this sense, also called *Anglo-French.*

An·glo-Sax·on (ăng'glō-săk'sən). *abbr.* **AS, A.S. 1.** A member of one of the Germanic peoples, the Angles, the Saxons, and the Jutes, who settled in Britain in the fifth and sixth centuries A.D. **2.** Any of the descendants of the Anglo-Saxons, who were dominant in England until the Norman Conquest of 1066. **3.** See **Old English. 4.** A person of English ancestry. **5.** Of or relating to Anglo-Saxons.

An·go·la (ăng-gō'lə, ăn-). *abbr.* **Ang.** A country of southwest Africa bordering on the Atlantic Ocean. The Portuguese established a coastal colony in 1575, though the Mbundu kingdom in central Angola was not conquered until 1902. The country became independent in 1975 after a long guerrilla war. Independence touched off a civil war in which Cuban and South African troops also took part until 1988. Elections in 1992 failed to end the fighting. Luanda is the capital and the largest city. ⊛ Pop. 8,140,000. —**An·go'lan** *adj. & n.*

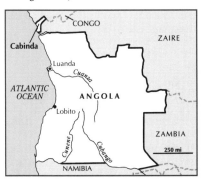

An·go·ra (ăng-gôr'ə, -gōr'ə, ăng'gər-ə). See **Ankara.**

An·gou·lême (äN-gōō-lām', -lĕm'). A city of western France north-northeast of Bordeaux. It was ceded to England in 1360 but was retaken by France in 1373. ⊛ Pop. 46,197.

An·gou·mois (äN'gōō-mwä'). A historical region and former province of western France in the Charente River valley. Occupied by Gallic peoples in pre-Roman times, it later was part of

Aquitaine, was briefly ceded to England (1360–1373), and became a French duchy in 1515.

An·guil·la (ăng-gwĭl'ə, ăn-). An island of the British West Indies in the northern Leeward Islands. Settled by the British in the 17th century, it was part of the self-governing colony of St. Kitts-Nevis-Anguilla until 1967, when it seceded unilaterally. A bid for full independence led to the landing of British troops in 1969.

An·hui (än'hwē') also **An·hwei** (-hwā', -wā'). A province of east-central China. It was made a separate province in the 17th century under the Manchu dynasty. Hefei is the capital. ⊛ Pop. 51,560,000.

An·jou (än'jōō', äN-zhōō'). **1.** A historical region and former province of northwest France in the Loire River valley. Ruled by the powerful counts of Anjou in the early Middle Ages, it was annexed to the French crown lands by Louis XI in the 1480's. **2.** A town of southern Quebec, Canada, a suburb of Montreal. ⊛ Pop. 37,346.

An·ka·ra (ăng'kər-ə, äng'-). Formerly **An·cy·ra** (ăn-sī'rə) and **An·go·ra** (ăng-gôr'ə, -gōr'ə, äng'gər-ə). The capital of Turkey, in the west-central part of the country at an elevation of about 915 m (3,000 ft). An important commercial center from ancient times until the late 19th century, the city declined until it replaced Istanbul as the capital in 1923. ⊛ Pop. 2,782,200.

An·ke·ny (ăng'kə-nē). A city of central Iowa, a suburb of Des Moines. ⊛ Pop. 18,482.

Ann (ăn), **Cape.** A peninsula of northeast Massachusetts projecting into the Atlantic Ocean northeast of Gloucester.

An·na·ba (ə-nä'bə, ä-nä'-). A city of northeast Algeria on the Mediterranean Sea near the Tunisian border. Founded by the Carthaginians, it was an early center of Christianity. ⊛ Pop. 239,975.

An Na·jaf (ăn năj'ăf'). A city of south-central Iraq on a lake near the Euphrates River. It is a starting point for the pilgrimage to Mecca. ⊛ Pop. 309,010.

An·nam (ə-năm', ăn'ăm'). A region and former kingdom of central Vietnam on the South China Sea between Tonkin and Cochin China. It was ruled by China from 111 B.C. until A.D. 939 and came under French control in the 19th century. —**An'na·mese'** (ăn'ə-mēz', -mēs'), **An'nam·ite'** *adj. & n.*

An·nan·dale (ăn'ən-dāl'). A city of northeast Virginia, a suburb of Alexandria and Washington, D.C. ⊛ Pop. 50,975.

An·nap·o·lis (ə-năp'ə-lĭs). The capital of Maryland, in the central part of the state on an inlet of Chesapeake Bay south-southeast of Baltimore. Settled in 1649, it was the site of the Annapolis Convention in 1786, which led to the federal

Constitutional Convention of 1787. The U.S. Naval Academy, founded in 1845, is in Annapolis. ⊕ Pop. 33,187.

Annapolis Roy·al (roi′əl). A town of western Nova Scotia, Canada, on an arm of the Bay of Fundy. One of the oldest settlements in Canada, it was founded as **Port Royal** by the French in 1605 and renamed by the British after 1710 in honor of Queen Anne.

An·na·pur·na (ăn′ə-pŏŏr′nə, -pûr′-). A massif of the Himalaya Mountains in north-central Nepal. It rises to 8,083.7 m (26,504 ft) at **Annapurna I** in the west. **Annapurna II,** in the east, is 7,942.5 m (26,041 ft) high.

Ann Ar·bor (är′bər). A city of southeast Michigan west of Detroit. A research and educational center, it is the seat of the University of Michigan (founded 1817). ⊕ Pop. 109,592.

An·ne·cy (ăn′ə-sē′, än-sē′). A city of southern France in the Alps on **Lake Annecy** east-northeast of Lyon. It is a popular resort and tourist center. ⊕ Pop. 49,965.

An·nis·ton (ăn′ĭ-stən). A city of northeast Alabama in the foothills of the Appalachian Mountains east-northeast of Birmingham. Founded in 1872 as an iron-manufacturing company town, it was opened to noncompany settlers in 1883. ⊕ Pop. 26,623.

A·no·ka (ə-nō′kə). A city of eastern Minnesota north-northwest of Minneapolis. It was originally a trading post and lumber town. ⊕ Pop. 15,634.

An·shan (än′shän′). A city of northeast China south-southwest of Shenyang. It has an enormous integrated iron and steel complex. ⊕ Pop. 2,478,650.

An·so·ni·a (ăn-sō′nē-ə, -sōn′yə). A city of southwest Connecticut west-northwest of New Haven. It was first settled in 1651. ⊕ Pop. 18,403.

An·ta·kya (än-täk′yä). See **Antioch** (sense 2).

An·tal·ya (än-täl′yä). A city of southwest Turkey on the **Gulf of Antalya,** an inlet of the Mediterranean Sea. The city is situated on a steep cliff and surrounded by an old wall. ⊕ Pop. 497,200.

An·ta·na·na·ri·vo (ăn′tə-năn′ə-rē′vō, än′tə-nä′nə-). Formerly **Ta·nan·a·rive** (tə-năn′ə-rēv′, tä-nä-nä-rēv′). The capital and largest city of Madagascar, in the east-central part of the country. It was founded in the 17th century as a walled citadel. ⊕ Pop. 347,466.

Ant·arc·ti·ca (ănt-ärk′tĭ-kə, -är′tĭ-). *abbr.* **Ant.** A continent lying chiefly within the Antarctic Circle and asymmetrically centered on the South Pole. Some 95 percent of Antarctica is covered by an icecap averaging 1.6 km (1 mi) in thickness. The region was first explored in the early 1800's, and although there are no permanent settlements, many countries have made territorial claims. The Antarctic Treaty of 1959, signed by 12 nations, prohibited military operations on the continent and provided for the interchange of scientific data. —**Ant·arc′tic** *adj. & n.*

Antarctic Archipelago. See **Palmer Archipelago.**

Antarctic Circle. The parallel of latitude approximately 66°33′ south. It forms the boundary between the South Temperate and South Frigid zones.

Antarctic Ocean. The waters surrounding Antarctica, actually the southern extensions of the Atlantic, Pacific, and Indian oceans.

Antarctic Peninsula also **Palm·er Peninsula** (pä′mər). A region of Antarctica extending about 1,931 km (1,200 mi) north toward South America.

An·te·ro (ăn-târ′ō), **Mount.** A peak, 4,352 m (14,269 ft) high, in the Sawatch Mountains of central Colorado.

An·tibes (äɴ-tēb′). A city of southeast France on the Riviera between Nice and Cannes. A seaport and fashionable resort, it is the center of one of Europe's largest flower-growing regions. ⊕ Pop. 62,859.

An·ti·cos·ti (ăn′tĭ-kô′stē, -kŏs′tē). An island of eastern Quebec, Canada, at the head of the Gulf of St. Lawrence. It was discovered by Jacques Cartier in 1534.

An·tie·tam (ăn-tē′təm). A creek of north-central Maryland emptying into the Potomac River. The bloody and inconclusive Civil War Battle of Antietam (or Sharpsburg, as it is often called in the South) was fought along its banks on September 17, 1862.

An·ti·gua and Bar·bu·da (ăn-tē′gə; bär-bōō′-də). A country in the northern Leeward Islands of the Caribbean Sea, comprising the island of Antigua and the smaller islands of Barbuda and Redonda. The country became independent in 1981. St. John's is the capital. ⊕ Pop. 72,000. —**An·ti′guan** *adj. & n.*

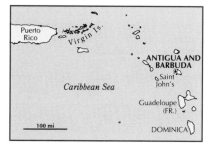

An·ti-Leb·a·non Range (ăn′tē-lĕb′ə-nən). A mountain range on the Syria-Lebanon border, rising to 2,815.8 ft (9,232 ft) at Mount Hermon.

An·til·les (ăn-tĭl′ēz). The islands of the West

Indies except for the Bahamas, separating the Caribbean Sea from the Atlantic Ocean and divided into the **Greater Antilles** to the north and the **Lesser Antilles** to the east.

An·ti·och (ăn′tē-ŏk′). **1.** An ancient town of Phrygia north of present-day Antalya, Turkey. It was a center of Hellenistic influence and was visited by Saint Paul in biblical times. **2.** also **An·ta·kya** (än-täk′yä). A city of southern Turkey on the Orontes River near the Mediterranean Sea. Founded c. 300 B.C. by Seleucus I, a Macedonian general under Alexander the Great and founder of the Seleucid dynasty, it was an important military and commercial center in the Roman era and an early center of Christianity. ⊛Pop. 137,200. **3.** A city of western California northeast of Oakland on the San Joaquin River near the mouth of the Sacramento River. It is a processing and shipping center. ⊛Pop. 62,195.

an·tip·o·des (ăn-tĭp′ə-dēz′). Any two places or regions that are on diametrically opposite sides of the earth. —**an·tip′o·dal, an·tip′o·de′an** *adj.*

An·tip·o·des (ăn-tĭp′ə-dēz′). **1.** Australia and New Zealand. Usually used informally. **2.** A group of rocky islands of the southern Pacific Ocean southeast of New Zealand, to which they belong. They were discovered by British seamen in 1800 and are so named because they are diametrically opposite Greenwich, England.

An·ti·sa·na (ăn′tĭ-sä′nə). A dormant volcano, about 5,760 m (18,885 ft) high, of north-central Ecuador in the Andes southeast of Quito.

An·to·fa·gas·ta (än′tō-fə-gä′stə). A city of northern Chile on the Pacific Ocean. It is a shipping center for minerals found in the area. ⊛Pop. 218,754.

An·to·ny (än-tə-nē′). A city of north-central France, a mainly residential suburb of Paris. ⊛Pop. 54,610.

An·tung (än′tŏong′). See **Dandong.**

Ant·werp (ăn′twərp) also **An·vers** (än-vâr′). A city of northern Belgium on the Scheldt River north of Brussels. One of Europe's busiest ports, it has been a center of the diamond industry since the 15th century. The first stock exchange was founded here in 1460. ⊛Pop. 470,349.

A·nu·ra·dha·pur·a (ŭn′ə-rä′də-pŏor′ə, ə-nŏor′-ə-). A town of north-central Sri Lanka north-northeast of Colombo. The ancient capital of Singhalese kings of Ceylon, it has extensive ruins and is a Buddhist pilgrimage center. ⊛Pop. 36,000.

An·vers (än-vâr′). See **Antwerp.**

An·yang (än′yäng′). **1.** A city of eastern China north-northeast of Zhengzhou. It was a capital of the Shang dynasty and one of the earliest centers of Chinese civilization. ⊛Pop. 616,803. **2.** A city of northwest South Korea, a suburb of Seoul. ⊛Pop. 481,291.

An·zhe·ro·Sud·zhensk (än-zhĕr′ə-sŏod-zhĕnsk′, -sŏod′zhĭnsk′). A city of south-central Russia northeast of Novosibirsk. It is one of the oldest coal-mining centers in the Kuznetsk Basin. ⊛Pop. 105,161.

An·zi·o (ăn′zē-ō, än′tsyô). A town of central Italy on the Tyrrhenian Sea south-southeast of Rome. In World War II Allied troops landed at Anzio on January 22, 1944. ⊛Pop. 27,094.

Ao·mo·ri (ou′mə-rē, ä′ô-môr′ē). A city of extreme northern Honshu, Japan, on **Aomori Bay.** Opened to foreign trade in 1906, it is now the chief port of northern Honshu. ⊛Pop. 288,291.

A·o·rang·i (ä′ō-räng′gē). See Mount **Cook** (sense 1).

A·pach·e (ə-păch′ē). **1.** *pl.* **Apache** or **-es.** A member of a Native American people inhabiting the southwest United States and northern Mexico. Various Apache tribes offered strong resistance to encroachment on their territory in the latter half of the 19th century. Present-day Apache populations are located in Arizona, New Mexico, and Oklahoma. **2.** Any of the Apachean languages of the Apaches.

A·pach·e·an (ə-păch′ē-ən). **1.** The subgroup of Athabaskan comprising the languages of the Apache and Navajo. **2.** A speaker of any of these languages.

Ap·a·lach·i·co·la (ăp′ə-lăch′ĭ-kō′lə). A river of northwest Florida flowing about 180 km (112 mi) generally southward from the Georgia border to **Apalachicola Bay,** an inlet of the Gulf of Mexico.

Ap·a·po·ris (ä′pə-pōr′ēs, -pôr′-). A river rising in south-central Colombia and flowing about 805 km (500 mi) southeast to the Japurá River on the Brazilian border.

A·pel·doorn (äp′əl-dôrn′, -dōrn′, -ä′pəl-). A city of east-central Netherlands north of Arnhem. It is a popular tourist center. ⊛Pop. 149,477.

Ap·en·nines (ăp′ə-nīnz′). A mountain system extending about 1,352 km (840 mi) from northwest Italy south to the Strait of Messina. The highest peak is Mount Corno, rising to 2,915.8 m (9,560 ft).

A·pi·a (ə-pē′ə, ä′pē-ä′). The capital of Western Samoa, on the northern coast of Upolo island in the southern Pacific Ocean. ⊛Pop. 32,099.

A·po (ä′pō). The highest mountain, 2,956.1 m (9,692 ft), of the Philippines, an active volcano on southeast Mindanao.

Ap·pa·la·chi·a (ăp′ə-lā′chē-ə, -chə, -lăch′ē-ə, -lăch′ə). A region of the eastern United States including the Appalachian Mountains.

Ap·pa·la·chi·an Mountains (ăp′ə-lā′chē-ən, -chən, -lăch′ē-ən, -lăch′ən, -lā′shē-ən, -lā′shən). A mountain system of eastern North America extending about 2,574 km (1,600 mi) southwest from Newfoundland, New Brunswick, and southern Quebec, Canada, to central Alabama. The range includes the Allegheny, Blue Ridge, and Cumberland mountains. Mount Mitchell in western North Carolina is the highest peak, rising to 2,038.6 m (6,684 ft).

Appalachian Trail. A hiking path of the eastern United States extending about 3,298 km (2,050 mi) from Mount Katahdin in central Maine to Springer Mountain in northern Georgia. It is the world's longest continuous mountain trail.

Ap·pi·an Way (ăp′ē-ən). An ancient Roman road between Rome and Capua, begun in A.D. 312 and later extended to Brindisi, with a total length of more than 563 km (350 mi).

Ap·ple·ton (ăp′əl-tən). A city of eastern Wisconsin on the Fox River southwest of Green Bay. The first hydroelectric plant in the United States was built here in 1882. ⊛ Pop. 65,695.

Ap·ple Valley (ăp′əl). A city of southeast Minnesota, a residential suburb of Minneapolis–St. Paul. ⊛ Pop. 34,598.

Ap·po·mat·tox (ăp′ə-măt′əks). A town of south-central Virginia east of Lynchburg. Confederate general Robert E. Lee surrendered to Union general Ulysses S. Grant at Appomattox Courthouse on April 9, 1865, ending the Civil War. The site is now a national historical park. ⊛ Pop. 1,345.

Appomattox River. A river rising in south-central Virginia and flowing about 220 km (137 mi) generally eastward to the James River near Petersburg.

A·pra Harbor also **Port A·pra** (ä′prə). A seaport of western Guam in the Mariana Islands of the western Pacific. It is the only good harbor on the island.

a·pron (ā′prən). An area covered by sand and gravel deposited at the front of a glacial moraine.

A·pu·lia (ə-pŏŏl′yə) also **Pu·glia** (pŏŏ′lyä). A region of southeast Italy bordering on the Adriatic Sea, Strait of Otranto, and Gulf of Taranto. Its southern portion forms the heel of the Italian "boot."

A·pu·re (ə-pŏŏr′ā). A river of west-central Venezuela originating in the Andes of Colombia and flowing about 805 km (500 mi) eastward to the Orinoco River.

A·pu·rí·mac (ä′pə-rē′mäk). A river of southern Peru rising in the Andes and flowing about 885 km (550 mi) generally northwest to join the Urubamba River and form the Ucayali River.

A·qa·ba (ä′kə-bə, ăk′ə-), **Gulf of.** An arm of the Red Sea between the Sinai Peninsula and northwest Saudi Arabia. It has long been of strategic importance in the Middle East.

A·quid·neck Island (ə-kwĭd′nĕk). See **Rhode Island**[1].

aq·ui·fer (ăk′wə-fər, ä′kwə-). An underground bed or layer of earth, gravel, or porous stone that yields water. —**a·quif′er·ous** (ə-kwĭf′ər-əs) *adj.*

A·qui·la (ăk′wə-lə, ä′kwē-lä). See **L'Aquila.**

A·qui·le·ia (ä′kwə-lā′ə, ä′kwē-lē′yä). A town of northeast Italy near the Adriatic Sea. It was founded by the Romans as a military outpost in 181 B.C. and was often destroyed by invaders, including Attila, king of the Huns, (A.D. 452).

Aq·ui·taine (ăk′wĭ-tān′). A historical region of southwest France between the Pyrenees and the Garonne River. The duchy of Aquitaine was joined with France after the marriage of Eleanor of Aquitaine to King Louis VII in 1137, but its possession was disputed after her subsequent marriage to Henry II of England.

Aq·ui·ta·ni·a (ăk′wĭ-tā′nē-ə). A Roman division of southwest Gaul extending from the Pyrenees to the Garonne River and roughly coextensive with the historical region of Aquitaine. Its Iberian peoples were conquered by Julius Caesar in 56 B.C. The region passed to the Franks in A.D. 507.

Ar·ab (ăr′əb). **1.** A member of a Semitic people inhabiting Arabia, whose language and Islamic religion spread widely throughout the Middle East and northern Africa from the seventh century. **2.** A member of an Arabic-speaking people. —**Ar′ab** *adj.*

A·ra·bi·a (ə-rā′bē-ə) also **A·ra·bi·an Peninsula** (-bē-ən), *abbr.* **Ar.** A peninsula of southwest Asia between the Red Sea and the Persian Gulf. Politically, it includes Saudi Arabia, Yemen, Oman, the United Arab Emirates, Qatar, Bahrain, and Kuwait. Arabia has an estimated one third of the world's oil reserves.

Arabian. *abbr.* **Ar., Arab. 1.** Of or concerning Arabia or the Arabs; Arab. **2.** A native or inhabitant of Arabia.

Arabian Desert. A desert of eastern Egypt between the Nile Valley and the Red Sea. Porphyry, granite, and sandstone found here have been used as building materials since ancient times.

Arabian Gulf. See **Persian Gulf.**

Arabian Peninsula. See **Arabia.**

Arabian Sea. The northwest part of the Indian Ocean between Arabia and western India. It has long been an important trade route between India and the West.

Ar·a·bic (ăr′ə-bĭk). **1.** Of or relating to Arabia, the Arabs, their language, or their culture. **2.**

abbr. **Ar., Arab.** A Semitic language consisting of numerous dialects that is the principal language of Arabia, Jordan, Syria, Iraq, Lebanon, Egypt, and parts of northern Africa.

A·ra·ca·ju (ä-rä′kä-zhōō′). A city of east-central Brazil near the Atlantic Ocean south-southeast of Recife. It is a commercial center in a cotton- and sugar-producing region. ◦ Pop. 401,676.

A·ra·ça·tu·ba (ä′rə-sə-tōō′bə). A city of southeast Brazil on the Tietê River northwest of São Paulo. It is a trade center in an agricultural area. ◦ Pop. 159,499.

A·rad (ä-räd′). A city of western Romania on the Mureşul River near the Hungarian border. Ruled by Turkey and later by Hungary, it became part of Romania in 1920. ◦ Pop. 188,609.

A·ra·fu·ra Sea (ä′rə-fōō′rə). A shallow part of the western Pacific Ocean between the Timor and Coral seas, separating New Guinea from Australia.

Ar·a·gon (ăr′ə-gŏn′). A region and former kingdom of northeast Spain. It was united with Castile in 1479 to form the nucleus of modern Spain. — **Ar′a·go·nese′** (ăr′ə-gə-nēz′, -nēs′) *adj. & n.*

A·ra·guaí·a or **A·ra·gua·ya** (är′ə-gwī′ə). A river rising in central Brazil and flowing about 2,092 km (1,300 mi) generally northward to the Tocantins River. There are numerous falls on the river.

A·rak (ə-räk′). A city of west-central Iran southwest of Tehran. It is a transportation hub noted for its carpets. ◦ Pop. 378,597.

Ar·al Sea (ăr′əl). An inland sea lying between southern Kazakstan and northwest Uzbekistan. Once the fourth-largest inland body of water in the world, it is fast disappearing because of diversion of its two sources, the Amu Darya and the Syr Darya.

Ar·am (âr′əm, ăr′-, ā′răm). In the Bible, an ancient country of southwest Asia, roughly coextensive with present-day Syria.

Ar·a·mae·an (ăr′ə-mē′ən). Variant of **Aramean.**

Ar·a·ma·ic (ăr′ə-mā′ĭk). A Semitic language, comprising several dialects, originally of the ancient Arameans but widely used by non-Aramean peoples throughout southwest Asia from the seventh century B.C. to the seventh century A.D. Also called *Aramean, Chaldean.* — **Ar′a·ma′ic** *adj.*

Ar·a·me·an or **Ar·a·mae·an** (ăr′ə-mē′ən). **1.** Of or relating to Aram, its inhabitants, their language, or their culture. **2.** One of a group of Semitic peoples inhabiting Aram and parts of Mesopotamia from the 11th to the 8th century B.C. **3.** See **Aramaic.**

Ar·an Islands (ăr′ən). Three small islands of western Ireland at the entrance to Galway Bay. The barren, primitive islands have many prehistoric and early Christian remains.

A·rap·a·ho also **A·rap·a·hoe** (ə-răp′ə-hō′). **1.** *pl.* **Arapaho** or **-hos** also **Arapahoe** or **-hoes.** A member of a Native American people formerly inhabiting eastern Colorado and southeast Wyoming, with present-day populations in Oklahoma and central Wyoming. Traditional Arapaho life was based on the buffalo-hunting culture of the Great Plains. **2.** The Algonquian language of the Arapahos.

A·rap·a·hoe Peak (ə-răp′ə-hō′). A mountain, 4,119.3 m (13,506 ft) high, of north-central Colorado in the Front Range of the Rocky Mountains east of Boulder.

Ar·a·rat (ăr′ə-răt′), **Mount.** A massif of extreme eastern Turkey near the Iranian border rising to about 5,168 m (16,945 ft). It is the traditional resting place of Noah's ark.

A·ras (ə-räs′). Formerly **A·rax·es** (ə-răk′sēz). A river rising in northeast Turkey and flowing about 965 km (600 mi) generally eastward.

A·rau·ca (ə-rou′kə). A river rising in northern Colombia in the Cordillera Oriental and flowing about 805 km (500 mi) eastward to the Orinoco River in central Venezuela.

Ar·au·ca·ni·an (ăr′ô-kä′nē-ən) also **A·rau·can** (ə-rô′kən). **1.** A member of a widespread group of South American Indian peoples of south-central Chile and the western pampas of Argentina. **2.** The language of the Araucanians, which constitutes an independent language family. — **Ar′-au·ca′ni·an** *adj.*

Ar·a·wak (ăr′ə-wäk′). **1.** *pl.* **Arawak** or **-waks.** A member of a South American Indian people formerly inhabiting much of the Greater Antilles and now living chiefly in certain regions of Guiana. **2.** The Arawakan language spoken by the Arawaks.

Ar·a·wa·kan (ăr′ə-wä′kən). **1.** *pl.* **Arawakan** or **-kans.** A member of a widespread group of Indian peoples living in an area of South America that includes parts of Colombia, Venezuela, Guiana, the Amazon basin of Brazil, Paraguay, Bolivia, Peru, and formerly most of the Greater Antilles. **2.** The largest and most important Indian linguistic family in South America, consisting of the languages spoken by the Arawakan peoples. — **Ar′a·wa′kan** *adj.*

A·rax·es (ə-răk′sēz). See **Aras.**

Ar·be·la (är-bē′lə). An ancient town of Assyria in present-day northern Iraq. Its name is sometimes given to the battle fought at Gaugamela, about 97 km (60 mi) away, in which Alexander the Great defeated Darius III in 331 B.C.

Ar·cade (är-kād′). A community of north-central California, a suburb of Sacramento. ⊛ Pop. 37,600.

Ar·ca·di·a (är-kā′dē-ə). **1.** also **Ar·ca·dy** (är′-kə-dē). A region of ancient Greece in the Peloponnesus. Its inhabitants, relatively isolated from the rest of the known civilized world, proverbially lived a simple, pastoral life. **2.** A city of southern California, a residential suburb of Los Angeles at the foot of the San Gabriel Mountains. ⊛ Pop. 48,290.

Ar·ca·di·an (är-kā′dē-ən). **1.** Of or relating to the ancient Greek region of Arcadia or its people, language, or culture. **2.** A native or inhabitant of Arcadia. **3.** The dialect of ancient Greek used in Arcadia.

Ar·ca·dy (är′kə-dē). See **Arcadia** (sense 1).

Arch·an·gel (ärk′ān′jəl). See **Arkhangelsk.**

ar·chi·pel·a·go (är′kə-pĕl′ə-gō′). *pl.* **-goes** or **-gos.** *abbr.* **arch. 1.** A large group of islands. **2.** A sea, such as the Aegean, containing a large number of scattered islands. — **ar′chi·pe·lag′·ic** (-pə-lăj′ĭk) *adj.*

Arc·tic (ärk′tĭk, är′tĭk). A region between the North Pole and the northern timberlines of North America and Eurasia. — **Arc′tic** *adj.*

Arctic Archipelago. A group of more than 50 large islands of Northwest Territories, Canada, in the Arctic Ocean between North America and Greenland.

Arctic Circle. The parallel of latitude approximately 66° 33′ north. It forms the boundary between the North Temperate and North Frigid zones.

Arctic Ocean. The waters surrounding the North Pole between North America and Eurasia. The smallest ocean in the world, it is covered by pack ice throughout the year.

Arctic Red River. A river rising in the Mackenzie Mountains of western Northwest Territories, Canada, and flowing about 499 km (310 mi) generally north-northwest to the Mackenzie River.

Ar·de·bil also **Ar·da·bil** (är′də-bēl′). A town of northwest Iran near the Caspian Sea. It was probably founded in the fifth century A.D. ⊛ Pop. 329,869.

Ar·den (är′dn). An unincorporated city of north-central California, a residential suburb of Sacramento. ⊛ Pop. 49,130.

Arden, Forest of. A wooded area, formerly very extensive, of central England west of Stratford-upon-Avon. It provided the setting for Shakespeare's *As You Like It.*

Ar·dennes (är-dĕn′). A plateau region of northern France, southeast Belgium, and northern Luxembourg east and south of the Meuse River. It was the scene of heavy fighting in World War I and World War II, notably during the Battle of the Bulge in December 1944 and January 1945.

Ard·more (ärd′môr, -mōr). A city of southern Oklahoma near the Texas border south-south-east of Oklahoma City. It is a commercial and industrial center. ⊛ Pop. 23,079.

A·re·ci·bo (ä′rə-sē′bō). A city of northern Puerto Rico on the Atlantic Ocean. It is a commercial and industrial center. ⊛ Pop. 48,779.

A·re·qui·pa (ăr′ə-kē′pə, ä′rĕ-kē′pä). A city of southern Peru at the foot of El Misti. Founded in 1540 on the site of an Incan village, it is the commercial center of southern Peru and northern Bolivia. ⊛ Pop. 624,500.

a·rête (ə-rāt′). A sharp, narrow mountain ridge or spur.

A·rez·zo (ä-rĕt′sō). A city of central Italy on the Arno River southeast of Florence. It was originally an Etruscan settlement and later a Roman military station and colony. ⊛ Pop. 91,535.

Ar·gen·teuil (är-zhäN-tœ′yə). A city of northern France, a residential and industrial suburb of Paris on the Seine River. It grew around a convent founded by Charlemagne in the seventh century. ⊛ Pop. 95,347.

Ar·gen·ti·na (är′jən-tē′nə). *abbr.* **Arg.** A country of southeast South America stretching about 3,701 km (2,300 mi) from its border with Bolivia to southern Tierra del Fuego, an island it shares with Chile. Europeans first explored the region in the early 1500's, and in 1776 Spain established a viceroyalty that included present-day Argentina, Uruguay, Paraguay, and Bolivia. Argentina achieved its independence from Spain in 1816, and alternated between constitutional government and extended periods of dictatorship, chiefly under Juan Manuel de Rosas (1829–1852) and Juan Domingo Perón (1946–1955). Argentina's failure to reclaim the Falkland Islands from Britain in 1982 contributed to considerable social and economic instability for the rest of the decade. Buenos Aires is the capital and the larg-

est city. ◉ Pop. 34,180,000. — **Ar·gen·tine**′ (-tēn′, -tīn′), **Ar·gen·tin**′**e·an** (-tĭn′ē-ən) *adj. & n.*

Ar·give (är′jīv′, -gīv′). **1.** Of or relating to Argos or the ancient region of Argolis. **2.** Of or relating to Greece or the Greeks. **3.** A Greek, especially an inhabitant of Argos or Argolis.

Ar·go·lis (är′gə-lĭs). An ancient region of southern Greece in the northeast Peloponnesus, dominated by the city of Argos.

Argolis, Gulf of. An inlet of the Aegean Sea on the eastern coast of the Peloponnesus in southern Greece.

Ar·gonne (är-gŏn′, är′gŏn). A wooded and hilly region of northeast France between the Meuse and Aisne rivers. The area was a major battleground during World War I.

Ar·gos (är′gŏs, -gəs). A city of ancient Greece in the northeast Peloponnesus near the head of the Gulf of Argolis. Inhabited from the early Bronze Age, it was one of the most powerful cities of ancient Greece until the rise of Sparta.

Ar·gun River (är-gōōn′) also **Er·gun He** (ĕr′-gōōn′ hĕ′, œr′gün′ hə′). A river of east-central Asia rising in northeast China and flowing about 1,529 km (950 mi) west then generally northeast along the Russia-China border.

Ǻr·hus also **Aar·hus** (ôr′hōōs′). A city of central Denmark, a commercial and industrial center on **Ǻrhus Bay**, an arm of the Kattegat. First mentioned in the mid-tenth century, it is one of the country's oldest cities. ◉ Pop. 250,404.

A·ri·ca (ə-rē′kə, ä-rē′kä). A city of northern Chile on the Pacific Ocean near the Peruvian border. Claimed by both Peru and Chile until 1929, it is a free port and popular resort. ◉ Pop. 177,330.

A·rik·a·ra (ə-rĭk′ər-ə). **1.** *pl.* **Arikara** or **-ras.** A member of a Native American people formerly inhabiting the Missouri River valley from Kansas into the Dakotas and now located in western North Dakota. Traditional Arikara life was based on agriculture and trade with the Plains Indians to the west. **2.** The Caddoan language of the Arikaras.

Ar·i·zo·na (ăr′ĭ-zō′nə). *abbr.* **AZ, Ariz.** A state of the southwest United States on the Mexican border. It was admitted as the 48th state in 1912. First explored by the Spanish in 1539, the area was acquired by the United States in 1848 through the Treaty of Guadalupe Hidalgo. Phoenix is the capital and the largest city. ◉ Pop. 3,677,985. — **Ar**′**i·zo**′**nan, Ar**′**i·zo**′**ni·an** *adj. & n.*

Ar·kan·sas (är′kən-sô′). *abbr.* **AR, Ark.** A state of the south-central United States bordered on the east by the Mississippi River. It was admitted as the 25th state in 1836. The region was first explored by members of Hernando de So-

to's expedition in 1541 and passed to the United States in 1803 as part of the Louisiana Purchase. Little Rock is the capital and the largest city. ◉ Pop. 2,362,239. — **Ar·kan**′**san** (är-kăn′-zən) *adj. & n.*

Ar·kan·sas River (är′kən-sô′, är-kăn′zəs). A river of the south-central United States rising in the Rocky Mountains in central Colorado and flowing about 2,333 km (1,450 mi) generally southeastward to the Mississippi River in southeast Arkansas. It was an important trade and travel route in the 19th century.

Ark·han·gelsk (är-kăn′gĕlsk, -кнän′-) or **Arch·an·gel** (ärk′ān′jəl). A city of northwest Russia on the Northern Dvina River near its mouth on the White Sea. Although icebound much of the year, it is a leading port and can generally be opened to navigation by icebreakers. ◉ Pop. 409,886.

Arl·berg (ärl′bûrg, -bĕrk). An Alpine pass, 1,813.5 m (5,946 ft) high, in western Austria. The rail tunnel crossing the pass was built in 1880–1884 and is 10 km (6.2 mi) long.

Arles (ärlz, ärl). **1.** A medieval kingdom of eastern and southeast France. It was formed in 933 and gradually split up after 1246. **2.** A city of south-central France on the Rhone River delta. A flourishing city in Roman times, it has an arena built in the second century A.D. that is now used for bullfights. ◉ Pop. 37,571.

Ar·ling·ton (är′lĭng-tən). **1.** A town of eastern Massachusetts, a residential suburb of Boston. ◉ Pop. 48,219. **2.** A city of northern Texas midway between Dallas and Fort Worth. It has a huge industrial park and is the site of the Pecan Bowl. ◉ Pop. 160,123. **3.** A county and unincorporated city of northern Virginia across the Potomac River from Washington, D.C. Mainly residential, it is the site of **Arlington National Cemetery,** where American war dead and other notables, including William Howard Taft and John F. Kennedy, are buried. The Tomb of the Unknown Soldier commemorates members of the Armed Forces who were killed in World War I, World War II, the Korean War, and the Vietnam War. ◉ Pop. 152,700.

Arlington Heights. A village of northeast Illinois, a manufacturing and residential suburb of Chicago. ◉ Pop. 75,460.

Ar·magh (är-mä′, är′mä′). An urban district of southern Northern Ireland. Reputedly founded by Saint Patrick (A.D. 389?–461?), it is the seat of both the Roman Catholic and Protestant primates of Ireland. ◉ Pop. 12,700.

Ar·ma·gnac (är′mən-yăk′). A historical region and former countship of southwest France in Gascony. Added to the French royal domain in 1607, the area is now noted for its viniculture.

Ar·me·ni·a[1] (är-mē′nē-ə, -mēn′yə). *abbr.* **Arm.**

1. A region and former kingdom of Asia Minor that included present-day Armenia and part of northeast Turkey and northwest Iran. Established in the 8th century B.C., it later came under Persian and Roman rule and was probably the first state to adopt Christianity as a national religion (c. A.D. 303). The Ottoman Turks invaded and held all of Armenia by the 16th century, but there were disputes over the eastern part, which Persia ceded to Russia in 1828. **2.** Formerly **Ar·me·ni·an Soviet Socialist Republic** (-mē′nē-ən, -mēn′yən). A country of Asia Minor east of Turkey and north of Iran. Acquired by Russia from Persia in 1828, it became a Soviet republic in 1921 and was a constituent republic of the U.S.S.R. from 1936 to 1991. Yerevan is the capital. ◉ Pop. 3,548,000.

Ar·me·nia[2] (är-mĕ′nē-ə, -nyə, -nyä). A city of west-central Colombia west of Bogotá. It is an industrial center and transportation hub. ◉ Pop. 192,409.

Ar·me·ni·an (är-mē′nē-ən, -mēn′yən). *abbr.* **Arm. 1.** Of or relating to Armenia or its people, language, or culture. **2. a.** A native or inhabitant of Armenia. **b.** A person of Armenian ancestry. **3.** The Indo-European language of the Armenians.

Armenian Soviet Socialist Republic. See **Armenia**[1] (sense 2).

Ar·men·tières (är′mən-tîrz′, -män-tyĕr′). A city of northern France west-northwest of Lille. It became known through the World War I song "Mademoiselle from Armentières." ◉ Pop. 24,834.

Ar·mi·jo (är-mē′hō). A community of central New Mexico, a suburb of Albuquerque. ◉ Pop. 18,900.

Ar·mor·ic (är-môr′ĭk, -mŏr′-) also **Ar·mor·i·can** (-ĭ-kən). **1.** Of or relating to the ancient region of Armorica or to its people, language, or culture. **2.** A native or inhabitant of Armorica. **3.** See **Breton** (sense 3).

Ar·mor·i·ca (är-môr′ĭ-kə, -mŏr′-). An ancient and literary name for the northwest part of France, especially Brittany.

Arn·hem (ärn′hĕm′, är′nəm). A city of eastern Netherlands on the lower Rhine River east-southeast of Utrecht. In World War II British airborne troops suffered a major defeat here in September 1944. ◉ Pop. 133,471.

Arn·hem Land (är′nəm). A region of northern Australia west of the Gulf of Carpentaria. The country's largest aboriginal reservation is here.

Ar·no (är′nō). A river of central Italy rising in the northern Apennines and flowing about 241 km (150 mi) to the Ligurian Sea. Flooding of the Arno has caused severe damage to art treasures in Florence.

Ar·nold (är′nəld). A city of eastern Missouri, a suburb of St. Louis. ◉ Pop. 18,828.

Arns·berg (ärnz′bərg, ärns′bĕrk). A city of west-central Germany south-southeast of Münster. It was founded in 1077 and received a municipal charter in 1237. ◉ Pop. 75,135.

A·roe Islands (ä′rōō). See **Aru Islands**.

A·roos·took (ə-rōōs′tək, -rōōs′-). A river rising in northern Maine and flowing about 225 km (140 mi) generally eastward to the St. John River in New Brunswick, Canada.

Ar·ran (ăr′ən). A granite island of western Scotland in the Firth of Clyde. It is a resort area noted for its scenery and its hunting and fishing.

Ar·ras (ăr′əs, ə-räs′). A city of northern France south-southwest of Lille. It was a famous woolen and tapestry center in the Middle Ages. ◉ Pop. 41,736.

Ar·roe Islands (ä′rōō). See **Aru Islands**.

ar·ron·disse·ment (ä-rôn′dēs-mäN′). **1.** The chief administrative subdivision of a department in France. **2.** A municipal subdivision in some large French cities.

ar·roy·o (ə-roi′ō). *pl.* **-os. 1.** A deep gully cut by an intermittent stream; a dry gulch. **2.** A brook; a creek.

Ar·tois (är-twä′). A historical region and former province of northern France near the English Channel between Picardy and Flanders. It was ruled at various times by Flanders, Burgundy, Austria, and Spain.

A·ru·ba (ə-rōō′bə). An island of the Netherlands Antilles north of the Venezuela coast. It is a popular Caribbean resort area.

A·ru Islands also **A·roe Islands** or **Ar·roe Islands** (ä′rōō). An island group of eastern Indonesia, part of the Moluccas in the Arafura Sea southwest of New Guinea. The islands were colonized by the Dutch after 1623.

A·ru·wi·mi (är′ə-wē′mē, är′-). A river of central Africa rising in northeast Zaire near Lake Albert and flowing about 1,287 km (800 mi) generally westward to the Congo River.

Ar·vad·a (är-văd′ə). A city of north-central Colorado, a residential suburb of Denver. ◉ Pop. 89,235.

Ar·y·an (âr′ē-ən, ăr′-). **1.** See **Indo-Iranian.** **2.** A member of the people who spoke the parent language of the Indo-European languages. **3.** A member of any people speaking an Indo-European language. **4.** Of or relating to Indo-Iranian. **5.** Of or relating to the Indo-European languages or the hypothetical language from which they are derived. **6.** Of or relating to a speaker of an Indo-European language.

A·sa·hi·ka·wa (ä′sə-hē-kä′wə, ä′sä-hē′kä-wä) also **A·sa·hi·ga·wa** (ä′sə-hē-gä′wə, ä′sä-hē′gä-wä). A city of west-central Hokkaido, Japan. It is the commercial, industrial, and transportation center of a fertile agricultural area. ◉ Pop. 362,176.

A·sa·ma (ə-sä′mə), **Mount.** A volcano, 2,543.7 m (8,340 ft) high, of central Honshu, Japan, near Nagano. One of the largest volcanoes in Japan, it erupted violently in 1783.

A·san·te (ə-sän′tē). Variant of **Ashanti**[1].

As·bur·y Park (ăz′bĕr′ē, -bə-rē). A city of eastern New Jersey on the Atlantic Ocean. It is a popular resort. ◉ Pop. 16,799.

As·cen·sion Island (ə-sĕn′shən). An island in the southern Atlantic northwest of St. Helena. Discovered by the Portuguese on Ascension Day in 1501, it was taken by the British in 1815 and has been administered by St. Helena since 1922.

A·schaf·fen·burg (ä-shä′fən-bərg, -bo͞ork′). A city of west-central Germany on the Main River. Once the site of a Roman garrison, it became part of Bavaria in 1814. ◉ Pop. 59,088.

A·sco·li Pi·ce·no (ä′skə-lē pĭ-chĕn′ō). A city of central Italy northeast of Rome. It has extensive Roman ruins. ◉ Pop. 54,193.

As·cot (ăs′kət). A village of south-central England southwest of London. The Royal Ascot horse races, initiated by Queen Anne in 1711, are held annually in June on Ascot Heath.

As·cu·lum (ăs′kyə-ləm). An ancient Roman town of southeast Italy south of present-day Foggia. Pyrrhus of Epirus defeated a Roman force here in 279 B.C. but suffered a heavy loss of troops.

A·shan·ti[1] (ə-shăn′tē, ə-shän′-) also **A·san·te** (-sän′tē). **1.** pl. **Ashanti** or **-tis** also **Asante** or **-tes.** A member of an Akan people of Ghana, formerly united in the Ashanti kingdom. **2.** The Twi language of the Ashantis.

A·shan·ti[2] (ə-shăn′tē, -shän′-). A region and former kingdom of western Africa in present-day central Ghana. The powerful Ashanti confederation of states, formed in the late 17th century, was defeated by the British in 1896 and annexed to the British Gold Coast colony in 1901.

Ash·dod (ăsh′dŏd′, äsh-dōd′). A city of southwest Israel on the Mediterranean Sea west of Jerusalem near the site of ancient **Ashdod,** an important Philistine city-state that was settled as early as the Bronze Age. ◉ Pop. 68,900.

Ashe·bor·o (ăsh′bûr-ō′, -bûr-ō). A city of central North Carolina in the Piedmont south of Greensboro. It is a manufacturing center. ◉ Pop. 15,252.

Ashe·ville (ăsh′vĭl′). A city of western North Carolina in the Blue Ridge west-northwest of Charlotte. A popular tourist center, it is the site of the writer Thomas Wolfe's home and of Biltmore, a magnificent mansion with extensive parks and gardens built by George Washington Vanderbilt. ◉ Pop. 61,607.

Ash·ke·lon (ăsh′kə-lŏn′, äsh′kĕ-lôn′). See **Ashqelon.**

Ash·ke·naz·i (äsh′kə-nä′zē) pl. **-naz·im** (-năz′-ĭm, -nä′zĭm). A member of the branch of European Jews, historically Yiddish-speaking, who settled in central and northern Europe as distinguished from the Sephardim of Spain and Portugal. —**Ash′ke·naz′ic** (-nä′zĭk) adj.

Ash·kha·bad (äsh′kä-bäd′, -кнä-bät′). The capital of Turkmenistan, in the south-central part of the country. It was founded as a fortress in 1881. A major earthquake in 1948 virtually destroyed the old city. ◉ Pop. 407,000.

Ash·land (ăsh′lənd). **1.** A city of northeast Kentucky on the Ohio–West Virginia border. Settled in 1786, it is a shipping point with varied industries. ◉ Pop. 23,622. **2.** A city of north-central Ohio southeast of Cleveland. It is a manufacturing center in an agricultural region. ◉ Pop. 20,079.

Ash·qe·lon or **Ash·ke·lon** (ăsh′kə-lŏn′, äsh′kĕ-lôn′). An ancient city of southwest Palestine on the Mediterranean Sea. Inhabited as early as the third millennium B.C., it was a seat of worship for the goddess Astarte.

Ash·ta·bu·la (ăsh′tə-byo͞o′lə). A city of northeast Ohio on Lake Erie northeast of Cleveland. It is an industrial center in an agricultural region. ◉ Pop. 21,633.

Ash·ton-un·der-Lyne (ăsh′tən-ŭn-dər-līn′). A borough of northwest England, an industrial suburb of Manchester. ◉ Pop. 218,800.

A·sia (ā′zhə, ā′shə). abbr. **As.** The world's largest continent. It occupies the eastern part of the Eurasian landmass and its adjacent islands and is separated from Europe by the Ural Mountains.

Asia Mi·nor (mī′nər). A peninsula of western Asia between the Black Sea and the Mediterranean Sea. It is generally coterminous with Asian Turkey and is usually considered synonymous with Anatolia.

A·sian (ā′zhən, ā′shən). abbr. **As. 1.** Of or relating to Asia or its peoples, languages, or cultures. **2.** A native or inhabitant of Asia. **3.** A person of Asian descent.

Asian American . A U.S. citizen or resident of Asian descent.

A·si·at·ic (ā'zhē-ăt'ĭk, -shē-, -zē-). Asian.

As·ma·ra (ăz-mä'rə). The capital of Eritrea, in the western part of the country at an altitude of about 2,227 m (7,300 ft). It was used as a base for the Italian invasion of Ethiopia (1935–1936). ◉ Pop. 358,100.

As·nières-sur-Seine (ä-nyĕr'sür-sān', -sĕn'). A city of north-central France, a residential suburb of Paris. ◉ Pop. 71,077.

A·so (ä'sō'), **Mount** also **A·so-san** (ä'sō-sän'). A volcanic mountain of central Kyushu, Japan. It is topped by one of the world's largest calderas, containing five volcanic cones, one of which is active. The highest cone rises to 1,593 m (5,223 ft).

As·pen (ăs'pən). A city of west-central Colorado in the Sawatch Range of the Rocky Mountains. Founded c. 1879 by silver prospectors, it is now a fashionable ski resort. ◉ Pop. 5,049.

As·sam (ă-săm'). A former kingdom of extreme northeast India, now a state separated from the rest of the country by Bangladesh. The kingdom was founded by invaders from Burma and China in the 13th century.

As·sam·ese (ăs'ə-mēz', -mēs'). **1.** Of or relating to Assam or its people, language, or culture. **2.** pl. **Assamese.** A native or inhabitant of Assam. **3.** The Indic language of the Assamese.

As·sa·teague Island (ăs'ə-tēg'). A long narrow island along the coast of Maryland and Virginia separating Chincoteague Bay from the Atlantic Ocean. It is a popular resort area.

As·sin·i·boin also **As·sin·i·boine** (ə-sĭn'ə-boin'). **1.** pl. **Assiniboin** or **-boins** also **Assiniboine** or **-boines.** A member of a Native American people formerly inhabiting southern Manitoba, now located in Montana, Alberta, and Saskatchewan. The Assiniboin became nomadic buffalo hunters after migrating to the northern Great Plains in the 18th century. **2.** The Siouan language of the Assiniboins. — **As·sin'i·boin'** adj.

Assiniboine . A river of south-central Canada rising in southeast Saskatchewan and flowing about 949 km (590 mi) generally southeastward and then eastward to the Red River at Winnipeg, Manitoba. Its valley is one of Canada's leading wheat-growing areas.

Assiniboine , Mount. A mountain, 3,620.4 m (11,870 ft) high, in the Canadian Rocky Mountains on the Alberta–British Columbia border near Banff.

As·si·si (ə-sē'zē, -sē, ə-sĭs'ē). A town of central Italy east-southeast of Perugia. Saint Francis of Assisi was born here in 1182 and died here

in 1226. The town is a religious and tourist center. ◉ Pop. 19,000.

As·syr·i·a (ə-sîr'ē-ə). An ancient empire and civilization of western Asia in the upper valley of the Tigris River. In its zenith between the ninth and seventh centuries B.C. the empire extended from the Mediterranean Sea across Arabia and Armenia.

As·syr·i·an (ə-sîr'ē-ən). abbr. **Assyr. 1.** Of or relating to Assyria or its people, language, or culture. **2.** A native or inhabitant of Assyria. **3.** See **Akkadian** (sense 2). **4.** The Assyrian dialects of Akkadian.

As·ti (ä'stē). A city of northwest Italy southeast of Turin. It is noted for its sparkling wines. ◉ Pop. 76,950.

As·to·ri·a (ă-stôr'ē-ə, -stōr'-). A city of northwest Oregon northwest of Portland near the mouth of the Columbia River. Fort Astoria, a fur-trading post established in 1811 by John Jacob Astor's Pacific Fur Company, was the first permanent American settlement along the Pacific coast. ◉ Pop. 9,998.

As·tra·khan (ăs'trə-kăn', ä-strä-кнän'). A city of southwest Russia on the Volga River delta. The Tartar city was conquered by Ivan the Terrible in 1556. ◉ Pop. 507,710.

as·tro·bleme (ăs'trə-blēm', -blēm'). A scar on the earth's surface left from the impact of a meteorite.

As·tu·ri·as (ăs-tŏor'ē-əs, -tyŏor'-, äs-tōo'-ryäs). A region and former kingdom of northwest Spain south of the Bay of Biscay. The original Iberian inhabitants were conquered by Rome in the second century B.C. — **As·tu'ri·an** adj. & n.

A·sun·ción (ä-sōon'syôn'). The capital and largest city of Paraguay, in the southern part of the country on the Paraguay River. It is Paraguay's chief port and industrial center. ◉ Pop. 546,637.

As·wan (ăs'wän, ăs-wän', äs-). A city of southern Egypt at the First Cataract of the Nile River near the **Aswan High Dam.** Construction of the dam, dedicated in 1971, required the relocation of some 90,000 people and numerous archaeological treasures. The city's population is 220,000.

As·yut (ä-syŏot'). A city of east-central Egypt on the Nile River. It is an industrial and trade center. ◉ Pop. 321,000.

At·a·ca·ma Desert (ăt'ə-kăm'ə, ä'tä-kä'mä). An arid region of northwest Chile. One of the driest areas in the world, it has yielded great nitrate and copper wealth.

A·tas·ca·de·ro (ə-tăs'kə-dâr'ō, ə-täs'-). An unincorporated community of southwest California north of San Luis Obispo. It was founded in 1913 as a model community. ◉ Pop. 23,138.

At·ba·ra (ăt′bər-ə, ät′-). A river of northeast Africa rising in northwest Ethiopia and flowing about 805 km (500 mi) to the Nile River in eastern Sudan.

A·tchaf·a·lay·a (ə-chăf′ə-lī′ə). A river of south-central Louisiana flowing about 362 km (225 mi) into **Atchafalaya Bay,** an inlet of the Gulf of Mexico.

At·chi·son (ăch′ĭ-sən). A city of northeast Kansas northwest of Kansas City. The city was an important outfitting point for westward travelers, especially after the foundation of the Atchison, Topeka, and Santa Fe Railroad in 1859. ⦾ Pop. 10,656.

Ath·a·bas·ca or **Ath·a·bas·ka** (ăth′ə-băs′kə). A river rising in the Rocky Mountains of southwest Alberta, Canada, and flowing about 1,231 km (765 mi) east and north to **Lake Athabasca** on the border of northern Alberta and Saskatchewan. The river and lake are important constituents of the Mackenzie River system.

Ath·a·bas·kan or **Ath·a·bas·can** (ăth′ə-băs′-kən) also **Ath·a·pas·can** (-păs′-). **1.** A group of related North American Indian languages including the Apachean languages and languages of Alaska, northwest Canada, and coastal Oregon and California. **2.** A member of an Athabaskan-speaking people. —**Ath′a·bas′kan** adj.

Ath·ens (ăth′ənz). **1.** The capital and largest city of Greece, in the eastern part of the country near the Saronic Gulf. It was at the height of its cultural achievements and imperial power in the fifth century B.C. during the time of Pericles. Athens became the capital of modern Greece in 1834, two years after the country achieved its independence from Turkey. ⦾ Pop. 885,737. **2.** A city of northeast Georgia east-northeast of Atlanta. It was founded in 1785 as the site of the University of Georgia (established 1801). ⦾ Pop. 45,734. **3.** A city of southeast Ohio in the foothills of the Appalachian Mountains west of Marietta. Settled c. 1797, it is a processing and manufacturing center. ⦾ Pop. 21,265.

Ath·os (ăth′ŏs, ā′thŏs, ä′thôs), **Mount.** A peak, about 2,034 m (6,670 ft) high, of northeast Greece. It is the site of the virtually independent monastic community of **Mount Athos,** originally founded in the tenth century.

A·ti·tlán (ä′tē-tlän′). A volcanic lake of southwest Guatemala. Among the lofty mountains nearby are three extinct volcanoes, including **Atitlán,** rising to 3,539.2 m (11,604 ft).

At·ka Island (ăt′kə, ät′-). An island of southwest Alaska in the Andreanof group of the central Aleutian Islands. It was the site of a major U.S. military base during World War II.

At·lan·ta (ăt-lăn′tə). The capital and largest city of Georgia, in the northwest part of the state. It was founded in 1837 at the end of the railroad line as Terminus and renamed Atlanta in 1845. Almost entirely burned on November 15, 1864, before the start of Union general William Tecumseh Sherman's march to the sea, the city was rapidly rebuilt and became the permanent state capital in 1877. ⦾ Pop. 394,017. —**At·lan′tan** n.

At·lan·tic (ăt-lăn′tĭk). abbr. **Atl. 1.** Of, in, near, upon, or relating to the Atlantic Ocean. **2.** Of, on, near, or relating to the eastern coast of the United States. **3.** Of or concerning countries bordering the Atlantic Ocean, especially those of Europe and North America.

Atlantic City. A city of southeast New Jersey on the Atlantic Ocean. It is a popular resort and convention center with a famous boardwalk. Legalized gambling was introduced in 1978. ⦾ Pop. 437,986.

Atlantic Intracoastal Waterway. A system of inland waterways including rivers, bays, and canals along the Atlantic coast of the United States. It extends from Cape Cod to southern Florida and forms part of the Intracoastal Waterway that affords protected passage from Massachusetts to southern Texas.

Atlantic Ocean. The world's second-largest ocean, divided into the **North Atlantic** and the **South Atlantic.** The Atlantic Ocean extends from the Arctic in the north to the Antarctic in the south between the eastern Americas and western Europe and Africa.

Atlantic Provinces. The eastern Canadian provinces of New Brunswick, Prince Edward Island, Nova Scotia, and Newfoundland.

Atlantic Standard Time. Standard time in the fourth time zone west of Greenwich, England, reckoned at 60° west and used, for example, in Puerto Rico and the Canadian Maritime Provinces. Also called Atlantic Time.

At·lan·tis (ăt-lăn′tĭs). Mythology. A legendary island in the Atlantic Ocean west of Gibraltar, said by Plato to have sunk beneath the sea during an earthquake.

at·las (ăt′ləs). pl. **-las·es.** A book or bound collection of maps, sometimes with supplementary illustrations and graphic analyses.

At·las Mountains (ăt′ləs). A system of ranges and plateaus of northwest Africa extending from southwest Morocco to northern Tunisia between the Sahara Desert and the Mediterranean Sea and rising to 4,167.8 m (13,665 ft).

a·toll (ăt′ôl′, -ŏl′, ā′tôl′, ā′tŏl′). A ringlike coral island and reef that nearly or entirely encloses a lagoon.

At·si·na (ăt-sē′nə). **1.** pl. **Atsina** or **-nas.** A member of a Native American people formerly inhabiting the plains of northern Montana and southern Saskatchewan, with a present-day population in north central Montana. **2.** The Algonquian language of the Atsinas, dialectally related to Arapaho. Also called *Gros Ventre.*

At·ta·wa·pis·kat (ăt′ə-wə-pĭs′kət). A river, about 748 km (465 mi) long, of northern Ontario, Canada, flowing from **Attawapiskat Lake** east and northeast into James Bay.

At·tic (ăt′ĭk). **1.** Of, relating to, or characteristic of ancient Attica, Athens, or the Athenians. **2.** The ancient Greek dialect of Attica, in which the bulk of classical Greek literature is written.

At·ti·ca (ăt′ĭ-kə). An ancient region of east-central Greece surrounding Athens. According to Greek mythology, the four Attic tribes were unified into a single state by the Athenian king Theseus.

At·tle·bor·o (ăt′l-bûr′ō, -bŭr′ō). A city of southeast Massachusetts northeast of Providence, Rhode Island. Its jewelry industry began in 1780. ⊛ Pop. 38,383.

At·tu (ăt′tōō′). An island of southwest Alaska, the westernmost of the Aleutians. In World War II it was occupied by the Japanese from June 1942 until June 1943.

At·wa·ter (ăt′wô′tər, -wŏt′ər). A city of central California west-northwest of Merced. It is a commercial center in an irrigated farming area. ⊛ Pop. 22,282.

Aube (ōb). A river of northeast France flowing about 225 km (140 mi) to the Seine River northnorthwest of Troyes.

Au·ber·vil·liers (ō′bər-vēl-yā′). A town of north-central France northeast of Paris. It is an important industrial center. ⊛ Pop. 67,719.

Au·burn (ô′bərn). **1.** A city of eastern Alabama north-northeast of Tuskegee. It is the seat of Auburn University (founded 1856). ⊛ Pop. 33,830. **2.** A city of southern Maine on the Androscoggin River opposite Lewiston. It was settled in 1765. ⊛ Pop. 24,309. **3.** A city of west-central New York in the Finger Lakes region west-southwest of Syracuse. Founded in 1793, it is a manufacturing center. ⊛ Pop. 31,258. **4.** A city of western Washington east-northeast of Tacoma. It is a center of the state's aircraft industry. ⊛ Pop. 33,102.

Auck·land (ôk′lənd). The largest city of New Zealand, on an isthmus of northwest North Island. It is a major port and an industrial center. ⊛ Pop. 316,900.

Augs·burg (ôgz′bûrg′, ouks′bōork′). A city of southern Germany west-northwest of Munich. Founded by Augustus as a Roman garrison c. 14 B.C., it was a major commercial and banking center in the 15th and 16th centuries. ⊛ Pop. 264,764.

Au·gus·ta (ô-gŭs′tə, ə-gŭs′-). **1.** A city of eastern Georgia on the South Carolina border north-northwest of Savannah. It is a popular re-sort known especially for its golf tournaments. ⊛ Pop. 44,639. **2.** The capital of Maine, in the southwest part of the state on the Kennebec River north-northeast of Portland. A trading post was established here in 1628. ⊛ Pop. 21,325.

Au·lis (ô′lĭs). An ancient port of east-central Greece in Boeotia. According to tradition, it was the embarkation point for the Greek fleet during the Trojan War.

Aul·nay-sous-Bois (ō-nä′sōō-bwä′). A town of north-central France, a suburb of Paris. ⊛ Pop. 75,996.

Au·nis (ō-nēs′). A historical region and former province of western France on the Atlantic Ocean. A part of Aquitaine, it was recovered from England in 1373 and incorporated into the French crown lands.

Au·rang·a·bad (ou-rŭng′gə-bäd′, -ə-bäd′). A town of western India east-northeast of Bombay. Founded in 1610, it is near the site of a mausoleum erected by the Mogul emperor Aurangzeb in honor of his empress. ⊛ Pop. 573,272.

Au·ri·gnac (ô′rēn-yäk′). A village of southern France at the foot of the Pyrenees. It is the site of caves containing prehistoric relics.

Au·ro·ra (ô-rôr′ə, ô-rōr′ə, ə-rôr′ə, ə-rōr′ə). **1.** A town of southern Ontario, Canada, north of Toronto. It is a manufacturing center. ⊛ Pop. 16,267. **2.** A city of north-central Colorado, a residential suburb of Denver. ⊛ Pop. 222,103. **3.** A city of northeast Illinois on the Fox River west of Chicago. It is an industrial center and was one of the first U.S. cities to use electricity for street lighting. ⊛ Pop. 99,581.

Ausch·witz (oush′vĭts′). See **Oświęcim.**

Aus·sie (ô′sē, ô′zē). *Informal.* A native or inhabitant of Australia. —**Aus′sie** *adj.*

Aus·ter·litz (ô′stər-lĭts′, ous′tər-). A town of southeast Czech Republic. Nearby, on December 2, 1805, Napoleon decisively defeated the Russian and Austrian armies of Czar Alexander I and Emperor Francis II.

Aus·tin (ô′stən, ŏs′tən). **1.** A city of southeast Minnesota near the Iowa border southwest of Rochester. It is a processing and manufacturing center. ⊛ Pop. 21,907. **2.** The capital of Texas, in the south-central part of the state. Austin was selected as the capital of the Republic of Texas in 1839 and became the permanent capital of the state of Texas in 1870. The main campus of the University of Texas (established 1881) is here. ⊛ Pop. 465,622.

Aus·tin·town (ô′stən-toun′). A community of northeast Ohio, a suburb of Youngstown. ⊛ Pop. 32,371.

Aus·tral·a·sia (ô′strə-lā′zhə, -shə). **1.** The islands of the southern Pacific Ocean, including

Australia, New Zealand, and New Guinea. **2.** Broadly, all of Oceania. **—Aus'tral·a'sian** *adj.* & *n.*

Aus·tra·lia (ô-strāl'yə). *abbr.* **Aus., Aust., Austl. 1.** The world's smallest continent, southeast of Asia between the Pacific and Indian oceans. **2.** A commonwealth comprising the continent of Australia, the island state of Tasmania, two external territories, and several dependencies. The first British settlement, a penal colony at Fort Jackson (now part of Sydney), was established in 1788. The present-day states grew as separate colonies; six of them formed a federation in 1901. In 1911 Northern Territory joined the commonwealth and the Capital Territory, site of Canberra, was created. Canberra is the capital and Sydney is the largest city. ⊛ Pop. 17,843,000.

Aus·tra·lian (ô-strāl'yən). *abbr.* **Aus., Aust., Austl. 1.** Of or relating to Australia or its peoples, languages, or cultures. **2.** *Ecology.* Of, relating to, or being the zoogeographic region that includes Australia and the islands adjacent to it, including New Guinea, New Zealand, Polynesia, and Tasmania. **3.** A native or inhabitant of Australia. **4.** A member of any of the aboriginal peoples of Australia. **5.** Any of the languages of the aboriginal peoples of Australia.

Australian Alps. A chain of mountain ranges of southeast Australia in the southern part of the Great Dividing Range. Mount Kosciusko, rising to 2,231.4 m (7,316 ft), is the highest elevation and the tallest peak in Australia.

Australian Antarctic Territory. A large section of Antarctica claimed by Australia since 1931. It extends from longitude 45° east to longitude 160° east not including Adélie Coast. The claim is disputed by the United States.

Aus·tra·loid (ô'strə-loid'). *Anthropology.* Of, relating to, or being a proposed human racial division traditionally distinguished by physical characteristics such as dark skin and dark curly hair, and including the aboriginal peoples of Australia along with various peoples of southeast

Asia, especially Melanesia and the Malay Archipelago. **—Aus'tra·loid'** *n.*

Aus·tra·sia (ô-strā'zhə, -shə). The eastern portion of the kingdom of the Franks from the sixth to the eighth century, including parts of eastern France, western Germany, and the Netherlands. It eventually became part of the Carolingian Empire. **—Aus·tra'sian** *adj.* & *n.*

Aus·tri·a (ô'strē-ə). *abbr.* **Aus., Aust.** A landlocked country of central Europe. A Roman and Carolingian territory, it was later a powerful empire ruled by the Hapsburg family. The empire was broken up in 1918, and the republic of Austria was annexed by Adolf Hitler in 1938. Full sovereignty was restored in 1955. Vienna is the capital and the largest city. ⊛ Pop. 8,031,000. **—Aus'tri·an** *adj.* & *n.*

Aus·tri·a-Hun·ga·ry (ô'strē-ə-hŭng'gə-rē). A former dual monarchy of central Europe consisting of Austria, Hungary, Bohemia, and parts of Poland, Romania, Slovenia, Croatia, and Italy. It was formed in 1867 after agitation by Hungarian nationalists within the Austrian empire and lasted until 1918. **—Aus'tro-Hun·gar'i·an** (ô'strō-hŭng-gâr'ē-ən) *adj.* & *n.*

Aus·tro-A·si·at·ic (ô'strō-ā'zhē-ăt'ĭk, -shē-, -zē-). A family of languages of southeast Asia once dominant in northeast India and Indochina, including Mon-Khmer and Munda. **—Aus'tro-A'si·at'ic** *adj.*

Aus·tro·ne·sia (ô'strō-nē'zhə, -shə). The islands of the Pacific Ocean, including Indonesia, Melanesia, Micronesia, and Polynesia.

Aus·tro·ne·sian (ô'strō-nē'zhən, -shən). **1.** Of or relating to Austronesia or its peoples, languages, or cultures. **2.** A family of languages that includes the Formosan, Indonesian, Malay, Melanesian, Micronesian, and Polynesian subfamilies.

Au·teuil (ō-toi', ō-tœ'yə). A former town between the Seine River and the Bois de Boulogne, now part of Paris. It was a favorite gathering place for French literary figures, including Molière and La Fontaine.

Au·vergne (ō-vûrn', ō-věrn'). A historical region and former province of central France traversed north to south by the **Auvergne Mountains,** a chain of extinct volcanoes. Auvergne became part of the French royal domain in 1615.

Av·a·lon Peninsula (ăv'ə-lŏn'). A large, irregularly shaped peninsula of southeast Newfoundland, Canada. Most of the province's population resides here.

A·vel·la·ne·da (ä-věl'yä-ně'dä, ä-vě'yä-, ä-vě'zhä-ně'*th*ä). A city of eastern Argentina near Buenos Aires. It is an important commercial and industrial center. ◉ Pop. 346,620.

A·vel·li·no (ä'věl-lē'nô). A city of southern Italy east-northeast of Naples. Although damaged by an earthquake in 1930, the old city retains much of its medieval aspect. ◉ Pop. 56,120.

Av·en·tine (ăv'ən-tīn', -tēn'). One of the seven hills of ancient Rome. It was turned over to the plebes, or common people, for settlement in 456 B.C. — **Av'en·tine'** *adj.*

A·ver·no (ä-věr'nō). Ancient name **A·ver·nus** (ə-vûr'nəs). A small crater lake of southern Italy near the Tyrrhenian Sea west of Naples. Because of its gloomy aspect and intense sulfuric vapors, now extinguished, the ancient Romans regarded it as the entrance to the underworld.

A·ver·sa (ä-věr'sä). A city of southern Italy near Naples. It is known for its sparkling white wines. ◉ Pop. 50,525.

A·ves·tan (ə-věs'tən). **1.** The eastern dialect of Old Iranian, in which the Avesta, a sacred text of Zoroastrianism, is written. **2.** Of or relating to the Avesta or Avestan.

A·vi·gnon (ä-vē-nyôn'). A city of southeast France on the Rhone River. It was the seat of the papacy from 1309 to 1378 and the residence of several antipopes from 1378 to 1417. ◉ Pop. 89,132.

Á·vi·la (ä'və-lə, ä'vē-lä). A town of central Spain west-northwest of Madrid. It is a religious and tourist center. ◉ Pop. 42,165.

A·vi·lés (ä'və-lās', ä'vē-lěs'). A town of northwest Spain on an inlet of the Bay of Biscay. It is a port and an industrial center. ◉ Pop. 89,992.

A·von (ā'vŏn, ā'vən, ăv'ən) also **Upper Avon.** A river of south-central England flowing 154.5 km (96 mi) to the Severn. It is known for its associations with Shakespeare.

A·wa·ji (ə-wä'jē) or **A·wa·ji·shi·ma** (ə-wä'jē-shē'mə). An island of Japan in the Inland Sea between southwest Honshu and Shikoku.

A·wash River (ä'wäsh') also **Ha·wash River** (hä'-). A river of eastern Ethiopia flowing about 805 km (500 mi) generally northeast to the Danakil Desert.

Ax·el Hei·berg (ăk'səl hī'bûrg'). An island of northern Northwest Territories, Canada, in the Arctic Ocean west of Ellesmere Island.

ax·is (ăk'sĭs). *pl.* **ax·es** (ăk'sēz'). *abbr.* **ax. 1.** A straight line about which a body or geometric object rotates or may be conceived to rotate. **2. a.** An alliance of powers, such as nations, to promote mutual interests and policies. **b. Axis.** The alliance of Germany and Italy in 1936, later including Japan and other nations, that opposed the Allies in World War II.

Ax·um (ăk'sōōm'). See **Aksum.**

Ayl·mer (āl'mər). A town of southwest Quebec, Canada, on the Ottawa River west of Hull. It is a resort community. ◉ Pop. 26,695.

Ay·ma·ra (ī'mä-rä', ī'mə-). **1.** *pl.* **Aymara** or **-ras.** A member of a South American Indian people inhabiting parts of highland Bolivia and Peru. **2.** The Aymaran language of the Aymaras.

Ay·ma·ran (ī'mä-rän'). **1.** A subgroup of the Quechumaran languages, the most important language being Aymara. **2.** Of or relating to the Aymaras or their language or culture.

Ayr (âr). A burgh of southwest Scotland at the mouth of the **Ayr River** on the Firth of Clyde. It is a resort and a fishing port. ◉ Pop. 48,600.

A·yut·thay·a (ä-yōō'tə-yä'). A city of south-central Thailand on an island in the Chao Phraya River north of Bangkok. It was founded c. 1350 and was the capital of a Siamese kingdom until 1767, when it was destroyed by the Burmese. ◉ Pop. 55,319.

A·za·ni·a (ə-zā'nē-ə, ə-zän'yə). South Africa. The term is often used by Black African nationalists. — **A·za'ni·an** *adj. & n.*

A·zer·bai·jan (ăz'ər-bī-jän', ä'zər-). *abbr.* **Azer., Azerb. 1.** A historical region in present-day northwest Iran and the country of Azerbaijan. It was settled by the Medes before the 8th century B.C. and later became a province of the Persian Empire. It became a separate kingdom after the death of Alexander the Great, but the region was much disputed and eventually conquered by Arabs (7th century), Turks (10th century), and Mongols (13th century). Persia (Iran) controlled the region after 1603. **2.** Formerly **Azerbaijan Soviet Socialist Republic** or **A·zer·bai·dzhan Soviet Socialist Republic** (ăz'ər-bī-

jän, ä′zər-). A country of Transcaucasia north of Iran. It constitutes the northern part of the historical region of Azerbaijan, which was ceded to Russia by Persia in 1813 and 1828. It was a constituent republic of the U.S.S.R. from 1936 to 1991. Baku is the capital. ◉ Pop. 7,472,000.

A·zer·bai·ja·ni (ăz′ər-bī-jä′nē, äz′ər-). **1.** Of or relating to Azerbaijan or its people, language, or culture. **2.** *pl.* **Azerbaijani** or **-nis.** A native or inhabitant of Azerbaijan. **3.** The Turkic language of Azerbaijan.

az·i·muth·al e·qui·dis·tant projection (ăz′-ə-mŭth′əl ē′kwĭ-dĭs′tənt, ĕk′wĭ-). A map projection of the earth designed so that a straight line from the central point on the map to any other point gives the shortest distance between the two points.

A·zores (ā′zôrz, ä′zōrz, ə-zôrz′, ə-zōrz′) also **A·ço·res** (ä-sôr′ĕsh). A group of volcanic islands in the northern Atlantic Ocean about 1,448 km (900 mi) west of mainland Portugal, of which they are administrative districts. Fishing, farming, and tourism are important to their economy. — **A·zor′e·an, A·zor′i·an** *adj. & n.*

A·zov (ăz′ôf, ä′zôf, ə-zôf′), **Sea of.** The northern arm of the Black Sea between southwest Russia and southeast Ukraine. The shallow sea has important fisheries.

Az·tec (ăz′tĕk′). **1.** A member of a people of central Mexico whose civilization was at its height at the time of the Spanish conquest in the early 16th century. **2.** The Nahuatl language of the Aztecs. **3.** also **Az·tec·an** (-tĕk′ən). Of or relating to the Aztecs or their language, culture, or empire.

A·zu·sa (ə-zōō′sə). A city of southern California east of Pasadena. It is a residential and industrial center in a citrus-growing region. ◉ Pop. 41,333.

B

Baal·bek (bäl′bĕk′, bā′əl-). Formerly **He·li·op·o·lis** (hē′lē-ŏp′ə-lĭs). A town of eastern Lebanon northeast of Beirut. It is the site of an ancient Phoenician city probably devoted to the worship of Baal and is now noted for its extensive Roman ruins. ◉ Pop. 24,000.

Ba·bel (bā′bəl, băb′əl). In the Bible, a city (now thought to be Babylon) in Shinar where construction of a heaven-reaching tower was interrupted when the builders became unable to understand one another's language.

Bab el Man·deb (bäb′ ĕl män′dĕb). A strate-gically important strait, 27.4 km (17 mi) wide, between the Arabian Peninsula and eastern Africa. It links the Red Sea with the Gulf of Aden.

Ba·bi·a Gó·ra (bä′bē-ə gŏŏr′ə). A peak, 1,726 m (5,659 ft) high, of the Beskids in the West Beskids on the border between Poland and Slovakia. It is the highest elevation in the range.

Ba·bian Jiang (bä′byän′ jyäng′). See **Black River** (sense 1).

Ba·bi Yar (bä′bē yär′, bä′byē). A ravine outside Kiev in north-central Ukraine where the Jews of the city were killed by German troops in 1941. The massacre is commemorated in Yevgeny Yevtushenko's 1961 poem "Babi Yar."

Ba·bu·yan Islands (bä′bōō-yän′). An island group of the Philippines separated from the northern coast of Luzon by the narrow **Babuyan Channel.** The group comprises 24 islands, including **Babuyan Island** in the northeast.

Bab·y·lon (băb′ə-lən, -lŏn′). **1.** The capital of ancient Babylonia in Mesopotamia on the Euphrates River. Established as capital c. 1750 B.C. and rebuilt in regal splendor by Nebuchadnezzar II after its destruction (c. 689 B.C.) by the Assyrians, Babylon was the site of the Hanging Gardens, one of the Seven Wonders of the World. **2.** A community of southeast New York on the southwest coast of Long Island. It is mainly residential. ◉ Pop. 12,388.

Bab·y·lo·ni·a (băb′ə-lō′nē-ə, -lŏn′yə). An ancient empire of Mesopotamia in the Euphrates River valley. It flourished under Hammurabi and Nebuchadnezzar II but declined after 562 B.C. and fell to the Persians in 539.

Bab·y·lo·ni·an (băb′ə-lō′nē-ən). *abbr.* **Bab. 1.** Of or relating to Babylonia or Babylon or their people, culture, or language. **2.** A native or inhabitant of Babylon or Babylonia. **3.** The form of Akkadian used in Babylonia.

Ba·ca·bal (bä′kä-bôl′). A city of northeast Brazil south-southwest of São Luís. It is a trade center in an agricultural area. ◉ Pop. 111,753.

Ba·cău (bə-kou′). A city of eastern Romania north-northeast of Bucharest. It is an industrial center in an oil-producing region. ◉ Pop. 206,995.

Back Bay (băk). An area of Boston, Massachusetts, largely consisting of filled-in land reclaimed from mud flats after the 1850's. It is noted for its many residences, long thoroughfares, and fine shops.

back·coun·try (băk′kŭn′trē). A sparsely inhabited rural region.

Back River. A river, about 965 km (600 mi) long, of central Northwest Territories, Canada. It rises in several lakes and flows northeast and north to an inlet south of Boothia Peninsula.

Ba·co·lod (bä-kō′lôd′). A city of northwest Negros Island in the south-central Philippines. It is a major port and processing center in a sugarcane region. ◉ Pop. 343,048.

Bac·tra (băk′trə). See **Balkh.**

Bac·tri·a (băk′trē-ə). An ancient country of southwest Asia in present-day northeast Afghanistan. It was an eastern province of the Persian Empire before its conquest by the Greeks in 328 B.C. The kingdom was destroyed c. 130 B.C. by nomadic tribes. —**Bac′tri·an** *adj. & n.*

Ba·da·joz (bä′də-hōz′, -*th*ä-hôth′). A city of southwest Spain on the Guadiana River near the Portugal border. An ancient fortress city, it rose to prominence under the Moors as the seat (1022–1094) of a vast independent emirate. ◉ Pop. 124,579.

Ba·da·lo·na (bä′də-lō′nə, -*th*ä-lô′nä). A city of northeast Spain, an industrial suburb of Barcelona on the Mediterranean Sea. ◉ Pop. 218,725.

Ba·den (bäd′n). A historical region of southwest Germany. In the 1840's it was a center of the German liberal movement.

Ba·den-Ba·den (bäd′n-bäd′n). A city of southwest Germany in the Black Forest near the French border. Founded as a Roman garrison in the third century A.D., it has long been one of Europe's most fashionable spas. ◉ Pop. 48,622.

Bad Hom·burg (bät′ hŏm′bûrg′, -bŏŏrk′). A city of west-central Germany at the foot of the Taunus Mountains near Frankfurt. It is a famous spa and resort. ◉ Pop. 50,647.

bad·lands (băd′lăndz′, -ləndz). Barren land characterized by roughly eroded ridges, peaks, and mesas.

Bad·lands also **Bad Lands** (băd′lăndz′, -ləndz). A heavily eroded arid region of southwest South Dakota and northwest Nebraska. The Badlands National Monument in South Dakota was established in 1939 to protect the area's colorful rock formations and prehistoric fossils.

Bad Salz·uf·len (bät sälts′ŏŏf-lən, zälts′-). A city of northwest Germany southwest of Hanover. Founded in 1048, it is a health resort with thermal springs. ◉ Pop. 50,494.

Baf·fin (băf′ĭn). A region of northeast Northwest Territories, Canada, including Baffin Island, the Queen Elizabeth and Parry islands, and Melville Peninsula.

Baffin Bay. An ice-clogged body of water between northeast Canada and Greenland. It connects with the Arctic Ocean to the north and west and with the Atlantic Ocean to the south by way of Davis Strait.

Baffin Island. An island of northeast Northwest Territories, Canada, west of Greenland. It is the fifth-largest island in the world.

Bagh·dad or **Bag·dad** (băg′dăd′). The capital

and largest city of Iraq, in the center of the country on the Tigris River. Founded in the eighth century, it was heavily damaged by U.S. forces during the Persian Gulf War (January–February 1991). ◉ Pop. 3,841,268.

Ba·gui·o (bä′gē-ō′). A city of northwest Luzon, Philippines. It is a mountain resort and the summer capital of the country. ◉ Pop. 169,565.

Ba·ha·mas (bə-hä′məz, -hä′-) also **Ba·ha·ma Islands** (-mə). An island country in the Atlantic Ocean east of Florida and Cuba comprising some 700 islands and islets and numerous cays. The country gained its independence from Great Britain in 1973. Nassau, on New Providence Island, is the capital and the largest city. ◉ Pop. 218,000. —**Ba·ha′mi·an** (-hä′mē-ən, -hä′-), **Ba·ha′man** (-hä′mən, -hä′-) *adj. & n.*

Ba·ha·sa Indonesia (bä-hä′sə). See **Indonesian** (sense 4).

Bahasa Malay also **Bahasa Me·la·yo** (mə-lä′-yōō). See **Malay** (sense 2).

Ba·ha·wal·pur (bə-hä′wəl-pŏŏr′, -hä′wəl-pŏŏr′). A region and former princely state of east-central Pakistan between the Sutlej River and the Indian border.

Ba·hi·a (bə-hē′ə, bä-ē′ə). See **Salvador.** —**Ba·hi′an** *adj. & n.*

Ba·hí·a Blan·ca (bə-hē′ə blăng′kə, bä-ē′ä vläng′kä). A city of eastern Argentina on the **Bahía Blanca,** an inlet of the Atlantic Ocean southwest of Buenos Aires. It is a major shipping and commercial center. ◉ Pop. 255,145.

Bah·rain or **Bah·rein** (bä-rān′). A country comprising an archipelago of low, sandy islands in the Persian Gulf between Qatar and Saudi Arabia. It was the first Arabian country to strike oil (1932). A British protectorate after 1861, Bahrain became independent in 1971. Manama, on

Bahrain Island, the largest in the archipelago, is the capital. ⊛ Pop. 549,000. — **Bah·rain′i** *adj.* & *n.*

Bahr el Gha·zal (bär′ ĕl′ gə-zäl′, bär′ ĕl′ gä-zäl′). A river of southwest Sudan flowing about 805 km (500 mi) east to Lake No, where it joins the Bahr el Jebel.

Bahr el Jeb·el (jĕb′əl). A river, about 956 km (594 mi) long, of southern Sudan. It is a section of the White Nile.

Ba·ia-Ma·re (bä′yə-mä′rə). A city of northwest Romania north of Cluj. It is an industrial center and popular health resort. ⊛ Pop. 150,018.

Bai·kal or **Bay·kal** (bī-kôl′, -kōl′), **Lake.** A lake of south-central Russia. Nearly 400 miles long, it is the largest freshwater lake in Eurasia and the world's deepest lake, with a maximum known depth of 1,742.2 m (5,712 ft).

Bai·ri·ki (bī-rē′kē). The administrative center of Kiribati, on Tarawa atoll in the northern Gilbert Islands of the west-central Pacific Ocean. ⊛ Pop. 1,956.

Ba·ja California (bä′hä) also **Low·er California** (lō′ər). A mountainous peninsula of western Mexico extending south-southeast between the Pacific Ocean and the Gulf of California south of the U.S. border. It was first explored by the Spanish in the 1530's.

Bak·er (bā′kər), **Mount.** A peak, 3,287.3 m (10,778 ft) high, of northwest Washington in the Cascade Range east of Bellingham. It is in a popular resort area.

Baker Lake. A lake of eastern Northwest Territories, Canada, near Chesterfield Inlet, an arm of Hudson Bay.

Ba·kers·field (bā′kərz-fēld′). A city of south-central California at the southern end of the fertile San Joaquin Valley north-northwest of Los Angeles. Gold was discovered in the region in 1855 and petroleum in 1899. ⊛ Pop. 105,611.

Bakh·ta·ran (bäk′tə-rän′, bäκн′tä-). Formerly **Ker·man·shah** (kĕr-män′shä′, -shô′). A city of western Iran west-southwest of Tehran.

Founded in the fourth century A.D., it was later a frontier fortress against the Ottoman Turks. ⊛ Pop. 665,636.

Ba·ku (bä-kōō′). The capital of Azerbaijan on the western shore of the Caspian Sea. Frequently under Persian rule, the city was annexed by Russia in 1806. It has been a center of oil production since the 1870's. In 1990 it was the scene of fierce fighting between Soviet forces and secessionist rebels. ⊛ Pop. 1,104,000.

Bal·a·kla·va also **Bal·a·cla·va** (băl′ə-klăv′ə, -klä′və). A section of Sevastopol in the Crimea of southern Ukraine. During the Crimean War Balaklava became famous for the doomed charge of the British Light Brigade against heavy Russian fire (October 25, 1854).

Bal·a·ton (băl′ə-tŏn′, bŏl′ŏ-tôn′), **Lake.** A lake of west-central Hungary southwest of Budapest. It is the largest lake in central Europe, with many tourist and health resorts.

Bald·win (bôld′wĭn). **1.** An unincorporated community of southeast New York on the southern shore of western Long Island. It is mainly residential. ⊛ Pop. 22,719. **2.** A borough of southwest Pennsylvania, a suburb of Pittsburgh on the Monongahela River. ⊛ Pop. 21,923.

Baldwin Park. A city of southern California, a residential suburb of Los Angeles near the San Gabriel Mountains. ⊛ Pop. 69,330.

Bal·e·ar·ic Islands (băl′ē-ăr′ĭk). An archipelago in the western Mediterranean Sea off the eastern coast of Spain. Noted for their scenery and mild climate, the islands are a major tourist center.

Ba·li (bä′lē). An island of southern Indonesia in the Lesser Sundas east of Java. Largely mountainous with a tropical climate and fertile soil, it is sometimes called the "Jewel of the East."

Ba·lik·pa·pan (bä′lĭk-pä′pän). A city of Indonesia in southeast Borneo on an inlet of Makassar Strait. It is a major port and oil center. ⊛ Pop. 280,675.

Ba·li·nese (bä′lə-nēz′, -nēs′). **1.** Of or relating to Bali or its people, language, or culture. **2.** *pl.* **Balinese.** A native or inhabitant of Bali. **3.** The Indonesian language of Bali.

Bal·kan (bôl′kən). **1.** Of or relating to the Balkan Peninsula or the Balkan Mountains. **2.** Of or relating to the Balkan States or their inhabitants.

Balkan Mountains also **Bal·kans** (bôl′kənz). A mountain system of southeast Europe extending about 563 km (350 mi) from eastern Yugoslavia through central Bulgaria to the Black Sea. The Balkans are a continuation of the Carpathian Mountains and rise to 2,377.2 m (7,794 ft).

Balkan Peninsula also **Balkans.** A peninsula of southeast Europe bounded by the Black Sea, the Sea of Marmara, and the Aegean, Mediterranean, Ionian, and Adriatic seas. The **Balkan States** include Albania, Bulgaria, continental Greece, southeast Romania, European Turkey, Yugoslavia, and the former Yugoslavian republics Slovenia, Croatia, Bosina and Herzegovina, and Macedonia. Formerly part of the Roman and Byzantine empires, the region fell to the Ottoman Turks by 1500. The Balkan Wars (1912–1913 and 1913), treaties signed after World War I, and nationalist movements in the early 1990's led to the present country boundaries.

Balkh (bälk). Formerly **Bac·tra** (băk′trə). An ancient city in present-day northern Afghanistan. One of the world's oldest settlements, it was the capital of Bactria and is the legendary birthplace of the prophet Zoroaster.

Bal·khash (băl-kăsh′, bäl-käsh′, -ĸнäsh′), **Lake.** A shallow lake of southeast Kazakstan. It has saline water in the east and fresh water in the west.

Bal·sas (bôl′səs, bäl′-). A river flowing about 724 km (450 mi) from south-central Mexico to the Pacific Ocean.

Balt (bôlt). **1.** A speaker of a Baltic language. **2.** A native or inhabitant of Lithuania, Latvia, or Estonia.

Bal·tic (bôl′tĭk). **1.** Of or relating to the Baltic Sea, the Baltic States, or a Baltic-speaking people. **2.** Of or relating to the branch of the Indo-European language family that contains Latvian, Lithuanian, and Old Prussian. **3.** The Baltic language branch.

Baltic Sea. An arm of the Atlantic Ocean in northern Europe bounded by Denmark, Sweden, Finland, Russia, Estonia, Latvia, Lithuania, Poland, and Germany. It opens to the North Sea via channels and canals, is mostly shallow, with relatively low salinity, and often freezes for three to five months of the year.

Baltic States. Estonia, Latvia, and Lithuania, on the eastern coast of the Baltic Sea. Formerly Russian provinces, they became independent countries after World War I and were incorporated into the U.S.S.R. as constituent republics in 1940. They became independent again in 1991.

Bal·ti·more (bôl′tə-môr′, -mōr′). A city of northern Maryland on an arm of Chesapeake Bay northeast of Washington, D.C. It has been a busy port since the 18th century. ◉ Pop. 736,014. **— Bal′ti·mor′e·an** *n.*

Bal·to-Sla·vic (bôl′tō-slä′vĭk, -slăv′ĭk). A subfamily of the Indo-European language family that consists of the Baltic and Slavic branches. **— Bal′to-Sla′vic** *adj.*

Ba·lu·chi (bə-lōō′chē) also **Ba·luch** (-lōōch′). **1.** *pl.* **Baluchi** or **-chis** also **Baluch** or **-lu·ches** (-lōō′chəz). A member of a traditionally nomadic

Muslim people of Baluchistan. **2.** The Iranian language of the Baluchis.

Ba·lu·chi·stan (bə-lōō′chĭ-stän′). A desert region of western Pakistan bounded by Iran, Afghanistan, and the Arabian Sea.

Ba·ma·ko (bä′mə-kō′). The capital and largest city of Mali, in the southwest on the Niger River. It was a leading center of Muslim learning under the Mali Empire (c. 11th–15th century). ◉ Pop. 658,275.

Bam·ba·ra (băm-bä′rä). **1.** *pl.* **Bambara** or **-ras.** A member of a people of the upper Niger River valley. **2.** The Mandingo language of the Bambaras, used as a lingua franca in Mali.

Bam·berg (băm′bûrg′, bäm′bĕrk′). A city of south-central Germany north-northwest of Nuremburg. An industrial and commercial center, it was the capital of a powerful ecclesiastical state from 1007 to 1802. ◉ Pop. 69,990.

Ba·na·ras (bə-när′əs, -ēz). See **Varanasi.**

Ba·nat (bə-nät′, bä′nät′). A region of southeast-central Europe extending across western Romania, northeast Serbia, and southern Hungary.

Ban·dar Se·ri Be·ga·wan (bŭn′dər sĕr′ē bə-gä′wən). The capital of Brunei, on the northern coast of Borneo. ◉ Pop. 49,902.

Ban·da Sea (băn′də, bän′-). An arm of the Pacific Ocean in eastern Indonesia southeast of Sulawesi and north of Timor. It includes the **Banda Islands,** a group of volcanic islands in the Moluccas south of Ceram.

Ban·djar·ma·sin (băn′jər-mä′sĭn, bän′-). See **Banjarmasin.**

Ban·dung (bän′dŏng′). A city of Indonesia in western Java southeast of Jakarta. Founded by the Dutch in 1810, it is an industrial and cultural center and a resort known for its cool, healthful climate. ◉ Pop. 1,462,637.

Banff (bămf). A town of southwest Alberta, Canada, in the Rocky Mountains near Lake Louise. It is a popular winter resort. ◉ Pop. 4,208.

Ban·ga·lore (băng′gə-lôr′, -lōr′). A city of south-central India west of Madras. Founded in 1537, it is a major industrial center and transportation hub. ◉ Pop. 2,660,088.

Bang·ka or **Ban·ka** (băng′kə). An island of western Indonesia in the Java Sea separated from Sumatra by the narrow **Strait of Bangka.** Tin was discovered here in the early 1700's.

Bang·kok (băng′kŏk′, băng-kŏk′) also **Krung Thep** (grŏong tĕp′). The capital and largest city of Thailand, in the southwest on the Chao Phraya River near the Gulf of Thailand. It is a leading port and industrial center with a major jewelry market. ◉ Pop. 5,876,000.

Bang·la·desh (băng′glə-dĕsh′, bäng′-). A country of southern Asia on the Bay of Bengal. Formerly part of Bengal, it became East Pakistan when India achieved independence in 1947. After a savage civil war with West Pakistan (1971), Bangladesh formed a separate nation. Dhaka is the capital and the largest city. ⊕ Pop. 117,787,000. — **Bang′la·desh′i** *adj. & n.*

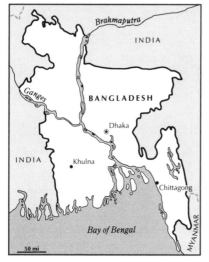

Ban·gor (băng′gôr, -gər). **1.** A municipal borough of eastern Northern Ireland on Belfast Lough. It is a seaport, resort, and yachting center. ⊕ Pop. 67,600. **2.** A city of south-central Maine on the Penobscot River. Settled in 1769, it was occupied by the British during the War of 1812. ⊕ Pop. 33,181.

Ban·gui (bäng-gē′, bäɴ-). The capital and largest city of Central African Republic, in the southern part of the country on the Ubangi River. It is a major port and trade center. ⊕ Pop. 473,817.

Bang·we·u·lu (băng′wē-ōō′lōō), **Lake.** A shallow lake bordered by swamps on a plateau of northeast Zambia. It was discovered by David Livingstone in 1868.

Ban·ja Lu·ka (bän′yə lōō′kə). A city of north-central Bosnia and Herzegovina northwest of Sarajevo. Ruled at various times by Turkey and Austria, Banja Luka became part of Yugoslavia after World War I. ⊕ Pop. 142,644.

Ban·jar·ma·sin also **Ban·djar·ma·sin** (băn′jər-mä′sĭn, bän′-). A city of Indonesia on a delta island of southern Borneo. An important deepwater port, Banjarmasin was part of a Hindu kingdom in the 14th century and passed to Muslim rulers in the 15th century. ⊕ Pop. 381,286.

Ban·jul (bän′jōōl′). Formerly **Bath·urst** (băth′-ərst). The capital and largest city of Gambia, on an island at the mouth of the Gambia River on the Atlantic Ocean. It was founded as a trading post by the British in 1816. ⊕ Pop. 49,181.

bank (băngk). **1.** A steep natural incline. **2.** An ar-

tificial embankment. **3.** often **banks.** The slope of land adjoining a body of water, especially adjoining a river, lake, or channel. **4.** often **banks.** A large elevated area of a sea floor.

Ban·ka (băng′kə). See **Bangka.**

Banks Island (băngks). An island of northwest Northwest Territories, Canada, in the Arctic Ocean west of Victoria Island. It is the westernmost island of the Arctic Archipelago.

Banks·town (băngks′toun′). A city of southeast Australia, a suburb of Sydney. ⊕ Pop. 153,600.

Ban·nock (băn′ək). **1.** *pl.* **Bannock** or **-nocks.** A member of a Native American people inhabiting southeast Idaho and western Wyoming. **2.** The variety of Northern Paiute spoken by the Bannocks.

Ban·nock·burn (băn′ək-bûrn′, băn′ək-bûrn′). A town of central Scotland north-northeast of Glasgow on the **Bannock River,** a tributary of the Forth. It was the site of Scottish king Robert the Bruce's defeat of the English under Edward II on June 23, 1314.

Ban·tu (băn′tōō). **1.** *pl.* **Bantu** or **-tus.** A member of any of a large number of linguistically related peoples of central and southern Africa. **2.** A group of over 400 closely related languages spoken in central, east-central, and southern Africa, belonging to the South Central subgroup of the Niger-Congo language family and including Swahili, Kinyarwanda, Kirundi, Zulu, and Xhosa. — **Ban′tu** *adj.*

Bao·ding also **Pao·ting** (bou′dĭng′). A city of northeast China south-southwest of Beijing. The city wall was built during the Ming period. ⊕ Pop. 594,966.

Bao·ji also **Pao·ki** (bou′jē′). A city of central China on the Wei He west of Xian. It is a thriving industrial center. ⊕ Pop. 452,286.

Bao·tou also **Pao·tow** (bou′tō′). A city of northern China on the Huang He (Yellow River) west of Hohhot. It is a major manufacturing center. ⊕ Pop. 1,075,920.

bar (bär). A ridge, as of sand or gravel, on a shore or streambed, that is formed by the action of tides or currents.

Ba·ra·cal·do (bär′ə-käl′dō, bä′rä-). A city of northern Spain, an industrial suburb of Bilbao. ⊕ Pop. 105,088.

Ba·ra·co·a (bär′ə-kō′ə, bä′rä-). A city of southeast Cuba on the coast near the eastern end of the island. It is the oldest settlement in Cuba. ⊕ Pop. 35,754.

Ba·ra·nof Island (băr′ə-nôf′, -nŏf′, bə-rä′-nəf). An island off southeast Alaska in the Alexander Archipelago. It was named after Aleksandr Baranov, who founded the town of Sitka on the island.

Ba·ra·no·vi·chi (bə-rä′nə-vĭch′ē). A city of southwest Belarus west of Bobruysk. Founded in 1870, it passed from Russia to Poland in 1920 and was incorporated into the U.S.S.R. in 1939. ⊛ Pop. 170,300.

Bar·ba·dos (bär-bā′dōs′, -dōz′, -dəs). *abbr.* **Barb.** A country occupying the easternmost island of the West Indies. Probably first visited by the Portuguese, the island was settled by the British in the early 1600's, became a separate colony in 1885, and gained full independence in 1966. Bridgetown is the capital and largest city. ⊛ Pop. 261,000. — **Bar·ba′di·an** *adj. & n.*

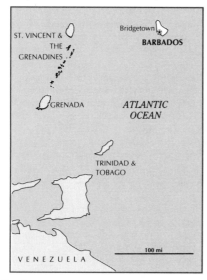

Bar·ba·ry (bär′bə-rē, -brē). A region of northern Africa on the Mediterranean coast between Egypt and the Atlantic Ocean. Settled by Berbers in the 2nd millennium B.C., it fell to the Arabs in the 7th century A.D. From the 16th to the 19th century it was used as a base by pirates who raided ships in the Mediterranean Sea and extracted tribute from the European powers trading in the area.

Barbary Coast. 1. The Mediterranean coastal area of Barbary and the Barbary States. **2.** A waterfront area of San Francisco, California, in the years after the 1849 gold rush. It was notorious for its gambling dens, saloons, brothels, and disreputable boarding houses.

Barbary States. The North African states of Algeria, Tunisia, Tripoli, and Morocco, especially from the 16th to the 19th century.

Bar·ber·ton (bär′bər-tən). A city of northeast Ohio, an industrial suburb of Akron. ⊛ Pop. 27,623.

Bar·bu·da (bär-bōō′də). An island of Antigua and Barbuda in the West Indies north of Antigua. It was privately owned from 1691 to 1872. — **Bar·bu′dan** *adj. & n.*

Bar·ce·lo·na (bär′sə-lō′nə). A city of northeast Spain on the Mediterranean Sea. Founded by the Carthaginians, it prospered under the Romans and Visigoths, fell to the Moors in 713, and was captured by Charlemagne's Frankish troops in 801. It has long been a center of Catalan separatism and radical political movements. ⊛ Pop. 1,770,296.

Ba·reil·ly also **Ba·re·li** (bə-rā′lē). A city of northern India east-southeast of Delhi. It was founded in the 16th century. ⊛ Pop. 587,211.

Bar·ents Sea (băr′ənts, bär′-). A shallow section of the Arctic Ocean north of Norway and northwest Russia. The North Atlantic Current keeps its southern ports ice-free all year.

Bar Harbor (bär). A town of southeast Maine on Mount Desert Island. It is a summer resort. ⊛ Pop. 2,768.

Ba·ri (bä′rē). A city of southeast Italy on the Adriatic Sea. Probably founded by Illyrians, it was controlled successively by the Greeks, Romans, Goths, Lombards, Byzantines, Normans, and Venetians and became part of the kingdom of Naples in 1557. ⊛ Pop. 341,273.

Ba·ri·sal (băr′ĭ-sôl′, bŭr′ĭ-säl′). A city of southern Bangladesh on the Ganges River delta. The phenomenon known as "the Barisal guns," unexplained sounds resembling distant thunder or cannon fire, may be seismic in origin. ⊛ Pop. 163,481.

Bar·let·ta (bär-lĕt′ə). A city of southern Italy on the Adriatic Sea west-northwest of Bari. It passed to the Goths after the fall of the Roman Empire. ⊛ Pop. 83,719.

Bar·na·ul (bär′nə-ōōl′). A city of south-central Russia on the Ob River south of Novosibirsk. It is an industrial center in a mining and agricultural region. ⊛ Pop. 595,298.

Barns·ley (bärnz′lē). A municipal borough of northern England north of Sheffield. It is a transportation and industrial center in a coal-mining area. ⊛ Pop. 225,800.

Barn·sta·ble (bärn′stə-bəl). A town of southeast Massachusetts on central Cape Cod. It is a resort community with many fine beaches. ⊛ Pop. 30,898.

Barn·sta·ple (bärn′stə-pəl). A municipal borough of southwest England on **Barnstaple Bay,** an inlet of the Bristol Channel. Incorporated in 1557, Barnstaple is a marketing town and tourist center. ⊛ Pop. 19,025.

Ba·ro·da (bə-rō′də). A city of west-central India southeast of Ahmadabad. Once the capital of the princely state of **Baroda,** it is noted for its public buildings, palaces, and Hindu temples. ⊛ Pop. 1,031,346.

Ba·rot·se·land (bə-rŏt′sē-lănd′). A former kingdom of central Africa, now the western part of Zambia.

Bar·qui·si·me·to (bär′kə-sə-mā′tō, -kē-sē-mĕ′tô). A city of northwest Venezuela west-southwest of Caracas. It was founded in 1552 and rebuilt after a major earthquake in 1812. ⊚ Pop. 692,599.

Bar·ra Man·sa (bä′rä mäɴ′sä). A city of southeast Brazil west-northwest of Rio de Janeiro. It is a rail junction and an industrial center. ⊚ Pop. 171,671.

bar·ran·ca (bə-răng′kə) also **bar·ran·co** (-kō). *Southwestern U.S.* **1.** A deep ravine or gorge. **2.** A bluff.

Bar·ran·ca·ber·me·ja (bä-räng′kä-vĕr-mĕ′hä). A city of northwest-central Colombia on the Magdalena River west-southwest of Bucaramanga. It is a river port. ⊚ Pop. 141,516.

Bar·ran·quil·la (băr′ən-kē′ə, -yä, bä′rän-). A city of northern Colombia on the Magdalena River near the Caribbean Sea. Founded in 1629, it is Colombia's chief port. ⊚ Pop. 917,486.

Bar·rei·ro (bä-rā′rōō). A city of western Portugal, an industrial suburb of Lisbon on the estuary of the Tagus River. ⊚ Pop. 50,863.

Bar·ren Grounds (băr′ən). A low-level treeless, sparsely inhabited region of northern Canada northwest of Hudson Bay and east of the Mackenzie River basin.

Bar·rie (băr′ē). A city of southern Ontario, Canada, on Lake Simcoe north-northwest of Toronto. It is a manufacturing center and summer resort. ⊚ Pop. 38,423.

bar·ri·er (băr′ē-ər). *Geology.* An ice barrier.

barrier reef. A long, narrow ridge of coral or rock parallel to and relatively near a coastline, separated from the coastline by a lagoon too deep for coral growth.

Bar·ring·ton (băr′ĭng-tən). A town of eastern Rhode Island southeast of Providence. It was part of Massachusetts until 1746. ⊚ Pop. 15,849.

Bar·row (băr′ō), **Point.** The northernmost point of Alaska, in the northwest on the Arctic Ocean. The nearby city of **Barrow** has research and government facilities. ⊚ Pop. 2,207.

Bar·row-in-Fur·ness (băr′ō-ĭn-fûr′nĭs). A borough of northwest England on a peninsula in an inlet of the Irish Sea northwest of Manchester. It is a shipbuilding center. ⊚ Pop. 72,800.

Bar·stow (bär′stō). A city of southeast California northeast of Los Angeles. It was founded in the 1880's as a silver-mining town. ⊚ Pop. 21,472.

Bar·tles·ville (bär′tlz-vĭl′). A city of northeast Oklahoma north of Tulsa. It is a trade center

in a ranching and oil-producing region. ⊚ Pop. 34,256.

Bart·lett (bärt′lĭt). A town of southwest Tennessee, a suburb of Memphis. ⊚ Pop. 17,076.

Ba·sel (bä′zəl) also **Basle** (bäl). A city of northern Switzerland on the Rhine River. It is one of the oldest intellectual centers in Europe. ⊚ Pop. 175,781.

Ba·shan (bā′shən). An ancient region of Palestine northeast of the Sea of Galilee.

Bash·kir·i·a (băsh-kîr′ē-ə). A region of southwest Russia in the southern Ural Mountains. It came under Russian control in the 16th century.

Ba·si·lan Islands (bä-sē′län′). A group of islands in the southern Philippines separated from southwest Mindanao by the narrow **Basilan Strait. Basilan Isand** is the largest island in the group.

Bas·il·don (băz′əl-dən, bā′zəl-). An urban district of southeast England east-northeast of London. It has varied light industries. ⊚ Pop. 161,699.

Ba·si·li·ca·ta (bə-zĭl′ĭ-kä′tə, bä-zē′lē-kä′tä). A region of southern Italy bordering on the Tyrrhenian Sea and the Gulf of Taranta. It forms the instep of the Italian "boot."

ba·sin (bā′sĭn). **1. a.** An artificially enclosed area of a river or harbor designed so that the water level remains unaffected by tidal changes. **b.** A small enclosed or partly enclosed body of water. **2.** A region drained by a single river system. **3.** *Geology.* **a.** A broad tract of land in which the rock strata are tilted toward a common center. **b.** A large, bowl-shaped depression in the surface of the land or ocean floor. —**ba′sin·al** *adj.*

Ba·sing·stoke (bā′zĭng-stōk′). A municipal borough of south-central England on the North Downs west-southwest of London. Mentioned as a royal manor in the Domesday Book, a census and survey of English lands made about 1086, it was long a market center for silk and woolen textiles. ⊚ Pop. 67,300.

Bas·ket Maker (băs′kĭt). **1.** Any of several early periods of Anasazi culture preceding the Pueblo periods and characterized by the use of wicker basketry, dry farming, and coiled pottery. **2.** A member of the Anasazi people who produced this culture.

Basle (bäl). See **Basel.**

Basque (băsk). **1.** A member of a people of unknown origin inhabiting the western Pyrenees and the Bay of Biscay in France and Spain. **2.** The language of the Basques, of no known linguistic affiliation. —**Basque** *adj.*

Basque Provinces. A region comprising three provinces of northern Spain on the Bay of Biscay. It borders on France in the northeast along the western Pyrenees.

Bas·ra (băs′rə, bŭs′-). A city of southeast Iraq on the Shatt al Arab near the Persian Gulf. It is the only port in the country. ◉ Pop. 406,296.

Basse·terre (băs-târ′, bäs-). The capital of St. Kitts and Nevis, on St. Kitts Island in the Leeward Islands of the West Indies. ◉ Pop. 14,161.

Basse-Terre (băs-târ′, bäs-). The capital of the French overseas department of Guadeloupe, on **Basse-Terre Island** in the Leeward Islands of the West Indies. ◉ Pop. 29,522.

Bass Strait (băs). A channel between Tasmania and southeast Australia connecting the Indian Ocean with the Tasman Sea. Its discovery in 1798 by the British explorer George Bass (died c. 1812) proved that Tasmania was not part of the Australian continent.

Bas·ti·a (băs′tē-ə, bä-stē′ə). A city of northeast Corsica, France, on the Tyrrhenian Sea. It is a commercial and tourist center. ◉ Pop. 44,020.

Bas·togne (bă-stōn′, bă-stôn′yə). A town of southeast Belgium near the Luxembourg border. It was a crucial point in the U.S. defensive line during the World War II Battle of the Bulge (December 1944–January 1945). ◉ Pop. 11,386.

Bas·trop (băs′trəp). A city of northeast Louisiana north-northeast of Monroe. It is an industrial center adjacent to a natural-gas field discovered in 1916. ◉ Pop. 15,527.

Ba·su·to·land (bə-sōō′tō-lănd′). See **Lesotho.**

Ba·taan (bə-tăn′, -tän′). A peninsula of western Luzon, Philippines, between Manila Bay and the South China Sea. After an extended siege U.S. and Philippine World War II troops surrendered to the Japanese in April 1942. U.S. forces recaptured the peninsula in February 1945.

Ba·tan Islands (bə-tän′). The northernmost island group of the Philippines, separated from southern Taiwan by a narrow channel.

Ba·ta·vi·a (bə-tā′vē-ə). **1.** A city of western New York west-southwest of Rochester. It is an industrial center in a farming region. ◉ Pop. 16,310. **2.** See **Jakarta.**

Bath (băth, bäth). A city of southwest England southeast of Bristol. Famous for its Georgian architecture and its hot mineral springs, tapped by the Romans in the first century A.D., it is a popular resort. ◉ Pop. 84,100.

Bath·urst (băth′ərst). **1.** A city of northern New Brunswick, Canada, on Chaleur Bay north-northeast of Fredericton. It is a popular beach resort. ◉ Pop. 15,705. **2.** See **Banjul.**

Bathurst Island. An island of northern Northwest Territories, Canada, in the Parry Islands northwest of Baffin Island.

bath·y·pe·lag·ic (băth′ə-pə-lăj′ĭk). Of, relating

to, or living in the depths of the ocean, especially between about 600 and 3,000 meters (2,000 and 10,000 feet).

Bat·on Rouge (băt′n rōōzh′). The capital of Louisiana, in the southeast-central part of the state on a bluff above the Mississippi River. Founded in 1719 as a French fort, it became the state capital in 1849 and was captured (May 1862) by Union admiral David Farragut during the Civil War. It is a major port of entry and oil-refining center. ◉ Pop. 219,531.

Bat·swa·na (bŏt-swä′nə). See **Tswana** (sense 1).

Bat·ter·y (băt′ə-rē) also **Battery Park.** A park at the southern tip of Manhattan Island at the upper end of New York Bay in southeast New York. It is the site of early Dutch and English fortifications and of Castle Clinton, built in 1808 for the defense of the harbor.

Bat·tle (băt′l). A town of southeast England, site of the Battle of Hastings (1066). William the Conqueror built Battle Abbey to commemorate his victory here. ◉ Pop. 4,987.

Battle Creek. A city of southern Michigan east of Kalamazoo. Breakfast cereals and other food products are important to its economy. ◉ Pop. 53,540.

Ba·tu·mi (bə-tōō′mē) also **Ba·tum** (-tōōm′). A city of southwest Georgia on the Black Sea near the Turkish border. On the site of an ancient Greek colony, it is an important petroleum refining and shipping center. ◉ Pop. 137,000.

Bat Yam (bät′ yäm′). A city of west-central Israel on the Mediterranean Sea near Tel Aviv–Jaffa. It is a resort and an industrial center. ◉ Pop. 144,200.

Bau·ru (bou-rōō′). A city of southeast Brazil northwest of São Paulo. It is a railroad junction and commercial center. ◉ Pop. 260,767.

Baut·zen (bout′sən). A city of eastern Germany on the Spree River east-northeast of Dresden. It was founded in the tenth century. ◉ Pop. 50,502.

Ba·var·i·a (bə-vâr′ē-ə). A region and former duchy of southern Germany. Conquered by the Romans in 15 B.C., the region became one of the five preeminent duchies of medieval Germany but was later overrun and ruled by numerous factions and powers.

Ba·var·i·an (bə-vâr′ē-ən). **1.** A native or inhabitant of Bavaria. **2.** The High German dialect of Bavaria and Austria. —**Ba·var′i·an** adj.

Bavarian Alps. A range of the Alps between southern Bavaria in Germany and the Tyrol in western Austria. It rises to 2,964.9 m (9,721 ft) at Zugspitze on the German border.

bay (bā). abbr. **b.** **1.** A body of water partially

enclosed by land but with a wide mouth, affording access to the sea. **2.** An area of land, such as an arm of prairie partially enclosed by woodland, that resembles in shape or formation a partially enclosed body of water.

Ba·ya·món (bä'yä-môn'). A town of northeast Puerto Rico, a residential and industrial suburb of San Juan. Founded in 1772, it is one of the oldest settlements on the island. ◦ Pop. 222,102.

Bay City (bā). **1.** A city of eastern Michigan on Saginaw Bay north-northwest of Detroit. It is a port of entry and industrial center. ◦ Pop. 38,936. **2.** A city of southeast Texas near the Colorado River and the Gulf of Mexico southwest of Houston. There are oil wells and sulfur mines in the area. ◦ Pop. 18,170.

Ba·yeux (bī-yōō', bā-, bä-yœ'). A town of northwest France near the English Channel. The famed Bayeux tapestry, housed in a museum here, depicts incidents in the Norman Conquest (1066) of England. ◦ Pop. 14,721.

Bay·kal (bī-kôl', -kŏl'), **Lake.** See Lake **Baikal.**

Bay of. For names of actual bays, see the specific element of the name; for example, **Biscay, Bay of; Pigs, Bay of.**

Ba·yonne[1] (bā-ōn', bä-yôn'). A town of southwest France near the Bay of Biscay and the Spanish border. French, Spanish, and Basque are all spoken here. ◦ Pop. 41,381.

Bay·onne[2] (bā-yōn'). A city of northeast New Jersey on a peninsula in Upper New York Bay across from Staten Island. First colonized by the Dutch, it passed to the English in 1664. ◦ Pop. 61,444.

bay·ou (bī'ōō, bī'ō). **1.** A body of water, such as a creek or small river, that is a tributary of a larger body of water. **2.** A sluggish stream that meanders through lowlands, marshes, or plantation grounds.

Bay·reuth (bī-roit', bī'roit). A city of east-central Germany northeast of Nuremberg. Richard Wagner lived here from 1872 to 1883 and designed the opera house used for the city's internationally famous music festivals. ◦ Pop. 71,811.

Bay Shore. An unincorporated community of southeast New York on the southern shore of Long Island. It is a residential town and fishing resort. ◦ Pop. 31,200.

Bay·town (bā'toun'). A city of southeast Texas at the head of Galveston Bay on the Houston Ship Channel. It is an oil-refining and industrial center. ◦ Pop. 63,850.

Bay Village. A city of northeast Ohio, a suburb of Cleveland on Lake Erie. ◦ Pop. 17,000.

beach (bēch). **1.** The shore of a body of water, especially when sandy or pebbly. **2.** The sand or pebbles on a shore.

Beach-la-Mar (bēch'lə-mär'). See **Bislama.**

Beach·y Head (bē'chē). Chalk cliffs, 175.4 m (575 ft) high, on the southeast coast of England. In 1690 Beachy Head was the scene of a French naval victory over Anglo-Dutch forces.

Bea·con Hill (bē'kən). An area of Boston, Massachusetts, noted for its historic residences, brick sidewalks, and picturesque mews.

Bea·cons·field (bē'kənz-fēld'). A town of southern Quebec, Canada, a residential suburb of Montreal on Montreal Island. ◦ Pop. 19,613.

Bear (bâr), **Mount.** A peak, 4,523.5 m (14,831 ft) high, in the Wrangell Mountains of southern Alaska near the British Columbia border.

Beard·more Glacier (bîrd'môr', -mōr'). A valley glacier, about 418 km (260 mi) long, in the Queen Maud Mountains of Antarctica. It was discovered by the British explorer Sir Ernest Shackleton in 1908.

Bear Mountain. A peak, 391.6 m (1,284 ft) high, of southeast New York overlooking the Hudson River. It is in a popular resort area.

Bé·arn (bā-ärn'). A historical region and former province of southwest France in the western Pyrenees. The region was autonomous until 1620.

Bear River. A river rising in northeast Utah and flowing about 563 km (350 mi) in a U-shaped course northwest through southwest Wyoming and southeast Idaho then south into Utah again. It empties into Great Salt Lake.

Be·as (bē'äs'). A river, about 402 km (250 mi) long, of northern India rising in the Himalaya Mountains. It is one of the five rivers of the Punjab that form a major tributary of the Indus River.

Beau·fort Sea (bō'fərt). A part of the Arctic Ocean north of northeast Alaska and northwest Canada extending from Point Barrow, Alaska, to the Canadian Arctic Archipelago. Covered with pack ice year-round, it was first explored in 1914.

Beau·jo·lais (bō'zhə-lā'). A hilly region of east-central France west of the Saône River between Mâcon and Lyon. It is noted for its wine.

Beau·mont (bō'mŏnt'). A city of southeast Texas north-northeast of Houston. A ship canal links the city with the Gulf of Mexico. ◦ Pop. 114,323.

Beau·port (bō-pôr'). A city of southern Quebec, Canada, a suburb of Quebec City on the St. Lawrence River. Settled in 1634, it is one of the oldest communities in Canada. ◦ Pop. 60,447.

Beau·vais (bō-vā'). A town of northern France north-northwest of Paris. Its tapestry works, established in the 17th century, were destroyed in June 1940 during World War II. ⊛ Pop. 52,365.

Bea·ver·creek (bē′vər-krēk′). A village of southwest Ohio, a residential suburb of Dayton. ⊛ Pop. 33,626.

Bea·ver·head Mountains (bē′vər-hĕd′). A section of the Bitterroot Range in the Rocky Mountains along the Continental Divide on the border between eastern Idaho and southwest Montana. It rises to 3,343.1 m (10,961 ft) at Garfield Mountain.

Bea·ver River (bē′vər). **1.** A river rising in central Alberta, Canada, and flowing about 491 km (305 mi) eastward into Saskatchewan then north to the headwaters of the Churchill River. **2.** A name for the North Canadian River as it flows about 450 km (280 mi) through northwest Oklahoma.

Bea·ver·ton (bē′vər-tən). A city of northwest Oregon west of Portland. It was founded in 1868. ⊛ Pop. 53,310.

Bêche-de-Mer (bĕsh′ də-mâr′). See **Bislama.**

Bech·u·a·na (bĕch′ōō-ä′nə). See **Tswana** (sense 1).

Bech·u·a·na·land (bĕch′wä′nə-lănd′, bĕch′-ōō-ä′-). See **Botswana.**

Beck·ley (bĕk′lē). A city of southern West Virginia southeast of Charleston. It is a trade center in a coal-mining region. ⊛ Pop. 18,296.

bed (bĕd). **1.** The bottom of a body of water, such as a stream. **2.** *Geology.* A rock mass of large horizontal extent bounded, especially above, by physically different material.

Bed·ford (bĕd′fərd). **1.** A municipal borough of south-central England on the Ouse River west of Cambridge. It was the site of a British victory over the Saxons in 571. ⊛ Pop. 74,500. **2.** A city of northeast Ohio, a residential suburb of Cleveland. ⊛ Pop. 14,822. **3.** A city of northern Texas northeast of Fort Worth. It was settled c. 1843. ⊛ Pop. 43,762.

Bed·loe's Island (bĕd′lōz). See **Liberty Island.**

Bed·ou·in also **Bed·u·in** (bĕd′ōō-ĭn, bĕd′wĭn). An Arab of any of the nomadic tribes of the Arabian, Syrian, Nubian, or Sahara deserts.

bed·rock (bĕd′rŏk′). The solid rock that underlies loose material, such as soil, sand, clay, or gravel.

Bed·u·in (bĕd′ōō-ĭn, bĕd′wĭn). Variant of **Bedouin.**

Bę·dzin (bĕn′jĕn′). A town of southern Poland northeast of Katowice. It was part of Russia from 1815 to 1919. ⊛ Pop. 77,100.

Bee·cher (bē′chər). A city of east-central Michigan, a suburb of Flint. ⊛ Pop. 17,178.

Beer·she·ba (bîr-shē′bə, bĕr-shĕv′ə). A city of southern Israel southwest of Jerusalem. In biblical times it marked the southern boundary of Palestine. ⊛ Pop. 138,100.

Bees·ton and Sta·ple·ford (bē′stən; stā′pəl-fərd). An urban district of central England, a suburb of Nottingham. ⊛ Pop. 65,400.

Bei·jing (bā′jĭng′) also **Pe·king** (pē′kĭng′, pā′-). Formerly (1928–1949) **Pei·ping** (pā′pĭng′). The capital of China, in the northeast part of the country. Founded c. 700 B.C., it served as Kublai Khan's capital (13th century) and the capital of China (1421–1911; 1949–). It is a major commercial and industrial city and the political, educational, and cultural center of the country. Pro-democracy demonstrations in 1989 were suppressed by the military, resulting in hundreds of deaths. ⊛ Pop. 7,362,426.

Bei·ra (bā′rə). A city of east-central Mozambique on the Mozambique Channel, an arm of the Indian Ocean. It is a commercial center and a popular resort. ⊛ Pop. 264,202.

Bei·rut (bā-rōōt′). The capital and largest city of Lebanon, in the western part of the country on the Mediterranean Sea. Founded by the Phoenicians, it was an important Greek and Roman trade center. The city became divided at the outbreak of the Lebanese civil war in the mid-1970's as a result of fighting between Muslim and Christian factions and was further destroyed in 1982 by an Israeli siege aimed at rooting out Palestinian guerrillas. Christian and Muslim militias withdrew from the city in 1990 and returned control of it to the government. ⊛ Pop. 474,870.

Be·ja (bā′jə). **1.** *pl.* **Beja** or **-jas.** A member of a people living primarily as pastoral nomads in the area between the Nile River and the Red Sea. **2.** The Cushitic language of the Beja.

Be·la·rus (bĕl′ə-rōōs′, bĕl′ə-rōōs′). Formerly **Bel·o·rus·sian Soviet Socialist Republic** (bĕl′ō-rŭsh′ən) or **Be·lo·rus·sia** (bĕl′ō-rŭsh′ə) also **Bye·lo·rus·sia** (byĕl′ō-). Popularly known as **White Russia.** A country of eastern Europe east of Poland and west of Russia. It was constituent re-

public of the Soviet Union from 1922 to 1991. Minsk is the capital. ⊛ Pop. 10,355,000.

Be·lau (bə-lou′). See **Palau.**

Be·la·ya (bĕl′ə-yə). A river of southwest Russia rising in the Ural Mountains and flowing about 1,416 km (880 mi) generally northwest to the Kama River.

Be·lém (bə-lĕm′, -lāN′). Formerly **Pa·rá** (pə-rä′). A city of northern Brazil in the Amazon delta. It is the chief port and commercial center of the vast Amazon River basin. ⊛ Pop. 1,244,688.

Bel·fast (bĕl′făst′, bĕl-făst′). The capital and largest city of Northern Ireland, in the eastern part of the country on **Belfast Lough,** an inlet of the North Channel of the Irish Sea. Conflict between Protestants and Catholics has divided the city since the 19th century. ⊛ Pop. 296,700.

Bel·fort (bĕl-fôr′). A city of northeast France commanding the strategic **Belfort Gap** between the Vosges and the Jura Mountains, thus dominating the land approaches from France, Germany, and Switzerland. ⊛ Pop. 51,206.

Bel·gae (bĕl′gī′, -jē′). A people who formerly inhabited northeast Gaul and areas of southeast England. Belgium is named for them.

Bel·gaum (bĕl-goum′). A town of southwest India south-southeast of Kolhapur. It is an agricultural market town. ⊛ Pop. 326,399.

Bel·gian (bĕl′jən). *abbr.* **Belg. 1.** Of or relating to Belgium or its people or culture. **2.** A native or inhabitant of Belgium.

Belgian Congo. See **Zaire.**

Belgian East Africa. The former Belgian trust territory of Ruanda-Urundi, now divided into the independent countries of Rwanda and Burundi.

Bel·gic (bĕl′jĭk). **1.** Of or relating to Belgium or the Belgians. **2.** Of or relating to the Belgae.

Bel·gium (bĕl′jəm). *abbr.* **Belg.** A country of northwest Europe on the North Sea. It has long been a strategic crossroads of Europe and the scene of heavy fighting in numerous wars. The country is culturally divided into Dutch-speaking Flanders in the north and French-speaking Wal-

lonia in the south. Brussels is the capital and the largest city. ⊛ Pop. 10,080,000.

Bel·go·rod (bĕl′gə-rŏd′, byĕl′gə-rət). A city of southwest Russia on the Donets River. It is a transportation and industrial center. ⊛ Pop. 314,425.

Bel·grade (bĕl′grād′, -grăd′, bĕl-grăd′) also **Be·o·grad** (bĕ′ô-gräd). The capital and largest city of Yugoslavia, in the north-central part of the country at the confluence of the Danube and Sava rivers. Founded in the third century B.C., it became the capital of the kingdom of Serbia in 1802 and the capital of Yugoslavia after World War I. ⊛ Pop. 1,136,786.

Bel·gra·vi·a (bĕl-grā′vē-ə). A fashionable residential district of southwest London, England, centered on Belgrave Square. It was laid out in the 1820's.

Be·li·tung (bə-lē′tŏŏng) also **Bil·li·ton** (bə-lē′tŏn′). An island of western Indonesia in the Java Sea between Sumatra and Borneo. It has important tin mines.

Be·lize (bə-lēz′). **1.** Formerly **British Honduras.** A country of Central America on the Caribbean Sea. A British colony in the late 19th century, it became self-governing in 1964 and independent in 1981. Belmopan is the capital. ⊛ Pop. 211,000. **2.** also **Belize City.** The largest city of Belize, in the eastern part of the country on the Caribbean Sea at the mouth of the **Belize River.** It was devastated by a hurricane in 1961. The capital was moved from here to Belmopan in 1970. ⊛ Pop. 39,771.

Bell (bĕl). A city of southern California, a suburb of Los Angeles. ⊛ Pop. 34,365.

Bel·la Coo·la (bĕl′ə kŏŏ′lə). **1.** *pl.* **Bella Coola** or **-las.** A member of a Native American people inhabiting the coast of British Columbia along the Bella Coola River, a short stream flowing westward into a channel of Queen Charlotte

Sound. **2.** The Salishan language of the Bella Coolas.

Bel·la·ry (bə-lär′ē). A town of south-central India north-northwest of Bangalore. It is a trade and administrative center. ● Pop. 245,391.

Bel·leau Wood (bĕ-lō′, bĕl′ō). A forest of northern France east of Château-Thierry. In World War I it was the site of a hard-fought victory over the Germans (June 1918) and now contains a cemetery dedicated to the Americans who died in the battle.

Belle Fourche (bĕl′ foosh′). A river rising in northeast Wyoming and flowing about 467 km (290 mi) to the Cheyenne River in western South Dakota.

Belle Glade. A city of southeast Florida on Lake Okeechobee west of West Palm Beach. It was rebuilt after a hurricane in 1928. ● Pop. 16,177.

Belle Isle, Strait of. A channel between southeast Labrador and northwest Newfoundland, Canada. It is the northern entrance to the Gulf of St. Lawrence.

Belle·ville (bĕl′vĭl′). **1.** A city of southeast Ontario, Canada, near Lake Ontario east-northeast of Toronto. Founded in 1790, it is a processing and manufacturing center. ● Pop. 34,881. **2.** A city of southwest Illinois southeast of East St. Louis. It is in a coal-mining region and has diverse industries. ● Pop. 42,785. **3.** A town of northeast New Jersey on the Passaic River near Newark. It was settled by the Dutch c. 1680. ● Pop. 34,213.

Belle·vue (bĕl′vyoo′). **1.** A city of eastern Nebraska, a suburb of Omaha on the Missouri River. ● Pop. 30,982. **2.** A city of west-central Washington on Lake Washington opposite Seattle. It is a manufacturing and residential community. ● Pop. 86,874.

Bell·flow·er (bĕl′flou′ər). A city of southern California, a suburb in the Los Angeles–Long Beach metropolitan area. ● Pop. 61,815.

Bell Gardens. A city of southern California, a suburb of Los Angeles. ● Pop. 42,355.

Bel·ling·ham (bĕl′ĭng-hăm′). A city of northwest Washington on **Bellingham Bay** south of the British Columbia, Canada, border. It is a port of entry with shipbuilding and processing industries. ● Pop. 52,179.

Bel·lings·hau·sen Sea (bĕl′ĭngz-hou′zən). An arm of the southern Pacific Ocean off the coast of Antarctica extending from Alexander I Island to Thurston Island.

Bell·more (bĕl′môr′, -mōr′). An unincorporated town of southeast New York on southwest Long Island. It is primarily residential. ● Pop. 16,438.

Bel·lo (bĕ′yô). A town of northwest-central Colombia, a suburb of Medellín. ● Pop. 211,203.

Bell·wood (bĕl′wood′). A village of northeast Illinois, a residential and manufacturing suburb of Chicago. ● Pop. 20,241.

Bel·mont (bĕl′mŏnt′). **1.** A city of western California, a residential suburb midway between San Francisco and San Jose. ● Pop. 24,127. **2.** A town of eastern Massachusetts, a residential suburb of Boston. ● Pop. 24,720.

Bel·mo·pan (bĕl′mō-păn′). The capital of Belize, in the north-central part of the country. It became the capital in 1970 after a hurricane devastated Belize City (1961). ● Pop. 44,087.

Bel·oeil (bə-līl′, bĕl-œy′). A town of southern Quebec, Canada, on the Richelieu River northeast of Montreal. It has varied light industries. ● Pop. 17,540.

Be·lo Ho·ri·zon·te (bĕl′ō hôr′ĭ-zôn′tē, bĕ′-loo ô′rĭ-zôn′thĭ). A city of eastern Brazil north of Rio de Janeiro. An important manufacturing and marketing center, it was built (1895–1897) as the first of Brazil's planned communities. ● Pop. 2,017,127.

Be·loit (bə-loit′). A city of southern Wisconsin on the Illinois border south-southeast of Madison. Beloit College was founded in 1846. ● Pop. 35,573.

Be·lo·rus·sia (bĕl′ō-rŭsh′ə) also **Bye·lo·rus·sia** (byĕl′ō-). Popularly known as **White Russia** (hwīt, wīt). **1.** A region of eastern Europe in present-day Belarus and Poland. Settled by Slavs in the 5th century, it became a part of the grand duchy of Lithuania in the 14th century and a part of the Russian empire in the 18th century. In 1921 the western part of the region was ceded to Poland, and the eastern part became the Belorussian Soviet Socialist Republic, now Belarus. **2.** See **Belarus.**

Bel·o·rus·sian (bĕl′ō-rŭsh′ən, byĕl′-). **1.** Of or relating to Belorussia or its people, language, or culture. **2.** A native or inhabitant of Belorussia. **3.** The Slavic language of the Belorussians.

Belorussian Soviet Socialist Republic See **Belarus.**

Bel·sen (bĕl′zən). In full **Ber·gen-Bel·sen** (bûr′gən-bĕl′sən, bĕr′gən-bĕl′zən). A village of northern Germany north of Hanover. It was the site of a Nazi concentration camp during World War II.

belt (bĕlt). A geographic region that is distinctive in a specific respect.

Be·lu·kha (bə-loo′kə, byĕ-loo′KHə). A peak, 4,508.8 m (14,783 ft) high, of the Altai Mountains in south-central Russia near the border of Kazakstan. It is the highest elevation in the range.

Bel·ve·dere Park (bĕl′vĭ-dîr′). A city of northwest Georgia, a suburb of Atlanta. ⊛ Pop. 18,089.

Bel·vi·dere (bĕl'vĭ-dîr '). A city of northern Illinois east of Rockford. It is a manufacturing center in a farming region. ⊛ Pop. 15,958.

Bem·ba (bĕm'bə). A Bantu language spoken in Zambia. Also called *Chibemba.*

Be·na·res (bə-när'əs, -ēz). See **Varanasi.**

bench (bĕnch). **1.** A level, narrow stretch of land interrupting a declivity. **2.** A level elevation of land along a shore or coast, especially one marking a former shoreline.

Bend (bĕnd). A city of central Oregon at the eastern foot of the Cascade Range east of Eugene. Lumbering and tourism are important to its economy. ⊛ Pop. 20,469.

Ben·de·ry (bĕn-dĕr'ē, bĭn-dyĕ'rē). A city of southern Moldova on the Dniester River northwest of Odessa, Ukraine. A historically strategic gateway to Bessarabia, the city has been controlled at various times by Turkey, Russia, Romania, and the Soviet Union. ⊛ Pop. 132,700.

Ben·di·go (bĕn'dĭ-gō'). A city of southeast Australia north-northwest of Melbourne. It was founded in 1851 during the Australian gold rush. ⊛ Pop. 31,841.

Be·ne·lux (bĕn'ə-lŭks'). An economic union of Belgium, the Netherlands, and Luxembourg, originally established as a customs union in 1948.

Be·ne·ven·to (bĕn'ə-vĕn'tō). A city of southern Italy northeast of Naples. In ancient times it was an important trade center on the Appian Way. ⊛ Pop. 51,900.

Ben·fleet (bĕn'flēt'). An urban district of southeast England on an inlet of the Thames estuary east of London. ⊛ Pop. 86,000.

Ben·gal (bĕn-gôl', bĕng-, bĕn'gəl, bĕng'-'). A region of eastern India and Bangladesh. It was a province of India until 1947, when the eastern part became East Pakistan, and later (1971) Bangladesh, and the western section was included in independent India. — **Ben'ga·lese'** (bĕn'gə-lēz', -lēs', bĕng'-) *adj.* & *n.*

Bengal, Bay of. An arm of the Indian Ocean bordered by Sri Lanka and India on the west, Bangladesh on the north, and Myanmar (Burma) and Thailand on the east.

Ben·ga·li (bĕn-gô'lē, bĕng-). **1.** Of or relating to Bengal or its people, language, or culture. **2.** *pl.* **-lis.** A native or inhabitant of Bengal. **3.** The modern Indic language of West Bengal and Bangladesh.

Ben·ga·si (bĕn-gä'zē, bĕng-). See **Benghazi.**

Beng·bu (bŭng'bōō') also **Peng·pu** (pŭng'pōō'). A city of eastern China northwest of Nanjing. It was a government base during the civil war (1946–1949). ⊛ Pop. 695,040.

Ben·gha·zi also **Ben·ga·si** (bĕn-gä'zē, bĕng-). A city of northeast Libya on the Gulf of Sidra. Inhabited since Greek and Roman times, it is a major port and was a capital of Libya from 1951 to 1972. ⊛ Pop. 367,600.

Be·ni (bĕ'nē). A river of central and northwest Bolivia rising in the Andes and flowing about 1,599 km (994 mi) to the Mamoré River.

Be·ni·cia (bə-nē'shə). A city of western California on an inlet of San Francisco Bay north-northeast of Oakland. It was the state capital from 1853 to 1854. ⊛ Pop. 15,376.

Be·nin (bə-nĭn', bĕ-nēn'). **1.** A former kingdom of western Africa, now part of Nigeria. It flourished from the 14th to the 17th century. **2.** Formerly **Da·ho·mey** (də-hō'mē, dä-ô-mā'). A country of western Africa. Originally made up of several ancient kingdoms colonized by France in the 19th century, it became independent in 1960 and was renamed Benin in 1975. Porto-Novo is the capital and Cotonou the largest city. ⊛ Pop. 5,387,000. **3.** also **Benin City.** A city of southern Nigeria on the **Benin River,** about 161 km (100 mi) long. The city is known for its bronze works of art. ⊛ Pop. 136,000.

Benin, Bight of. A wide indentation of the Gulf of Guinea in western Africa.

Ben Lo·mond (bĕn lō'mənd). A mountain, 973.6 m (3,192 ft) high, of south-central Scotland on the eastern shore of Loch Lomond.

Ben Ne·vis (nē'vĭs, nĕv'ĭs). The highest mountain of Great Britain, rising to 1,343.8 m (4,406 ft) in the Grampian Mountains of western Scotland near Loch Linnhe.

Ben·ning·ton (bĕn'ĭng-tən). A town of southwest Vermont west of Brattleboro. It is a tourist center and the seat of Bennington College (established 1925). ⊛ Pop. 16,451.

Ben·sen·ville (bĕn′sən-vĭl′). A village of northeast Illinois near Chicago. ⦿ Pop. 17,767.

ben·thos (bĕn′thŏs′). The bottom of a sea or a lake. —**ben′thic** (-thĭk), **ben·thon′ic** (bĕn-thŏn′ĭk) *adj.*

Ben·ton (bĕn′tən). A city of central Arkansas southwest of Little Rock. There are bauxite deposits in the area. ⦿ Pop. 18,177.

Be·nue (bān′wā) also **Bin·ue** (bĭn′-). A river of western Africa rising in Cameroon and flowing about 1,078 km (670 mi) to the Niger River in central Nigeria.

Ben·xi (bŭn′shē′) also **Pen·ki** (-jē′). A city of northeast China south-southeast of Shenyang. It was founded as a metallurgical center in 1915. ⦿ Pop. 937,805.

Be·o·grad (bĕ′ô-gräd). See **Belgrade**.

Be·rar (bā-rär′, bə-). A region of west-central India. It was one of the early kingdoms of the Deccan.

Ber·ber (bûr′bər). **1.** A member of a North African, primarily Muslim people living in settled or nomadic tribes from Morocco to Egypt. **2.** Any of the Afro-Asiatic languages of the Berbers. —**Ber′ber** *adj.*

Berch·tes·ga·den (bĕrk′təs-gäd′n, bĕrкн′-). A town of southeast Germany in the Bavarian Alps. It is a popular winter and summer resort. The site of Adolf Hitler's wartime villa is on a peak overlooking the town. ⦿ Pop. 8,126.

Be·re·a (bə-rē′ə). A city of northeast Ohio, a suburb of Cleveland. ⦿ Pop. 19,051.

Be·re·zi·na (bə-rĕ′zĭ-nə, byə-ryĕ-zyĭ-nä′). A river of Belarus rising in the north-central part of the country and flowing about 611 km (380 mi) generally southward to the Dnieper River.

Be·rez·ni·ki (bə-rĕz′nĭ-kē, byə-ryôz′nyĭ-kē′). A city of western Russia on the Kama River. It is an important industrial center. ⦿ Pop. 197,324.

berg (bûrg). A mass of floating or stationary ice; an iceberg.

Ber·ga·ma (bər-gä′mə, bûr′gə-). A town of western Turkey north of Izmir. It occupies the site of ancient Pergamum. ⦿ Pop. 34,716.

Ber·ga·mo (bĕr′gə-mō′). A city of northern Italy in the foothills of the Alps northeast of Milan. Originally a Gallic settlement, it later became a Lombard duchy. ⦿ Pop. 115,655.

Ber·gen (bûr′gən, bĕr′-). A city of southwest Norway on inlets of the North Sea. Founded c. 1070, it was the largest and most important city of medieval Norway. ⦿ Pop. 218,144.

Ber·gen-Bel·sen (bûr′gən-bĕl′sən, bĕr′gən-bĕl′zən). See **Belsen**.

Ber·gen·field (bûr′gən-fēld′). A borough of northeast New Jersey east of Paterson. It has varied light industries. ⦿ Pop. 24,458.

Ber·gisch-Glad·bach (bĕr′gĭsh-glät′bäk′, -bäкн′). A town of western Germany near Cologne. Chartered in 1856, it is an industrial center. ⦿ Pop. 104,991.

Ber·ing Sea (bâr′ĭng, bĕr′-, bîr′-). A northward extension of the Pacific Ocean between Siberia and Alaska, lying north of the Aleutian Islands and connected with the Arctic Ocean by the Bering Strait. It was first explored in the 17th century.

Bering Standard Time. Standard time in the 11th time zone west of Greenwich, England, reckoned at 165° west and used, for example, in the Midway Islands. Also called *Bering Time.*

Bering Strait. A narrow stretch of water separating Alaska from Siberia and connecting the Arctic Ocean with the Bering Sea. It is believed that during prehistoric times the strait formed a land bridge by which the original inhabitants of North America arrived from Asia.

Bering Time. See **Bering Standard Time**.

Berke·ley (bûrk′lē). **1.** A city of western California on San Francisco Bay north of Oakland. Founded as Oceanview on land purchased from a Spanish family in 1853, it was renamed Berkeley in 1866. A branch of the University of California is here (established 1872). ⦿ Pop. 102,724. **2.** A city of eastern Missouri, an industrial suburb of St. Louis. ⦿ Pop. 12,450.

Berk·ley (bûrk′lē). A city of southeast Michigan, a residential suburb of Detroit. ⦿ Pop. 16,960.

Berk·shire Hills (bûrk′shîr′, -shər) also **Berk·shires** (bûrk′shîrz′, -shərz). A region of wooded hills in western Massachusetts rising to 1,064.8 m (3,491 ft). There are numerous resorts, state parks, and forests in the area.

Ber·lin. 1. (bûr-lĭn′). The capital and largest city of Germany, in the northeast part of the country. Divided between 1945 and 1990 into **East Berlin** and **West Berlin,** it was the center of the Prussian state and after 1871 was the capital of the German Empire. The division of the city grew out of the zones of occupation established at the end of World War II. The **Berlin Wall,** a wire and concrete barrier, was erected by the East German government in August 1961 and dismantled in November 1989. ⦿ Pop. 3,475,392. **2.** (bûr′lĭn). A city of central Connecticut, an industrial suburb of Hartford. ⦿ Pop. 16,787.

berm also **berme** (bûrm). **1. a.** A narrow ledge or shelf, as along the top or bottom of a slope. **b.** The shoulder of a road. **c.** A raised bank or path, such as one along a canal. **2.** A terrace formed by wave action along the backshore of a beach.

Ber·me·jo (bər-mā′hō, bĕr-). A river of northern Argentina rising near the Bolivian border and flowing about 1,046 km (650 mi) generally southeast to the Paraguay River at the Paraguay border.

Ber·mu·da (bər-myōō′də). A self-governing British colony comprising about 300 coral islands in the Atlantic Ocean southeast of Cape Hatteras. The first settlement was made in 1609 by British colonists shipwrecked on their way to Virginia. Tourism is crucial to its economy. Hamilton, on **Bermuda Island,** the largest in the archipelago, is the capital. ⊛ Pop. 63,000. — **Ber·mu′di·an, Ber·mu′dan** *adj. & n.*

Bern or **Berne** (bûrn, bĕrn). The capital of Switzerland, in the west-central part of the country on the Aare River. Founded as a military post in 1191, it became part of the Swiss Confederation in 1353 and its capital in 1848. ⊛ Pop. 129,692.

Ber·nese Alps (bûr′nēz, -nēs, bûr-nēz′, -nēs′). A range of the Alps in south-central Switzerland rising to 4,276.7 m (14,022 ft).

Ber·ni·ci·a (bər-nĭsh′ē-ə, -nĭsh′ə, bĕr-). A sixth-century A.D. Anglian kingdom in present-day northeast England. It was later part of the kingdom of Northumbria.

Ber·ni·na Alps (bər-nē′nə, bĕr-). A mountain group of southeast Switzerland in the Rhaetian Alps on the Swiss-Italian border. The highest elevation is **Piz Bernina,** rising to 4,051.6 m (13,284 ft). **Bernina Pass** connects Switzerland and Italy by road and rail.

Ber·ry (bĕ-rē′). A historical region and former province of central France. Purchased by the French crown in 1101, it became an independent duchy in 1360 and reverted to the crown in 1601.

Ber·wyn (bûr′wĭn). A city of northeast Illinois, a residential suburb of Chicago. ⊛ Pop. 45,426.

Be·san·çon (bĭ-zän-sōn′). A city of eastern France east of Dijon. It is an industrial center noted for the manufacture of clocks and watches. ⊛ Pop. 113,835.

Bes·kids (bĕs′kĭdz′, bĕs-kēdz′). A mountain range of the western Carpathians extending about 322 km (200 mi) along the Polish-Slovak border and rising to 1,726 m (5,659 ft) at Babia Góra. The range is divided into the **East Beskids** and the **West Beskids.**

Bes·sa·ra·bi·a (bĕs′ə-rā′bē-ə). A region of Moldova and western Ukraine. As the gateway from Russia into the Danube River valley, it was for centuries an invasion route from Asia to Europe. The region became part of Russia in 1812 but declared itself independent in 1918 and later voted for union with Romania, which was forced to cede it to the U.S.S.R. in 1940. — **Bes′sa·ra′bi·an** *adj. & n.*

Bes·se·mer (bĕs′ə-mər). A city of north-central Alabama south-southwest of Birmingham.

Founded as a mining town, it was named after Sir Henry Bessemer. ⊛ Pop. 33,497.

Beth·a·ny (bĕth′ə-nē). **1.** A village of ancient Palestine at the foot of the Mount of Olives near Jerusalem. According to the New Testament, it was the site of the resurrection of Lazarus. **2.** A city of central Oklahoma west of Oklahoma City. It was settled in 1906. ⊛ Pop. 20,075.

Beth·el (bĕth′əl). **1.** A town of ancient Palestine north of Jerusalem. It is now a major archaeological site. **2.** A town of southwest Connecticut southeast of Danbury. It has varied light industries. ⊛ Pop. 17,541.

Bethel Park. 1. A borough of southwest Pennsylvania, an industrial suburb of Pittsburgh. ⊛ Pop. 33,823. **2.** A town of southwest Connecticut southeast of Danbury. It has varied light industries. ⊛ Pop. 17,541.

Be·thes·da (bə-thĕz′də). An unincorporated city of west-central Maryland, a residential suburb of Washington, D.C. The National Institutes of Health and Naval Medical Center are here. ⊛ Pop. 62,936.

Beth·le·hem (bĕth′lĭ-hĕm′, -lē-əm). **1.** A town in the West Bank south of Jerusalem. It is the traditional birthplace of Jesus. ⊛ Pop. 25,000. **2.** A city of eastern Pennsylvania on the Lehigh River north-northwest of Philadelphia. It is an important steel-producing center. ⊛ Pop. 71,428.

Beth·page (bĕth-pāj′). An unincorporated village of southeast New York on southwest Long Island. It is mainly residential. ⊛ Pop. 15,761.

Beth·sa·i·da (bĕth-sā′ĭ-də). A town of ancient Palestine on the northeast shore of the Sea of Galilee.

Bet·si·a·mi·tes (bĕt′sē-ə-mē′tēz). A river rising in the highlands of eastern Quebec, Canada, and flowing about 386 km (240 mi) generally southeast to the St. Lawrence River.

Bet·ten·dorf (bĕt′n-dôrf′). A city of eastern Iowa, an industrial suburb of Davenport on the Mississippi River. ⊛ Pop. 28,132.

Bev·er·ly (bĕv′ər-lē). A city of northeast Massachusetts northeast of Boston. It was settled in 1626. The schooner *Hannah,* the first ship of the Continental Navy, was outfitted here (1775). ⊛ Pop. 38,195.

Beverly Hills. A city of southern California surrounded by Los Angeles. It adjoins Hollywood and is famous as a fashionable residential area for show business personalities. ⊛ Pop. 31,971.

Bé·ziers (bāz-yā′). A city of southern France southwest of Montpellier. An ancient Gallic fortress, it is an industrial center with an important trade in wines. ⊛ Pop. 76,647.

Bez·wa·da (bĕz-wä′də). See **Vijayawada.**

Bha·gal·pur (bä′gəl-pŏŏr′). A city of northeast

India on the Ganges River north-northwest of Calcutta. It has remains of Buddhist monasteries. ⊛ Pop. 253,225.

Bhat·pa·ra (bät-pä′rə). A city of northeast India on the Hooghly River north of Calcutta. Once a center of Sanskrit learning, it is now part of a vast industrial complex. ⊛ Pop. 304,952.

Bhav·na·gar (bou-nŭg′ər, bäv-). A city of western India on the Gulf of Cambay south of Ahmadabad. It is a manufacturing center and major port. ⊛ Pop. 402,338.

Bhi·lai·na·gar (bĭ-lī′nə-gər) or **Bhi·lai** (bĭ-lī′). A city of east-central India east of Nagpur. It is the site of a large state-owned steel industry built with Soviet assistance. ⊛ Pop. 386,159.

Bho·lan Pass (bō-län′). See **Bolan Pass.**

Bho·pal (bō-päl′). A city of central India north-northwest of Nagpur. Founded in the early 18th century, it is an industrial and trade center. In 1984 a toxic gas leak at an insecticide plant killed more than 2,000 people. ⊛ Pop. 1,062,771.

Bhu·ba·nes·war (boo′bə-nĕsh′wər). A city of east-central India southwest of Calcutta. It is known for its Hindu and Buddhist shrines. ⊛ Pop. 411,542.

Bhu·tan (boo-tăn′, -tän′). *abbr.* **Bhu.** An isolated country of central Asia in the eastern Himalaya Mountains. Long under the influence of Great Britain and India, the kingdom became fully independent in the 1980's. Thimphu is the capital and the largest city. ⊛ Pop. 1,614,000.

Bhu·tan·ese (boo′tə-nēz′, -nēs′). **1.** Of or relating to Bhutan or its people, language, or culture. **2.** *pl.* **Bhutanese.** A native or inhabitant of Bhutan. **3.** The Sino-Tibetan language of Bhutan.

Bi·a·fra (bē-ăf′rə, -ä′frə). A region of eastern Nigeria on the **Bight of Biafra,** an arm of the Gulf of Guinea stretching from the Niger River delta to northern Gabon. It formed a secessionist state from May 1967 to January 1970. **— Bi·a′fran** *adj. & n.*

Bi·ak (bē-yäk′). The largest of the Schouten Islands of Indonesia, off the northwest coast of New Guinea. In World War II it was the scene of heavy fighting from May 27 to June 20, 1944.

Bia·ly·stok (bē-ä′lĭ-stôk′, byä′wĭ-). A city of

northeast Poland near the border of Belarus. About half the city's population was killed by Nazi occupation forces (1941–1944). Today it is an industrial and transportation center. ⊛ Pop. 272,137.

Biar·ritz (bē′ə-rĭts′, bē′ə-rĭts′). A city of southwest France on the Bay of Biscay near the Spanish border. It is a fashionable resort. ⊛ Pop. 26,598.

Bid·de·ford (bĭd′ə-fərd). A city of southwest Maine on the Saco River southwest of Portland. The first permanent settlement was established in 1630. ⊛ Pop. 20,710.

Biel (bēl) also **Bi·enne** (bē-ĕn′). A city of northwest Switzerland at the northeast end of the **Lake of Biel** at the foot of the Jura Mountains. It is noted for its clocks. ⊛ Pop. 52,600.

Bie·le·feld (bē′lə-fĕlt′). A city of northwest Germany east of Münster. It is an industrial center long known for its fine linens. ⊛ Pop. 324,674.

Biel·la (bē-ĕl′ə). A city of northwest Italy west-northwest of Milan. It is a manufacturing center famous for its textiles. ⊛ Pop. 53,572.

Biel·sko-Bia·la (byĕl′skô-byä′lä, -byä′wä). A city of southern Poland south of Katowice. Founded in the 13th century, it passed to Austria in 1772 and was returned to Poland in 1919. ⊛ Pop. 184,108.

Bi·enne (bē-ĕn′). See **Biel.**

Bier·stadt (bîr′stät′), **Mount.** A peak, 4,288.3 m (14,000 ft) high, of north-central Colorado in the Front Range of the Rocky Mountains.

Big Bend (bĭg). A region of southwest Texas on the Mexican border in a triangle formed by a bend in the Rio Grande. The area includes deep river canyons, desert wilderness, mountains rising to 2,386.6 m (7,825 ft), archaeological remains, and rare forms of plant and animal life.

Big Black River. A river rising in north-central Mississippi and flowing about 531 km (330 mi) generally southwest to the Mississippi River below Vicksburg.

Big Blue River. A river rising in southeast Nebraska and flowing about 483 km (300 mi) east and southeast to the Kansas River in northeast Kansas near Manhattan.

Big Diomede Island. See **Diomede Islands.**

Big·horn Mountains (bĭg′hôrn′). A section of the Rocky Mountains of northern Wyoming and southern Montana rising to 4,018.4 m (13,175 ft) at Cloud Peak in Wyoming.

Bighorn River. A river rising in west-central Wyoming and flowing about 742 km (461 mi) north to join the Yellowstone River in southern Montana northeast of Billings.

bight (bīt). **1.** A bend or curve, especially in a

shoreline. **2.** A wide bay formed by such a bend or curve.

Big Muddy River. A river of southwest Illinois flowing about 217 km (135 mi) to the Mississippi River north-northwest of Cairo.

Big Sandy Creek. A river rising in central Colorado and flowing about 322 km (200 mi) east-northeast and southeast to the Arkansas River.

Big Sioux River. A river rising in northeast South Dakota and flowing about 676 km (420 mi) southward, partly along the South Dakota–Iowa border, to the Missouri River at Sioux City, Iowa.

Big Spring. A city of west-central Texas west-southwest of Abilene. It is a trade center in an agricultural region. ● Pop. 23,093.

Big Sur (sûr). A rugged, picturesque resort region along the Pacific coast of California south of Carmel and Monterey.

Bi·har (bē-här′). A region of east-central India crossed by the Ganges River. Buddha spent his early days in the area.

Bi·ha·ri (bĭ-hä′rē). **1.** *pl.* **Bihari** or **-ris.** A native or inhabitant of Bihar. **2.** The Indic language of the Bihari.

Bi·ka·ner (bē′kə-nîr′, -nâr′). A city of northwest India in the Thar Desert near the Pakistan border west-southwest of Delhi. It has several 16th-century Rajput palaces built of red sandstone. ● Pop. 416,289.

Bi·ki·ni (bĭ-kē′nē). An atoll in the Ralik Chain of the Marshall Islands in the west-central Pacific Ocean. The area was the site of U.S. nuclear tests between 1946 and 1958, including the first aerial detonation of a hydrogen bomb (May 21, 1956).

Bil·ba·o (bĭl-bä′ō, -bou′). A city of northern Spain near the Bay of Biscay. Founded c. 1300, it is a major port and industrial center. ● Pop. 365,269.

Bille·ric·a (bĭl-rĭk′ə, bĕl′ə-). A town of northeast Massachusetts south of Lowell. Settled in 1637, it is primarily residential. ● Pop. 37,609.

Bil·lings (bĭl′ĭngz). A city of southern Montana on the Yellowstone River east-southeast of Helena. A trade and manufacturing center, it is the largest city in the state. ● Pop. 81,151.

Bil·li·ton (bə-lē′tŏn′). See **Belitung.**

Bi·lox·i¹ (bə-lŭk′sē, -lŏk′-). **1.** *pl.* **Biloxi** or **-is.** A member of a Native American people formerly inhabiting territory around Biloxi Bay in southeast Mississippi on the Gulf of Mexico. **2.** The extinct Siouan language of the Biloxis.

Bi·lox·i² (bə-lŭk′sē, -lŏk′-). A city of southeast Mississippi on a peninsula between **Biloxi Bay** and Mississippi Sound on the Gulf of Mexico. Old Biloxi was settled by the French in 1699. ● Pop. 46,319.

Bim·i·nis (bĭm′ə-nēz). A group of small islands of the western Bahamas in the Straits of Florida. According to legend, the islands are the site of the Fountain of Youth sought by the Spanish explorer Juan Ponce de León (1460–1521).

Bing·ham·ton (bĭng′əm-tən). A city of south-central New York near the Pennsylvania border south-southeast of Syracuse. It was settled in 1787. ● Pop. 53,008.

Bin·ue (bĭn′wā). See **Benue.**

Bí·o-Bí·o (bē′ō-bē′ō). A river of central Chile flowing about 386 km (240 mi) generally northwest from the Andes to the Pacific Ocean near Concepción.

Bi·o·ko (bē-ō′kō). Formerly **Fer·nan·do Po** (fər-năn′dō pō′). An island of Equatorial Guinea in the Gulf of Guinea.

bi·o·sphere (bī′ə-sfîr′). The part of the earth and its atmosphere in which living organisms exist or that is capable of supporting life.

Bir·ken·head (bûr′kən-hĕd′). A borough of northwest England at the mouth of the Mersey River near Liverpool. It has extensive docks and is a shipbuilding center. ● Pop. 99,075.

Bir·ming·ham (bûr′mĭng-hăm′). **1.** A city of central England northwest of London. It is a major industrial center and transportation hub. ● Pop. 1,012,351. **2.** A city of north-central Alabama northeast of Tuscaloosa. The largest city in the state, it is in a mining and industrial region. ● Pop. 265,968. **3.** A city of southeast Michigan, a residential suburb of Detroit. ● Pop. 19,997.

Bis·cay (bĭs′kā). **Bay of.** An arm of the Atlantic Ocean indenting the western coast of Europe from Brittany in northwest France southward to northwest Spain.

Bis·cayne Bay (bĭs-kān′, bĭs′kān′). A narrow inlet of the Atlantic Ocean in southeast Florida.

bise (bēz). A cold north wind of the Swiss Alps and nearby regions of France and Italy.

Bish·kek (bĭsh′kĕk, bēsh′-). Formerly **Frun·ze** (frōōn′zə). The capital of Kyrgyzstan in the north-central part on the Chu River west-southwest of Almaty, Kazakhstan. Built on the sight of a fort established in 1846, it was taken by the Russians in 1862. ● Pop. 627,800.

Bisk (bĭsk, bēsk). See **Biysk.**

Bis·la·ma (bĭs-lä′mə). A lingua franca that combines Malay and English, spoken in the southwest Pacific, especially in the Papua New Guinea area. Also called *Beach-la-Mar, Bêche-de-Mer.*

Bis·marck (bĭz′märk′). The capital of North Dakota, in the south-central part of the state on hills overlooking the Missouri River. It was originally a camp for laborers building the Northern Pacific Railroad. ● Pop. 49,256.

Bismarck Archipelago. A group of volcanic

islands and islets of Papua New Guinea in the southwest Pacific Ocean. The islands were discovered by Dutch explorers in the early 1700's.

Bismarck Sea. A section of the southwest Pacific Ocean northeast of New Guinea and northwest of New Britain. During World War II it was the site of a major naval battle (March 2–3, 1943) in which the Japanese fleet was completely destroyed.

Bis·sau (bĭ-sou′). The capital and largest city of Guinea-Bissau, on an estuary of the Atlantic Ocean. Founded by the Portuguese in 1687, the city has been a free port since 1869. ◉ Pop. 109,486.

Bi·thyn·i·a (bĭ-thĭn′ē-ə). An ancient country of northwest Asia Minor in present-day Turkey. Originally inhabited by Thracians, it was absorbed into the Roman Empire by the end of the first century B.C. — **Bi·thyn′i·an** adj. & n.

Bi·to·la (bēt′l-yä′, bē′tôl-yä′). A city of southern Macedonia near the Greek border. It was a major agricultural center in Roman times and an important military and commercial center in the 15th and 16th centuries. ◉ Pop. 72,900.

Bit·ter·root Range (bĭt′ər-rōōt′, -rŏŏt′). A rugged chain of the Rocky Mountains along the Idaho-Montana border. It rises to 3,474.9 m (11,393 ft) at Scott Peak.

Bitterroot River. A river rising in southwest Montana and flowing about 193 km (120 mi) northward to the Clark Fork River near Missoula in west-central Montana.

Bi·wa (bē′wä). A lake of southern Honshu, Japan, west of Nagoya. It is the largest lake in the country and a popular scenic resort area.

Bi·ysk (bē′ĭsk, bēsk) or **Bisk** (bĭsk, bēsk). A city of south-central Russia east-southeast of Barnaul. It was founded as a fortress in 1709. ◉ Pop. 232,529.

Bi·zer·te (bĭ-zûr′tē, bē-zĕrt′). A city of northern Tunisia on the Mediterranean Sea northwest of Tunis. It was founded by the Phoenicians and is today a major port and naval base. ◉ Pop. 62,856.

Black·burn (blăk′bûrn′). A borough of northwest England north-northwest of Manchester. The city's textile industry dates to the early 17th century. ◉ Pop. 139,528.

Blackburn, Mount. A peak, 5,039.5 m (16,523 ft) high, of the Wrangell Mountains in southern Alaska.

Black Country (blăk). A highly industrialized region of west-central England centered on Birmingham. It was named for the grime accumulated from factory smoke and other industrial pollutants.

Black English. The range of varieties of English spoken by American Black people.

Black·foot (blăk′fŏŏt′). **1.** pl. **Blackfoot** or **-feet.** A member of a Native American confederacy located on the northern Great Plains, composed of the Blackfoot, Blood, and Piegan tribes. Traditional Blackfoot life was based on nomadic buffalo hunting. **2.** A member of the northernmost tribe of the Blackfoot confederacy, inhabiting central Alberta. **3.** The Algonquian language of the Blackfeet, Bloods, and Piegans. **4.** See **Sihasapa.** — **Black′foot′** adj.

Blackfoot Sioux. See **Sihasapa.**

Black Forest. A mountainous region of southwest Germany between the Rhine and Neckar rivers. It is a year-round resort area that is famous for its clock and toy industries.

Black Hills. A group of rugged mountains of southwest South Dakota and northeast Wyoming rising to 2,208.8 m (7,242 ft) at Harney Peak. The Black Hills are a major recreational area.

Black Mountains. A range of the Blue Ridge in western North Carolina rising to 2,038.6 km (6,684 ft) at Mount Mitchell.

Black·pool (blăk′pōōl′). A borough of northwest England on the Irish Sea north of Liverpool. It is a popular seaside resort. ◉ Pop. 153,614.

Black River. 1. or in China **Ba·bian Jiang** (bä′byän′ jyäng′) and in Vietnam **Song Da** (sông′ dä′). A river of southeast Asia rising in southern China and flowing about 805 km (500 mi) generally southeast to the Red River in northern Vietnam. **2.** A river rising in southeast Missouri and flowing about 483 km (300 mi) to the White River in northeast Arkansas. **3.** A river of northern New York rising in the Adirondack Mountains and flowing about 193 km (120 mi) to **Black River Bay,** an inlet of Lake Ontario. **4.** A river rising in central Wisconsin and flowing about 257 km (160 mi) generally southwest to the Mississippi River at La Crosse.

Blacks·burg (blăks′bûrg′). A town of southwest Virginia in the Allegheny Mountains west of Roanoke. Virginia Polytechnic Institute and State University (established 1872) is located here. ◉ Pop. 34,590.

Black Sea. An inland sea between Europe and Asia. The Black Sea is connected with the Aegean Sea by the Bosporus, the Sea of Marmara, and the Dardanelles.

Black·town (blăk′toun′). A city of southeast Australia, a suburb of Sydney. ◉ Pop. 192,200.

Black Volta. A river of western Africa rising in western Burkina Faso and flowing about 1,352 km (840 mi) to the White Volta in Ghana.

Black War·ri·or River (wôr′ē-ər, wŏr′-). A river rising in north-central Alabama and flowing about 286 km (178 mi) generally southwest to the Tombigbee River.

Bla·go·vesh·chensk (blä′gə-věsh′chěnsk, blə-gə-vyěsh′chĭsk). A city of eastern Russia at the confluence of the Amur and Zeya rivers. It is a port and railroad hub. ⊛ Pop. 212,179.

Blaine (blān). A city of eastern Minnesota, an industrial suburb of St. Paul. ⊛ Pop. 38,975.

Blanc (blängk, bläɴ), **Mont.** The highest peak of the Alps, rising to 4,810.2 m (15,771 ft) in the Savoy Alps of southeast France on the Italian border.

Blan·ca Peak (blăng′kə). A mountain, 4,375.2 m (14,345 ft) high, in the Sangre de Cristo Mountains of southern Colorado. It is the highest elevation in the range.

Blan·tyre (blăn-tīr′). A city of southern Malawi. It is the largest city and chief commercial center of the country. ⊛ Pop. 331,588.

Blar·ney (blär′nē). A village of southern Ireland near Cork. Blarney Castle (dating from the 15th century) is the site of the Blarney Stone, said to impart powers of eloquence and persuasion.

Bli·da (blē′də). A town of northern Algeria at the foot of the Atlas Mountains southwest of Algiers. It was built on the site of a Roman military base. ⊛ Pop. 138,240.

Block Island (blŏk). An island off southern Rhode Island at the eastern entrance to Long Island Sound. Visited by Dutch explorers in 1614, it was settled in 1661.

Bloem·fon·tein (blōōm′fŏn-tān′). A city of central South Africa east-southeast of Kimberley. It is unofficially called the judicial capital of the country because the appellate division of the national supreme court sits here. ⊛ Pop. 104,381.

Blois (blwä). A town of central France on the Loire River northeast of Tours. It was the seat of the powerful counts of Blois and a favorite residence of French royalty. ⊛ Pop. 47,243.

Blood (blŭd). **1.** *pl.* **Blood** or **-Bloods.** A member of a tribe of the Blackfoot confederacy inhabiting southern Alberta.

Bloom·field (blōōm′fēld′). **1.** A town of north-central Connecticut, north-northwest of Hartford. ⊛ Pop. 19,483. **2.** A town of northeast New Jersey, an industrial and residential suburb of Newark. It was settled c. 1660. ⊛ Pop. 45,061.

Bloo·ming·ton (blōō′mĭng-tən). **1.** A city of central Illinois east-southeast of Peoria. It is a commercial and industrial center. ⊛ Pop. 51,972. **2.** A city of south-central Indiana south-southwest of Indianapolis. Indiana University (established 1820) is located here. ⊛ Pop. 60,633. **3.** A city of eastern Minnesota, a suburb of Minneapolis. ⊛ Pop. 86,335.

Blooms·bur·y (blōōmz′běr′-ē, -bə-rē, -brē). A residential district of north-central London, England, made famous by its association with an influential group of writers, artists, and intellectuals, including Virginia Woolf, E.M. Forster, and John Maynard Keynes, in the early 20th century.

Blue·field (blōō′fēld′). A city of southern West Virginia in the Allegheny Mountains south-southeast of Charleston. It is a trade and shipping center in a coal-mining region. ⊛ Pop. 12,756.

Blue·grass also **Blue·grass Country** or **Blue·grass Region** (blōō′grăs′). A region of central Kentucky noted for its lushly growing bluegrass and the breeding of thoroughbred horses.

Blue Island (blōō). A city of northeast Illinois, a residential and industrial suburb of Chicago. ⊛ Pop. 21,203.

Blue Mountains. **1.** A range of northeast Oregon and southeast Washington consisting of an uplifted, eroded part of the Columbia Plateau. It rises to 2,777.3 m (9,106 ft) at Rock Creek Butte in Oregon. **2.** A range of eastern Jamaica rising to 2,252 m (7,388 ft) at **Blue Mountain Peak.** It is a coffee-growing area.

Blue Nile. A river of northeast Africa. It is the chief headstream of the Nile and flows about 1,609 km (1,000 mi) from northwest Ethiopia to Sudan. At Khartoum it merges with the White Nile to form the Nile River proper.

Blue Ridge also **Blue Ridge Mountains.** A range of the Appalachian Mountains extending from southern Pennsylvania to northern Georgia. It rises to 2,038.6 m (6,684 ft) at Mount Mitchell in the Black Mountains of western North Carolina.

Blue Springs. A city of western Missouri, a suburb of Kansas City. ⊛ Pop. 40,153.

bluff (blŭf). **1.** A steep headland, promontory, riverbank, or cliff. **2.** Having a broad, steep front. **— bluff′ly** *adv.* **— bluff′ness** *n.*

Blu·me·nau (blōō′mĭ-nou′). A town of southern Brazil southwest of São Paulo. It was founded by German immigrants in the 1850's. ⊛ Pop. 211,862.

Blyth (blī, blīth). A municipal borough of northeast England on the North Sea at the mouth of the **Blyth River.** It is an industrial center and a seaport. ⊛ Pop. 78,200.

Blythe·ville (blī′vəl, blīth′vĭl′). A city of northeast Arkansas near the Mississippi River north of Memphis, Tennessee. It is a trade center in a cotton-growing area. ⊛ Pop. 22,906.

Bo·bruysk also **Bo·bruisk** (bə-brōō′ĭsk). A city of southern Belarus southeast of Minsk. It was founded in the 16th century. ⊛ Pop. 226,000.

Bo·ca Ra·ton (bō′kə rə-tōn′). A city of southeast Florida on the Atlantic Ocean south of Palm Beach. It is a resort and industrial center. ⊛ Pop. 61,492.

Bo·cholt (bō′kŏlt, -кнôlt). A city of west-central Germany near the Netherlands border northwest of Essen. It is a manufacturing center. ⊛ Pop. 65,710.

Bo·chum (bō′kəm, -кнo͞om). A city of west-central Germany in the Ruhr Valley east of Essen. Chartered in 1321, it is an industrial and commercial center. ⊛ Pop. 401,058.

Bo·den·see (bōd′n-zā′). See Lake of **Constance**.

Boe·o·tia (bē-ō′shə, -shē-ə). An ancient region of Greece north of Attica and the Gulf of Corinth. The cities of the region formed the **Boeotian League** in the seventh century B.C. but were usually under the dominance of Thebes. **—Boe·o′tian** adj. & n.

Boer (bōr, bôr, bo͞or). A Dutch colonist or descendant of a Dutch colonist in South Africa.

Bo·ga·lu·sa (bō′gə-lo͞o′sə). A city of southeast Louisiana near the Mississippi border northnortheast of New Orleans. It was founded in 1906. ⊛ Pop. 14,280.

Bo·gor (bō′gôr′). A city of western Java, Indonesia, south of Jakarta. It is a resort and agricultural research center with notable botanical gardens. ⊛ Pop. 247,409.

Bo·go·tá (bō′gə-tä′). The capital and largest city of Colombia, in the central part of the country on a high plain in the eastern Andes. It was a center of Chibcha culture before the Spanish established a settlement here in 1538. ⊛ Pop. 5,025,989.

Bo Hai also **Po Hai** (bō′ hī′). An inlet of the Yellow Sea on the northeast coast of China west of the Shandong and Liaodong peninsulas.

Bo·he·mi·a (bō-hē′mē-ə). A historical region and former kingdom of present-day western Czech Republic. The Czechs, a Slavic people, settled in the area between the 1st and 5th centuries A.D. A later principality was independent until the 15th century, when it passed to Hungary and then to the Hapsburg dynasty of Austria. Bohemia became the core of the newly formed state of Czechoslovakia in 1918.

Bo·he·mi·an (bō-hē′mē-ən). **1.** A native or inhabitant of Bohemia. **2.** A Gypsy. **3.** The Czech dialects of Bohemia. **—Bo·he′mi·an** adj.

Bohemian Forest. A mountain range along the border of southeast Germany and western Czech Republic. The region is known for its glassmaking and woodcarving.

Bo·hol (bō-hôl′). An island in the Visayan Islands of central Philippines north of Mindanao in the **Bohol Sea**. The **Bohol Strait** separates Bohol from Cebu.

Bois de Bou·logne (bwä′ də bo͞o-lōn′, -lôn′-yə). A park in Paris, France, bordering on the suburb of Neuilly-sur-Seine. A popular recreation area since the 17th century, it is the site of Auteuil and Longchamps racecourses.

Boi·se (boi′sē, -zē). The capital and largest city of Idaho, in the southwest part of the state on the **Boise River,** about 257 km (160 mi) long. The city was founded in 1863 after gold was discovered in the river valley. ⊛ Pop. 102,160.

Bo·kha·ra (bō-kär′ə, -här′ə, -кнä′rə). See **Bukhara**.

Bok·mål (bo͞ok′môl′, bōk′-). See **Dano-Norwegian**.

Bo·lan Pass also **Bho·lan Pass** (bō-län′). A mountain pass of western Pakistan at an altitude of 1,793.4 m (5,880 ft). The strategic pass has long been a gateway to India.

Bo·ling·brook (bō′lĭng-bro͞ok′). A village of northeast Illinois, a suburb of Chicago. ⊛ Pop. 40,843.

Bo·lí·var (bō′lə-vär′, bŏl′ə-, bō-lē′vär), **Pico.** A mountain, 5,005.4 m (16,411 ft) high, of western Venezuela in the Cordillera Mérida south of Lake Maracaibo. It is the highest elevation in the range and in the country.

Bo·liv·i·a (bə-lĭv′ē-ə, bō-). abbr. **Bol.** A landlocked country of western South America. Once a part of the Incan Empire, the area was conquered by Spain in the 16th century. It was named Bolivia after Simón Bolívar, the South American revolutionary leader who helped win its independence from Spain in 1825. Much territory, including an outlet to the Pacific Ocean, was lost to Chile, Brazil, and Paraguay during the late 19th and early 20th centuries as a result of border wars. Subject to political instability since independence, the government was taken over by the military in 1964 and was not returned to civilian control until 1982. Sucre is the legal capital and the seat of the judiciary. La Paz is the administrative center and the largest city. ⊛ Pop. 7,237,000. **—Bo·liv′i·an** adj. & n.

Bo·lo·gna (bə-lōn′yə). A city of north-central Italy at the foot of the Apennines north-northeast of Florence. It was originally an Etruscan town and became a Roman colony in the second century B.C. Its famed university was founded as a law school in A.D. 425. ⊕ Pop. 404,322. —**Bo·lo′gnan**, **Bo′lo·gnese′** (bō′lə-nēz′, -nēs′, -lən-yēz′, -yēs′) *adj. & n.*

bol·son (bōl-sōn′). *Chiefly Southwestern U.S.* A flat, arid valley surrounded by mountains and draining into a shallow central lake.

Bol·ton (bōl′tən). A borough of northwest England northwest of Manchester. It was a center of the woolen trade from the 14th to the 18th century. ⊕ Pop. 264,880.

Bol·za·no (bōl-zä′nō, bôl-tsä′nô). A city of northern Italy near the Austrian border northnorthwest of Venice. It is a tourist center and health resort noted for its Alpine scenery. ⊕ Pop. 98,233.

Bom·bay (bŏm-bā′). A city of west-central India on coastal **Bombay Island** and adjacent Salsette Island. It is India's main port and commercial center. ⊕ Pop. 9,925,891.

Bo·mu (bō′mōō). A river of central Africa rising in southeast Central African Republic and flowing about 805 km (500 mi) generally west along the boundary with Zaire to merge with the Uele and form the Ubangi River.

Bon (bŏn, bôN), **Cape.** A peninsula of northeast Tunisia extending into the Mediterranean Sea across from Sicily.

Bo·na (bō′nə), **Mount.** A peak, 5,032.5 m (16,500 ft) high, of southern Alaska at the southern end of the Wrangell Mountains near the Canadian border. It is the highest elevation in the range.

Bo·naire (bô-nâr′). An island of the Netherlands Antilles in the Caribbean Sea off the northern coast of Venezuela. Tourism is important to its economy.

Bo·nam·pak (bō-näm′päk). A ruined Mayan city near present-day Tuxtla Gutiérrez in southern Mexico. The ruins, with temples and wellpreserved frescoes, were discovered in 1946.

Bo·nan·za Creek (bə-năn′zə). A stream of western Yukon Territory, Canada, flowing about 32 km (20 mi) to the Klondike River near Dawson. The first gold strike in the Yukon occurred here in 1896.

Bo·nin Islands (bō′nĭn). An archipelago of volcanic islands in the western Pacific Ocean south of Japan. The islands formed a major Japanese military stronghold in World War II.

Bonn (bŏn, bôn). A city of west-central Germany on the Rhine River. Founded as a Roman garrison in the first century A.D., it was the capital of West Germany from 1949 to 1990. In 1991 Berlin was designated the official seat of the reunified German government with the move to be completed by the year 2000, but some government offices will remain in Bonn. ⊕ Pop. 296,859.

Bon·ne·ville Salt Flats (bŏn′ə-vĭl′). A plain of northwest Utah west of Great Salt Lake in the bed of prehistoric **Lake Bonneville.** The flats are often used for speed-test trials.

Boo·thi·a Peninsula (bōō′thē-ə). The northernmost tip of the North American mainland, in northeast Northwest Territories, Canada. It is connected with the Canadian mainland by the narrow **Isthmus of Boothia** and separated from Baffin Island to the east by the **Gulf of Boothia,** an arm of the Arctic Ocean.

Boo·tle (bōōt′l). A borough of northwest England, a suburb of Liverpool at the mouth of the Mersey River. ⊕ Pop. 62,463.

Bo·phu·tha·tswa·na (bō′pōō-tät-swä′nə). A former autonomous Black homeland of northern South Africa. It was granted nominal independence in December 1977 and was dissolved and reintegrated into South Africa by the 1993 interim constitution.

bo·ra (bôr′ə, bōr′ə). A violent, cold, northeasterly winter wind on the Adriatic Sea.

Bo·ra Bo·ra (bôr′ə bôr′ə, bōr′ə bōr′ə). A volcanic island of French Polynesia in the Leeward group of the Society Islands in the southern Pacific Ocean.

Bo·rah Peak (bôr′ə, bōr′ə). A mountain, 3,861.9 m (12,662 ft) high, in the Lost River Range of central Idaho. It is the highest elevation in the state.

Bo·rås (bōō-rôs′). A city of southwest Sweden east of Göteborg. It was founded in 1632. ⊕ Pop. 102,840.

Bor·deaux (bôr-dō′). A city of southwest France on the Garonne River. It was under English rule from 1154 to 1453 and was the seat of the French government in 1914 and again in 1940. Bordeaux is the trading center of a notable wine-producing region. ⊕ Pop. 210,467.

bor·der (bôr′dər). The line or frontier area separating political divisions or geographic regions; a boundary. —**bor′der·er** *n.*

bor·der·land (bôr′dər-lănd′). Land located on or near a frontier.

Bor·der States (bôr′dər). The slave states of Delaware, Maryland, Virginia, Kentucky, and Missouri that were adjacent to the free states of the North during the Civil War. Virginia joined the Confederacy in 1861, causing its western counties to form the new state of West Virginia. It and other Border States remained tied to the Union despite strong Southern sympathies.

Bor·ger (bôr′gər). A city of northern Texas in the Panhandle northeast of Amarillo. Oil was discovered in the area in 1925. ⊕ Pop. 15,675.

Bor·ne·o (bôr′nē-ō′). An island of the western Pacific Ocean in the Malay Archipelago between the Sulu and Java seas southwest of the Philippines. It is the third-largest island in the world. The sultanate of Brunei is on the northwest coast; the rest of the island is divided between Indonesia and Malaysia. — **Bor′ne·an** *adj. & n.*

Born·holm (bôrn′hōm′, -hōlm′, -hôlm′). An island of eastern Denmark in the Baltic Sea near Sweden. It was held for varying periods by Denmark, Sweden, and Lübeck merchants before becoming part of Denmark in the 1600's.

Bor·nu (bôr′nōō). A region and former Muslim kingdom of western Africa occupying a vast plain in present-day northeast Nigeria. Founded in the 11th century, the kingdom reached the height of its power in the late 16th century. The region became part of Nigeria in 1902.

Bo·ro·bu·dur (bôr′ə-bə-dōōr′, bōr′-). A ruined Buddhist shrine in central Java, Indonesia. Dating probably from the ninth century, the ruins include intricately carved stone blocks illustrating episodes in the life of Buddha.

Bo·ro·di·no (bôr′ə-dē′nō, bŏr′-, bə-rə-dyē-nô′). A village of western Russia west of Moscow. Nearby, Napoleon I, emperor of the French (1804–1814), defeated the Russian troops defending Moscow on September 7, 1812.

bor·ough (bûr′ō, bŭr′ō). *abbr.* **bor. 1.** A self-governing incorporated town in some U.S. states, such as New Jersey. **2.** One of the five administrative units of New York City. **3.** A civil division of the state of Alaska that is the equivalent of a county in most other U.S. states. **4.** *Chiefly British.* **a.** A town having a municipal corporation and certain rights, such as self-government. **b.** A town that sends a representative to Parliament. **5.** A medieval group of fortified houses that formed a town having special privileges and rights.

Bos·ni·a (bŏz′nē-ə). **1.** A region that forms the northern part of Bosnia and Herzegovina. It was settled by Serbs in the 7th century and became an independent state in the 12th century. Bosnia was controlled after 1463 by Turkey and after 1878 by the Austro-Hungarian Empire, which formally annexed Bosnia in 1908. After World War II Bosnia was united with Herzegovina to form a constituent republic of Yugoslavia. **2.** See **Bosnia and Herzegovina.** — **Bos′ni·an** *adj. & n.*

Bosnia and Her·ze·go·vi·na (hĕrt′sə-gō-vē′nə, hûrt′-) or **Bosnia-Herzegovina.** Commonly known as **Bosnia.** A country of the northwest Balkan Peninsula. It was a constituent republic of Yugoslavia from 1946 to 1991, when it declared its independence. In 1992 the country erupted in war when Bosnian Serbs, with the help of the largely Serbian Yugoslav army,

attempted to create a separate state within Bosnia and Herzegovina and gained control of a large portion of the country. Bosnian Muslims and Croats joined forces and in 1995 retook much of the territory that had been lost to the Serbs. An agreement reached in November 1995 by Balkan leaders in Dayton, Ohio, called for the creation of two substates, a Muslim-Croat federation to govern one half of the country and a Bosnian Serb republic to constitute the other half, both of which would be united under a newly created national presidency, assembly, court, and central bank ◉ Pop. 3,527,000.

Bos·po·rus (bŏs′pər-əs). A narrow strait separating European and Asian Turkey and joining the Black Sea with the Sea of Marmara. It has been an important trade route since ancient times.

Bos·sier City (bō′zhər). A city of northwest Louisiana, an industrial suburb of Shreveport on the opposite bank of the Red River. ◉ Pop. 52,721.

Bos·ton (bô′stən, bŏs′tən). The capital and largest city of Massachusetts, in the eastern part of the state on **Boston Bay,** an arm of Massachusetts Bay. Founded in the 17th century, it was a leading center of agitation against England in the 18th century and a stronghold of abolitionist thought in the 19th century. Today it is a major commercial, financial, and educational hub. ◉ Pop. 574,283. — **Bos·to′ni·an** (bô-stō′nē-ən, bŏ-) *adj. & n.*

Bos·worth Field (bŏz′wərth). A locality in central England near Leicester. It was the site of the final battle (August 22, 1485) of the Wars of the Roses, in which Henry Tudor (afterward Henry VII) defeated Richard III, the last king of the Plantagenet line. Richard was killed in the battle.

Bot·a·ny Bay (bŏt′n-ē). An inlet of the Tasman Sea in southeast Australia south of Sydney. It was visited by Capt. James Cook in 1770 and named by Sir Joseph Banks, the botanist in his crew, for the wide variety of exotic flora found on its shores.

Both·ni·a (bŏth′nē-ə), **Gulf of.** An arm of the Baltic Sea between Sweden and Finland. It is icebound for nearly half the year.

Bot·swa·na (bŏt-swä′nə). Formerly **Bech·u·a·na·land** (bĕch′wä′nə-lănd′, bĕch′ oō-ä′-). A country of south-central Africa. Originally inhabited by the San and later (18th century) by the Tswana, the region became a British protectorate after 1885 and gained full independence in 1966. Gaborone is the capital and the largest city. ⊛ Pop. 1,443,000.

ANGOLA ZAMBIA
Zambezi
NAMIBIA
ZIMBABWE
BOTSWANA
Limpopo
Gaborone ✲
SOUTH AFRICA
250 mi

bot·tom (bŏt′əm). *abbr.* **bot. 1.** The solid surface under a body of water. **2.** often **bottoms.** Low-lying alluvial land adjacent to a river. Also called *bottomland.*

Bot·trop (bŏt′rŏp′, bôt′rôp′). A city of northwest Germany in the Ruhr Valley northwest of Essen. It developed as a coal-mining center after the 1860's. ⊛ Pop. 119,676.

Boua·ké (bwä′kā). A town of central Ivory Coast. It was once a crossroads for caravan trade. ⊛ Pop. 329,850.

Bou·cher·ville (boō′shər-vĭl′, boō′shä-vēl′). A town of southern Quebec, Canada, an industrial suburb of Montreal on the St. Lawrence River. ⊛ Pop. 29,704.

Bou·gain·ville (boō′gən-vĭl′, boō-găn-vēl′). A volcanic island of Papua New Guinea in the Solomon Islands of the southwest Pacific Ocean. It was explored by Louis de Bougainville, a French navigator, in 1768.

Boul·der (bōl′dər). A city of north-central Colorado northwest of Denver. It is a major Rocky Mountains resort and the seat of the University of Colorado (opened 1877). ⊛ Pop. 83,312.

Bou·logne (boō-lōn′, -lôn′yə) also **Bou·logne-sur-Mer** (-sûr-mĕr′). A city of northern France on the English Channel north-northwest of Amiens. Of Celtic origin, it is the leading fishing port of France. ⊛ Pop. 47,653.

Bou·logne-Bil·lan·court (boō-lôn′yə-bē-yän-koōr′). A city of north-central France, an industrial suburb of Paris. ⊛ Pop. 101,569.

Bou·logne-sur-Mer (boō-lôn′sûr-mĕr′, -lôn′-yə-). See **Boulogne.**

bound·a·ry (boun′də-rē, -drē). **1.** Something that indicates a border or limit. **2.** The border or limit so indicated.

Boun·da·ry Peak (boun′də-rē, -drē). A mountain, 4,008.6 m (13,143 ft) high, of southwest Nevada near the California border. It is the highest elevation in the state.

Boun·ti·ful (boun′tə-fəl). A city of north-central Utah, a residential suburb of Salt Lake City. ⊛ Pop. 36,659.

Bour·bon·nais (boōr-bôn-nā′). A historical region and former province of central France in the Massif Central. It was held by the counts (later dukes) of Bourbon until 1527, when Francis I added it to the French crown lands.

Bourges (boōrzh). A city of central France south-southeast of Orléans. It was a Roman provincial capital under Augustus and the site of a notable university that was founded by Louis XI in 1463 but abolished during the French Revolution. ⊛ Pop. 76,432.

Bour·gogne (boōr-gôn′yə). See **Burgundy.**

bourn also **bourne** (bôrn, bōrn, boōrn). A small stream; a brook.

Bourne·mouth (bôrn′məth, bōrn′-, boōrn′-). A borough of southern England on an inlet of the English Channel southwest of Southampton. It is a popular resort and fine-arts center. ⊛ Pop. 159,876.

Bou·vet Island (boō′vā). A Norwegian dependency in the southern Atlantic Ocean near the Antarctic Circle south-southwest of the Cape of Good Hope.

bow (bō). An oxbow.

Bow·er·y (bou′ə-rē, bou′rē). A section of lower Manhattan in New York City. The street that gives the area its name was once the road to Peter Stuyvesant's *bouwerij,* or farm. At various times the Bowery has been notorious for its saloons, petty criminals, and derelicts.

Bow·ie (boō′ē). A city of west-central Maryland northeast of Washington, D.C. It is primarily residential. ⊛ Pop. 37,589.

bowl (bōl). A bowl-shaped topographic depression.

Bowl·ing Green (bō′lĭng grēn′). **1.** A city of southern Kentucky southeast of Owensboro. It was occupied by the Confederates from the start of the Civil War until 1862. ⊛ Pop. 40,641. **2.** A city of northwest Ohio south-southwest of Toledo. Bowling Green State University (established 1910) is located here. ⊛ Pop. 28,176.

Boyne (boin). A river of eastern Ireland flowing

about 113 km (70 mi) to the Irish Sea. In the Battle of the Boyne on July 1, 1690, the armies of King William III defeated the forces of James II, who fled to France.

Boyn·ton Beach (boin'tən). A city of southeast Florida on the Atlantic Ocean north of Boca Raton. It is a seaside resort. ◉ Pop. 46,194.

Boz·ca·a·da (bōz'jä-ä-dä'). An island of Turkey in the northeast Aegean Sea south of the Dardanelles. According to tradition, it was the site of a Greek naval station during the Trojan War.

Boze·man (bōz'mən). A city of southwest Montana east-southeast of Butte. Settled in the 1860's, it is a gateway to Yellowstone National Park. ◉ Pop. 22,660.

Bra·bant (brə-bănt', -bänt', brä'bənt, -bänt'). A region and former duchy of northwest Europe. It became an independent duchy in 1190 and is now divided between the southern Netherlands and north-central Belgium.

Brack·nell (brăk'nəl). A town of southeast England. It was designated as a new town in 1949 to alleviate overcrowding in London. ◉ Pop. 50,100.

Bra·den·ton (brād'n-tən). A city of west-central Florida on an inlet of Tampa Bay south of Tampa. Hernando de Soto is believed to have landed near here in 1539. ◉ Pop. 43,779.

Brad·ford (brăd'fərd). A borough of north-central England west of Leeds. Its worsted industry dates from the Middle Ages. ◉ Pop. 479,996.

Bra·ga (brä'gə). A city of northwest Portugal north-northeast of Oporto. Said to have been founded by the Carthaginians, it was an important settlement in Roman times. ◉ Pop. 63,033.

Brah·ma·pu·tra (brä'mə-pōō'trə). A river of southern Asia rising in the Himalaya Mountains of southwest Xizang (Tibet) and flowing about 2,896 km (1,800 mi) generally southwest through northeast India to join the Ganges River and form a vast delta in central Bangladesh.

Brǎ·i·la (brə-ē'lə). A city of southeast Romania on the Danube River near the Ukrainian border. It was taken by the Turks c. 1550 and finally awarded to Romania in 1829. ◉ Pop. 236,344.

Brain·tree (brān'trē'). A town of eastern Massachusetts, a residential and industrial suburb of Boston. ◉ Pop. 33,836.

Bramp·ton (brămp'tən). A city of southern Ontario, Canada, an industrial suburb of Toronto. ◉ Pop. 149,030.

Bran·den·burg (brăn'dən-bûrg', brän'dən-bōōrk'). **1.** A historical region and former duchy of north-central Germany around which the kingdom of Prussia developed. The region is now divided between Poland and Germany. **2.** A city of northeast Germany on the Havel River west-southwest of Berlin. It is an industrial center. ◉ Pop. 95,133.

Bran·don (brăn'dən). **1.** A city of southwest Manitoba, Canada, on the Assiniboine River west of Winnipeg. It is an industrial and transportation center. ◉ Pop. 36,242. **2.** An unincorporated village of west-central Florida, a residential suburb of Tampa. ◉ Pop. 57,985.

Bran·dy·wine (brăn'dē-wīn'). A creek of southeast Pennsylvania and northern Delaware. It was the site of a major defeat of the Continental Army on September 11, 1777, thus allowing British troops to enter Philadelphia on September 27.

Brant·ford (brănt'fərd). A city of southern Ontario, Canada, southwest of Toronto. It was named for the Mohawk leader Joseph Brant, who is buried nearby. Alexander Graham Bell performed some of his early experiments in sound transmission here in the 1870's. ◉ Pop. 74,315.

Bras d'Or Lake (brä' dôr'). An arm of the Atlantic Ocean indenting deeply into Cape Breton Island in southeast Canada.

Bra·sí·lia (brə-zĭl'yə). The capital of Brazil, in the central plateau northwest of Rio de Janeiro. The city, laid out in the shape of an airplane, was officially inaugurated in 1960. ◉ Pop. 1,598,415.

Bra·şov (brä-shôv'). A city of central Romania in the foothills of the Transylvanian Alps north-northwest of Bucharest. It was founded in 1211 by the Teutonic Knights. ◉ Pop. 324,104.

Bra·ti·sla·va (brăt'ĭ-slä'və, brä'tĭ-). The capital of largest city of Slovakia, in the southwest part of the country on the Danube River near the Austrian and Hungarian borders. It was the capital of Hungary from 1541 to 1784. ◉ Pop. 445,089.

Bratsk (brätsk). A city of south-central Russia on the Angara River north-northwest of Irkutsk. It has hydroelectric power installations. ◉ Pop. 260,201.

Brat·tle·bor·o (brăt'l-bûr'ō, -bər-ə, -bŭr'ō). A town of southeast Vermont on the Connecticut River and the New Hampshire border. It was chartered in 1753 and is now a winter resort center. ◉ Pop. 12,241.

Braun·schweig (broun'shvīk'). See **Brunswick** (sense 2).

Bra·zil (brə-zĭl'). *abbr.* **Braz.** A country of eastern South America. The largest country in the continent, it was ruled by Portugal from 1500 to 1822, when it became a separate empire ruled by Pedro I, son of King John VI of Portugal. In 1889, following the abolition of slavery, Pedro II, son of Pedro I, was forced to abdicate and a republic was established. A coup in 1964 brought to power a military regime, which returned the government to civilian control in

1985. Corruption charges and the failure to end hyperinflation forced Fernando Collor de Mello (elected 1989) to resign in 1992. Brasília replaced Rio de Janeiro as the capital in 1960; São Paulo is the largest city. ⊕ Pop. 153,725,000. — **Bra·zil′i·an** *adj. & n.*

Braz·os (brăz′əs). A river of northern Texas flowing about 1,400 km (870 mi) generally southeast to the Gulf of Mexico southwest of Galveston.

Braz·za·ville (brăz′ə-vĭl′, brä-zä-vēl′). The capital and largest city of Congo, in the southern part of the country on the Congo River across from Kinshasa, Zaire. Founded by the French in the 1880's, it is a trade center and major port. ⊕ Pop. 596,200.

Bre·a (brā′ə). A city of southern California north of Anaheim. It is a residential community with varied light industries. ⊕ Pop. 32,873.

Bre·da (brā-dä′). A city of southern Netherlands south-southeast of Dordrecht. It was founded in the 11th century. Charles II of England lived here before the Restoration in 1660. ⊕ Pop. 128,655.

Breed's Hill (brēdz). A hill in Charlestown, a section of Boston, Massachusetts. It was the site of the Battle of Bunker Hill on June 17, 1775.

Bre·men (brĕm′ən, brā′mən). A city of northwest Germany on the Weser River southwest of Hamburg. It is a major port and was a leading member of the Hanseatic League in the Middle Ages. ⊕ Pop. 551,604.

Bre·mer·ha·ven (brĕm′ər-hä′vən, -hā′-, brā′-mər-hä′fən). A city of northwest Germany at the mouth of the Weser River near the North Sea. It has a deep natural harbor and is an important shipping center. Transatlantic service to the United States was inaugurated here in 1847. ⊕ Pop. 131,492.

Brem·er·ton (brĕm′ər-tən). A city of west-

central Washington on an arm of Puget Sound west of Seattle. It was laid out in 1891 after its selection as the site of a U.S. naval shipyard. ⊕ Pop. 38,142.

Bren·ner Pass (brĕn′ər). An Alpine pass, 1,371 m (4,495 ft) high, connecting Innsbruck, Austria, with Bolzano, Italy. It has been a strategic trade and invasion route since Roman times.

Brent·wood (brĕnt′wŏŏd′). **1.** An urban district of southeast England east-northeast of London. A grammar school in the district dates from the mid-16th century. ⊕ Pop. 72,700. **2.** An unincorporated town of southeast New York on central Long Island. It is mainly residential. ⊕ Pop. 45,218.

Bre·scia (brĕsh′ə). A city of northern Italy east of Milan. It was a Gallic town, a Roman stronghold, and a free city from 936 to 1426. ⊕ Pop. 200,722.

Bres·lau (brĕs′lou). See **Wroclaw.**

Brest (brĕst). **1.** A city of northwest France on an inlet of the Atlantic Ocean. Its large landlocked harbor was built in 1631 by Cardinal Richelieu as a military base and arsenal. ⊕ Pop. 147,888. **2.** Formerly **Brest-Li·tovsk** (-lĭ-tôfsk′). A city of southwest Belarus on the Bug River near the border of Poland. The Treaty of Brest-Litovsk, a separate peace treaty between Russia and the German coalition in World War I, was signed here on March 3, 1918. ⊕ Pop. 287,200.

Bre·tagne (brə-tän′yə). See **Brittany.**

Bret·on (brĕt′n). *abbr.* **Bret. 1.** Of or relating to Brittany or its people, language, or culture. **2.** A native or inhabitant of Brittany. **3.** The Celtic language of Brittany. In this sense, also called *Armoric.*

Bri·ansk (brē-änsk′). See **Bryansk.**

Bri·dal·veil Falls also **Bri·dal Veil Falls** (brīd′-l-vāl′). A waterfall, 189.1 m (620 ft) high, in Yosemite National Park in central California.

Bridge·port (brĭj′pôrt′, -pōrt′). A city of southwest Connecticut on Long Island Sound southwest of New Haven. Settled in 1639, it grew as a fishing community and is today the leading industrial center of the state. ⊕ Pop. 141,686.

Bridge·ton (brĭj′tən). **1.** A city of eastern Missouri on the Missouri River northwest of St. Louis. It is a manufacturing center. ⊕ Pop. 17,779. **2.** A city of southwest New Jersey near the mouth of the Delaware River south of Philadelphia. Settled by Quakers c. 1686, it is now highly industrialized. ⊕ Pop. 18,942.

Bridge·town (brĭj′toun′). The capital of Barbados, in the West Indies. It was founded by the British in 1628. ⊕ Pop. 7,466.

Bridge·wa·ter (brĭj′wô′tər, -wŏt′ər). A town of eastern Massachusetts south of Boston. It had an iron industry in colonial times. ● Pop. 21,249.

Bri·enz (brē-ĕnts′), **Lake of.** A lake of central Switzerland near Interlaken. It is noted for its scenic beauty.

Brig·ham City (brĭg′əm). A city of northern Utah north of Ogden. It was founded as Box Elder in 1851 and renamed in 1856 to honor Brigham Young. ● Pop. 15,644.

Brigh·ton (brīt′n). A borough of southeast England on the English Channel south of London. It became a fashionable resort after 1783 when the Prince of Wales (later George IV) began to patronize it. The Royal Pavilion, in a combination of Chinese and Mogul styles, was designed by the noted architect John Nash (1752–1835). ● Pop. 154,370.

brim (brĭm). The rim or uppermost edge of a natural basin.

Brin·di·si (brĭn′dĭ-zē, brēn′-). A city of southern Italy on the Adriatic Sea southeast of Bari. It was an ancient center of trade with the eastern Mediterranean and an embarkation point for the Crusaders during the Middle Ages. ● Pop. 88,947.

Bris·bane (brĭz′bən, -bān′). A city of eastern Australia on the **Brisbane River,** about 346 km (215 mi) long, near its mouth on Moreton Bay, an inlet of the Pacific Ocean. It was settled (1824) as a penal colony. ● Pop. 1,421,600.

Bris·tol (brĭs′təl). **1.** A city of southwest England west of London. It has been an important trading center since the 12th century. ● Pop. 397,585. **2.** A city of central Connecticut north of Waterbury. Its clockmaking industry dates from 1790. ● Pop. 60,640. **3.** A town of eastern Rhode Island on Narragansett Bay southeast of Providence. In the 18th and 19th centuries its port was a base for slave trading, privateering, whaling, and shipbuilding. ● Pop. 21,625. **4.** Two cities on the Tennessee-Virginia line east-northeast of Kingsport, Tennessee. The communities, though politically independent, are an economic unit and share a main thoroughfare along the state boundary. ● Pop. 23,421 (Tennessee) and 18,426 (Virginia).

Bristol Bay. An arm of the Bering Sea in southwest Alaska between the mainland and the Alaska Peninsula. It is a rich salmon-fishing area.

Bristol Channel. An inlet of the Atlantic Ocean stretching west from the Severn River and separating Wales from southwest England. It is a major shipping route.

Brit·ain¹ (brĭt′n). The island of Great Britain during pre-Roman, Roman, and early Anglo-Saxon times before the reign of Alfred the Great

(871–899). The name is derived from *Brittania,* which the Romans used for the portion of the island that they occupied.

Brit·ain² (brĭt′n). *abbr.* **Brit., Br.** See **United Kingdom.**

Bri·tan·nic (brĭ-tăn′ĭk). British.

Brit·ish (brĭt′ĭsh). *abbr.* **Brit., Br. 1. a.** Of or relating to Great Britain or its people, language, or culture. **b.** Of or relating to the United Kingdom or the Commonwealth of Nations. **2.** Of or relating to the ancient Britons. **3.** The people of Great Britain. **4.** British English. **5.** The Celtic language of the ancient Britons.

British America. See **British North America.**

British Antarctic Territory. A British territory of the extreme Southern Hemisphere, including the South Orkney and South Shetland island groups in the southern Atlantic Ocean and Graham Land on the Antarctic Peninsula.

British Cam·e·roons (kăm′ə-rōōnz′). A former British trust territory of western Africa, divided in 1961 between Nigeria and Cameroon.

British Columbia. *abbr.* **BC, B.C.** A province of western Canada bordering on the Pacific Ocean. It joined the confederation in 1871. The coastal area was first explored by Capt. James Cook in 1778. Victoria Island was a separate colony from 1849 until 1866, when it was combined with the mainland territory. Victoria is the capital and Vancouver the largest city. ● Pop. 2,744,467.

British Commonwealth. See **Commonwealth of Nations.**

British East Africa. The former British territories of eastern Africa, including Kenya, Uganda, Tanganyika, and Zanzibar.

British Empire. The geographic and political units formerly under British control, including dominions, colonies, dependencies, trust territories, and protectorates. It can be dated back to the late 16th century when private commercial ventures with royal charters began establishing overseas posts in order to supply European markets with commodities such as spices, tea, fur, sugar, and tobacco, At the height of its power in the late 19th and early 20th centuries, the empire comprised about one quarter of the world's land area and population and encompassed territories on every continent, including the British Isles, British North America, British West Indies, British Guiana, British West Africa, British East Africa, India, Australia, and New Zealand.

British English. The English language used in England as distinguished from that used elsewhere.

British Guiana. See **Guyana.**

British Honduras. See **Belize** (sense 1).

British India. The part of the Indian subcontinent under direct British administration until India's independence (1947).

British Indian Ocean Territory. A British colony comprising small islands in the western Indian Ocean. It was formed in 1965 by agreement with Mauritius and Seychelles.

British Isles. A group of islands off the northwest coast of Europe comprising Great Britain, Ireland, and adjacent smaller islands.

British North America also **British America.** The former British possessions in North America north of the United States. The term was once used to designate Canada.

British Solomon Islands. A former British protectorate in the Solomon and Santa Cruz islands of the southwest Pacific Ocean.

British Somaliland. A former British protectorate of eastern Africa in present-day northwest Somalia on the Gulf of Aden. It was combined with Italian Somaliland in 1960 to form Somalia.

British Togoland. A former British protectorate of western Africa. It became part of Ghana in 1957.

British Virgin Islands. A British colony in the eastern Caribbean east of Puerto Rico and the U.S. Virgin Islands. Road Town, on Tortola Island, is the capital. ● Pop. 12,034.

British West Africa. The former British territories of western Africa, including Nigeria, Gambia, Sierra Leone, Gold Coast, Togoland, and Cameroons.

British West Indies. *abbr.* **B.W.I.** The islands of the West Indies that were formerly under British control, including Jamaica, Barbados, Trinidad, Grenada, Antigua, St. Lucia, and the Bahamas.

Brit·on (brĭt′n). **1.** A native or inhabitant of Great Britain. **2.** One of a Celtic people inhabiting Britain at the time of the Roman invasion.

Brit·ta·ny (brĭt′n-ē) also **Bre·tagne** (brə-tän′-yə). A historical region and former province of northwest France on a peninsula between the English Channel and the Bay of Biscay. It was settled c. 500 by Britons driven out of their homeland by the Anglo-Saxons. The region was formally incorporated into France in 1532.

Brit·ton·ic (brĭ-tŏn′ĭk) also **Bry·thon·ic** (-thŏn′-). The branch of the Celtic languages that includes Welsh, Breton, and Cornish.

Brive-la-Gail·larde (brēv-lä-gä-yäd′) also **Brive** (brēv). A city of southwest-central France south-southeast of Limoges. It grew around a medieval church. ● Pop. 51,511.

Br·no (bûr′nō). A city of southeast Czech Republic southeast of Prague. Founded in the tenth century, it became a free imperial city in 1243. ● Pop. 389,762.

Broad River (brôd). A river rising on the eastern slope of the Blue Ridge in western North Carolina and flowing about 241 km (150 mi) southeast then south to Columbia, South Carolina, where it joins the Saluda River to form the Congaree.

Broads (brôdz). A low-lying region of eastern England with wide, shallow lakes interconnected by rivers and small streams. The Broads is a wildlife sanctuary and recreational center.

Broad·way (brôd′wā′). **1.** A thoroughfare of New York, the longest street in the world. It begins at the southern tip of Manhattan and extends about 241 km (150 mi) north to Albany. **2.** The principal theater and amusement district of New York City, on the West Side of midtown Manhattan centered on Broadway.

Brock·en (brŏk′ən). A granite peak, 1,142.8 m (3,747 ft) high, of the Harz Mountains in central Germany. According to legend it is the site of the witches' Sabbath on Walpurgis Night, the eve of May Day.

Brock·ton (brŏk′tən). A city of eastern Massachusetts south of Boston. It was settled in 1700. ● Pop. 92,788.

Brock·ville (brŏk′vĭl′). A city of southeast Ontario, Canada, on the St. Lawrence River south of Ottawa. ● Pop. 19,896.

Bro·ken Arrow (brō′kən). A city of northeast Oklahoma, a suburb of Tulsa. ● Pop. 58,043.

Bronx (brŏngks). A borough of New York City in southeast New York on the mainland north of Manhattan. It was first settled by Jonas Bronck (died c. 1643), a Dane in the service of the Dutch West India Company, and became part of Greater New York in 1898. ● Pop. 1,203,789.

Bronze Age (brŏnz). A period of human culture between the Stone Age and the Iron Age, characterized by weapons and implements made of bronze.

brook (brŏŏk). See **creek.**

Brook·field (brŏŏk′fēld′). **1.** A village of northeast Illinois, a residential suburb of Chicago. ● Pop. 18,876. **2.** A city of southeast Wisconsin, a suburb of Milwaukee. ● Pop. 35,184.

Brook·line (brŏŏk′līn′). A town of eastern Massachusetts, a residential suburb of Boston. ● Pop. 54,718.

Brook·lyn (brŏŏk′lĭn). A borough of New York City in southeast New York on western Long Island. Dutch colonists first settled the area in 1636 and 1637 and in 1645 established the hamlet of Breuckelen. Renamed Brooklyn by the English, the expanded community became part of Greater New York City in 1898. ● Pop. 2,300,664.

Brooklyn Center. A city of southeast Minnesota, a suburb of Minneapolis. ● Pop. 28,887.

Brooklyn Park. A city of southeast Minnesota, a suburb of Minneapolis. ● Pop. 56,381.

Brook Park (brŏŏk). A city of northeast Ohio, a suburb of Cleveland. ◉ Pop. 22,865.

Brook·side (brŏŏk′sīd′) also **Brookside Park.** A community of northern Delaware southwest of Wilmington. It is mainly residential. ◉ Pop. 15,307.

Brooks Range (brŏŏks). A mountain chain of northern Alaska within the Arctic Circle. The northernmost section of the Rocky Mountains, it rises to about 2,763 m (9,060 ft) in the eastern part of the range.

Broom·all (brŏŏ′môl). An unincorporated village of southeast Pennsylvania. It is a suburb west of Philadelphia. ◉ Pop. 10,930.

Broom·field (brŏŏm′fēld′). A city of north-central Colorado, a suburb of Denver. ◉ Pop. 24,638.

Bros·sard (brô-sär′, -särd′). A town of southern Quebec, Canada, a residential suburb of Montreal on the St. Lawrence River. ◉ Pop. 52,232.

Browns·ville (brounz′vĭl′, -vəl). A city of southern Texas on the Rio Grande near its mouth on the Gulf of Mexico. It is a major port of entry served by a deepwater channel that accommodates oceangoing ships. ◉ Pop. 98,962.

Brown·wood (broun′wŏŏd′). A city of central Texas west of Waco. It is an industrial center in an agricultural region. ◉ Pop. 18,387.

Bruges (brŏŏzh). A city of northwest Belgium connected by canal with the North Sea. It was founded in the 9th century and was a leading member of the Hanseatic League in the 13th century. Today the old city is a popular tourist center known as "the City of Bridges." ◉ Pop. 117,100.

Bru·lé (brŏŏ-lā′). *pl.* **Brulé** or **-lés**. A member of a Native American people constituting a subdivision of the Teton Sioux, inhabiting northwest Nebraska and southwest South Dakota.

Bru·nei (brŏŏ-nī′). A sultanate of northwest Borneo on the South China Sea. Formerly a self-governing British protectorate, it became fully independent on January 1, 1984. Bandar Seri Begawan is the capital. ◉ Pop. 280,000.

Bruns·wick (brŭnz′wĭk). **1.** A region and former duchy of north-central Germany. Established in the 13th century, the duchy became independent in 1918 before joining the Weimar Republic. **2.** also **Braun·schweig** (broun′-shvīk′). A city of north-central Germany east-southeast of Hanover. Reputedly founded in 861, it is an industrial and commercial center. ◉ Pop. 256,267. **3.** A city of southeast Georgia south-southwest of Savannah near the Atlantic coast. It is a port of entry. ◉ Pop. 16,433. **4.** A town of southwest Maine on the Androscoggin River northeast of Portland. Bowdoin College (established 1794) is here. ◉ Pop. 14,683. **5.** A city of northeast Ohio, a suburb of Cleveland and Akron. ◉ Pop. 28,230.

Brus·sels (brŭs′əlz). The capital and largest city of Belgium, in the central part of the country. Officially bilingual (Flemish and French), it became the capital in 1830. ◉ Pop. 136,488.

Brut·ti·um (brŏŏt′ē-əm, brŭt′-). An ancient region of southern Italy roughly occupying present-day Calabria in the toe of the Italian "boot."

Bry·an (brī′ən). A city of east-central Texas northwest of Houston. It is an industrial community and a research center. ◉ Pop. 55,002.

Bry·ansk also **Bri·ansk** (brē-änsk′). A city of western Russia southwest of Moscow. It was part of Lithuania until the 16th century. ◉ Pop. 456,202.

Bryth·on (brĭth′ən, -ŏn′). **1.** An ancient Celtic Briton of Cornwall, Wales, or Cumbria. **2.** One who speaks a Brittonic language.

Bry·thon·ic (brĭ-thŏn′ĭk). **1.** Of or relating to the Brythons or their language or culture. **2.** Variant of **Brittonic.**

Bu·bas·tis (byŏŏ-băs′tĭs). An ancient city of northeast Egypt in the Nile delta. It was a religious center for the worship of the cat-headed god Bast.

Bu·ca·ra·man·ga (bŏŏ′kə-rə-mäng′gə, -kä-rä-mäng′gä). A city of north-central Colombia in the Cordillera Oriental of the Andes. Founded in 1622, it is a leading commercial center. ◉ Pop. 351,687.

Bu·cha·rest (bŏŏ′kə-rĕst′, byŏŏ′-). The capital and largest city of Romania, in the southeast part of the country on a tributary of the Danube River. Founded in the 14th century, it soon became a fortress and commercial center on the trade route to Constantinople. ◉ Pop. 2,343,824.

Bu·chen·wald (bŏŏ′kən-wôld′, -ӄᴇn-vält′). A village of central Germany near Weimar. It was the site of a Nazi concentration camp during World War II.

Bu·co·vi·na (bŏŏ′kə-vē′nə). See **Bukovina.**

Bu·da·pest (bŏŏ′də-pĕst′, -pĕsht′). The capital

and largest city of Hungary, in the north-central part of the country on the Danube River. It was formed in 1873 by the union of Buda on the right bank of the river with Pest on the left bank. The city was the center of the Hungarian uprising against the Communist government in 1956. ⊕Pop. 2,002,121.

Bue·na Park (bwā'nə). A city of southern California west-northwest of Anaheim. Knott's Berry Farm, a re-created gold rush town, is here. ⊕ Pop. 68,784.

Bue·na·ven·tu·ra (bwā'nə-vĕn-tŏor'ə, -tyŏor'ə, bwĕ'nä-vĕn-tŏo'rä). A city of western Colombia on **Buenaventura Bay**, an inlet of the Pacific Ocean. The city was originally settled in the 1540's. ⊕Pop. 165,829.

Bue·na Vis·ta (bwā'nə vĭs'tə, bwĕ'nä vēs'-tä). A locality in northern Mexico just south of Saltillo. In the Mexican War U.S. forces led by Zachary Taylor defeated a Mexican army commanded by General Santa Anna on February 22–23, 1847.

Bue·nos Ai·res (bwā'nəs âr'ēz, ī'rĭz, bwĕ'-nôs ī'rĕs). The capital and largest city of Argentina, in the eastern part of the country on the Río de la Plata. Founded by the Spanish in 1536, it became the national capital in 1862. The highly industrialized city is also a major port. ⊕Pop. 2,960,976.

Buf·fa·lo (bŭf'ə-lō'). A city of western New York at the eastern end of Lake Erie on the Canadian border. It is a major Great Lakes port of entry and an important manufacturing and milling center. ⊕ Pop. 328,123.

Buffalo Grove. A village of northeast Illinois, a suburb of Chicago. ⊕ Pop. 36,427.

Bug (bŏŏg, bŏŏk). **1.** also **Western Bug.** A river of eastern Europe rising in southwest Ukraine and flowing about 772 km (480 mi) through Poland to the Vistula River near Warsaw. **2.** also **Southern Bug.** A river of southern Ukraine rising in the southwest part and flowing about 853 km (530 mi) generally southeast to the Black Sea.

Bu·gan·da (bŏŏ-găn'də, byŏŏ-). A region and former kingdom of eastern Africa on the northern shore of Lake Victoria in present-day Uganda. It was a British protectorate from 1894 until 1962, when it joined independent Uganda.

Bu·jum·bu·ra (bŏŏ'jəm-bŏŏr'ə). The capital and largest city of Burundi, in the western part of the country on Lake Tanganyika. Originally called Usumbura, it was renamed when Burundi became independent in 1962. ⊕ Pop. 235,440.

Bu·kha·ra (bŏŏ-kär'ə, -här'ə, -кнä'rə) also **Bo·kha·ra** (bō-). A city of southern Uzbekistan west of Samarkand. It is one of the oldest cultural and trade centers of Asia and was capital of the former emirate of **Bukhara** from the 16th to the 19th century. ⊕ Pop. 228,000.

Bu·ko·vi·na also **Bu·co·vi·na** (bŏŏ'kə-vē'nə). A historical region of eastern Europe in western Ukraine and northeast Romania. A part of the Roman province of Dacia, it was overrun by barbarian hordes after the third century A.D. The area was later controlled by Kiev, the Ottoman Empire, and Austria.

Bu·la·wa·yo (bŏŏ'lə-wä'yō, -wä'-). A city of southwest Zimbabwe near the Botswana border. It was founded by the British in 1893. ⊕ Pop. 621,742.

Bul·gar (bŭl'gär', bŏŏl'-). See **Bulgarian** (sense 2).

Bul·gar·i·a (bŭl-gâr'ē-ə, bŏŏl-). *abbr.* **Bulg.** A country of southeast Europe on the Black Sea. Settled in the 6th century A.D. by Slavic tribes, it was ruled by Turkey from the late 14th century until 1908, when it became an independent kingdom. The monarchy was overthrown after the Soviet Union occupied Bulgaria in 1944 and Communists took control of the government. Communist rule came to an end in 1989, and a new constitution established a parliamentary republic in 1991. Sofia is the capital and the largest city. ⊕ Pop. 8,443,000.

Bul·gar·i·an (bŭl-gâr'ē-ən, bŏŏl-). *abbr.* **Bulg.**
1. Of or relating to Bulgaria or its people, language, or culture. **2.** A native or inhabitant of Bulgaria. Also called *Bulgar.* **3.** The Slavic language of the Bulgarians.

Bull Run (bŏŏl). A small stream of northeast Virginia southwest of Washington, D.C., near Manassas. It was the site of two important Civil War battles (July 21, 1861, and August 29–30, 1862), both Confederate victories. They are also known as the Battles of Manassas.

Bun·ker Hill (bŭng'kər). A low elevation, 32.6 m (107 ft) high, in Charlestown, a section of Boston, Massachusetts. The first major Revolutionary War battle took place on nearby Breed's Hill on June 17, 1775.

bu·ran (bŏŏ-rän'). A violent windstorm of the

Eurasian steppes, accompanied in summer by dust and in winter by snow.

Bur·bank (bûr′băngk′). **1.** A city of southern California near Los Angeles. There are several motion picture and television studios here. ⊛ Pop. 93,643. **2.** A city of northeast Illinois, a suburb of Chicago. ⊛ Pop. 27,600.

Bur·gas (bŏŏr-gäs′). A city of southeast Bulgaria on the Black Sea. It is one of the country's several major ports. ⊛ Pop. 195,986.

Bur·gos (bŏŏr′gōs′). A city of northern Spain on a high plateau south-southwest of Bilbao. Founded c. 884, it was the capital of the kingdom of Castile in the 11th century and of Francisco Franco's regime during the Spanish Civil War (1936–1939). ⊛ Pop. 161,700.

Bur·gun·dy (bûr′gən-dē) also **Bour·gogne** (bŏŏr-gôn′yə). A historical region and former province of eastern France. The area was first organized into a kingdom by the Burgundii in the 5th century A.D. At the height of its later power in the 14th and 15th centuries, Burgundy controlled vast territories in present-day Netherlands, Belgium, and northeast France. It was incorporated into the French crown lands by Louis XI in 1477. — **Bur·gun′di·an** (bər-gŭn′dē-ən) *adj. & n.*

Bur·ki·na Fa·so (bər-kē′nə fä′sō). Formerly **Upper Volta.** A landlocked country of western Africa. It was a French protectorate from 1896 until 1960, when it gained its independence. The name of the country was officially changed on August 4, 1984. Ouagadougou is the capital and the largest city. ⊛ Pop. 9,889,000.

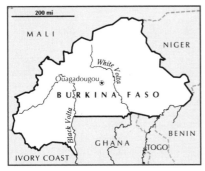

Bur·lin·game (bûr′lĭn-gām′, -lĭng-). A city of western California on the western shore of San Francisco Bay. It is mainly residential. ⊛ Pop. 26,801.

Bur·ling·ton (bûr′lĭng-tən). **1.** A city of southern Ontario, Canada, a suburb of Hamilton on Lake Ontario. ⊛ Pop. 114,853. **2.** A city of southeast Iowa on hills overlooking the Mississippi River. Settled in the 1830's, it was the temporary capital of Iowa Territory (1838–1840). ⊛ Pop. 27,208. **3.** A town of northeast

Massachusetts, a residential suburb of Boston. ⊛ Pop. 23,302. **4.** A city of north-central North Carolina east of Greensboro. It is a textile center in an industrialized area. ⊛ Pop. 39,498. **5.** A city of northwest Vermont on Lake Champlain west-northwest of Montpelier. The largest city in the state, it was the site of a military and naval base during the War of 1812. ⊛ Pop. 39,127.

Bur·ma (bûr′mə). See **Myanmar.**

Bur·man (bûr′mən). Variant of **Burmese.**

Burma Road. A highway extending about 1,126 km (700 mi) generally northeastward through mountainous country from northeast Burma to Kunming, China. It was a vital transportation route for wartime supplies to the Chinese government from 1938 to 1946.

Bur·mese (bər-mēz′, -mēs′) also **Bur·man** (bûr′mən). *abbr.* **Bur.** **1.** Of or relating to Burma (now Myanmar) or its people, language, or culture. **2.** *pl.* **Burmese** also **-mans.** A native or inhabitant of Burma. **3.** The Sino-Tibetan language of Burma.

Bur·na·by (bûr′nə-bē). A city of southwest British Columbia, Canada, a suburb of Vancouver. ⊛ Pop. 136,494.

Burn·ley (bûrn′lē). A borough of northwest England north of Manchester. It grew as a coal-mining and textile center. ⊛ Pop. 93,700.

Burns·ville (bûrnz′vĭl′). A city of southeastern Minnesota, a suburb of Minneapolis. ⊛ Pop. 51,288.

Bur·sa (bûr′sə, bŏŏr-sä′). A city of northwest Turkey west of Ankara. It dates from the third century B.C. and was a capital of the Ottoman Turks in the 1300's. ⊛ Pop. 996,600.

Bur·ton (bûr′tn). A city of southeast-central Michigan, a suburb of Flint. ⊛ Pop. 27,617.

Burton upon Trent or **Burton on Trent** (trĕnt′). A borough of west-central England south-southwest of Derby. It is the center of a brewing industry begun by Benedictine monks who built an abbey on the site in 1002. ⊛ Pop. 48,500.

Bu·ru (bŏŏr′ŏŏ). An island of eastern Indonesia in the Moluccas west of Ceram.

Bu·run·di (bŏŏ-rŏŏn′dē, -rŏŏn′-). A country of east-central Africa with a coastline on Lake Tanganyika. It was inhabited originally by the Twa, a Pygmy people, and later also by Hutus and Tutsis, the latter gaining political and economic dominance in the 19th century. The area formed a part of German East Africa and of Belgian-ruled Ruanda-Urundi before it became an independent kingdom in 1962. The years since independence have been marked by political instability as a result of fighting between the Hutus and Tutsis and power struggles among the Tutsis. Bujumbura is the capital and the largest city. ⊛ Pop. 6,134,000. — **Bu·run′-di·an** *adj. & n.*

Bur·y (bĕr′ē). A borough of northwest England north-northwest of Manchester. It was founded on the site of a Saxon settlement and has been a textile center since the 14th century. ⊛ Pop. 181,390.

Bury Saint Ed·munds (ĕd′məndz). A municipal borough of east-central England east of Cambridge. In 903 the remains of King Edmund were interred in the town's monastery (founded c. 630), which became a famous shrine and Benedictine abbey. ⊛ Pop. 28,914.

Bush·man (boͦosh′mən). *pl.* **-men. 1.** See **San. 2. bushman.** *Australian.* One who lives or travels in the wilderness, especially in the outback.

Bu·sto Ar·si·zio (boͦo′stō är-sē′tsyō). A city of northern Italy northwest of Milan. It is a center of Italy's cotton industry. ⊛ Pop. 76,769.

Bute (byoͦot). An island of southwest Scotland in the Firth of Clyde.

But·ler (bŭt′lər). A city of western Pennsylvania north of Pittsburgh. It is a manufacturing center in a highly industrialized region. ⊛ Pop. 15,714.

butte (byoͦot). *Chiefly Western U.S.* A hill that rises abruptly from the surrounding area and has sloping sides and a flat top.

Butte (byoͦot). A city of southwest Montana south-southwest of Helena. It has been a mining center since its settlement in the 1860's and enjoyed its greatest importance after the discovery of copper deposits in 1880. ⊛ Pop. 37,205.

Bu·zău (bə-zou′, boͦo-zŭ′oͦo). A city of southeast Romania northeast of Bucharest. It is an important transportation hub. ⊛ Pop. 149,032.

Buz·zards Bay (bŭz′ərdz). An inlet of the Atlantic Ocean in southeast Massachusetts connected with Cape Cod Bay by the Cape Cod Canal.

Byb·los (bĭb′ləs, -lŏs′). An ancient city of Phoenicia north-northeast of present-day Beirut, Lebanon. It was the chief city of Phoenicia in the second millennium B.C. and was noted for its papyruses.

Byd·goszcz (bĭd′gôsh, -gôshch). A city of north-central Poland northeast of Poznań. Chartered in 1346, it developed during the Middle Ages around the site of a prehistoric fort. ⊛ Pop. 382,004.

Bye·lo·rus·sia (byĕl′ō-rŭsh′ə). See **Belarus.** — **Byel′o·rus′sian** *adj. & n.*

By·tom (bē′tôm′, bĭ′-). A city of southwest Poland northwest of Katowice. It became part of Prussia in 1742 and was incorporated into Poland in 1945. ⊛ Pop. 231,848.

Byz·an·tine (bĭz′ən-tēn′, -tīn′, bĭ-zăn′tĭn). **1. a.** Of or relating to the ancient city of Byzantium. **b.** Of or relating to the Byzantine Empire. **2.** A native or inhabitant of Byzantium or the Byzantine Empire.

Byzantine Empire. The eastern part of the later Roman Empire, dating from A.D. 330 when Constantine I rebuilt Byzantium and made it his capital. Its extent varied greatly over the centuries, but its core remained the Balkan Peninsula and Asia Minor. The empire finally collapsed when Constantinople fell to the Ottoman Turks in 1453.

By·zan·ti·um (bĭ-zăn′shē-əm, -tē-əm). **1.** The Byzantine Empire. **2.** An ancient city of Thrace on the site of present-day Istanbul, Turkey. It was founded by the Greeks in the seventh century B.C. and taken by the Romans in A.D. 196. Constantine I ordered the rebuilding of the city in 330 and renamed it Constantinople.

C

Ca·ba·na·tuan (kä′bə-nə-twän′, -bä-nä-). A city of central Luzon, Philippines, north of Manila. It was the site of a World War II Japanese prison camp for American and Filipino soldiers who had been captured at Bataan and Corregidor. ⊛ Pop. 38,400.

Ca·bi·mas (kə-bē′məs, kä-vē′mäs). A town of northwest Venezuela on the northeast shore of Lake Maracaibo. It is a center for oil producing and refining. ⊛ Pop. 182,845.

Ca·bin·da (kə-bĭn′də). A territory of Angola forming an exclave on the Atlantic Ocean between Congo and Zaire. It was separated from Angola proper when the Belgian Congo (now Zaire) acquired a corridor to the sea along the lower Congo River.

Ca·bo·clo or **ca·bo·clo** (kə-bô′kloͦo, -klō). *pl.* **-clos.** A person, especially a Brazilian, whose descent is traced entirely or partially to the Indian peoples inhabiting Brazil.

Cab·ot Strait (kăb′ət). A channel between

southwest Newfoundland and northern Cape Breton Island, Canada, connecting the Gulf of St. Lawrence with the Atlantic Ocean.

Cá·ce·res (kä'sə-räs', -thĕ-rĕs'). A city of west-central Spain southwest of Madrid. An important Roman settlement, it was ruled by the Moors from 1142 to 1229. ◉ Pop. 69,734.

Cache la Pou·dre (kăsh' lə poō'dər, -drə). A river of northern Colorado flowing about 201 km (125 mi) to the South Platte River.

Cad·do (kăd'ō). **1.** *pl.* **Caddo** or **-dos.** A member of a Native American confederacy composed of numerous small tribes formerly inhabiting the Red River area of Louisiana, Arkansas, and eastern Texas and now located in central Oklahoma. **2.** The Caddoan language of the Caddos.

Cad·do·an (kăd'ō-ən). A family of North American Indian languages formerly spoken in the Dakotas, Kansas, Nebraska, Texas, Oklahoma, Arkansas, and Louisiana, and presently in North Dakota and Oklahoma.

Cá·diz (kə-dĭz', kā'dĭz, kä'-, kä'thĕth, -thēs). A city of southwest Spain northwest of Gibraltar on the **Gulf of Cádiz,** an inlet of the Atlantic Ocean. Cádiz was founded c. 1100 B.C. by Phoenicians and passed to the Carthaginians (c. 500 B.C.), Romans (third century A.D.), Moors (711), and the kingdom of Castile (1262). Its port was a base for Spanish treasure ships after the conquest of the Americas. ◉ Pop. 152,187.

Cae·li·an (sē'lē-ən). One of the seven hills of ancient Rome. The most southeasterly of the hills, it was densely populated until much of it was devastated by a fire in A.D. 27. —**Cae'li·an** *adj.*

Caen (kän). A city of northern France southwest of Le Havre. A Huguenot stronghold in the 16th and 17th centuries, it is the burial place of William the Conqueror. ◉ Pop. 112,872.

Caer·nar·von (kär-när'vən). A municipal borough of northwest Wales on a narrow strait of the Irish Sea opposite Anglesey Island. The investiture of Charles as Prince of Wales took place in the castle here in 1969. ◉ Pop. 9,506.

Cae·sa·re·a (sē'zə-rē'ə, sĕs'ə-, sĕz'ə-). **1.** also **Caesarea Pal·e·sti·nae** (păl'ĭ-stī'nē). An ancient seaport of Palestine south of present-day Haifa, Israel. It was founded (30 B.C.) by Herod the Great and later became the capital of Roman Judea. The city was destroyed by Muslims in 1265. **2.** also **Caesarea Phil·ip·pi** (fĭl'ĭ-pī, fĭ-lĭp'ī). An ancient city of northern Palestine near Mount Hermon in present-day southwest Syria. It was built in the first century A.D. on the site of a center for the worship of Pan. **3.** also **Caesarea Maz·a·ca** (măz'ə-kə). An ancient city of Cappadocia on the site of present-day Kayseri in central Turkey. The

chief city of the region, it was destroyed by Persians in A.D. 260.

Ca·glia·ri (käl'yə-rē'). A city of Sardinia, Italy, on the southern coast on the **Gulf of Cagliari,** an inlet of the Mediterranean Sea. The city was taken by the Romans in 238 B.C. ◉ Pop. 203,254.

Ca·guas (kä'gwäs'). A city of east-central Puerto Rico south-southeast of San Juan. It is an industrial center in an agricultural region. ◉ Pop. 134,562.

Ca·ha·ba (kə-hô'bə, -hä'-). A river rising in the Appalachian Mountains of north-central Alabama near Birmingham and flowing about 322 km (200 mi) generally south to the Alabama River near Selma.

Ca·ho·ki·a (kə-hō'kē-ə). A village of southwest Illinois, a residential suburb of East St. Louis. Nearby are the **Cahokia Mounds,** a group of approximately 85 prehistoric Native American earthworks, including Monks' Mound, which at 30.5 m (100 ft) is the largest mound in the United States. ◉ Pop. 17,550.

Ca·huil·la (kə-wē'ə). **1.** *pl.* **Cahuilla** or **-las.** A member of a Native American people inhabiting parts of southeast California. **2.** The Uto-Aztecan language of the Cahuillas.

Cai·cos Islands (kā'kəs, -kōs). One of the island groups constituting the Turks and Caicos Islands in the Atlantic Ocean southeast of the Bahamas.

Cairn·gorm Mountains (kârn'gôrm'). A range of the Grampian Mountains in central Scotland rising to 1,310.3 m (4,296 ft) at Ben Macdhui. It is a popular winter sports area.

Cai·ro. 1. (kī'rō). The capital and largest city of Egypt, in the northeast part of the country on the Nile River. Old Cairo was built c. 642 as a military camp; the new city was founded c. 968 by the Fatimid dynasty and reached its greatest prosperity under the Mameluke sultans (13th–16th century). ◉ Pop. 800,000. **2.** (kā'rō). A town of extreme southern Illinois near the confluence of the Mississippi and Ohio rivers. It was named after Cairo, Egypt, because of its similar deltalike setting. ◉ Pop. 4,846.

Caith·ness (kāth'nĕs, kāth-nĕs'). A historical region and former county of northeast Scotland. Settled by the Picts, it was overrun by the Vikings in the ninth century and did not revert to Scottish rule until 1202.

Ca·jun also **Ca·jan** (kā'jən). **1.** A member of a group of people in southern Louisiana descended from French colonists exiled from Acadia in the 18th century. **2.** often **Cajan.** A member of a group living in southern Alabama and southeast Mississippi, of mixed white, Black, and Native American ancestry. **3.** Of or relating to the Cajuns or their culture.

Ca·la·bri·a (kə-lā′brē-ə, kä-lä′brē-ä). A region of southern Italy forming the toe of the Italian "boot." Founded as a Greek colony, it was taken by the Romans in 268 B.C. and by the Byzantine Empire in the ninth century A.D. It later became part of the kingdom of Naples and was conquered by Giuseppe Garibaldi in 1860.

Ca·lah (kā′lə) also **Ka·lakh** (kä′läкн). An ancient city of Assyria on the Tigris River south of present-day Mosul, Iraq. It was probably built in the 13th century B.C.

Ca·lais (kă-lā′, kăl′ā). A city of northern France on the Strait of Dover opposite Dover, England. The city fell to the English in 1347 after a siege of 11 months and was retaken by the French in 1558. ⊛ Pop. 76,527.

Ca·la·mi·an Islands (kä′lə-mē-än′, -myän′). An island group of the west-central Philippines between Mindoro and Palawan.

Cal·ca·sieu (kăl′kə-shōō′). A river rising in west-central Louisiana and flowing about 322 km (200 mi) east, southeast, then southwest to the Gulf of Mexico. Near its outlet it passes through **Lake Calcasieu.**

Cal·cut·ta (kăl-kŭt′ə). A city of eastern India on the Hooghly River in the Ganges delta. Founded c. 1690 as a British East India Company trading post, it is India's largest city and a major port and industrial center. In the notorious Black Hole of Calcutta more than 120 British soldiers died of suffocation (1756) after being imprisoned overnight in the small, stifling dungeon by the nawab of Bengal. ⊛ Pop. 4,399,819.

cal·de·ra (kăl-dâr′ə, -dîr′ə, kôl-). A large crater formed by volcanic explosion or by collapse of a volcanic cone.

Cald·well (kôld′wĕl′, -wəl, kŏld′-). A city of southwest Idaho on the Boise River west of Boise. It was built on the site of an Oregon Trail camping ground. ⊛ Pop. 18,400.

Cal·e·don (kăl′ĭ-dən). A town of southeast Ontario, Canada, a residential suburb of Toronto. ⊛ Pop. 26,645.

Cal·e·do·ni·a (kăl′ĭ-dō′nē-ə, -dōn′yə). Roman Britain north of the Antonine Wall, which was built c. A.D. 140–142 during the reign of the Roman emperor Antoninus Pius and which stretched from the Firth of Forth to the Firth of Clyde. Today it is a poetic term for all of Scotland. — **Cal′e·do′ni·an** adj. & n.

Caledonian Canal. A waterway, about 97 km (60 mi) long, cutting diagonally across northern Scotland from Loch Linnhe on the southwest to Moray Firth on the northeast. Opened in 1822, it is used today mainly by pleasure craft.

Cal·ga·ry (kăl′gə-rē). A city of southern Alberta, Canada, south of Edmonton. Site of the annual Calgary Stampede, a famous rodeo dating

from 1912, the city is the center of Canada's petroleum industry. The 1988 Winter Olympics were held here. ⊛ Pop. 710,677. — **Cal·gar′i·an** (-gâr′ē-ən, -găr′-) n.

Ca·li (kä′lē). A city of western Colombia on the **Cali River** southwest of Bogotá. It was founded in 1536. ⊛ Pop. 1,369,331.

Cal·i·cut (kăl′ĭ-kŭt′) also **Ko·zhi·kode** (kō′zhĭ-kōd′). A city of southwest India on the Malabar Coast southwest of Bangalore. It was the site of the Portuguese explorer Vasco da Gama's first landfall in India (1498) and was later occupied by Portuguese, British, French, and Danish trading colonies. ⊛ Pop. 419,831.

Cal·i·for·nia (kăl′ĭ-fôr′nyə, -fôr′nē-ə). abbr. **CA, Cal., Calif.** A state of the western United States on the Pacific Ocean. It was admitted as the 31st state in 1850. The area was colonized by the Spanish and formally ceded to the United States by the Treaty of Guadalupe Hidalgo (1848). California is often called the Golden State because of its sunny climate and the discovery of gold during the 1800's. Sacramento is the capital and Los Angeles the largest city. ⊛ Pop. 29,839,250. — **Cal′i·for′nian** adj. & n.

California, Gulf of. An arm of the Pacific Ocean in northwest Mexico separating Baja California from the mainland.

California Current. A cold current originating in the northern Pacific Ocean and passing southward and then southwestward along the western coast of North America.

Ca·li·na·go (kăl′ĭ-nä′gō, kä′lĭ-). **1.** pl. **Calinago** or **-gos.** A member of a Caribbean Indian people inhabiting the Lesser Antilles. **2.** The language of the Calinagos.

Cal·la·o (kə-yä′ō, käyou′). A city of west-central Peru on the Pacific Ocean near Lima. Founded in 1537, it is Peru's largest port. ⊛ Pop. 515,200.

Ca·lo·o·can (kăl′ə-ō′kän, kä′lä-). A city of southwest Luzon, Philippines, a suburb of Manila. ⊛ Pop. 642,670.

Ca·loo·sa·hatch·ee (kə-lōō′sə-hăch′ē). A river of southern Florida, about 120 km (75 mi) long, flowing west from south-central Florida to the Gulf of Mexico. It is connected to Lake Okeechobee by the **Caloosahatchee Canal** and forms the western part of the Cross-Florida Waterway.

Cal·pe (kăl′pē). Ancient Gibraltar. Calpe was one of the Pillars of Hercules at the entrance to the Mediterranean Sea.

Cal·ta·nis·set·ta (kăl′tə-nĭ-sĕt′ə, kăl′tä-nēs-sĕt′tä). A city of central Sicily, Italy, southeast of Palermo. It is a sulfur-producing and agricultural center. ⊛ Pop. 54,000.

Cal·u·met (kăl′yə-mĕt′, -mĭt). A major industrial region of northeast Illinois and northwest Indiana on Lake Michigan adjacent to Chicago.

Calumet City. A city of northeast Illinois, an industrial suburb of Chicago. ⊛ Pop. 37,840.

Cal·va·ry (kăl′və-rē, kăl′vrē) also **Gol·go·tha** (gŏl′gə-thə, gŏl-gŏth′ə). A hill outside ancient Jerusalem where Jesus was crucified.

Cal·y·don (kăl′ĭ-dŏn′, -dən). An ancient city of west-central Greece north of the Gulf of Patras. According to legend, the Calydonian boar, a gigantic beast sent by the goddess Artemis to devastate the city, was slain by Meleager, the son of the king of Calydon. —**Cal′y·do′ni·an** (-dō′nē-ən, -dōn′yən) *adj. & n.*

Cam (kăm). A river, about 64 km (40 mi) long, of east-central England. It flows past Cambridge to join the Ouse River south of Ely.

Ca·ma·güey (kăm′ə-gwā′, kä′mä-). A city of east-central Cuba. Founded in 1514, it is the island's third largest city. ⊛ Pop. 291,426.

Cam·a·ril·lo (kăm′ə-rē′ō). A city of southern California west of Los Angeles. It is a manufacturing center in a farming area. ⊛ Pop. 52,303.

Cam·bay (kăm-bā′), **Gulf of.** An inlet of the Arabian Sea on the northwest coast of India.

Cam·bo·di·a (kăm-bō′dē-ə) or **Kam·pu·che·a** (kăm′pōō-chē′ə). Formerly (1970–1975) **Khmer Republic** (kmär). A country of southeast Asia on the Gulf of Thailand. Part of the Khmer Empire (6th–15th century), it was later controlled by the neighboring kingdoms of Siam and Annam. Cambodia became part of French Indochina in the 19th century and proclaimed its independence as the Kingdom of Cambodia in 1953. A major battleground of the Vietnam War (1954–1975), Cambodia underwent extreme political and social disruption under the Khmer Rouge, a communist faction led by Pol Pot. Occupation by Vietnam (1978–1989) was followed by a UN-sponsored interim government and, in 1993, by restoration of a constitutional monarchy under the former head of state Norodom Sihanouk. Phnom Penh is the capital and the largest city. ⊛ Pop. 9,568,000. —**Cam·bo′di·an** *adj. & n.*

Cam·bri·a (kăm′brē-ə). Wales during Roman times. The term is now used poetically.

Cam·bri·an (kăm′brē-ən). **1.** Of or relating to Wales; Welsh. **2.** A native of Wales; a Welshman or Welsh woman.

Cambrian Mountains. A rugged upland plateau extending north to south through central Wales.

Cam·bridge (kăm′brĭj). **1.** A city of southeast Ontario, Canada, west-northwest of Hamilton. ⊛ Pop. 77,183. **2.** A municipal borough of east-central England on the Cam River north-north-east of London. It is an ancient market town and the site of Cambridge University, established in the 12th to 13th century. ⊛ Pop. 113,836. **3.** A city of eastern Massachusetts on the Charles River opposite Boston. Settled in 1630 as New Towne, it is known for its research and educational facilities, including Harvard University (founded in 1636), Radcliffe College (1879), and Massachusetts Institute of Technology (1861). ⊛ Pop. 95,802.

Cam·den (kăm′dən). **1.** A city of southern Arkansas south-southwest of Little Rock. It is a manufacturing and transportation center. ⊛ Pop. 14,380. **2.** A city of western New Jersey on the Delaware River opposite Philadelphia. Walt Whitman lived here from 1873 to 1892. ⊛ Pop. 87,492.

Cam·er·on (kăm′ər-ən, kăm′rən), **Mount.** A peak, 4,342.6 m (14,238 ft) high, in the Rocky Mountains of central Colorado.

Cam·e·roon (kăm′ə-rōōn′) also **Came·roun** (käm-rōōn′). A country of west-central Africa on the Bight of Biafra. Comprising the former French Cameroons and the southern part of British Cameroons, it became independent in 1960. A one-party regime was instituted in 1966, with nominal multiparty rule established in 1992. Yaoundé is the capital and Douala the largest city. ⊛ Pop. 12,871,000.

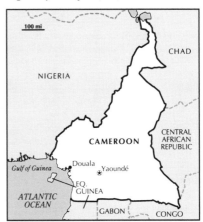

Cam·e·roons (kăm′ə-rōōnz′). A region and former German protectorate of west-central Africa. After World War I the territory was divided into British Cameroons and French Cameroons.

Came·roun (kăm-rōōn'). See **Cameroon.**

Cam·pa·gna di Ro·ma (kăm-pän'yə dē rō'-mə, -mä, käm-). A low-lying region surrounding Rome, Italy. It was a favorite residential area during ancient times but was largely abandoned for centuries because of the prevalance of malaria. Much of the region was reclaimed and repopulated in the 19th and 20th centuries.

Cam·pa·ni·a (kăm-pā'nē-ə, -pān'yə, käm-pä'-nyä). A region of southern Italy on the Tyrrhenian Sea. Inhabited in ancient times by Italic tribes, Greek colonists, Etruscans, and Samnites, it was conquered by Rome in the fourth century B.C. Campania joined Italy in 1860 as part of the kingdom of Naples.

Camp·bell (kăm'bəl). A city of west-central California southwest of San Jose. It has an electronics industry. ● Pop. 36,048.

Campbell River. A city of southwest British Columbia, Canada, on Vancouver Island and the Strait of Georgia northwest of Vancouver. ● Pop. 15,370.

Camp Da·vid (kămp' dā'vĭd). A presidential retreat in the Catoctin Mountains of northern Maryland north-northwest of Washington, D.C. It was established by Franklin D. Roosevelt in 1942 as Shangri-La. Dwight D. Eisenhower renamed it Camp David in honor of his grandson.

Cam·pe·che (kăm-pē'chē, käm-pě'chě). A city of southeast Mexico on the **Bay of Campeche,** a section of the Gulf of Mexico west of Yucatán. Founded in 1540, Campeche was frequently sacked by buccaneers in the 17th century. ● Pop. 128,434.

Cam·pi·na Gran·de (kăm'pē-nə grăn'də, -dē, kän-pē'nə grän'də). A city of extreme eastern Brazil northwest of Recife. It is a commercial and financial center. ● Pop. 326,106.

Cam·pi·nas (kăm-pē'nəs, kän-). A city of southeast Brazil north-northwest of São Paulo. It grew as the center of a coffee-producing region in the 19th century. ● Pop. 846,434.

cam·po (kăm'pō, käm'-). *pl.* **-pos.** A large grassy plain in South America, with scattered bushes and small trees.

Cam·po·bel·lo Island (kăm'pə-běl'ō). An island of southwest New Brunswick, Canada, off the coast of Maine. A popular resort area, the island became part of Canada in 1817.

Cam·po Gran·de (kăm'pō grän'də, -dē, kän'-pōō grän'də). A city of southwest Brazil west-northwest of São Paulo. It is a major processing and shipping center. ● Pop. 525,463.

Cam·pos (kăm'pəs, kän'pōōs). A city of southeast Brazil on the Paraíba River northeast of Rio

de Janeiro. It was founded in the 17th century. ● Pop. 178,457.

Camp Springs. A city of west-central Maryland, a suburb of Washington, D.C. It is just west of Andrews Air Force Base. ● Pop. 16,392.

Cam·ranh Bay or **Cam Ranh Bay** (kăm'răn', käm'rän'). An inlet of the South China Sea in southeast Vietnam. Formerly a French naval base, it was the site of a large U.S. military installation during the Vietnam War.

Ca·na (kā'nə). A village of northern Palestine near Nazareth. In the New Testament, Jesus performed his first miracle here, changing water into wine.

Ca·naan (kā'nən). An ancient region made up of Palestine or the part of it between the Jordan River and the Mediterranean Sea. In the Bible it was referred to as the Promised Land.

Ca·naan·ite (kā'nə-nīt'). **1.** A member of a Semitic people inhabiting Canaan from late prehistoric times and who were conquered by the Israelites around 1000 B.C. **2.** The Semitic language of the Canaanites. **3.** Of or relating to ancient Canaan or its people, language, or culture.

Can·a·da (kăn'ə-də). *abbr.* **Can.** A country of northern North America. Eastern Canada was settled by both English and French colonists and was ceded to England in 1763 after the Seven Years' War. The Dominion of Canada was formed in 1867 and extended to the western provinces in 1905; Newfoundland formally joined the federation in 1949. The Statute of Westminster (1931) confirmed Canada's status as an independent nation within the Commonwealth. Ottawa is the capital and Montreal the largest city. ● Pop. 29,248,000. —**Ca·na'di·an** (kə-nā'dē-ən) *adj. & n.*

Canadian Falls also **Horse·shoe Falls** (hôrs'-shōō', hôrsh'-). A section, about 48 m (158 ft) high, of Niagara Falls within Ontario, Canada.

Canadian French. The French language as used in Canada.

Canadian River. A river rising in northeast New Mexico and flowing about 1,458 km (906 mi) eastward across the Texas Panhandle to the Arkansas River in eastern Oklahoma.

Canadian Shield. See **Laurentian Plateau.**

ca·nal (kə-năl′). An artificial waterway or artificially improved river used for travel, shipping, or irrigation.

Ca·nal Zone (kə-năl′) also **Pan·a·ma Canal Zone** (păn′ə-mä′, -mô′). *abbr.* **CZ, C.Z.** A strip of land, about 16 km (10 mi) wide, across the Isthmus of Panama. Formerly administered by the United States for the operation of the Panama Canal, it was turned over to Panama in 1979.

Can·an·dai·gua Lake (kăn′ən-dā′gwə). A glacial lake of west-central New York. One of the Finger Lakes, it is in a popular resort area.

Ca·nar·y Islands (kə-nâr′ē). A group of Spanish islands in the Atlantic Ocean off the northwest coast of Africa. The Canaries have been part of Spain since 1479 and are a major tourist center.

Ca·nav·er·al (kə-năv′ər-əl, -năv′rəl), **Cape.** Formerly (1963–1973) **Cape Ken·ne·dy** (kĕn′ĭ-dē). A sandy promontory extending into the Atlantic Ocean from a barrier island on the east-central coast of Florida. It is the site of NASA's Kennedy Manned Space Flight Center, the launching area for U.S. space missions.

Can·ber·ra (kăn′bər-ə, -bĕr′ə). The capital of Australia, in the southeast part of the country. Settled in 1824, it replaced Melbourne as the capital in 1908. ● Pop. 298,200.

Can·cún (kăn-kōōn′, käng-). An island community of southeast Mexico off the northeast tip of the Yucatán Peninsula. It is a popular Caribbean resort. ● Pop. 33,273.

Can·di·a¹ (kăn′dē-ə). A name used by Italian colonizers (13th–17th century) for the island of Crete.

Can·di·a² (kăn′dē-ə). See **Iráklion.**

Ca·ney Fork (kā′nē). A river rising in central Tennessee and flowing about 232 km (144 mi) west then north to the Cumberland River.

Can·i·a·pis·cau also **Kan·i·a·pis·kau** (kăn′ē-ə-pĭs′kō, -kou). A river of northern Quebec, Canada, rising in **Lake Caniapiscau** (or **Lake Kaniapiskau**) and flowing about 925 km (575 mi) generally northward to the Larch River.

Can·nae (kăn′ē). An ancient town of southeast Italy where Carthaginians under Hannibal defeated the Romans in 216 B.C.

Cannes (kăn, kănz, kän). A city of southeast France on the Mediterranean Sea near Nice. It is a fashionable resort and the site of an annual international film festival. ● Pop. 72,259.

Can·nock (kăn′ək). An urban district of west-central England north-northwest of Birmingham. It is the center of a mining area based at

Cannock Chase, a nearby moorland. ● Pop. 84,900.

Ca·no·as (kə-nō′əs, kä-nô′äs). A city of southern Brazil, a suburb of Pôrto Alegre. ● Pop. 279,107.

ca·ñon (kăn′yən). Variant of **canyon.**

Ca·no·pus (kə-nō′pəs). An ancient city of northern Egypt east of Alexandria. It was the site of a great temple honoring Serapis, god of the lower world, or abode of the dead.

Ca·nos·sa (kə-nōs′ə, kä-nôs′sä). A village of north-central Italy in the Apennines. In January 1077 the Holy Roman emperor Henry IV did penance in the castle here to obtain a pardon from his excommunication by Pope Gregory VII.

Can·so (kăn′sō), **Strait of** or **Gut of.** A narrow channel between Cape Breton Island and the northeast mainland of Nova Scotia, Canada.

Can·ta·bri·an Mountains (kăn-tā′brē-ən). A range of northern Spain extending about 483 km (300 mi) along the coast of the Bay of Biscay from the Pyrenees to Cape Finisterre. It rises to 2,649.8 m (8,688 ft) at Torre de Cerredo.

Can·ta·brig·i·an (kăn′tə-brĭj′ē-ən). **1.** Of or relating to Cambridge, England, or Cambridge, Massachusetts. **2.** Relating to Cambridge University. **3.** A native or resident of Cambridge, England, or Cambridge, Massachusetts. **4.** A student or graduate of Cambridge University.

Can·ter·bur·y (kăn′tər-bĕr′ē, -brē, -tə-). **1.** A city of southeast Australia, a suburb of Sydney. ● Pop. 128,000. **2.** A borough of southeast England on the Stour River east-southeast of London. Canterbury Cathedral (11th–16th century) is the seat of the archbishop and primate of the Anglican Communion. Built on the site of an abbey founded by Saint Augustine c. 600, it was the scene of the murder of the Roman Catholic archbishop Thomas à Becket (1170) and later a popular pilgrimage site. ● Pop. 36,000.

Can·ti·gny (kän-tē-nyē′). A village of northern France south of Amiens. It was the site of the first U.S. offensive (May 1918) in World War I.

can·ton (kăn′tən, -tŏn′). **1.** A small territorial division of a country, especially one of the states of Switzerland. **2.** A subdivision of an arrondissement in France. —**can′ton·al** (kăn′tə-nəl, kăn-tŏn′əl) *adj.*

Can·ton (kăn′tən). **1.** A town of eastern Massachusetts, a residential and industrial suburb of Boston. ● Pop. 18,530. **2.** A city of northeast Ohio south-southeast of Akron. It was the home of President William McKinley. ● Pop. 84,161. **3.** (kăn′tŏn′, kăn′tŏn′). See **Guangzhou.**

Can·ton·ese (kăn′tə-nēz′, -nēs′). The dialect of Chinese spoken in and around Guangzhou (formerly Canton), China. —**Can′ton·ese′** *adj.*

Can·ton Island (kăn′tən). A coral atoll of the Phoenix Islands in the central Pacific Ocean southwest of Honolulu, Hawaii. An important aviation way station, it was placed under Anglo-American control in 1939.

Can·ton River (kăn′tŏn′, kăn′tŏn′). See **Zhu Jiang.**

can·yon also **ca·ñon** (kăn′yən). A narrow chasm with steep cliff walls, cut into the earth by running water; a gorge.

Can·yon de Chel·ly (kăn′yən də shā′). A canyon in northeast Arizona containing the ruins of spectacular Anasazi cliff dwellings built between A.D. 350–1300.

Cap de la Ma·de·leine or **Cap-de-la-Ma·de·leine** (kăp′ də lä măd-lān′, -lĕn′). A city of southern Quebec, Canada, on the St. Lawrence River northeast of Montreal. It is a manufacturing center with a shrine that is an important pilgrimage site. ⊕ Pop. 32,626.

cape (kāp). *abbr.* **c., C.** A point or head of land projecting into a body of water.

Cape (kāp) or **Cape of.** For names of actual capes, see the specific element of the names, for example, **Hatteras, Cape; Good Hope, Cape of.** Other geographic names beginning with *Cape* are entered under **Cape,** for example, **Cape Coral,** Florida; **Cape York Peninsula.**

Cape Bret·on Island (brĕt′n, brĭt′n). An island forming the northeast part of Nova Scotia, Canada. It was under French sovereignty from 1632 to 1763.

Cape Cod Canal (kŏd). A waterway, about 28 km (17.5 mi) long, of southeast Massachusetts connecting Buzzards Bay with **Cape Cod Bay,** the southern part of Massachusetts Bay. The canal was built (1910–1914) to shorten the water route between New York and Boston.

Cape Cor·al (kôr′əl, kŏr′-). A city of southwest Florida on the estuary of the Caloosahatchee River southwest of Fort Myers. It grew rapidly during the 1970's. ⊕ Pop. 74,991.

Cape Fear River. A river rising in central North Carolina and flowing about 325 km (202 mi) southeast to the Atlantic Ocean north of Cape Fear.

Cape Gi·rar·deau (jə-rär′dō, -rä′-). A city of southeast Missouri on the Mississippi River south-southeast of St. Louis. It was founded in 1793. ⊕ Pop. 34,438.

Cape Province. Officially Cape of Good Hope Province; formerly (before 1910) Cape Colony. *abbr.* **C.P.** A province and historical region of southern South Africa on the Atlantic and Indian oceans. Settled by the Dutch in 1652, it was ceded to Great Britain in 1814 and became part of the Union of South Africa in 1910.

Ca·per·na·um (kə-pûr′nē-əm). A city of an-cient Palestine on the northwest shore of the Sea of Galilee. It was Jesus's home for much of his ministry and the site of many events in the New Testament. A nearby elevation is said to have been the setting for the Sermon on the Mount.

Cape Town or **Cape·town** (kāp′toun′). The legislative capital of South Africa, in the extreme southwest part of the country on the Atlantic Ocean. It was founded in 1652 as a supply station for the Dutch East Indies Company. ⊕ Pop. 854,616.

Cape Verde (vûrd). *abbr.* **C.V.** An island country of the Atlantic Ocean west of Senegal. The islands were settled by the Portuguese in the mid-15th century, became a colony in 1495 and an overseas province in 1951, and gained independence in 1975. Praia, on São Tiago Island, is the capital. ⊕ Pop. 381,000. **—Cape Ver′de·an** (vûr′dē-ən) *adj. & n.*

Cape York Peninsula. A peninsula of northeast Australia between the Gulf of Carpentaria and the Coral Sea.

Cap Hai·tien (kăp′ hā′shən) or **Cap-Ha·ï·tien** (kä-pä-ē-syăN′). A city of northern Haiti on the Atlantic Ocean. Founded c. 1670, it is a tourist center. ⊕ Pop. 64,406.

cap·i·tal (kăp′ĭ-tl). *abbr.* **cap.** A town or city that is the official seat of government in a political entity, such as a state or nation.

Cap·i·to·line (kăp′ĭ-tə-līn′). The highest of the seven hills of ancient Rome. It was the historic and religious center of the city.

Cap·i·tol Peak (kăp′ĭ-tl). A mountain, 4,309.7 m (14,130 ft) high, in the Rocky Mountains of west-central Colorado.

Cap·pa·do·cia (kăp′ə-dō′shə, -shē-ə). An ancient region of Asia Minor in present-day east-central Turkey. Heart of a Hittite state and later a Persian satrapy, it was annexed by the Romans in A.D. 17. **—Cap′pa·do′cian** *adj. & n.*

Ca·pri (kə-prē′, kăp′rē, kä′prē). An island of southern Italy on the southern edge of the Bay of Naples. A popular resort since Roman times, it is famous for its Blue Grotto, a picturesque cave indenting the island's high, precipitous coast.

Ca·pri·vi Strip (kə-prē′vē). A panhandle area of northeast Namibia. It passed from Great Britain to Germany in 1890 in order to give German South-West Africa access to the Zambezi River.

Cap·si·an (kăp′sē-ən). Of, relating to, or being a Paleolithic culture of northern Africa and southern Europe.

Cap·u·a (kăp′yōō-ə, kä′pwä). A town of southern Italy north of Naples. The ancient Roman city of **Capua** was located nearby on the Appian Way. ⊛ Pop. 18,053.

Ca·ra·cas (kə-rä′kəs). The capital and largest city of Venezuela, in the northern part of the country near the Caribbean coast. Founded by the Spanish in 1567, it grew rapidly during the oil boom of the 1950's, and is the country's commercial, industrial, and cultural hub. ⊛ Pop. 1,964,846.

Car·bon·dale (kär′bən-dāl′). A city of southern Illinois southeast of East St. Louis. It is the seat of a branch of Southern Illinois University (established 1869). ⊛ Pop. 27,033.

Car·cas·sonne (kär′kə-sôn′, -sōn′, -kä-). A city of southern France southeast of Toulouse. Its medieval stronghold is a major tourist attraction. ⊛ Pop. 41,153.

Car·che·mish (kär′kə-mĭsh′, kär-kē′mĭsh). An ancient Hittite and Assyrian city on the Euphrates River in present-day southern Turkey. The Babylonian king Nebuchadnezzar II defeated the Egyptians here in 605 B.C.

Cár·de·nas (kär′dn-äs′, -thĕ-näs′). A city of northern Cuba on the **Bay of Cárdenas,** an inlet of the Straits of Florida. Cárdenas is a processing and shipping center. ⊛ Pop. 59,532.

Car·diff (kär′dĭf). The capital and largest city of Wales, in the southeast part of the country on Bristol Channel. It was a prosperous coal-shipping port in the 19th and early 20th centuries. ⊛ Pop. 298,697.

Car·di·gan Bay (kär′dĭ-gən). A wide-mouthed inlet of St. George's Channel on the western coast of Wales.

car·di·nal point (kär′dn-əl, kärd′nəl). One of the four principal directions on a compass: north, south, east, or west.

Car·i·a (kâr′ē-ə). An ancient region of southwest Asia Minor with a coastline on the Aegean Sea. It was settled by Dorian and Ionian colonists and conquered by Alexander the Great in 334 B.C. — **Car′i·an** adj. & n.

Car·ib (kăr′ĭb). **1.** also **Car·i·ban** (kăr′ə-bən, kə-rē′bən′). pl. **Carib** or **-ibs** also **-bans.** A member of a group of Indian peoples of northern South America, the Lesser Antilles, and the eastern coast of Central America. The Caribs were expanding from the South American mainland into the eastern Caribbean islands and pushing the Arawaks northward at the time of the Spanish arrival in the late 15th century. **2.** Any of the languages of the Caribs. — **Car′ib** adj.

Car·i·ban (kăr′ə-bən, kə-rē′bən). **1.** Variant of **Carib** (sense 1). **2.** A language family comprising the Carib languages. — **Car′i·ban** adj.

Car·ib·be·an (kăr′ə-bē′ən, kə-rĭb′ē-ən). **1.** Of or relating to the Caribbean Sea, its islands, or its Central or South American coasts or to the peoples or cultures of this region. **2.** Of or relating to the Caribs or their language or culture. **3.** A Carib.

Caribbean Sea. An arm of the western Atlantic Ocean bounded by the coasts of Central and South America and the West Indies. It has been an important shipping route since the opening of the Panama Canal in 1914. Its many islands and tropical climate make the Caribbean a major tourist area.

Car·i·boo Mountains (kăr′ə-bōō′). A range of eastern British Columbia, Canada, parallel to and west of the Rocky Mountains. It rises to 3,583.8 m (11,750 ft) at Mount Sir Wilfred Laurier. Gold was discovered in the western foothills in 1860.

Ca·rin·thi·a (kə-rĭn′thē-ə). A region and former duchy of central Europe in southern Austria. It was part of the Hapsburg domains after 1335. — **Ca·rin′thi·an** adj.

Car·i·o·ca (kăr′ē-ō′kə). A native or inhabitant of Rio de Janeiro, Brazil. — **Car′i·o′can** adj.

Car·lisle (kär-līl′, kär′līl′). **1.** A borough of northwest England near the Scottish border. Mary Queen of Scots was imprisoned in Carlisle's 11th-century castle from May to July 1568. ⊛ Pop. 102,878. **2.** A borough of southern Pennsylvania west-southwest of Harrisburg. It was a headquarters for George Washington during the Whiskey Rebellion of 1794. ⊛ Pop. 18,419.

Carls·bad (kärlz′băd′). **1.** A city of southern California on the Pacific Ocean north-northwest of San Diego. It is a health resort and manufacturing center. ⊛ Pop. 63,126. **2.** A city of southeast New Mexico on the Pecos River near the Texas border. Large deposits of potash were discovered in the vicinity in 1931. ⊛ Pop. 24,952. **3.** (also kärls′bät′). See **Karlovy Vary.**

Carlsbad Caverns. A group of limestone caverns in the Guadalupe Mountains of southeast New Mexico including spectacular stalactite and stalagmite formations.

Carls·ru·he (kärlz′rōō′ə, kärls′-). See **Karlsruhe.**

Car·mar·then (kär-mär′thən). A municipal borough of southern Wales. One of the oldest towns in Wales, it was built on the site of a Roman fort. ◉ Pop. 12,302.

Car·mel. 1. (kär-mĕl′) also **Car·mel-by-the-Sea** (-bī-*th*ə-sē′). A city of western California on Carmel Bay at the southern end of the Monterey Peninsula. It is an artists' and writers' colony and a popular tourist spot. ◉ Pop. 4,407. **2.** (kär′məl). A city of central Indiana, a suburb of Indianapolis. ◉ Pop. 25,380.

Car·mel (kär′məl), **Mount.** A limestone ridge of northwest Israel extending about 24 km (15 mi) from the Plain of Esdraelon northwest to the Mediterranean Sea. It rises to approximately 546 m (1,790 ft).

Car·mi·chael (kär′mī′kəl). An unincorporated community of north-central California, a residential suburb of Sacramento. ◉ Pop. 48,702.

Car·nac (kär′năk, kär-näk′). A small village in northwest France on the coast of Brittany. It is famous for its prehistoric megalithic monuments that extend in parallel rows. — **Car·na′cian** (-nā′shən) *adj.*

Car·nic Alps (kär′nĭk). A range of the eastern Alps in southern Austria and northeast Italy rising to about 2,782 m (9,121 ft).

Car·ni·o·la (kär′nē-ō′lə, kärn-yō′-). A mountainous region of southwest Slovenia. The earliest inhabitants, a Celtic people, were displaced by the Romans, who in turn were overrun by Slovenes in the sixth century A.D. — **Car′ni·o′lan** *adj. & n.*

Car·ol City (kär′əl). An unincorporated community of southeast Florida northwest of Miami Beach. It is mainly residential. ◉ Pop. 53,331.

Car·o·li·na[1] (kăr′ə-lī′nə). An English colony of southeast North America, first settled in 1653 and divided into North Carolina and South Carolina in 1729.

Ca·ro·li·na[2] (kä′rô-lē′nä). A city of northeast Puerto Rico east-southeast of San Juan. It is a processing center and has a textile industry. ◉ Pop. 147,835.

Car·o·li·nas (kăr′ə-lī′nəz). The colonies (after 1729) or present-day states of North Carolina and South Carolina.

Car·o·line Islands (kăr′ə-līn′). An archipelago of the western Pacific Ocean east of the Philippines. The islands were controlled successively by Spain, Germany, and Japan before being included in the U.S. Trust Territory of the Pacific Islands (1947–1978). All of the islands except Palau joined the Federated States of Micronesia.

Car·o·lin·i·an (kăr′ə-lĭn′ē-ən). **1.** Of or relating to Carolina or the Carolinas. **2.** A native or inhabitant of Carolina or the Carolinas.

Carol Stream. A village of northeast Illinois, a suburb of Chicago. ◉ Pop. 31,716.

Ca·ro·ní (kär′ə-nē′). A river rising in southeast Venezuela near the Guyana border and flowing approximately 885 km (550 mi) northward to join the Orinoco River.

Car·pa·thi·an Mountains (kär-pā′thē-ən). A major mountain system of central Europe in Slovakia, southern Poland, western Ukraine, and northeast Romania. Extending in an arc about 2,253 km (1,400 mi) long, the range links the Alps with the Balkan Mountains and is a popular year-round resort area.

Car·pen·tar·i·a (kär′pən-târ′ē-ə), **Gulf of.** A wide inlet of the Arafura Sea indenting the northern coast of Australia.

Car·pen·ters·ville (kär′pən-tərz-vĭl′). A village of northeast Illinois west-northwest of Chicago. It was settled in 1834. ◉ Pop. 23,049.

Car·pi (kär′pē). A city of northern Italy north of Modena. It is a rail junction and processing center. ◉ Pop. 52,400.

Car·ran·tuo·hill (kăr′ən-tōō′əl). The highest mountain of Ireland, rising to 1,041.3 m (3,414 ft) in the southwest part of the country in Macgillicuddy's Reeks.

Car·ra·ra (kə-rär′ə, kär-rä′rä). A city of northern Italy near the Ligurian Sea east of Genoa. It is famous for the white marble quarried nearby that was favored by Michelangelo, the Italian sculptor, painter, and architect who created some of the greatest works of art of all time. ◉ Pop. 68,460.

Car·roll·ton (kăr′əl-tən). A city of northern Texas, a residential and industrial suburb of Dallas. ◉ Pop. 82,169.

Car·son (kär′sən). A city of southern California, a residential and industrial suburb of Los Angeles. ◉ Pop. 83,995.

Carson City. The capital of Nevada, in the western part of the state near the California border. It was laid out in 1858 on the site of an earlier trading post and named in honor of Kit Carson. ◉ Pop. 40,443.

Carson River. A river rising in western Nevada near Carson City and flowing 201 km (125 mi) northeast to **Carson Sink,** an intermittent lake.

Car·ta·ge·na (kär′tə-gā′nə, -jē′-, -hē′nä). **1.** A city of northwest Colombia on the **Bay of Cartagena,** an inlet of the Caribbean Sea. Founded in 1533, Cartagena was once the richest port on the Spanish Main. ◉ Pop. 513,986. **2.** A city of southeast Spain on the Mediterranean Sea south-southeast of Murcia. It was settled c. 225 B.C. and soon became the chief Carthaginian sea base in Spain. ◉ Pop. 168,023.

Car·ter·et (kär′tə-rĕt′). A borough of northeast New Jersey south of Elizabeth opposite Staten Island. It is an industrial center. ◉ Pop. 19,025.

Car·thage (kär′thĭj). An ancient city and state

of northern Africa on the Bay of Tunis northeast of modern Tunis. It was founded by the Phoenicians in the ninth century B.C. and became the center of Carthaginian power in the Mediterranean after the sixth century B.C. The city was destroyed by the Romans at the end of the Third Punic War (146 B.C.) but was rebuilt by Julius Caesar and later (A.D. 439–533) served as capital of the Vandals before its virtual annihilation by the Arabs (698). —**Car'tha·gin'i·an** (kär'thə-jĭn'ē-ən) *adj. & n.*

car·to·gram (kär'tə-grăm'). A presentation of statistical data in geographical distribution on a map.

car·tog·ra·phy (kär-tŏg'rə-fē). The art or technique of making maps or charts. —**car·tog'-ra·pher** *n.* —**car'to·graph'ic** (kär'tə-grăf'ĭk), **car'to·graph'i·cal** *adj.*

Ca·rua·ru (kär'wä-rōō'). A city of northeastern Brazil west of Recife. It is a manufacturing and processing center. ◉ Pop. 213,573.

Car·y (kâr'ē). A town of east-central North Carolina, an industrial suburb of Raleigh. ◉ Pop. 43,858.

Cas·a·blan·ca (kăs'ə-blăng'kə, kä'sə-bläng'-kə). A city of northwest Morocco on the Atlantic Ocean south-southwest of Tangier. Founded by the Portuguese in the 16th century, it became a center of French influence in Africa after 1907. It is now Morocco's largest city. ◉ Pop. 2,943,000.

cas·cade (kă-skād'). A waterfall or a series of small waterfalls over steep rocks.

Cas·cade Range (kă-skād'). A mountain chain of western Canada and the United States extending about 1,126 km (700 mi) south from British Columbia through western Washington and Oregon to northern California, where it joins the Sierra Nevada. Mount Rainier, 4,395.1 m (14,410 ft), is the highest peak and one of many snow-capped volcanic cones in the range.

Cas·co Bay (kăs'kō). A deep inlet of the Atlantic Ocean in southwest Maine. The bay, with its wooded, hilly islands, is a popular vacation area.

Ca·ser·ta (kə-zĕr'tə, kä-zĕr'tä). A city of southern Italy north-northeast of Naples. German World War II forces in Italy surrendered to the Allies here on April 29, 1945. It is an agricultural and commercial center. ◉ Pop. 66,754.

Cash·mere (kăsh'mîr', kăsh-mîr'). See **Kashmir.**

Ca·so·ri·a (kə-sôr'ē-ə, kä-). A city of southern Italy, a suburb of Milan. ◉ Pop. 68,355.

Cas·per (kăs'pər). A city of east-central Wyoming on the North Platte River northwest of Cheyenne. It was founded in 1888 with the coming of the railroad and grew rapidly after the discovery of oil nearby. ◉ Pop. 46,742.

Cas·pi·an Sea (kăs'pē-ən). A saline lake between southeast Europe and western Asia. Its water level is decreasing because of dam construction on the Volga River, which feeds the lake.

Cas·sel (kăs'əl, kä'səl). See **Kassel.**

Cas·sel·ber·ry (kăs'əl-bĕr'ē). A city of east-central Florida, a suburb of Orlando. ◉ Pop. 18,911.

Cas·si·no (kə-sē'nō, käs-). A town of central Italy in the Apennines northwest of Naples. In World War II the town and nearby Benedictine monastery of Monte Cassino were reduced to rubble during fierce German-Allied fighting (February–May 1944). ◉ Pop. 26,300.

Cas·tel Gan·dol·fo (kä-stĕl' gän-dôl'fō). A town of central Italy on Lake Albano southeast of Rome. It is the site of the papal summer residence. ◉ Pop. 3,600.

Cas·tel·lam·ma·re di Sta·bia (kä-stĕl'ə-mär'-ä dĭ stäb'yə, kä-stĕl'läm-mä'rĕ dē stä'byä). A city of southern Italy on the Bay of Naples west of Salerno. A summer resort and spa, it has thermal mineral springs known since Roman times. ◉ Pop. 70,317.

Cas·tel·lón de la Pla·na (kăs'təl-yōn' də lä plä'nə, kä'stĕl-yôn' dĕ lä plä'nä). A city of eastern Spain on the Mediterranean Sea north-northeast of Valencia. A port and manufacturing center, it was captured from the Moors in 1233. ◉ Pop. 136,816.

Cas·tile (kăs-tēl'). A region and former kingdom of central and northern Spain. Autonomous from the tenth century, it joined with Aragon after the marriage of Isabella and Ferdinand in 1469, thus forming the nucleus of modern Spain.

Cas·til·ian (kă-stĭl'yən). **1.** A native or inhabitant of Castile. **2. a.** The Spanish dialect of Castile. **b.** The standard literary and official form of Spanish, which is based on this dialect. **3.** Of or relating to Castile or its people, language, or culture.

Cas·tle Peak (kăs'əl). A mountain, 4,350.8 m (14,265 ft) high, in the Elk Mountains of west-central Colorado. It is the highest elevation in the range.

Cas·tries (kăs'trēz', -trēs'). The capital of St. Lucia, in the Windward Islands of the British West Indies. It was founded by the French in 1650. ◉ Pop. 51,994.

Cas·trop-Rau·xel (käs'trôp-rouk'səl). A city of western Germany in the Ruhr Valley south-southwest of Münster. It is a commercial and industrial center. ◉ Pop. 76,428.

Cas·tro Valley (kăs'trō). An unincorporated community of western California southeast of Oakland. It is mainly residential. ◉ Pop. 48,619.

Cat·a·lan (kăt'l-ăn', -ən, kăt'l-än'). **1.** Of or

relating to Catalonia or its people, language, or culture. **2.** A native or inhabitant of Catalonia. **3.** The Romance language spoken especially in Catalonia, the Balearic Islands, Andorra, and the Roussillon region of France.

Cat·a·li·na Island (kăt′l-ē′nə). See **Santa Catalina Island.**

Cat·a·lo·nia (kăt′l-ōn′yə, -ō′nē-ə). A region of northeast Spain bordering on France and the Mediterranean Sea. In the late 19th and early 20th centuries it was a center of socialist and anarchist activity. Catalan separatists established an autonomous republic (1932–1938) that opposed General Francisco Franco's loyalist forces during the Spanish Civil War (1936–1939). —**Cat′-a·lo′nian** adj. & n.

Ca·ta·nia (kə-tän′yə, -tä′nē-ə, kä-tä′nyä). A city of eastern Sicily, Italy on the **Gulf of Catania,** an inlet of the Ionian Sea. Founded in the eighth century B.C., Catania was a flourishing Greek community and later a Roman colony. ◉ Pop. 330,037.

Ca·tan·za·ro (kä′tän-zär′ō, -dzär′ō). A city of southern Italy near the Ionian Sea. It was founded in the tenth century. ◉ Pop. 93,464.

cat·a·ract (kăt′ə-răkt′). A large or high waterfall or steep rapids in a river.

Ca·taw·ba (kə-tô′bə). **1.** pl. **Catawba** or **-bas.** A member of a Native American people formerly inhabiting territory along the Catawba River in North and South Carolina and now located in western South Carolina. **2.** The Siouan language of the Catawbas.

Catawba River. A river rising in the Blue Ridge of western North Carolina and flowing about 402 km (250 mi) generally southward into South Carolina, where it is called the Wateree River.

catch·ment (kăch′mənt, kĕch′-). **1.** A structure, such as a basin or reservoir, used for collecting or draining water. **2.** A catchment area.

catchment area. The area drained by a river or body of water. Also called *catchment basin.*

Ca·thay (kă-thā′). A medieval name for China popularized by the Venetian traveler Marco Polo in accounts of his travels through Asia. It usually applied only to the area north of the Chang Jiang (Yangtze River).

Ca·toc·tin Mountains (kə-tŏk′tĭn). A section of the Blue Ridge in northern Maryland extending from the Pennsylvania border south to Virginia. Camp David is located in the northern part.

Ca·tons·ville (kāt′nz-vĭl′). An unincorporated community of north-central Maryland, a suburb of Baltimore. ◉ Pop. 35,233.

Cats·kill Mountains (kăt′skĭl′). A range of the Appalachian Mountains in southeast New York just west of the Hudson River. The mountains, rising to 1,282.2 m (4,204 ft), include many popular resort areas.

Cau·ca (kou′kə). A river rising in the Cordillera Central of western Colombia and flowing about 965 km (600 mi) northward to the Magdalena River.

Cau·ca·sian (kô-kā′zhən, -kăzh′ən). **1.** *Anthropology.* Of, relating to, or being a proposed human racial division traditionally distinguished by physical characteristics such as very light to brown skin pigmentation and straight to wavy or curly hair, and including peoples indigenous to Europe, northern Africa, western Asia, and India. **2.** Of or relating to the Caucasus region or its peoples, languages, or cultures. **3.** Of or relating to any of the non-Turkic, non-Slavic, non-Indo-European languages of the Caucasus. **4.** *Anthropology.* A member of the Caucasian racial division. **5.** A native or inhabitant of the Caucasus region.

Cau·ca·soid (kô′kə-soid′) *Anthropology.* **1.** Of or relating to the Caucasian racial division. **2.** A member of the Caucasian racial division.

Cau·ca·sus (kô′kə-səs) also **Cau·ca·sia** (kô-kā′zhə, -shə). A region between the Black and Caspian seas that includes southeast Russia, Georgia, Azerbaijan, and Armenia, and that forms part of the traditional boundary between Europe and Asia. Inhabited before 2000 B.C., it was the scene of countless invasions over the millenniums. The region's vast oil resources were a major German objective in World War II.

Caucasus Mountains. A range from the north to the southeast in the Caucasus. Mount Elbrus, 5,645.6 m (18,510 ft), is the highest elevation.

cave (kāv). A hollow or natural passage under or into the earth with an opening to the surface.

cav·ern (kăv′ərn). **1.** A large cave. **2.** A large underground chamber, as in a cave.

Ca·vi·te (kə-vē′tē, kä-vē′tě). A city of southwest Luzon, Philippines, on Manila Bay southwest of Manila. It has been an important naval base since Spanish times. The American facilities here were virtually destroyed in bombing raids by the Japanese on December 10, 1941. ◉ Pop. 103,422.

Cawn·pore (kôn′pôr′, -pōr′). See **Kanpur.**

Ca·xi·as (kə-shē′əs). A city of northeast Brazil east-northeast of Teresina. It is an agricultural processing center. ◉ Pop. 146,730.

Caxias do Sul (də sŏŏl′). A city of southern Brazil north of Pôrto Alegre. Founded in 1875, it is an industrial center in a wine-producing region. ◉ Pop. 290,969.

cay (kē, kā). A small, low island composed largely of coral or sand.

Cay·enne (kī-ĕn′, kā-). The capital of French Guiana, on **Cayenne Island** at the mouth of the **Cayenne River.** Founded by the French in 1643, it was the center of a penal colony from the 1850's until the 1940's. ⊛ Pop. 41,164.

Cay·man Islands (kā-măn′, kā′mən). A British-administered island group in the Caribbean Sea northwest of Jamaica, including **Grand Cayman, Little Cayman,** and **Cayman Brac.** The islands were discovered by Columbus in 1503. Georgetown, on Grand Cayman, is the capital. ⊛ Pop. 30,000.

Ca·yu·ga (kā-yōō′gə, kī-). **1.** *pl.* **Cayuga** or **-gas.** A member of a Native American people formerly inhabiting the shores of Cayuga Lake in west-central New York, with present-day populations in Ontario, western New York, Wisconsin, and Oklahoma. The Cayugas are one of the five original tribes of the Iroquois confederacy. **2.** The Iroquoian language of the Cayugas.

Cayuga Lake. A lake of west-central New York. The longest of the Finger Lakes, it is a popular resort area.

Cay·use (kī-yōōs′, kī′yōōs′). **1.** *pl.* **Cayuse** or **-us·es.** A member of a Native American people inhabiting northeast Oregon and southeast Washington. **2. a.** The extinct traditional language of the Cayuse, not closely related to any other. **b.** The dialect of Nez Perce spoken by the Cayuse in the 19th and 20th centuries.

Ce·bu (sĕ-bōō′). An island of the central Philippines in the Visayan Islands between Leyte and Negros. Magellan landed on the island in 1521. The city of **Cebu** is an important harbor on the eastern coast. The city's population is 688,196.

Ce·dar Falls (sē′dər). A city of northeast Iowa, a manufacturing suburb of Waterloo on the Cedar River. ⊛ Pop. 36,322.

Cedar Rapids. A city of east-central Iowa on the Cedar River west-northwest of Davenport. It is a major commercial, industrial, and transportation center. ⊛ Pop. 108,751.

Cedar River. A river rising in southeast Minnesota and flowing about 531 km (330 mi) southeastward to the Iowa River in southeast Iowa.

Ce·la·ya (sə-lī′ə, sĕ-lä′yä). A city of central Mexico northwest of Mexico City. Founded in 1571, it is the center of an agricultural and cattle-raising area. ⊛ Pop. 141,675.

Cel·e·bes (sĕl′ə-bēz′, sə-lē′bēz′, sĕ-lä′bĕs) also **Su·la·we·si** (sōō′lä-wä′sē). An irregularly shaped island of central Indonesia on the equator east of Borneo. The Portuguese first visited Celebes in 1512 but were ousted by the Dutch in the 1600's. The island is noted for its rare species of fauna.

Celebes Sea. A section of the western Pacific Ocean between Celebes and the southern Philippines. It is connected with the Java Sea by Makassar Strait.

Ce·les·tial Empire (sə-lĕs′chəl). An old name for China or the Chinese Empire.

Cel·le (sĕl′ə, tsĕl′ə). A city of northern Germany south of Hamburg. Founded in 1292, it is a manufacturing center. ⊛ Pop. 70,754.

Celt (kĕlt, sĕlt) also **Kelt** (kĕlt). **1.** One of an Indo-European people originally of central Europe and spreading to western Europe, the British Isles, and southeast to Galatia during pre-Roman times, especially a Briton or Gaul. **2.** A speaker of a modern Celtic language or a descendant of such a speaker, especially a modern Gael, Welshman, Cornishman, or Breton.

Celt·i·ber·i·an (kĕl′tĭ-bĕr′ē-ən, sĕl′-). **1.** One of an ancient Celtic people of northern Spain. **2.** The language of this people, known from place and personal names and from inscriptions. **3.** Of or relating to the Celtiberians or to their language or culture.

Celt·ic (kĕl′tĭk, sĕl′-) also **Kelt·ic** (kĕl′-). *abbr.* **C. 1.** A subfamily of the Indo-European language family comprising the Brittonic and the Goidelic branches. **2.** Of or relating to the Celtic people and languages.

Ce·nis (sə-nē′), **Mont.** A mountain pass, about 2,083.5 m (6,831 ft) high, in the Alps on the French-Italian border. It was long important as an invasion route.

Cen·ter·each (sĕn′tə-rēch′). A community of southeast New York on central Long Island. It is mainly residential. ⊛ Pop. 26,720.

Cen·ter·ville (sĕn′tər-vĭl′). A city of southwest Ohio, a suburb of Dayton. ⊛ Pop. 21,082.

Cen·tral African Republic (sĕn′trəl). Formerly (1976–1979) **Central African Empire.** A country of central Africa. Part of French Equatorial Africa after the 1890's, it became independent in 1960. In 1966 Colonel Jean-Bédel Bokassa rescinded the national constitution and later declared himself emperor (1977–1979). Further political instability in the 1980's preceded the restoration of free multiparty elec-

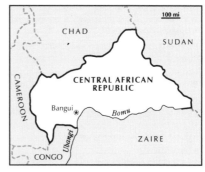

tions in 1992. Bangui is the capital and the largest city. ⊛ Pop. 2,395,000.

Central America. *abbr.* **C.A.** A region of southern North America extending from the southern border of Mexico to the northern border of Colombia. It separates the Caribbean Sea from the Pacific Ocean and is linked to South America by the Isthmus of Panama. —**Central American** *adj. & n.*

Central Asian U.S.S.R. A region of the southern U.S.S.R. stretching from the Caspian Sea to just beyond the Irtysh River and including the present-day countries of Kazakstan, Turkmenistan, Uzbekistan, Tajikistan, and Kyrgyzstan.

Central Falls. A city of northeast Rhode Island, an industrial suburb of Providence. ⊛ Pop. 17,637.

Cen·tra·lia (sĕn-trāl′yə). A city of south-central Illinois east of East St. Louis. It was founded in 1853. ⊛ Pop. 14,274.

Central I·slip (ī′slĭp). A community of southeast New York on central Long Island. It is mainly residential. ⊛ Pop. 26,028.

Central Kar·roo (kə-rōō′). See **Karroo.**

Central Park. An extensive recreational area of New York City extending north to south in central Manhattan. The land, acquired in 1856, was developed according to plans drawn up by the landscape artists Frederick Law Olmsted and Calvert Vaux.

Central Provinces. The Canadian provinces of Ontario and Quebec.

Central Standard Time. *abbr.* **CST, C.S.T.** Standard time in the sixth time zone west of Greenwich, England, reckoned at 90° W and used in the central United States. Also called *Central Time.*

Central Valley. A rich agricultural valley of central California between the Sierra Nevada and the Coast Ranges.

Ceph·a·lo·ni·a (sĕf′ə-lō′nē-ə, -lōn′yə) also **Ke·fal·li·ní·a** (kĕ′fä-lē-nē′ä). The largest of the Ionian Islands off the western coast of Greece. It was held by the British from 1809 to 1864.

Ce·ram (sā′räm′, sĕ-räN′). An island of eastern Indonesia in the Moluccas west of New Guinea. It borders on the **Ceram Sea,** a section of the western Pacific Ocean.

Cer·re·do (sə-rā′dō, sĕ-rĕ′thô), **Torre de.** See **Torre de Cerredo.**

Cer·ri·tos (sə-rē′təs). A city of southern California, a suburb of Los Angeles. ⊛ Pop. 53,240.

Cer·ro de Pun·ta (sĕr′ō də pōōn′tə, -tä). A mountain, 1,338.6 m (4,389 ft) high, of central Puerto Rico in the Cordillera Central. It is the highest elevation on the island.

Cerro Gor·do (gôr′dō). A mountain pass of southeast Mexico between Veracruz and Mexico City. It was the site of a U.S. victory (April 18, 1847) in the Mexican War.

Ce·se·na (chə-zā′nə, chĕ-zĕ′nä). A city of north-central Italy east-northeast of Florence. It flourished under the Malatesta family (1379–1465), who founded its Renaissance-style library. ⊛ Pop. 67,600.

Čes·ké Bu·dě·jo·vi·ce (chĕs′kĕ bōōd′yə-yô-vĭ-tsĕ). A city of southwest Czech Republic on the Vltava River south of Prague. It was founded in the 13th century. ⊛ Pop. 93,520.

Ceu·ta (syōō′tə, thĕ′ōō-tä, sĕ′-). A Spanish city of northwest Africa, an enclave in Morocco on the Strait of Gibraltar. A flourishing trade city under the Arabs, it was taken by the Portuguese in 1415 and passed to Spain in 1580. ⊛ Pop. 68,882.

Cé·vennes (sā-vĕn′). A mountain range of southern France west of the Rhone River. Its highest elevation is 1,754.7 m (5,753 ft).

Cey·lon (sĭ-lŏn′, sā-). See **Sri Lanka.** —**Cey′lo·nese′** (-nēz′, -nēs′) *adj. & n.*

Cha·co (chä′kō). See **Gran Chaco.**

Chad (chăd). A country of north-central Africa. Formerly part of French Equatorial Africa, it became independent in 1960. Since independence the country has been plagued by internal strife, especially between the Muslim north and Christian and animist south, triggering numerous changes in government. Chad has also been embroiled in a long-standing conflict with Libya, which has intermittently invaded and controlled parts of northern Chad. N'Djamena is the capital and the largest city. ⊛ Pop. 4,405,000. —**Chad′i·an** *adj. & n.*

Chad, Lake. A shallow lake of north-central Africa in Chad, Cameroon, Niger, and Nigeria. It was first explored by Europeans in 1823.

Chad·ic (chăd′ĭk). A branch of the Afro-Asiatic language family, spoken in west-central Africa and including Hausa as its best-known member.

Chaer·o·ne·a (kĕr′ə-nē′ə, kîr′-). An ancient city of eastern Greece. Philip of Macedon defeated a confederation of Greek states here in 338 B.C.

Cha·gres (chä′grĕs). A river rising in central Panama, flowing southwest to Gatún Lake (formed by a dam on the river), then draining northwest to the Caribbean Sea.

chain (chān). A range of mountains.

Chal·ce·don (kăl′sĭ-dŏn′, kăl-sēd′n). An ancient Greek city of northwest Asia Minor on the Bosporus near present-day Istanbul. Founded in 685 B.C., it passed to Rome in A.D. 74.

Chal·cid·i·ce (kăl-sĭd′ĭ-sē) also **Khal·ki·dhi·kí** (käl-kē′*th*ē-kē′, ᴋʜäl-). A mountainous peninsula of northeast Greece projecting into the northern Aegean Sea with three fingerlike extensions. —**Chal·cid′i·an** adj. & n.

Chal·cis (kăl′sĭs) also **Khal·kís** (käl-kēs′, ᴋʜäl-). An ancient city of southeast Greece on the western coast of Euboea. It was a prosperous trading center after the eighth century B.C., establishing outposts in Italy, Syria, Sicily, and mainland Greece.

Chal·de·a or **Chal·dae·a** (kăl-dē′ə). An ancient region of southern Mesopotamia. Settled c. 1000 B.C., it reached the height of its power under Nebuchadnezzar II, king of Babylonia from 605 to 562 B.C. The Chaldean empire was destroyed by Persians in 539 B.C.

Chal·de·an also **Chal·dae·an** (kăl-dē′ən) or **Chal·dee** (kăl′dē′). **1.** Of or relating to Chaldea or its people, language, or culture. **2.** A member of an ancient Semitic people who ruled in Babylonia. **3.** See **Aramaic.** —**Chal·da′ic** (-dā′-ĭk) adj. & n.

Cha·leur Bay (shə-lo͝or′, -lûr′). An inlet of the Gulf of St. Lawrence between eastern Quebec and northern New Brunswick, Canada. It is an important fishing ground.

Chal·mette (shăl-mĕt′). A village of extreme southeast Louisiana on the east bank of the Mississippi River just below New Orleans. It is a processing center. ◉ Pop. 31,860.

Châ·lons-sur-Marne (shä-lôn′sûr′märn′, -sür-). A city of northeast France east of Paris. The Huns under Attila were defeated near here by Roman and Visigothic troops in A.D. 451. ◉ Pop. 51,137.

Cha·lon-sur-Saône (shä-lôɴ′sûr-sōn′, -sür-). A city of east-central France north of Mâcon. It is an inland port and a manufacturing center. ◉ Pop. 56,194.

Cham·bers·burg (chăm′bərz-bûrg′). A borough of southern Pennsylvania southwest of Harrisburg. It was burned by the Confederate cavalry in July 1864 after the townspeople refused to pay an indemnity of $100,000 in gold. ◉ Pop. 16,647.

Cham·bé·ry (shäɴ-bā-rē′). A city of eastern France east-southeast of Lyon. It is a manufacturing center in a popular tourist area. ◉ Pop. 53,427.

Cham·bly (shăm′blē, shäɴ-blē′). A city of southern Quebec, Canada, on the Richelieu River east of Montreal. Its fort, built by the French in 1665, was captured by the British in 1760 and held briefly by the Americans during the Revolutionary War. ◉ Pop. 12,190.

Cham·bord (shäɴ-bôr′). A village of north-central France northeast of Tours. It is noted for its magnificent Renaissance château built by Francis I.

Cha·mi·zal (shăm′ĭ-zäl′, chäm′ĭ-säl′). An area on the northern bank of the Rio Grande near El Paso, Texas. It became part of the United States after the river shifted course in the 19th century and was returned to Mexico in 1963.

Cha·mo·nix (shăm′ə-nē′, shä-mô-). A valley of eastern France at the foot of Mont Blanc. It is a major winter sports resort and was the site of the 1924 Winter Olympics.

Cham·pagne (shăm-pān′, shäɴ-pän′yə). A historical region and former province of northeast France. It was incorporated into the French royal domain in 1314. The sparkling wine champagne was first produced here c. 1700.

Cham·paign (shăm-pān′). A city of east-central Illinois adjoining Urbana. It was founded in 1855 with the coming of the railroad and is a commercial and industrial center in a fertile farm area. ◉ Pop. 63,502.

Cham·pi·gny-sur-Marne (shäɴ-pē-nyē′sûr-märn′, -sür-). A city of northern France, a suburb of Paris. ◉ Pop. 76,176.

Cham·plain (shăm-plān′), **Lake.** A lake of northeast New York, northwest Vermont, and southern Quebec, Canada. It was the site of important battles in the French and Indian War, the American Revolution, and the War of 1812. The region has many popular resorts.

Champs É·ly·sées (shäɴ zā-lē-zā′). A broad tree-lined thoroughfare of Paris, France, leading from the Place de la Concorde to the Arc de Triomphe.

Chan·cel·lors·ville (chăn′sə-lərz-vĭl′, -slərz-). A former town of northeast Virginia west of Fredericksburg. It was the site of a major Civil War battle (May 2–4, 1863) in which the Confederates under Robert E. Lee defeated the

Union forces commanded by Joseph Hooker. The Confederate general Stonewall Jackson was mortally wounded in the battle.

Chan Chan (chän′ chän′). A ruined pre-Incan city of northern Peru, probably built after A.D. 800. It may once have had a population of 200,000.

Chan·chiang (jän′jyäng′). See **Zhanjiang.**

Chan·di·garh (chŭn′dē-gər, chŭn′dĭ-gŭr′). A city of northern India north of Delhi. It was laid out by a European team of architects led by Le Corbusier (1887–1965). ◉ Pop. 504,094.

Chan·dler (chănd′lər). A city of south-central Arizona southeast of Phoenix. It is a residential community and winter resort. ◉ Pop. 90,533.

Chang·chow (chäng′jō′). See **Changzhou.**

Chang·chun (chäng′cho͞on′). Formerly **Hsin·king** (shĭn′kĭng′, -gĭng′). A city of northeast China south-southwest of Harbin. It was the capital of the Japanese puppet state of Manchukuo from 1932 until 1945. Changchun is the capital of Jilin province. ◉ Pop. 2,980,870.

Chang Jiang (chäng′ jyäng′) or **Yang·tze River** (yăng′sē′, -tsē′, yäng′dzə′). The longest river of China and of Asia, flowing about 5,551 km (3,450 mi) from Xizang (Tibet) to the East China Sea. The river has been an important trade and transportation route since ancient times.

Chang·sha (chäng′shä′). A city of southern China on the Xiang Jiang west-southwest of Shanghai. It was founded in the early third century B.C. and was long noted as a literary center. Changsha is the capital of Hunan province. ◉ Pop. 1,328,950.

Chang·zhou also **Chang·chow** (chäng′jō′). A city of eastern China on the Grand Canal westnorthwest of Shanghai. It is an industrial center in an agricultural region. ◉ Pop. 729,893.

Chan·kiang (chän′kyäng′, jän′jyäng′). See **Zhanjiang.**

chan·nel (chăn′əl). *abbr.* **chan. 1.** The bed of a stream or river. **2.** The deeper part of a river or harbor, especially a deep navigable passage. **3.** A broad strait, especially one that connects two seas.

Chan·nel Islands (chăn′əl). A group of British islands in the English Channel off the coast of Normandy, France. Settled by Norse mariners, the islands became part of the duchy of Normandy in the tenth century and passed to England with the Norman Conquest of 1066.

Chan·nel·view (chăn′əl-vyo͞o′). A community of southeast Texas, a suburb of Houston. ◉ Pop. 25,564.

Chan·til·ly (shăn-tĭl′ē, shäN-tē-yē′). A village of northern France north of Paris. It was long noted for its fine porcelain and delicate lace. ◉ Pop. 10,065.

Chao Phra·ya (chou prä-yä′). A river of Thailand formed by the Nan and Ping rivers and flowing about 225 km (140 mi) southward past Bangkok to the Gulf of Thailand.

Cha·pa·la (chə-pä′lə). A lake of west-central Mexico southeast of Guadalajara. It is the largest lake in the country and a popular resort area.

Chap·el Hill (chăp′əl). A town of north-central North Carolina at the edge of the Piedmont west-northwest of Raleigh. It is the seat of the University of North Carolina (chartered 1789). ◉ Pop. 38,719.

Cha·pul·te·pec (chə-po͞ol′tə-pĕk′). A rocky hill south of Mexico City, Mexico. It was the site of a major American victory (September 12–13, 1847) during the Mexican War.

Char·dzhou (chär-jō′, chĭr-). A city of eastern Turkmenistan on the Amu Darya southwest of Tashkent, Uzbekistan. It is an inland port and a manufacturing center. ◉ Pop. 164,000.

Cha·rente (shə-ränt′, shä-räNt′). A river of France rising in the foothills of the Massif Central and flowing about 354 km (220 mi) westward to the Bay of Biscay.

Cha·ri (shä′rē, shä-rē′). See **Shari.**

Char·ing Cross (chăr′ĭng). A district of London, England, where King Edward I erected (c. 1290) the last of a series of crosses in memory of his wife, Eleanor of Castile.

Char·i·ton (shăr′ĭ-tn). A river rising in southern Iowa and flowing about 451 km (280 mi) east then south to the Missouri River in northern Missouri.

Char·le·roi (shär′lə-roi′, shär-lə-rwä′). A city of southern Belgium south of Brussels. It was founded in 1666 and is now a commercial center and rail junction. ◉ Pop. 206,928.

Charles·bourg (chärlz′bûrg′, shärl-bo͞or′). A city of southern Quebec, Canada, near Quebec City. It was settled in 1659. ◉ Pop. 68,326.

Charles River (chärlz). A river, about 97 km (60 mi) long, of eastern Massachusetts flowing into Boston harbor and separating Boston from Cambridge.

Charles·ton (chärl′stən). **1.** A city of eastern Illinois east-southeast of Decatur. It is a trade and processing center. ◉ Pop. 20,398. **2.** A city of southeast South Carolina northeast of Savannah. Charleston has been a major commercial and cultural center since colonial times. ◉ Pop. 80,414. **3.** The capital and largest city of West Virginia, in the west-central part of the state. The city grew around the site of Fort Lee in the late 1780's. ◉ Pop. 57,287.

Charleston Peak. A mountain, 3,635.3 m (11,919 ft) high, of southeast Nevada in the Spring Mountains west of Las Vegas.

Charles·town (chärlz′toun′). A former city of eastern Massachusetts, the oldest part of Boston. It was settled c. 1629. The Battle of Bunker Hill was fought here on June 17, 1775.

Char·le·ville-Mé·zières (shärl-vēl′mä-zyĕr′). A city of northeast France on the Meuse River east-northeast of Paris. Mézières was founded in the ninth century and Charleville in 1606. The cities merged in 1966. ● Pop. 58,667.

Char·lotte (shär′lət). A city of southern North Carolina near the South Carolina border south-southwest of Winston-Salem. Settled c. 1750 and named for the wife of King George III of England, it is the largest city in the state. ● Pop. 395,934.

Charlotte A·ma·lie (ə-mäl′yə). The capital of the U.S. Virgin Islands, on St. Thomas Island in the West Indies east of Puerto Rico. It was called St. Thomas from 1921 to 1937 and is a commercial center and popular tourist resort. ● Pop. 11,842.

Char·lottes·ville (shär′ləts-vĭl′). An independent city of central Virginia northwest of Richmond. It is the seat of the University of Virginia (founded 1819). Thomas Jefferson's estate, Monticello, is nearby. ● Pop. 40,341.

Char·lotte·town (shär′lət-toun′). The capital and largest city of Prince Edward Island, Canada, on the southern coast of the island. It was founded by the French c. 1720. ● Pop. 15,282.

chart (chärt). **1.** A map showing information, such as water depths, of use to navigators. **2.** An outline map on which specific information, such as scientific data, can be plotted.

Char·tres (shärt, shär′trə). A city of northern France southwest of Paris. Its 13th-century cathedral is a masterpiece of Gothic architecture noted for its stained glass and asymmetrical spires. ● Pop. 37,119.

Cha·ryb·dis (kə-rĭb′dĭs). *Greek Mythology.* A whirlpool off the Sicilian coast, opposite the cave of Scylla.

chasm (kăz′əm). A deep, steep-sided opening in the earth's surface; an abyss or a gorge. —**chas′mal** (kăz′məl) *adj.*

Châ·teau·guay (shăt′ə-gā′, shä-tō-gā′). A town of southern Quebec, Canada, southwest of Montreal. It is a port of entry and manufacturing center. ● Pop. 36,928.

Châ·teau·roux (shä-tō-rōō′). A city of central France southeast of Tours. It is a commercial center with textile and food-processing industries. ● Pop. 51,942.

Châ·teau-Thier·ry (shä-tō-tyĕ-rē′). A town of northern France on the Marne River east-northeast of Paris. It was the site of the second Battle of the Marne (June 3–4, 1918), which ended the last major German offensive in World War I. ● Pop. 14,557.

Chat·ham (chăt′əm). **1.** A city of southeast Ontario, Canada, on the Thames River east-northeast of Windsor. It is an industrial center in an agricultural region. ● Pop. 40,952. **2.** A municipal borough of southeast England east of London. Elizabeth I established the first dockyard here in 1588. ● Pop. 142,800.

Chatham Islands. An island group of New Zealand in the southwest Pacific Ocean east of South Island. The islands were discovered by Europeans in 1791.

Chat·ta·hoo·chee (chăt′ə-hōō′chē). A river rising in northern Georgia and flowing about 702 km (436 mi) generally southwest then south to the Flint River on the Georgia-Florida border.

Chat·ta·noo·ga (chăt′ə-nōō′gə). A city of southeast Tennessee on the Georgia border southeast of Nashville. A major rail junction and port of entry on the Tennessee River, it was strategically important during the Civil War and was finally taken by Union forces in November 1863. ● Pop. 152,466.

Chau·tau·qua Lake (shə-tô′kwə, chə-). A lake of extreme southwest New York. The Chautauqua movement of adult education, offering a range of cultural, religious, and recreational activies, was founded in 1874 at the resort village of **Chautauqua** on the northwest shore of the lake.

Cheap·side (chēp′sīd′). A street and district in the City of London, England. It was the market center of medieval London and the site of the Mermaid Tavern, a gathering place for Elizabethan poets and playwrights.

Che·bok·sa·ry (chĭ-bŏk-sär′ē). A city of west-central Russia on the Volga River west of Kazan. It is a commercial and cultural center. ● Pop. 445,707.

Che·chen (chĕch′ən, chə-chĕn′). **1.** A member of a Muslim people of Chechnya. **2.** The Caucasian language of the Chechens, closely related to Ingush.

Chech·nya (chĕch′nē-ə, chĕch-nyä′). A region of southwest Russia in the northern Caucasus bordering on Georgia. Conquered by Russia in the 19th century, it later formed a part of the Chechen-Ingush Autonomous Soviet Socialist Republic. Around the time of the breakup of the Soviet Union in the early 1990's, a strong nationalist movement developed, and the republic declared its independence in November of 1991. Russian troops invaded Chechnya in late 1994, and fighting continued until May 1996, when Russia and Chechnya signed an accord that called for an end to the hostilities and the opening of negotiations on Chechnya's future political status. Aslan Maskhadov, former Soviet colonel and chief of staff of the Chechen military, won the presidential election in January 1997.

Cheek·to·wa·ga (chēk'tə-wä'gə). An unincorporated community of western New York east of Buffalo. It is mainly residential. ●Pop. 84,387.

Che·ju (chĕ'jōō'). An island of South Korea separated from the southwest coast of the mainland by **Cheju Strait,** a channel linking the Yellow Sea and Korea Strait.

Che·kiang (chŭ'kyäng', jə'gyäng'). See **Zhejiang.**

Che·lan (shə-lăn'), Lake. A narrow lake of north-central Washington in the Cascade Range. It is the third-deepest freshwater lake in the United States.

Chelms·ford (chĕmz'fərd). **1.** A municipal borough of southeast England northeast of London. The Italian engineer and inventor Guglielmo Marconi began the world's first broadcasting service here in 1920. ●Pop. 58,500. **2.** A town of northeast Massachusetts near Lowell. It is chiefly residential. ●Pop. 32,388.

Chel·sea (chĕl'sē). **1.** A district of western London, England, on the north bank of the Thames River, popular since the 18th century with writers and artists. **2.** A city of eastern Massachusetts, a suburb of Boston. It was settled in 1624 and set off from Boston in 1739. ●Pop. 28,710.

Chel·ten·ham (chĕlt'nəm, chĕl'tən-əm). A municipal borough of west-central England south of Birmingham. It has been a popular resort since the discovery of mineral springs in 1716. ●Pop. 106,708.

Che·lya·binsk (chĕl-yä'bĭnsk, chĭ-lyä'-). A city of southwest Russia south of Yekaterinburg. Founded in 1736 as a Russian frontier outpost, it is a major metallurgical and industrial center. ●Pop. 1,129,661.

Che·lyus·kin (chĕl-yōō'skĭn, chĭ-lyōō'-), Cape. A cape of north-central Russia on the Taimyr Peninsula. It is the northernmost point of Asia.

Chem·nitz (kĕm'nĭts). Formerly **Karl-Marx-Stadt** (kärl-märk'shtät'). A city of east-central Germany southeast of Leipzig. Chartered in 1143, it prospered as a textile center after the late 17th century. ●Pop. 279,520.

Che·nab (chə-näb'). A river, about 1,086 km (675 mi) long, of northern India and eastern Pakistan. It is one of the five rivers of the Punjab.

Cheng·chow (jŭng'jō', jœng'-). See **Zhengzhou.**

Cheng·du also **Cheng·tu** (chŭng'dōō'). A city of south-central China west-northwest of Chongqing. Founded before 770 B.C., it is one of China's oldest cities. ●Pop. 3,483,834.

Cher (shĕr). A river of central France flowing about 354 km (220 mi) to the Loire River near Tours.

Cher·bourg (shâr'bŏŏrg', shĕr-bŏŏr'). A city

of northwest France on the English Channel. The site has been occupied since ancient times and was frequently contested by the French and English because of its strategic location. ●Pop. 28,442.

Che·re·po·vets (chĕr'ə-pə-vĕts', chĭ-rĭ-pŭ-vyĕts'). A city of west-central Russia north of Moscow. It grew around a monastery established in the 14th century. ●Pop. 318,196.

Cher·kas·sy (chər-kä'sē). A city of central Ukraine on the Dnieper River south-southeast of Kiev. It was an important Cossack outpost before passing to Russia in the 1790's. ●Pop. 307,600.

Cher·ni·gov (chər-nē'gəf, -nyē'-). A city of north-central Ukraine north-northeast of Kiev. First mentioned in 907, it was the capital of the Chernigov principality in the 11th century and later passed to Lithuania, Poland, and Russia. ●Pop. 310,500.

Cher·no·byl (chər-nō'bəl, chyĭr-nô'bĭl). A city of north-central Ukraine north-northwest of Kiev. It was the site of a major nuclear power plant accident on April 16, 1986. ●Pop. (in 1986) 12,000.

Cher·nov·tsy (chər-nôft'sē, chyĭr-nŭf-tsĭ'). A city of southwest Ukraine in the foothills of the Carpathian Mountains near the Romanian border. It was a center of the Ukrainian nationalist movement in the 19th and early 20th centuries. ●Pop. 261,200.

Cher·o·kee (chĕr'ə-kē', chĕr'ə-kē'). **1.** pl. **Cherokee** or **-kees.** A member of a Native American people formerly inhabiting the southern Appalachian Mountains from the western Carolinas and eastern Tennessee to northern Georgia, with present-day populations in northeast Oklahoma and western North Carolina. The Cherokees were forcibly removed to Indian Territory in the 1830's after conflict with American settlers over rights to traditional lands. **2.** The Iroquoian language spoken by the Cherokees. —**Cher'o·kee'** adj.

Cherokee Strip or **Cherokee Outlet.** A plot of land in present-day northern Oklahoma. Purchased from the Cherokee Nation by the United States in 1891, it was opened to settlement in 1893.

Cher·ry Hill (chĕr'ē). An urban township of west-central New Jersey east-southeast of Camden. It is mainly residential. ●Pop. 69,319.

cher·so·nese (kûr'sə-nēz', -nēs'). A peninsula.

Chert·sey (chûrt'sē). An urban district of southeast England on the southern bank of the Thames River. It has engineering works. ●Pop. 73,100.

Ches·a·peake (chĕs'ə-pēk'). An independent city of southeast Virginia south of Norfolk. Its vast area includes residential communities, farm-

land, and a section of the Dismal Swamp.
⊛ Pop. 151,976.

Chesapeake Bay. An inlet of the Atlantic
Ocean separating the Delmarva Peninsula from
mainland Maryland and Virginia. Explored and
charted by John Smith in 1608, it is an important
link in the Intracoastal Waterway.

Chesh·ire (chĕsh′ər, -îr′). A town of south-
central Connecticut north of New Haven. It is
mainly residential. ⊛ Pop. 25,684.

Ches·hunt (chĕs′ənt). An urban district of
southeast England, a residential suburb of London. ⊛ Pop. 79,700.

Ches·ter (chĕs′tər). **1.** A borough of west-central England on the Dee River south-southeast of Liverpool. The Romans built a fort here
to defend the river crossing into Wales and
named the settlement Deva. Chester is known
for its Rows, a double tier of shops and houses
along its main streets. ⊛ Pop. 58,100. **2.** A city
of southeast Pennsylvania on the Delaware
River, an industrial suburb of Philadelphia. Established as Upland, it was the site of William
Penn's first landing in America (1682) and is the
oldest city in the state. ⊛ Pop. 41,856.

Ches·ter·field (chĕs′tər-fēld′). A city of north-
central England south of Sheffield. It is an important industrial center. ⊛ Pop. 101,171.

Ches·ter-le-Street (chĕs′tər-lĭ-strēt′). An urban district of northeast England south-southeast of Newcastle. It is in a mining area. ⊛ Pop.
51,800.

Chev·i·ot Hills (chĕv′ē-ət, shĭv′-, chē′vē-). A
range of hills extending about 56 km (35 mi)
along the border between England and Scotland.
The Cheviot, 816.2 m (2,676 ft), is the highest
elevation.

Chev·y Chase (chĕv′ē chās′). A village of
west-central Maryland, a residential suburb of
Washington, D.C. ⊛ Pop. 2,675.

Che·wa (chä′wä). A Bantu language spoken in
Malawi, closely related to Nyanja.

Chey·enne¹ (shī-ĕn′, -ăn′). **1.** *pl.* **Cheyenne**
or **-ennes.** A member of a Native American
people, divided after 1832 into the Northern
and Southern Cheyenne, inhabiting respectively
southeast Montana and southern Colorado, with
present-day populations in Montana and Oklahoma. The Cheyennes became nomadic buffalo
hunters after migrating to the Great Plains in
the 18th century and figured prominently in the
resistance by Plains Indians to white encroachment. **2.** The Algonquian language of the Cheyennes. **—Chey·enne′** *adj.*

Chey·enne² (shī-ăn′, -ĕn′). The capital of Wyoming, in the southeast part of the state near
the Nebraska and Colorado borders. It was
founded in 1867 as a division point for the Union
Pacific Railroad. ⊛ Pop. 50,008.

Cheyenne River. A river rising in eastern Wyoming and flowing about 848 km (527 mi) east
then northeast to the Missouri River in central
South Dakota.

Chi·ai or **Chia-i** (jē-ī′, jyä′ē′). A city of southwest Taiwan north of Kaohsiung. It is an agricultural market center. ⊛ Pop. 252,376.

Chia-ling (jyä′lĭng′). See **Jialing.**

Chia·mus·su (jyä′mōō′sōō′). See **Jiamusi.**

Chi·ba (chē′bä′). A city of east-central Honshu,
Japan, on the northeast shore of Tokyo Bay. It is
a manufacturing center. ⊛ Pop. 850,631.

Chib·cha (chĭb′chə). **1.** *pl.* **Chibcha** or **-chas.**
A member of an extinct Indian people once inhabiting central Colombia. **2.** The extinct language of the Chibchas.

Chib·chan (chĭb′chən). **1.** A member of a
widely scattered Indian people of Colombia and
Central America. **2.** A language family comprising the Chibchan languages.

Chi·bem·ba (chĭ-bĕm′bə). See **Bemba.**

Chi·ca·go (shĭ-kä′gō, -kô′-). The largest city of
Illinois, in the northeast part of the state on
Lake Michigan. It is a major port and the commercial, financial, industrial, and cultural center
of the Middle West. The city was nearly destroyed by a disastrous fire in 1871. ⊛ Pop.
2,783,726. **—Chi·ca′go·an** *n.*

Chicago Heights. A city of northeast Illinois
south of Chicago. It is an industrial center.
⊛ Pop. 33,072.

Chicago River. A river formed at Chicago by
the junction of northern and southern branches
that total about 55 km (34 mi) in length. It is an
important link in the Illinois Waterway.

Chi·ca·no (chĭ-kä′nō, shĭ-). **1.** *pl.* **-nos.** A
Mexican-American. **2.** Of or relating to Mex-
ican-Americans or their culture.

Chich·a·gof Island (chĭch′ə-gôf′, -gŏf′). An
island of southeast Alaska in the northern Alexander Archipelago. It was named after a Russian
admiral.

Chi·chén It·zá (chē-chĕn′ ē-tsä′, ēt′sə). An
ancient Mayan city of central Yucatán in Mexico.
It was founded c. A.D. 514 and abandoned in
1194. There are extensive well-preserved ruins
on the site.

Chich·es·ter (chĭch′ĭ-stər). A municipal borough of southern England near the English
Channel east of Southampton. Called Regnum
by the Romans, it was a major port in the Middle Ages. ⊛ Pop. 24,300.

Chick·a·mau·ga (chĭk′ə-mô′gə). A city of extreme northwest Georgia south of Chattanooga,
Tennessee. Confederate troops led by Braxton
Bragg defeated Union forces here on September
19–20, 1863. ⊛ Pop. 2,149.

Chick·a·saw (chĭk′ə-sô′). **1.** *pl.* **Chickasaw**

or **-saws. 1.** A member of a Native American people formerly inhabiting northeast Mississippi and northwest Alabama, now located in south-central Oklahoma. The Chickasaws were forcibly removed to Indian Territory in the 1830's. **2.** The Muskogean language of the Chickasaws. —**Chick′a·saw′** *adj.*

Chick·a·sa·whay (chĭk′ə-sô′wā). A river, about 338 km (210 mi) long, of southeast Mississippi flowing generally south to join the Leaf River and form the Pascagoula River.

Chick·a·sha (chĭk′ə-shā′). A city of central Oklahoma southwest of Oklahoma City. It is a trade and processing center. ◉ Pop. 14,988.

Chi·cla·yo (chĭ-klä′yō, chē-). A city of northwest Peru north-northwest of Lima. Situated on the coastal desert between the Andes and the Pacific Ocean, the city may go years at a time without rainfall. ◉ Pop. 448,400.

Chi·co (chē′kō). A city of northern California northwest of Oroville. Chico is a processing and packing center in an almond-growing region. ◉ Pop. 40,079.

Chic·o·pee (chĭk′ə-pē). A city of southwest Massachusetts on the Connecticut River near Springfield. It was founded c. 1641 and set off from Springfield in 1848. ◉ Pop. 56,632.

Chi·cou·ti·mi (shĭ-kōō′tə-mē). A city of south-central Quebec, Canada, on the Saguenay River north of Quebec City. The site of a Jesuit mission established in 1676, it is today a commercial and industrial center. ◉ Pop. 60,064.

Chie·ti (kyā′tē). A city of central Italy near the Adriatic coast. It occupies the site of an ancient Roman settlement and is a commercial and industrial center. ◉ Pop. 55,207.

Chig·well (chĭg′wĕl, -wəl). An urban district of southeast England, a residential suburb of London. ◉ Pop. 51,290.

Chi·hua·hua (chə-wä′wä, chē-). A city of northern Mexico south of Ciudad Juárez. It is the rail and commercial center for the vast northern section of the country. ◉ Pop. 385,603.

Chil·e (chĭl′ē, chē′lē). A country of southwest South America with a long Pacific coastline. Originally inhabited by Araucanian Indian peoples, it was colonized by Spain in 1541 and declared its independence in 1818. One of the most politically stable and economically prosperous of South American countries, Chile annexed mineral-rich territory from Bolivia and Peru following the War of the Pacific (1879–1884). The election of a Marxist president, Salvador Allende Gossens, in 1970 triggered a U.S.-backed military coup led by General Augusto Pinochet in 1973. The government was restored to civilian control in 1990. Santiago, in the central part of the country, is the capital and largest city. ◉ Pop. 13,994,000. —**Chil′e·an** *adj. & n.*

Chi·lin (jē′lĭn′). See **Jilin.**

Chil·lán (chē-yän′). A city of central Chile east-northeast of Concepción. Founded in the 16th century, it was twice destroyed by earthquakes (1835 and 1939). ◉ Pop. 145,972.

Chil·li·coth·e (chĭl′ĭ-kŏth′ē, -kô′thē). A city of south-central Ohio south of Columbus. It became capital of the Northwest Territory in 1800 and served as Ohio's capital from 1803 to 1810 and from 1812 to 1816. ◉ Pop. 21,923.

Chil·li·wack (chĭl′ə-wăk′). A city of southwest British Columbia, Canada, on the Fraser River east of Vancouver. ◉ Pop. 40,642.

Chi·lo·é (chĭl′ō-ā′, chē′lô-ĕ′). An island off central Chile. It is the largest of the Chilean islands and the only one to be successfully settled.

Chil·tern Hills (chĭl′tərn). A range of chalk hills in south-central England northeast of the upper Thames River.

Chi·lung (jē′lōōng′, chē′-). See **Keelung.**

Chim·bo·ra·zo (chĭm′bə-rä′zō, -rä′-, chēm′-bô-rä′sô). An extinct volcano, 6,271.1 m (20,561 ft) high, in central Ecuador. The highest elevation of the Cordillera Real, it was first scaled in 1880.

Chim·bo·te (chĭm-bō′tē, chēm-bô′tĕ). A city of western Peru on the Pacific Ocean north-northwest of Callao. It suffered severe earthquake damage in 1970. ◉ Pop. 314,700.

Chim·kent (chĭm-kĕnt′). A city of south-central Kazakstan north of Tashkent, Uzbekistan. Founded in the 12th century, it was taken by Russia in 1864. ⊛ Pop. 404,000.

Chi·na (chī′nə). *abbr.* **Ch., Chin.** A country of eastern Asia. China is the third largest (after Russia and Canada) and the most populous country in the world, and its ancient civilization traditionally dates to c. 2700 B.C. Some of China's most notable dynasties include the Shang (1766?–1122? B.C.), Chou (1122?–221? B.C.), Han (206 B.C.–A.D. 220), Tang (618–907), Ming (1368–1644), and Qing, or Manchu, (1644–1912). After a bitter civil war (1946–1949), Mao Zedong established a Communist people's republic on the mainland, and the defeated Nationalists under Chiang Kai-shek fled to Taiwan. Mao's 1958 economic program known as the "Great Leap Forward" ended in failure, and his Cultural Revolution (1966–1969), aimed at eliminating counterrevolutionary elements, initiated a period of great political and social disruption. After Mao's death (1976), Deng Xiaoping adopted policies to modernize the economy and established diplomatic relations with the U.S. (1979). In 1989 in Beijing, a massive demonstration by students calling for democratic reforms was suppressed by the army and hundreds were killed. Deng was succeeded after his death (1997) by Jiang Zemin. Beijing is the capital and Shanghai the largest city. ⊛ Pop. 1,208,841,000.

China **Republic of.** See **Taiwan.**

China Sea The western part of the Pacific Ocean extending along the eastern coast of Asia from southern Japan to the Malay Peninsula. It is divided by Taiwan into the **East China Sea** and the **South China Sea.**

Chin·chow (jĭn′jō′). See **Jinzhou.**

Chin·co·teague Bay (shĭng′kə-tēg′, chĭng′-). A long, narrow bay off northeast Virginia and southeast Maryland. **Chincoteague Island** is at the southern end of the bay.

Chin·dwin (chĭn′dwĭn′). A river rising in northern Myanmar (Burma) and flowing about 1,158 km (720 mi) south to the Irrawaddy River.

Chi·nese (chī-nēz′, -nēs′). *abbr.* **Chin. 1.** Of or relating to China or its peoples, languages, or cultures. **2.** *pl.* **Chinese. a.** A native or inhabitant of China. **b.** A person of Chinese ancestry. **c.** See **Han. 3. a.** A branch of the Sino-Tibetan language family that consists of the various dialects spoken by the Chinese people. **b.** Any of the dialects spoken by the Chinese people.

Ching·hai (chĭng′hī′). See **Qinghai.**

Chin Hills (chĭn). A range of hills in western Myanmar (Burma) rising to about 3,055.5 m (10,018 ft).

Chin·ju (jĭn′jōō′). A city of southern South Korea west of Pusan. It is a transportation center in an agricultural region. ⊛ Pop. 255,695.

Chin·kiang (chĭn′kyäng′, jĭn′gyäng′). See **Zhenjiang.**

Chi·no (chē′nō). A city of southern California east of Los Angeles. It was founded in 1887. ⊛ Pop. 59,682.

Chi·nook (shĭ-nŏŏk′, chĭ-). **1. a.** *pl.* **Chinook** or **-nooks.** A member of a Native American people formerly inhabiting the lower Columbia River valley and adjoining coastal regions of Washington and Oregon, now located in western Washington. The Chinooks traded widely throughout the Pacific Northwest. **b.** The Chinookan language of the Chinook. **2.** *pl.* **Chinook** or **-nooks.** A member of any various Chinookan-speaking peoples formerly inhabiting the Columbia River valley eastward to The Dalles and now located in southern Washington and northern Oregon. **3. chinook. a.** A moist, warm wind blowing from the sea on the northwest U.S. coast. **b.** A warm, dry wind that descends from the eastern slopes of the Rocky Mountains, causing a rapid rise in temperature.

Chi·nook·an (shĭ-nŏŏk′ən, chĭ-). A North American Indian language family of Washington and Oregon. —**Chi·nook′an** *adj.*

Chinook Jargon. A pidgin language combining words from Nootka, Chinook, Salishan languages, French, and English, formerly used as a lingua franca in the Pacific Northwest.

Chin·wang·tao (chĭn′wäng′tou′). See **Qinhuangdao.**

Chiog·gia (kē-ō′jə, kyôd′jä). A city of northeast Italy on an island in the Venetian lagoon. It is connected with the mainland by a bridge. ⊛ Pop. 38,200.

Chi·os (kī′ŏs′, -ōs′, kē′-, κHē′ôs) also **Khí·os** (kē′ôs, κHē′-). An island of Greece in the Aegean Sea off the western coast of Turkey. It was noted in antiquity for its school of epic poets.

Chip·e·wy·an (chĭp′ə-wī′ən). **1.** *pl.* **Chipewyan** or **-ans.** A member of a Native American people made up of numerous autonomous bands inhabiting a large area of northern Canada north of the Churchill River. Formerly nomadic caribou hunters, the Chipewyans became settled fur traders during the 18th century. **2.** The Athabaskan language of the Chipewyans.

Chip·pe·wa (chĭp′ə-wô′, -wä′, -wā′, -wə). *pl.* **Chippewa** or **-was.** See **Ojibwa.**

Chir·i·ca·hua (chĭr′ĭ-kä′wə). *pl.* **Chiricahua** or **-huas.** A member of a formerly nomadic Apache tribe inhabiting southern New Mexico, southeast Arizona, and northern Mexico, with present-day populations in Oklahoma and New Mexico.

Chippewa River. A river rising in the lake region of northern Wisconsin and flowing about 290 km (180 mi) generally south to the Mississippi River.

Chis·holm Trail (chĭz′əm). A former cattle trail from San Antonio, Texas, north to Abilene, Kansas. It was important from the 1860's to the 1880's, when it fell into disuse following the expansion of the railroads and the introduction of barbed-wire fencing

Chi·ta (chĭ-tä′). A city of southeast Russia east of Irkutsk. Founded in 1653, it is a manufacturing center on the Trans-Siberian railroad. ⊛ Pop. 364,903.

Chit·ta·gong (chĭt′ə-gông′, -gŏng′). A city of southeast Bangladesh near the Bay of Bengal. It is the country's chief port and an industrial center. ⊛ Pop. 1,363,998.

Chka·lov (chə-kä′ləf, chkä′-). See **Orenburg.**

Choc·taw (chŏk′tô). **1.** *pl.* **Choctaw** or **-taws.** A member of a Native American people formerly inhabiting central and southern Mississippi and southwest Alabama, with present-day populations in Mississippi and southeast Oklahoma. The Choctaws were forcibly removed to Indian Territory in the 1830's. **2.** The Muskogean language of the Choctaws.

Choc·taw·hatch·ee (chŏk′tə-hăch′ē). A river rising in southern Alabama and flowing about 225 km (140 mi) south into northwest Florida, where it empties into **Choctawhatchee Bay,** an inlet of the Gulf of Mexico.

Choi·seul (shwä-zœl′). One of the Solomon Islands in the southwest Pacific Ocean southeast of Bougainville Island. It was under German control from 1886 to 1899.

Cho·let (shō-lā′). A city of western France east-southeast of Nantes. It is an industrial center. ⊛ Pop. 55,524.

Cho·lu·la (chə-lōō′lə, chô-lōō′lä). A town of east-central Mexico west of Puebla. Site of an ancient Toltec center and a city sacred to the Aztecs, it was destroyed by the Spanish explorer and conquistador Hernando Cortés in 1519. ⊛ Pop. 26,748.

Cho·mo Lha·ri (chō′mō lär′ē). A peak, 7,318.8 m (23,996 ft) high, of the southeast Himalaya Mountains on the Bhutan-China border.

Chong·jin (chông′jĭn′, chœng′-). A city of northeast North Korea on the Sea of Japan. It is a port and an industrial center. ⊛ Pop. 490,000.

Chong·qing (chông′chĭng′, chōōng′-) also **Chung·king** (chōōng′kĭng′, jōōng′gĭng′). A city of south-central China on the Chang Jiang (Yangtze River). It was the capital of China from 1937 to 1946. ⊛ Pop. 3,122,704.

Chon·ju (chôn′jōō′, chœn′-). A city of southwest South Korea south of Seoul. It is a marketing and transportation center in a rice-growing region. ⊛ Pop. 366,997.

Cho O·yu (chō′ ō-yōō′). A peak, 8,158.8 m (26,750 ft) high, of the central Himalaya Mountains on the Nepal-China border.

Chor·ley (chôr′lē). A municipal borough of northwest England west-northwest of Manchester. It is a manufacturing center. ⊛ Pop. 54,700.

cho·rog·ra·phy (kə-rŏg′rə-fē). **1.** The technique of mapping a region or district. **2.** A description or map of a region. — **cho·rog′-ra·pher** *n.* — **cho′ro·graph′ic** (kôr′ə-grăf′-ĭk, kōr′-), **cho′ro·graph′i·cal** *adj.* — **cho′ro·graph′i·cal·ly** *adv.*

Chor·ril·los (chô-rē′ōs). A city of west-central Peru, a residential suburb of Lima. ⊛ Pop. 141,881.

Cho·rzów (hô′zhōōf). A city of southern Poland northwest of Katowice. It is a mining center. ⊛ Pop. 131,468.

Cho·sen (chō′sĕn′). A name used for Korea since the second millennium B.C.

chott also **shott** (shŏt). **1.** The depression surrounding a salt marsh or lake, especially in North Africa. **2.** The bed of a dried salt marsh.

Christ·church (krīst′chûrch′). A city of eastern South Island, New Zealand, near the Pacific coast. It is an important manufacturing center. ⊛ Pop. 293,700.

Chris·ti·a·ni·a (krĭs′tē-ăn′ē-ə, -ä′nē-ə, krĭs′-chē-). See **Oslo.**

Chris·tian·sted (krĭs′chən-stĕd′). The chief city of St. Croix in the U.S. Virgin Islands. Tourism is the leading industry. ⊛ Pop. 2,914.

Christ·mas Island (krĭs′məs). **1.** An Australian-administered island in the eastern Indian Ocean south of Java. It was annexed by Great Britain in 1888 and came under Australian sovereignty in 1958. **2.** The largest of the Line Islands in the central Pacific Ocean near the equator. Discovered by James Cook in 1777, the island is now part of Kiribati.

Chu (chōō). A river of southern Kazakhstan flowing about 1,126 km (700 mi) eastward into Issyk-Kul.

Chu·but (chə-bōōt′, chōō-). A river rising in the Andes of southwest Argentina and flowing about 805 km (500 mi) eastward to the Atlantic Ocean.

Chu·gach Mountains (chōō′gäch′, -gäsh′). A range of southern Alaska extending eastward from Cook Inlet to the Canadian border. Mount Marcus Baker, 4,018.7 m (13,176 ft), is the highest elevation.

Chuk·chi also **Chuk·chee** (chōōk′chē). **1.** *pl.* **Chukchi** or **-chis** also **Chukchee** or **-chees.** A member of a people of northeast Siberia. **2.** The language of the Chukchi, noted for being pronounced differently by men and women.

Chukchi Peninsula. A peninsula of extreme northeast Russia across the Bering Strait from northwest Alaska. It borders on the **Chukchi Sea,** a section of the Arctic Ocean.

Chu Kiang (chōō′ kyäng′, jōō′ gyäng′). See **Zhu Jiang.**

Chu·la Vis·ta (chōō′lə vĭs′tə). A city of southern California south of San Diego. It is an industrial center. ⊛ Pop. 135,163.

Chu·lym also **Chu·lim** (chə-lĭm′, chōō-). A river of south-central Russia flowing about 1,730 km (1,075 mi) north and west to the Ob River.

Chu·mash (chōō′măsh). *pl.* **Chumash** or **-mash·es.** A member of a group of Hokan-speaking Native American peoples formerly inhabiting the southern California coastal region around and the channel islands off Santa Barbara, with a small present-day population near Santa Barbara.

Chung·king (chŏong′kĭng′, jŏong′gĭng′). See **Chongqing.**

Chur·chill (chûr′chĭl′, chûrch′hĭl′), **Mount.** A peak, about 4,769.6 m (15,638 ft) high, in the Wrangell Mountains of southern Alaska.

Churchill Falls. Formerly **Grand Falls** (grănd). A waterfall, 74.7 m (245 ft) high, of the upper Churchill River in southwest Labrador, Canada. There is an enormous hydroelectric power plant at the falls.

Churchill River. 1. A river of eastern Canada flowing about 965 km (600 mi) across Labrador to the Atlantic Ocean. **2.** A river rising in northwest Saskatchewan, Canada, and flowing about 1,609 km (1,000 mi) eastward across Saskatchewan and northern Manitoba then northeast to Hudson Bay. It was formerly an important fur-trading route.

Church Slavonic (chûrch). See **Old Church Slavonic.**

chute (shōōt). A waterfall or rapid.

Chu·vash¹ (chōō-väsh′). **1.** *pl.* **Chuvash** or **-vash·es.** A member of a people located in the middle Volga River valley, chiefly in the Chuvash region. **2.** The Turkic language spoken by the Chuvash.

Chu·vash² (chōō′väsh′, chyōō-väsh′). A region of western Russia in the Volga River valley.

Conquered by the Mongols in the 13th and 14th centuries, it came under Russian rule in 1552.

Cí·bo·la (sē′bə-lə). A vaguely defined historical region generally thought to be in present-day northern New Mexico. It included seven pueblos, the fabled Seven Cities of Cibola, which were sought by the earliest Spanish explorers for their supposed riches.

Cic·e·ro (sĭs′ə-rō′). A town of northeast Illinois, an industrial and residential suburb of Chicago. ⊛ Pop. 67,436.

Cien·fue·gos (syěn-fwä′gōs). A city of south-central Cuba on **Cienfuegos Bay,** a narrow-necked inlet of the Caribbean Sea. The city is a port and a trade and processing center. ⊛ Pop. 129,665.

Ci·li·cia (sĭ-lĭsh′ə). An ancient region of southeast Asia Minor along the Mediterranean Sea south of the Taurus Mountains. The area was conquered by Alexander the Great and later became part of the Roman Empire. It was the site of an independent Armenian state from 1080 to 1375. — **Ci·li′cian** *adj. & n.*

Cilician Gates. A mountain pass in the Taurus Mountains of southern Turkey. The pass has served for centuries as a natural highway linking Anatolia with the Mediterranean coast.

Cim·ar·ron (sĭm′ə-rŏn′, -rōn′). A river rising in northeast New Mexico and flowing approximately 1,123 km (698 mi) eastward across southwest Kansas to the Arkansas River in northern Oklahoma.

Cin·cin·na·ti (sĭn′sə-năt′ē, -năt′ə). A city of extreme southwest Ohio on the Ohio River. Founded in 1788, it is a port of entry and an industrial, commercial, and cultural center for an extensive area in Ohio and Kentucky. ⊛ Pop. 364,040.

Ci·ni·sel·lo Bal·sa·mo (chē′nĭ-zěl′ō bôl′sə-mō′, chē′nē-zěl′lô bäl′sä-mô′). A city of northern Italy, a suburb of Milan. ⊛ Pop. 80,323.

Cin·na·min·son (sĭn′ə-mĭn′sən). A community of southwest New Jersey near the Delaware River northeast of Camden. The destructive Japanese beetle was first discovered here in 1916. ⊛ Pop. 14,583.

Cinque Ports (sĭngk′). A group of seaports of southeast England (originally Hastings, Romney, Hythe, Dover, and Sandwich) that formed a maritime and defensive association in the 11th century. They reached the height of their significance in the Anglo-French conflicts of the 14th century.

Ci·pan·go (sĭ-păng′gō). A poetic name for Japan, used by the Venetian traveler Marco Polo (1254–1324).

Cir·cas·sia (sər-kăsh′ə, -ē-ə). A historical region of southwest Russia on the northeast coast of the Black Sea north of the Caucasus Mountains. It was ceded to Russia by the Ottoman Turks in 1829.

Cir·cas·sian (sər-kăsh′ən, -kăsh′ē-ən). **1.** A native or inhabitant of Circassia. **2.** The non-Indo-European language of the Circassians. **3.** Of or relating to Circassia or its people, language, or culture.

cir·cle (sûr′kəl). *abbr.* **cir, circ.** A territorial or administrative division, especially of a province, in some European countries.

cir·cum·po·lar (sûr′kəm-pō′lər). Located or found in one of the Polar Regions.

Ci·re·bon (chĭr′ə-bôn′). A city of south-central Indonesia on the northern coast of Java east-northeast of Bandung. It is a port on the Java Sea. ◉ Pop. 223,776.

cirque (sûrk). A steep hollow, often containing a small lake, occurring at the upper end of a mountain valley. Also called *cwm.*

cis·al·pine (sĭs-ăl′pīn′). Relating to, living on, or coming from the southern side of the Alps.

Cis·al·pine Gaul (sĭs-ăl′pīn′). A section of ancient Gaul south and east of the Alps in present-day Italy.

cis·at·lan·tic (sĭs′ət-lăn′tĭk). Situated on this side of the Atlantic Ocean.

Cis·cau·ca·sia (sĭs′kô-kā′zhə, -shə). A steppeland of southwest Russia in the Caucasus north of the main range of the Caucasus Mountains.

Cis·kei (sĭs′kī). A former Black homeland of southeast South Africa. It was granted nominal independence in 1980 and was reabsorbed into South Africa under the 1993 interim constitution.

cis·mon·tane (sĭs-mŏn′tān′). Situated on this side of the mountains, especially the Alps.

Ci·thae·ron (sĭ-thîr′ən). A mountain, 1,410 m (4,623 ft) high, of southeast Greece. It was considered sacred to Dionysus and the Muses.

Ci·tlal·té·petl (sē′tläl-tā′pĕt-l) also **Mount O·ri·za·ba** (ôr′ĭ-zä′bə, ōr′-, ô′rē-sä′vä). An extinct volcanic peak, 5,702.6 m (18,697 ft) high, of southern Mexico between Mexico City and Veracruz. It is the highest elevation in the country.

Cit·rus Heights (sĭt′rəs). A community of north-central California, a largely residential suburb of Sacramento. ◉ Pop. 107,439.

cit·y (sĭt′ē). *abbr.* **C. 1.** A center of population, commerce, and culture; a town of significant size and importance. **2. a.** An incorporated municipality in the United States with definite boundaries and legal powers set forth in a charter granted by the state. **b.** A Canadian municipality of high rank, usually determined by population but varying by province. **c.** A large incorporated town in Great Britain, usually the

seat of a bishop, with its title conferred by the Crown. **3.** An ancient Greek city-state.

Ci·u·dad Bo·lí·var (sē′ōō-däd′ bə-lē′vär, syōō-*thäth*′ bô-lē′vär). A city of east-central Venezuela on the Orinoco River southeast of Caracas. It was founded in 1764 on the narrows (or *angosturas*) of the river and was popularly known as Angostura. ◉ Pop. 253,112.

Ciudad de Nau·cal·pan de Juá·rez (dĕ nou-käl′pän dĕ hwä′rĕs). A city of south-central Mexico, an industrial suburb of Mexico City. ◉ Pop. 723,723.

Ciudad Gua·ya·na (gwə-yä′nə, gwä-yä′nä). A city of eastern Venezuela on the Orinoco River. It was founded in 1961 as a planned community. ◉ Pop. 523,578.

Ciudad Juá·rez (wär′ĕz, hwä′rĕs) also **Juárez.** A city of northern Mexico on the Rio Grande opposite El Paso, Texas. The two cities are connected by bridge. ◉ Pop. 544,496.

Ciudad Ma·de·ro (mə-dĕr′ō, mä-*thĕ*′rô). A city of eastern Mexico on the Gulf of Mexico. It is a suburb of Tampico. ◉ Pop. 132,444.

Ciudad O·bre·gón (ō′brĕ-gŏn′, ô-vrĕ-gôn′). A city of northwest Mexico south-southeast of Hermosillo. It is a trade and processing center in an agricultural region. ◉ Pop. 165,520.

Ciudad O·je·da (ō-hĕ′də, -*th*ä). A city of northwest Venezuela on the eastern shore of Lake Maracaibo. It is a petroleum-refining center. ◉ Pop. 129,000.

Ciudad Re·al (rĕ-äl′). A city of central Spain in a fertile area south of Madrid. It was founded by Alfonso X of Castile (1226?–1284). ◉ Pop. 53,546.

Ciudad Tru·jil·lo (trōō-hē′yō). See **Santo Domingo.**

Ciudad Vic·to·ri·a (vĭk-tôr′ē-ə, -tōr′-, vĕk-tô′ryä). A city of east-central Mexico south-southeast of Monterrey. It was founded in 1750. ◉ Pop. 140,161.

Ci·vi·ta·vec·chia (chē′vē-tä-vĕk′yä). A city of west-central Italy on the Tyrrhenian Sea west-northwest of Rome. Its harbor is the chief port of Rome. ◉ Pop. 45,836.

Clac·ton (klăk′tən) also **Clac·ton-on-Sea** (-ŏn-sē′, -ôn-). An urban district of southeast England on the North Sea. It is a resort situated on high cliffs overlooking the sea. ◉ Pop. 44,000.

Clac·to·ni·an (klăk-tō′nē-ən). *Archaeology.* Of or relating to a lower Paleolithic culture of northwest Europe.

Clac·ton-on-Sea (klăk′tən-ŏn-sē′, -ôn-). See **Clacton.**

Clare·mont (klâr′mŏnt′). A city of southern California northeast of Pomona. It is mainly residential and the site of the associated Claremont Colleges. ◉ Pop. 32,503.

Clark (klärk). An unincorporated community of northeast New Jersey southwest of Elizabeth. It is mainly residential. ⊕ Pop. 14,629.

Clark Fork. A river rising in southwest Montana near Butte and flowing about 579 km (360 mi) generally north then northwest to Pend Oreille Lake in the Idaho Panhandle.

Clarks·burg (klärks′bûrg′). A city of northern West Virginia south-southeast of Wheeling. It was an important Union supply base during the Civil War. ⊕ Pop. 18,059.

Clarks·dale (klärks′dāl′). A city of northwest Mississippi near the Arkansas border. It is a manufacturing center. ⊕ Pop. 19,717.

Clarks·ville (klärks′vĭl′). **1.** A town of southern Indiana on the Ohio River opposite Louisville, Kentucky. It was founded in 1784 by the explorer George Rogers Clark. ⊕ Pop. 19,833. **2.** A city of northwest Tennessee on the Cumberland and Red rivers northwest of Nashville. An important tobacco market, it is also a manufacturing center. ⊕ Pop. 75,494.

Claw·son (klô′sən). A city of southeast Michigan, an industrial suburb of Detroit. ⊕ Pop. 13,874.

Clear·field (klîr′fēld′). A city of northern Utah south of Ogden. It is a trade center in an irrigated agricultural area. ⊕ Pop. 21,435.

Clear·wa·ter (klîr′wô′tər, -wŏt′ər). A city of west-central Florida west of Tampa. It is a residential and resort community. ⊕ Pop. 98,784.

Clearwater Mountains. A range of north-central Idaho between the Salmon River and the Bitterroot Range. The highest point is about 2,745 m (9,000 ft).

Clearwater River. **1.** A river, about 209 km (130 mi) long, of northwest Saskatchewan and northeast Alberta, Canada. It joins the Athabasca River at Fort McMurray. **2.** A river rising in the Bitterroot Range of northern Idaho and flowing about 306 km (190 mi) generally west to join the Snake River at Lewiston. Gold was discovered along the river in 1860.

Cle·burne (klē′bərn). A city of northeast Texas south of Fort Worth. It is a market center in an agricultural region. ⊕ Pop. 22,205.

Cler·mont-Fer·rand (klĕr-môN′fə-räN′, -fĕ-). A city of central France west of Lyon. Clermont was founded in Roman times and merged with Montferrand, an 11th-century town, in 1731. ⊕ Pop. 136,180.

Cleve·land (klēv′lənd). **1.** A city of northeast Ohio on Lake Erie. A port of entry and industrial center, the city was laid out in 1796 by Moses Cleveland (1754–1806). ⊕ Pop. 505,616. **2.** A city of southeast Tennessee east-northeast of Chattanooga. It is a trade center with varied industries. ⊕ Pop. 30,354.

Cleveland, Mount. A peak, about 3,192.1 m (10,466 ft) high, of northwest Montana. It is the highest point in the Lewis Range of the Rocky Mountains.

Cleveland Heights. A city of northeast Ohio, a suburb of Cleveland. ⊕ Pop. 54,052.

Cleves (klēvz). See **Kleve.**

Cli·chy (klē-shē′). A city of north-central France, a suburb of Paris. It was a royal residence of the Merovingians, a Frankish ruling dynasty, in the seventh century. ⊕ Pop. 46,895.

cliff (klĭf). A high, steep, or overhanging face of rock. — **cliff′y** *adj.*

cliff dweller. A member of certain Anasazi groups of the southwest United States who built rock or adobe dwellings on sheltered ledges in the sides of cliffs. — **cliff dwelling** *n.*

Cliff·side Park (klĭf′sīd′). A borough of northeast New Jersey on the Palisades overlooking the Hudson River opposite New York City. It is mainly residential and has varied light industries. ⊕ Pop. 20,393.

Clif·ton (klĭf′tən). A city of northeast New Jersey near Paterson. It was formerly part of Passaic. ⊕ Pop. 71,742.

Clinch River (klĭnch). A river rising in southwest Virginia and flowing about 483 km (300 mi) generally southwest across eastern Tennessee to the Tennessee River.

Cling·mans Dome (klĭng′mənz). A mountain, 2,026.1 m (6,643 ft) high, in the Great Smoky Mountains on the Tennessee–North Carolina border. It is the highest elevation of the range and the highest point in Tennessee.

Clin·ton (klĭn′tən). **1.** A city of east-central Iowa on the Mississippi River northeast of Davenport. It is a manufacturing and trade center in an agricultural region. ⊕ Pop. 29,201. **2.** An unincorporated village of central Maryland southeast of Washington, D.C. Andrews Air Force Base is nearby. ⊕ Pop. 19,987.

Cloud Peak (kloud). A mountain, 4,018.4 m (13,175 ft) high, in the Bighorn Mountains of north-central Wyoming. It is the highest elevation in the range.

Clo·vis¹ (klō′vĭs). **1.** A city of central California in the foothills of the Sierra Nevada near Fresno. It is a trade and processing center. ⊕ Pop. 50,323. **2.** A city of eastern New Mexico near the Texas border. It is a trade center in a wheat and cattle area. ⊕ Pop. 30,954.

Clo·vis² (klō′vĭs). Of or relating to a prehistoric human culture widespread throughout North America from about 12,000 to 9,000 B.C., distinguished by sharp, fluted projectile points made of chalcedony or obsidian. The culture is named after Clovis, New Mexico, where the first artifacts were unearthed in 1932.

Cluj·Na·po·ca (klo͞ozh'nä-pô'kä). A city of west-central Romania northwest of Bucharest. It was founded by German colonists in the 12th century and became part of Romania in 1920. ◉ Pop. 321,850.

Clu·ny (klo͞o'nē, klo͞o-nē', klü-). A town of east-central France north-northwest of Lyon. Its abbey, the center of an influential religious order, was founded in 910. ◉ Pop. 4,335.

Clyde (klīd). A river of southwest Scotland flowing about 171 km (106 mi) northwest to the **Firth of Clyde,** an estuary of the North Channel. The river is navigable to Glasgow for oceangoing vessels.

Clyde·bank (klīd'băngk'). A burgh of west-central Scotland on the north bank of the Clyde River. Many large ocean liners, including the *Queen Mary,* were built in its shipyards. ◉ Pop. 52,385.

Cni·dus also **Cni·dos** (nī'dəs). An ancient Greek city of Asia Minor in present-day southwest Asiatic Turkey. It was noted for its wealth and its magnificent buildings and statuary.

Cnos·sos or **Cnos·sus** (nŏs'əs). See **Knossos.**

coast (kōst). **1. a.** Land next to the sea; the seashore. **b. Coast.** The Pacific Coast of the United States. **2.** *Obsolete.* The frontier or border of a country. — **coast'al** (kō'stəl) *adj.*

coast·land (kōst'lănd'). The land along a coast.

coast·line (kōst'līn'). The shape, outline, or boundary of a coast.

Coast Mountains. A range of western British Columbia, Canada, and southeast Alaska extending about 1,609 km (1,000 mi) parallel to the Pacific coast. The mountains slope precipitously to the Pacific Ocean, where the shoreline is deeply indented by fjords. Mount Waddington, 3,996.7 m (13,104 ft), is the highest elevation in the range.

Coast Ranges. A series of mountain ranges of extreme western North America extending from southeast Alaska to Baja California along the coastline of the Pacific Ocean.

Coast Salish. The Salish-speaking Native American peoples inhabiting the northwest Pacific coast from the Strait of Georgia to southwest Washington.

Coat·bridge (kōt'brĭj'). A burgh of south-central Scotland east of Glasgow. It is a manufacturing center with iron and steel industries. ◉ Pop. 50,700.

Coats Land (kōts). A region of western Antarctica along the southeast shore of the Weddell Sea.

Co·at·za·co·al·cos (kō-ät'sə-kō-äl'kəs, kô-ä'-tsä-kô-äl'kôs). A city of eastern Mexico on the Gulf of Campeche at the mouth of the **Coatza-**coalcos River, about 282 km (175 mi) long. The city is an important commercial center. ◉ Pop. 127,170.

Cobh (kōv). An urban district of southern Ireland on Cork Harbor. It is a popular seaside resort. ◉ Pop. 6,587.

Co·blenz (kō'blĕnts'). See **Koblenz.**

Co·burg (kō'bûrg'). A city of central Germany north of Nuremberg. It was first mentioned in the 11th century. ◉ Pop. 44,239.

Co·cha·bam·ba (kō'chə-bäm'bə, kô'chä-bäm'-bä). A city of west-central Bolivia north-northwest of Sucre. Founded in 1574 as Orpeza, it was renamed in 1786. ◉ Pop. 448,756.

Co·chin (kō'chĭn). A region and former princely state of southwest India on the Malabar Coast of the Arabian Sea. The city of **Cochin** was visited by Vasco da Gama in 1502 and colonized by the Portuguese in the following year. It was taken by the Dutch in 1663 and occupied by the British in 1795. ◉ Pop. 513,249.

Cochin China. A region of southern Indochina including the rich delta area of the Mekong River. Originally a part of the Khmer Empire, it fell to the Annamese in the 18th century and to the French in the 19th century. It forms the southern part of present-day Vietnam.

Cock·eys·ville (kŏk'ēz-vĭl'). A community of northern Maryland, a manufacturing suburb of Baltimore. ◉ Pop. 18,668.

cock·ney (kŏk'nē). **1.** often **Cockney.** A native of the East End of London. **2.** The dialect or accent of the natives of the East End of London. **3.** Of or relating to cockneys or their dialect.

Co·co (kō'kō). A river rising in northern Nicaragua and flowing about 483 km (300 mi) northeast along the Nicaragua-Honduras border to the Caribbean Sea.

Co·coa (kō'kō). A city of east-central Florida east-southeast of Orlando. It is a tourist center in a citrus-growing region. ◉ Pop. 17,722.

Co·cos Islands (kō'kōs) also **Kee·ling Islands** (kē'lĭng). An island group in the eastern Indian Ocean southwest of Sumatra. Discovered in 1609, the islands were settled by the British in 1826 and are today administered by Australia.

Cod (kŏd), **Cape.** A hook-shaped peninsula of southeast Massachusetts extending east and north into the Atlantic Ocean. Fishing, whaling, and shipping were important here until the late 1800's; the economy today is based largely on tourism.

Coeur d'A·lene (kôr' də-lān', kôrd'l-ān', kûrd'-). A city of northern Idaho on **Coeur D'Alene Lake** in the Panhandle east of Spokane, Washington. The city is the gateway to a popular resort area. ◉ Pop. 24,563.

Cof·fey·ville (kô′fē-vĭl′, kŏf′ē-). A city of southeast Kansas near the Oklahoma border. It was settled as a cattle-shipping point after the coming of the railroad in the 1870's. ◉ Pop. 12,917.

Co·gnac (kôn′yăk′, kŏn-, kô-nyäk′). A city of western France on the Charente River north-northeast of Bordeaux. It is famous for its distilleries, which have manufactured and exported cognac since the 18th century. ◉ Pop. 20,660.

Co·hoes (kə-hōz′). A city of east-central New York on the Hudson River north of Albany. It was settled by the Dutch in 1665 and is a manufacturing center. ◉ Pop. 16,825.

Coim·ba·tore (koim′bə-tōr′, -tôr′). A city of southern India south-southwest of Bangalore. It is a manufacturing center and an agricultural market. ◉ Pop. 816,321.

Co·im·bra (kō-ĭm′brə, kwĭm′-, kwēN′-). A city of central Portugal north-northeast of Lisbon. It is noted for its university, founded in Lisbon in the 1290's and transferred to Coimbra in 1540. ◉ Pop. 74,616.

Col·ches·ter (kōl′chĕs′tər, -chĭ-stər). A municipal borough of southeast England near the North Sea. It was an important pre-Roman city and the site of the first Roman colony in Britain. ◉ Pop. 149,087.

Col·chis (kŏl′kĭs). An ancient region on the Black Sea south of the Caucasus Mountains. It was the site of Jason's legendary quest for the Golden Fleece.

Cold Harbor (kōld). A locality in eastern Virginia east-northeast of Richmond. Confederate forces defeated Union troops here in two Civil War battles (1862 and 1864).

Cold·wa·ter River (kōld′wô′tər, -wŏt′ər). A river, 354 km (220 mi) long, of northwest Mississippi flowing generally south to the Tallahatchie River.

Col·lege Park (kŏl′ĭj). **1.** A city of northwest Georgia, a residential suburb of Atlanta. ◉ Pop. 20,457. **2.** A city of central Maryland north-northeast of Washington, D.C. It is the seat of the main campus of the University of Maryland (established 1807). ◉ Pop. 21,927.

College Station. A city of east-central Texas northwest of Houston. Texas Agricultural and Mechanical University (opened 1876) is here. ◉ Pop. 52,456.

Col·lings·wood (kŏl′ĭngz-wŏŏd′). A borough of southwest New Jersey southeast of Camden. Founded by Quakers in 1682, it is a residential suburb of Philadelphia. ◉ Pop. 15,289.

Col·lins·ville (kŏl′ĭnz-vĭl′). A city of southwest Illinois east-northeast of East St. Louis. It was formerly a coal-mining center. ◉ Pop. 22,446.

col·lu·vi·um (kə-lōō′vē-əm). A loose deposit of rock debris accumulated through the action of gravity at the base of a cliff or slope. —**col·lu′vi·al** adj.

Col·mar also **Kol·mar** (kōl′mär, kôl-mär′). A city of eastern France between the Vosges Mountains and the Rhine River. It became a free imperial city in 1226. ◉ Pop. 62,483.

Co·logne (kə-lōn′) also **Köln** (kœln). A city of western Germany on the Rhine River north of Bonn. It was a Roman settlement called Colonia Agrippina after A.D. 50 and passed under Frankish control in the 5th century. During the 15th century it flourished as a member of the Hanseatic League. ◉ Pop. 962,517.

Co·lombes (kə-lōm′, kô-lôNb′). A city of north-central France, an industrial suburb of Paris on the Seine River. ◉ Pop. 78,777.

Co·lom·bi·a (kə-lŭm′bē-ə). abbr. **Col.** A country of northwest South America with coastlines on the Pacific Ocean and the Caribbean Sea. It was settled by the Spanish after they defeated the Chibchas in the late 1530's and later formed the core of the viceroyalty of New Granada. The area gained its independence from Spain in 1821 under the leadership of Simón Bolívar, but the modern state of Colombia did not emerge until after Venezuela and Ecuador (1830) and later Panama (1903) had become separate nations. The country's political history has been turbulent, marked by power struggles between Conservatives and Liberals and civil war. In the 1990's the government launched an official military campaign against the powerful illegal drug cartels that had operated with relative impunity during the 1970's and 1980's. Bogotá is the capital and the largest city. ◉ Pop. 26,525,670. —**Co·lom′bi·an** adj. & n.

Caribbean Sea
Cartagena
PANAMA
VENEZUELA
Medellín
PACIFIC OCEAN
Cauca
Magdalena
Bogotá
Orinoco
COLOMBIA
Putumayo
ECUADOR
BRAZIL
PERU
250 mi

Co·lom·bo (kə-lŭm′bō). The capital and largest city of Sri Lanka, on the western coast of the island on the Indian Ocean. The city was probably known to Greco-Roman, Arab, and Chinese traders more than 2,000 years ago. It became capital of the crown colony of Ceylon in 1802 and of independent Ceylon in 1948. ● Pop. 615,000.

Co·lón (kə-lŏ′, kô-lôn′). A city of northern Panama at the Caribbean entrance to the Panama Canal. The city was founded as Aspinwall in 1850 by Americans working on the Panama Railroad and was renamed in 1890. ● Pop. 59,840.

Co·lo·ni·al Heights (kə-lō′nē-ə). A city of southeast Virginia south of Richmond. It was Robert E. Lee's headquarters during the Battle of Petersburg (1864). ● Pop. 16,064.

col·o·ny (kŏl′ə-nē) *pl.* **col·o·nies. 1. a.** A group of emigrants or their descendants who settle in a distant territory but remain subject to or closely associated with the parent country. **b.** A territory thus settled. **2.** *abbr.* **col.** A region politically controlled by a distant country; a dependency.

Col·o·phon (kŏl′ə-fŏn′). An ancient Greek city of Asia Minor northwest of Ephesus. It was famous for its cavalry.

Col·o·ra·do (kŏl′ə-răd′ō, -rä′dō). *abbr.* **CO, Col., Colo.** A state of the west-central United States. It was admitted as the 38th state in 1876. First explored by the Spanish in the 16th and 17th centuries, the region was added to the United States through the Louisiana Purchase (1803) and a cession by Mexico (1848). The Colorado Territory was organized in 1861. Denver is the capital and the largest city. ● Pop. 3,307,912. — **Col′o·ra′dan** *adj. & n.*

Colorado Desert. An arid region of southeast California west of the Colorado River.

Colorado River. 1. also **Co·lo·ra·do** (kô′lô-rä′dô, -thô). A river of central Argentina rising in the Andes and flowing about 853 km (530 mi) southeast to the Atlantic Ocean. **2.** A river of the southwest United States rising in the Rocky Mountains and flowing about 2,333 km (1,450 mi) southwest through the **Colorado Plateau** of western Colorado, southeast Utah, and western Arizona to the Gulf of California in northwest Mexico. The most spectacular of its many gorges is the Grand Canyon. **3.** A river rising in northwest Texas and flowing about 1,438 km (894 mi) southeast to an inlet of the Gulf of Mexico.

Colorado Springs. A city of central Colorado at the foot of Pikes Peak south of Denver. It is a tourist center near the site of the U.S. Air Force Academy (established 1958). ● Pop. 281,140.

Co·los·sae (kə-lŏs′ē). An ancient city of central Asia Minor. It was the site of an early Christian church. — **Co·los′sian** (-lŏsh′ən) *adj.& n.*

Co·los·sus of Rhodes (kə-lŏs′əs). A huge statue of Apollo located at the entrance to the harbor of Rhodes. Built c. 280 B.C. and later destroyed by an earthquake, it was about 37 m (120 ft) high and was one of the Seven Wonders of the World.

Col·ton (kōl′tən). A city of southern California, a suburb of San Bernardino. ● Pop. 40,213.

Co·lum·bi·a¹ (kə-lŭm′bē-ə). **1.** A community of north-central Maryland west-southwest of Baltimore. It is mainly residential. ● Pop. 75,883. **2.** A city of central Missouri north-northwest of Jefferson City. The University of Missouri (established 1839) is here. ● Pop. 69,101. **3.** The capital and largest city of South Carolina, in the central part of the state. It was chosen as the site of the new state's capital in 1786. ● Pop. 98,052. **4.** A city of west-central Tennessee south-southwest of Nashville. It was first settled in 1807. ● Pop. 28,583.

Co·lum·bi·a² (kə-lŭm′bē-ə). The United States.

Columbia, Cape. A cape on the northern coast of Ellesmere Island. It is the northernmost point of Canada.

Columbia, District of. See **District of Columbia.**

Columbia Heights. A city of eastern Minnesota, a residential suburb of Minneapolis. ● Pop. 18,910.

Co·lum·bi·an (kə-lŭm′bē-ən). **1.** Of or relating to the United States. **2.** Of or relating to Christopher Columbus.

Columbia River. A river rising in southeast British Columbia, Canada, and flowing about 1,947 km (1,210 mi) south then west through the **Columbia Plateau** and along the Washington-Oregon border to its outlet on the Pacific Ocean. It was named by the American explorer Robert Gray in 1792.

Co·lum·bus (kə-lŭm′bəs). **1.** A city of western Georgia on the Chattahoochee River southsouthwest of Atlanta. Settled in 1828 on the site of a Creek village, it is a port of entry and major industrial center. ● Pop. 179,278. **2.** A city of south-central Indiana south-southeast of Indianapolis. It was a supply depot for Union troops during the Civil War. ● Pop. 31,802. **3.** A city of northeast Mississippi near the Alabama border. There are many antebellum houses in the area. ● Pop. 23,799. **4.** A city of east-central Nebraska at the confluence of the Loup and Platte rivers west of Omaha. It is a trade, processing, and manufacturing center. ● Pop. 19,480. **5.** The capital of Ohio, in the central part of the state. Laid out in 1812, it is a major industrial, commercial, and cultural center. ● Pop. 632,910.

Col·ville (kōl′vĭl′, kŏl′-). A river rising in the Brooks Range of northwest Alaska and flowing about 603 km (375 mi) east and north across the tundra to the Arctic Ocean.

Co·man·che (kə-măn′chē). **1.** *pl.* **Comanche** or **-ches.** A member of a Native American people formerly ranging over the southern Great Plains from western Kansas to northern Texas and now located in Oklahoma. The Comanches became nomadic buffalo hunters after migrating south from Wyoming in the 18th century. **2.** The Uto-Aztecan language of the Comanches. —**Co·man′che** *adj.*

Com·ba·hee (kŭm-bē′, kŭm′bē). A river, about 225 km (140 mi) long, of southern South Carolina flowing generally southeast to the Atlantic Ocean.

Com·mack (kō′măk, kŏm′ăk). An unincorporated community of southeast New York on central Long Island. It is chiefly residential. ◉ Pop. 36,124.

Com·merce City (kŏm′ərs). A city of north-central Colorado, an industrial suburb of Denver. ◉ Pop. 16,466.

Com·mon Market (kŏm′ən). See **European Economic Community.**

com·mon·wealth (kŏm′ən-wĕlth′). **1.** The people of a nation or state; the body politic. **2.** *abbr.* **comm.** A nation or state governed by the people; a republic. **3. Commonwealth. a.** Used to refer to some U.S. states, namely, Kentucky, Massachusetts, Pennsylvania, and Virginia. **b.** Used to refer to a self-governing, autonomous political unit voluntarily associated with the United States, namely, Puerto Rico and the Northern Mariana Islands. **4.** often **Commonwealth.** The Commonwealth of Nations. **5.** The English state and government from the death of Charles I in 1649 to the restoration of the monarchy in 1660, including the Protectorate of 1653 to 1659.

Commonwealth of Independent States *abbr.* **CIS** An association of former Soviet republics that was established in December 1991 by Russia, Ukraine, and Belarus to help ease the dissolution of the Soviet Union and coordinate interrepublican affairs. Other members include Armenia, Azerbaijan, Georgia, Kazakstan, Kyrgyzstan, Moldova, Tajikistan, Turkmenistan, and Uzbekistan.

Commonwealth of Nations also **Brit·ish Commonwealth** (brĭt′ĭsh). An association comprising the United Kingdom, its dependencies, and many former British colonies that are now sovereign states with a common allegiance to the British Crown, including Canada, Australia, India, and many countries in the West Indies and Africa. It was formally established by the Statute of Westminster in 1931.

Com·mu·nism Peak (kŏm′yə-nĭz′əm) also **Mount Communism.** A mountain, 7,500 m

(24,590 ft) high, of northeast Tajikistan, in the Pamirs near the Chinese border. It is the highest elevation in the country.

Co·mo (kō′mō). A resort city of northern Italy near the Swiss border at the southwest end of **Lake Como.** The city was a Roman colony and became an independent commune in the 11th century. ◉ Pop. 95,183.

Com·o·rin (kŏm′ər-ĭn), **Cape.** A cape at the southernmost point of India projecting into the Indian Ocean.

Com·o·ros (kŏm′ə-rōz′). A country comprising the three main islands and numerous islets of the **Comoro Islands** in the Indian Ocean off southeast Africa between Mozambique and Madagascar. Settled by peoples from Africa, Indonesia, and Arabia, the islands were ceded to the French between 1841 and 1909 and declared their independence from France in 1975, although Mayotte, the largest of the group, voted to retain its status as a French territory. Moroni, on Grande Comoro Island, is the capital. ◉ Pop. 630,000.

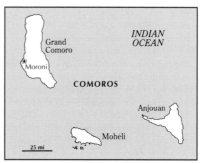

com·pass (kŭm′pəs, kŏm′-). **1.** A device used to determine geographic direction, usually consisting of a magnetic needle or needles horizontally mounted or suspended and free to pivot until aligned with the magnetic field of Earth. **2.** Another device, such as a radio compass or a gyrocompass, used for determining geographic direction.

compass card. A freely pivoting circular disk carrying the magnetic needles of a compass and marked with the 32 points of the compass and the 360 degrees of the circle.

Com·piégne (kōmp-yān′, kôN-pyěn′yə). A city of northern France on the Oise River northeast of Paris. The armistice ending World War I was signed in a railroad car in a nearby forest on November 11, 1918. Adolf Hitler demanded that the same car be used for the formal surrender of France in 1940. ◉ Pop. 40,384.

Comp·ton (kŏmp′tən). A city of southern California, a residential and industrial suburb of Los Angeles and Long Beach. ◉ Pop. 90,454.

Com·stock Lode (kŏm′stŏk′, kŭm′-). A rich vein of gold and silver discovered in 1859 at Virginia City in western Nevada. Because of wasteful mining techniques, it was largely abandoned by 1898.

Con·a·kry (kŏn′ə-krē). The capital and largest city of Guinea, in the southwest part of the country on the Atlantic Ocean. It is on an island connected with the mainland by a causeway. ⊛ Pop. 600,000.

Con·cep·ción (kən-sĕp′sē-ōn′, -sĕp′shən, kôn′-sĕp-syôn′). A city of west-central Chile near the Pacific coast south-southwest of Santiago. Founded in 1550, it has frequently suffered severe earthquake damage. ⊛ Pop. 306,464.

con·ces·sion (kən-sĕsh′ən). A grant of a tract of land made by a government or other controlling authority in return for stipulated services or a promise that the land will be used for a specific purpose. — **con·ces′sion·al** adj. — **con·ces′-sion·ar′y** (-sĕsh′ə-nĕr′ē) adj.

Con·chos (kŏn′chōs, kôn′chôs). A river of northwest Mexico flowing about 563 km (350 mi) northeast to the Rio Grande.

Con·cord (kŏng′kərd). **1.** A city of west-central California northeast of Oakland. It is a residential and manufacturing community. ⊛ Pop. 111,348. **2.** A town of eastern Massachusetts on the **Concord River** west-northwest of Boston. An early battle of the Revolutionary War was fought here on April 19, 1775. In the 19th century the town was noted as an intellectual and literary center. ⊛ Pop. 17,076. **3.** A community of east-central Missouri, a suburb of St. Louis. ⊛ Pop. 19,859. **4.** The capital of New Hampshire, in the south-central part of the state on the Merrimack River. It became the capital in 1808. ⊛ Pop. 36,006. **5.** A city of south-central North Carolina northeast of Charlotte. Gold was discovered in the area in 1799. ⊛ Pop. 27,347.

con·do·min·i·um (kŏn′də-mĭn′ē-əm). **1.** Joint sovereignty, especially joint rule of territory by two or more nations, or a plan to achieve it. **2.** A politically dependent territory. — **con′do·min′i·al** (-ē-əl) adj.

Con·es·to·ga (kŏn′ĭ-stō′gə). pl. **Conestoga** or **-gas.** See **Susquehannock** (sense 1).

Co·ney Island (kō′nē). A resort district of Brooklyn, New York, on the Atlantic Ocean, famous for its boardwalk and amusement park featuring souvenir stands, thrilling rides, and numerous eating places.

con·fed·er·a·cy (kən-fĕd′ər-ə-sē). **1. a.** A union of persons, parties, or states; a league. **b.** The persons, parties, or states joined in such a union. **2. Confederacy.** The 11 Southern states that seceded from the United States in 1860 and 1861.

con·flu·ence (kŏn′flōō-əns). **1.** A flowing together of two or more streams. **2.** The point of juncture of such streams. **3.** The combined stream formed by this juncture.

con·flu·ent (kŏn′flōō-ənt). **1.** Flowing together; blended into one. **2.** One of two or more confluent streams. **3.** A tributary.

con·for·mal (kən-fôr′məl). Of or relating to a map projection in which small areas are rendered with true shape.

Con·go (kŏng′gō). **1.** A country of west-central Africa with a short coastline on the Atlantic Ocean. It was part of French Equatorial Africa before becoming independent in 1960. In 1970 a Marxist state was established, and the country was renamed the People's Republic of Congo. In the early 1990's Marxism-Leninism was abandoned and a new constitution was adopted. Brazzaville is the capital and the largest city. ⊛ Pop. 2,516,000. **2.** See **Zaire.** — **Con′go·lese′** (-lēz′, -lēs′) adj. & n.

Congo Free State. See **Zaire.**

Congo River also **Zaire River** (zī′îr, zä-îr′). A river of central Africa flowing about 4,666 km (2,900 mi) north, west, and southwest through Zaire to the Atlantic Ocean. Its remotest tributaries rise in northern Zambia. For much of its latter course the river forms the border between Zaire and Congo.

con·ic projection (kŏn′ĭk) or **con·i·cal projection** (-ĭ-kəl). A method of projecting maps of parts of the earth's spherical surface on a surrounding cone, which is then flattened to a plane surface having concentric circles as parallels of latitude and radiating lines from the apex as meridians.

Con·nacht (kŏn′ət, -əKHt) also **Con·naught** (-ôt′). A historical region of west-central Ireland. An ancient native kingdom, it was dominated by the O'Connor family in the 11th and 12th centuries.

Con·nect·i·cut (kə-nĕt′ĭ-kət). abbr. **CT, Conn., Ct.** A state of the northeast United States. It was admitted as one of the original Thirteen

Colonies in 1788. Connecticut's coastline was first explored by Dutch navigators after 1614, and in 1635 colonists from Massachusetts Bay began to settle in the Connecticut River valley. The Fundamental Orders, a constitution based on the consent of the governed, was adopted by the colony in 1639. Hartford is the capital and Bridgeport the largest city. ◉ Pop. 3,295,669.

Connecticut River. A river of the northeast United States flowing about 655 km (407 mi) from northern New Hampshire southward along the border of Vermont and New Hampshire and through central Massachusetts and Connecticut to its outlet on Long Island Sound.

Con·ne·ma·ra (kŏn'ə-mär'ə). A region of western Ireland on the coast of the Atlantic Ocean. The area is noted for its peat bogs and mountainous terrain.

Con·ners·ville (kŏn'ərz-vĭl'). A city of east-central Indiana east of Indianapolis. Founded in 1813 it is now a rail and manufacturing center. ◉ Pop. 15,550.

Con·roe (kŏn'rō). A city of southeast Texas north of Houston. Oil was discovered in the area in 1932. ◉ Pop. 27,610.

Con·stance (kŏn'stəns). See **Konstanz.**

Constance, Lake of also **Bo·den·see** (bōd'n-zā'). An Alpine lake bordering on southern Germany, northern Switzerland, and western Austria.

Con·stan·ţa (kən-stän'sə, kôn-stän'tsä). A city of southeast Romania on the Black Sea east of Bucharest. Founded in the seventh century B.C. as a Greek colony, it is the country's main seaport. ◉ Pop. 348,985.

Con·stan·tine (kŏn'stən-tēn', kôn-stăn-tēn'). A city of northeast Algeria east of Algiers. It was founded by Carthaginians and was the capital and commercial center of Numidia. Destroyed in warfare in A.D. 311, it was rebuilt by the Roman emperor Constantine I (ruled 306–337 B.C.) and named in his honor. ◉ Pop. 344,454.

Con·stan·ti·no·ple (kŏn'stăn-tə-nō'pəl). See **Istanbul.**

con·ti·nent (kŏn'tə-nənt). **1.** *abbr.* **cont.** One of the principal land masses of the earth, usually regarded as including Africa, Antarctica, Asia, Australia, Europe, North America, and South America. **2. Continent.** The mainland of Europe. Used with *the.*

con·ti·nen·tal (kŏn'tə-nĕn'tl). **1.** Of, relating to, or characteristic of a continent. **2.** often **Continental.** Of or relating to the mainland of Europe; European. **3. Continental.** Of or relating to the American colonies during and immediately after the American Revolution (1775–1783). **4.** often **Continental. a.** An inhabitant of a continent. **b.** An inhabitant of the mainland

of Europe; a European. **5.** A native of the continental United States living or working in Puerto Rico or the U.S. Virgin Islands. **6. Continental.** A soldier in the American army during the American Revolution. — **con′ti·nen′tal·ism** *n.* — **con′ti·nen′tal·ist** *n.* — **con′ti·nen·tal′i·ty** (-nĕn-tăl′ĭ-tē) *n.*

continental divide. An extensive stretch of high ground from each side of which the river systems of a continent flow toward different drainage areas.

Continental Divide. A series of mountain ridges extending from Alaska to Mexico that forms the watershed of North America. Most of it runs along peaks of the Rocky Mountains and is often called the **Great Divide** in the United States.

continental drift. The movement, formation, or re-formation of continents described by the theory of plate tectonics.

continental shelf. A submerged border of a continent that slopes gradually and extends to a point of steeper descent to the ocean bottom.

continental slope. The descent from the continental shelf to the ocean bottom.

con·tour (kŏn'tŏŏr'). A contour line.

contour line. A line on a map that joins points of equal elevation.

contour map. A map showing elevations and surface configuration by means of contour lines.

con·ur·ba·tion (kŏn'ər-bā'shən). A predominantly urban region including adjacent towns and suburbs; a metropolitan area.

Con·way (kŏn'wā'). **1.** A city of central Arkansas north-northwest of Little Rock. It is a trade and industrial center in an agricultural region. ◉ Pop. 26,481. **2.** A community of east-central Florida, a suburb of Orlando. ◉ Pop. 16,000.

Cooch Be·har (kōōch' bə-här'). A former princely state of northeast India. Once a powerful part of Assam, it came under British rule in 1772.

Cook (kŏŏk), **Mount. 1.** also **A·o·rang·i** (ä'ō-räng'gē). The highest mountain, 3,766.4 m (12,349 ft), of New Zealand, on South Island in the Southern Alps. **2.** A peak, 4,196.8 m (13,760 ft) high, in the St. Elias Mountains on the border between Alaska and Yukon Territory, Canada.

Cooke·ville (kŏŏk'vĭl'). A city of central Tennessee east of Nashville. It is a farm trade center. ◉ Pop. 21,744.

Cook Inlet. An inlet of the Gulf of Alaska in southern Alaska west of the Kenai Peninsula. It is a major fishing ground for salmon and herring and has the largest tidal bore in the United States.

Cook Islands. An island group of the southern Pacific Ocean southeast of Samoa. Probably first inhabited by Polynesians more than 1,500 years ago, the islands were sighted by Capt. James Cook in 1773. They are now self-governing under the sovereignty of New Zealand.

Cook Strait. A narrow channel separating North Island and South Island in New Zealand. It was discovered by Capt. James Cook in 1770.

Coon Rapids (kōōn). A city of eastern Minnesota, a suburb of Minneapolis–St. Paul. ⊛ Pop. 52,978.

Coo·pers·town (kōō′pərz-toun′). A residential village of east-central New York west-southwest of Schenectady. It was founded in 1787 by William Cooper, the father of James Fenimore Cooper (1789–1851), who used the region as the setting for his *Leatherstocking Tales*. The National Baseball Hall of Fame and Museum is here. ⊛ Pop. 2,180.

Coo·sa (kōō′sə). A river rising in northwest Georgia and flowing about 460 km (286 mi) southwest through eastern Alabama to join the Tallapoosa River near Montgomery and form the Alabama River.

cop (kŏp). *Chiefly British.* A summit or crest, as of a hill.

Co·pán (kō-pän′). A ruined Mayan city of western Honduras that flourished from c. 300 B.C. to A.D. 900. The ruins include the Hieroglyphic Stairway with nearly 2,000 glyphs.

Co·pen·ha·gen (kō′pən-hā′gən, -hä′-). The capital and largest city of Denmark, in the extreme eastern part of the country on the eastern coast of Sjaelland. It was a trading and fishing center by the 11th century and became the capital in 1443. ⊛ Pop. 619,288.

Co·piague (kō′pāg′, -pĕg). An unincorporated community of southeast New York on the southern shore of Long Island. It is mainly residential. ⊛ Pop. 20,769.

Cop·per·as Cove (kŏp′ər-əs). A city of central Texas southwest of Waco. It is a trade center in an agricultural area. ⊛ Pop. 24,079.

Cop·per·mine (kŏp′ər-mīn′). A river of northern Northwest Territories, Canada, flowing about 845 km (525 mi) northward to the Arctic Ocean.

Cop·per River (kŏp′ər). A river rising in the Wrangell Mountains of southern Alaska and flowing about 483 km (300 mi) southward through the Chugach Mountains to the Gulf of Alaska.

Copt (kŏpt). **1.** An Egyptian belonging to or descended from the people of ancient or pre-Islamic Egypt. **2.** A member of the Coptic Church, the Christian church of Egypt.

Cop·tic (kŏp′tĭk). *abbr.* **Copt., Cop. 1.** The Afro-Asiatic language of the Copts, which survives only as a liturgical language of the Coptic

Church. **2.** Of or relating to the Copts, the Coptic Church, or the Coptic language.

Cor·al Ga·bles (kôr′əl gā′bəlz, kŏr′-). A city of southeast Florida on Biscayne Bay southwest of Miami. It is mainly residential. ⊛ Pop. 40,091.

cor·al reef (kôr′əl, kŏr′-). An erosion-resistant marine ridge or mound consisting chiefly of compacted coral together with algal material and biochemically deposited magnesium and calcium carbonates.

Coral Sea. An arm of the southwest Pacific Ocean bounded by Vanuatu, northeast Australia, and southeast New Guinea. It was the scene of a U.S. World War II naval victory in May 1942.

Coral Springs. A city of southeast Florida, a suburb of Fort Lauderdale. ⊛ Pop. 79,443.

Co·ran·tijn (kôr′ən-tīn′, kôr′-). See **Courantyne.**

Cor·by (kôr′bē). An urban district of central England southeast of Leicester. It is a center for iron and steel production. ⊛ Pop. 52,400.

Cor·co·va·do (kôr′kə-vä′dō, kôr′kô-vä′dōō). A mountain, 704.6 m (2,310 ft) high, of southeast Brazil overlooking Rio de Janeiro. A popular tourist attraction, it has a cable railroad and is surmounted by an enormous concrete statue of Christ the Redeemer.

Cor·cy·ra (kôr-sī′rə). See **Corfu.**

cor·dil·le·ra (kôr′dl-yâr′ə, kôr′dĭl′ər-ə). An extensive chain of mountains or mountain ranges, especially the principal mountain system of a continent. **—cor′dil·le′ran** (-yâr′ən) *adj.*

Cor·dil·le·ra Cen·tral (kôr′dĭl-yĕr′ə sĕn-träl′, -thē-yĕ′rä). **1.** The central of three ranges of the Andes in western Colombia. **2.** A mountain range of central Dominican Republic. **3.** A range of the Andes extending northwest and southeast in north-central Peru. **4.** A mountain range of northern Luzon, Philippines. **5.** A range of south-central Puerto Rico.

Cordillera de Ta·la·man·ca (dā tä′lä-mäng′-kä, thĕ). A mountain range of southern Costa Rica extending southeast into western Panama.

Cordillera Mé·ri·da (mĕr′ĭ-də, mĕ′rē-thä). A mountain range of western Venezuela extending northeast and southwest. Pico Bolívar, 5,005.4 m (16,411 ft), is the highest elevation.

Cordillera Oc·ci·den·tal (ŏk′sĭ-dĕn-täl′, ôk′-sē-thĕn-). A range of the western Andes with branches in western Colombia and along the Pacific coast of Peru.

Cordillera O·rien·tal (ôr′ē-ĕn-täl′, ô′ryĕn-). A range of the eastern Andes with branches in central Bolivia, western Colombia, and southeast Peru. Its highest elevation is Salcantay, 6,275.4 m (20,575 ft), in Peru.

Cordillera Re·al (rā-äl′). A range of the Andes

with separate branches in western Bolivia and central Ecuador.

Cor·dil·le·ras (kôr′dĭl-yĕr′əz, kôr′thē-yĕ′räs). The entire complex of mountain ranges in western North America and South America, extending from Alaska to Cape Horn.

Cór·do·ba (kôr′də-bə, -və, -thô-vä). **1.** A city of north-central Argentina northwest of Buenos Aires. The country's second largest city, it was founded in 1573. ◉ Pop. 1,148,305. **2.** A city of southern Spain on the Guadalquivir River east-northeast of Seville. Probably established by Carthaginians, it was later ruled by Romans and Visigoths. Under the Moors (711–1236) it was renowned as a cultural and intellectual center. ◉ Pop. 305,894. — **Cor′do·van** (-vən) *adj. & n.*

Cor·fu (kôr′fōō, -fyōō, kôr-fōō′) also **Kér·ki·ra** (kĕr′kē-rä′). Formerly **Cor·cy·ra** (kôr-sī′rə). An island of Greece in the Ionian Islands off the northwest coast of the mainland. Settled c. 700 B.C., the island was controlled by Rome, Byzantium, Sicily, Venice, and Great Britain before being ceded to Greece in 1864.

Cor·inth (kôr′ĭnth, kŏr′-) also **Kó·rin·thos** (kô′rĭn-thôs′). A city of southern Greece in the northeast Peloponnesus on the Gulf of Corinth. It is near the site of the ancient city of **Corinth,** which was founded in Homeric times and was a rich, influential maritime power in the seventh and sixth centuries B.C. ◉ Pop. 22,658.

Corinth, Gulf of. Formerly **Gulf of Le·pan·to** (lĭ-păn′tō, lĕ′pän-tô). An inlet of the Ionian Sea between the Peloponnesus and central Greece.

Corinth, Isthmus of. A narrow isthmus connecting central Greece with the Peloponnesus. It lies between the Gulf of Corinth and the Saronic Gulf and is crossed by the **Corinth Canal,** constructed from 1881 to 1893.

Co·rin·thi·an (kə-rĭn′thē-ən). **1.** Of or relating to ancient Corinth or its people or culture. **2.** A native or inhabitant of Corinth.

Cork (kôrk). A city of southern Ireland near the head of **Cork Harbor,** an inlet of the Atlantic Ocean. Cork was occupied by the Danes in the ninth century and by Oliver Cromwell in 1649. ◉ Pop. 127,253.

Corn Belt (kôrn). An agricultural region of the central United States primarily in Iowa and Illinois but also including parts of Indiana, Minnesota, South Dakota, Nebraska, Kansas, Missouri, and Ohio. The chief products of the area are corn and corn-fed livestock.

Cor·nel·lá (kôr′nĕl-yä′, -nĕ-yä′). A city of northeast Spain, a suburb of Barcelona. ◉ Pop. 90,270.

Cor·ner Brook (kôr′nər). A city of west-central Newfoundland, Canada, on an estuary

emptying into the Gulf of St. Lawrence. Located in a lumbering region, it is an important paper-producing center. ◉ Pop. 24,339.

Corn·ing (kôr′nĭng). A city of southern New York near the Pennsylvania border west of Elmira. It is noted for its glassworks dating from 1868 and its glass museum. ◉ Pop. 11,938.

Cor·nish (kôr′nĭsh). **1.** Of or relating to Cornwall, its people, or the Cornish language. **2.** The Brythonic language of Cornwall, which has been extinct since the late 18th century.

Cor·nish·man (kôr′nĭsh-mən). A man who is a native or inhabitant of Cornwall, England.

Cor·nish·wom·an (kôr′nĭsh-wŏŏm′ən). A woman who is a native or inhabitant of Cornwall, England.

Cor·no (kôr′nō), **Mount.** The highest peak, 2,915.8 m (9,560 ft), of the Apennines, in central Italy.

Corn·wall (kôrn′wôl′). **1.** A region of extreme southwest England on a peninsula bounded by the Atlantic Ocean and English Channel. Its tin and copper mines were known to ancient Greek traders. **2.** A city of southeast Ontario, Canada, on the St. Lawrence River and the New York border southeast of Ottawa. It is a manufacturing center. ◉ Pop. 46,144.

Co·ro (kôr′ō, kōr′ō). A city of northwest Venezuela near the Caribbean Sea east-northeast of Maracaibo. It was founded in 1527 by the Spanish, who mortgaged it to a German banking house from 1528 to 1546. ◉ Pop. 137,040.

Cor·o·man·del Coast (kôr′ə-măn′dl). A region of southeast India bounded by the Bay of Bengal and the Eastern Ghats. The coast is known for its monsoons and turbulent waters.

Co·ro·na (kə-rō′nə). A city of southern California southwest of Riverside. It is a manufacturing center in a citrus-growing area. ◉ Pop. 76,095.

Cor·o·na·do (kôr′ə-nä′dō, kŏr′-). A city of southern California on a narrow spit west of San Diego between San Diego Bay and the Pacific Ocean. It is a popular resort. ◉ Pop. 26,540.

Cor·pus Chris·ti (kôr′pəs krĭs′tē). A city of southern Texas on **Corpus Christi Bay,** an arm of the Gulf of Mexico. Founded (1838) as a trading post, the city is highly industrialized and has a large shrimp-fishing fleet. ◉ Pop. 257,453.

Cor·reg·i·dor (kə-rĕg′ĭ-dôr′, -dōr′, kôr-rĕ′hē-thôr′). An island of the northern Philippines at the entrance to Manila Bay. Despite a heroic defense, Filipino and U.S. troops were forced to surrender the fortified island to Japan in May 1942. U.S. paratroopers recaptured the island in March 1945.

cor·ri·dor (kôr′ĭ-dər, -dôr′, kŏr′-). **1. a.** A tract of land forming a passageway, such as one that allows an inland country access to the sea through another country. **b.** A restricted tract of land for the passage of trains. **c.** Restricted airspace for the passage of aircraft. **2.** A thickly populated strip of land connecting two or more urban areas.

cor·rie (kôr′ē, kŏr′ē). A round hollow in a hillside; a cirque.

Cor·ri·en·tes (kôr′ē-ĕn′tĕs). A city of northeast Argentina on the Paraná River and the Paraguay border. It was founded in 1588. ⊛ Pop. 257,766.

Cor·si·ca (kôr′sĭ-kə). An island of France in the Mediterranean Sea north of Sardinia. Napoleon Bonaparte (1769–1821) was born on the island, which was ceded to France by Genoa in 1768. —**Cor′si·can** adj. & n.

Cor·si·ca·na (kôr′sĭ-kăn′ə). A city of northeast Texas south-southeast of Dallas. It is in an oil-producing region. ⊛ Pop. 22,911.

Cort·land (kôrt′lənd). A city of central New York south of Syracuse. It was settled in 1792. ⊛ Pop. 19,801.

Cor·val·lis (kôr-văl′ĭs). A city of western Oregon on the Willamette River south-southwest of Salem. It is the seat of Oregon State University (established 1858). ⊛ Pop. 44,757.

Cos (kŏs, kôs). See **Kos.**

co·seis·mal (kō-sīz′məl, -sīs′-) also **co·seis·mic** (-mĭk). **1.** Relating to or designating a line connecting the points on a map that indicate the places simultaneously affected by an earthquake shock. **2.** A coseismal line.

Co·sen·za (kō-zĕn′sə, kô-zĕn′tsä). A city of southern Italy southeast of Naples. Cosenza has frequently suffered severe earthquake damage. ⊛ Pop. 87,140.

cos·mog·ra·phy (kŏz-mŏg′rə-fē). **1.** The study of the visible universe that includes geography and astronomy. **2.** A general description or depiction of the world or universe. —**cos·mog′ra·pher** n. —**cos′mo·graph′ic** (-mə-grăf′ĭk), **cos′mo·graph′i·cal** adj. —**cos′mo·graph′i·cal·ly** adv.

Cos·sack (kŏs′ăk). A member of a people of southern European Russia and adjacent parts of Asia, noted as cavalrymen especially during czarist times. —**Cos′sack′** adj.

Cos·ta Bra·va (kŏs′tə brä′və, kô′stə, kō′-, kôs′tä brä′vä). The northeast coast of Spain, on the Mediterranean Sea from Barcelona to the French border. It has been a popular tourist area since the end of World War II.

Cos·ta del Sol (kŏs′tə dĕl sōl′, kô′stə, kô′stä thĕl sôl′). The southern coast of Spain northeast of Gibraltar. It is a popular resort and retirement area.

Cos·ta Me·sa (kŏs′tə mā′sə, kō′stə). A city of southern California south-southwest of Santa

Ana. It has an electronics industry and is noted as a cultural center. ⊛ Pop. 96,357.

Cos·ta Ri·ca (kŏs′tə rē′kə, kô′stə, kō′-, kô′stä rē′kä). abbr. **C.R.** A country of Central America between Panama and Nicaragua. Although Christopher Columbus touched at Costa Rica in 1502, Spanish conquest of the area did not begin until 1563. The country achieved independence from Spain in 1821 as part of Mexican territory and declared itself a sovereign republic in 1838. Costa Rica has a long tradition of stable democratic government and has no official army, only a Civil Guard. San José is the capital and the largest city. ⊛ Pop. 3,071,000. —**Cos′ta Ri′can** (rē′kən) adj. & n.

Côte d'A·zur (kōt′ də-zōōr′, dä-zür′). The Mediterranean coast of southeast France. It is known for its fashionable resorts.

Côte d'Ivoire (dē-vwär′). See **Ivory Coast.**

Co·ten·tin (kō-täN-tăN′). A peninsula of northwest France extending into the English Channel east of the Channel Islands. It was the scene of heavy fighting during World War II after the Allied invasion in June 1944.

Côte Saint Luc (sānt lōōk′, sənt, săN lük′). A city of southern Quebec, Canada, a residential suburb of Montreal. ⊛ Pop. 27,531.

co·tid·al (kō-tīd′l). Of or being a line that passes through each location on a coastal map where tides occur at the same time of day.

Co·to·nou (kōt′n-ōō′). A city of southern Benin on the Gulf of Guinea. The largest city in the country, it is a seaport and commercial center. ⊛ Pop. 536,827.

Co·to·pax·i (kō′tə-păk′sē, kô′tô-päk′sē). A volcano, about 5,900.8 m (19,347 ft) high, in the Andes of central Ecuador. The symmetrical snowcapped cone is one of the highest volcanoes in the world.

Cots·wold Hills (kŏt′swōld′). A range of southwest England extending about 80 km (50 mi) northeast from Bristol and rising to approximately 329 m (1,080 ft).

Cot·tage Grove (kŏt′ĭj). A city of eastern Minnesota, a suburb of St. Paul. ◉ Pop. 22,935.

Cott·bus also **Kott·bus** (kŏt′bəs, kôt′boͦos′). A city of east-central Germany near the Polish border. It developed as a market center in the late 12th century. ◉ Pop. 128,121.

Cot·ti·an Alps (kŏt′ē-ən). A range of the Alps between northwest Italy and southeast France. It rises to 3,843.6 m (12,602 ft) at Mount Viso.

Cot·ton Belt (kŏt′n). An agricultural region of the southeast United States extending through North Carolina, South Carolina, Georgia, Alabama, Mississippi, Tennessee, Arkansas, Louisiana, Texas, and Oklahoma and including small sections of Missouri, Kentucky, Florida, and Virginia. Originally dependent on cotton, the region now has highly diversified agriculture.

Cot·ton·wood (kŏt′n-woͦod′). A river, about 225 km (140 mi) long, of southwest Minnesota flowing eastward to the Minnesota River.

cou·lee (koͦo′lē). 1. *Western U.S.* A deep gulch or ravine with sloping sides, often dry in summer. 2. *Louisiana & Southern Mississippi.* **a.** A streambed, often dry according to the season. **b.** A small stream, bayou, or canal. 3. *Upper Midwest.* A valley with hills on either side. 4. A stream or sheet of lava.

cou·loir (koͦol-wär′). A deep mountainside gorge or gully, especially in the Swiss Alps.

Coun·cil Bluffs (koun′səl). A city of southwest Iowa on the Missouri River opposite Omaha, Nebraska. It was settled as Kanesville in 1846 and renamed in 1852. ◉ Pop. 54,315.

coun·try (kŭn′trē). 1. **a.** A nation or state. **b.** The territory of a nation or state; land. **c.** The people of a nation or state; populace. 2. The land of a person's birth or citizenship. 3. A region, territory, or large tract of land distinguishable by features of topography, biology, or culture. 4. A district outside of cities and towns; a rural area.

coun·ty (koun′tē). *abbr.* **co**; **co.** 1. An administrative subdivision of a state in the United States. 2. **a.** A territorial division exercising administrative, judicial, and political functions in Great Britain and Ireland. **b.** The territory under the jurisdiction of a count or earl. 3. The people living in a county. —**coun′ty** *adj.*

county seat. A town or city that is the administrative center of its county.

county town. *Chiefly British.* A county seat. Also called *shire town.*

Cour·an·tyne also **Co·ran·tijn** (kōr′ən-tīn′, kôr′-). A river rising in southeast Guyana and flowing about 724 km (450 mi) to the Atlantic Ocean. It forms the Guyana-Suriname border in its lower course.

Cour·be·voie (koͦor-bə-vwä′, koͦor-). A city of north-central France, an industrial suburb of Paris on the Seine River. ◉ Pop. 59,830.

Cour·land also **Kur·land** (koͦor′lənd). A historical region and former duchy of southern Latvia between the Baltic Sea and the Western Dvina River. It passed to Russia in 1795 and was largely incorporated into Latvia in 1918.

Cour·trai (koͦor-trā′, koͦor-). See **Kortrijk.**

cove (kōv). 1. A small sheltered bay in the shoreline of a sea, river, or lake. 2. **a.** A recess or small valley in the side of a mountain. **b.** A cave or cavern. 3. A narrow gap or pass between hills or woods.

Cov·ent Garden (kŭv′ənt, kŏv′-). An area in London long noted for its produce market (established in 1671) and its royal theater (first built in 1731–1732). The market was moved to a site on the Thames River in 1974.

Cov·en·try (kŭv′ĭn-trē). 1. A city of central England east-southeast of Birmingham. Famous as the home of Lady Godiva in the 11th century, Coventry was severely damaged in air raids during World War II (November 1940). ◉ Pop. 304,097. 2. A town of west-central Rhode Island southwest of Providence. It was settled in 1643 and was formerly a noted lacemaking center. ◉ Pop. 31,083.

Co·vi·na (kō-vē′nə). A city of southern California east of Los Angeles. It has a large citrus-processing industry. ◉ Pop. 43,207.

Cov·ing·ton (kŭv′ĭng-tən). A city of extreme northern Kentucky on the Ohio River opposite Cincinnati. Settled in 1812 on the site of an earlier tavern and ferry landing, it is a manufacturing center east of the Greater Cincinnati International Airport. ◉ Pop. 43,264.

Cowes (kouz). A town on the northern coast of the Isle of Wight off southern England. It is the headquarters of the Royal Yacht Club and the site of annual regattas. ◉ Pop. 19,663.

Cow·litz (kou′lĭts). A river rising in the Cascade Range of southwest Washington and flowing about 209 km (130 mi) west and south to the Columbia River.

Co·zu·mel (kō′zə-mĕl′, -soͦo-). An island off the coast of southeast Mexico near Cancún. It is a growing resort area.

Crac·ow also **Kra·ków** (krăk′ou, krä′kou, -koͦof). A city of southern Poland on the Vistula River south-southeast of Warsaw. Founded in the eighth century A.D., it was the national capital from 1305 to 1595. ◉ Pop. 750,588.

crag (krăg). A steeply projecting mass of rock forming part of a rugged cliff or headland. —**crag′ged** (krăg′ĭd) *adj.* —**crag′gy** *adj.*

Cra·io·va (krə-yō′və, krä-yô′vä). A city of southwest Romania west of Bucharest. Built on the site of a Roman settlement, it was destroyed by an earthquake in 1790 and burned by the Turks in 1802. ⊕ Pop. 303,033.

Cran·brook (krăn′brŏŏk′). A city of southeast British Columbia, Canada, near the Alberta and Idaho borders. It is a trade center in a lumbering and mining region. ⊕ Pop. 15,915.

Cran·ford (krăn′fərd). A community of northeast New Jersey west of Elizabeth. Mainly residential, it has varied industries. ⊕ Pop. 22,624.

Cran·ston (krăn′stən). A city of east-central Rhode Island south of Providence. It was settled in 1636. ⊕ Pop. 76,060.

cra·ter (krā′tər). **1.** A bowl-shaped depression at the mouth of a volcano or geyser. **2. a.** A bowl-shaped depression in a surface made by an explosion or the impact of a body, such as a meteoroid. **b.** A pit; a hollow.

Cra·ter Lake (krā′tər). A lake of southwest Oregon in a volcanic crater of the Cascade Range. At 589.3 m (1,932 ft) deep, it is the second-deepest lake in North America and the deepest in the United States. The lake and surrounding parkland are popular tourist attractions.

cra·ter·let (krā′tər-lĭt). A small crater.

Craw·ley (krô′lē). An urban district of southeast England near London. It was designated a new town in 1946 to help alleviate overcrowding in London. ⊕ Pop. 72,700.

Cré·cy (krĕs′ē, krā-sē′) or **Cré·cy-en-Pon·thieu** (-äɴ-pôɴ-tyœ′). A town of northern France northwest of Amiens. It was the site of the first decisive battle of the Hundred Years' War (August 26, 1346), in which Edward III of England defeated Philip VI of France.

Cree (krē). **1.** *pl.* **Cree** or **Crees.** A member of a Native American people inhabiting a large area from eastern Canada west to Alberta and the Great Slave Lake. Formerly located in central Canada, the Crees expanded westward and eastward in the 17th and 18th centuries, the western Crees adopting the Plains Indian life and the eastern Crees retaining their woodland culture. **2.** The Algonquian language spoken by the Crees.

creek (krēk, krĭk). *abbr.* **cr. 1.** A small stream, often a shallow or intermittent tributary to a river. Also called *brook.* **2.** A channel or stream running through a salt marsh. **3.** *Chiefly British.* A small inlet in a shoreline, extending farther inland than a cove.

Creek (krēk). **1. a.** *pl.* **Creek** or **Creeks.** A member of a Native American people formerly inhabiting eastern Alabama, southwest Georgia, and northwest Florida and now located in central Oklahoma and southern Alabama. The Creeks were forcibly removed to Indian Territory in the 1830's. **b.** The Muskogean language of the Creeks. **2.** *pl.* **Creek** or **Creeks.** A member of a

Native American confederacy made up of the Creek and various smaller southeast tribes. Also called *Muskogee.*

Cre·mo·na (krə-mō′nə, krĕ-mô′nä). A city of northern Italy on the Po River east-southeast of Milan. Originally a Roman colony, it was an independent commune in the Middle Ages until its surrender to Milan in 1334. ⊕ Pop. 80,758.

Cre·ole (krē′ōl′). **1.** A person of European descent born in the West Indies or Spanish America. **2. a.** A person descended from or culturally related to the original French settlers of the southern United States, especially Louisiana. **b.** The French dialect spoken by these people. **3.** A person descended from or culturally related to the Spanish and Portuguese settlers of the Gulf States. **4.** often **creole.** A person of mixed Black and European ancestry who speaks a creolized language, especially one based on French or Spanish. **5.** A Black slave born in the Americas as opposed to one brought from Africa. **6. creole.** A creolized language. **7.** Haitian Creole. **8.** Of or relating to the Creoles.

cre·o·lized language (krē′ə-līzd′). A language derived from a pidgin but more complex in grammar and vocabulary than the ancestral pidgin because it has become the native tongue of a community.

Cres·tone Needle (krĕs′tōn). A mountain, about 4,330.1 m (14,197 ft) high, in the Sangre de Cristo Mountains of south-central Colorado.

Crestone Peak. A mountain, about 4,359.7 m (14,294 ft) high, in the Sangre de Cristo Mountains of south-central Colorado.

Crete (krēt). An island of southeast Greece in the eastern Mediterranean Sea. Its Minoan civilization, centered at the city of Knossos on the northern coast, was one of the earliest in the world and reached the height of its wealth and power c. 1600 B.C. Crete subsequently fell to the Greeks, Romans, Byzantines, Arabs, Venetians, and Ottoman Turks. The islanders proclaimed their union with modern Greece in 1908. —**Cre′tan** *adj. & n.*

Crete, Sea of. A section of the southern Aegean Sea between Crete and the Cyclades Islands.

Cré·teil (krā-tā′). A city of north-central France, an industrial suburb of Paris on the Marne River. ⊕ Pop. 71,693.

Crewe (krōō) also **Crewe and Nant·wich** (nănt′wĭch′). A municipal borough of west-central England southeast of Liverpool. It is an important railroad junction. ⊕ Pop. 109,534.

Cri·me·a (krī-mē′ə, krĭ-). A region and peninsula of southern Ukraine on the Black Sea and Sea of Azov. In ancient times it was colonized by Greeks and Romans and later overrun by Ostrogoths, Huns, and Mongols. Conquered by the Ottoman Turks in 1475, the area was annexed by Russia in 1783. The peninsula was the scene of the Crimean War (1853–1856), in which a coalition of English, French, and Turkish troops defeated the Russians, although Crimea itself did not change hands. It became (1921) an autonomous Russian republic, which was dissolved following German occupation (1941–1944). In 1954 it became a Ukrainian oblast. — **Cri·me'an** adj.

Crip·ple Creek (krĭp'əl). A city of central Colorado in the Rocky Mountains southwest of Colorado Springs. After 1891 it was the center of a thriving gold-producing area but declined as deposits were exhausted. ⊛ Pop. 584.

Croat (krō'ăt', krōt). **1.** A native or inhabitant of Croatia. **2.** Serbo-Croatian as used in Croatia, distinguished from Serbian primarily by its being written in the Latin alphabet. Also called *Croatian.*

Cro·a·tia (krō-ā'shə, -shē-ə). A country of southern Europe along the northeast Adriatic coast. It was settled by Croats in the 7th century, became a kingdom in the 10th century, and reached the height of its power in the 11th century before being conquered by Hungary in 1091. Most of Croatia came under Turkish rule in the 16th and 17th centuries before it was reunited with Hungary in 1867. After the collapse of the Austro-Hungarian Empire in 1918, Croatia became a part of the Kingdom of Serbs, Croats, and Slovenes, which later became Yugoslavia. Croatia was occupied (1941–1945) by Axis powers, who set up a Fascist government. Croatia declared its independence from Yugoslavia in 1991, which led to fighting with Serbia and civil war in which Croatia lost a portion of its territory to Serb forces. A 1995 peace agreement formally ended the conflict among the former Yugoslav republics. ⊛ Pop. 4,504,000.

Cro·a·tian (krō-ā'shən). **1.** See **Croat. 2.** Of or relating to Croatia or its people, language, or culture.

Croc·o·dile River (krŏk'ə-dīl'). See **Limpopo.**

Cro-Mag·non (krō-măg'nən, -măn'yən). An early form of modern human being *(Homo sapiens)* inhabiting Europe in the late Paleolithic Era and characterized by a broad face and tall stature. It is known from skeletal remains first found in a cave in southern France. — **Cro-Mag'non** adj.

Cros·by (krôz'bē) also **Great Crosby** (grāt). A municipal borough of northwest England on Liverpool Bay. It is primarily residential. ⊛ Pop. 53,660.

Cross-Flo·ri·da Waterway (krôs'flôr'ĭ-də, -flôr'-, krôs'-). See Lake **Okeechobee.**

Cro·to·ne (krə-tō'nē, krô-tô'nĕ). Formerly **Cro·to·na** (krə-tō'nə). A city of southern Italy on the Ionian Sea northeast of Reggio di Calabria. It was founded c. 708 B.C. as a colony of Magna Graecia and reached the height of its power after 510 B.C. ⊛ Pop. 58,281.

Crow (krō). **1.** pl. **Crow** or **Crows.** A member of a Native American people formerly inhabiting an area of the northern Great Plains between the Platte and Yellowstone rivers, now located in southeast Montana. The Crows became nomadic buffalo hunters after migrating west from the Missouri River in North Dakota in the 18th century. **2.** The Siouan language of the Crows. Also called *Absaroke.*

Crow·ley (krou'lē). A city of southern Louisiana west of Lafayette. It is the trade and shipping center of a rice-growing region. ⊛ Pop. 13,983.

crown colony (kroun). A British colony in which the government in London has some control of legislation, usually administered by an appointed governor.

Crown Point (kroun). **1.** A city of northwest Indiana, a mainly residential suburb of Gary. ⊛ Pop. 17,728. **2.** A village of northeast New York on the western shore of Lake Champlain. It was the site of a French fort captured by the British in 1759 during the French and Indian War. In the American Revolution it was taken by the Green Mountain Boys, retaken by the British in 1777, and abandoned the same year after the defeat at Saratoga. ⊛ Pop. 900.

crust (krŭst). *Geology.* The exterior portion of the earth that lies above the Mohorovičić discontinuity.

Cru·zan (krōō-zăn', krōō'zăn). A native or inhabitant of St. Croix in the U.S. Virgin Islands. — **Cru'zan** adj.

Crys·tal (krĭs'təl). A city of eastern Minnesota, a suburb of Minneapolis. ⊛ Pop. 23,788.

Crystal Lake. A city of northeast Illinois, a suburb of Chicago. First settled in 1836, it was long a summer resort. ⊛ Pop. 24,512.

Ctes·i·phon (tĕs'ə-fŏn', tē'sə-). An ancient

city of central Iraq on the Tigris River southeast of Baghdad. As the residence of Parthian kings it was renowned for its splendor. The Arabs captured and plundered the city in 637.

Cuan·do also **Kwan·do** (kwän′dō). A river rising in central Angola and flowing about 965 km (600 mi) generally southeast and east to the Zambezi River.

Cuan·za also **Kwan·za** (kwän′zə). A river rising in central Angola and flowing about 965 km (600 mi) generally northwest to the Atlantic Ocean.

Cu·ba (kyōō′bə). An island country in the Caribbean Sea south of Florida. Originally settled by Arawak Indians, it was discovered by Columbus in 1492 and remained an important Spanish colony until the achievement of independence, with U.S. support, in 1898. Fulgencio Batista dominated the Cuban government from 1933 to 1959, when he was ousted by guerrilla leader Fidel Castro, who soon after established a Communist state. The United States broke off relations in 1961, and the two governments became further antagonized following the abortive Bay of Pigs invasion (1961) and a missile crisis (1962) in which U.S. ships quarantined Cuba to keep Soviet missiles from being installed on the island. Waves of emigrants and refugees left the island, principally for the United States, from the early 1960's until the 1980's. Limited diplomatic ties were reestablished between Cuba and the United States in 1977. Cuba has remained a Marxist-Leninist state despite the end of the cold war, though the government has permitted some private economic activity in the 1990's. Havana is the capital and the largest city. ◉ Pop. 10,960,000. —**Cu′ban** *adj. & n.*

Cu·ban·go (kōō-bäng′gō). See **Okavango.**

Cú·cu·ta (kōō′kə-tə, -kōō-tä′). A city of northeast Colombia near the Venezuelan border. Established in 1733 and rebuilt after a devastating earthquake in 1875, it is a transportation and industrial center. ◉ Pop. 383,584.

Cud·a·hy (kŭd′ə-hē). **1.** A city of southern California southeast of Los Angeles. It is a process-

ing and manufacturing center. ◉ Pop. 22,8117. **2.** A city of southeast Wisconsin, suburb of Milwaukee on Lake Michigan. ◉ Pop. 18,659.

Cuen·ca (kwĕng′kə, -kä). A city of south-central Ecuador southeast of Guayaquil. Founded in 1557, it is known as "the Marble City" for its fine buildings. ◉ Pop. 194,981.

Cuer·na·va·ca (kwĕr-nə-vä′kə, -nä-vä′kä). A city of south-central Mexico in the **Cuernavaca Valley** near Mexico City. It is an industrial city and a popular tourist and health resort. ◉ Pop. 281,294.

cues·ta (kwĕs′tə). A ridge with a gentle slope on one side and a cliff on the other.

Cu·ia·bá (kōō′yə-bä′). A city of west-central Brazil west of Brasília on the **Cuiabá River,** about 483 km (300 mi) long. The city was founded during the gold rush of the early 18th century. ◉ Pop. 401,303.

Cu·le·bra Cut (kōō-lā′brə). See **Gaillard Cut.**

Culebra Peak. A mountain, 4,284.3 m (14,047 ft) high, in the Sangre de Cristo Mountains of extreme south-central Colorado.

Cu·lia·cán (kōōl′yə-kän′). A city of western Mexico west-northwest of Durango on the **Culiacán River,** about 282 km (175 mi) long. The city was founded in 1531 and figured prominently as a departure point for early Spanish expeditions to the north. ◉ Pop. 304,826.

Cul·lo·den Moor (kə-lŏd′n, -lôd′n). A moor in northern Scotland east of Inverness. It was the site of the final defeat (April 16, 1746) by English forces of the Highland Jacobites, who had sought to restore the thrones of England and Scotland to the descendants of James II, the last Stuart king to rule England and Scotland.

Cul·ver City (kŭl′vər). A city of southern California, a residential and manufacturing suburb of Los Angeles. Its motion-picture industry dates to c. 1915. ◉ Pop. 38,793.

Cu·mae (kyōō′mē). An ancient city and Greek colony of south-central Italy near present-day Naples. Founded c. 750 B.C., it is the earliest known Greek settlement in Italy. Cumae adopted Roman culture after the second century B.C. and gradually declined as neighboring cities rose to power.

Cu·ma·ná (kōō′mä-nä′). A city of northeast Venezuela on the Caribbean Sea east of Caracas. It was founded in 1521 to exploit nearby pearl fisheries. ◉ Pop. 232,228.

Cum·ber·land (kŭm′bər-lənd). A city of northwest Maryland in the Panhandle on the Potomac River and the West Virginia border. It is an industrial and shipping center in a coal-mining area. ◉ Pop. 23,706.

Cumberland Gap. A natural passage through the Cumberland Plateau near the junction of the Kentucky, Virginia, and Tennessee borders. It was discovered in 1750 and used by Daniel Boone in 1775 as a strategic point along his Wilderness Road, the principal route of westward migration for the next half century.

Cumberland Plateau or **Cumberland Mountains.** The southwest section of the Appalachian Mountains, extending from southern West Virginia through Virginia, Kentucky, and Tennessee into northern Alabama.

Cumberland River. A river rising in southeast Kentucky and flowing about 1,105 km (687 mi) in a winding course southwest into northern Tennessee then northwest to the Ohio River near Paducah in southwest Kentucky.

Cum·bri·a (kŭm′brē-ə). An ancient Celtic kingdom of northwest England. The southern part came under Anglo-Saxon control c. 944; the northern portion passed to Scotland in 1018. —**Cum′bri·an** adj. & n.

Cumbrian Mountains. A range of hills in northwest England rising to 979.1 m (3,210 ft) at Scafell Pike.

Cu·nax·a (kyōō-năk′sə). An ancient town of Babylonia northwest of Babylon. It was the site of a battle (401 B.C.) in which Artaxerxes II of Persia defeated his brother Cyrus the Younger, leading to the retreat of Greek troops to the Black Sea described by Xenophon, a Greek soldier and writer, in his *Anabasis.*

Cu·ne·ne also **Ku·ne·ne** (kōō-nā′nə). A river rising in west-central Angola and flowing about 1,207 km (750 mi) south and west to the Atlantic Ocean. It forms the Angola-Namibia border in its lower course.

Cu·ne·o (kōō′nē-ō′, -nĕ-ô). A city of northwest Italy west of Genoa. It is an industrial and agricultural center. ● Pop. 55,385.

Cu·per·ti·no (kōō′pər-tē′nō, kyōō′-). A city of western California west of San Jose. It has an electronics industry. ● Pop. 40,263.

Cu·ra·çao (kōōr′ə-sou′, -sō′, kyōōr′-, kōōr′-ə-sou′, -sō′, kyōōr′-). An island of the Netherlands Antilles in the southern Caribbean Sea off the northwest coast of Venezuela. It was discovered in 1499 and settled by the Spanish in 1527. The Dutch gained control in 1634, although the British held the island during the Napoleonic Wars (1807–1815). Oil refining and tourism are the major industries.

Cu·ri·ti·ba (kōōr′ĭ-tē′bə). A city of southeast Brazil southwest of São Paulo. It was founded in 1654 but did not grow rapidly until the late l9th and early 20th centuries when German, Italian, and Slavic immigrants began to develop the surrounding area. ● Pop. 1,313,094.

Cus·co (kōō′skō). See **Cuzco.**

Cush also **Kush** (kŭsh, kōōsh). **1.** An ancient region of northeast Africa where the biblical descendants of Cush, a grandson of Noah, are supposed to have settled. It is often identified with Ethiopia. **2.** An ancient kingdom of Nubia in northern Sudan. It flourished from the 11th century B.C. to the 4th century A.D., when its capital fell to the Ethiopians.

Cush·it·ic (kōō-shĭt′ĭk). A branch of the Afro-Asiatic language family spoken in Somalia, Ethiopia, and northern Kenya and including Beja, Oromo, and Somali. —**Cush·it′ic** adj.

Cut·ler Ridge (kŭt′lər). A community of extreme southeast Florida on Biscayne Bay southsouthwest of Miami. ● Pop. 21,268.

Cut·tack (kŭt′ək). A city of eastern India southwest of Calcutta. Founded in the tenth century, it was long noted for gold and silver filigree work. ● Pop. 403,418.

Cux·ha·ven (kōōks-hä′fən). A city of northwest Germany at the mouth of the Elbe River. It is a North Sea fishing port and a summer resort. ● Pop. 56,977.

Cuy·a·ho·ga Falls (kī′ə-hō′gə, kə-hō′-, -hô′-, -hä′-). A city of northeast Ohio on the **Cuyahoga River,** about 129 km (80 mi) long. The city is a residential and industrial suburb of Akron. ● Pop. 48,950.

Cuz·co also **Cus·co** (kōō′skō). A city of southern Peru in the Andes east-southeast of Lima. It was built on the site of an ancient city, which was supposedly founded in the 11th century by Manco Capac, the first ruler of the Incas, and which was plundered by the Spanish conquistador Francisco Pizarro in 1533. It is a trade center. ● Pop. 302,700.

cwm (kōōm). See **cirque.**

Cyc·la·des (sĭk′lə-dēz′) also **Ki·klá·dhes** (kē-klä′thĕs). A group of islands of southeast Greece in the southern Aegean Sea. The name was used in ancient times for the islands surrounding the small island of Delos.

Cym·ric (kĭm′rĭk, sĭm′-). **1.** Of or relating to the Cymry. **2.** See **Welsh** (sense 3).

Cym·ry (kĭm′rē, sĭm′-). **1.** The Brythonic Celts of Wales, Cornwall, and Brittany. **2.** The Welsh.

Cyn·os·ceph·a·lae (sĭn′ə-sĕf′ə-lē, sī′nə-). Two hills of southeast Thessaly in northeast Greece. The Theban general Pelopidas was killed in battle here (364 B.C.). Later (197 B.C.) the Roman general Flaminius decisively defeated Philip V of Macedon at Cynoscephalae.

Cy·press (sī′prĭs). A city of southern California, a suburb of Long Beach. ● Pop. 42,655.

Cyp·ri·an (sĭp′rē-ən). **1.** Of or relating to Cyprus; Cypriot. **2.** See **Cypriot** (sense 1).

Cyp·ri·ot (sĭp′rē-ət, -ŏt′) also **Cyp·ri·ote** (-ōt′, -ət). **1.** A native or inhabitant of Cyprus. Also called *Cyprian.* **2.** The ancient or modern

Greek dialect of Cyprus. **3.** Of or relating to Cyprus or its people or culture. **4.** Of or relating to Cypriot Greek as used on Cyprus.

Cy·prus (sī′prəs). An island country in the eastern Mediterranean Sea south of Turkey. Site of an ancient Neolithic culture, the island was settled by Phoenicians c. 800 B.C. and thereafter fell successively to the Assyrians, Egyptians, Persians, Macedonian Greeks, Egyptians again, and finally Romans (58 B.C.) The Byzantines controlled it from A.D. 395 until 1191, when it was captured by Richard I of England during the Third Crusade. Venice annexed it in 1489, Turkey conquered it in 1571, and Great Britain proclaimed its sovereignty in 1914. Cyprus became independent in 1960, but large-scale fighting between Greek and Turkish Cypriots led to the installment of a UN peacekeeping force on the island in 1965. In 1974 Turkey invaded Cyprus and established a separate Turkish state in the northern part. Negotiations to end the division of the island have been unsuccessful. Nicosia, in the central part of the island, is the capital and the largest city. ⊛ Pop. 734,000.

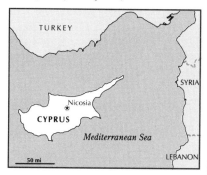

Cyr·e·na·ic (sĭr′ə-nā′ĭk, sī′rə-). **1.** Of or relating to Cyrenaica or Cyrene. **2.** A native or inhabitant of Cyrenaica or Cyrene.

Cyr·e·na·i·ca (sĭr′ə-nā′ĭ-kə, sī′rə-). An ancient region of northeast Libya bordering on the Mediterranean Sea. It was colonized by the Greeks in the seventh century B.C. and became a Roman province in the first century B.C.

Cy·re·ne (sī-rē′nē). An ancient Greek city of Cyrenaica. Founded c. 630 B.C., it was noted as an intellectual center with distinguished schools of medicine and philosophy.

Cy·ril·lic (sə-rĭl′ĭk). Of, relating to, or constituting the old Slavic alphabet ascribed to Saint Cyril (827–869), at present used in modified form for Russian, Bulgarian, certain other Slavic languages, and other languages of the former Soviet Union.

Cy·the·ra (sĭ-thîr′ə, sĭth′ər-ə) also **Kí·thi·ra** (kē′thē-rä′). An island of southern Greece in the Mediterranean Sea south of the Peloponnesus. Southernmost of the Ionian Islands, it was the chief center for the worship of Aphrodite.

Czech (chĕk). **1.** A native or inhabitant of Czech Republic or Czechoslovakia, especially a Bohemian, Moravian, or Silesian. **2.** The Slavic language of the Czechs. —**Czech** *adj.*

Czech·o·slo·va·ki·a (chĕk′ə-slə-vä′kē-ə, -ō-slō-). *abbr.* **Czech.** A former country of central Europe. It was formed in 1918 from Czech-speaking and Slovak-speaking territories of the Austro-Hungarian Empire, although disparate ethnic elements led to internal conflicts before World War II. Communists gained control of the government after the war and stayed in control until 1989 when demands for democratic political reform forced Communist leaders to resign. In 1993 the country was divided into Czech Republic and Slovakia. —**Czech′o·slo′-vak, Czech′o·slo·va′ki·an** *adj. & n.*

Czech Republic. A country of central Europe east of Germany and south of Poland. It was a part of Czechoslovakia from 1918 until January 1993. Prague is the capital and largest city. ⊛ Pop. 10,333,000.

Czę·sto·cho·wa (chĕn′stə-kō′və, chĕN′stô-hô′vä). A city of southern Poland north of Katowice. Heavily industrialized, its monastery is a famous pilgrimage site. ⊛ Pop. 258,266.

D

Dą·bro·wa Gór·ni·cza (dôm-brô′və gŏŏr-nē′chə). A city of southern Poland northeast of Katowice. It has been a coal-mining center since the 1790's. ⊛ Pop. 137,249.

Dac·ca (dăk′ə, dä′kə). See **Dhaka.**

Da·chau (dä′kou′, -кнou′). A city of southeast Germany north-northwest of Munich. It was the site of a Nazi concentration camp built in 1935 and captured by the Allies in April 1945. ⊛ Pop. 33,141.

Da·ci·a (dā′shē-ə, -shə). An ancient region and

Roman province corresponding roughly to present-day Romania. Inhabited before the Christian era by a Thracian people with an advanced material culture, the region was abandoned to the Goths after A.D. 270. —**Da'ci·an** *adj. & n.*

Da·ges·tan (dä'gĭ-stän, də-gyĭ-). An autonomous republic of southwest Russia bordering on the Caspian Sea. Settled in the first millennium B.C., it was ceded to Russia by Persia in 1813.

Da·ho·mey (də-hō'mē, dä-ô-mā'). See **Benin** (sense 2). —**Da·ho'me·an** (də-hō'mē-ən), **Da·ho'man** (-mən) *adj. & n.*

Dai·ren (dī'rĕn'). See **Dalian.**

Dai (dī). Variant of **Tai.**

Da·kar (də-kär', dăk'är'). The capital and largest city of Senegal, in the western part of the country on the Atlantic Ocean. A busy port, it grew around a French fort built in 1857 and was the capital of French West Africa from 1902 to 1959. ◉ Pop. 1,641,358.

Da·ko·ta (də-kō'tə). **1.** *pl.* **Dakota** or **-tas.** A member of any of the Sioux peoples, especially any of the peoples of the Santee branch. **2.** The Siouan language of the Dakotas. —**Da·ko'tan** *adj. & n.*

Da·ko·tas (də-kō'təz). The Dakota Territory or (after 1889) the states of North Dakota and South Dakota.

Dakota Territory. A territory of the north-central United States organized in 1861 and divided into the states of North Dakota and South Dakota in 1889. The territory included much of present-day Montana until 1864 and Wyoming until 1868.

dale (dāl). A valley.

Dale City (dāl). A community of northeast Virginia southwest of Alexandria. It is mainly residential. ◉ Pop. 23,000.

Dal·ian (däl'yän') also **Ta·lien** (tä'lyĕn'). Formerly **Dai·ren** (dī'rĕn'). A city of northeast China on the Liaodong Peninsula and the Bo Hai. A major seaport, it was opened to foreign commerce in 1901 and occupied by the Japanese during the Russo-Japanese War (1904–1905). Dalian and Lüshun form the conurbation of Lüda. ◉ Pop. 3,473,832.

Dal·las (däl'əs). A city of northeast Texas on the Trinity River east of Fort Worth. It was founded by French settlers in 1841 and became a cotton market in the 1870's. Present-day industries include oil, aerospace, electronics, and banking. ◉ Pop. 1,006,877.

dalles (dălz). The rapids of a river that runs between the steep walls of a gorge.

Dalles (dălz), **The.** A city of northern Oregon on the Columbia River east of Portland. An important stop on the Oregon Trail in the 1800's, it is now a busy inland port. ◉ Pop. 10,800.

Dal·ma·ti·a (dăl-mā'shə). A historical region of the northwest Balkan Peninsula on the Adriatic Sea in present-day Croatia. Subdued by the Romans in the 1st century B.C., it was divided between the kingdoms of Serbia and Croatia in the 10th century and held by numerous powers after the 15th century. —**Dal·ma'tian** *adj. & n.*

Dal·ton (dôl'tən). A city of northwest Georgia southeast of Chattanooga, Tennessee. It is an industrial center. ◉ Pop. 21,761.

Da·ly City (dā'lē). A city of western California, a suburb of San Francisco. It was settled in 1906 by refugees from the San Francisco earthquake. ◉ Pop. 92,311.

Da·man (də-män'). A former Portuguese colony of northwest India on the eastern shore of the Gulf of Cambay. It was acquired by the Portuguese in 1588 and annexed by India in 1962.

Daman and Diu. A union territory of northwest India on the Arabian Sea. It comprises two former Portuguese colonies, which were annexed by India in 1962 and administered jointly with Goa from 1962 to 1987, when Goa became a separate state.

Da·man·hur (dăm'ən-hŏŏr', dä'män-hŏŏr'). A city of northeast Egypt on the Nile River delta northwest of Cairo. In ancient times it was known as Hermopolis Parva. ◉ Pop. 222,000.

Da·mas·cus (də-măs'kəs). The capital and largest city of Syria, in the southwest part of the country. Inhabited since prehistoric times, the city became a thriving commercial center under the Romans and was a Saracen stronghold during the Crusades in the 11th, 12th, and 13th centuries. ◉ Pop. 1,549,000. —**Dam'a·scene'** (dăm'ə-sēn') *adj. & n.*

Dam·a·vand (dăm'ə-vănd', dä'mä-vänd) also **Dem·a·vend** (dĕm'ə-vĕnd'). A peak, 5,774.9 m (18,934 ft) high, in the Elburz Mountains of northern Iran northeast of Tehran. It is the highest elevation in the range.

Dam·i·et·ta (dăm'ē-ĕt'ə) also **Dum·yat** (dŏŏm-yät'). A city of northeast Egypt on the Nile River delta north-northeast of Cairo. It was conquered by Crusaders in 1219. ◉ Pop. 118,100.

Dan·a·kil (dăn'ə-kĭl', də-nä'kēl). A desert region of northeast Ethiopia, southern Eritrea, and northern Djibouti bordering on the Red Sea. It is part of the Great Rift Valley.

Da Nang or **Da·nang** (də năng', dä' näng'). Formerly **Tou·rane** (tŏŏ-rän'). A city of central Vietnam on the South China Sea. It was the site of an important U.S. military base during the Vietnam War (1954–1975). ◉ Pop. 382,674.

Dan·bur·y (dăn'bĕr'ē, -bə-rē) A city of southwest Connecticut northwest of Bridgeport. Settled in 1685, it was largely destroyed by the British in 1777 during the American Revolution. ◉ Pop. 65,585.

Dan·dong (dän'dông') also **Tan·tung** (tän'-tŏŏng') or **An·tung** (än'tŏŏng'). A city of northeast China on the Yalu River opposite North Korea. It is a seaport and manufacturing center. ◉ Pop. 660,518.

Dane (dān). **1.** A native or inhabitant of Denmark. **2.** A person of Danish ancestry.

Dan·ish (dā′nĭsh). *abbr.* **Dan., Da. 1.** Of or relating to Denmark, the Danes, their language, or their culture. **2.** The North Germanic language of the Danes.

Da·no-Nor·we·gian (dā′-nō-nôr-wē′jən). An official literary form of Norwegian based on written Danish. Also called *Bokmål, Riksmål.*

Dan River (dăn). A river, about 290 km (180 mi) long, of southern Virginia and northern North Carolina flowing south and east to the Roanoke River.

Dan·ube (dăn′yōōb). A river of south-central Europe rising in southwest Germany and flowing about 2,848 km (1,770 mi) southeastward through Austria, Hungary, Yugoslavia, and Romania to the Black Sea. It has been a major trade route since the Middle Ages. **— Dan·u′-bi·an** *adj.*

Dan·vers (dăn′vərz). A town of northeast Massachusetts north-northeast of Boston. It was settled in the 1630's and set off from Salem in 1752. ◉ Pop. 24,174.

Dan·ville (dăn′vĭl′). **1.** A city of western California, a suburb of Oakland. ◉ Pop. 31,306. **2.** A city of eastern Illinois east-northeast of Decatur. It is a commercial center in an agricultural region. ◉ Pop. 33,828. **3.** An independent city of southern Virginia on the Dan River near the North Carolina border. Founded in 1793, it was the last capital of the Confederacy in 1865. ◉ Pop. 53,056.

Dan·zig (dăn′sĭg, dän′tsĭk). See **Gdańsk.**

Danzig Free City. A former state (1919–1939) on the Gulf of Gdańsk surrounding and including the city of Gdańsk.

Dard (därd) also **Dar·dic** (där′dĭk). A group of Indic languages spoken in the upper Indus River valley.

Dar·dan (där′dn) or **Dar·da·ni·an** (där-dā′nē-ən). *Archaic.* A Trojan. **— Dar′dan** *adj.*

Dar·da·nelles (där′dn-ĕlz′). Formerly **Hel·les·pont** (hĕl′ĭ-spŏnt′). A strait connecting the Aegean Sea with the Sea of Marmara. In ancient times it was the scene of the legendary exploits of Hero and Leander.

Dar·dic (där′dĭk). Variant of **Dard.**

Dar es Sa·laam (där′ ĕs sə-läm′). The de facto capital and largest city of Tanzania, in the eastern part of the country on an arm of the Indian Ocean. It was founded in 1862 by the sultan of Zanzibar. The name means "haven of peace." ◉ Pop. 1,096,000.

Dar·fur (där-fōōr′). A region and former sultan-ate of western Sudan. Occupied since prehistoric times, the area fell to the Egyptians in 1874 and later to the British, who incorporated it into their holdings in the Sudan.

Dar·i·en (dăr′ē-ĕn′, dâr′-, dăr′ē-ən, dâr′-). A town of southwest Connecticut northwest of Stamford. Settled c. 1641, it is mainly residential. ◉ Pop. 18,196.

Da·ri·én (dâr′ē-ĕn′, där-yĕn′). A region of eastern Panama on the **Gulf of Darién,** a wide bay of the Caribbean Sea between eastern Panama and northwest Colombia. In 1513 the Spanish explorer Vasco Núñez de Balboa led an expedition across the **Isthmus of Darién** (now the Isthmus of Panama) and became the first European to view the Pacific Ocean from the New World.

Dar·jee·ling (där-jē′lĭng). A town of northeast India in the lower Himalaya Mountains on the Sikkim border. At an altitude of 2,287.5 m (7,500 ft), it is a popular tourist center with commanding views of Mount Kanchenjunga and Mount Everest. ◉ Pop. 57,603.

Dark Continent (därk). A former name for Africa, so used because its hinterland was largely unexplored and therefore mysterious until the 19th century. The British journalist and explorer Henry M. Stanley was probably the first to use the term in his 1878 account *Through the Dark Continent.*

Dar·ling Range (där′lĭng). An upland region of southwest Australia extending along the Pacific coast north and south of Perth.

Darling River. A river rising in the Great Dividing Range of southeast Australia and flowing about 2,739 km (1,702 mi) generally southwest to the Murray River. It is the longest river in Australia but has a sporadic flow.

Dar·ling·ton (där′lĭng-tən). A borough of northeast England south of Newcastle. It is a railroad center. ◉ Pop. 100,163.

Darm·stadt (därm′stăt, -shtät′). A city of southwest Germany southeast of Frankfurt. It was chartered in 1330. ◉ Pop. 139,754.

Dart·ford (därt′fərd). A municipal borough of southeast England east-southeast of London. The Peasants' Revolt led by Wat Tyler began here in June 1381. ◉ Pop. 77,900.

Dart·moor (därt′mōōr′, -môr′, -mōr′). An upland region of southwest England noted for its bare granite tors. There are remains of numerous Bronze Age settlements.

Dart·mouth (därt′məth). **1.** A city of southern Nova Scotia, Canada, on an inlet of the Atlantic Ocean opposite Halifax. It was founded by the British in the 1750's. ◉ Pop. 62,277. **2.** A town of southeast Massachusetts on Buzzards Bay southwest of New Bedford. Formerly a shipbuilding center, it is now a tourist resort. ⊛ Pop. 27,244.

Dar·win (där′wĭn). A city of northern Australia on **Port Darwin,** an inlet of the Timor Sea. It was founded as Palmerston in 1869 and renamed in 1911. ⊛ Pop. 65,200.

Dasht-e-Ka·vir (däsht′ē-kə-vîr′, däsht′ē-kä-vîr′). A salt desert of north-central Iran southeast of the Elburz Mountains.

Dasht-e-Lut (däsht′ē-lōōt′). A sand and stone desert of eastern Iran extending southward from the Dasht-e-Kavir.

date line (dāt). The International Date Line.

Da·tong (dä′tông′) also **Ta·tung** (tä′tŏŏng′). A city of northeast China west of Beijing. It is an important industrial and railroad center. ⊛ Pop. 1,277,310.

da·tum (dā′təm, dăt′əm, dä′təm). A point, line, or surface used as a reference, as in surveying, mapping, or geology.

Dau·gav·pils (dou′gəf-pĭlz′, -gäf-pēlz′). A city of southeast Latvia southeast of Riga. Founded in the 13th century, it was held by Lithuania and Poland before being ceded to Russia in 1771. ⊛ Pop. 124,000.

Dau·phi·né (dō-fē-nā′). A historical region and former province of southeast France bordering on Italy. After 1349 it became controlled by the eldest son of the king of France.

Da·vao (dä′vou′). A city of southeast Mindanao, Philippines, on **Davao Gulf,** an inlet of the Pacific Ocean. Davao is a major port and commercial center. ⊛ Pop. 960,910.

Dav·en·port (dăv′ĭn-pôrt′, -pōrt′). A city of eastern Iowa on the Mississippi River opposite Moline and Rock Island, Illinois. It grew rapidly after the first railroad bridge across the Mississippi was completed in 1856. ⊛ Pop. 95,333.

Da·vie (dā′vē). A town of southeast Florida southwest of Fort Lauderdale. It is in a citrus-growing area. ⊛ Pop. 47,217.

Da·vis (dā′vĭs). A city of central California west of Sacramento. A branch of the University of California (established 1908) is here. ⊛ Pop. 46,209.

Davis Strait. A strait of the northern Atlantic Ocean between southeast Baffin Island and southwest Greenland.

Daw·son (dô′sən). A town of western Yukon Territory, Canada, at the confluence of the Yukon and Klondike rivers. A boom town during the Klondike gold rush of the late 1890's, it was the territorial capital from 1898 to 1951. ⊛ Pop. 697.

Dawson Creek. A city of eastern British Columbia, Canada, near the Alberta border. It is the southern terminus of the Alaska Highway. ⊛ Pop. 11,373.

Day·ak (dā′ăk′) or **Dy·ak** (dī′-). **1.** *pl.* **Dayak** or **-aks** also **Dyak** or **-aks.** A member of any of various Indonesian peoples inhabiting Borneo. **2.** The language of the Dayaks.

Day·ton (dāt′n). A city of southwest Ohio north-northeast of Cincinnati. Now a manufacturing center, it was the home of the aviation pioneers Orville and Wilbur Wright. ⊛ Pop. 182,044.

Day·to·na Beach (dā-tō′nə). A city of northeast Florida on the Atlantic coast north-northeast of Orlando. Automobile speed trials and races have been held on its hard, white beach since the early 1900's. ⊛ Pop. 54,176.

Dead Sea (dĕd). A salt lake, about 397 m (1,300 ft) below sea level, between Israel and Jordan. It is one of the saltiest bodies of water known and is the lowest point on the earth.

Dear·born (dîr′bôrn′, -bərn). A city of southeast Michigan west of Detroit. Greenfield Village, the restored birthplace of the automobile manufacturer Henry Ford (1863–1947), is here. ⊛ Pop. 60,838.

Dearborn Heights. A city of southeast Michigan, a suburb of Detroit. ⊛ Pop. 60,838.

Death Valley (dĕth). An arid desert basin of eastern California and western Nevada. It includes the lowest point, 86 m (282 ft) below sea level, in the Western Hemisphere.

Deau·ville (dō′vĭl, dō-vēl′). A city of northwest France on the English Channel. It is a fashionable resort with a noted racecourse. ⊛ Pop. 4,682.

de·bouch·ment (dĭ-bouch′mənt, -bōōsh′-). A debouchure.

de·bou·chure (dĭ-bōō′shŏŏr′). An opening or mouth, as of a river or stream.

De·bre·cen (dĕb′rĭt-sĕn′, -rĕ-tsĕn′). A city of eastern Hungary near the Romanian border east of Budapest. First known in the 13th century, it was the provisional capital from 1944 to 1945. ⊛ Pop. 217,497.

De·cap·o·lis (dĭ-kăp′ə-lĭs). A confederacy in northeast Palestine of ten Roman-controlled cities settled by Greeks. It was formed after 63 B.C. and dominated by Damascus.

De·ca·tur (dĭ-kā′tər). **1.** A city of northern Alabama on the Tennessee River north of Birmingham. Most of the original city was destroyed during the Civil War. ⊛ Pop. 48,761. **2.** A city of northwest Georgia, a residential suburb of Atlanta. ⊛ Pop. 17,336. **3.** A city of central Illinois east of Springfield. Abraham Lincoln practiced law here. ⊛ Pop. 83,885.

Dec·can (dĕk′ən). A plateau of south-central India between the Eastern Ghats and the Western Ghats. The name is also used for the entire Indian peninsula south of the Narmada River.

Ded·ham (dĕd′əm). A town of eastern Massachusetts, a mainly residential suburb of Boston on the Charles River. ⊛ Pop. 23,782.

Dee (dē). **1.** A river rising in the Cairngorm Mountains of eastern Scotland and flowing about 145 km (90 mi) eastward to the North Sea through an artificial channel at Aberdeen. It is known for its scenic beauty and salmon fisheries. **2.** A river of northern Wales and western England flowing about 113 km (70 mi) partially along the Welsh-English border to the Irish Sea.

deep (dēp). **1. a.** A deep place in land or in a body of water. **b.** A vast, immeasurable extent. **2.** The ocean.

Deep River (dēp). A river rising in north-central North Carolina and flowing about 201 km (125 mi) southeast and east to join the Haw River and form the Cape Fear River.

Deep South. A region of the southeast United States, usually comprising the states of Alabama, Georgia, Louisiana, Mississippi, and South Carolina.

Deer·field (dîr′fēld′). A village of northeast Illinois, a residential suburb of Chicago. ⊛ Pop. 17,327.

Deerfield Beach. A city of southeast Florida on the Atlantic Ocean north of Fort Lauderdale. It is in a truck-farming area. ⊛ Pop. 46,325.

Deer Park (dîr). **1.** An unincorporated community of southeast New York on central Long Island north of Babylon. It is mainly residential. ⊛ Pop. 28,840. **2.** A city of southeast Texas east of Houston. It is an industrial center in a truck-farming area. ⊛ Pop. 27,652.

De·fi·ance (dĭ-fī′əns). A city of northwest Ohio southwest of Toledo. Fort Defiance was built on the site by the American Revolutionary general Anthony Wayne in 1794. ⊛ Pop. 16,768.

de·gree (dĭ-grē′). A unit of latitude or longitude, equal to 1/360 of a great circle.

Deh·ra Dun (dā′rə dōōn′). A city of northern India north-northeast of Delhi. It is a trade center and has a forestry college. ⊛ Pop. 270,159.

De Kalb (dĭ kălb′). A city of northern Illinois south-southeast of Rockford. It is a manufacturing center in a farming region. ⊛ Pop. 34,925.

Del·a·go·a Bay (dĕl′ə-gō′ə). An inlet of the Indian Ocean in southern Mozambique. The bay was discovered by the Portuguese in 1502 and explored after 1544. Portugal's claim to the area was upheld in 1875 after a dispute with Great Britain.

De Land (dĭ lănd′). A city of northeast Florida west-southwest of Daytona Beach. It is a winter resort. ⊛ Pop. 16,491.

De·la·no (də-lā′nō). A city of south-central California in the San Joaquin Valley north-northwest of Bakersfield. It is a processing and shipping center. ⊛ Pop. 22,762.

Del·a·ware[1] (dĕl′ə-wâr′). **1.** *pl.* **Delaware** or **-wares.** A member of a group of closely related Native American peoples formerly inhabiting the Delaware and Hudson river valleys and the area between, with present-day populations in Oklahoma, Kansas, Wisconsin, and Ontario. The Delawares formed a variety of political alliances in their westward migration after losing their lands to white settlement in the 17th and 18th centuries. Also called *Lenape, Lenni Lenape.* **2.** One or both of the Algonquian languages of the Delawares. — **Del′a·war′e·an** *adj.*

Del·a·ware[2] (dĕl′ə-wâr′). **1.** *abbr.* **DE, Del.** A state of the eastern United States on the Atlantic Ocean. It was admitted as the first of the original Thirteen Colonies in 1787. Settled by the Dutch in 1631 and by Swedes in 1638, the region passed to England in 1664. It was part of William Penn's Pennsylvania grant from 1682 until 1776. Dover is the capital and Wilmington the largest city. ⊛ Pop. 668,696. **2.** A city of central Ohio north of Columbus. Rutherford B. Hayes, the 19th President of the United States, was born here in 1822. ⊛ Pop. 20,030.

Delaware Bay. An estuary of the Delaware River emptying into the Atlantic Ocean between eastern Delaware and southern New Jersey.

Delaware River. A river rising in the Catskill Mountains of southeast New York and flowing about 451 km (280 mi) generally southward along the New York–Pennsylvania border and the Pennsylvania–New Jersey border to northern Delaware, where it enters Delaware Bay. The Dutch explorers named it the South River to distinguish it from the North River, an estuary of the Hudson River.

Del City (dĕl). A city of central Oklahoma, a residential suburb of Oklahoma City. ⊛ Pop. 23,928.

Delft (dĕlft). A city of southwest Netherlands southeast of The Hague. Fine pottery has been produced here since the 16th century. ⊛ Pop. 86,733.

Del·hi (dĕl′ē). A city of north-central India on the Jumna River. Important since ancient times, the old city was rebuilt by Shah Jahan, Mogul emperor of India, in the 17th century with high stone walls enclosing the Red Fort that contained the imperial Mogul palace. The new part of Delhi became the capital of British India in 1912 and of independent India in 1947. ⊛ Pop. 7,206,704.

dell (dĕl). A small, secluded, wooded valley.

Del·mar·va Peninsula (dĕl-mär′və). A peninsula of the eastern United States separating Chesapeake Bay from Delaware Bay and the Atlantic Ocean. It includes all of Delaware and parts of eastern Maryland and Virginia.

Del·men·horst (dĕl′mĭn-hôrst′). A city of

northwest Germany, an industrial suburb of Bremen. ⊛ Pop. 70,671.

De·los (dē′lŏs′, dĕl′ōs). An island of southeast Greece in the southern Aegean Sea. It is the smallest of the Cyclades Islands and was traditionally considered sacred to the god Apollo.

Del·phi (dĕl′fī′). An ancient town of central Greece near Mount Parnassus. Dating to at least the seventh century B.C., Delphi was the seat of a famous oracle of Apollo, the god of prophecy, music, medicine, and poetry in Greek mythology.

Del·phic (dĕl′fĭk) also **Del·phi·an** (-fē-ən). *Greek Mythology.* Of or relating to Delphi or to the oracle of Apollo at Delphi.

Del·ray Beach (dĕl′rā′). A city of southeast Florida on the Atlantic Ocean north of Boca Raton. Settled in 1901, it is a tourist resort. ⊛ Pop. 47,181.

Del Ri·o (dĕl rē′ō). A city of southwest Texas on the Rio Grande west of San Antonio. Founded in 1868, it is a market and shipping center in an agricultural region. ⊛ Pop. 30,705.

del·ta (dĕl′tə). **1.** A usually triangular alluvial deposit at the mouth of a river. **2.** A similar deposit at the mouth of a tidal inlet, caused by tidal currents. —**del·ta′ic** (-tā′ĭk), **del′tic** *adj.*

Dem·a·vend (dĕm′ə-vĕnd′). See **Damavand.**

deme (dēm). Any of the townships or local governments of ancient Attica.

Dem·o·crat (dĕm′ə-krăt′), **Mount.** A peak, 4,315.1 m (14,148 ft) high, of central Colorado in the Park Range of the Rocky Mountains.

De·na·li (də-nä′lē). See Mount **McKinley.**

dene (dēn). *Chiefly British.* A sandy tract or dune by the seashore.

Den Hel·der (dən hĕl′dər). A city of northwest Netherlands on the North Sea. It is the country's most important naval base. ⊛ Pop. 63,826.

Den·i·son (dĕn′ĭ-sən). A city of northern Texas near the Oklahoma border north-northeast of Dallas. An industrial center, it was founded (1872) as a railroad junction on the site of a stagecoach stop. Dwight D. Eisenhower was born here in 1890. ⊛ Pop. 21,505.

Den·mark (dĕn′märk′). *abbr.* **Den.** A country of northern Europe on Jutland and adjacent islands including Sjaelland, Fyn, and Bornholm. It was unified in the 10th century by the Viking king Harold Bluetooth (died c. 985), who converted the people to Christianity. Denmark controlled England briefly in the 11th century and was united with Sweden and Norway in 1397. The union with Sweden lasted until 1523, and the union with Norway until 1814. The country was occupied (1940–1945) by German forces during World War II. Copenhagen is the capital and the largest city. ⊛ Pop. 5,205,000.

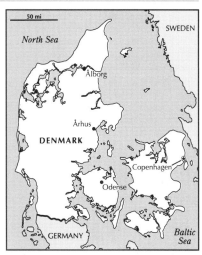

Denmark Strait. A channel between Greenland and Iceland connecting the Arctic Ocean with the northern Atlantic Ocean.

Den·ton (dĕn′tən). A city of northeast Texas north-northwest of Dallas. It is a trade and agricultural center. ⊛ Pop. 66,270.

Den·ver (dĕn′vər). The capital and largest city of Colorado, in the north-central part of the state on the South Platte River. It was settled by gold prospectors in 1858 and became territorial capital in 1867. ⊛ Pop. 467,610.

de·part·ment (dĭ-pärt′mənt). *abbr.* **dept., dpt., dep., D. 1.** A principal administrative division of a government. **2.** An administrative district in France. —**de′part·men′tal** (-mĕn′tl) *adj.*

de·pend·en·cy also **de·pend·an·cy** (dĭ-pĕn′-dən-sē). *abbr.* **dep.** A territory under the jurisdiction of a state of which it does not form an integral part.

De·pew (dĭ-pyoo′). A village of western New York, an industrial suburb of Buffalo. ⊛ Pop. 17,673.

de·pres·sion (dĭ-prĕsh′ən). An area that is sunk below its surroundings; a hollow.

Der·by (där′bē). A city of central England west of Nottingham. Settled by the Romans, it is a trade and manufacturing center with a pottery industry dating from the 18th century. ⊛ Pop. 228,648.

Der·ry (dĕr′ē). See **Londonderry.**

Des·chutes (dā-shoot′, də-shoots′). A river rising in the Cascade Range of west-central Oregon and flowing about 402 km (250 mi) generally north to the Columbia River near The Dalles.

Des·er·et (dĕz′ə-rĕt′). An area proposed by the Mormons in 1849 as an independent state or a state of the Union. Deseret would have included much of the southwest United States, with a capital at Salt Lake City. Congress refused to recognize the provisional state and created the Utah Territory in 1850.

des·ert (dĕz′ərt). A dry, often sandy region of little rainfall, extreme temperatures, and sparse vegetation.

Des Moines (dĭ moin′). The capital and largest city of Iowa, in the south-central part of the state on the Des Moines River. Fort Des Moines was built on the site in 1843, and the surrounding settlement became a city in 1851. It was chosen as state capital in 1857. ⊛ Pop. 193,187.

Des Moines River. A river rising in southwest Minnesota and flowing about 861 km (535 mi) generally southeastward across Iowa to the Mississippi River.

Des·na (də-snä′, dyə-). A river rising east of Smolensk in western Russia and flowing about 885 km (550) generally south to the Dnieper River above Kiev, Ukraine.

De So·to (dĭ sō′tō). A city of northeast Texas, a suburb of Dallas. ⊛ Pop. 30,544.

Des Plaines (dĕs plānz′). A city of northeast Illinois, a suburb of Chicago on the Des Plaines River. ⊛ Pop. 53,223.

Des Plaines River. A river rising in southeast Wisconsin and flowing about 241 km (150 mi) generally southward to the Kankakee River in northeast Illinois.

Des·sau (dĕs′ou). A city of east-central Germany north of Leipzig. It was the site of the Bauhaus school of design headed by the architect Walter Gropius from 1925 to 1932. ⊛ Pop. 103,738.

Det·mold (dĕt′mōld′, -môlt′). A city of west-central Germany east of Münster. Charlemagne, king of the Franks, defeated the Saxons nearby in 783. ⊛ Pop. 66,282.

de·tri·tus (dĭ-trī′təs). Loose fragments or grains that have been worn away from rock. —**de·tri′tal** (-trīt′l) *adj.*

De·troit (dĭ-troit′). A city of southeast Michigan opposite Windsor, Ontario, on the **Detroit River,** about 51 km (32 mi) long. Founded by French settlers in 1701, Detroit became known as "the automobile capital of the world" in the early 20th century. ⊛ Pop. 1,027,974.

Deur·ne (dûr′nə). A city of northern Belgium, a manufacturing suburb of Antwerp. ⊛ Pop. 80,766.

De·va·na·ga·ri (dā′və-nä′gə-rē). The alphabet in which Sanskrit and many modern Indian languages are written.

De·ven·ter (dā′vən-tər). A city of east-central Netherlands on the Ijssel River east-northeast of Utrecht. A member of the Hanseatic League, it was a noted center of piety and learning during the Middle Ages. ⊛ Pop. 64,823.

Dev·il's Island (dĕv′ĭlz). An island in the Caribbean Sea off French Guiana. A French penal colony after the 1850's, it was used mainly for political prisoners, including Alfred Dreyfus, a French army officer of Jewish descent who was falsely accused of treason and sequestered here from 1894 until 1899.

Dev·on (dĕv′ən). A region of southwest England bordering on the English Channel. Occupied in Paleolithic times, it became part of Wessex in the eighth century.

Devon Island. An island of northeast Northwest Territories, Canada, between Baffin and Ellesmere islands.

Dezh·nev (dĕzh′nəf, dĕzh′nē-ôf′, dĭzh-nyôf′), **Cape** also **East Cape** (ēst). A cape of extreme northeast Russia on the Bering Strait opposite Alaska. It is the easternmost point of Asia.

Dha·ka also **Dac·ca** (dăk′ə, dä′kə). The capital and largest city of Bangladesh, in the east-central part of the country. It was the Mogul capital of Bengal in the 17th century and came under British rule in 1765. After India achieved independence in 1947, Dhaka was made the capital of East Pakistan, which became Bangladesh in 1971. ⊛ Pop. 3,397,187.

Dhau·la·gi·ri (dou′lə-gîr′ē). A peak, 8,177 m (26,810 ft) high, in the Himalaya Mountains of west-central Nepal. It was first scaled in 1960.

Dhe·gi·ha (dā′jē-hä′). **1.** A branch of the Siouan linguistic family comprising the Omaha, Ponca, Osage, Kansa, and Quapaw languages. **2.** *pl.* **Dhegiha** or **-has.** A member of any of the peoples speaking Dhegiha.

Dhu·li·a (dōō′lē-ə, dōōl′yə). A city of west-central India northeast of Bombay. It is an important cotton market. ⊛ Pop. 278,317.

Di·a·man·ti·na (dī′ə-mən-tē′nə). A river, about 901 km (560 mi) long, of east-central Australia flowing generally southwest as a tributary of the Warburton River.

Di·a·mond Head (dī′ə-mənd, dī′mənd). A promontory, 232.1 m (761 ft) high, on the southeast coast of Oahu, Hawaii.

Dick·in·son (dĭk′ĭn-sən). A city of southwest North Dakota west of Bismarck. It is a processing and shipping center in an agricultural region. ⊛ Pop. 16,097.

Dien Bien Phu (dyĕn′ byĕn′ fōō′). A town of northwest Vietnam near the Laos border. The French military base here fell to Communist and nationalist Vietminh troops on May 7, 1954, after a 56-day siege, leading to the end of France's involvement in Indochina.

Di·eppe (dē-ĕp′, dyĕp′). A city of northeast France on the English Channel north of Rouen. It is a port for channel steamers and a beach resort. Allied forces led a disastrous commando attack on the city (August 19, 1942) to test the strength of German defenses. ● Pop. 35,957.

Di·jon (dē-zhōn′). A city of eastern France north of Lyon. It is an industrial center and a transportation hub noted for its foodstuffs, including mustard and cassis. ● Pop. 146,723.

di·lu·vi·al (dĭ-lōō′vē-əl) also **di·lu·vi·an** (-ən). Of, relating to, or produced by a flood.

Di·nar·ic Alps (dĭ-năr′ĭk). A range of the northwest Balkan Peninsula extending about 644 km (400 mi) along the eastern coast of the Adriatic Sea in Croatia and Bosnia and Herzegovina. The partially submerged western part of the system forms numerous islands along the coast.

din·gle (dĭng′gəl). A small, wooded valley; a dell.

Dins·la·ken (dĭns′lä′kən). A city of western Germany near the Rhine River north of Duisburg. Chartered in 1273, it is an industrial center. ● Pop. 60,430.

Di·o·mede Islands (dī′ə-mēd′). Two rocky islands in the Bering Strait between Alaska and Siberia. **Little Diomede** belongs to the United States; **Big Diomede**, to Russia. The islands were discovered and named by the Danish explorer Vitus Bering in 1728.

dip (dĭp). **1.** Magnetic dip. **2.** A hollow or depression.

Dis·ap·point·ment (dĭs′ə-point′mənt), **Cape.** A cape of southwest Washington on the northern side of the mouth of the Columbia River. It was named in 1788 by a British sea captain who was searching for the fabled River of the West and was disappointed when he did not discover a wide river mouth.

Dis·mal Swamp or **Great Dis·mal Swamp** (dĭz′məl). A swampy region of southeast Virginia and northeast North Carolina. The heavily forested area has been greatly reduced by drainage. George Washington surveyed the Dismal Swamp in 1763.

dis·trib·u·tar·y (dĭ-strĭb′yə-tĕr′ē). A branch of a river that flows away from the main stream.

dis·trict (dĭs′trĭkt). *abbr.* **dist. 1.** A division of an area, as for administrative purposes. **2.** A region or locality marked by a distinguishing feature. —**dis′trict·wide′** *adv. & adj.*

Dis·trict of Columbia (dĭs′trĭkt′). *abbr.* **DC, D.C.** A federal district of the eastern United States on the Potomac River between Virginia and Maryland. Coextensive with the city of Washington, it was established by congressional acts of 1790 and 1791 on a site selected by George Washington.

Di·u (dē′ōō). An island of western India in the Arabian Sea northwest of Bombay. A Portuguese possession after 1535, Diu was invaded by India in 1961 and annexed the following year. It is now part of the union territory of Daman and Diu.

di·vide (dĭ-vīd′). A ridge of land; a watershed.

Di·vi·nó·po·lis (dē′vē-nô′pōō-lēs). A city of southeast Brazil west-southwest of Belo Horizonte. It is a railroad junction and an agricultural trade center. ● Pop. 151,382.

Dix·ie (dĭk′sē). A region of the southern and eastern United States, usually comprising the states that joined the Confederacy during the Civil War. The term was popularized in the minstrel song "Dixie's Land," written by Daniel D. Emmett (1815–1904) in 1859.

Dix·on (dĭk′sən). A city of northern Illinois south-southwest of Rockford. Founded in 1830, it is a manufacturing center. ● Pop. 15,144.

Di·yar·ba·kir (dĭ-yär′bə-kîr′, dē-yär′bŭk-ər). A city of southeast Turkey on the Tigris River. It was a Roman colony called Amida from A.D. 230 to 363 and was finally captured by the Ottoman Turks in 1515. ● Pop. 448,300.

Dja·kar·ta (jə-kär′tə). See **Jakarta.**

Dji·bou·ti (jĭ-bōō′tē). **1.** Formerly **A·fars and Is·sas** (ə-färs′; ī′səs). A country of eastern Africa on the Gulf of Aden. The area was acquired by France during the mid-19th century and organized as a French colony, French Somaliland, in 1896. Later it was granted territorial status (1946) and renamed the French Territory of Afars and Issas (1967). The country took the name of its capital city in 1977 when it became independent. ● Pop. 566,000. **2.** The capital and largest city of Djibouti, in the southeast part of the country on an inlet of the Gulf of Aden. It was founded by the French in 1888. ● Pop. 120,000.

Djok·ja·kar·ta (jŏk′yə-kär′tə). See **Jogjakarta.**

Dne·pro·dzer·zhinsk (nĕp′rō-dər-zhĭnsk′, dnyĭ′prə-dzĭr-zhĭnsk′). A city of east-central Ukraine on the Dnieper River south-southwest of Kharkov. It is a port and major industrial center. ⦿Pop. 285,600.

Dne·pro·pe·trovsk (nĕp'rō-pə-trôfsk', dnyĭ'-prə-pyĭ-trôfsk'). A city of east-central Ukraine on the Dnieper River south-southwest of Kharkov. Founded in 1787 on the site of a Cossack village, it has a huge iron and steel industry. ⦿Pop. 1,189,900.

Dnie·per (nē'pər, dnyĕ'pər). A river rising near Smolensk in west-central Russia and flowing about 2,285 km (1,420 mi) southward through Belarus and Ukraine to the Black Sea. It has been a major commercial waterway since the ninth century.

Dnies·ter (nē'stər, dnyĕ'stər). A river rising in western Ukraine and flowing about 1,368 km (850 mi) generally southeast through eastern Moldova then back into Ukraine, where it empties into the Black Sea near Odessa. It formed the Soviet-Romanian border from 1918 to 1940.

Do·dec·a·nese (dō-dĕk'ə-nēz', -nēs'). An island group of southeast Greece in the Aegean Sea between Turkey and Crete. The name means "12 islands," although there are also several islets. The islands were held by Turkey from 1522 until 1912.

Dodge City (dŏj). A city of southwest Kansas on the Arkansas River west of Wichita. Laid out on the Santa Fe Trail in 1872, it soon became a wild and rowdy cow town whose residents included such legendary frontiersmen as Wyatt Earp and Bat Masterson. ⦿Pop. 21,129.

Do·do·ma (dō'də-mä, -dō-). The official capital of Tanzania, in the central part of the country. ⦿Pop. 46,000.

Do·do·na (də-dō'nə). An ancient city of northwest Greece. It was a center of Pelasgian worship dedicated to Zeus, the principal god and ruler of the heavens in Greek mythology.

Dog·ger Bank (dô'gər, dŏg'ər). An extensive sandbank of the central North Sea between Great Britain and Denmark. It is a major breeding ground for fish.

Dog·rib (dôg'rĭb', dŏg'-). **1.** *pl.* **Dogrib** or **-ribs.** A member of a Native American people inhabiting an area between the Great Bear and Great Slave lakes in the Northwest Territories of Canada. **2.** The Athabaskan language of this people.

Do·ha (dō'hə, -hä). The capital of Qatar, on the Persian Gulf. It was a tiny village before oil production began in 1949. ⦿Pop. 217,294.

dol·drums (dōl'drəmz', dôl'-, dŏl'-). **1.** A region of the ocean near the equator, characterized by calms, light winds, or squalls. **2.** The weather conditions characteristic of these regions of the ocean.

Dol·lard des Or·meaux or **Dol·lard-des-Or·meaux** (dō-yär'dā-zôr-mō'). A town of south-

ern Quebec, Canada, a residential suburb of Montreal. ⦿Pop. 39,940.

Do·lo·mite Alps (dō'lə-mīt', dŏl'ə-). A range of the eastern Alps in northeast Italy rising to 3,344.3 m (10,965 ft). The dolomitic limestone peaks of the range are famous for their vivid coloring at sunrise and sunset.

Dol·ton (dōl'tən). A village of northern Illinois south of Chicago. It is a manufacturing center in a truck-farming area. ⦿Pop. 23,930.

Dom·i·ni·ca (dŏm'ə-nē'kə, də-mĭn'ĭ-kə). An island country of the eastern Caribbean between Guadeloupe and Martinique. The largest of the Windward Islands, it was discovered by Christopher Columbus in 1493, became a British colony in the early 1800's, and gained its independence in 1978. Roseau is the capital. ⦿Pop. 71,000. —**Dom'i·ni'can** *adj. & n.*

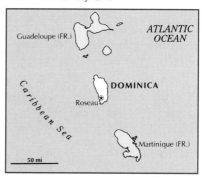

Do·min·i·can (də-mĭn'ĭ-kən). **1.** Of or relating to the Dominican Republic or its people. **2.** A native or inhabitant of the Dominican Republic. **3.** A person of Dominican ancestry.

Dominican Republic. A country of the West Indies on the eastern part of the island of Hispaniola. Originally inhabited by Arawaks, it was discovered by Columbus in 1492 and remained a Spanish colony until 1795, when it was ceded to France. The area was conquered in 1801 by Haitians under the revolutionary leader Toussaint L'Ouverture and was ruled by Haiti after 1821. The country became independent from Haiti in 1844 but has had a turbulent history, including two U.S. military occupations (1916–1924 and 1965–1966) and many years of dictatorship (1930–1961) under Rafael Trujillo Molina. Santo Domingo is the capital and the largest city. ⦿Pop. 7,760,000.

do·min·ion (də-mĭn′yən). *abbr.* **dom. 1.** A territory or sphere of influence or control; a realm. **2.** often **Dominion.** One of the self-governing nations within the Commonwealth of Nations.

Dom·ré·my-la-Pu·celle (dôN-rā-mē-lä-pü-sĕl′). A village of northeast France on the Meuse River east of Troyes. Saint Joan of Arc (1412?–1431) was born here.

Don·bas (dŏn′bäs). See **Donets Basin.**

Don·cas·ter (dŏng′kə-stər). A borough of north-central England northeast of Sheffield. A manufacturing center, it is the site of the famous annual St. Leger horse race. ⊛ Pop. 292,729.

Do·nets (də-nĕts′, dŭ-nyĕts′). A river rising in western Russia and flowing about 1,046 km (650 mi) through eastern Ukraine to join the Don River.

Donets Basin also **Don·bas** (dŏn′bäs). A major industrial region of eastern Ukraine and southeast Russia north of the Sea of Azov and west of the Donets River. Developed after the 1870's, it is one of the densest industrial concentrations in the world.

Do·netsk (də-nĕtsk′, dŭ-nyĕts′). A city of eastern Ukraine east-southeast of Kiev. Founded c. 1870, it is the leading industrial center of the region. ⊛ Pop. 1,121,400.

Don·ner Pass (dŏn′ər). A pass, 2,162.1 m (7,089 ft) high, in the Sierra Nevada of eastern California near Lake Tahoe. It is named after the Donner Party of westward migrants whose survivors supposedly practiced cannibalism after being trapped in a snowstorm near here in October 1846.

Don River (dŏn). A river of western Russia flowing about 1,963 km (1,220 mi) generally south then west into the northeast Sea of Azov. It is linked with the Volga River by a canal near Volgograd.

Doon (do͞on). A river, about 48 km (30 mi) long, of southeast Scotland flowing through **Loch Doon** to the Firth of Clyde south of Ayr. The river is immortalized in the poetry of Robert Burns.

Door Peninsula (dôr). A peninsula of eastern Wisconsin between Green Bay and Lake Michigan. It is a cherry-growing region.

Dor·ches·ter (dôr′chĕs′tər, -chĭ-stər). A municipal borough of southern England west of Poole. An agricultural market, it was the model for Casterbridge in Thomas Hardy's novels. ⊛ Pop. 14,049.

Dor·dogne (dôr-dōn′, -dôn′yə). A river rising in the Auvergne Mountains of south-central France and flowing about 483 km (300 mi) southwest to join the Garonne River north of Bordeaux and form the Gironde estuary.

Dor·drecht (dôr′drĕkt′, -drĕкнt′) also **Dort** (dôrt). A city of southwest Netherlands on the Meuse River southeast of Rotterdam. Founded in the 11th century, it is a railroad junction and river port. ⊛ Pop. 113,041.

Do·ri·an (dôr′ē-ən, dōr′-). One of a Hellenic people that invaded Greece around 1100 B.C. and remained culturally and linguistically distinct within the Greek world. —**Do′ri·an** *adj.*

Dor·ic (dôr′ĭk, dŏr′-). *abbr.* **Dor.** A dialect of ancient Greek spoken in the Peloponnesus, Crete, certain of the Aegean Islands, Sicily, and southern Italy.

Dor·is (dôr′ĭs, dōr′-, dŏr′-). An ancient region of central Greece. It was the traditional homeland of the Dorians.

Dor·ma·gen (dôr′mä-gən, dōr′-). A city of west-central Germany south of Düsseldorf. It is a manufacturing center. ⊛ Pop. 56,985.

Dor·set (dôr′sĭt). A region of southwest England on the English Channel. Part of the Anglo-Saxon kingdom of Wessex, it was used as the setting for many of Thomas Hardy's novels.

Dor·sten (dôr′stən, dōr′-). A city of west-central Germany north of Essen. Founded in the 11th century, it was heavily bombed during World War II. ⊛ Pop. 72,020.

Dort (dôrt). See **Dordrecht.**

Dort·mund (dôrt′mənd, -mo͞ont′). A city of west-central Germany north-northeast of Cologne. First mentioned c. 885, it flourished from the 13th to the 17th century as a member of the Hanseatic League. ⊛ Pop. 601,966.

Dor·val (dôr-väl′). A town of southern Quebec, Canada, a residential suburb of Montreal on the southern shore of Montreal Island. ⊛ Pop. 17,722.

Dos Her·ma·nas (dōs′ hər-mä′nəs, dôs′ ĕr-mä′näs). A city of southwest Spain, an industrial suburb of Seville. ⊛ Pop. 60,563.

Do·than (dō′thən). A city of southeast Alabama near the Florida border. Settled in 1885, it is a trading center for a large agricultural area. ⊛ Pop. 53,589.

Dou·ai (do͞o-ā′). Formerly **Dou·ay** (do͞o-ā′). A town of northern France northeast of Amiens. Under the patronage of Philip II of Spain a Roman Catholic college for English priests was established here and produced the first English translation of the Old Testament in the early 1600's. ⊛ Pop. 42,576.

Dou·a·la also **Du·a·la** (do͞o-ä′lä). The largest city of Cameroon, in the southwest part of the country on the Bight of Biafra. It is the country's chief port. ⊛ Pop. 1,029,731.

Dou·ay (do͞o-ā′). See **Douai.**

Doubs (do͞o). A river rising in the Jura Mountains of eastern France and flowing about 434 km (270 mi) northeast to and along the French-Swiss border, into Switzerland, then back into France, where it meanders in a generally southwest course to the Saône River.

Doug·las (dŭg′ləs). A municipal borough of southeast Isle of Man, England, on the Irish Sea. It is a popular seaside resort and the most important city on the island. ◉ Pop. 20,368.

Dou·ro (dôr′ oō, dō′ roō) also **Due·ro** (dwĕr′ ō). A river rising in north-central Spain and flowing about 772 km (480 mi) westward then southwestward along the Spanish-Portuguese border. It enters the Atlantic Ocean at Oporto.

Do·ver (dō′ vər). **1.** A municipal borough of southeast England on the Strait of Dover opposite Calais, France. Site of a Roman lighthouse, it has been a strategic port since medieval times. The chalk cliffs rising above the city have caves and tunnels originally used by smugglers. ◉ Pop. 33,700. **2.** The capital of Delaware, in the central part of the state. Founded in 1683 on orders from the English Quaker colonizer William Penn, it became capital in 1777. ◉ Pop. 27,630. **3.** A city of southeast New Hampshire northwest of Portsmouth. It was the first permanent settlement in New Hampshire (c. 1623). ◉ Pop. 25,042.

Dover, Strait of. A narrow channel at the eastern end of the English Channel between southeast England and northern France.

Down East also **down East** (doun ēst′). New England, especially Maine. —**Down East′er, down-East′er** (doun-ē′stər) n. —**Down East′ern** adj.

Dow·ners Grove (dou′nərz). A village of northeast Illinois, a manufacturing suburb of Chicago. ◉ Pop. 46,858.

Dow·ney (dou′nē). A city of southern California, a residential and industrial suburb of Los Angeles. ◉ Pop. 91,444.

Down·ing Street (dou′nĭng). A thoroughfare of Westminster in London, England, off Whitehall. No. 10 Downing Street is the official residence of the first lord of the Treasury, who is usually but not necessarily the prime minister of Great Britain. Nearly all prime ministers have lived at No. 10 since the time of Robert Walpole, regarded as Britain's first prime minister, in the early 1700's.

Downs (dounz). Two roughly parallel ranges of chalk hills in southeast England. The **North Downs** extend about 161 km (100 mi) from west to east; the **South Downs,** about 105 km (65 mi). Both are sheep-rearing areas.

down under. Informal. To or in Australia or New Zealand.

Dra·cut (drā′kət). A town of northeast Massachusetts on the Merrimack River near the New Hampshire border. It was settled in 1664. ◉ Pop. 25,594.

drain·age basin (drā′nĭj). An area drained by a river system.

Dra·kens·burg Mountains (drä′kənz-bûrg′). A range of eastern South Africa, Lesotho, and Swaziland rising to 3,484.6 m (11,425 ft).

Drake Passage (drāk). A strait between Cape Horn and Antarctica connecting the southern Atlantic and Pacific oceans. It is named after the English navigator Sir Francis Drake, whose ships were blown southward into its waters after passing through the Strait of Magellan in 1578.

Dram·men (drä′mən). A city of southeast Norway southwest of Oslo. It is a commercial and fishing port with varied industries. ◉ Pop. 50,605.

Dran·cy (dräɴ-sē′). A city of north-central France, an industrial suburb of Paris. ◉ Pop. 60,183.

Dra·va or **Dra·ve** (drä′və) also **Drau** (drou). A river rising in the Carnic Alps of southern Austria and flowing about 724 km (450 mi) eastward through northeast Slovenia and northern Croatia to the Danube River.

Dra·vid·i·an (drə-vĭd′ē-ən). **1.** A large family of languages spoken especially in southern India and northern Sri Lanka that includes Tamil, Telugu, Malayalam, and Kannada. **2.** A member of any of the peoples that speak one of the Dravidian languages, especially a member of one of the pre-Indo-European peoples of southern India. —**Dra·vid′i·an, Dra·vid′ic** (-vĭd′ĭk) adj.

draw (drô). A small natural depression that water drains into; a shallow gully.

Dray·ton Plains (drāt′n). A community of southeast Michigan, a suburb of Pontiac. ◉ Pop. 18,000.

Dres·den (drĕz′dən). A city of east-central Germany on the Elbe River east-southeast of Leipzig. An industrial and cultural center, it was severely damaged in bombing raids during World War II. Its china industry was moved to Meissen in the early 18th century. ◉ Pop. 479,273.

Drex·el Hill (drĕk′səl). A community of southeast Pennsylvania, a residential suburb of Philadelphia. ◉ Pop. 29,744.

Drin (drēn). A river, about 282 km (175 mi) long, of Albania flowing north and west to the Adriatic Sea.

Dri·na (drē′nə, -nä). A river, about 459 km (285 mi) long, rising in eastern Bosnia and Herzegovina and flowing generally north to the Sava River.

Dro·ghe·da (drô′ĭ-də, drŏ′hĭ-). A municipal borough of eastern Ireland on the Boyne River. Oliver Cromwell, the English leader of the Parliamentarian victory in the English Civil War, stormed the town in 1649 and massacred its royalist inhabitants. ◉ Pop. 23,247.

drum·lin (drŭm′lĭn). An elongated hill or ridge of glacial drift.

Drum·mond·ville (drŭm′ənd-vĭl′). A city of southern Quebec, Canada, northeast of Montreal. It is an industrial center. ◉ Pop. 27,374.

Dry Tor·tu·gas (drī tôr-tōō′gəz). An island group of southern Florida west of Key West. Famed for their marine life, the islands were named *Tortugas* ("turtles") by the Spanish explorer Juan Ponce de León in 1513.

Du·a·la (dōō-ä′lä). See **Douala**.

Duar·te (dwär′tē). A city of southern California east of Pasadena. It is mainly residential with varied light industries. ◉ Pop. 20,688.

Du·bai (dōō-bī′). A city and sheikdom of eastern United Arab Emirates on the Persian Gulf. Oil was discovered here in the 1960's. ◉ Pop. 265,702.

Du·bawnt (dōō-bônt′). A river, about 933 km (580 mi) long, of southeast Northwest Territories, Canada, flowing through **Dubawnt Lake** and into Baker Lake.

Dub·lin (dŭb′lĭn). **1.** The capital and largest city of Ireland, in the east-central part of the country on the Irish Sea. A Danish stronghold until 1014, Dublin was later captured by the English (1170) and made the center of the Pale. It was the scene of the Black Monday massacre of English residents in 1209 and of much bloodshed connected with the movement to secure Irish independence from Britain in the 19th and early 20th centuries, including the bloody Easter Rebellion of April 24, 1916. The city also became the center of a Gaelic renaissance and was the birthplace of the Irish cultural and political movement Sinn Fein in the early 20th century. ◉ Pop. 533,929. **2.** An unincorporated town of western California, a residential suburb in the San Francisco–Oakland area. ◉ Pop. 23,229. **3.** A city of central Georgia east-southeast of Macon. It is a commercial center in a lumbering area. ◉ Pop. 16,312. — **Dub′lin·er** *n.*

Du·brov·nik (dōō′brôv-nĭk′). Formerly **Ra·gu·sa** (rə-gōō′zə, rä-gōō′zä). A city of extreme southern Croatia on a promontory jutting into the Adriatic Sea. A popular tourist resort, it was a center of Serbo-Croatian culture and literature in medieval times. ◉ Pop. 31,106.

Du·buque (də-byōōk′). A city of eastern Iowa on the Mississippi River opposite the Illinois-Wisconsin border. It was first settled permanently in 1833 and is the oldest city in the state. ◉ Pop. 57,546.

Dud·ley (dŭd′lē). A borough of west-central England west-northwest of Birmingham. It had thriving iron, coal, and limestone industries until the 1870's. ◉ Pop. 311,478.

Due·ro (dwĕr′ō). See **Douro**.

Duis·burg (dōōs′bûrg′, dōōz′-, düs′bŏork′). A city of west-central Germany at the confluence of the Rhine and Ruhr rivers. It is a major inland port and a steel-producing center. ◉ Pop. 536,797.

Du·luth (də-lōōth′). A city of northeast Minnesota on Lake Superior opposite Superior, Wisconsin. Permanent settlement began here in the 1850's. The city's fine harbor accommodates oceangoing vessels. ◉ Pop. 85,493.

Dum·fries (dŭm-frēs′). A burgh of southern Scotland south-southwest of Edinburgh. The poet Robert Burns (1759–1796) is buried here. ◉ Pop. 31,800.

Du·mont (dōō′mŏnt′, dyōō′-). A borough of northeast New Jersey, a residential suburb of Hackensack. It was settled by the Dutch in 1677. ◉ Pop. 17,187.

Dum·yat (dōōm-yät′). See **Damietta**.

Dun·bar (dŭn-bär′). A burgh of southeast Scotland on the North Sea east of Edinburgh. Oliver Cromwell, the English leader of the Parliamentarian victory in the English Civil War, defeated the Covenanters, a group of Scottish Presbyterians, here on September 3, 1650. ◉ Pop. 4,609.

Dun·can (dŭng′kən). A city of southern Oklahoma south-southwest of Oklahoma City. It is the center of an oil-producing region. ◉ Pop. 21,732.

Dun·can·ville (dŭng′kən-vĭl′). A city of northeast Texas, a residential suburb of Dallas. ◉ Pop. 35,748.

Dun·dalk (dŭn′dôk). An unincorporated community of northeast Maryland, a residential and industrial suburb of Baltimore. ◉ Pop. 71,293.

Dun·das (dŭn′dəs). A town of southeast Ontario, Canada, a manufacturing suburb of Hamilton. ◉ Pop. 19,586.

Dun·dee (dŭn-dē′). A burgh of east-central Scotland on the northern bank of the Firth of Tay. In the 17th century it was a stronghold of the Covenanters, a group of Scottish Presbyterians, in the religious wars of the Scottish Reformation. ◉ Pop. 170,120.

dune (dōōn, dyōōn). A hill or ridge of wind-blown sand.

Dun·e·din (dŭn-ēd′n). **1.** A city of southeast South Island, New Zealand. A major port, it was settled by Scottish Presbyterians in 1848. ◉ Pop. 117,100. **2.** A city of west-central Florida on the Gulf of Mexico west of Tampa. It is a popular winter resort. ◉ Pop. 34,012.

Dun·ferm·line (dŭn-fûrm′lĭn). A burgh of east-central Scotland northwest of Edinburgh. It was long a favorite residence of Scottish kings. The American industrialist Andrew Carnegie was born here (1835) and gave the town its library. ◉ Pop. 53,800.

Dun·kirk (dŭn′kûrk′). **1.** also **Dun·kerque** (dœN-kěrk′). A city of northern France on the North Sea. In World War II more than 330,000 Allied troops were evacuated from its beaches in the face of enemy fire (May–June 1940). ◉ Pop. 73,120. **2.** A city of western New York on Lake Erie southwest of Buffalo. It is in a grape-growing region. ◉ Pop. 15,310.

Dun Laoghai·re (dŭn lâr′ə). A borough of east-central Ireland on the Irish Sea southeast of Dublin. It is a resort and a yachting and fishing center. ◉ Pop. 54,496.

Dun·more (dŭn′môr′, -mōr′). A borough of northeast Pennsylvania, an industrial suburb of Scranton. ◉ Pop. 15,403.

Du·que de Ca·xi·as (dōō′kē də kə-shē′əs, dōō′kǐ dǐ kä-shē′äs). A city of southeast Brazil, a commercial and residential suburb of Rio de Janeiro on Guanabara Bay. ◉ Pop. 665,343.

Du·ran·go (dōō-răng′gō). A city of north-central Mexico north-northwest of Guadalajara. Founded as a mining town c. 1560, it was an important political and religious center during the early history of northern Mexico. ◉ Pop. 257,915.

Dur·ban (dûr′bən). A city of eastern South Africa on **Durban Bay**, an inlet of the Indian Ocean. First visited by the Portuguese navigator Vasco da Gama in 1497, the site was settled after the arrival of the British in 1824. Durban is a major seaport and year-round resort. ◉ Pop. 715,669.

Dü·ren (dōōr′ən, dür′-). A city of west-central Germany southwest of Cologne. It was a center of the Frankish Carolingian culture, which lasted from the 8th through the 10th century. ◉ Pop. 84,631.

Dur·ga·pur (dōōr′gə-pōōr′, -gä-). A city of northeast India northwest of Calcutta. Its steel plant, completed in 1962, was built with British aid. ◉ Pop. 425,836.

Dur·ham (dûr′əm). A city of north-central North Carolina east of Greensboro. Settled c. 1750, it is the seat of Duke University (founded 1838). ◉ Pop. 136,611.

Dur·rës (dōōr′əs). A city of western Albania on the Adriatic Sea. Founded as a Greek colony c. 625 B.C., it is the country's chief seaport. ◉ Pop. 72,400.

Du·shan·be (dōō-shăm′bə, -shäm′-, -shŭn-byĕ′). The capital of Tajikistan, in the western part of the country south of Tashkent, Uzbekistan. It is a major industrial and commercial center in a rich agricultural area. ◉ Pop. 602,000.

Düs·sel·dorf (dōōs′əl-dôrf′, düs′-). A city of west-central Germany on the Rhine River north-northwest of Cologne. Chartered in 1288,

it has been a leading industrial center since the 1870's. The poet Heinrich Heine was born here in 1797. ◉ Pop. 514,936.

dust bowl (dŭst). A region reduced to aridity by drought and dust storms.

Dutch (dŭch). *abbr.* **D., Du. 1. a.** Of or relating to the Netherlands or its people or culture. **b.** Of or relating to the Dutch language. **2.** *Archaic.* **a.** German. **b.** Of or relating to any of the Germanic peoples or languages. **3.** Of or relating to the Pennsylvania Dutch. **4. a.** The people of the Netherlands. **b.** *Archaic.* A Germanic people. **c.** The Pennsylvania Dutch. **5. a.** The official West Germanic language of the Netherlands. **b.** *Archaic.* One or more of the West Germanic languages of Germany, Switzerland, and the Low Countries. **c.** See **Pennsylvania Dutch** (sense 2).

Dutch East Indies. See **Indonesia.**

Dutch Guiana. See **Suriname.**

Dutch·man (dŭch′mən). **1. a.** A man who is a native or inhabitant of the Netherlands. **b.** A man of Dutch ancestry. **2. a.** *Archaic.* A member of any of the Germanic peoples of central or northern Europe. **b.** *Regional.* A person of German ancestry.

Dutch West Indies. See **Netherlands Antilles.**

Dutch·wom·an (dŭch′wŏŏm′ən). **1.** A woman who is a native or inhabitant of the Netherlands. **2.** A woman of Dutch ancestry.

Dvi·na (dvē-nä′). **1.** also **Northern Dvina.** A river, about 748 km (465 mi) long, of northwest Russia flowing north and northeast into **Dvina Bay**, an arm of the White Sea. **2.** also **Western Dvina.** A river, about 1,022 km (635 mi) long, rising in west-central Russia and flowing southwest and west through Belarus and Latvia to the Gulf of Riga.

Dy·ak (dī′ăk′). Variant of **Dayak.**

Dy·ers·burg (dī′ərz-bûrg′). A city of northwest Tennessee north-northeast of Memphis. It is a manufacturing and processing center. ◉ Pop. 16,317.

Dzer·zhinsk (dər-zhǐnsk′, dzǐr-). A city of west-central Russia on the Oka River west of Kazan. It is a chemical and industrial center. ◉ Pop. 286,479.

Dzham·bul (jäm-bōōl′). A city of south-central Kazakstan near the border of Kyrgyzstan. Founded in the seventh century, it was ruled by Turks in the eighth and ninth centuries and passed to Russia in 1864. ◉ Pop. 317,000.

Dzun·gar·i·a (dzōōng-gâr′ē-ə, zōōng-). A vast historical region of northwest China. It was a Mongol kingdom from the 11th to the 14th century and was conquered by the Chinese in the 1750's.

E

Ea·gan (ē'gən). A city of eastern Minnesota, a suburb of Minneapolis–St. Paul on the Minnesota River. ◉ Pop. 47,409.

Ea·gle Pass (ē'gəl). A city of southwest Texas on the Rio Grande west-southwest of San Antonio. It was a way station on the route to California during the gold rush of 1848–1849. ◉ Pop. 20,651.

east (ēst). *abbr.* **E, E., e, e. 1. a.** The cardinal point on the mariner's compass 90° clockwise from due north and directly opposite west. **b.** The direction of the earth's axial rotation. **2.** An area or a region lying in the east. **3.** often **East. a.** The eastern part of the earth, especially eastern Asia. **b.** The eastern part of a region or country. **4.** often **East. a.** The region of the United States east of the Allegheny Mountains and north of the Mason-Dixon Line. **b.** The former Communist bloc of countries in Asia and especially in Eastern Europe. **5.** To, toward, or in the east. **6.** Originating in or coming from the east. **— east′ern, East′ern** *adj.*

East Anglia. A region and Anglo-Saxon kingdom of eastern England. Settled by Angles in the late fifth century A.D., it was a powerful kingdom by the late sixth century but became a dependency of Mercia for long periods after 650. The Danes controlled the region from 886 to 917, after which it became an English earldom.

East Asia. A region of Asia coextensive with the Far East. **— East Asian** *adj. & n.*

East Berlin. See **Berlin. — East Berliner** *n.*

East Beskids. See **Beskids.**

East·bourne (ēst'bôrn', -bōrn'). A borough of southeast England on the English Channel south-southeast of London. It is a popular resort. ◉ Pop. 77,300.

East Brunswick. A community of central New Jersey south of New Brunswick. It is mainly residential. ◉ Pop. 43,548.

east by north. *abbr.* **EbN. 1.** The direction or point on the mariner's compass halfway between due east and east-northeast, or 78°45′ east of due north. **2.** Toward or from east by north.

east by south. *abbr.* **EbS. 1.** The direction or point on the mariner's compass halfway between due east and east-southeast, or 101°15′ east of due north. **2.** Toward or from east by south.

East Cape. See Cape **Dezhnev.**

East·ches·ter (ēst'chĕs'tər). A community of southeast New York, a residential suburb of New York City. ◉ Pop. 18,537.

East Chicago. A city of northwest Indiana on Lake Michigan in the Calumet region south-southeast of Chicago, Illinois. It is an industrial center. ◉ Pop. 33,892.

East China Sea. An arm of the western Pacific Ocean bounded by China, South Korea, Taiwan, and the Ryukyu and Kyushu islands. It has rich fishing grounds.

East Cleveland. A city of northeast Ohio, a residential suburb of Cleveland. ◉ Pop. 33,096.

East Coast. A region of the eastern United States along the Atlantic coast, especially the urban corridor from Boston to Washington, D.C.

East Detroit. A city of southeast Michigan, a residential suburb of Detroit. ◉ Pop. 35,283.

East End. A section of eastern London north of the Thames River. It was long a densely populated working-class and immigrant area centered around the docks and warehouses, although most of the Victorian-built slums described by British writers Charles Dickens and Henry Mayhew were obliterated by bombing raids during World War II.

Eas·ter Island (ē'stər). Known locally as **Ra·pa Nu·i** (rä'pə nōō'ē). An island of Chile (since 1888) in the southern Pacific Ocean about 3,701 km (2,300 mi) west of the mainland. Inhabited by Polynesians since the fifth century A.D. and discovered by Dutch explorers on Easter Day, 1722, the island is famous for its hieroglyphic tablets and colossal heads carved from volcanic rock. The ancient remains have inspired many legends and theories, though it is now generally accepted that they were produced by the Polynesian inhabitants during a period from roughly 1000 to 1600.

Eastern Empire. The Byzantine Empire.

Eastern Europe. The countries of eastern Europe, especially those that were allied with the U.S.S.R. in the Warsaw Pact, which was established in 1955 and dissolved in 1991.

Eastern Ghats. See **Ghats.**

Eastern Hemisphere. The half of the earth comprising Europe, Africa, Asia, and Australia.

Eastern Highlands. See **Great Dividing Range.**

Eastern Shore. A region of Maryland and Virginia east of Chesapeake Bay.

Eastern Shoshone. See **Shoshone** (sense 1c).

Eastern Sioux. See **Santee.**

Eastern Standard Time. *abbr.* **EST, E.S.T.** Standard time in the fifth time zone west of Greenwich, England, reckoned at 75° west and used, for example, in the eastern part of North America. Also called *Eastern Time.*

East Frisian Islands. See **Frisian Islands.**

East Germanic. The subdivision of the Germanic languages that includes Gothic.

East Germany. Officially **German Democratic Republic.** A former country of northern Europe on the Baltic Sea. It was formed in 1949 from the zone of Germany occupied by Soviet troops after World War II. It was reunified with West Germany in 1990. — **East German** *adj. & n.*

East·hamp·ton (ēst-hămp'tən). A town of west-central Massachusetts north-northwest of Springfield. It was settled in 1664. ⊛ Pop. 15,537.

East Hartford. A town of north-central Connecticut on the Connecticut River opposite Hartford. It was settled c. 1640. ⊛ Pop. 50,452.

East Ha·ven (hā'vən). A town of southern Connecticut on Long Island Sound east of New Haven. It is a residential community and summer resort. ⊛ Pop. 26,144.

East Indies. Indonesia. The term is sometimes used to refer to all of Southeast Asia. Historically, it referred chiefly to India. — **East Indian** *adj. & n.*

East Kil·bride (kĭl-brīd'). A town of south-central Scotland southeast of Glasgow. It was established in 1946 as a new town to absorb the growing population of Glasgow. ⊛ Pop. 70,600.

East·lake (ēst'lāk'). A city of northeast Ohio, a residential suburb of Cleveland on Lake Erie. ⊛ Pop. 21,161.

East Lansing. A city of south-central Michigan, a residential suburb of Lansing. It is the seat of Michigan State University (founded 1855). ⊛ Pop. 50,677.

East·leigh (ēst'lē). A municipal borough of southern England north-northeast of Southampton. Its industries include railroad shops. ⊛ Pop. 109,576.

East Liverpool. A city of eastern Ohio on the West Virginia border south of Youngstown. It has been a ceramics center since the 1830's. ⊛ Pop. 13,654.

East Los Angeles. An unincorporated community of southern California, a residential suburb of Los Angeles. ⊛ Pop. 126,379.

East·main (ēst'mān'). A river rising in central Quebec, Canada, and flowing about 821 km (510 mi) eastward to James Bay.

East Meadow. An unincorporated community of southeast New York on west-central Long Island southeast of Mineola. It is mainly residential. ⊛ Pop. 36,909.

East Moline. A city of northwest Illinois, a residential and industrial suburb of Moline on the Mississippi River. ⊛ Pop. 20,147.

east-north·east (ēst'nôrth'ēst'). *abbr.* **ENE.**
1. The direction or point on the mariner's compass halfway between due east and northeast, or 67°30' east of due north. **2.** To, toward, of, facing, or in the east-northeast.

East North·port (nôrth'pôrt', -pōrt'). An unincorporated community of southeast New York on north-central Long Island east of Huntington. It is mainly residential. ⊛ Pop. 20,411.

East·on (ē'stən). **1.** A town of southeast Massachusetts southwest of Brockton. It was settled in 1694. ⊛ Pop. 19,807. **2.** A city of eastern Pennsylvania north of Philadelphia. Founded in 1751, it was formerly a coal-receiving port. ⊛ Pop. 26,276.

East Orange. A city of northeast New Jersey, a residential suburb of Newark. ⊛ Pop. 73,552.

East Pakistan. A former region of southern Asia on the Bay of Bengal. Originally part of Bengal, it was held by the British from c. 1775 and then by Pakistan from 1947 to 1971, when it achieved independence as Bangladesh.

East Palo Alto. A community of western California on San Francisco Bay southeast of San Mateo. It is mainly residential. ⊛ Pop. 18,191.

East Peoria. A city of north-central Illinois, a manufacturing suburb of Peoria on the Illinois River. ⊛ Pop. 21,378.

East Point. A city of northwest Georgia, an industrial suburb of Atlanta. ⊛ Pop. 34,402.

East Providence. A city of eastern Rhode Island, an industrial suburb of Providence. ⊛ Pop. 50,380.

East Prussia. A historical region and former province of Prussia on the Baltic Sea in present-day Poland and Russia. Between World War I and World War II it was separated from Germany by the Polish Corridor and the Free City of Danzig (Gdańsk). After World War II the area was divided between Poland and the U.S.S.R.

East Ridge. A city of southeast Tennessee, a suburb of Chattanooga on the Georgia border. ⊛ Pop. 21,101.

East River. A narrow tidal strait connecting Upper New York Bay with Long Island Sound and separating the boroughs of Manhattan and the Bronx from Brooklyn and Queens.

East Saint Louis. A city of southwest Illinois on the Mississippi River opposite St. Louis, Missouri. It is a railroad center with varied industries. ⊛ Pop. 40,944.

East Siberian Sea. An arm of the Arctic Ocean extending from Wrangel Island to the New Siberian Islands.

East Side. A section of New York City on Manhattan Island east of Fifth Avenue. The northern part, approximately between 57th Street and 96th Street, is also known as the **Upper East Side** and includes many fashionable shops and residences. The **Lower East Side,** south of 14th Street, was long a home to immigrants from eastern Europe.

east-south·east (ēst'south'ēst'). *abbr.* **ESE.**

1. The direction or point on the mariner's compass halfway between due east and southeast, or 112°30′ east of due north. **2.** To, toward, of, facing, or in the east-southeast.

Eau Claire (ō klâr′). A city of west-central Wisconsin at the mouth of the **Eau Clair River,** about 113 km (70 mi) long. Founded in the 1840's, the city grew as the center of a lumbering region. ⊛ Pop. 56,856.

E·bers·wal·de (ā′bərz-väl′də). A city of northeast Germany northeast of Berlin. It was chartered in 1257. ⊛ Pop. 53,473.

Eb·la (ĕb′lə, ē′blə). An ancient city of southwest Asia near the site of present-day Aleppo, Syria. The cuneiform Ebla Tablets, discovered from 1974 to 1975, describe a thriving third-millennium B.C. civilization centered around the city.

Eb·la·ite (ĕb′lə-īt′, ē′blə-). The Semitic language of ancient Ebla.

Eb·ro (ē′brō, ĕb′rō, ĕ′vrô). A river rising in the Cantabrian Mountains of northern Spain and flowing about 925 km (575 mi) to the Mediterranean Sea southwest of Barcelona.

E·ca·te·pec de Mo·re·los (ā-kä′tə-pĕk′ də mô-rĕl′əs, ĕ-kä′tä-pĕk′ dĕ mô-rĕl′ôs). A city of central Mexico near Mexico City. An industrial center, it occupies the site of an Aztec kingdom established in the 12th century. ⊛ Pop. 741,821.

Ec·ba·ta·na (ĕk-băt′n-ə). A city of ancient Media on the site of present-day Hamadan in western Iran. It was captured by Cyrus the Great, king of Persia, in 549 B.C. and by Alexander the Great, king of Macedonia, in 330 B.C.

Ec·ua·dor (ĕk′wə-dôr′). *abbr.* **Ec., Ecua.** A country of northwest South America on the Pacific Ocean. Once a part of the Incan Empire, it was conquered by the Spanish in 1534 and later became subject to Peru and New Granada. The area achieved independence from Spain in 1822 and joined Venezuela, Panama, and Colombia to form Greater Colombia until 1830, when that

union collapsed and Ecuador became a separate country. The 19th and 20th centuries were marked by border disputes with Colombia and Peru, many changes of government as a result of political infighting between the Conservative and Liberal factions, and periods of military rule. Ecuador adopted a new constitution in 1979. Quito is the capital and Guayaquil the largest city. ⊛ Pop. 11,221,000. — **Ec′ua·dor′i·an** *adj. & n.*

E·dam (ē′dəm, ē′dăm′, ā-däm′). A town of western Netherlands on the Ijsselmeer. Chartered in 1357, it has a famous cheese market. ⊛ Pop. 24,019.

Ed·dy·stone Rocks (ĕd′ĭ-stən). A rocky islet of southwest England in the English Channel south of Plymouth. It has been the site of a strategic lighthouse since the 1690's.

E·de. 1. (ā′də). A city of central Netherlands northwest of Arnhem. It is an industrialized commune. ⊛ Pop. 71,952. **2.** (ā′dā, ā-dā′). A city of western Nigeria northeast of Ibadan. A center of Yoruba culture, it is in a cocoa-growing region. ⊛ Pop. 216,400.

E·den (ēd′n). A city of northern North Carolina near the Virginia border north of Greensboro. It is a processing and shipping center in an agricultural area. ⊛ Pop. 15,238.

Eden Prairie. A city of eastern Minnesota, a suburb of Minneapolis. ⊛ Pop. 39,311.

E·der (ā′dər). A river rising in central Germany and flowing about 177 km (110 mi) generally eastward to the Fulda River.

E·des·sa (ĭ-dĕs′ə). An ancient city of Mesopotamia on the site of present-day Urfa in southeast Turkey. A major Christian center after the third century A.D., it fell to the Arabs in 639 and was captured by Crusaders in 1097.

Edge·wood (ĕj′wŏod′). A community of northeast Maryland on an inlet of Chesapeake Bay northeast of Baltimore. A U.S. Army arsenal is nearby. ⊛ Pop. 23,903.

E·di·na (ĭ-dī′nə). A city of eastern Minnesota, a residential suburb of Minneapolis. ⊛ Pop. 46,070.

Ed·in·burg (ĕd′n-bûrg′). A city of southern Texas near the Mexican border west-northwest of Brownsville. It is a processing center in an agricultural region. ⊛ Pop. 29,885.

Ed·in·burgh (ĕd′n-bûr′ə, -bŭr′ə, -brə). The capital of Scotland, in the eastern part of the country on the Firth of Forth. The city grew up around a castle built in the 11th century by King Malcolm III, successor to Macbeth, and it became the capital of Scotland in 1437. Edinburgh lost much of its political importance after the accession of James VI to the throne of England in 1603 and the Act of Union with England in 1707, but it later became an important literary and cultural center. The city is the site of an annual international festival of the arts. ◉Pop. 441,620.

E·dir·ne (ĕ-dîr′nĕ). Formerly **A·dri·a·no·ple** (ā′-drē-ə-nō′pəl). A city of northwest Turkey northwest of Istanbul. It was founded c. A.D. 125 by the Roman emperor Hadrian on the site of an earlier Thracian town and was conquered at various times by Visigoths, Bulgarians, Crusaders, Turks, and Russians. Held by Greece after 1920, it was restored to Turkey in 1923. ◉Pop. 71,914.

Ed·i·son (ĕd′ĭ-sən). A community of central New Jersey northeast of New Brunswick. It is mainly residential. ◉Pop. 88,680.

Ed·is·to (ĕd′ĭ-stō′). A river, about 241 km (150 mi) long, of southern South Carolina flowing southeast to the Atlantic Ocean.

E·dith Ca·vell (ē′dĭth kăv′əl, kə-vĕl′), **Mount.** A peak, 3,365.1 m (11,033 ft) high, in the Rocky Mountains of southwest Alberta, Canada.

Ed·mond (ĕd′mənd). A city of central Oklahoma north of Oklahoma City. It is a trade center in an oil-producing area. ◉Pop. 52,315.

Ed·monds (ĕd′məndz). A city of northwest Washington on Puget Sound north of Seattle. It was settled in 1866. ◉Pop. 30,744.

Ed·mon·ton (ĕd′mən-tən). The capital and largest city of Alberta, Canada, in the central part of the province north of Calgary. It was founded in 1795 as a fort and trading post of the Hudson's Bay Company. ◉Pop. 616,741.

E·do (ĕd′ō). See **Tokyo.**

E·dom (ē′dəm). An ancient country of Palestine between the Dead Sea and the Gulf of Aqaba. According to the Bible, the original inhabitants were descendants of Esau, the eldest son of Isaac and Rebecca.

E·dom·ite (ē′də-mīt′). A member of a Semitic people inhabiting Edom in ancient times. — **E′-dom·it′ish** *adj.*

Ed·ward, (ĕd′wərd), **Lake.** A lake in the Great Rift Valley of central Africa on the Zaire-Uganda border. It was discovered by the British journalist and explorer Henry M. Stanley in 1889.

E·fa·te (ā-fä′tē, ĕ-fä′tĕ). A volcanic island of central Vanuatu in the New Hebrides. Vila, the capital of Vanuatu, is on the island.

ef·flu·ent (ĕf′lōō-ənt). A stream flowing out of a body of water.

Ef·ik (ĕf′ĭk). **1.** *pl.* **Efik** or **-iks.** A member of a people inhabiting southern Nigeria. **2.** The Niger-Congo language of the Efik people, closely related to Ibibio. — **Ef′ik** *adj.*

Eg·a·di Islands (ĕg′ə-dē) also **Ae·ga·de·an Isles** (ē-gā′dē-ən) or **Ae·ga·tes** (-tēz). An island group of southwest Italy in the Mediterranean Sea west of Sicily. A Roman naval victory over

the Carthaginians, achieved in a battle fought in the waters off the islands in 241 B.C., ended the First Punic War.

E·ger (ā′gər). A city of northeast Hungary on the **Eger River,** about 311 km (193 mi) long. The city was occupied by the Turks from 1596 to 1687. ◉Pop. 64,702.

E·gypt (ē′jĭpt). Formerly (1958–1961) **United Arab Republic.** A country of northeast Africa on the Mediterranean Sea. One of the earliest known civilizations, ancient Egypt is known for its hieroglyphic writing and its achievements in agriculture, art, and architecture, including the Great Pyramids at Giza. It reached its height during the XVIII dynasty (1570–1342? B.C.) and declined after the seventh century B.C., falling to the Assyrians, Greeks, Romans, and (A.D. 639) the Arabs, under whom Egypt became an Islamic, Arabic-speaking country. Later domination by the Ottoman Turks and by French and British forces kept it weak, and Egypt, though nominally independent after 1922, remained a British protectorate until 1936. A military coup in 1952 overthrew King Farouk I's constitutional monarchy and brought to power Colonel Gamal Abdel Nasser, who nationalized the Suez Canal (1956) and formed the short-lived United Arab Republic (1958–1961) with Syria. Clashes with Israel, notably in 1956–1957 and 1967, led to the loss of the Sinai Peninsula and the Gaza Strip. Nasser was succeeded (1970) by Anwar el-Sadat, who signed a peace treaty with Israel (1979) resulting in Egypt's temporary suspension from the Arab League. Control of the Sinai was returned to Egypt by 1982. Cairo is the capital and the largest city. ◉Pop. 48,503,000.

E·gyp·tian (ĭ-jĭp′shən). **1.** A native or inhabitant of Egypt. **2.** The now extinct Afro-Asiatic language of the ancient Egyptians. **3.** Of or relating to Egypt or its people or culture. **4.** Of or relating to the language spoken by the ancient Egyptians.

Ei·fel (ī′fəl). A hilly region of western Germany west of the Rhine River. The barren area has limestone moors and crater lakes.

Eind·ho·ven (īnt′hō′vən). A city of southern Netherlands southeast of Rotterdam. Chartered in 1232, it was a major Allied objective in World War II. ⊛ Pop. 195,632.

Eir·e (âr′ə, ī′rə, âr′ē, ī′rē). See **Ireland**².

Ei·sen·ach (ī′zən-äk′, -äкн′). A city of central Germany west of Erfurt. Johann Sebastian Bach was born in Eisenach in 1685, and Martin Luther studied here from 1498 to 1501. ⊛ Pop. 50,895.

El Al·a·mein (ĕl ăl′ə-mān′, ä′lə-) also **Al Al·a·mayn** (ăl ăl′ə-mān′, ä′lə-). A town of northern Egypt on the Mediterranean Sea. In a decisive battle of World War II the British forces under Bernard Montgomery defeated Erwin Rommel's German troops here in November 1942.

E·lam (ē′ləm) also **Su·si·a·na** (sōō′zē-ä′nə, -ăn′-ə). An ancient country of southwest Asia in present-day southwest Iran. It was established east of the Tigris River before 3000 B.C. and was known for its warlike people, traditionally thought to be descended from Noah's son Shem.

E·la·mite (ē′lə-mīt′). **1.** A native or inhabitant of Elam. **2.** The language of the ancient Elamites, of no known linguistic affiliation.

El·ba (ĕl′bə). An island of Italy in the Tyrrhenian Sea between Corsica and the mainland. Napoleon Bonaparte spent his first period of exile here (May 1814–February 1815) after he was deposed as emperor of France.

El·be (ĕl′bə, ĕlb). A river of Czech Republic and Germany flowing about 1,167 km (725 mi) to the North Sea. It has been a major waterway since Roman times.

El·bert (ĕl′bərt), **Mount**. A peak, 4,402.1 m (14,433 ft) high, in the Sawatch Range of central Colorado. It is the highest elevation in the range and also the highest of the U.S. Rocky Mountains outside Alaska.

El·bląg (ĕl′blông′, -blôngk′). A city of northern Poland east-southeast of Gdańsk. It was founded by the Teutonic Knights in 1237 and passed through various hands before becoming part of Poland after World War II. ⊛ Pop. 126,546.

El·brus (ĕl-brōōs′), **Mount**. A peak, 5,645.6 m (18,510 ft) high, in the Caucasus Mountains of northwest Georgia. It is the highest elevation in the range.

El·burz Mountains (ĕl-bōōrz′). A range of northern Iran rising to 5,774.9 m (18,934 ft) at Mount Damavand, which is the highest point in the country.

El Ca·jon (kə-hōn′). A city of southern Califor-nia, an industrial and residential suburb of San Diego. ⊛ Pop. 88,693.

El Cap·i·tan (kăp′ĭ-tăn′). A peak, 2,308.5 m (7,569 ft) high, in the Sierra Nevada of central California. Its dramatic exposed monolith rises some 1,098 m (3,600 ft) above the floor of the Yosemite Valley.

El Cen·tro (sĕn′trō). A city of southern California in the Imperial Valley near the Mexican border. It is a shipping point for fruits and vegetables. ⊛ Pop. 31,384.

El Cer·ri·to (sə-rē′tō). A city of western California on San Francisco Bay north of Oakland. It is mainly residential. ⊛ Pop. 22,731.

El·che (ĕl′chĕ). A city of southeast Spain southwest of Alicante. An ancient Roman colony, it was held by the Moors from the 8th to the 13th century. ⊛ Pop. 188,062.

El·da (ĕl′də, -dä). A city of southeast Spain west-northwest of Alicante. It is a manufacturing center in an agricultural area. ⊛ Pop. 55,322.

El Di·en·te Peak (dē-ĕn′tē). A mountain, 4,318.5 m (14,159 ft) high, in the Rocky Mountains of southwest Colorado.

El Do·ra·do (də-rä′dō). **1.** (də-rä′dō). A vaguely defined historical region and city of the New World, often thought to be in northern South America. Fabled for its great wealth of gold and precious jewels, it was eagerly sought after by 16th- and 17th-century explorers, including Sir Walter Raleigh. **2.** A city of southern Arkansas near the Louisiana border south-southwest of Little Rock. Oil was discovered nearby in 1921. ⊛ Pop. 23,146.

E·le·a (ē′lē-ə) also **Ve·li·a** (vē′lē-ə). An ancient Greek colony of southern Italy near the Gulf of Salerno. Reputedly founded by the Greek philosopher Xenophanes, it was the center of the Eleatic school of philosophy.

E·lec·tric Peak (ĭ-lĕk′trĭk). A mountain, about 3,402.3 m (11,155 ft) high, in the Gallatin Range of southern Montana near the Wyoming border. It is the highest elevation in the range.

El·e·phan·ti·ne (ĕl′ə-făn-tī′nē). An island of southeast Egypt in the Nile River below the First Cataract near Aswan. In ancient times it was a military post guarding the southern frontier of Egypt. The Elephantine papyruses, dating from the fifth century B.C. and describing a Jewish colony, were discovered here in 1903.

E·leu·sis (ĭ-lōō′sĭs). An ancient city of eastern Greece near Athens, site of the Eleusinian mysteries, religious rites honoring the goddesses Persephone and Demeter. —**El′eu·sin′i·an** (ĕl′-yōō-sĭn′ē-ən) adj. & n.

el·e·va·tion (ĕl′ə-vā′shən). abbr. **el., elev.** The height above sea level.

El Fer·rol (fə-rôl', fĕ-) also **El Ferrol del Cau·dil·lo** (dĕl' kou-dē'ō, -thē'ô). A city of northwest Spain on the Atlantic Ocean. An important naval station since the 18th century, it was occupied by the British and then the French in the early 1800's. ⊛ Pop. 90,410.

El·gin (ĕl'jĭn). A city of northeast Illinois on the Fox River west-northwest of Chicago. It is a trade and industrial center. ⊛ Pop. 77,010.

El·gon (ĕl'gŏn'), **Mount.** An extinct volcano, 4,324.3 m (14,178 ft) high, on the Kenya-Uganda border.

E·lis (ē'lĭs). A region and city of ancient Greece in the western Peloponnesus. The plain of Olympia, in the southern part of the area, was the site of the original Olympic games.

E·lis·a·beth·ville (ĭ-lĭz'ə-bəth-vĭl'). See **Lubumbashi.**

E·liz·a·beth (ĭ-lĭz'ə-bəth). A city of northeast New Jersey south of Newark. Settled as Elizabethtown in 1664, it was the capital of New Jersey until 1686 and is today a residential suburb of New York City. ⊛ Pop. 110,002.

E·liz·a·beth·town (ĭ-lĭz'ə-bəth-toun'). A city of central Kentucky south of Louisville. It has many antebellum houses. ⊛ Pop. 18,167.

Elk Grove Village (ĕlk). A village of northeast Illinois, an industrial suburb of Chicago. ⊛ Pop. 33,429.

Elk·hart (ĕl'kärt', ĕlk'härt'). A city of northern Indiana east of South Bend. It was settled in 1824. ⊛ Pop. 43,627.

Elk Mountains. A range of the Rocky Mountains in west-central Colorado rising to 4,350.8 m (14,265 ft) at Castle Peak.

Elk River. 1. A river rising in the Cumberland Mountains of south-central Tennessee and meandering about 322 km (200 mi) generally west-southwest into northern Alabama. **2.** A river, approximately 277 km (172 mi) long, of central West Virginia.

El·len (ĕl'ən), **Mount.** A peak, 3,514.2 m (11,522 ft) high, of southern Utah.

Elles·mere Island (ĕlz'mîr'). An island of northern Northwest Territories, Canada, in the Arctic Ocean separated from Greenland by a narrow passage. It was sighted by the English explorer William Baffin in 1616.

Ellesmere Port. A municipal borough of northwest England on the Mersey River south-southeast of Liverpool. It has oil refineries and various light industries. ⊛ Pop. 82,500.

El·lice Islands (ĕl'ĭs). See **Tuvalu.**

El·li·cott City (ĕl'ĭ-kət). An unincorporated community of north-central Maryland west of Baltimore. It is a trade and manufacturing center. ⊛ Pop. 41,396.

El·li·ot Lake (ĕl'ē-ət). A community of south-

central Ontario, Canada, west-southwest of Sudbury. ⊛ Pop. 16,723.

El·lis Island (ĕl'ĭs). An island of Upper New York Bay southwest of Manhattan. It was the chief immigration station of the United States from 1892 to 1943, during which time more than 12 million immigrants entered the country through its doors. Officially closed in 1954, the site was designated a National Monument in 1965, and the main building was opened as a public museum in 1990.

Ells·worth Land (ĕlz'wûrth'). A high plateau of western Antarctica south of the Antarctic Peninsula. It includes the **Ellsworth Mountains,** rising to 5,142.3 m (16,860 ft) at Vinson Massif.

El Man·su·ra (măn-sŏŏr'ə). A city of northern Egypt on a branch of the Nile River. It is a commercial and industrial center. ⊛ Pop. 371,000.

Elm·hurst (ĕlm'hûrst'). A city of northeast Illinois, a residential and industrial suburb of Chicago. ⊛ Pop. 42,029.

El·mi·ra (ĕl-mī'rə). A city of southern New York near the Pennsylvania border west of Binghamton. The author and humorist Mark Twain is buried here. ⊛ Pop. 33,724.

El Mis·ti (mē'stē). A dormant volcano, 5,825.8 m (19,101 ft) high, in the Cordillera Occidental of southern Peru. It has a perfect snowcapped cone and has long figured in Peruvian legends and poetry.

El·mont (ĕl'mŏnt). An unincorporated community of southeast New York on western Long Island southwest of Mineola. It is mainly residential. ⊛ Pop. 28,612.

El Mon·te (mŏn'tē). A city of southern California east of Los Angeles. It is an industrial center in an area noted for its walnut groves. ⊛ Pop. 106,209.

Elm·wood Park (ĕlm'wŏŏd'). **1.** A village of northeast Illinois, a residential suburb of Chicago. ⊛ Pop. 23,206. **2.** A borough of northeast New Jersey southeast of Paterson. It was originally called East Paterson. ⊛ Pop. 17,623.

El Ni·ño (nēn'yō). *Oceanography.* A warming of the ocean surface off the western coast of South America that occurs every 4 to 12 years when upwelling of cold, nutrient-rich water does not occur. It causes plankton and fish to die and affects weather over much of the Pacific Ocean.

El O·beid (ō-bād'). See **Al Ubayyid.**

El Pas·o (păs'ō). A city of extreme western Texas on the Rio Grande opposite Ciudad Juárez, Mexico. The surrounding area was first settled by Spanish missionaries, soldiers, and traders in the 17th century. ⊛ Pop. 515,342.

El Re·no (rē'nō). A city of central Oklahoma west of Oklahoma City. It is a processing center and railroad junction. ⊛ Pop. 15,414.

El Sal·va·dor (săl'və-dôr', säl'vä-*thôr'*). A country of Central America bordering on the Pacific Ocean. Conquered by Spain in 1524, the region gained its independence in 1821, joined (1825–1838) a federation of Central American states, and became a separate republic in 1839. The increasing importance of coffee cultivation led to the rise of a landholding system that resulted in grossly unequal distribution of land and wealth, which in turn led to civil and political unrest in the 20th century. A military dictatorship under Maximiliano Hernández Martínez (1931–1944) was followed by a succession of military governments. In 1980 war broke out between leftist guerrilla and rightist government forces, which did not end until 1992. San Salvador is the capital and the largest city. ◉ Pop. 4,949,000. —**El Sal'va·dor'i·an** (săl'və-dôr'ē-ən, -dôr'-) *adj. & n.*

El·si·nore (ĕl'sə-nôr', -nōr'). See **Helsingør.**

El To·ro (tôr'ō). A community of southern California southeast of Santa Ana. It is mainly residential. ◉ Pop. 62,685.

E·ly (ē'lē), **Isle of.** A region of east-central England with extensive drained fens. The name *Isle* comes from the high ground amid the fens; *Ely* probably refers to the eels formerly found in the fens. The city of **Ely** is noted for its cathedral, dating from the 11th century and one of the largest in England. The city's population is 10,268.

E·ly·ri·a (ĭ-lîr'ē-ə). A city of northern Ohio west-southwest of Cleveland. Settled in 1817, it is an industrial center. ◉ Pop. 56,746.

Em·barras River also **Em·barrass River** (ăm'-brô). A river rising in eastern Illinois and flowing approximately 298 km (185 mi) generally south and southeast to the Wabash River in southwest Indiana.

em·bay·ment (ĕm-bā'mənt). **1.** A bay or bay-like shape. **2.** The formation of a bay.

em·bou·chure (äm'bōō-shŏor'). The mouth of a river.

em·branch·ment (ĕm-brănch'mənt). A branching out, as of a mountain range or river.

Em·den (ĕm'dən). A city of northwest Germany at the mouth of the Ems River west-northwest of Bremen. Founded in the ninth century, it was an important naval base during World War II. ◉ Pop. 50,164.

E·mi·lia-Ro·ma·gna (ĕ-mēl'yə-rō-mä'nyä). A region of northern Italy bordering on the Adriatic Sea. Named for the Aemilian Way, a Roman road laid out in 187 B.C. that connected Piacenza with Rimini, the area was conquered by the Lombards in the fifth century A.D. and became part of the kingdom of Italy in 1861.

em·pire (ĕm'pīr'). *abbr.* **emp. 1.** A political unit having an extensive territory or comprising a number of territories or nations and ruled by a single supreme authority. **2.** The territory included in such a unit.

Em·po·ri·a (ĕm-pôr'ē-ə, -pōr'-). A city of east-central Kansas southwest of Topeka. Founded in 1856, it was the home of the noted newspaper editor William Allen White from 1895 to 1944. ◉ Pop. 25,512.

Emp·ty Quar·ter (ĕmp'tē kwôr'tər). See **Rub al Khali.**

Ems (ĕmz, ĕms). A river of northwest Germany flowing about 335 km (208 mi) to the North Sea at the Netherlands border.

en·clave (ĕn'klāv', ŏn'-). A country or part of a country lying wholly within the boundaries of another.

En·der·by Land (ĕn'dər-bē). A region of Antarctica between Queen Maud Land and Wilkes Land. First explored in 1831 and 1832, it is claimed by Australia.

En·field (ĕn'fēld'). A town of northern Connecticut near the Massachusetts border. It was settled c. 1680 as part of Massachusetts and annexed by Connecticut in 1749. ◉ Pop. 45,532.

En·ga·dine (ĕng'gə-dēn'). A valley of the Inn River in eastern Switzerland. Divided into the **Upper Engadine** in the southwest and the **Lower Engadine** in the northeast, it is a noted resort area.

Eng·land (ĭng'glənd). *abbr.* **Eng.** A division of the United Kingdom, the southern part of the island of Great Britain. Originally settled by Celtic peoples, it was subsequently conquered by Romans, Angles, Saxons, Jutes, Danes, and Normans. Acts of union joined England with Wales in 1536, with Scotland in 1707 to create the political entity of Great Britain, and with Ireland in 1801 to form the United Kingdom. London is the capital and the largest city of both England and the United Kingdom. ◉ Pop. 46,220,955.

En·gle·wood (ĕng'gəl-wŏod'). **1.** A city of north-central Colorado, a residential and industrial suburb of Denver on the South Platte River. ◉ Pop. 29,387. **2.** A city of northeast

New Jersey east of Paterson. Settled by the Dutch in the 17th century, it is a residential suburb of New York City. ⊛ Pop. 24,850.

Eng·lish (ĭng′glĭsh). *abbr.* **E, E., Eng. 1.** Of, relating to, or characteristic of England or its people or culture. **2.** Of or relating to the English language. **3.** The people of England. **4.** The West Germanic language of England, the United States, Canada, Australia, and other countries that are or have been under English influence or control. **— Eng′lish·ness** *n.*

English Channel. An arm of the Atlantic Ocean between western France and southern England. It opens into the North Sea and is traversed by a train-ferry service. A tunnel beneath the English Channel, known as the "Chunnel," connecting Folkstone, England and Calais, France, was opened in 1994.

Eng·lish·man (ĭng′glĭsh-mən). **1.** A man who is a native or inhabitant of England. **2.** A man of English descent.

Eng·lish·wom·an (ĭng′glĭsh-wŏŏm′ən). **1.** A woman who is a native or inhabitant of England. **2.** A woman of English descent.

E·nid (ē′nĭd). A city of north-central Oklahoma north-northwest of Oklahoma City. It is a trade and processing center. ⊛ Pop. 45,309.

En·i·we·tok (ĕn′ə-wē′tŏk, ə-nē′wĭ-). An atoll in the Ralik Chain of the Marshall Islands in the west-central Pacific Ocean. It was the site of U.S. atomic tests from 1948 to 1954.

En·sche·da or **En·sche·de** (ĕn′skə-dā′, -sкнə-). A city of eastern Netherlands near the German border. It is a rail junction and a textile center. ⊛ Pop. 147,486.

En·se·na·da (ĕn′sə-nä′də). A city of northwest Mexico on the Pacific Ocean. It is a port and manufacturing center as well as a popular resort. ⊛ Pop. 120,483.

En·teb·be (ĕn-tĕb′ə, -tĕb′ē). A town of southern Uganda on Lake Victoria. At its airport in 1976 Israeli commando forces rescued most of the hostages held aboard an Air France plane by Palestinian hijackers. ⊛ Pop. 21,289.

En·ter·prise (ĕn′tər-prīz′). A city of southeast Alabama south-southeast of Montgomery. It is a processing and manufacturing center. ⊛ Pop. 20,123.

E·nu·gu (ā-nōō′gōō). A city of southeast Nigeria east of the Niger River. Enugu developed as a coal-mining center in the early 1900's. ⊛ Pop. 222,600.

en·vi·rons (ĕn-vī′rənz, -vī′ərnz). A surrounding area, especially of a city.

E·o·lus (ē-ō′ləs), **Mount.** A peak, 4,295.3 m (14,083 ft) high, in the San Juan Mountains of southwest Colorado.

ep·ei·rog·e·ny (ĕp′ī-rŏj′ə-nē). Uplift or depression of the earth's crust, affecting large areas of land or ocean bottom. **— e·pei′ro·gen′ic** (ĭ-pī′rō-jĕn′ĭk) *adj.* **— e·pei′ro·gen′i·cal·ly** *adv.*

É·per·nay (ā-pĕr-nā′). A city of north-central France on the Marne River east-northeast of Paris. It is a production and distributing center for the champagne wines of the district. ⊛ Pop. 27,668.

E·phe·sian (ĭ-fē′zhən). **1.** A native or inhabitant of ancient Ephesus. **2.** Of or relating to the ancient city of Ephesus or its people, language, or culture.

Eph·e·sus (ĕf′ĭ-səs). An ancient city of Greek Asia Minor in present-day western Turkey. Its temple, dedicated to the Greek goddess Artemis, or in Roman times Diana, was one of the Seven Wonders of the World. Saint Paul visited the city on his missionary journeys.

ep·i·cen·ter (ĕp′ĭ-sĕn′tər). The point on the earth's surface directly above the focus of an earthquake. **— ep′i·cen′tral** *adj.*

Ep·i·dau·rus (ĕp′ĭ-dôr′əs). An ancient city of Greece on the northeast coast of the Peloponnesus. Its temple of Asclepius, the Greek god of medicine, was renowned for its magnificent sculpture.

ep·i·gene (ĕp′ə-jēn′). Formed, originating, or occurring on or just below the surface of the earth.

É·pi·nay-sur-Seine (ā-pē-nā′sûr-sĕn′, -sür-). A city of north-central France, an industrial suburb of Paris. ⊛ Pop. 50,314.

E·pi·rus (ĭ-pī′rəs). An ancient country on the Ionian Sea in present-day northwest Greece and southern Albania. It flourished in the 3rd century B.C. and was later a Roman province. An independent state after A.D. 1204, Epirus was conquered by the Turks in the 15th century.

ep·o·nym (ĕp′ə-nĭm′). A person whose name is or is thought to be the source of the name of something, such as a city, country, or era. For example, *Romulus* is the eponym of *Rome.* **— ep′o·nym′ic** *adj.*

Ep·ping Forest (ĕp′ĭng). A former royal hunting preserve of southeast England northeast of London. It is now a public park.

Ep·som and Ew·ell (ĕp′səm; yōō′əl). A municipal borough of southeast England near London. The Derby is run annually at Epsom Downs racetrack. Epsom salts were originally produced at the mineral springs nearby. ⊛ Pop. 69,000.

e·qua·tor (ĭ-kwā′tər). **1.** The imaginary great circle around the earth's surface, equidistant from the poles and perpendicular to the earth's axis of rotation. It divides the earth into the Northern and Southern hemispheres.

e·qua·to·ri·al (ē′kwə-tôr′ē-əl, -tōr′-, ĕk′wə-).
1. Of, relating to, or resembling the earth's
equator. **2.** Relating to conditions that exist at
the earth's equator. **— e′qua·to′ri·al·ly** *adv.*

equatorial current. One of the surface currents drifting westward through the oceans at
the equator.

E·qua·to·ri·al Guinea (ē′kwə-tôr′ē-əl, -tōr′-,
ĕk′wə-). A country of west-central Africa including islands in the Gulf of Guinea. Originally
inhabited by Pygmy peoples, it was discovered
by Portugal in 1472 and settled in the following
centuries by Bantu speakers. The largest island,
now called Bioko, was ceded to Spain by Portugal in 1778, and the mainland territory, Río
Muni, came under Spanish rule in 1885. The colony became known as Spanish Guinea, and it
gained independence from Spain in 1968. The
first president, who had assumed dictatorial
powers, was overthrown by a military junta in
1979. Nominally a multiparty democracy, the
1993 elections were largely boycotted in protest
against unfair election laws. Malabo is the capital
and the largest city. ◉ Pop. 389,000.

Er·bil (îr′bĭl, ĕr′-). See **Irbil.**

Er·e·bus (ĕr′ə-bəs), **Mount.** A volcanic peak,
3,796.6 m (12,448 ft) high, on Ross Island in
Antarctica.

E·re·tri·a (ĕ-rē′trē-ə). An ancient city of Greece
on the southern coast of Euboea. Founded as an
Ionian colony, it was destroyed by the Persians
in 490 B.C.

E·re·van (yĕ′rĭ-vän′). See **Yerevan.**

Er·furt (ĕr′fərt, -fŏŏrt′). A city of central Germany southwest of Leipzig. Site of an episcopal
see founded by Saint Boniface in the eighth century, it was later a free imperial city and a member of the Hanseatic League. ◉ Pop. 200,799.

Er·gun He (ĕr′gōōn′ hĕ′, œr′gün hə′). See
Argun River.

E·rie[1] (îr′ē). **1.** *pl.* **Erie** or **Eries.** A member of
a Native American people formerly inhabiting
the southern shore of Lake Erie in northern
Ohio, northwest Pennsylvania, and western New
York. The Erie ceased to exist as a people after

being defeated by the Iroquois in the mid-17th
century. **2.** The Iroquoian language of the
Eries.

E·rie[2] (îr′ē). A city of northwest Pennsylvania on
Lake Erie southwest of Buffalo, New York. A
port of entry, it was laid out in 1795 on the site
of Fort Presque Isle, built by the French in
1753. ◉ Pop. 108,718.

Erie, Lake. One of the Great Lakes, bounded by
southern Ontario, western New York, northwest Pennsylvania, northern Ohio, and southeast Michigan. A vital part of the Great Lakes–
St. Lawrence Seaway system, it is linked with
the Hudson River by the New York State Barge
Canal.

Erie Canal. An artificial waterway extending
about 579 km (360 mi) across central New York
from Albany to Buffalo. Constructed from 1817
to 1825 and enlarged numerous times after
1835, it is now part of the New York State
Barge Canal.

Er·in (ĕr′ĭn). A poetic name for Ireland.

Er·i·tre·a (ĕr′ĭ-trē′ə). A country of northeast
Africa bordering on the Red Sea. Once a part of
the Ethiopian empire of Aksum, it became an
Italian colony in 1890 and was named after the
Roman term for the Red Sea, *Mare erythraeum.*
Captured by the British during World War II,
Eritrea later became a federated part (1952) and
then a province (1962) of Ethiopia. After nearly
two decades of fighting by secessionist rebel forces, Eritrea gained its independence in 1993. Asmara is the capital and largest city. ◉ Pop.
3,437,000. **— Er′i·tre′an** *adj. & n.*

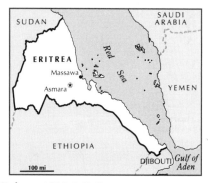

E·ri·van (yĕ′rĭ-vän′). See **Yerevan.**

Er·lang·en (ĕr′läng′ən). A city of south-central
Germany north-northeast of Nuremberg. Char-
tered in 1398, it passed to Bavaria in 1810.
◉ Pop. 102,383.

Er·na·ku·lum (ĕr-nä′kə-ləm). A city of southwest India on the Malabar Coast west of Madu-
rai. It has a Jewish sector that may date to the
second or third century A.D. ◉ Pop. 213,811.

Er Rif (ĕr rĭf′). A hilly region along the coast of
northern Morocco. The Berber peoples of the

area remained fiercely independent until they were subdued by French and Spanish forces (1925–1926).

Erse (ûrs). **1.** See **Irish Gaelic. 2.** See **Scottish Gaelic. — Erse** *adj.*

Er·y·man·thos or **Er·y·man·thus** (ĕr′ə-măn′-thəs, -thŏs, ĕ-rē′män-thôs′). A mountain range of southern Greece in the northwest Peloponnesus. The tallest peak is **Mount Erymanthos,** about 2,225 m (7,295 ft) high. In Greek legend, the range was the haunt of the ferocious Erymanthian boar, which was ultimately slain by Hercules. — **Er′y·man′thi·an** *adj.*

Erz·ge·bir·ge (ĕrts′gə-bîr′gə). A mountain range extending about 153 km (95 mi) along the border of Germany and Czech Republic. It rises to 1,244.4 m (4,080 ft).

Er·zu·rum (ĕr′zə-rōōm′). A city of eastern Turkey east of Ankara. It was known in the fifth century A.D. as an important Byzantine frontier post. ◉ Pop. 250,100.

Es·bjerg (ĕs′bē-ĕrg′, -byĕr′). A city of southwest Denmark on the North Sea. It is a commercial and industrial center with major fisheries. ◉ Pop. 80,534.

Es·cam·bi·a (ə-skăm′bē-ə). A river rising in southeast Alabama as the Conecuh River and flowing about 372 km (231 mi) southwest to join **Escambia Creek,** about 121 km (75 mi) long, and then southward into northwest Florida, where it empties into **Escambia Bay,** an arm of the Gulf of Mexico near Pensacola.

es·carp (ĭ-skärp′). A steep slope or cliff; an escarpment.

es·carp·ment (ĭ-skärp′mənt). A steep slope or long cliff that results from erosion or faulting and separates two relatively level areas of differing elevations.

Esch·wei·ler (ĕsh′vī′lər). A city of west-central Germany northeast of Aachen. It is an industrial center in a coal-mining area. ◉ Pop. 52,869.

Es·con·di·do (ĕs′kən-dē′dō). A city of southern California north of San Diego. It is in an area that specializes in grapes and citrus fruit. ◉ Pop. 108,635.

Es·co·ri·al (ĕ-skôr′ē-əl, ĕ-skōr′-, ĕs′kô-rē-äl′). A monastery and palace of central Spain near Madrid. Built from 1563 to 1584, it was commissioned by the Spanish king Philip II to commemorate a victory over the French.

Es·dra·e·lon (ĕs′drā-ē′lŏn, -drə-, ĕz′-), **Plain of.** A fertile plain of northern Israel extending from the coastal lowlands near Mount Carmel to the Jordan River valley.

Es·fa·han (ĕs′fə-hän′). See **Isfahan.**

E·sher (ē′shər). An urban district of southeast England southwest of London. It is mainly residential. ◉ Pop. 63,970.

es·ker (ĕs′kər). A long, narrow ridge of coarse gravel deposited by a stream flowing in or under a decaying glacial ice sheet. Also called *os.*

Es·kils·tu·na (ĕs′kĭl-styōō′nə, -nä). A city of southeast Sweden west of Stockholm. It was chartered in 1659. ◉ Pop. 88,664.

Es·ki·mo (ĕs′kə-mō′). *abbr.* **Esk. 1.** *pl.* **Eskimo** or **-mos.** A member of a group of peoples inhabiting the Arctic coastal regions of North America and parts of Greenland and northeast Siberia. Eskimos are generally considered a Native American people in Alaska and Canada. **2.** Any of the languages of the Eskimo peoples. — **Es′ki·mo′an** *adj.*

Es·ki·şe·hir (ĕs′kĭ-shə-hîr′). A city of west-central Turkey west of Ankara. An industrial center, it has hot mineral springs and Phrygian ruins nearby. ◉ Pop. 451,000.

Es·pe·ran·to (ĕs′pə-răn′tō, -rän′-). An artificial international language with a vocabulary based on word roots common to many European languages and a regularized system of inflection. — **Es′pe·ran′tist** *adj. & n.*

Es·pí·ri·tu San·to (ĕ-spîr′ĭ-tōō sän′tō). An island of Vanuatu in the southern Pacific Ocean. In World War II it was the site of U.S. military bases after March 1942.

es·pla·nade (ĕs′plə-näd′, -nād′). A flat, open stretch of pavement or grass, especially one designed as a promenade along a shore.

Es·poo (ĕs′pō, -pô). A town of southern Finland, a suburb of Helsinki. ◉ Pop. 180,851.

Es·qui·line (ĕs′kwə-līn′, -lĭn). One of the seven hills of ancient Rome. Nero's Golden House and Trajan's *Thermae,* or hot baths, were in the area.

Es·qui·malt (ĭ-skwī′môlt). A community of southwest British Columbia, Canada, on Vancouver Island and the Strait of Juan de Fuca just west of Victoria. It is a port and naval base. ◉ Pop. 15,870.

Es·qui·mau (ĕs′kə-mō′). *pl.* **Esquimau** or **-maux** (-mōz′). An Eskimo.

Es·sen (ĕs′ən). A city of west-central Germany near the confluence of the Ruhr and Rhine rivers north of Cologne. Founded in the ninth century, it is a major iron and steel center that was largely rebuilt after heavy bombing during World War II. ◉ Pop. 622,380.

Es·se·qui·bo (ĕs′ĭ-kwē′bō). A river rising on the Brazilian border of southern Guyana and flowing about 965 km (600 mi) generally northward to the Atlantic Ocean.

Es·sex (ĕs′ĭks). **1.** A historical region and Anglo-Saxon kingdom of southeast England. Probably settled by Saxons in the early sixth century, the kingdom was long dominated by Mercia and later by Wessex before and after it was controlled by the Danes from 886 to 917. There are important Roman and Saxon remains in the area. **2.** A community of northeast Maryland, a manufacturing suburb of Baltimore. ● Pop. 40,872.

Ess·ling·en (ĕs′lĭng-ən). A city of southwest Germany on the Neckar River southeast of Stuttgart. Founded in the 8th century, it was a free imperial city from the 13th century until 1802. ● Pop. 86,996.

Es·to·ni·a (ĕ-stō′nē-ə). Formerly **Es·to·ni·an Soviet Socialist Republic** (-nē-ən). *abbr.* **Est.** A country of north-central Europe west of Russia, bordering on the Baltic Sea. Settled before the 1st century A.D., it was held successively between the 13th and the 18th centuries by the Danes, German Livonian Knights, Swedes, and Russians. Estonia became an independent republic in 1918 but was annexed by the Soviet Union in 1940. Occupied by Germany in 1941, it reverted to Soviet control in 1944. A growing nationalist movement in the 1980's led to the adoption of a constitution (1988) and the abolition of the Communist Party's monopoly on power (1990). Full independence was gained in 1991, and a new constitution was ratified in 1992. Tallinn is the capital. ● Pop. 1,499,000.

Es·to·ni·an (ĕ-stō′nē-ən). **1.** Of or relating to Estonia or its people, language, or culture. **2.** A native or inhabitant of Estonia. **3.** The Finno-Ugric language of Estonia.

Estonian Soviet Socialist Republic. See **Estonia.**

Es·tre·ma·du·ra (ĕs′trə-mə-dōōr′ə, ĕs′trä-mä-*thōō*′rä). **1.** A historical region and former province of western Portugal surrounding Lisbon. **2.** A historical region of west-central Spain bordering on Portugal. Reconquered from the Moors in the 12th and 13th centuries, it was frequently a battlefield in the Spanish territorial wars with Portugal and in the Peninsular War fought between France and Great Britain (1808–1814). — **Es′tre·ma·du′ran** *adj. & n.*

es·tu·a·rine (ĕs′chōō-ə-rīn′, -rēn′). Of, relating to, or found in an estuary.

es·tu·ar·y (ĕs′chōō-ĕr′ē). **1.** The part of the wide lower course of a river where its current is met by the tides. **2.** An arm of the sea that extends inland to meet the mouth of a river. — **es′tu·ar′i·al** (-âr′ē-əl) *adj.*

e·te·sian (ĭ-tē′zhən). Occurring annually. Used of the prevailing northerly summer winds of the Mediterranean. — **e·te′sian** *n.*

E·thi·o·pi·a (ē′thē-ō′pē-ə). Formerly **Ab·ys·sin·i·a** (ăb′ĭ-sĭn′ē-ə), *abbr.* **Eth.** A country of northeast Africa. A kingdom was established around Aksum in the 1st century A.D., which was converted to Christianity in the 4th century and declined in the 7th century following the rise of Islam in neighboring territories. After a long period of disorder the area was finally reunited in 1889 by Emperor Menelik II, who repelled an Italian invasion (1895) and later greatly expanded Ethiopia by conquest. Italy invaded again (1935) and held the country until 1941, when it was liberated by British forces. Under Emperor Haile Selassie (crowned 1930) Ethiopia annexed Eritrea in 1962, touching off a long war with secessionist rebels, which resulted in Eritrea's becoming indpendent in 1993. After Haile Selassie was deposed by the military in 1974, Ethiopia was declared a socialist state. Under Colonel Mengistu Haile Mariam, who came into power in 1977 and later established a Marxist state, the country suffered enormous hardship from war and famine. Mengistu was overthrown in 1991, and a new government was established in 1995. Addis Ababa is the capital and the largest city. ● Pop. 32,775,000.

E·thi·o·pi·an (ē′thē-ō′pē-ən). **1.** Of or relating to Ethiopia or its peoples or cultures. **2.** Of or relating to the zoogeographic region that includes Africa and most of Arabia. **3.** A native or inhabitant of Ethiopia.

E·thi·op·ic (ē′thē-ŏp′ĭk, -ō′pĭk). **1.** The Afro-Asiatic language of ancient Ethiopia that is still used as a liturgical language in the Christian

Church in Ethiopia. **2.** Of or relating to Ethiopic. **3.** Of or relating to Ethiopia; Ethiopian.

Ethiopian Jew. A member of a Jewish population residing in northern Ethiopia since at least the sixth century A.D. Most Ethiopian Jews were removed to Israel in 1991 by means of an airlift organized by the Israeli government.

Et·na also **Aet·na** (ĕt′nə), **Mount.** An active volcano, 3,325.1 m (10,902 ft) high, of eastern Sicily. Its first known eruption occurred in 475 B.C.

E·ton (ēt′n). An urban district of southeast-central England on the Thames River opposite Windsor. Its college, the largest and most famous of England's public schools, was founded by Henry VI in 1440. ⊛ Pop. 3,523.

E·tru·ri·a (ĭ-tro͝or′ē-ə). An ancient country of west-central Italy in present-day Tuscany and parts of Umbria. It was the center of the Etruscan civilization, which spread throughout much of Italy before being supplanted by Rome in the third century B.C. — **E·tru′ri·an** *adj. & n.*

E·trus·can (ĭ-trŭs′kən). **1.** Of or relating to ancient Etruria or its people, language, or culture. **2.** A native or inhabitant of ancient Etruria. **3.** The extinct language of the Etruscans, of unknown linguistic affiliation.

Eu·boe·a (yo͞o-bē′ə) also **Ev·voia** (ĕv′yä). An island of central Greece in the Aegean Sea east of the mainland. It was settled by Ionian and Thracian colonists and was later controlled by Athens, Rome, Byzantium, Venice, and Turkey before becoming part of Greece in 1830.

Eu·clid (yo͞o′klĭd). A city of northeast Ohio, a manufacturing suburb of Cleveland on Lake Erie. ⊛ Pop. 54,875.

Eu·gene (yo͞o-jēn′). A city of western Oregon on the Willamette River south of Salem. It is the seat of the University of Oregon (founded 1872). ⊛ Pop. 112,669.

Eu·less (yo͞o′lĭs). A city of northeast Texas, a suburb of Fort Worth. ⊛ Pop. 38,149.

Eu·phra·tes (yo͞o-frā′tēz). A river of southwest Asia flowing about 2,735 km (1,700 mi) from central Turkey through Syria and into Iraq, where it joins the Tigris River to form the Shatt al Arab. Its waters were a major source of irrigation for the flourishing civilizations of ancient Mesopotamia.

Eur·a·sia (yo͝o-rā′zhə). The land mass comprising the continents of Europe and Asia. — **Eur·a′sian** *adj. & n.*

Eu·re·ka (yo͝o-rē′kə). A city of northwest California on Humboldt Bay, an arm of the Pacific Ocean. Lumbering, fishing, and tourism are important to its economy. ⊛ Pop. 27,025.

eu·ri·pus (yo͝o-rī′pəs). A sea channel characterized by turbulent and unpredictable currents.

Eu·rope (yo͝or′əp). *abbr.* **Eur.** The sixth-largest

continent, extending west from the Dardanelles, Black Sea, and Ural Mountains. It is technically a vast peninsula of the Eurasian land mass.

Eu·ro·pe·an (yo͝or′ə-pē′ən) *abbr.* **Eur. 1.** A native or inhabitant of Europe. **2.** A person of European desent. **3.** Of or relating to Europe or its peoples, languages, or cultures.

European Community. *abbr.* **EC** An organization that resulted from the consolidation in 1967 of three western European treaty organizations, the European Economic Community, the European Coal and Steel Community, and the European Atomic Energy Community. Its members are the same as those of the European Economic Community, and its goals are the economic and eventual political union of its members. The EC operates with a governing body that has four main branches including a European parliament and a court, and representatives are either elected or appointed to these bodies. Athough the parliament holds monthly sessions in Strasbourg, France, most of the EC's offices are in Brussels, Belgium.

European Economic Community. Known informally as the **Common Market.** *abbr.* **EEC** A treaty organization established in 1958 to reduce internal tariff barriers and promote trade and cooperation among the countries of western Europe, specifically Belgium, France, Italy, Luxembourg, the Netherlands, and West Germany. The United Kingdom, Ireland, and Denmark joined in 1973, Greece in 1981, Spain and Portugal in 1986, and Austria, Finland, and Sweden in 1995. In 1967 the EEC was merged with two other treaty organizations, the European Coal and Steel Community and the European Atomic Energy Community to form the European Community.

European Union. *abbr.* **EU** A supranational union established in 1993 after the ratification of the Maastricht Treaty by the members of the European Community (EC), which forms its core. In establishing the EU, the treaty expanded the political scope of the EC, especially in the area of foreign and security policy, and provided for the creation of a central European bank and the adoption of a common currency by the end of the 20th century.

European U.S.S.R. A region of the U.S.S.R. west of the Ural Mountains and the Caspian Sea.

eu·sta·sy (yo͞o′stə-sē). A worldwide change in sea level. — **eu·stat′ic** (-stăt′ĭk) *adj.*

Ev·ans (ĕv′ənz), **Mount.** A peak, 4,350.5 m (14,264 ft) high, of north-central Colorado in the Front Range of the Rocky Mountains.

Ev·ans·ton (ĕv′ən-stən). A city of northeast Illinois on Lake Michigan north of Chicago. Mainly residential, it is the seat of Northwestern University (chartered 1851). ⊛ Pop. 73,233.

Ev·ans·ville (ĕv′ənz-vĭl′). A city of extreme southwest Indiana on the Ohio River and the Kentucky border. It is the shipping and commercial center for a coal, oil, and farm region. ⊛ Pop. 126,272.

E·ven·ki (ĭ-wĕng′kē, ĭ-vĕng′-) also **E·wen·ki** (ĭ-wĕng′kē). **1.** *pl.* **Evenki** or **-kis** also **Ewenki** or **-kis.** A member of a people inhabiting a large area of eastern Siberia in Russia and northern Nei Monggol (Inner Mongolia) in China. **2.** The Tungusic language of the Evenki. Also called *Tungus.*

Ev·er·est (ĕv′ər-ĭst, ĕv′rĭst), **Mount.** A mountain, 8,853.5 m (29,028 ft) high, of the central Himalaya Mountains on the border of Xizang (Tibet) and Nepal. The highest elevation in the world, it was first scaled in 1953 by members of an expedition including Sir Edmund Hillary and Tenzing Norgay.

Ev·er·ett (ĕv′ər-ĭt, ĕv′rĭt). **1.** A city of eastern Massachusetts, an industrial suburb of Boston. ⊛ Pop. 35,701. **2.** A city of northwest Washington on Puget Sound north of Seattle. It is a port and has lumbering, paper, and aircraft industries. ⊛ Pop. 69,961.

ev·er·glade (ĕv′ər-glād′). A tract of marshland, usually under water and covered in places with tall grass.

Ev·er·glades (ĕv′ər-glādz′). A subtropical swamp area of southern Florida including **Everglades National Park.** It is noted for its wildlife, especially crocodiles, alligators, and egrets.

Ev·er·green Park (ĕv′ər-grēn′). A village of northeast Illinois, a residential suburb of Chicago. ⊛ Pop. 20,874.

Év·reux (ā-vrœ′). A town of northern France west-northwest of Paris. Founded in Roman times, it alternated between French and English control in the 15th century. ⊛ Pop. 46,045.

Ev·voia (ĕv′yä). See **Euboea.**

E·we (ā′wā′, ā′vā′). **1.** *pl.* **Ewe** or **Ewes.** A member of a people inhabiting southeast Ghana, southern Togo, and southern Benin. **2.** The Gbe language of the Ewe people.

E·wen·ki (ĭ-wĕng′kē). Variant of **Evenki.**

Ew·ing (yōō′ĭng). A community of west-central New Jersey north-northwest of Trenton. It is mainly residential. ⊛ Pop. 34,185.

ex·clave (ĕk′sklāv′). A part of a country that is isolated from the main part and is surrounded by foreign territory.

Ex·e·ter (ĕk′sĭ-tər). **1.** A borough of southwest England northeast of Plymouth. It has been important since Roman times because of its strategic location. ⊛ Pop. 105,087. **2.** A town of southeast New Hampshire southwest of Ports-

mouth. Settled in 1638, it is the site of Phillips Exeter Academy (opened 1783). ⊛ Pop. 12,481.

Ex·moor (ĕk′smŏŏr′, -smôr′, -smōr′). A moorland plateau of Cornwall in southwest England. It is a popular tourist area with notable prehistoric ruins.

ex·ter·ri·to·ri·al (ĕks′tĕr-ĭ-tôr′ē-əl, -tōr′-). Extraterritorial. — **ex′ter·ri·to′ri·al′i·ty** (-ăl′ĭ-tē) *n.* — **ex′ter·ri·to′ri·al·ly** *adv.*

ex·tra·ter·ri·to·ri·al (ĕk′strə-tĕr′ĭ-tôr′ē-əl, -tōr′-). Located outside territorial boundaries.

ex·urb (ĕk′sûrb′). A region lying beyond the suburbs of a city, especially one inhabited principally by wealthy people. — **ex·ur′ban** *adj.*

ex·ur·ban·ite (ĕk-sûr′bə-nīt′, ĕg-zûr′-). A resident of an exurb.

ex·ur·bi·a (ĕk-sûr′bē-ə, ĕg-zûr′-). A typically exurban area.

Eyre (âr), **Lake.** A shallow salt lake of south-central Australia. It is the largest lake in the country and the lowest point on the continent.

Eyre Peninsula. A peninsula of southern Australia between Spencer Gulf and the Great Australian Bight.

F

Fa·en·za (fä-ĕn′zə). A city of north-central Italy southwest of Ravenna. It is noted for its richly colored pottery, produced here since the 12th century. ⊛ Pop. 39,700.

Faer·oe Islands or **Far·oe Islands** (fâr′ō). A group of volcanic islands in the northern Atlantic Ocean between Iceland and the Shetland Islands. Originally settled by Celtic peoples, the islands passed to Denmark in 1380.

Faer·o·ese or **Far·o·ese** (fâr′ō-ēz′, -ēs′). **1.** A member of the Scandinavian people inhabiting the Faeroe Islands. **2.** The North Germanic language spoken by the inhabitants of the Faeroe Islands. — **Fae′ro·ese′** *adj.*

Fa·ial also **Fa·yal** (fə-yäl′, fä-). An island of the central Azores in the northern Atlantic Ocean. The island was originally colonized by Flemish settlers in the 16th century.

Fair·banks (fâr′băngks′). A city of central Alaska north-northeast of Anchorage. It was founded in 1902 as a gold-mining camp. ⊛ Pop. 30,843.

Fair·born (fâr′bôrn′). A city of southwest Ohio northeast of Dayton. It was formed in 1950 by the consolidation of two former villages. ⊛ Pop. 31,300.

Fair·fax (fâr′făks′). An independent city of

northeast Virginia, a residential suburb of Washington, D.C. ⊛ Pop. 19,622.

Fair·field (fâr′fēld′). **1.** A city of southeast Australia, a suburb of Sydney. ⊛ Pop. 143,500. **2.** A city of western California north-northeast of Oakland. It was founded in 1859. ⊛ Pop. 77,211. **3.** A town of southwest Connecticut on Long Island Sound southwest of Bridgeport. Settled in 1639, it is mainly residential and has varied light industries. ⊛ Pop. 53,418. **4.** A city of southwest Ohio north of Cincinnati. It is an industrial center. ⊛ Pop. 39,729.

Fair·ha·ven (fâr′hā′vən). A town of southeast Massachusetts on Buzzards Bay opposite New Bedford. It was formerly a whaling port. ⊛ Pop. 16,132.

Fair Isle (fâr). A small island between the Orkney Islands and the Shetland Islands of northern Scotland. Fair Isle is famous for its knitted woolen garments with distinctive colored patterns.

Fair Lawn. A borough of northeast New Jersey across the Passaic River from Paterson. ⊛ Pop. 30,548.

Fair·mont (fâr′mŏnt′). A city of northern West Virginia near the Pennsylvania border northeast of Clarksburg. It was settled in 1793 around Prickett's Fort (built 1774). ⊛ Pop. 20,210.

Fair Oaks. **1.** An unincorporated community of central California east-northeast of Sacramento. It is in a citrus-growing region. ⊛ Pop. 26,867. **2.** A locality just east of Richmond, Virginia, where Union troops defeated the Confederates at the Battle of Seven Pines (May 31–June 1, 1862).

Fair·view Park (fâr′vyōō′). A city of northeast Ohio, a residential suburb of Cleveland. ⊛ Pop. 18,028.

Fair·weath·er (fâr′wĕth′ər), **Mount.** A peak, 4,666.5 m (15,300 ft) high, on the border between southeast Alaska and western British Columbia, Canada.

Fai·sa·la·bad (fī′sä-lə-bäd′). Formerly **Ly·all·pur** (lī′əl-pŏŏr′). A city of northeast Pakistan west of Lahore. Founded in 1892, it is a cloth and grain market. ⊛ Pop. 1,104,209.

Fa·la·sha (fə-lä′shə, fä-). *pl.* **Falasha** or **-shas.** An Ethiopian Jew.

Fa·lis·can (fə-lĭs′kən). **1.** A member of an ancient Italic people of southern Etruria. **2.** The language of this people, closely related to Latin and known from place and personal names and from inscriptions. **3.** Of or relating to the Faliscans or their language or culture.

Fal·kirk (fôl′kûrk′). A burgh of central Scotland west of Edinburgh. At the Battle of Falkirk (1298), said to be the first battle in which the longbow proved decisive, the troops of the English king Edward I defeated the Scots. ⊛ Pop. 142,610.

Falk·land Islands (fôk′lənd, fôlk′-). A group of islands in the southern Atlantic Ocean east of the Strait of Magellan. Controlled by Great Britain since the 1830's, the islands are also claimed by Argentina and were occupied briefly by Argentinian troops in 1982 before being reoccupied by British forces.

fall line (fôl). **1.** A line connecting the waterfalls of nearly parallel rivers that marks a drop in land level. **2.** The natural line of descent, as for skiing, between two points on a slope.

Fall River (fôl). A city of southeast Massachusetts on the Rhode Island border west-northwest of New Bedford. Formerly a thriving textile center, it now has various diversified industries. It was the home of Lizzie Borden, a woman infamously accused and acquitted of the ax murder of her parents (1892). ⊛ Pop. 92,703.

Fal·mouth (făl′məth). A town of southeast Massachusetts on southwest Cape Cod. Once a whaling and shipbuilding center, it is now a popular summer resort and the site of Woods Hole Oceanographic Institution. ⊛ Pop. 27,960.

False Bay (fôls). An inlet of the Atlantic Ocean southwest of Cape Town, South Africa.

Fal·ster (fäl′stər, fôl′-). An island of southeast Denmark in the Baltic Sea off the southern tip of Sjaelland, with which it is connected by bridge.

Fa·ma·gu·sta (fä′mə-gōō′stə, făm′ə-). A city of eastern Cyprus on the **Bay of Famagusta,** an inlet of the Mediterranean Sea. Famagusta was a refugee center for Christians after Acre fell to the Saracens (1291). ⊛ Pop. 50,000.

Fang (făng, fäng, fäɴ). **1.** *pl.* **Fang** or **Fangs.** A member of a people inhabiting Gabon, Equatorial Guinea, and Cameroon. **2.** The Bantu language of the Fang.

Fan·te or **Fan·ti** (făn′tē, fän′-). **1.** *pl.* **Fante** or **-tes** or **Fanti** or **-tis.** A member of a people inhabiting Ghana. **2.** The variety of Akan spoken by this people.

Far East (fär). The countries and regions of eastern and southeast Asia, especially China, Japan, North Korea, South Korea, and Mongolia. —**Far′ East′ern** *adj.*

Far Eastern U.S.S.R. The easternmost region of the U.S.S.R., bordering on the Pacific Ocean.

Fare·ham (fâr′əm). An urban district of southern England on Portsmouth harbor north-northwest of Portsmouth. It is a shipbuilding center. ⊛ Pop. 100,987.

Fare·well (fâr-wĕl′, fâr′wĕl′), **Cape.** The southernmost point of Greenland.

Far·go (fär′gō). A city of eastern North Dakota on the Red River east of Bismarck. Founded with the coming of the railroad in 1871, it is the largest city in the state. ⊕ Pop. 74,111.

Far·i·bault (făr'ə-bō'). A city of southeast Minnesota south of Minneapolis. A manufacturing center, it was built on the site of a trading post established in 1826. ⊕ Pop. 17,085.

Fa·ri·da·bad (fə-rē'də-bäd'). A city of north-central India south-southeast of New Delhi. It is a grain and cotton market. ⊕ Pop. 617,717.

Far·mers Branch (fär'mərz). A town of northeast Texas, a residential and industrial suburb of Dallas. ⊕ Pop. 24,250.

Far·ming·ton (fär'mĭng-tən). **1.** A town of central Connecticut southwest of Hartford. Settled in 1640, it is chiefly residential. ⊕ Pop. 20,608. **2.** A city of northwest New Mexico south-southwest of Durango, Colorado. It is the trade center of an irrigated farming area. ⊕ Pop. 33,997.

Farmington Hills. A city of southeast Michigan, a residential suburb of Detroit. ⊕ Pop. 74,652.

Far·oe Islands (fâr'ō). See **Faeroe Islands.**

Far·o·ese (fâr'ō-ēz', -ēs'). Variant of **Faeroese.**

Fars (färz, färs) or **Far·si·stan** (fär'sĭ-stän', -stän'). A historical region of southern Iran along the Persian Gulf. It was more or less identical with the ancient province of Pars, which formed the nucleus of the Persian Empire. The Arabs changed the name after they conquered the region in the seventh century.

Far·si (fär'sē). **1.** The modern Iranian language, dating from about the ninth century A.D., that is the national language of Iran and is written in an Arabic alphabet; Persian. **2. a.** A speaker of Farsi. **b.** A member of the predominant ethnic group of Iran.

Far·si·stan (fär'sĭ-stän', -stän'). See **Fars.**

Far West. A region of the United States originally comprising all territories west of the Mississippi River. It is now generally restricted to the area west of the Great Plains. — **Far Western** adj.

Fá·ti·ma (făt'ə-mə). A village of west-central Portugal north-northeast of Lisbon. It became a pilgrimage site after the reported appearance of the Virgin Mary to three children in 1917.

fau·bourg (fō'bŏŏr', -bŏŏrg'). *New Orleans.* A district of metropolitan New Orleans lying outside the original city limits.

fault (fôlt). *Geology.* A fracture in the continuity of a rock formation caused by a shifting or dislodging of the earth's crust, in which adjacent surfaces are differentially displaced parallel to the plane of fracture. Also called *shift.*

Fa·yal (fə-yäl', fä-). See **Faial.**

Fay·ette·ville (fā'ĭt-vĭl', -vəl). **1.** A city of

northwest Arkansas in the Ozark Plateau north-northeast of Fort Smith. It is an agricultural trade center and the site of the University of Arkansas (established 1871). ⊕ Pop. 42,099. **2.** A city of south-central North Carolina southsouthwest of Raleigh. Founded by Scottish colonists in 1739, it was a Tory, or Loyalist, center during the American Revolution. The city is an agricultural and industrial center. ⊕ Pop. 75,695.

Fear (fîr), **Cape.** A promontory on Smith Island off the coast of southeast North Carolina at the mouth of the Cape Fear River.

Feath·er River (fĕth'ər). A river of central California flowing about 161 km (100 mi) southwest to the Sacramento River near Sacramento.

fed·er·al district also **Fed·er·al District** (fĕd'ər-əl, fĕd'rəl). An area, such as the District of Columbia, that is reserved as the site of the national capital of a federation.

Fed·er·at·ed Malay States (fĕd'ə-rā'tĭd). A former federation of British-protected Malayan states, part of present-day Malaysia.

feed·er (fē'dər). A tributary stream.

Fei·ra de San·ta·na (fā'rə də săn-tän'ə, fā'rä dĭ sän-täN'nä). A city of eastern Brazil westnorthwest of Salvador. It is a distribution center for a large agricultural region. ⊕ Pop. 405,848.

fell (fĕl). *Chiefly British.* **1.** A stretch of high open country; a moor. **2.** A barren or stony hill.

fen (fĕn). Low, flat, swampy land; a bog.

Fens (fĕnz). A lowland district of eastern England west and south of the Wash. Early attempts by the Romans to drain the area were abandoned by Anglo-Saxon times. Modern-day reclamation of the Fens began in the 17th century.

Fer·ga·na also **Fer·gha·na** (fər-gä'nə, fyĭr-gə-nä'). A city of eastern Uzbekistan southwest of Andizhan. It is the center of the fertile **Fergana Valley,** a densely populated agricultural and industrial region controlled by Russia after 1876. ⊕ Pop. 198,000.

Fer·gu·son (fûr'gə-sən). A city of eastern Missouri, a residential suburb of St. Louis with varied industries. ⊕ Pop. 22,286.

Fer·nan·do de No·ro·nha (fər-năn'dō də nə-rōn'yə, fĕr-näN'dŏŏ də nô-rô'nyə). An island group in the Atlantic Ocean off the northeast coast of Brazil. A federal territory of Brazil since 1942, the islands are used as a military base and penal colony.

Fer·nan·do Po (fər-năn'dō pō'). See **Bioko.**

Fern·dale (fûrn'dāl'). A city of southeast Michigan, a residential suburb of Detroit. ⊕ Pop. 25,084.

Fer·ra·ra (fə-rär'ə, fĕ-rä'rä). A city of northern Italy southwest of Venice. In the early 13th century the Este family established a powerful principality here and made it a flourishing center of Renaissance learning and the arts. ⊕ Pop. 137,336.

Fer·tile Cres·cent (fûr′tl krĕs′ənt). A region of the Middle East arching across the northern part of the Syrian Desert and extending from the Nile River valley to the Tigris and Euphrates rivers. The civilizations of Egypt, Phoenicia, Assyria, and Babylonia developed in this area, which was also the site of numerous migrations and invasions.

Fez (fĕz) also **Fès** (fĕs). A city of north-central Morocco northeast of Casablanca. The oldest part of the city was founded in the 9th century and reached the height of its influence in the mid-14th century. ⊕ Pop. 564,000.

Fez·zan (fə-zän′). A region of southwest Libya. It was under Turkish control from the 16th century until 1912.

Fich·tel·ge·bir·ge (fĭk′təl-gə-bîr′gə, fĭкн′-). A mountain range of east-central Germany near the border of Czech Republic. The region is a popular resort area.

Fie·so·le (fē-ā′zə-lē, fyĕ′zô-lĕ). A town of central Italy. An important Etruscan city, it was conquered by the Romans in 283 B.C. and is now primarily a tourist center, with villas and gardens on a hill overlooking the Arno River and the city of Florence. ⊕ Pop. 14,774.

Fife (fīf). A region of eastern Scotland between the Firths of Forth and Tay. It was once a Pict kingdom.

Fi·ji (fē′jē). An island country of the southwest Pacific Ocean comprising about 320 islands, the largest of which are Viti Levu and Vanua Levu. Populated by Melanesian and later Polynesian groups, the islands were discovered by the Dutch navigator Abel Tasman in 1643 and visited by the British navigator and explorer Capt. James Cook in 1774. Great Britain annexed the Fiji Islands in 1874, and they gained their independence in 1970. A military takeover in 1987 was aimed at keeping ethnic Indians, who make up roughly half of the present population, from

exercising political power. A new constitution (1992) solidified the monopoly of ethnic Fijians over land ownership and government office. Suva, on the island of Viti Levu, is the capital. ⊕ Pop. 784,000.

Fi·ji·an (fē′jē-ən). **1.** A native or inhabitant of Fiji. **2.** The Austronesian language of Fiji. **3.** Of or relating to Fiji or its people, language, or culture.

Filch·ner Ice Shelf (fĭlk′nər). An area of Antarctica bordering on Coats Land at the head of Weddell Sea. It was discovered in 1912.

Fil·i·pi·no (fĭl′ə-pē′nō). **1.** pl. **-nos.** A native or inhabitant of the Philippines. **2.** Used as the name for the Austronesian language that is based on Tagalog, draws its lexicon from other Philippine languages, and is the official language of the Philippines. **3.** Of or relating to the Philippines or its peoples, languages, or cultures.

Find·lay (fĭnd′lē). A city of northwest Ohio south of Toledo. It is a manufacturing center in an agricultural region. ⊕ Pop. 35,703.

Fin·gal's Cave (fĭng′gəlz). A cavern of western Scotland on Staffa Island in the Inner Hebrides. The cave is noted for its unusual beauty.

Fin·ger Lakes (fĭng′gər). A group of 11 elongated glacial lakes in west-central New York, including Cayuga and Seneca, the largest and deepest of the lakes. The region is a major grape-growing area with many resorts and recreational facilities.

Fin·is·terre (fĭn′ĭ-stâr′, fē′nē-stĕr′rĕ), **Cape.** A rocky promontory of extreme northwest Spain on the Atlantic Ocean. Off the cape the British won two naval victories over the French (1747 and 1805).

Fin·land (fĭn′lənd). abbr. **Fin.** A country of northern Europe bordering on the Gulf of Bothnia and the Gulf of Finland. Controlled from the 13th century by Sweden and after 1809 by Rus-

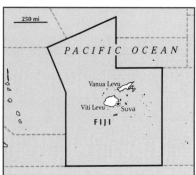

sia, it became independent in 1919. Finland lost territory to the Soviet Union during World War II and was forced to sign a treaty (1948) pledging to defend the Finnish-Soviet border from attack. The socialist governments of the postwar years sought to remain politically neutral while maintaining ties with the West. Finland abandoned socialism in 1991 and held popular elections in 1994. Helsinki is the capital and the largest city. ◉ Pop. 5,095,000. **—Fin'land·er** *n.*

Finland, Gulf of. An arm of the Baltic Sea bordered by Finland, Russia, and Estonia. An important shipping lane, the shallow gulf is usually frozen from December to March.

Fin·lay River (fĭn'lē). A river of northern British Columbia, Canada, flowing about 402 km (250 mi) to the Peace River.

Finn (fĭn). **1.** A native or inhabitant of Finland. **2.** One who speaks Finnish or a Finnic language.

Fin·nic (fĭn'ĭk). **1.** Of or relating to Finland or the Finns. **2.** A branch of Finno-Ugric that includes Finnish, Estonian, and Lapp.

Finn·ish (fĭn'ĭsh). *abbr.* **Fin. 1.** Of or relating to Finland or its people, language, or culture. **2.** The Finno-Ugric language of the Finns.

Fin·no-U·gric (fĭn'ō-ōō'grĭk, -yōō'-) also **Fin·no-U·gri·an** (-ōō'grē-ən, -yōō'-). **1.** A subfamily of the Uralic language family that includes Finnish, Hungarian, and other languages of northern and eastern Europe and northwest Russia. **2.** Of or relating to the Finns and the Ugrians. **3.** Of or relating to Finno-Ugric.

Fin·ster·aar·horn (fĭn'stər-är'hôrn'). A peak, 4,276.7 m (14,022 ft) high, of the Bernese Alps in south-central Switzerland. It is the highest elevation in the range.

fiord (fyôrd, fyōrd). Variant of **fjord.**

Fire Island (fīr). A narrow barrier island off the southern shore of Long Island in southeast New York. It has many resort communities, a state park, and a nationally protected seashore area that includes the Sunken Forest, with unusual plant and animal life.

Fi·ren·ze (fē-rĕn'dzĕ). See **Florence** (sense 1).

First World also **first world** (fûrst). The industrialized non-Communist countries of the world.

Fi·ro·za·bad (fĭ-rō'zä-bäd'). A city of north-central India southeast of Delhi. It is a manufacturing center in a cotton and grain area. ◉ Pop. 215,128.

firth (fûrth). *Scots.* A long, narrow inlet of the sea.

Fish·ers Island (fĭsh'ərz). A small island off the northeast tip of Long Island in southeast New York. It was developed as a resort in 1925.

Fitch·burg (fĭch'bûrg'). A city of north-central Massachusetts north of Worcester. It was settled in 1740. ◉ Pop. 41,194.

Fiu·me (fyōō'mä, -mĕ). See **Rijeka.**

Five Forks (fīv). A crossroads in southeast Virginia southwest of Petersburg where the last important Civil War battle was fought on April 1, 1865. The Union victory led to the fall of Petersburg, the capture of Richmond, and the surrender of Confederate general Robert E. Lee to Union general Ulysses S. Grant at Appomattox Courthouse on April 9.

fjeld (fyĕld). A high, barren plateau in the Scandinavian countries.

fjord or **fiord** (fyôrd, fyōrd). A long, narrow, deep inlet of the sea between steep slopes.

Flag·staff (flăg'stăf'). A city of north-central Arizona northeast of Prescott. It is a health resort in a lumbering and ranching area and the site of Lowell Observatory (founded 1894). ◉ Pop. 45,857.

Fla·min·i·an Way (flə-mĭn'ē-ən). An ancient Roman road that was the principal artery between Rome and Cisalpine Gaul. It was begun in 220 B.C. by the Roman general Gaius Flaminius (died 217).

Flan·ders (flăn'dərz). A historical region of northwest Europe including parts of northern France, western Belgium, and southwest Netherlands along the North Sea. For many centuries it enjoyed virtual independence and great prosperity as a center of the cloth industry. The Hapsburg wars in the Low Countries caused the eventual division of the region, which suffered heavy damage during both World Wars.

flat (flăt) or **flats** (flăts). A stretch of level ground.

Flat·head (flăt'hĕd'). **1. a.** *pl.* **Flathead** or **-heads.** A member of a Native American people inhabiting western Montana and northern Idaho, now located principally on Flathead Lake. **b.** The Salishan language of the Flatheads. **2.** See **Interior Salish.**

Flathead River. A river rising in southeast British Columbia, Canada, and flowing about 386 km (240 mi) generally southward across the Montana border to **Flathead Lake** then south and west to the Clark Fork River. The lake is surrounded by mountains and is a popular recreation region.

flat·land (flăt'lănd', -lənd). **1.** Land that varies little in elevation. **2. flatlands.** A geographic area composed chiefly of land that varies little in elevation. **—flat'land'er** *n.*

Flat·ter·y (flăt'ə-rē), **Cape.** A headland of northwest Washington at the entrance to the Strait of Juan de Fuca. It was discovered by the British navigator and explorer Capt. James Cook in 1778.

Flem·ing (flĕm'ĭng). **1.** A native or inhabitant of Flanders. **2.** A Belgian who speaks Flemish.

Flem·ish (flĕm'ĭsh). *abbr.* **Flem. 1.** Of or relating to Flanders, the Flemings, or their language or culture. **2.** The West Germanic language of the Flemings. **3.** The Flemings.

Flens·burg (flĕnz'bûrg, flĕns'boork'). A city of northern Germany on **Flensburg Fjord,** an arm of the Baltic Sea at the Danish border. Founded c. 1200, the city is a port and shipbuilding center. ◉ Pop. 86,873.

Fletsch·horn (flĕch'hôrn'). A peak, about 3,999 m (13,110 ft) high, in the Pennine Alps of southern Switzerland near the Italian border.

Flin·ders Range (flĭn'dərz). A mountain range of south-central Australia east of Lake Torrens. The highest peak is 1,189.5 m (3,900 ft).

Flinders River. An intermittent river of northeast Australia flowing about 837 km (520 mi) northwest to the Gulf of Carpentaria.

Flint (flĭnt). A city of southeast-central Michigan north-northwest of Detroit. Founded on the site of a fur-trading post established in 1819, it became an automobile-manufacturing center in the early 1900's. ◉ Pop. 140,761.

Flint River. A river of western Georgia flowing about 531 km (330 mi) generally southward to join the Chattahoochee River and form the Apalachicola River at the Florida border.

Flod·den (flŏd'n). A hill of northern England near the Scottish border. It was the site of the Battle of Flodden Field (September 9, 1513) in which the English defeated the Scots under James IV, who was killed in the slaughter.

flood·plain also **flood plain** (flŭd'plān'). A plain bordering a river and subject to flooding.

floor (flôr, flōr). The ground or lowermost surface, as of a forest or an ocean.

Flo·ral Park (flôr'əl, flōr'-). A village of southeast New York on western Long Island, a residential suburb of New York City with a commercial flower industry. ◉ Pop. 15,947.

Flor·ence (flôr'əns, flōr'-). **1.** also **Fi·ren·ze** (fē-rĕn'dzĕ). A city of central Italy on the Arno River east of Pisa. Originally an Etruscan settlement, then a Roman town, Florence was a powerful city-state under the Medici family during the Italian Renaissance (14th–16th century), with a brilliant artistic flowering led by Giotto, Michelangelo, Leonardo da Vinci, Dante, and Raphael. Florence became the capital of newly-unified Italy (1865–1871) until the government was moved to Rome. ◉ Pop. 402,316. **2.** A city of northwest Alabama on the Tennessee River west-northwest of Decatur. Founded in 1818, it is highly industrialized. ◉ Pop. 36,426. **3.** An unincorporated community of southern California, a residential and manufacturing suburb of Los Angeles. ◉ Pop. 38,000. **4.** A city of north-central Kentucky southwest of Cincinnati, Ohio, in a farming region. ◉ Pop. 18,624. **5.** A city of northeast South Carolina east-northeast of Columbia. It has been a transportation center since the Civil War. ◉ Pop. 29,813.

Flor·en·tine (flôr'ən-tēn, -tīn, flōr'-). **1.** Of or relating to Florence, Italy. **2.** A native or inhabitant of Florence, Italy.

Flo·res (flôr'ĭs, -ēz, flōr'-). An island of eastern Indonesia in the Lesser Sunda Islands on the **Flores Sea,** between the eastern end of the Java Sea and the western end of the Banda Sea south of Celebes. The island came under Dutch influence in the 17th century, although the Portuguese held the eastern end until 1851.

Flo·ri·a·nó·po·lis (flôr'ē-ə-nŏp'ə-lĭs, flōr-, flô'ryə-nô'poo-lēs'). A city of southeast Brazil on an island just off the coast. It is a port linked to the mainland by a suspension bridge. ◉ Pop. 254,941.

Flor·i·da (flôr'ĭ-də, flōr'-). *abbr.* **FL, Fla.** A state of the southeast United States bordering on the Atlantic Ocean and the Gulf of Mexico. It was admitted as the 27th state in 1845. The peninsula was discovered by Spanish explorer Juan Ponce de León in 1513 and became the center of a Spanish settlement that included the southeast part of the present-day United States. Spain finally ceded the area in 1819. Tallahassee is the capital and Jacksonville the largest city. ◉ Pop. 13,003,362. — **Flo·rid'i·an** (flə-rĭd'ē-ən), **Flor'i·dan** (-ĭd-n) *adj.*

Florida, Straits of also **Florida Strait.** A sea passage between Cuba and the Florida Keys, linking the Gulf of Mexico with the Atlantic Ocean.

Florida Keys. A chain of small coral and limestone islands and reefs extending about 241 km (150 mi) in a southwestward arc from south of Miami to Key West. The Keys are popular tourist resorts noted for their fishing and tropical vegetation.

Florida Strait. See Straits of **Florida.**

Flor·in (flôr'ĭn, flōr'-). A community of central California, a mainly residential suburb of Sacramento. ◉ Pop. 24,330.

Flor·is·sant (flôr'ĭ-sənt, flōr'-). A city of eastern Missouri, a residential suburb of St. Louis. It was settled by French farmers and fur trappers in the 1760's. ◉ Pop. 51,206.

flume (floom). **1.** A narrow gorge, usually with a stream flowing through it. **2.** An open artificial channel or chute carrying a stream of water, as for furnishing power or conveying logs.

Flush·ing (flŭsh'ĭng). **1.** A section of New York City in northern Queens on western Long Island. Flushing Meadow was the site of two world's fairs (1939–1940 and 1964–1965) and the temporary headquarters of the United Nations (1946–1949). **2.** See **Vlissingen.**

flu·vi·al (floo′vē-əl). **1.** Of, relating to, or inhabiting a river or stream. **2.** Produced by the action of a river or stream.

flu·vi·a·tile (floo′vē-ə-tīl′). Fluvial.

flu·vi·o·ma·rine (floo′vē-ō-mə-rēn′). Relating to or being deposits, especially near the mouth of a river, formed by the combined action of river and sea.

Fly River (flī). A river, about 1,046 km (650 mi) long, rising in western Papua New Guinea and flowing generally southeastward to the Gulf of Papua.

Foc·şa·ni (fôk-shän′, -shä′nē). A town of east-central Romania northwest of Brăila. Situated at the foot of the Transylvanian Alps, it is a market and industrial center. ● Pop. 101,414.

foehn also **föhn** (fœn, fān). A warm, dry wind coming off the lee slopes of a mountain range, especially off the northern slopes of the Alps.

Fog·gia (fô′jə). A city of southern Italy northeast of Naples. It is a transportation and industrial center and a major wheat market. ● Pop. 155,042.

föhn (fœn, fān). Variant of **foehn.**

Fol·som (fōl′səm). Of or relating to a culture that flourished in western North America east of the Rocky Mountains during the late Pleistocene period (11,000 to 2 million years ago), notable chiefly for the use of grooved, leaf-shaped flint projectile points.

Fon (fŏn). **1.** *pl.* **Fon** or **Fons.** A member of a people of Benin and neighboring parts of Nigeria. **2.** The Gbe language of the Fon.

Fond du Lac (fŏn′ də lăk′, dyə). A city of eastern Wisconsin at the southern end of Lake Winnebago south-southeast of Oshkosh. Settled on the site of a French trading post (established 1785), it is an industrial center in a dairy-farming region. ● Pop. 37,757.

Fon·ga·fa·le (fŏn′gə-fä′lē). The capital of Tuvalu, on Funafuti Island in the southern Pacific Ocean. ● Pop. 2,191.

Fon·se·ca (fôn-sā′kə, -sĕ′kä), **Gulf of.** An inlet of the Pacific Ocean in western Central America bordered by El Salvador, Honduras, and Nicaragua.

Fon·taine·bleau (fŏn′tĭn-blō′, fôN-tĕn-blō′). A town of northern France southeast of Paris. Its chateau, which was built by King Francis I (ruled 1515–1547), was long a royal palace and is now the summer residence of the president of France. The revocation of the Edict of Nantes, a document that defined the rights of the French Protestants, was signed here in 1685. ● Pop. 15,679.

Fon·tan·a (fŏn-tăn′ə). A city of southern California west of San Bernardino. It is an industrial center in a citrus-growing area. ● Pop. 87,535.

Fonte·nay-sous-Bois (fôNt-nā′soo-bwä′). A city of north-central France, a manufacturing suburb of Paris. ● Pop. 52,627.

Foo·chow (foo′jō′, -chou′). See **Fuzhou.**

foot·hill (foot′hĭl′). A hill near the base of a mountain or mountain range.

For·a·ker (fôr′ə-kər, fôr′-), **Mount.** A peak, 5,307 m (17,400 ft) high, in the Alaska Range of south-central Alaska.

For·bid·den City (fər-bĭd′n, fôr-). A walled enclosure of central Beijing, China, containing the palaces of 24 emperors in the Ming and Qing dynasties (1420–1911). Formerly closed to the public (hence its name), it is now a vast museum and a major tourist attraction.

ford (fôrd, fōrd). A shallow place in a body of water, such as a river, where one can cross by walking or riding on an animal or in a vehicle.

fore·land (fôr′lənd, fōr′-). A projecting land mass; a promontory.

fore·shore (fôr′shôr′, fōr′shōr′). **1.** The part of a shore that lies between high and low watermarks. **2.** The part of a shore between the water and occupied or cultivated land.

Fo·rest (fô-rĕ′). See **Vorst.**

For·est Hills (fôr′ĭst, fŏr′-). A residential section of New York City in central Queens on western Long Island. Until 1978 the U.S. Open Championship matches were held at the West Side Tennis Club here.

Forest Park. 1. A city of northwest Georgia, an industrial suburb of Atlanta. ● Pop. 16,925. **2.** A village of northeast Illinois west of Chicago. It is mainly residential. ● Pop. 14,918. **3.** A city of southwest Ohio, a residential suburb of Cincinnati. ● Pop. 18,609.

For·est·ville (fôr′ĭst-vĭl′, fŏr′-). An unincorporated community of central Maryland, a residential suburb of Washington, D.C., near Andrews Air Force Base. ● Pop. 16,731.

For·lì (fôr-lē′). A city of northern Italy southeast of Bologna. A Roman trade center, it became a free commune in the 11th century and part of the Papal States in 1504. It is an industrial center. ● Pop. 109,228.

For·mo·sa (fôr-mō′sə). See **Taiwan.**

Formosa Strait also **Tai·wan Strait** (tī′wän′). An arm of the Pacific Ocean between Taiwan and China. It links the East China Sea with the South China Sea.

For·ta·le·za (fôr′tl-ā′zə, -tə-lĕ′-). A city of northeast Brazil northwest of Natal on the Atlantic Ocean. Founded in 1609, it is a thriving port and industrial center. ● Pop. 1,765,794.

Fort Col·lins (fôrt kŏl′ĭnz, fōrt). A city of northern Colorado north-northeast of Boulder. It is a trade, shipping, and processing center. ● Pop. 87,758.

Fort-de-France (fôr-də-fräNs'). The capital and largest city of Martinique, on the western coast of the island on **Fort-de-France Bay,** an inlet of the Caribbean Sea. Settled by the French in 1762, Fort-de-France is a popular resort. ⊛ Pop. 99,844.

Fort Dodge. A city of central Iowa on the Des Moines River north-northwest of Des Moines. It was settled in the 1840's. ⊛ Pop. 25,894.

Fort Erie. A town of southern Ontario, Canada, on the Niagara River opposite Buffalo, New York. It is on the site of a fort established in 1764, captured in 1813 by the Americans in the War of 1812, and destroyed by them in 1814 after a siege by British troops. ⊛ Pop. 24,096.

Forth (fôrth, fōrth). A river of south-central Scotland flowing about 187 km (116 mi) eastward to the **Firth of Forth,** a wide inlet of the North Sea.

Fort-La·my (fôr-lä-mē'). See **N'Djamena.**

Fort Lau·der·dale (lô'dər-dāl'). A city of southeast Florida on the Atlantic coast north of Miami Beach. It is a yachting and fishing resort and has long been a favorite vacation spot for college students during spring break. ⊛ Pop. 149,377.

Fort Lee (lē). A borough of northeast New Jersey on the Hudson River opposite Manhattan. Settled around 1700, it was an early center of the motion-picture industry. ⊛ Pop. 31,997.

Fort Mc·Mur·ray (mĭk-mûr'ē, -mŭr'ē). A city of northeast Alberta, Canada, at the conjunction of the Athabasca and Clearwater rivers. ⊛ Pop. 31,000.

Fort My·ers (mī'ərz). A city of southwest Florida on an estuary of the Caloosahatchee River north-northeast of Cape Coral. It is a shipping and tourist center. ⊛ Pop. 45,206.

Fort Nelson. A river, about 418 km (260 mi) long, of northeast British Columbia, Canada.

Fort Pierce (pîrs). A city of east-central Florida on the Indian River lagoon north-northwest of Palm Beach. It is a distribution center in a cattle and farming region. ⊛ Pop. 36,830.

Fort Smith (smĭth). 1. A region of southwest Northwest Territories, Canada, including Great Slave Lake and most of Great Bear Lake. 2. A city of western Arkansas on the Oklahoma border west-northwest of Little Rock. It was founded as a military post in 1817. ⊛ Pop. 72,798.

Fort Thom·as (tŏm'əs). A city of northern Kentucky, a residential suburb of Covington. ⊛ Pop. 16,032.

Fort Wal·ton Beach (wôl'tən). A city of northwest Florida in the Panhandle east of Pensacola. It is a year-round resort on the Gulf of Mexico. ⊛ Pop. 21,471.

Fort Wayne. A city of northeast Indiana northeast of Indianapolis. A French trading post and fort were built on the site in the late 17th century, and an American fort was established by the American Revolutionary general Anthony Wayne in 1794. ⊛ Pop. 173,072.

Fort Worth (wûrth). A city of northeast Texas west of Dallas. Built on the site of a military post established in the 1840's, it is a major industrial center and distribution point. ⊛ Pop. 447,619.

Fos·ter City (fô'stər, fŏs'tər). A city of western California, a suburb of San Mateo. ⊛ Pop. 28,176.

Fos·tor·i·a (fô-stôr'ē-ə, -stōr'-, fŏs-tôr'-, -tōr'). A city of northwest Ohio south-southeast of Toledo. It is a trade and shipping center in an agricultural region. ⊛ Pop. 14,983.

fount (fount). A fountain.

foun·tain (foun'tən). A spring, especially the source of a stream.

foun·tain·head (foun'tən-hĕd'). A spring that is the source or head of a stream.

Foun·tain Valley (foun'tən). A city of southern California southeast of Los Angeles. It is mainly residential. ⊛ Pop. 53,691.

Four Cor·ners (fôr kôr'nərz). A location in the southwest United States where the boundaries of four states—Colorado, New Mexico, Arizona, and Utah—meet. It is the only point in the United States where such a junction occurs.

Fourth World also **fourth world** (fôrth, fōrth). The least-developed countries of the Third World, especially those in Africa and Asia.

Fou·ta Djal·lon also **Fu·ta Jal·lon** (fōō'tə jə-lōn', fōō'tä jä-lôn'). A mountainous region of northwest Guinea. The headwaters of the Gambia, Niger, and Senegal rivers rise here.

Fox (fŏks). 1. pl. **Fox** or **Fox·es.** A member of a Native American people formerly inhabiting various parts of southern Michigan, southern Wisconsin, northern Illinois, and eastern Iowa, with present-day populations in central Iowa and with the Sauk in Oklahoma. 2. The Algonkian language of the Fox.

Foxe Basin (fŏks). An arm of the Atlantic Ocean between the Melville Peninsula and Baffin Island in Northwest Territories, Canada.

Fox Islands (fŏks). A group of islands of southwest Alaska in the eastern Aleutian Islands off the southwest tip of the Alaska Peninsula.

Fox River. 1. A river rising in southeast Wisconsin and flowing about 354 km (220 mi) south-southwest to the Illinois River in northeast Illinois. 2. A river of central and eastern Wisconsin flowing about 282 km (175 mi) generally northeastward through Lake Winnebago and into Green Bay.

Fra·ming·ham (frā'mĭng-hăm'). A town of

east-central Massachusetts west-southwest of Boston. Settled in 1650, it is a commercial and industrial center. ⊛Pop. 64,994.

Fran·ca (fräɴ′kä). A city of southeast Brazil north of São Paulo. It is a shipping and manufacturing center in a farming region. ⊛Pop. 232,855.

France (frăns). *abbr.* **Fr.** A country of western Europe on the Atlantic Ocean and the English Channel. It was settled by the Franks after the retreat of the Romans, who had conquered Celtic Gaul in 58–51 B.C. Charlemagne made it the center of his Empire of the West after A.D. 800. In the Middle Ages France was split into numerous fiefdoms and kingdoms, most of which were incorporated into the royal domain by the time of Louis XI (reigned 1461–1483). Under Louis XIV (1643–1715) France became the greatest power in Europe, but warfare and social and economic backwardness depleted the treasury, and widespread discontent led to the French Revolution (1789) and the end of monarchic rule. The First Republic (1792–1804) was followed by the First Empire (1804–1815) under Napoleon Bonaparte, a period of constitutional monarchy (1814–1848), and a succession of republics broken by the Second Empire under Louis Napoleon (1852–1870). France saw heavy fighting in World War I, and much of its territory was occupied by the Germans in World War II. Paris is the capital and the largest city. ⊛Pop. 54,334,871.

Franche-Com·té (fränsh-kôn-tā′). A historical region and former province of eastern France. The region was first occupied by a Celtic tribe in the fourth century B.C. and became part of France after 1676. Until that time its control was continually disputed by France, Germany, Burgundy, Switzerland, and Spain.

Fran·co-A·mer·i·can (frăng′kō-ə-měr′ĭ-kən). **1.** An American of French or French-Canadian descent. **2.** Of or relating to the Franco-

Americans. **3.** Of or relating to France and America.

Fran·co·ni·a (frăng-kō′nē-ə, -kōn′yə, frăn-). A region and former duchy of southern Germany. It was one of the five primary duchies of medieval Germany. —**Fran·co′ni·an** *adj. & n.*

Fran·co·phone or **fran·co·phone** (frăng′kə-fōn′). **1.** A French-speaking person, especially in a region where two or more languages are spoken. **2.** French-speaking. —**Fran′co·phon′-ic** (-fŏn′ĭk) *adj.*

Frank (frăngk). A member of any of the Germanic tribes of the Rhine region in the early Christian era, especially one of the Salian Franks who conquered Gaul about A.D. 500 and established an extensive empire under the Merovingian (c. A.D. 450–751) and Carolingian (751–987) dynasties. Frankish power reached its peak under the Carolingian emperor Charlemagne (742?–814), whose capital was at Aix-la-Chapelle.

Frank·fort (frăngk′fərt). **1.** A city of central Indiana north-northwest of Indianapolis. It is a trade and processing center. ⊛Pop. 14,754. **2.** The capital of Kentucky, in the north-central part of the state northwest of Lexington. First visited by the frontiersman Daniel Boone in 1770, it was chosen as capital in 1792. ⊛Pop. 25,968.

Frank·furt (frăngk′fərt, frängk′fŏŏrt′). **1.** also **Frankfurt an der O·der** (än dər ō′dər). A city of eastern Germany on the Oder River and the Polish border. It was chartered in 1253 and became a prosperous member of the Hanseatic League in the 14th century. ⊛Pop. 84,072. **2.** also **Frankfurt am Main** (äm mīn′). A city of west-central Germany on the Main River. Founded in the first century B.C. by the Romans, it was the virtual capital of Germany from 1816 to 1866. It is now an industrial, commercial, and financial center. ⊛Pop. 659,803.

Frank·ish (frăng′kĭsh). **1.** Of or relating to the Franks or their language. **2.** The West Germanic language of the Franks.

Frank·lin (frăngk′lĭn). **1.** A town of southeast Massachusetts near the Rhode Island border southwest of Boston. It was settled in 1660. ⊛Pop. 22,095. **2.** A city of southeast Wisconsin, a residential suburb of Milwaukee. ⊛Pop. 21,855.

Franklin D. Roosevelt Lake. A reservoir of northeast Washington formed in the Columbia River by Grand Coulee Dam.

Franklin Park. A village of northeast Illinois, a residential suburb of Chicago. ⊛Pop. 18,485.

Franklin Square. A community of southeast New York on southeast Long Island. It is mainly residential. ⊛Pop. 28,205.

Franks Peak (frăngks). A mountain, 4,007.7 m (13,140 ft) high, in the Absaroka Range of the Rocky Mountains in northwest Wyoming. It is the highest elevation in the range.

Franz Jo·sef Land (fränz jō′zəf länd, -səf, fränts yō′zĕf länt). An archipelago in the Arctic Ocean north of Novaya Zemlya. First explored by an Austrian expedition in 1873, the islands were claimed by the U.S.S.R. in 1926.

Fra·ser River (frā′zər). A river of British Columbia, Canada, flowing about 1,368 km (850 mi) from the Rocky Mountains near the Alberta boundary to the Strait of Georgia at Vancouver. It was discovered by the Canadian explorer Sir Alexander Mackenzie in 1793 and named later for the Canadian navigator Simon Fraser.

Fred·er·ick (frĕd′rĭk, -ər-ĭk). A city of northern Maryland west of Baltimore. It is a processing center in a farming region. ◉ Pop. 40,148.

Fred·er·icks·burg (frĕd′rĭks-bûrg′, -ər-ĭks-). An independent city of northeast Virginia north of Richmond. In the Battle of Fredericksburg (December 1862) Ambrose Burnside's Union forces were defeated by Robert E. Lee's smaller Confederate army in one of the bloodiest battles of the Civil War. ◉ Pop. 19,027.

Fred·er·ic·ton (frĕd′rĭk-tən, -ər-ĭk-). The capital of New Brunswick, Canada, in the south-central part of the province northwest of St. John. It was founded in 1783 and became provincial capital in 1785. ◉ Pop. 43,723.

Fred·er·iks·berg (frĕd′rĭks-bûrg′, -ər-ĭks-, frĕ′thə-rĕks-bärkн′). A city of eastern Denmark, a suburb of Copenhagen on Sjaelland Island. ◉ Pop. 88,114.

Free·port (frē′pôrt′, -pōrt′). 1. A city of northwest Bahamas on Grand Bahama Island. It is a tourist center. ◉ Pop. 25,000. 2. A city of northwest Illinois west of Rockford. The second of seven debates in the U.S. senatorial campaign between Abraham Lincoln and Stephen Douglas was held here in 1858. ◉ Pop. 25,840. 3. A village of southeast New York on the southern shore of Long Island. It is mainly residential. ◉ Pop. 39,894.

Free·town (frē′toun′). The capital and largest city of Sierra Leone, in the western part of the country on the Atlantic Ocean. It was settled in 1792 by freed slaves sent from England by British abolitionists. ◉ Pop. 469,776.

Frei·berg (frī′bûrg′, -bĕrk′). A city of east-central Germany east-northeast of Chemnitz. It was founded in the 12th century as a silver-mining camp. ◉ Pop. 51,290.

Frei·burg (frī′bûrg′, -bŏŏrk′) also **Freiburg im Breis·gau** (ĭm brīs′gou′). A city of southwest Germany near the Rhine River at the edge of the Black Forest. Founded in 1120, it is a manu-facturing, cultural, and tourist center. ◉ Pop. 197,384.

Fre·mont (frē′mŏnt′). 1. A city of western California on San Francisco Bay southeast of Oakland. It is a manufacturing and shipping center. ◉ Pop. 173,339. 2. A city of east-central Nebraska on the Platte River west-northwest of Omaha. It is a processing center in an agricultural region. ◉ Pop. 23,680. 3. A city of northern Ohio southeast of Toledo. A government trading post was established on the site in 1795. ◉ Pop. 17,648.

French (frĕnch). *abbr.* **Fr., F. 1.** Of, relating to, or characteristic of France or its people or culture. **2.** Of or relating to the French language. **3.** The Romance language of France, parts of Switzerland and Belgium, and other countries formerly under French influence or control. **4.** The people of France.

French Broad (brôd). A river rising in the Blue Ridge of western North Carolina and flowing about 338 km (210 mi) north and northwest to eastern Tennessee, where it joins the Holston River to form the Tennessee River.

French Cameroons. A region and former French protectorate of west-central Africa. It was ceded to France by Germany in 1919 and joined with the southern portion of British Cameroons to form the independent country of Cameroon in 1960.

French-Ca·na·di·an also **French Ca·na·di·an** (frĕnch′kə-nā′dē-ən). A Canadian of French descent. — **French′-Ca·na′di·an** *adj.*

French Equatorial Africa. Formerly **French Congo.** A former federation of west-central Africa (1910–1958) comprising the present-day countries of Chad, Gabon, Congo, and Central African Republic.

French Guiana. A French overseas department of northeast South America on the Atlantic Ocean. Settlement by the French began in 1604, but the area was largely ignored until penal colonies (now closed) were established in the 19th century. Cayenne is the capital and the largest city. ◉ Pop. 72,012.

French·man (frĕnch′mən). A man who is a native or inhabitant of France.

French Polynesia. A French overseas territory in the south-central Pacific Ocean comprising some 120 islands, including the Society and Marquesas islands and the Tuamotu Archipelago. It was organized as a territory in 1903. Papeete, on the island of Tahiti, is the capital. ◉ Pop. 166,753.

French West Africa. A former federation of French territories in western Africa (1895–1959) comprising the present-day countries of Benin, Guinea, Ivory Coast, Mali, Mauritania, Niger, Senegal, and Burkina Faso.

French West Indies. The French overseas departments of Guadeloupe and Martinique in the Lesser Antilles.

French·wom·an (frĕnch'wŏŏm'ən). A woman who is a native or inhabitant of France.

fresh·et (frĕsh'ĭt). A stream of fresh water that empties into a body of salt water.

fresh·wa·ter (frĕsh'wô'tər, -wŏt'ər). **1.** Of, relating to, living in, or consisting of water that is not salty. **2.** Situated away from the sea; inland.

Fres·no (frĕz'nō). A city of central California south-southeast of Sacramento. It is a major processing and distribution center in the fertile San Joaquin Valley. ● Pop. 354,202.

Frid·ley (frĭd'lē). A city of eastern Minnesota, a suburb of Minneapolis on the Mississippi River. ● Pop. 28,335.

Frie·drichs·ha·fen (frē'drĭks-hä'fən, -drĭKHS-). A city of southern Germany on the Lake of Constance. The Zeppelin aircraft works were located here during World War I. ● Pop. 51,094.

Friend·ly Islands (frĕnd'lē). See **Tonga.**

Frie·sian (frē'zhən). Variant of **Frisian.**

Fries·land (frēz'lənd, -lănd', frēs'-). A region of northern Europe on the North Sea between the Scheldt and Weser rivers. The Frisians, a Germanic people, were conquered by the Franks in the eighth century. A portion of the area is now a province, also called Friesland, of the northern Netherlands.

Frig·id Zone (frĭj'ĭd). Either of two extreme latitude zones of the earth, the **North Frigid Zone,** between the North Pole and the Arctic Circle, or the **South Frigid Zone,** between the South Pole and the Antarctic Circle.

Frim·ley and Cam·ber·ley (frĭm'lē; kăm'-bər-lē). An urban district of southern England southwest of London. The village of Sandhurst, site of the Royal Military College, is in the district. ● Pop. 52,600.

Fri·o (frē'ō). A river of southern Texas flowing about 354 km (220 mi) south and southeast to the Nueces River.

Fri·sian (frĭzh'ən, frē'zhən) also **Frie·sian** (frē'zhən). *abbr.* **Fris., Frs. 1.** A native or inhabitant of the Frisian Islands or Friesland. **2.** The West Germanic language of the Frisians. It is the language most closely related to English. —**Fri'sian** *adj.*

Frisian Islands. A chain of islands in the North Sea off the coast of the Netherlands, Germany, and Denmark. The **West Frisian Islands** belong to the Netherlands. The **East Frisian Islands** and most of the **North Frisian Islands** are part of Germany; the other North Frisians are Danish.

frith (frĭth). *Scots.* A firth.

Fri·u·li (frē'ə-lē', frē-ōō'lē). A historical region

and former duchy of Italy in present-day northeast Italy and Slovenia. Occupied by the Romans in the second century B.C., it became a Lombard duchy in the sixth century A.D. and was conquered by various peoples and states before being ceded to Italy in 1866 (the western part) and 1919 (the eastern part). Eastern Friuli was awarded to Yugoslavia by treaty in 1947.

Fri·u·li-Ve·ne·zia Giu·lia (frē'ə-lē'və-nĕt'-sē-ə jōōl'yə, frē-ōō'lē-vĕ-nĕt'syä). A region of northeast Italy bounded by Austria in the north and Slovenia in the east. It was formed in 1947.

Fro·bish·er Bay (frō'bĭ-shər). An arm of the Atlantic Ocean extending into extreme southeast Baffin Island in Northwest Territories, Canada. It was discovered by the English explorer Sir Martin Frobisher in 1576 and until 1860 was thought to be a strait separating Baffin Island from another island.

Front Range (frŭnt). A range of the Rocky Mountains in north-central Colorado. It rises to 4,352.4 m (14,270 ft) at Grays Peak.

fron·tier (frŭn-tîr', frŏn-, frŭn'tîr', frŏn'-). **1. a.** An international border. **b.** The area along an international border. **2.** A region just beyond or at the edge of a settled area.

Frost·belt also **Frost Belt** (frôst'bĕlt', frŏst'-). The north-central and northeast United States.

Fro·ward (frō'wərd, -ərd), **Cape.** The southernmost point of mainland South America, in southern Chile on the Strait of Magellan.

Frun·ze (frōōn'zə). See **Bishkek.**

Fu·chou (fōō'jō', -chou'). See **Fuzhou.**

Fu·chu (fōō'chōō'). A city of east-central Honshu, Japan, a mainly residential suburb of Tokyo. ● Pop. 215,048.

Fuer·te·ven·tu·ra (fōō-ĕr'tē-vĕn-tōōr'ə, fwĕr'-tĕ-vĕn-tōō'rä). An island in the Canary Islands off the northwest coast of Africa. It has many extinct volcanoes.

Fu·jai·rah (fə-jī'rə, fōō-jī'rä). A sheikdom of the United Arab Emirates on the Gulf of Oman. It joined the federation in 1971. ● Pop. 32,191.

Fu·ji (fōō'jē). A city of central Honshu, Japan, at the foot of Mount Fuji. It is an important communications and industrial center. ● Pop. 228,069.

Fuji, Mount also **Fu·ji·ya·ma** (fōō'jē-yä'mə, -mä) or **Fu·ji·no·ya·ma** (-nō-) or **Fu·ji·san** (-sän'). The highest peak, 3,778.6 m (12,389 ft), in Japan, in central Honshu west-southwest of Tokyo. A dormant volcano and an almost perfectly symmetrical snow-capped cone, it is a sacred mountain and traditional pilgrimage site. Its last major eruption was in 1707.

Fu·jian¹ (fōō'jyän', fü'-) also **Fu·kien** (-kyĕn'). A province of southeast China on the East China Sea and the Formosa Strait. Agriculture and fishing are important to its economy. Fuzhou is the capital. ● Pop. 27,130,000.

Fu·jian² (fōō'jyän', fü'-) also **Fu·kien** (-kyĕn'). A dialect of Chinese spoken in Fujian province, eastern Guangdong province, and Taiwan.

Fu·ji·no·ya·ma (fōō'jē-nō-yä'mə, -mä). See Mount **Fuji.**

Fu·ji·san (fōō'jē-sän'). See Mount **Fuji.**

Fu·ji·sa·wa (fōō'jē-sä'wə, -wä). A city of east-central Honshu, Japan, an industrial and residential suburb of Tokyo. ● Pop. 362,088.

Fu·ji·ya·ma (fōō'jē-yä'mə, -mä). See Mount **Fuji.**

Fu·kien¹ (fōō'kyĕn'). See **Fujian¹.**

Fu·kien² (fōō'kyĕn'). See **Fujian².**

Fu·ku·i (fōō-kōō'ē). A city of central Honshu, Japan, north-northwest of Nagoya. A major textile center since the tenth century, it was rebuilt after a disastrous earthquake in June 1948. ● Pop. 254,667.

Fu·ku·o·ka (fōō'kōō-ō'kə, -kä). A city of northwest Kyushu, Japan, on an inlet of the Sea of Japan. It is an industrial and educational center. ● Pop. 1,268,626.

Fu·ku·shi·ma (fōō'kə-shē'mə, -kōō-shē'mä). A city of north-central Honshu, Japan, north-northeast of Tokyo. It is a trade and transportation center. ● Pop. 282,654.

Fu·ku·ya·ma (fōō'kə-yä'mə, -kōō-yä'mä). A city of southwest Honshu, Japan, on the Inland Sea east of Kure. It is a commercial, industrial, and communications center. ● Pop. 370,873.

Fu·la·ni (fōō'lä'nē, fōō-lä'-) also **Fu·la** (fōō'lə). **1.** *pl.* **Fulani** or **-nis** also **Fula** or **-las.** A member of a pastoral, largely Muslim people inhabiting parts of West Africa from northern Nigeria to Mali and the Atlantic coast. **2.** The West Atlantic language of this people.

Ful·da (fōōl'də). A city of central Germany south-southeast of Kassel on the **Fulda River,** about 217 km (135 mi) long. The city grew around a Benedictine abbey founded in 744. ● Pop. 55,441.

Ful·ler·ton (fōōl'ər-tən). A city of southern California southeast of Los Angeles. Founded in 1887, it has varied industries. ● Pop. 114,144.

Ful·ton (fōōl'tən). A city of central Missouri east-southeast of Columbia. On March 5, 1946, British statesman Winston Churchill delivered his Iron Curtain speech here at Westminster College (established 1851). ● Pop. 10,033.

fu·ma·role (fyōō'mə-rōl'). A hole in a volcanic area from which hot smoke and gases escape. —**fu'ma·rol'ic** (-rŏl'ĭk) *adj.*

Fu·na·ba·shi (fōō'nə-bä'shē, -nä-). A city of east-central Honshu, Japan, a suburb of Tokyo on Tokyo Bay. ● Pop. 539,740.

Fu·na·fu·ti (fōō'nə-fōō'tē). An atoll of Tuvalu in the southern Pacific Ocean. Discovered in 1819, it is the site of Fongafale, the capital of Tuvalu.

Fun·dy (fŭn'dē), **Bay of.** An inlet of the Atlantic Ocean in southeast Canada between New Brunswick and Nova Scotia noted for its tidal bore and its exceptionally high tides.

Fürth (fōōrt, fürt). A city of south-central Germany, a suburb of Nuremberg. It was supposedly founded by Charlemagne, king of the Franks, in the late eighth century. ● Pop. 108,097.

Fu·san (fōō'sän'). See **Pusan.**

Fu·shun (fōō'shōōn', fü'shün'). A city of northeast China east of Shenyang. Highly industrialized, it was formerly controlled by Russia and Japan. ● Pop. 1,388,011.

Fu·sin (fōō'shĭn', fü'-). See **Fuxin.**

Fu·ta Jal·lon (fōō'tə jə-lōn', fōō'tä jä-lôN'). See **Fouta Djallon.**

Fu·tu·na Islands (fə-tōō'nə, fōō-) also **Hoorn Islands** (hôrn, hōrn). An island group of the southwest Pacific Ocean northeast of Fiji. Part of the French overseas territory of Wallis and Futuna, the islands were annexed by France in 1887.

Fu·xin also **Fu·sin** (fōō'shĭn', fü'-). A city of northeast China west-northwest of Shenyang. It is a mining center. ● Pop. 743,165.

Fu·zhou (fōō'jō') also **Foo·chow** or **Fu·chou** (fōō'jō', -chou'). A city of southeast China on the Min River delta. An ancient walled city, it was a treaty port following the Opium War (1839–1842) with Great Britain. Fuzhou has been the capital of Fujian province since the tenth century. ● Pop. 1,395,739.

Fyn (fĭn, fün). An island of south-central Denmark west of Sjaelland. Its chief products are dairy goods and cereals.

G

Ga (gä). **1.** *pl.* **Ga** or **Gas.** A member of a people of southeast Ghana. **2.** The Kwa language of the Ga.

Ga·bon (gă-bōN'). A country of west-central Africa on the Atlantic Ocean. It was probably inhabited by Pygmy peoples before the migration of Bantu speakers into the region. Visited by the Portuguese in 1472, it was settled by the French in 1841 and became part of French Equatorial Africa in 1910. Gabon achieved independence from France in 1960, and a one-party state was established in 1968. Growing discontent with repressive government policies during the 1980's led to the adoption (1990) of a transitional constitution that legalized opposition parties and called for free elections, which were held in 1990 and 1993 amid charges of fraud. Following rioting and dissension in 1994, a new constitution was approved in 1995. Libreville is the capital and the largest city. ⊛ Pop. 1,283,000.

Ga·bo·rone (gä'bə-rōn', -rō'nē). The capital of Botswana, in the southeast part of the country near the South African border. It was founded c. 1890. ⊛ Pop. 133,468.

Gad·a·ra (găd'ər-ə). An ancient city of Palestine southeast of the Sea of Galilee. It was one of the Greek cities of the Decapolis. —**Gad'a·rene'** (găd'ə-rēn', găd'ə-rēn') adj. & n.

Gads·den (gădz'dən). A city of northeast Alabama northeast of Birmingham. It is an industrial center. ⊛ Pop. 42,523.

Gadsden Purchase. An area in extreme southern New Mexico and Arizona south of the Gila River. It was purchased by the United States from Mexico in 1853 to ensure territorial rights for a practicable southern railroad route to the Pacific Coast.

Gael (gāl). **1.** A Gaelic-speaking Celt of Scotland, Ireland, or the Isle of Man. **2.** A Scottish Highlander.

Gael·ic (gā'lĭk). **1.** Of or relating to the Gaels or their culture or languages. **2.** Goidelic. **3.** Any of the Goidelic languages.

Ga·e·ta (gä-ā'tə, -ē'tä). A city of west-central Italy northwest of Naples on the **Gulf of Gaeta,** an inlet of the Tyrrhenian Sea. Gaeta was a favorite resort of the ancient Romans and a prosperous duchy from the 9th to the 12th century, when it was conquered by the Normans. ⊛ Pop. 22,605.

Ga·han·na (gə-hăn'ə). A city of central Ohio, a suburb of Columbus. ⊛ Pop. 27,791.

Gail·lard Cut (gĭl-yärd', gā'lärd'). Formerly **Cu·le·bra Cut** (kōō-lā'brə). An excavation, about 13 km (8 mi) long and 14 m (45 ft) deep, through Culebra Mountain, a hill in the Canal Zone, Panama. The cut forms the southeast section of the Panama Canal.

Gaines·ville (gānz'vĭl', -vəl). **1.** A city of north-central Florida southwest of Jacksonville.

The University of Florida (founded 1853) is important to its economy. ⊛ Pop. 84,770. **2.** A city of north-central Georgia northeast of Atlanta in the foothills of the Blue Ridge. It is a trade and industrial center. ⊛ Pop. 17,885.

Gai·thers·burg (gā'thərz-bûrg'). A city of west-central Maryland north-northwest of Washington, D.C. It is a residential city with light industries. ⊛ Pop. 39,542.

Ga·lá·pa·gos Islands (gə-lä'pə-gəs, -läp'ə-). A group of volcanic islands lying along the equator in the Pacific Ocean about 1,045 km (650 mi) west of the mainland of Ecuador, to which they belong. The islands are famous for their rare species of fauna, including the giant tortoises for which they are named. Charles Darwin visited the islands in 1835 and collected a wealth of scientific data that contributed to his theory of natural selection. Tourism is now strictly regulated to protect the endangered species unknown outside the archipelago.

Ga·la·ţi (gä-läts', -lät'sē) or **Ga·latz** (gä'läts'). A city of eastern Romania on the lower Danube River northeast of Bucharest. Founded in the Middle Ages, it is a major inland port. ⊛ Pop. 324,234.

Ga·la·tia (gə-lā'shə, -shē-ə). An ancient country of central Asia Minor in the region surrounding modern Ankara, Turkey. Settled by Celtic tribes in the third century B.C., it came under Roman control in 189 B.C. and became a Roman province in 25 B.C. —**Ga·la'tian** adj. & n.

Ga·latz (gä'läts'). See **Galați.**

Ga·le·na (gə-lē'nə). A city of extreme northwest Illinois west-northwest of Rockford. A prosperous river port until the 1860's, it was the home of Union general and U.S. President Ulysses S. Grant, whose residence is now a museum. ⊛ Pop. 3,876.

Gales·burg (gālz'bûrg'). A city of northwest-central Illinois west-northwest of Peoria. The poet Carl Sandburg (1878–1967) was born here. ⊛ Pop. 33,530.

Ga·li·bi (gə-lē'bē). **1.** pl. **Galibi** or **-bis.** A member of the Carib people of French Guiana. **2.** The language of the Galibi.

Ga·li·cia (gə-lĭsh'ə, -ē-ə). **1.** A historical region of central Europe in southeast Poland and western Ukraine. An independent principality after 1087, it was conquered by the Russians in the 12th century and later passed to Poland and Austria. The territory was returned to Poland after World War I, and the eastern portion was ceded to the U.S.S.R. after World War II. **2.** A region and ancient kingdom of northwest Spain on the Atlantic Ocean south of the Bay of Biscay. Originally inhabited by Celts, Galicia was exploited by the Romans for its mineral resources and later became a Goth kingdom and a stronghold of the Moors.

Ga·li·cian¹ (gə-lĭsh′ən). **1.** Of or relating to Polish Galicia or its people, language, or culture. **2.** A native or inhabitant of Polish Galicia.

Ga·li·cian² (gə-lĭsh′ən). **1.** Of or relating to Spanish Galicia or its people, language, or culture. **2.** A native or inhabitant of Spanish Galicia. **3.** The Portuguese dialect spoken in Spanish Galicia.

Gal·i·lee (găl′ə-lē′). A region of northern Israel. The northernmost part of Palestine and the ancient kingdom of Israel, Galilee was the center of Jesus's ministry. — **Gal′i·le′an, Gal′i·lae′an** adj. & n.

Galilee, Sea of. Formerly **Lake Ti·be·ri·as** (tī-bîr′ē-əs). A freshwater lake of northeast Israel. About 214 m (700 ft) below sea level, it is fed and drained by the Jordan River.

Gal·la (găl′ə). pl. **Galla** or **-las.** See **Oromo.**

Gal·la·tin (găl′ĭ-tn). A city of northern Tennessee northeast of Nashville. It is a trade center in a tobacco-growing region. ⦿ Pop. 18,794.

Gallatin Range. A section of the Rocky Mountains in northwest Wyoming and southwest Montana rising to 3,402.3 m (11,155 ft) at Electric Peak.

Gallatin River. A river rising in the Gallatin Range of northwest Wyoming and flowing about 201 km (125 mi) generally northwest to join the Jefferson and Madison rivers and form the Missouri River in southwest Montana.

Galle (găl, gäl). A city of southern Sri Lanka on the Indian Ocean. It was a trade center for the Chinese and Arabs by 100 B.C. and later flourished as a Portuguese and Dutch port. It passed to the British in 1796. ⦿ Pop. 109,000.

Gal·li·a (găl′ē-ä). See **Gaul².**

Gal·lic (găl′ĭk). Of or relating to Gaul or France; French.

Gal·li·nas (gä-yē′näs), **Point.** A cape of northern Colombia, the northernmost point of South America.

Gal·lip·o·li (gə-lĭp′ə-lē). A city of northwest Turkey on the **Gallipoli Peninsula** at the eastern end of the Dardanelles. The peninsula was the scene of heavy fighting (1915) between Allied and Turkish forces in World War I. The city's population is 16,715.

Gal·lo·way (găl′ə-wā′). A region of southwest Scotland. The **Mull of Galloway,** a promontory on a peninsula on its southwest coast, is the southernmost point in Scotland.

Gal·lup (găl′əp). A city of northwest New Mexico near the Arizona border. It is a trade center in a ranching and mining area. ⦿ Pop. 19,154.

Gal·ves·ton (găl′vĭ-stən). A city of southeast Texas south-southeast of Houston on **Galveston Island** at the entrance to **Galveston Bay,** an arm

of the Gulf of Mexico. The Spanish explorer Cabeza de Vaca may have been shipwrecked on the island in 1528. ⦿ Pop. 59,070.

Gal·way (gôl′wā′). A region of west-central Ireland bordering on **Galway Bay,** an inlet of the Atlantic Ocean. The city of **Galway** was incorporated in the late 14th century and is today an important industrial and tourist center. The city's population is 37,835.

Gam·bi·a (găm′bē-ə) or **The Gambia.** A country of western Africa lying along the Gambia River and surrounded, except for a short coastline on the Atlantic Ocean, by Senegal. Once a part of the Mali Empire, the area became a British crown colony in 1843 and a British protectorate in 1894. Gambia achieved independence in 1965 and declared itself a republic in 1970. From 1982 until 1989 it formed with Senegal the Confederation of Senegambia, an economic and military union under which both countries maintained their sovereignty. Relatively stable since independence, the government was rocked by a military coup in 1994 that deposed the president, suspended the constitution, and banned political parties. Banjul is the capital and largest city. ⦿ Pop. 1,081,000. — **Gam′bi·an** adj. & n.

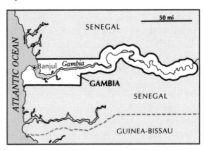

Gambia River. A river of western Africa flowing about 1,126 km (700 mi) from northern Guinea through southeast Senegal and Gambia to the Atlantic Ocean at Banjul.

Gam·bier Islands (găm′bîr′). An island group of French Polynesia in the south-central Pacific Ocean.

Gan·der (găn′dər). A town of northeast Newfoundland, Canada. Its airport was strategically important during World War II and was long used as a refueling stop for transatlantic flights. ⦿ Pop. 10,404.

Gan·ges (găn′jēz′) also **Gan·ga** (gŭng′gə). A river of northern India and Bangladesh rising in the Himalaya Mountains and flowing about 2,510 km (1,560 mi) eastward through a vast plain to the Bay of Bengal. The river is considered sacred by Hindus.

Gan Jiang (gän′ jyäng′) also **Kan River** (kän′). A river of southeast China flowing about 885 km

(550 mi) generally north into the Chang Jiang (Yangtze River) north of Nanchang.

Gan·nett Peak (găn′ĭt). A mountain, 4,210.2 m (13,804 ft) high, in the Wind River Range of the Rocky Mountains in west-central Wyoming. It is the highest point in the state.

Gan·su (gän′sōō′) also **Kan·su** (kän′sōō′, gän′-). A province of north-central China. It was long a corridor for the Silk Road to Turkistan, India, and Persia. Lanzhou is the capital. ◉ Pop. 20,410,000.

gap (găp). An opening through mountains; a pass.

Garb·sen (gärb′sən). A city of north-central Germany, a suburb of Hanover. ◉ Pop. 57,292.

Gar·da (gär′də), **Lake.** A lake of northern Italy east of Milan. Its shoreline is dotted with resorts and vineyards.

Gar·de·na (gär-dē′nə). A city of southern California, an industrial suburb of Los Angeles. ◉ Pop. 49,847.

Gar·den City (gär′dn). 1. A city of southwest Kansas west-northwest of Dodge City. It is a trade and industrial center in an irrigated farming area. ◉ Pop. 24,097. 2. A city of southeast Michigan, a chiefly residential suburb of Detroit. ◉ Pop. 31,846. 3. A village of southeast New York on western Long Island. Roosevelt Field, the starting point for Charles A. Lindbergh's 1927 transatlantic flight, is here. ◉ Pop. 21,686.

Garden Grove. A city of southern California, a residential suburb of Long Beach and Los Angeles. ◉ Pop. 143,050.

Gar·di·ners Island (gärd′nərz, gär′dn-ərz). An island of southeast New York in **Gardiners Bay** between two peninsulas of eastern Long Island. Settled in 1639, it is a reputed burial place of Captain Kidd's pirate treasure.

Gard·ner (gärd′nər). A city of north-central Massachusetts west of Fitchburg. Its furniture industry dates from c. 1805. ◉ Pop. 20,125.

Gar·field (gär′fēld′). A city of northeast New Jersey on the Passaic River southeast of Paterson. It was settled by the Dutch in 1679. ◉ Pop. 26,727.

Garfield Heights. A city of northeast Ohio, an industrial suburb of Cleveland. ◉ Pop. 31,739.

Garfield Mountain. A peak, 3,343.1 m (10,961 ft) high, in the Bitterroot Range of the Rocky Mountains in southwest Montana. It is the highest elevation of the range.

Gar·land (gär′lənd). A city of northeast Texas, an industrial suburb of Dallas. ◉ Pop. 180,650.

Gar·misch-Par·ten·kir·chen (gär′mĭsh-pär′-tn-kîr′kən, -кнən). A city of south-central Germany in the foothills of the Bavarian Alps. A noted resort, it was the site of the 1936 Winter Olympics. ◉ Pop. 28,049.

Ga·ronne (gä-rôn′). A river of southwest France flowing about 563 km (350 mi) generally northwest from the Spanish Pyrenees to join the Dordogne River north of Bordeaux and form the Gironde estuary.

Gar·y (gâr′ē, găr′ē). A city of northwest Indiana on Lake Michigan near the Illinois border. Founded on land purchased by the U.S. Steel Corporation in 1905, it is a highly industrialized port of entry. ◉ Pop. 116,646.

Gas·con (găs′kən). 1. A native or inhabitant of Gascony. 2. Of or relating to Gascony, the Gascons, or their language or culture.

Gas·con·ade (găs′kə-nād′). A river rising in the Ozark Plateau of south-central Missouri and flowing about 426 km (265 mi) generally northeast to the Missouri River east of Jefferson City.

Gas·co·ny (găs′kə-nē). A historical region and former province of southwest France. Settled originally by Basque peoples, it was conquered by the Romans and later by the Visigoths and Franks. A new wave of Basque invaders from south of the Pyrenees established the duchy of Vasconia in the sixth century A.D. In 1052 Gascony passed to the duchy of Aquitaine, and after serving as a major battlefield during the Hundred Years' War between England and France (1337–1453), it finally became part of the French royal domain in 1607.

Gash·er·brum (gŭsh′ər-brōōm′, -brōōm′). A series of four peaks in the Karakoram Range of the Himalaya Mountains in northern Kashmir. **Gasherbrum I** is the highest, at 8,073.4 m (26,470 ft), although **Gasherbrum IV,** 7,930 m (26,000 ft), has been called more difficult than Everest for mountain climbers. The other two peaks are 8,039.8 m (26,360 ft) and 7,957.5 m (26,090 ft) high.

Gas·pé (găs-pā′). A city of eastern Quebec, Canada, on **Gaspé Bay,** an inlet of the Gulf of St. Lawrence near the eastern tip of the Gaspé Peninsula. Fishing, lumbering, and tourism are important to its economy. ◉ Pop. 17,261.

Gaspé Peninsula. A peninsula of eastern Quebec, Canada, between Chaleur Bay and the mouth of the St. Lawrence River. Mountainous and heavily wooded, the peninsula is known for its picturesque coastal villages as well as its hunting and fishing. The French explorer Jacques Cartier landed here in 1534.

Gas·to·ni·a (gă-stō′nē-ə). A city of southern North Carolina near the South Carolina border west of Charlotte. It is a textile center. ◉ Pop. 54,732.

gat (găt). A narrow passage extending inland from a shore; a channel.

Gates (gāts). A community of western New York, a suburb of Rochester. ◉ Pop. 29,756.

Gates·head (gāts'hĕd'). A borough of northeast England on the Tyne River opposite Newcastle. Dating probably to Saxon times, it has an iron and steel industry that developed in the 19th century. ⊛ Pop. 202,850.

Gath (găth). An ancient city of Palestine east-northeast of Gaza. It was one of the five Philistine city-kingdoms and the home of Goliath, the giant Philistine warrior slain by David in the Bible.

Gat·i·neau (găt'n-ō', gä-tē-nō'). A town of southwest Quebec, Canada, northeast of Hull near the mouth of the **Gatineau River,** about 386 km (240 mi) long. The river rises in the Laurentian Plateau and flows generally southwest to the Ottawa River. The city is an industrial center. ⊛ Pop. 74,988.

Ga·tún Lake (gə-tōōn', gä-). An artificial lake of central Panama formed by the impounding of the Chagres River. It is a major link in the Panama Canal system.

Gau·ga·me·la (gô'gə-mē'lə). An ancient village of Assyria northeast of Nineveh. Alexander the Great defeated the Persians under Darius III here in 331 B.C.

Gaul[1] (gôl). **1.** A Celt of ancient Gaul. **2.** A French person.

Gaul[2] (gôl). Formerly **Gal·li·a** (găl'ē-ä). An ancient region of western Europe south and west of the Rhine River, west of the Alps, and north of the Pyrenees, corresponding roughly to modern-day France and Belgium. The Romans extended the designation to include northern Italy, particularly after Julius Caesar's conquest of the area in the Gallic Wars (58–51 B.C.).

Gaul·ish (gô'lĭsh). The Celtic language of ancient Gaul.

Ga·var·nie (găv'ər-nē', gä-vär-). A waterfall, about 422 m (1,384 ft) high, of southwest France in the Pyrenees south of Lourdes. Nearby is the **Cirque de Gavarnie,** a vast natural amphitheater with steep walls up to 1,708 m (5,600 ft) high.

Gäv·le (yĕv'lĕ). A city of eastern Sweden on the Gulf of Bothnia north-northwest of Stockholm. Chartered in 1446, it has a thriving export trade. ⊛ Pop. 67,300.

Ga·ya (gə-yä', gī'ə). A city of northeast India south of Patna. The surrounding area is sacred to Buddhist and Hindu pilgrims. ⊛ Pop. 291,675.

Ga·za (gä'zə, găz'ə, gā'zə). A city of southwest Asia in the **Gaza Strip,** a narrow coastal area along the Mediterranean Sea adjoining Israel and Egypt. The territory was part of the British mandate for Palestine (1917–1948), passed to Egypt in 1949, and was occupied by Israel in 1967. Palestinian autonomy was prom-

ised in the 1979 Israeli-Egyptian peace treaty, and limited autonomy was granted in a 1993 Israeli-Palestinian accord, which also called for negotiations to determine the future of the territory within five years. The city of Gaza was one of the five major Philistine city-kingdoms. ⊛ Pop. 118,272.

Ga·zi·an·tep (gä'zē-än-tĕp'). Formerly **Ain·tab** (īn-täb'). A city of southern Turkey north of Aleppo, Syria. An ancient Hittite center, it was strategically important during the Crusades. The surrounding area is known for its textiles and pistachio nuts. ⊛ Pop. 716,000.

Gbe (bĕ, gbĕ). A closely related group of languages, including Ewe and Fon, that are spoken in coastal Ghana, Togo, Benin, and Nigeria.

Gdańsk (gə-dänsk', -dänsk', -dĭnsk') also **Danzig** (dăn'sĭg, dän'tsĭk). A city of northern Poland near the mouth of the Vistula River on the **Gulf of Gdańsk,** an inlet of the Baltic Sea. It is a major port and shipbuilding center. An old Slavic settlement, Gdańsk was a part of the Hanseatic League after the 13th century and was later ruled by Poland and Prussia before it was made a free city again by the Treaty of Versailles (1919). Hitler's demand that Gdańsk be returned to Germany led to his invasion of Poland and the beginning of World War II (September 1939). The city was liberated by the Russians in 1945 and subsequently restored to Poland. In 1980 strikes begun by the shipyard workers in Gdańsk led to the formation of the illegal trade union Solidarity and major political changes within the Polish government. ⊛ Pop. 465,395.

Gdy·ni·a (gə-dĭn'ē-ə, -dĭn'yə). A city of northern Poland on the Gulf of Gdańsk northwest of Gdańsk. It has been a major Baltic port since the 1930's. ⊛ Pop. 251,463.

Ge·bel Mu·sa (jĕb'əl mōō'sə, -sä). See **Jebel Musa.**

Gee·chee (gē'chē). **1.** *Southeastern U.S.* Gullah. **2.** The local dialect of English spoken in Charleston, South Carolina.

Gee·long (jə-lông'). A city of southeast Australia southwest of Melbourne. It is a manufacturing center with a thriving tourist industry. ⊛ Pop. 151,900.

Ge·la (jĕ'lä). A city of southern Sicily, Italy, on the Mediterranean Sea. Founded c. 688 B.C. by Greek colonists from Crete and Rhodes, it reached the height of its prosperity in the fifth century B.C. The dramatist Aeschylus (525–456 B.C.) lived here. ⊛ Pop. 74,789.

Gel·der·land (gĕl'dər-lănd', кНĕl'dər-länt'). A region and former duchy of east-central Netherlands. The duchy was formed in 1339 and passed to the Hapsburgs in 1543. It became part of the Netherlands in 1579, although a portion of the territory was ceded to Prussia in the 18th century.

Gel·sen·kir·chen (gĕl′zən-kîr′kən, -KHən). A city of west-central Germany in the Ruhr Valley northeast of Essen. It is a major industrial and coal-mining center. • Pop. 295,037.

Gen·er·al San Mar·tín (jĕn′ər-əl săn märtēn′, hĕn′ĕ-räl′ sän). A city of eastern Argentina, a manufacturing suburb of Buenos Aires. • Pop. 407,506.

Gen·e·see (jĕn′ĭ-sē′, jĕn′ĭ-sē′). A river rising in northern Pennsylvania and flowing about 241 km (150 mi) generally northward across western New York to Lake Ontario.

Ge·ne·va (jə-nē′və). 1. A city of southwest Switzerland located on Lake Geneva and bisected by the Rhone River. Originally an ancient Celtic settlement, it was a focal point of the Reformation after the arrival of the Protestant theologian John Calvin in 1536. Geneva was the headquarters of the League of Nations (1920–1946) and is still the site of many international organizations. • Pop. 170,861. 2. A city of west-central New York at the northern end of Seneca Lake west-southwest of Syracuse. It is a manufacturing center in an agricultural region. • Pop. 14,143.

Geneva, Lake also **Lake Le·man** (lē′mən, ləmăn′). A lake on the Swiss-French border between the Alps and the Jura Mountains. It is traversed east to west by the Rhone River.

Ge·ne·van (jə-nē′vən) also **Gen·e·vese** (jĕn′əvēz′, -vēs′). 1. Of or relating to Geneva, Switzerland, or its inhabitants. 2. A native or inhabitant of Geneva, Switzerland.

Genk (gĕngk). A city of northeast Belgium north of Liège. It is a commercial and industrial center. • Pop. 61,808.

Gen·o·a (jĕn′ō-ə). A city of northwest Italy on the **Gulf of Genoa,** an arm of the Ligurian Sea. An ancient settlement, Genoa flourished under the Romans and also enjoyed great prosperity during the Crusades. Today, it is Italy's chief port and a major commercial and industrial center. • Pop. 675,659. — **Gen′o·ese′** (-ēz′, -ēs′), **Gen′o·vese′** (-vēz′, -vēs′) adj. & n.

Gent (gĕnt, KHĕnt). See **Ghent.**

Gen·tof·te (gĕn′tŭf′tə). A city of eastern Denmark, a mainly residential suburb of Copenhagen on Sjaelland Island. • Pop. 67,112.

ge·od·e·sy (jē-ŏd′ĭ-sē). The geologic science of the size and shape of the earth. — **ge′o·des′·ic** (jē′ə-dĕs′ĭk, -dē′sĭk), **ge′o·det′ic** (-dĕt′ĭk), **ge′o·det′i·cal** adj. — **ge·od′e·sist** n.

geodetic survey. A survey of a large area of land in which corrections are made to account for the curvature of the earth.

ge·o·graph·ic (jē′ə-grăf′ĭk) also **ge·o·graph·i·**

cal (-ĭ-kəl). abbr. **geog.** 1. Of or relating to geography. 2. Concerning the topography of a specific region. — **ge′o·graph′i·cal·ly** adv.

ge·og·ra·phy (jē-ŏg′rə-fē). abbr. **geog.** 1. The study of the earth and its features and of the distribution of life on the earth, including human life and the effects of human activity. 2. The physical characteristics, especially the surface features, of an area. — **ge·og′ra·pher** n.

ge·oid (jē′oid′). The hypothetical surface of the earth that coincides everywhere with mean sea level. — **ge·oid′al** (-oid′l) adj.

ge·o·mag·net·ic equator (gē′ō-măg-nĕt′ĭk). The imaginary great circle on the earth's surface formed by the intersection of a plane passing through the earth's center perpendicular to the axis connecting the north and south magnetic poles.

Geor·die (jôr′dē). *Chiefly British.* 1. A native or inhabitant of Newcastle upon Tyne, England, or its environs. 2. The dialect of English spoken by Geordies.

George V Coast also **George V Land** (jôrj). A section of the coastal area of Antarctica between Wilkes Land and Victoria Land. It is claimed by Australia.

George, Lake. 1. A lake of northeast Florida formed by a widening of the St. Johns River. 2. A glacial lake of northeast New York in the foothills of the Adirondack Mountains south of Lake Champlain. Discovered in 1646, it was the site of numerous battles during the French and Indian War (1754–1763) and the American Revolution (1775–1783). Today the lake is the center of a large recreational area.

George River. A river of northeast Quebec, Canada, rising on the Quebec-Labrador border and flowing about 563 km (350 mi) northward to Ungava Bay.

Geor·ges Bank (jôr′jĭz). A submerged sandbank in the Atlantic Ocean east of Cape Cod, Massachusetts. Controlled by the United States and Canada, it is a highly productive fishing ground.

George·town (jôrj′toun′). 1. also **George Town.** The capital of the Cayman Islands, on Grand Cayman in the West Indies west of Jamaica. It is an international banking center. • Pop. 7,617. 2. The capital and largest city of Guyana, in the northern part of the country on the Atlantic Ocean. Founded by the British in 1781, it was called Stabroek while it was controlled by the Dutch and was renamed Georgetown in 1812. • Pop. 78,500. 3. A section of western Washington, D.C. Settled c. 1665, it was incorporated as a town in 1789 but lost its charter in 1871 and was annexed by Washington, D.C., in 1878. It is known for its fashionable old houses and private gardens.

George Town. 1. also **Pi·nang** or **Pe·nang** (pə-năng′, pē′näng′). A city of western Malaysia on Pinang Island in the Strait of Malacca. It is a leading seaport. ● Pop. 250,578. **2.** See **Georgetown** (sense 1).

Geor·gia (jôr′jə). **1.** Formerly **Geor·gian Soviet Socialist Republic** (-jən). A country in the Caucasus on the Black Sea. It developed as a kingdom c. 4th century B.C. and reached the height of its prosperity and cultural flowering in the 12th and 13th centuries. Ruled by both Turkey and Persia at various times, Georgia was acquired by Russia between 1801 and 1829. The region was briefly independent (1918–1921), but was invaded by the Red Army in 1921 and proclaimed a Soviet republic. It was joined with Armenia and Azerbaijan to form the Transcaucasian Soviet Federated Socialist Republic from 1922 until 1936, when it became a separate constituent republic. Georgia declared its independence in 1991, since which time it has been beset by ethnic and civil strife, including conflicts with separatists in Abkhazia and South Ossetia. The capital is Tbilisi. ● Pop. 5,450,000. **2.** *abbr.* **GA, Ga.** A state of the southeast United States. It was admitted as one of the original Thirteen Colonies in 1788. Georgia was founded in 1732 by a group led by the British philanthropist James Oglethorpe and named for King George II. Atlanta is the capital and the largest city. ● Pop. 6,508,419.

Georgia, Strait of. A channel between Vancouver Island, Canada, and mainland British Columbia and northern Washington State. Part of the Inside Passage to Alaska, the strait links Puget Sound with Queen Charlotte Sound.

Geor·gian (jôr′jən). **1.** Of or relating to the U.S. state of Georgia or its inhabitants. **3.** Of or relating to the country of Georgia or its people, language, or culture. **4.** A native or inhabitant of the U.S. state of Georgia. **5. a.** A native or inhabitant of the country of Georgia. **b.** The non-Indo-European language of the Georgians.

Georgian Bay. An extension of Lake Huron in southeast Ontario, Canada. Many of its small, wooded islands are summer resorts.

Georgian Soviet Socialist Republic. See **Georgia** (sense 1).

Geor·gi·na (jôr-jē′nə). An intermittent river, about 1,126 km (700 mi) long, of the Simpson Desert in north-central Australia.

Ge·ra (gĕr′ə). A city of east-central Germany south-southwest of Leipzig. Chartered in the early 13th century, it is an industrial and transportation center. ● Pop. 122,974.

Ger·man (jûr′mən). *abbr.* **Ger. 1.** Of, relating to, or characteristic of Germany or its people. **2.** Of or relating to the German language. **3. a.** A native or inhabitant of Germany. **b.** A person of German ancestry. **4.** The West Germanic language of Germany, Austria, and part of Switzerland. In this sense, also called *High German.*

German East Africa. A former German protectorate of eastern Africa comprising much of what is now Tanzania, Rwanda, and Burundi. The protectorate was declared in 1885 and lasted until the Germans surrendered the territory after World War I.

Ger·ma·ni·a (jər-mā′nē-ə, -mān′yə). **1.** An ancient region of central Europe north of the Danube and east of the Rhine. It was never under Roman control. **2.** A part of the Roman Empire west of the Rhine River corresponding to present-day northeast France and sections of Belgium and the Netherlands.

Ger·man·ic (jər-măn′ĭk). **1. a.** Of, relating to, or characteristic of Germany or its people, language, or culture. **b.** Of or relating to the Teutons. **c.** Of or relating to speakers of a Germanic language. **2.** Of, relating to, or constituting the Germanic languages. **3.** A branch of the Indo-European language family that comprises North Germanic, West Germanic, and the extinct East Germanic.

German Southwest Africa. A former German colony of southwest Africa. It was annexed by Germany in 1885 and awarded to South Africa as the mandate of South-West Africa (now Namibia) by the League of Nations in 1919.

Ger·man·town (jûr′mən-toun′). **1.** A residential section of Philadelphia, Pennsylvania. Settled in 1683, it was the site of a Revolutionary War battle (October 4, 1777) in which George Washington's troops unsuccessfully attacked the British encampment. The original township was annexed by Philadelphia in 1854. **2.** A town of extreme southwest Tennessee, a suburb of Memphis. ● Pop. 32,893.

Ger·ma·ny (jûr′mə-nē). *abbr.* **Ger.** A country of north-central Europe bordered on the north by the Baltic and North seas. Occupied since c. 500 B.C. by Germanic tribes, it was by the sixth century part of the vast empire created by the Franks, and it later became a loose federation of principalities and the nucleus of the Holy Roman Empire. Religious strife and dynastic feuds weakened the imperial state, which was broken up by Napoleon in 1806. After 1815 Germany became a confederation, then an empire centered around Prussia (1871–1918). The Weimar Republic, proclaimed after Germany's defeat in World War I, collapsed after the rise of Adolf Hitler and the Nazis. Hitler's invasion of Poland (1939) led to World War II, during which Germany invaded and occupied a number of European countries. After Germany surrendered to the Allies in 1945, it was divided up into four occupation zones controlled by the United States, France, Great Britain, and the Soviet Union. Dissension between the Soviet Union and the other three occupying countries led to the formation (1949) of the Federal Republic of Germany (West Germany) out of the U.S., French, and British zones, and the German Democratic Republic (East Germany) out of the Soviet zone. The reunification of Germany occurred in 1990 after the fall of the Communist government in East Germany. Berlin is the capital and largest city and Bonn the seat of government. ◉ Pop. 81,410.000.

Ge·ro·na (jə-rō'nə, hĕ-rô'nä). A city of northeast Spain northeast of Barcelona. Dating from pre-Roman times, it was ruled by the Moors from c. 713 to 785 and from 795 to 1015. ◉ Pop. 67,259.

Ge·ta·fe (hĕ-tä'fĕ). A town of central Spain south of Madrid. It is an industrial and agricultural center. ◉ Pop. 139,190.

Geth·sem·a·ne (gĕth-sĕm'ə-nē). In the New Testament, a garden east of Jerusalem near the foot of the Mount of Olives. It was the scene of Jesus's agony and betrayal.

Get·tys·burg (gĕt'ēz-bûrg'). A town of southern Pennsylvania east-southeast of Chambersburg. It was the site of a major Union victory (July 1–3, 1863) in the Civil War, which checked Robert E. Lee's invasion of the North. The battle and Abraham Lincoln's famous Gettysburg Address (delivered at the dedication of a cemetery here on November 19, 1863) are commemorated by a national park. President Dwight D. Eisenhower's farm, a national historic site, is also in Gettysburg. ◉ Pop. 7,025.

gey·ser (gī'zər). A natural hot spring that intermittently ejects a column of water and steam into the air.

Ge·zer (gē'zər). An ancient city of Canaan on the coastal Plain of Sharon northwest of Jerusalem. Excavations here have revealed many levels of prehistoric cultures.

Ge·zi·ra (jə-zîr'ə), **El.** A region of east-central Sudan between the Blue Nile and the White Nile.

Gha·gha·ra (gä'gə-rä') or **Gha·ghra** (gä'grə, -grä) also **Gog·ra** (gŏg'rə, -rä). A river rising in southwest Xizang (Tibet) and flowing about 965 km (600 mi) south through the Himalaya Mountains in Nepal then southeast into northern India, where it joins the Ganges River.

Gha·na (gä'nə, găn'ə). **1.** A medieval African kingdom of Mande-speaking peoples in what is now eastern Senegal, southwest Mali, and southern Mauritania. It was probably founded in the 6th century A.D. and prospered because of its location astride the trans-Saharan caravan routes. The kingdom declined after the 11th century. **2.** A country of western Africa on the Gulf of Guinea. It was inhabited in precolonial times by a number of ancient kingdoms, including an inland Ashanti kingdom and various Fante states along the coast. Trade with European states flourished after contact with the Portuguese in the 15th century. In 1874 the British created the crown colony of Gold Coast, extending control over the Ashanti kingdom by 1901. Ghana gained its independence in 1957, with Kwame Nkrumah as prime minister. It became a republic in 1960 and a one-party state in 1964. Nkrumah was deposed in 1966, since which time there has been a succession of coups and military governments. In 1992 a new constitution providing for a multiparty system was approved and free elections were held. Accra is the capital and the largest city. ◉ Pop. 16,944,000. —**Gha'na·ian, Gha'ni·an** adj. & n.

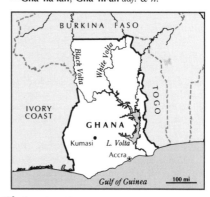

Ghats (gôts). Two mountain ranges of southern India. The **Eastern Ghats** extend about 1,448 km (900 mi) along the coast of the Bay of Bengal. The **Western Ghats** extend about 1,609 km (1,000 mi) along the coast of the Arabian Sea. The ranges are separated by the Deccan Plateau of south-central India.

Gha·zi·a·bad (gä′zē-ə-bäd′). A city of north-central India northeast of New Delhi. An agricultural market, the city was the scene of fighting during the Indian Mutiny (1857–1858), an uprising of Indian colonial soldiers against British rule in India. ◉ Pop. 454,156.

Ghent (gĕnt) also **Gent** (gĕnt, кнĕnt). A city of western Belgium west-northwest of Brussels. Founded in the seventh century, it was a medieval wool-producing center and remained virtually independent until its capture by the Hapsburgs in 1584. ◉ Pop. 230,446.

Gi·ant's Causeway (jī′ənts). A basaltic formation on the northern coast of Northern Ireland. It consists of thousands of columns of volcanic origin forming three natural platforms. According to legend, it was once a bridge for giants crossing between Ireland and Scotland.

Gib·e·on (gĭb′ē-ən). An ancient village of Palestine near Jerusalem. In the Bible, its inhabitants were condemned by Joshua to serve as manual laborers for the Israelites. — **Gib′e·o·nite′** *n.*

Gi·bral·tar (jə-brôl′tər). *abbr.* **Gib.** A British colony at the northwest end of the **Rock of Gibraltar,** a peninsula on the south-central coast of Spain in the **Strait of Gibraltar,** connecting the Mediterranean Sea and the Atlantic Ocean between Spain and northern Africa. Gibraltar was captured by Arabs in 711 and passed to the Spanish in 1462. Great Britain took control in 1704 during the War of the Spanish Succession, although Spain has made repeated claims to regain the territory. ◉ Pop. 31,874.

Gib·son Desert (gĭb′sən). A desert of west-central Australia bounded by the Great Sandy Desert on the north and Great Victoria Desert on the south. The area includes a number of salt lakes.

Gies·sen (gē′sən). A city of west-central Germany north of Frankfurt. Chartered in 1248, it is a manufacturing center in a mining area. ◉ Pop. 70,743.

Gi·fu (gē′foo′). A city of central Honshu, Japan, north-northwest of Nagoya. A manufacturing center, the city was rebuilt after a devastating earthquake and fire in 1891. ◉ Pop. 409,558.

Gi·jón (hē-hōn′). A city of northwest Spain on the Bay of Biscay west of Santander. Of pre-Roman origin, it is a major port and industrial center. ◉ Pop. 259,067.

Gi·ku·yu (gĭ-koo′yoo). Variant of **Kikuyu.**

Gi·la River (hē′lə). A river rising in the mountains of western New Mexico and flowing about 1,014 km (630 mi) generally westward across

southern Arizona to the Colorado River at Yuma in the southwest corner of the state.

Gil·bert Islands (gĭl′bərt). A group of islands of western Kiribati in the central Pacific Ocean. Inhabited by a mixture of Polynesian and Melanesian peoples, the islands were first visited by the British in 1765, made a protectorate in 1892 and later became part of the **Gilbert and Ellice Islands Colony** (1915–1976). Full independence as the principal islands of Kiribati was achieved in 1979.

Gil·e·ad (gĭl′ē-əd). A mountainous region of ancient Palestine east of the Jordan River in what is now northwest Jordan.

gill (gĭl). *Chiefly British.* **1.** A ravine. **2.** A narrow stream.

Gil·ling·ham (jĭl′ĭng-əm). A municipal borough of southeast England north of Maidstone. The Royal School of Military Engineering is here. ◉ Pop. 95,900.

Gil·roy (gĭl′roi′). A city of western California southeast of San Jose. Located in the fertile Santa Clara Valley, the city is a trade center with varied industries. ◉ Pop. 31,487.

Gin·za (gĭn′zə). A major shopping and entertainment district of Tokyo, Japan.

Gip·sy (jĭp′sē). Variant of **Gypsy.**

Gi·ronde (jə-rŏnd′, zhē-rōɴd′). An estuary of southwest France formed by the Garonne and Dordogne rivers and opening into the Bay of Biscay.

Giur·giu (joor′joo′). A city of southern Romania on the Danube River south of Bucharest. Founded in the tenth century by Genoese merchants on the site of a Roman settlement, it was ruled by the Turks after 1417. ◉ Pop. 62,710.

Gi·za (gē′zə). A city of northern Egypt, an industrial suburb of Cairo on the Nile River. The Great Pyramids and the Sphinx are nearby. ◉ Pop. 2,144,000.

Glace Bay (glās). A town of northeast Nova Scotia, Canada, on the Atlantic coast of Cape Breton Island. It is a mining center and fishing port. The first transatlantic wireless message was transmitted from nearby Table Head in 1902. ◉ Pop. 21,466.

gla·cier (glā′shər). A huge mass of ice slowly flowing over a land mass, formed from compacted snow in an area where snow accumulation exceeds melting and sublimation. — **gla′cial, gla′ciered** *adj.*

Gla·cier Bay (glā′shər). A narrow inlet of the Pacific Ocean in southeast Alaska northwest of Juneau. It is surrounded by towering mountain peaks and spectacular glaciers.

Glacier Peak. A mountain, 3,215 m (10,541 ft) high, of northwest-central Washington in the Cascade Mountains east-northeast of Everett.

gla·cis (glă-sē′, glăs′ē, glā′sĭs). A gentle slope; an incline.

Glad·beck (glăd′bĕk′, glät′-). A city of west-central Germany in the Ruhr River valley west-northwest of Dortmund. It is an industrial center. ⊛ Pop. 76,812.

Glad·stone (glăd′stōn′, -stən). A city of western Missouri, an industrial suburb surrounded by Kansas City. ⊛ Pop. 26,243.

Glå·ma (glô′mə) also **Glom·ma** (-mə, -mä). A river of eastern Norway flowing about 587 km (365 mi) generally southward to the Skagerrak.

Glas·gow (glăs′kō, -gō, glăz′-). A city of southwest Scotland on the Clyde River. Founded in the late sixth century, Glasgow is a major port, an industrial center, and the largest city in Scotland. ⊛ Pop. 681,470.

Glas·ton·bur·y (glăs′tən-bĕr′ē). **1.** A municipal borough of southwest England south-southwest of Bristol. There are extensive remains of an Iron Age village nearby. Glastonbury is the traditional site of King Arthur's Isle of Avalon. ⊛ Pop. 6,773. **2.** A city of central Connecticut southeast of Hartford. Settled in 1650, it is a manufacturing center. ⊛ Pop. 27,901.

Glas·we·gian (glăs-wē′jən, glăz-). **1.** Of or relating to Glasgow, Scotland. **2.** A native or resident of Glasgow, Scotland.

glen (glĕn). A valley.

Glen Bur·nie (glĕn bûr′nē). A community of north-central Maryland south of Baltimore. It is mainly residential. ⊛ Pop. 37,305.

Glen Cove. A city of southeast New York on northwest Long Island north of Mineola. Chiefly residential, it also has light industries. ⊛ Pop. 24,149.

Glen·dale (glĕn′dāl′). **1.** A city of south-central Arizona, an industrial suburb of Phoenix in an irrigated agricultural area. ⊛ Pop. 148,134. **2.** A city of southern California, an industrial suburb of Los Angeles. It is located on part of the first Spanish land grant in the area (1784). ⊛ Pop. 180,038.

Glendale Heights. A village of northeast Illinois, a mainly residential suburb west of Chicago. ⊛ Pop. 27,973.

Glen·do·ra (glĕn-dôr′ə, -dōr′ə). A city of southern California at the foot of the San Gabriel Mountains east-northeast of Los Angeles. The city grew as a fruit-shipping center but is now mainly residential. ⊛ Pop. 47,828.

Glen El·lyn (ĕl′ĭn). A village of northeast Illinois, a residential suburb of Chicago. ⊛ Pop. 24,944.

Glens Falls (glĕnz). A city of eastern New York on the Hudson River north-northeast of Saratoga Springs. Settled c. 1762, it is a manufacturing center. ⊛ Pop. 15,023.

Glen·side (glĕn′sīd′). A community of southeast Pennsylvania, a manufacturing suburb of Philadelphia. ⊛ Pop. 8,704.

Glen·view (glĕn′vyōō′). A village of northeast Illinois, a chiefly residential suburb of Chicago. ⊛ Pop. 37,093.

Glit·ter·tind·en (glĭt′ər-tĭn′ən). A peak, 2,473.6 m (8,110 ft) high, of south-central Norway. It is the highest elevation in Scandinavia.

Gli·wi·ce (glĭ-vēt′sə, glē-vē′tsĕ). A city of south-central Poland west-northwest of Katowice. Chartered in 1276, it was ceded by Austria to Prussia in 1742 and assigned to Poland by the Potsdam Conference in 1945. ⊛ Pop. 214,762.

glob·al (glō′bəl). **1.** Having the shape of a globe; spherical. **2.** Of, relating to, or involving the entire earth; worldwide. **— glob′al·ly** *adv.*

globe (glōb). **1.** A body with the shape of a sphere, especially a representation of the earth in the form of a hollow ball. **2.** The earth.

Glom·ma (glô′mə, -mä). See **Glåma.**

Glouces·ter (glŏs′tər, glô′stər). **1.** A borough of southwest-central England on the Severn River west-northwest of London. On the site of the Roman city Glevum, it was the Saxon capital of Mercia and is today a market town and industrial center. ⊛ Pop. 104,805. **2.** A city of northeast Massachusetts on Cape Ann and the Atlantic Ocean northeast of Boston. Its sheltered harbor has been used by fishing fleets for three centuries. ⊛ Pop. 28,716.

Glov·ers·ville (glŭv′ərz-vĭl′). A city of east-central New York northwest of Schenectady. Its glove-making industry dates to the late 18th century. ⊛ Pop. 16,656.

Gniez·no (gnyĕz′nō, -nô). A city of central Poland east-northeast of Poznań. Polish kings were crowned here from 1025 to 1320. The city passed to Prussia in 1793 and was restored to Poland in 1919. ⊛ Pop. 67,400.

Go·a (gō′ə). A state of west-central India on the Malabar Coast. Formerly a Portuguese colony (1510–1961), it was annexed by India in 1962 and formed a constituent part of the union territory **Goa, Daman, and Diu** until 1987.

Goat Island (gōt). An island of western New York in the Niagara River dividing Niagara Falls into the American and Canadian falls.

Go·bi (gō′bē). A large, generally cold desert of southeast Mongolia and northern China. It consists mainly of shallow alkaline basins.

Go·da·va·ri (gō-dä′və-rē). A river of central India flowing about 1,448 km (900 mi) from the Western Ghats southeast across the Deccan Plateau to the Bay of Bengal.

Go·doy Cruz (gō-doi′ krōōz′, krōōs′, gô-*thoi*′). A city of western Argentina, a manufacturing suburb of Mendoza. ⊛ Pop. 141,553.

Godt·håb or **Godt·haab** (gôt′hôp′) also **Nuuk** (nōōk). The capital and largest town of Greenland, on the southwest coast of the island on **Godthåb Fjord.** It was founded in 1721 by a Norwegian missionary. ◉ Pop. 12,483.

God·win Aus·ten (gŏd′wĭn ô′stən), **Mount.** See **K2.**

Gog·ra (gŏg′rə, -rä). See **Ghaghara.**

Goi·â·ni·a (goi-än′ē-ə, -ä′nē-ə). A city of south-central Brazil southwest of Brasília. It is a shipping and processing center in an agricultural and cattle-raising region. ◉ Pop. 920,840.

Goi·del·ic (goi-dĕl′ĭk). **1.** A branch of the Celtic languages that includes Irish Gaelic, Scottish Gaelic, and Manx. **2.** Of or relating to the Gaels. **3.** Of, relating to, or characteristic of Goidelic.

Go·lan Heights (gō′län′). An upland region between northeast Israel and southwest Syria northeast of the Sea of Galilee. Fortified by Syria after 1948, the area was captured by Israel in the 1967 Arab-Israeli War and formally annexed by that country in 1981.

Gol·con·da (gŏl-kŏn′də). A ruined city of south-central India west of Hyderabad. Capital of an ancient kingdom (c. 1364–1512), it was later one of the five Muslim kingdoms of the Deccan until its capture by the Hindustani emperor Aurangzeb's forces in 1687. Golconda was once known for the diamonds found nearby and cut in the city.

Gold Coast (gōld). **1.** A section of coastal western Africa along the Gulf of Guinea on the southern shore of Ghana. It was named for the large quantities of gold formerly found in the area and brought to the coast for sale. **2.** A former British colony (1874–1957) in the southern part of the Gold Coast, now part of Ghana.

Gold·en Gate (gōl′dən). A strait in western California connecting the Pacific Ocean and San Francisco Bay. Discovered in 1579 by the English explorer Sir Francis Drake, it was known as the Golden Gate long before the name gained new popularity during the gold rush of 1849. The Golden Gate Bridge, which spans the strait between San Francisco and Marin County, was completed in 1937.

Golden Horn. An inlet of the Bosporus in northwest Turkey forming Istanbul's harbor.

Golden Valley. A city of southeast Minnesota, a suburb of Minneapolis. It is largely residential with some light industry. ◉ Pop. 20,971.

Golds·bor·o (gōldz′bûr′ō). A city of east-central North Carolina southeast of Raleigh. It is a manufacturing center and marketplace for a tobacco-growing region. ◉ Pop. 40,709.

Go·le·ta (gō-lē′tə). A city of southern California on the Pacific Ocean west of Santa Barbara. It is a trade center for an agricultural region. ◉ Pop. 28,100.

Gol·go·tha (gŏl′gə-thə, gŏl-gŏth′ə). See **Calvary.**

Go·mel (gō′məl, gô′-, gô′myĭl). A city of southeast Belarus north of Kiev, Ukraine. First mentioned in 1142, it was controlled alternately by Russia and Poland, passing finally to Russia in 1772. ◉ Pop. 503,000.

Gó·mez Pa·la·ci·o (gō′mĕz pə-lä′sē-ō, gō′-mĕs pä-lä′syô). A city of north-central Mexico west of Monterrey. It is a processing and transportation center in an agricultural region. ◉ Pop. 116,967.

Go·mor·rah (gə-môr′ə, -mŏr′ə). An ancient city of Palestine near Sodom, possibly covered by the waters of the Dead Sea. According to the Bible, the city was destroyed by fire because of its wickedness.

Go·na·ïves (gō′nə-ēv′, gô-nä-). A city of western Haiti on an arm of the Caribbean Sea northnorthwest of Port-au-Prince. Haitian independence was proclaimed here in 1804. ◉ Pop. 34,209.

Gond (gŏnd). A member of a Dravidian people inhabiting central India.

Gon·dar (gŏn′dər, -där′) also **Gon·der** (-dər). A city of northwest Ethiopia on Lake Tana. It was the capital of Ethiopia, from 1635 until 1867. ◉ Pop. 166,593.

Gon·di (gŏn′dē). The Dravidian language of the Gonds.

Gond·wa·na·land (gŏnd-wä′nə-lănd′). The protocontinent of the Southern Hemisphere, a hypothetical landmass that according to the theory of plate tectonics broke up into India, Australia, Antarctica, Africa, and South America.

Good Hope (gōōd′ hōp′), **Cape of.** A promontory on the southwest coast of South Africa south of Cape Town. It was circumnavigated in 1488 by the Portuguese navigator Bartolomeu Dias, who named it Cape of Storms.

Good·win Sands (gōōd′wĭn). A stretch of dangerous shoals in the Strait of Dover off the southeast coast of England.

Goose Creek (gōōs). A city of southeast South Carolina, a suburb of Charleston. ◉ Pop. 24,692.

Göp·ping·en (gœp′ĭng-ən). A city of southwest Germany east-southeast of Stuttgart. Chartered in the mid-12th century, the city was twice devastated by fire (1425 and 1782). ◉ Pop. 51,713.

Go·rakh·pur (gôr′ək-pōōr′, gōr′-). A city of northern India east of Lucknow. It was founded c. 1400. ◉ Pop. 505,566.

Gor·ky or **Gor·ki** (gôr′kē). See **Nizhny Novgorod.**

Gör·litz (gûr′lĭts′, gœr′-). A city of east-central Germany east of Dresden on the Polish border. It was founded c. 1200 and grew as a cloth-weaving center. A small part of the city on the eastern bank of the Neisse River was awarded to Poland after World War II. ● Pop. 80,216.

Gor·lov·ka (gôr-lôf′kə, gôr′ləf-kə). A city of southeast Ukraine in the Donets Basin north of Donetsk. It is a major coal-mining and industrial center. ● Pop. 336,100.

Gor·zów Wiel·ko·pol·ski (gô′zhōōf vyĕl′kə-pôl′skē). A city of western Poland on the Warta River west-northwest of Poznań. Founded as a German city in 1257, it was assigned to Poland by the Potsdam Conference of 1945. ● Pop. 124,555.

Go·shen (gō′shən). 1. A region of ancient Egypt on the eastern delta of the Nile River. According to the Bible, it was inhabited by the Israelites from the time of Jacob until the Exodus. 2. A city of northern Indiana east-southeast of South Bend. It is a manufacturing center in a farming region. ● Pop. 23,797.

Go·siute (gō′shōōt). 1. pl. **Gosiute** or **-siutes.** A member of a Native American people inhabiting an area southwest of Great Salt Lake. b. A member of this people. 2. The Uto-Aztecan language of this people, a dialect of Shoshone.

Gos·lar (gôs′lär′). A city of central Germany southeast of Hanover at the foot of the Harz Mountains. It was founded in the tenth century as a mining settlement and was a free imperial city until 1802, when it passed to Prussia. ● Pop. 50,516.

Gos·port (gŏs′pôrt′, -pōrt′). A municipal borough of southern England west of Portsmouth. Formerly a victualing station for the Royal Navy, it was an embarkation point for the invasion of France in 1944. ● Pop. 77,400.

Gö·ta Canal (yœ′tə). A system of rivers, lakes, and canals of southern Sweden extending west to east from the Kattegat at the mouth of the **Göta River,** about 93 km (58 mi) long, to the Baltic Sea.

Gö·te·borg (yœ′tə-bôr′ē). A city of southwest Sweden on the Kattegat at the starting point of the Göta Canal system. Founded in 1604, it is a port and industrial center. ● Pop. 433,811.

Goth (gŏth). A member of a Germanic people, traditionally from Gotland in southeast Sweden, whose two branches, the Ostrogoths and the Visigoths, harassed and invaded the Roman Empire in the early centuries of the Christian era.

Go·tha (gō′thə, -tä). A city of central Germany west of Erfurt. First mentioned in the tenth century, it is an industrial and cultural center. The *Almanach de Gotha,* a record of Europe's aristo-

cratic and royal houses, was first published here in 1763. ● Pop. 57,662.

Goth·am (gŏth′əm). New York City. The nickname was popularized by the American writer Washington Irving and others in *Salmagundi,* a series of satirical sketches (1807–1808). —**Goth′am·ite′** (-ə-mīt′) n.

Goth·ic (gŏth′ĭk). abbr. **Goth. 1. a.** Of or relating to the Goths or their language. **b.** Germanic; Teutonic. **2.** The extinct East Germanic language of the Goths.

Got·land (gŏt′lənd, gôt′lŭnd). A region of southeast Sweden comprising several islands in the Baltic Sea, including **Gotland Island.** Inhabited since the Stone Age, Gotland is traditionally the original homeland of the Goths.

Göt·tin·gen (gœt′ĭng-ən). A city of central Germany northeast of Kassel. Chartered in 1210, the city is noted for its university, founded in the 1730's. ● Pop. 128,419.

Gott·wald·ov (gôt′väl-dôf′). See **Zlin.**

Gou·da (gou′də, gōō′-, кнou′dä). A city of western Netherlands northeast of Rotterdam. Chartered in 1272, it is noted for its cheese market. ● Pop. 60,026.

Go·ver·na·dor Va·la·da·res (gŭv′ər-nə-dôr′ väl′ə-där′ĭs, gô′vĕr-nä-dôr′ vä′lä-där′ĭs). A city of eastern Brazil northeast of Belo Horizonte. It is a processing center in a lumbering and agricultural region. ● Pop. 230,403.

Gov·er·nors Island (gŭv′ər-nərz). An island of southeast New York in Upper New York Bay south of Manhattan. A U.S. military base since about 1800, the island was used by the British as a residence for the colonial governor of New York in the 17th and 18th centuries. There were plans in 1997 to transfer control of the island to New York for public use.

gra·ben (grä′bən). A usually elongated depression between geologic faults.

Gra·ham Island (grā′əm). An island off western British Columbia, Canada, in the Pacific Ocean. It is the largest and northernmost of the Queen Charlotte Islands.

Graham Land. A region of Antarctica near the tip of the Antarctic Peninsula. Part of the British Antarctic Territory, it is also claimed by Argentina and Chile.

Gra·ian Alps (grā′ən, grī′ən). A section of the western Alps on the border between southeast France and northwest Italy. The highest elevation is Gran Paradiso, 4,063.5 m (13,323 ft), in the Italian section of the range.

Grain Coast (grān). A historical region of western Africa along the coast of the Atlantic Ocean, roughly identical with present-day Liberia. It was named for its once-thriving trade in grains of paradise, an aromatic seed used medicinally and as a flavoring.

Gram·pi·an Mountains (grăm'pē-ən). A mountain range of central Scotland extending northeast to southwest and forming a natural barrier between the Highlands and the Lowlands. Ben Nevis, 1,343.8 m (4,406 ft), is the highest point.

Gra·na·da (grə-nä'də, grä-nä'thä). A city of southern Spain southeast of Córdoba. Founded by the Moors in the eighth century, it became the center of an independent kingdom in 1238. The city was captured by Castilian troops in 1492, ending Moorish control in Spain. ◉ Pop. 256,784.

Gran·by (grăn'bē). A city of southern Quebec, Canada, east of Montreal. It is a manufacturing center. ◉ Pop. 38,069.

Gran Cha·co (grän' chä'kō). A lowland plain of central South America divided among Paraguay, Bolivia, and Argentina. The arid plain is largely uninhabited.

Grand Ba·ha·ma (grănd bə-hä'mə, -hā'-). An island of the Bahamas in the Atlantic Ocean east of West Palm Beach, Florida.

Grand Banks. An extensive area of shoals in the western Atlantic Ocean off southeast Newfoundland, Canada. The mingling of the cold Labrador Current and the warmer Gulf Stream along with the shallowness of the water make the area a major source of food fish.

Grand Canal. **1.** An inland waterway, about 1,609 km (1,000 mi) long, of eastern China extending from Tianjin in the north to Hangzhou in the south. Begun in the 5th to 6th century B.C., it was extended in the 7th century A.D. and completed in the 13th century. It is the world's longest artificial waterway. **2.** The principal waterway of Venice, Italy. Crossed by the Rialto and other bridges, the canal is lined with impressive palazzos and other buildings.

Grand Canary. One of the Canary Islands in the Atlantic Ocean east-southeast of Tenerife Island. It is the principal island of the group.

Grand Canyon. A gorge of the Colorado River in northwest Arizona. It is up to 1.6 km (1 mi) deep, from 6.4 to 29 km (4 to 18 mi) wide, and more than 321.8 km (200 mi) long. The eroded walls of the canyon record many centuries of geologic time.

Grand Cayman. See **Cayman Islands.**

Grand Cou·lee (kōō'lē). A gorge, about 48 km (30 mi) long, of north-central Washington, carved by the Columbia River. It is fed by water from the **Grand Coulee Dam** (built 1933–1942).

Gran·de (grän'də, grän'dĭ), **Rio. 1.** A river, about 1,046 km (650 mi) long, flowing from southeast Brazil generally northwest to the Paranaíba River, with which it forms the Paraná River. **2.** See **Rio Grande.**

Grande Prairie (grănd). A city of western Alberta, Canada, northwest of Edmonton. It is a trade center in a farming region. ◉ Pop. 24,263.

Grande-Terre (grän'târ', gränd-). An island of eastern Guadeloupe in the Leeward Islands of the West Indies.

Grand Falls. See **Churchill Falls.**

Grand Forks (fôrks). A city of eastern North Dakota on the Red River north of Fargo. Established as a fur-trading post in 1801, it is the seat of the University of North Dakota (founded 1883). ◉ Pop. 49,425.

Grand Island. A city of southeast-central Nebraska west of Lincoln. It was settled on the Platte River in 1857 and moved to its present location on the railroad line in 1866. ◉ Pop. 39,386.

Grand Junction. A city of western Colorado at the junction of the Gunnison and Colorado rivers near the Utah border. It is a trade and manufacturing center in an irrigated farming region. ◉ Pop. 29,034.

Grand Ma·nan Island (mə-năn'). An island of southern New Brunswick, Canada, in the Bay of Fundy. Settled by Loyalists after the American Revolution, it is a popular summer resort. **Grand Manan Channel** separates the island from the coast of Maine.

Grand'·Mère (grän-měr'). A city of southern Quebec, Canada, north of Trois Rivières. It is a manufacturing center with pulp and paper mills. ◉ Pop. 15,442.

Grand Prairie. A city of northeast Texas halfway between Dallas and Fort Worth. Located in a highly urbanized area, the city has an aerospace industry and is the site of an enormous amusement park. ◉ Pop. 99,616.

Grand Pré (grän' prā', grän'). A village of western Nova Scotia, Canada, on an arm of the Bay of Fundy. Settled by Acadians, it is the setting for Henry Wadsworth Longfellow's poem *Evangeline* (1847).

Grand Rap·ids (grănd răp'ĭdz). A city of west-central Michigan on the Grand River west-northwest of Lansing. Built on the site of an Ottawa village, it has been a furniture-manufacturing center since the mid-1800's. ◉ Pop. 189,126.

Grand River. 1. A river of southeast Ontario, Canada, flowing about 265 km (165 mi) south and southeast to Lake Erie. **2.** A river rising in southeast Iowa and flowing about 483 km (300 mi) southeast across northwest Missouri to the Missouri River. **3.** A river, about 418 km (260 mi) long, of southern Michigan flowing north and northwest to Lake Michigan. **4.** A river of northern South Dakota formed by the confluence of its northern and southern forks and flowing about 322 km (200 mi) eastward to the Missouri River. The North Fork rises in southwest North Dakota.

Grand Te·ton (tē′tŏn′, tēt′n). A mountain, 4,198.6 m (13,766 ft) high, of the Teton Range in northwest Wyoming. It is the highest elevation in the range.

Grand Trav·erse Bay (trăv′ərs). An arm of Lake Michigan in northwest Michigan. It is noted for its boating and fishing.

Grand Turk. The chief island of the Turks and Caicos Islands in the Atlantic Ocean southeast of the Bahamas. The town of **Grand Turk** (population 3,146) is the capital of the island group.

Grand·view (grănd′vyoō′). A city of western Missouri bordered on three sides by Kansas City. It is a trade and manufacturing center in a farming region. ⊛ Pop. 24,967.

Gran·ite City (grăn′ĭt). A city of southwest Illinois, an industrial suburb of East St. Louis on the Mississippi River. ⊛ Pop. 32,862.

Granite Peak. A mountain, 3,903.7 m (12,799 ft) high, of southern Montana northeast of Yellowstone National Park. It is the highest elevation in the state.

Gran Pa·ra·di·so (grän′ pä-rä-dē′zō). A peak, 4,063.5 m (13,323 ft) high, of the Graian Alps in northwest Italy. It is the highest elevation in the range.

Grants Pass (grănts). A city of southwest Oregon on the Rogue River west-northwest of Medford. It is an important lumbering center with varied industries. ⊛ Pop. 17,488.

Gras·mere (grăs′mîr′). A lake of northwest England in the Lake District. Dove Cottage, in the former village of **Grasmere,** was the home of the poet William Wordsworth from 1799 to 1808. The cottage is now a museum.

Grasse (grăs, gräs). A town of southeast France west of Nice. Probably founded in Roman times, it was an independent republic in the 12th century. The city has long been noted for its perfume industry. ⊛ Pop. 24,553.

grass·land (grăs′lănd′). An area, such as a prairie or meadow, of grass or grasslike vegetation.

Graves (gräv′). A region of southwest France in the Garonne River valley. The area is known for its fine table wines.

Graves·end (grāvz′ĕnd′). A municipal borough of southeast England on the Thames River east of London. Known as "the Gateway to the Port of London," it is an industrial and shipping center. Pocahontas (1595?–1617), daughter of Chief Powhatan of the Powhatan confederacy in Virginia, is buried here. ⊛ Pop. 96,300.

Grays Harbor (grāz). An inlet of the Pacific Ocean in western Washington. It is the shipping point for a lumbering area.

Grays Peak. A mountain, 4,352.4 m (14,270 ft) high, in the Front Range of the Rocky Mountains in central Colorado. It is the highest elevation in the range.

Graz (gräts). A city of southeast Austria on the Mur River south-southwest of Vienna. It was probably founded in the 12th century. ⊛ Pop. 237,810.

Great Abaco (grāt′). The largest island of the Abaco and Cays group in the northern Bahamas.

Great Alföld. See **Alföld.**

Great Australian Bight. A wide bay of the Indian Ocean on the southern coast of Australia. Much of the coastline consists of high cliffs extending inland as the Nullarbor Plain.

Great Barrier Reef. The largest coral reef in the world, about 2,011 km (1,250 mi) long, off the northeast coast of Australia. Its vividly colored banks are known for their exotic fish and crustaceans.

Great Basin. A desert region of the western United States comprising most of Nevada and parts of Utah, California, Idaho, Wyoming, and Oregon. The soldier and politician John C. Frémont explored and named the area (1843–1845).

Great Bear Lake. A lake of northwest mainland Northwest Territories, Canada. The **Great Bear River,** about 113 km (70 mi) long, flows westward from the lake to the Mackenzie River.

Great Bend (bĕnd). A city of central Kansas on the Arkansas River northwest of Wichita. Located on the old Santa Fe Trail, it is a shipping center for oil and wheat. ⊛ Pop. 15,427.

Great Britain. *abbr.* **G.B., Gr. Brit., Gt. Brit. 1.** An island off the western coast of Europe comprising England, Scotland, and Wales. It is separated from the mainland by the English Channel and from Ireland by the Irish Sea. **2.** See **United Kingdom.**

great circle. **1.** A circle described by the intersection of the surface of a sphere with a plane passing through the center of the sphere. **2.** A segment of such a circle representing the shortest distance between two terrestrial points.

Great Com·o·ro (kŏm′ə-rō′). The largest of the Comoro Islands, in the northern Mozambique Channel of the Indian Ocean.

Great Crosby. See **Crosby.**

Great Dismal Swamp. See **Dismal Swamp.**

great divide. A large or major watershed of a landmass.

Great Divide. See **Continental Divide.**

Great Di·vid·ing Range (dĭ-vī′dĭng) also **Eastern Highlands.** A chain of mountains curving along the eastern coast of Australia.

great·er also **Great·er** (grā′tər). Of, relating to, or being a city considered together with its populous suburbs.

Greater Antilles. An island group of the northern West Indies including Cuba, Jamaica, Hispaniola, and Puerto Rico.

Greater Sunda Islands. See **Sunda Islands.**

Great Falls. A city of central Montana on the Missouri River north-northeast of Helena. At the center of extensive hydroelectric power installations, Great Falls is popularly known as "Electric City." ⊛ Pop. 55,097.

Great Grimsby. See **Grimsby** (sense 2).

Great Indian Desert. See **Thar Desert.**

Great Karroo. See **Karroo.**

Great Lakes. A group of five freshwater lakes of central North America between the United States and Canada, including Lakes Superior, Huron, Erie, Ontario, and Michigan. French traders first sighted the lakes in the early 17th century. Today the Great Lakes connect Midwestern ports with the Atlantic Ocean via the St. Lawrence Seaway.

Great Miami River. See **Miami River.**

Great Namaqualand. See **Namaqualand.**

Great Ouse River. See **Ouse River** (sense 1).

Great Pee Dee. See **Pee Dee.**

Great Plains. A vast grassland region of central North America extending from the Canadian provinces of Alberta, Saskatchewan, and Manitoba southward to Texas. It was largely uninhabited before the arrival (16th century) of the Spanish and the introduction of the horse, which enabled Indian tribes living elsewhere to expand into the area. Waves of settlers came following the Homestead Act of 1862, provoking the Indian Wars of the late 19th century. In the 1930's the plowing of parts of the prairie led to dust bowl conditions and the depopulation of some areas. Much of the land was later rehabilitated and is now used for cattle ranching and wheat farming.

Great Rift Valley. A geologic depression of southwest Asia and eastern Africa extending from the Jordan River valley to Mozambique. The region is marked by a series of faults caused by volcanic action.

Great Russian. A member of the Russian-speaking people constituting the largest ethnic group in Russia.

Great Saint Ber·nard Pass (bər-närd′). An Alpine pass, 2,473.6 m (8,110 ft) high, on the Italian-Swiss border.

Great Salt Lake. A shallow body of salt water of northwest Utah between the Wasatch Range on the east and the **Great Salt Lake Desert** on the west. The lake is a remnant of prehistoric Lake Bonneville, which covered an extensive area of the Great Basin. Great Salt Lake Desert is barren and uncultivated.

Great Sandy Desert. A vast arid area of northwest Australia north of the Gibson Desert.

Great Sark. See **Sark.**

Great Slave Lake. A lake of southern Northwest Territories, Canada. The British fur trader Samuel Hearne (1745–1792) discovered the lake in 1771 while exploring for the Hudson's Bay Company.

Great Smoky Mountains. A range of the Appalachian Mountains on the North Carolina–Tennessee border rising to 2,026.1 m (6,643 ft) at Clingmans Dome. The mountains, named for the smokelike haze that often envelops them, are noted for their luxuriant vegetation.

Great South Bay. An arm of the Atlantic Ocean between the southern shore of Long Island and offshore barrier islands.

Great Victoria Desert. An arid region of south-central Australia sloping to the Nullarbor Plain on the south.

Great Wall of China. A line of fortifications extending about 2,414 km (1,500 mi) across northern China. Built in the third century B.C. by some 300,000 laborers (mainly criminals, conscript soldiers, and slaves), the wall proved ineffective against invaders and is today a major tourist attraction.

Gre·cian (grē′shən). **1.** Greek. **2.** A native or inhabitant of Greece.

Grec·o-Ro·man (grĕk′ō-rō′mən, grē′kō-). Of or relating to both Greece and Rome.

Greece (grēs). Formerly **Hel·las** (hĕl′əs). *abbr.* **Gr. 1.** A country of southeast Europe on the southern Balkan Peninsula and including numerous islands in the Mediterranean, Aegean, and Ionian seas. Settled by Achaeans, Aeolians, Ionians, and Dorians by 1000 B.C., the region grew and flourished as an amalgam of independent city-states, and by the 8th century B.C. a network of colonies existed throughout the Mediterranean. Greek culture reached a high point in the 5th century B.C. before succumbing to Sparta in the Peloponnesian War (431–404 B.C.). The area was later controlled by the Roman and Byzantine empires before being absorbed into the Ottoman Empire from 1456 until 1829, when Greece gained its independence and established a constitutional monarchy. During the late 19th and early 20th centuries Greece gained much territory, including Thessaly (1881), parts of Macedonia and Thrace (1912–1913), Crete (1913), and many of the Aegean islands. The period between the World Wars was marked by great political turmoil, and during World War II the country was occupied by Germany (1941–1944). After a civil war between communists and royalists, the monarchy was reestablished in 1949, which lasted until 1967 when a military coup removed the king and imposed martial law. In 1975 a new constitution was adopted making Greece a democratic republic. Athens is the capital and the largest city. ⊛ Pop. 9,740,417. **2.** A community of western New York, an industrial and residential suburb of Rochester. ⊛ Pop. 15,632.

Greek (grēk). *abbr.* **Gr., Gk. 1. a.** The Indo-European language of the Greeks. Greek, the sole member of the Hellenic branch, consists of several groups of ancient and modern regional, social, and literary dialects and is divided into several historical periods. **b.** Greek language and literature from the middle of the eighth century B.C. to the end of the third century A.D., especially the Attic Greek of the fifth and fourth centuries B.C. **2. a.** A native or inhabitant of Greece. **b.** A person of Greek ancestry. **3.** Of or relating to Greece or its people, language, or culture.

Gree·ley (grē′lē). A city of north-central Colorado north-northeast of Denver. It was founded in 1870 as a cooperative farm and temperance center and named for its patron, the American journalist and politician Horace Greeley. ⊛ Pop. 60,536.

Green Bay (grēn). A city of eastern Wisconsin on **Green Bay,** an arm of Lake Michigan. Founded as a trading post in 1634, the city is a port of entry with varied industries. ⊛ Pop. 96,466.

green·belt (grēn′bĕlt′). A belt of recreational parks, farmland, or uncultivated land surrounding a community.

Green·belt (grēn′bĕlt′). A city of central Maryland, a residential suburb of Washington, D.C. It was planned and built by the federal government as an experimental model community. ⊛ Pop. 21,096.

Green·dale (grēn′dāl′). A village of southeast Wisconsin, a suburb of Milwaukee. It was founded in the 1930's as a planned community built by the federal government. ⊛ Pop. 15,128.

Green·field (grēn′fēld′). **1.** A town of northwest Massachusetts north of Northampton. The

first cutlery factory in America was established here in the early 1800's. ⊛ Pop. 18,666. **2.** A city of southeast Wisconsin, a residential suburb of Milwaukee. ⊛ Pop. 33,403.

Greenfield Park. A town of southern Quebec, Canada, a residential suburb of Montreal on the opposite bank of the St. Lawrence River. ⊛ Pop. 18,527.

Green·land (grēn′lənd, -lănd′). An island of Denmark in the northern Atlantic Ocean off northeast Canada. It lies mostly within the Arctic Circle and is the largest island in the world. Inhabited by Inuit peoples as early as 3000 B.C., it was discovered by the Norwegian navigator Eric the Red in the tenth century A.D., became a Danish colony in 1815, and was granted home rule in 1979. —**Green·land′ic** (-lăn′dĭk) *adj.*

Greenland Sea. A section of the southern Arctic Ocean off the eastern coast of Greenland.

Green Mountains. A range of the Appalachian Mountains extending from southern Quebec, Canada, through Vermont to western Massachusetts. The range rises to 1,339.9 m (4,393 ft) at Mount Mansfield in north-central Vermont.

Green·ock (grē′nək, grĕn′ək). A burgh of southwest Scotland on the Firth of Clyde. It is a port and manufacturing center. ⊛ Pop. 56,194.

Green River. 1. A river rising in central Kentucky and flowing about 595 km (370 mi) generally northwest to the Ohio River near Evansville, Indiana. **2.** A river, about 1,175 km (730 mi) long, rising in western Wyoming and flowing through northwest Colorado and eastern Utah to the Colorado River.

Greens·bor·o (grēnz′bûr′ə, -bûr′ō). A city of north-central North Carolina east of Winston-Salem. Settled in 1749, it is a textile center. ⊛ Pop. 183,521.

Greens·burg (grēnz′bûrg′). A city of southwest Pennsylvania east-southeast of Pittsburgh. It was settled in the late 1700's and incorporated as a city in 1928. ⊛ Pop. 16,318.

Green·ville (grēn′vĭl′). **1.** A city of western Mississippi on the Mississippi River north of Vicksburg. It is a trade, processing, and industrial center in a fertile agricultural region. ⊛ Pop. 45,226. **2.** A city of eastern North Carolina southeast of Rocky Mount. Founded in 1786, the city grew as a tobacco market. ⊛ Pop. 44,972. **3.** A city of northwest South Carolina northwest of Columbia. Located in the Piedmont near the Blue Ridge, it was laid out in 1797 and is today a resort and manufacturing center. ⊛ Pop. 58,282. **4.** A city of northeast Texas northeast of Dallas. It is a manufacturing center in a cotton-producing area. ⊛ Pop. 23,071.

Green·wich. 1. (grĕn′ĭch, grĭn′ĭj) A borough of Greater London in southeast England on the Thames River. It is the site of the original Royal Observatory, through which passes the prime meridian, or longitude 0°. ⊛ Pop. 214,836. 2. (grĕn′ĭch, grĭn′-, grēn′wĭch). A town of southwest Connecticut on Long Island Sound near the New York border. Settled in 1640, it is mainly residential. ⊛ Pop. 58,441.

Green·wich time (grĕn′ĭch, grĭn′ĭj). See **universal time.**

Green·wich Village (grĕn′ĭch, -ĭj, grĭn′-). A mainly residential section of lower Manhattan in New York City. Settled during colonial times, the area began to attract notice as an artists' and writers' community after 1910.

Green·wood (grēn′wŏŏd′). 1. A city of central Indiana, a residential suburb of Indianapolis. ⊛ Pop. 26,265. 2. A city of west-central Mississippi east of Greenville. It is a trade center for a cotton-growing region. ⊛ Pop. 18,906. 3. A city of western South Carolina west-northwest of Columbia. The city was settled in 1824 on the site of a trading post established in 1751. ⊛ Pop. 20,807.

Greifs·wald (grīfs′vält′). A city of northeast Germany near the Baltic Sea southeast of Stralsund. Chartered in 1250, it is an industrial and commercial center. ⊛ Pop. 62,991.

Gre·na·da (grə-nā′də). A country in the Windward Islands of the West Indies comprising the island of **Grenada** and the southern Grenadines. Originally inhabited by Arawaks, who were later driven out by the Caribs, the island of Grenada was discovered by Columbus in 1498 and settled by the French in the mid-17th century. It became a British colony in 1783, was granted self-government in 1967, and achieved independence in 1974. A coup in 1979 brought a Marxist government to power, and concern over Cuban influence led to an invasion by primarily U.S.

troops in October 1983, after which democratic rule was restored. St. George's, on Grenada, is the capital and the largest city. ⊛ Pop. 92,000.

Gren·a·dines (grĕn′ə-dēnz′). An archipelago in the Windward Islands of the eastern Caribbean Sea. The southern islands are part of Grenada; the other islands are part of St. Vincent and the Grenadines.

Gre·no·ble (grə-nō′bəl, -nôbl′). A city of southeast France on the Isère River southsouthwest of Chambéry. An ancient Roman city, Grenoble is a noted tourist and skiing center and was the site of the 1968 Winter Olympics. ⊛ Pop. 150,815.

Gresh·am (grĕsh′əm). A city of northwest Oregon, a mainly residential suburb of Portland. ⊛ Pop. 68,235.

Gret·na (grĕt′nə). A city of southeast Louisiana on the Mississippi River opposite New Orleans. It is a manufacturing center. ⊛ Pop. 17,208.

Gretna Green. A village of southern Scotland on the English border. It was famous as a place for runaway marriages from 1754 until 1856, when the Scottish law was changed to require a 21-day residence period for one of the parties before issuance of a license.

Gre·ven·broich (grā′vən-broik′, -broiкн′). A city of west-central Germany northwest of Cologne. It is a railroad junction and manufacturing center. ⊛ Pop. 56,580.

Grif·fin (grĭf′ĭn). A city of west-central Georgia south-southeast of Atlanta. It is a textile and food-processing center in a farming region. ⊛ Pop. 21,347.

Grif·fith (grĭf′ĭth). A town of extreme northwest Indiana south of Hammond. It is mainly residential. ⊛ Pop. 17,916.

Grims·by (grĭmz′bē). 1. A town of southern Ontario, Canada, on Lake Ontario east-southeast of Hamilton. Grimsby is a manufacturing center. ⊛ Pop. 15,797. 2. Officially **Great Grimsby.** A borough of eastern England near the mouth of the Humber River southeast of Hull. It is a major fishing port and has varied industries. ⊛ Pop. 91,800.

Grim·sel Pass (grĭm′zəl). An Alpine pass, 2,183.5 m (7,159 ft) high, of southern Switzerland between the Rhone and Aare river valleys.

Gris-Nez (grē-nā′), **Cape.** A promontory of northern France extending into the Strait of Dover near Calais. It is the nearest point to the island of Great Britain.

Grod·no (grôd′nō, -nə, grŏd′-). A city of western Belarus on the Neman River near the Polish border. Capital of an independent principality until 1398, Grodno was ruled at various times by Lithuania, Poland, and Russia. ⊛ Pop. 295,400.

Gro·ning·en (grō′nĭng-ən, кнrō′-). A city of northeast Netherlands north-northeast of Apeldoorn. An important trade and transportation center, it was captured by the Dutch in 1594. ● Pop. 170,287.

Groote Ey·landt (grōōt′ ī′lənd). An island of northern Australia in the western part of the Gulf of Carpentaria. Manganese is mined on the island.

Grosse Pointe Farms (grōs′ point′). A city of southeast Michigan, a residential suburb of Detroit. ● Pop. 10,092.

Grosse Pointe Woods. A city of southeast Michigan, a residential suburb of Detroit. ● Pop. 17,715.

Gros·se·to (grō-sā′tō, grôs-sĕ′tô). A city of central Italy northwest of Rome. It is a market town near the site of Rusellae, an Etruscan town abandoned in the 12th century. ● Pop. 61,500.

Gross·glock·ner (grōs′glŏk′nər). A peak, 3,799.4 m (12,457 ft) high, of southern Austria in the Hohe Tauern range of the Alps. It is the highest elevation in the range and the highest point of the country.

Gros Ventre (grō′ vänt′). **1.** See **Atsina. 2.** See **Hidatsa.**

Gros Ventre River. A river rising in the Wind River Range of western Wyoming and flowing about 161 km (100 mi) westward to the Snake River.

grot (grŏt). A grotto.

Grot·on (grŏt′n). A town of southeast Connecticut on the Thames River opposite New London. Settled c. 1650, it is a port and the site of a U.S. submarine base. ● Pop. 45,144.

grot·to (grŏt′ō). A small cave or cavern.

ground (ground). **1. a.** The solid surface of the earth. **b.** The floor of a body of water, especially the sea. **2.** Soil; earth. **3.** often **grounds.** An area of land used for a particular purpose.

Grove City (grōv). A city of central Ohio south-southwest of Columbus. It is in a diversified farming area. ● Pop. 19,661.

Groves (grōvz). A city of southeast Texas east of Port Arthur near the Louisiana border. It is mainly residential. ● Pop. 16,513.

Groz·ny or **Groz·nyy** (grôz′nē). The capital of Chechnya in southwest Russia. In the center of a rich oil-producing area, it was a major objective of German forces during World War II. As a result of fighting (1994–1995) between Russian troops and Chechen secessionists, the city was largely destroyed. The city's population in 1993 was 353,961.

Gru·dziadz (grōō′jônts′). A city of north-central Poland on the Vistula River northeast of Bydgoszcz. Founded by the Teutonic Knights, it passed to Poland in 1466 and was ruled by Prussia from 1772 to 1919. ● Pop. 102,589.

Gua·da·la·ja·ra (gwŏd′l-ə-här′ə, gwä′t͟hä-lä-hä′rä). **1.** A city of west-central Mexico west-northwest of Mexico City. At an altitude of more than 1,525 m (5,000 ft), it is noted for its glassware and pottery. ● Pop. 1,626,152. **2.** A city of central Spain northeast of Madrid. Built on the site of a flourishing Roman colony, it was held by the Moors from 714 to 1081. ● Pop. 58,436.

Gua·dal·ca·nal (gwŏd′l-kə-năl′). A volcanic island of the western Pacific Ocean, the largest of the Solomon Islands. Visited by the Spanish navigator Álvaro de Mendaña de Neira in 1568 and by the English navigator John Shortland in 1788, the island became a British protectorate in 1893 and was occupied by the Japanese in World War II, leading to an invasion by U.S. troops in August 1942. After fierce jungle fighting, the island was captured by the Allies in February 1943.

Gua·dal·qui·vir (gwŏd′l-kwĭv′ər, gwä′t͟häl-kē-vîr′). A river of southern Spain flowing about 644 km (400 mi) west and southwest to the Gulf of Cádiz.

Gua·da·lupe Hi·dal·go (gwäd′l-ōōp′ hĭ-däl′-gō, gwä′t͟hä-lōō′pĕ ē-t͟häl′gô). Officially (since 1931) **Gus·ta·vo A. Ma·de·ro** (gōō-stä′vō ä′ mə-dâr′ō, gōō-stä′vô ä′ mä-t͟hĕ′rô). A city of south-central Mexico, a suburb of Mexico City. The Virgin of Guadalupe, revered throughout Mexico, is said to have appeared to an Indian convert in this vicinity in 1531, and the basilica erected in her honor is a popular pilgrimage site. On February 2, 1848, a treaty ending the Mexican War (1846–1848) was signed here. ● Pop. 88,537.

Gua·da·lupe Mountains (gwŏd′l-ōōp′, gwŏd′-l-ōō′pē). A mountain range of southern New Mexico and western Texas rising to **Guadalupe Peak,** 2,668.4 m (8,749 ft) high, in Texas. The peak is the highest point in Texas.

Guadalupe River. A river, about 402 km (250 mi) long, of southeast Texas flowing southeast to the San Antonio River near its mouth on San Antonio Bay.

Gua·de·loupe (gwŏd′l-ōōp′, gwŏd′l-ōōp′). An overseas department of France comprising the islands of Grande-Terre and Basse-Terre and smaller islands in the Leeward Islands of the West Indies. Inhabited by Arawaks and later (15th century) by Caribs, the islands were discovered by Columbus in 1493 and first colonized by the French in 1635. Basse-Terre is the capital. ● Pop. 421,000.

Gua·dia·na (gwä-dyä′nə, -t͟hyä′nä). A river rising in south-central Spain and flowing about 821 km (510 mi) west and south partly along the Spanish-Portuguese border to the Gulf of Cádiz.

Guam (gwäm). *abbr.* **GU.** An unincorporated

territory of the United States, the largest and most southerly of the Mariana Islands in the western Pacific Ocean. Discovered by the Portuguese navigator Ferdinand Magellan in 1521, the island was ceded by Spain to the United States in 1898. Agana is the capital. ⊛ Pop. 156,974. — **Gua·ma′ni·an** (gwä-mä′nē-ən) adj. & n.

Gua·na·ba·ra Bay (gwä′nə-bär′ə). An inlet of the Atlantic Ocean on the southeast coast of Brazil. The city of Rio de Janeiro is on its southwest shore.

Guang·dong (gwäng′dông′) also **Kwang·tung** (kwäng′tŏŏng′, gwäng′dŏŏng′). A province of southeast China on the South China Sea. It has been part of China since c. 200 B.C. Guangzhou is the capital. ⊛ Pop. 62,530,000.

Guang·xi Zhuang·zu (gwäng′shē′ jwäng′-dzŏō′) also **Kwang·si Chuang** (kwäng′sē′ chwäng′). An autonomous region of southern China on the Vietnamese border. Nanning is the capital. ⊛ Pop. 38,730,000.

Guang·zhou (gwäng′jō′) also **Kwang·chow** (kwäng′chō′). Formerly **Can·ton** (kăn′tŏn′, kăn′tŏn′). A city of southern China on a delta near the South China Sea. The capital of Guangdong province, it became a treaty port open to foreign trade after the Opium War (1839–1842). ⊛ Pop. 3,918,010.

Guan·tá·na·mo (gwän-tä′nə-mō′). A city of southeast Cuba north of **Guantánamo Bay,** an inlet of the Caribbean Sea. A U.S. naval station was established on the bay in 1903. The city was founded by French settlers from Haiti in the 19th century. ⊛ Pop. 206,311.

Gua·po·ré (gwä′pə-rā′, -pŏŏ-rě′, -pô-). A river of South America rising in western Brazil and flowing about 1,609 km (1,000 mi) northwest and partly along the Brazil-Bolivia border to the Mamoré River.

Gua·ra·ni (gwä′rə-nē′). **1.** pl. **Guarani** or **-nis.** A member of a South American Indian people of Paraguay, northern Argentina, and southern Brazil. **2.** The Tupi-Guaranian language of the Guaranis.

Gua·rul·hos (gwä-rŏŏ′lyŏŏs). A city of southeast Brazil, an industrial suburb of São Paulo. ⊛ Pop. 786,355.

Gua·te·ma·la (gwä′tə-mä′lə). **1.** abbr. **Guat.** A country of northern Central America. The area has been inhabited since around 1500 B.C. by Mayan Indians, whose great cities, such as Tikal, were mostly built during the Classic Period (A.D. 300–900). Maya civilization was already in decline by the time of the Spanish conquest in 1524. After independence from Spain (1821) Guatemala joined in a federation of Central American states (1825–1838), becoming a separate republic in 1839. A U.S.-backed coup

in 1954 initiated a period of military repression, sparking a leftist insurgency that lasted from the 1960's to the 1990's and resulted in more than 100,000 deaths. A formal peace was declared in December 1996. Guatemala is the capital and the largest city. ⊛ Pop. 10,322,000. **2.** also **Guatemala City.** The capital and largest city of Guatemala, in the south-central part of the country. Founded on its present site in 1776, it was rebuilt after major earthquakes in 1917 and 1918. ⊛ Pop. 1,675,589. — **Gua′te·ma′lan** adj. & n.

Gua·via·re (gwäv-yär′ē, -yä′rě). A river of central and eastern Colombia flowing about 1,046 km (650 mi) east from the Andes to the Orinoco River on the Colombia-Venezuela boundary.

Gua·ya·quil (gwī′ə-kēl′). The largest city and principal port of Ecuador, in the western part of the country near the **Gulf of Guayaquil,** an inlet of the Pacific Ocean. Founded in 1535, the city was frequently subject to pirate attacks in the 17th century. ⊛ Pop. 1,508,444.

Guay·na·bo (gwī-nä′bō). A city of northeast Puerto Rico, a manufacturing suburb of San Juan. ⊛ Pop. 65,075.

Guelph (gwělf). A city of southern Ontario, Canada, west of Toronto. It is an industrial center in a farming area. ⊛ Pop. 71,207.

Guer·ni·ca (gwâr′nĭ-kə, gěr-nē′kä) also **Guer·nica y Lu·no** (ē lŏŏ′nō). A town of north-central Spain northeast of Bilbao. Its April 1937 bombing by German planes during the Spanish Civil War inspired one of Picasso's most famous paintings. ⊛ Pop. 12,100.

Guern·sey (gûrn′zē). An island of southern Great Britain, one of the Channel Islands in the English Channel off the coast of northwest France.

Gui·an·a (gē-ăn′ə, -ä′nə, gī-). A region of northeast South America including southeast

Venezuela, part of northern Brazil, and French Guiana, Suriname, and Guyana.

Guiana Highlands. A mountainous tableland region of northern South America extending from southeast Venezuela into Guyana and northern Brazil.

Gui·do·ni·a (gwē-dō′nē-ə, -dô′nyä). A city of west-central Italy northeast of Rome. It was heavily damaged in World War II. ⊛Pop. 50,990.

Gui·enne or **Guy·enne** (gē-ĕn′). A historical region and former province of southwest France. Part of England after the marriage of Eleanor of Aquitaine to King Henry II of England in 1152, it was reconquered by France in 1453.

Guild·ford (gĭl′fərd). A municipal borough of southeast England southwest of London. It is a market town with varied industries. ⊛Pop. 58,600.

Guil·ford (gĭl′fərd). A town of southern Connecticut east of New Haven. It was settled in 1639. ⊛Pop. 19,848.

Gui·lin (gwē′lĭn′) also **Kwei·lin** (kwā′-). A city of southeast China northwest of Guangzhou. The original city dates back to the sixth century A.D. ⊛Pop. 557,346.

Guin·ea (gĭn′ē). *abbr.* **Guin.** A country of western Africa on the Atlantic Ocean. Inhabited by Fulani, Malinke, and Susu peoples, parts of present-day Guinea belonged to the medieval kingdom of Ghana and later to the Mali Empire. The area was explored by the Portuguese in the 15th century. France gained control of it in the 19th century, and the colony was named French Guinea in 1893, becoming part of French West Africa in 1895. Gaining its independence in 1958, Guinea was established as a Marxist state. A military regime took over in 1984 and paved the way for democratic reforms by loosening state control of the economy and providing for constitutional rule in the 1990's. Conakry is the capital and the largest city. ⊛Pop. 6,501,000. **—Guin′-e·an** *adj. & n.*

Guinea, Gulf of. A broad inlet of the Atlantic Ocean formed by the great bend in the west-central coast of Africa. It includes the Bights of Benin and Biafra.

Guin·ea-Bis·sau (gĭn′ē-bĭ-sou′). A country of western Africa on the Atlantic Ocean. Populated by Fulani, Malinke, and other West African peoples, it was first visited by the Portuguese in the 15th century and became the colony of Portuguese Guinea in 1879. After more than ten years of fighting by secessionist guerrillas, the country achieved independence in 1974. In 1991 the ruling party approved a multiparty system and free elections were held in 1994. Bissau is the capital and the largest city. ⊛Pop. 1,050,000.

Gui·yang (gwē′yäng′) also **Kwei·yang** (kwā′-). A city of southwest China east-northeast of Kunming. The capital of Guizhou province, it is a major transportation and industrial center. ⊛Pop. 1,664,709.

Gui·zhou (gwē′jō′) also **Kwei·chow** (kwā′-chō′). A province of southeast China. It passed under Chinese suzerainty in the 10th century and became a province in the 17th century. Guiyang is the capital. ⊛Pop. 29,680,000.

Gu·ja·rat (gōo′jə-rät′, gōoj′ə-). A region of western India bordering on the Arabian Sea. An independent kingdom after 1401, it was annexed by the Mogul Empire in 1572.

Gu·ja·ra·ti (gōo′jə-rä′tē, gōoj′ə-). **1.** The Indic language of Gujarat. **2.** *pl.* **Gujarati** or **-tis.** A native or inhabitant of Gujarat.

Guj·ran·wa·la (gōoj′rən-wä′lə, gōoj′-). A city of northeast Pakistan north of Lahore. It was an early center of Sikh influence. ⊛Pop. 658,753.

Gul·bar·ga (gŭl′bər-gä′). A city of south-central India west of Hyderabad. It is a manufacturing center in an agricultural area. ⊛Pop. 304,099.

gulch (gŭlch). A small ravine, especially one cut by a torrent.

gulf (gŭlf). *abbr.* **g., G.** A large area of a sea or ocean partially enclosed by land, especially a long landlocked portion of sea opening through a strait.

Gulf Intracoastal Waterway (gŭlf). An inland waterway of bays, canals, and rivers from northwest Florida to Brownsville, Texas. It is approximately 1,770 km (1,100 mi) long.

Gulf of. For names of actual gulfs, see the specific element of the name; for example, **Mexico, Gulf of; Lions, Gulf of.**

Gulf·port (gŭlf′pôrt′, -pōrt′). A city of southeast Mississippi on an arm of the Gulf of Mexico west of Biloxi. Settled in 1891 as a railroad terminus, it developed as a port after 1902. ◉ Pop. 40,775.

Gulf States. **1.** The countries bordering the Persian Gulf in southwest Asia, including Iran, Iraq, Kuwait, Saudi Arabia, Bahrain, Qatar, United Arab Emirates, and Oman. **2.** The states of the southern United States with coastlines on the Gulf of Mexico. They are Florida, Alabama, Mississippi, Louisiana, and Texas.

Gulf Stream. A warm ocean current of the northern Atlantic Ocean off eastern North America. It originates in the Gulf of Mexico and, as the Florida Current, passes through the Straits of Florida and then flows northward along the southeast coast of the United States. North of Cape Hatteras the Gulf Stream veers northeastward away from the coast into the Atlantic Ocean, where it splits to form the North Atlantic Drift, which flows northeastward to northwest Europe and Iceland, and the Canary Current, which flows southeastward to the Iberian Peninsula and northwest Africa.

Gul·lah (gŭl′ə). **1.** One of a group of people of African ancestry inhabiting the Sea Islands and coastal areas of South Carolina, Georgia, and northern Florida. **2.** The creolized language of the Gullahs, based on English but including vocabulary elements and grammatical features from several African languages and spoken in isolated communities from Georgetown in eastern South Carolina to northern Florida.

gul·ly (gŭl′ē). A deep ditch or channel cut in the earth by running water following a prolonged downpour.

Gunn·bjørn (gŏon′byôrn′), **Mount.** The highest peak, 3,702.4 m (12,139 ft), of Greenland, near the southeast coast.

Gun·ni·son (gŭn′ĭ-sən). A river, about 290 km (180 mi) long, of west-central Colorado flowing southwest, west, and northwest into the Colorado River at Grand Junction.

Gun·tur (gŏon-tŏor′). A city of southeast India east-southeast of Hyderabad. Founded by the French in the 18th century, it was officially ceded to the British in 1823. ◉ Pop. 471,051.

Guo·yu (gwô′yōō′) also **Kuo·yu** (kwôo′-). See **Mandarin.**

Gur·kha (gŏor′kə). **1.** A member of a Rajput ethnic group predominant in Nepal. **2.** A member of this people serving in the British or Indian armies.

Gu·ryev (gŏor′yəf). A city of western Kazakstan at the mouth of the Ural River on the Caspian Sea. Founded in 1645 as a military outpost, it was a fishing port until the development of the region's petroleum resources in the 1930's. ◉ Pop. 151,000.

Gus·ta·vo A. Ma·de·ro (gōō-stä′vō ä′ mə-dâr′ō, gōō-stä′vô ä′ mä-thě′rô). See **Guadalupe Hidalgo.**

Gü·ters·loh (gōō′tərz-lō′, gü′tərs-). A city of northwest Germany south-southwest of Bielefeld. It was chartered in 1825 and has diverse industries. ◉ Pop. 78,414.

Guy·a·na (gī-ăn′ə, -ä′nə). Formerly **Brit·ish Gui·a·na** (brĭt′ĭsh gē-ăn′ə, -ä′nə, gī-). *abbr.* **Guy.** A country of northeast South America on the Atlantic Ocean. The region was settled in the early 17th century by the Dutch, who competed with the English and French over the next two centuries for control of the Guiana coast. The Congress of Vienna (1815) awarded most of the western portions of Guiana to Great Britain, who founded the colony of the British Guiana in 1831. It was granted home rule in 1953 and gained full independence in 1966, becoming a republic in 1970. For most of the 20th century the country has been politically divided between the majority of East Indians, descendants of indentured servants imported during the 19th century, and a large Black minority. Georgetown is the capital and the largest city. ◉ Pop. 825,000. —**Guy′a·nese′** (-nēz′, -nēs′) *adj. & n.*

Guy·enne (gē-ĕn′). See **Guienne.**

guy·ot (gē′ō). A flat-topped seamount.

Gwa·li·or (gwä′lē-ôr′). A city of north-central India south of Agra. It lies at the foot of a medieval Hindu fort, within which are elaborately carved palaces and temples. ⊛ Pop. 690,765.

Győr (dyûr, dyœr). A city of northwest Hungary near the Slovakian border. On the site of a Roman military outpost evacuated in the fourth century A.D., it was later a Magyar stronghold (ninth century) and a royal free town (after 1743). ⊛ Pop. 130,752.

Gyp·sy also **Gip·sy** (jĭp′sē). **1.** A member of a nomadic people that arrived in Europe in migrations from northern India around the 14th century, now also living in North America and Australia. Many Gypsy groups have preserved elements of their traditional culture, including an itinerant existence, tribal organization, and the Romany language. **2.** See **Romany** (sense 2).

Gyum·ri (gē-oōm′rē, gyoōm-rē′). Formerly **Le·nin·a·kan** (lĕn′ĭ-nə-kän′, lyĭ-nĭ-). A city of northwest Armenia south-southeast of Tbilisi, Georgia. Founded on the site of a Turkish fortress, it was called Leninakan from 1924 to 1990. ⊛ Pop. 206,600.

H

Haar·lem (här′ləm). A city of western Netherlands near the North Sea west of Amsterdam. Chartered in 1245, it is an industrial city best known as a flower-growing center and distribution point for bulbs, especially tulips. ⊛ Pop. 149,764.

Haar·lem·mer·meer (här′lə-mər-mâr′). A city of western Netherlands west-northwest of Amsterdam in an agricultural region. ⊛ Pop. 103,232.

hab·i·tant (hăb′ĭ-tənt). **1.** An inhabitant. **2.** also **ha·bi·tan** (ă′bē-tän′). An inhabitant of French descent living in Canada, especially Quebec, or in Louisiana.

ha·boob (hə-boōb′). A penetrating sandstorm or dust storm with violent winds, occurring chiefly in Arabia, North Africa, and India.

Ha·chi·no·he (hä′chē-nō′hĕ). A city of northern Honshu, Japan, on the Pacific Ocean. It is an important fishing and commercial port. ⊛ Pop. 241,229.

Ha·chi·o·ji (hä′chē-ō′jē). A city of east-central Honshu, Japan, west of Tokyo. It has been noted for its weaving industry since the early 18th century. ⊛ Pop. 488,187.

Ha·ci·en·da Heights (hä′sē-ĕn′də). A community of southern California, a suburb of Los Angeles. ⊛ Pop. 49,422.

Hack·en·sack (hăk′ən-săk′). A city of northeast New Jersey east-southeast of Paterson on the **Hackensack River,** about 64 km (40 mi) long. The city is an industrial and residential suburb of New York City. ⊛ Pop. 37,049.

ha·dal (hād′l). Of or relating to the deepest regions of the ocean, below about 6,000 meters (20,000 feet).

Ha·dri·an's Wall (hā′drē-ənz). An ancient Roman wall, 118.3 km (73.5 mi) long, across northern England. Built by the emperor Hadrian c. A.D. 122–126 and extended by the emperor Severus a century later, the wall marked the northern defensive boundary of Roman Britain. Fragmentary ruins of the wall remain.

Ha·fun (hä-foōn′), **Cape.** A promontory of northeast Somalia on the Indian Ocean. It is the easternmost point of Africa.

Ha·gen (hä′gən). A city of west-central Germany northeast of Cologne. Chartered in 1746 and famous for its textiles in the late 18th century, it became an industrial and manufacturing center after 1870. ⊛ Pop. 214,877.

Hag·ers·town (hā′gərz-toun′). A city of northern Maryland northwest of Frederick. It is a manufacturing center in an agricultural region. ⊛ Pop. 35,445.

Hague (hāg), **The** also **'s Gra·ven·ha·ge** (skrä′vən-hä′gə, sкнrä′vən-hä′кнə). The de facto capital of the Netherlands, in the western part of the country near the North Sea. The Hague grew around a palace built c. 1250 by William of Holland (1228–1256) and is today the seat of the country's legislature and supreme court and of the International Court of Justice. ⊛ Pop. 444,392.

Hai·da (hī′də). **1.** *pl.* **Haida** or **-das.** A member of a Native American people inhabiting the Queen Charlotte Islands of British Columbia, Canada, and Prince of Wales Island in Alaska. **2.** Any or all of the language varieties spoken by the Haida. — **Hai′dan** *adj.*

Hai·fa (hī′fə). A city of northwest Israel on the **Bay of Haifa,** an inlet of the Mediterranean Sea. Located at the foot of Mount Carmel, the city probably dates from the third century A.D. and is now a major port and industrial center. ⊛ Pop. 248,200.

Haight-Ash·bu·ry (hāt′ăsh′bĕr-ē, -bə-rē′). A section of central San Francisco. In the 1960's it was a famous gathering place for hippies and followers of the drug culture.

Hai·kou (hī′kou′, -kō′). A city of southern China on Hainan Island in the South China Sea. It is a seaport and an industrial center. ⊛ Pop. 410,050.

Hai·nan (hī'nän'). An island of southern China in the South China Sea, separated from Leizhou Peninsula by a narrow strait.

Hai·naut (hā-nō', ĕ-nō'). A historical region of southwest Belgium and northern France. It originated in the ninth century and was later joined, through royal marriages, with Flanders and Holland. Parts of Hainaut were annexed by France in the 1600's.

Hai·phong (hī'fŏng'). A city of northeast Vietnam on the Red River delta near the Gulf of Tonkin. Established in 1874, it was shelled by the French in 1946 and heavily bombed by U.S. forces from 1965 to 1968 and again in 1972 during the Vietnam War. ● Pop. 783,133.

Hai·ti (hā'tē). **1.** A country of the West Indies comprising the western part of the island of Hispaniola and two offshore islands. Originally inhabited by Arawak Indians, the region became a French colony (Saint-Dominque) in 1697. A period of violent slave revolts and social turmoil at the end of the 18th century culminated in the establishment (1800) of the first Black-ruled government in the Americas under the leadership of Toussaint L'Ouverture (1743?–1803), a former slave, who abolished slavery and helped drive the Spanish and English from Hispaniola. Haiti became an independent republic in 1804. Chronic instability led to a prolonged occupation (1915–1934) by U.S. Marines. The repressive regimes of François ("Papa Doc") Duvalier, who ruled from 1957–1971, and his son Jean-Claude ("Baby Doc"), who fled the island in 1986, were followed by the democratic election (1991) and subsequent ouster of Jean-Bertrand Aristide. Aristide returned to Haiti in 1994 under the protection of U.S. troops serving as an interim replacement for the disbanded Haitian military. Port-au-Prince is the capital and largest city. ● Pop. 7,041,000. **2.** See **Hispaniola.**

Hai·tian (hā'shən, -tē-ən). **1.** Of or relating to Haiti or its people or culture. **2.** A native or inhabitant of Haiti. **3.** Haitian Creole.

Haitian Creole. A language spoken by the majority of Haitians, based on French and various African languages.

Ha·ko·da·te (hä'kô-dä'tĕ). A city of southwest Hokkaido, Japan, on Tsugaru Strait. Its excellent harbor was first opened to foreign traders in 1854. ● Pop. 304,286.

Ha·le·a·ka·la Crater (hä'lē-ä'kə-lä'). An enormous volcanic crater, 829.6 m (2,720 ft) deep, of eastern Maui, Hawaii. The mountain itself is 3,057 m (10,023 ft) high.

Hale·thorpe (hăl'thôrp). A community of northern Maryland, a residential suburb of Baltimore. ● Pop. 20,163.

Hal·i·car·nas·sus (hăl'ĭ-kär-năs'əs). An ancient Greek city of southwest Asia Minor on the Aegean Sea in present-day Turkey. In the fourth century B.C. Queen Artemisia built a magnificent tomb here for her husband, King Mausolus. His mausoleum was considered one of the Seven Wonders of the World.

Hal·i·fax (hăl'ə-făks'). **1.** The capital and largest city of Nova Scotia, Canada, in the south-central part of the province on the Atlantic Ocean. Founded in 1749, it served as an important naval base in the American Revolution, the War of 1812, and both World Wars. ● Pop. 328,699. **2.** A borough of northeast England northeast of Manchester. It is an industrial center. ● Pop. 192,500.

Hal·lan·dale (hăl'ən-dāl'). A city of southeast Florida on the Atlantic Ocean south of Fort Lauderdale. It is a processing center for fruits and vegetables. ● Pop. 30,996.

Hal·le (hä'lə). A city of central Germany on the Saale River west-northwest of Leipzig. First mentioned in the ninth century, it was an important member of the Hanseatic League in the Middle Ages. ● Pop. 295,372.

Hal·le-Neu·stadt (hä'lə-noi'shtät). A city of central Germany, a suburb of Halle. ● Pop. 91,510.

Hall·statt (hôl'stăt', häl'shtät'). Of or relating to a dominant Iron Age culture of central and western Europe, probably chiefly Celtic, that flourished ninth–fifth century B.C.

Hal·ma·he·ra (hăl'mə-hĕr'ə, häl'mä-hĕ'rä). An island of eastern Indonesia between New Guinea and Celebes. Irregular in shape, it is the largest of the Moluccas. Japanese installations on the island were a frequent target for Allied bombing raids in 1944.

Häl·sing·borg or **Hel·sing·borg** (hĕl'sĭng-bôrg', hĕl'sĭng-bôr'ē). A city of southwest Sweden on the Oresund opposite Sjaelland. It belonged to Denmark until the mid-1600's. ● Pop. 110,614.

Hal·tem·price (hôl'təm-prīs'). An urban district of east-central England near Hull. It was named for an Augustinian canonry founded in the district in 1322. ● Pop. 53,633.

Hal·tom City (hôl′təm). A city of northeast Texas, a residential and industrial suburb of Fort Worth. ⊛ Pop. 32,856.

Hal·ton Hills (hôl′tən). A town of southeast Ontario, Canada, a suburb of Toronto. ⊛ Pop. 35,190.

Ha·ma or **Ha·mah** (hä′mä). A city of western Syria south-southwest of Aleppo. Settled probably in the Bronze Age, it was a Hittite center in the second millennium B.C. and is frequently mentioned in the Bible as Hamath. ⊛ Pop. 273,000.

Ham·a·dan (hăm′ə-dăn′, -dän′). A city of western Iran west-southwest of Tehran. An ancient city, it was captured by Alexander the Great in 330 B.C. and later ruled by Seleucid kings, Romans, Byzantines, and Arabs (after A.D. 645). ⊛ Pop. 406,070.

Ha·mah (hä′mä). See **Hama.**

Ha·ma·ma·tsu (hä′mə-mät′sōō). A city of southern Honshu, Japan, east-southeast of Nagoya. It is an industrial and transportation center. ⊛ Pop. 560,660.

Ham·burg (hăm′bûrg′, häm′bŏŏrg′, -bŏŏrk′). A city of northern Germany on the Elbe River northeast of Bremen. Founded by Charlemagne, king of the Franks, as a defensive citadel in the early ninth century, the city quickly grew in commercial importance and in 1241 formed an alliance with Lübeck that became the basis for the Hanseatic League. Today Hamburg is a major port and financial, industrial, and cultural center. ⊛ Pop. 1,702,887.

Ham·den (hăm′dən). A town of southern Connecticut, a residential and manufacturing suburb of New Haven. ⊛ Pop. 52,434.

Ha·meln (hä′məln) also **Ham·e·lin** (hăm′ə-lĭn, hăm′lĭn). A city of northern Germany on the Weser River southwest of Hanover. An ancient Saxon settlement, it is a manufacturing and tourist center famous as the setting for the legend of the Pied Piper. ⊛ Pop. 55,992.

Ham·il·ton (hăm′əl-tən). **1.** The capital of Bermuda, on Bermuda Island. Founded in 1790, it is an important tourist resort. ⊛ Pop. 1,100. **2.** A city of southeast Ontario, Canada, at the western end of Lake Ontario southwest of Toronto. It is an industrial center and a thriving port. ⊛ Pop. 318,499. **3.** A burgh of south-central Scotland southeast of Glasgow in a coal and iron region. ⊛ Pop. 51,900. **4.** A city of southwest Ohio north of Cincinnati. It was settled on the site of Fort Hamilton, built in 1791. ⊛ Pop. 61,368.

Hamilton, Mount. A peak, 1,285 m (4,213 ft) high, of western California east of San Jose. It is the site of Lick Observatory, built 1876–1888 and directed by the University of California.

Hamilton Inlet. A deep inlet of the northern Atlantic Ocean in southeast Labrador connecting with Lake Melville. It was first explored in 1586.

Ham·ite (hăm′īt′). A member of a group of peoples of northern and northeast Africa, including the Berbers, Tuareg, and the ancient Egyptians and their descendants.

Ha·mit·ic (hă-mĭt′ĭk). **1.** Of or relating to the Hamites or their languages or cultures. **2.** A presumed language family formerly thought to include Egyptian and the Berber, Cushitic, and Chadic languages.

Ham·i·to-Se·mit·ic (hăm′ĭ-tō-sə-mĭt′ĭk). Former designation for Afro-Asiatic. No longer in technical use.

Hamm (hăm, häm). A city of west-central Germany in the Ruhr district south-southeast of Münster. Founded c. 1226, it was an active member of the Hanseatic League after 1417. ⊛ Pop. 182,390.

Ham·mer·fest (hăm′ər-fĕst′, hä′mər-). A town of northern Norway on an island in the Arctic Ocean. It is the northernmost town of Europe, with uninterrupted daylight from May 17 to July 29. ⊛ Pop. 7,208.

Ham·mond (hăm′ənd). **1.** A city of northwest Indiana on the Illinois border west of Gary. It is highly industrialized. ⊛ Pop. 84,236. **2.** A city of southeast Louisiana east of Baton Rouge. It is the seat of Southeastern Louisiana University (founded 1925). ⊛ Pop. 15,871.

Hamp·ton (hămp′tən). **1.** A historic section of London, England. It includes Hampton Court Palace, built by Cardinal Wolsey in 1515 and appropriated by Henry VIII in 1526. George II was the last to use it as a royal residence, and much of the palace is now open to the public. **2.** An independent city of southeast Virginia opposite Norfolk on **Hampton Roads,** the outlet of three rivers into Chesapeake Bay. Settled by colonists from Jamestown in 1610, the city was sacked by the British in the War of 1812 and was almost burned to the ground by Confederates in 1861 to prevent its occupation by Union troops during the American Civil War. ⊛ Pop. 137,048.

Ham·tramck (hăm-trăm′ĭk). A city of southeast Michigan surrounded by Detroit. The city is known primarily for automobile manufacturing. ⊛ Pop. 18,372.

Han (hän). A member of the principal ethnic group of China, constituting about 93 percent of the population, especially as distinguished from Manchus, Mongols, Huis, and other minority nationalities. Also called *Chinese, Han Chinese.*

Ha·nau (hä′nou′). A city of central Germany on the Main River east of Frankfurt. Chartered in 1303, it is a center of the country's jewelry industry. ⊛ Pop. 84,373.

Han Chinese. See **Han.**

Han·dan also **Han·tan** (hän′dän′). A city of east-central China located south-southwest of Beijing. It is a flourishing industrial center. ⊛ Pop. 1,769,315.

Han·dies Peak (hăn′dēz). A mountain, 4,284.6 m (14,048 ft) high, in the San Juan Mountains of southwest Colorado.

Han·ford (hăn′fərd). A city of central California south-southeast of Fresno. It is a trade and processing center for the San Joaquin Valley. ⊛ Pop. 30,897.

Hang·zhou (häng′jō′) also **Hang·chow** or **Hang·chou** (hăng′chou′, häng′jō′). A city of eastern China at the head of **Hangzhou Bay,** an inlet of the East China Sea. Founded in 606, the city was the capital of a powerful kingdom from 907 to 960. It was later described by the Venetian explorer Marco Polo (1254–1324) as one of the finest and noblest cities in the world. Today it is a modern industrial center and the capital of Zhejiang province. ⊛ Pop. 2,589,504.

Han·ni·bal (hăn′ə-bəl). A city of northeast Missouri on the Mississippi River northwest of St. Louis. It is famous as the boyhood home of Mark Twain. ⊛ Pop. 18,004.

Han·no·ver (hăn′ō′vər, hä-nō′-). See **Hanover.**

Ha·noi (hă-noi′, hə-). The capital of Vietnam, in the northern part of the country on the Red River. Founded before the seventh century, it became the capital of French Indochina after 1887 and the capital of North Vietnam after 1954. The city was bombed heavily during the Vietnam War. ⊛ Pop. 1,089,760.

Han·o·ver or **Han·no·ver** (hăn′ō′vər, hä-nō′). **1.** A former kingdom and province of northwest Germany. It was an electorate of the Holy Roman Empire from 1692 to 1805. The kingdom lasted from 1815 to 1866, when Hanover became a province of Prussia (later Germany). **2.** A city of northwest Germany southeast of Bremen. Chartered in 1241, it became part of the Hanseatic League in 1386. Hanover was badly damaged during World War II (1939–1945) but has been extensively rebuilt. ⊛ Pop. 524,823.

Han·o·ve·ri·an (hăn′ō-vîr′ē-ən). **1.** Of, relating to, or characteristic of the royal family of Hanover. **2.** Of, belonging to, or characteristic of the kingdom or province of Hanover.

Hanover Park. A village of northeast Illinois, a suburb of Chicago. ⊛ Pop. 32,895.

Han River (hän). A river, about 1,126 km (700 mi) long, of east-central China flowing generally southeast to the Chang Jiang (Yangtze River).

Han·se·at·ic League (hăn′sē-ăt′ĭk). A former economic and defensive confederation of free towns in northern Germany and neighboring areas. Traditionally dated to a protective alliance

formed by Lübeck and Hamburg in 1241, it reached the height of its power in the 14th century and held its last official assembly in 1669.

Han·tan (hän′dän′). See **Handan.**

Ha·o·ra (hä′ô-rä, -rə). See **Howrah.**

Haps·burg also **Habs·burg** (hăps′bûrg′, häps′-bŏŏrk′). A royal German family that supplied rulers to a number of European states from the late Middle Ages until the 20th century. The Hapsburgs reached the height of their power under Charles V of Spain. When Charles abdicated (1558), the empire was divided between the Spanish and Austrian lines. The Spanish branch ceased to rule after 1700 and the Austrian branch after 1918.

Ha·ran or **Har·ran** (hä-rän′). An ancient city of Mesopotamia in present-day southeast Turkey. It was an important trading post and a religious center devoted to the Assyrian moon god.

Ha·rap·pa (hə-răp′ə). A locality in the Indus River valley of the Punjab in Pakistan. Archaeological finds dating back to the third millennium B.C. include the remains of a well-laid-out city and indicate a possible link between Indian and Sumerian cultures.

Ha·ra·re (hə-rär′ā). Formerly **Salis·bur·y** (sôlz′-bĕr′ē, -brē). The capital and largest city of Zimbabwe, in the northeast part of the country. Founded by the British in 1890, it is a manufacturing and tobacco-processing center. The name was changed in 1982 to honor a 19th-century African leader. ⊛ Pop. 1,189,103.

Har·bin (här′bĭn′). A city of northeast China north of Jilin. It grew after Russia was granted a trade concession in 1896 and the completion of the railroad to Port Arthur (now Lüshun) in 1898. The city is the capital of Heilongjiang province. ⊛ Pop. 3,597,404.

har·bor (här′bər). *abbr.* **h., H.** A sheltered part of a body of water deep enough to provide anchorage for ships.

har·bour (här′bər). *Chiefly British.* Variant of **harbor.**

Har·dwar (här′dwär′, hûr′-). A city of northern India on the Ganges River north-northeast of Delhi. It is a Hindu pilgrimage center. ⊛ Pop. 147,305.

Ha·ri Rud (här′ē rōōd′). A river, about 1,126 km (700 mi) long, of northwest Afghanistan, northeast Iran, and southern Turkmenistan.

Har·lem (här′ləm). A section of New York City in northern Manhattan bordering on the Harlem and East rivers. Peter Stuyvesant established the Dutch settlement of Nieuw Haarlem here in 1658. A rapid influx of Black people beginning c. 1910 made it one of the largest Black communities in the United States. In the 1920's a flowering of Black art and literature was known as the

Harlem Renaissance. After World War II many Hispanics settled in East (or Spanish) Harlem. —**Har′lem·ite′** *n.*

Har·lin·gen (här′lĭn-jən). A city of extreme southern Texas northwest of Brownsville. It is a processing and shipping center for the lower Rio Grande valley. ⊛ Pop. 48,735.

Har·low (här′lō). An urban district of southeast England northeast of London. It was designated as a new town in 1946 to alleviate overpopulation in London. ⊛ Pop. 79,400.

har·mat·tan (här′mə-tăn′, här-măt′n). A dry, dusty wind that blows along the northwest coast of Africa.

Har·ney Peak (här′nē). A mountain, 2,208.8 m (7,242 ft) high, of southwest South Dakota. It is the highest elevation of the Black Hills and the highest point in the state.

Har·pers Fer·ry (här′pərz fĕr′ē). A locality of extreme northeast West Virginia. It was the scene of the abolitionist John Brown's rebellion (1859), in which he briefly seized the U.S. arsenal here. The town changed hands a number of times during the Civil War (1861–1865).

Har·per Woods (här′pər). A city of southeast Michigan, a suburb of Detroit. ⊛ Pop. 14,903.

Har·ran (hä-rän′). See Haran.

Har·ris·burg (hăr′ĭs-bûrg′). The capital of Pennsylvania, in the southeast-central part of the state west-northwest of Philadelphia. Settled in the early 1700's as Harris' Ferry, it was renamed in 1785 and became the capital in 1812. ⊛ Pop. 53,430.

Har·ri·son (hăr′ĭ-sən). A village of southeast New York, a residential suburb of New York City. ⊛ Pop. 23,308.

Har·ri·son·burg (hăr′ĭ-sən-bûrg′). An independent city of north-central Virginia northwest of Charlottesville. It is a processing center in an agricultural region. ⊛ Pop. 30,707.

Har·ro·gate (hăr′ə-gət, -gāt′). A municipal borough of north-central England north of Leeds. It is a popular health resort with mineral springs used for therapeutic treatment since 1596. ⊛ Pop. 67,000.

Har·row (hăr′ō). A mainly residential district of northeast Greater London. It is the site of the public school Harrow, founded in 1571. ⊛ Pop. 206,632.

Hart·ford (härt′fərd). The capital of Connecticut, in the north-central part of the state on the Connecticut River. Settled 1635–1636 by Massachusetts colonists on the site of a Dutch trading post, it became the nucleus of the Con-

necticut Colony in 1639. From 1701 to 1875 it was joint capital with New Haven. ⊛ Pop. 139,739.

Har·tle·pool (härt′lē-pōōl′, här′tl-). A borough of northeast England on the North Sea south-southeast of Newcastle. It is a seaport with iron and steel industries. ⊛ Pop. 94,600.

Har·vard (här′vərd), **Mount.** A peak, 4,398.1 m (14,420 ft) high, in the Sawatch Range of the Rocky Mountains in central Colorado.

Har·vey (här′vē). A city of northeast Illinois, an industrial suburb of Chicago. ⊛ Pop. 29,771.

Harz Mountains (härts). A mountain range of central Germany extending about 97 km (60 mi) between the Weser and the Elbe. The range rises to 1,142.8 m (3,747 ft) and has many mineral springs and resort areas.

Has·selt (häs′əlt). A city of northeast Belgium east of Brussels. Chartered in 1232, it was the site of a Dutch defeat of Belgian nationalists in 1831. ⊛ Pop. 65,437.

Has·tings (hā′stĭngz). **1.** A borough of southeast England on the English Channel at the entrance to the Strait of Dover. Hastings is near the site of William the Conqueror's victory over the Anglo-Saxons under Harold II (October 14, 1066). ⊛ Pop. 75,900. **2.** A city of southern Nebraska south of Grand Island. It is a manufacturing center. ⊛ Pop. 22,837.

Hatch·ie (hăch′ē). A river rising in northern Mississippi and flowing about 290 km (180 mi) generally northwest to the Mississippi River north of Memphis, Tennessee.

Hat·ter·as Island (hăt′ər-əs). A long barrier island off the eastern coast of North Carolina between Pamlico Sound and the Atlantic Ocean, with **Cape Hatteras** projecting from the southeast part. The cape experiences frequent storms that drive ships landward and has been called "the Graveyard of the Atlantic."

Hat·ties·burg (hăt′ēz-bûrg′). A city of southeast Mississippi southeast of Jackson. Once a lumbering center, it now has varied industries. ⊛ Pop. 41,882.

Hat·ting·en (hä′tĭng-ən). A city of west-central Germany, an industrial suburb of Essen on the Ruhr River. ⊛ Pop. 54,887.

haugh (hôкн). *Scots.* A low-lying meadow in a river valley.

Hau·ra·ki Gulf (hou-rä′kē, -răk′ē). An inlet of the southern Pacific Ocean on the northern coast of North Island, New Zealand.

Hau·sa (hou′sə, -zə). **1.** *pl.* **Hausa** or **-sas.** A member of a predominantly Muslim people inhabiting northern Nigeria and southern Niger. **2.** A Chadic language spoken by the Hausa, widely used as a trade language in West Africa.

Ha·van·a (hə-văn′ə). The capital and largest

city of Cuba, in the northwest part of the island country on the Gulf of Mexico. Founded on its present site in 1519, it became the capital of Spanish Cuba in 1552. The demolition of the U.S. battleship *Maine* in Havana's harbor in February 1898 was the immediate cause of the Spanish-American War. ⊛ Pop. 2,160,368. — **Ha·van′an** *adj. & n.*

Hav·ant and Wa·ter·loo (hăv′ənt; wô′tər-lōō′, wŏt′ər-). An urban district of southern England near the English Channel east of Southampton. It is a manufacturing center. ⊛ Pop. 117,517.

Ha·va·su·pai (hä′və-sōō′pī). **1.** *pl.* **Havasupai** or **-pais.** A member of a Native American people inhabiting an area southeast of the Grand Canyon. **2.** The Yuman language of the Havasupais, closely related to Hualapai.

Ha·vel (hä′fəl). A river, about 346 km (215 mi) long, of eastern Germany flowing through Berlin to the Elbe River.

Have·lock (hăv′lŏk′). A city of southeast North Carolina east of Fayetteville. It processes cotton and tobacco. ⊛ Pop. 20,268.

ha·ven (hā′vən). A harbor or an anchorage; a port.

Hav·er·hill (hāv′rəl, hā′vər-əl). A city of northeast Massachusetts on the Merrimack River northeast of Lowell. It grew as a shoe-producing center but now has varied light industries. ⊛ Pop. 51,418.

Ha·ví·řov (hä′və-rôf′, -vîr-zhôf′). A town of northern Czech Republic southeast of Ostrava. It was founded in the 1950's. ⊛ Pop. 90,013.

Ha·wai·i (hə-wä′ē, -wī′ē, -wä′yə). *abbr.* **HI.** A state of the United States in the central Pacific Ocean comprising the Hawaiian Islands. The islands became a U.S. territory in 1900, which was admitted as the 50th state in 1959. Honolulu, on Oahu, is the capital and the largest city. ⊛ Pop. 1,115,274.

Ha·wai·ian (hə-wä′yən). **1. a.** A member or descendent of the indigenous Polynesian people of the Hawaiian Islands. **b.** A native or inhabitant of the Hawaiian Islands, the state of Hawaii, or Hawaii Island. **2.** The Polynesian language of Hawaii. — **Ha·wai′ian** *adj.*

Hawaiian Islands. Formerly **Sand·wich Islands** (sănd′wĭch, săn′-), *abbr.* **H.I.** A group of volcanic and coral islands in the central Pacific Ocean coextensive with the state of Hawaii. There are eight major islands and more than a hundred minor ones. The islands were settled by Polynesians in the sixth century A.D. and visited by the British explorer Capt. James Cook in 1778. They were ruled by native Hawaiian monarchs from 1795 until 1893, when Queen Liliuokalani was deposed. A republic was pro-

claimed the following year, but petitions for annexation by the United States were finally approved in 1898. Pearl Harbor, on the island of Oahu, became an important center of U.S. naval power in the Pacific.

Hawaii Island. The largest and southernmost of the Hawaiian Islands. It is the top of an enormous submarine mountain and has several volcanic peaks.

Hawaii Standard Time. Standard time in the tenth time zone west of Greenwich, England, reckoned at 150° west and used, for example, in Hawaii and the western Aleutian Islands. Also called *Hawaii Time.*

Ha·wash River (hä′wäsh′). See **Awash River.**

Hawke Bay (hôk). A large inlet of the southern Pacific Ocean on the east-central coast of North Island, New Zealand.

Haw·orth (hou′ərth, härth). A village of northern England west-northwest of Bradford. In the 19th century, the Brontës, a family of novelists and poets, lived in the parsonage, which now houses a library and museum devoted to family memorabilia.

Haw River (hô). A river, about 209 km (130 mi) long, rising in north-central North Carolina and flowing generally southeast to join the Deep River and form the Cape Fear River.

Haw·thorne (hô′thôrn′). **1.** A city of southern California, an industrial and residential suburb of Los Angeles. ⊛ Pop. 71,349. **2.** A borough of northeast New Jersey north-northeast of Paterson. It is primarily residential with varied light industries. ⊛ Pop. 17,084.

Hayes River (hāz). A river, about 483 km (300 mi) long, of eastern Manitoba, Canada, flowing northeast to Hudson Bay.

Hay River (hā). A river of northwest Canada rising in northeast British Columbia and flowing about 853 km (530 mi) generally northeast across northwest Alberta to Great Slave Lake in southern Northwest Territories.

Hays (hāz). A city of central Kansas west of Salina. Founded near the site of Fort Hays, established in 1865, the city has a large agricultural experiment station. ⊛ Pop. 17,767.

Hay·ward (hā′wərd). A city of western California southeast of Oakland. Food processing is among its important industries. ⊛ Pop. 115,189.

Ha·zel Park (hā′zəl). A city of southeast Michigan, a residential suburb of Detroit. ⊛ Pop. 20,051.

Haz·let (hāz′lĭt). A community of east-central New Jersey east-southeast of New Brunswick. ⊛ Pop. 23,013.

Ha·zle·ton (hā′zəl-tən). A city of east-central Pennsylvania south of Wilkes-Barre. It is an industrial center. ⊛ Pop. 24,730.

head·land (hĕd′lənd, -lănd′). A point of land, usually high and with a sheer drop, extending out into a body of water; a promontory.

head wall (hĕd). A steep slope or precipice rising at the head of a valley or glacial cirque.

head·wa·ter (hĕd′wô′tər, -wŏt′ər) also **headwaters** (-wô′tərz, -wŏt′ərz). The water from which a river rises; a source.

Heard Island (hûrd). An island of the southern Indian Ocean near the coast of Antarctica. First discovered by an American navigator in 1853, it was placed under Australian administration in 1947.

heart·land (härt′lănd′). A central region, especially one that is politically, economically, or militarily vital to a nation.

Heart River (härt). A river, about 290 km (180 mi) long, of southwest North Dakota flowing eastward to the Missouri River near Bismarck.

He·bei (hœ′bā′) also **Ho·pei** or **Ho·peh** (hō′pā′, hŭ′bā′). A province of northeast China bordering on the Bo Hai. One of the earliest regions of Chinese settlement, Hebei has many prehistoric sites. Shijiazhuang is the capital. ⊕ Pop. 55,480,000.

He·bra·ic (hĭ-brā′ĭk) also **He·bra·i·cal** (-ĭ-kəl). Of, relating to, or characteristic of the Hebrews or their language or culture. **—He·bra′i·cal·ly** *adv.*

He·brew (hē′brōō). *abbr.* **Heb., Hebr. 1.** A member or descendant of a northern Semitic people, claiming descent from the Biblical patriarchs Abraham, Isaac, and Jacob; an Israelite; a Jew. **2. a.** The Semitic language of the ancient Hebrews. **b.** Any of the various later forms of this language, especially the language of the Israelis. **—He′brew** *adj.*

Heb·ri·des (hĕb′rĭ-dēz′) also **West·ern Islands** (wĕs′tərn). An island group of western and northwest Scotland in the Atlantic Ocean, divided into the **Inner Hebrides,** closer to the Scottish mainland, and the **Outer Hebrides,** to the northwest. The original Celtic inhabitants were conquered by Scandinavians, particularly Norwegians, who ruled the islands until 1266. Native Scottish chieftains controlled the Hebrides until the 16th century, when the islands passed to the kingdom of Scotland. **—Heb′ri·de′an** *adj. & n.*

He·bron (hĕb′rŏn′, -rôn′, hē′brən). A city of the West Bank south-southwest of Jerusalem. Sacred to both Jews and Arabs as the home and burial place of the patriarch Abraham and his family and (to Jews) as King David's capital for seven years, the city has figured in every war in Palestine and has a history of Jewish-Arab violence. Hebron was occupied by Israel in 1967. Israeli troops withdrew from most of the city,

which came under Palestinian control, in January 1996. ⊕ Pop. 43,000.

Hec·ate Strait (hĕk′ət, -ə-tē). A channel of western British Columbia, Canada, separating the Queen Charlotte Islands from coastal islands off the mainland of the province.

Hed·jaz (hē-jăz′). See **Hejaz.**

Heer·len (hâr′lən). A city of southeast Netherlands east-northeast of Maastricht near the German border. It is a manufacturing center in a coal-mining area. ⊕ Pop. 93,283.

He·fei (hœ′fā′) also **Ho·fei** (hŭ′-). A city of east-central China west of Nanjing. A rapidly growing industrial center, it is the capital of Anhui province. ⊕ Pop. 1,099,523.

He·gang (hœ′gäng′) also **Ho·kang** (hŭ′käng′, -gäng′). A city of extreme northeast China northeast of Harbin near the Russian border. It is a manufacturing center. ⊕ Pop. 647,021.

Hei·del·berg (hīd′l-bûrg′, -bĕrk′). A city of southwest Germany on the Neckar River northnorthwest of Stuttgart. First mentioned in the 12th century, it was the capital of the Palatinate until the early 18th century. Its university was established in 1386. ⊕ Pop. 139,429.

Heil·bronn (hīl′brŏn′, -brôn′). A city of southwest Germany on the Neckar River north of Stuttgart. On the site of a 9th-century Carolingian palace, it became a free imperial city in the 14th century. ⊕ Pop. 122,396.

Hei·long·jiang (hā′lông′jyäng′) also **Hei·lung·kiang** (hā′lōōng′kyäng′). A province of extreme northeast China bordering on Russia. It was under Japanese control from 1932 to 1945. Harbin is the capital. ⊕ Pop. 33,110,000.

Hei·long Jiang (hā′lông′ jyäng′). See **Amur River.**

Hei·lung·kiang (hā′lōōng′kyäng′). See **Heilongjiang.**

He·jaz also **Hed·jaz** (hē-jăz′). A region of northwest Saudi Arabia on the Gulf of Aqaba and the Red Sea. It includes the holy cities of Mecca and Medina.

Hek·la (hĕk′lə). An active volcano, 1,492.1 m (4,892 ft) high, of southwest Iceland. In medieval Icelandic folklore, Hekla was believed to be one of the gateways to purgatory.

Hel·e·na (hĕl′ə-nə). The capital of Montana, in the west-central part of the state northnortheast of Butte. It was founded in 1864 after the discovery of gold at Last Chance Gulch. Helena became the territorial capital after 1874 and the state capital in 1889. ⊕ Pop. 24,569.

Hel·go·land (hĕl′gō-länd′, -länt′). An island of northwest Germany, one of the North Frisian Islands in **Helgoland Bay,** an inlet of the North Sea southwest of Jutland. The island belonged to Denmark and Great Britain before being ceded to Germany in 1890. Helgoland is a popular tourist resort.

Hel·i·con (hĕl′ĭ-kŏn′, -kən). A mountain, 1,749.2 m (5,735 ft) high, of central Greece. It was the legendary abode of the Muses, the daughters of Zeus who presided over the difference arts and sciences, and was sacred to the god Apollo.

He·li·op·o·lis (hē′lē-ŏp′ə-lĭs). **1.** An ancient city of northern Egypt in the Nile River delta north of modern Cairo. It was the center of worship of the sun god Ra until the rise of Thebes (c. 2100 B.C.). Its importance as a historical repository with famed schools of philosophy and astronomy declined after the founding of Alexandria in the fourth century B.C. Two of its obelisks, both known as Cleopatra's Needle, are now in London and in New York City's Central Park. **2.** See **Baalbek.**

Hel·las (hĕl′əs). See **Greece.**

Hel·lene (hĕl′ēn′) also **Hel·le·ni·an** (hĕ-lē′nē-ən). A Greek.

Hel·len·ic (hĕ-lĕn′ĭk). **1.** Of or relating to the ancient Hellenes, their language, or their history; Greek. **2.** The branch of the Indo-European language family that consists only of Greek.

Hel·le·nism (hĕl′ə-nĭz′əm). The civilization and culture of ancient Greece.

Hel·le·nist (hĕl′ə-nĭst). A person living in Hellenistic times who adopted the Greek language and culture, especially a Jew exiled from Israel in the Diaspora.

Hel·le·nis·tic (hĕl′ə-nĭs′tĭk) also **Hel·le·nis·ti·cal** (-tĭ-kəl). **1.** Of or relating to the Hellenists. **2.** Of or relating to postclassical Greek history and culture from the death of Alexander the Great (323 B.C.) to the accession of Augustus, first emperor (27 B.C.–A.D. 14) of Rome.

Hel·les·pont (hĕl′ĭ-spŏnt′). See **Dardanelles.**

Hell Gate (hĕl). A narrow channel of the East River in New York City between Manhattan and Long Island. It was named by the Dutch navigator Adriaen Block (fl. 1610–1624), who passed through it into Long Island Sound in 1614.

Hells Canyon (hĕlz). A gorge of the Snake River on the Idaho-Oregon border. It is about 201 km (125 mi) long and has a maximum depth of approximately 2,410 m (7,900 ft).

Hel·mand (hĕl′mənd). A river, about 1,287 km (800 mi) long, rising in the Hindu Kush and flowing southwest across Afghanistan to a marshy lake on the Iranian border.

Hel·mond (hĕl′mônt′). A city of southeast Netherlands east-northeast of Eindhoven. It is a manufacturing center. ◉ Pop. 60,582.

Hel·sing·borg (hĕl′sĭng-bôrg′, hĕl′sĭng-bôr′-ē). See **Hälsingborg.**

Hel·sing·ør (hĕl′sĭng-ûr′, -œr′) also **El·si·nore** (ĕl′sə-nôr′, -nōr′). A city of eastern Denmark north of Copenhagen on northern Sjaelland Island and the Oresund. Known since the 13th century, it is famous as the setting for Shakespeare's *Hamlet,* and performances of the play are often presented at the restored castle. ◉ Pop. 56,161.

Hel·sin·ki (hĕl′sĭng′kē, hĕl-sĭng′-). The capital and largest city of Finland, in the southern part of the country on the Gulf of Finland. Founded in 1550 by Gustavus I of Sweden, it was moved to its present site in 1640. Helsinki passed to Russia along with Finland in 1809 and became capital of Finland in 1812, retaining that status when the country proclaimed its independence in 1917. ◉ Pop. 505,051.

Hel·ve·tia (hĕl-vē′shə, -shē-ə). An ancient region of central Europe occupying a plateau between the Alps and the Jura Mountains. It was named by the Romans for its predominantly Celtic inhabitants. Helvetia corresponded roughly to the western part of modern Switzerland, and the name is still used in poetic references and on the country's postage stamps.

Hel·ve·tian (hĕl-vē′shən). **1.** Of or relating to Helvetia or the Helvetii. **2.** Swiss. **3.** One of the Helvetii. **4.** A Swiss.

Hel·ve·ti·i (hĕl-vē′shē-ī′). A Celtic people inhabiting western Switzerland during the time of Julius Caesar (first century B.C.).

Hem·el Hemp·stead (hĕm′əl hĕmp′stĭd). A municipal borough of southeast England northwest of London. It is a market town and residential suburb with varied light industries. ◉ Pop. 80,900.

Hem·et (hĕm′ĭt). A city of southern California east of Santa Ana. Ancient rock paintings and carvings have been found here. ◉ Pop. 36,094.

hem·i·sphere (hĕm′ĭ-sfîr′). Either the northern or southern half of the earth as divided by the equator or the eastern or western half as divided by a meridian. — **hem′i·spher′ic** (-sfîr′-ĭk, -sfĕr′-), **hem′i·spher′i·cal** *adj.*

Hemp·stead (hĕmp′stĕd′, -stĭd). A village of southeast New York on western Long Island southeast of Mineola. Settled c. 1643, it is the seat of Hofstra University (founded 1935). ◉ Pop. 49,453.

He·nan (hœ′nän′) also **Ho·nan** (hō′-). A province of east-central China. It is one of the oldest inhabited regions in China and the site of many Stone Age remains. Zhengzhou is the capital. ◉ Pop. 77,130,000.

Hen·der·son (hĕn′dər-sən). **1.** A city of northwest Kentucky on the Ohio River south of Evansville, Indiana. Settled in the late 1700's, it was the home of the ornithologist and artist John J. Audubon from 1810 to 1819. ◉ Pop. 25,945.

2. A city of southeast Nevada southeast of Las Vegas. Founded in 1942, it is in a desert area surrounded by mountains. ⊛ Pop. 64,942.

Hen·der·son·ville (hĕn′dər-sən-vĭl′). A city of northern Tennessee northeast of Nashville. It is a popular resort. ⊛ Pop. 32,188.

Heng·e·lo (hĕng′ə-lō′). A city of eastern Netherlands near the German border northwest of Enscheda. It is an industrial center. ⊛ Pop. 76,855.

Heng·yang (hŭng′yäng′, hœng′-). A city of southeast China south-southwest of Wuhan. It is an important transportation hub and industrial center. ⊛ Pop. 1,814,936.

Hen·ley (hĕn′lē) or **Hen·ley-on-Thames** (-ŏn-tĕmz′, -ôn-). A municipal borough of south-central England west of London. It is the site of a famed annual rowing regatta that was established in 1839. ⊛ Pop. 10,976.

Hen·ry (hĕn′rē), **Cape**. A promontory of southeast Virginia at the entrance to Chesapeake Bay east of Norfolk.

hep·tar·chy also **Hep·tar·chy** (hĕp′tär′kē). The informal confederation of the Anglo-Saxon kingdoms from the fifth to the ninth century, consisting of Kent, Sussex, Wessex, Essex, Northumbria, East Anglia, and Mercia.

Her·a·cle·a (hĕr′ə-klē′ə). An ancient Greek city of southern Italy near the Gulf of Taranto. In 280 B.C. it was the site of a victory over the Romans by Pyrrhus, king of Epirus.

He·rat (hĕ-rät′). A city of northwest Afghanistan on the Hari Rud west of Kabul. Located at a strategic position on an ancient trade route, it was ruled by numerous conquerors, primarily the Persians. Herat became part of Afghanistan in 1881. ⊛ Pop. 177,300.

Her·cu·la·ne·um (hûr′kyə-lā′nē-əm). An ancient city of south-central Italy on the Bay of Naples. A popular resort during Roman times, it was completely destroyed by the eruption of Mount Vesuvius (A.D. 79). Important ruins have been unearthed since the early 1700's.

Here·ford (hûr′fərd). A city of northwest Texas in the Panhandle southwest of Amarillo. It is a processing center in a farming and cattle-raising area. ⊛ Pop. 14,745.

He·re·ro (hə-râr′ō, hĕr′ə-rō′). **1.** *pl.* **Herero** or **-ros.** A member of a pastoral people inhabiting Namibia and Botswana. **2.** The Bantu language of this people.

Her·ford (hĕr′fôrt′). A city of northeast Germany east-northeast of Münster. It is a manufacturing center. ⊛ Pop. 59,941.

Her·mon (hûr′mən), **Mount**. The highest peak, 2,815.8 m (9,232 ft), of the Anti-Lebanon Range on the Syria-Lebanon border. It was sacred to the worshipers of Baal, an ancient Semitic deity,

and is considered the traditional site of Jesus's transfiguration.

Her·mo·sa Beach (hər-mō′sə). A city of southern California on the Pacific Ocean south-southwest of Los Angeles. It is a resort and residential suburb. ⊛ Pop. 18,219.

Her·mo·sil·lo (ĕr′mô-sē′ô). A city of northwest Mexico near the Gulf of California west of Chihuahua. Established c. 1700, it is a trade center in an agricultural and mining area. ⊛ Pop. 297,175.

Her·ne (hĕr′nə). A city of west-central Germany in the Ruhr district east-northeast of Essen. It is an industrial center in a mining area. ⊛ Pop. 180,539.

Her·ten (hĕr′tn). A city of west-central Germany north of Essen. It is an industrial center in a mining area. ⊛ Pop. 68,423.

Her·ze·go·vi·na (hĕrt′sə-gō-vē′nə, hûrt′-). A region comprising the southern part of Bosnia and Herzegovina. Largely independent after the 10th century, it was conquered by Bosnia in the 14th century and by Turkey in the 15th century, since which time it has frequently been joined administratively with Bosnia. Bosnia and Herzegovina were united to form a constituent republic of Yugoslavia from 1946 to 1991. **—Her′ze·go·vi′ni·an** *adj. & n.*

Hes·pe·ri·an (hĕ-spîr′ē-ən). Of or relating to the west.

Hesse (hĕs). A region and former grand duchy of west-central Germany. In medieval times the territory was expanded west to the Rhine River and south to the Main River, but after 1567 it was divided into four separate regions ruled by various branches of the Hesse family.

Hes·sian (hĕsh′ən). **1.** Of or relating to Hesse or its inhabitants. **2.** A native or inhabitant of Hesse.

Hi·a·le·ah (hī′ə-lē′ə). A city of southeast Florida northwest of Miami. It is a manufacturing center and the site of a noted racetrack (established 1931), which encircles a flamingo-filled lake. ⊛ Pop. 188,004.

Hib·bing (hĭb′ĭng). A city of northeast Minnesota in the Mesabi Range northwest of Duluth. Established as a lumber camp in 1893, the town was moved (1919–1921) several miles south to make room for a huge open-pit iron mine. ⊛ Pop. 18,046.

Hi·ber·ni·a (hī-bûr′nē-ə). The Latin and poetic name for the island of Ireland. **—Hi·ber′ni·an** *adj. & n.*

Hi·ber·no-Eng·lish (hī-bûr′nō-ĭng′glĭsh). See **Irish English**.

Hick·o·ry (hĭk′ə-rē, hĭk′rē). A city of west-central North Carolina northwest of Charlotte.

Located at the foot of the Blue Ridge, it is a manufacturing center. ◉ Pop. 28,301.

Hicks·ville (hĭks′vĭl). A community of southeast New York on western Long Island northeast of Mineola. Founded in 1648, it is mainly residential. ◉ Pop. 40,174.

Hi·dat·sa (hē-dät′sä). **1.** *pl.* **Hidatsa** or **-sas.** A member of a Native American people inhabiting an area along the Missouri River in western North Dakota. **2.** The Siouan language of this people. Also called *Gros Ventre.*

Hi·er·ap·o·lis (hī-ə-răp′ə-lĭs). An ancient city of northwest Asia Minor in present-day Turkey. The Roman city was known for its baths fed by hot springs. Hierapolis was also an early center of Christianity.

Hi·ga·shi·o·sa·ka (hē-gä′shē-ō-sä′kä). A city of southern Honshu, Japan, a residential and industrial suburb of Osaka. ◉ Pop. 515,375.

high-coun·try (hī′kŭn′trē). Of, relating to, or being country that is above the piedmont and below the timberline.

High German (hī). *abbr.* **HG, H.G. 1.** German as indigenously spoken and written in central and southern Germany. **2.** See **German** (sense 4).

high·land (hī′lənd). **1.** Elevated land. **2. highlands.** A mountainous or hilly section of a country. **3.** Of, relating to, or characteristic of a highland. **—high′land·er** *n.*

High·land (hī′lənd). A town of northwest Indiana, a residential and industrial suburb in the Chicago-Gary metropolitan area. ◉ Pop. 23,696.

Highland Park. 1. A city of northeast Illinois, a residential suburb of Chicago on Lake Michigan. ◉ Pop. 30,575. **2.** A city of southeast Michigan surrounded by Detroit. It grew mainly after Henry Ford established an automobile factory here in 1909. ◉ Pop. 20,121.

High·lands (hī′ləndz). A mountainous region of central and northern Scotland extending northwest and including the Grampian Mountains. Famous for its rugged beauty, the area maintained a highly distinctive culture, based on the Scottish Gaelic language and the clan system, until well into the 19th century. **—High′land** *adj.* **—High′land·er** *n.*

High Point. A city of north-central North Carolina southwest of Greensboro. Settled before 1750, it is a furniture-manufacturing center. ◉ Pop. 69,496.

High Wyc·ombe (wĭk′əm). A municipal borough of southeast-central England west-north-west of London. It is an industrial center. ◉ Pop. 68,900.

Hil·den (hĭl′dən). A city of west-central Germany, an industrial suburb of Düsseldorf. ◉ Pop. 53,297.

Hil·des·heim (hĭl′dəs-hīm′, -dĕs-). A city of central Germany south-southeast of Hanover. A member of the Hanseatic League, it passed to Hanover in 1813 and to Prussia in 1866. ◉ Pop. 106,303.

hill (hĭl). A well-defined natural elevation smaller than a mountain. **—hill′y** *adj.*

hill·crest (hĭl′krĕst′). The summit line of a hill.

Hill·crest Center (hĭl′krĕst′). A community of south-central California, a suburb of Bakersfield. ◉ Pop. 30,000.

Hillcrest Heights. A community of west-central Maryland, a suburb of Washington, D.C. ◉ Pop. 17,136.

hill·ock (hĭl′ək). A small hill.

Hills·bor·o (hĭlz′bûr′ō, -bûr′ō). A city of northwest Oregon west of Portland. It was settled in the 1840's. ◉ Pop. 37,520.

hill·side (hĭl′sīd′). The side or slope of a hill, situated between the foot and the summit.

Hill·side (hĭl′sīd′). A community of northeast New Jersey north of Elizabeth. It has varied light industries. ◉ Pop. 21,044.

hill·top (hĭl′tŏp′). The crest or top of a hill.

Hi·lo (hē′lō). A city of Hawaii on the eastern coast of Hawaii Island on **Hilo Bay,** an inlet of the Pacific Ocean. Settled in the 1820's by American missionaries, the city is a trade and shipping center whose economy depends heavily on sugar exports and tourism. ◉ Pop. 37,808.

Hil·ton Head Island (hĭl′tən hĕd′). An island off the southern coast of South Carolina in the Sea Islands of the Atlantic Ocean. It is a popular tourist resort. The town of **Hilton Head Island,** on the northeast coast, has a population of 23,694.

Hil·ver·sum (hĭl′vər-səm). A city of central Netherlands southeast of Amsterdam. It is a manufacturing and broadcasting center. ◉ Pop. 84,379.

Him·a·la·ya Mountains (hĭm′ə-lā′ə, hĭ-mäl′-yə). A mountain system of south-central Asia extending about 2,414 km (1,500 mi) through Kashmir, northern India, southern Xizang (Tibet), Nepal, Sikkim, and Bhutan. The Himalayas include nine of the world's ten highest peaks, including Mount Everest. **—Him′a·la′yan** *adj.* & *n.*

Hi·me·ji (hē′mĕ-jē′, hē-mĕ′jē). A city of southwest Honshu, Japan, west-northwest of Kobe. An industrial center, it has a large Buddhist shrine. ◉ Pop. 463,197.

Him·yar·ite (hĭm′yə-rīt′). **1.** A member of an ancient tribe of southwest Arabia. **2.** The Semitic language of the ancient Himyarites. **3.** Of or relating to the Himyarites, their language, or their culture. **—Him′yar·it′ic** (-rĭt′ĭk) *adj.*

Hinck·ley (hĭngk′lē). An urban district of central England east-northeast of Birmingham. Hosiery and shoes are among its manufactures. ⊛ Pop. 55,600.

Hin·di (hĭn′dē). *abbr.* **Hind. 1.** A group of vernacular Indic dialects spoken in northern India. **2.** The literary and official language of northern India that is based on these dialects. It is written in Devanagari and uses Sanskrit as a resource language. — **Hin′di** *adj.*

Hin·doo (hĭn′dōō). *Archaic.* Variant of **Hindu.**

Hin·du (hĭn′dōō). **1.** An adherent of Hinduism. **2.** A native of India, especially northern India. **3.** Of or relating to Hinduism. **4.** Of or relating to the Hindus and their culture.

Hindu Kush (kōōsh, kŭsh). A mountain range of southwest Asia extending more than 805 km (500 mi) westward from northern Pakistan to northeast Afghanistan. It is crossed by several high-altitude passes used as invasion and trade routes since ancient times. The highest elevation is Tirich Mir, 7,695.2 m (25,230 ft) high, in Pakistan.

Hin·du·stan (hĭn′dōō-stän′, -stăn′). A historical region of India considered at various times to include only the upper Ganges River plateau or all of northern India from the Himalaya Mountains to the Deccan Plateau and from the Punjab to Assam. The term has also been applied to the entire Indian subcontinent.

Hin·du·sta·ni (hĭn′dōō-stä′nē, -stăn′ē). *abbr.* **Hind. 1.** A group of Indic dialects that includes Urdu and Hindi. **2.** Of or relating to Hindustan, its people, or the Hindustani language.

Hing·ham (hĭng′əm). A town of eastern Massachusetts on Massachusetts Bay southeast of Boston. It is a residential suburb and summer resort. ⊛ Pop. 19,821.

Hins·dale (hĭnz′dāl′). A village of northeast Illinois, a residential suburb of Chicago. ⊛ Pop. 16,029.

hin·ter·land (hĭn′tər-lănd′). **1.** The land directly adjacent to and inland from a coast. **2. a.** A region remote from urban areas; backcountry. **b.** A region situated beyond metropolitan centers of culture.

Hip·po (hĭp′ō) also **Hippo Re·gi·us** (rē′jē-əs). An ancient city of northwest Africa in present-day northeast Algeria south of Annaba. Saint Augustine was its bishop from A.D. 396 to 430.

Hip·po·crene (hĭp′ə-krēn′, hĭp′ə-krē′nē). *Greek Mythology.* A fountain on Mount Helicon, Greece, sacred to the Muses and regarded as a source of poetic inspiration.

Hippo Re·gi·us (rē′jē-əs). See **Hippo.**

Hi·ra·ka·ta (hē′rä-kä′tä, hē-rä′kä-tä′). A city of southern Honshu, Japan, a suburb north-

east of Osaka in an agricultural and lumbering area. ⊛ Pop. 396,867.

Hi·ra·tsu·ka (hĭ-rät′sə-kä′, hē′rä-tsōō′kä). A city of central Honshu, Japan, on an inlet of the Pacific Ocean southwest of Yokohama. It is a commercial and industrial center. ⊛ Pop. 251,991.

Hi·ro·shi·ma (hîr′ə-shē′mə, hĭ-rō′shə-mə). A city of southwest Honshu, Japan, on the Inland Sea west of Osaka. Founded in the 16th century, it was destroyed in World War II by the first atomic bomb used in warfare (August 6, 1945). The rebuilt city is an important commercial and industrial center. ⊛ Pop. 1,102,047.

His·pan·ic (hĭ-spăn′ĭk). **1.** Of or relating to Spain or Spanish-speaking Latin America. **2.** Of or relating to a Spanish-speaking people or culture. **3.** A Spanish-speaking person. **4.** A U.S. citizen or resident of Latin-American or Spanish descent.

Hispanic American. 1. A U.S. citizen or resident of Hispanic descent. **2.** A Spanish American. — **His·pan′ic-A·mer′i·can** (hĭ-spăn′-ĭk-ə-mĕr′ĭ-kən) *adj.*

His·pan·io·la (hĭs′pən-yō′lə). Formerly **Hai·ti** (hā′tē). An island of the West Indies east of Cuba, divided between Haiti and the Dominican Republic. Originally inhabited by Arawak Indians, it was discovered by Columbus in 1492 and was originally called Española. The western part (now Haiti) was ceded to France by Spain in 1697.

His·pa·no (hĭ-spăn′ō, -spä′nō). *pl.* **-nos. 1.** A native or resident of Spanish descent living in the southwest United States. **2.** A Hispanic.

Hispano American. A Hispanic American. — **His·pa′no-A·mer′i·can** (hĭ-spän′ō-ə-mĕr′ĭ-kən) *adj.*

Hi·ta·chi (hĭ-tä′chē). A city of east-central Honshu, Japan, on the Pacific Ocean northeast of Tokyo. It is the center of an important industrial area. ⊛ Pop. 201,831.

Hit·tite (hĭt′īt′). *abbr.* **Hitt. 1.** A member of an ancient people living in Anatolia and northern Syria about 2000–1200 B.C. **2.** The Indo-European language of the Hittites. **3.** Of or relating to the Hittites, their language, or their culture.

Hi·va O·a (hē′və ō′ə). A volcanic island of the southern Pacific Ocean in the southeast Marquesas Islands of French Polynesia. The French painter Paul Gauguin is buried here.

Hi·was·see (hī-wŏs′ē). A river rising in northeast Georgia and flowing about 241 km (150 mi) northward across southwest North Carolina and into southeast Tennessee, where it joins the Tennessee River.

Hka·ka·bo Ra·zi (kä′kə-bō rä′zē). A mountain, 5,885.3 m (19,296 ft) high, of northern Myanmar (Burma) near the Chinese border. It is the highest peak in the country.

Hmong (hmông). **1.** *pl.* **Hmong** or **Hmongs.** A member of a people inhabiting the mountainous regions of southern China and adjacent areas of Vietnam, Laos, and Thailand. **2.** The Miao-Yao language of the Hmong. Also called *Miao.*

Ho·bart. 1. (hō′bärt). A city of southeast Tasmania, Australia, on an inlet of the Tasman Sea. It was founded in 1804 as a penal colony. ● Pop. 47,920. **2.** (hō′bərt). A city of northwest Indiana southeast of Gary. Mainly residential, it also has varied light industries. ● Pop. 21,822.

Hobbs (hŏbz). A city of southeast New Mexico near the Texas border southeast of Roswell. Oil and natural gas were discovered in the area in 1927. ● Pop. 29,115.

Ho·bo·ken (hō′bō′kən). A city of northeast New Jersey on the Hudson River opposite Manhattan. Now a railroad hub and busy seaport, it was a resort and amusement center for New Yorkers before the mid-19th century. ● Pop. 33,397.

Ho Chi Minh City (hō′chē′ mĭn′). Formerly **Sai·gon** (sī′gŏn′). The largest city of Vietnam, in the southern part of the country near the South China Sea. An ancient Khmer settlement, it became the capital of Cochin China (1862–1954) and subsequently of South Vietnam. The city was used as the headquarters of U.S. military operations during the Vietnam War (1954–1975) and was heavily damaged by fighting in 1968. ● Pop. 3,015,743.

Ho·dei·da (hō-dā′də). A city of western Yemen on the Red Sea. It is a major port and industrial center. ● Pop. 246,068.

Hoek van Hol·land (hōōk′ vän hô′länt). See **Hook of Holland.**

Hof (hōf, hôf). A city of east-central Germany near the Czech border north-northeast of Bayreuth. First mentioned in the early 13th century, it passed to Prussia in 1792 and Bavaria in 1810. ● Pop. 51,183.

Ho·fei (hŭ′fā′). See **Hefei.**

Hoff·man Estates (hôf′mən). A village of northeast Illinois, a suburb of Chicago. ● Pop. 46,561.

hog·back (hôg′băk′, hŏg′-). A sharp ridge with steeply sloping sides, produced by erosion of the broken edges of highly tilted strata.

Ho·he Tau·ern (hō′ə tou′ərn). A range of the eastern Alps in southern Austria near the Italian border. Grossglockner, 3,799.4 m (12,457 ft), is the highest peak.

Hoh·hot (hō′hōt′) also **Hu·he·hot** (hōō′hä-). A city of northern China west-northwest of Beijing. An industrial city, it is also the capital of Nei

Monggol (Inner Mongolia) autonomous region. ● Pop. 938,470.

Ho·ho·kam (hə-hō′kəm). A Native American culture flourishing from about the 3rd century B.C. to the mid-15th century A.D. in south-central Arizona, noted for the construction of an extensive system of irrigation canals.

Ho·kan (hō′kən). A proposed grouping of a number of Native American language families of western North America.

Ho·kang (hŭ′käng′, -gäng′). See **Hegang.**

Hok·kai·do (hŏ-kī′dō, hô′kī-dō′). An island of Japan north of Honshu. It is the second largest of the Japanese islands but the least populated. Hokkaido became part of Japan in the medieval period (c. 1600) and was called Yezo or Ezo until 1868.

Hol·guín (ôl-gēn′). A city of eastern Cuba north-northwest of Santiago de Cuba. It is a commercial and transportation center. ● Pop. 239,000.

Hol·i·day (hŏl′ĭ-dā′). A community of west-central Florida on the Gulf of Mexico northwest of Tampa. ● Pop. 15,400.

Hol·la·day (hŏl′ə-dā′). A community of north-central Utah, a suburb of Salt Lake City. ● Pop. 22,189.

Hol·land (hŏl′ənd). **1.** A city of southwest Michigan southwest of Grand Rapids. Founded in 1847 by Dutch settlers, it is a manufacturing center and summer resort. ● Pop. 30,745. **2.** See **Netherlands.**

hol·low (hŏl′ō) also **hol·ler** (hŏl′ər). *Appalachian Mountains.* A small valley between mountains.

Hol·ly·wood (hŏl′ē-wōōd′). **1.** A district of Los Angeles, California. Consolidated with Los Angeles in 1910, it has long been a film and entertainment center. **2.** A city of southeast Florida on the Atlantic Ocean north of Miami Beach. It is a resort and retirement community with varied light industries. ● Pop. 121,697.

holm (hōm, hōlm). *Chiefly British.* An island in a river.

Ho·lon (hō-lōn′, кнô-lôn′). A city of west-central Israel near Tel Aviv–Jaffa. It was established in 1941. ● Pop. 162,800.

Hol·stein (hōl′stīn′, -stēn′). A region and former duchy of northern Germany at the base of the Jutland Peninsula. It became a duchy under the suzerainty of the Holy Roman Empire in 1474 and was often controlled by Denmark in the years that followed.

Hol·ston (hōl′stən). A river, about 225 km (140 mi) long, rising in two forks in western Virginia and northeast Tennessee and flowing southwest to join the French Broad River and form the Tennessee River at Knoxville.

Ho·ly Cross (hō′lē krôs′, krŏs′), **Mount of the.** A peak, 4,271.5 m (14,005 ft) high, in the Sawatch Range of the Rocky Mountains in west-central Colorado.

Holy Island or **Lin·dis·farne** (lĭn′dĭs-färn′). An island off the coast of northeast England near the Scottish border. At low tide the island is connected with the mainland by a stretch of sand. Saint Aidan (died 651) established Celtic Christianity in England by founding a church and a monastery here in 635. Danes destroyed the settlement in 793.

Holy Land. The biblical region of Palestine.

Hol·yoke (hōl′yōk′). A city of southwest Massachusetts on the Connecticut River north of Springfield. Settled in 1745, it is a manufacturing center specializing in paper products. ⊛ Pop. 43,704.

Holy Roman Empire *abbr.* **H.R.E.** A loosely federated European political entity that began with the papal coronation of the German king Otto I as the first emperor in 962 and lasted until Emperor Francis II's renunciation of the title at the instigation of Napoleon I in 1806. The empire was troubled from the beginning by papal-secular squabbles over authority and after the 13th century by the rising ambitions of nationalistic states in Europe. By 1273 the empire consisted primarily of the Hapsburg domains in Austria and Spain.

home·land (hōm′lănd′). **1.** One's native land. **2.** A state, region, or territory that is closely identified with a particular people or ethnic group. **3.** Any of the ten regions established by South Africa in the 1970's as independent or semiautonomous territorial states for the Black population. The Black homelands were dissolved and reincorporated into South Africa when the interim constitution took effect in April 1994.

Home·stead (hōm′stĕd′). A city of southeast Florida southwest of Miami. It is a trade center for a citrus-growing area. ⊛ Pop. 26,866.

Home·wood (hōm′wŏŏd′). **1.** A city of central Alabama, a residential suburb of Birmingham. ⊛ Pop. 22,922. **2.** A village of northeast Illinois, a manufacturing and residential suburb of Chicago. ⊛ Pop. 19,278.

hom·o·lo·graph·ic projection (hŏm′ə-lə-grăf′ĭk). A map projection reproducing the ratios of areas as they exist on the earth's surface.

ho·mol·o·sine projection (hō-mŏl′ə-sīn′, -sĭn, hə-). A map of the earth's surface laid out on the basis of sinusoidal curves, with the interruptions over ocean areas distorted so that the continents appear with minimal distortion.

Homs (hômz, hôms). A city of west-central Syria north of Damascus. Birthplace of the Ro-

man emperor Heliogabalus (A.D. 204–222), it was taken by the Arabs in 636. Egypt controlled the city from 1831 to 1840. ⊛ Pop. 558,000.

Ho·nan (hō′nän′). See **Henan.**

Hon·du·ras (hŏn-dŏŏr′əs, -dyŏŏr′-). *abbr.* **Hond.** A country of northern Central America. Originally inhabited by a Mayan civilization, Honduras was colonized by the Spanish in the early 1500's and gained its independence along with Mexico in 1821. Part of a short-lived confederation of Central American states, Honduras became a separate republic in 1838. The country has experienced frequent coups and sporadic conflict with neighboring states. A new constitution adopted in 1982 established free elections but did little to diminish the power of the military. Tegucigalpa is the capital and the largest city. ⊛ Pop. 5,770,000. — **Hon·du′ran** *adj. & n.*

Honduras, Gulf of. An inlet of the western Caribbean Sea bordering on Belize, Honduras, and Guatemala.

Hong Ha (hông′ hä′). See **Red River** (sense 1).

Hong Kong (hŏng′kŏng′, -kŏng′, hông′kông′, -kông′). A region on the southeast coast of China southeast of Guangzhou, including Hong Kong Island and adjacent areas. Formerly a British crown colony, Hong Kong was occupied by the British during the Opium War (1839–1842) and ceded to them by the Treaty of Nanking (1842). Other portions of the colony were acquired in 1860 and in 1898 by a 99-year lease. A free port and an important center of international commerce and banking for most of the 20th century, it reverted to Chinese sovereignty in 1997. Victoria is the capital. ⊛ Pop. 6,061,000.

Hong·shui He also **Hung·shui He** (hŏŏng′-shwā′ hə′). A river, about 1,448 km (900 mi) long, rising in southwest China and flowing generally southeast to join the Xiang Jiang. It is navigable for small craft.

Ho·ni·a·ra (hō′nē-är′ə). The capital of the Solomon Islands, on the northwest coast of Guadalcanal. ⊛ Pop. 16,125.

Hon·o·lu·lu (hŏn′ə-lŏŏ′lŏŏ). The capital and

largest city of Hawaii, on the southeast coast of Oahu. Honolulu's harbor was first entered by Europeans in 1794. Settlement of the area began in 1816, and the city soon gained prominence as a whaling and sandalwood port. From 1845 to 1893 it was the residence of the native Hawaiian monarchs. Today it is a major tourist center. ⊛ Pop. 365,272.

Hon·shu (hŏn'shōō). The largest island of Japan, in the central part of the country between the Sea of Japan and the Pacific Ocean.

Hood (hŏŏd), **Mount.** A volcanic peak, 3,426.7 m (11,235 ft) high, in the Cascade Range of northwest Oregon. It is the highest elevation in the state.

hoo·doo (hōō'dōō). *Geology.* A column of eccentrically shaped rock, produced by differential weathering.

Hoogh·ly (hōō'glē). A channel, about 257 km (160 mi) long, of the Ganges River in eastern India. The westernmost channel on the Ganges River delta, it connects Calcutta with the Bay of Bengal.

hook (hŏŏk). **1.** A sharp bend or curve in a river. **2.** A point or spit of land with a sharply curved end.

Hook of Hol·land (hŏŏk; hŏl'ənd) also **Hoek van Hol·land** (hōōk' vän hô'länt). A cape and harbor of southwest Netherlands on the North Sea west of Rotterdam, for which it serves as a port.

Hoorn (hôrn, hōrn). A city of western Netherlands on an inlet of the Ijsselmeer north-northeast of Amsterdam. Founded in 1311, it is a commercial and processing center for an agricultural region. ⊛ Pop. 50,473.

Hoorn Islands. See **Futuna Islands.**

Hoo·ver (hōō'vər). A city of north-central Alabama, a suburb of Birmingham. ⊛ Pop. 39,788.

Ho·pat·cong (hə-păt'kŏng', -kông'). A borough of north-central New Jersey on **Lake Hopatcong** northwest of Morristown. The city and lake are summer resorts. ⊛ Pop. 15,586.

Ho·pei or **Ho·peh** (hō'pā', hŭ'bā'). See **Hebei.**

Hope·well[1] (hōp'wĕl', -wəl). An early Native American culture centered in the Ohio River valley from about the second century B.C. to the fourth century A.D., noted for the construction of extensive earthworks and large conical burial mounds and for its highly developed arts and crafts.

Hope·well[2] (hōp'wĕl'). An independent city of southeast Virginia south-southeast of Richmond. It was founded in 1913 as a munitions center. ⊛ Pop. 23,101.

Ho·pi (hō'pē). **1.** *pl.* **Hopi** or **-pis.** A member of a Pueblo people occupying a number of mesatop pueblos on reservation land in northeast Ar-

izona. The Hopis are noted for their sophisticated dry-farming techniques, a rich ceremonial life, and fine craftsmanship in basketry, pottery, silverwork, and weaving. **2.** The Uto-Aztecan language of the Hopi.

Hop·kins (hŏp'kĭnz). A city of southeast Minnesota, an industrial suburb of Minneapolis. ⊛ Pop. 16,534.

Hop·kins·ville (hŏp'kĭnz-vĭl'). A city of southwest Kentucky west-southwest of Bowling Green. It is a tobacco and livestock market. ⊛ Pop. 29,809.

Hor·muz (hôr-mōōz', hôr'mŭz'), **Strait of** also **Strait of Or·muz** (ôr-mōōz', ôr'mŭz'). A strategic waterway linking the Persian Gulf with the Gulf of Oman. The narrow strait controls oceangoing traffic to and from the oil-rich Gulf States.

Horn (hôrn), **Cape.** A headland of extreme southern Chile in the Tierra del Fuego archipelago. The southernmost point of South America, it was first rounded in 1616 by the Dutch navigator Willem Schouten (died 1625), who named it after his birthplace, Hoorn. It is notorious for its storms and heavy seas.

hor·ni·to (hôr-nē'tō). A low mound of volcanic origin, sometimes emitting smoke or vapor.

horse latitudes (hôrs). Either of two belts of latitudes located over the oceans at about 30° to 35° north and south, having high barometric pressure, calms, and light, changeable winds.

Hor·sens (hôr'sənz, -səns). A city of central Denmark on the eastern Jutland Peninsula at the head of **Horsens Fjord,** an inlet of the Kattegat. A fortified medieval town, Horsens is now a commercial and industrial center. ⊛ Pop. 54,717.

Horse·shoe Falls (hôrs'shōō', hôrsh'-). See **Canadian Falls.**

horst (hôrst). A mass of the earth's crust that lies between two faults and is higher than the surrounding land.

Hor·ton River (hôr'tn). A river, about 443 km (275 mi) long, of northern Northwest Territories, Canada, flowing northwest into Franklin Bay, an inlet of the Beaufort Sea.

Hos·pi·ta·let (hŏs'pĭt-l-ĕt', ôs'pē-tä-lĕt'). A city of northeast Spain, an industrial suburb of Barcelona. ⊛ Pop. 272,578.

hot spot also **hot·spot** (hŏt'spŏt'). An area in which there is unusually dangerous unrest or hostile action.

Hot Springs (hŏt). A city of west-central Arkansas west-southwest of Little Rock. It is a health resort noted for its 47 thermal springs. The Spanish explorer Hernando de Soto first visited the site in 1541. ⊛ Pop. 32,462.

Hou·ma (hō'mə, hōō'-). A city of southeast

Louisiana on the Intracoastal Waterway southwest of New Orleans. It is a processing center for seafood and sugar. ⊛ Pop. 30,495.

hour (our). *abbr.* **hr, h.** A unit of measure of longitude or right ascension, equal to 15° or 1/24 of a great circle.

Hou·sa·ton·ic (hoo′sə-tŏn′ĭk). A river rising in the Berkshire Hills of western Massachusetts and flowing about 209 km (130 mi) generally south through western Connecticut to Long Island Sound.

Hous·ton (hyoo′stən). A city of southeast Texas northwest of Galveston. Founded in 1836 and named for Sam Houston, who served as president (1836–1838 and 1841–1844) of the Republic of Texas, it is a major industrial, commercial, and financial hub, the center of the U.S. aerospace industry, and a deep-water port connected with Galveston Bay and the Gulf of Mexico by the **Houston Ship Channel.** Houston is also the largest city in Texas. ⊛ Pop. 1,690,180. — **Hous·to′ni·an** (-stō′nē-ən) *n.*

Hove (hōv). A municipal borough of southeast England on the English Channel west of Brighton. It is a residential seaside resort. ⊛ Pop. 88,500.

How·rah (hou′rə, -rä) also **Ha·o·ra** (hä′ô-rä, -rə). A city of eastern India on the Hooghly River opposite Calcutta. It is a major industrial center. ⊛ Pop. 950,435.

Hoy·ers·wer·da (hoi′ərz-vĕr′də, -dä, -ərs-). A city of east-central Germany north-northeast of Dresden. It was chartered in 1371 and today has a major glassmaking industry. ⊛ Pop. 70,698.

Hra·dec Krá·lo·vé (rä′dĕts krä′lə-və, -lô-vě, hrä′-). A city of northern Czech Republic east of Prague. Founded in the tenth century, it was a leading town of medieval Bohemia. ⊛ Pop. 100,822.

Hsian (shyän). See **Xi'an.**

Hsiang Kiang (shyäng′ kyäng′). See **Xiang Jiang.**

Hsin·king (shĭn′gĭng′). See **Changchun.**

Huai·nan (hwī′nän′). A city of east-central China west-northwest of Nanjing. It grew after 1949 as the center of a coal-mining region. ⊛ Pop. 1,228,052.

Hua·la·pai or **Wa·la·pai** (wä′lə-pī′). **1.** *pl.* **Hualapai** or **-pis.** A member of a Native American people inhabiting northwest Arizona south of the Grand Canyon. **2.** The Yuman language of the Hualapais.

Hual·la·ga (wä-yä′gä). A river rising in the Andes of west-central Peru and flowing about 1,126 km (700 mi) generally northward to the Marañón River.

Huang He (hwäng′ hə′) also **Hwang Ho** (hō′)

or **Yel·low River** (yĕl′ō). A river of northern China rising in the Kunlun Mountains and flowing about 4,827 km (3,000 mi) generally eastward to the Bo Hai. It is named for the vast quantities of yellow silt it carries to its delta. The river is sometimes called "China's Sorrow" because of the devastating floods that once occurred regularly in its lower course.

Huas·ca·rán (wäs′kə-rän′, -kä-). An extinct volcano, 6,770.4 m (22,198 ft) high, in the Andes of west-central Peru. It is the highest peak in the country.

Hub·bard (hŭb′ərd). **Mount.** A peak, 4,559.8 m (14,950 ft) high, in the Coast Mountains of southeast Alaska.

Hu·bei (hoo′bā′, hü′-) also **Hu·pei** or **Hu·peh** (-pā′). A province of east-central China. It is a major agricultural region watered by the Chang Jiang (Yangtze River). Wuhan is the capital. ⊛ Pop. 49,310,000.

Hu·ber Heights (hyoo′bər). A community of southwest Ohio, a suburb of Dayton. ⊛ Pop. 38,696.

Hu·bli-Dhar·war (hoob′lē-där-wär′). A city of southwest India northwest of Bangalore. It was formed from two municipalities in 1961. ⊛ Pop. 648,298.

Hud·ders·field (hŭd′ərz-fēld′). A borough of north-central England northeast of Manchester. First settled in Roman times, it is an industrial center specializing in textiles. ⊛ Pop. 125,800.

Hud·ding·e (hü′dĭng-ĕ). A city of eastern Sweden, a manufacturing suburb of Stockholm. ⊛ Pop. 69,581.

Hud·son (hŭd′sən). A town of east-central Massachusetts northeast of Worcester. It is an industrial community. ⊛ Pop. 17,233.

Hudson Bay. An inland sea of east-central Canada connected to the Atlantic Ocean by **Hudson Strait,** lying between southern Baffin Island and northern Quebec. James Bay is the southern extension of Hudson Bay, which was explored and named by the English navigator Henry Hudson in 1610.

Hudson River. A river rising in the Adirondack Mountains of northeast New York and flowing about 507 km (315 mi) generally southward to Upper New York Bay at New York City. The Italian explorer Giovanni da Verrazano first sighted the river in 1524, but it was not explored until the English navigator Henry Hudson's 1609 voyage.

Hue (hyoo-ā′, hwä). A city of central Vietnam near the South China Sea northwest of Da Nang. Probably dating from the 3rd century A.D., it became the capital of the kingdom of Annam in the 16th century. Hue was taken by the French in 1883 and became part of South Vietnam in 1954. It was nearly destroyed during heavy fighting in the Vietnam War (1954–1975) but has since been rebuilt. ⊛ Pop. 219,149.

Huel·va (wĕl′və, -vä). A city of southwest Spain near the Gulf of Cádiz and the Portuguese border. Founded by Carthaginians, it was colonized by the Romans, who built a still-used aqueduct to supply water to the settlement. ⊛ Pop. 144,053.

Hu·gue·not (hyōō′gə-nŏt′). A French Protestant of the 16th and 17th centuries. When their political and religious freedom was curtailed in the late 17th century, many Huguenots fled to Protestant Europe and to America. —**Hu′gue·not′ic** adj. —**Hu′gue·not′ism** n.

Hu·he·hot (hōō′hä-hōt′). See Hohhot.

Hui (hwē) also **Hwei** (hwā). pl. **Hui** or **Huis** also **Hwei** or **Hweis.** A member of a Muslim people of northwest China, descended chiefly from the Han and constituting an important minority of the Chinese population; a Chinese Muslim.

Hull (hŭl). **1.** A city of southwest Quebec, Canada, opposite Ottawa, Ontario. It has a hydroelectric station and pulp, paper, and lumber mills. ⊛ Pop. 56,225. **2.** also **King·ston-up·on-Hull** (kĭng′stən-ə-pŏn-hŭl′, -pôn-). A borough of northeast-central England on the northern shore of the Humber estuary at the influx of the **Hull River.** Chartered in 1299, the city has been a major seaport since the late 1700's. ⊛ Pop. 267,889.

Hum·ber (hŭm′bər). An estuary of the Trent and Ouse rivers in northeast-central England. It is navigable for large vessels as far inland as Hull.

Hum·boldt Bay (hŭm′bōlt′). A sheltered inlet of the Pacific Ocean in northwest California.

Humboldt Current. A cold ocean current of the South Pacific, flowing north along the western coast of South America. Approximately every ten years complex weather conditions result in the disruption of the Humboldt Current, and nutrients from the ocean floor do not rise to the surface, and the fish starve, which phenomenon is known as El Niño. Also called *Peru Current.*

Humboldt Peak. A mountain, 4,289.5 m (14,064 ft) high, in the Sangre de Cristo Mountains of south-central Colorado.

Humboldt River. A river rising in the mountains of northeast Nevada and meandering about 467 km (290 mi) generally west and southwest to the **Humboldt Sink,** a lake in western Nevada. The river was an important route for early settlers.

hum·mock (hŭm′ək). **1.** A low mound or ridge of earth; a knoll. **2.** also **ham·mock** (hăm′ək). A tract of forested land that rises above an adja-

cent marsh in the southern United States. **3.** A ridge or hill of ice in an ice field. —**hum′-mock·y** adj.

Hum·phreys Peak (hŭm′frēz′, hŭmp′-). A mountain, 3,853.1 m (12,633 ft) high, in the San Francisco Peaks of north-central Arizona. It is the highest point in the state.

Hun (hŭn). A member of a nomadic people of north-central Asia known for their invasions of China (third century B.C.) and Europe (fourth and fifth centuries A.D.). Famed for their fierceness and horsemanship, the Huns reached the height of their European conquests under Attila (406?–453). —**Hun′nish** adj.

Hu·nan (hōō′nän′). A province of southeast-central China. Under Chinese rule since the third century B.C., the province is noted for its timber and mineral resources. Changsha is the capital. ⊛ Pop. 56,220,000.

hun·dred (hŭn′drĭd). abbr. **h., H.** An administrative division of some counties in England and the United States. —**hun′dred** adj.

Hun·gar·i·an (hŭng-gâr′ē-ən). abbr. **Hung. 1.** Of or relating to Hungary or its people, language, or culture. **2.** A native or inhabitant of Hungary. **3.** The Finno-Ugric language of the Magyars that is the official language of Hungary. In this sense, also called *Magyar.*

Hun·ga·ry (hŭng′gə-rē). abbr. **Hung.** A country of central Europe. Conquered by Magyars in the late ninth century, the area was converted to Christianity by Saint Stephen, who was the first king (997?–1038) of Hungary. It passed to the Ottoman Turks after 1526 and later fell under Hapsburg control, subsequently becoming part of the dual monarchy of Austria-Hungary from 1867 until 1918, when it achieved independence again. A Communist regime was established in 1949, and with the aid of the Soviet Union an anti-Communist uprising was suppressed in 1956. Economic reforms aimed at decentralizing the economy were introduced in 1968, as were political reforms in the 1980's, culminating in the adoption (1989) of a new constitution and the end (1991) of Soviet military occupation. Buda-

pest is the capital and the largest city. ● Pop. 10,261,000.

Hung·nam (hŏong′näm′). A city of east-central North Korea on the Sea of Japan north-northeast of Seoul, South Korea. Heavily bombed in the Korean War, it is now an industrial center. ● Pop. 260,000.

Hung·shui He (hŏong′shwā′ hœ). See **Hong-shui He.**

Hunk·pa·pa (hŭngk′pä′pä). *pl.* **Hunkpapa** or **-pas.** A member of a Native American people constituting a subdivision of the Teton Sioux, formerly inhabiting an area from the western Dakotas to southeast Montana, with a present-day population along the border between North and South Dakota. The Hunkpapas figured prominently in the resistance to white encroachment on the northern Great Plains in the late 19th century.

Hun·ting·ton (hŭn′tĭng-tən). **1.** A city of northeast Indiana southwest of Fort Wayne. It is a trade and industrial center. ● Pop. 16,389. **2.** A city of western West Virginia on the Ohio River west of Charleston. Founded in 1871 as a railroad terminus, it has glass and chemical industries. ● Pop. 54,844.

Huntington Beach. A city of southern California on the Pacific Ocean southeast of Long Beach. Aerospace, metallurgical, and food-processing industries are important to its economy. ● Pop. 185,055.

Huntington Park. A city of southern California, a residential and industrial suburb of Los Angeles. ● Pop. 56,065.

Huntington Station. A community of southeast New York on the northern shore of western Long Island. It is chiefly residential with varied light industries. ● Pop. 28,247.

Hunts·ville (hŭnts′vĭl′). **1.** A city of northern Alabama east-northeast of Decatur. Settled in 1805, it is a major center for space research. ● Pop. 163,319. **2.** A city of east-central Texas north of Houston. The general and politician Sam Houston's gravesite and restored home are here. ● Pop. 27,925.

Hu·on Gulf (hyōō′ən, -ŏn). An inlet of the Solomon Sea on the eastern coast of New Guinea.

Hu·pei or **Hu·peh** (hōō′pā′, hü′-). See **Hubei.**

Hu·ron (hyōōr′ən, -ŏn′). **1.** *pl.* **Huron** or **-rons.** A member of a Native American confederacy formerly inhabiting southeast Ontario around Lake Simcoe, with small present-day populations in Quebec and northeast Oklahoma, where they are known as Wyandot. The Huron traded extensively throughout eastern Canada until the confederacy was destroyed by war with the Iroquois in the mid-17th century. **2.** The Iroquoian language of the Huron.

Huron, Lake. The second largest of the Great Lakes, between southeast Ontario, Canada, and eastern Michigan. Part of the Great Lakes–St. Lawrence Seaway system, it is navigable for oceangoing vessels, although winter ice in the shallower sections impedes free passage. The French explorer Samuel de Champlain first sighted the lake in 1615.

Hurst (hûrst). A city of northeast Texas, an industrial and residential suburb of Fort Worth. ● Pop. 33,574.

Hürth (hürt). A city of west-central Germany south-southeast of Cologne. It is an industrial center in a coal-mining area. ● Pop. 50,437.

Hutch·in·son (hŭch′ĭn-sən). A city of south-central Kansas on the Arkansas River northwest of Wichita. It is a commercial and industrial center in an agricultural and oil-producing area. ● Pop. 39,308.

Huy·ton-with-Ro·by (hīt′n-wĭth-rō′bē, -wĭth-). An urban district of northwest England, a residential suburb of Liverpool. ● Pop. 174,100.

Hwang Ho (hwäng′ hō′). See **Huang He.**

Hwei (hwā). Variant of **Hui.**

Hy·an·nis (hī-ăn′ĭs). A town of southeast Massachusetts on Nantucket Sound in south-central Cape Cod. It is a popular summer resort. The summer White House was located nearby while John F. Kennedy was President (1961–1963). ● Pop. 14,120.

Hyde Park[1] (hīd). A large public park in west-central London, England. A royal deer park under King Henry VIII, it was opened to the public in 1635 and is famous for its soapbox orators.

Hyde Park[2] (hīd). A village of southeast New York on the eastern bank of the Hudson River north of Poughkeepsie. It is the birth and burial place of President Franklin D. Roosevelt (1882–1945). ● Pop. 2,550.

Hy·der·a·bad (hī′dər-ə-băd′, -bäd′, hī′drə-). **1.** A city of south-central India east-southeast of Bombay. Center of a former Mogul kingdom and Indian state, the city was founded in 1589 and is today a commercial center and transportation hub. ● Pop. 2,964,638. **2.** A city of southern Pakistan on the Indus River northeast of Karachi. Founded in 1768, it was occupied by the British in 1839. The city is noted for its handicrafts. ● Pop. 751,529.

hy·drog·ra·phy (hī-drŏg′rə-fē). **1.** The scientific description and analysis of the physical conditions, boundaries, flow, and related characteristics of the earth's surface waters. **2.** The mapping of bodies of water. —**hy·drog′ra·pher** *n.* —**hy′dro·graph′ic** (hī′drə-grăf′ĭk) *adj.* —**hy′dro·graph′i·cal·ly** *adv.*

hy·dro·sphere (hī′drə-sfîr′). **1.** The waters of the earth's surface as distinguished from those of the lithosphere and the atmosphere. **2.**

The water vapor in the earth's atmosphere. —**hy·dro·spher·ic** (-sfîr′ĭk, -sfēr′-) *adj.*

Hy·ères (ē-âr′, yâr). A city of southeast France on the Mediterranean Sea east of Toulon. A medieval port, Hyères is now a resort. The small **Hyères Islands** lie just off the coast. ⊛ Pop. 32,191.

hy·e·tal (hī′ĭ-tl). Of or relating to rain or rainy regions.

Hy·met·tus (hī-mĕt′əs). A mountain ridge, rising to about 1,028 m (3,370 ft), in east-central Greece near Athens. Marble has been quarried here since antiquity. Hymettus is also famous for its honey.

hyp·sog·ra·phy (hĭp-sŏg′rə-fē). **1. a.** The scientific study of the earth's topologic configuration above sea level, especially the measurement and mapping of land elevations. **b.** A representation or description of the earth's topologic features above sea level, as on a map. **2.** Hypsometry. —**hyp·so·graph·ic** (hĭp′sə-grăf′ĭk), **hyp·so·graph·i·cal** *adj.*

hyp·som·e·try (hĭp-sŏm′ĭ-trē). The measurement of elevation relative to sea level. —**hyp·-so·met·ric** (hĭp′sə-mĕt′rĭk), **hyp·so·met·ri·cal** *adj.* —**hyp·so·met′ri·cal·ly** *adv.* —**hyp·som′-e·trist** *n.*

I

Ia·și (yäsh, yä′shē). A city of northeast Romania north-northeast of Bucharest. It was the capital of the country until 1861 and temporarily during World War I. ⊛ Pop. 337,643.

I·ba·dan (ē-bäd′n, ē-bä′dän). The second largest city of Nigeria, in the southwest part north-northwest of Lagos. Founded in the 1830's as a military camp, it developed into a powerful Yoruba city-state and is now a major commercial and industrial center. ⊛ Pop. 1,009,400.

I·ba·gué (ē-bä-gĕ′). A city of west-central Colombia west of Bogotá. It grew rapidly in the 1890's as the result of a coffee boom. ⊛ Pop. 280,638.

I·ba·ra·ki (ē′bä-rä′kē, ē-bä′rä-kē). A city of southern Honshu, Japan, a residential suburb of Osaka. ⊛ Pop. 255,500.

I·be·ri·a (ī-bîr′ē-ə). **1.** An ancient country of Transcaucasia roughly equivalent to the eastern part of present-day Georgia. Iberia was allied to Rome, then ruled by a Persian dynasty, and became a Byzantine province in the sixth century A.D. **2.** See **Iberian Peninsula**.

I·be·ri·an (ī-bîr′ē-ən). **1.** Of or relating to ancient Iberia in Transcaucasia or its peoples, languages, or cultures. **2. a.** Of or relating to the Iberian Peninsula or its modern peoples, languages, or cultures. **b.** Of or relating to the ancient peoples that inhabited the Iberian Peninsula or their languages or cultures. **3.** A native or inhabitant of ancient Iberia in Transcaucasia. **4. a.** A native or inhabitant of the Iberian Peninsula. **b.** A member of one of the ancient peoples that inhabited the Iberian Peninsula. **5.** Any of the languages of these peoples.

Iberian Peninsula also **I·be·ri·a** (ī-bîr′ē-ə). A peninsula of southwest Europe occupied by Spain and Portugal. It is separated from the rest of Europe by the Pyrenees and from Africa by the Strait of Gibraltar.

I·bib·i·o (ĭ-bĭb′ē-ō). **1.** *pl.* **Ibibio** or **-os.** A member of a people of southeast Nigeria, noted for their woodcarving. **2.** The South Central Niger-Congo language of the Ibibio, closely related to Efik.

I·bi·za also **I·vi·za** (ē-bē′sə, ē-vē′thä). A Spanish island of the Balearic Islands in the western Mediterranean Sea southwest of Majorca. The island attracts tourists and artists and has Roman, Phoenician, and Carthaginian ruins.

I·bo (ē′bō) also **Ig·bo** (ĭg′bō). **1.** *pl.* **Ibo** or **I·bos** also **Igbo** or **Ig·bos.** A member of a people inhabiting southeast Nigeria. **2.** The South Central Niger-Congo language of the Ibo.

I·ca (ē′kə, ē′kä). A city of southwest Peru south-southeast of Lima. Settled by the Spanish in 1563, it is now a commercial center. The surrounding area was inhabited by Inca peoples in pre-Columbian times. ⊛ Pop. 153,700.

I·car·i·a (ĭ-kâr′ē-ə, ī-kâr′-). See **Ikaria**.

ice age (īs). **1.** A cold period marked by episodes of extensive glaciation alternating with episodes of relative warmth. **2. Ice Age.** The most recent glacial period, which occurred during the Pleistocene epoch, between 11,000 and 2 million years ago.

ice barrier. *Geology.* A section of the Antarctic ice shelf that extends beyond the coastline, resting partly on the ocean floor.

ice·berg (īs′bûrg′). A massive floating body of ice broken away from a glacier. Only about 10 percent of its mass is above the surface of the water.

ice·blink (īs′blĭngk′). A coastal ice cliff.

ice·cap or **ice cap** (īs′kăp′). An extensive dome-shaped or platelike perennial cover of ice and snow that spreads out from a center and covers a large area, especially of land.

ice·fall (īs′fôl′). The part of a glacier resembling a frozen waterfall that flows down a steep slope.

ice field. A large, level expanse of floating ice

that is more than eight kilometers (five miles) in its greatest dimension.

ice foot. A belt or ledge of ice that forms along the shoreline in Arctic regions.

Ice·land (īs′lənd). *abbr.* **Ice., Icel.** An island country in the North Atlantic near the Arctic Circle. Norse settlers arrived c. 850–875, and Christianity was introduced c. 1000. Iceland became a feudal state and passed to Norway in 1262 and, with Norway, to Denmark in 1380. During the 19th century a revival of national culture and the birth of a strong independence movement led to the adoption (1874) of a constitution and limited home rule. In 1918 Iceland became a sovereign state still nominally under the Danish king, which lasted until the Icelanders voted for full independence in 1944. The 1970's were marked by conflicts with the British over the extent of Iceland's territorial waters and fishing rights. In 1980 Vigdís Finnbogadóttir became the first democratically elected woman head of state. Reykjavík is the capital and the largest city. ☉ Pop. 266,000. — **Ice′land·er** *n.*

Ice·land·ic (īs-lăn′dĭk). *abbr.* **Ice., Icel. 1.** Of or relating to Iceland or its people, language, or culture. **2.** The North Germanic language of Iceland.

I·ce·ni (ī-sē′nī′). An ancient Celtic tribe of eastern Britain who under Queen Boudicca fought unsuccessfully against the Romans about A.D. 60. — **I·ce′nic** (-nĭk) *adj.*

ice pack. A floating mass of compacted ice fragments.

ice·scape (īs′skāp′). A wide view or vista of a region of ice and snow.

I·chi·ha·ra (ē-chē′hä-rä′). A city of east-central Honshu, Japan, on Tokyo Bay opposite Tokyo. It is an industrial center. ☉ Pop. 270,332.

I·chi·ka·wa (ē-chē′kä-wä′). A city of east-central Honshu, Japan, an industrial suburb of Tokyo. ☉ Pop. 447,165.

I·chi·no·mi·ya (ē′chē-nō′mē-ä′, -yä′). A city of central Honshu, Japan, a textile-manufacturing suburb of Nagoya. ☉ Pop. 266,648.

I·da (ī′də), **Mount.** A peak, 2,457.7 m (8,058 ft) high, of central Crete. It is the highest elevation on the island and in ancient times was closely associated with the worship of the god Zeus.

I·da·ho (ī′də-hō′). *abbr.* **ID, Id.** A state of the northwest United States. It was admitted as the 43rd state in 1890. First explored by the Lewis and Clark expedition in 1805, the region was held jointly by Great Britain and the United States from 1818 to 1846. Idaho became a separate territory in 1863. Boise is the capital and the largest city. ☉ Pop. 1,011,986. — **I′da·ho′an** *adj. & n.*

Idaho Falls. A city of southeast Idaho northnortheast of Pocatello. The site was originally a miner's fording point over the Snake River. ☉ Pop. 43,929.

Ie·per (yā′pər) also **Y·pres** (ē′prə). A city of western Belgium near the French border south of Ostend. A famous cloth-weaving center in medieval times, it was the site of three major World War I battles (1914, 1915, and 1917). ☉ Pop. 21,200.

I·fe (ē′fā). A city of southwest Nigeria east of Ibadan. Center of a powerful Yoruba kingdom until the late 17th century, it is an agricultural market with varied industries. ☉ Pop. 209,100.

If·ni (ēf′nē). A former Spanish possession on the Atlantic coast of southwest Morocco. It was ceded to Spain in 1860, but overseas control was nominal until 1934. Ifni was returned to Morocco in 1969.

Ig·bo (ĭg′bō). Variant of **Ibo.**

I·go·rot (ĭg′ə-rŏt′, ē′gə-). **1.** *pl.* **Igorot** or **-rots.** A member of any of several peoples of the mountains of northern Luzon in the Philippines. **2.** Any of the Austronesian languages spoken by the Igorot.

I·gua·çú also **I·guas·sú** (ē′gwə-sōō′). A river, about 1,199 km (745 mi) long, of southern Brazil flowing west to the Paraná River at the Argentina-Paraguay-Brazil border. Just above the border it forms **Iguaçú Falls,** consisting of a series of cataracts averaging 61 m (200 ft) high and separated by rocky crags and islands.

Ij·mui·den (ī-mī′dən). A city of west-central Netherlands on the North Sea at the entrance to the North Sea Canal west of Amsterdam. It is a seaport and fishing center. ☉ Pop. 58,287.

Ijs·sel or **IJs·sel** (ī′səl). A river, about 113 km (70 mi) long, of eastern Netherlands flowing from the Lower Rhine River northward to the Ijsselmeer.

Ijs·sel·meer or **IJs·sel·meer** (ī′səl-mâr′, -mār′). A shallow, dike-enclosed lake of northwest Netherlands. It was formed from the Zuider Zee by the construction of two dams (completed in 1932). Much fertile farmland has been reclaimed from the lake since that time.

I·ka·ri·a (ē'kä-rē'ä) also **I·car·i·a** (ĭ-kâr'ē-ə, ī-kâr'-). An island of southeast Greece in the Aegean Sea west of Samos. According to Greek legend, Icarus plummeted into the sea near the island after he flew too close to the sun, which melted his wax wings.

Île-de-France (ēl'də-fräɴs'). A historical region and former province of north-central France in the Paris basin. The name came into use in the 14th century, but the region was known much earlier. In 987 with the choice of Hugh Capet, Count of Paris, as the French king, the Île-de-France became the nucleus of the crown lands.

I·le·sha (ĭ-lĕsh'ə). A city of southwest Nigeria east-northeast of Ibadan. Formerly a caravan trade center, it is now an agricultural market. ● Pop. 266,700.

I·li (ē'lē'). A river, about 1,287 km (800 mi) in total length, of northwest China and southeast Kazakstan flowing west and northwest into Lake Balkhash.

Il·i·am·na Lake (ĭl'ē-ăm'nə). A lake of southwest Alaska at the base of the Alaska Peninsula. Noted for sport fishing, it is the largest lake in the state. Nearby is **Iliamna Peak,** a volcano rising to 3,054.9 m (10,016 ft).

Il·i·on (ĭl'ē-ən, -ŏn'). See **Troy** (sense 1).

Il·i·um (ĭl'ē-əm). See **Troy** (sense 1).

Il·lam·pu (ē-yäm'poo). A peak, 6,366.3 m (20,873 ft) high, in the Andes of western Bolivia northwest of La Paz.

Il·li·ma·ni (ē'yē-mä'nē). A mountain, 6,461.1 m (21,184 ft) high, in the Andes of western Bolivia east of La Paz. It was first scaled in 1898.

Il·li·nois¹ (ĭl'ə-noi', -noiz'). **1.** *pl.* **Illinois.** A member of a confederacy of Native American peoples formerly inhabiting southern Wisconsin, northern Illinois, and parts of eastern Iowa and Missouri, with present-day descendants mostly in Oklahoma. **2.** The Algonquian language of the Illinois.

Il·li·nois² (ĭl'ə-noi', -noiz'). *abbr.* **IL, Ill.** A state of the north-central United States. It was admitted as the 21st state in 1818. The area was explored by the French in the late 1600's, ceded by France to the British in 1763, and ceded by them to the newly formed United States in 1783. Springfield is the capital and Chicago the largest city. ● Pop. 11,466,682. —**Il'li·nois'-an** (-noi'ən, -zən) *adj. & n.*

Illinois River. A river rising in northeast Illinois and flowing about 439 km (273 mi) generally southwest to the Mississippi River in west-central Illinois.

Illinois Waterway. A system of rivers and ca-

nals of northern and western Illinois, linking Chicago and Lake Michigan with the Mississippi River. It includes the Chicago, Des Plaines, and Illinois rivers.

Il·lyr·i·a (ĭ-lîr'ē-ə) also **Il·lyr·i·cum** (-ĭ-kəm). An ancient region of the Balkan Peninsula on the Adriatic coast. Occupied in prehistoric times by an Indo-European-speaking people, the area became the Roman province of Illyricum after the final conquest of the Illyrians in 35–33 B.C. The name was revived by Napoleon I of France for the provinces of Illyria (1809–1815) and retained for the kingdom of Illyria, a division of Austria from 1816 to 1849.

Il·lyr·i·an (ĭ-lîr'ē-ən). **1.** Of or relating to ancient Illyria or its peoples, languages, or cultures. **2.** A member of one of the ancient peoples that inhabited Illyria. **3.** Any of the Indo-European languages of these peoples.

Il·lyr·i·cum (ĭ-lîr'ĭ-kəm). See **Illyria.**

I·lo·ca·no also **I·lo·ka·no** (ē'lō-kä'nō). **1.** *pl.* **Ilocano** or **-nos** also **Ilokano** or **-nos.** A member of an agricultural people of northern Luzon in the Philippines. **2.** The Austronesian language of the Ilocano. **3.** Of or relating to the Ilocano or their language or culture.

I·lo·i·lo (ē'lō-ē'lō). A city of southeast Panay, Philippines, on **Iloilo Strait,** an inlet of the Sulu Sea. Iloilo is a major port noted for its delicate, handwoven fabrics. ● Pop. 302,200.

I·lo·ka·no (ē'lō-kä'nō). Variant of **Ilocano.**

I·lo·rin (ē'lə-rēn', ĭ-lôr'ən). A city of southwest Nigeria north-northeast of Lagos. Capital of a Yoruba kingdom c. 1800–1825, it is now an industrial center and agricultural market. ● Pop. 355,400.

Im·per·a·triz (ĭm-pĕr'ä-trĭs). A city of northeast Brazil on the Tocantins River southeast of Belém. It is a shipping center. ● Pop. 276,440.

Im·pe·ri·al Beach (ĭm-pîr'ē-əl). A city of southern California on the Pacific Ocean at the Mexican border. It is a residential and resort community. ● Pop. 26,512.

Imperial Valley. A fertile, irrigated region of southeast California and northeast Baja California, Mexico. Mostly below sea level, it includes the Salton Sea.

I·na·ri (ĭn'ə-rē, ē'när'ē), **Lake.** A lake of northern Finland with an outlet to the Arctic Ocean. The island-studded lake is a tourist attraction.

In·ca (ĭng'kə). *pl.* **Inca** or **-cas. 1. a.** A member of the group of Quechuan peoples of highland Peru who established an empire from northern Ecuador to central Chile before the Spanish conquest (1533). **b.** A ruler or high-ranking member of the Inca empire. **2.** A member of any of the peoples ruled by the Incas.

In·ca·ic (ĭn-kā′ĭk). Incan.

In·can (ĭng′kən). **1.** Of or relating to the Incas, their civilization, or their language. **2.** An Inca. **3.** Quechua.

inch (ĭnch). *Scots.* A small island.

In·chon (ĭn′chŏn′). A city of northwest South Korea on an inlet of the Yellow Sea southwest of Seoul. It was opened to foreign trade in 1883. ⊛ Pop. 2,116,794.

In·de·pend·ence (ĭn′dĭ-pĕn′dəns). A city of western Missouri, a suburb of Kansas City. A starting point for the Santa Fe and Oregon trails during the 19th century, it was the home of President Harry S. Truman (1884–1972). His gravesite and presidential library are here. ⊛ Pop. 112,301.

In·di·a (ĭn′dē-ə). **1.** A peninsula and subcontinent of southern Asia south of the Himalaya Mountains, occupied by India, Nepal, Bhutan, Sikkim, Pakistan, and Bangladesh. It was the site of one of the oldest civilizations in the world, centered in the Indus River valley in present-day Pakistan from about 2500 to 1500 B.C. **2.** A country of southern Asia occupying most of the Indian subcontinent. Aryans from the northwest invaded c. 1500 B.C., pushing Dravidian and other peoples to the south and developing Hinduism, the socioreligious system that is the basis for India's culture. Later Buddhism spread widely after it was adopted as the state religion by the emperor Asoka, who unified most of India in the 3rd century B.C. Indian culture experienced a golden age in the 4th and 5th centuries A.D. before being invaded c. 1000 by Muslims and later by the Mongol conqueror Baber, who established the Mogul empire (1526–1857). India was visited (1497–1498) by the Portuguese explorer Vasco da Gama, opening India to European trade. The British expanded their colonial interests in the 18th century and finally assumed authority over India in 1857, with Queen Victoria taking the title of empress in 1876.

In the 20th century increasing unrest under the leadership of Mohandas Gandhi led to the division (1947) of British India into the separate Hindu and Muslim countries of India and Pakistan. Since independence conflict between Hindus and Muslims, rival claims to the princely state of Jammu and Kashmir, and the civil war in Pakistan have led to hostilities (1947–1948, 1965, 1971) between the two countries. New Delhi is the capital and Calcutta the largest city. ⊛ Pop. 918,570,000.

In·di·an (ĭn′dē-ən). *abbr.* **Ind. 1.** Of or relating to India or the East Indies or to their peoples, languages, or cultures. **2.** Of or relating to any of the Native American peoples. **3.** A native or inhabitant of India or of the East Indies. **4.** See **Native American. 5.** Any of the languages of the Native Americans.

In·di·an·a (ĭn′dē-ăn′ə). **1.** *abbr.* **IN, Ind.** A state of the north-central United States. It was admitted as the 19th state in 1816. The area was controlled by France until 1763 and then by Great Britain until 1783. The Indiana Territory was formed in 1800. Indianapolis is the capital and the largest city. ⊛ Pop. 5,564,228. **2.** A borough of west-central Pennsylvania eastnortheast of Pittsburgh. It is an industrial center. ⊛ Pop. 15,174. — **In′di·an′an, In′di·an′- i·an** *adj. & n.*

In·di·an·ap·o·lis (ĭn′dē-ə-năp′ə-lĭs). The capital and largest city of Indiana, in the central part of the state. It was settled in 1820 as the site of a new state capital, which was moved here in 1825. ⊛ Pop. 741,952.

Indian Ocean. A body of water extending from southern Asia to Antarctica and from eastern Africa to southeast Australia.

Indian River. A lagoon extending about 265 km (165 mi) along the coast of east-central Florida.

Indian Territory. A region and former territory of the south-central United States, mainly in present-day Oklahoma. It was set aside by the government as a homeland for forcibly displaced Native Americans in 1834. The western section was opened to general settlement in 1889 and became part of the Oklahoma Territory in 1890. The two territories were merged in 1907 to form the state of Oklahoma.

In·dic (ĭn′dĭk). **1.** Of or relating to India or its peoples or cultures. **2.** Of, relating to, or constituting the Indo-European languages of the Indian subcontinent and Sri Lanka. **3.** A branch of the Indo-European language family that comprises the languages of the Indian subcontinent and Sri Lanka. Also called *Sanskritic.*

In·dies (ĭn′dēz). *abbr.* **Ind. 1.** See **East Indies. 2.** See **West Indies.**

In·di·gir·ka (ĭn′dĭ-gîr′kə). A river, about 1,789

km (1,112 mi) long, of northeast Russia flowing northward to the East Siberian Sea.

In·di·o (ĭn'dē-ō'). A city of southeast California east of Santa Ana. It is a resort and processing center in a farming region. ● Pop. 36,793.

In·do-Ar·y·an (ĭn'dō-âr'ē-ən, -är'-). **1.** Of, relating to, or being any of the peoples of the Indian subcontinent who speak an Indo-European language. **2.** Indo-Iranian. **3.** A member of any of the Indo-Aryan peoples. **4.** The Indo-Iranian languages.

In·do·chi·na (ĭn'dō-chī'nə). **1.** A peninsula of southeast Asia comprising Vietnam, Laos, Cambodia, Thailand, Myanmar (Burma), and the mainland territory of Malaysia. The area was influenced in early times by India (particularly the Hindu culture) and China. **2.** The former French colonial empire in southeast Asia, including much of the eastern part of the Indochinese peninsula. French influence extended from roughly 1862 to 1954, when the French were defeated by Vietnamese nationalist forces at Dien Bien Phu. — **In'do·chi'nese'** (-nēz', -nēs') *adj. & n.*

In·do-Eu·ro·pe·an (ĭn'dō-yŏor'ə-pē'ən). **1. a.** A family of languages consisting of most of the languages of Europe as well as those of Iran, the Indian subcontinent, and other parts of western Asia. **b.** Proto-Indo-European. Also called *Indo-Germanic.* **2.** A member of any of the peoples speaking an Indo-European language. — **In'do-Eu'ro·pe'an** *adj.*

In·do-Ger·man·ic (ĭn'dō-jər-măn'ĭk). See **Indo-European** (sense 1). — **In'do-Ger·man'-ic** *adj.*

In·do-Hit·tite (ĭn'dō-hĭt'īt'). **1.** A language family that includes Indo-European and Anatolian. **2.** The hypothetical parent language of Indo-European and Anatolian.

In·do-I·ra·ni·an (ĭn'dō-ĭ-rā'nē-ən). **1.** A subfamily of the Indo-European language family that comprises the Indic and Iranian branches. **2.** A member of any of the peoples speaking an Indo-Iranian language. Also called *Aryan.* — **In'do-I·ra'ni·an** *adj.*

In·do·ne·sia (ĭn'də-nē'zhə, -shə, -dō-). Formerly the **Neth·er·lands East Indies** (nĕth'ər-ləndz) or **Dutch East Indies** (dŭch). A country of southeast Asia in the Malay Archipelago comprising Sumatra, Java, Celebes, the Moluccas, parts of Borneo, New Guinea, and Timor, and many smaller islands. The islands were first inhabited by Austronesian-speaking peoples from the Asian mainland. By the 7th and 8th centuries, Hindu and Buddhist kingdoms closely allied to India had developed on Java and Sumatra. Arab traders arrived in the 14th century and introduced Islam, which became the dominant religion by the end of the 16th century. The Portu-

guese were the first Europeans to establish (1511) trading posts, but the territory came to be dominated by the Dutch East Indies Company from 1602 to 1798, when authority was turned over to the government of the Netherlands, and it became known as the Netherlands, or Dutch, East Indies. The Indonesian independence movement began in the early 20th century, and after the Japanese occupation of the islands during World War II, the nationalist leader Sukarno declared (1945) Indonesia's independence, which was finally achieved in 1949. After an attempted Communist coup, General Suharto led an anti-Communist military takeover of the government and replaced Sukarno as president in 1967. President Suharto was reelected to a sixth consecutive term in 1993. Jakarta, on Java, is the capital and the largest city. ● Pop. 192,217,000.

In·do·ne·sian (ĭn'də-nē'zhən, -shən). *abbr.* **Indon. 1.** A native or inhabitant of Indonesia. **2.** A native or inhabitant of the Malay Archipelago. **3.** A subfamily of Austronesian that includes Malay, Tagalog, and the languages of Indonesia. **4.** A dialect of Malay that is the official language of Indonesia. In this sense, also called *Bahasa Indonesia.* **5.** Of or relating to Indonesia, the Indonesians, or their languages or cultures.

In·dore (ĭn-dôr', -dōr'). A city of west-central India north-northeast of Bombay. Founded in 1715, it is a commercial and industrial center. ● Pop. 1,091,674.

In·dus (ĭn'dəs). A river of south-central Asia rising in southwest Xizang (Tibet) and flowing about 3,057 km (1,900 mi) northwest through northern India and southwest through Pakistan to the Arabian Sea. Its valley was the site of an advanced civilization lasting c. 2500 to 1500 B.C.

In·gle·wood (ĭng'gəl-wŏod'). A city of southern California, a residential and industrial suburb of Los Angeles. Population 109,602.

In·gol·stadt (ĭng'gəl-shtät', -gôl-). A city of southeast Germany on the Danube River north of Munich. Chartered c. 1250, it is a commercial and industrial center. ● Pop. 109,666.

In·gush (ĭn-gŏosh'). **1.** *pl.* **Ingush** or **-gush·es.** A member of a Muslim people of Ingushetia. **2.** The Caucasian language of the Ingushes.

In·gu·she·ti·a (ĭn'gŏo-shē'tē-ə, ĭng'-). An autonomous republic of southwest Russia in the northern Caucasus west of Chechnya. Conquered by Russia in the 19th century, it became the Ingush Autonomous Region (1924) and later formed a part of the Chechen-Ingush Autonomous Soviet Socialist Republic (1936). In the early 1990's a strong nationalist movement developed in Chechnya, which declared its independence from the Soviet Union in November of 1991. Opting to remain an autonomous republic within the Russian Soviet Federated Socialist Republic, Ingushetia approved separation from Chechnya in a referendum (November 30–December 1, 1991) and became an autonomous republic within the Russian Federation the following year.

Ink·ster (ĭngk′stər). A city of southeast Michigan, a residential suburb of Detroit. ⊛ Pop. 30,772.

in·land (ĭn′lənd). **1.** Of, relating to, or located in the interior part of a country or region. **2.** *Chiefly British.* Operating or applying within the borders of a country or region; domestic. **3.** In, toward, or into the interior of a country or region. **4.** The interior of a country or region. — **in′land′er** *n.*

In·land Empire (ĭn′lənd, -lănd′). A region of the northwest United States between the Cascade Range and the Rocky Mountains, comprising eastern Washington, eastern Oregon, northern Idaho, and western Montana. Farming, lumbering, livestock raising, and mining are important to the area.

Inland Passage. See **Inside Passage.**

Inland Sea. An arm of the Pacific Ocean in southern Japan between Honshu, Shikoku, and Kyushu. Linked to the Sea of Japan by a narrow channel, the sea is famous for its scenic beauty.

in·let (ĭn′lĕt′, -lĭt). **1.** A recess, such as a bay or cove, along a coast. **2.** A stream or bay leading inland, as from the ocean; an estuary. **3.** A narrow passage of water, as between two islands or two peninsulas.

Inn (ĭn). A river of eastern Switzerland, western Austria, and southeast Germany flowing about 515 km (320 mi) generally northeastward to the Danube River. Its lower course forms part of the German-Austrian border.

In·ner Hebrides (ĭn′ər). See **Hebrides.**

Inner Mongolia. See **Nei Monggol.**

Inns·bruck (ĭnz′brŏŏk′, ĭns′-). A city of southwest Austria west-southwest of Salzburg. Established as a fortified town c. 1180, it is an industrial, commercial, and transportation center famed as a summer and winter resort. The Winter Olympics were held here in 1964 and 1976. ⊛ Pop. 118,112.

In·nu·it (ĭn′yŏŏ-ĭt). Variant of **Inuit.**

In·side Passage (ĭn′sīd′) also **In·land Passage** (ĭn′lənd). A natural protected waterway extending about 1,529 km (950 mi) from Puget Sound to Skagway, Alaska. It threads through the Alexander Archipelago and is known for its snow-capped mountains, waterfalls, and glaciers.

in·ter·coast·al (ĭn′tər-kōs′təl). Relating to, involving, or connecting two or more coastlines.

in·ter·con·ti·nen·tal (ĭn′tər-kŏn′tə-nĕn′tl). Extending or taking place between or among continents.

in·ter·fluve (ĭn′tər-flōōv′). The region of higher land between two rivers that are in the same drainage system. — **in′ter·flu′vi·al** *adj.*

in·te·ri·or (ĭn-tîr′ē-ər). **1.** Situated away from a coast or border; inland. **2.** The inland part of a political or geographic entity. **3.** The internal affairs of a country or nation.

In·te·ri·or Salish (ĭn-tîr′ē-ər). A group of Salish-speaking Native American peoples inhabiting parts of British Columbia, northern Washington, northern Idaho, and western Montana. Also called *Flathead.*

in·ter·is·land (ĭn′tər-ī′lənd). Relating to, involving, or connecting two or more islands.

In·ter·la·ken (ĭn′tər-lä′kən, ĭn′tər-lä′-). A town of west-central Switzerland southeast of Bern. It is a popular resort in the Bernese Alps. ⊛ Pop. 4,852.

in·ter·na·tion·al (ĭn′tər-năsh′ə-nəl). *abbr.* **int., intl. 1.** Of, relating to, or involving two or more nations. **2.** Extending across or transcending national boundaries. — **in′ter·na′tion·al′i·ty** (-shə-năl′ĭ-tē) *n.* — **in′ter·na′tion·al·ly** *adv.*

In·ter·na·tion·al Date Line (ĭn′tər-năsh′ə-nəl dāt′). An imaginary line through the Pacific Ocean roughly corresponding to 180° longitude, to the east of which, by international agreement, the calendar date is one day earlier than to the west.

in·ter·re·gion·al (ĭn′tər-rē′jə-nəl). Relating to, involving, or connecting two or more regions.

in·ter·state (ĭn′tər-stāt′). Involving, existing between, or connecting two or more states.

in·ter·trop·i·cal (ĭn′tər-trŏp′ĭ-kəl). **1.** Between or within the tropics. **2.** Of or relating to the tropics.

in·ter·vale (ĭn′tər-vəl). *New England.* A tract of low-lying land, especially along a river.

In·tra·coas·tal Waterway (ĭn′trə-kōs′təl). A system of artificial and natural channels and canals along the Atlantic and Gulf coasts of the eastern and southeast United States. It includes the Atlantic Intracoastal Waterway and the Gulf Intracoastal Waterway and affords sheltered passage for commercial and pleasure craft.

in·tra·state (ĭn′trə-stāt′). Relating to or existing within the boundaries of a state.

In·u·it also **In·nu·it** (ĭn'yōō-ĭt). **1.** *pl.* **Inuit** or **-its** also **Innuit** or **-its.** A member of any of the Eskimo peoples of North America and especially of Arctic Canada and Greenland. **2.** Any or all of the Eskimo languages of the Inuit.

I·nu·vik (ĭ-nōō'vĭk). A region of northwest Northwest Territories, Canada. It is crossed by the Mackenzie River.

In·ver Grove Heights (ĭn'vər). A city of southeast Minnesota, a residential suburb of St. Paul. ◉ Pop. 22,477.

In·ver·ness (ĭn'vər-nĕs'). A burgh of northern Scotland on the Moray Firth at the terminus of the Caledonian Canal. Thought to have been a Pict stronghold, it was chartered c. 1200. ◉ Pop. 39,700.

I·o·na (ī-ō'nə). An island of western Scotland in the southern Inner Hebrides. An early center of Celtic Christianity, it is a popular tourist site.

I·o·ni·a (ī-ō'nē-ə). An ancient region of western Asia Minor along the coast of the Aegean Sea. Greek settlers established colonies here before 1000 B.C. The seaports of Ionia flourished from c. 8th century B.C. until the Turkish conquest of the 15th century A.D.

I·o·ni·an (ī-ō'nē-ən). **1.** A native or inhabitant of Ionia. **2.** One of a Hellenic people of Mycenaean origin that inhabited Attica, the Peloponnesus along the Saronic Gulf, Euboea, the Cyclades, and Ionia. — **I·o'ni·an** *adj.*

Ionian Islands. A chain of islands of western Greece in the Ionian Sea. Colonized by the ancient Greeks, the islands subsequently came under the rule of Rome, Byzantium, Venice, France, Russia, and Great Britain before being ceded to Greece in 1864.

Ionian Sea. An arm of the Mediterranean Sea between western Greece and southern Italy. It is linked with the Adriatic Sea by the Strait of Otranto.

I·on·ic (ī-ŏn'ĭk). **1.** Of or relating to Ionia or the Ionians. **2.** The ancient Greek dialect of Ionia.

I·o·wa¹ (ī'ə-wə). **1.** *pl.* **Iowa** or **-was.** A member of a Native American people formerly inhabiting parts of Iowa and southwest Minnesota, with present-day descendants in Nebraska, Kansas, and Oklahoma. **2.** The Siouan language of the Iowa. — **I'o·wa** *adj.*

I·o·wa² (ī'ə-wə). *abbr.* **IA, Ia.** A state of the north-central United States. It was admitted as the 29th state in 1846. Part of the Louisiana Purchase of 1803, Iowa was organized as a separate territory in 1838. The Mound Builders lived in the area in prehistoric times. Des Moines is the capital and the largest city. ◉ Pop. 2,787,424. — **I'o·wan** *adj. & n.*

Iowa City. A city of eastern Iowa on the Iowa River south-southeast of Cedar Rapids. It is the seat of the University of Iowa (established 1847). ◉ Pop. 59,738.

Iowa River. A river rising in northern Iowa and flowing 529 km (329 mi) southeast to the Mississippi River in the southeast part of the state.

I·poh (ē'pō). A city of western Malaysia north-northwest of Kuala Lumpur. It is a commercial center in a tin-mining area. ◉ Pop. 382,633.

Ips·wich (ĭp'swĭch'). A borough of eastern England near the North Sea northeast of London. It was a commercial and pottery-making center from the 7th to the 12th century and was later (16th century) important in the woolen trade. ◉ Pop. 114,806.

I·qa·lu·it (ĭ-kăl'ōō-ĭt). A town of eastern Northwest Territories, Canada, on Baffin Island at the head of Frobisher Bay. It has been designated the capital of Nunavut when it becomes a territory (April 1999). ◉ Pop. 3,552.

I·qui·que (ĭ-kē'kĕ). A city of northwest Chile on the Pacific Ocean south of the Peruvian border. Founded in the 16th century, it was ceded to Chile by Peru in 1883. ◉ Pop. 148,511.

I·qui·tos (ĭ-kē'tōs, ē-kē'tôs). A city of northeast Peru on the Amazon River northeast of Lima. It grew after a boom in wild rubber in the early 20th century. ◉ Pop. 293,100.

I·rá·kli·on (ĭ-rä'klē-ôn') also **Can·di·a** (kăn'dē-ə). A city of southern Greece on the northern coast of Crete. It was founded by Saracens in the ninth century and passed to the Byzantines, Venetians, and Ottoman Turks before becoming part of Greece in 1913. ◉ Pop. 102,398.

I·ran (ĭ-răn', ĭ-rän', ī-răn'). Formerly **Per·sia** (pûr'zhə, -shə). A country of southwest Asia bordering on Iraq to the west and Afghanistan and Pakistan to the east. Inhabited c. 2000 B.C. by Medes and Persians, the region came to form the core of the Persian Empire, which was founded c. 550 B.C. by Cyrus the Great. It was conquered (333–331 B.C.) by Alexander the Great but returned to Persian control under the

Sassanid dynasty (A.D. 224–651). Arab conquerors introduced Islam in the 7th century. After invasions by Turks (10th century) and Mongols (13th–14th centuries), Persia was reestablished under the Safavid dynasty (1502–1736), which made the Shiite form of Islam the state religion. Weakened by territorial losses to neighboring states, Persia came under the sway of European powers, especially Great Britain and Russia, which occupied the country until after World War I. Reza Khan established the Pahlevi dynasty in 1925, abdicating in favor of his son, Mohammed Reza Pahlevi, in 1941. Despite U.S. support, the increasingly unpopular regime was overthrown in 1979 in a revolution led by the Shiite leader Ayatollah Khomeini (1900–1989), who established an Islamic republic. A prolonged border war with Iraq (1980–1988) resulted in deaths estimated at well over a million. The name of the country was officially changed to Iran in 1935. Tehran is the capital and the largest city. ◉ Pop. 59,778,000.

I·ra·ni·an (ĭ-rā′nē-ən, ĭ-rä′-, ī-rā′-). **1.** Of or relating to Iran or its people, language, or culture. **2.** A native or inhabitant of Iran. **3.** A branch of the Indo-European language family that includes Persian, Kurdish, Pashto, and other languages of Iran, Afghanistan, and western Pakistan.

I·ra·pua·to (îr′ə-pwä′tō, ē′rä-). A city of central Mexico east of Guadalajara. It is the commercial center of a mining and agricultural area. ◉ Pop. 170,138.

I·raq (ĭ-răk′, ĭ-räk′). A country of southwest Asia sharing major borders with Syria to the northwest, Saudi Arabia to the southwest, and Iran to the east. Site of a number of ancient Mesopotamian civilizations, including Sumer, Akkad, Assyria, and Babylonia, the region fell to Cyrus the Great of Persia (6th century B.C.), Alexander the Great (4th century B.C.), Arabs (7th century), and later to the Ottoman Turks (16th century). It was established as an independent kingdom in 1921 under a British man-

date, which lasted from 1920 until 1932. Following a military coup in 1958, the monarchy was overthrown and Iraq became a republic. Under Saddam Hussein, who became president in 1979, Iraq engaged in a bloody border war with Iran (1980–1988), invaded neighboring Kuwait (1990), and fought the Persian Gulf War (1991), in which Iraqi forces were defeated by a coalition of allies under U.S. command. Baghdad is the capital and largest city. ◉ Pop. 19,925,000.

I·ra·qi (ĭ-răk′ē, ĭ-rä′kē). **1.** Of or relating to Iraq or its people, language, or culture. **2.** *pl.* **-qis.** A native or inhabitant of Iraq. **3.** The modern dialect of Arabic spoken in Iraq.

Ir·bil (îr′bĭl) also **Er·bil** (îr′bĭl, ĕr′-). A city of northern Iraq north of Baghdad. Built on the site of ancient Arbela, it is a trade center. ◉ Pop. 485,968.

Ire·land¹ (īr′lənd). An island in the northern Atlantic Ocean west of Great Britain, divided between the independent Republic of Ireland and Northern Ireland, which is a part of the United Kingdom. It was invaded by Celts c. 500 B.C. and by the Christian era was divided into five kingdoms, namely Ulster, Connacht, Leinster, Meath, and Munster. In the 5th century A.D. the people were converted to Christianity by Saint Patrick, and Irish monasteries became great centers of learning. Norse invaders established trading towns on the coast beginning in the 8th century but were defeated (1014) by forces under King Brian Boru. The Pope granted all of Ireland to England in the 12th century, but it wasn't until the 17th century that English control became well established. Ireland was joined with Great Britain by the Act of Union (1801) to form the United Kingdom of Great Britain and Ireland, but Irish resistance to British rule continued. The 19th century was also marked by the Great Potato Famine (1845–1849), in which nearly a million Irish died and many more emigrated to the United States. After the Easter Rebellion (1916) and a civil war (1919–1921) the island was split into the independent Irish Free State (now Ireland) and Northern Ireland.

Ire·land² (īr′lənd). Formerly **I·rish Free State** (ī′rĭsh) also **Eir·e** (âr′ə, ī′rə, âr′ē, ī′rē). *abbr.* **Ire.** A country occupying most of the island of Ireland. The Irish Free State was established by treaty with Great Britain as a dominion within the Commonwealth of Nations in 1922, and it officially became the sovereign state of Eire in 1937. Full independence came in 1949 when the Republic of Ireland was proclaimed, and the country withdrew from the Commonwealth. Anglo-Irish conflict flared up again in the late 1960's, however, with fighting between Protestants and Catholics in Northern Ireland aggravated by the terrorist activities of the Irish Republican Army, which is headquartered in the Republic and seeks the unification of Ireland. The country elected its first woman president in 1990. ⊛ Pop. 3,571,000.

Ireland, Northern. See **Northern Ireland.**

I·ri·an Ja·ya (ĭr′ē-än′ jä′yə, jī′ə). Formerly **Neth·er·lands New Guinea** (nĕth′ər-ləndz) or **Dutch New Guinea** (dŭch). A province of Indonesia occupying the western half of New Guinea and about 12 offshore islands. Ceded to Indonesia by the Netherlands in 1963, it was renamed Irian Jaya in 1973.

I·rish (ī′rĭsh). *abbr.* **Ir.** **1.** Of or relating to Ireland or its people, language, or culture. **2.** The people of Ireland. **3. a.** See **Irish Gaelic. b.** See **Irish English.**

Irish English. English as spoken by the Irish. Also called *Anglo-Irish, Hiberno-English, Irish.*

Irish Free State. See **Ireland².**

Irish Gaelic. The Goidelic language of Ireland. Also called *Erse, Irish.*

I·rish·man (ī′rĭsh-mən). A man of Irish birth or ancestry.

I·rish·ry (ī′rĭsh-rē). The Irish people, especially those of Celtic descent.

Irish Sea. An arm of the northern Atlantic Ocean between Ireland and Great Britain.

I·rish·wom·an (ī′rĭsh-woom′ən). A woman of Irish birth or ancestry.

Ir·kutsk (ĭr-kōōtsk′). A city of south-central Russia near the southern end of Lake Baikal. It is an industrial center and a major stop on the Trans-Siberian Railroad (completed 1905), which links European Russia with the Pacific Ocean. ⊛ Pop. 629,747.

I·ron Age (ī′ərn). The period in human cultural development succeeding the Bronze Age, characterized by the introduction of iron metallurgy and in Europe beginning around the eighth century B.C.

I·ron·de·quoit (ĭ-rŏn′dĭ-kwoit′, -kwŏt′). A town of western New York west of Rochester. It was settled in 1791. ⊛ Pop. 52,322.

Iron Gate. A narrow gorge of the Danube River on the border of Yugoslavia and Romania. Created by a gap between the Carpathian and Balkan mountains, the gorge is bypassed by a ship canal (opened in 1896) to allow navigation by large river craft.

Ir·o·quoi·an (ĭr′ə-kwoi′ən). **1.** A family of North American Indian languages of the eastern part of Canada and the United States that includes Cayuga, Mohawk, Oneida, Onondaga, Seneca, Tuscarora, Cherokee, Erie, Huron, and Wyandot. **2.** A member of an Iroquoian-speaking people. **3.** Of or constituting the Iroquoian language family.

Ir·o·quois (ĭr′ə-kwoi′). **1.** *pl.* **Iroquois.** A member of a Native American confederacy inhabiting New York State and originally composed of the Mohawk, Oneida, Onondaga, Cayuga, and Seneca peoples, known as the Five Nations. After 1722 the confederacy was joined by the Tuscaroras to form the Six Nations. Also called *Iroquois League.* **2.** Any or all of the languages of the Iroquois. — **Ir′o·quois′** *adj.*

Ir·ra·wad·dy (ĭr′ə-wŏd′ē, -wô′dē). A river of Myanmar (Burma) flowing about 1,609 km (1,000 mi) southward to the Bay of Bengal and the Andaman Sea. It is the chief river of the country.

Ir·tysh or **Ir·tish** (ĭr-tĭsh′). A river of northwest China, eastern Kazakstan, and central Russia flowing about 4,264 km (2,650 mi) generally northwest to the Ob River. It is navigable for much of its course.

I·rún (ē-rōōn′). A city of northern Spain near the Bay of Biscay and the French border. It is a commercial and industrial center. ⊛ Pop. 54,877.

Ir·vine. **1.** (ûr′vĭn). A burgh of southwest Scotland on the estuary of the **Irvine River** southwest of Glasgow. It is an industrial center. ⊛ Pop. 54,600. **2.** (ûr′vīn′). A city of southern California southeast of Santa Ana. A branch of the University of California (opened 1965) is here. ⊛ Pop. 110,330.

Ir·ving (ûr′vĭng). A town of northeast Texas, an industrial suburb of Dallas. ⊛ Pop. 155,037.

Ir·ving·ton (ûr′vĭng-tən). A town of northeast New Jersey, a residential and industrial suburb of Newark. It was settled in 1692 as Camptown and renamed in 1852 in honor of the writer Washington Irving (1783–1859). ⊛ Pop. 59,774.

Is·a·bel·a Island (ĭz′ə-bĕl′ə). The largest of the Galápagos Islands of Ecuador, in the Pacific Ocean on the equator.

i·sal·lo·bar (ī-săl′ə-bär′). A line on a weather map connecting places having equal changes in atmospheric pressure within a given period of time.

Is·chi·a (ĭs′kē-ə, ē′skyä). An island of southern Italy in the Tyrrhenian Sea at the entrance to the Bay of Naples. Known as "the Emerald Isle," it is a tourist center and health resort noted for its warm mineral springs.

I·se Bay (ē′sä, ē′sĕ′). An arm of the Pacific Ocean on the south-central coast of Honshu, Japan. The city of **Ise,** near the entrance to the bay, has several ancient Shinto shrines built in a distinctive archaic style of architecture. ◉ Pop. 102,980.

Ise·lin (ĭz′lĭn). A community of east-central New Jersey northwest of Perth Amboy. ◉ Pop. 16,141.

I·sère (ē-zâr′). A river, about 290 km (180 mi) long, of southeast France rising in the Graian Alps near the Italian border and flowing west and southwest to the Rhone River.

I·ser·lohn (ē′zər-lōn′, ē′zər-lōn′). A city of west-central Germany northeast of Cologne. Founded in the 13th century, it is a manufacturing center. ◉ Pop. 89,951.

Is·fa·han (ĭs′fə-hän′) or **Es·fa·han** (ĕs′-). A city of central Iran south of Tehran. An ancient town and capital of Persia from 1598 to 1722, it was long noted for its fine carpets and silver filigree. Today it has textile and steel mills. ◉ Pop. 1,220,595.

I·shi·ka·ri Bay (ĭsh′ĭ-kär′ē). An inlet of the Sea of Japan on the western coast of Hokkaido, Japan. The **Ishikari River,** about 443 km (275 mi) long, flows generally southwest from the mountainous interior of the island into the bay.

I·shim (ĭ-shĭm′). A river, about 1,818 km (1,130 mi) long, rising in the steppe region of Kazakstan and flowing generally northwest then northeast to the Irtysh River in south-central Russia.

I·sis (ī′sĭs). The upper Thames River in south-central England in the vicinity of Oxford. The name is used locally and in literature.

Is·kar (ĭs′kər). See **Iskŭr.**

Is·ken·de·run (ĭs-kĕn′də-rōōn′, -kĕn′dĕ-rōōn′). Formerly **Al·ex·an·dret·ta** (ăl′ĭg-zăn-drĕt′ə). A city of southern Turkey on an inlet of the eastern Mediterranean Sea. Founded by Alexander the Great to celebrate his victory over the Persians in 333 B.C., it is Turkey's chief port on the Mediterranean. ◉ Pop. 156,800.

Is·kŭr also **Is·kar** (ĭs′kər). A river of western Bulgaria rising in the Rhodope Mountains and flowing about 402 km (250 mi) generally north and northeast to the Danube River.

Is·lam·a·bad (ĭs-lä′mə-bäd′, ĭz-läm′ə-bäd′). The capital of Pakistan, in the northeast part of the country northeast of Rawalpindi. Construction began on the city in 1960, and it replaced Karachi as the capital in 1967. ◉ Pop. 201,000.

is·land (ī′lənd). *abbr.* **is., i., Is., I., isl.** A land mass, especially one smaller than a continent, entirely surrounded by water.

Is·la Vis·ta (ī′lə vĭs′tə). A community of southern California on the Pacific Ocean west of Santa Barbara. ◉ Pop. 20,395.

Is·lay (ī′lā, ī′lə). An island of the southern Inner Hebrides of western Scotland. Farming, fishing, and distilling are important to its economy.

isle (īl). *abbr.* **i., I.** An island, especially a small one.

Isle au Haut (ī′lə-hō′, ē′lə-). An island of south-central Maine at the entrance to Penobscot Bay.

Isle of (īl). For names of actual isles, see the specific element of the name; for example, **Wight, Isle of.**

Isle Roy·ale (roi′əl). An island of northern Michigan in Lake Superior near the coast of Ontario. French fur traders named the island in 1671. Native Americans mined the island's copper for centuries before ceding the island to the United States in 1843. It is now a tourist center.

is·let (ī′lĭt). A very small island.

Is·ma·i·li·a (ĭz′mä-ə-lē′ə, ĭs′-). A city of northeast Egypt on the Suez Canal. It was founded in 1863 by the French engineer Ferdinand de Lesseps as a base of operations during the building of the canal. ◉ Pop. 255,000.

i·so·cli·nal (ī′sə-klī′nəl) or **i·so·clin·ic** (-klĭn′-ĭk). **1.** Having the same magnetic inclination or dip. **2.** See **isoclinic line.** —**i′so·cli′nal·ly** *adv.*

isoclinic line. A line drawn on a map connecting points of equal magnetic dip. Also called *isoclinal.*

i·so·gon·ic line (ī′sə-gŏn′ĭk). A line on a map connecting points of equal magnetic declination.

i·so·gram (ī′sə-grăm′). See **isoline.**

i·so·hel (ī′sō-hĕl′). A line drawn on a map connecting points that receive equal amounts of sunlight.

i·so·hy·et (ī′sō-hī′ĭt). A line drawn on a map connecting points that receive equal amounts of rainfall.

i·so·line (ī′sə-līn′). A line on a map, chart, or graph connecting points of equal value. Also called *isogram.*

i·som·e·try (ī-sŏm′ĭ-trē). **1.** Equality of measure. **2.** Equality of elevation above sea level.

i·sos·ta·sy (ī-sŏs′tə-sē). Equilibrium in the earth's crust such that the forces tending to elevate land masses balance the forces tending to depress land masses.

i·so·therm (ī′sə-thûrm′). A line drawn on a weather map or chart linking all points of equal or constant temperature.

Is·ra·el (ĭz′rē-əl). **1.** An ancient Hebrew kingdom of Palestine founded by Saul c. 1025 B.C.

After 933 it split into the Northern Kingdom, or kingdom of Israel, and the kingdom of Judah to the south. Israel was overthrown by the Assyrians in 721. **2.** *abbr.* **Isr.** A country of southwest Asia on the eastern Mediterranean Sea. In 1947 the United Nations recommended the partition of Palestine, then under British mandate, into Jewish and Arab states. When the British withdrew from the area in 1948, Jewish leaders proclaimed the state of Israel in their portion of the divided territory. Neighboring Arab states rejected the partition and attacked, but in the ensuing war (1948–1949) Israel was able to enlarge its territory by half. Other wars broke out, notably in 1956, 1967, and 1973. In the Six-Day War of 1967 Israel expanded its territory again, occupying the Gaza Strip, the West Bank, Jerusalem's Old City, the Golan Heights, and the Sinai Peninsula. The Golan Heights and Jerusalem were later annexed, and the Sinai Peninsula was returned to Egypt in 1982, after the signing (1979) of a peace agreement between Israel and Egypt. Ongoing fighting with the Palestinian Liberation Organization resulted in an Israeli invasion of Lebanon in 1982. Israel eventually withdrew its troops from the Beirut area, but maintains a security zone in southern Lebanon. A 1993 Israeli-Palestinian accord granted limited Palestinian autonomy in the Gaza Strip, and a similar accord calling for Palestinian self-rule in the West Bank was signed in 1994. Jerusalem is

the capital and Tel Aviv–Jaffa the largest city. ● Pop. 5,383,000.

Is·rae·li (ĭz-rā′lē). *abbr.* **Isr.** **1.** Of or relating to modern-day Israel or its people. **2.** A native or inhabitant of modern-day Israel.

Is·ra·el·ite (ĭz′rē-ə-līt′). **1.** A native or inhabitant of the ancient Northern Kingdom of Israel. **2.** A descendant of the biblical patriarch Jacob; a Jew. **3.** also **Is·ra·el·it·ic** (ĭz′rē-ə-lĭt′ĭk). Of or relating to Israel, the Israelites, or their culture.

Is·sus (ĭs′əs). An ancient town of southeast Asia Minor near modern-day Iskenderun, Turkey. Alexander the Great defeated Darius III of Persia here in 333 B.C.

Is·syk-Kul (ĭs′ĭk-kōōl′, ē-sĭ′kōōl′). A lake of northeast Kyrgyzstan in the Tien Shan near the northwest Chinese border.

Is·tan·bul (ĭs′tän-bōōl′, -tän-, ĭ-stän′bōōl). Formerly **Con·stan·ti·no·ple** (kŏn′stän-tə-nō′-pəl). The largest city of Turkey, in the northwest part of the country on both sides of the Bosporus at its entrance into the Sea of Marmara. Founded c. 660 B.C. as Byzantium, it was renamed Constantinople in A.D. 330 by the Roman emperor Constantine the Great (A.D. 285?–337), who made it the capital of the Eastern Roman, or Byzantine, Empire. The city was sacked by Crusaders in 1204 and taken by the Turks in 1453. Istanbul was chosen as the official name in 1930. ● Pop. 7,615,500.

isth·mi (ĭs′mī′). A plural of **isthmus.**

isth·mi·an (ĭs′mē-ən). Of, relating to, or forming an isthmus. **2.** Of or relating to the Isthmus of Corinth, especially to the biennial Pan-Hellenic games held there in antiquity.

isth·mus (ĭs′məs). *pl.* **-mus·es** or **-mi** (-mī′). *abbr.* **isth.** A narrow strip of land connecting two larger masses of land.

Is·tri·a (ĭs′trē-ə). A peninsula of northwest Croatia projecting into the northeast Adriatic Sea. The original Istrian inhabitants were overthrown by the Romans in the second century B.C. Istria was subsequently occupied by Austria, Venice, and Italy. All but the area surrounding Trieste was awarded to Yugoslavia in 1946. —**Is′tri·an** *adj. & n.*

I·ta·bu·na (ē′tə-bōō′nə). A city of eastern Brazil south-southeast of Salvador. It is a cacao-producing center. ● Pop. 185,165.

I·ta·güí (ē′tä-gwē′). A city of northwest-central Colombia, a manufacturing suburb of Medellín. ● Pop. 139,050.

I·tal·ian (ĭ-tăl′yən). *abbr.* **It., Ital.** **1.** Of or relating to Italy or its people, language, or culture. **2. a.** A native or inhabitant of Italy. **b.** A person of Italian descent. **3.** The Romance language of the Italians, which is also an official language of Switzerland.

Italian East Africa. A former federation of

Italian-held territories in eastern Africa, including Ethiopia, Eritrea, and part of present-day Somalia. It was formed in 1936 and lasted until the British World War II invasion of 1941.

Italian Somaliland. A former Italian colony of eastern Africa comprising the eastern and southern portions of present-day Somalia. It became part of Italian East Africa in 1936 and was invaded by British troops in 1941. In 1960 Italian Somaliland was combined with British Somaliland to form Somalia.

I·tal·ic (ĭ-tăl′ĭk, ī-tăl′-). **1.** Of or relating to ancient Italy or its peoples or cultures. **2.** A branch of the Indo-European language family that includes Latin, Faliscan, Oscan, Umbrian, and other languages or dialects.

It·a·ly (ĭt′l-ē). **1.** A peninsula of southern Europe projecting into the Mediterranean Sea between the Tyrrhenian and Adriatic seas. **2.** *abbr.* **It.** A country of southern Europe comprising the peninsula of Italy, Sardinia, Sicily, and several smaller islands. It was settled by Indo-European peoples during the 2nd millenium B.C., including the Italic ancestors of the Latins. Etruscan civilization flourished from the 8th to the 5th century B.C., when it was gradually supplanted by the rise of Rome. By 270 B.C. most of the peninsula had come under Roman control, and Italy became the center of European power and culture until the decline of the western Roman Empire in the 5th century A.D. A succession of invaders including the Lombards, Franks, Germans, and Normans set up kingdoms on Italian territory during the Middle Ages. The rise of wealthy city-states such as Florence, Siena, and Padua produced the Renaissance in the 14th century, but Italy remained a battleground for conflicts among other European powers until Napleonic times. Growing nationalism in the 19th century eventually resulted in unification (1861–1870) under King Victor Emmanuel II. Italy became a fascist state under Benito Mussolini, whose regime (1922–1943) made colonial conquests in Ethiopia (1936) and Albania (1939). It joined with Germany in World War II, surrendering to the Allies in 1943. Reconstituted as a republic in 1946, it has experienced frequent turnovers of coalition governments since that time. Rome is the capital and the largest city. ⊛ Pop. 57,193,000.

I·tas·ca (ī-tăs′kə). A lake of northwest Minnesota. It was identified in 1832 as the source of the Mississippi River.

Ith·a·ca (ĭth′ə-kə). **1.** A city of southwest-central New York on Cayuga Lake south-southwest of Syracuse. It is the seat of Cornell University (chartered 1865). ⊛ Pop. 29,541. **2.** See **Itháki.**

I·thá·ki (ē-thä′kē) also **Ith·a·ca** (ĭth′ə-kə). An island of western Greece in the Ionian Islands. According to tradition, it was the home of Odysseus, the hero of Homer's *Odyssey.*

I·tsu·ku·shi·ma (ĭt′sōō-kōō′shĭ-mə). An island of southwest Japan in the Inland Sea southwest of Hiroshima. It is noted for its ancient Shinto shrine and scenic beauty.

It·u·rae·a (ĭch′ə-rē′ə). An ancient country of northeast Palestine. The area was first inhabited by Arabians and later passed to Judea and Rome. —**It′u·rae′an** *adj. & n.*

I·va·no-Fran·kovsk (ĭ-vä′nō-fräng-kôfsk′, ē-vä′nə-frŭn-). A city of southwest Ukraine southwest of Kiev. Chartered in 1662 as Stanislov, it passed to Austria in 1772 and to Poland in 1919. It was incorporated into the Ukrainian S.S.R. in 1939. ⊛ Pop. 230,400.

I·va·no·vo (ĭ-vä′nə-və). A city of western Russia northeast of Moscow. It has long been a textile-producing center. ⊛ Pop. 474,102.

I·vi·za (ē-bē′sə, ē-vē′thä). See **Ibiza.**

I·vo·ry Coast (ī′və-rē, īv′rē). Officially **Côte d'I·voire** (kōt′ dē vwär′). A country of western Africa on the Gulf of Guinea. Divided into various isolated kingdoms at the time of European

discovery in the 15th century, the region soon became an important source of ivory and slaves for European traders. Ivory Coast was created as a French colony in 1893 and became nominally part of French West Africa in 1904, though French control over the interior was not established until after World War I. In 1947 the northern part joined with other French territories to form Upper Volta, now Burkina Faso. Ivory Coast gained its independence in 1960 and was ruled as a one-party state until 1990. Yamoussoukro is the capital and Abidjan is the largest city and de facto administrative center. ⊛ Pop. 13,695,000. — **I·vo′ri·an** (ī-vôr′ē-ən, ī-vōr′-), **I·voir′i·an** (ē-vwär′ē-ən) *adj. & n.*

I·vry-sur-Seine (ē-vrē′sōōr-sän′, -sür-sĕn′). A city of north-central France, a suburb of Paris on the Seine River. ⊛ Pop. 55,699.

I·wa·ki (ĭ-wä′kē). A city of eastern Honshu, Japan, on the Pacific Ocean north-northeast of Tokyo. It is an industrial center. ⊛ Pop. 359,098.

I·wo (ē′wō). A city of southwest Nigeria east-northeast of Ibadan. It was the capital of a Yoruba kingdom from the 17th to the 19th century. ⊛ Pop. 255,100.

I·wo Ji·ma (ē′wə jē′mə, ē′wō). The largest of the Volcano Islands of Japan in the northwest Pacific Ocean east of Taiwan. The island was the scene of severe fighting during World War II.

Ix·elles (ēk-sĕl′). A city of central Belgium, an industrial suburb of Brussels. ⊛ Pop. 76,146.

I·zal·co (ĭ-zäl′kō, ē-säl′-). A volcano, about 2,388 m (7,828 ft) high, of western El Salvador. Having erupted some 50 times between 1770 and 1966, it is sometimes called "the Lighthouse of the Pacific."

I·zhevsk (ē-zhĕfsk′, ē-zhĭfsk′). Formerly **U·sti·nov** (ōō-stĭn′ôf). A city of west-central Russia northeast of Kazan. Its ironworks date to 1760. ⊛ Pop. 652,424.

Iz·mir (ĭz-mîr′). Formerly **Smyr·na** (smûr′nə). A city of western Turkey on the **Gulf of Izmir,** an inlet of the Aegean Sea. Settled during the Bronze Age, Izmir is now a major port and an industrial center. ⊛ Pop. 1,985,300.

J

Jab·al·pur (jŭb′əl-pōōr′) also **Jub·bul·pore** (-pôr′, -pōr′). A city of central India south-southeast of Delhi. It is a manufacturing center and rail junction. ⊛ Pop. 741,927.

Ja·ca·re·í (zhä′kä-rĭ-ē′). A city of southeast Brazil, a textile-manufacturing suburb of São Paulo. ⊛ Pop. 163,843.

Jack·son (jăk′sən). **1.** A city of south-central Michigan on the Grand River south of Lansing. It is an industrial and commercial center. ⊛ Pop. 37,446. **2.** The capital and largest city of Mississippi, in the west-central part of the state. Originally a small trading post, it was chosen as capital in 1821 and named in honor of President Andrew Jackson (1767–1845). ⊛ Pop. 196,637. **3.** A city of western Tennessee northeast of Memphis. Settled in 1819, it is a processing and educational center. ⊛ Pop. 48,949.

Jackson Hole. A fertile valley of northwest Wyoming in the Rocky Mountains east of the Teton Range. It was named after a fur trapper, David Jackson, who stayed in the region during the winter of 1828–1829.

Jack·son·ville (jăk′sən-vĭl′). **1.** A city of central Arkansas northeast of Little Rock. A U.S. Air Force base is nearby. ⊛ Pop. 29,101. **2.** A city of northeast Florida on the St. Johns River near the Atlantic Ocean and the Georgia border. Settled in 1816, it is a major port and manufacturing center and the largest city in Florida. ⊛ Pop. 672,971. **3.** A city of west-central Illinois west of Springfield. Laid out in 1825, it has varied industries. ⊛ Pop. 19,324. **4.** A city of eastern North Carolina near the Atlantic Ocean north-northeast of Wilmington. Camp Lejeune, a U.S. Marine Corps training base, is nearby. ⊛ Pop. 30,013.

Jacksonville Beach. A city of northeast Florida, a mainly residential suburb of Jacksonville on the Atlantic Ocean. ⊛ Pop. 17,839.

Ja·én (hä-ĕn′). A city of southern Spain northwest of Granada. It is a distribution center in a lead-mining region. Pop. 104,892.

Jaf·fa (jăf′ə, yä′fə). A former city of west-central Israel on the Mediterranean Sea. An ancient Phoenician city, it was taken by the Israelites in the 6th century A.D. and later fell to the Arabs (636), Crusaders (12th century), and Ottoman Turks (16th century). Jaffa was inhabited mainly by Arabs until the state of Israel was proclaimed in 1948. Since 1950 the city has been part of Tel Aviv–Jaffa.

Jaff·na (jäf′nə). A city of extreme northern Sri Lanka on Palk Strait. It was the center of an ancient Tamil culture until the Portuguese conquest of 1617. ⊛ Pop. 129,000.

Jai·pur (jī′pōōr′). A city of northwest India south-southwest of Delhi. The center of a former state established in the 12th century, Jaipur was founded in 1728 and is noted for its walls and fortifications and the pink color of many of its houses. ⊛ Pop. 1,458,483.

Ja·kar·ta or **Dja·kar·ta** (jə-kär′tə). Formerly **Ba·ta·vi·a** (bə-tā′vē-ə). The capital and largest city of Indonesia, on the northeast coast of Java. Founded c. 1619 by the Dutch, it became an important center of the Dutch East India Company and was renamed Jakarta after Indonesia became independent in 1949. ● Pop. 7,885,519.

Ja·la·pa (hə-lä′pə, hä-lä′pä) also **Jalapa En·rí·quez** (ĕn-rē′kĕs). A city of east-central Mexico east of Mexico City. Built on the site of a pre-Columbian city, Jalapa was captured by the Spanish conquistador Hernando Cortés in 1519. It is now an agricultural trade center and a mountain resort. ● Pop. 204,594.

Ja·mai·ca (jə-mā′kə). *abbr.* **Jam.** An island country in the Caribbean Sea south of Cuba. Originally inhabited by Arawaks, it was discovered by Columbus in 1494 and settled by the Spanish beginning in 1509. The British captured the island in 1655, and it was formally ceded to Great Britain in 1670, becoming a crown colony in 1865. A leading producer of sugar in the 18th century and of bauxite in the 20th, Jamaica gained an increasing measure of autonomy after the adoption of a new constitution in 1884, and the country became fully independent in 1962. Kingston is the capital and the largest city. ● Pop. 2,496,000. **—Ja·mai′can** *adj. & n.*

James Bay (jāmz). The southern arm of Hudson Bay, in Northwest Territories, Canada, between northeast Ontario and western Quebec. It was first sighted by the English navigator Henry Hudson in 1610 but named for the English captain Thomas James (1593?–1635?), who explored much of the bay in 1631.

James River. **1.** A river rising in central North Dakota and flowing about 1,142 km (710 mi) generally south across South Dakota to the Missouri River. **2.** A river, about 547 km (340 mi) long, rising in central Virginia and flowing eastward to Chesapeake Bay. The river is navigable to Richmond for large craft.

James·town (jāmz′toun′). **1.** The capital of St. Helena in the southern Atlantic Ocean. ● Pop. 1,516. **2.** A city of western New York on Chautauqua Lake near the Pennsylvania border. It is the trade center of a farming and grape-producing region. ● Pop. 34,681. **3.** A city of southeast-central North Dakota on the James River east of Bismarck. Settled in 1872 when

Fort Seward was established nearby, it is an agricultural market center. ● Pop. 15,571. **4.** A former village of southeast Virginia, the first permanent English settlement in America. It was founded in May 1607 and named for the reigning English monarch, James I. The "Starving Time" of 1609 to 1610 nearly wiped out the colony, and only the timely arrival of Baron De La Warr, the first governor of the Virginia colony, with supplies convinced the survivors to remain. Jamestown became the capital of Virginia after 1619 but was almost entirely destroyed during Bacon's Rebellion (1676) and further declined after the removal of the capital to Williamsburg (1698–1700).

Jam·mu (jŭm′ōō). A city of northern India near the Pakistan border south of Srinagar. Formerly the seat of a Rajput dynasty, it was later captured by the Sikhs. ● Pop. 206,135.

Jammu and Kash·mir (kăsh′mîr′, kăsh-mîr′). Popularly known as **Kashmir.** A former princely state in present-day northern India and Pakistan. Under the nominal control of the British from 1846–1947, it was partitioned between India and Pakistan after fierce fighting (1947–1948). Both India and Pakistan have continued to claim jurisdiction over the the whole territory.

Jam·na·gar (jäm-nŭg′ər). A city of western India on the Gulf of Kutch southwest of Ahmadabad. Founded in 1540, it is a port city noted for its silk, embroidery, and marble. ● Pop. 341,637.

Jam·shed·pur (jäm′shĕd-pōōr′). A city of eastern India west-northwest of Calcutta. It developed as a steel-producing center after 1911. ● Pop. 460,577.

Janes·ville (jānz′vĭl′). A city of southern Wisconsin north of Beloit. It is an industrial and commercial center. ● Pop. 52,133.

Jan May·en Island (yän mī′ən). An island of Norway in the Greenland Sea between northern Norway and Greenland. Discovered by the English navigator Henry Hudson in 1607, it was annexed by Norway in 1929.

Ja·pan (jə-păn′). A country occupying an archipelago off the eastern coast of mainland Asia. Traditionally settled c. 660 B.C., Japan's recorded history began in the 5th century A.D., by which time the foundations for a centralized state were established. In the next few centuries Japanese society was much influenced by Chinese culture, from which it borrowed and adapted its writing system. During the feudal period (12th–19th centuries) real power was held by the shoguns, local warriors whose dominance was finally ended by the restoration of the emperor Mutsuhito (Meiji) in 1868. Feudalism was abolished, and the country was opened to Western trade and industrial technology. Expansionist policies led to Japan's participation in World War II, which ended after atomic bombs were dropped on Hiroshima and Nagasaki (August 1945). During the subsequent occupation by U.S. forces, a new constitution went into effect (1947), and Japan was granted full sovereignty over the main islands in 1951 and other islands in 1968 and 1972. Today the country is highly industrialized and noted for its advanced technology. Tokyo is the capital and the largest city. ◉ Pop. 124,961,000.

Japan, Sea of. An enclosed arm of the western Pacific Ocean between Japan and the Asian mainland. It is connected with the East China Sea, the Pacific Ocean, and the Sea of Okhotsk by several straits.

Japan Current. A warm ocean current flowing northeast from the Philippine Sea past southeast Japan to the North Pacific Ocean. Also called *Kuroshio Current.*

Jap·a·nese (jăp′ə-nēz′, -nēs′). *abbr.* **J. 1.** Of or relating to Japan or its people, language, or culture. **2.** *pl.* **Japanese a.** A native or inhabitant of Japan. **b.** A person of Japanese ancestry. **3.** The language of the Japanese, written in kana, a Japanese syllabic script, mixed with Chinese characters.

Japan Trench. A depression in the floor of the North Pacific Ocean off northeast Japan. It extends from the Bonin Islands north to the Kuril Islands and reaches depths of more than 9,000 m (30,000 ft).

Ja·pu·rá (zhä′pōō-rä′). A river rising in the Andes of southwest Colombia and flowing about 2,816 km (1,750 mi) southeast across northwest Brazil to the Amazon River.

Jat (jät). A member of a peasant caste residing in the Punjab and other areas of northern India and

Pakistan, comprising Muslim, Hindu, and Sikh groups.

Ja·va (jä′və, jăv′ə). An island of Indonesia separated from Borneo by the **Java Sea,** an arm of the western Pacific Ocean. Center of an early Hindu-Javanese civilization, Java was converted to Islam before the arrival of Europeans (mainly the Dutch) in the late 16th century.

Jav·a·nese (jăv′ə-nēz′, -nēs′, jä′və-). *abbr.* **Jav. 1.** Of or relating to Java or its people, language, or culture. **2.** *pl.* **Javanese.** A native or inhabitant of Java, especially a member of the Javanese-speaking majority population. **3.** The Austronesian language of the principal ethnic group of Java.

Ja·va·rí (zhä′və-rē′). A river rising in eastern Peru and flowing about 965 km (600 mi) northeast along the Peru-Brazil border to the Amazon River.

Je·bel Mu·sa also **Ge·bel Mu·sa** (jĕb′əl mōō′-sə, -sä). A mountain, about 851 m (2,790 ft) high, of northern Morocco on the Strait of Gibraltar. With Gibraltar it forms the so-called Pillars of Hercules.

Jebel Toub·kal (tōōb-käl′). A mountain, about 4,167.8 m (13,665 ft) high, of central Morocco in the Atlas Mountains. It is the highest peak in the range.

Jef·fer·son (jĕf′ər-sən). An unincorporated community of southeastern Louisiana on the Mississippi River west of New Orleans. ◉ Pop. 14,521.

Jefferson, Mount. A peak, 3,201.6 m (10,497 ft) high, in the Cascade Range of northwest Oregon southeast of Portland.

Jefferson City. The capital of Missouri, in the central part of the state on the Missouri River. It was chosen as the capital when Missouri was admitted to the Union in 1821. ◉ Pop. 35,481.

Jefferson River. A river, about 402 km (250 mi) long, of southwest Montana. It is a headwater of the Missouri River.

Jef·fer·son·town (jĕf′ər-sən-toun′). A city of north-central Kentucky, a mainly residential suburb of Louisville. ◉ Pop. 15,795.

Jef·fer·son·ville (jĕf′ər-sən-vĭl′). A city of southern Indiana on the Ohio River opposite Louisville, Kentucky. It was founded in 1802 on the site of a frontier fort. ◉ Pop. 21,220.

Je·le·nia Gó·ra (yā-lĕn′yə gōōr′ə, yĕ-lĕ′nyä gōō′rä). A city of southwest Poland west-southwest of Poznań. Chartered in 1312, it passed to Prussia in 1741 and was assigned to Poland by the Potsdam Conference of 1945. ◉ Pop. 90,400.

Je·na (yā′nə). A city of central Germany southwest of Leipzig. The French emperor Napoleon

I decisively defeated the Prussians here on October 14, 1806. ⊛ Pop. 100,093.

Jen·i·son (jĕn′ĭ-sən). A community of west-central Michigan, a suburb of Grand Rapids. ⊛ Pop. 17,882.

Jen·nings (jĕn′ĭngz). A city of eastern Missouri, a residential suburb of St. Louis. ⊛ Pop. 15,905.

Je·qui·tin·hon·ha (zhə-kēt′n-yōn′yə, zhĭ-kwē′-tĭ-nyô′nyä). A river, about 805 km (500 mi) long, of eastern Brazil flowing northeast and east to the Atlantic Ocean.

Je·rez (hĕ-rĕs′, -rĕth′) also **Jerez de la Fron·te·ra** (də lä frŭn-tĕr′ə, *th*ĕ lä frôn-tĕ′rä). A city of southwest Spain northeast of Cádiz. Noted for its sherry and cognac, it was held by the Moors from 711 to 1264. ⊛ Pop. 183,316.

Jer·i·cho (jĕr′ĭ-kō′). An ancient city of Palestine near the northwest shore of the Dead Sea. A stronghold commanding the valley of the lower Jordan River, it was, according to the Bible, captured and destroyed by the Hebrew leader Joshua.

Jer·sey (jûr′zē). The largest of the Channel Islands in the English Channel. It was annexed by the Normans in 933, and French influence has persisted since autonomy was granted in 1204.

Jersey City. A city of northeast New Jersey on the Hudson River opposite lower Manhattan. Settled before 1650 by the Dutch, it came under English control in 1664 and is today a port of entry and a major distribution center. ⊛ Pop. 228,537.

Je·ru·sa·lem (jə-rōō′sə-ləm, -zə-). The capital of Israel, in the east-central part of the country in the West Bank. Of immense religious and historical importance, the city was occupied as far back as the fourth millennium B.C. and became the capital of King David c. 1000 B.C. Destroyed by Nebuchadnezzar II, king of Babylonia, in the sixth century B.C., it was later ruled by Greeks, Romans, Persians, Arabs, Crusaders, and Turks and by Great Britain under a League of Nations mandate. Israeli forces took control of the city in 1967. Jerusalem is considered a holy city to Jews, Muslims, and Christians. ⊛ Pop. 561,900.

Jew (jōō). **1.** An adherent of Judaism as a religion or culture. **2.** A member of the widely dispersed people originally descended from the ancient Hebrews and sharing an ethnic heritage based on Judaism. **3.** A native or inhabitant of the ancient kingdom of Judah. — **Jew′ish** *adj.*

Jew·ry (jōō′rē). **1.** The Jewish people. **2.** A section of a medieval city inhabited by Jews; a ghetto.

Jhan·si (jän′sē). A city of north-central India south-southeast of Delhi. The city grew around a walled Mogul fort built in 1613. ⊛ Pop. 300,850.

Jhe·lum (jā′ləm). A river, about 772 km (480 mi) long, of northern India and northeast Pakistan. It is the westernmost of the five rivers of the Punjab.

Jia·ling also **Chia·ling** (jyä′lĭng′) or **Kia·ling** (kyä′-, jyä′-). A river, about 965 km (600 mi) long, of central China flowing east and south to the Chang Jiang (Yangtze River) at Chongqing.

Jia·mu·si (jyä′mōō′sē′, -mü′-) also **Chia·mus·su** (-mōō′sōō′) or **Kia·mu·sze** (kyä′mōō′sōō′). A city of extreme northeast China east-northeast of Harbin. It is an industrial center and a river port. ⊛ Pop. 744,584.

Jiang·su (jyäng′sōō′, -sü′) also **Kiang·su** (kyäng′-). A province of eastern China bordering on the Yellow Sea. Densely populated and highly industrialized, it became a separate province in the 18th century. Nanjing is the capital. ⊛ Pop. 62,130,000.

Jiang·xi (jyäng′shē′) also **Kiang·si** (kyäng′-). A province of southeast China. In early times it served as a corridor for north-south migration and communications. Nanchang is the capital. ⊛ Pop. 34,600,000.

Jiao·zuo (jyou′dzwō′) also **Tsiao·tso** (-jō′). A city of east-central China north-northwest of Zhengzhou. It is a coal-mining center. ⊛ Pop. 1,578,461.

Ji·ca·ril·la (hē′kə-rē′yə, -rēl′yə). *pl.* **Jicarilla** or **-las.** A member of an Apache tribe formerly inhabiting southeast Colorado and northern New Mexico and ranging eastward to the Great Plains, with a present-day population in northern New Mexico.

Jid·da (jĭd′ə). A city of west-central Saudi Arabia on the Red Sea. Ruled by the Turks until 1916, Jidda has long been used as a port by Muslim pilgrims making the journey to Mecca. ⊛ Pop. 1,300,000.

Ji·lin also **Chi·lin** (jē′lĭn′) or **Ki·rin** (kē′rĭn′). **1.** A province of northeast China bordering on North Korea. Extensive timberlands have long been important to the province's economy. Changchun is the capital. ⊛ Pop. 22,980,000. **2.** A city of northeast China east of Changchun. Founded in 1673, it is now a commercial and industrial center. ⊛ Pop. 2,251,848.

Ji·nan also **Tsi·nan** (jē′nän′). A city of eastern China on the Huang He (Yellow River) south of Tianjin. Opened to foreign commerce in 1904, it is the capital of Shandong province. ⊛ Pop. 2,403,946.

Jing·de·zhen (jĭng′də′jœn′) also **King·teh·chen** (kĭng′tə′chœn′). A city of southeast China southwest of Shanghai. Established in the sixth century A.D., it has an important pottery industry. ⊛ Pop. 369,995.

Jin·men (jĭn′mœn′). See **Quemoy.**

Jin·zhou also **Chin·chow** (jĭn'jō'). A city of northern China east-northeast of Beijing. It is a commercial center. ● Pop. 736,297.

Ji·va·ro (hē'və-rō'). **1.** *pl.* **Jivaro** or **-ros.** A member of a South American Indian people of eastern Ecuador and northeast Peru. **2.** The language of this people.

Ji·xi (jē'shē') also **Ki·si** (kē'sē', -shē'). A city of northeast China near the Russian border east of Harbin. ● Pop. 835,496.

João Pes·so·a (zhwoᴜɴ' pə-sō'ə). A city of northeast Brazil near the Atlantic Ocean north of Recife. Founded in 1585, it has excellent examples of colonial architecture. ● Pop. 497,306.

Jodh·pur (jŏd'pər, jōd'pŏŏr'). A city of western India southwest of Delhi. Center of a former principality founded in the 13th century, it is an important wool market. ● Pop. 666,279.

Jog·ja·kar·ta (jŏg'yə-kär'tə, jôk'jä-) also **Yog·ya·kar·ta** (yŏg'yə-, jôk'jä-) or **Djok·ja·kar·ta** (jŏk'yə-). A city of southern Java, Indonesia, east-southeast of Jakarta. Founded in 1749, it is a major cultural center known for its dance and drama festivals. ● Pop. 398,727.

Jo·han·nes·burg (jō-hăn'ĭs-bûrg', -hä'nĭs-). The largest city of South Africa, in the northeast part of the country northwest of Durban. Founded in 1886 after the discovery of gold nearby, it is a major industrial center. ● Pop. 703,980.

John Day (jŏn' dā'). A river, about 452 km (281 mi) long, of northern Oregon flowing west and north to the Columbia River.

John o'Groat's (ə-grōts'). A location on the northeast coast of Scotland, traditionally considered the northernmost point of Great Britain.

John·son City (jŏn'sən). **1.** A village of south-central New York east of Binghamton. It has tanneries and other industries. ● Pop. 16,890. **2.** A city of northeast Tennessee east-northeast of Knoxville. Settled in the 1760's, it is a railroad junction and manufacturing center. ● Pop. 49,381.

John·ston (jŏn'stən). A town of north-central Rhode Island, a manufacturing suburb of Providence. ● Pop. 24,907.

Johns·town (jŏnz'toun'). A city of southwest Pennsylvania east of Pittsburgh. A devastating flood on May 31, 1889, killed more than 2,000 people and destroyed much of the town. ● Pop. 28,134.

Jo·hor Ba·ha·ru (jə-hôr' bə-hä'rōō, jə-hôr') also **Jo·hore Bah·ru** (bä'rōō). A city of Malaysia on the southern tip of the Malay Peninsula opposite Singapore Island. The city is connected with Singapore by a causeway across the narrow **Johore Strait.** ● Pop. 328,646.

Join·vi·le also **Join·vil·le** (zhoiɴ-vē'lĕ). A city of

southern Brazil north-northeast of Pôrto Alegre. Founded c. 1850 by German immigrants, it is an industrial center. ● Pop. 346,332.

Jo·li·et (jō'lē-ĕt', jō'lē-ĕt'). A city of northeast Illinois southwest of Chicago. It is an industrial center and a river port. ● Pop. 76,836.

Jo·li·ette (zhō'lē-ĕt'). A city of southern Quebec, Canada, north of Montreal. It was founded in 1841 by descendants of the French-Canadian explorer Louis Jolliet (1645–1700). ● Pop. 16,987.

Jones·bor·o (jōnz'bûr'ō, -bûr'ə, -bŭr'ō). A city of northeast Arkansas northeast of Little Rock. It is the seat of Arkansas State University (founded 1909). ● Pop. 46,535.

Jön·kö·ping (yœn'chœ'pĭng). A city of southern Sweden southwest of Stockholm. Chartered in 1284, it was burned by its citizens in 1612 to prevent the Danes from sacking it. ● Pop. 112,802.

Jon·quière (zhōɴ-kyĕr'). A city of southern Quebec, Canada, on the Saguenay River north of Quebec City. Pulp and paper mills are important to its economy. ● Pop. 60,354.

joo·al (zhōō-äl'). *Chiefly Canadian & Maine.* Variant of **joual.**

Jop·lin (jŏp'lĭn). A city of southwest Missouri near the Kansas border west of Springfield. It was founded in 1839. ● Pop. 40,961.

Jor·dan (jôr'dn). Formerly known as **Trans·jor·dan** (trăns'-, trănz'-). A country of southwest Asia in northwest Arabia. Inhabited since biblical times, the area was conquered by the Seleucid dynasty (fourth century B.C.), Romans (first century A.D.), Arabs (seventh century), and Ottoman Turks, who held it from 1516 until World War I. As Transjordan it became part of the British mandate of Palestine in 1920 and achieved

independence in 1946. The country was renamed Jordan in 1949 after acquiring the territory west of the Jordan River during the Arab-Israeli War of 1948. The West Bank was later occupied by Israeli forces (1967), and Jordan renounced (1974) its claim to the area. Jordan joined Middle East peace talks in 1991 and signed a peace agreement with Israel in 1994. Amman is the capital and the largest city. ◉ Pop. 5,198,000. — **Jor·da′ni·an** (jôr-dā′nē-ən) *adj. & n.*

Jordan River. A river of southwest Asia rising in Syria and flowing about 322 km (200 mi) south through the Sea of Galilee to the northern end of the Dead Sea.

jou·al also **joo·al** (zhoo-äl′). *Chiefly Canadian & Maine.* A dialect of Canadian French characterized by nonstandard pronunciations and grammar and by English vocabulary and syntax.

Juan de Fu·ca (wän də foo′kə, fyoo′-, hwän), **Strait of.** A strait between northwest Washington State and Vancouver Island, British Columbia, Canada, linking Puget Sound and the Strait of Georgia with the Pacific Ocean. Discovered by an English captain in 1787, it was named for a Spanish sailor who reputedly had discovered it in 1592.

Juan Fer·nán·dez Islands (fər-năn′dəs, fĕr-nän′dĕs). An island group belonging to Chile, in the southeast Pacific Ocean west of Valparaiso, Chile. Alexander Selkirk, a Scottish sailor and the inspiration for Defoe's *Robinson Crusoe,* lived on one of the islands from 1704 to 1709.

Juá·rez (wär′ĕz, hwä′rĕs). See **Ciudad Juárez.**

Jua·zei·ro do Nor·te (zhwä-zā′roo doo nôr′-tĭ). A city of northeast Brazil south of Fortaleza. It is the center of a fertile agricultural region. ◉ Pop. 173,320.

Ju·ba (joo′bə, -bä). A river of southern Ethiopia and southern Somalia flowing about 1,609 km (1,000 mi) to the Indian Ocean.

Jub·bul·pore (jŭb′əl-pôr′, -pōr′). See **Jabalpur.**

Jú·car (hoo′kär). A river, about 483 km (300 mi) long, flowing from eastern Spain to the Mediterranean Sea south of Valencia.

Ju·dae·a (joo-dē′ə, -dā′ə). See **Judea.**

Ju·dah (joo′də). An ancient kingdom of southern Palestine between the Mediterranean and the Dead Sea. It lasted from the division of Palestine in 931 B.C. until the destruction of Jerusalem in 586 B.C.

Ju·de·a also **Ju·dae·a** (joo-dē′ə, -dā′ə). An ancient region of southern Palestine in present-day southern Israel and southwest Jordan. In the time of Jesus it was a kingdom ruled by the Herods and part of the Roman province of Syria. — **Ju·de′an** *adj. & n.*

Ju·de·o-Span·ish (joo-dā′ō-spăn′ĭsh). See **Ladino** (sense 1).

Ju·dith River (joo′dĭth). A river, about 200 km (124 mi) long, flowing from central Montana northward to the Missouri River.

Juiz de Fo·ra (zhwēzh′ də fôr′ə). A city of southeast Brazil north of Rio de Janeiro. It is an industrial and commercial center. ◉ Pop. 385,734.

Ju·juy (hoo-hwē′). A city of northern Argentina north of San Miguel de Tucumán. It is a manufacturing and trade center. ◉ Pop. 124,950.

Jul·ian Alps (jool′yən). A range of the eastern Alps in Slovenia and northeast Italy. The heavily forested range rises to 2,864 m (9,390 ft).

Jul·lun·dur (jŭl′ən-dər). A city of northwest India north-northwest of Delhi. It was the capital of an ancient kingdom of the same name and came under British jurisdiction in 1846. ◉ Pop. 509,510.

Jum·na (jŭm′nə). A river of northern India rising in the Himalaya Mountains and flowing about 1,384 km (860 mi) generally southeast to the Ganges River at Allahabad.

Junc·tion City (jŭngk′shən). A city of northeast-central Kansas west of Topeka. It is the rail and trade center of an agricultural and dairy region. ◉ Pop. 20,604.

Jun·dia·í (zhoon′dyə-ē′). A city of southeast Brazil north-northwest of São Paulo. Established in the 17th century, it is an agricultural center and a railroad junction. ◉ Pop. 288,644.

Ju·neau (joo′nō′). The capital of Alaska, in the Panhandle northeast of Sitka. It was settled by gold miners in 1880 and designated territorial capital in 1900 (effective 1906) and state capital in 1959. ◉ Pop. 26,751.

Jung·frau (yoong′frou′). A mountain, 4,160.8 m (13,642 ft) high, in the Bernese Alps of south-central Switzerland. It was first scaled in 1811.

Ju·ni·at·a (joo′nē-ăt′ə). A river, about 241 km (150 mi) long, of south-central Pennsylvania flowing eastward to the Susquehanna River.

Ju·ra Mountains (joor′ə, zhü-rä′). A range extending about 241 km (150 mi) along the French-Swiss border and rising to 1,723.9 m (5,652 ft). The area is a popular year-round resort region.

Ju·ru·á (zhoo-roo-ä′). A river of eastern Peru and northwest Brazil flowing about 1,931 km (1,200 mi) northeast to the Amazon River.

Jute (joot). A member of a Germanic people who invaded Britain in the fifth and sixth centuries A.D. and settled in the south and southeast and on the Isle of Wight.

Jut·land (jŭt′lənd). A peninsula of northern Europe comprising mainland Denmark and northern Germany. The name is usually applied only to the Danish section of the peninsula. The largest naval battle of World War I was fought by

British and German fleets off the western coast of Jutland on May 31–June 1, 1916.

Jy·väs·ky·lä (yōō′və-skōō′lə, yü′väs-kü′lä). A city of south-central Finland north-northeast of Helsinki. Chartered in 1837, it has a papermaking industry. ⊛ Pop. 64,834.

K

K2 (kā′tōō′) also **Mount God·win Aus·ten** (gŏd′-wĭn ô′stən). A peak in the Karakoram Range of northern India. At 8,616.3 m (28,250 ft), it is the second-highest mountain in the world. It was designated K2 in 1856 because it was the second Karakoram peak to be measured for height and was later (1888) named for Henry Haversham Godwin-Austen (1834–1923), a British soldier and surveyor.

Ka·bul (kä′bŏol, kə-bōol′). The capital and largest city of Afghanistan, in the eastern part of the country near the border with Pakistan on the **Kabul River,** about 483 km (300 mi) long. Strategically located and more than 3,000 years old, the city became the capital of Afghanistan in the 1700's. ⊛ Pop. 1,424,400.

Ka·byle (kə-bīl′). **1.** *pl.* **Kabyle** or **-byles.** A member of a Berber people of northeast Algeria. **2.** The Berber language of this people.

Ka·du·na (kə-dōō′nə). A city of northwest-central Nigeria northeast of Lagos. Founded by the British in 1913, the city has cotton mills, beverage plants, and furniture factories. ⊛ Pop. 202,000.

Kae·song (kā′sông′). A city of southern North Korea near the South Korean border. It is intersected by the 38th parallel and changed hands several times during the Korean War (1950–1953). ⊛ Pop. 240,000.

Kaf·ir also **Kaf·fir** (kăf′ər). See **Nuristani.**

Kaf·i·ri (kăf′ə-rē, kə-fîr′ē). The Dardic language of the Nuristani.

Ka·fu·e (kə-fōō′ä). A river rising along the Zambia-Zaire border and meandering about 965 km (600 mi) through central Zambia to the Zambezi River.

Ka·go·shi·ma (kä′gô-shē′mə). A city of southern Kyushu, Japan, on **Kagoshima Bay,** an inlet of the East China Sea. Satsuma porcelain ware is produced in the city, which is also a major port. ⊛ Pop. 539,911.

Ka·ho·o·la·we (kä-hō′ō-lä′wē, -wä, -vä). An island of south-central Hawaii southwest of Maui. The low and unfertile island has been used as a prison and a military target range.

Kai·e·teur Falls (kī′ĭ-tōŏr′). A waterfall, 250.7 m (822 ft) high, in the Potaro River of central Guyana.

Kai·feng (kī′fŭng′). A city of east-central China south-southwest of Beijing. Founded in the third century B.C., it is a commercial, agricultural, and industrial center. ⊛ Pop. 693,148.

Kai·las (kī-läs′). A peak, 6,718.2 m (22,027 ft) high, in the Himalaya Mountains of southwest China. It is the highest elevation of the **Kailas Range** and according to Hindu legend was the dwelling place of the god Shiva.

Kai·lu·a (kī-lōō′ə). An unincorporated community of Hawaii, a suburb of Honolulu on the southeast coast of Oahu on **Kailua Bay,** an inlet of the Pacific Ocean. ⊛ Pop. 36,818.

Kai·sers·lau·tern (kī′zərs-lou′tərn). A city of southwest Germany southwest of Frankfurt. First mentioned in 882, it was chartered in 1276. ⊛ Pop. 102,370.

Ka·ki·na·da (kä′kə-nä′də). A city of southeast India on the Bay of Bengal north-northeast of Madras. It is primarily an agricultural marketplace. ⊛ Pop. 279,980.

Ka·ko·ga·wa (kä′kô-gä′wə). A city of southern Honshu, Japan, west of Kobe. It is an industrial center. ⊛ Pop. 249,390.

Ka·la·ha·ri Desert (kä′lə-här′ē). An arid plateau region of southern Botswana, eastern Namibia, and western South Africa. It is covered largely with reddish sand and studded with dry lake beds.

Ka·lakh (kä′läкн). See **Calah.**

Kal·a·ma·zoo (kăl′ə-mə-zōō′). A city of southwest Michigan south of Grand Rapids. First settled in 1829, it is a manufacturing center. ⊛ Pop. 80,277.

Kal·gan (käl′gän′). See **Zhangjiakou.**

Kal·goor·lie (kăl-gŏŏr′lē). A town of southwest Australia east-northeast of Perth. Gold was discovered in the area in the late 1800's. ⊛ Pop. 10,100.

Ka·li·man·tan (käl′ə-măn′tän′, kä′lē-män′tän). The part of Indonesia occupying most of the island of Borneo.

Ka·li·nin (kə-lē′nĭn, kəl-yē′-). See **Tver.**

Ka·li·nin·grad (kə-lē′nĭn-grăd′, -gräd′, -lyĭ-nĭn-grät′). Formerly **Kö·nigs·berg** (kā′nĭgz-bûrg′, kœ′nĭкнs-bĕrk′). A city of extreme western Russia on the Baltic Sea near the Polish border. It was founded in 1255 by the Teutonic Knights and joined the Hanseatic League in 1340. As Königsberg it was an important Prussian city and the birthplace of the German philosopher Immanuel Kant (1724). Transferred to the U.S.S.R. in 1945, the city was renamed Kaliningrad in 1946. ⊛ Pop. 413,491.

Ka·lisz (kä′lĭsh). A city of central Poland west of

Lódź. An ancient settlement dating possibly to the second century A.D., it passed to Prussia in 1793, Russia in 1815, and was restored to Poland in 1919. ⊛ Pop. 106,359.

Kal·li·thé·a (kăl′ĭ-thā′ə, kä′lē-thā′ä). A city of east-central Greece, an industrial suburb of Athens. ⊛ Pop. 117,319.

Kal·mar (käl′mär′, käl′-). A city of southeast Sweden on **Kalmar Sound,** an arm of the Baltic Sea between the Swedish mainland and Öland. An important trade center since the eighth century, the city was the site of the Union of Kalmar (1397), which joined Sweden, Denmark, and Norway into a single monarchy that lasted until 1523. ⊛ Pop. 30,300.

Kal·myk¹ (kăl′mĭk, kăl-mĭk′) also **Kal·muck** or **Kal·muk** (kăl′mŭk, kăl-mŭk′). **1.** A member of a Buddhist Mongol people now located primarily in the Kalmyk region. **2.** The Mongolian language of this people.

Kal·myk² (kăl′mĭk, kăl-mĭk′). A region of southwest Russia on the Caspian Sea. Settled in the early 17th century by Kalmyk people from central China, it came under Russian control after 1646.

Ka·lu·ga (kə-lōō′gə). A city of west-central Russia southwest of Moscow. Dating to the 14th century, it is an industrial center and a river port. ⊛ Pop. 343,967.

Ka·ma (kä′mə). A river of west-central Russia rising in the central Ural Mountains and flowing about 2,031 km (1,262 mi) to the Volga River. It is the chief tributary of the Volga.

Ka·ma·ku·ra (kä′mə-kōōr′ə). A city of southeast Honshu, Japan, on an arm of the Pacific Ocean south of Yokohama. Probably founded in the seventh century, it is a resort, residential suburb, and religious center. ⊛ Pop. 172,638.

Ka·mar·ha·ti (kä′mär-hä′tē). A city of northeast India, an industrial suburb of Calcutta on the Hooghly River. ⊛ Pop. 266,889.

Kam·chat·ka (kăm-chăt′kə, -chät′-, kəm-chyät′-). A peninsula of eastern Russia between the Sea of Okhotsk and the Bering Sea. It was first explored in the 18th century.

kame (kām). A short ridge or mound of sand and gravel deposited during glacial melting.

Ka·met (kŭm′ät′). A mountain, 7,761.3 m (25,447 ft) high, in the northwest Himalaya Mountains on the India-China border. It was first scaled in 1931.

Kam·loops (kăm′lōōps′). A city of southern British Columbia, Canada, northeast of Vancouver. It was founded in the early 1800's as a trading post and flourished after the discovery of gold in 1860. ⊛ Pop. 64,048.

Kam·pa·la (käm-pä′lə). The capital and largest city of Uganda, in the southern part of the country on Lake Victoria. It grew around a fort established in 1890. ⊛ Pop. 458,503.

Kam·pu·che·a (kăm′pōō-chē′ə). See **Cambodia.**

Ka·nan·ga (kə-näng′gə). A city of south-central Zaire east-southeast of Kinshasa. Founded in 1884, it is the trade center of an agricultural region. ⊛ Pop. 298,693.

Kan·a·rese (kăn′ə-rēz′, -rēs′). **1.** *pl.* **Kanarese.** A member of a Kannada-speaking people of southwest India. **2.** See **Kannada.** —**Kan′-ar·ese′** *adj.*

Ka·na·ta (kə-nä′tä). A city of eastern Ontario, Canada, a suburb of Ottawa on the Ottawa River. ⊛ Pop. 19,728.

Ka·na·za·wa (kä′nä-zä′wə). A city of western Honshu, Japan, on the Sea of Japan north of Nagoya. It was ruled by powerful daimios, or feudal lords, during the feudal period (16th–19th century). ⊛ Pop. 446,325.

Kan·chen·jun·ga (kŭn′chən-jŭng′gə, -jōōng′-, kän′-). A mountain, 8,603.4 m (28,208 ft) high, in the Himalaya Mountains on the India-Nepal border. It is the third-highest mountain in the world.

Kan·da·har also **Qan·da·har** (kŭn′də-här′, kän′-). A city of southeast Afghanistan near the Pakistan border southwest of Kabul. Perhaps founded by Alexander the Great in the fourth century B.C., the city has long been important for its strategic location on the trade routes of central Asia. ⊛ Pop. 225,500.

Kan·dy (kăn′dē). A city of central Sri Lanka east-northeast of Colombo. The last capital of the ancient kings of Ceylon, it is a resort and religious center. ⊛ Pop. 104,000.

Ka·ne·o·he (kä′nē-ō′ē, -nä-ō′hä). A city of Hawaii in eastern Oahu on **Kaneohe Bay,** an inlet of the Pacific Ocean. The city is a residential community. ⊛ Pop. 35,448.

Kan·i·a·pis·kau (kăn′ē-ə-pĭs′kō, -kou). See **Caniapiscau.**

Kan·ka·kee (kăng′kə-kē′). A city of northeast Illinois on the Kankakee River south-southwest of Chicago. It is an industrial and shipping center. ⊛ Pop. 27,575.

Kankakee River. A river rising in northern Indiana and flowing 362 km (225 mi) southwest to join the Des Plaines River and form the Illinois River in northeast Illinois.

Kan·kan (kän-kän′). A city of eastern Guinea on a tributary of the Niger River. It is the commercial center of a farming area. ⊛ Pop. 229,000.

Kan·na·da (kä′nə-də). The principal Dravidian language of Mysore, a region of southern India. Also called *Kanarese.*

Kan·nap·o·lis (kə-năp′ə-lĭs). An unincorporated community of south-central North Carolina north-northeast of Charlotte. It was founded c. 1905 as a planned company town by a manufacturer of household linens. ⊛ Pop. 29,696.

Ka·no (kä′nō). A city of north-central Nigeria northeast of Lagos. A powerful Hausa citystate, particularly in the 17th and 18th centuries, it was taken by the British in 1903. It is now the chief industrial city of northern Nigeria. ⊛ Pop. 475,000.

Kan·pur (kän′pŏŏr) also **Cawn·pore** (kôn′pôr′, -pōr′). A city of northern India on the Ganges River southeast of Delhi. During the Indian Mutiny, a disgruntled pension-seeker slaughtered the entire British garrison, including women and children (July 1857). ⊛ Pop. 1,874,409.

Kan River (kăn). See **Gan Jiang.**

Kan·sa (kăn′zə, -sə). **1.** *pl.* **Kansa** or **-sas.** A member of a Native American people formerly inhabiting eastern and central Kansas, with a present-day population in eastern Oklahoma. **2.** The Siouan language of the Kansa. Also called *Kaw.*

Kan·san (kăn′zən). **1.** Of or relating to Kansas. **2.** A native or resident of Kansas.

Kan·sas¹ (kăn′zəz, -səz). A plural of **Kansas.**

Kan·sas² (kăn′zəs). *abbr.* **KS, Kans.** A state of the central United States. It was admitted as the 34th state in 1861. Organized as a territory by the Kansas-Nebraska Act of 1854, which provided it would be classified as a free or slave state on the basis of popular sovereignty, it became a virtual battleground, known as Bleeding Kansas, for free and slave factions (1854–1859). Kansas was finally admitted as a free state. Topeka is the capital and Wichita the largest city. ⊛ Pop. 2,485,600.

Kansas City. 1. A city of northeast Kansas on the Missouri River adjacent to Kansas City, Missouri. It is an industrial center. ⊛ Pop. 149,767. **2.** A city of western Missouri on the Missouri River west-northwest of St. Louis. Established as a fur-trading post in the 1820's, it is a commercial, industrial, and cultural center. ⊛ Pop. 435,146.

Kansas River. Locally known as **Kaw River** (kô). A river formed by the confluence of the Republican and Smoky Hill rivers and flowing about 272 km (169 mi) eastward to the Missouri River at Kansas City.

Kan·su (kän′sŏŏ′, gän′-). See **Gansu.**

Ka·nu·ri (kə-nŏŏr′ē). **1.** *pl.* **Kanuri** or **-ris.** A member of a Muslim people in the Bornu region west of Lake Chad in northeast Nigeria. **2.** The Nilo-Saharan language of this people.

Kao·hsiung (kou′shyŏŏng′, gou′-). A city of southwest Taiwan on Formosa Strait. It was developed as a manufacturing center by the Japa-nese, who occupied Taiwan from 1895–1945, and is now the country's leading port. ⊛ Pop. 1,248,175.

Ka·pu·as (kä′pŏŏ-äs′). A river, about 1,142 km (710 mi) long, of western Kalimantan, Borneo, flowing westward to the South China Sea.

Ka·ra·chi (kə-rä′chē). A city of southern Pakistan on the Arabian Sea. Developed as a trading center in the early 18th century, it passed to the British in 1843 and was the capital of the newly independent country of Pakistan from 1947 until 1959. ⊛ Pop. 5,180,562.

Ka·ra·gan·da (kär′ə-gən-dä′, kə-rə-). A city of central Kazakstan north-northeast of Tashkent, Uzbekistan. Founded in 1857 as a copper-mining settlement, it is now the center of a coal industry. ⊛ Pop. 596,000.

Ka·raj (kə-räj′). A city of northern Iran northwest of Tehran. It is an agricultural trade center with a chemicals industry. ⊛ Pop. 588,287.

Ka·ra·ko·ram Range also **Ka·ra·ko·rum Range** (kär′ə-kôr′əm, -kōr′-, kär′-). A mountain system of northern Pakistan and India and southwest China. An extension of the Hindu Kush, it rises to 8,616.3 m (28,250 ft) at K2, the second-highest mountain in the world.

Ka·ra·ko·rum (kär′ə-kôr′əm, -kōr′-, kär′-). A ruined ancient Mongol city in central Mongolia. Inhabited by Turkic tribes from the first century A.D., it became Genghis Khan's capital c. 1220 but was abandoned by Kublai Khan in 1267.

Karakorum Range. See **Karakoram Range.**

Ka·ra Kum (kär′ə kŏŏm′). A desert region of Turkmenistan between the Caspian Sea and the Amu Darya. A canal provides water for irrigated agriculture in the southern section.

Kara Sea A section of the Arctic Ocean between Novaya Zemlya and the Siberian mainland. Icebound much of the year, it is connected with the Barents Sea by **Kara Strait.**

Kar·ba·la (kär′bə-lə) also **Ker·be·la** (kûr′-). A city of central Iraq south-southwest of Baghdad. It is a pilgrimage site for Shiite Muslims. ⊛ Pop. 296,705.

Ka·re·li·a (kə-rē′lē-ə, -rēl′yə, -ryě′lē-yə). A region of northeast Europe mainly in northwest Russia between the Gulf of Finland and the White Sea. First mentioned in the ninth century, the area later came under Swedish domination and was annexed by Russia in 1721.

Ka·re·li·an (kə-rē′lē-ən, -rēl′yən). **1.** Of or relating to Karelia or its people, language, or culture. **2.** A native or inhabitant of Karelia. **3.** The Finnic language spoken in Karelia.

Karelian Isthmus. A land bridge of northwest Russia between Lake Ladoga and the Gulf of Finland.

Ka·ren (kə-rěn′). **1.** *pl.* **Karen** or **-rens.** A member of a Thai people inhabiting southern and eastern Myanmar (Burma). **2.** Any of the Tibeto-Burman languages of this people.

Ka·ri·ba (kə-rē′bə), **Lake.** A lake of south-central Africa on the Zambia-Zimbabwe border. It is formed by the **Kariba Dam** (completed 1958) on the Zambezi River, which supplies electricity to the copper mining region of north-central Zambia and to parts of Zimbabwe. The creation of the lake forced the relocation of about 50,000 people.

Kar·kheh (kər-kā′, -ĸнā′). A river, about 563 km (350 mi) long, of western Iran and southeast Iraq flowing southwest to marshlands bordering the Tigris River.

Karl-Marx-Stadt (kärl-märk′shtät′). See **Chemnitz.**

Kar·lo·vy Va·ry (kär′lə-vē vär′ē) also **Carls·bad** or **Karls·bad** (kärlz′băd′, kärls′bät′). A city of northwest Czech Republic west-north-west of Prague. Chartered in the 14th century, it has medicinal sulfur springs and has long been popular as a spa. ⊛ Pop. 58,541.

Karls·ru·he also **Carls·ru·he** (kärlz′rōō′ə, kärls′-). A city of southwest Germany on the Rhine River west-northwest of Stuttgart. Founded in 1715, it was badly damaged in World War II. The rebuilt city is an industrial, judicial, and cultural center. ⊛ Pop. 277,998.

Karl·stad (kärl′städ′). A city of southwest Sweden on Lake Vänern west of Stockholm. Chartered in 1584, it was destroyed by fire in 1865. The treaty ending the union of Norway and Sweden was signed here in 1905. ⊛ Pop. 74,324.

Kar·nak (kär′năk′). A village of east-central Egypt on the right bank of the Nile River on part of the site of ancient Thebes. Its pharaonic remains include the Great Temple of Amen, the chief Egyptian deity.

Kar·ok (kə-rŏk′). **1.** *pl.* **Karok** or **-oks.** A member of a Native American people inhabiting northwest California, closely related in culture to the Yurok. **2.** The Hokan language of the Karoks.

ka·roo also **kar·roo** (kə-rōō′). An arid plateau of southern Africa.

Ka·roo (kə-rōō′). See **Karroo.**

Kár·pa·thos (kär′pə-thŏs′, -pä-thôs′). An island of southeast Greece in the Dodecanese Islands of the Aegean Sea between Crete and Rhodes. It was controlled at various times by Venice, Turkey, and Italy before passing to Greece in 1947.

kar·roo (kə-rōō′). Variant of **karoo.**

Kar·roo also **Ka·roo** (kə-rōō′). A semiarid plateau region of southwest South Africa. It is divided into the **North Karroo,** along the Orange River; the **Great¡** or **Central, Karroo;** and the **Little Karroo,** near the coast.

Kars (kärs). A city of northeast Turkey near the Armenian border. Capital of an Armenian principality in the 9th and 10th centuries, it was destroyed by the Mongol conqueror Tamerlane c. 1386, rebuilt by Ottoman Turks in the 16th century, and ceded to Russia in 1878. It was returned to Turkey in 1921. ⊛ Pop. 58,799.

karst (kärst). An area of irregular limestone in which erosion has produced fissures, sinkholes, underground streams, and caverns. —**karst′ic** (kär′stĭk) *adj.*

Ka·run (kə-rōōn′, kä-). A river of western Iran flowing about 724 km (450 mi) west and south into the Shatt al Arab on the Iraq border.

Kar·vi·ná (kär′vē-nä′). A city of northeast Czech Republic east of Ostrava. It was held by Poland from 1938 to 1945. ⊛ Pop. 76,428.

Ka·sai (kə-sī′). A river of northeast Angola and western Zaire flowing 1,931 km (1,200 mi) to the Congo River on the Zaire-Congo border.

Ka·shi·wa (kä′shē-wä′). A city of east-central Honshu, Japan, an industrial suburb of Tokyo. ⊛ Pop. 316,725.

Kash·mir (kăsh′mîr′, kăsh-mîr′). **1.** also **Cash·mere** (kăsh′mîr′, kăsh-mîr′). A historical region of northern India and Pakistan. Conquered by the Mogul emperor Akbar in 1586, it later came under the control of Afghanistan (1757) and a Sikh empire (1819). After 1846 it was a part of the princely state of Jammu and Kashmir. **2.** See **Jammu and Kashmir.**

Kash·mir·i (kăsh-mîr′ē, kăzh-). **1.** *pl.* **Kashmiri** or **-is.** A native or inhabitant of Kashmir. **2.** A Dardic language of Jammu and Kashmir.

Kas·kas·ki·a (kəs-kăs′kē-ə). *pl.* **Kaskaskia** or **-as.** A member of a Native American people forming part of the Illinois confederacy.

Kaskaskia River. A river, about 483 km (300 mi) long, rising in east-central Illinois and flowing southwestward to the Mississippi River.

Kas·sel also **Cas·sel** (kăs′əl, kä′səl). A city of central Germany south-southwest of Hanover on the Fulda River. Chartered in 1198, it was a munitions center in World War II and was frequently bombed by the Allies. It is a rail and industrial center. ⊛ Pop. 202,158.

Ka·su·gai (kä-sōō′gī). A city of central Honshu, Japan, an industrial suburb of Nagoya. ⊛ Pop. 273,116.

Ka·tah·din (kə-täd′n), **Mount.** A mountain, about 1,607 m (5,268 ft) high, of north-central Maine in the **Katahdin Range.** It is the highest elevation in the state and the northern terminus of the Appalachian Trail.

Ka·tan·ga (kə-täng′gə, -tăng′-). See **Shaba.** —**Kat′an·gese′** (kăt′äng-gēz′, -gēs′, -äng-) *adj. & n.*

Ka·tha·rev·u·sa (kä′thä-rĕv′ōō-sä′). The puristic, archaizing form of Modern Greek, which contains morphological and lexical features borrowed from Koine.

Ka·thi·a·war (kä'tē-ə-wär'). A peninsula of western India projecting into the Arabian Sea between the Gulfs of Kutch and Cambay.

Kath·man·du (kăt'măn-dōō', kät'män-). See **Katmandu.**

Kat·mai (kăt'mī'), **Mount.** An active volcano, about 2,048 m (6,715 ft) high, in the Aleutian Range of southern Alaska at the eastern end of the Alaska Peninsula. It is located in a national monument that includes the Valley of the Ten Thousand Smokes.

Kat·man·du also **Kath·man·du** (kăt'măn-dōō', kät'män-). The capital and largest city of Nepal, in the central part of the country in the eastern Himalaya Mountains. It was founded c. 723 and was a Gurkha capital from 1768 until the late 18th century. ⊛ Pop. 235,160.

Ka·to·wi·ce (kä'tə-vēt'sə, -tô-vē'tsě). A city of southern Poland west-northwest of Cracow. Chartered in 1865, it is an important mining and industrial center. ⊛ Pop. 366,465.

Kat·te·gat (kăt'ĭ-găt'). A strait of the North Sea between southwest Sweden and eastern Jutland, Denmark. It connects with the North Sea through the Skagerrak.

Kau·ai (kou'ī', kou-ī'). An island of Hawaii northwest of Oahu. It was an independent royal domain when visited by the British navigator and explorer Capt. James Cook in 1778 and became part of the kingdom of Hawaii in 1810.

Kau·nas (kou'nəs, -näs). A city of central Lithuania on the Neman River south of Riga. Founded in the 11th century, it was a medieval trading post and a Lithuanian stronghold against the Teutonic Knights. Russia acquired the city in the third partition of Poland (1795). ⊛ Pop. 421,600.

Ka·vál·la (kə-văl'ə, kä-vä'lä). A city of northeast Greece on an inlet of the Aegean Sea. Held by the Ottoman Turks from 1387 to 1913, it is a center for tobacco processing and shipping. ⊛ Pop. 56,375.

Kaw (kô). See **Kansa.**

Ka·wa·goe (kə-wä'goi, -gô-ě). A city of east-central Honshu, Japan, northwest of Tokyo. Its manufactures include silk textiles. ⊛ Pop. 316,313.

Ka·wa·gu·chi (kä'wə-gōō'chē). A city of east-central Honshu, Japan, an industrial suburb of Tokyo. ⊛ Pop. 451,345.

Ka·war·tha Lakes (kə-wôr'thə). A series of lakes· in southeast Ontario, Canada, connected with Lake Simcoe by the Trent Canal system. The lakes are popular as a summer resort area.

Ka·wa·sa·ki (kä'wə-sä'kē). A city of east-

central Honshu, Japan, an industrial suburb of Tokyo on Tokyo Bay. ⊛ Pop. 1,199,707.

Kaw River. See **Kansas River.**

Kay·se·ri (kī'zə-rē', -sə-). A city of central Turkey southeast of Ankara. The modern city was founded in the fourth century A.D. It is an important commercial center. ⊛ Pop. 454,000.

Ka·zak also **Ka·zakh** (kə-zäk', -zäk'). **1.** *pl.* **Kazak** or **-zaks** also **Kazakh** or **-zakhs.** A member of a pastoral Muslim people inhabiting Kazakstan and parts of Xinjiang Uygur in China. **2.** The Turkic language of this people.

Ka·zak·stan (kä'zäk-stän', kə-zäk'-, kə-zŭkH-stän'). Formerly **Ka·zakh Soviet Socialist Republic** (kə-zäk') or **Ka·zakh·stan** (kä'zäk-stän', kə-zäk'-, kə-zŭkH-stän'). A country of west-central Asia south of Russia and northeast of the Caspian Sea. The original Turkic inhabitants were overrun by the Mongols in the 13th century and ruled by various khanates until the Russian conquest of 1730 to 1853. The region became an autonomous republic of the U.S.S.R. in 1920 and was a constituent republic from 1936 to 1991. Almaty is the capital and largest city. ⊛ Pop. 17,027,000.

Ka·zan (kə-zăn', -zän'). A city of west-central Russia on the Volga River east of Moscow. Founded in 1401, the modern city became the capital of a powerful Tartar khanate in 1455 but was conquered by Czar Ivan IV in 1552. In the 18th century it was an outpost of Russian colonization to the east. ⊛ Pop. 1,085,944.

Ka·zan·lŭk (kä'zän-lŭk') or **Ka·zan·lik** (-lĭk'). A city of central Bulgaria east of Sofia. The center of a region famed for its rose fields, it developed in the 17th century as a manufacturing center for attar of roses. ⊛ Pop. 62,000.

Ka·zan River (kə-zăn'). A river, about 732 km (455 mi) long, of southeast Northwest Territories, Canada, flowing north-northeast through a series of lakes to Baker Lake.

Kaz·bek (käz-běk'), **Mount.** An extinct volcano, 5,042.3 m (16,532 ft) high, of northern Georgia in the central Caucasus. Towering above a nearby pass, it is the subject of many legends.

Kaz·vin (kăz-vēn′). See **Qazvin.**

Ke·a·la·ke·ku·a Bay (kā-ä′lə-kə-kōō′ə). An inlet of the Pacific Ocean on the western coast of Hawaii Island. The British navigator and explorer Capt. James Cook landed here (January 1779) during his second voyage to the islands and was killed (February 14) during a beach fight with the islanders.

Kear·ney (kär′nē). A city of south-central Nebraska on the Platte River west-southwest of Grand Island. It is a trade and industrial center in an agricultural region. ● Pop. 24,396.

Kearns (kûrnz). An unincorporated community of northern Utah, a mainly residential suburb of Salt Lake City. ● Pop. 28,374.

Kear·ny (kär′nē). A town of northeast New Jersey on the Passaic River opposite Newark. It is a port and an industrial center. ● Pop. 34,874.

Kech·ua (kěch′wə, -wä′). Variant of **Quechua.**

Kecs·ke·mét (kěch′kě-māt′). A city of central Hungary southeast of Budapest. Known since the fourth century A.D., it is a manufacturing center and transportation hub. ● Pop. 105,399.

Ke·di·ri (kā-dîr′ē). A city of eastern Java, Indonesia, southwest of Surabaya. It has a sugar industry. ● Pop. 221,830.

Kee·ling Islands (kē′lǐng). See **Cocos Islands.**

Kee·lung (kē′lōōng′) also **Chi·lung** (jē′-, chē′-). A city of northern Taiwan on the East China Sea. It is a port for the capital city of Taipei. ● Pop. 349,686.

Keene (kēn). A city of southwest New Hampshire west of Manchester. It was first settled in 1736. ● Pop. 22,430.

Kee·wa·tin (kē-wāt′n). A region of southeast Northwest Territories, Canada. It includes the eastern section of the mainland and various islands in Hudson Bay. The district was originally created as a much larger region in 1876.

Ke·fal·li·ní·a (kě′fä-lē-nē′ä). See **Cephalonia.**

Kef·la·vík (kyěb′lə-vēk′, kěf′-). A town of southwest Iceland on the Atlantic Ocean west-southwest of Reykjavík. Its international airport was built by the U.S. military during World War II. ● Pop. 6,907.

Kei·zer (kī′zər). An unincorporated community of northwest Oregon, a mainly residential suburb of Salem. ● Pop. 21,884.

Ke·low·na (kə-lō′nə). A city of southern British Columbia, Canada, on Okanagan Lake east-northeast of Vancouver. It is a tourist resort and trade center for a farming and lumbering area. ● Pop. 75,950.

Kelt (kělt). Variant of **Celt.**

Kelt·ic (kěl′tǐk). Variant of **Celtic.**

Ke·me·ro·vo (kěm′ə-rō′və, kyě′mər-ə-və). A city of south-central Russia east-northeast of Novosibirsk. It is an industrial center in a coal-mining region. ● Pop. 512,778.

Ke·mi·jo·ki (kěm′ē-yô′kē). A river, about 555 km (345 mi) long, of northern Finland flowing generally southwest to the Gulf of Bothnia.

Kemp·ten (kěmp′tən). A city of south-central Germany southwest of Munich. Of Celtic origin, it was a flourishing Roman colony and a free imperial city from 1289 to 1803. ● Pop. 56,691.

Ke·nai Peninsula (kē′nī′). A peninsula of south-central Alaska between Cook Inlet and the Gulf of Alaska.

Ken·dall (kěn′dl). A community of southeast Florida, a suburb of Miami. ● Pop. 87,271.

Ken·il·worth (kěn′əl-wûrth′). An urban district of central England southeast of Birmingham. It is famous for the ruins of Kenilworth Castle, founded c. 1120 and celebrated in Sir Walter Scott's novel *Kenilworth* (1821). Queen Elizabeth I (1533–1603) gave the castle to her favorite, the courtier and politician Robert Dudley, Earl of Leicester. ● Pop. 19,315.

Ken·more (kěn′môr′, -mōr′). A village of western New York on the Niagara River north of Buffalo. It is mainly residential. ● Pop. 17,180.

Ken·ne·bec (kěn′ə-běk′). A river, about 257 km (160 mi) long, of west-central and southern Maine flowing south to the Atlantic Ocean.

Ken·ne·dy (kěn′ĭ-dē), **Cape.** See Cape **Canaveral.**

Kennedy, Mount. A peak, 4,241 m (13,905 ft) high, in the St. Elias Mountains of Yukon Territory, Canada, near the Alaskan border. Discovered in 1935, it was named for President John F. Kennedy and climbed for the first time in 1965.

Ken·ner (kěn′ər). A city of southeast Louisiana, an industrial suburb of New Orleans on the Mississippi River. ● Pop. 72,033.

Ken·ne·wick (kěn′ə-wǐk′). A city of southern Washington on the Columbia River west-northwest of Walla Walla. The Hanford Works, a nuclear plant built during World War II, is nearby. ● Pop. 42,155.

Ke·no·sha (kə-nō′shə). A city of extreme southeast Wisconsin on Lake Michigan south of Milwaukee. Founded in 1835, it is an industrial center and a port of entry. ● Pop. 80,352.

Kent (kěnt). **1.** A region and former kingdom of southeast England. Jutes settled in the area in the fifth century A.D., displacing the original inhabitants and establishing one of the seven kingdoms of the Anglo-Saxon Heptarchy. Converted to Christianity in 597, the people of Kent later became subject to the kingdoms of Mercia and Wessex. **2.** A city of northeast Ohio east-northeast of Akron. Kent State University (founded 1910) is in the city and was the site of a 1970 demonstration against the Vietnam War in which four students were killed by members of the National Guard. ⊚ Pop. 28,835. **3.** A city of west-central Washington south of Seattle. A newly urbanized community in a former farming region, it is a food-processing center with an aerospace industry. ⊚ Pop. 37,960.

Kent·ish (kĕn′tĭsh). **1.** Of or relating to Kent, England, or its inhabitants. **2.** The dialect of English spoken in Kent.

Ken·tuck·y (kən-tŭk′ē). *abbr.* **KY, Ken., Ky.** A state of the east-central United States. It was admitted as the 15th state in 1792. Daniel Boone's Transylvania Company made the first permanent settlement in the area in 1775. By the Treaty of Paris (1783) the territory became part of the United States. Frankfort is the capital and Louisville the largest city. ⊚ Pop. 3,698,969. —**Ken·tuck′i·an** *adj. & n.*

Kentucky River. A river, about 417 km (259 mi) long, of north-central Kentucky flowing northwest to the Ohio River.

Kent·wood (kĕnt′wŏŏd′). A city of western Michigan, a suburb of Grand Rapids. ⊚ Pop. 37,826.

Ken·ya (kĕn′yə, kēn′-). A country of east-central Africa bordering on the Indian Ocean. The site of many early hominid fossils, Kenya has been inhabited during historic times by various Cushitic, Nilotic, and Bantu peoples including the Kikuyu and the Masai. The coast was settled by Arab traders in the 8th century A.D. and later (16th–18th century) by the Portuguese. Kenya became a British protectorate in 1890 and a crown colony in 1920. A terrorist revolt against British rule in the 1950's, known as the Mau Mau emergency, was instrumental in preparing the way for independence in 1963 under Jomo Kenyatta (1893?–1978). After Kenyatta's death the country came under one-party rule, which was officially ended in 1991, although the reelection of President Daniel arap Moi in multiparty elections in 1992 was disputed by the opposition. Nairobi is the capital and the largest city. ⊚ Pop. 29,292,000. —**Ken′yan** *adj. & n.*

Kenya, Mount. An extinct volcano, 5,202.7 m (17,058 ft), in central Kenya. It is the second-highest peak in Africa.

Ker·be·la (kûr′bə-lə). See **Karbala.**

Kerch (kĕrch, kyĕrch). A city of southern Ukraine on **Kerch Strait,** a shallow waterway connecting the Black Sea with the Sea of Azov and bordered on the west by the **Kerch Peninsula.** The city was founded by Greek colonists in the sixth century B.C. and eventually passed to Russia after the first Russo-Turkish War (1768–1774). ⊚ Pop. 180,500.

Ker·e·san (kĕr′ĭ-sən). Any of a group of languages spoken by certain Pueblo peoples, including the Acomas. —**Ker′e·san** *adj.*

Ker·gue·len Islands (kûr′gə-lən, -lĕn′). A French-administered island group in the southern Indian Ocean southeast of South Africa. The largest island, **Kerguelen,** was discovered by a French navigator in 1772 and is used mainly as a research station.

Kér·ki·ra (kĕr′kē-rä′). See **Corfu.**

Ker·kra·de (kĕr′krä′də). A city of southeast Netherlands on the German border north of Aachen. Its coal-mining industry dates to the 12th century. ⊚ Pop. 53,231.

Ker·man (kər-män′, kĕr-). A city of east-central Iran southeast of Tehran. It is famous for its carpets. ⊚ Pop. 349,626.

Ker·man·shah (kĕr-män′-shä′, -shô′). See **Bakhtaran.**

Kern River (kûrn). A river rising in the Sierra Nevada of eastern California and flowing about 249 km (155 mi) south and southwest to the southern San Joaquin Valley.

Kerr·ville (kûr′vĭl′, -vəl). A city of southwest Texas northwest of San Antonio. Settled in 1846, it is a health and vacation resort. ⊚ Pop. 17,384.

Ker·u·len (kĕr′ŏŏ-lĕn). A river rising in northeast Mongolia and flowing about 1,263 km (785 mi) south then east to a lake in northeast China.

Ketch·i·kan (kĕch′ĭ-kăn′). A city of southeast Alaska on an island in the Alexander Archipelago. A supply point for miners during the gold rush of the 1890's, it is now a major port and tourist center on the Inside Passage. ⊚ Pop. 8,263.

Ket·ter·ing (kĕt′ər-ĭng). A city of southwest Ohio, an industrial suburb of Dayton. ⊚ Pop. 60,569.

ket·tle (kĕt′l). *Geology.* A depression left in a mass of glacial drift, formed by the melting of an isolated block of glacial ice.

Ket·tle River (kĕt′l). A river, about 257 km

SUDAN
ETHIOPIA
L. Turkana
UGANDA
SOMALIA
KENYA
L. Victoria
Nairobi
TANZANIA
Mombasa
INDIAN OCEAN
100 mi

(160 mi) long, of southern British Columbia, Canada, and northeast Washington flowing generally southward to the Columbia River.

Keu·ka Lake (kyōō'kə, kā-yōō'-). A lake of west-central New York, one of the Finger Lakes west of Seneca Lake. It is the center of a resort and wine-making region.

Kew (kyōō). A district of western Greater London in southeast England. The famed Royal Botanic Gardens were established in 1759 and presented to the nation in 1841.

Ke·wee·naw Peninsula (kē'wə-nô'). A peninsula of northwest Michigan extending into Lake Superior and bordered on the south by **Keweenaw Bay.**

key (kē). A low offshore island or reef, especially in the Gulf of Mexico; a cay.

Key Lar·go (kē lär'gō). A narrow island off southern Florida. It is the largest of the Florida Keys.

Key West . A city of extreme southern Florida on the island of **Key West,** the westernmost of the Florida Keys in the Gulf of Mexico. Fishing and tourism are important to its economy. ◉ Pop. 24,832.

Kha·ba·rovsk (kə-bär'əfsk, кнə-). A city of southeast Russia on the Amur River near the Chinese border. Located on the site of a fort established in 1652, it prospered after the coming of the railroad in 1905. ◉ Pop. 607,669.

Khal·ki·dhi·kí (käl-kē'thē-kē', кнäl-). See **Chalcidice.**

Khal·kís (käl-kēs', кнäl-). See **Chalcis.**

kham·sin (kăm-sēn'). A generally southerly hot wind from the Sahara that blows across Egypt from late March to early May.

Khan·ba·lik (kän'bə-lēk'). An ancient city of Mongol China on the site of modern Beijing. Rebuilt by Kublai Khan from 1264 to 1267 on the site of an earlier city, Khanbalik was called Cambaluc by Marco Polo, who described its magnificence in the account of his travels.

Khan·ka (kăng'kə), **Lake.** A lake of southeast Russia and northeast China north of Vladivostok. Most of it lies in Russian territory.

Khar·kov (kär'kôf', кнär'kəf). A city of northeast Ukraine east of Kiev. Founded in 1656, it was an important 17th-century frontier headquarters of Ukrainian Cossacks who were loyal to the Russian czars. Today Kharkov is a leading industrial center and transportation hub. ◉ Pop. 1,621,600.

Khar·toum also **Khar·tum** (kär-tōōm'). The capital and largest city of Sudan, in the east-central part of the country at the confluence of the Blue Nile and the White Nile. Khartoum was founded c. 1821 as an Egyptian army camp

and was destroyed by Mahdists, followers of the Muslim religious leader Muhammad Ahmad (1844–1885), in 1885 after a long siege. Leading an Anglo-Egyptian force, Lord Kitchener retook the city in 1898 and oversaw its rebuilding. ◉ Pop. 924,505.

Khas·ko·vo (käs'kə-və, кнäs'-). A city of southern Bulgaria east-southeast of Plovdiv. Tobacco growing and processing are important to its economy. ◉ Pop. 91,000.

Kha·tan·ga (kə-täng'gə, -tăng'-, кнä-tän'-). A river, about 1,150 km (715 mi) long, of north-central Russia flowing southeast then north to the **Khatanga Gulf,** an arm of the Laptev Sea.

Kher·son (kĕr-sôn', кнyĭr-). A city of south-central Ukraine on the Dnieper River near the Black Sea east-northeast of Odessa. Kherson was founded in 1778 as a naval base. ◉ Pop. 368,300.

Khí·os (kē'ôs, кнē'-). See **Chios.**

Khir·bet Qumran (kîr'bĕt). See **Qumran.**

Khmel·nit·sky (kə-məl-nĭt'skē, кнmyĭl-nyĕt'-). A city of west-central Ukraine west-southwest of Kiev. Founded in the 15th century, Khmelnitsky became part of Russia in 1795. ◉ Pop. 249,500.

Khmer (kmâr). **1.** *pl.* **Khmer** or **Khmers.** A member of a people of Cambodia whose civilization reached its height from the 9th to the 15th century. **2.** The Mon-Khmer language that is the official language of Cambodia. — **Khmer, Khmer'i·an** *adj.*

Khmer Republic . See **Cambodia.**

Khoi·khoin (koi'koi'ĭn) or **Khoi·khoi** (koi'koi). **1.** *pl.* **Khoikhoin** or **-khoins** or **Khoikhoi** or **-khois.** A member of a pastoral people of Namibia and South Africa. **2.** Any of the Khoisan languages of the Khoikhoin, including Nama.

Khoi·san (koi'sän'). A family of languages of southern Africa, including those of the Khoikhoin and the San.

Kho·per (kə-pyôr', кнŏ-). A river, about 1,006 km (625 mi) long, of southwest Russia flowing generally south to the Don River.

Khu·jand or **Khu·dzhand** (kōō-jänd'). Formerly **Le·nin·a·bad** (lĕn'ĭ-nə-bäd', lyĭ-nĭ-nə-bät'). A city of northwest Tajikistan on the Syr Darya south of Tashkent, Uzbekistan. Located on an ancient caravan route, it is one of the oldest towns of central Asia and marked the farthest eastward expansion of Alexander the Great. Russia annexed the city in 1866, and it was known as Leninabad from 1936 to 1992. Khujand is a major silk and textiles production center. ◉ Pop. 160,000.

Khul·na (kōōl'nə). A city of southwest Bangladesh near the Ganges River delta. It is a trade and processing center for a large swampy, forested region. ◦ Pop. 545,849.

Khy·ber Pass (kī′bər). A narrow pass, about 53 km (33 mi) long, through mountains on the border between eastern Afghanistan and northern Pakistan. It has long been a strategic trade and invasion route. The highest point of the pass is about 1,068 m (3,500 ft).

Kia·ling (kyä′lĭng′, jyä′-). See **Jialing.**

Ki·a·mich·i (kī′ə-mĭsh′ē). A river, about 161 km (100 mi) long, of southeast Oklahoma flowing southwest then southeast to the Red River on the Texas border.

Kia·mu·sze (kyä′mōō′sōō′). See **Jiamusi.**

Kiang·si (kyäng′shē′). See **Jiangxi.**

Kiang·su (kyäng′sōō′, -sü′). See **Jiangsu.**

Kick·a·poo (kĭk′ə-pōō′). **1.** *pl.* **Kickapoo** or **-poos.** A member of a Native American people formerly inhabiting southern Wisconsin and northern Illinois, with small present-day populations in Kansas, Oklahoma, and northern Mexico. **2.** The Algonquian language spoken by the Kickapoos.

Kickapoo River. A river, about 161 km (100 mi) long, of southwest Wisconsin flowing south-southwest to the Wisconsin River.

Kid·der·min·ster (kĭd′ər-mĭn′stər). A municipal borough of west-central England west-southwest of Birmingham. Carpets have been manufactured here since 1735. ◦ Pop. 91,600.

Kiel (kēl). A city of northern Germany on **Kiel Bay,** an arm of the Baltic Sea. Chartered in 1242, Kiel joined the Hanseatic League in 1284, passed to Denmark in 1773, and was annexed by Prussia in 1866. German sailors mutinied here in 1918, setting off a socialist revolution. ◦ Pop. 248,931.

Kiel Canal also **Nord-Ost·see Ka·nal** (nört-ôst′zä kä-näl′). An artificial waterway, 98.1 km (61 mi) long, of northern Germany connecting the North Sea with the Baltic Sea. Built (1887–1895) to facilitate movement of the German fleet, it was widened and deepened from 1905 to 1914.

Kiel·ce (kyĕl′tsĕ). A city of southeast-central Poland south of Warsaw. Founded in 1173, it was controlled by Austria (from 1795) and Russia (from 1815) before reverting to Poland in 1919. ◦ Pop. 214,445.

Ki·ev (kē′ĕf, -ĕv, kyĕ′yĭf). The capital of Ukraine, in the north-central part of the country on the Dnieper River. One of the oldest cities of northern Europe, it was the center of the first Russian state, which included most of present-day Ukraine and Belarus and part of northwest Russia. It fell to the Mongols in the 13th century and later became a part of the Russian Empire (1686) and the Soviet Union (1920). During World War II the city was occupied (1941–1944)

by German forces, and thousands of its residents were massacred. ◦ Pop. 2,642,700.

Ki·ga·li (kĭ-gä′lē, kē-). The capital and largest city of Rwanda, in the central part of the country east of Lake Kivu. ◦ Pop. 156,700.

Ki·klá·dhes (kē-klä′thĕs). See **Cyclades.**

Ki·kon·go (kē-kŏng′gō). See **Kongo** (sense 2).

Ki·ku·yu (kĭ-kōō′yōō) also **Gi·ku·yu** (gĭ-kōō′-yōō). **1.** *pl.* **Kikuyu** or **-yus** also **Gikuyu** or **-yus.** A member of a people of central and southern Kenya. **2.** The Bantu language of the Kikuyu.

Ki·lau·e·a (kē′lou-ā′ə). An active volcanic crater on the southeast slope of Mauna Loa in south-central Hawaii Island. It is one of the largest and most spectacular craters in the world.

Kil·i·man·ja·ro (kĭl′ə-mən-jär′ō), **Mount.** The highest mountain in Africa, in northeast Tanzania near the Kenya border, rising in two snow-capped peaks to 5,896 m (19,340 ft) and 5,354 m (17,564 ft). The higher of the two peaks was first climbed in 1889.

Kil·lar·ney (kĭ-lär′nē), **Lakes of.** Three small lakes of southwest Ireland near the market town of **Killarney.** Studded with islands, the lakes are a popular tourist attraction noted for their scenic beauty. The town's population is 7,693.

Kil·leen (kĭ-lēn′). A city of central Texas southwest of Waco. Founded in 1882, it has some light industry. ◦ Pop. 63,535.

Kil·mar·nock (kĭl-mär′nək). A burgh of southwest Scotland south-southwest of Glasgow. It is an industrial town in a mining region and the site of a monument to Robert Burns, whose poems were first published in Kilmarnock in 1786. ◦ Pop. 51,800.

Kim·ber·ley (kĭm′bər-lē). A city of central South Africa west-northwest of Bloemfontein. Founded in 1871 after the discovery of a rich trove of diamonds nearby, Kimberley also has some manufacturing industries. ◦ Pop. 70,920.

Kim·bun·du (kĭm-bōōn′dōō). See **Mbundu** (sense 4).

King of Prussia (kĭng). A community of southeast Pennsylvania, a suburb of Philadelphia. ◦ Pop. 18,200.

King's English (kĭngz). English speech or usage that is considered standard or accepted; Received Standard English.

King's Lynn. A municipal borough of eastern England on the Ouse River near the Wash. Dating from Saxon times, it was formerly one of the chief ports in England. ◦ Pop. 33,340.

Kings Peak (kĭngz). A peak, 4,116.9 m (13,498 ft) high, of the Uinta Mountains in northeast Utah. It is the highest elevation in the range.

Kings·port (kĭngz′pôrt′, -pōrt′). A city of northeast Tennessee near the Virginia border east-northeast of Knoxville. Its industries include printing and bookbinding. ◉ Pop. 36,365.

Kings River. A river, about 201 km (125 mi) long, of central California rising in headstreams that flow through the gorges of **Kings Canyon** in the Sierra Nevada.

King·ston (kĭng′stən). **1.** A city of southeast Ontario, Canada, on Lake Ontario near the head of the St. Lawrence River. Built on the site of Fort Frontenac, a crucial defense point in the French and Indian Wars, it was the capital of Canada from 1841 to 1844. ◉ Pop. 52,616. **2.** The capital of Jamaica, in the southeast part of the island on the Caribbean Sea. It was founded c. 1692 and became the capital in 1872. ◉ Pop. 103,962. **3.** A city of southeast New York on the Hudson River north of Poughkeepsie. Permanently established in 1652, it was the capital of New York State until the British burned the town in October 1777. ◉ Pop. 23,095. **4.** A borough of northeast-central Pennsylvania on the Susquehanna River opposite Wilkes-Barre. It is mainly residential. ◉ Pop. 14,507.

King·ston-up·on-Hull (kĭng′stən-ə-pŏn-hŭl′, -pôn-). See **Hull** (sense 2).

Kings·town (kĭngz′toun′). The capital of St. Vincent and the Grenadines in the West Indies, on the southwest coast of St. Vincent Island. A botanic garden, the oldest of its kind in the Western Hemisphere, was established here in 1763. ◉ Pop. 18,378.

Kings·ville (kĭngz′vĭl′, -vəl). A city of southern Texas southwest of Corpus Christi. It is the headquarters for the King Ranch, one of the largest ranches in the world. ◉ Pop. 25,276.

Kings·wood (kĭngz′wŏŏd′). An urban district of southwest England, a mainly residential suburb of Bristol. ◉ Pop. 84,200.

King·teh·chen (kĭng′tə′chœn′). See **Jingdezhen.**

King Wil·liam Island (wĭl′yəm). An island of central Northwest Territories, Canada, in the Arctic Ocean between Boothia Peninsula and Victoria Island. It was first explored in 1831.

Kin·sha·sa (kĭn-shä′sə). Formerly **Le·o·pold·ville** (lē′ə-pōld-vĭl′, lā′-). The capital and largest city of Zaire, in the western part of the country on the Congo River. Founded in 1881 by the British explorer Henry M. Stanley, who named it after his patron, Leopold II of Belgium, it became capital of the Belgian Congo in 1926 and was the scene of the revolt (June 1960) that led to Zaire's independence. In 1966 its name was changed to Kinshasa, after the name of an early village that occupied the site. ◉ Pop. 2,664,309.

Kin·ston (kĭn′stən). A city of east-central North Carolina southeast of Raleigh. It is a tobacco market. ◉ Pop. 25,295.

Kin·yar·wan·da (kĭn′yär-wän′də). A Bantu language of Rwanda, closely related to Kirundi and an official language of Rwanda.

Ki·o·ga or **Ky·o·ga** (kē-ō′gə), **Lake.** An irregularly shaped lake of central Uganda. The shallow lake is noted for its papyrus swamps.

Ki·o·wa (kī′ə-wô′, -wä′, -wā′). **1.** *pl.* **Kiowa** or **-was.** A member of a Native American people formerly inhabiting the southern Great Plains, with a present-day population in southwest Oklahoma. The Kiowas migrated onto the plains in the late 17th century from an earlier territory in western Montana. **2.** The Tanoan language of the Kiowas.

Kiowa Apache. 1. *pl.* **Kiowa Apache** or **-es.** A member of a Native American people of the southern Great Plains who formed an integral part of the Kiowa tribe and shared its culture and history although speaking an unrelated Athabaskan language. **2.** The Athabaskan language of the Kiowa Apaches.

Kir·ghiz or **Kir·giz** (kîr-gēz′). See **Kyrgyz.**

Kir·ghi·zia or **Kir·gi·zia** (kîr-gē′zhə, -zhē-ə, -gyē′zĭ-yə). See **Kyrgyzstan.**

Kir·ghiz Soviet Socialist Republic or **Kir·giz Soviet Socialist Republic** (kîr′gēz′, kîr-gēz′, kîr-gyēs′). See **Kyrgyzstan.**

Ki·ri·ba·ti (kēr′ə-bä′tē, kîr′ə-băs′). An island country of the west-central Pacific Ocean near the equator. It includes the former Gilbert Islands, Ocean Island, and the Phoenix and Line islands. The islands were settled by Austronesian peoples before the 1st century A.D. and later (14th century) by groups from Fiji and Tonga. Together with the Ellice Islands they became a British protectorate (1892–1916) and subsequently a crown colony under the name the Gilbert and Ellice Island Colony. The area, especially Tarawa atoll, saw heavy fighting during World War II. Following the attainment of self-rule in 1971, the Ellice Islands gained independence (1978) as Tuvalu and the remaining islands (1979) as Kiribati. Bairiki, on Tarawa atoll, is the administrative center. ◉ Pop. 56,213.

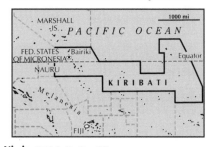

Ki·rin (kē′rĭn′). See **Jilin.**

Kirk·land (kûrk′lənd). A city of west-central Washington on Lake Washington northeast of

Seattle. It is a residential community with some light industry. ⊛ Pop. 40,052.

Kirk·pat·rick (kûrk-păt′rĭk), **Mount.** A mountain, 4,531.1 m (14,856 ft) high, of Antarctica near the edge of the Ross Ice Shelf.

Kirks·ville (kûrks′vĭl′). A city of northern Missouri northwest of Hannibal. It is a manufacturing center in a coal-mining area. ⊛ Pop. 17,152.

Kir·kuk (kîr-kōōk′). A city of northeast Iraq southeast of Mosul. Built on the site of a settlement dating to 3000 B.C., it is an agricultural market in an oil-producing region. ⊛ Pop. 418,624.

Kirk·wall (kûrk′wôl′, -wəl). A burgh of northern Scotland on Mainland Island in the central Orkney Islands. In early times it was important as a trading post on the northern route to Scandinavia. ⊛ Pop. 5,713.

Kirk·wood (kûrk′wŏŏd′). A city of eastern Missouri, a commercial and residential suburb of St. Louis. ⊛ Pop. 27,291.

Ki·rov (kē′rôf′, kyē′rəf). A city of west-central Russia east-northeast of Moscow. Founded c. 1174, it became the center of a medieval principality that was conquered by Ivan III in 1489. ⊛ Pop. 490,964.

Ki·ro·va·bad (kĭ-rō′və-băd′, kyĭ′rə-və-bät′). A city of western Azerbaijan southeast of Tbilisi, Georgia. An important textile and wine center in medieval times, Kirovabad was annexed by Russia in 1804. ⊛ Pop. 261,000.

Ki·ro·vo·grad (kĭ-rō′və-grăd′, kyĭ′rə-va-grät′). A city of central Ukraine south-southeast of Kiev. It is primarily an agricultural trade center. ⊛ Pop. 280,300.

Ki·run·di (kē-rōōn′dē). A Bantu language of Burundi, closely related to Kinyarwanda and an official language of Burundi.

Ki·san·ga·ni (kē′sän-gä′nē, kĭ-zäng′gä-nē). Formerly **Stan·ley·ville** (stăn′lē-vĭl′). A city of northern Zaire on the Congo River northeast of Kinshasa. It was founded in 1883 by the British explorer Henry M. Stanley. ⊛ Pop. 317,581.

Kish (kĭsh). An ancient city of Mesopotamia in the Euphrates River valley of present-day central Iraq. Its extensive ruins have yielded valuable archaeological evidence about Sumerian culture.

Ki·shi·nev (kĭsh′ə-nĕf′, -nôf′, kyĭ′shĭ-nyôf′). The capital of Moldova, in the southern part of the country near the Romanian border northwest of Odessa. It was founded as a monastery center in the early 15th century. ⊛ Pop. 667,100.

Ki·si (kē′sē′, -shē′). See **Jixi**.

Kis·ka Island (kĭs′kə). An island of southwest Alaska near the western end of the Aleutian Is-

lands. During World War II it was held by the Japanese from June 1942 until August 15, 1943.

Kis·sim·mee (kĭ-sĭm′ē). A city of central Florida south of Orlando. Shipbuilding and fruit packing are among its industries. ⊛ Pop. 30,050.

Kissimmee River. A river of central Florida flowing about 225 km (140 mi) south-southeast through **Lake Kissimmee** to Lake Okeechobee.

Kist·na (kĭst′nə) or **Krish·na** (krĭsh′-). A river of southern India rising in the Western Ghats and flowing about 1,287 km (800 mi) eastward to the Bay of Bengal.

Ki·swa·hi·li (kē′swä-hē′lē). See **Swahili** (sense 2).

Ki·ta·kyu·shu (kē-tä′kyōō-shōō). A city of northern Kyushu, Japan, on the channel connecting the Inland Sea with the Korea Strait. It is one of Japan's most important manufacturing centers. ⊛ Pop. 1,019,996.

Kit Car·son Mountain (kĭt kär′sən). A peak, 4,320.3 m (14,165 ft) high, in the Sangre de Cristo Mountains of south-central Colorado.

Kitch·e·ner (kĭch′nər, kĭch′ə-nər). A city of southern Ontario, Canada, west-southwest of Toronto. Settled by Mennonites (1806) and by Germans who named it Berlin in 1825, it was renamed in honor of the British soldier and statesman Lord Kitchener in 1916. ⊛ Pop. 168,282.

Kí·thi·ra (kē′thē-rä′). See **Cythera.**

Ki·tik·me·ot (kĭ-tĭk′mē-ŏt′). A region of central Northwest Territories, Canada, including a portion of the northern mainland and Victoria and King William islands.

Kit·ter·y (kĭt′ə-rē). A town of extreme southwest Maine opposite Portsmouth, New Hampshire. The oldest town in Maine (settled c. 1623), it has long been a shipbuilding center. ⊛ Pop. 5,151.

Kit·ty Hawk (kĭt′ē hôk′). A village of northeast North Carolina on a sandy peninsula between Albemarle Sound and the Atlantic Ocean. Nearby is Kill Devil Hill, which is the site of the Wright brothers' first two successful flights (December 17, 1903).

Ki·twe (kē′twä′). A city of north-central Zambia near the Zaire border. It was founded in 1936 as a copper-mining center. ⊛ Pop. 338,207.

Ki·vu (kē′vōō), **Lake.** A lake on the Zaire-Rwanda border north of Lake Tanganyika. It is situated at an altitude of 1,461 m (4,790 ft) and is Africa's highest lake.

Ki·zil Ir·mak also **Ki·zil-Ir·mak** (kĭ-zĭl′ îr-mäk′). A river of north-central Turkey flowing about 1,150 km (715 mi) southwest, west, north, and then northeast to the Black Sea.

Kla·gen·furt (klä′gən-fōŏrt′). A city of southern Austria southwest of Graz. It was chartered in 1279 and is today a manufacturing center and noted ski resort. ⊛ Pop. 87,321.

Klai·pe·da (klī′pĭ-də, -pĕ-dä). Formerly **Me·mel** (mā′məl). A city of western Lithuania on the Baltic Sea. Settled as early as the seventh century, the site was conquered in 1252 by Teutonic Knights, who built a fortress and named it Memelburg. It was an important trading town of the Hanseatic League and was later held by Sweden, Prussia, and Russia before becoming (1924) part of an autonomous region within Lithuania. Occupied by Germany during World War II, it was taken by Soviet forces in 1945 and made part of the Lithuanian S.S.R. ⊛ Pop. 204,300.

Klam·ath (klăm′əth). **1.** *pl.* **Klamath** or **-aths.** A member of a Native American people inhabiting an area of the Cascade Range in south-central Oregon and northern California, with close cultural ties to the Modocs. **2.** The Penutian language of the Klamaths.

Klamath Falls. A city of southern Oregon near the California border east-southeast of Medford. It is a resort center in a lumber, livestock, and agriculture area. ⊛ Pop. 17,737.

Klamath River. A river flowing about 423 km (263 mi) generally southwest from Upper Klamath Lake in southwest Oregon through northwest California to the Pacific Ocean.

Kle·ve (klā′və) also **Cleves** (klēvz). A city of west-central Germany west-southwest of Münster. It was the seat of a historical duchy and passed subsequently to Brandenburg, Prussia, France, and Prussia again. ⊛ Pop. 44,223.

Klon·dike (klŏn′dīk′). A region of Yukon Territory, Canada, just east of Alaska and traversed by the **Klondike River,** about 145 km (90 mi) long. Gold was discovered here in August 1896, leading to the gold rush of 1897–1898 in which more than 25,000 people sought their fortune in the frozen north. Small quantities of gold are still mined in the area.

kloof (klo͞of). *South African.* A deep ravine.

Knick·er·bock·er (nĭk′ər-bŏk′ər). **1.** A descendant of the Dutch settlers of New York. **2.** A native or inhabitant of New York.

Knife River (nīf). A river, about 265 km (165 mi) long, of west-central North Dakota flowing east to the Missouri River.

knob (nŏb). A usually prominent rounded hill or mountain.

knoll (nōl). A small rounded hill; a hillock.

Knos·sos also **Cnos·sos** or **Cnos·sus** (nŏs′əs). An ancient city of northern Crete near present-day Iráklion. It was the center of Minoan civilization, which reached its peak c. 2200 to 1500 B.C., and is the site of the ruins of a great palace dating from that time. It is also the traditional site in Greek mythology of the palace of King Minos and the labyrinth built by Daedalus.

Knox·ville (nŏks′vĭl′, -vəl). A city of eastern Tennessee on the Tennessee River northeast of Chattanooga. Settled c. 1785, it twice served as the state capital (1796–1812 and 1817–1819). ⊛ Pop. 165,121.

Ko·be (kō′bē′, -bā′). A city of southern Honshu, Japan, on Osaka Bay south-southwest of Kyoto. A port and manufacturing center, it was almost entirely rebuilt after World War II. ⊛ Pop. 1,509,395.

Ko·blenz also **Co·blenz** (kō′blĕnts′). A city of west-central Germany at the confluence of the Rhine and Moselle rivers southeast of Bonn. Founded as a Roman frontier station, it was prominent during Carolingian times (eighth–tenth century) as a residence of Frankish kings. ⊛ Pop. 109,907.

Ko·chi (kō′chē). A city of southern Shikoku, Japan, on an inlet of the Pacific Ocean. It is a port and fish-processing center. ⊛ Pop. 319,243.

Ko·di·ak Island (kō′dē-ăk′). An island of southern Alaska in the Gulf of Alaska east of the Alaska Peninsula. Explored in 1763 by a Russian fur trader, the island was the site of the first permanent Russian settlement in the area (1784).

Ko·fu (kō′fo͞o). A city of central Honshu, Japan, west of Tokyo. The seat of several powerful lords during the feudal era, it is now an industrial center. ⊛ Pop. 199,841.

Koi·ne (koi-nā′, koi′nā′). **1.** A dialect of Greek that developed primarily from Attic and became the common language of the Hellenistic world, from which later stages of Greek are descended. **2. koine.** A lingua franca. **3.** A regional dialect or language that becomes the standard language over a wider area, losing its most extreme local features.

Ko·kand (kō-kănd′). A city of eastern Uzbekistan southeast of Tashkent. It was the center of a powerful khanate in the 18th century and was finally conquered by Russia in 1876. ⊛ Pop. 176,000.

Ko·ko·mo (kō′kə-mō′). A city of central Indiana north of Indianapolis. Founded in the 1840's, it is a manufacturing center. ⊛ Pop. 44,962.

Ko·ko Nor (kō′kō′ nôr′, nōr′). See **Qinghai Hu.**

Ko·la Peninsula (kō′lə). A peninsula of northwest Russia projecting eastward from Scandinavia between the White Sea and the Barents Sea.

Kol·ding (kôl′dĭng). A city of south-central Denmark on the eastern coast of Jutland. Founded in the tenth century, it is a port and tourist center. ⊛ Pop. 56,519.

Kol·ha·pur (kō′lə-po͞or′). A city of southwest

India south-southeast of Bombay. It was formerly the center of an important Deccan state. ◦ Pop. 406,370.

Kol·mar (kōl′mär, kôl-mär′). See **Colmar.**

Köln (kœln). See **Cologne.**

Kol·we·zi (kōl-wĕz′ē). A city of southeast Zaire near the Zambia border. It is a center for copper and cobalt mining. ◦ Pop. 416,122.

Ko·ly·ma (kə-lē′mə, kə-lē-mä′). A river of northeast Russia rising in the Kolyma Mountains and flowing about 2,148 km (1,335 mi) generally north and northeast to the East Siberian Sea. Its upper course crosses rich gold fields.

Kolyma Mountains. A range of northeast Russia extending about 1,126 km (700 mi) north and south to the east of the Kolyma River and roughly parallel to the coast of Siberia.

Ko·man·dor·ski Islands (kŏm′ən-dôr′skē) also **Ko·man·dor·ski·ye Islands** (-skē-yě). An island group of northeast Russia in the Bering Sea east of the Kamchatka Peninsula. Fishing, hunting, and whaling are the main occupations of the islanders.

Ko·ma·ti (kə-mä′tē). A river flowing about 805 km (500 mi) through northeast South Africa, northern Swaziland, and southern Mozambique to an inlet of the Indian Ocean.

Kom·so·molsk (kŏm′sə-môlsk′). A city of southeast Russia north of Vladivostok. It was laid out and settled in 1932 by members of Komsomol, the Communist youth organization. ◦ Pop. 314,110.

Kon·go (kŏng′gō). **1.** *pl.* **Kongo** or **-gos.** A member of a people living in west-central Africa along the lower Congo River. **2.** A Bantu language of the Kongo used as a lingua franca in southern Congo, western Zaire, and northern Angola. In this sense, also called *Kikongo.*

Kon·ia (kôn-yä′). See **Konya.**

Kö·nigs·berg (kā′nĭgz-bûrg′, kœ′nĭкнs-běrk′). See **Kaliningrad.**

Kon·stanz (kôn′stänts′) also **Con·stance** (kŏn′-stəns). A city of southwest Germany on the Lake of Constance south of Stuttgart. Thought to have been founded c. A.D. 300, it is a tourist center with varied industries. ◦ Pop. 68,605.

Kon·ya also **Kon·ia** (kôn-yä′). A city of southwest-central Turkey south of Ankara. Built on the site of an ancient Phrygian city, Konya was a powerful Seljuk sultanate from the 11th to the 13th century. ◦ Pop. 576,000.

Koo·te·nay River also **Koo·te·nai River** (kōōt′-n-ā′). A river, about 655 km (407 mi) long, flowing from southeast British Columbia, Canada, south through northwest Montana, northwest through northern Idaho, and then north again into British Columbia, where it widens to form **Kootenay Lake** before joining the Columbia River.

Kor·do·fan·i·an (kô′də-făn′ē-ən). A small group of related languages spoken in Sudan and forming part of the Niger-Kordofanian language family.

Ko·re·a (kə-rē′ə, kô-, kō-). *abbr.* **Kor.** A peninsula and former country of eastern Asia between the Yellow Sea and the Sea of Japan. Site of an ancient civilization dating to the 12th century B.C., the peninsula was united as a kingdom in the 7th century A.D. and despite a Mongol invasion (13th century) remained unified until the Japanese occupation of 1910 to 1945. After World War II the Soviet- and U.S.-occupied territories formed separate republics, and a Soviet-backed invasion of the south led to the Korean War (1950–1953). The peninsula is now divided between North Korea and South Korea.

Korea Bay. An inlet of the Yellow Sea between northeast China and western North Korea.

Ko·re·an (kə-rē′ən, kô-, kō-). *abbr.* **Kor. 1.** A native or inhabitant of Korea. **2.** The language of the Koreans, possibly in the Altaic family. **3.** Of or relating to Korea or its people, language, or culture.

Korea Strait. A channel between southeast South Korea and southwest Japan. It connects the East China Sea with the Sea of Japan.

Kó·rin·thos (kô′rĭn-thôs′). See **Corinth.**

Ko·ri·ya·ma (kôr′ē-ä′mə, -yä′mä). A city of north-central Honshu, Japan, north of Tokyo. It is a major commercial and communications center. ◦ Pop. 322,255.

Ko·ror (kôr′ôr). The capital of Palau on the island of Koror. From 1921 to 1945 it served as the administrative capital for all the Pacific islands under Japanese mandate. ◦ Pop. 10,500.

Kort·rijk (kôrt′rĭk′) also **Cour·trai** (kōōr-trā′, kōōr-). A city of western Belgium west of Brussels. It was the most important cloth-manufacturing town of medieval Flanders and is still a textile center. ◦ Pop. 76,081.

Kos also **Cos** (kŏs, kôs). An island of southeast Greece in the northern Dodecanese Islands at the entrance to the **Gulf of Kos,** an inlet of the Aegean Sea on the southwest coast of Turkey. Hippocrates, the Greek physician known as "the Father of Medicine," founded a medical school on the island in the fifth century B.C. Kos became part of modern Greece in 1947.

Kos·ci·us·ko (kŏs′ē-ŭs′kō, kŏs′kē-), **Mount.** The highest mountain of Australia, in the southeast part of the country in the Australian Alps. It rises to 2,231.4 m (7,316 ft).

Ko·shi·ga·ya (kō-shē′gä-yä′, kō′shē-gä′yä). A city of east-central Honshu, Japan, a mainly residential suburb of Tokyo. ◦ Pop. 294,966.

Ko·ši·ce (kô′shĭ-tsě). A city of eastern Slovakia northeast of Budapest, Hungary. Chartered in

1241, it was an important trade center during the Middle Ages. ◉ Pop. 236,984.

Ko·so·vo (kô′sə-vō′). A province of southern Yugoslavia in the Serbian republic. Settled by Slavs in the seventh century, the area was under Turkish rule from 1389 to 1913 and became part of Yugoslavia after World War I. An autonomous region within Serbia after World War II, Kosovo was stripped of its autonomy in 1990 by Serbia, which imposed direct rule. Kosovo's Albanian majority reacted by pressing for complete independence, electing a shadow government (1992), and boycotting Serbian elections (1992).

Kos·tro·ma (kŏs′trə-mä′). A city of northwest Russia on the Volga River northeast of Moscow. Founded in 1152, it was annexed by Moscow in 1364. ◉ Pop. 281,497.

Ko·ta (kō′tə). A city of northwest India southsouthwest of Delhi. Enclosed by a massive wall, it is an agricultural market and has many fine temples. ◉ Pop. 537,371.

Kott·bus (kŏt′bəs, kôt′bŏŏs′). See **Cottbus**.

Kot·ze·bue Sound (kŏt′sə-byŏŏ′). An inlet of the Chukchi Sea in northwest Alaska north of Seward Peninsula.

Kow·loon (kou′lŏŏn′). A city of Hong Kong on the southeast coast of China on **Kowloon Peninsula** opposite Hong Kong Island. The city was ceded to the British in 1860. ◉ Pop. 799,123.

Koy·u·kuk (kī′ə-kŭk′). A river, about 805 km (500 mi) long, of northern Alaska flowing generally southwest from the Brooks Range to the Yukon River.

Ko·zhi·kode (kō′zhĭ-kōd′). See **Calicut**.

Kra (krä), **Isthmus of**. A strip of land, about 64 km (40 mi) wide at its narrowest point, linking the Malay Peninsula with the Asian mainland.

Kra·ji·na (krī′ē-nə). A region of southern Croatia bordering on western Bosnia and Herzegovina. Inhabited primarily by ethnic Serbs since the 15th century, the region opposed Croatia's secession from the former Yugoslavia and set up (1990) an autonomous Serbian state. It was retaken by Croatia in 1995, resulting in the mass exodus of thousands of Serbs.

Kra·ka·tau (krăk′ə-tou′, krä′kə-) or **Kra·ka·to·a** (-tō′ə). A volcanic island of Indonesia between Sumatra and Java. A violent explosion in August 1883 blew the island apart and caused a tidal wave that killed more than 36,000 people.

Kra·ków (krăk′ou, krä′kou, -kŏŏf). See **Cracow**.

Kra·ma·torsk (krä′mə-tôrsk′, krə-). A city of eastern Ukraine in the Donets Basin southsoutheast of Kharkov. It is an iron and steel center. ◉ Pop. 202,600.

Kras·no·dar (krăs′nə-där′, krə-snə-där′). A

city of southwest Russia in the northern Caucasus south of Rostov. Founded by Cossacks on orders from Catherine the Great in 1794, it is now an industrial center. ◉ Pop. 635,856.

Kras·no·yarsk (krăs′nə-yärsk′, krə-snə-). A city of south-central Russia on the upper Yenisey River east of Novosibirsk. It was founded as a Cossack fortress in 1628. ◉ Pop. 916,525.

Kre·feld (krā′fĕld′, -fĕlt′). A city of westcentral Germany on the Rhine River northnorthwest of Cologne. Chartered in 1373, it has long been important as a textile center. ◉ Pop. 249,565.

Kre·men·chug (krĕm′ən-chŏŏk′, -chŏŏg′, kryĭ′-mĭn-chŏŏk′). A city of east-central Ukraine on the Dnieper River southeast of Kiev. It was founded as a fortress in 1571. ◉ Pop. 244,500.

Krish·na (krĭsh′nə). See **Kistna**.

Kris·tian·sand (krĭs′chən-sănd′, krĭs′tyän-sän′). A city of extreme southern Norway on the Skagerrak southwest of Oslo. Founded in 1641, it is a commercial and passenger port. ◉ Pop. 61,834.

Kri·voi Rog or **Kri·voy Rog** (krĭ-voi′ rōg′, rôk′). A city of south-central Ukraine northeast of Odessa. Located in a rich iron-producing region, it is highly industrialized. ◉ Pop. 729,400.

Krung Thep (grŏŏng tĕp′). See **Bangkok**.

Kua·la Lum·pur (kwä′lə lŏŏm-pŏŏr′). The capital and largest city of Malaysia, on the southwest Malay Peninsula northwest of Singapore. Founded by tin miners in 1857, it is the commercial and industrial center of the country. ◉ Pop. 1,145,075.

Ku·ban (kŏŏ-băn′, -bän′). A river of southwest Russia flowing about 917 km (570 mi) north and west to the Sea of Azov.

Ku·ban·go (kŏŏ-băng′gō). See **Okavango**.

Ku·fic (kŏŏ′fĭk, kyŏŏ′-). Relating to or being an angular form of the Arabic alphabet used in making fine copies of the Koran.

Kui·by·shev (kwē′bə-shĕf′, -shĕv′, kŏŏ′ē-bə-shĭf′). See **Samara**.

Ku·ma·mo·to (kŏŏ′mə-mō′tō). A city of western Kyushu, Japan, east of Nagasaki. It was an important castle town during the feudal period. ◉ Pop. 639,699.

Ku·ma·si (kŏŏ-mä′sē). A city of south-central Ghana northwest of Accra. Founded c. 1700, it is a commercial and transportation center in a cocoa-producing region. ◉ Pop. 348,880.

Ku·ne·ne (kŏŏ-nä′nə). See **Cunene**.

Kun·lun (kŏŏn′lŏŏn′). A mountain system of western China extending from the Karakoram Range eastward along the northern edge of the Xizang (Tibet) plateau. Its highest point is 7,729 m (25,341 ft).

Kun·ming (kŏŏn′mĭng′). A city of southern

China southwest of Chongqing. The Chinese terminus of the Burma Road during World War II, Kunming is the capital of Yunnan province. ⊛ Pop. 1,611,969.

Kuo·pio (kwô′py-ô′). A city of south-central Finland north-northeast of Helsinki. Chartered in 1782, it is a winter sports center in a lumbering area. ⊛ Pop. 77,371.

Kuo·yu (kwô′yōō′). Variant of **Guoyu.**

Ku·ra (kōō-rä′). A river of northeast Turkey and southern Azerbaijan flowing about 1,514 km (941 mi) generally northeast and southeast to the Caspian Sea south of Baku.

Ku·ra·shi·ki (kōō-rä′shē-kē). A city of western Honshu, Japan, an industrial suburb of Okayama on the Inland Sea. ⊛ Pop. 418,450.

Kurd (kûrd, kōōrd). A member of a pastoral and agricultural people inhabiting the transnational region of Kurdistan.

Kurd·ish (kûr′dĭsh, kōōr′-). **1.** Of or relating to the Kurds or their language or culture. **2.** The Iranian language of the Kurds.

Kurd·i·stan (kûr′dĭ-stăn′, kōōr′dĭ-stän′). An extensive plateau region of southwest Asia. The area was conquered by Arabs in the 7th century, at which time the Kurds were converted to Islam. Since the dissolution of the Ottoman Empire after World War I, it has been divided among southeast Turkey, northeast Iraq, and northwest Iran, with smaller sections in Syria and Armenia. Numerous uprisings in various parts of the transnational region in the 20th century, including a brief rebellion in northern Iraq following the Persian Gulf War (1991), have been unsuccessful in gaining either autonomy or independence for the Kurdish population.

Ku·re (kōō′rě′). A city of southwest Honshu, Japan, on an arm of the Inland Sea southeast of Hiroshima. It is a naval base and major port. ⊛ Pop. 211,616.

kur·gan (kōōr-gän′, -gän′). **1.** A type of tumulus or barrow characteristic of a culture located on the steppes of southern Russia about 5000 B.C. and later spreading to the Danube, northern Europe, and northern Iran from around 3500 B.C. **2. Kurgan. a.** The culture that produced these tumuli or barrows. **b.** A member of the people or peoples sharing this culture. The earliest Kurgans are considered by some to be speakers of Proto-Indo-European. — **Kur·gan′** adj.

Kur·gan (kōōr-gän′). A city of western Russia southeast of Yekaterinburg. Founded in the 17th century, it is a trade center in a rich agricultural area. ⊛ Pop. 360,205.

Ku·ril Islands also **Ku·rile Islands** (kōōr′ĭl, kōō-rēl′). An island chain of extreme eastern Russia extending about 1,207 km (750 mi) in the Pacific Ocean between Kamchatka Peninsula and northern Hokkaido, Japan. The volcanic, largely uninhabited islands were held by Japan from 1875 to 1945. — **Ku·ril′i·an** adj. & n.

Kur·land (kōōr′lənd). See **Courland.**

Kur·nool (kər-nōōl′). A city of south-central India northwest of Madras. A market town, Kurnool was captured by Muslims in 1565 and ceded to the British in 1800. ⊛ Pop. 236,800.

Ku·ro·shi·o Current (kōō-rō′shē-ō′). See **Japan Current.**

Kursk (kōōrsk). A city of western Russia southwest of Moscow. First mentioned in 1095, it was destroyed by the Mongols in 1240 and rebuilt as a fortress in 1586. ⊛ Pop. 433,991.

Ku·ru·me (kōō-rōō′mě). A city of northwest Kyushu, Japan, northeast of Nagasaki. Textiles, especially a blue-figured cotton fabric, are important to its economy. ⊛ Pop. 232,846.

Kush (kŭsh, kōōsh). See **Cush.**

Ku·shi·ro (kōōsh′ə-rō′, kōō-shē′rô). A city of southeast Hokkaido, Japan, bordering on the Pacific Ocean. It is the island's only ice-free trading port. ⊛ Pop. 202,297.

Kus·ko·kwim (kŭs′kə-kwĭm′). A river of southwest Alaska flowing about 965 km (600 mi) southwest to **Kuskokwim Bay,** an inlet of the Bering Sea.

Ku·ta·i·si (kōō-tī′sē, kōō′tə-yē′syĭ). A city of western Georgia west-northwest of Tbilisi. The capital of ancient Colchis in the eighth century, it was taken by the Russians after 1773. ⊛ Pop. 236,000.

Kutch (kŭch). See **Rann of Kutch.**

Kutch, Gulf of. An inlet of the Arabian Sea in western India adjoining the Rann of Kutch.

Ku·te·nai (kōōt′n-ā′, -n-ē′). **1.** pl. **Kutenai** or **-nais.** A member of a Native American people inhabiting parts of southeast British Columbia, northeast Washington, and northern Idaho. **2.** The language of the Kutenais.

Ku·wait (kōō-wāt′). **1.** A country of the northeast Arabian Peninsula at the head of the Persian Gulf. Settled by Arab tribes in the early 18th century, it became a British protectorate in 1897 and an independent kingdom in 1961. Iraq

invaded and occupied the country in August 1990, sparking the Persian Gulf War (January–February 1991), which ended with Iraqi troops being driven out by a coalition of Arab and Western forces. With its major oil reserves, discovered in 1938, it has one of the highest per capita incomes in the world. The city of Kuwait is its capital. ⦾Pop. 1,620,000. **2.** also **Kuwait City.** The capital of Kuwait, in the east-central part of the country on the Persian Gulf. It was heavily damaged during the Persian Gulf War. ⦾Pop. 151,060. **— Ku·wait'i** (-wā'tē) *adj. & n.*

Kuy·by·shev (kwē'bə-shĕf', -shĕv', kōō'ē-bə-shĭf). See **Samara.**

Kuz·netsk Basin (kōōz-nĕtsk', -nyĕtsk'). A coal-producing region of west-central Russia extending from Tomsk southward to Novokuznetsk. The area's mineral resources were first exploited in the mid-19th century.

Kwa (kwä). Any of several West African languages belonging to the South Central Niger-Congo language family, including Efik, Ewe, Ibibio, Ibo, and Yoruba. **— Kwa** *adj.*

Kwa·ja·lein (kwä'jə-lən, -lān'). An atoll in the Marshall Islands of the western Pacific Ocean. It was used as a Japanese air and naval base during World War II.

Kwa·ki·u·tl (kwä'kē-ōōt'l). **1.** *pl.* **Kwakiutl** or **-tls.** A member of a Native American people inhabiting parts of coastal British Columbia and northern Vancouver Island. **2.** The Wakashan language of the Kwakiutls.

Kwan·do (kwän'dō). See **Cuando.**

Kwang·chow (kwäng'chō'). See **Guangzhou.**

Kwang·ju (kwäng'jōō', gwäng'-). A city of southwest South Korea south-southeast of Seoul. It is an agricultural market and a commercial center. ⦾Pop. 1,214,347.

Kwang·si Chuang (kwäng'sē' chwäng'). See **Guangxi Zhuangzu.**

Kwang·tung (kwäng'tōong', gwäng'dōong'). See **Guangdong.**

Kwan·tung (kwän'tōong', gwän'dōong'). A former coastal territory of northeast China in southern Manchuria. It was leased to Russia in 1898 and controlled by Japan from 1905 to 1945.

Kwan·za (kwän'zə). See **Cuanza.**

Kwei·chow (kwā'chō'). See **Guizhou.**

Kwei·lin (kwā'lĭn'). See **Guilin.**

Kwei·yang (kwā'yäng'). See **Guiyang.**

Ky·o·ga (kē-ō'gə), **Lake.** See Lake **Kioga.**

Kyo·to (kē-ō'tō, kyō'-). A city of west-central Honshu, Japan, north-northeast of Osaka. Founded in the eighth century, it has long been a cultural, artistic, and religious center. Kyoto was Japan's capital from 794 until 1869, although its political importance declined after the rise (1192) of the feudal warlords known as shoguns. ⦾Pop. 1,452,240.

Kyr·gyz also **Kir·ghiz** or **Kir·giz** (kîr-gēz'). **1.** *pl.* **Kyrgyz** or **-gyz·es** also **Kirghiz** or **-ghiz·es** or **Kirgiz** or **-giz·es.** A member of a traditionally nomadic Mongolian people living principally in Kyrgyzstan. **2.** The Turkic language of the Kyrgyz.

Kyr·gyz·stan (kîr'gē-stän', kîr' gē-stän', -gyē-). Formerly **Kir·ghiz Soviet Socialist Republic** or **Kir·giz Soviet Socialist Republic** (kîr'gēz', kîr-gēz', kîr-gyēs') also **Kir·ghi·zia** or **Kir·gi·zia** (-gē'zhə, -zhē-ə, -gyē'zĭ-yə). A country of west-central Asia bordering on southeast Kazakstan and northwest China. The region was inhabited probably before the 13th century by the Kyrgyz and was annexed by Russia in 1864. It became an autonomous republic of the Soviet Union in 1926 and a constituent republic in 1936. Kyrgyzstan declared its independence in 1991 following the collapse of the Soviet Union. Bishkek is the capital and the largest city. ⦾Pop. 4,596,000.

Kyu·shu (kē-ōō'shōō, kyōō'-). The southernmost of the major islands of Japan, in the southwest on the East China Sea and the Pacific Ocean.

Ky·zyl-Kum (kĭ-zĭl'kōom'). A desert of north-central Uzbekistan and south-central Kazakstan southeast of the Aral Sea between the Amu Darya and the Syr Darya.

L

La Baie (lä bā'). A city of south-central Quebec, Canada, on the Saguenay River southeast of Chicoutimi. ⦾Pop. 20,935.

La·bé (lä-bā'). A city of west-central Guinea northeast of Conakry. It is a trade center for an agricultural region. ⦾Pop. 253,000.

Lab·ra·dor (lăb'rə-dôr'). *abbr.* **Lab.** The mainland territory of Newfoundland, Canada, on the northeast portion of the Labrador Peninsula. Its coastline was visited by Norse seamen as early as the tenth century. The area later became a possession of the Hudson's Bay Company and was claimed by Quebec until 1927, when it was

awarded to Newfoundland. — **Lab′ra·dor′e·an,**
Lab′ra·dor′i·an *adj. & n.*

Labrador Current. A cold ocean current flow-ing southward from Baffin Bay along the coast of Labrador and turning east after intersecting with the Gulf Stream.

Labrador Peninsula. A peninsula of eastern Canada between Hudson Bay and the Atlantic Ocean. It is divided between Quebec and New-foundland provinces.

Labrador Sea. An arm of the northern Atlantic Ocean between eastern Canada and southwest Greenland.

La·bu·an (lə-bo͞o′ən, lä′bo͞o-än′). An island of Malaysia off the northeast coast of Borneo. At one time a British crown colony (after 1848), it became part of Malaysia in 1963.

La Ca·na·da-Flint·ridge (lä′ kən-yä′də-flïnt′-rïj′). An unincorporated community of south-west California northwest of Pasadena. It is pri-marily residential. ⊛ Pop. 19,378.

Lac·ca·dive Islands (lăk′ə-dīv′, lä′kə-dēv′). A group of islands and coral reefs in the Arabian Sea off the southwest coast of India. The islands are now part of the region of Lakshadweep.

Lac·e·dae·mon (lăs′ĭ-dē′mən). See **Sparta.** — **Lac′e·dae·mo′ni·an** (-də-mō′nē-ən) *adj. & n.*

La·chine (lə-shēn′, lä-). A city of southern Que-bec, Canada, on Montreal Island and the St. Lawrence River. It was first settled as an estate by the French explorer Sieur La Salle in 1668 and named for his futile dream of finding a west-ward passage to China. ⊛ Pop. 37,521.

La·chish (lā′kĭsh). An ancient city of southern Palestine southwest of Jerusalem. It was proba-bly inhabited as early as 3200 B.C.

Lach·lan (lăk′lən). A river, about 1,483 km (922 mi) long, of southeast Australia flowing north-west then southwest to the Murrumbidgee River.

Lack·a·wan·na (lăk′ə-wŏn′ə). A city of west-ern New York on Lake Erie south of Buffalo. It is an industrial center. ⊛ Pop. 20,585.

La·co·ni·a (lə-kō′nē-ə). **1.** An ancient region of southern Greece in the southeast Peloponne-sus. It was dominated by Sparta until the rise of the second Achaean League in the third and second centuries B.C. **2.** A city of central New Hampshire north of Concord. Settled in 1761, it is a summer and winter resort. ⊛ Pop. 15,743.

La Co·ru·ña (lä′ kə-ro͞on′yə, kô-ro͞o′nyä). A city of northwest Spain on the Atlantic Ocean west of Oviedo. Perhaps predating Roman times, it was the point of departure for the Spanish Armada (1588). ⊛ Pop. 248,293.

La Crosse (lə krôs′, krŏs′). A city of western

Wisconsin on the Mississippi River northwest of Madison. It was founded on the site of a French fur-trading post established in the late 18th cen-tury. ⊛ Pop. 51,003.

la·cus·trine (lə-kŭs′trĭn). **1.** Of or relating to lakes. **2.** Living or growing in or along the edges of lakes.

La·din (lə-dēn′). **1.** See **Romansch. 2.** A per-son who is a native speaker of Ladin.

La·di·no (lə-dē′nō). **1.** A Romance language with elements borrowed from Hebrew that is spoken by Sephardic Jews especially in the Bal-kans. Also called *Judeo-Spanish.* **2.** also **ladino.** *pl.* **-nos.** In Central America, a Spanish-speaking or acculturated Indian; a mestizo.

La·do·ga (lä′də-gə), **Lake.** A lake of northwest Russia northeast of St. Petersburg. It is the larg-est lake in Europe.

La·fa·yette (läf′ē-ĕt′, lä′fē-, -fä-). **1.** A city of western California, a residential suburb in the San Francisco Bay area. ⊛ Pop. 23,501. **2.** A city of west-central Indiana on the Wabash River northwest of Indianapolis. It is the seat of Pur-due University (founded 1869). ⊛ Pop. 43,764. **3.** A city of south-central Louisiana west-south-west of Baton Rouge. Settled by Acadians, it is a commercial and shipping center. ⊛ Pop. 94,440.

La·gash (lā′găsh). An ancient city of Sumer in southern Mesopotamia. It flourished c. 2400 B.C., and after the fall of Akkad (2180), when the rest of Mesopotamia was in disorder, it en-joyed a cultural flowering noted for its sculpture and literature.

la·goon (lə-go͞on′). A shallow body of water, es-pecially one separated from a sea by sandbars or coral reefs.

La·gos (lā′gŏs′, lä′gōs). The largest city of Nigeria, in the southwest part of the country on the Gulf of Guinea. An old Yoruba town, it served as the capital of Nigeria from indepen-dence in 1960 until 1991, when the capital was officially moved to Abuja. Lagos remains the economic and commercial center of the country. ⊛ Pop. 1,404,000.

La Grange (lə grānj′). **1.** A city of western Georgia north of Columbus. Incorporated in 1828, it is an industrial center. ⊛ Pop. 25,597. **2.** A village of northeast Illinois, a residential suburb of Chicago. ⊛ Pop. 15,362.

La·gu·na Beach (lə-go͞o′nə). A city of south-ern California southeast of Long Beach. It is a seaside resort with a noted art colony. ⊛ Pop. 23,170.

Laguna Hills. A city of southern California southeast of Santa Ana. ⊛ Pop. 46,731.

La Ha·bra (lə hä′brə). A city of southern Cali-fornia, a processing and manufacturing suburb of Los Angeles. ⊛ Pop. 51,266.

La Hague (lə hāg′), **Cape.** A promontory of northwest France at the northwest tip of the Cotentin Peninsula on the English Channel.

la·har (lä′här′). **1.** A landslide or mudflow of volcanic fragments on the flanks of a volcano. **2.** The deposit produced by such a landslide.

La·hon·tan (lə-hŏn′tən), **Lake.** An extinct lake with surviving remnants in western Nevada and northeast California. It was formed by heavy precipitation caused by Pleistocene glaciers but largely disappeared after the end of the epoch, about 11,000 years ago.

La·hore (lə-hôr′, -hōr′). A city of northeast Pakistan near the Indian border southeast of Rawalpindi. The city reached the height of its grandeur as a Mogul capital in the 16th century and retains many splendid architectural examples from that period. ◉ Pop. 2,952,689.

Lah·ti (lä′tē, läkH′-). A city of southern Finland north-northeast of Helsinki. It is a lake port with woodworking industries. ◉ Pop. 94,347.

La Jol·la (lə hoi′ə). An unincorporated resort district of San Diego, California, on the Pacific Ocean. Scripps Institute of Oceanography is located in the area.

lake (lāk). *abbr.* **l., L. 1.** A large inland body of fresh water or salt water. **2.** A scenic pond, as in a park.

Lake or **Lake of** (lāk) or **Loch** (lŏk, lôкH). For the names of actual lakes, see the specific element of the name; for example, **Erie, Lake; Lucerne, Lake of; Lomond, Loch.**

lake·bed (lāk′bĕd′). The floor of a lake.

Lake Charles (chärlz). A city of southwest Louisiana east of Beaumont, Texas. It is a deepwater port and the center of a petrochemical industry. ◉ Pop. 70,580.

Lake Dis·trict (lāk′ dĭs′trĭkt). A scenic area of northwest England including the Cumbrian Mountains and some 15 lakes. It is a popular tourist attraction for its associations with the 19th-century Lake Poets, notably William Wordsworth, Samuel Coleridge, and Robert Southey.

Lake For·est (fôr′ĭst, fŏr′-). A city of northeast Illinois, a residential suburb of Chicago on Lake Michigan. ◉ Pop. 17,836.

Lake Hav·a·su City (hăv′ə-sōō′). A city of west-central Arizona on the California border. London Bridge, transported from England, is a popular tourist attraction. ◉ Pop. 24,363.

Lake·hurst (lāk′hûrst). A borough of east-central New Jersey southeast of Trenton. The dirigible *Hindenburg* was destroyed by fire at the naval air station here (May 6, 1937). ◉ Pop. 3,078.

Lake Jackson. A city of southeast Texas southwest of Galveston. It is mainly residential. ◉ Pop. 22,776.

Lake·land (lāk′lənd). A city of central Florida east-northeast of Tampa. It is a winter resort and processing center in a citrus-growing region. ◉ Pop. 70,576.

Lake Oswego. A city of northwest Oregon, a residential suburb of Portland. ◉ Pop. 30,576.

Lake Placid. A village of northeast New York in the Adirondack Mountains southwest of Plattsburg. A popular year-round resort, it was the site of the Winter Olympics in 1932 and 1980. ◉ Pop. 2,485.

Lake·side (lāk′sīd′). **1.** A community of southern California, a residential and resort suburb of San Diego. ◉ Pop. 23,921. **2.** A community of east-central Virginia, a suburb of Richmond. ◉ Pop. 12,081.

Lake Suc·cess (sək-sĕs′). An unincorporated village of southeast New York on northwest Long Island northwest of Mineola. It was the temporary headquarters of the United Nations from 1946 to 1951.

Lake·wood (lāk′wŏŏd′). **1.** A city of southern California, a residential and industrial suburb of Long Beach. ◉ Pop. 73,557. **2.** A city of north-central Colorado, a residential suburb of Denver. ◉ Pop. 126,481. **3.** An unincorporated township of east-central New Jersey southwest of Asbury Park. It is a health resort in a pine forest and lake region. ◉ Pop. 26,095. **4.** A city of northeast Ohio, a residential and industrial suburb of Cleveland on Lake Erie. ◉ Pop. 59,718. **5.** also **Lakewood Center.** A community of west-central Washington, a residential suburb of Tacoma. ◉ Pop. 58,412.

Lake Worth (wûrth). A city of southeast Florida south of West Palm Beach. It is a resort center. ◉ Pop. 28,564.

La·ko·ta (lə-kō′tə). *pl.* **Lakota** or **-tas.** See **Teton.**

Lak·shad·weep (lək-shäd′wēp′, lŭk′shə-dwēp′). A region of southwest India comprising the Laccadive, Minicoy, and Amindivi islands.

La Lí·ne·a (lä lē′nē-ə). A city of southwest Spain on the Bay of Gibraltar southeast of Cadíz. There is a military garrison in the city. ◉ Pop. 58,945.

Lal·lan (lăl′ən) also **Lal·lans** (-ənz). *Scots.* **1.** The Lowlands of Scotland. **2.** Scots as spoken in southern and eastern Scotland. —**Lal′lan** *adj.*

La Lou·vière (lä lōō-vyĕr′). A city of southwest Belgium south of Brussels. It is a manufacturing commune. ◉ Pop. 76,534.

La Man·cha (lä män′chə). A region of south-central Spain. The high, mostly barren plateau is famous as the setting for Cervantes's *Don Quixote* (1605–1615).

La Marque (lə märk′). A city of southeast

Texas southeast of Houston. It is primarily residential. ⊛ Pop. 14,120.

La Me·sa (lə mā′sə). A city of southern California, a residential suburb of San Diego. ⊛ Pop. 52,931.

La·mi·a (lə-mē′ə, lä-mē′ä). A city of east-central Greece northwest of Athens. Founded c. fifth century B.C., it was the site of the Lamian War (323–322 B.C.) between the confederated Greeks and the Macedonian general Antipater, who was besieged in the city for several months before his ultimate victory. ⊛ Pop. 41,667. —**La·mi′an** *adj. & n.*

La Mi·ra·da (lä′ mə-rä′də). A city of southern California southeast of Los Angeles. It is primarily residential. ⊛ Pop. 40,452.

La·nai (lə-nī′). An island of central Hawaii west of Maui. It developed as a pineapple-growing area after 1922.

Lan·ca·shire (lăng′kə-shîr′, -shər). A historical region of northwest England on the Irish Sea. It was part of the kingdom of Northumbria in Anglo-Saxon times and became a county palatine in 1351. Long noted for its textiles, the area grew rapidly after the Industrial Revolution in the late 18th century.

Lan·cas·ter (lăng′kə-stər, -kăs′tər, lăn′-). **1.** A municipal borough of northwest England north of Liverpool. Chartered in 1193, it was built on the site of a Roman frontier station. ⊛ Pop. 133,610. **2.** An unincorporated community of southern California northeast of Los Angeles. It is a trade center for an irrigated farming area. ⊛ Pop. 97,291. **3.** A city of south-central Ohio southeast of Columbus. The birthplace of Union general William Tecumseh Sherman (1820–1891) has been preserved. ⊛ Pop. 34,507. **4.** A city of southeast Pennsylvania west of Philadelphia. A trade center in a rich farming region, it was settled by German Mennonites c. 1709 and was the meeting place of the Continental Congress in 1777. ⊛ Pop. 55,551.

Lancaster Sound. An arm of Baffin Bay between northern Baffin Island and southern Devon Island in Northwest Territories, Canada.

Lan·chow (lăn′jō′). See **Lanzhou.**

land (lănd). *abbr.* **l. 1.** The solid ground of the earth. **2. a.** Ground or soil. **b.** A topographically or functionally distinct tract. **3. a.** A nation; a country. **b.** The people of a nation, district, or region. **c. lands.** Territorial possessions or property. **4.** Public or private landed property; real estate. **5.** An area or a realm. **6.** *Law.* **a.** A tract that may be owned, together with everything growing or constructed on it. **b.** A landed estate.

land bridge. A neck of land that connects two landmasses; an isthmus.

land·form (lănd′fôrm′). One of the features that make up the earth's surface, such as a plain, mountain, or valley.

land·mass (lănd′măs′). A large unbroken area of land.

Land's End or **Lands End** (lăndz′ ĕnd′). A peninsula of southwest England on the coast of Cornwall. It is the westernmost point of the country.

Lands·hut (länts′hōōt′). A city of southeast Germany on the Isar River northeast of Munich. It was founded in 1204 and suffered heavy damage during the Thirty Years' War (1618–1648). ⊛ Pop. 56,230.

Lands·mål (länts′môl′). See **New Norwegian.**

Lang·ley (lăng′lē). A city of southern British Columbia, Canada, near the Washington border east-southeast of Vancouver. It is in a diversified farming area. ⊛ Pop. 15,124.

Langley, Mount. A peak, 4,227.9 m (14,026 ft) high, in the Sierra Nevada range of southern California.

Lan·go·bard (lăng′gə-bärd′). See **Lombard¹** (sense 1). —**Lan′go·bar′dic** *adj.*

Lan·gue·doc (läng-dôk′, läng-). A historical region and former province of south-central France on an arm of the Mediterranean Sea west of the Rhone River. Named after the Romance language of its inhabitants, it was conquered by the Franks in the eighth century and incorporated into the French royal domain in 1271.

langue d'oc (läng dôk′, läng). The Romance language spoken in and around Provence and Roussillon, surviving in Provençal.

langue d'o·ïl (doïl′, doï′, dô-ēl′). The Romance language of Gaul north of the Loire River, on which modern French in based.

Lans·dale (lănz′dāl′). A borough of southeast Pennsylvania north of Philadelphia. It has varied industries. ⊛ Pop. 16,362.

Lan·sing (lăn′sĭng). **1.** A village of northeast Illinois, a suburb of Chicago near the Indiana border. ⊛ Pop. 28,086. **2.** The capital of Michigan, in the south-central part of the state northwest of Detroit. It is an automobile-manufacturing center and became the state capital in 1847. ⊛ Pop. 127,321.

La·nús (lə-nōōs′, lä-). A city of eastern Argentina, an industrial suburb of Buenos Aires. ⊛ Pop. 466,755.

Lan·zhou also **Lan·chow** (lăn′jō′). A city of central China on the Huang He (Yellow River) north of Chengdu. A major oil-refining center, it is the capital of Gansu province. ⊛ Pop. 1,617,761.

Lao (lou). **1.** *pl.* **Lao** or **Laos.** A member of a Buddhist people inhabiting the area of the Mekong River in Laos and Thailand. **2.** The Tai language of the Lao. **3.** Of or relating to the Lao or their language or culture.

La·od·i·ce·a (lā-ŏd′ĭ-sē′ə, lā′ə-dĭ-). An ancient city of western Asia Minor in present-day western Turkey. Built by the Seleucids in the third century B.C., it was a prosperous Roman market town on the trade route from the East and an early center of Christianity.

La·os (lous, lā′ŏs′). A country of southeast Asia sharing major borders with Thailand to the west and Vietnam to the east. Originally part of the Khmer Empire, the region became a powerful Lao kingdom (14th–15th century) that later came under Siamese control before being incorporated into French Indochina in 1893. Laos gained independence from the French in 1953, but a Communist uprising in the north soon drew the country into a civil war that after 1965 was greatly influenced by the escalating war in neighboring Vietnam. A coalition government established after the 1973 cease-fire was taken over by the Communists in 1975, and ties with Vietnam were strengthened. Laos abandoned communist economic policies in the 1990's but retained tight party control over the government. Vientiane is the capital and the largest city. ☮ Pop. 4,742,000.

La·o·tian (lā-ō′shən, lou′shen). **1.** Of or relating to Laos or its people, language, or culture. **2.** Of or relating to the Lao people. **3.** A native or inhabitant of Laos. **4.** A Lao.

La Pal·ma¹ (lə päl′mə, lä päl′mä). An island of Spain in the northwest Canary Islands.

La Pal·ma² (lə päl′mə). A city of southern California, a suburb of Los Angeles. ☮ Pop. 15,663.

La Paz (lə päz′, lä päs′). The administrative capital and largest city of Bolivia, in the western part of the country near Lake Titicaca. Built on the site of an Inca village, it is the highest capital in the world, lying at an altitude of about 3,660 m (12,000 ft) above sea level. ☮ Pop. 784,976.

La Pé·rouse Strait (lä pā-rōōz′). A channel of the western Pacific Ocean between Sakhalin Island and northern Hokkaido, Japan, connecting the Sea of Okhotsk with the Sea of Japan.

La·place or **La Place** (lə-plās′). A village of southeast Louisiana on the Mississippi River west-northwest of New Orleans. It is a trade center in a truck farm and sugar cane area. ☮ Pop. 24,194.

Lap·land (lăp′lănd′, -lənd). A region of extreme northern Europe including northern Norway, Sweden, and Finland and the Kola Peninsula of northwest Russia. It is largely within the Arctic Circle. —**Lap′land·er** *n.*

La Pla·ta (lä plä′tä). A city of east-central Argentina southeast of Buenos Aires. Founded in 1882, it is an industrial center. ☮ Pop. 520,647.

La Pla·ta Peak (lə plä′tə). A mountain, 4,380.1 m (14,361 ft) high, in the Sawatch Range of the Rocky Mountains in central Colorado.

La Porte (lə pôrt′, pōrt′). **1.** A city of northwest Indiana west-southwest of South Bend. Settled in 1832, it is a manufacturing center. ☮ Pop. 21,507. **2.** A city of southeast Texas on Galveston Bay east of Houston. It is a popular summer resort. ☮ Pop. 27,910.

Lapp (lăp). **1.** A member of a people of nomadic herding tradition inhabiting Lapland. Also called *Sami.* **2.** Any of the Finnic languages of the Lapps. —**Lap′pish** (lăp′ĭsh) *adj.*

Lap·peen·ran·ta (lăp′ān-răn′tə, lä′pĕn-rän′-tä). A city of southeast Finland near the Russian border northeast of Helsinki. Chartered in 1649, it was an important border fortress after 1721. ☮ Pop. 53,966.

Lap·tev Sea (lăp′tĕf′, -tĕv′, läp′tyĭf). A section of the Arctic Ocean north of eastern Russia between the Taimyr Peninsula and the New Siberian Islands. It is icebound most of the year.

La Pu·en·te (lä′ pōō-ĕn′tē, pwĕn′tä). A city of southern California, a residential suburb of Los Angeles. ☮ Pop. 36,955.

L'A·qui·la (lăk′wə-lə, lä′kwē-lä) also **A·qui·la** (ăk′wə-lə, ä′kwē-lä). A city of central Italy northeast of Rome. It is a trade and industrial center. ☮ Pop. 63,465.

Lar·a·mie (lăr′ə-mē). A city of southeast Wyoming west-northwest of Cheyenne. Settled in 1868 with the coming of the railroad, it is the seat of the University of Wyoming (founded 1886). ☮ Pop. 26,687.

Laramie River. A river of northern Colorado and southeast Wyoming flowing about 348 km (216 mi) generally north and northeast to the North Platte River.

Larch River (lärch). A river, about 434 km (270 mi) long, of northern Quebec, Canada, flowing northeast to join the Caniapiscau River.

La·re·do (lə-rā′dō). A city of southern Texas on the Rio Grande south-southwest of San Antonio. Established by Spanish settlers in 1755, it is a major port of entry and a retail, tourist, and industrial center. ☮ Pop. 122,899.

Lar·go (lär′gō). A city of western Florida on the Gulf of Mexico northwest of St. Petersburg. It is a resort and processing center in a citrus-growing area. ◉ Pop. 65,674.

Lá·ri·sa (lä′rē-sä) or **La·ris·sa** (lə-rĭs′ə). A city of eastern Greece near the Aegean Sea. The chief city of ancient Thessaly, it was later part of the Byzantine Empire, Serbia, and Ottoman Turkey (until 1881). ◉ Pop. 102,048.

La Ro·chelle (lä′ rə-shĕl′, rô-). A city of western France on the Bay of Biscay southwest of Tours. It was a Huguenot stronghold in the 16th century. ◉ Pop. 75,840.

La Salle (lə săl′, lä). A city of southern Quebec, Canada, on Montreal Island and the St. Lawrence River. It is a residential suburb of Montreal. ◉ Pop. 76,299.

Las·caux (lă-skō′). A cave of southwest France in the Dordogne River valley. The cave, discovered in 1940 and now closed to the public, contains important Paleolithic paintings, primarily of animals.

Las Cru·ces (läs krōō′sĭs). A city of southern New Mexico on the Rio Grande north-northwest of El Paso, Texas. Irrigated farming and the nearby White Sands Missile Range are important to its economy. ◉ Pop. 62,126.

La Seyne-sur-Mer (lä sān′sûr-mĕr′, -sür-). A city of southeast France on the Mediterranean Sea southwest of Toulon. It is a shipbuilding center. ◉ Pop. 57,659.

Las Pal·mas (läs päl′mäs). The chief city of the Canary Islands of Spain, on the northeast coast of Grand Canary Island. It was founded in the late 15th century. ◉ Pop. 359,611.

La Spe·zia (lä spĕt′sē-ə, spĕ′tsyä). A city of northwest Italy east-southeast of Genoa on the **Gulf of La Spezia,** an arm of the Ligurian Sea. The city is a major seaport and year-round resort. ◉ Pop. 101,701.

Las·sen Peak (lăs′ən). A dormant volcano, about 3,188.2 m (10,453 ft) high, in the Cascade Range of northern California.

Las Ve·gas (läs vā′gəs). A city of southeast Nevada near the California and Arizona borders. It is a major tourist center known for its casinos. ◉ Pop. 258,295.

Late Greek (lāt). The Greek language as used from the fourth to the ninth century A.D.

Late Hebrew. The Hebrew language as used from the 12th to the 18th century.

Late Latin. The Latin language as used from the third to the seventh century A.D.

Lat·in (lăt′n). *abbr.* **Lat., L. 1. a.** The Indo-European language of the ancient Latins and Romans. Latin, the most important member of the Italic branch of Indo-European, is divided into several historical periods and social dialects and

was the most important cultural language of western Europe until the end of the 17th century. **b.** The Latin language and literature from the end of the third century B.C. to the end of the second century A.D. **2.** A member of a Latin people, especially a native or inhabitant of Latin America. **3.** A native or resident of ancient Latium. **4.** Of, relating to, or composed in Latin. **5. a.** Of or relating to ancient Rome, its people, or its culture. **b.** Of or relating to Latium, its people, or its culture. **6. a.** Of or relating to the languages that developed from Latin, such as Italian, French, Spanish, and Portuguese, or to the peoples that speak them. **b.** Of or relating to the peoples, countries, or cultures of Latin America.

La·ti·na (lə-tē′nə, lä-tē′nä). A city of west-central Italy southeast of Rome. It is a commercial and industrial center. ◉ Pop. 81,000.

Latin America. The countries of the Western Hemisphere south of the United States, especially those speaking Spanish, Portuguese, or French.

Latin American. 1. A native or inhabitant of Latin America. **2.** A person of Latin-American descent. —**Lat′in-A·mer′i·can** *adj.*

La·ti·no (lə-tē′nō, lă-). *pl.* **-nos. 1.** A Latin American. **2.** A person of Hispanic, especially Latin-American, descent.

Latin Quar·ter (kwôr′tər). A section of Paris on the southern bank of the Seine River. Centered around the Sorbonne, it has attracted students for many centuries.

lat·i·tude (lăt′ĭ-tōōd′, -tyōōd′). *abbr.* **lat. 1.** The angular distance north or south of the earth's equator, measured in degrees along a meridian, as on a map or globe. **2.** A region of the earth considered in relation to its distance from the equator. —**lat′i·tu′din·al** (-tōōd′n-əl, -tyōōd′-) *adj.* —**lat′i·tu′di·nal·ly** *adv.*

La·ti·um (lā′shē-əm, -shəm). An ancient country of west-central Italy bordering on the Tyrrhenian Sea. It was dominated by Rome after the third century B.C.

Lat·vi·a (lăt′vē-ə). Formerly **Lat·vi·an Soviet Socialist Republic** (-vē-ən). *abbr.* **Lat.** A country of north-central Europe on the Baltic Sea. The original inhabitants, the Letts, were conquered and Christianized in the 13th century by German knights, the Livonian Brothers of the Sword, who ruled the area until 1561, when it passed to Poland. Latvia came under Russian control in the 18th century and had become agriculturally and industrially prosperous by the end of the 19th century. It became independent after World War I but was annexed by and made a constituent republic of the U.S.S.R. in 1940. Occupied (1941–1944) by Germany during World War II, Latvia was retaken by the

U.S.S.R., from which it declared its independence in 1990. Riga is the capital. ⊛ Pop. 2,548,000.

Lat·vi·an (lăt′vē-ən). *abbr.* **Lat. 1.** Of or relating to Latvia or its people, language, or culture. **2.** A native or inhabitant of Latvia. **3.** The Baltic language of the Latvians. In this sense, also called *Lettish.*

Latvian Soviet Socialist Republic. See **Latvia.**

Lau·der·dale Lakes (lô′dər-dāl′). A city of southeast Florida, a residential suburb of Fort Lauderdale. ⊛ Pop. 27,341.

Lau·der·hill (lô′dər-hĭl′). A city of southeast Florida, a residential suburb of Fort Lauderdale. Population 49,708.

Laur·a·sia (lô-rā′zhə, -shə). The protocontinent of the Northern Hemisphere, a hypothetical landmass that according to the theory of plate tectonics broke up into North America, Europe, and Asia.

Lau·rel (lôr′əl, lŏr′-). A city of southeast Mississippi southwest of Meridian. Oil was discovered in the area in 1944. ⊛ Pop. 18,827.

Lau·ren·tian (lô-rĕn′shən). Of, relating to, or being in the vicinity of the St. Lawrence River.

Laurentian Mountains. A range of southern Quebec, Canada, north of the St. Lawrence and Ottawa rivers. Rising to 960.8 m (3,150 ft), the mountains are a year-round recreational area.

Laurentian Plateau or **Laurentian Highlands** also **Ca·na·di·an Shield** (kə-nā′dē-ən). A plateau region of eastern Canada extending from the Great Lakes and the St. Lawrence River northward to the Arctic Ocean. The highland formation also covers much of Greenland and forms the Adirondack Mountains in the United States.

Lau·sanne (lō-zăn′, -zän′). A city of western Switzerland on the northern shore of Lake Geneva. Originally a Celtic settlement, Lausanne became a center of Calvinism after the 1530's and was home to Voltaire, Edward Gibbon, and Jean Jacques Rousseau in the 18th century. ⊛ Pop. 117,303.

La·val (lə-văl′, lä-väl′). **1.** A city of southern Quebec, Canada, on an island opposite Montreal, of which it is a residential suburb. ⊛ Pop. 314,398. **2.** A town of northwest France east of Rennes. Founded in the 9th century, it has been noted for its linen products since the 14th century. ⊛ Pop. 50,360.

La Verne (lə vûrn′). A city of southern California east of Los Angeles. It is mainly residential. ⊛ Pop. 30,897.

Lawn·dale (lôn′dāl′). A city of southern California southwest of Los Angeles near the Pacific Ocean. It is mainly residential. ⊛ Pop. 27,331.

Law·rence (lôr′əns, lŏr′-). **1.** A city of central Indiana, a residential suburb of Indianapolis. ⊛ Pop. 26,763. **2.** A city of northeast Kansas on the Kansas River east-southeast of Topeka. It was founded in 1854 by the New England Emigrant Aid Society and was the scene of a proslavery raid (1856) that sparked retaliatory killings by the abolitionist John Brown. ⊛ Pop. 65,608. **3.** A city of northeast Massachusetts on the Merrimack River north-northeast of Lowell. Laid out as an industrial town in 1845, it soon became one of the world's greatest centers for woolen textiles. Many of the old mills have now been renovated. ⊛ Pop. 70,207.

Law·ton (lôt′n). A city of southwest Oklahoma southwest of Oklahoma City. It is a commercial and trade center. ⊛ Pop. 80,561.

Lay·san Island (lī′sän′). An island of Hawaii in the Leeward Islands northwest of Niihau.

Lay·ton (lāt′n). A city of northern Utah south of Ogden. It is a processing center in an irrigated farming region. ⊛ Pop. 41,784.

lea (lē, lā) also **ley** (lā, lē). A grassland; a meadow.

Leaf River (lēf). A river, about 290 km (180 mi) long, of southeast Mississippi flowing generally south to Hattiesburg.

League City (lēg). A city of southeast Texas southeast of Houston. The aeronautics industry is important to its economy. ⊛ Pop. 30,159.

League of Nations. A world organization established in 1920 to promote international cooperation and peace. It was first proposed in 1918 by President Woodrow Wilson, although the United States never joined the League. Essentially powerless, it was officially dissolved in 1946.

Leal·man (lēl′mən). A community of west-central Florida, a suburb of St. Petersburg. ⊛ Pop. 19,875.

Leam·ing·ton (lĕm′ĭng-tən). Officially **Royal Leamington Spa.** A municipal borough of central England northeast of Warwick. It is a health resort with mineral springs. ⊛ Pop. 42,953.

Leav·en·worth (lĕv′ən-wûrth′). A city of northeast Kansas on the Missouri River northwest of Kansas City. Settled in 1854 by pro-slavery partisans from Missouri, it is near Fort Leavenworth, the site of a federal penitentiary. ⊛ Pop. 38,495.

Leb·a·nese (lĕb'ə-nēz', -nēs'). *abbr.* **Leb. 1.** Of or relating to Lebanon, its people, or their culture. **2.** A native or inhabitant of Lebanon.

Leb·a·non (lĕb'ə-nən, -nŏn'). **1.** *abbr.* **Leb.** A country of southwest Asia on the Mediterranean Sea bordering on Syria to the north and west and Israel to the south. It was the site of ancient Phoenicia, which was gradually absorbed into the Persian Empire. Conquered by Alexander the Great in the 4th century B.C., the region later came under Roman control and was Christianized before the Arab conquest of the 7th century. It became part of the Ottoman Empire in the early 16th century and was a French League of Nations mandate after World War I. Lebanon proclaimed its independence in 1941, but full self-government was not achieved until 1945. Civil war broke out in 1975 between Christians and Muslims, and Israel invaded in 1978 and 1982 in an effort to root out Palestinian terrorists. In 1989 Christian and Muslim representatives signed a peace accord providing for a new constitution, which increased the political power of the Muslim majority. The civil war came to an end in 1991 with the disbanding of all militias, but Israeli and Syrian forces continued to occupy parts of the country. Beirut is the capital and the largest city. ⊛ Pop. 2,915,000. **2.** A city of southeast Pennsylvania east-northeast of Harrisburg. It is an industrial center in the Pennsylvania Dutch farm country. ⊛ Pop. 24,800.

Mediterranean Sea
Tripoli
Orontes
LEBANON
Beirut
Sidon
SYRIA
Jordan
Tyre
Golan Heights
25 mi
ISRAEL

Lebanon Mountains. A range of Lebanon extending about 161 km (100 mi) parallel to the Mediterranean coast and rising to about 3,090 m (10,131 ft).

Lec·ce (lĕch'ā, lĕt'chĕ). A city of extreme southeast Italy east of Taranto. A Greek and Roman town, Lecce was a semi-independent county from 1053 to 1463. ⊛ Pop. 91,625.

Lec·co (lĕk'ō). A city of northern Italy on Lake Como north-northeast of Milan. It is a manufacturing center. ⊛ Pop. 100,233.

Lech (lĕk, lĕкн). A river rising in western Austria and flowing about 249 km (155 mi) generally north past Augsburg to the Danube River in southern Germany.

ledge (lĕj). **1.** A cut or projection forming a shelf on a cliff or rock wall. **2.** An underwater ridge or rock shelf. — **ledg'y** *adj.*

lee (lē). **1.** *Nautical.* The side away from the direction from which the wind blows; the side sheltered from the wind. **2.** *Nautical.* Of or relating to the side sheltered from the wind. **3.** Located in or facing the path of an oncoming glacier. Used of a geologic formation.

Leeds (lēdz). A borough of north-central England northeast of Manchester. Incorporated in 1626, it is a major commercial, transportation, communications, and industrial center. ⊛ Pop. 724,524.

Lee's Summit (lēz). A city of western Missouri southeast of Kansas City. It is a manufacturing center within the Kansas City metropolitan area. ⊛ Pop. 46,418.

Leeu·war·den (lā'vär-dn, lā'ü-wär'dn). A city of northern Netherlands northeast of the Ijsselmeer. Chartered in 1435, it was noted for its manufacture of gold and silver articles from the 16th to the 18th century. ⊛ Pop. 85,435.

Lee·ward Islands (lē'wərd). **1.** The northern group of the Lesser Antilles in the West Indies, extending from the Virgin Islands southeast to Guadeloupe. Inhabited by Caribs when Columbus discovered them in 1493, the islands were hotly contested by the Spanish, French, and British in the 17th and 18th centuries. **2.** A chain of small islets of Hawaii in the central Pacific Ocean west-northwest of the main islands. The Leewards constitute a government bird sanctuary.

Left Bank (lĕft). A district of Paris on the southern, or left, bank of the Seine River. It has long been noted for its artistic and bohemian atmosphere.

Le·ga·nés (lē'gä-nĕs'). A city of central Spain, an industrial and residential suburb of Madrid. ⊛ Pop. 171,589.

Leg·horn (lĕg'hôrn', -ərn) or **Li·vor·no** (lē-vôr'nō). A city of northwest Italy on the Ligurian Sea southeast of Genoa. A fortified town in the Middle Ages, Leghorn was developed into a flourishing community by the Medici, an Italian noble family. ⊛ Pop. 167,445.

Leg·ni·ca (lĕg-nēt'sə). A city of southwest Poland west of Wroclaw. Chartered in 1252, it was acquired by Prussia in 1742 and was the site of Frederick the Great's victory over the Austrians (August 15, 1760). ⊚ Pop. 105,637.

Le Ha·vre (lə hä′vrə, häv′). A city of northern France on the English Channel west-northwest of Paris. It has been a major port since the 16th century. ⊚ Pop. 195,932.

Le·high River (lē′hī′). A river, about 166 km (103 mi) long, of eastern Pennsylvania flowing generally southeast to the Delaware River.

Leices·ter (lĕs′tər). A borough of central England east-northeast of Birmingham. Built on the site of a Roman settlement, it is an important industrial center in a mining and sheep-raising district. ⊚ Pop. 289,286.

Lei·den also **Ley·den** (līd′n). A city of southwest Netherlands northeast of The Hague. Dating from Roman times, Leiden has had an important textile industry since the 16th century. Its university, founded in 1575, was a noted center for the study of theology, science, and medicine in the 17th and 18th centuries. ⊚ Pop. 114,365.

Lein·ster (lĕn′stər). A historical region of southeast Ireland. Its wealth and accessibility made it an early prey to Danish and Anglo-Saxon invasions.

Leip·zig (līp′sĭg, -sĭk, -tsĭk). A city of east-central Germany south-southwest of Berlin. Originally a Slavic settlement called Lipsk, it developed by the early Middle Ages into a major commercial and cultural center. At the so-called Battle of the Nations (October 16–19, 1813), Austrian, Russian, and Prussian forces decisively defeated the French emperor Napoleon I. ⊚ Pop. 490,851.

Lei·sure City (lē′zhər). An unincorporated community of southeast Florida southwest of Miami. It is a resort center near Biscayne Bay. ⊚ Pop. 19,379.

Leith (lēth). A district of Edinburgh, Scotland, on the southern shore of the Firth of Forth. It is a noted seaport and shipbuilding center.

Lei·zhou Peninsula (lā′jō′) also **Lui·chow Peninsula** (lwē′jō′). A peninsula of southern China between the Gulf of Tonkin and the South China Sea. A narrow strait separates it from the island of Hainan.

Le·man (lē′mən, lə-mäN′), **Lake**. See Lake **Geneva.**

Le Mans (lə mäN′). A city of northwest France west-southwest of Paris. Settled in pre-Roman times, it is famous for its annual (since 1906) 24-hour sports car races. ⊚ Pop. 145,439.

Le·may (lə-mā′, lē-). A community of east-central Missouri, a suburb on the southern border of St. Louis. ⊚ Pop. 18,005.

Lem·nos (lĕm′nŏs, -nōs, lēm′nŏs) also **Lím·nos** (lēm′nôs). An island of northeast Greece in the Aegean Sea off the coast of Turkey northwest of Lesbos. Occupied in ancient times by Greeks,

the island was later held by Persians, Romans, Byzantines, and Ottoman Turks. It became part of modern Greece in 1913.

Lem·on Grove (lĕm′ən). An unincorporated community of southern California, a residential suburb of San Diego. ⊚ Pop. 23,984.

Le·na (lē′nə, lyĕ′-). A river of eastern Russia rising near Lake Baikal and flowing about 4,296 km (2,670 mi) northeast and north to the Laptev Sea. Its delta is some 402 km (250 mi) wide.

Len·a·pe (lĕn′ə-pē). *pl.* **Lenape** or **-pes.** See **Delaware**[1] (sense 1).

Le·nex·a (lə-nĕk′sə). A city of eastern Kansas, a suburb of Kansas City. ⊚ Pop. 34,034.

Len·i Len·a·pe (lĕn′ē lĕn′ə-pē). Variant of **Lenni Lenape.**

Le·nin·a·bad (lĕn′ĭ-nə-bäd′, lyĭ-nĭ-nəbät′). See **Khujand.**

Le·nin·a·kan (lĕn′ĭ-nə-kän′, lyĭ-nĭ-). See **Gyumri.**

Len·in·grad (lĕn′ĭn-grăd′, lyĭ-nĭn-grät′). See **Saint Petersburg.**

Le·nin Peak (lĕn′ĭn, lyĕ′nyĭn). A mountain, 7,138.5 m (23,405 ft) high, in the Trans Alai on the Kyrgyzstan-Tajikistan border. It is the highest peak in the range.

Len·ni Len·a·pe or **Len·i Len·a·pe** (lĕn′ē lĕn′-ə-pē). See **Delaware.**

Len·nox (lĕn′əks). An unincorporated community of southern California, an industrial suburb of Los Angeles. ⊚ Pop. 18,445.

Leom·in·ster (lĕm′ĭn-stər). A city of north-central Massachusetts south-southeast of Fitchburg. It is a manufacturing center. ⊚ Pop. 38,145.

Le·ón (lā-ōn′). **1.** A historical region and former kingdom of northwest Spain. United first with Asturias (eighth–ninth century), it was conquered by Castile in 1037, became independent in 1157, and was rejoined with Castile in 1230. **2.** A city of central Mexico east-northeast of Guadalajara. It was founded in the 1570's and today is a commercial and industrial center in a rich mining area. ⊚ Pop. 593,002. **3.** A city of western Nicaragua northwest of Managua. Founded in 1524 on Lake Managua, it was moved to its present site after a severe earthquake in 1610. ⊚ Pop. 92,764. **4.** A city of northwest Spain at the foot of the Cantabrian Mountains south-southeast of Oviedo. Reconquered from the Moors in 882, it is now a popular tourist center. ⊚ Pop. 143,496.

Le·o·ne (lā-ō′nā), **Monte.** A peak, 3,563.3 m (11,683 ft) high, of the Lepontine Alps on the Swiss-Italian border near the Simplon Pass. It is the highest elevation in the range.

Le·o·pold·ville (lē′ə-pōld-vĭl′, lā′-). See **Kinshasa.**

Le·pan·to (lĭ-păn′tō, lĕ′pän-tô), **Gulf of.** See Gulf of **Corinth.**

Lep·cha (lĕp′chə). **1.** *pl.* **Lepcha** or **-chas.** A member of a Buddhist people living in Sikkim. **2.** The Tibeto-Burman language of the Lepcha.

Le·pon·tic (lĭ-pŏn′tĭk). An ancient Indo-European language of northeast Italy and southern Switzerland, known from inscriptions dated from the third century B.C. — **Le·pon′tic** *adj.*

Le·pon·tine Alps (lĭ-pŏn′tīn′). A range of the central Alps in southern Switzerland and along the Swiss-Italian border. The highest point is Monte Leone, rising to 3,563.3 m (11,683 ft).

Lep·tis Mag·na (lĕp′tĭs măg′nə). An ancient city of northern Africa in present-day Libya east of Tripoli. Founded by Phoenicians, it flourished as a port during Roman times and is today noted for its impressive ruins.

Lé·ri·da (lā′rĭ-də, lĕ′rē-*th*ä). A city of northeast Spain west of Barcelona. Julius Caesar defeated Pompey's generals here in 49 B.C. During the Spanish Civil War it was a key defense point for Barcelona but fell to the Nationalists (April 1938) after a nine-month battle. ⊕ Pop. 87,800.

Les·bi·an (lĕz′bē-ən). **1.** A native or inhabitant of Lesbos. **2.** The ancient Greek dialect of Lesbos. **3.** Of or relating to Lesbos.

Les·bos (lĕz′bŏs, -bōs) also **Lés·vos** (-vôs). An island of eastern Greece in the Aegean Sea near the northwest coast of Turkey. An important Aeolian settlement, Lesbos was noted for its lyric poets, including Sappho, in the seventh century B.C. After occupation by various powers, the island was annexed by Greece in 1913.

Le·so·tho (lə-sō′tō, -sōō′tōō). Formerly **Ba·su·to·land** (bə-sōō′tō-lănd′). A country of southern Africa forming an enclave within east-central South Africa. Originally inhabited by the San, the area was populated by a variety of Sotho peoples in the 18th century. In the early 19th century encroachment by neighboring Zulus led to the establishment (c. 1820) of a central Sotho kingdom under Moshesh I (died 1870). The territory, known as Basutoland, became a British protectorate in 1868 and later (1884) a self-governing crown colony, remaining under British control after the creation of the Union of

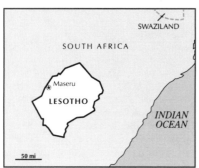

South Africa in 1910. Full independence as the Kingdom of Lesotho was granted in 1966. Maseru is the capital. ⊕ Pop. 1,996,000.

Less·er Antilles (lĕs′ər). An island group of the eastern West Indies extending in an arc from Curaçao to the Virgin Islands.

Lesser Slave Lake. A lake of central Alberta, Canada, drained by the **Lesser Slave River,** a tributary of the Athabasca River.

Lesser Sunda Islands. See **Sunda Islands.**

Lés·vos (lĕz′vôs). See **Lesbos.**

Leth·bridge (lĕth′brĭj′). A city of southern Alberta, Canada, south-southeast of Calgary. It is a commercial center in an irrigated farming region. ⊕ Pop. 54,072.

Lett (lĕt). A member of a Baltic people constituting the main population of Latvia.

Let·tish (lĕt′ĭsh). **1.** Of or relating to the Letts or their language or culture. **2.** See **Latvian** (sense 3).

Leuc·tra (lōōk′trə). A village of ancient Greece southwest of Thebes. It was the site of a major Spartan defeat by the Thebans (371 B.C.).

Leu·ven (lĕv′ən). See **Louvain.**

Lev·al·loi·si·an (lĕv′ə-loi′zē-ən). Of or relating to a western European stage in lower Paleolithic culture, characterized by a distinctive method of striking off flake tools from pieces of flint.

Le·val·lois-Per·ret (lə-väl-wä′pĕ-rā′). A city of north-central France, a residential and industrial suburb of Paris on the Seine River. ⊕ Pop. 53,500.

Le·vant (lə-vănt′). The countries bordering on the eastern Mediterranean Sea from Turkey to Egypt. — **Le′van·tine′** (lĕv′ən-tīn′, -tēn′, lə-văn′-) *adj. & n.*

le·vant·er (lə-văn′tər). **1.** A strong easterly wind of the Mediterranean area. **2. Levanter.** A native or inhabitant of the Levant.

lev·ee (lĕv′ē). **1.** An embankment raised to prevent a river from overflowing. **2.** A small ridge or raised area bordering an irrigated field.

Le·ven (lē′vən), **Loch.** A lake of eastern Scotland north-northwest of Edinburgh. Mary Queen of Scots was imprisoned on an island in the lake from 1567 to 1568.

Le·ver·ku·sen (lā′vər-kōō′zən). A city of west-central Germany, an industrial center on the Rhine River north of Cologne. ⊕ Pop. 161,761.

Lé·vis-Lau·zon (lē′vĭs-lō-zôN′, lä-vē′-). A city of southern Quebec, Canada, on the St. Lawrence River opposite Quebec City. Settled in the mid-17th century, the city of Lévis and neighboring Lauzon developed separately and were merged in 1989. It is a port and shipbuilding center. ⊕ Pop. 17,895.

Lev·it·town (lĕv′ĭt-toun′). **1.** An unincorporated community of southeast New York on western Long Island east-southeast of Mineola. It was founded in 1947 as a low-cost housing development for World War II veterans. ⊛ Pop. 53,286. **2.** A community of southeast Pennsylvania near the Delaware River northeast of Philadelphia. ⊛ Pop. 55,362.

Lew·es River (lōō′ĭs). The upper course of the Yukon River above its junction with the Pelly River in southern Yukon Territory, Canada. It is about 544 km (338 mi) long.

Lew·is Range (lōō′ĭs). A section of the Rocky Mountains in northwest Montana rising to 3,192.1 m (10,466 ft) at Mount Cleveland.

Lew·is·ton (lōō′ĭ-stən). **1.** A city of northwest Idaho on the border south-southeast of Spokane, Washington. A commercial and industrial center in a timber, grain, and livestock region, it was the first capital (1863–1864) of the Idaho Territory. ⊛ Pop. 28,082. **2.** A city of southwest Maine on the Androscoggin River north of Portland. Settled in 1770, it became a textile center in the early 19th century. ⊛ Pop. 39,757.

Lew·is·ville (lōō′ĭs-vĭl′, lōō′ē-). A city of northeast Texas, an industrial and residential suburb in the Dallas–Fort Worth metropolitan area. ⊛ Pop. 46,521.

Lewis with Har·ris (hăr′ĭs). An island of northwest Scotland. The largest and northernmost of the Outer Hebrides, it is noted for its tweeds.

Lex·ing·ton (lĕk′sĭng-tən). **1.** A city of northeast-central Kentucky east-southeast of Louisville. A noted center for the raising of thoroughbred horses, it was named in 1775 after the Battle of Lexington. ⊛ Pop. 204,165. **2.** A town of northeast Massachusetts, a residential suburb of Boston. The Battle of Lexington (April 19, 1775) marked the beginning of the American Revolution. ⊛ Pop. 28,974. **3.** A city of central North Carolina south of Winston-Salem. It is a trade and processing center in a farming region. ⊛ Pop. 16,581.

ley (lā, lē). Variant of **lea.**

Ley·den (līd′n). See **Leiden.**

Ley·land (lā′lənd). An urban district of northwest England north-northeast of Liverpool. It is an industrial center. ⊛ Pop. 97,700.

Ley·te (lā′tē, -tĕ). An island of the east-central Philippines in the Visayan Islands north of Mindanao. It was discovered in 1521 by the Portuguese navigator Ferdinand Magellan.

Leyte Gulf. An inlet of the western Pacific Ocean in the Philippines south of Samar and east of Leyte. An invasion force led by the American general Douglas MacArthur decisively defeated the Japanese here on October 25–26, 1944.

Lha·sa (lä′sə, läs′ə). A city of southwest China, the capital of Xizang (Tibet). Because of its remoteness and exclusivity as the center of Ti-

betan Buddhism, Lhasa was long closed to foreign visitors and known as "the Forbidden City." ⊛ Pop. 139,822.

Lho·tse (lō′tsĕ′). A peak, 8,506.5 m (27,890 ft) high, of the central Himalaya Mountains on the Nepal-Xizang (Tibet) border.

Lian·yun·gang (lyän′yōōn′gäng′, -yœn′-) also **Lien·yün·kang** (lyŭn′yün′käng′). A city of eastern China near the Yellow Sea south-southwest of Qingdao. It is an industrial center. ⊛ Pop. 537,355.

Liao·dong (lyou′dŭng′) also **Liao·tung** (-tōōng′), **Gulf of.** The northern part of the Bo Hai in northeast China. It borders on the **Liaodong Peninsula,** a land area projecting southwest into the Yellow Sea.

Liao He (lyou′ hə′). A river of northeast China flowing about 1,448 km (900 mi) northeast and southwest to the Gulf of Liaodong.

Liao·ning (lyou′nĭng′). A province of northeast China on the Bo Hai and Korea Bay. It was under Japanese control from 1932 until 1945. Shenyang is the capital. ⊛ Pop. 36,860,000.

Liao·tung (lyou′tōōng′), **Gulf of.** See Gulf of **Liaodong.**

Liao·yang (lyou′yäng′). A city of northeast China south-southwest of Shenyang. One of the oldest cities in Manchuria, it was the site of a Russian victory (August–September 1904) in the Russo-Japanese War. ⊛ Pop. 639,553.

Liao·yu·an (lyou′yōō′än′, -ywän′). A city of northeast China south of Changchun. It is a coal-mining center with iron and steel works. ⊛ Pop. 411,073.

Li·ard (lē′ərd, lē-ärd′). A river rising in southeast Yukon Territory, Canada, and flowing about 1,215 km (755 mi) southeast into northern British Columbia then northeast to the Mackenzie River in southwest Northwest Territories.

Li·be·rec (lĭb′ə-rĕts′). A city of north-central Czech Republic north-northeast of Prague. Founded c. 1350, it has been a textile center since the 16th century. ⊛ Pop. 101,048.

Li·be·ri·a (lī-bîr′ē-ə). A country of western Africa on the Atlantic Ocean. It was founded

(1821) through the efforts of the American Colonization Society and settled mainly by freed slaves from 1822 to the 1860's. Liberia is the oldest independent country in Africa (established 1847). After years of relative stability, a military coup led by Samuel K. Doe in 1980 ended more than 100 years of rule by Liberians of American descent and initiated a period of despotic government and violent unrest. After Doe's capture and execution in 1990, a full-scale civil war broke out between rival ethnic factions, and despite a cease-fire secured by West African peacekeeping forces in 1991, sporadic fighting continued at various levels during the following years. An agreement reached between the rebel leaders in August 1996 called for a new cease-fire to be followed by elections in 1997. Monrovia is the capital and the largest city. ⊛ Pop. 2,700,000. —**Li·be′ri·an** *adj. & n.*

Lib·er·ty (lĭb′ər-tē). A city of western Missouri, an industrial suburb of Kansas City. ⊛ Pop. 20,459.

Liberty Island. Formerly **Bed·loe′s Island** (bĕd′lōz). An island of southeast New York in Upper New York Bay southwest of Manhattan. The Statue of Liberty was placed on the island in 1885, using the star-shaped Fort Wood (built in 1841) as a base. Congress officially renamed the island in 1956.

Lib·er·ty·ville (lĭb′ər-tē-vĭl′). A village of northeast Illinois southwest of Waukegan. It is an industrial center. ⊛ Pop. 19,174.

Li·bre·ville (lē′brə-vĭl′, -vēl′). The capital and largest city of Gabon, in the northwest part of the country on the Gulf of Guinea. Founded as a French trading post in 1843, it was named Libreville after freed slaves settled there (1848). ⊛ Pop. 235,700.

Lib·y·a (lĭb′ē-ə). A country of northern Africa on the Mediterranean Sea. Controlled at various times by Carthage, Rome, Arabia, and Spain, the area was part of the Ottoman Empire from 1551 to 1911. It was subsequently seized by Italy and became an Italian colony during World War II, gaining independence as a kingdom in

1951. In 1969 Colonel Muammar al-Qaddafi took power in a coup d'état, establishing a socialist dictatorship whose policies were openly opposed to Israel and frequently at odds with other Western democracies. The United States conducted limited air strikes against Libya in 1986 in retaliation for suspected support of international terrorism. An ongoing territorial dispute with Chad was turned over to international arbitration in 1990. Tripoli is the capital and the largest city. ⊛ Pop. 4,899,000.

Lib·y·an (lĭb′ē-ən). **1.** Of or relating to Libya or its people, language, or culture. **2.** A native or inhabitant of Libya. **3.** A Berber language of ancient northern Africa.

Libyan Desert. A desert of northeast Africa in Egypt, Libya, and Sudan. It is the northeast section of the Sahara Desert.

Lich·field (lĭch′fēld′). A municipal borough of west-central England north-northeast of Birmingham. The writer Samuel Johnson was born here in 1709. ⊛ Pop. 25,800.

Lick·ing River (lĭk′ĭng). A river of northeast Kentucky flowing about 515 km (320 mi) northwest to the Ohio River at Covington.

Li·di·ce (lĭd′ĭ-sē, -chā′, lyĭ′dĭ-tsĕ). A village of northwest Czech Republic west-northwest of Prague. In reprisal for the murder of a Nazi official, German forces killed its male population, deported the women and children to concentration camps, and burned the village to the ground (June 9–10, 1942).

Li·do (lē′dō). An island reef of northeast Italy separating the lagoon of Venice from the Adriatic Sea. The town of **Lido,** at the northern end of the island, is a fashionable resort.

Liech·ten·stein (lĭk′tən-stīn′, lĭкн′tən-shtīn′). *abbr.* **Liech.** A small Alpine principality in central Europe between Austria and Switzerland. It was created as a principality within the Holy Roman Empire in 1719 and became independent in 1866. Vaduz is the capital. ⊛ Pop. 31,000.

Li·ège (le-azh′, lyezh). A city of eastern Belgium near the Dutch and German borders. First mentioned in 558, it was a noted intellectual center

in the Middle Ages. Liège was held by France from 1794 to 1815 and by the Netherlands from 1815 to 1830. ◉ Pop. 195,201.

Lien·yün·kang (lyŭn′yün′käng′). See **Lianyungang.**

Lie·pa·ja (lē-ĕp′ə-yə, lyĕ′pä-yä). A city of southwest Latvia on the Baltic Sea southwest of Riga. Founded by the Teutonic Knights in 1263, it passed to Russia in 1795, was briefly the capital of the Latvian provisional government (1918), and was annexed by the U.S.S.R. along with the rest of Latvia after World War II. ◉ Pop. 106,442.

Liè·vre (lē-ĕv′rə, lyĕv′-). A river, about 322 km (200 mi) long, of southern Quebec, Canada, flowing generally southwest to the Ottawa River.

life zone (līf). *Ecology.* A geographic region or area defined by its characteristic life forms.

Li·gu·ri·a (lĭ-gyŏŏr′ē-ə). A region of northwest Italy on the **Ligurian Sea,** an arm of the Mediterranean Sea between northwest Italy and Corsica. Named for an ancient pre-Indo-European people, the Ligurii, the region was subdued by the Romans in the 2nd century B.C. and was later (16th–19th century) controlled by Genoa. A small section of the coastline surrounding Genoa formed the **Ligurian Republic** from 1797 until 1815. — **Li·gu′ri·an** *adj. & n.*

Lille (lēl). A city of northern France northeast of Paris near the Belgian border. Founded c. 1030, it was the medieval capital of Flanders and is now a commercial, cultural, and manufacturing center. ◉ Pop. 172,149.

Li·long·we (lĭ-lông′wā). The capital of Malawi, in the south-central part of the country. It was founded in the 1940's as an agricultural market town. ◉ Pop. 233,973.

Li·ma. 1. (lē′mə). The capital and largest city of Peru, in the west-central part of the country near the Pacific Ocean. Founded by the Spanish conquistador Francisco Pizarro in 1535, it was the capital of Spain's New World empire until the 19th century. The city was largely rebuilt after earthquakes in 1687 and 1746. ◉ Pop. 6,414,500. **2.** (lī′mə). A city of northwest Ohio south-southwest of Toledo. It is a processing and marketing center for a rich farming area. ◉ Pop. 45,549.

Lim·burg (lĭm′bûrg′, -bœrкн′). A former duchy of northwest Europe. Founded in the 11th century, it was incorporated into the Netherlands in 1815 and divided into the Dutch and Belgian provinces of Limburg in 1839.

Li·mei·ra (lĭ-mā′rä). A city of southeast Brazil northwest of São Paulo. Citrus fruits and silkworm cultivation are important to its economy. ◉ Pop. 207,416.

Lim·er·ick (lĭm′ər-ĭk, lĭm′rĭk). A borough of southwest Ireland on the Shannon River estuary. It was an important Norse settlement in the 9th and 10th centuries and was taken by the English in the late 12th century. The city is noted for its fine lace. ◉ Pop. 60,736.

li·mes (lī′mēz). *pl.* **lim·i·tes** (lĭm′ĭ-tēz). A fortified boundary or border, especially of the Roman Empire.

Lím·nos (lēm′nôs). See **Lemnos.**

Li·moges (lē-mōzh′). A city of west-central France on the Vienne River, northeast of Bordeaux. Its ceramic industry dates to the 18th century. ◉ Pop. 133,469.

Li·mou·sin (lē-mōō-zăN′). A historical region and former province of central France west of the Auvergne Mountains. It was included in the dowry given by Eleanor of Aquitaine to Henry II of England in 1152 and was eventually reconquered by France (1370–1374).

Lim·po·po (lĭm-pō′pō) also **Croc·o·dile River** (krŏk′ə-dīl′). A river of southeast Africa rising in northeast South Africa and flowing 1,770 km (1,100 mi) in a northeast-southeast arc to the Indian Ocean in southern Mozambique.

Li·na·res (lĭ-när′ĭs, lē-nä′rĕs). A city of southern Spain east-northeast of Córdoba. It is a center for lead and silver mining. ◉ Pop. 51,800.

Lin·coln (lĭng′kən). **1.** A borough of eastern England northeast of Nottingham. Located on the site of Roman, Saxon, and Danish settlements, it was first chartered in 1157. ◉ Pop. 75,900. **2.** A city of central Illinois north-north-east of Springfield. It was mapped out (1853) with the aid of Abraham Lincoln, who practiced law here from 1847 to 1859. ◉ Pop. 15,418. **3.** The capital of Nebraska, in the southeast part of the state southwest of Omaha. Founded in 1864 as Lancaster, the city was renamed when it was chosen as the state capital in 1867. ◉ Pop. 191,972.

Lincoln, Mount. A peak, 4,357.2 m (14,286 ft) high, in the Rocky Mountains of central Colorado. It is the highest elevation of the Park Range.

Lincoln Park. A city of southeast Michigan, a residential suburb of Detroit. ◉ Pop. 41,832.

Lin·den (lĭn′dən). A city of northeast New Jersey, an industrial center adjacent to Elizabeth. ◉ Pop. 36,701.

Lin·den·hurst (lĭn′dən-hûrst′). A village of southeast New York on southern Long Island near Babylon. It is mainly residential. ◉ Pop. 26,879.

Lin·den·wold (lĭn′dən-wōld′). A borough of southwest New Jersey southeast of Camden. It was settled in 1742. ◉ Pop. 18,734.

Lin·des·nes (lĭn′dĭs-nĕs′). A cape of extreme southern Norway projecting into the North Sea.

Lin·dis·farne (lĭn'dĭs-färn'). See **Holy Island.**

Lin·e·ar A (lĭn'ē-ər). An undeciphered writing system used in Crete from the 18th to the 15th century B.C.

Linear B. A syllabic script used in Mycenaean Greek documents chiefly from Crete and Pylos, mostly from the 14th to the 12th century B.C.

Line Islands (līn). A group of islands in the central Pacific Ocean south of Hawaii and astride the equator. First visited in 1798 by American sailors, the islands are now part of Kiribati.

Lin·ga·la (lĭng-gä'lə). A creole based on Bantu, widely spoken as a lingua franca in Zaire.

Lin·ga·yen Gulf (lĭng'gä-yĕn'). An inlet of the South China Sea on the western coast of Luzon, Philippines. It was captured by the Japanese in December 1941 and retaken by American forces in January 1945.

lin·gua fran·ca (lĭng'gwə frăng'kə). **1.** A medium of communication between peoples of different languages. **2.** A mixture of Italian with Provençal, French, Spanish, Arabic, Greek, and Turkish, formerly spoken on the eastern Mediterranean coast.

Lin·kö·ping (lĭn'chœ'pĭng). A city of southeast Sweden southwest of Stockholm. It was a noted intellectual and religious center during the Middle Ages. ● Pop. 126,377.

links (lĭngks). *Scots.* Relatively flat or undulating sandy turf-covered ground usually found along a seashore.

linn (lĭn). *Scots.* **1.** A waterfall. **2.** A steep ravine or precipice.

Linn·he (lĭn'ē), **Loch.** An inlet of the Atlantic Ocean on the western coast of Scotland. It is part of the Caledonian Canal waterway.

Linz (lĭnts). A city of northern Austria on the Danube River west of Vienna. Originally a Roman settlement, it was a provincial capital of the Holy Roman Empire in the late 15th century. ● Pop. 203,044.

Li·ons (lī'ənz), **Gulf of.** A wide inlet of the Mediterranean Sea on the southern coast of France.

Li·pan (lĭ-pän'). **1.** *pl.* **Lipan** or **-pans.** A member of an Apache tribe formerly inhabiting western Texas, with a present-day population in southern New Mexico. **2.** The Apachean language of this tribe.

Lip·a·ri Islands (lĭp'ə-rē, lē'pä-). Formerly **Ae·o·li·an Islands** (ē-ō'lē-ən). A group of volcanic islands of Italy off the northeast coast of Sicily in the Tyrrhenian Sea. The islands have been inhabited since the Neolithic Period.

Li·petsk (lē'pĕtsk', lyē'pyĭtsk). A city of west-central Russia south-southeast of Moscow. Originally founded in the 13th century, it was rebuilt in 1707 as a metallurgical center by orders of Peter the Great. ● Pop. 465,753.

Lipp·stadt (lĭp'stät', -shtät'). A city of west-central Germany east-northeast of Dortmund. Founded in 1168, it became a member of the Hanseatic League in 1280 and was sold to Prussia in 1850. ● Pop. 60,106.

Lis·bon (lĭz'bən). The capital and largest city of Portugal, in the western part of the country on the Tagus River estuary. An ancient Iberian settlement, it was held by the Phoenicians and Carthaginians, taken by the Romans in 205 B.C., and conquered by the Moors c. A.D. 714. Reconquered by the Portuguese in 1147, it flourished in the 16th century during the heyday of colonial expansion in Africa and India. The city was devastated by a major earthquake in 1755. ● Pop. 663,315.

lith·o·sphere (lĭth'ə-sfîr'). **1.** The solid part of the earth. **2.** The rocky crust of the earth.

Lith·u·a·ni·a (lĭth'ōō-ā'nē-ə). Formerly **Lith·u·a·ni·an Soviet Socialist Republic** (-nē-ən). *abbr.* **Lith.** A country of north-central Europe on the Baltic Sea. Settled perhaps as early as 1500 B.C., the area was unified in the 13th century and became one of the largest states of medieval Europe, stretching as far as the Black Sea. Lithuania merged with Poland in 1569 but was absorbed into Russia by three partitions of Poland (1772, 1793, and 1795). The independent country of Lithuania existed from 1918 to 1940, when it became a constituent republic of the U.S.S.R. Germany occupied (1941–1944) the country during World War II, after which Soviet rule was resumed. In 1990 Lithuania declared its independence, which was recognized by the Soviet government and Western nations in 1991. Vilnius is the capital. ● Pop. 3,721,000.

Lith·u·a·ni·an (lĭth'ōō-ā'nē-ən). *abbr.* **Lith. 1.** Of or relating to Lithuania or its people, language, or culture. **2. a.** A native or inhabitant of Lithuania. **b.** A person of Lithuanian ancestry. **3.** The Baltic language of the Lithuanians.

Lithuanian Soviet Socialist Republic. See **Lithuania.**

Lit·tle Alföld (lĭt'l). See **Alföld.**

Little America. A U.S. base for explorations in

Antarctica on the Ross Ice Shelf. The American explorer Richard E. Byrd established and named the settlement in 1929.

Little Bighorn River. A river, about 145 km (90 mi) long, rising in the Bighorn Mountains of northern Wyoming and flowing north to the Bighorn River in southern Montana. Sioux and Cheyenne warriors defeated the forces of Gen. George A. Custer in the Little Bighorn valley on June 25, 1876.

Little Cayman. See **Cayman Islands.**

Little Colorado River. A river of northeast Arizona flowing about 507 km (315 mi) northwest to the Colorado River just above the Grand Canyon.

Little Diomede Island. See **Diomede Islands.**

Little Fork River (fôrk). A river of northern Minnesota flowing about 212 km (132 mi) northward to the U.S.-Canadian border.

Little Ka·na·wha River (kə-nô′wə). A river rising in central West Virginia and flowing about 257 km (160 mi) north and northwest to the Ohio River.

Little Karroo. See **Karroo.**

Little Minch. See **Minch.**

Little Missouri River. **1.** A river, about 233 km (145 mi) long, of southwest Arkansas flowing generally southeast to the Ouachita River. **2.** A river of the northern United States rising in northeast Wyoming and flowing about 901 km (560 mi) through southeast Montana and northwest South Dakota to the Missouri River in western North Dakota.

Little Namaqualand. See **Namaqualand.**

Little Pee Dee River. A river, about 169 km (105 mi) long, of southern North Carolina and northern South Carolina flowing south then southeast to the Pee Dee River.

Little Rock. The capital and largest city of Arkansas, in the central part of the state on the Arkansas River. It became territorial capital in 1821 and state capital in 1836. Federal troops were sent to the city in 1957 to enforce a 1954 U.S. Supreme Court ruling against segregation in the public schools. ◉ Pop. 175,795.

Little Saint Ber·nard Pass (sānt′ bər-närd′). A mountain pass through the Savoy Alps between Italy and France south of Mont Blanc. It rises to 2,189.9 m (7,180 ft).

Little Sark. See **Sark.**

Little Sioux River. A river rising in southwest Minnesota and flowing about 356 km (221 mi) generally southwest to the Missouri River in northwest Iowa.

Little Tennessee River. A river, about 217 km (135 mi) long, of northeast Georgia, south-

west North Carolina, and eastern Tennessee, where it joins the Tennessee River.

Lit·tle·ton (lĭt′l-tən). A city of north-central Colorado, a residential and industrial suburb of Denver. ◉ Pop. 33,685.

Little Wabash River. A river, about 322 km (200 mi) long, of eastern Illinois flowing southeast to the Wabash River.

lit·to·ral (lĭt′ər-əl). **1.** Of or on a shore, especially a seashore. **2.** A coastal region; a shore.

Liu·zhou (lyoō′jō′) also **Liu·chow** (-chō′). A city of southern China north-northeast of Nanning. It is an industrial and transportation center with a large integrated iron and steel complex. ◉ Pop. 751,311.

Liv·er·more (lĭv′ər-môr′, -mōr′). A city of western California east-southeast of Oakland. There are wineries in the area. ◉ Pop. 56,741.

Liv·er·pool (lĭv′ər-poōl′). A borough of northwest England on the Mersey River near its mouth on the Irish Sea. First colonized by the Norse in the late eighth century, Liverpool received a charter from King John in 1207. Today it is highly industrialized and a major port. ◉ Pop. 476,969.

Liv·ing·ston (lĭv′ĭng-stən). A community of northeast New Jersey northwest of Newark. It is in a truck-farming area. ◉ Pop. 26,609.

Li·vo·ni·a (lĭ-vō′nē-ə, -vōn′yə). **1.** A region of north-central Europe in southern Estonia and northern Latvia. Originally settled by the Livs, a Finnic people, the area was conquered in the 13th century by German knights, the Livonian Brothers of the Sword, who converted the inhabitants to Christianity. After the dissolution of the Livonian Order (1561), Livonia was contested by Poland, Russia, and Sweden, finally becoming a Russian province in 1783. In 1918 Livonia was divided between Estonia and Latvia. **2.** A city of southeast Michigan, an industrial suburb of Detroit. ◉ Pop. 100,850.

Li·vo·ni·an (lĭ-vō′nē-ən). **1.** Of or relating to the region of Livonia or its people or culture. **2.** A native or inhabitant of the region of Livonia.

Li·vor·no (lē-vôr′nō). See **Leghorn.**

Liz·ard Point or **Liz·ard Head** (lĭz′ərd). A cape of southwest England at the southern tip of **The Lizard,** a peninsula extending southward into the English Channel. It is the southernmost point of Great Britain.

Lju·blja·na (loō′blē-ä′nə, lyoō′blyä-nä). The capital and largest city of Slovenia, in the central part of the country on the Sava River westnorthwest of Zagreb, Croatia. Founded by Augustus in 34 B.C., it came under Hapsburg rule in A.D. 1277 and passed to the former Yugoslavia in 1919. ◉ Pop. 281,821.

lla·no (lä′nō, lăn′ō). *pl.* **-nos.** A large, grassy, almost treeless plain, especially one in Latin America.

Lla·no Es·ta·ca·do (lăn′ō ĕs′tə-kä′dō, lä′nō). An extensive, semiarid plateau region of the southern Great Plains in southeast New Mexico, western Texas, and northwest Oklahoma. The grazing lands also have resources of oil and natural gas.

Lloyd·min·ster (loid′mĭn′stər). A city on the Alberta-Saskatchewan border, Canada, east of Edmonton. The city, chartered by both provinces, is in a farming and ranching region with oil and natural gas deposits. ⊛Pop. 15,031.

Llu·llai·lla·co (yoo′yĭ-yä′kō). An extinct volcano, 6,727.4 m (22,057 ft) high, in the Andes of northern Chile near the Argentine border.

Lo·an·da (lō-än′də). See **Luanda.**

Lo·bi·to (lō-bē′tō). A city of west-central Angola on **Lobito Bay,** an inlet of the Atlantic Ocean. It is the country's chief port. ⊛Pop. 120,000.

Lo·car·no (lō-kär′nō). A town of southern Switzerland at the northern end of Lake Maggiore. First mentioned in 749, it passed to Milan in 1342 and was taken by the Swiss in 1512. The Locarno Pact between Germany and various European powers was signed here on December 1, 1925, in an effort to promote peace and maintain existing territorial borders. The city is today a popular resort. ⊛Pop. 14,300.

loch (lŏкн, lŏk). *Scots.* **1.** A lake. **2.** An arm of the sea similar to a fjord.

Loch (lŏk, lôкн). See **Lake.**

Lock·port (lŏk′pôrt′, -pōrt′). A city of western New York north-northeast of Buffalo. An industrial center, the city was built around a series of locks on the Erie Canal. ⊛Pop. 24,426.

Lodge·pole Creek (lŏj′pōl′). A river, about 341 km (212 mi) long, rising in southeast Wyoming and flowing generally east through southwest Nebraska to the South Platte River at the Colorado border.

Lo·di (lō′dī′). **1.** A city of central California north of Stockton. It is a processing center in a rich farming area. ⊛Pop. 51,874. **2.** A borough of northeast New Jersey northeast of Passaic. The city has varied industries. ⊛Pop. 22,355.

Lódź (lŏdz, wooch). A city of central Poland west-southwest of Warsaw. Chartered in 1423, it passed to Prussia in 1793 and to Russia in 1815. It became part of Poland after World War I. ⊛Pop. 846,514.

Lo·gan (lō′gən). A city of northern Utah north of Ogden. Settled in the 1850's, it is the seat of Utah State University (chartered 1888). ⊛Pop. 32,762.

Logan, Mount. A peak, 5,954.8 m (19,524 ft)

high, of the St. Elias Mountains in southwest Yukon Territory, Canada, near the Alaska border. It is the highest elevation in Canada.

Lo·gans·port (lō′gənz-pôrt′, -pōrt′). A city of north-central Indiana north-northwest of Kokomo. It is an agricultural trade center with diversified industries. ⊛Pop. 17,731.

Lo·gro·ño (lə-grōn′yə, lô-grô′nyô). A city of northern Spain on the Ebro River north-northeast of Madrid. Wood and metal products, textiles, and wine are important to its economy. ⊛Pop. 122,607.

Loir (lwär). A river, about 311 km (193 mi) long, of northwest France flowing generally westward to the Sarthe River.

Loire (lwär). The longest river of France, rising in the Cévennes and flowing about 1,014 km (630 mi) north, northwest, and west to the Bay of Biscay.

Lol·land (lŏl′ənd, lô′län). An island of southeast Denmark in the Baltic Sea south of Sjaelland.

Lo·ma·mi (lō-mä′mē). A river of Zaire flowing about 1,448 km (900 mi) northward to the Congo River.

Lo·mas de Za·mo·ra (lō′mäs də zə-môr′ə, -môr′ə, *th*ĕ sä-mô′rä). A city of eastern Argentina, an industrial suburb of Buenos Aires. ⊛Pop. 572,769.

Lom·bard[1] (lŏm′bərd, -bärd′, lŭm′-). **1.** A member of a Germanic people that invaded northern Italy in the sixth century A.D. and established a kingdom in the Po River valley. Also called *Langobard.* **2.** A native or inhabitant of Lombardy. **—Lom·bar·dic** (-bär′dĭk) *adj.*

Lom·bard[2] (lŏm′bärd′). A village of northeast Illinois, a residential suburb of Chicago. ⊛Pop. 39,408.

Lom·bar·dy (lŏm′bər-dē, lŭm′-). A region of northern Italy bordering on Switzerland. First inhabited by a Gallic people, it became the center of the kingdom of the Lombards in the sixth century A.D. and part of Charlemagne's empire in 774. The Lombard League of cities defeated the Holy Roman emperor Frederick I in 1176.

Lom·bok (lŏm-bŏk′). An island of south-central Indonesia in the Lesser Sunda Islands east of Bali, from which it is separated by the **Lombok Strait.** The island was first visited by the Dutch in 1674.

Lo·mé (lō-mā′). The capital and largest city of Togo, in the southern part of the country on the Gulf of Guinea. It is Togo's administrative, communications, and transportation center. ⊛Pop. 369,926.

Lo·mi·ta (lō-mē′tə). A city of southern California, a residential suburb of Los Angeles. ⊛Pop. 19,382.

Lo·mond (lō′mənd), **Loch.** A lake in south-central Scotland. Surrounded by mountains, it is the largest lake in Scotland and a popular tourist region for its associations with the 18th-century outlaw Rob Roy.

Lom·poc (lŏm'pŏk'). A city of southern California west-northwest of Santa Barbara. Vandenburg Air Force Base is nearby. ⊛ Pop. 37,649.

Lon·don (lŭn'dən). **1.** A city of southeast Ontario, Canada, southwest of Toronto. Settled in 1826, it is an industrial city whose streets and bridges are named after those of London, England. ⊛ Pop. 402,124. **2.** The capital and largest city of the United Kingdom, on the Thames River in southeast England. Greater London consists of 32 boroughs surrounding the City of London, built on the site of a Roman outpost named Londinium. Its growth as an important trade center dates from 886, under the rule of Alfred the Great. During the Elizabethan period (1558–1603) London achieved new heights of wealth, power, and influence and has continued to dominate its country's political, economic, and cultural life. The old city was devastated by the plague in 1665 and by the Great Fire of 1666; the modern city was damaged severely by bombs during World War II. ⊛ Pop. 6,904,600.

Lon·don·der·ry (lŭn'dən-dĕr'ē, lŭn'dən-dĕr'-ē) also **Der·ry** (dĕr'ē). A borough of northwest Northern Ireland northwest of Belfast. Built on the site of an abbey founded by Saint Columba in 546, it is a port and manufacturing center. ⊛ Pop. 68,000.

Lon·dri·na (lôn-drē'nə). A city of southern Brazil east of São Paulo. Founded in 1932, it is a trade and processing center. ⊛ Pop. 389,959.

Long Beach (lông' bēch', lŏng'). **1.** A city of southern California on an arm of the Pacific Ocean southeast of Los Angeles. It is a thriving port and year-round resort and convention center. The city's main growth occurred after the discovery of oil in 1921. ⊛ Pop. 429,433. **2.** A city of southeast New York on an island off southern Long Island. It is a residential and resort community. ⊛ Pop. 33,510.

Long Branch (lông' brănch', lŏng'). A city of east-central New Jersey on the Atlantic Ocean north of Asbury Park. It has been a popular ocean resort since the 19th century. ⊛ Pop. 28,658.

Long Island. *abbr.* **L.I.** A long, narrow island of southeast New York bordered on the south by the Atlantic Ocean. **Long Island Sound,** an arm of the Atlantic, separates it from Connecticut on the north. The western part of Long Island includes two boroughs of New York City. The rest of the island has seen tremendous industrial and residential growth since 1945, although there are still countless resort communities along its shoreline.

lon·gi·tude (lŏn'jĭ-tōōd', -tyōōd', lôn'-). *abbr.* **long.** Angular distance on the earth's surface, measured east or west from the prime meridian at Greenwich, England, to the meridian passing through a position, expressed in degrees (or hours), minutes, and seconds. **—lon'gi·tu'di·nal** *adj.*

Long·mea·dow (lông'mĕd'ō, lŏng'-). A town of southwest Massachusetts, a residential suburb of Springfield on the Connecticut River. ⊛ Pop. 15,467.

Long·mont (lông'mŏnt', lŏng'-). A city of north-central Colorado north-northeast of Boulder. It is a trade and processing center for an irrigated farming region. ⊛ Pop. 42,942.

Longs Peak (lôngz, lŏngz). A mountain, 4,347.8 m (14,255 ft) high, in the Front Range of the Rocky Mountains in north-central Colorado. It is named after the American explorer Stephen Harriman Long (1784–1864).

Lon·gueil (lông-gāl'). A city of southern Quebec, Canada, on the St. Lawrence River opposite Montreal. It is an industrial center. ⊛ Pop. 129,874.

Long·view (lông'vyōō', lŏng'-). **1.** A city of northeast Texas west of Shreveport, Louisiana. The city produces varied manufactures. ⊛ Pop. 70,311. **2.** A city of southwest Washington on the Columbia River north of Vancouver. A port of entry, it has a large lumber and pulp industry. ⊛ Pop. 31,499.

Look·out (lŏŏk'out'), **Cape.** A point on a sandy reef off eastern North Carolina southwest of Cape Hatteras. A lighthouse was built here in 1859.

Loop (lōōp). The central business district of Chicago, Illinois. The Loop was originally named for a loop in the elevated railroad tracks.

Lop Nur (lŏp' nŏŏr') also **Lop Nor** (nôr'). A marshy depression of northwest China. Once a large salt lake, the area has been used since 1964 for nuclear testing.

Lo·rain (lə-rān', lô-). A city of northern Ohio on Lake Erie west of Cleveland. Settled in 1807, it is now highly industrialized. ⊛ Pop. 71,245.

Lord Howe Island (lôrd' hou'). A volcanic island of Australia in the Tasman Sea east-northeast of Sydney. Explored by the British in 1788, it was settled in 1834.

Lo·rette·ville (lə-rĕt'vĭl', lô-). A city of southern Quebec, Canada, a manufacturing suburb of Quebec City. ⊛ Pop. 15,060.

Lo·rient (lô-ryäɴ'). A city of northwest France on the Bay of Biscay southeast of Brest. Established as a port in the 17th century, it was developed as a naval base by Napoleon I, emperor of the French (1804–1814). ⊛ Pop. 62,554.

Lorne also **Lorn** (lôrn), **Firth of.** An inlet of the

Atlantic Ocean on the western coast of Scotland between Mull Island and the mainland.

Lor·raine (lô-rān', lô-, lō-rĕn'). A historical region and former province of northeast France. Originally part of a kingdom belonging to Charlemagne's grandson Lothair I (795?–855), the region passed to France in 1766 but was ceded with Alsace to Germany after the Franco-Prussian War (1871). The area was returned to France by the Treaty of Versailles (1919).

Los Al·a·mos (lôs ăl'ə-mōs', lŏs). An unincorporated community of north-central New Mexico northwest of Santa Fe. It was chosen in 1942 as a nuclear research site to produce the first atomic bombs. The Atomic Energy Commission governed the town from 1947 to 1962. ◉ Pop. 11,455.

Los Al·tos (ăl'təs, -tōs). A city of western California south of Palo Alto. It is mainly residential. ◉ Pop. 26,303.

Los An·ge·les (ăn'jə-ləs, -lēz', ăng'gə-ləs). *abbr.* **L.A., LA.** A city of southern California on the Pacific Ocean in a widespread metropolitan area. The so-called City of the Angels was founded by the Spanish in 1781 and served several times as a colonial capital. Its real growth began after the coming of the railroads in the 1870's and 1880's and the discovery of oil in the 1890's. Today it is a major shipping, manufacturing, communications, financial, and distribution center noted for its entertainment industry. ◉ Pop. 3,485,398.

Los Ga·tos (găt'əs). A city of west-central California, a health resort and residential suburb of San Jose. ◉ Pop. 27,357.

Los Mo·chis (mō'chĭs, mô'chēs). A city of northwest Mexico near the Gulf of California south-southeast of Hermosillo. It is a resort in a farming area. ◉ Pop. 122,531.

Los Te·ques (tĕ'kĕs). A city of northern Venezuela, a residential and industrial suburb of Caracas. ◉ Pop. 162,145.

Lost River Range (lôst, lŏst). A chain of mountains in east-central Idaho rising to 3,861.9 m (12,662 ft) at Borah Peak, the highest elevation in the state.

Lot (lŏt, lôt). A river of southern France rising in the Cévennes and flowing about 483 km (300 mi) westward to the Garonne River.

lough (lŏKH, lŏk). *Irish.* **1.** A lake. **2.** A bay or an inlet of the sea.

Lou·is·burg or **Lou·is·bourg** (lōo'ĭs-bûrg'). A town of Nova Scotia, Canada, on eastern Cape Breton Island. It is near the site of the fortress of Louisbourg, built c. 1712–1740 by the French to guard the entrance to the Gulf of St. Lawrence. In 1758 the fort fell to a British land and sea attack, which reduced it to rubble. A na-

tional historical park here includes reconstructed portions of the complex.

Lou·ise (lōo-ēz'), **Lake.** A lake of southwest Alberta, Canada, in the Rocky Mountains near Banff. Surrounded by high peaks and glaciers, it is noted for its scenic beauty.

Lou·i·si·an·a (lōo-ē'zē-ăn'ə, lōo'zē-). *abbr.* **LA, La.** A state of the southern United States on the Gulf of Mexico. It was admitted as the 18th state in 1812. Part of the vast region claimed by the explorer La Salle for France in 1682, it was first successfully settled in 1718 with the foundation of New Orleans. Control of the area passed to the United States in 1803, and the Territory of Orleans was created in 1804 when the northern part was split off to form the District of Louisiana (later the Territory of Louisiana and the Missouri Territory). Baton Rouge is the capital and New Orleans the largest city. ◉ Pop. 4,238,216.

Louisiana French. French as spoken by the descendants of the original French settlers of Louisiana.

Louisiana Purchase. A territory of the western United States extending from the Mississippi River to the Rocky Mountains between the Gulf of Mexico and the Canadian border. It was purchased from France on April 30, 1803, for $15 million and officially explored by the Lewis and Clark expedition (1804–1806).

Lou·is·ville (lōo'ē-vĭl', -ə-vəl). The largest city of Kentucky, in the north-central part of the state on the Ohio River west of Lexington. On the site of a fort built by the military leader George Rogers Clark in 1778, it is a port of entry and a major industrial, financial, and marketing center. ◉ Pop. 269,063.

Loup River (lōop). A river of east-central Nebraska rising in three branches and flowing a total length of about 451 km (280 mi) eastward to the Platte River.

Lourdes (lōord, lōordz). A town of southwest France at the foot of the Pyrenees. It is noted for its Roman Catholic shrine marking the site where the Virgin Mary is said to have appeared to Saint Bernadette in 1858. ◉ Pop. 17,425.

Lou·ren·ço Mar·ques (lə-rĕn'sō mär'kĕs, lô-rĕN'sōo mär'kĕsh). See **Maputo.**

Lou·vain (lōo-văn') also **Leu·ven** (lĕv'ən). A city of central Belgium east of Brussels. First mentioned in the 9th century, it was a center of the wool trade in the Middle Ages but declined in the late 14th century because of civil strife. Its famed university dates from the 15th century. ◉ Pop. 85,068.

Love·land (lŭv'lənd). A city of northern Colorado south of Fort Collins. It is a food-processing center with varied industries. ◉ Pop. 37,352.

Low Countries (lō). A region of northwest Europe comprising Belgium, the Netherlands, and Luxembourg.

Low·ell (lō′əl). A city of northeast Massachusetts on the Merrimack River northwest of Boston. Settled in 1653, it was once a major textile center and now has diversified industries. It was the birthplace of the painter James Abbott McNeill Whistler (1834–1903) and the writer Jack Kerouac (1922–1969). ⊛ Pop. 103,439.

Low·er California (lō′ər). See **Baja California.**

Lower Canada. The southern, mainly French-speaking portion of Quebec, Canada, from 1791 until 1841, when it was reunited with Upper Quebec to form the present-day province of Quebec.

Lower East Side. See **East Side.**

Lower Egypt. The part of ancient Egypt comprising the Nile River delta. It was united with Upper Egypt c. 3100 B.C.

Lower Engadine. See **Engadine.**

Lower Klamath. A lake of northern California formerly connected with Upper Klamath Lake in soutern Oregon.

Lower Michigan. See **Lower Peninsula.**

Lower New York Bay. See **New York Bay.**

Lower Palatinate. See **Palatinate.**

Lower Peninsula also **Lower Michigan.** The section of Michigan between Lakes Michigan and Huron and south of the Straits of Mackinac.

Lower Rhine. The portion of the Rhine River between Bonn, Germany, and the North Sea.

Lower Tunguska. See **Tunguska.**

Lowes·toft (lō′stəf, -stôft′, -stŏft′). A municipal borough of extreme eastern England on the North Sea east-southeast of Norwich. A seaside resort, it is famous for the fine bone china produced here in the latter half of the 18th century. ⊛ Pop. 55,800.

Low German. 1. The German dialects of northern Germany. Also called *Plattdeutsch.* 2. The continental West Germanic languages except High German.

low·land (lō′lənd). 1. An area of land that is low in relation to the surrounding country. 2. Relating to or characteristic of low, usually level land.

Low·lands (lō′ləndz). A region of Scotland lying south of the Highlands. —**Low′land** *adj.* —**Low′land·er** *n.*

low·ly·ing (lō′lī′ĭng). Lying close to water or ground level.

Loy·al·ty Islands (loi′əl-tē). A group of coral islands of the southwest Pacific Ocean northwest of New Caledonia, of which they are an administrative division.

Lo·yang (lō′yäng′). See **Luoyang.**

Lu·an·da (lōō-än′də) also **Lo·an·da** (lō-än′də). The capital and largest city of Angola in the northwest part of the country on the Atlantic Ocean. Founded by the Portuguese in 1575, it has a fine natural harbor and diversified industries. ⊛ Pop. 1,200,000.

Lu·ang·wa (lōō-äng′wä). A river, about 805 km (500 mi) long, of eastern Zambia flowing southwest to the Zambezi River.

Lu·ba (lōō′bə). 1. *pl.* **Luba** or **-bas.** A member of a Bantu people inhabiting southeast Zaire. 2. The Bantu language of this people. In this sense, also called *Tshiluba.*

Lub·bock (lŭb′ək). A city of northwest Texas south of Amarillo. Settled in 1879, it is an industrial center in an agricultural region. ⊛ Pop. 186,206.

Lü·beck (lōō′bĕk′, lü′-). A city of north-central Germany northeast of Hamburg. A major Baltic port and industrial center, the present city dates from 1143 and was the leading town of the Hanseatic League after its designation as a free city in 1226. It retained that status until 1937. ⊛ Pop. 217,269.

Lu·blin (lōō′blən, -blēn′). A city of eastern Poland southeast of Warsaw. Chartered in 1317, it passed to Austria in 1795 and Russia in 1815. ⊛ Pop. 352,163.

Lu·bum·ba·shi (lōō′bŏŏm-bä′shē). Formerly **E·lis·a·beth·ville** (ĭ-lĭz′ə-bəth-vĭl′). A city of southeast Zaire near the border of Zambia. Founded in 1910, it was the center of a secessionist state during the civil war in Zaire (1960–1963). ⊛ Pop. 564,830.

Lu·ca·ni·a (lōō-kä′nē-ə, -kän′yə), **Mount.** A peak, 5,229.8 m (17,147 ft) high, of the St. Elias Mountains in southwest Yukon Territory, Canada, near the Alaskan border.

Luc·ca (lōō′kə). A city of northwest Italy west of Florence. On the site of an ancient Ligurian settlement and a Roman colony, it became a free commune in the 12th century and was later an independent republic. ⊛ Pop. 91,097.

Lu·cerne (lōō-sûrn′, lü-sĕrn′). A city of central Switzerland on the northern shore of the **Lake of Lucerne,** an irregularly shaped lake surrounded by mountains. The city developed around a monastery founded in the eighth century and is a major resort. ⊛ Pop. 59,724.

Luck·now (lŭk′nou). A city of north-central India east-southeast of Delhi. It was once the capital of the kingdom of Oudh (1775–1856), and during the Indian Mutiny of 1857 the British garrison there was besieged for five months. ⊛ Pop. 1,619,115.

Lü·da also **Lü·ta** (lōō′dä′, lü′-). An industrial conurbation of northeast China on Korea Bay at the southern end of the Liaodong Peninsula. It includes the cities of Lüshun and Dalian. ⊛ Pop. 3,473,832.

Lü·den·scheid (lōōd'n-shīt', lüd'-). A city of west-central Germany east of Düsseldorf. Chartered in 1287, it is an industrial center. ⊛ Pop. 73,496.

Lu·dhi·a·na (lōō'dē-ä'nə). A city of northwest India north-northwest of Delhi. It is an industrial center and a railroad junction. ⊛ Pop. 1,042,740.

Lud·low (lüd'lō). A town of southwest Massachusetts, a suburb of Springfield. It was set off from Springfield in 1774. ⊛ Pop. 18,820.

Lud·wigs·burg (lōōd'vĭgz-bûrg', lōōt'vĭKHS-bōōrk'). A city of southwest Germany north of Stuttgart. It grew around a baroque 18th-century castle built in imitation of the palace of Versailles, France. ⊛ Pop. 77,054.

Lud·wigs·ha·fen (lōōd'vĭgz-hä'fən, lōōt'vĭKHS-). A city of southwest Germany on the Rhine River opposite Mannheim. Founded as a fortress in the early 17th century, it is now a major transshipment point and a leading center of the country's chemical industry. ⊛ Pop. 168,130.

Luf·kin (lŭf'kĭn). A city of eastern Texas north-northeast of Houston. It is a commercial and industrial center. ⊛ Pop. 30,206.

Lu·gansk (lōō-gänsk', -gänsk'). Formerly **Vo·ro·shi·lov·grad** (vôr'ə-shē'ləf-gräd', və-rə-shē-ləf--grät'). A city of eastern Ukraine in the Donets Basin southeast of Kharkov. A coal-mining center, it was founded c. 1795. ⊛ Pop. 505,100.

Lu·go (lōō'gō). A city of northwest Spain west-southwest of Oviedo. It is a trade center with well-preserved Roman walls dating from the third century B.C. ⊛ Pop. 62,300.

Lui·chow Peninsula (lwē'jō'). See **Leizhou Peninsula.**

Lui·se·ño (lwē-sān'yō). **1.** *pl.* **Luiseño** or **-ños.** A member of a Native American people inhabiting the coastal area of California south of Los Angeles, associated during Spanish times with the missions of San Luis Rey and San Juan Capistrano. **2.** The Uto-Aztecan language of the Luiseño.

Lu·le·å (lōō'lĕ-ô', lü'-). A city of northeast Sweden on the Gulf of Bothnia. Chartered in 1621, it was rebuilt after a devastating fire in 1887. ⊛ Pop. 66,811.

Lu·le·älv (lōō'lĕ-ôlv', lü'lə-ĕlv'). A river, about 443 km (275 mi) long, of northern Sweden flowing southeast to the Gulf of Bothnia.

Lum·ber River (lŭm'bər). A river, about 201 km (125 mi) long, of south-central North Carolina and northeast South Carolina flowing southeast and south to the Little Pee Dee River.

Lum·ber·ton (lŭm'bər-tən). A city of southern North Carolina south of Fayetteville. It is a tobacco market with lumber and textile mills. ⊛ Pop. 18,601.

lu·nar·scape (lōō'nər-skāp'). A landscape reminiscent of the moon's surface.

Lund (lŭnd). A city of southern Sweden north of Malmö. It was the largest town in Sweden during the Middle Ages and today is an educational center. ⊛ Pop. 81,199.

Lun·dy Isle (lŭn'dē). An island off the southwest coast of England at the mouth of the Bristol Channel. Inhabited from prehistoric times, it was a stronghold for pirates and smugglers from the Middle Ages until the 18th century.

Lü·ne·burg (lōō'nə-bûrg', lü'nə-bōōrk'). A city of north-central Germany south-southeast of Hamburg. Dating from the tenth century, it was an important member of the Hanseatic League. ⊛ Pop. 60,194.

Lü·nen (lōō'nən, lü'-). A city of west-central Germany east-northeast of Essen. It is an industrial center in a coal-mining region. ⊛ Pop. 84,084.

lu·nette (lōō-nĕt'). A broad, low-lying, typically crescent-shaped mound of sandy or loamy matter that is formed by the wind, especially along the windward side of a lake basin.

Luo·yang (lwō'yäng') also **Lo·yang** (lō'-). A city of east-central China east-northeast of Xi'an. A cultural and industrial center, it was the capital of several ancient dynasties, including the Han and Tang. ⊛ Pop. 1,202,192.

Lu·sa·ka (lōō-sä'kə). The capital and largest city of Zambia, in the south-central part of the country. It was founded by Europeans in 1905. ⊛ Pop. 982,362.

Lu·sa·ti·a (lōō-sā'shē-ə, -shə). A region of central Europe in eastern Germany and southwest Poland. Settled by descendants of the Wends, it changed hands frequently among Saxony, Bohemia, and Brandenburg before passing to Prussia in 1815. —**Lu·sa'tian** *adj. & n.*

Lü·shun (lōō'shōōn', lü'-). Formerly **Port Arthur** (pôrt' är'thər, pōrt). A city of northeast China at the tip of the Liaodong Peninsula. A major port and naval base, it is part of the conurbation of Lüda.

Lu·si·ta·ni·a (lōō'sĭ-tā'nē-ə). An ancient region and Roman province of the Iberian Peninsula. It corresponded roughly to modern-day Portugal. —**Lu'si·ta'ni·an** *adj. & n.*

Lü·ta (lōō'dä', lü'-). See **Lüda.**

Lu·ther·ville-Ti·mo·ni·um (lōō'thər-vĭl'tĭ-mō'nē-əm). An unincorporated community of northern Maryland. It is a residential suburb of Baltimore. ⊛ Pop. 16,442.

Lu·ton (lōōt'n). A borough of southeast England north-northwest of London. A millinery industry was established here during the reign (1603–1625) of King James I. ⊛ Pop. 178,642.

Lutsk (lōōtsk). A city of northwest Ukraine

northeast of Lvov. First mentioned in 1085, it was the capital of an independent principality in the 12th century and an important trade center from the 14th to the 16th century. ⊛ Pop. 214,500.

Lu·wi·an (lōō′wē-ən, -vē-ən) or **Lu·vi·an** (-vē-ən). **1.** An Indo-European language of the Anatolian family, attested in documents from the second millennium B.C. and now extinct. **2.** A speaker of Luwian. **3.** Of or relating to the Luwians, their culture, or their language.

Lux·em·bourg also **Lux·em·burg** (lŭk′səm-bûrg′). **1.** *abbr.* **Lux.** A country of northwest Europe bordering on Belgium, Germany, and France. It was one of the largest fiefs of the Holy Roman Empire and was raised to the status of duchy in 1354. Passing successively to Burgundy, Spain, Austria, and France between 1443 and 1797, it was made a grand duchy of the Netherlands by the Congress of Vienna (1814–1815). In 1839 the greater part of it passed to Belgium. The remainder became autonomous in 1848 and was declared a neutral and independent territory in 1867. The country was occupied by Germany during World War I and World War II, since which time it has played an active role in promoting the unification of Europe. Luxembourg is the capital. ⊛ Pop. 401,000. **2.** also **Luxembourg City.** The capital of Luxembourg, in the southern part of the country. It developed around a heavily fortified tenth-century castle. ⊛ Pop. 75,833.

Lux·or (lŭk′sôr′, lōōk′-). A city of central Egypt on the eastern bank of the Nile River. Built partially on the site of ancient Thebes, it includes the Temple of Luxor built in the reign (1411?–1375 B.C.) of Amenhotep III and added to significantly by Rameses II (reigned 1304–1237 B.C.), who had colossal statues of himself erected at the complex. ⊛ Pop. 146,000.

Lu·zon (lōō-zŏn′). An island of the northwest Philippines. It is the largest, most populous, and most important island in the archipelago.

Lvov (lvôf). A city of west-central Ukraine near the Polish border. Founded in 1256, it was cap-

tured by Poland in 1340, passed to Austria in 1772, and was retaken by Poland in 1918. The city was formally ceded to the U.S.S.R. in 1945. ⊛ Pop. 742,000.

Ly·all·pur (lī′əl-pōōr′). See **Faisalabad.**

Lyc·i·a (lĭsh′ē-ə, lĭsh′ə). An ancient country and Roman province of southwest Asia Minor on the Aegean Sea. Ruled from early times by Persia and Syria, it was annexed by Rome in the first century A.D.

Ly·ci·an (lĭsh′ē-ən, lĭsh′ən). **1.** Of or relating to Lycia or its people, language, or culture. **2.** A language of the extinct Anatolian branch of Indo-European, found in inscriptions down to the beginning of the third century B.C. in southwest Turkey. **3.** A speaker of Lycian.

Lyd·i·a (lĭd′ē-ə). An ancient country of west-central Asia Minor on the Aegean Sea in present-day northwest Turkey. Noted for its wealth and the magnificence of its capital, Sardis, it may have been the earliest kingdom to use minted coins (seventh century B.C.).

Lyd·i·an (lĭd′ē-ən). **1.** Of or relating to Lydia or its people, language, or culture. **2.** A language of the extinct Anatolian branch of Indo-European, found in inscriptions of the fourth century B.C. in western Turkey. **3.** A speaker of Lydian.

Ly·ell (lī′əl), **Mount.** A peak, 3,994 m (13,095 ft) high, of the Sierra Nevada in the east-central part of California.

Lyn·brook (lĭn′brōōk′). A village of southeast New York on southwest Long Island east of Queens. It is mainly residential. ⊛ Pop. 19,208.

Lynch·burg (lĭnch′bûrg′). An independent city of southwest-central Virgina east-northeast of Roanoke. Located in the foothills of the Blue Ridge, it is an educational center with varied industries. ⊛ Pop. 66,049.

Lynd·hurst (lĭnd′hûrst′). **1.** An unincorporated community of northeast New Jersey, an industrial suburb of Newark. ⊛ Pop. 20,326. **2.** A city of northeast Ohio, a residential suburb of Cleveland. ⊛ Pop. 18,092.

Lynn (lĭn). A city of northeast Massachusetts, a residential and industrial suburb of Boston. It was formerly an important shoe-making center. ⊛ Pop. 81,245.

Lynn Canal. An inlet of the Pacific Ocean in southeast Alaska connecting Skagway with Juneau. It was a major route to the goldfields during the Alaskan gold rush (1896–1898).

Lynn·wood (lĭn′wŏŏd′). A city of west-central Washington, an industrial and residential suburb of Seattle. ⊛ Pop. 28,695.

Lyn·wood (lĭn′wŏŏd′). A city of southern California, an industrial and residential suburb of Los Angeles. ⊛ Pop. 61,945.

Ly·on or **Ly·ons** (lē-ōN′, lyôN). A city of east-central France at the confluence of the Rhone and Saône rivers south of Mâcon. Founded in 43 B.C. as a Roman colony, it was the principal city of Gaul and an important religious center after the introduction of Christianity. Its silk industry dates to the 15th century. ◉ Pop. 415,479.

Ly·on·nais (lē-ô-nĕ′). A historical region and former province of east-central France. It was a county during medieval times and became part of the French royal domain in the 14th century.

Ly·ons (lē-ŏN′, lyôN). See **Lyon.**

Lys (lēs). A river rising in northern France and flowing about 217 km (135 mi) northeast along the French-Belgian border to the Scheldt River.

M

maar (mär). A flat-bottomed, roughly circular volcanic crater of explosive origin that is often filled with water.

Maas (mäs). A section of the Meuse River flowing westward through the southern Netherlands to a joint delta with the Rhine River.

Maa·sai (mä-sī′, mä′sī). Variant of **Masai** (sense 2).

Maas·tricht (mäs′trĭkt′, -trĭKHt′). A city of extreme southeast Netherlands on the Maas River near the Belgian border. Founded on the site of a Roman settlement, the city was a strategic fortress and was frequently captured or beseiged, as in 1579 by the Spanish and in 1673 and 1794 by the French. The Treaty of European Union (known as the Maastricht Treaty) was signed in 1992 following a summit conference here. ◉ Pop. 118,194.

Ma·ble·ton (mā′bəl-tən). A community of northwest Georgia, a suburb of Atlanta. ◉ Pop. 25,725.

Ma·cao also **Ma·cau** (mə-kou′). A Portuguese overseas province comprising **Macao Peninsula** and two offshore islands in the South China Sea west of Hong Kong. A Portuguese trading post was established here in 1557 and became a free port in 1849. It is now a tourist center known for its casinos. The province will come under Chinese control on December 20, 1999. The city of **Macao,** coextensive with the peninsula, is the capital. ◉ Pop. 398,000.

Mac·e·don (măs′ĭ-dən, -dŏn′) also **Mac·e·do·ni·a** (măs′ĭ-dō′nē-ə, -dŏn′yə). An ancient kingdom of northern Greece originally occupying territory north of Thessaly and northwest of the Aegean Sea. It was the center of a powerful empire under Philip II and his son Alexander the Great (fourth century B.C.) and contributed sig-

nificantly to the spread of Hellenistic civilization. The Romans annexed it, and it became the first Roman province (146 B.C.).

Macedonia. 1. A region of southeast Europe on the Balkan Peninsula roughly coextensive with ancient Macedon and now divided among Greece, Bulgaria, and The Former Yugoslav Republic of Macedonia. After the fall of the Alexandrian empire, it was held by Romans, Byzantines, Bulgars, Serbs, and Turks. The present division was largely determined after the Second Balkan War (1913). 2. Officially **The Former Yugoslav Republic of Macedonia.** A country of the central Balkan Peninsula bordered by Albania, Yugoslavia, Bulgaria, and Greece. It was a constituent republic of the former Yugoslavia until it declared its independence in September 1991. Greece, fearing future territorial disputes between Macedonia and Greek Macedonia, objected to the name and, as a result, other nations did not immediately recognize the new country's sovereignty. It was eventually recognized by the UN under its current official name in 1993. Skopje is the capital and largest city. ◉ Pop. 2,142,000. 3. See **Macedon.**

Mac·e·do·ni·an (măs′ĭ-dō′nē-ən). *abbr.* **Maced.** 1. Of or relating to ancient or modern Macedonia or its peoples, languages, or cultures. 2. A native or inhabitant of ancient or modern Macedonia. 3. The language of ancient Macedonia, of uncertain affiliation within Indo-European. 4. The Slavic language of modern Macedonia, closely related to Bulgarian.

Ma·cei·ó (măs′ā-ō′, mä′sā-). A city of northeast Brazil on the Atlantic Ocean south-southwest of Recife. It is a commercial and distribution center. ◉ Pop. 628,241.

Mac·gil·li·cud·dy's Reeks (mə-gĭl′ĭ-kŭd′ēz rēks′). A mountain range of extreme southwest Ireland. It rises to 1,041.3 m (3,414 ft) at Carrantuohill, which is the island's highest peak.

Ma·cha·la (mä-chä′lä). A city of southwest Ecuador south of Guayaquil. It is a processing center in a gold-mining region. ◉ Pop. 144,197.

Ma·chi·da (mə-chē′də, mä-chē′dä). A city of

east-central Honshu, Japan, an industrial and residential suburb of Tokyo. ⊛ Pop. 358,891.

Ma·chu Pic·chu (mä′chōō pēk′chōō, pē′-). An ancient Inca fortress city in the Andes northwest of Cuzco, Peru. Its extensive ruins, including elaborate terraces, were discovered in 1911.

Mac·ken·zie District (mə-kĕn′zē). A former district of western and central Northwest Territories, Canada, now divided mainly between Inuvik and Fort Smith districts.

Mackenzie Mountains. A range of the northern Rocky Mountains in eastern Yukon Territory and western Northwest Territories, Canada, rising to 2,973.8 m (9,750 ft).

Mackenzie River. A river of northwest Canada rising in Great Slave Lake in southern Northwest Territories and flowing about 1,802 km (1,120 mi) generally northwest to a vast delta on **Mackenzie Bay,** an arm of the Beaufort Sea. It was first navigated by the Canadian explorer Sir Alexander Mackenzie in 1789.

Mack·i·nac Island (măk′ə-nô′). An island of northern Michigan in the **Straits of Mackinac,** a passage connecting Lakes Huron and Michigan between the Upper and Lower peninsulas. The island was long the center of an important fur-trading area and is now a resort.

Ma·comb (mə-kōm′). A city of western Illinois west-southwest of Peoria. It is known for its pottery and clay products. ⊛ Pop. 19,952.

Ma·con (mā′kən). A city of central Georgia southeast of Atlanta. Settled in the early 1820's, it is a processing, industrial, and educational center in an extensive farming area. ⊛ Pop. 106,612.

Mâ·con (mä-kôN′). A city of east-central France on the Saône River north of Lyon. A Huguenot stronghold in the 16th century, it is noted for its fine Burgundy wines. ⊛ Pop. 38,404.

Mac·quar·ie (mə-kwär′ē, -kwôr′ē). A river of southeast Australia flowing about 949 km (590 mi) northwest to the Darling River.

Mad·a·gas·car (măd′ə-găs′kər). Formerly **Mal·a·gas·y Republic** (măl′ə-găs′ē). abbr. **Mad., Madag.** An island country in the Indian Ocean off the southeast coast of Africa comprising the island of **Madagascar** and several small islands. Originally peopled by Indonesian and African groups around the end of the first century B.C., the islands were first visited by Muslim traders from eastern Africa in the ninth century and by the Portuguese in 1500. The French established settlements in 1642, declaring Madagascar a protectorate in 1885, though complete control was not achieved until 1904. The country gained full independence as the Malagasy Republic in 1960 and was renamed Madagascar in 1975 following a military takeover. Civil unrest in the 1990's led to the nation's first free elections in 1993. Antananarivo is the capital and the largest city. ⊛ Pop. 14,303,000. — **Mad′a·gas′can** adj. & n.

Ma·dei·ra (mə-dîr′ə, -dĕr′ə). A river of northwest Brazil rising on the Bolivian border and flowing about 3,315 km (2,060 mi) generally northeast to the Amazon River near Manaus. It is the most important tributary of the Amazon.

Madeira Islands. An archipelago of Portugal in the northeast Atlantic Ocean west of Morocco. Only two of the volcanic islands are inhabited. The island of **Madeira** is a tourist center noted for its wine. — **Ma·dei′ran** adj. & n.

Ma·de·ra (mə-dĕr′ə). A city of central California in the San Joaquin Valley northwest of Fresno. It is an industrial and processing center. ⊛ Pop. 29,281.

Mad·i·son (măd′ĭ-sən). **1.** A borough of northeast New Jersey southeast of Morristown. It is mainly residential. ⊛ Pop. 15,850. **2.** The capital of Wisconsin, in the south-central part of the state west of Milwaukee. It was chosen as territorial capital in 1836 and settled the same year. The main branch of the University of Wisconsin (founded 1848) is here. ⊛ Pop. 191,262.

Madison Heights. A city of southeast Michigan, a suburb of Detroit. ⊛ Pop. 32,196.

Madison River. A river of southwest Montana flowing about 294 km (183 mi) generally northward to join the Jefferson and Gallatin rivers and form the Missouri River.

Mad·i·son·ville (măd′ĭ-sən-vĭl′). A city of western Kentucky north of Hopkinsville. It is a processing center in a coal and farm area. ⊛ Pop. 16,200.

Ma·dras (mə-drăs′, -dräs′). A city of southeast India on the Coromandel Coast of the Bay of Bengal. Founded in 1639 as Fort St. George by the British East India Company, Madras was held by the French from 1746 to 1748. It is today a major industrial, commercial, and cultural center with a thriving harbor (constructed 1862–1901). ◉ Pop. 3,841,396.

Ma·dre de Di·os (mä′drä dä dē-ōs′, mä′thrĕ thĕ dyôs′). A river, about 1,126 km (700 mi) long, of southeast Peru and northwest Bolivia flowing northeast from the Andes to the Beni River.

Ma·drid (mə-drĭd′). The capital and largest city of Spain, on the central plateau north-northeast of Toledo. Built on the site of a Moorish fortress captured in the 10th century, it became the capital in 1561 during the reign of Philip II and grew in importance and magnificence under the Bourbons in the 18th century. Madrid was a Loyalist stronghold during the Spanish Civil War (1936–1939). ◉ Pop. 2,976,064.

Ma·du·rai (mä′də-rī′, măd′yŏō-rī′). A city of southern India south-southwest of Madras. Known as "the City of Festivals and Temples," it is a Hindu pilgrimage site and an educational and cultural center with varied industries. ◉ Pop. 940,989.

Mae·an·der (mē-ăn′dər). An ancient name for the Menderes River of western Turkey.

Ma·e·ba·shi (mä′ĕ-bä′shē). A city of central Honshu, Japan, northwest of Tokyo. Located in a mountainous region with volcanic soil, the city is a leading center for silk production. ◉ Pop. 287,912.

Maf·i·keng (mä′fĭ-kĭng′). Formerly **Maf·e·king** (-kĕng′). A town of north-central South Africa west of Pretoria. The relief (May 17, 1900) of a 217-day-long siege of the British garrison here was a celebrated event of the Boer War. ◉ Pop. 6,500.

Ma·ga·dha (mä′gə-də). An ancient kingdom of northeast India. It was especially powerful from the fourth century B.C. to the fifth century A.D., particularly under the emperor Asoka (third century B.C.).

Mag·da·le·na (măg′də-lā′nə, mäg′thä-lĕ′nä). A river rising in the Andes of southwest Colombia and flowing about 1,601 km (1,000 mi) generally northward to the Caribbean Sea near Barranquilla.

Mag·de·burg (măg′də-bûrg′, mäg′də-bŏŏrk′). A city of central Germany on the Elbe River west-southwest of Berlin. Known as early as 805, it was chartered in the 13th century and became one of the chief cities of the Hanseatic League. Magdeburg was severely damaged during World War II. ◉ Pop. 270,546.

Ma·gel·lan (mə-jĕl′ən), **Strait of.** A channel separating South America from Tierra del Fuego and other islands south of the continent and connecting the southern Atlantic and Pacific oceans. The Portuguese navigator Ferdinand Magellan sailed through the strait in October and November 1520.

Mag·gio·re (mə-jôr′ē, -jōr′ē, mäd-jô′rĕ), **Lake.** A lake of northern Italy and southern Switzerland. Nearly surrounded by peaks of the Lepontine Alps, it is a major resort area.

Ma·ghreb or **Ma·ghrib** (mŭg′rəb). A region of northwest Africa comprising the coastlands and the Atlas Mountains of Morocco, Algeria, and Tunisia.

Ma·gle·mo·si·an (mä′glə-mō′zē-ən). *Archaeology.* Of or relating to a Mesolithic forest culture of northern Europe.

Mag·na Grae·cia (măg′nə grē′shə). The ancient Greek seaport colonies of southern Italy and Sicily from the eighth to the fourth century B.C. Cumae and Tarantum (modern Taranto) remained significant after the decline of the other colonies.

mag·net·ic dec·li·na·tion (măg-nĕt′ĭk dĕk′-lə-nā′shən). The angle between magnetic north and true north at a particular location. Also called *magnetic variation.*

magnetic dip. The angle that a magnetic needle makes with the horizontal plane at any specific location. Magnetic dip is 0° at the magnetic equator and 90° at each of the magnetic poles. Also called *magnetic inclination.*

magnetic equator. A line connecting all points on the earth's surface at which a magnetic needle balances horizontally without dipping. Also called *aclinic line.*

magnetic in·cli·na·tion (ĭn′klə-nā′shən). See **magnetic dip.**

magnetic meridian. A line passing through both magnetic poles of the earth.

magnetic north. *abbr.* **MN.** The direction of the earth's magnetic pole, to which the north-seeking pole of a magnetic needle points when free from local magnetic influence.

magnetic pole. **1.** Either of two limited regions in a magnet at which the magnet's field is most intense, each of which is designated by the approximate geographic direction to which it is attracted. **2.** Either of two variable points on the earth, close to but not coinciding with the geographic poles, where the earth's magnetic field is most intense and toward which a compass needle points.

magnetic var·i·a·tion (vâr′ē-ā′shən, văr′-). See **magnetic declination.**

Mag·ni·to·gorsk (măg-nē′tə-gôrsk′, məg-nyĭ-tə-gôrsk′). A city of southwest Russia in the Ural Mountains south-southwest of Chelyabinsk. It was developed in the early 1930's as a leading center for heavy industry. ⊛ Pop. 438,808.

Mag·yar (măg′yär′, mäg′-, mŭd′-). **1.** A member of the principal ethnic group of Hungary. **2.** See **Hungarian** (sense 2). —**Mag′yar** *adj.*

Ma·hal·la el Ku·bra (mə-hăl′ə ĕl kōō′brə). A city of northern Egypt in the Nile River delta north of Cairo. It is a textile center with processing mills for rice and flour. ⊛ Pop. 408,000.

Ma·ha·na·di (mə-hä′nə-dē). A river of central India flowing about 885 km (550 mi) north and generally east to the Bay of Bengal.

Ma·ha·rash·tra (mä′hə-räsh′trə). A historical region of west-central India. It was controlled by the Muslim rulers of India from the early 14th to the mid-17th century and incorporated by the British into the province of Bombay in the 19th century. The Marathi-speaking section of the region became a separate state in 1960.

Ma·hi·can (mə-hē′kən) also **Mo·hi·can** (mō-, mə-). **1.** *pl.* **Mahican** or **-cans** also **Mohican** or **-cans.** A member of a Native American confederacy of subtribes formerly inhabiting the upper Hudson River valley from Albany south to the Catskill Mountains and north to Lake Champlain. Present-day descendants live in Oklahoma and Wisconsin. **2.** The Algonquian language of the Mahicans.

Ma·hón (mə-hōn′, mä-ôn′). A city of Spain on eastern Minorca. Probably founded by the Carthaginians, it was held by the Moors from the 8th to the 13th century. After passing to various powers, it came under Spanish control in 1802. ⊛ Pop. 22,926.

Mah·ra·ti (mə-rä′tē, -răt′ē). Variant of **Marathi.**

Mah·rat·ta (mə-rä′tə, -răt′ə). Variant of **Maratha.**

Mah·rat·ti (mə-rä′tē, -răt′ē). Variant of **Marathi.**

Maid·stone (mād′stən, -stōn′). A municipal borough of southeast England east-southeast of London. First chartered in 1549, it is a papermaking and brewing center. ⊛ Pop. 138,507.

Mai·du (mī′dōō). **1.** *pl.* **Maidu** or **-dus.** A member of a Native American people inhabiting northeast California south of Lassen Peak. **2.** The Penutian language of the Maidus.

Mai·du·gu·ri (mī-dōō′gōō-rē). A city of northeast Nigeria east of Kano. Maiduguri is a leather-processing center in the Lake Chad region. ⊛ Pop. 225,100.

main (mān). **1.** A mainland. **2.** The open ocean.

Main (mān, mīn). A river rising in eastern Germany and flowing about 499 km (310 mi) generally westward to the Rhine River at Mainz.

Maine (mān). **1.** A historical region and former province of northwest France south of Normandy. United with Anjou in 1126, it passed to England when Henry Plantagenet became king in 1154. Maine reverted to the French crown in 1481. **2.** *abbr.* **ME, Me.** A state of the northeast United States. It was admitted as the 23rd state in 1820. First explored by Europeans in 1602, the region was annexed by Massachusetts in 1652. Maine's northern boundary with New Brunswick was settled by a treaty with Great Britain in 1842. Augusta is the capital and Portland the largest city. ⊛ Pop. 1,233,223.

main·land (mān′lănd′, -lənd). The principal landmass of a continent. —**main′land′er** *n.*

Main·land Island (mān′lənd) also **Po·mo·na** (pə-mō′nə). The largest of the Orkney Islands off the northern coast of Scotland. It is known for its numerous Pictish remains including mounds, underground dwellings, and standing stones.

Main Line (mān′). A group of suburbs of southeast Pennsylvania. The fashionable area was named after the chief railroad line traveling west from Philadelphia.

Mainz (mīnts). A city of west-central Germany at the confluence of the Rhine and Main rivers west-southwest of Frankfurt. Built on the site of a Roman camp founded in the 1st century B.C., it is an important industrial and commercial city. Johann Gutenburg, considered the inventor of movable type, established a printing industry here in the 15th century. ⊛ Pop. 185,487.

Mai·sons-Al·fort (mā-zôɴ′äl-fôr′). A city of north-central France, an industrial suburb of Paris on the Marne River. ⊛ Pop. 51,065.

Ma·jor·ca (mə-jôr′kə, -yôr′-) also **Mal·lor·ca** (mä-yôr′kä, -lyôr′-). An island of Spain in the western Mediterranean Sea off the east-central coast of the mainland. The largest of the Balearic Islands, it was the center of an independent kingdom from 1276 until 1343. Tourism is its major industry. —**Ma·jor′can** *adj. & n.*

Ma·ju·ro (mə-jōōr′ō). The capital of the Marshall Islands, an atoll of the southern Ratak chain. ⊛ Pop. 20,000.

Mak·a·lu (mŭk′ə-lōō′). A mountain, 8,476 m (27,790 ft) high, in the Himalaya Mountains of northeast Nepal. It was first scaled in 1955.

Ma·kas·sar or **Ma·ka·sar** (mə-kăs′ər). See **Ujung Pandang.**

Makassar Strait. A strait between Borneo and Celebes connecting the Java Sea with the Celebes Sea.

Ma·ka·ti (mä′kə-tē′). A city of southwest Luzon, Philippines, a suburb of Manila. ⊛ Pop. 408,991.

Ma·ke·yev·ka (mə-kē′əf-kə, -kyĕ′-). A city of eastern Ukraine northeast of Donetsk. It is a major metallurgical and coal-mining center. ⊚ Pop. 425,600.

Ma·khach·ka·la (mə-käch′kə-lä′, -кнəch-). A city of southwest Russia on the western coast of the Caspian Sea. Founded in 1844, it is an oil-refining and a transshipment center. ⊚ Pop. 325,140.

Mal·a·bar Coast (măl′ə-bär′). A region of southwest India bordering on the Arabian Sea and bounded on the east by the Western Ghats.

Mal·a·bo (măl′ə-bō′, mä-lä′bō). Formerly **San·ta Is·a·bel** (săn′tə ĭz′ə-bĕl′, sän′tä ē-sä-bĕl′). The capital and largest city of Equatorial Guinea, on Bioko in the Gulf of Guinea. It was founded by the British in 1827. ⊚ Pop. 30,710.

Ma·lac·ca (mə-lăk′ə, -lä′kə), **Strait of.** A channel between Sumatra and the Malay Peninsula connecting the Andaman Sea with the South China Sea.

Má·la·ga (măl′ə-gə, mä′lä-gä′). A city of southern Spain northeast of Gibraltar. Founded by Phoenicians in the 12th century B.C., it was held successively by Carthaginians, Romans, Visigoths, and Moors (after 711). Málaga was conquered by Ferdinand and Isabella's troops in 1487. ⊚ Pop. 523,450.

Mal·a·gas·y (măl′ə-găs′ē). **1.** *pl.* **Malagasy** or **-gas·ies.** A native or inhabitant of Madagascar. **2.** The Austronesian language of the Malagasy. **3.** Of or relating to Madagascar, the Malagasy, or their language or culture.

Malagasy Republic. See **Madagascar.**

Ma·lang (mə-läng′). A city of eastern Java, Indonesia, south of Surabaya. It developed as an industrial center after 1914. ⊚ Pop. 511,780.

Mä·lar·en (mä′lär′ən). A lake of southeast Sweden. Stockholm is located on both sides of the strait that connects the lake with the Baltic Sea.

Ma·la·tya (mä′lə-tyä′). A city of east-central Turkey in the Taurus Mountains. It was the capital of a Hittite kingdom c. 1100 B.C. and was long a strategic frontier outpost. Malatya was annexed by the Ottoman Empire in 1516. ⊚ Pop. 319,700.

Ma·la·wi (mə-lä′wē). Formerly **Ny·as·a·land** (nī-ăs′ə-lănd′, nyä′sä-). A country of southeast Africa sharing major borders with Zambia to the west and Mozambique to the south. Center of the widespread Malawi kingdom from the 15th to the late 18th century, the region became a British protectorate in 1891 and was known as Nyasaland from 1907 until 1964. It joined Northern and Southern Rhodesia (now Zambia and Zimbabwe) in a federation from 1953 to 1963 and became independent as Malawi in 1964. Protests against one-party rule in the early 1990's resulted in a 1993 referendum laying

the groundwork for a multiparty democracy. Lilongwe is the capital and Blantyre the largest city. ⊚ Pop. 9,461,000. — **Ma·la′wi·an** *adj. & n.*

Malawi, Lake. See Lake **Nyasa.**

Ma·lay (mə-lā′, mā′lā′). *abbr.* **Mal. 1.** A member of a people inhabiting Malaysia, the northern Malay Peninsula, and parts of the western Malay Archipelago. **2.** The Austronesian language of the Malays. In this sense, also called *Bahasa Malay.* **3.** Of, relating to, or characteristic of the Malays or their language. **4.** Of or relating to Malaysia, the Malay Peninsula, or the Malay Archipelago. — **Ma·lay′an** *adj. & n.*

Ma·la·ya (mə-lā′ə, mā-). See **Malay Peninsula.**

Mal·a·ya·lam (măl′ə-yä′ləm). A Dravidian language spoken in the state of Kerala on the Malabar Coast of southwest India.

Malay Archipelago. An island group of southeast Asia between Australia and the Asian mainland and separating the Indian and Pacific oceans. It includes the islands of Indonesia, the Philippines, and Malaysia.

Ma·lay·o-Pol·y·ne·sian (mə-lā′ō-pŏl′ə-nē′-zhən)′. A subgroup of the Austronesian language family. — **Ma·lay′o-Pol′y·ne′sian** *adj.*

Malay Peninsula also **Ma·la·ya** (mə-lā′ə, mā-). A peninsula of southeast Asia comprising southwest Thailand, western Malaysia, and the island of Singapore.

Ma·lay·sia (mə-lā′zhə, -shə). A country of southeast Asia consisting of the southern Malay Peninsula and the northern part of the island of Borneo. Malays probably moved into the peninsula c. 2000 B.C., eventually reaching northern Borneo and displacing the indigenous Dayaks toward the interior. Later migrations of Chinese, Indians, and Thais formed the main part of Malaysia's multiethnic population. The peninsula was converted to Islam in the 15th century and was first visited by Europeans in the 16th century. By the 20th century Great Britain had established protectorates throughout the lower peninsula which were later joined to form the Union (1946) and subsequently the Federation (1948) of Malaya, an entity that gained independence within the Commonwealth in 1957. The Federation of Malaysia was created in 1963, comprising federated Malaya along with Singapore, Sabah, and Sarawak, with Singapore gaining separate independence in 1965. Kuala Lumpur is the capital and the largest city. ⊕ Pop. 19,489,000. — **Ma·lay′sian** *adj. & n.*

Mal·den (môl′dən). A city of northeast Massachusetts, a residential and manufacturing suburb of Boston. ⊕ Pop. 53,884.

Mal·dives (môl′dīvz, -dēvz, măl′-). Formerly **Mal·dive Islands** (-dīv, -dēv). An island country in the Indian Ocean southwest of Sri Lanka, consisting of 19 atolls made up of more than 2,000 coral islands. Settled by various groups from southern Asia, the islands were converted to Islam in the 12th century and came under European influence beginning with the arrival of the Portuguese in the 16th century. They became a self-governing British protectorate in 1887 and gained independence as a sultanate (1965) and

subsequently a republic (1968). Male is the capital. ⊕ Pop. 246,000. — **Mal·div′i·an** (-dĭv′ē-ən), **Mal·di′van** *adj. & n.*

Ma·le (mä′lē). The capital of the Maldives, on **Male,** the chief atoll of the island country. ⊕ Pop. 46,334.

Mal·e·cite (măl′ə-sīt′) or **Mal·i·seet** (-sēt′). **1.** *pl.* **Malecite** or **-cites** or **Maliseet** or **-seets.** A member of a Native American people inhabiting the St. John River valley in New Brunswick and northeast Maine. The Malecites helped form the Abenaki confederacy in the mid-18th century. **2.** The Algonquian language of the Malecites.

Ma·le·gaon (mä′lĭ-goun′, -gouɴ′). A town of west-central India northeast of Bombay. It has a weaving industry. ⊕ Pop. 342,595.

Ma·li (mä′lē). A country of western Africa. Several powerful states, including the Mali (flourished 14th century) and Songhai (flourished 15th–16th century) empires, dominated the region in medieval times. Following a Moroccan invasion in 1590, political control remained fragmented until French forces conquered the area in the late 19th century and made it part of French West Africa. Growing nationalism led to a referendum (1958) creating the autonomous Sudanese Republic, which joined briefly with Senegal to form the Mali Federation before achieving full independence in 1960. In 1992 one-party rule was ended and Mali held its first democratic elections. Bamako is the capital and the largest city. ⊕ Pop. 10,462,000. — **Ma′li·an** *adj. & n.*

Ma·lines (mə-lēnz′, mä-lēn′). See **Mechlin.**

Ma·lin·ke (mə-lĭng′kē). **1.** *pl.* **Malinke** or **-kes.** A member of a Mandingo people of Senegal and Gambia. **2.** The Mandingo language spoken by this people.

Mal·i·seet (măl′ə-sēt′). Variant of **Malecite.**

Mal·lor·ca (mä-yôr′kä, -lyôr′-). See **Majorca.**

Mal·mö (măl′mō, mäl′mœ). A city of southern Sweden on the Oresund opposite Copenhagen. An important trade and shipping center during the Hanseatic period, it passed from Denmark to Sweden in 1658. ⊛ Pop. 236,684.

Mal·ta (môl′tə). An island country in the Mediterranean Sea south of Sicily, comprising the island of **Malta** and two smaller islands. Occupied successively by Phoenicians, Greeks, Carthaginians, Romans, Saracens, and Normans, Malta was granted to the Knights Hospitalers in 1530 and passed to France in 1798 and Great Britain in 1800. During World War II it was heavily attacked by German and Italian aircraft, but it was never invaded. The country became independent in 1964 but has remained part of the British Commonwealth. Valletta, on Malta Island, is the capital. ⊛ Pop. 364,000.

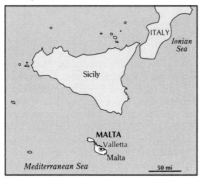

Mal·tese (môl-tēz′, -tēs′). **1.** Of or relating to Malta or its people, language, or culture. **2.** *pl.* **Maltese.** A native or inhabitant of Malta. **3.** The Semitic language of the people of Malta.

Mal·vern Hills (môl′vərn, mô′-). A range of hills of west-central England rising to 425.5 m (1,395 ft). The scenic hills are a popular resort area.

Ma·mar·o·neck (mə-măr′ə-nĕk′). A village of southeast New York, a residential and industrial suburb of New York City. ⊛ Pop. 17,325.

Mam·be·ra·mo (măm′bə-rä′mō). A river, about 805 km (500 mi) long, of western New Guinea flowing northwest into the Pacific Ocean.

Ma·mo·ré (mä-mə-rā′). A river, about 965 km (600 mi) long, of northern Bolivia flowing partly along the Brazilian border to join the Beni River and form the Madeira River.

Man (măn), **Isle of.** An island of Great Britain in the Irish Sea off the northwest coast of England. Occupied in the 9th century by Vikings, it passed from Norway to Scotland in 1266 and to the earls of Salisbury and of Derby in the 14th century. Parliament purchased the island in 1765, and it remains an autonomous possession of the British crown.

Ma·na·do (mə-nä′dō). A town of northeast Celebes, Indonesia. Established by the Dutch in 1657, it is a major seaport. ⊛ Pop. 217,519.

Ma·na·gua (mə-näg′wə, mä-nä′gwä). The capital and largest city of Nicaragua, in the western part of the country on the southern shore of Lake Managua. The city, designated as the capital in the 1850's, has frequently been damaged by earthquakes. ⊛ Pop. 644,588. — **Ma·na′-guan** *adj. & n.*

Ma·na·ma (mə-năm′ə, mă-) or **Al Ma·na·mah** (ăl mə-năm′ə, mă-). The capital and largest city of Bahrain, on the Persian Gulf. A free port, it became capital in 1971. ⊛ Pop. 136,999.

Ma·nas·sas (mə-năs′əs). An independent city of northeast Virginia west of Alexandria. The Civil War Battles of Bull Run (called the Battles of Manassas by the Confederates) were fought nearby in July 1861 and August 1862. ⊛ Pop. 27,957.

Ma·naus (mə-nous′, mä-). A city of northwest Brazil on the Río Negro near its junction with the Amazon River. Founded in the 1660's, Manaus was a prosperous center of the wild-rubber trade in the late 19th century and today is the chief commercial hub of the upper Amazon basin. ⊛ Pop. 1,010,544.

Man·ches·ter (măn′chĕs′tər, -chĭ-stər). **1.** A borough of northwest England east-northeast of Liverpool. Founded on the site of Celtic and Roman settlements, it was first chartered in 1301. Greater Manchester is densely populated and highly industrialized. The **Manchester Ship Canal** (completed in 1894) affords access for oceangoing vessels. ⊛ Pop. 432,038. **2.** A town of north-central Connecticut east of Hartford. It was settled in 1672. ⊛ Pop. 51,618. **3.** The largest city of New Hampshire, in the southeast part of the state on the Merrimack River north of Nashua. Incorporated as Derryfield in 1751 and renamed in 1810, it was an important textile center from the mid-1800's until the 1930's. ⊛ Pop. 99,567.

Man·chu (măn′chōō, măn-chōō′). **1.** *pl.* **Manchu** or **-chus.** A member of a people native to Manchuria who ruled China during the Qing dynasty. **2.** The Tungusic language of the Manchu. **3.** Of or relating to the Manchu or their language or culture.

Man·chu·kuo (măn′chōō′kwō′) also **Man·chu·guo** (-gwō′). A former state of eastern Asia in Manchuria and eastern Nei Monggol (Inner Mongolia). It was established as a puppet state (1932) after the Japanese invaded Manchuria in 1931 and was returned to Chinese sovereignty in 1945.

Man·chu·ri·a (măn-chŏŏr′ē-ə). A region of northeast China comprising the modern-day provinces of Heilongjiang, Jilin, and Liaoning. It was the homeland of the Manchu people who conquered China in the 17th century and was hotly contested by the Russians and the Japanese in the late 19th and early 20th centuries. Chinese Communists gained control of the area in 1948. — **Man·chu′ri·an** *adj. & n.*

Man·chu-Tun·gus (măn′chōō-tŏŏng-gōōz′, -tŭn-, măn-chōō′-). See **Tungusic.** —**Man′-chu-Tun·gus′ic** *adj.*

Man·cu·ni·an (măn-kyōō′nē-ən, -kyōōn′yən). **1.** Of or relating to Manchester, England. **2.** A native or inhabitant of Manchester, England.

Man·dae·an (măn-dē′ən). Variant of **Mandean.**

Man·da·lay (măn′dl-ā′, măn′dl-ā′). A city of central Myanmar (Burma) on the Irrawaddy River north of Yangon (Rangoon). Capital of the kingdom of Burma from 1860 to 1885, when it was annexed by the British, it was heavily damaged in World War II. ◉ Pop. 532,949.

Man·dan¹ (măn′dăn′). **1.** *pl.* **Mandan** or **-dans.** A member of a Native American people formerly living in villages along the Missouri River in south-central North Dakota, with present-day descendants on Lake Sakakawea in west-central North Dakota. **2.** The Siouan language of the Mandans.

Man·dan² (măn′dən, -dăn). A city of south-central North Dakota across the Missouri River from Bismarck. It is a distribution and manufacturing center in an agricultural region. ◉ Pop. 15,177.

Man·da·rin (măn′də-rĭn). The official national standard spoken language of China, which is based on the principal dialect spoken in and around Beijing. Also called *Guoyu, Putonghua.*

Man·de (män′dā′). **1.** A branch of the Niger-Congo language family, spoken in the upper Niger River valley. **2.** *pl.* **Mande** or **-des.** A member of a Mande-speaking people.

Man·de·an also **Man·dae·an** (măn-dē′ən). **1.** A member of a Gnostic sect originating in Jordan and still existing in Iraq. **2.** A form of Aramaic used by the Mandeans. —**Man·de′an** *adj.*

Man·de·kan (măn-dē′kən, män-dā′-). See **Mandingo** (sense 2).

Man·din·go (măn-dĭng′gō). **1.** *pl.* **Mandingo** or **-gos** also **-goes.** A member of any of various peoples inhabiting a large area of the upper Niger River valley of western Africa. **2.** A group of closely related Mande languages including Bambara, Malinke, and Maninka, widely spoken in western Africa. In this sense, also called *Mandekan.*

Man·hat·tan (măn-hăt′n). **1.** A city of northeast Kansas west of Topeka. It is a processing and educational center. ◉ Pop. 37,712. **2.** A borough of New York City in southeast New York, mainly on **Manhattan Island** at the north end of New York Bay. Peter Minuit of the Dutch West Indies Company bought the island in 1626 from the Manhattans, a Wappinger subtribe, supposedly for some $24 worth of merchandise. The settlement of New Amsterdam, renamed New York when the English assumed control in 1664, quickly spread from the southern tip

of the island, eventually becoming the financial, commercial, and cultural center of the United States. ◉ Pop. 1,487,536. —**Man·hat′tan·ite′** (-īt′) *n.*

Manhattan Beach. A city of southern California, a residential and industrial suburb of Los Angeles. ◉ Pop. 32,063.

Ma·nil·a (mə-nĭl′ə). The capital and largest city of the Philippines, on southwest Luzon Island and **Manila Bay,** an inlet of the South China Sea. Founded in 1571, the city was controlled by Spain until it was seized by U.S. troops in 1898 during the Spanish-American War. It was held by the Japanese from 1942 to 1945 during World War II. ◉ Pop. 1,728,441.

Ma·nin·ka (mə-nĭng′kā, -kē). **1.** *pl.* **Maninka** or **-kas.** A member of a Mandingo people inhabiting Senegal and Mali. **2.** The Mandingo language of this people.

Man·i·to·ba (măn′ĭ-tō′bə). *abbr.* **MB, Man.** A province of south-central Canada. It was admitted to the confederation in 1870. Originally part of a 1670 grant to the Hudson's Bay Company, it was largely settled by immigrants in the late 19th and early 20th centuries. Winnipeg is the capital and the largest city. ◉ Pop. 1,026,241. —**Man′i·to′ban** *adj. & n.*

Manitoba, Lake. A lake of southern Manitoba, Canada. It is a remnant of the glacial age Lake Agassiz.

Man·i·tou·lin Islands (măn′ĭ-tōō′lĭn). A group of islands of southern Ontario, Canada, in northern Lake Huron. The principal island, **Manitoulin,** is the largest lake island in the world.

Man·i·to·woc (măn′ĭ-tə-wŏk′). A city of eastern Wisconsin on Lake Michigan north of Sheboygan. Its shipbuilding industry dates from the 1840's. ◉ Pop. 32,520.

Ma·ni·za·les (măn′ĭ-zä′lĭs, -zäl′ĭs, mä′nē-sä′-lĕs). A city of west-central Colombia west of Bogotá. It is a commercial center in an important coffee-producing region. ◉ Pop. 283,365.

Man·ka·to (măn-kā′tō). A city of southern Minnesota south-southwest of Minneapolis. It is a trade and processing center in a farm and dairy region. ◉ Pop. 31,477.

Man·nar (mə-när′), **Gulf of.** An inlet of the Indian Ocean between southern India and Sri Lanka. It has important pearl fisheries.

Mann·heim (măn′hīm′, män′-). A city of southwest Germany at the confluence of the Rhine and Neckar rivers north-northwest of Stuttgart. First mentioned in the 8th century, it was chartered in 1607 and became an important musical and theatrical center in the 18th century. ◉ Pop. 318,025.

Man·re·sa (män-rā′sə, -rĕ′sä). A city of northeast Spain north-northwest of Barcelona. Metallurgical and textile industries are important to its economy. ◉ Pop. 66,951.

Mans·field (mănz′fēld′). **1.** A municipal borough of central England north of Nottingham. It is an industrial center in a coal-mining region. ◉ Pop. 102,145. **2.** A town of northeast Connecticut east-northeast of Hartford. It is an agricultural and manufacturing community. ◉ Pop. 21,103. **3.** A city of north-central Ohio west-southwest of Akron. First surveyed in 1808, it now manufactures a wide variety of products. ◉ Pop. 50,627.

Mansfield, Mount. The highest peak, 1,339.9 m (4,393 ft), of the Green Mountains in north-central Vermont. It is a winter sports area.

Man·te·ca (măn-tē′kə). A city of central California south of Stockton. It is a trade and processing center in a diversified agricultural area. ◉ Pop. 40,773.

Man·ti·ne·a (măn′tə-nē′ə). An ancient city of southern Greece in the eastern Peloponnesus. Thebes defeated Sparta here in 362 B.C.

Man·tu·a (măn′chōō-ə, -tōō-ə). A city of northern Italy south-southwest of Verona. Originally an Etruscan settlement, it was ceded to Austria in 1714 and was finally returned to Italy in 1866. ◉ Pop. 60,932. — **Man′tu·an** adj. & n.

Manx (măngks). **1.** Of or relating to the Isle of Man or its people, language, or culture. **2.** pl. **Manx.** The people of the Isle of Man. **3.** The extinct Goidelic language of the Manx.

Manx·man (măngks′mən). A man who is a native or inhabitant of the Isle of Man.

Manx·wo·man (măngks′wŏŏm′ən). A woman who is a native or inhabitant of the Isle of Man.

Mao·ri (mou′rē). **1.** pl. **Maori** or **-ris.** A member of a people of New Zealand, of Polynesian-Melanesian descent. **2.** The Austronesian language of the Maori. **3.** Of or relating to the Maori or their language or culture.

map (măp). **1.** A representation, usually on a plane surface, of a region of the earth or heavens. **2.** To make a map of. **3.** To explore or make a survey of (a region) for the purpose of making a map. — **map′pa·ble** adj. — **map′-mak′er** n.

Ma·ple Grove (mā′pəl). A city of southeast Minnesota, a suburb of Minneapolis. ◉ Pop. 38,736.

Maple Heights. A city of northeast Ohio, a residential suburb of Cleveland. ◉ Pop. 27,089.

Maple Shade. A community of south-central New Jersey east of Camden. It is a manufacturing center in a truck-farming region. ◉ Pop. 19,211.

Ma·ple·wood (mā′pəl-wŏŏd′). **1.** A city of southeast Minnesota, a residential suburb of St. Paul. ◉ Pop. 30,954. **2.** A community of north-

east New Jersey east of Newark. It is mainly residential. ◉ Pop. 21,756.

Ma·pu·to (mə-pōō′tō). Formerly **Lou·ren·ço Mar·ques** (lə-rĕn′sō mär′kĕs, lô-rĕn′sŏŏ mär′-kĕsh). The capital and largest city of Mozambique, in the extreme southern part of the country on the Indian Ocean. Founded in the late 18th century, it was renamed (1976) after the country gained its independence (1975). ◉ Pop. 882,601.

Ma·ra·cai·bo (măr′ə-kī′bō, mä′rä-kī′vô). A city of northwest Venezuela south of the Gulf of Venezuela at the outlet of **Lake Maracaibo,** the largest lake of South America. Founded in 1571, the city is a major port on a dredged channel allowing access for oceangoing vessels. It developed rapidly after the discovery of oil reserves in 1917. ◉ Pop. 1,207,513.

Ma·ra·cay (mär′ə-kī′). A city of northern Venezuela west-southwest of Caracas. It is a cattle center. ◉ Pop. 384,782.

Mar·ais des Cygnes (mĕr′ də zēn′). A river rising in east-central Kansas and flowing about 241 km (150 mi) generally southeast to the Osage River in western Missouri.

Mar·a·jó (măr′ə-zhō′, mä′rä-). An island of northern Brazil in the Amazon delta. It is noted for its prehistoric mounds.

Ma·ra·ñón (mär′ən-yōn′, mä′rä-nyôn′). A river flowing about 1,609 km (1,000 mi) from west-central to northeast Peru, where it joins the Ucayali River to form the Amazon.

Ma·raş (mə-räsh′). A city of south-central Turkey in the Taurus Mountains northeast of Adana. A Hittite city-state c. 1000 B.C., it was captured by Arabs in A.D. 638 and annexed by the Ottoman Empire in the early 16th century. ◉ Pop. 242,200.

Ma·ra·tha also **Mah·rat·ta** (mə-rä′tə, -răt′ə). pl. **Maratha** or **-thas** also **Mahratta** or **-tas.** A member of a Hindu people inhabiting Maharashtra in west-central India.

Ma·ra·thi also **Mah·ra·ti** or **Mah·rat·ti** (mə-rä′tē, -răt′ē). The principal Indic language of Maharashtra.

Mar·a·thon (măr′ə-thŏn′). A village and plain of ancient Greece northeast of Athens. It was the site of a major victory over the Persians in 490 B.C.

Mar·bel·la (mär-bĕl′ə, -vĕ′lyä). A city of southern Spain on the Mediterranean Sea southwest of Málaga. It is a noted tourist resort. ◉ Pop. 39,000.

Mar·ble·head (mär′bəl-hĕd′, mär′bəl-hĕd′). A town of northeast Massachusetts northeast of Boston. Founded in the 17th century, it is a boating center and resort. ◉ Pop. 19,971.

Mar·burg (mär′bûrg′, -bŏŏrk′). A city of west-central Germany north of Frankfurt. Europe's first Protestant university was founded here in 1527. ◉ Pop. 76,260.

march (märch). **1.** The border of a country or an area of land. **2.** A tract of land bordering on two countries and claimed by both.

Marche¹ (märsh). A historical region and former province of central France. So called because of its location as a northern border fief of the duchy of Aquitaine, it became part of the French crown lands in 1531.

Mar·che² (mär′kā) or **Mar·ches** (-chĭz). A region of east-central Italy extending from the eastern slopes of the Apennines to the Adriatic Sea. Colonized by Rome in the 3rd century B.C., it was under papal control for much of the period from the 16th to the 19th century.

Mar·cus Ba·ker (mär′kəs bā′kər), **Mount.** A peak, 4,018.7 m (13,176 ft) high, in the Chugach Mountains of southeast Alaska. It is the highest elevation in the range.

Mar del Pla·ta (mär′ dĕl plä′tə, thĕl plä′tä). A city of east-central Argentina on the Atlantic Ocean south-southeast of Buenos Aires. It is a popular resort with a fishing industry. ◉ Pop. 519,707.

Mar·gate (mär′gāt′). **1.** A municipal borough of southeast England east of London. A popular seaside resort, it also has light industries. ◉ Pop. 121,900. **2.** A city of southeast Florida northwest of Fort Lauderdale. It is a resort community. ◉ Pop. 42,985.

Mar·i·an·a Islands (măr′ē-ăn′ə, mâr′-, mä′-rē-ä′nä). An island group in the western Pacific Ocean east of the Philippines. Guam, the largest island of the group, is independent of the others, which are known formally as the **Commonwealth of the Northern Mariana Islands.** The Marianas were discovered by the Portuguese navigator Ferdinand Magellan in 1521 and held by Spain until 1898. They were sold to Germany in 1899 (when Guam was ceded to the United States) and later became a Japanese mandate (1919–1944). The islands were part of the Trust Territory of the Pacific Islands from 1947–1978, when they became a commonwealth under U.S. sovereignty.

Mar·i·an·as Trench (măr′ē-ăn′əz, mâr′-, mä′-rē-ä′näs). A depression with a maximum depth of 11,040.4 m (36,198 ft) in the floor of the western Pacific Ocean south and east of Guam.

Ma·ri·as (mə-rī′əs). A river of northwest Montana flowing about 338 km (210 mi) generally southeast to the Missouri River.

Ma·ri·bor (mär′ĭ-bôr′). A city of eastern Slovenia on the Drava River near the Austrian border. It is an industrial center. ◉ Pop. 131,492.

Mar·i·co·pa (măr′ĭ-kō′pə). **1.** pl. **Maricopa** or **-pas.** A member of a Native American people sharing reservation lands with the Pimas in south-central Arizona. **2.** The Yuman language of the Maricopas.

Ma·rie Byrd Land (mə-rē′ bûrd′). A region of western Antarctica east of the Amundsen Sea. It was discovered and claimed for the United States by Richard E. Byrd in 1929.

Mar·i·et·ta (măr′ē-ĕt′ə, mâr′-). **1.** A city of northwest Georgia northwest of Atlanta. It is a residential community with an aircraft industry. ◉ Pop. 44,129. **2.** A city of southeast Ohio on the Ohio River southeast of Zanesville. Founded in 1788, it is the oldest permanent settlement in the state. ◉ Pop. 15,026.

Ma·ri·ki·na (mär′ĭ-kē′nə). A city of southwest Luzon, Philippines, a suburb of Manila. ◉ Pop. 248,183.

Ma·rí·lia (mə-rēl′yə, mä-rē′lyä). A city of southeast Brazil west-northwest of São Paulo. It is a trade and processing center in an agricultural region. ◉ Pop. 160,872.

Ma·ri·na (mə-rē′nə). A city of western California on Monterey Bay west of Salinas. It is a resort community. ◉ Pop. 26,436.

Ma·rin·gá (mä′rĭn-gä′). A city of southeast Brazil northwest of Curitiba. It is a coffee-processing center. ◉ Pop. 240,135.

Mar·i·on (măr′ē-ən, mâr′-). **1.** A city of northeast-central Indiana northwest of Muncie. It is a trade, processing, and industrial center. ◉ Pop. 32,618. **2.** A city of east-central Iowa, a suburb of Cedar Rapids. ◉ Pop. 20,403. **3.** A city of central Ohio north of Columbus. The home and burial place of President Warren G. Harding, it is a manufacturing center. ◉ Pop. 34,075.

Mar·i·time Alps (măr′ĭ-tīm′). A range of the southwest Alps on the French-Italian border near the Mediterranean Sea. The highest elevation is 3,299.2 m (10,817 ft).

Maritime Provinces. The Canadian provinces of Nova Scotia, New Brunswick, and Prince Edward Island, bordering on the Atlantic Ocean. They were politically distinct from Canada until the confederation of 1867. —**Mar′i·tim′er** *n.*

Ma·ri·tsa (mə-rēt′sə). A river of western Bulgaria and western Turkey flowing about 483 km (300 mi) southeast then south to the Aegean Sea.

Ma·ri·u·pol (mä′rē-ōō′pŏl′). Formerly **Zhda·nov** (zhdä′nəf). A city of southeast Ukraine on the Sea of Azov. It is a major port. ◉ Pop. 522,900.

Mark·ham (mär′kəm). **1.** A town of southern Ontario, Canada, north-northeast of Toronto. It is a processing center. ◉ Pop. 77,037. **2.** A city of northeast Illinois, a suburb of Chicago. ◉ Pop. 13,136.

Markham, Mount. A peak, 4,353 m (14,272 ft) high, of Victoria Land, Antarctica. It was discovered in 1902.

Marl (märl). A city of west-central Germany in the Ruhr Valley north of Essen. First mentioned in the ninth century, it is now highly industrialized. ⊛ Pop. 87,231.

Marl·bor·ough or **Marl·bo·ro** (märl′bûr′ō, -bər-ə, -bŭr′ō). A city of east-central Massachusetts east-northeast of Worcester. Settled in 1657, it was nearly destroyed in 1676 during King Philip's War. ⊛ Pop. 31,813.

Mar·ma·ra (mär′mər-ə), **Sea of.** A sea of northwest Turkey located between Europe and Asia. It is connected to the Black Sea through the Bosporus and to the Aegean Sea through the Dardanelles.

Mar·mo·la·da (mär′mə-lä′də, -mô-lä′dä). A peak, 3,344.3 m (10,965 ft) high, in the Dolomite Alps of northeast Italy. It is the highest elevation in the range.

Marne (märn). A river, about 523 km (325 mi) long, of northeast France flowing in an arc generally northwest to the Seine River near Paris. It was the scene of heavy fighting in World War I (1914 and 1918) and World War II (1944).

Ma·ro·ni (mə-rō′nē) also **Ma·ro·wij·ne** (mär′-ə-vī′nə). A river of northern South America flowing about 724 km (450 mi) northward along the Suriname–French Guiana border to the Atlantic Ocean.

ma·roon also **Ma·roon** (mə-rōōn′). **1.** A fugitive Black slave in the West Indies in the 17th and 18th centuries. **2.** A descendant of such a slave.

Maroon Peak. A mountain, 4,317.6 m (14,156 ft) high, in the Elk Mountains of west-central Colorado.

Mar·que·san (mär-kā′zən, -sən). **1.** A native or inhabitant of the Marquesas Islands. **2.** The Austronesian language of the Marquesans. **3.** Of or relating to the Marquesas Islands or their people, language, or culture.

Mar·que·sas Islands (mär-kā′zəz, -səz, -səs). A volcanic archipelago in the southern Pacific Ocean, part of French Polynesia. The southern islands were discovered by a Spanish navigator in 1595; the northern group, by an American seafarer in 1791. France took possession of the islands in 1842.

Mar·quette (mär-kĕt′). A city of northwest Michigan on the Upper Peninsula and Lake Superior. It is a shipping center for iron ore and various manufactures. ⊛ Pop. 21,977.

Mar·ra·kesh or **Mar·ra·kech** (mär′ə-kĕsh′, mə-rä′kĕsh). A city of west-central Morocco in the foothills of the Atlas Mountains. Founded in 1062, it is a commercial center and a popular resort noted for its leatherwork. ⊛ Pop. 602,000.

Mar·re·ro (mə-rär′ō, -rĕr′ō). A community of southeast Louisiana, a suburb of New Orleans on the Mississippi River. ⊛ Pop. 36,671.

Mar·sa·la (mär-sä′lə). A city of western Sicily on the Mediterranean Sea. Founded by the Carthaginians c. 397 B.C., it is noted for its wine. ⊛ Pop. 46,300.

Mar·seille also **Mar·seilles** (mär-sā′). A city of southeast France on an arm of the Mediterranean Sea west-northwest of Toulon. The oldest city of France, it was founded c. 600 B.C. by Greeks from Asia Minor and overrun by barbarian tribes in the 5th and 6th centuries A.D. Marseille became independent in the 13th century and passed to France in 1481. Today it is an industrial center and a major seaport. ⊛ Pop. 800,309.

Mar·shall (mär′shəl). A city of northeast Texas west of Shreveport, Louisiana. It is a manufacturing center in a resort region. ⊛ Pop. 23,682.

Marshall Islands. A self-governing island group in the central Pacific Ocean. Inhabited by Micronesian peoples, the islands were sighted by Spanish explorers in the early 16th century and were governed by Spain and later Germany until their seizure in 1914 by the Japanese, who were given a mandate over them in 1920. After 1947 they became part of the U.S. Trust Territory of the Pacific Islands, during which time the United States carried out numerous nuclear tests on Enewetok and Bikini atolls. In 1983 the U.S. government paid the Marshall Islands $183.7 million in compensation for damages caused by the testing. Self-governing after 1979, the islands attained free-association status with the United States in 1986. Majuro is the capital. ⊛ Pop. 58,363.

Mar·shall·town (mär′shəl-toun′). A city of central Iowa northeast of Des Moines. It is a transportation and trade center. ⊛ Pop. 25,178.

Marsh·field (märsh′fēld′). **1.** A town of southeast Massachusetts on Massachusetts Bay southeast of Boston. The burial place of the American politician Daniel Webster (1782–1852), it is now a resort community. ⊛ Pop. 21,531. **2.** A city of central Wisconsin southwest of Wausau. It is a processing center in a dairy region. ⊛ Pop. 19,291.

Mar·ston Moor (mär′stən). A site in northern

England west of York. The first Parliamentarian victory of the English Civil War occurred here on July 2, 1644.

Mar·ta·ban (mär′tə-băn′, -bän′), **Gulf of.** An arm of the Andaman Sea off southern Myanmar (Burma).

Mar·tha's Vine·yard (mär′thəz vĭn′yərd). An island of southeast Massachusetts off the southwest coast of Cape Cod. Settled in 1642, it was a whaling and fishing center in the 18th and early 19th centuries and is now a popular resort area.

Mar·ti·nez (mär-tē′nəs). **1.** A city of western California northeast of Oakland. It is a manufacturing and processing center. ☉ Pop. 31,808. **2.** A community of eastern Georgia, a suburb of Augusta. ☉ Pop. 33,731.

Mar·ti·nique (mär′tĭ-nēk′, -tn-ēk′). *abbr.* **Mart.** An island and overseas department of France in the Windward Islands of the West Indies. Inhabited first by Arawaks and later by Caribs, the island was visited by Columbus in 1502 but was not settled by Europeans until the French established a colony in 1635. Martinique became a French department in 1946. Fort-de-France is the capital. ☉ Pop. 375,000.

Mar·tins·ville (mär′tnz-vĭl′). An independent city of southern Virginia in the foothills of the Blue Ridge near the North Carolina border. It was founded in 1793. ☉ Pop. 16,162.

Mar·y·land (mĕr′ə-lənd). *abbr.* **MD, Md.** A state of the east-central United States. It was admitted as one of the original Thirteen Colonies in 1788. The colony was founded by Lord Baltimore in 1634 as a refuge for English Roman Catholics. Annapolis is the capital and Baltimore the largest city. ☉ Pop. 4,798,622. **—Mar′y·land·er** *n.*

Mar·y·ville (mâr′ē-vĭl′, mĕr′ĭ-vəl, -vĭl′). A city of eastern Tennessee south of Knoxville. Settled around a fort built in 1785, it is an aluminum-producing center. ☉ Pop. 19,208.

Ma·sa·da (mə-sä′də, -tsä-dä′). An ancient mountaintop fortress in southeast Israel on the southwest shore of the Dead Sea. In A.D. 73, after a two-year siege, members of the Zealot Jewish sect who lived there committed mass suicide rather than surrender to the Romans.

Ma·sai (mä-sī′, mä′sī). **1.** *pl.* **Masai** or **-sais.** A member of a chiefly pastoral people of Kenya and parts of Tanzania. **2.** also **Maa·sai.** The Nilotic language of this people. **—Ma·sai′** *adj.*

Ma·san (mä′sän′). A city of southeast South Korea west of Pusan. Its port was opened to foreign trade in 1899. ☉ Pop. 493,731.

Mas·ba·te (mäs-bä′tē, -tĕ). An island of the central Philippines south of Luzon. Its gold mines have been worked for centuries.

Mas·ca·rene Islands (măs′kə-rēn′). A group of islands in the Indian Ocean east of Madagascar. Mauritius and the French island of Réunion are in the group.

Mas·couche (mä-skōōsh′). A city of southern Quebec, Canada, a suburb of Montreal on the upper bank of the St. Lawrence River. ☉ Pop. 20,345.

Mas·er·u (măz′ə-rōō′, mä′sə-rōō′). The capital of Lesotho, in the western part of the country. It was founded in 1869. ☉ Pop. 14,686.

Ma·sher·brum (mŭsh′ər-brōōm′). A peak, 7,826.3 m (25,660 ft) high, in the Karakoram Range of the Himalaya Mountains in Kashmir. It was first scaled in 1960.

Mash·had (mäsh-häd′). See **Meshed.**

Mas·keg (măs′kĕg′). Variant of **muskeg.**

Ma·son City (mā′sən). A city of north-central Iowa north-northeast of Des Moines. It is a trade and industrial center in an agricultural region. ☉ Pop. 29,040.

Ma·son-Dix·on Line (mā′sən-dĭk′sən). The boundary between Pennsylvania and Maryland, regarded as the division between free and slave states before the Civil War (1861–1865). It was established between 1763 and 1767 by the British surveyors Charles Mason (1730–1787) and Jeremiah Dixon (died 1777).

Mas·sa (mä′sə). A city of north-central Italy near the Ligurian Sea north of Leghorn. It was the capital of an independent principality and duchy from the 15th to the 19th century. ☉ Pop. 65,726.

Mas·sa·chu·sett also **Mas·sa·chu·set** (măs′ə-chōō′sĭt, -zĭt). **1.** *pl.* **Massachusett** or **-setts** also **Massachuset** or **-sets.** A member of a Native American people formerly located along Massachusetts Bay from Plymouth north to Salem. Reduced by epidemics, the Massachusetts ceased to exist as a people during the 17th century. **2.** The Algonquian language spoken by the Massachusetts.

Mas·sa·chu·setts (măs′ə-chōō′sĭts). *abbr.* **MA, Mass.** A state of the northeast United States. It was admitted as one of the original Thirteen Colonies in 1788. The first settlement was made by the Pilgrims of the *Mayflower* in 1620. Governed by the Massachusetts Bay Company from 1629 until 1684, the colony was a leader in the move for independence from Great Britain and the site of the first battles of the Revolutionary War in 1775. Boston is the capital and the largest city. ☉ Pop. 6,029,051.

Massachusetts Bay. An inlet of the Atlantic Ocean off eastern Massachusetts extending from Cape Ann in the north to Cape Cod in the south.

Mas·sa·pe·qua (măs-ə-pē′kwə). An unincorporated community of southeast New York on the southern coast of Long Island southeast of Mineola. It is chiefly residential. ◉ Pop. 22,018. The village of **Massapequa Park** is to the east; its population is 18,044.

mas·sif (mă-sēf'). **1.** A large mountain mass or compact group of connected mountains forming an independent portion of a range. **2.** A large section or block of the earth's crust that is more rigid than the surrounding rock and has been moved or displaced as a unit.

Mas·sif Cen·tral (mă-sēf' sĕn-träl', säN-). A mountainous plateau of south-central France. It includes the Cévennes and the Auvergne Mountains, which rise to the plateau's highest point, 1,887.3 m (6,188 ft).

Mas·sil·lon (măs'ə-lən, -lŏn'). A city of northeast Ohio west of Canton. It is an industrial center with varied manufactures. ◉ Pop. 31,007.

Mas·sive (măs'ĭv), **Mount.** A peak, 4,398.4 m (14,421 ft) high, in the Sawatch Range of the Rocky Mountains in central Colorado.

Ma·su·ri·a (mə-zŏŏr'ē-ə). A historical region of northeast Poland. Ruled by the Teutonic Knights after the 14th century and later part of East Prussia, it was assigned to Poland by the Potsdam Conference of 1945. — **Ma·su'ri·an** *adj.*

Mat·a·be·le (mä'tä-bĕl'ā). See **Ndebele**.

Mat·a·be·le·land (mä'tə-bĕl'ā-lănd'). A region of western Zimbabwe. Inhabited by the Ndebele people after 1827, it came under the control of the British South Africa Company in 1889.

Mat·a·gor·da Bay (măt'ə-gôr'də). An inlet of southeast Texas separated from the Gulf of Mexico by the **Matagordo Peninsula**, a narrow sand spit.

Ma·ta·mo·ros (măt'ə-môr'əs, -mōr'-, mä'tä-mô'rôs). A city of northeast Mexico near the mouth of the Rio Grande opposite Brownsville, Texas. It was captured by Zachary Taylor's forces in 1846 during the Mexican War. ◉ Pop. 188,745.

Ma·tan·zas (mə-tăn'zəs, mä-tän'säs). A city of northwest-central Cuba east of Havana. It was founded in 1693 and was once a haven for pirates. ◉ Pop. 120,988.

Mat·a·pan (măt'ə-păn'), **Cape.** See Cape **Taínaron**.

Ma·ta·ró (mä'tə-rō', -tä-). A city of northeast Spain on the Mediterranean Sea northeast of Barcelona. It is a port and manufacturing center. ◉ Pop. 101,510.

Ma·te·ra (mə-tĕr'ə). A city of southern Italy in the Apennines south of Bari. It is an agricultural and industrial center. ◉ Pop. 51,000.

Ma·thu·ra (mŭt'ər-ə) also **Mut·tra** (mŭt'rə). A city of north-central India northwest of Agra. An important repository of ancient Indian art, it is a Hindu pilgrimage site revered as the reputed birthplace of Krishna, the principal avatar of the Hindu deity Vishnu. ◉ Pop. 226,691.

Mat·su (mät'sŏŏ'). An island in the East China Sea off the southeast coast of mainland China. It remained a Nationalist stronghold after the Chinese Communist revolution of 1949 and is now administered, along with Quemoy, by Taiwan.

Ma·tsu·do (mä-tsŏŏ'dō). A city of east-central Honshu, Japan, a suburb of Tokyo, with several ironworks factories. ◉ Pop. 463,517.

Ma·tsu·ya·ma (mä'tsŏŏ-yä'mä). A city of western Shikoku, Japan, on the Inland Sea. A port and distribution center, it was an important fortress town during the feudal period. ◉ Pop. 454,374.

Mat·tag·a·mi (mə-tăg'ə-mē). A river, about 443 km (275 mi) long, of eastern Ontario, Canada, rising in **Mattagami Lake** and flowing north to the Moose River.

Mat·ta·po·ni (măt'ə-pə-nī'). A river, about 201 km (125 mi) long, of eastern Virginia flowing southeast to the York River.

Mat·ter·horn (măt'ər-hôrn', mä'tər-). A mountain, 4,481.1 m (14,692 ft) high, in the Pennine Alps on the Italian-Swiss border. It was first scaled in 1865.

Mat·toon (mə-tŏŏn'). A city of east-central Illinois southeast of Decatur. Founded in 1854, it is a processing and industrial center in a farm and dairy region. ◉ Pop. 18,441.

Ma·tu·rín (mä'tə-rēn', -tŏŏ-). A city of northeast Venezuela east-southeast of Caracas. It was founded in 1710 by Capuchin missionaries. ◉ Pop. 207,382.

Mau·á (mou-ä'). A city of southeast Brazil, a suburb of São Paulo. ◉ Pop. 294,631.

Mau·i (mou'ē). An island of Hawaii northwest of Hawaii Island. It is the second-largest island in the state, with an economy based chiefly on sugar cane, pineapples, and tourism.

Mau·mee (mô-mē', mô'mē). A city of northwest Ohio, a residential suburb of Toledo. It was settled on the site of Fort Miami, a British port surrendered to the Americans in the War of 1812. ◉ Pop. 15,561.

Maumee River. A river rising in northeast Indiana and flowing about 209 km (130 mi) east and northeast to Lake Erie at Toledo, Ohio.

Mau·na Ke·a (mou'nə kā'ə, mô'nə kē'ə). An active volcano, about 4,208 m (13,796 ft) high, of north-central Hawaii Island. It is the highest peak in the islands.

Mauna Lo·a (lō'ə). An active volcano, 4,172.4 m (13,680 ft) high, in the south-central part of Hawaii Island.

Mau·re·ta·ni·a (môr'ĭ-tā'nē-ə, -tān'yə, mär'-). An ancient district of the Roman Empire in present-day Morocco and Algeria. Settled by a Berber people, it was ruled by Rome from c. 100 B.C. to the fifth century A.D. — **Mau're·ta'ni·an** *adj. & n.*

Mau·ri·ta·ni·a (môr′ĭ-tā′nē-ə, -tān′yə, mär′-).
A country of northwest Africa bordering on the
Atlantic Ocean. Southern Mauritania was part of
the ancient empire of Ghana, and the northern
part was settled by Berbers around 1000 A.D.
The region later formed part of the Mali Empire
(flourished 14th century) and was visited by
Portuguese and other European traders beginning in the 15th century. French influence became dominant in the early 1800's, with Mauritania being declared a French protectorate in
1903 and a separate colony within French West
Africa in 1920. Independence was gained in
1960. Mauritania was granted control of part of
Western Sahara in 1976 but renounced its claims
in 1979 after clashes with guerrilla forces seek-
ing independence for the Saharan territory.
Nouakchott is the capital and the largest city.
⊛ Pop. 2,211,000. **—Mau′ri·ta′ni·an** *adj. & n.*

Mau·ri·tius (mô-rĭsh′əs, -ē-əs). An island
country in the southwest Indian Ocean comprising the island of **Mauritius** and several small dependencies in the Mascarene Islands. Originally
uninhabited, the islands were probably known to
Arab and Malay traders in the Middle Ages.
Mauritius was controlled by the Dutch (1598–
1710), the French (1715–1810), and the British
(after 1814) before achieving independence in
1968 as a constitutional monarchy. It became a
republic in 1992. Port Louis is the capital and
the largest city. ⊛ Pop. 1,104,000. **—Mau·ri′-
tian** *adj. & n.*

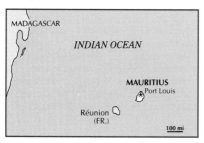

May (mā), **Cape.** A peninsula of southern New
Jersey between the Atlantic Ocean and Dela-
ware Bay. The southern tip forms **Cape May
Point.**

Ma·ya (mä′yə). **1.** *pl.* **Maya** or **-yas. a.** A
member of a Mesoamerican Indian people inhabiting southeast Mexico, Guatemala, and Belize,
whose civilization reached its height around A.D.
300–900. The Mayas are noted for their architecture and city planning, their mathematics and
calendar, and their hieroglyphic writing system.
b. A modern-day descendant of this people. **2.**
Any of the Mayan languages, especially Quiché
and Yucatec. **—Ma′ya** *adj.*

Ma·ya·güez (mī′ə-gwěz′, mä′yä-gwěs′). A
city of western Puerto Rico west-southwest of
San Juan. It is a port of entry and manufacturing
center. ⊛ Pop. 101,209.

Ma·yan (mä′yən). **1.** Of or relating to the Mayas, their culture, their languages, or the language group to which it belongs. **2.** A Maya.
3. A linguistic stock of Central America that includes Quiché and Yucatec.

May·fair (mā′fâr′). A fashionable district in the
West End of London, England. It was named after an annual fair held in the district until 1708.

May·field Heights (mā′fēld′). A city of northeast Ohio, a residential suburb of Cleveland.
⊛ Pop. 19,847.

Ma·yon (mä-yōn′), **Mount.** An active volcano,
2,461.4 m (8,070 ft) high, of southeast Luzon,
Philippines. It is considered one of the world's
most perfect cones.

Ma·yotte (mä-yôt′). An island of the eastern
Comoros in the Mozambique Channel of the Indian Ocean. It remained a French territory after
the other islands declared their independence in
1975.

May·wood (mā′wŏŏd′). **1.** A city of southern
California, a residential and industrial suburb of
Los Angeles. ⊛ Pop. 27,850. **2.** A village of
northeast Illinois, a residential suburb of Chicago. ⊛ Pop. 27,139.

Ma·za·tlán (mä′sət-län′). A city of western
Mexico on the Pacific Ocean northwest of Gua-
dalajara. It is a seaport and tourist center.
⊛ Pop. 199,830.

Mba·bane (əm-bä-bän′, -bä′nē). The capital of
Swaziland, in the northwest part of the country.
It is a commercial center for an agricultural re-
gion. ⊛ Pop. 38,290.

Mbu·ji Ma·yi (əm-bŏŏ′jē mä′yē). A city of
south-central Zaire east of Kinshasa. It is a
commercial center in a diamond-mining region.
⊛ Pop. 486,235.

Mbun·du (əm-bŏŏn′dŏŏ). *pl.* **Mbundu** or **-dus.**
1. A member of a Bantu people inhabiting southern and central Angola. Also called *Ovimbundu.*
2. The Bantu language of this people. Also

called *Umbundu*. **3.** A member of a Bantu people inhabiting northern Angola. Also called *Ndongo*. **4.** The Bantu language of this people. Also called *Kimbundu*.

Mc·Al·es·ter (mĭ-kăl′ĭ-stər). A city of southeast Oklahoma southeast of Oklahoma City. It is a distribution center in a stock-raising area. ◉ Pop. 16,370.

Mc·Al·len (mĭ-kăl′ən). A city of southern Texas on the Rio Grande west-northwest of Brownsville. It is a processing and shipping center for a citrus-growing region. ◉ Pop. 84,021.

Mc·Clure Strait (mə-klŏŏr′). An arm of the Beaufort Sea in western Northwest Territories, Canada, between Banks Island and Melville Island. Icebreakers cut through the strait for the first time in 1954.

Mc·Kees·port (mĭ-kēz′pôrt′, -pōrt′). A city of southwest Pennsylvania east-southeast of Pittsburgh. It is an industrial center. ◉ Pop. 26,016.

Mc·Kin·ley (mə-kĭn′lē), **Mount** also **De·na·li** (də-nä′lē). A peak, 6,197.6 m (20,320 ft) high, in the Alaska Range of south-central Alaska. The highest point in North America, it was first scaled in 1913.

Mc·Kin·ney (mə-kĭn′ē). A city of northeast Texas north-northeast of Dallas. It is a distribution center for an agricultural region. ◉ Pop. 21,283.

Mc·Lean (mə-klān′, -klēn′). A community of northern Virginia, a residential suburb in the Washington, D.C. area. ◉ Pop. 38,168.

Mc·Mur·do Sound (mĭk-mûr′dō). An inlet of the Ross Sea in Antarctica off the coast of Victoria Land. A U.S. research and exploration base is here.

Mde·wa·kan·ton (əm-dē-wô′kən-tōn′, mĕd′-ē-wô′-). *pl.* **Mdewakanton** or **-tons.** A member of a Sioux people of the Santee division.

mead (mēd). *Archaic.* A meadow.

Mead (mēd), **Lake.** A reservoir of southeast Nevada and northwest Arizona formed by Hoover Dam on the Colorado River. It is the center of a large recreational area.

Mead·ville (mēd′vĭl′). A city of northwest Pennsylvania south of Erie. It is an industrial center in an agricultural area. ◉ Pop. 14,318.

Meath (mēth). A historical region and county of eastern Ireland. It was one of the five ancient kingdoms of Ireland, and Tara Hill, in central Meath, was the capital of the early Irish kings.

Mec·ca (mĕk′ə). A city of western Saudi Arabia near the coast of the Red Sea. The birthplace of the prophet Muhammad, it is the holiest city of Islam and a pilgrimage site for all devout believers of the faith. ◉ Pop. 689,010.

Mech·lin (mĕk′lĭn) also **Mech·e·len** (mĕk′ə-

lən, mĕкн′-) or **Ma·lines** (mə-lēnz′, mä-lēn′). A city of north-central Belgium north-northeast of Brussels. Founded in the early Middle Ages, it enjoyed its greatest prosperity during the 15th and early 16th centuries. ◉ Pop. 77,010.

Meck·len·burg (mĕk′lən-bûrg′, -bŏŏrk′). A historical region of northeast Germany on the Baltic Sea. It was originally occupied c. sixth century A.D. by Slavic peoples who were then displaced by Germanic settlements. After 1621 Mecklenburg was divided into two duchies, which were raised to grand duchies (1815) and joined the German Confederation (1867) and the German Empire (1871). Reunited in 1934, the region later comprised three districts of East Germany (1952–1990).

Me·dan (mā-dän′). A city of Indonesia on northern Sumatra north-northwest of Padang. It is a shipping and trade center for an agricultural region. ◉ Pop. 1,378,955.

Mede (mēd). A member of an Iranian people, closely related to the Persians, inhabiting ancient Media.

Me·del·lín (mĕd′l-ēn′, mĕ′*th*ĕ-yēn′). A city of northwest-central Colombia northwest of Bogotá. Founded in 1675, it is a coffee market in a mining region at an altitude of about 1,525 m (5,000 ft). ◉ Pop. 1,473,351.

Med·ford (mĕd′fərd). **1.** A city of northeast Massachusetts, a residential and industrial suburb of Boston. Settled in 1630, it is the seat of Tufts University (chartered 1852). ◉ Pop. 57,407. **2.** A city of southwest Oregon west of Klamath Falls near the California border. It is a summer resort and processing center in a fruit and lumber area. ◉ Pop. 46,951.

Me·di·a (mē′dē-ə). An ancient country of southwest Asia in present-day northwest Iran. Settled by an Indo-European people, it became part of the Assyrian Empire and was conquered c. 550 B.C. by Cyrus the Great, king of Persia, who added it to the Persian Empire. **—Me′di·an** *adj. & n.*

Med·i·cine Bow Mountains (mĕd′ĭ-sĭn bō′). A range of the eastern Rocky Mountains in southeast Wyoming and northern Colorado. It rises to 3,664 m (12,013 ft) at **Medicine Bow Peak** in south-central Wyoming.

Medicine Bow River. A river, about 193 km (120 mi) long, of southern Wyoming flowing north and west to the North Platte River.

Medicine Hat (hăt). A city of southeast Alberta, Canada, near the Saskatchewan border southeast of Calgary. Founded in 1883, it is a trade center in a farming and ranching region with natural gas reserves. ◉ Pop. 40,380.

Me·di·e·val Greek (mē′dē-ē′vəl, mĕd′ē-). *abbr.* **Med. Gr.** The Greek language as used from about 800 to about 1500.

Medieval Latin. *abbr.* **Med. Lat.** The Latin language as used from about 700 to about 1500.

me·di·na (mĭ-dē′nə). The old section of an Arab city in North Africa.

Me·di·na (mĭ-dē′nə). **1.** A city of western Saudi Arabia north of Mecca. Muhammad lived here after fleeing from Mecca in 622. The Mosque of the Prophet, containing Muhammad's tomb, is a holy site for Muslim pilgrims. ◉ Pop. 290,000. **2.** A city of northeast Ohio west-northwest of Akron. It is a processing and marketing center. ◉ Pop. 19,231.

med·i·ter·ra·ne·an (mĕd′ĭ-tə-rā′nē-ən, -rān′-yən). Surrounded nearly or completely by dry land. Used of large bodies of water, such as lakes or seas.

Med·i·ter·ra·ne·an (mĕd′ĭ-tə-rā′nē-ən). *abbr.* **Medit.** The region surrounding the Mediterranean Sea. Some of the most ancient civilizations flourished in the region, which was dominated for millenniums by Phoenicia, Carthage, Greece, Sicily, and Rome. — **Med′i·ter·ra′ne·an** *adj.*

Mediterranean Sea. An inland sea surrounded by Europe, Asia, Asia Minor, the Near East, and Africa. It connects with the Atlantic Ocean through the Strait of Gibraltar; with the Black Sea through the Dardanelles, the Sea of Marmara, and the Bosporus; and with the Red Sea through the Suez Canal.

Mé·doc (mā-dŏk′, -dôk′). A region of southwest France north of Bordeaux between the Bay of Biscay and the Gironde River estuary. It is noted for its vineyards.

Mee·rut (mā′rət, mîr′ət). A city of north-central India northeast of Delhi. A Mogul city after the 14th century, it was the site of the first uprising (May 1857) against the British in the Indian Mutiny. ◉ Pop. 753,778.

meg·a·lop·o·lis (mĕg′ə-lŏp′ə-lĭs) also **me·gap·o·lis** (mĭ-găp′ə-lĭs, mĕ-). A region made up of several large cities and their surrounding areas in sufficient proximity to be considered a single urban complex. — **meg′a·lop·o·lis′tic** *adj.* — **meg′a·lo·pol′i·tan** (-lō-pŏl′ĭ-tən) *adj.*

Meg·a·ra (mĕg′ər-ə). An ancient city of east-central Greece. It was the capital of Megaris, a small Dorian state between the Saronic Gulf and the Gulf of Corinth. Megara flourished as a maritime center from the eighth to the fifth century B.C. It is the probable birthplace of the mathematician Euclid.

Me·gid·do (mĭ-gĭd′ō). An ancient city of northwest Palestine on the southern edge of the Plain of Esdraelon. Megiddo was the scene of many battles throughout early history because of its strategic position on the route connecting Egypt with Mesopotamia.

Mehl·ville (mĕl′vĭl′). A community of east-central Missouri, a suburb of St. Louis. ◉ Pop. 27,557.

Meis·sen (mī′sən). A city of east-central Germany on the Elbe River northwest of Dresden. Its porcelain industry dates to the early 18th century. ◉ Pop. 38,710.

Mek·nes (mĕk-nĕs′). A city of northern Morocco west-southwest of Fez. A capital of Moroccan sultans after c. 1672, it was once known as "the Versailles of Morocco" for its palatial buildings and splendid gardens. ◉ Pop. 401,000.

Me·kong (mā′kông′, -kŏng′). A river of southeast Asia flowing about 4,183 km (2,600 mi) from southeast China to the South China Sea through a vast delta in southern Vietnam. The delta, a major rice-growing area, was the scene of heavy fighting during the Vietnam War (1954–1975).

Mel·a·ne·sia (mĕl′ə-nē′zhə, -shə). A division of Oceania in the southwest Pacific Ocean comprising the islands northeast of Australia and south of the equator. It includes the Solomon Islands, Vanuatu, New Caledonia, the Bismarck Archipelago, various other island groups, and sometimes New Guinea.

Mel·a·ne·sian (mĕl′ə-nē′zhən, -shən). **1.** Of or relating to Melanesia or its peoples, languages, or cultures. **2.** A member of any of the indigenous peoples of Melanesia. **3.** A subfamily of the Austronesian languages that includes the languages of Melanesia.

Mel·bourne (mĕl′bərn). **1.** A city of southeast Australia southwest of Canberra. Settled in 1835, it was the seat of the Australian federal government from 1901 to 1927. The Summer Olympics were held here in 1956. ◉ Pop. 3,189,200. **2.** A city of east-central Florida on Indian River south of Cocoa Beach. It is a winter resort with varied light industries. ◉ Pop. 59,646.

Me·lil·la (mā-lēl′yä). A Spanish city on the Mediterranean coast of northeast Morocco. Conquered by Spain c. 1496, it was the site of the army revolt that triggered the Spanish Civil War in 1936. ◉ Pop. 56,247.

Me·los (mē′lôs). See **Milos.**

Mel·rose (mĕl′rōz′). A city of northeast Massachusetts, a residential suburb of Boston. ◉ Pop. 28,150.

Melrose Park. A village of northeast Illinois, an industrial suburb of Chicago. ◉ Pop. 20,859.

Mel·ville (mĕl′vĭl′), **Lake.** A saltwater lake of Newfoundland, Canada, in southeast Labrador. It receives the Churchill River in Goose Bay, its southwest arm.

Melville Island. **1.** An island of northern Australia in the Timor Sea. **2.** An island of northern Northwest Territories, Canada, in the Queen

Elizabeth Islands north of Victoria Island. It was discovered by the British explorer Sir William Parry in 1819.

Melville Peninsula. A peninsula of eastern Northwest Territories, Canada, between Foxe Basin and an arm of the Gulf of Boothia. It is separated from Baffin Island by a narrow strait.

Me·mel (mā′məl). See **Klaipeda.**

Mem·phis (mĕm′fĭs). **1.** An ancient city of Egypt south of Cairo. Reputedly founded by Menes, the first king of united Egypt, it retained its primacy until the conquest of Egypt by Alexander the Great. Its remains include two huge statues of Ramses II (ruled 1304–1237 B.C.) and an extensive necropolis. **2.** A city of southwest Tennessee on the Mississippi River near the Mississippi border. Established and named (1819) by Andrew Jackson on the site of a fort built in 1797, it was an important Union base after its capture by federal troops in 1862 during the Civil War. Memphis is today a major port and a tourist center famous for its associations with blues music. ⊛Pop. 610,337.

Men·den (mĕn′dən). A city of west-central Germany east-southeast of Dortmund. It is an industrial center. ⊛Pop. 51,959.

Men·de·res (mĕn′də-rĕs′). A river of western Turkey flowing about 402 km (250 mi) southwest and west to the Aegean Sea. In ancient times it was called the Maeander and was legendary for its winding course.

Men·do·ci·no (mĕn′də-sē′nō), **Cape.** A promontory of northwest California south-southwest of Eureka. First sighted by a Spanish explorer in 1542, it is the westernmost extremity of the state.

Men·do·za (mĕn-dō′zə, -dô′sä). A city of western Argentina east-northeast of Santiago, Chile. Founded c. 1560, it was part of Chile until 1776. ⊛Pop. 121,739.

Men·lo Park (mĕn′lō). **1.** A city of western California southeast of San Francisco. It is mainly residential. ⊛Pop. 28,040. **2.** An unincorporated community of central New Jersey north of New Brunswick. A memorial tower marks the site of the laboratory where Thomas Edison perfected the incandescent light bulb in 1879.

Me·nom·i·nee (mə-nŏm′ə-nē). **1.** *pl.* **Menominee** or **-nees.** A member of a Native American people formerly inhabiting an area along the Menominee River, with a present-day population in northeast Wisconsin. **2.** The Algonquian language of the Menominees.

Menominee River. A river rising in the Upper Peninsula of northwest Michigan and flowing about 190 km (118 mi) southeast along the Michigan-Wisconsin border to Green Bay.

Me·nom·o·nee Falls (mə-nŏm′ə-nē). A village of southeast Wisconsin, a manufacturing suburb of Milwaukee. ⊛Pop. 26,840.

Me·nor·ca (mə-nôr′kə, mĕ-nôr′kä). See **Minorca.**

Men·tor (mĕn′tər). A city of northeast Ohio, a residential suburb of Cleveland on Lake Erie. ⊛Pop. 47,358.

Me·o (mē-ou′). Variant of **Miao.**

Meq·uon (mĕk′wŏn′). A city of southeast Wisconsin, a suburb of Milwaukee. ⊛Pop. 18,885.

Mer·a·mec River (mĕr′ə-măk′). A river rising in southeast-central Missouri and flowing about 322 km (200 mi) northeast to the Mississippi River below St. Louis.

Mer·ca·tor projection (mər-kā′tər). A cylindrical map projection in which the meridians and parallels of latitude appear as lines crossing at right angles and in which areas appear greater farther from the equator.

Mer·ced (mər-sĕd′). A city of central California in the San Joaquin Valley northwest of Fresno. It is a trade and tourist center in a farm and dairy region. ⊛Pop. 56,216.

Mer·ce·da·rio (mĕr′sə-där′ē-ō, -sĕ-*th*ä′ryô). A mountain, 6,774.4 m (22,211 ft) high, in the Andes of western Argentina on the border with Chile.

Merced River. A river, about 241 km (150 mi) long, of central California flowing west to the San Joaquin River.

Mer·cer Island (mûr′sər). A city of west-central Washington, coextensive with **Mercer Island** in Lake Washington near Seattle. It is primarily residential. ⊛Pop. 20,816.

Mer·cer·ville (mûr′sər-vĭl′). A community of west-central New Jersey, a suburb of Trenton. ⊛Pop. 26,873.

Mer·ci·a (mûr′shē-ə, -shə). An Anglo-Saxon kingdom of central England. It was settled by Angles c. A.D. 500 and enjoyed its greatest influence during the rule (757–796) of Offa. In 874 the kingdom was overrun by the Danes and split between Wessex and the part of England controlled by the Danes.

Mer·ci·an (mûr′shē-ən, -shən). **1.** Of or relating to Mercia or its people, dialect, or culture. **2.** A native or inhabitant of Mercia. **3.** The Old English dialect of Mercia.

Mé·ri·da (mĕr′ĭ-də, mĕ′rē-*th*ä). A city of southeast Mexico on the Yucatán Peninsula. It was founded in 1542 on the site of a ruined Mayan city. ⊛Pop. 400,142.

Mer·i·den (mĕr′ĭ-dən). A city of south-central Connecticut north-northeast of New Haven. Settled in 1661, it is known for its silver industry, which dates to the 18th century. ⊛Pop. 59,479.

me·rid·i·an (mə-rĭd′ē-ən). *abbr.* **m., M., mer.**
1. An imaginary great circle on the earth's surface passing through the North and South geographic poles. All points on the same meridian have the same longitude. **2.** Either half of such a great circle from pole to pole.

Me·rid·i·an (mə-rĭd′ē-ən). A city of eastern Mississippi near the Alabama border east of Jackson. It was razed by the Union general William T. Sherman's troops in February 1864. ◉ Pop. 41,036.

Mé·ri·gnac (mā-rē-nyäk′). A city of southwest France, an industrial suburb of Bordeaux. ◉ Pop. 51,306.

Mer·lo (mĕr′lō). A city of eastern Argentina, a suburb of Buenos Aires. ◉ Pop. 293,059.

Mer·o·ë also **Mer·o·we** (mĕr′ō-ē′). An ancient city of northern Sudan on the Nile River north of Khartoum. It was the capital of a Cush dynasty from 530 B.C. to A.D. 350 and was noted for its iron smelting and casting.

Mer·rick (mĕr′ĭk). An unincorporated community of southeast New York on southwest Long Island southeast of Mineola. It is mainly residential. ◉ Pop. 23,042.

Mer·rill·ville (mĕr′əl-vĭl′). A town of northwest Indiana, a suburb of Gary. ◉ Pop. 27,257.

Mer·ri·mack (mĕr′ə-măk′). A town of southern New Hampshire on the Merrimack River south of Manchester. It has varied light industries. ◉ Pop. 22,156.

Merrimack River. A river rising in south-central New Hampshire and flowing about 177 km (110 mi) south into northeast Massachusetts then northeast to the Atlantic Ocean. It was long used as a source of power for textile mills.

Mer·ritt Island (mĕr′ĭt). A city of east-central Florida on **Merritt Island** between the mainland and Cape Canaveral. ◉ Pop. 32,886.

Mer·sey (mûr′zē). A river of northwest England flowing about 113 km (70 mi) generally westward to the Irish Sea at Liverpool. Its large estuary is navigable for oceangoing vessels.

Mer·sin (mĕr-sēn′). A city of southern Turkey on the Mediterranean Sea west-southwest of Adana. It is a rail terminus and major port. ◉ Pop. 523,000.

Mer·thyr Tyd·fil (mûr′thər tĭd′vĭl). A borough of southern Wales north-northwest of Cardiff. It is a manufacturing center in a coal-mining region. ◉ Pop. 60,200.

me·sa (mā′sə). A broad, flat-topped elevation with one or more clifflike sides, common in the southwest United States.

Me·sa (mā′sə). A city of south-central Arizona east of Phoenix. It is a winter resort and trade center with varied industries. ◉ Pop. 288,091.

Me·sa·bi Range (mə-sä′bē). A series of low hills in northeast Minnesota. Extensive iron ore deposits were discovered here in 1887.

Mes·ca·le·ro (mĕs′kə-lâr′ō). *pl.* **Mescalero** or **-ros.** A member of an Apache tribe formerly inhabiting southern New Mexico, western Texas, and north-central Mexico, with a present-day population in southern New Mexico.

Me·shed (mĕ-shĕd′) also **Mash·had** (mäsh-häd′). A city of northeast Iran near the Turkmenistan and Afghanistan borders. It was long an important trade center on caravan routes from Tehran to India. ◉ Pop. 1,964,489.

Mes·o·a·mer·i·ca (mĕz′ō-ə-mĕr′ĭ-kə, mĕs′-). A region extending south and east from central Mexico to include parts of Guatemala, Belize, Honduras, and Nicaragua. In pre-Columbian times it was inhabited by diverse civilizations, including the Mayan and the Olmec. — **Mes′o·a·mer′i·can** *adj. & n.*

Mes·o·lith·ic (mĕz′ə-lĭth′ĭk, mĕs′-). **1.** Of, relating to, or being the cultural period of the Stone Age between the Paleolithic and Neolithic ages, marked by the appearance of the bow and cutting tools. **2.** The Mesolithic Age.

Mes·o·po·ta·mi·a (mĕs′ə-pə-tā′mē-ə). An ancient region of southwest Asia between the Tigris and Euphrates rivers in modern-day Iraq. Probably settled before 5000 B.C., the area was the home of numerous early civilizations, including Sumer, Akkad, Babylonia, and Assyria. It declined in importance after Mongol invaders destroyed its extensive irrigation system in A.D. 1258. — **Mes′o·po·ta′mi·an** *adj. & n.*

Mes·quite (mə-skēt′, mĕ-). A city of northeast Texas, an industrial and residential suburb of Dallas. ◉ Pop. 101,484.

Mes·se·ne (mĭ-sē′nē). An ancient Greek city in the southwest Peloponnesus. It was founded c. 369 B.C. under Theban auspices as a new capital for the region of Messenia.

Mes·se·ni·a (mĭ-sē′nē-ə, -sēn′yə). An ancient region of southwest Greece in the Peloponnesus on the Ionian Sea. It fought a series of wars against Sparta c. 736 to 371 B.C. The Romans conquered the area in 146 B.C. — **Mes·sen′i·an** *adj. & n.*

Mes·si·na (mĭ-sē′nə, mĕ-). A city of northeast Sicily, Italy, on the **Strait of Messina,** a channel separating Sicily from mainland Italy. Founded in the eighth century B.C. by Greek colonists, Messina was decimated by the plague in 1743 and suffered severe earthquakes in 1783 and 1908. The strait's rocks, currents, and whirlpools may have been the inspiration for the legend of Scylla and Charybdis. ◉ Pop. 272,461.

mes·ti·zo (mĕs-tē′zō). *pl.* **-zos** or **-zoes.** A person of mixed racial ancestry, especially of mixed European and Native American ancestry.

Me·ta (mā'tə, mĕ'tä). A river, about 1,102 km (685 mi) long, of northeast Colombia flowing partially along the border with Venezuela.

Met·ai·rie (mĕt'ə-rē). A community of southeast Louisiana, the largest suburb of New Orleans. ● Pop. 149,428.

Met·a·pon·tum (mĕt'ə-pŏn'təm). An ancient city of southeast Italy on the Gulf of Taranto. It was settled by Greeks c. 700 B.C. Pythagoras taught here in the sixth century.

Me·thu·en (mə-thōō'ən, -thyōō'-). A town of northeast Massachusetts on the New Hampshire border northeast of Lowell. It was settled c. 1642. ● Pop. 39,990.

mé·tis (mā-tēs'). *pl.* **métis**. **1.** A mestizo. **2.** often **Métis**. A person of mixed Native American and French-Canadian ancestry.

met·ro (mĕt'rō) *Informal.* **1.** Metropolitan. **2.** A metropolitan area.

met·ro·plex also **Metroplex** (mĕt'rə-plĕks'). A large metropolitan region, especially one encompassing two or more cities and their surrounding suburbs.

me·trop·o·lis (mĭ-trŏp'ə-lĭs). **1.** A major city, especially the chief city of a country or region. **2.** A city or an urban area regarded as the center of a specific activity. **3.** The mother city or country of an overseas colony, especially in ancient Greece.

met·ro·pol·i·tan (mĕt'rə-pŏl'ĭ-tən). *abbr.* **met.** **1. a.** Of, relating to, or characteristic of a major city. **b.** Of or constituting a large city or urbanized area, including adjacent suburbs and towns. **2.** Of, relating to, or constituting the home territory of an imperial or colonial state. **3.** A citizen of a metropolis, especially one who displays urbane characteristics, attitudes, and values.

Metz (mĕts, mĕs). A city of northeast France on the Moselle River north of Nancy. Settled before Roman times, it prospered as a free imperial city after the 12th century and was annexed by France in 1552. The city was ruled by Germany from 1871 to 1918. ● Pop. 119,598.

Meuse (myōōz, mœz). A river of western Europe flowing about 901 km (560 mi) from northeast France through southern Belgium and the southeast Netherlands to the North Sea. Its valley was the scene of severe fighting during World Wars I and II.

Mex·i·cal·i (mĕk'sĭ-kăl'ē, mĕ'hē-kä'lē). A city of northwest Mexico near the California border east of Tijuana. It is a distribution and processing center in an irrigated agricultural region. ● Pop. 341,559.

Mex·i·can (mĕk'sĭ-kən). *abbr.* **Mex.** **1.** A native or inhabitant of Mexico. **2.** Of or relating to Mexico or its people, language, or culture.

Mexican Spanish. The Spanish language as used in Mexico.

Mex·i·co (mĕk'sĭ-kō'). *abbr.* **Mex.** A country of south-central North America. Southern Mexico was the site of various advanced civilizations beginning with the Olmec (c. 1300–400 B.C.) and including the Maya, Zapotec, Toltec, Mixtec, and Aztec cultures. The Spanish conquistador Hernando Cortés conquered the Aztecs in 1521, and the region became the viceroyalty of New Spain in 1535, eventually extending northward to include the present-day southwestern United States. Mexico gained its independence in 1821. War with the United States (1846–1848) following the U.S. annexation of Texas ended with the further cession of all lands north of the Rio Grande. A period of revolution and civil warfare in the early 20th century resulted in the constitution of 1917, whose economic and political reforms, though not always enforced, remained the basis of succeeding governments. Mexico City is the capital and the largest city. ● Pop. 93,008,000.

Mexico, Gulf of. An arm of the Atlantic Ocean in southeast North America bordering on eastern Mexico, the southeast United States, and Cuba. It connects with the Atlantic Ocean through the Straits of Florida and with the Caribbean Sea through the Yucatán Channel.

Mexico City. The capital and largest city of Mexico, at the southern end of the central plateau. Situated at an altitude of 2,379 m (7,800 ft), it was founded on the site of an ancient Aztec capital destroyed by the Spanish conquistador Cortés in 1521. The 1968 Summer Olympics were held here. ● Pop. 8,235,744.

Mi·am·i¹ (mī-ăm'ē, -ăm'ə). **1.** *pl.* **Miami** or **-is.** A member of a Native American people originally of the Green Bay area of Wisconsin, with various groups later inhabiting parts of southern Michigan and northern Ohio, Indiana, and Illinois. Present-day populations are in northern Indiana and northeast Oklahoma. **2.** The variety of Illinois spoken by the Miamis.

Mi·am·i² (mī-ăm'ē, -ăm'ə). A city of southeast Florida on Biscayne Bay south of Fort Lauderdale. Settled in the 1870's near the site of a fort built in 1836, it expanded greatly during the land boom of the 1920's and again after World War II. Today it is an important resort and cruise center for the Caribbean. ● Pop. 358,548.

Miami Beach. A city of southeast Florida across from Miami on an island between Biscayne Bay and the Atlantic Ocean. It was long famous for its gold coast strip of fashionable hotels, palatial estates, and recreational facilities. ● Pop. 92,639.

Miami River or **Great Miami River** (grāt). A river rising in western Ohio and flowing about 257 km (160 mi) generally southwest to the Ohio River at the Indiana border.

Mi·am·is·burg (mī-ăm′ēz-bûrg′). A city of southwest Ohio south of Dayton. It is an industrial center. ● Pop. 17,834.

Miao (myou′) also **Me·o** (mē-ou′). See **Hmong.**

Miao-Yao (myou′ you′). A small group of languages of uncertain affinity, including Hmong and Yao, spoken in southern China, northern Laos, Thailand, and Vietnam.

Mic·co·su·kee (mĭk′ə-soō′kē). Variant of **Mikasuki.**

Mich·i·gan (mĭsh′ĭ-gən). *abbr.* **MI, Mich.** A state of the north-central United States. It was admitted as the 26th state in 1837. French explorers first visited the area in 1618, and the French retained nominal control until the end of the French and Indian Wars (1763), when the region passed to Great Britain. It was ceded to the United States in 1783, although the British held some areas until 1796. The Michigan Territory was organized in 1805 with Detroit as its capital. Lansing is the state capital (since 1847) and Detroit the largest city. ● Pop. 9,328,784. —**Mich′i·gan′der** (-găn′dər) *adj. & n.*

Michigan, Lake. The third largest of the Great Lakes, between Wisconsin and Michigan. It is the only one of the lakes entirely within the United States. Lake Michigan is connected with the Mississippi River by the Illinois Waterway and with Lake Huron through the Straits of Mackinac. The St. Lawrence Seaway links it with the Atlantic Ocean.

Michigan City. A city of northwest Indiana on Lake Michigan northeast of Gary. It is a manufacturing and resort center. ● Pop. 33,822.

Mic·mac (mĭk′măk′). **1.** *pl.* **Micmac** or **-macs.** A member of a Native American people inhabiting Nova Scotia, New Brunswick, Prince Edward Island, and the Gaspé Peninsula of Quebec. **2.** The Algonquian language spoken by the Micmacs.

Mi·cro·ne·si·a (mī′krō-nē′zhə, -shə). A division of Oceania in the western Pacific Ocean comprising the islands east of the Philippines

and north of the equator. It includes the Caroline, Marshall, Mariana, and Gilbert islands.

Micronesia, Federated States of. A group of associated islands in the Caroline Islands of the western Pacific Ocean. Originally inhabited by Austronesian-speaking peoples, they were controlled in turn by Spain, Germany, and Japan prior to their capture by U.S. forces during World War II. The group was administered as part of the U.S. Trust Territory of the Pacific Islands after 1947 and became self-governing under a compact of free association with the United States in 1986. Palikir, on Pohnpei (Ponape) Island, is the capital. ● Pop. 104,000.

Mi·cro·ne·sian (mī′krə-nē′zhən, -shən). **1.** Of or relating to Micronesia or its peoples, languages, or cultures. **2.** A member of any of the peoples inhabiting Micronesia. **3.** A subfamily of the Austronesian language family that includes the languages of Micronesia.

Mid-At·lan·tic States (mĭd′ăt-lăn′tĭk). See **Middle Atlantic States.**

Mid·dle America (mĭd′l). A region of southern North America comprising Mexico, Central America, and sometimes the West Indies. —**Middle American** *adj. & n.*

Middle Atlantic States also **Mid-At·lan·tic States** (mĭd′ăt-lăn′tĭk). The U.S. states of New York, Pennsylvania, New Jersey, and usually Delaware and Maryland.

Mid·dle·bor·ough or **Mid·dle·bor·o** (mĭd′l-bûr′ō, -bŭr′ō). A town of southeast Massachusetts north of New Bedford. It is a processing and manufacturing center. ● Pop. 16,404.

Mid·dle·burg Heights (mĭd′l-bûrg′). A city of northeast Ohio, a suburb of Cleveland. ● Pop. 16,218.

Middle Dutch. The Dutch language from the middle of the 12th through the 15th century.

Middle East also **Mid·east** (mĭd-ēst′). An area roughly comprising the countries of southwest Asia and northeast Africa. In the 20th century the region has been the continuing scene of political and economic turmoil. —**Middle Eastern** *adj.* —**Middle Easterner** *n.*

Middle English. *abbr.* **ME, M.E.** The English language from about 1100 to 1500.

Middle High German. High German from the 11th through the 15th century.

Middle Irish. Irish from the 10th through the 13th century.

Middle Loup. A river rising in central Nebraska and flowing about 354 km (220 mi) east and southeast to join the North Loup and South Loup rivers and form the Loup River.

Middle Low German. Low German from the middle of the 13th through the 15th century.

Middle Pal·i·sade (păl′ĭ-sād′). A mountain, 4,273.7 m (14,012 ft) high, of the Sierra Nevada in east-central California.

Middle River. A community of northern Maryland, an industrial suburb of Baltimore. ⊛ Pop. 24,616.

Mid·dles·brough (mĭd′lz-brə). A borough of northeast England at the mouth of the Tees River. It has iron, steel, and chemical works. ⊛ Pop. 150,600.

Mid·dle·town (mĭd′l-toun′). **1.** A city of central Connecticut on the Connecticut River south of Hartford. It is an industrial center and the seat of Wesleyan University (chartered 1831). ⊛ Pop. 42,762. **2.** A community of eastern New Jersey northwest of Red Bank. It was settled in 1665. ⊛ Pop. 62,298. **3.** A city of southeast New York west-southwest of Newburgh. A summer resort, it is also an industrial center. ⊛ Pop. 24,160. **4.** A city of southwest Ohio north-northeast of Cincinnati. Founded in 1802, it has a steel industry. ⊛ Pop. 46,022. **5.** A town of southeast Rhode Island on Narragansett Bay north of Newport. It is a summer resort. ⊛ Pop. 19,460.

Middle Welsh. Welsh from the 12th through the 15th century.

Middle West. See **Midwest.** — **Middle Western** adj. — **Middle Westerner** n.

Mid·east (mĭd-ēst′). See **Middle East.** — **Mid·east′ern** adj. — **Mid·east′ern·er** n.

Mi·di (mē-dē′). The south of France.

Mid·i·an·ite (mĭd′ē-ə-nīt′). A member of an ancient tribe of Midian in northwest Arabia. — **Mid′i·an·ite′** adj.

mid·land (mĭd′lənd). **1.** The middle or interior part of a country or region. **2.** Of or in a midland.

Mid·land (mĭd′lənd). **1.** A city of central Michigan west of Bay City. Chemical industries are important to its economy. ⊛ Pop. 38,053. **2.** A city of west-central Texas west-southwest of Abilene. It is an industrial center in a cattle-ranching area. ⊛ Pop. 89,443.

Mid·lands (mĭd′ləndz). A region of central England. It roughly corresponds to the Anglo-Saxon kingdom of Mercia and is today a highly industrialized area.

Mid·lo·thi·an (mĭd-lō′thē-ən). A region of southeast Scotland on the Firth of Forth surrounding Edinburgh. "The Heart of Midlothian" was a popular name for the former Tolbooth Prison in Edinburgh and was used by the British author Sir Walter Scott as the title of his 1818 novel.

mid-o·cean ridge (mĭd′ō′shən). A series of mountain ranges on the ocean floor, more than 84,000 kilometers (52,000 miles) in length, extending through the North and South Atlantic, the Indian Ocean, and the South Pacific. According to the plate tectonics theory, volcanic rock is added to the sea floor as the mid-ocean ridge spreads apart.

Mid·way Islands (mĭd′wā′). Two small islands and a surrounding coral atoll in the central Pacific Ocean northwest of Honolulu. Discovered in 1859, they were annexed by the United States in 1867 and remain a U.S. territory with an important naval base. A decisive World War II Allied victory in the Battle of Midway (June 3–6, 1942) was a major turning point in the war in the Pacific.

Mid·west (mĭd-wĕst′) or **Mid·dle West** (mĭd′-l). A region of the north-central United States around the Great Lakes and the upper Mississippi River valley. It is generally considered to include Ohio, Indiana, Illinois, Michigan, Wisconsin, Minnesota, Iowa, Missouri, Kansas, and Nebraska. The area is known for its rich farmlands and highly industrialized centers. — **Mid·west′ern** adj. — **Mid·west′ern·er** n.

Midwest City. A city of central Oklahoma, a residential suburb of Oklahoma City. ⊛ Pop. 52,267.

Mik·a·su·ki also **Mic·co·su·kee** (mĭk′ə-sōō′-kē). **1.** pl. **Mikasuki** or **-kis** also **Miccosukee** or **-kees.** A member of a Native American people formerly inhabiting northwest Florida, now forming part of the Seminole people of southern Florida. **2.** The Muskogean language of the Mikasukis.

Mí·ko·nos (mē′kô-nôs′). See **Mykonos.**

Mi·lan (mĭ-lăn′, -län′). A city of northern Italy northeast of Genoa. Probably of Celtic origin, it was taken by the Romans in 222 B.C. and has been an important commercial, financial, cultural, and industrial center since medieval times because of its strategic location. ⊛ Pop. 1,371,008. — **Mil′a·nese′** (mĭl′ə-nēz′, -nēs′) adj. & n.

Mi·le·sian¹ (mĭ-lē′zhən, -shən). **1.** Of or relating to Miletus or its inhabitants. **2.** A native or inhabitant of Miletus.

Mi·le·sian² (mĭ-lē′zhən, -shən). **1.** Mythology. A member of a people who invaded Ireland and became the ancestors of the Irish. **2.** A native or inhabitant of Ireland. **3.** Of or relating to Ireland; Irish.

Mi·let·us (mĭ-lē′təs). An ancient Ionian city of

western Asia Minor in present-day Turkey. Occupied by Greeks c. 1000 B.C., it became an important trading and colonizing settlement and also flourished as a center of learning. The city declined after its harbor silted up early in the Christian era.

Mil·ford (mĭl'fərd). **1.** A city of southwest Connecticut on Long Island Sound southwest of New Haven. Founded in 1639, it was a shipbuilding center until the early 19th century. Today it is mainly residential with various light industries. ☙ Pop. 48,168. **2.** A city of south-central Massachusetts southeast of Worcester. It is an industrial center. ☙ Pop. 25,355.

Mi·li·la·ni Town (mē'lē-lä'nē). A community of south-central Oahu, Hawaii, a suburb of Honolulu. ☙ Pop. 29,359.

Milk River (mĭlk). A river rising in the Rocky Mountains of northwest Montana and flowing about 1,006 km (625 mi) northward to southern Alberta then east and south back to northern Montana, where it joins the Missouri River.

Mill·brae (mĭl'brā'). A city of western California south of San Francisco. It is mainly residential. ☙ Pop. 20,412.

Mill·burn (mĭl'bərn). A community of northeast New Jersey, a residential suburb west of Newark. ☙ Pop. 18,630.

Mill·creek (mĭl'krēk'). A community of north-central Utah, a suburb of Salt Lake City. ☙ Pop. 24,150.

Mill·ing·ton (mĭl'ĭng-tən). A city of southwest Tennessee north of Memphis. It is a manufacturing center in a farming area. ☙ Pop. 17,866.

Mill·ville (mĭl'vĭl'). A city of southern New Jersey west of Atlantic City. Settled in the 18th century, it has varied light industries. ☙ Pop. 25,992.

Mi·los also **Me·los** (mē'lôs) or **Mi·lo** (mē'lō, mī'-). An island of southeast Greece in the Cyclades Islands of the Aegean Sea. It was a flourishing trade and obsidian-mining center in ancient times but lost importance when bronze replaced obsidian as a material for tools and weapons. The famous statue *Venus de Milo* was discovered here in 1820.

Mil·pi·tas (mĭl-pē'təs). A city of western California southeast of San Francisco Bay and north of San Jose. It is an industrial and residential suburb in a truck-farming region. ☙ Pop. 50,686.

Mil·ton (mĭl'tən). **1.** A town of southeast Ontario west-southwest of Toronto. It is an industrial center. ☙ Pop. 28,067. **2.** A town of eastern Massachusetts, a residential suburb of Boston. ☙ Pop. 25,725.

Milton Keynes (kēnz). A town of south-central England northeast of Oxford. It was designated

as a new town in 1967 to alleviate overcrowding in London. ☙ Pop. 184,440.

Mil·wau·kee (mĭl-wô'kē). A city of southeast Wisconsin on Lake Michigan. Established as a fur-trading post in 1795, it was a major center of German immigration during the last half of the 19th century and was long noted for its breweries and meat-packing plants. It is the largest city in the state. ☙ Pop. 628,088.

Mil·wau·kie (mĭl-wô'kē). A city of northwest Oregon, a trade and manufacturing suburb of Portland on the Willamette River. ☙ Pop. 18,692.

Mim·bres (mĭm'brĭs). The final period of the Mogollon culture, from the 9th to the 13th century, noted for its distinctive pottery bowls painted with black-on-white designs.

Mi·nas Basin (mī'nəs). An arm of the Bay of Fundy extending into west-central Nova Scotia, Canada. It is connected with the bay by the **Minas Channel.**

Mi·na·ti·tlán (mē'nə-tĭ-tlän', -nä-tē-). A town of southeast Mexico southeast of Veracruz. It has a petroleum refinery. ☙ Pop. 106,765.

Minch (mĭnch). A channel, divided into **North Minch** and **Little Minch,** separating northwest Scotland from the Outer Hebrides.

Min·da·na·o (mĭn'də-nä'ō, -nou'). An island of the southern Philippines northeast of Borneo. It borders the **Mindanao Sea** on the west.

Min·den (mĭn'dən). **1.** A city of northwest Germany on the Weser River south of Bremen. Settled in Roman times, it was founded c. 800 as a bishopric by Charlemagne. Minden joined the Hanseatic League in the 13th century and passed to Prussia in 1814. ☙ Pop. 75,419. **2.** A city of northwest Louisiana east-northeast of Shreveport. It is a shipping center in a lumber and natural gas area. ☙ Pop. 13,661.

Min·do·ro (mĭn-dôr'ō, -dōr'ō). An island of the west-central Philippines south of Luzon. It was first visited by Spaniards in 1570.

Min·e·o·la (mĭn'ē-ō'lə). A village of southeast New York on west-central Long Island. It is a residential community. ☙ Pop. 18,994.

Mi·nho (mē'nyōō) or **Mi·ño** (-nyô). A river flowing about 338 km (210 mi) from northwest Spain south and southwest to the Atlantic Ocean. Its lower course forms part of the border between Spain and Portugal.

Min·i·con·jou also **Min·ne·con·jou** (mĭn'ĭ-kŏn'jōō). *pl.* **Miniconjou** or **-jous** also **Minneconjou** or **-jous.** A member of a Native American people constituting a subdivision of the Teton Sioux, formerly inhabiting an area from the Black Hills to the Platte River, with a present-day population in west-central South Dakota.

Mi·ni·coy Island (mĭn'ĭ-koi'). An island in the Arabian Sea off the southwest coast of India. It is part of the region of Lakshadweep.

Min·nan (mĭ-nän′). The dialect of Chinese spoken on most of Taiwan, in southern Fujian province, and in parts of Guangzhou and Hainan. Minnan is the vernacular of most traditional Chinese communities outside China.

Min·ne·ap·o·lis (mĭn′ē-ăp′ə-lĭs). A city of southeast Minnesota on the Mississippi River adjacent to St. Paul. The largest city in the state, it was a leading lumbering center in the 19th century and today is a port of entry and major industrial hub. ⊛ Pop. 368,383.

Min·ne·con·jou (mĭn′ĭ-kŏn′jōō). Variant of **Miniconjou.**

Min·ne·so·ta (mĭn′ĭ-sō′tə). *abbr.* **MN, Minn.** A state of the northern United States bordering on Lake Superior and on Manitoba and Ontario, Canada. It was admitted as the 32nd state in 1858. Occupied by the Santee Sioux and first explored by the French in the mid-17th century, the area became part of the United States through the Treaty of Paris (1783) and the Louisiana Purchase (1803). St. Paul is the capital and Minneapolis is the largest city. ⊛ Pop. 4,387,029. — **Min′ne·so′tan** *adj. & n.*

Minnesota River. A river, about 534 km (332 mi) long, of southern Minnesota flowing southeast and northeast to the Mississippi River near St. Paul.

Min·ne·ton·ka (mĭn′ĭ-tŏng′kə). A city of southeast Minnesota, a residential suburb of Minneapolis. ⊛ Pop. 48,370.

Mi·ño (mē′nyô). See **Minho.**

Mi·no·an (mĭ-nō′ən). **1.** Of or relating to the advanced Bronze Age culture that flourished in Crete from about 3000 to 1100 B.C. **2.** A native or inhabitant of ancient Crete.

Mi·nor·ca (mĭ-nôr′kə) also **Me·nor·ca** (mə-nôr′kə, mĕ-nôr′kä). A Spanish island in the Balearics of the western Mediterranean Sea. Held by the British and the French at various times during the 18th century, it was a Loyalist stronghold in the Spanish Civil War. — **Mi·nor′can** *adj. & n.*

Mi·not (mī′nŏt′). A city of northwest-central North Dakota north-northwest of Bismarck. It is a commercial and distribution center in an agricultural area. ⊛ Pop. 34,544.

Minsk (mĭnsk, myēnsk). The capital and largest city of Belarus, in the central part of the country. First mentioned in 1067, it was ruled from the 13th to the 18th century by various powers, including Lithuania, Russia, Poland, and Sweden. Minsk passed to Russia in 1793 and was occupied (1941–1943) by German forces in World War II. ⊛ Pop. 1,654,800.

min·ute (mĭn′ĭt). *abbr.* **min., min.** A unit of angular measurement equal to one sixtieth of a degree, or 60 seconds. Also called *minute of arc.*

Mi·que·lon (mĭk′ə-lŏn′, mēk-lôN′). An island

in the Atlantic Ocean off the southern coast of Newfoundland. It is part of the French overseas department of St. Pierre and Miquelon.

Mir·a·mar (mîr′ə-mär′). A city of southeast Florida south of Fort Lauderdale. It is a resort community. ⊛ Pop. 40,663.

Mish·a·wa·ka (mĭsh′ə-wô′kə, -wŏk′ə). A city of northern Indiana, an industrial suburb of South Bend. ⊛ Pop. 42,608.

Mish·na·ic Hebrew (mĭsh-nā′ĭk). The Hebrew language as used from the fifth century B.C. to the late seventh century A.D. Also called *Rabbinic Hebrew.*

Mis·ki·to (mĭ-skē′tō). **1.** *pl.* **Miskito** or **-tos.** A member of an American Indian people inhabiting the Caribbean coast of northeast Nicaragua and southeast Honduras. **2.** The language of the Miskito. Also called *Mosquito.*

Mis·kolc (mĭsh′kôlts′). A city of northeast Hungary northeast of Budapest. A major industrial center, it was invaded by Mongols in the 13th century, by Turks in the 16th and 17th centuries, and by German imperial forces in the 17th and 18th centuries. ⊛ Pop. 190,330.

Mis·sion (mĭsh′ən). A city of southern Texas near the Rio Grande west-northwest of Brownsville. It is a distribution center in an oil and farm region. ⊛ Pop. 28,653.

Mis·sion·ar·y Ridge (mĭsh′ə-nĕr′ē). A range of hills in southeast Tennessee and northwest Georgia. It was the site of an important Union victory (November 25, 1863) in the Civil War.

Mission Vie·jo (vē-ā′hō). A community of southern California southeast of Irvine. It is mainly residential. ⊛ Pop. 72,820.

Mis·sis·sau·ga (mĭs′ĭ-sô′gə). A town of southern Ontario, Canada, a suburb of Toronto on Lake Ontario. ⊛ Pop. 463,388.

Mis·sis·sip·pi (mĭs′ĭ-sĭp′ē). *abbr.* **MS, Miss.** A state of the southeast United States. It was admitted as the 20th state in 1817. The first settlers in the region (1699) were French, and the area became part of Louisiana. It passed to the British (1763–1779) and then to the Spanish before being ceded to the United States in 1783. The Mississippi Territory, organized in 1798 and enlarged in 1804 and 1813, also included the present state of Alabama. Jackson is the capital and the largest city. ⊛ Pop. 2,586,443.

Mis·sis·sip·pi·an (mĭs′ĭ-sĭp′ē-ən). **1.** Of or relating to the state or residents of Mississippi or to the Mississippi River. **2.** A native or resident of Mississippi.

Mississippi River. The chief river of the United States, rising in the lake region of northern Minnesota and flowing about 3,781 km (2,350 mi) generally southward to enter the Gulf of Mexico through a huge delta in southeast Louisiana. Probably discovered by the Spanish explorer Hernando de Soto in 1541, it was explored by Jacques Marquette, a French missionary, and Louis Jolliet, a French-Canadian explorer, in 1673. The French explorer La Salle claimed the entire region for France after he descended to the river's mouth in 1682.

Mississippi Sound. An arm of the Gulf of Mexico bordering on southeast Louisiana, southern Mississippi, southwest Alabama, and a chain of small offshore islands. It is part of the Intracoastal Waterway.

Mis·sou·la (mĭ-zōō′lə). A city of western Montana west-northwest of Helena. It is a processing and trade center in a farming and lumbering region and the seat of the University of Montana (founded 1893). ◉ Pop. 42,918.

Mis·sou·ri[1] (mĭ-zōōr′ē). **1.** *pl.* **Missouri** or **-ris.** A member of a Native American people formerly inhabiting north-central Missouri, with present-day descendants living with the Oto in north-central Oklahoma. **2.** The Siouan language of the Missouri.

Mis·sou·ri[2] (mĭ-zōōr′ē, -zōōr′ə). *abbr.* **MO, Mo.** A state of the central United States. It was admitted as the 24th state in 1821. Under Spanish control from 1762 to 1800, the area passed to the United States through the Louisiana Purchase of 1803. Organized as a territory in 1812, Missouri's application for admission as a slaveholding state in 1817 sparked a bitter controversy over the question of extending slavery into new territories. The Missouri Compromise of 1820 provided for the admission of Maine as a free state and Missouri as a slave state in the following year. Jefferson City is the capital and St. Louis the largest city. ◉ Pop. 5,137,804. — **Mis·sou′ri·an** *adj. & n.*

Missouri City. A city of southeast Texas, a suburb of Houston. ◉ Pop. 36,176.

Missouri River. A river of the United States rising in the Rocky Mountains as various headstreams that join to form the Missouri proper in southwest Montana. The longest river in the United States, it flows about 4,127 km (2,565 mi) in a meandering course to the Mississippi River north of St. Louis, Missouri. French explorers first reached the river in the late 17th century, and the American explorers Lewis and Clark followed it on their journey westward (1804–1806).

Mis·tas·si·ni (mĭs′tə-sē′nē), **Lake.** A lake of south-central Quebec, Canada, draining westward into James Bay by way of the Rupert River.

Mis·ti (mē′stē), **El.** See **El Misti.**

mis·tral (mĭs′trəl, mĭ-sträl′). A dry, cold northerly wind that blows in squalls toward the Mediterranean coast of southern France.

Mi·tan·ni (mĭ-tän′ē, -tä′nē). An ancient king-

dom of northwest Mesopotamia extending from the bend in the Euphrates River nearly to the Tigris River. Founded probably by Aryans, the kingdom was established c. 1475 B.C. and lasted until c. 1275, when it fell to the Hittites. — **Mi·tan′ni·an** *adj. & n.*

Mitch·ell (mĭch′əl), **Mount.** A peak, 2,038.6 m (6,684 ft) high, in the Appalachian Mountains of western North Carolina. It is the highest point east of the Mississippi River.

Mi·to (mē′tō). A city of east-central Honshu, Japan, northeast of Tokyo. The center of an important shogunate after 1600, it is now a commercial and industrial center. ◉ Pop. 246,851.

Mi·wok (mē′wŏk). **1.** *pl.* **Miwok** or **-woks.** A member of a Native American people formerly composed of numerous groups inhabiting central California from the Sierra Nevada foothills to the San Francisco Bay area, with a small number of present-day descendants in the same region. **2.** Any of the Penutian languages of this people.

Mix·tec (mēs′tĕk). **1.** *pl.* **Mixtec** or **-tecs. a.** A member of a Mesoamerican Indian people of southern Mexico whose civilization was overthrown by the Aztecs in the 16th century. **b.** A modern-day descendant of this people. **2.** The language of the Mixtecs.

Mi·ya·za·ki (mē-yä′zä-kē, mē′yä-zä′kē). A city of southeast Kyushu, Japan, southeast of Kumamoto on an arm of the Pacific Ocean. It is an industrial and resort center. ◉ Pop. 293,590.

Mo·ab (mō′ăb). An ancient kingdom east of the Dead Sea in present-day southwest Jordan. According to the Bible, its inhabitants were descendants of Lot, whose wife was turned into a pillar of salt when she looked back as they fled Sodom. Archaeological exploration has traced settlement in the area to at least the 13th century B.C.

Mo·ab·ite (mō′ə-bīt′). **1.** A native or inhabitant of Moab. **2.** The Semitic language of Moab. — **Mo′a·bite′, Mo′a·bit′ish** *adj.*

Mo·bile (mō-bēl′, mō′bēl′). A city of southwest Alabama at the mouth of the **Mobile River,** about 61 km (38 mi) long, on the north shore of **Mobile Bay,** an arm of the Gulf of Mexico. Founded c. 1710, the city was held by the French, British, and Spanish until it was seized by U.S. forces in 1813. In the Battle of Mobile Bay (August 1864) Adm. David Farragut defeated a major Confederate flotilla and secured Union control of the area. ◉ Pop. 196,278.

Mo·bu·to Lake (mō-bōō′tō). See Lake **Albert.**

Mo·chi·ca (mō-chē′kə) or **Mo·che** (mō′chä, -chĕ). A pre-Incan civilization that flourished on the northern coast of Peru from about 200 B.C. to A.D. 600, known especially for its pottery vessels modeled into naturalistic human and animal figures.

Mo·de·na (môd′n-ə, mô′dĕ-nä). A city of northern Italy west-northwest of Bologna. An ancient Etruscan settlement and later (after 183 B.C.) a Roman colony, Modena became a free commune in the 12th century A.D. and passed under the control of the powerful Este family in 1288. ◉ Pop. 176,148.

Mod·ern English (mŏd′ərn). English since about 1500. Also called *New English.*

Modern Greek. Greek since the early 16th century. Also called *New Greek.*

Modern Hebrew. 1. The Hebrew language as used from 1948 to the present. 2. See **New Hebrew.**

Mo·des·to (mə-dĕs′tō). A city of central California southeast of Stockton. Founded in 1870, it is a processing and trade center in a farming and fruit-growing region of the San Joaquin Valley. ◉ Pop. 164,730.

Mo·doc (mō′dŏk). 1. *pl.* **Modoc** or **-docs.** A member of a Native American people inhabiting an area of the Cascade Range in south-central Oregon and northern California. 2. The dialect of Klamath spoken by the Modocs.

Moers also **Mörs** (mœrs). A city of west-central Germany west of Essen. Chartered in 1300, it is a market and industrial center. ◉ Pop. 106,631.

Moe·sia (mē′shə, -shē-ə). An ancient region of southeast Europe south of the Danube River in what is now Yugoslavia and northern Bulgaria. Originally inhabited by Thracians, it was conquered by the Romans c. 29 B.C. and occupied by Goths in the fourth century A.D.

Moes·kroen (mōōs′krōōn′). See **Mouscron.**

mo·fette also **mof·fette** (mō-fĕt′). An opening in the earth from which carbon dioxide and other gases escape, usually marking the last stage of volcanic activity.

Mog·a·dish·u (mŏg′ə-dĭsh′ōō, -dē′shōō). The capital and largest city of Somalia, on the Indian Ocean. Settled by Arab colonists in the ninth or tenth century, it was occupied in 1871 by the sultan of Zanzibar, who leased it to the Italians in 1892. After 1905 it became the capital of Italian Somaliland. ◉ Pop. 400,000.

Mo·ghul (mōō-gŭl′). Variant of **Mogul** (sense 1).

Mo·gi das Cru·zes (mōō-zhē′ däs krōō′zĭs). A city of southeast Brazil east of São Paulo. Founded in 1611, it is an industrial center. ◉ Pop. 273,255.

Mo·gi·lev (mŏg′ə-lĕf′, mə-gĭ-lyôf′). A city of east-central Belarus on the Dnieper River east of Minsk. Founded around a castle built in 1267, the city changed hands frequently before it passed to Russia in the First Partition of Poland (1772). ◉ Pop. 363,600.

Mo·gol·lon (mō′gə-yōn′). A Native American culture flourishing from the 2nd century B.C. to the 13th century A.D. in southeast Arizona and southwest New Mexico, especially noted for its development of pottery.

Mogollon Plateau. A tableland, 2,135–2,440 m (7,000–8,000 ft) high, of east-central Arizona. Its southern edge is the rugged escarpment **Mogollon Rim.**

Mo·gul (mō′gəl, mō-gŭl′). 1. also **Mo·ghul** (mōō-gŭl′). a. A member of the force that under the Mongol conqueror Baber invaded India in 1526. b. A member of the Muslim dynasty founded by Baber that ruled India until 1857. 2. A Mongol or Mongolian. —**Mo′gul, mo′gul** *adj.*

Mo·hács (mō′hăch′, -häch′). A city of southern Hungary on the Danube River near the Croatian and Yugoslavian borders. It was the site of a Turkish victory (1526) that led to more than 150 years of Ottoman rule over the Hungarians. ◉ Pop. 18,100.

Mo·ha·ve also **Mo·ja·ve** (mō-hä′vē). 1. *pl.* **Mohave** or **-ves** also **Mojave** or **-ves.** A member of a Native American people inhabiting lands along the lower Colorado River on the Arizona-California border. 2. The Yuman language of the Mohaves.

Mohave Desert. See **Mojave Desert.**

Mo·hawk (mō′hôk′). 1. *pl.* **Mohawk** or **-hawks.** A member of a Native American people formerly inhabiting northeast New York along the Mohawk and upper Hudson river valleys north to the St. Lawrence River, with present-day populations chiefly in southern Ontario and extreme northern New York. The Mohawks were the easternmost member of the Iroquois confederacy. 2. The Iroquoian language of the Mohawks.

Mohawk River. A river of east-central New York flowing about 225 km (140 mi) south and southeast to the Hudson River. Long an important route to the West, it is now used mainly by pleasure craft.

Mo·he·gan (mō-hē′gən). 1. *pl.* **Mohegan** or **-gans.** A member of a Native American people formerly inhabiting eastern Connecticut, with present-day descendants in southeast Connecticut and Wisconsin. The Mohegans broke away from the Pequot in the early 17th century under the leadership of Uncas. 2. The Algonquian language of the Mohegans. —**Mo·he′gan** *adj.*

Mo·hen·jo-Da·ro (mō-hĕn′jō-där′ō). A ruined prehistoric city of Pakistan in the Indus River valley northeast of Karachi. Its remains date to c. 3000 B.C.

Mo·hi·can (mō-hē′kən, mə-). Variant of **Mahican.**

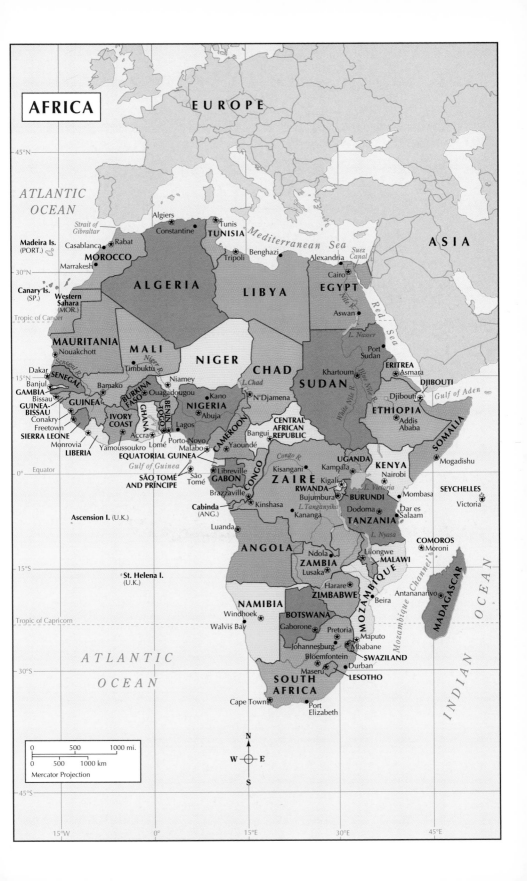

AFRICA

EUROPE

ASIA

ATLANTIC
OCEAN

Mediterranean Sea

Madeira Is.
(PORT.)

Algiers
Tunis
Constantine **TUNISIA**
Tripoli Benghazi
Alexandria *Suez Canal*
Casablanca *Rabat*
MOROCCO
Marrakesh
Cairo

Canary Is.
(SP.)

Western
Sahara
(MOR.)

Tropic of Cancer

Aswan

L. Nasser

ALGERIA

LIBYA

EGYPT

Red Sea

Nile R.

MAURITANIA
Nouakchott

MALI

NIGER

CHAD

Port
Sudan

ERITREA
Asmara

DJIBOUTI

Gulf of Aden

Dakar
Senegal R.
Timbuktu
Niger R.
Niamey
Khartoum

SENEGAL
GAMBIA Banjul
Bissau
**GUINEA-
BISSAU**
Conakry
Freetown
SIERRA LEONE
Monrovia
LIBERIA

Bamako
**BURKINA
FASO**
Ouagadougou
Kano
N'Djamena
NIGERIA
Abuja

L. Chad

SUDAN

White Nile R.
Blue Nile R.

Djibouti

ETHIOPIA
Addis
Ababa

SOMALIA

GUINEA
**IVORY
COAST**
GHANA
TOGO
BENIN
Accra
Lagos
Porto-Novo
Malabo
Lomé
Yamoussoukro
CAMEROON
**CENTRAL
AFRICAN
REPUBLIC**
Bangui
Yaoundé

Mogadishu

0° Equator

EQUATORIAL GUINEA
Gulf of Guinea
São Tomé
**SÃO TOMÉ
AND PRÍNCIPE**

Libreville
GABON
CONGO
Brazzaville
Kinshasa

Congo R.
Kisangani
ZAIRE

UGANDA
Kampala
Kigali
RWANDA
Bujumbura
BURUNDI
L. Victoria
Nairobi
KENYA
Dodoma
TANZANIA
Dar es
Salaam
Mombasa

SEYCHELLES
Victoria

Ascension I. (U.K.)

Luanda

Cabinda
(ANG.)
Kananga
L. Tanganyika
L. Nyasa

15°S

St. Helena I.
(U.K.)

ANGOLA

Ndola
ZAMBIA
Lusaka
Lilongwe
MALAWI

COMOROS
Moroni

Harare
ZIMBABWE
Beira
Antananarivo

MOZAMBIQUE

Mozambique Channel

MADAGASCAR

NAMIBIA
Windhoek
Walvis Bay

BOTSWANA
Gaborone
Pretoria
Johannesburg
Maputo
Mbabane
SWAZILAND
Bloemfontein
Maseru
Durban
LESOTHO

Tropic of Capricorn

ATLANTIC
OCEAN

**SOUTH
AFRICA**
Cape Town
Port
Elizabeth

INDIAN
OCEAN

| 0 | 500 | 1000 mi. |
| 0 | 500 | 1000 km |

Mercator Projection

N
W E
S

ATLANTIC
OCEAN

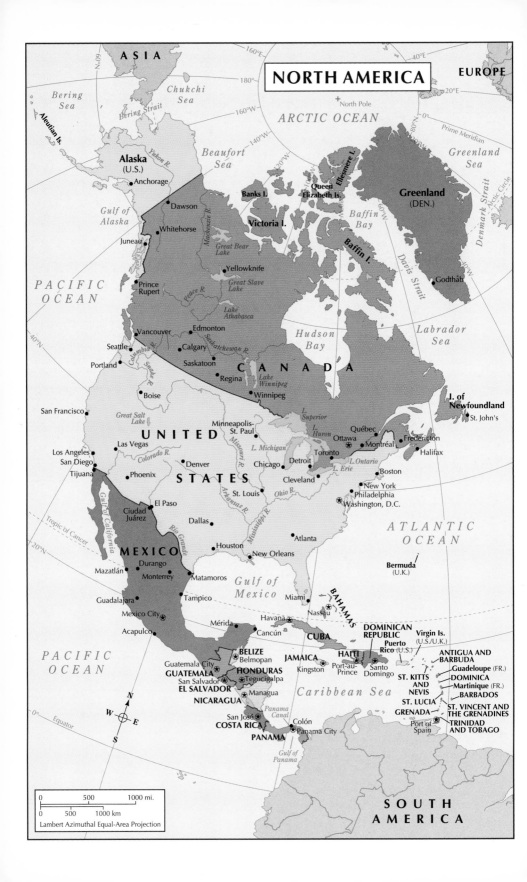

NORTH AMERICA

ASIA

EUROPE

Bering Sea

Chukchi Sea

Aleutian Is.

Bering Strait

ARCTIC OCEAN

North Pole +

20°E

Greenland Sea

Prime Meridian

Alaska
(U.S.)
• Anchorage

Beaufort Sea

Banks I.

**Queen
Elizabeth Is.**

Ellesmere I.

Arctic Circle

Gulf of Alaska

• Dawson

Yukon R.

Victoria I.

Baffin Bay

Greenland
(DEN.)

Denmark Strait

• Whitehorse

Mackenzie R.

Baffin I.

Juneau •

Great Bear Lake

Davis Strait

• Godthåb

PACIFIC
OCEAN

• Yellowknife

Great Slave Lake

Hudson Bay

Labrador Sea

Prince
Rupert •

Peace R.

Lake Athabasca

40°N

Vancouver •

• Edmonton

Saskatchewan R.

C A N A D A

I. of
Newfoundland

Seattle •

• Calgary

• St. John's

Portland •

• Saskatoon

Columbia R.

• Regina

Lake Winnipeg

Snake R.

• Boise

• Winnipeg

L. Superior

San Francisco •

Great Salt Lake

U N I T E D

Minneapolis-
St. Paul •

L. Huron

• Québec

Fredericton •

Las Vegas •

Missouri R.

L. Michigan

Ottawa ⊛

• Montréal

Halifax •

Los Angeles •

Denver •

S T A T E S

Chicago •

Toronto •

L. Ontario

San Diego •

• Phoenix

Colorado R.

Detroit •

L. Erie

• Boston

Tijuana •

Cleveland •

• New York

El Paso •

• St. Louis

Arkansas R.

Ohio R.

Philadelphia •
Washington, D.C. ⊛

Ciudad
Juárez •

• Dallas

Rio Grande

Mississippi R.

ATLANTIC
OCEAN

Tropic of Cancer

20°N

MEXICO

• Durango

Houston •

• Atlanta

Mazatlán •

Monterrey •

• New Orleans

Bermuda
(U.K.)

Guadalajara •

• Tampico

Matamoros •

Gulf of Mexico

Miami •

BAHAMAS

PACIFIC
OCEAN

Mexico City ⊛

• Mérida

Havana •

Nassau •

**DOMINICAN
REPUBLIC**

Virgin Is.
(U.S./U.K.)

Acapulco •

Cancún •

CUBA

HAITI

Puerto
Rico
(U.S.)

**ANTIGUA AND
BARBUDA**

Guatemala City ⊛

BELIZE
Belmopan

JAMAICA

Port-au-
Prince •

• Santo
Domingo

Guadeloupe (FR.)

GUATEMALA

HONDURAS

Kingston •

**ST. KITTS
AND
NEVIS**

DOMINICA

San Salvador •

⊛ Tegucigalpa

Martinique (FR.)

EL SALVADOR

BARBADOS

⊛ Managua

ST. LUCIA

NICARAGUA

Caribbean Sea

**ST. VINCENT AND
THE GRENADINES**

GRENADA

0°
Equator

Panama Canal

San José •

Colón •

COSTA RICA

PANAMA

Panama City •

Port of
Spain •

**TRINIDAD
AND TOBAGO**

N
W ✦ E
S

Gulf of Panama

SOUTH
AMERICA

0   500   1000 mi.
0   500   1000 km
Lambert Azimuthal Equal-Area Projection

WORLD MAP

80°N
160°W 140°W 120°W 100°W 80°W 60°W
ARCTIC OCEAN
Beaufort Sea
Baffin Bay
Green (DE

Mt. McKinley ▲ Yukon R.
60°N
Bering Sea
Gulf of Alaska
NORTH AMERICA
Hudson Bay
Laurentian Plateau
Aleutian Islands
ROCKY MOUNTAINS
Great Plains
Great Lakes
Ottawa
APPALACHIAN MTS.
New York
40°N
Mt. Whitney ▲
Mississippi R.
Azo (PO

PACIFIC OCEAN
Los Angeles
Bermuda (U.K.)
ATLANTIC OCEAN
Tropic of Cancer
Gulf of Mexico
20°N
Hawaiian Is. (U.S.)
Mexico City
CUBA Hispaniola
C VE

Caribbean Sea
P O L Y N E S I A
Equator
0°
GUIANA HIGHLANDS
Amazon R.

Galápagos Is. (EC.)
Amazon Basin
ANDES
SOUTH AMERICA
20°S
Atacama Desert
Paraná R.
Rio de Janei

Tropic of Capricorn
Easter I. (CHILE)
Mt. Aconcagua ▲
Pampas

PACIFIC OCEAN
Buenos Aires
40°S
PATAGONIA
Falkland Is. (U.K.)
So Geo (L

Cape Horn
60°S
Antarctic Circle
Ross Sea
Wedde Sea
80°S

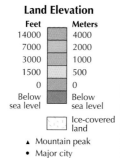

Land Elevation

Feet	Meters
14000	4000
7000	2000
3000	1000
1500	500
0	0
Below sea level	Below sea level

Ice-covered land

▲ Mountain peak

● Major city

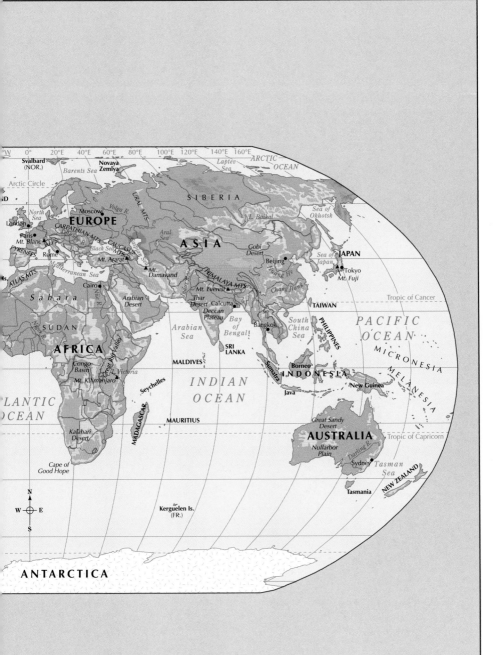

W   0°   20°E   40°E   60°E   80°E   100°E   120°E   140°E   160°E   ARCTIC
Svalbard   Novaya   Laptev   OCEAN
(NOR.)   Zemlya   Sea
Arctic Circle
Barents Sea
ND   S I B E R I A
North   Moscow   Volga R.   L. Baikal   Sea of
Sea   URAL MTS.   Okhotsk
London   EUROPE   Aral   JAPAN
Paris   CARPATHIAN MTS.   Sea   A S I A   Gobi   Tokyo
Mt. Blanc ALPS   Black Sea CAUCASUS MTS.   Desert Beijing Sea of   Mt. Fuji
PYRENEES Rome   Mt. Ararat   Japan
ATLAS MTS. Mediterranean Sea Mt.   HIMALAYA MTS. Huang He   Tropic of Cancer
          Cairo   Damavand   Mt. Everest   Chang Jiang
Sahara   Arabian   Thar   Calcutta   TAIWAN   PACIFIC
          SUDAN   Desert   Desert Deccan   OCEAN
                              Plateau Bay   Bangkok South   MICRONESIA
AFRICA   Arabian   of   China
Congo   Sea   Bengal   SRI   Sea   PHILIPPINES
Basin Great Rift Valley   MALDIVES LANKA   Borneo   MELANESIA
Mt. Kilimanjaro L. Victoria   INDIAN   Sumatra INDONESIA
          Seychelles   OCEAN   Java   New Guinea
LANTIC   Great Sandy
OCEAN   MADAGASCAR   MAURITIUS   Desert   AUSTRALIA
          Kalahari   Nullarbor   Tropic of Capricorn
          Desert   Plain   Darling R.
Cape of   Sydney Tasman
Good Hope   Sea
                    N   NEW ZEALAND
              W ⊙ E   Kerguelen Is.   Tasmania
                    S   (FR.)

ANTARCTICA

0   1,500   3,000 mi.

0   1,500   3,000 km
Robinson Projection

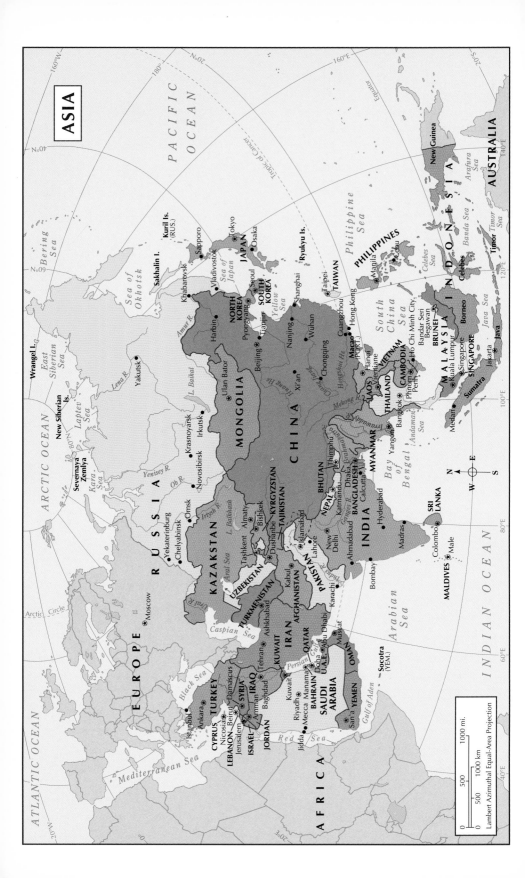

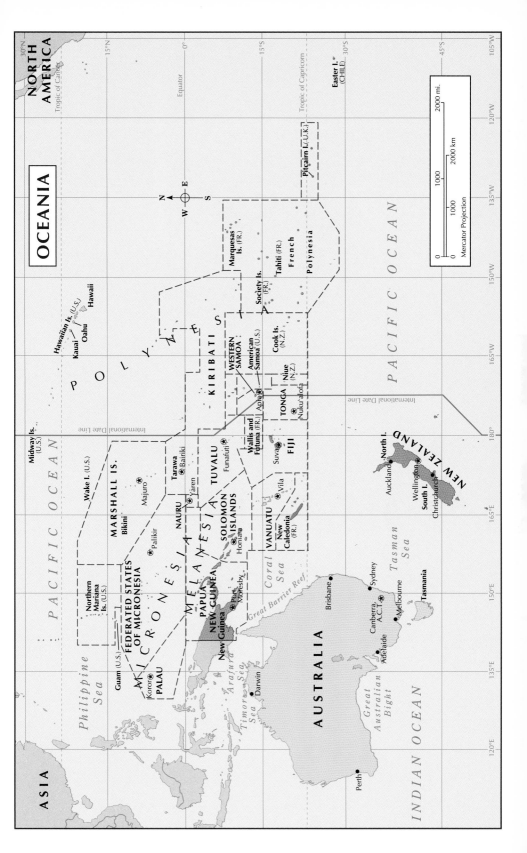

OCEANIA

ASIA

NORTH AMERICA

PACIFIC OCEAN

Philippine Sea

Midway Is. (U.S.)

Wake I. (U.S.)

Hawaiian Is. (U.S.)
Kauai
Oahu
Hawaii

MARSHALL IS.
Majuro
Bikini

FEDERATED STATES OF MICRONESIA
Palikir

Northern Mariana Is. (U.S.)

Guam (U.S.)

PALAU
Koror

M I C R O N E S I A

NAURU
Yaren

KIRIBATI
Tarawa
Bairiki

TUVALU
Funafuti

P O L Y N E S I A

Marquesas Is. (FR.)

Society Is. (FR.)
Tahiti (FR.)
French Polynesia

WESTERN SAMOA
Apia
American Samoa (U.S.)

Cook Is. (N.Z.)

Niue (N.Z.)

TONGA
Nuku'alofa

Wallis and Futuna (FR.)

FIJI
Suva

M E L A N E S I A

PAPUA NEW GUINEA
New Guinea
Port Moresby

SOLOMON ISLANDS
Honiara

VANUATU
Vila

New Caledonia (FR.)

Coral Sea

Arafura Sea

Timor Sea

AUSTRALIA
Darwin
Brisbane
Sydney
Canberra, A.C.T.
Adelaide
Melbourne
Tasmania
Perth

Great Barrier Reef

Great Australian Bight

Tasman Sea

NEW ZEALAND
North I.
Auckland
Wellington
South I.
Christchurch

PACIFIC OCEAN

INDIAN OCEAN

Easter I. (CHILE)

Pitcairn I. (U.K.)

Tropic of Cancer

Equator

Tropic of Capricorn

International Date Line

N
W E
S

Mercator Projection

0   1000   2000 km
0   1000   2000 mi.

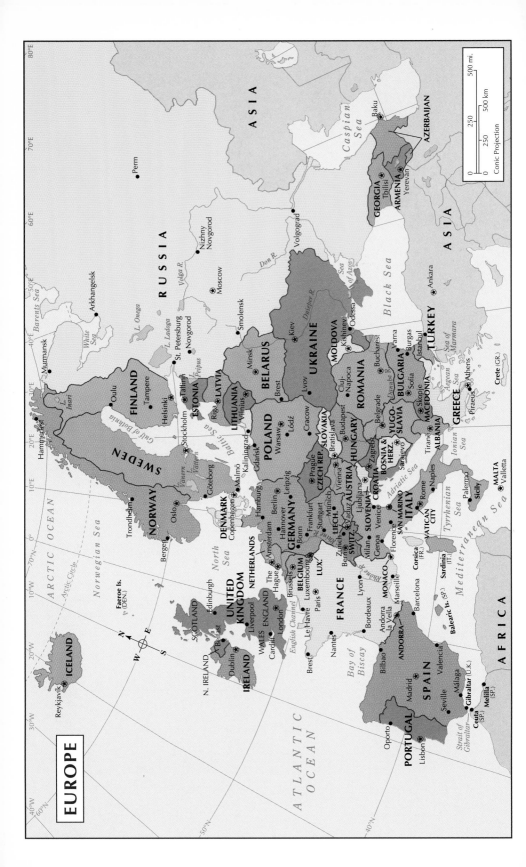

Mo·ho (mō′hō′). *Geology.* The Mohorovičić discontinuity.

Mo·ho·ro·vi·čić discontinuity (mō′hə-rō′-və-chĭch). *Geology.* The boundary between the earth's crust and the underlying mantle, averaging 8 kilometers (5 miles) in depth under the oceans and 32 kilometers (20 miles) in depth under the continents.

Mo·ja·ve (mō-hä′vē). Variant of **Mohave.**

Mojave Desert also **Mo·ha·ve Desert** (mō-hä′vē). An arid region of southern California southeast of the Sierra Nevada. Once part of an ancient inland sea, the desert was formed by volcanic action and by materials deposited by the Colorado River.

Mok·po (mŏk′pō′, môk′-). A city of southwest South Korea on an inlet of the Yellow Sea. Its port was opened to foreign trade in 1897. ◉ Pop. 243,064.

Mol·da·vi·a (mŏl-dā′vē-ə, -dāv′yə, môl-). A historical region of eastern Romania east of Transylvania. Part of the Roman province of Dacia, it became a principality in the 14th century and passed to the Ottoman Empire in 1504, although it was continually attacked and often virtually controlled by numerous other powers. In 1861 Moldavia united with Walachia to form the nucleus of modern Romania.

Mol·do·va (mŏl-dō′və, môl-). Formerly **Mol·da·vi·an Soviet Socialist Republic** (-dā′vē-ən, -dāv′yən) also **Moldavia.** A country of eastern Europe bordering on Romania. Comprised of lands acquired by Russia from the Romanian region of Moldavia in 1791, 1793, and 1812 and (after 1940) part of Bessarabia, it was established as an autonomous republic of the U.S.S.R. in 1924 and became a constituent republic in 1940. Moldova declared its independence in 1991. Kishinev is the capital and largest city. ◉ Pop. 4,350,000. **— Mol·da′vi·an** *adj. & n.*

Mo·len·beek-Saint-Jean (mō′lən-bāk′săn-zhän′). A city of central Belgium, a manufacturing suburb of Brussels. ◉ Pop. 71,891.

Mol·fet·ta (mŏl-fĕt′ə, môl-fĕt′tä). A city of southeast Italy west-northwest of Bari on the Adriatic Sea. It is a port and manufacturing center. ◉ Pop. 65,951.

Mo·line (mō-lēn′). A city of northwest Illinois on the Mississippi River across from Davenport, Iowa. Settled in 1847, it is a transportation and industrial center. ◉ Pop. 43,202.

Mo·li·se (mô′lĭ-zā′). A region of south-central Italy bordering on the Adriatic Sea. Conquered by the Romans in the 4th century B.C., it was ruled by a Lombard duchy from the 6th to the 11th century A.D.

Mo·lo·kai (mŏl′ə-kī′, mō′lə-). An island of central Hawaii between Oahu and Maui. The Belgian missionary Father Damien (1840–1889) established a leper colony on the northern coast in 1860.

Mo·lo·po (mə-lō′pō). An intermittent river of South Africa flowing about 965 km (600 mi) generally westward to the Orange River. It forms part of the border with Botswana.

Mo·luc·cas (mə-lŭk′əz). Formerly **Spice Islands** (spīs). A group of islands of eastern Indonesia between Celebes and New Guinea. Discovered in the early 16th century, the islands were settled by the Portuguese but taken in the 17th century by the Dutch, who used them as the basis for their monopoly of the spice trade. **— Mo·luc′can** *adj. & n.*

Mom·ba·sa (mŏm-bäs′ə, -bä′sä). A city of southeast Kenya mainly on **Mombasa Island,** in the Indian Ocean north of Zanzibar. Visited by the Portuguese explorer Vasco da Gama on his first voyage to India (1498), the island-city was ruled successively by Portugal, Oman, Zanzibar, and Great Britain until the early 20th century. ◉ Pop. 442,369.

Mon (mŏn). **1.** *pl.* **Mon** or **Mons.** A member of a Buddhist people inhabiting an area of eastern Myanmar (Burma) and adjacent parts of Thailand. **2.** The Mon-Khmer language of the Mon.

Mon·a·co (mŏn′ə-kō′, mə-nä′kō). A principality on the Mediterranean Sea consisting of an enclave in southeast France. Probably settled by Phoenicians in ancient times, it has been ruled by the Grimaldi family since the 13th century (first by the Genovese line and later, after 1731, by a French line). Monaco was at various times under the protection of Spain, Sardinia, and France but regained its sovereignty in 1861. Prince Rainier III (born 1923) succeeded his grandfather, Louis II, on the latter's death in 1949. The village of **Monaco,** or **Monaco-Ville,**

is the capital. ⊛ Pop. 31,700. **— Mon′a·can** *adj. & n.*

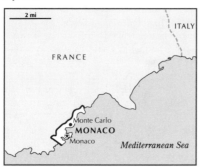

mo·nad·nock (mə-năd′nŏk′). A mountain or rocky mass that has resisted erosion and stands isolated in an essentially level area.

Mo·na Passage (mō′nə). A strait lying between Puerto Rico and the Dominican Republic connecting the northern Atlantic Ocean with the Caribbean Sea. **Mona Island,** in the passage, was discovered by Columbus in 1493 and is today part of Puerto Rico.

Mon·ca·lie·ri (môn′kə-lyĕr′ē, -kä-). A city of northwest Italy on the Po River south of Turin. It is a commercial and industrial center. ⊛ Pop. 61,740.

Mön·chen·glad·bach (mŭn′kən-glät′bäk, mœn′-ᴋнən-glät′bäᴋн). A city of west-central Germany west-southwest of Düsseldorf. Established around a Benedictine abbey founded c. 972, the city was chartered in 1336. ⊛ Pop. 265,312.

Mon·clo·va (môn-klō′və, -vä). A city of northeast Mexico northwest of Monterrey. It is a trade and processing center in a farming and mining region. ⊛ Pop. 115,786.

Monc·ton (mŭngk′tən). A city of southeast New Brunswick, Canada, northeast of Saint John. Originally settled by Acadians, it was resettled by Germans in 1763. ⊛ Pop. 54,743.

Mo·né·gasque (mô-nā-găsk′). A native or inhabitant of Monaco; a Monacan. **— Mo·né·gasque′** *adj.*

Mon·gol (mŏng′gəl, -gōl′, mŏn′-). 1. A member of any of the traditionally nomadic peoples of Mongolia. 2. See **Mongolian** (sense 5). 3. *Anthropology.* A member of the Mongoloid racial division. 4. Of or relating to Mongolia, the Mongols, or their language or culture. 5. *Anthropology.* Of or relating to the Mongoloid racial division.

Mon·go·li·a (mŏng-gō′lē-ə, -gōl′yə, mŏn′-). 1. An ancient region of east-central Asia comprising modern-day Nei Monggol (Inner Mongolia) and the country of Mongolia. In the 13th century Genghis Khan, leader of the Mongols, united all the tribes of the area and forged a great empire that eventually stretched from China to the Danube River and into Persia. After the 17th century China and Russia contended for control of the area, with the southern part eventually joining China. 2. Formerly **Out·er Mongolia** (out′ər). A country of north-central Asia situated between Russia and China. Originally part of the Mongol Empire, the area was under Chinese control from 1691 to 1911 and from 1919 to 1921, when it formed a separate state under the protection of the U.S.S.R. China continued to claim the region until 1945, when a Chinese-Soviet treaty allowed Outer Mongolia to become a nominally independent country, though closely allied with the U.S.S.R. in its ongoing border disputes with China. In 1990 a reformist government instituted considerable political, economic, and religious freedoms, opening the way for free democratic elections in 1993 that gave the country its first non-Communist government. Ulan Bator is the capital and the largest city. ⊛ Pop. 2,363,000.

Mon·go·li·an (mŏng-gō′lē-ən, -gōl′yən, mŏn′-). 1. Of or relating to Mongolia, the Mongols, or their language or culture. 2. A native or inhabitant of Mongolia. 3. A member of the Mongol people. 4. *Anthropology.* A member of the Mongoloid racial division. 5. **a.** A subfamily of the Altaic language family, Mongolian and Kalmyk being the most important members. **b.** Any of the various spoken and written dialects and languages of the Mongols living in Mongolia and China. In this sense, also called *Mongol.*

Mon·gol·oid (mŏng′gə-loid′, mŏn′-). 1. *Anthropology.* Of, relating to, or being a proposed human racial division traditionally distinguished by physical characteristics such as yellowish-brown skin pigmentation, straight black hair, dark eyes with pronounced epicanthic folds, and prominent cheekbones and including peoples indigenous to central and eastern Asia. 2. Characteristic of or resembling a Mongol. 3. *Anthropology.* A member of the Mongoloid racial division.

Mon-Khmer (mŏn′kmĕr′). A subfamily of the Austro-Asiatic language family that includes Mon, Khmer, and other languages of southeast Asia.

Mo·non·ga·he·la River (mə-nŏng′gə-hē′lə).

A river rising in northern West Virginia and flowing about 206 km (128 mi) generally north into southwest Pennsylvania, where it joins the Allegheny River at Pittsburgh to form the Ohio River.

Mon·roe (mən-rō′). **1.** A city of northeast-central Louisiana east of Shreveport. Founded in 1785, it is an industrial center. ⊕ Pop. 54,909. **2.** A city of southeast Michigan on Lake Erie southwest of Detroit. It was settled c. 1778 and today is a manufacturing and shipping center for an area noted for its nurseries. ⊕ Pop. 22,902.

Mon·roe·ville (mən-rō′vĭl′). A borough of southwest Pennsylvania, a residential suburb of Pittsburgh. ⊕ Pop. 29,169.

Mon·ro·vi·a (mən-rō′vē-ə). **1.** The capital and largest city of Liberia, in the northwest part of the country on the Atlantic Ocean. It was founded in 1822 as a haven for freed slaves and named after President James Monroe. ⊕ Pop. 421,053. **2.** A city of southern California. It is an industrial and residential suburb of Los Angeles in the foothills of the San Gabriel Mountains. ⊕ Pop. 35,761.

Mons (môns). A city of southwest Belgium near the French border southwest of Brussels. Founded on the site of a Roman camp, it was an important cloth market in the 14th century. ⊕ Pop. 91,868.

mon·soon (mŏn-sōōn′). **1.** A wind system that influences large climatic regions and reverses direction seasonally. **2. a.** A wind from the southwest or south that brings heavy rainfall to southern Asia in the summer. **b.** The rain that accompanies this wind. —**mon·soon′al** *adj.*

Mon·tag·nais (mŏn′tən-yā′). **1.** *pl.* **Montagnais.** A member of a Native American people inhabiting an extensive area in Quebec and Labrador. **2.** The Algonquian language of the Montagnais and Naskapis.

Mon·ta·gnard also **mon·ta·gnard** (mŏn′tən-yärd′). **1.** A member of a people inhabiting the mountains and highlands of southern Vietnam near the border of Cambodia. **2.** Of or relating to the Montagnards or their culture.

Mon·tan·a (mŏn-tăn′ə). *abbr.* **MT, Mont.** A state of the northwest United States bordering on Canada. It was admitted as the 41st state in 1889. Most of the area passed to the United States through the Louisiana Purchase of 1803 and was explored by Lewis and Clark in 1805 and 1806. Split for many years among other western territories, the region was organized as the Montana Territory in 1864. Helena is the capital and Billings is the largest city. ⊕ Pop. 803,655. —**Mon·tan′an** *adj. & n.*

mon·tane (mŏn-tān′, mŏn′tān′). Of, growing in, or inhabiting mountain areas.

Mon·tauk (mŏn′tôk′). *pl.* **Montauk** or **-tauks.** **1.** A member of a Native American people formerly inhabiting the eastern end of Long Island in New York. **2.** The Algonquian language of the Montauks, dialectally related to Mohegan and Pequot. **3.** A member of any of various Algonquian peoples of eastern and central Long Island connected with the Montauks.

Montauk Point. The eastern extremity of Long Island, in southeast New York. It is a popular resort area.

Mont Blanc (mônt blăngk, môɴ bläɴ′). See Mont **Blanc.**

Mont·clair (mŏnt-klâr′). **1.** A city of southern California northeast of Pomona. It is a residential community in a citrus-growing area. ⊕ Pop. 28,434. **2.** A town of northeast New Jersey, a residential suburb of New York City. ⊕ Pop. 37,729.

Mon·te Al·bán (mŏn′tĕ äl-bän′). A ruined Zapotec city of southern Mexico near Oaxaca. Excavations (begun in 1931) have revealed that an advanced culture flourished here c. 200 B.C.

Mon·te·bel·lo (mŏn′tə-bĕl′ō). A city of southern California, a residential and industrial suburb of Los Angeles. ⊕ Pop. 59,564.

Mon·te Car·lo (mŏn′tē kär′lō). A town of Monaco on the Mediterranean Sea and the French Riviera. It is a noted resort famed for its casino and luxurious hotels. ⊕ Pop. 13,150.

Mon·te·go Bay (mŏn-tē′gō). A town of northwest Jamaica on the Caribbean Sea. Visited by Columbus in 1494, it is today a port and popular resort area. ⊕ Pop. 70,285.

Mon·te·ne·gro (mŏn′tə-nē′grō, -nĕg′rō). A constituent republic of Yugoslavia, in the southwest part of the country bordering on the Adriatic Sea. An ancient Balkan state, it did not come under Turkish control until the end of the 15th century, and from 1910 to 1918 it was an independent kingdom. Montenegro then joined the newly formed Kingdom of the Serbs, Croats, and Slovenes, which became Yugoslavia after 1929. In 1991 four of the six Yugoslav republics declared independence, leaving Montenegro and Serbia to form a new Yugoslav state in 1992.

Mon·te·rey (mŏn′tə-rā′). A city of western California south of San Francisco on **Monterey Bay,** an inlet of the Pacific Ocean. First settled in 1770 around a Franciscan mission, Monterey was a Spanish colonial capital for much of the time from 1774 to 1846, when it was taken by U.S. naval forces. The city and scenic **Monterey Peninsula** attract many tourists to the area. ⊕ Pop. 31,954.

Monterey Park. A city of southern California, a residential suburb of Los Angeles. ⊕ Pop. 60,738.

Mon·te·rí·a (môn′tə-rē′ə). A city of northwest Colombia south-southwest of Cartagena. It is an inland river port and a trade and manufacturing center. ● Pop. 162,056.

Mon·ter·rey (mŏn′tə-rā′, môn′tĕ-). A city of northeast Mexico east of Matamoros. Founded in 1579, the city was captured (September 1846) during the Mexican War by U.S. forces under Zachary Taylor, who later became the 12th President of the United States (1848–1850). ● Pop. 1,090,099.

Mon·tes Cla·ros (môn′tĭs klä′rŏŏs). A city of east-central Brazil north of Belo Horizonte. It is a trade and shipping center in an agricultural region. ● Pop. 249,565.

Mon·te·vi·de·o (mŏn′tə-vĭ-dā′ō, -vĭd′ē-ō′, môn′tĕ-vē-*the*′ô). The capital and largest city of Uruguay, in the southern part of the country on the Río de la Plata estuary. Founded by the Spanish c. 1726 on the site of a captured Portuguese fort, it became the capital after Uruguay became a fully independent country in 1828. ● Pop. 1,360,258.

Mont·fer·rat (mŏnt-fə-rät′). A historical region of northwest Italy south of the Po River. Claimed by both a noble family of Mantua and the house of Savoy after 1612, it was finally awarded to Savoy by the Peace of Utrecht (1713).

Mont·gom·er·y (mŏnt-gŭm′ə-rē, -gŭm′rē). The capital of Alabama, in the southeast-central part of the state south-southeast of Birmingham. Designated the state capital in 1847, the city boomed as a cotton market and port on the Alabama River. From February to May 1861 it served as the first capital of the Confederate States of America. ● Pop. 187,106.

Montgomery Village. A community of central Maryland, a suburb of Washington, D.C. ● Pop. 16,600.

Mon·ti·cel·lo (mŏn′tĭ-chĕl′ō, -sĕl′ō). An estate of central Virginia southeast of Charlottesville. Designed by Thomas Jefferson, it was begun in 1770 and was his home for 56 years. Owned by other families from shortly after Jefferson's death until 1923, it is now a national shrine.

mon·ti·cule (mŏn′tĭ-kyōōl′). A minor cone of a volcano.

Mont·mar·tre (môn-mär′trə). A hill and district of northern Paris, France, on the Right Bank. It is noted for its nightlife and for its associations with artists such as Vincent Van Gogh (1853–1890), Henri de Toulouse-Lautrec (1864–1901), and Maurice Utrillo (1883–1955). The original village of Montmartre was annexed by Paris in 1860.

Mont·par·nasse (môn-pär-näs′). A district of south-central Paris, France, on the Left Bank.

Its cafés have long been famous as gathering places for artists, writers, and intellectuals.

Mont·pel·ier (mŏnt-pēl′yər). The capital of Vermont, in the north-central part of the state. Founded in 1780, it became the state capital in 1805. ● Pop. 8,247.

Mont·pel·lier (môn-pĕl-yā′). A city of southern France west-northwest of Marseille. Founded in the eighth century, it was purchased by Philip VI of France in 1349. The city was later a Huguenot center and was besieged and captured by Louis XIII in 1622. It is a commercial and tourist center. ● Pop. 208,103.

Mon·tre·al (mŏn′trē-ôl′) or **Mont·ré·al** (môn′-rā-äl′). A city of southern Quebec, Canada, on **Montreal Island** in the St. Lawrence River. Named after Mount Royal, a hill at its center, it was founded by the French as Ville Marie de Montréal in 1642 and grew rapidly as a fur-trading center and starting point for western exploration. The English captured the city in 1760. Today Montreal is Canada's largest city, a major port, and a cultural, commercial, and industrial hub. ● Pop. 1,017,666.

Montreal North or **Mont·ré·al-Nord** (môn′rā-äl-nôr′). A town of southern Quebec, Canada, a suburb of Montreal on Montreal Island. ● Pop. 94,914.

Mon·treuil (môn-trœ′yə). A town of north-central France, an industrial suburb of Paris. ● Pop. 93,368.

Mont Roy·al (môn rwä-yäl′) or **Mount Roy·al** (roi′əl). A town of southern Quebec, Canada, a suburb of Montreal on Montreal Island. ● Pop. 19,247.

Mont-Saint-Mi·chel (môn-săn-mē-shĕl′). A small island off the coast of northwest France in an arm of the English Channel. Crowned by a strongly fortified abbey founded c. 708, it is a major tourist attraction.

Mont·ser·rat (mŏnt′sə-răt′). An island in the Leeward Islands of the British West Indies northwest of Guadeloupe. Discovered and named by Columbus in 1493, it was colonized by the English after 1632 but held by the French at various periods before being awarded to Great Britain in 1783.

Mont·ville (mŏnt′vĭl′). A town of southeast Connecticut north-northwest of New London on the Thames River. It was settled in 1670 and incorporated in 1786. ● Pop. 16,673.

Mon·za (mōn′zə, môn′tsä). A city of northern Italy north-northeast of Milan. An ancient capital of Lombardy, it is now a major industrial center with diversified manufactures. ● Pop. 121,151.

moor (mŏŏr). A broad area of open land, often high but poorly drained, with patches of heath and peat bogs.

Moor (mŏŏr). **1.** A member of a Muslim people

of mixed Berber and Arab descent, now living chiefly in northwest Africa. **2.** One of the Muslims who invaded Spain in the 8th century and established a civilization in Andalusia that lasted until the late 15th century. —**Moor′ish** *adj.*

Moore (mŏŏr, môr). A city of central Oklahoma, an industrial suburb of Oklahoma City. ◉ Pop. 40,318.

Moores·town (môrz′toun′, mŏŏrz′-, môrz′-). A community of southwest-central New Jersey east of Camden. It was a headquarters for Hessian troops in 1776. ◉ Pop. 13,695.

Moor·head (mŏŏr′hĕd′, môr′-). A city of western Minnesota on the Red River opposite Fargo, North Dakota. Founded in 1871, it is a trade center in an agricultural region. ◉ Pop. 32,295.

moor·land (mŏŏr′lănd′). Land consisting of moors.

Moose·head Lake (mŏŏs′hĕd′). A lake of west-central Maine north of Augusta. It is the center of a popular resort area.

Moose Jaw (mŏŏs′ jô′). A city of south-central Saskatchewan, Canada, west of Regina. It was founded in 1882 and is a processing center for an agricultural and oil-producing area. ◉ Pop. 33,941.

Moose River. A river, about 547 km (340 mi) long, of northeast Ontario, Canada, flowing northeast to James Bay as the estuary of the Abitibi, Mattagami, and other rivers.

Mo·rad·a·bad (mə-rä′də-bäd′, môr′ə-də-bäd′). A city of north-central India east-northeast of Delhi. Founded in 1625, it is an important railjunction, agricultural market, and manufacturing center. ◉ Pop. 429,214.

Mor·a·ga (mə-rä′gə). A city of western California east of Oakland. It is mainly residential. ◉ Pop. 15,852.

mo·raine (mə-rān′). An accumulation of boulders, stones, or other debris deposited by a glacier. —**mo·rain′al, mo·rain′ic** *adj.*

mo·rass (mə-răs′, mô-). An area of low-lying, soggy ground.

Mo·ra·va (môr′ə-və, mô′rä-vä). **1.** A river rising in eastern Czech Republic and flowing about 386 km (240 mi) generally southward to the Danube River near Bratislava, Slovakia. **2.** A river of eastern Yugoslavia rising in two forks and flowing about 209 km (130 mi) generally north-northwest to the Danube River east of Belgrade.

Mo·ra·vi·a (mə-rā′vē-ə, mô-). A region of central and eastern Czech Republic. Settled by a Slavic people at the end of the sixth century A.D., it became an independent kingdom in 870 but fell to the Magyars in 906 and later to the Bohemians. In 1526 Moravia came under the rule of the Austrian Hapsburgs. It was incorporated into Czechoslovakia in 1918.

Mo·ra·vi·an (mə-rā′vē-ən). **1.** A native or inhabitant of Moravia. **2.** A group of Czech dialects spoken in Moravia. **3.** A member of a Protestant denomination founded in Saxony in 1722 by Hussite emigrants from Moravia. **4.** Of or relating to Moravia or its people, dialects, or culture. **5.** Of or relating to the Moravian denomination.

Moravian Gate or **Moravian Gap.** A mountain pass of central Europe between the Sudetes and the western Carpathian Mountains. It was long a strategic trade and communications route.

Mor·ay Firth (mûr′ē). An inlet of the North Sea on the northeast coast of Scotland. It is the northern outlet of the Caledonian Canal system.

Mor·do·vi·a (môr-dō′vē-ə) or **Mord·vin·i·a** (môrd-vĭn′ē-ə). Formerly the **Mor·do·vi·an Autonomous Soviet Socialist Republic** (-vē-ən) or **Mord·vin·i·an Autonomous Soviet Socialist Republic** (-ē-ən). An autonomous republic of west-central Russia. Settled by a Finno-Ugric people first mentioned in the sixth century A.D., the region was annexed by Russia in 1552, and was made an A.S.S.R. in 1934. In 1992 it became a signatory to the treaty that created the Russian Federation.

Mo·reau River (môr′ō, môr′ō). A river of northwest South Dakota flowing about 402 km (250 mi) eastward to the Missouri River.

Mo·re·lia (mə-rāl′yə, mô-rĕ′lyä). A city of southwest Mexico west-northwest of Mexico City. Founded in 1541 as Valladolid, it was renamed in 1828 after the revolutionary hero José María Morelos y Pavón (1765–1815). ◉ Pop. 297,544.

Mor·gan City (môr′gən). A city of southern Louisiana south of Baton Rouge. Settled in 1850, it is a trade center in a bayou area with shrimp and oyster industries. ◉ Pop. 14,531.

Morgan Hill. A city of western California southeast of San Jose. It is a processing center. ◉ Pop. 23,928.

Mor·gan·town (môr′gən-toun′). A city of northern West Virginia on the Monongahela River near the Pennsylvania border. It is a shipping and industrial center. ◉ Pop. 25,879.

Mo·ri·o·ka (môr′ē-ō′kə). A city of northern Honshu, Japan, south-southeast of Aomori. It is a commercial and cultural center known for its ironware. ◉ Pop. 283,398.

Mo·ris·co (mə-rĭs′kō). *pl.* **-cos** or **-coes**. A Moor, especially a Spanish Moor.

Mo·ro (môr′ō, môr′ō). **1.** *pl.* **Moro** or **-ros**. A member of any of the predominantly Muslim Malay tribes of the southern Philippines. **2.** Any of the Austronesian languages of the Moro.

Mo·roc·co (mə-rŏk′ō). *abbr.* **Mor.** A country of northwest Africa on the Mediterranean Sea and the Atlantic Ocean. Inhabited from ancient times by Berbers, the region was the site of Phoenician and Carthaginian settlements and became a Roman province in the 1st century A.D. Arab conquerors introduced Islam in the 7th century. The country was united (11th–13th century), under the Almoravids and Almohads, Berber-Muslim dynasties whose influence reached from Spain to Senegal. European encroachment was limited prior to the French establishment of a protectorate over most of the region in 1912. Morocco achieved independence as a kingdom in 1956. Its claims to territory in Western Sahara have been actively opposed since the 1970's by the Polisario Front, a guerrilla nationalist movement based in Algeria. Rabat is the capital and Casablanca the largest city. ⊛ Pop. 26,590,000. —**Mo·roc′can** *adj. & n.*

Moro Gulf. An inlet of the Celebes Sea southwest of Mindanao, Philippines.

Mo·rón (mô-rôn′). A city of eastern Argentina, an industrial suburb of Buenos Aires. ⊛ Pop. 641,541.

Mo·ro·ni (mə-rō′nē, mô-). The capital of the Comoros, on Great Comoro Island at the northern end of the Mozambique Channel. ⊛ Pop. 20,112.

Mor·ris Jes·up (môr′ĭs jĕs′əp, mŏr′-), **Cape.** A cape of northern Greenland on the Arctic Ocean. It is the northernmost point of land in the world.

Mor·ris·town (môr′ĭs-toun′, mŏr′-). **1.** A town of northern New Jersey west-northwest of Newark. The Continental Army encamped here during the winters of 1776–1777 and 1779–1780. ⊛ Pop. 16,189. **2.** A city of northeast Tennessee east-northeast of Knoxville. Settled in 1783, it is a manufacturing and processing center. ⊛ Pop. 21,385.

Mor·ro Castle (môr′ō, mŏr′ō). A fort at the entrance to the harbor of Havana, Cuba. Built

by the Spanish (1589–1597) to protect the city from buccaneers, it was captured by the British in 1762 and bombarded by American forces during the Spanish-American War (1898).

Mörs (mœrs). See **Moers.**

Mor·ton Grove (môr′tn). A village of northeast Illinois, a mainly residential suburb of Chicago. ⊛ Pop. 22,408.

Mos·cow (mŏs′kou, -kō). **1.** The capital and largest city of Russia, in the west-central part of the country on the **Moscow River,** flowing about 499 km (310 mi) eastward to the Oka River. Inhabited since Neolithic times and first mentioned in Russian chronicles in 1147, Moscow became the capital of the principality of Muscovy and by the 15th century was the capital of the Russian state and the seat of the metropolitan (later patriarch) of the Russian Orthodox Church. The capital was transferred to St. Petersburg in 1712 but returned to Moscow by the Soviets in 1918. It was the site of the 1980 Summer Olympics. ⊛ Pop. 8,526,750. **2.** A city of northwest Idaho on the Washington border north of Lewiston. It is the seat of the University of Idaho (chartered 1889). ⊛ Pop. 18,519.

Mo·selle (mō-zĕl′) also **Mo·sel** (mō′zəl). A river rising in the Vosges Mountains of northeast France and flowing 547 km (340 mi) north then northeast to the Rhine River in western Germany. The German valley of the river is noted for its old castles and celebrated vineyards.

Mos·lem (mŏz′ləm, mŏs′-). Variant of **Muslim.**

Mos·qui·to (mə-skē′tō). See **Miskito.**

Mosquito Coast. A region of eastern Nicaragua and northeast Honduras. A British protectorate from 1655 to 1860, it then became an autonomous state known as the Mosquito Kingdom. Nicaragua appropriated it in 1894, and in 1960 the northern part was awarded to Honduras by the International Court of Justice.

Mos·so·ró (mŏŏ-sŏŏ-rô′). A city of northeast Brazil west-northwest of Natal. It is a shipping center in a mining and agricultural region. ⊛ Pop. 191,959.

Moss Point (môs, mŏs). A city of extreme southeast Mississippi east of Biloxi. Fishing is important to its economy. ⊛ Pop. 18,998.

Most (môst). A city of northwest Czech Republic near the German border northwest of Prague. It dates to at least the 11th century. It is a railway junction and industrial center in a coal-mining region. ⊛ Pop. 63,634.

Mo·star (mô′stär′). A city of southern Bosnia and Herzegovina. In the 16th century it became the chief Turkish administrative and commercial center in Herzegovina. Mostar passed to Austria in 1878 and to Yugoslavia after World War II. In 1993 ethnic Croats proclaimed the city the capital of the breakaway Croat republic Herzeg-Bosna, initiating a period of hostilities between Muslims and Croats, who finally reached an agreement on joint government of the city in 1996. Many structures, including a historic 16th century bridge, were destroyed in the early 1990's as a result of fighting between Muslims, Croats, and Serbs. ◉ Pop. 110,377.

Mó·sto·les (mô′stô-lĕs′). A city of central Spain, an industrial suburb of Madrid. ◉ Pop. 192,018.

Mo·sul (mō-sōōl′, mō′səl). A city of northern Iraq on the Tigris River north-northwest of Baghdad. An important center on the historical caravan route across northern Mesopotamia, it became part of the Ottoman Empire in the 16th century. Mosul was awarded to Iraq by the League of Nations in 1925. ◉ Pop. 664,221.

moth·er tongue (mŭ*th*′ər tŭng′). **1.** One's native language. **2.** A parent language.

Moth·er·well and Wish·aw (mŭ*th*′ər-wĕl′, -wəl; wĭsh′ô). A burgh of south-central Scotland on the Clyde River southeast of Glasgow. Consolidated in 1920, it has various heavy industries. ◉ Pop. 143,730.

Moul·mein (mōōl-mān′, mōl-). A city of southern Myanmar (Burma) on the Gulf of Martaban east of Yangon (Rangoon). The chief town of British Burma from 1826 to 1852, it is a port and commercial center. ◉ Pop. 219,991.

Moul·trie (mōl′trē). A city of southern Georgia southeast of Albany. It grew as a lumbering town and is now a processing center. ◉ Pop. 14,865.

Mound Builder (mound). A member of any of various Native American peoples flourishing from around the 5th century B.C. to the 16th century A.D. especially in the Ohio and Mississippi valleys, practicing settled agriculture and known for their often large burial and effigy mounds.

mount (mount). *abbr.* **mt., Mt.** A mountain or hill. Used especially as part of a proper name.

moun·tain (moun′tən). *abbr.* **mt., Mt., mtn., Mtn.** A natural elevation of the earth's surface having considerable mass, generally steep sides, and a height greater than that of a hill. —**moun′tain·y** *adj.*

Moun·tain Brook (moun′tən). A city of north-central Alabama, a residential suburb of Birmingham. ◉ Pop. 19,810.

moun·tain·ous (moun′tə-nəs). Having many mountains.

mountain range. A series of mountain ridges alike in form, direction, and origin.

Mountain Standard Time. *abbr.* **MST, M.S.T.** Standard time in the seventh time zone

west of Greenwich, England, reckoned at 105° west and used in the Rocky Mountain states of the United States. Also called *Mountain Time.*

Mountain View. A city of western California on San Francisco Bay northwest of San Jose. It is a manufacturing center with research facilities. ◉ Pop. 67,460.

Mount Ath·os (mount ăth′ŏs, ā′thŏs, ä′thôs). See **Athos.**

Mount Clem·ens (klĕm′ənz). A city of southeast Michigan north-northeast of Detroit. It is a health resort known for its mineral waters. ◉ Pop. 18,405.

Mount De·sert Island (dĭ-zûrt′). An island in the Atlantic Ocean off the southern coast of Maine. Named by 17th-century French explorers for its *Monts Deserts,* or "wilderness peaks," it is a popular summer resort.

Mount·lake Terrace (mount′lāk′). A city of northwest Washington south of Everett. It is mainly residential. ◉ Pop. 19,320.

Mount Lebanon. A community of southwest Pennsylvania, a residential suburb of Pittsburgh. ◉ Pop. 33,362.

Mount Pleasant. A city of central Michigan west-northwest of Saginaw. Oil was discovered nearby in 1928. ◉ Pop. 23,285.

Mount Pros·pect (prŏs′pĕkt′). A village of northeast Illinois, an industrial suburb of Chicago. ◉ Pop. 53,170.

Mount Royal. See **Mont Royal.**

Mount Vernon¹. An estate of northeast Virginia on the Potomac River near Washington, D.C. It was the home of George Washington from 1752 until his death in 1799. The mansion, built in 1743 by Lawrence Washington, George's half-brother, has been restored and is open to the public.

Mount Vernon². **1.** A city of south-central Illinois east-southeast of East St. Louis. It is a trade and industrial center in a farming region. ◉ Pop. 16,988. **2.** A city of southeast New York adjacent to the Bronx. Primarily residential, it was laid out as a planned community in the 1850's. ◉ Pop. 67,153.

Mous·cron (mōō-skrôn′) also **Moes·kroen** (mōōs′krōōn′). A city of western Belgium near the French border west-southwest of Brussels. It was founded as a frontier station. ◉ Pop. 54,402.

Mo·zam·bique (mō′zəm-bēk′, -zăm-). *abbr.* **Moz.** A country of southeast Africa on the Mozambique Channel. The interior was inhabited by Bantu peoples since the 1st century A.D., while the coast was settled by Arab traders beginning in the 8th century. The Portuguese colonized the area in the early 16th century and governed it as part of their India holdings until 1752, when a separate administrative unit was formed. As Portuguese East Africa it became an overseas province in 1951, but increasing nationalist feeling and guerrilla activity forced Portugal to grant Mozambique its independence in 1975. A devastating civil war between the new Marxist government and opposition guerrilla forces lasted until 1992, with UN-sponsored multiparty elections following in 1994. Maputo is the capital and the largest city. ⊛ Pop. 16,614,000. —**Mo′zam·bi′can** (-bē′-kən) *adj. & n.*

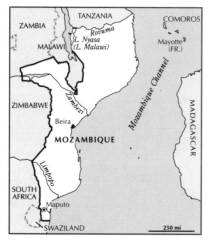

Mozambique Channel. An arm of the Indian Ocean between Madagascar and the mainland of southeast Africa.

Moz·ar·ab (mō-zăr′əb). One of a group of Spanish Christians who adopted certain aspects of Arab culture under Muslim rule but practiced a modified form of Christian worship. —**Moz·ar′a·bic** *adj.*

Mu·dan·jiang (mōō′dän′jyäng′) also **Mu·tan·chiang** (-tän′chyäng′). A city of northeast China southeast of Harbin. It is a railroad junction and industrial center. ⊛ Pop. 750,585.

mud flat (mŭd′ flăt′). Low-lying muddy land that is covered by water at high tide and exposed at low tide.

Muk·den (mōōk′dən, -dĕn′, mōōk′-). See **Shen·yang.**

Mul·ha·cén (mōō′lä-sän′, -thĕn′). A mountain, 3,480.4 m (11,411 ft) high, of southern Spain in the Sierra Nevada east of Granada. It is the highest point in the country.

Mül·heim (mōōl′hīm, myōōl′-, mül′-). A city of west-central Germany on the Ruhr River east of Duisburg. First mentioned in 1093, it passed to Prussia in 1815 and is today a highly industrialized city with diverse manufactures. ⊛ Pop. 177,175.

Mul·house (mə-lōōz′, mü-). A city of northeast France south of Colmar. Dating from at least

803, it became a free imperial city in 1308, allied itself with the Swiss from the 15th to the 18th century, and in 1798 voted to join France. ⊛ Pop. 108,358.

Mull (mŭl). An island of western Scotland in the Inner Hebrides. It is separated from the mainland on the northeast by the **Sound of Mull.**

Mul·tan (mōōl-tän′). A city of east-central Pakistan southwest of Lahore. Conquered c. 326 B.C. by Alexander the Great, it was captured by the Mongolian conqueror Tamerlane in 1398 and was under British jurisdiction from 1849 until 1947. ⊛ Pop. 732,070.

Mult·no·mah Falls (mŭlt-nō′mə). A waterfall, 189.1 m (620 ft) high, in a tributary of the Columbia River east of Portland, Oregon.

Mun·cie (mŭn′sē). A city of east-central Indiana northeast of Indianapolis. Established on the site of an earlier Delaware settlement, it was the setting for Robert and Helen Lynd's pioneering sociological study *Middletown* (1929). ⊛ Pop. 71,035.

Mun·de·lein (mŭn′dl-īn′). A village of northeast Illinois southwest of Waukegan. It was incorporated as Area in 1909 and renamed in 1925. ⊛ Pop. 21,215.

Mu·nich (myōō′nĭk). A city of southeast Germany near the Bavarian Alps southeast of Augsburg. Founded in 1158, it has long been the center of Bavaria. Adolf Hitler organized the Nazi Party here after World War I and signed the Munich Pact, widely regarded as a symbol of appeasement, with Great Britain, France, and Italy in 1938. The city was largely rebuilt after extensive Allied bombing in World War II. Munich was the site of the 1972 Summer Olympics. It is a major commercial, industrial, and cultural center. ⊛ Pop. 1,255,623.

Mun·see (mŭn′sē). **1.** One of the two Algonquian languages of the Delaware peoples, spoken in northern New Jersey, downstate New York, and western Long Island. **2.** *pl.* **Munsee** or **-sees.** A speaker of this language.

Mun·ster (mŭn′stər). **1.** A historical region and province of southwest Ireland. It was one of the kingdoms of ancient Ireland. **2.** A town of northwest Indiana, a suburb of Gary on the Illinois border. ⊛ Pop. 19,949.

Mün·ster (mōōn′stər, mŭn′-, mün′-). A city of west-central Germany north-northeast of Cologne. Founded c. 800 as a Carolingian episcopal see, the city was a prominent member of the Hanseatic League after the 14th century. Today it is an industrial center and a canal port. ⊛ Pop. 267,367.

Mur (mōōr) also **Mu·ra** (mōōr′ə). A river, about 483 km (300 mi) long, of south-central Austria, northeast Slovenia, and northern Croatia, where it flows into the Drava River.

Mur·chi·son River (mûr′chĭ-sən). An intermittent river of western Australia flowing about 708 km (440 mi) generally southwest to the Indian Ocean.

Mur·cia (mûr′shə, -shē-ə, mōōr′thyä). **1.** A region and former kingdom of southeast Spain on the Mediterranean Sea. Settled by Carthaginians, it was conquered by the Moors in the 8th century and became an independent Moorish kingdom in the 11th century. It was annexed by Castile in 1266. **2.** A city of southeast Spain north-northwest of Cartagena. Originally a Roman settlement, it was the capital of the ancient kingdom of Murcia. ⊛ Pop. 331,898.

Mu·re·şul (mōōr′ə-sōōl′, mōō′rĕ-shōōl′) or **Mu·reş** (mōō′rĕsh). A river rising in the Carpathian Mountains of north-central Romania and flowing about 756 km (470 mi) generally westward into southern Hungary.

Mur·frees·bor·o (mûr′frēz-bûr′ō, -bûr′ō). A city of central Tennessee southeast of Nashville. The state capital from 1819 to 1825, it was the site of a hard-fought Union victory in the Battle of Murfreesboro (December 31, 1862–January 2, 1863). ⊛ Pop. 44,922.

Mur·gab also **Mur·ghab** (mōōr-gäb′). A river rising in northeast Afghanistan and flowing about 853 km (530 mi) west and northwest to the Kara Kum Desert in southeast Turkmenistan.

Mur·mansk (mōōr-mänsk′, mōōr′mənsk). A city of northwest Russia on the northern Kola Peninsula on an inlet of the Barents Sea. A major ice-free port, it was the terminus of an important supply line to the Soviet Union in World Wars I and II. ⊛ Pop. 453,590.

Mu·rom (mōōr′əm). A city of west-central Russia on the Oka River southwest of Gorky. One of the oldest cities in Russia, it was first mentioned in a chronicle of 862. ⊛ Pop. 124,715.

Mur·ray (mûr′ē). A city of north-central Utah, a residential suburb of Salt Lake City. ⊛ Pop. 31,282.

Mur·ray River (mûr′ē). A river of southeast Australia rising in the Australian Alps and flowing about 2,589 km (1,609 mi) northwest then south to an arm of the Indian Ocean south of Adelaide.

Mur·rum·bidg·ee (mûr′əm-bĭj′ē). A river of southeast Australia rising in the Australian Alps and flowing about 1,689 km (1,050 mi) westward to the Murray River.

Mur·rys·ville (mûr′ēz-vĭl′, mûr′-). A borough of southwest Pennsylvania, a suburb of Pittsburgh. ⊛ Pop. 17,240.

Mus·cat (mŭs′kăt′, -kət, mŭs-kăt′). The capital of Oman, in the northern part of the country on the Gulf of Oman. Held by Portugal from 1508 to 1648, it became the capital of Oman in 1741. ⊛ Pop. 30,000.

Muscat and Oman. See **Oman.**

Mus·ca·tine (mŭs′kə-tēn′). A city of southeast Iowa on the Mississippi River west-southwest of Davenport. Founded in 1833, it grew as a river port and lumber center. ⊛ Pop. 22,881.

Mus·co·vite (mŭs′kə-vīt′). **1.** A native or resident of Moscow or Muscovy. **2.** Of or relating to Moscow, Muscovy, or the Muscovites.

Mus·co·vy (mŭs′kə-vē). A historical region and former principality in west-central Russia. Centered on Moscow, it was founded c. 1280 and existed as a separate entity until the 16th century, when it was united with another principality to form the nucleus of the early Russian empire. The name was then used for the expanded territory.

Mu·shin (mōō′shĭn′). A city of southwest Nigeria, an industrial and residential suburb of Lagos. ⊛ Pop. 234,500.

mus·keg (mŭs′kĕg′) also **mas·keg** (măs′-). A swamp or bog formed by an accumulation of sphagnum moss, leaves, and decayed matter resembling peat.

Mus·ke·go (mŭ-skē′gō). A city of southeast Wisconsin, a residential suburb of Milwaukee. ⊛ Pop. 16,813.

Mus·ke·gon (mŭ-skē′gən). A city of southwest Michigan west-northwest of Grand Rapids at the mouth of the **Muskegon River,** which flows about 365 km (227 mi) from west-central Michigan southwest to Lake Michigan. The city was founded on the site of a fur-trading post established c. 1810. ⊛ Pop. 40,283.

Mus·kho·ge·an (mŭs-kō′gē-ən). Variant of **Muskogean.**

Mus·king·um River (mə-skĭng′əm, -gəm). A river of eastern Ohio flowing about 179 km (111 mi) south and southeast to the Ohio River at Marietta.

Mus·ko·ge·an also **Mus·kho·ge·an** (mŭs-kō′-gē-ən). A family of Native American languages of the southeast United States that includes Choctaw, Chickasaw, Creek, and Alabama.

Mus·ko·gee¹ (mŭs-kō′gē). See **Creek.**

Mus·ko·gee² (mə-skō′gē). A city of eastern Oklahoma on the Arkansas River southeast of Tulsa. Founded in 1872, it is a trade and industrial center. ⊛ Pop. 37,708.

Mus·lim (mŭz′ləm, mōōz′-, mŭs′-, mōōs′-) or **Mos·lem** (mŏz′ləm, mŏs′-). A believer in or adherent of Islam. — **Mus′lim** adj.

Mus·sel·shell (mŭs′əl-shĕl′). A river of central Montana flowing about 483 km (300 mi) east then north to the Missouri River.

Mu·tan·chiang (mōō′tän′chyäng′). See **Mudanjiang.**

Mut·tra (mŭt′rə). See **Mathura.**

Muz·tag or **Muz·tagh** (mōōs-tä′, -täg′). A mountain, 7,286.8 m (23,891 ft) high, in the Kunlun Range of western China near the Indian border.

Muz·tag·a·ta also **Muz·tagh A·ta** (mōōs-tä′ə-tä′, mōōs-täg′-). A mountain, about 7,550.9 m (24,757 ft) high, of the **Muztagata Range** in western China near Tajikistan.

Muz·tagh (mōōs-tä′, -täg′). See **Muztag.**

Mwe·ru (mwä′rōō), **Lake.** A lake of central Africa on the Zaire-Zambia border west of the southern end of Lake Tanganyika.

Myan·mar (myän-mär′) or **Myan·ma** (-mä′). Formerly **Bur·ma** (bûr′mə). A country of southeast Asia on the Bay of Bengal and the Andaman Sea. Site of ancient Mon and Burman kingdoms, Burma was a province of British India from 1886 until 1937, when it became a separate colony. During World War II the Japanese invaded (1941) and occupied Burma until it was liberated by the Allied forces in 1945. Burma achieved independence from the British in 1948, since which time the country has had major problems with Communist insurgents and separatist ethnic groups. The civilian government was overthrown by a military coup in 1962 and again in 1988. Elections held in 1990 were overwhelmingly won by the opposition National League for Democracy, but the government declared the results invalid and jailed or put under house arrest many of the party's leaders, including Nobelist Aung San Suu Kyi, who was finally released in 1995. The country was renamed Myanmar in 1989. Yangon (formerly Rangoon) is the capital and the largest city. ● Pop. 45,555,000.

Myc·a·le (mĭk′ə-lē). A promontory of western Asia Minor opposite Samos. In 479 B.C. it was the site of a major Greek victory over the Persian fleet.

My·ce·nae (mī-sē′nē). An ancient Greek city in the northeast Peloponnesus that flourished during the Bronze Age as the center of an early civ-

ilization. It was the legendary capital of Agamemnon, the Greek leader in the Trojan War.

My·ce·nae·an (mī′sə-nē′ən). **1.** Of or relating to Mycenae or its inhabitants. **2.** Of, relating to, or being the Aegean civilization that spread its influence from Mycenae to many parts of the Mediterranean region from about 1580 to 1120 B.C. **3.** Of, relating to, or being the archaic dialect of Greek written in the Linear B script. **4.** A native or inhabitant of Mycenae. **5.** Mycenaean Greek.

Myk·o·nos (mĭk′ə-nŏs′, -nōs′, mē′kô-nôs′) also **Mí·ko·nos** (mē′kô-nôs′). An island of southeast Greece in the Cyclades Islands of the Aegean Sea. It is a popular resort.

My Lai (mē′ lī′). A village of southern Vietnam where more than 300 unarmed civilians, including women and children, were massacred by U.S. troops (March 1968) during the Vietnam War.

My·ra (mī′rə). An ancient Lycian city of southern Asia Minor. A major seaport, it was one of the chief cities of the region.

Myr·tle Beach (mûr′tl). A city of eastern South Carolina on the Atlantic Ocean east of Columbia. It is a popular resort. ● Pop. 24,848.

My·si·a (mĭsh′ē-ə). An ancient region of northwest Asia Minor. Mysia passed successively to Lydia, Persia, Macedon, Syria, Pergamum, and Rome. —**My′si·an** adj. & n.

My·sore (mī-sôr′, -sōr′). A city of southern India southwest of Bangalore. Inhabited before the 3rd century B.C., it was the center of a Muslim state after the late 16th century and was occupied by the British in 1831. Today it is an important industrial city. ● Pop. 480,692.

N

Nab·a·tae·a (năb′ə-tē′ə). An ancient kingdom of southwest Asia in present-day Jordan. It flourished from the fourth century B.C. to A.D. 106, when it was conquered by Rome. The "rose-red city" of Petra was its capital.

Nab·a·tae·an also **Nab·a·te·an** (năb′ə-tē′ən). **1.** A subject or inhabitant of the ancient kingdom of Nabataea. **2.** The Aramaic dialect of the Nabataeans. —**Nab′a·tae′an** adj.

Na·blus (näb′ləs, nä′bləs) also **Nab·u·lus** (näb′-ə-lōōs′). A city in the West Bank north of Jerusalem. An ancient Canaanite town, it was the biblical home of Jacob and the chief city of Samaria. ● Pop. 64,000.

Nack·a (nä′kə, -kä). A city of eastern Sweden,

an industrial suburb of Stockholm near the Baltic Sea. ⊛ Pop. 59,009.

Nac·og·do·ches (năk′ə-dō′chĭz). A city of eastern Texas east of Waco. Settled in 1779 on the site of a Spanish mission founded in 1716, it is today a processing and manufacturing center. ⊛ Pop. 30,872.

Na-Den·e also **Na·Dé·né** (nä-dĕn′ē). A proposed phylum of North American Indian languages including Athabaskan, Tlingit, and also possibly Haida. — **Na-Den′e** *adj.*

Na·fud (nă-fōōd′). See **Nefud.**

Na·ga Hills (nä′gə). A region on the India-Myanmar (Burma) border. Its people were subdued by the British from 1865 to 1880.

Na·ga·no (nä-gä′nō). A city of central Honshu, Japan, northwest of Tokyo. It is a religious center with diverse industries in a silk-producing region. ⊛ Pop. 352,378.

Na·ga·sa·ki (nä′gə-sä′kē, năg′ə-săk′ē). A city of western Kyushu, Japan, on **Nagasaki Bay,** an inlet of the East China Sea. The first Japanese port to be opened to foreign trade in the 16th century, Nagasaki was devastated by the second atomic bomb used in World War II (August 9, 1945). ⊛ Pop. 441,308.

Na·go·ya (nə-goi′ə, nä′gô-yä′). A city of central Honshu, Japan, at the head of Ise Bay east of Kyoto. A fortress town in the 16th century, it was rebuilt after heavy bombing in World War II. ⊛ Pop. 2,158,713.

Nag·pur (näg′pōōr′). A city of central India northeast of Bombay. Founded in the 18th century, it passed to the British in 1853 and is today an important commercial and industrial center. ⊛ Pop. 1,624,752.

Na·ha (nä′hä). A city of southwest Okinawa, Japan, in the Ryukyu Islands on the East China Sea. It is a port and the commercial center of the islands. ⊛ Pop. 301,679.

Na·hua·tl (nä′wät′l). **1.** *pl.* **Nahuatl** or **-tls.** A member of any of various Indian peoples of central Mexico, including the Aztecs. **2.** The Uto-Aztecan language of the Nahuatl.

Nai·ro·bi (nī-rō′bē). The capital and largest city of Kenya, in the south-central part of the country. Founded in 1899, it became the seat of government for British East Africa in 1905 and capital of independent Kenya in 1963. ⊛ Pop. 1,162,189.

Najd (näjd). See **Nejd.**

Nal·chik (näl′chĭk). A city of southwest Russia southeast of Rostov. Founded as a fortress town c. 1818, it is now an industrial center and a health resort. ⊛ Pop. 236,305.

Nam (näm, năm). Vietnam.

Na·ma (nä′mä, -mə). **1.** *pl.* **Nama** or **-mas.** A member of a Khoikhoin people of southwest Africa. **2.** The Khoikhoin language of the Nama.

Na·ma·land (nä′mə-lănd′). See **Namaqualand.**

Na·man·gan (nä′mən-gän′, nə-mən-). A city of eastern Uzbekistan east of Tashkent. It has textile and food-processing industries. ⊛ Pop. 312,000.

Na·ma·qua·land (nə-mä′kwə-lănd′) or **Na·ma·land** (nä′mə-). A mostly arid region of southwest Africa divided by the Orange River into **Great Namaqualand** in Namibia and **Little Namaqualand** in South Africa.

Na·mib Desert (nä′mĭb). A dry region of southwest Africa extending along the coast of Namibia between the Atlantic Ocean and the interior plateau.

Na·mib·i·a (nə-mĭb′ē-ə). Formerly **South-West Africa** (south′wĕst′). A country of southwest Africa on the Atlantic Ocean. The Portuguese and Dutch explored the Namibian coast in the early 15th century, and English and German missionaries followed in the 18th and 19th centuries. A German protectorate after 1884, the region was occupied in 1915 by South Africa, which governed it under a League of Nations mandate (1920–1945) but refused to acknowledge the UN trusteeship that replaced the mandate. A campaign to make the country independent on terms favorable to South Africa was opposed by SWAPO, a nationalist guerrilla movement based in Angola, and in 1988 South Africa agreed to a UN timetable for full independence, which was achieved in 1990. Windhoek is the capital. ⊛ Pop. 1,500,000. — **Na·mib′i·an** *adj. & n.*

Nam·oi (năm′oi′). A river, about 846 km (526 mi) long, of southeast Australia flowing generally northwest to a tributary of the Darling River.

Nam·pa (năm′pə). A city of southwest Idaho west-southwest of Boise. It is a processing and shipping center for an irrigated farming region. ⊛ Pop. 28,365.

Na·mur (nă-mōōr′, nä-mür′). A city of south-central Belgium on the Meuse River southeast of Brussels. Strategically located, it has been the scene of numerous sieges and battles, notably in the 17th century and in World Wars I and II. ⊕ Pop. 103,935.

Nan (nän). A river of western Thailand flowing about 563 km (350 mi) generally southward to join the Ping River and form the Chao Phraya.

Na·nai·mo (nə-nī′mō). A city of southwest British Columbia, Canada, on Vancouver Island and the Strait of Georgia west of Vancouver. The Hudson's Bay Company erected a blockhouse here in 1833. ⊕ Pop. 47,069.

Nan·chang (nän′chäng′). A city of southeast China on the Gan Jiang southeast of Wuhan. Dating from the 12th century, it is the capital of Jiangxi province. ⊕ Pop. 1,262,031.

Nan·cy (năn′sē, näN-sē′). A city of northeast France east of Paris. The capital of the duchy and region of Lorraine, the city passed to France in 1766. It was heavily bombed in World War II. ⊕ Pop. 96,317.

Nan·da De·vi (nŭn′də dā′vē). A peak, 7,821.7 m (25,645 ft) high, of the Himalaya Mountains in northern India. It was first scaled in 1936.

Nan·ga Par·bat (nŭng′gə pŭr′bət). A peak, 8,131.3 m (26,660 ft) high, of the Himalaya Mountains in northwest Kashmir.

Nan·jing (nän′jĭng′) also **Nan·king** (nän′kĭng′, nän′-). A city of east-central China on the Chang Jiang (Yangtze River) northwest of Shanghai. The capital of China from the third to the sixth century A.D. and again from 1368 to 1421, it was opened to foreign trade by the Treaty of Nanking in 1842. It was Sun Yat-sen's capital from 1912 to 1927 and Chiang Kai-shek's capital from 1928 to 1937, when it was captured by the Japanese. Reclaimed by Chinese forces in 1946, it is now the capital of Jiangsu province. ⊕ Pop. 2,610,594.

Nan Ling (nän′ lĭng′). A mountain range of southeast China running east to west along the northern border of Guangdong province.

Nan·ning (nän′nĭng′). A city of extreme southern China west of Guangzhou. The capital of Guangxi Zhuangzu, it is highly industrialized. ⊕ Pop. 1,159,099.

Nan Shan (nän′ shän′). See **Qilian Shan.**

Nan·terre (näN-tĕr′). A city of north-central France, an industrial suburb of Paris on the Seine River. ⊕ Pop. 88,578.

Nantes (nănts, näNt). A city of western France on the Loire River west of Tours. Dating to pre-Roman times, it was captured by Norse raiders in the ninth century and later fell to the dukes of Brittany. The Edict of Nantes, granting limited religious and civil liberties to the Huguenots, was issued in 1598 by Henry IV of France and revoked in 1685 by Louis XIV. ⊕ Pop. 244,514.

Nan·ti·coke[1] (năn′tĭ-kōk′). **1.** pl. **Nanticoke** or **-cokes.** A member of a Native American peo-

ple formerly inhabiting Delaware and eastern Maryland between Chesapeake Bay and the Atlantic coast. **2.** The Algonquian language of the Nanticokes.

Nan·ti·coke[2] (năn′tĭ-kōk′). A city of southeast Ontario, Canada, on Lake Erie south-southeast of Hamilton. Created in 1974 by an amalgamation of seven municipalities, it is a beach resort and has a large fishing fleet. ⊕ Pop. 19,816.

Nan·tong also **Nan·tung** (nän′tŏong′). A city of east-central China on the northern bank of the Chang Jiang (Yangtze River) estuary east of Nanjing. It is an industrial center. ⊕ Pop. 1,602,029.

Nan·tuck·et (năn-tŭk′ĭt). An island of southeast Massachusetts south of Cape Cod, from which it is separated by **Nantucket Sound,** an arm of the Atlantic Ocean. Settled in 1659, the island was part of New York from 1660 to 1692, when it was ceded to Massachusetts. It was a whaling center until the mid-1850's and is now a popular resort. **— Nan·tuck′et·er** n.

Nan·tung (nän′tŏong′). See **Nantong.**

Nap·a (năp′ə). A city of western California north of Oakland. It is a center of the **Napa Valley,** a mountainous region that is famous for its vineyards. ⊕ Pop. 61,842.

Nap·a·ta (năp′ə-tə). An ancient city of Nubia near the Fourth Cataract of the Nile River in modern-day Sudan. Napata flourished during the eighth century B.C.

Na·per·ville (nā′pər-vĭl′). A city of northeast Illinois, a manufacturing and residential suburb of Chicago. ⊕ Pop. 85,351.

Na·ples (nā′pəlz). **1.** also **Na·po·li** (nä′pô-lē). A city of south-central Italy on the **Bay of Naples,** an arm of the Tyrrhenian Sea. Founded by Greeks c. 600 B.C., Naples was conquered by the Romans in the fourth century B.C. and eventually became an independent duchy (eighth century A.D.) and capital of the kingdom of Naples (1282–1860). The city is a major seaport and a commercial, cultural, and tourist center. ⊕ Pop. 1,054,601. **2.** A city of southwest Florida on the Gulf of Mexico south of Fort Myers. It is a resort and has a shrimp-fishing industry. ⊕ Pop. 19,505.

Na·po (nä′pō). A river of northeast Ecuador and northern Peru flowing about 1,126 km (700 mi) east and southeast to the Amazon River.

Na·po·li (nä′pô-lē). See **Naples** (sense 1).

Na·ra (när′ə). A city of south-central Honshu, Japan, east of Osaka. An ancient cultural and religious center, it was founded in 706 and was the first permanent capital of Japan (710–784). ⊕ Pop. 355,869.

Nar·ba·da (nər-bŭd′ə). See **Narmada.**

Nar·bonne (när-bŏn′, -bôn′). A city of southern France near the Mediterranean coast southwest of Montpellier. Thought to have been the first Roman colony established in Transalpine Gaul (118 B.C.), it was an important seaport until its harbor silted up in the 14th century. It is now the commercial center of a wine-growing region. ◉ Pop. 41,565.

Na·rew also **Na·rev** (nä′rəf). A river rising in western Belarus and flowing about 442 km (275 mi) to northeast Poland and then generally west and southwest to the Western Bug River near its confluence with the Vistula River.

Nar·ma·da (nər-mŭd′ə) also **Nar·ba·da** (-bŭd′-ə). A river of central India flowing about 1,247 km (775 mi) westward to the Gulf of Cambay. Sacred to Hindus, it is said to have sprung from the body of the god Shiva.

Nar·ra·gan·sett also **Nar·ra·gan·set** (năr′ə-găn′sĭt). **1.** *pl.* **Narragansett** or **-setts** also **Narraganset** or **-sets.** A member of a Native American people formerly inhabiting Rhode Island west of Narragansett Bay, with present-day descendants in the same area. The Narragansetts were nearly exterminated during King Philip's War in 1675–1676. **2.** The Algonquian language of the Narragansetts.

Narragansett Bay. A deep inlet of the Atlantic Ocean in eastern Rhode Island. There are many good harbors and resort areas along its shores.

nar·row (năr′ō) or **nar·rows** (-ōz). **1.** A body of water with little width that connects two larger bodies of water. **2.** A part of a river or an ocean current that is not wide.

Nar·rows (năr′ōz). A strait of southeast New York between Brooklyn and Staten Island in New York City and connecting Upper and Lower New York Bay. The Narrows is spanned by the Verrazano-Narrows Bridge, completed in 1964 and one of the longest suspension bridges in the world.

Nase·by (nāz′bē). A village of central England near Northampton. Nearby on June 14, 1645, Oliver Cromwell's Parliamentarian forces decisively defeated Royalist troops led by Charles I and Prince Rupert.

Nash·u·a (năsh′ōō-ə). A city of southern New Hampshire on the Merrimack River south of Manchester. Settled c. 1655, it developed as a textile center in the early 19th century. ◉ Pop. 79,662.

Nash·ville (năsh′vĭl′). The capital of Tennessee, in the north-central part of the state northeast of Memphis. Founded in 1779 as Fort Nashborough, it was renamed in 1784 and became the permanent capital in 1843. Nashville is a port of entry and major commercial center known especially for its music industry. ◉ Pop. 488,374.

Na·sik (nä′sĭk). A town of west-central India northeast of Bombay. It is a Hindu pilgrimage

center noted for its brass and copper ware. ◉ Pop. 656,925.

Nas·ka·pi (năs′kə-pē). **1.** *pl.* **Naskapi** or **-pis.** A member of a Native American people inhabiting northern Quebec and Labrador. **2.** The variety of Montagnais spoken by the Naskapis.

Nas·sau (năs′ô′). **1.** A region and former duchy of central Germany north and east of the Main and Rhine rivers. The region became a duchy in 1806 and was absorbed by Prussia in 1866. Members of the original dynasty subsequently ruled Luxembourg and the Netherlands (as the house of Orange). **2.** The capital and largest city of the Bahamas, on the northeast coast of New Providence Island in the Atlantic Ocean east of Miami, Florida. Settled in the 17th century, it was a haven for pirates in the 18th century. ◉ Pop. 172,196.

Nas·ser (năs′ər), **Lake.** A lake of southeast Egypt and northern Sudan. It was formed in the 1960's by the construction of the Aswan High Dam on the Nile river. The rising waters of the lake submerged many historic sites.

Nass River (năs). A river of western British Columbia, Canada, flowing about 380 km (236 mi) southwest through the Coast Mountains to the Pacific Ocean north of Prince Rupert.

Na·tal (nə-tăl′, -täl′, -tôl′). **1.** A region of southeast Africa on the Indian Ocean. First sighted by the Portuguese explorer Vasco da Gama on Christmas Day 1497 and named *Terra Natalis,* it was acquired by the British in the 1820's and 1830's and settled by the Boers after 1836. Natal became a British colony in 1843 and was later a separate colony (after 1856) and then a founding province of the country of South Africa (1910). **2.** A city of northeast Brazil on the Atlantic Ocean north of Recife. Founded in the late 1590's, it was occupied by the Dutch from 1633 to 1654. The city grew rapidly in World War II as a base for flights connecting with Africa. ◉ Pop. 606,681.

Na·tash·quan or **Na·tash·kwan** (nə-tăsh′kwən). A river of eastern Canada rising in southern Labrador and flowing about 388 km (241 mi) southward across eastern Quebec to the Gulf of St. Lawrence.

Natch·ez¹ (năch′ĭz). **1.** *pl.* **Natchez.** A member of a Native American people formerly located along the lower Mississippi River near present-day Natchez. The Natchez ceased to exist as a people after war with the French in the early 18th century. **2.** The language of the Natchez.

Natch·ez² (năch′ĭz). A city of southwest Mississippi on the Mississippi River south-southwest of Vicksburg. Founded as a fortified settlement in 1716, it was held successively by France, Great Britain, Spain, and the United

States. Natchez prospered especially as the southern terminus of the **Natchez Trace,** an old road connecting the city with Nashville, Tennessee, that was commercially and strategically important in the late 18th and early 19th centuries. ◉ Pop. 19,460.

Natch·i·toches (năk′ĭ-tŏsh′). A city of northwest-central Louisiana southeast of Shreveport. It was founded c. 1714 as a French military and trading post. ◉ Pop. 16,609.

Na·tick¹ (nā′tĭk). The variety of Massachusett presumed to have been spoken in the mission town of Natick, Massachusetts, and used in the Massachusett Bible.

Na·tick² (nā′tĭk). A town of northeast Massachusetts, a residential and industrial suburb of Boston. ◉ Pop. 30,510.

na·tion (nā′shən). **1.** A relatively large group of people organized under a single, usually independent government; a country. **2.** The government of a sovereign state. **3.** A people who share common customs, origins, history, and frequently language; a nationality. **4. a.** A federation or tribe, especially one composed of Native Americans. **b.** The territory occupied by such a federation or tribe. — **na′tion·hood′** *n.*

Na·tion·al City (năsh′ə-nəl, năsh′nəl). A city of southern California, a residential and industrial suburb of San Diego on San Diego Bay. ◉ Pop. 54,249.

Na·tive American (nā′tĭv). A member of any of the aboriginal peoples of the Western Hemisphere. The ancestors of the Native Americans are generally considered to have entered the Americas from Asia by way of the Bering Strait sometime during the late glacial epoch. Also called *American Indian, Amerindian, Indian.* — **Native American** *adj.*

Nau·cra·tis (nô′krə-tĭs). An ancient city of Egypt in the Nile River delta southeast of Alexandria. Greek colonists probably settled here in the seventh century B.C.

Nau·ga·tuck (nô′gə-tŭk′). A town of west-central Connecticut south of Waterbury on the **Naugatuck River,** about 105 km (65 mi) long. It is an industrial center. ◉ Pop. 30,625.

Na·u·ru (nä-ōō′rōō). Formerly **Pleas·ant Island** (plĕz′ənt). An island country of the central Pacific Ocean just south of the equator and west of Kiribati. Inhabited by a population of mainly Polynesian ancestry, Nauru was discovered by the British in 1798 and became a German protectorate in 1888. Australians occupied the atoll in 1914 and administered it, except during a period of Japanese occupation (1942–1945), until it became independent in 1968. There is no official capital, but government offices are located in Yaren. ◉ Pop. 11,000. — **Na·u′ru·an** *adj. & n.*

Nav·a·jo also **Nav·a·ho** (năv′ə-hō′, nä′və-). **1.** *pl.* **Navajo** or **-jos** also **Navaho** or **-hos.** A member of a Native American people inhabiting extensive reservation lands in Arizona, New Mexico, and southeast Utah. The most populous of contemporary Native American groups in the United States, the Navajos are noted as stockbreeders and skilled weavers, potters, and silversmiths. **2.** The Apachean language of the Navajos. — **Nav′a·jo′** *adj.*

Navajo Mountain. A peak, 3,168.3 m (10,388 ft) high, of south-central Utah on the Arizona border.

Na·varre (nə-vär′, nä-). A historical region and former kingdom of southwest Europe in the Pyrenees of northern Spain and southwest France. Inhabited from early times by ancestors of the Basques, it was ruled by a Basque dynasty from the 9th to the 13th century. The southern part was annexed to Spain (1512–1515), while the northern part remained an independent kingdom until it was incorporated into the French crown lands in 1589.

Nav·a·so·ta (năv′ə-sō′tə). A river of east-central Texas flowing about 209 km (130 mi) southward to the Brazos River.

Nax·os or **Náx·os** (năk′sŏs, -sōs, -səs, näk′sôs). An island of southeast Greece in the Aegean Sea. The largest of the Cyclades, it was famous in ancient times as a center of Dionysian worship. The island belonged to Venice and then Turkey before it became part of independent Greece in 1829.

Naz·a·rene (năz′ə-rēn′, năz′ə-rēn′). **1.** A native or inhabitant of Nazareth. **2.** A member of a sect of early Christians of Jewish origin who retained many of the prescribed Jewish observances. **3.** A member of an American Protestant denomination, the Church of the Nazarene, that follows many of the doctrines of early Methodism. **4.** Of or relating to Nazareth or its inhabitants.

Naz·a·reth (năz′ər-əth). A town of northern Israel southeast of Haifa. Settled in prehistoric times, it is first mentioned in the New Testament as the boyhood home of Jesus. The modern town is a trade center and pilgrimage site. ◉ Pop. 46,300.

Nde·be·le (ən′də-bĕl′ā). **1.** *pl.* **Ndebele** or

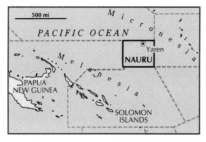

-les. A member of a Zulu people of southwest Zimbabwe. **2.** The Nguni language of the Ndebele. Also called *Matabele*.

N'Dja·me·na or **N'dja·me·na** or **Ndja·me·na** (ən-jä′mə-nə). Formerly **Fort-La·my** (fôr-lä-mē′). The capital and largest city of Chad, in the southwest part of the country on the Shari River. Founded by the French in 1900, it was renamed in 1973. ⊛ Pop. 303,000.

Ndo·la (ən-dō′lə). A city of north-central Zambia north of Lusaka on the border with Zaire. It is a commercial and manufacturing center in a copper-mining region. ⊛ Pop. 376,311.

Ndong·o (ən-dông′gō). See **Mbundu** (sense 3).

Ne·a·pol·i·tan (nē′ə-pŏl′ĭ-tən). **1.** Of, belonging to, or characteristic of Naples, Italy. **2.** A native or resident of Naples, Italy.

Ne·arc·tic (nē-ärk′tĭk, -är′tĭk). Of or designating the biogeographic region that includes the Arctic and Temperate areas of North America and Greenland.

Near East (nîr). A region of southwest Asia generally thought to include Turkey, Lebanon, Israel, Iraq, Jordan, Saudi Arabia, and the other countries of the Arabian Peninsula. Egypt and Sudan in northeast Africa are sometimes considered part of the region. — **Near Eastern** *adj.*

Near Islands. A group of islands of southwest Alaska. The westernmost of the Aleutian Islands, they were occupied by Japan from June 1942 until May–June 1943. Attu is the chief island of the group.

Ne·bras·ka (nə-brăs′kə). *abbr.* **NE, Nebr.** A state of the central United States in the Great Plains. It was admitted as the 37th state in 1867. The region became part of the United States through the Louisiana Purchase of 1803 and was made a separate territory by the Kansas-Nebraska Act of 1854. Its present boundaries were established in 1861. Lincoln is the capital and Omaha the largest city. ⊛ Pop. 1,584,617.

Ne·bras·kan (nə-brăs′kən). **1.** Of or relating to Nebraska. **2.** A native or resident of Nebraska.

Ne·chak·o (nə-chăk′ō). A river, about 462 km (287 mi) long, of central British Columbia, Canada, flowing northeast then east to the Fraser River at Prince George.

Nech·es (nĕch′ĭz). A river of eastern Texas flowing about 669 km (416 mi) south and southeast to Sabine Lake.

Neck·ar (nĕk′ər, -är). A river of southwest Germany rising in the Black Forest and flowing about 337 km (228 mi) generally north and west to the Rhine River at Mannheim.

Ne·der·land (nē′dər-lănd′). A city of southeast Texas between Beaumont and Port Arthur.

Founded by Dutch settlers, it is an industrial and residential community. ⊛ Pop. 16,192.

Need·ham (nē′dəm). A town of eastern Massachusetts, a mainly residential suburb of Boston. ⊛ Pop. 27,557.

Nee·nah (nē′nə). A city of eastern Wisconsin on Lake Winnebago north-northeast of Oshkosh. Settled c. 1840, it now includes paper and paper products among its manufactured goods. ⊛ Pop. 23,219.

Ne·fud (nĕ-fōōd′) also **Na·fud** (nä-). A desert region of northern Saudi Arabia. It is noted for its red sand and sudden violent winds.

Ne·gev (nĕg′ĕv) also **Ne·geb** (-ĕb). A hilly desert region of southern Israel comprising more than half of the country. The scene of much fighting between Israeli and Egyptian forces after the partition of Palestine in 1948, it has various mineral resources and many Kibbutzim.

Ne·gri·to (nĭ-grē′tō). *pl.* **-tos** or **-toes.** A member of any of various peoples of short stature inhabiting parts of Malaysia, the Philippines, and southeast Asia.

Ne·gro (nē′grō). *pl.* **-groes. 1.** A member of a major human racial division traditionally distinguished by physical characteristics such as brown to black pigmentation and often tightly curled hair, especially one of various peoples of sub-Saharan Africa. **2.** A person of Negro descent. — **Ne′gro** *adj.*

Ne·gro (nā′grō, nĕ′grô, -grōō), **Río. 1.** A river rising in central Argentina and flowing about 644 km (400 mi) eastward to the Atlantic Ocean. **2.** A river rising in southern Brazil and flowing about 805 km (500 mi) generally southwest to the Uruguay River in central Uruguay. **3.** A river of northwest South America flowing about 2,253 km (1,400 mi) from eastern Colombia to the Amazon River near Manaus, Brazil. Part of its course forms a section of the Colombia-Venezuela border.

Ne·groid (nē′groid′) *Anthropology.* **1.** Of, relating to, or being a proposed human racial division traditionally distinguished by physical characteristics such as brown to black pigmentation and often tightly curled hair and including peoples indigenous to sub-Saharan Africa. **2.** A member of this racial division.

Ne·gros (nā′grōs, nĕ′grôs). An island of the central Philippines in the Visayan Islands between Panay and Cebu. Sugar cane is important to its economy.

Nei Mong·gol (nā′ mŏn′gōl′, mŏng′-) also **In·ner Mongolia** (ĭn′ər). An autonomous region of northeast China. Originally the southern section of Mongolia, it was annexed by the Manchus in 1635 and became an integral part of China in 1911. Hohhot is the capital. ⊛ Pop. 20,070,000.

Neis·se (nī′sə). A river, about 225 km (140 mi)

long, rising in northern Czech Republic and flowing generally north along the border of Germany and Poland to the Oder River.

Nei·va (nā'və, -vä). A city of south-central Colombia on the Magdalena River south-southwest of Bogotá. It is a processing center in a cattle-ranching and coffee-growing region. ⊕Pop. 179,908.

Nejd (nĕjd) also **Najd** (nä̆jd). A vast plateau region of the central Arabian Peninsula. Formerly a separate kingdom, it was the nucleus for the modern state of Saudi Arabia.

Nel·lore (nĕ-lôr', -lōr'). A town of southeast India north of Madras. One of the chief ports along the Coromandel Coast, it is also a market and processing center. ⊕Pop. 316,606.

Nel·son River (nĕl'sən). A river of Manitoba, Canada, flowing about 644 km (400 mi) generally north and northeast from Lake Winnipeg to Hudson Bay. Discovered by European explorers in 1612, the river was long an important route for fur traders.

Nem·an (nĕm'ən, nyĕ'mən) also **Nie·men** (nē'-mən, nyĕ'-). A river of western Belarus flowing about 933 km (580 mi) west then north and west to the Baltic Sea.

Ne·me·a (nē'mē-ə). A valley of northern Argolis in ancient Greece. Its temple of Zeus was the site of the Nemean games, one of four Pan-Hellenic festivals, after 573 B.C. — **Ne'me·an** *adj. & n.*

Nen·ets (nĕn'ĕts). 1. *pl.* **Nenets.** A member of a reindeer-herding people of extreme northwest Russia along the coast of the White, Barents, and Kara seas. 2. The Uralic language of this people. Also called *Samoyed.*

Nen Jiang (nŭn' jyäng') also **Nen Chiang** (chyäng'). A river, about 1,191 km (740 mi) long, of northeast China flowing generally southward to the Songhua River.

Ne·o·lith·ic (nē'ə-lĭth'ĭk). Of, relating to, or being the cultural period of the Stone Age beginning around 10,000 B.C. in the Middle East and later elsewhere, characterized by the development of agriculture and the making of polished stone implements.

Ne·o·sho (nē-ō'shō, -shə). A river rising in east-central Kansas and flowing about 740 km (460 mi) southeast and south to the Arkansas River in eastern Oklahoma.

Ne·pal (nə-pôl', -päl', -pă̆l', nä-). *abbr.* **Nep.** A country of central Asia in the Himalaya Mountains between India and southwest China. Site of a flourishing civilization by the 4th century A.D., the region was divided in the medieval era into a number of principalities, one of which, Gurkha, became dominant in the 18th century. Gurkha expansion into northern India led to border wars with Great Britain (1814–1816), and

Nepal afterwards adopted a policy of seclusion from foreign contact. The Rana family came to dominate the government in 1846 and continued to do so until 1951. A British-Nepalese treaty of 1923 affirmed Nepal's full sovereignty, and a limited constitutional monarchy was established in 1951. The king, however, dissolved the parliament and banned political parties in 1960. In 1990 mass pro-democracy protests led to the abolition of the existing government and the reestablishment of a constitutional monarchy. Katmandu is the capital and the largest city. ⊕Pop. 21,360,000.

Nep·al·ese (nĕp'ə-lēz', -lēs'). 1. *pl.* **Nepalese.** A native or inhabitant of Nepal. 2. The Nepali language. 3. Of or relating to Nepal or its people, language, or culture.

Ne·pal·i (nə-pô'lē, -pä'-, -pă̆l'ē). 1. *pl.* **-is.** A native or inhabitant of Nepal. 2. The Indic language of Nepal, closely related to Hindi. 3. Of or relating to Nepal or its people, language, or culture.

Ne·pe·an (nə-pē'ən). A city of southeast Ontario, Canada, a suburb of Ottawa on the Ottawa River. Its industries include computer technology and brewing. ⊕Pop. 84,361.

Nep·tune (nĕp'tōōn', -tyōōn'). A community of east-central New Jersey south of Asbury Park. It is an industrial center in a coastal resort area. ⊕Pop. 28,366.

ness (nĕs). A cape or headland.

Ness (nĕs), **Loch.** A lake of north-central Scotland. It drains through the **Ness River** into the Moray Firth and is part of the Caledonian Canal system. The Loch Ness Monster is reputed to inhabit its deep waters.

Neth·er·lands (nĕ*th*'ər-ləndz). Often called **Hol·land** (hŏl'ənd). *abbr.* **Neth.** A country of northwest Europe on the North Sea. Inhabited by Germanic tribes during Roman times, the region passed to the Franks (4th–8th century), the Holy Roman Empire (10th century), the dukes of Burgundy (14th–15th century), and then to the house of Hapsburg. The northern part of the region formed the Union of Utrecht in 1579 and achieved its independence as the United Provinces in 1648 after the Thirty Years'

War. In the 17th century the country enjoyed great commercial prosperity and expanded its territories in the East and West Indies and elsewhere, although it lost this supremacy to Great Britain and France in the 18th century. The kingdom of the Netherlands, proclaimed at the Congress of Vienna (1814–1815), included Belgium until 1830. Despite its neutrality in World War II, the country was invaded and occupied by the Nazis (1940–1945). In 1948, after a 50-year reign, Queen Wilhelmina abdicated to her daughter Juliana, who abdicated to her daughter Beatrix in 1980. Amsterdam is the constitutional capital and the largest city; The Hague is the seat of government. ◉ Pop. 15,380,000. — **Neth′-er·land′ish** (-lăn′dĭsh) *adj.*

Netherlands Antilles. Formerly **Dutch West Indies** (dŭch). An autonomous territory of the Netherlands consisting of several islands in the Caribbean Sea, including Curaçao and Bonaire off the coast of Venezuela, and Saba, St. Eustatius, and the southern portion of St. Martin in the northern Windward Islands. Willemstad, on Curaçao, is the capital. ◉ Pop. 192,056.

Netherlands East Indies. See **Indonesia.**

Net·til·ling Lake (nĕch′ə-lĭng). A freshwater lake of south-central Baffin Island in the eastern Northwest Territories, Canada. It is frozen for most of the year.

Ne·tza·hual·có·yotl (nĕ-tsä′wäl-kō′yōt′l). A city of south-central Mexico, a suburb of Mexico City. ◉ Pop. 1,342,230.

Neu·bran·den·burg (noi-brän′dən-bûrg′, -bŏŏrk′). A city of northeast Germany north of Berlin. Founded in 1248, it is an industrial center. ◉ Pop. 82,451.

Neu·châ·tel (nŏŏ′shə-tĕl′, nyŏŏ′-, nœ-shä-), **Lake of.** A narrow lake of northwest Switzerland near the French border. It is in a picturesque region with notable vineyards.

Neuil·ly (nœ-yē′) or **Neuil·ly-sur-Seine** (-yē-sŏŏr-sĕn′, -sür-). A city of north-central France, a residential and industrial suburb of Paris. ◉ Pop. 64,170.

Neu·mün·ster (noi-mün′stər). A city of north-

ern Germany south-southwest of Kiel. Founded in the 12th century, it is a transportation and industrial center. ◉ Pop. 78,743.

Neun·kir·chen (noin′kîr-kən, -кнən). A city of southwest Germany northeast of Saarbrücken. It is a center for heavy industry in a coal-mining area. ◉ Pop. 50,382.

Neuse (nŏŏs, nyŏŏs). A river of east-central North Carolina flowing about 442 km (275 mi) generally southeast to Pamlico Sound.

Neuss (nois). A city of west-central Germany across the Rhine River from Düsseldorf. Built on the site of a Roman camp, it was chartered in the 12th century and held by France from 1794 to 1815, when it passed to Prussia. ◉ Pop. 148,560.

Neus·tri·a (nŏŏ′strē-ə, nyŏŏ′-). The western part of the kingdom of the Merovingian Franks from the sixth to the eighth century, in present-day northwest France. It engaged in almost constant warfare with Austrasia, the eastern portion of the realm. After 912 the name was applied to Normandy. — **Neu′stri·an** *adj. & n.*

Neu·tral (nŏŏ′trəl, nyŏŏ′-). **1.** A confederacy of Iroquoian-speaking Native American peoples formerly inhabiting the northern shore of Lake Erie. The Neutrals were destroyed by the Iroquois in the mid-17th century. **2.** *pl.* **Neutral** or **-trals.** A member of this people.

Neu·wied (noi-vēd′, -vēt′). A city of west-central Germany on the Rhine River southeast of Bonn. It developed around a palace built in 1648. ◉ Pop. 58,795.

Ne·va (nē′və, nyĭ-vä′). A river of northwest Russia flowing about 74 km (46 mi) from Lake Ladoga to the Gulf of Finland. St. Petersburg is located in its delta.

Ne·vad·a (nə-văd′ə, -vä′də). *abbr.* **NV, Nev.** A state of the western United States. It was admitted as the 36th state in 1864. Part of the area ceded by Mexico to the United States in 1848, it was made into a separate territory in 1861 after an influx of settlers who were drawn by the discovery (1859) of the Comstock Lode. Carson City is the capital and Las Vegas the largest city. ◉ Pop. 1,206,152. — **Ne·vad′an, Ne·vad′i·an** *adj. & n.*

Ne·vis (nē′vĭs, nĕv′ĭs). One of the Leeward Islands of the eastern West Indies in the Caribbean Sea. Discovered by Columbus in 1493, it was colonized by the English after 1628 and is now part of St. Kitts and Nevis.

New Albany (nŏŏ, nyŏŏ). A city of southern Indiana on the Ohio River opposite Louisville, Kentucky. A shipbuilding center in the 19th century, it now produces various goods and processes and ships agricultural products. ◉ Pop. 36,322.

New Amsterdam. A settlement established in

1624 by the Dutch at the mouth of the Hudson River on the southern end of Manhattan Island. It was the capital of New Netherland from 1626 to 1664, when it was captured by the British and renamed New York.

New·ark (nōō′ərk, nyōō′-). **1.** A city of western California south-southeast of Oakland. On the eastern coast of San Francisco Bay, it is largely residential. ☉ Pop. 37,861. **2.** A city of northwest Delaware west-southwest of Wilmington. Settled c. 1694, it is the seat of the University of Delaware (established 1743). ☉ Pop. 25,098. **3.** A city of northeast New Jersey on **Newark Bay,** an inlet of the Atlantic Ocean, opposite Jersey City and west of New York City. It was settled by Puritans in 1666 and is today a heavily industrialized port of entry. ☉ Pop. 275,221. **4.** A city of central Ohio east of Columbus. It is an industrial and processing center in an area marked by notable earthworks erected by the Mound Builders. ☉ Pop. 44,389.

New Bed·ford (běd′fərd). A city of southeast Massachusetts on Buzzards Bay east-southeast of Fall River. Settled in the mid-1600's, it was a major whaling port in the first half of the 19th century. Fishing and diversified manufacturing are important to its economy. ☉ Pop. 99,922.

New Ber·lin (bûr-lĭn′). A city of southeast Wisconsin. It is primarily a residential suburb of Milwaukee. ☉ Pop. 33,592.

New Bern (bûrn). A city of eastern North Carolina on the Neuse River southeast of Raleigh. Settled in 1710 by Swiss and German colonists, it was an early colonial capital as the seat of royal governors (1770–1774) and as the site of the first provincial convention (1774). ☉ Pop. 17,363.

New Braun·fels (broun′fəlz). A city of south-central Texas northeast of San Antonio. It was founded by German immigrants and has a textile industry. ☉ Pop. 27,334.

New Brighton. A city of southeast Minnesota, a suburb of Minneapolis–St. Paul. It is primarily residential with some light industry. ☉ Pop. 22,207.

New Britain[1]. A volcanic island of Papua New Guinea, in the southwest Pacific Ocean. The largest island in the Bismarck Archipelago, it was first visited and named by the English navigator William Dampier in 1700 and was controlled by Germany after 1884 and by Australia from 1920 until 1975, when Papua New Guinea achieved independence.

New Britain[2]. A city of central Connecticut south-southwest of Hartford. Tin and brass industries were established here in the 18th century. ☉ Pop. 75,491.

New Brunswick. **1.** *abbr.* **NB, N.B.** A province of eastern Canada on the Gulf of St. Lawrence. Part of French Acadia and then the province of Nova Scotia, it became a separate province in 1784 after an influx of Loyalists from the newly independent United States. New Brunswick joined Nova Scotia, Quebec, and Ontario to form the confederated Dominion of Canada in 1867. Fredericton is the capital and St. John the largest city. ☉ Pop. 696,405. **2.** A city of central New Jersey on the Raritan River southwest of Newark. Settled in 1681, it served as headquarters for both the British and Continental armies during the American Revolution (1775–1783). ☉ Pop. 41,711.

New·burgh (nōō′bûrg′, nyōō′-). A city of southeast New York on the Hudson River south-southwest of Poughkeepsie. Founded c. 1709, it was Commander George Washington's headquarters from April 1782 until August 1783 during the American Revolution. ☉ Pop. 26,454.

New·bur·y·port (nōō′bə-rē-pôrt′, -pōrt′, nyōō′-). A city of northeast Massachusetts at the mouth of the Merrimack River east-northeast of Lawrence. Settled in 1635, it was a shipbuilding and whaling port in early times and is now a resort community with varied light industries. ☉ Pop. 16,317.

New Caledonia. A French overseas territory in the southwest Pacific Ocean consisting of the island of **New Caledonia** and several smaller islands. The island of New Caledonia was discovered and named by the British navigator Capt. James Cook in 1774 and annexed by France in 1853. It was a penal colony from 1864 to 1894. Nouméa is the territorial capital. ☉ Pop. 145,368.

New Canaan. A town of southwest Connecticut north-northeast of Stamford. It is mainly residential. ☉ Pop. 17,864.

New Castile. A historical region of central Spain that combined with Old Castile to the north to form the kingdom of Castile. It was united with Aragon after the marriage of Ferdinand and Isabella (1469).

New·cas·tle (nōō′kăs′əl, nyōō′-). **1.** A town of southern Ontario, Canada, on Lake Ontario east of Toronto. It was established in a dairy and farm region. ☉ Pop. 32,229. **2.** or **New·cas·tle-un·der·Lyme** (-ŭn′dər-līm′). A municipal borough of west-central England south-southwest of Stoke. It has brick, tile, and clothing industries. ☉ Pop. 123,009. **3.** or **Newcastle upon Tyne.** A borough of northeast England on the Tyne River north of Leeds. Built on the site of a Roman military station, it became a coal-shipping port in the 13th century and was the principal center for coal exports after the 16th century. ☉ Pop. 285,310.

New Castle. **1.** A city of east-central Indiana south of Muncie. It is a trade center in an agricultural region. There are prehistoric mounds in the area. ⊛ Pop. 17,753. **2.** A city of western Pennsylvania north-northwest of Pittsburgh. Coal, iron ore, and limestone deposits are important to its economy. ⊛ Pop. 28,334.

New·cas·tle-un·der-Lyme (no͞o′kăs′əl-ŭn′dər-līm′, nyo͞o′-). See **Newcastle** (sense 2).

Newcastle upon Tyne. See **Newcastle** (sense 3).

New City. An unincorporated community of southeast New York on the western side of the Hudson River north of New York City. It is mainly residential. ⊛ Pop. 33,673.

New Delhi. The capital of India, in the north-central part of the country south of Delhi. It was constructed between 1912 and 1929 to replace Calcutta as the capital of British India and officially inaugurated in 1931. New Delhi is also a trade center and transportation hub with various manufactures. ⊛ Pop. 301,297.

New England. *abbr.* **NE, N.E.** A region of the northeast United States comprising the states of Maine, New Hampshire, Vermont, Massachusetts, Connecticut, and Rhode Island. **— New Eng′land·er** *n.*

New England Range. A mountain range and plateau of southeast Australia in the northern part of the Great Dividing Range.

New English. See **Modern English.**

New Forest. A region of southern England. Set aside as a hunting ground by William the Conqueror in 1079, it is mostly administrated as public parkland.

New·found·land (no͞o′fən-lənd, -lănd′, -fənd-, nyo͞o′-). *abbr.* **NF, Newf., Nfld.** A province of eastern Canada including the island of **Newfoundland** and nearby islands and the mainland area of Labrador with its adjacent islands. Newfoundland joined the confederation in 1949. Vikings probably visited the region c. 1000, but the area was not known to European fishermen and explorers until the Italian-born explorer John Cabot's voyages in the late 15th century. England claimed Newfoundland in 1583, although the claims were disputed by France until the Treaty of Paris (1763). The province of Quebec continued to claim Labrador until 1927. St. John's is the capital and the largest city. ⊛ Pop. 567,681. **— New′found·land·er** *n.*

New France. The possessions of France in North America from the 16th century until the Treaty of Paris (1763), when the French holdings were awarded to Great Britain and Spain. At its greatest extent it included much of southeast Canada, the Great Lakes region, and the Mississippi Valley. British and French rivalry for control of the territory led to the four conflicts known collectively in the New World as the French and Indian Wars (1689–1763).

New Georgia Island. An island of the Solomon Islands in the southwest Pacific Ocean. It was occupied by the Japanese in 1942 and recaptured by the Allies in August 1943.

New Gra·na·da (grə-nä′də). A former Spanish colony and viceroyalty of northern South America including present-day Colombia, Ecuador, Panama, and Venezuela. It was under Spanish rule from the 1530's to 1819.

New Greek. See **Modern Greek.**

New Guinea. An island in the southwest Pacific Ocean north of Australia. The western half is part of Indonesia, and the eastern half forms the major portion of Papua New Guinea. Inhabited by Papuan, Negrito, and Melanesian peoples, it was probably first sighted by the Portuguese in 1511 and named for the Guinea coast of western Africa. **— New Guinean** *adj. & n.*

New Guinea, Trust Territory of. A former trust territory of Australia consisting of northeast New Guinea, the Bismarck Archipelago, and Bougainville in the Solomon Islands. It was placed under Australian jurisdiction after World War II and was gradually broken up between 1963 and 1973.

New Hamp·shire (hămp′shər, -shîr′, hăm′-). *abbr.* **NH, N.H.** A state of the northeast United States between Vermont and Maine. It was admitted as one of the original Thirteen Colonies in 1788. First explored in 1603, it was settled by colonists from Massachusetts during the 1620's and 1630's and became a separate colony in 1741. New Hampshire was the first colony to declare its independence from Great Britain and the first to establish its own government (January 1776). Concord is the capital and Manchester the largest city. ⊛ Pop. 1,113,915. **— New Hamp′shir·ite′** *n.*

New Har·mo·ny (här′mə-nē). A village of southwest Indiana on the Wabash River west-northwest of Evansville. It was founded in 1814 by the Harmony Society led by George Rapp and was the site (1825–1828) of a utopian community established by the British social reformer Robert Owen. The colony was known for its progressive educational, intellectual, and scientific ideas. ⊛ Pop. 846.

New Ha·ven (hā′vən). A city of southern Connecticut on Long Island Sound northeast of Bridgeport. Settled (1637–1638) by Puritans, it was the center of a theocratic colony that was joined with Connecticut in 1664. From 1701 to 1875 it was joint capital with Hartford. New Haven is the seat of Yale University, which was founded in 1701 and moved here permanently in 1716. ⊛ Pop. 130,474.

New Hebrew. The Hebrew language as used from the mid-18th century until 1948. Also called *Modern Hebrew.*

New Hebrides. See **Vanuatu.**

New Hope (hōp). A city of southeast Minnesota, a primarily residential suburb of Minneapolis. ⦿ Pop. 21,853.

New Iberia. A city of southern Louisiana southwest of Baton Rouge. Settled by Acadians after c. 1765, it is a processing and shipping center. ⦿ Pop. 31,828.

New·ing·ton (nōo′ĭng-tən, nyōo′-). A town of north-central Connecticut southwest of Hartford. It is mainly residential. ⦿ Pop. 29,208.

New Ireland. A volcanic island of the southwest Pacific Ocean in the Bismarck Archipelago. First sighted by Europeans in 1616, it was thought to be part of the island of New Britain until 1797. New Ireland was a German protectorate from 1884 to 1914 and now belongs to Papua New Guinea.

New Jersey. *abbr.* **NJ, N.J.** A state of the east-central United States on the Atlantic Ocean. It was admitted as one of the original Thirteen Colonies in 1787. The region was settled by Dutch and Swedish colonists in the 1620's and 1630's, was ceded to the English as part of New Netherland in 1664, and became a royal province in 1702. The colony was strategically important in the American Revolution (1775–1783) and was the site of a number of major battles, including the engagements at Trenton, Princeton, and Monmouth. Trenton is the capital and Newark is the largest city. ⦿ Pop. 7,748,634. — **New Jer′sey·ite′** *n.*

New Ken·sing·ton (kĕn′zĭng-tən). A city of southwest Pennsylvania on the Allegheny River east-northeast of Pittsburgh. Aluminum products were first manufactured here in 1892. ⦿ Pop. 15,894.

New Kingdom. Ancient Egypt during the XVIII–XX Dynasties, from c. 1580 to 1090 B.C. The New Kingdom was noted for its territorial expansion and richness of art and architecture under rulers such as Amenhotep III (reigned 1411?–1375 B.C.) and Rameses II (reigned 1304–1237 B.C.).

New Latin. Latin as used since about 1500.

New London. A city of southeast Connecticut at the mouth of the Thames River near Long Island Sound. Laid out by John Winthrop, the first govenor of Massachusetts Bay Colony, in 1646, it was an important whaling center during the 19th century and is today the site of a U.S. submarine base. ⦿ Pop. 28,540.

New·ly Independent States (nōo′le, nyōo′-). *abbr.* **NIS** The countries that were formerly (before 1991) constituent republics of the U.S.S.R., including Armenia, Azerbaijan, Belarus, Georgia, Kazakstan, Kyrgyzstan, Moldova, Tajikistan, Turkmenistan, Ukraine, and Uzbekistan. The term can also include Russia and sometimes Estonia, Latvia, and Lithuania.

New·mar·ket (nōo′mär′kĭt, nyōo′-). **1.** A town of southeast Ontario, Canada, north of Toronto. It is an industrial community. ⦿ Pop. 29,753. **2.** An urban district of eastern England east of Cambridge. Newmarket has been a center for horseracing since the early 17th century. ⦿ Pop. 16,235.

New Mexico. *abbr.* **NM, N.M., N.Mex.** A state of the southwest United States on the Mexican border. It was admitted as the 47th state in 1912. Site of prehistoric cultures that long preceded the Pueblo civilization encountered by the Spanish in the 16th century, the region was governed as a province of Mexico after 1821 and ceded to the United States by the Treaty of Guadalupe Hidalgo in 1848. The original territory (established 1850) included Arizona and part of Colorado and was enlarged by the Gadsden Purchase of 1853. Sante Fe is the capital and Albuquerque the largest city. ⦿ Pop. 1,521,779. — **New Mexican** *adj.*

New Milford. 1. A town of western Connecticut on the Housatonic River north-northeast of Danbury. Founded in the early 1700's, it is a manufacturing center in a summer resort region. ⦿ Pop. 23,629. **2.** A borough of northeast New Jersey east-northeast of Paterson. Settled in 1695 by French Huguenots, it is primarily residential. ⦿ Pop. 15,990.

New Neth·er·land (nĕth′ər-lənd). A Dutch colony in North America along the Hudson and lower Delaware rivers. The first settlement was made at Fort Orange (now Albany, New York) in 1624, although the colony centered on New Amsterdam at the tip of Manhattan Island after 1625–1626. New Netherland was annexed by the English and renamed New York in 1664.

New Norwegian. A Norwegian national standard language based on the spoken, especially rural dialects, devised in 1853 and recognized as a second national language in 1885. Also called *Landsmål, Nynorsk.*

New Or·leans (ôr′lē-ənz, ôr′lənz, ôr-lēnz′). A city of southeast Louisiana between the Mississippi River and Lake Pontchartrain. Founded in 1718, it became the capital of a French colony in 1722 and passed to the United States as part of the Louisiana Purchase of 1803. French influence continued to dominate the city, however, especially in the Vieux Carré and in the celebration of Mardi Gras. New Orleans is the largest city in Louisiana. ⦿ Pop. 496,938. — **New Or·lea′ni·an** (ôr-lē′nē-ən, -lēn′yən) *n.*

New Philadelphia. A city of northeast central Ohio south of Canton. Ceramics and machinery are among its manufactures. ⦿ Pop. 15,698.

New·port (nōō′pôrt′, -pōrt′, nyōō′-). **1.** A municipal borough of southern England. It is the administrative and commercial center of the Isle of Wight in the English Channel. ⊛ Pop. 23,570. **2.** A city of northern Kentucky on the Ohio River opposite Cincinnati, Ohio. Laid out in 1791, it is an industrial center. ⊛ Pop. 18,871. **3.** A city of southeast Rhode Island at the mouth of Narragansett Bay south-southeast of Providence. Settled in 1639, it was an important economic center in pre-Revolutionary times and in the 19th century became a fashionable summer resort where the wealthy built palatial "cottages" such as the Breakers and Marble House. The mansions and restored colonial buildings still attract tourists to the city, as do its tennis museum and yachting facilities. ⊛ Pop. 28,227. **4.** A borough of southeast Wales on an inlet of the Severn estuary northeast of Cardiff. It is an industrial and a manufacturing center. ⊛ Pop. 137,037.

Newport Beach. A city of southern California on the Pacific Ocean south of Santa Ana. It is a popular seaside and yachting resort. ⊛ Pop. 66,643.

Newport News (nōōz, nyōōz). An independent city of southeast Virginia at the mouth of the James River off Hampton Roads north-northwest of Norfolk. Settled c. 1620, it is a railroad terminus and a port, with an important shipbuilding industry dating back to the 1880's. ⊛ Pop. 170,045.

New Providence. An island of the Bahamas in the West Indies. Nassau is on the island, which is a popular tourist resort.

New River. A river of the southeast United States flowing about 515 km (320 mi) from the Blue Ridge in northwest North Carolina northeast across southwest Virginia then northwest to the Allegheny Plateau in south-central West Virginia.

New Ro·chelle (rə-shĕl′, rō-). A city of southeast New York on Long Island Sound east of Mount Vernon. Settled by Huguenots in 1688, it is mainly residential with some light industry. ⊛ Pop. 67,265.

New Siberian Islands. An archipelago of northeast Russia in the Arctic Ocean between the Laptev and East Siberian seas. Discovered in the 1770's, they are used for meteorological and other scientific stations.

New Spain. 1. A former Spanish viceroyalty (1521–1821) in North America, including the southwest United States, Mexico, Central America north of Panama, and some West Indian islands. It also included the islands of the Philippines and was administered from Mexico City. **2.** The former Spanish possessions in the New World. At its greatest extent, New Spain comprised South America (except Brazil), Central America, Mexico, the West Indies, Florida, and much of the land west of the Mississippi River.

New Sweden. A Swedish colony in North America on the Delaware River. Founded in 1638, it included parts of present-day Pennsylvania, New Jersey, and Delaware. The Dutch under Peter Stuyvesant took the colony in 1655.

New·ton (nōōt′n, nyōōt′n). **1.** A city of south-central Iowa east-northeast of Des Moines. It is an industrial center. ⊛ Pop. 14,789. **2.** A city of south-central Kansas north of Wichita. Russian Mennonites settled here in the early 1870's. ⊛ Pop. 16,700. **3.** A city of eastern Massachusetts, a mainly residential suburb of Boston. The city comprises a number of villages, including **Newton Corner, Newton Center, Newton Upper Falls,** and **Newton Lower Falls.** ⊛ Pop. 82,585.

New·town (nōō′toun′, nyōō′-). A town of southwest Connecticut on the Housatonic River east-northeast of Danbury. It is a manufacturing center in an agricultural region. ⊛ Pop. 20,779.

New·town·ab·bey (nōōt′n-ăb′ē, nyōōt′-). An urban district of eastern Northern Ireland, an industrial and residential suburb of Belfast. ⊛ Pop. 72,400.

New Westminster. A city of southwest British Columbia, Canada, a suburb of Vancouver on the Fraser River. It was the capital of the province from 1860 to 1866. ⊛ Pop. 38,550.

New World (wûrld). The Western Hemisphere. The term was first used by the Italian historian Peter Martyr (1457–1526), whose *De Rebus Oceanicis et Novo Orbe* (1516) chronicled the discovery of America.

New York. *abbr.* **NY, N.Y. 1.** A state of the northeast United States. It was admitted as one of the original Thirteen Colonies in 1788. First explored by the French explorer Samuel de Champlain and the English navigator Henry Hudson, the region was claimed by the Dutch in 1624 but fell to the English in 1664–1667. The building of the Erie Canal and railroad lines in the 1820's and 1830's led to development of the western part of the state and great economic prosperity, establishing New York City as the financial center of the nation. Albany is the capital and New York City the largest metropolis. ⊛ Pop. 18,044,505. **2.** or **New York City.** A city of southern New York on New York Bay at the mouth of the Hudson River. Founded by the Dutch as New Amsterdam, it was renamed by the English in honor of the Duke of York. It is the largest city in the country and a financial, cultural, trade, shipping, and communications center. Originally consisting only of Manhattan Island, it was rechartered in 1898 to include the five present-day boroughs of Manhattan, the

Bronx, Brooklyn, Queens, and Staten Island. ⊛ Pop. 7,322,564. **— New York′er** *n.*

New York Bay. An arm of the Atlantic Ocean at the mouth of the Hudson River between western Long Island and northeast New Jersey. It is divided into **Upper New York Bay** and **Lower New York Bay** by the Narrows.

New York City. *abbr.* **NYC, N.Y.C.** See **New York** (sense 2).

New York State Barge Canal. A system of inland waterways, about 845 km (525 mi) long, traversing New York State and connecting the Great Lakes with the Hudson River and Lake Champlain. Authorized in 1903 as a modification and expansion of the Erie Canal, it was begun in 1905 and completed in 1918.

New Zea·land (zē′lənd). *abbr.* **N.Z.** An island country in the southern Pacific Ocean southeast of Australia. Maori groups probably migrated to New Zealand from Polynesia beginning before A.D. 1400. Discovered by the Dutch navigator Abel Tasman in 1642, the islands were visited and explored by the British navigator Capt. James Cook four times between 1769 and 1777. The British established their first permanent settlement in 1840 and claimed the region as a crown colony, separating it administratively from Australia in 1841. New Zealand attained self-governing status in 1852 and dominion status 1907. Britain granted full autonomy in 1931, although the nation did not formally declare its independence until 1947. Wellington is the capital and Auckland is the largest city. ⊛ Pop. 3,493,000. **— New Zea′land·er** *n.*

Ne·ya·ga·wa (ně′yə-gä′wə). A city of southern Honshu, Japan, a commercial suburb of Osaka. ⊛ Pop. 257,137.

Nez Perce (něz′ pûrs′, něs′) also **Nez Per·cé** (pər-sā′). **1.** *pl.* **Nez Perce** or **Per·ces** also

Nez Percé or **Per·cés.** A member of a Native American people formerly inhabiting the lower Snake River and its tributaries in western Idaho, northeast Oregon, and southeast Washington, with present-day populations in western Idaho and northeast Washington. **2.** The Sahaptian language of the Nez Perces.

Nga·mi (ang-gä′mē), **Lake.** A lake of northern Botswana north of the Kalahari Desert. The marshy lake covered an extensive area during the Pleistocene epoch (about 11,000 to 2 million years ago) but was greatly reduced in size during the 1880's, when papyrus growth blocked the mouth of its main tributary.

Ngu·ni (ang-gōō′nē). **1.** *pl.* **Nguni** or **-nis.** A member of peoples of southern and southeast Africa, including the Swazi, Ndebele, Xhosa, and Zulu. **2.** Any of the Bantu languages of the Nguni.

Ni·ag·a·ra Falls¹ (nī-ăg′rə, -ər-ə). Falls in the Niagara River located between the cities of Niagara Falls, New York, and Niagara Falls, Ontario, Canada. The falls are divided by Goat Island into the American Falls, 50.9 m (167 ft) high, and the Canadian, or Horseshoe, Falls, 48.2 m (158 ft) high.

Ni·ag·a·ra Falls² (nī-ăg′rə, -ər-ə). **1.** A city of southeast Ontario, Canada, on the Niagara River opposite Niagara Falls, New York. It is a port of entry and an important industrial center. ⊛ Pop. 70,960. **2.** A city of western New York on the Niagara River north-northwest of Buffalo. Occupied by the French in the 1680's, captured by the British in 1759, and settled by Americans in 1805, it was held by the British during the War of 1812. Tourism is a mainstay of its economy. ⊛ Pop. 61,840.

Niagara River. A river flowing about 55 km (34 mi) from Lake Erie to Lake Ontario. It forms part of the boundary between western New York and Ontario, Canada.

Nia·mey (nē-ä′mā, nyä-mā′). The capital and largest city of Niger, in the southwest part of the country on the Niger River. It is an important commercial center. ⊛ Pop. 399,100.

Ni·cae·a (nī-sē′ə). An ancient city of Bithynia in northwest Asia Minor. Dating from the fourth century B.C., it flourished during Roman times. The Nicene Creed was adopted at an ecumenical council convened here by Constantine I, emperor of Rome, in A.D. 325. **— Ni·cae′an** *adj.*

Nic·a·ra·gua (nĭk′ə-rä′gwə). *abbr.* **Nic.** A country of Central America on the Caribbean Sea and the Pacific Ocean. Various Indian peoples, including the Miskito, inhabited the area when Columbus visited in 1502. Spanish settlement began in 1524, and the colony was ruled as a part of Guatemala until 1821, when the entire region won its independence from Spain. Nicara-

gua became a separate republic in 1838. Chronic political instability and U.S. interest in a possible canal route through Nicaraguan territory led to the almost continual presence of U.S. Marines in the country from 1912 to 1933. Sandinista guerrilla opposition eventually toppled the dictatorial Somoza family (ruled 1937–1979), but the ensuing Marxist government was hindered in carrying out its programs by armed conflict with U.S.-backed Contra forces. Opposition candidate Violeta Barrios de Chamorro defeated the Sandinista leader Daniel Ortega Saavedra in the 1990 presidential elections, though a number of Sandinista officials retained their posts under the new coalition government. Managua is the capital and the largest city. ⊛ Pop. 4,401,000. — **Ni′-ca·ra′guan** adj. & n.

Nicaragua, Lake. The largest lake of Central America, in southwest Nicaragua. The freshwater lake contains fish, such as tuna and sharks, usually found only in salt water because it was part of the Caribbean Sea until land masses rose around it in prehistoric times.

Nice (nēs). A city of southeast France on the Mediterranean Sea northeast of Cannes. Controlled by various royal houses after the 13th century, the city was finally ceded to France in 1860. It is the leading resort city of the Côte d′Azur and is known for its beaches, casinos, and luxurious hotels. ⊛ Pop. 342,903.

Nic·o·bar Islands (nĭk′ə-bär′). An island group in the Bay of Bengal northwest of Sumatra. They are part of the union territory of the Andaman and Nicobar Islands belonging to India.

Nic·o·me·di·a (nĭk′ə-mē′dē-ə). An ancient city of northwest Asia Minor near the Bosporus in present-day Turkey. It flourished from 264 B.C. until it was sacked by Goths in A.D. 258. Diocletian (A.D. 245?–313?) chose it for the capital of his Eastern Roman Empire, but it was soon superseded by Byzantium.

Nic·o·si·a (nĭk′ə-sē′ə). The capital and largest city of Cyprus, in the north-central part of the island. Founded probably before the seventh century B.C., it fell to the Venetians in 1489 and the Turks in 1571. It became the capital when

Cyprus gained independence in 1960. ⊛ Pop. 186,400.

Ni·co·ya (nĭ-kō′yə, nē-kô′yä), **Gulf of.** An inlet of the Pacific Ocean between **Nicoya Peninsula** and the northwest mainland of Costa Rica.

Nie·men (nē′mən, nyě′-). See **Neman.**

Ni·ger (nī′jər, nē-zhâr′). A country of west-central Africa. The Tuareg and Hausa established states in the late Middle Ages, and the region was dominated by the Songhai and Bornu empires in the 16th century. Niger came under the French sphere of influence after the Conference of Berlin (1884–1885) and was made a separate colony within French West Africa in 1922. A growing nationalist movement led to full independence in 1960. Drought in the Sahel region (1968–1975) caused severe social disruption and near famine, and an army coup in 1974 initiated a period of military rule that lasted until the country's first multiparty elections were held in 1993. A second coup in 1996 ended Niger's brief experience with a democratically elected government. Niamey is the capital and the largest city. ⊛ Pop. 8,846,000.

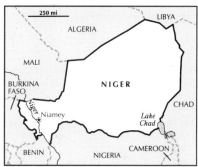

Ni·ger-Con·go (nī′jər-kŏng′gō). A large and widely dispersed language family of sub-Saharan Africa that includes the Mande, West Atlantic, and Central Niger-Congo branches.

Ni·ge·ri·a (nī-jîr′ē-ə). abbr. **Nig.** A country of western Africa on the Gulf of Guinea. A variety of states were established in the region prior to European discovery, including the Bornu, Benin, and Songhai empires. Exploited by Portuguese, British, French, and Dutch traders in the 17th and 18th centuries, southern Nigeria was claimed by the British after the Conference of Berlin (1884–1885) and was consolidated with the predominantly Muslim north into one colony in 1914. Full independence was attained in 1960, but regional conflict and political turmoil led to civil war (1967–1970) in which Ibo-dominated Biafra attempted unsuccessfully to secede. The military remained in power during most of the following years, with national elections in 1992 and 1993 being annulled by the government. A constitutional conference in 1994 called for a return to civilian rule, but the government of Gen. Sani Abacha rejected the scheduled change-over and postponed any democratic political reforms. Abuja is the official capital (since 1991), but many government offices remain in Lagos, the former capital and largest city. ◉ Pop. 108,467,000. — **Ni·ge′ri·an** *adj. & n.*

Ni·ger-Kor·do·fan·i·an (nī′jər-kôr′də-făn′ē-ən, -făn′yən). The largest language family of sub-Saharan Africa, consisting of the Niger-Congo and Kordofanian branches.

Niger River. A river of western Africa rising in Guinea and flowing about 4,183 km (2,600 mi) in a wide arc through Mali, Niger, and Nigeria to the Gulf of Guinea.

Ni·i·ga·ta (nē′ē-gä′tə, -tä). A city of northwest Honshu, Japan, on the Sea of Japan north-northwest of Tokyo. It is a leading port with a major chemical industry. ◉ Pop. 490,237.

Ni·i·ha·u (nē′ē-hou′, nē′hou′). An island of northwest Hawaii west of Kauai Island. It is used mainly for cattle grazing.

Nij·me·gen (nī′mā′gən, -кнən). A city of eastern Netherlands on the Waal River near the German border. Founded in Roman times, it flourished under Charlemagne (eighth–ninth century) and later became a free imperial city and a member of the Hanseatic League. ◉ Pop. 147,005.

Nik·ko (nĭk′ō, nē′kō). A town of central Honshu, Japan, north of Tokyo. It is a pilgrimage center famed for its ornate temples and shrines. ◉ Pop. 21,705.

Ni·ko·la·yev (nĭk′ə-lä′yəf, nyĭ-kə-). A city of southern Ukraine at the mouth of the Western Bug River northeast of Odessa. Founded c. 1784 as a fortress, it later became a shipbuilding center and is now a major seaport and rail junction. ◉ Pop. 515,400.

Ni·ko·pol (nĭ-kô′pəl, nyē′kə-). A city of southern Ukraine on the Dnieper River. It is an industrial center in a rich manganese-mining area. ◉ Pop. 160,300.

Nile (nīl). The longest river in the world, flowing about 6,677 km (4,150 mi) through eastern Af-

rica from its most remote sources in Burundi to a delta on the Mediterranean Sea in northeast Egypt. The main headstreams, the **Blue Nile** and the **White Nile**, join at Khartoum in Sudan to form the Nile proper. Between Khartoum and Aswan, Egypt, the river is interrupted five times by cataracts, or rapids. The river has been used for irrigation in Egypt since at least 4000 B.C., a function now regulated largely by the Aswan High Dam.

Niles (nīlz). **1.** A village of northeast Illinois, an industrial suburb of Chicago on the Chicago River. ◉ Pop. 28,284. **2.** A city of northeast Ohio north-northwest of Youngstown. It is an iron and steel center. ◉ Pop. 21,128.

Ni·ló·po·lis (nĭ-lô′pōo-lĭs). A city of southeast Brazil, an industrial suburb of Rio de Janeiro. ◉ Pop. 157,936.

Ni·lo-Sa·har·an (nī′lō-sə-hăr′ən, -hä′rən). A language family of sub-Saharan Africa spoken in the interior from Nigeria to Kenya and including Kanuri, Nubian, and the Nilotic languages.

Ni·lot·ic (nī-lŏt′ĭk). **1.** Of or relating to the Nile or the Nile Valley. **2.** Of or relating to the peoples who speak Nilotic languages. **3.** A large group of Nilo-Saharan languages, spoken in southern Sudan, Uganda, Kenya, and northern Tanzania and including Masai.

Nîmes (nēm). A city of southern France northeast of Montpellier. Thought to have been founded by Greek colonists, it was one of the leading cities of Roman Gaul and has many important ruins dating from the first and second centuries A.D. ◉ Pop. 128,549.

Nim·rud (nĭm-rōod′). An ancient city of Assyria south of present-day Mosul, Iraq.

Nin·e·veh (nĭn′ə-və). An ancient city of Assyria on the Tigris River opposite the site of present-day Mosul, Iraq. As capital of the Assyrian Empire, it enjoyed great influence and prosperity, especially under the two kings Sennacherib and Ashurbanipal (seventh century B.C.). The city was captured and destroyed by Babylonia and its allies in 612 B.C.

Ning·bo (nĭng′bō′) also **Ning·po** (-pō′). A city of eastern China east-southeast of Hangzhou on Hangzhou Bay. Built on a site occupied since the eighth century, it was used as a trading post by the Portuguese from 1520 to 1545 and became a treaty port in 1842. ◉ Pop. 3,350,851.

Ning·xia Hui·zu (nĭng′shyä′ hwē′dzōo′) also **Ning·sia Hui** (hwē′). An autonomous region of northern China. Formerly a province, it was incorporated into Gansu in 1954 but reconstituted as a region in 1958. Yinchuan is the capital. ◉ Pop. 4,150,000.

Ni·ño (nēn′yō). El Niño.

Ni·o·brar·a (nī′ə-brâr′ə). A river, about 692

km (430 mi) long, rising in eastern Wyoming and flowing generally eastward to the Missouri River in northeast Nebraska.

Niort (nyôr). A city of western France southeast of Nantes. Settled since Roman times, it was a Huguenot stronghold in the 16th and 17th centuries and now has numerous varied industries. ◉ Pop. 58,203.

Nip·i·gon (nĭp′ĭ-gŏn′), **Lake.** A lake of southwest-central Ontario, Canada, north of Lake Superior. It is a popular resort center.

Nip·is·sing (nĭp′ĭ-sĭng′), **Lake.** A lake of southeast Ontario, Canada, between Georgian Bay and the Ottawa River.

Nip·pon (nĭ-pŏn′, nĭp′ŏn, nē-pôn′). Japan. The name was derived from the Chinese characters for "the place where the sun comes from," or the Land of the Rising Sun.

Nip·pon·ese (nĭp′ə-nēz′, -nēs′). Japanese.

Nip·pur (nĭ-pŏŏr′). An ancient city of Babylonia on the Euphrates River southeast of Babylon. It was an important religious center in Sumerian times.

Niš also **Nish** (nĭsh). A city of southeast Yugoslavia near the Morava River. The birthplace (A.D. 284?) of the Roman emperor Constantine the Great, it was held at various times by Bulgarians, Hungarians, Turks, and Serbians. ◉ Pop. 175,555.

Ni·shi·no·mi·ya (nĭsh′ə-nō′mē-ä, nē′shē-nô′-mē-yä′). A city of southern Honshu, Japan, on Osaka Bay east of Kobe. It is a resort and an industrial center. ◉ Pop. 424,719.

Nis·ka·yu·na (nĭs′kə-yōō′nə). A town of east-central New York, a suburb between Albany and Schenectady. There are research laboratories in the town. ◉ Pop. 19,048.

Ni·te·rói (nē′tə-roi′). A city of southeast Brazil on Guanabara Bay opposite Rio de Janeiro. Founded in 1671, it is a residential and industrial center. ◉ Pop. 435,658.

Ni·tra (nē′trə). A city of western Slovakia on the **Nitra River,** a tributary of the Danube. Dating from Roman times, Nitra was a religious center after the ninth century and became a free city in 1248. ◉ Pop. 83,338.

Ni·u·e (nē-ōō′ā). An island dependency of New Zealand in the south-central Pacific Ocean east of Tonga. Visited by the British explorer Capt. James Cook in 1774, it became internally self-governing in 1974. Alofi is the capital. ◉ Pop. 3,578.

Ni·ver·nais (nĭv′ər-nā′, nē-vĕr-nĕ′). A historical region and former province of central France. A countship after the ninth century, it passed to various noble families before being incorporated into the royal domain by Louis XIV in 1669.

Nizh·ne·var·tovsk (nĭzh′nə-vär-tôfsk′, nyĭzh-). A city of central Russia on the Ob River. A huge oil field was discovered nearby in 1965 and led to the rapid growth of the former village during the 1970's. ◉ Pop. 244,519.

Nizh·niy Ta·gil (nĭzh′nē tə-gēl′, nyē′zhnē tə-gyēl′). A city of central Russia in the east-central Ural Mountains. Founded in 1725, it is a leading metallurgical center. ◉ Pop. 430,990.

Nizh·ny Nov·go·rod (nĭzh′nē nŏv′gə-rŏd′, nyē′zhnē nôv′gə-rət). Formerly **Gor·ky** or **Gor·ki** (gôr′kē). A city of western Russia on the Volga River west of Kazan. Founded as a frontier post in 1221, it was formerly famous for its annual trade fairs (1817–1930). The city was renamed Gorky from 1932 until 1991 in honor of the Russian writer Maksim Gorky, who was born here in 1868. ◉ Pop. 1,425,316.

No (nō), **Lake.** A lake of south-central Sudan. Formed by the flood waters of the White Nile, it varies in size seasonally.

No·a·tak (nō-ä′tək, -täk). A river of northwest Alaska rising in the Brooks Range and flowing about 644 km (400 mi) westward to Kotzebue Sound.

No·gal·es (nō-găl′ĭs, -gä′lĭs). A city of southern Arizona south of Tucson on the Mexican border adjacent to **Nogales,** Mexico. Both cities are ports of entry and tourist centers. Nogales, Arizona, has a population of 19,489; Nogales, Mexico, has 14,254 inhabitants.

Nol·i·chuck·y (nŏl′ə-chŭk′ē). A river, about 241 km (150 mi) long, rising in the Blue Ridge of western North Carolina and flowing northwest and west to the French Broad River in eastern Tennessee.

nom·ar·chy (nŏm′är′kē). Any of the administrative provinces of the modern Greek state.

nome (nōm). **1.** A province of Pharaonic, Hellenistic, and Roman Egypt. **2.** A nomarchy.

Nome (nōm). A city of western Alaska on Norton Sound and the southern coast of Seward Peninsula. It was founded as a gold-mining camp in 1896 and was an important center of the Alaskan gold rush from 1899 to 1903. ◉ Pop. 3,500.

Noot·ka (nōōt′kə, nŏŏt′-). **1.** pl. **Nootka** or **-kas.** A member of a Native American people inhabiting Vancouver Island in British Columbia and Cape Flattery in northwest Washington. **2.** The Wakashan language of the Nootka.

Nootka Sound. An inlet of the Pacific Ocean on the western coast of Vancouver Island in southwest British Columbia, Canada. It was explored by the British navigator Capt. James Cook in 1778.

Nor·co (nôr′kō, nōr′-). A city of southern California west-southwest of Riverside. It is an industrial center in an agricultural region. ◉ Pop. 23,302.

Nor·der·stedt (nôr′dər-stĕt′, -shtĕt′). A city of northern Germany, a suburb of Hamburg. ⊛ Pop. 66,680.

Nor·dic (nôr′dĭk). Of, relating to, or characteristic of Scandinavia or its peoples, languages, or cultures.

Nord·kyn (nôr′kən, -kün), Cape. The northernmost point of the European mainland, in northern Norway east of North Cape.

Nord-Ost·see Ka·nal (nört-ôst′zä kä-näl′). See **Kiel Canal.**

Nor·folk (nôr′fək, -fôk). **1.** A historical region of eastern England bordering on the North Sea. Settled in prehistoric times, it was part of the Anglo-Saxon kingdom of East Anglia. Its name means the "northern people," as opposed to the "southern people" of Suffolk. **2.** A city of northeast Nebraska northwest of Omaha. It is a processing and trade center in an agricultural region. ⊛ Pop. 21,476. **3.** An independent city of southeast Virginia on Hampton Roads southeast of Richmond. Founded in 1682 and today the largest city of Virginia, it has been a major naval base since the American Revolution. ⊛ Pop. 261,229.

Norfolk Island. An island territory of Australia in the southern Pacific Ocean northeast of Sydney. Visited by the British explorer Capt. James Cook in 1774, it was formerly a British penal colony.

Nor·i·cum (nôr′ĭ-kəm, nŏr′-). An ancient country and province of the Roman Empire south of the Danube River in present-day Austria west of Vienna. It was incorporated into the Roman Empire in the first century B.C. and prospered as a frontier colony until it was overrun by various Germanic peoples in the fifth century A.D.

No·rilsk (nə-rēlsk′). A city of north-central Russia. Founded in 1935, it is the center of an important mining region. ⊛ Pop. 170,065.

Nor·mal (nôr′məl). A town of central Illinois north-northeast of Bloomington. It is the seat of Illinois State University (founded 1857). ⊛ Pop. 40,023.

Nor·man[1] (nôr′mən). *abbr.* **Norm., Nor. 1. a.** A member of a Scandinavian people who settled in northern France in the tenth century. **b.** A descendant of this people, especially one ruling or inhabiting England from the time of the Norman Conquest (1066). **2.** A native or inhabitant of Normandy. **3.** Of or relating to Normandy, the Normans, their culture, or their language.

Nor·man[2] (nôr′mən). A city of central Oklahoma south of Oklahoma City. The University of Oklahoma opened here in 1892. ⊛ Pop. 80,071.

Nor·man·dy (nôr′mən-dē). A historical region and former province of northwest France on the English Channel. Part of ancient Gaul, the region was successively conquered by the Romans, Franks, and Norse; passed to England after the Norman Conquest (1066) and during the Hundred Years' War (1337–1453); and was restored to France in 1450. Its beaches were the focal point of Allied landings on D-day (June 6, 1944) in World War II.

Norman French. The dialect of Old French used in medieval Normandy.

Nor·ridge (nôr′ĭj, nŏr′-). A village of northeast Illinois, a suburb of Chicago. ⊛ Pop. 14,459.

Nor·ris·town (nôr′ĭs-toun′, nŏr′-). A borough of southeast Pennsylvania on the Schuylkill River northwest of Philadelphia. Settled in the early 1700's, it is a trade and manufacturing center. ⊛ Pop. 30,749.

Norr·kö·ping (nôr′chœ′pĭng). A city of southeast Sweden on **Norrköping Bay,** an inlet of the Baltic Sea southwest of Stockholm. The city was chartered in 1384 and is today a major manufacturing center with a thriving textile industry. ⊛ Pop. 120,798.

Norse (nôrs). *abbr.* **N. 1.** Of or relating to medieval Scandinavia or its peoples, languages, or cultures. **2.** Of or relating to Norway or its people, language, or culture. **3.** Of, relating to, or being the branch of the North Germanic languages that includes Norwegian, Icelandic, and Faeroese. **4. a.** The people of Scandinavia; the Scandinavians. **b.** The people of Norway; the Norwegians. **c.** Speakers of Norwegian, Icelandic, and Faeroese. **5. a.** See **North Germanic. b.** Any of the West Scandinavian languages, especially Norwegian.

Norse·man (nôrs′mən). A member of any of the peoples of medieval Scandinavia.

north (nôrth). *abbr.* **N, N., n, n., No., no., Nor. 1. a.** The direction along a meridian 90° counterclockwise from east; the direction to the left of sunrise. **b.** The cardinal point on the mariner's compass located at 0°. **2.** An area or a region lying in the north. **3.** often **North. a.** The northern part of the earth. **b.** The northern part of a region or country. **4. North.** The northern part of the United States, especially the states that fought for the Union in the Civil War. **5.** To, toward, of, facing, or in the north. **6.** Originating in or coming from the north. —**north′ern, North′ern** *adj.*

North Adams. A city of northwest Massachusetts north-northeast of Pittsfield. It was settled c. 1737. ⊛ Pop. 16,797.

North Africa. A region of northern Africa generally considered to include the modern-day countries of Morocco, Algeria, Tunisia, and Libya. —**North African** *adj. & n.*

North America. *abbr.* **N.A.** The northern continent of the Western Hemisphere, extending northward from the Colombia-Panama border and including Central America, Mexico, the islands of the Caribbean Sea, the United States, Canada, the Arctic Archipelago, and Greenland. —**North American** *adj. & n.*

North·amp·ton (nôrth-hămp′tən). **1.** A borough of central England north-northwest of London. Its Norman castle was the meeting place for parliaments from the 12th to the 14th century. ⊛Pop. 158,900. **2.** A city of west-central Massachusetts on the Connecticut River north of Springfield. It is the seat of Smith College (founded 1875). ⊛Pop. 29,289.

North Andover. A town of northeast Massachusetts on the Merrimack River east-northeast of Lowell. It was a textile center in the 19th century. ⊛Pop. 22,792.

North Arlington. A borough of northeast New Jersey, a residential and industrial suburb of Newark on the Passaic River. ⊛Pop. 13,790.

North Atlanta. A community of northwest Georgia, a suburb of Atlanta. ⊛Pop. 22,800.

North Atlantic Current or **North Atlantic Drift.** The northern extension of the Gulf Stream in the northern Atlantic Ocean. It warms the coast and affects the climate of northwest Europe.

North Atlantic Ocean. The northern part of the Atlantic Ocean, extending northward from the equator to the Arctic Ocean.

North Attleboro. A town of southeast Massachusetts north-northeast of Providence, Rhode Island. It was settled in 1669 and has long been a jewelry-manufacturing center. ⊛Pop. 16,178.

North Bay. A city of southeast Ontario, Canada, on Lake Nipissing east-southeast of Sudbury. It is a trade center in a lumber and mining region. ⊛Pop. 51,268.

North Bellmore. An unincorporated community of southeast New York on Long Island near Hempstead. It is mainly residential. ⊛Pop. 23,600.

North Ber·gen (bûr′gən). A community of northeast New Jersey north of Jersey City and across the Hudson River from Manhattan Island. ⊛Pop. 47,019.

North·brook (nôrth′brook′). A village of northeast Illinois, a residential and industrial suburb of Chicago. ⊛Pop. 32,308.

North Brunswick. A community of central New Jersey, a residential and industrial outgrowth of New Brunswick. ⊛Pop. 31,287.

north by east. *abbr.* **NbE. 1.** The direction or point on the mariner's compass halfway between due north and north-northeast, or 11°15′ east of due north. **2.** Toward or from north by east.

north by west. *abbr.* **NbW. 1.** The direction or point on the mariner's compass halfway between due north and north-northwest, or 11°15′ west of due north. **2.** Toward or from north by west.

North Canadian River. A river rising in northeast New Mexico and flowing about 1,223 km (760 mi) generally southeast to the Canadian River in eastern Oklahoma.

North Cape. 1. The northernmost point of North Island, New Zealand, projecting into the southern Pacific Ocean. **2.** A promontory on an island of northern Norway west of Cape Nordkyn. It is considered the northernmost important extremity of the continent of Europe.

North Car·o·li·na (kăr′ə-lī′nə). *abbr.* **NC, N.C.** A state of the southeast United States bordering on the Atlantic Ocean. It was admitted as one of the original Thirteen Colonies in 1789. First settled c. 1653, it was part of the province of Carolina until 1691 and became a separate colony in 1711 and a royal colony in 1729. North Carolina seceded in May 1861 and was readmitted to the Union in 1868. The state has long been a center of tobacco growing and processing. Raleigh is the capital and Charlotte the largest city. ⊛Pop. 6,657,630. —**North Car′o·lin′i·an** (-lĭn′ē-ən) *adj. & n.*

North Channel. A strait between Scotland and Northern Ireland. It connects the Atlantic Ocean with the Irish Sea.

North Charleston. A city of southeast South Carolina, a residential and commercial suburb of Charleston. ⊛Pop. 70,218.

North Chicago. A city of northeast Illinois, an industrial suburb of Waukegan on Lake Michigan. ⊛Pop. 34,978.

North Country. 1. The northern section of England north of the Humber estuary. **2.** A geographic and economic region comprising Alaska and the Yukon Territory of Canada.

North Dakota. *abbr.* **ND, N.D., N.Dak.** A state of the north-central United States bordering on Canada. It was admitted as the 39th state in 1889. Acquired through the Louisiana Purchase (1803) and a border treaty with Great Britain (1818), the region became part of the Dakota Territory in 1861. It was set off from South Dakota when statehood was achieved. Bismarck is the capital and Fargo the largest city. ⊛Pop. 641,364. —**North Dakotan** *adj. & n.*

North Downs. See **Downs.**

north·east (nôrth-ēst′, nôr-ēst′). *abbr.* **NE. 1.** The direction or point on the mariner's compass halfway between due north and due east, or 45° east of due north. **2.** An area or a region lying in the northeast. **3. Northeast.** A region of the northeast United States, generally including the New England states, New York, and sometimes Pennsylvania and New Jersey. **4.** To, toward, of, facing, or in the northeast. **5.** Originating in or coming from the northeast. —**north·east′ern** *adj.*

northeast by east. *abbr.* **NEbE. 1.** The direction or point on the mariner's compass halfway between northeast and east-northeast, or 56°15′ east of due north. **2.** Toward or from northeast by east.

northeast by north. *abbr.* **NEbN. 1.** The direction or point on the mariner's compass halfway between northeast and north-northeast, or 33°45′ east of due north. **2.** Toward or from northeast by north.

Northeast Passage. A water route along the northern coast of Europe and Asia between the Atlantic and Pacific oceans. A goal of navigators since the 15th century, it was first traversed by the Swedish explorer Nils A.E. Nordenskjöld in 1878 to 1880.

Northern Dvina. See **Dvina** (sense 1).

Northern Hemisphere. The half of the earth north of the equator.

Northern Ireland. *abbr.* **N.Ire.** A division of the United Kingdom in the northeast section of the island of Ireland. The province occupies much of the ancient Irish kingdom of Ulster and is often known by that name. It was colonized by the British in the 17th century and became a part of the United Kingdom in 1920. Civil strife between the Protestant majority of Northern Ireland and the largely Catholic population of the Republic of Ireland has erupted frequently since the late 1960's. Belfast is the capital and the largest city. ⊛ Pop. 1,488,077.

Northern Kingdom. See **Israel.**

Northern Mariana Islands. A commonwealth in political union with the United States comprising most of the Mariana Islands (except Guam) in the western Pacific Ocean. The Islands were occupied (1944) by U.S. forces during World War II and became part of the U.S. Trust Territory of the Pacific Islands from 1947 to 1978, when they became internally self-governing. The largest island, which serves as the capital, is Saipan. ⊛ Pop. 52,284.

Northern Paiute. 1. See **Paiute** (sense 1). **2.** The Uto-Aztecan language of the Northern Paiute.

Northern Shoshone. See **Shoshone** (sense 1a).

Northern Sporades. See **Sporades.**

North Fork. A river rising in the Ozark Plateau of southern Missouri and flowing about 161 km (100 mi) southward to the White River in northern Arkansas.

North Fort Myers. A community of southwest Florida on the Caloosahatchee River opposite Fort Myers. ⊛ Pop. 30,027.

North Frigid Zone. See **Frigid Zone.**

North Frisian Islands. See **Frisian Islands.**

North Germanic. A subdivision of the Ger-

manic languages that includes Norwegian, Icelandic, Swedish, Danish, and Faeroese. Also called *Norse, Scandinavian.*

North·glenn (nôrth-glĕn′). A city of north-central Colorado, a residential suburb of Denver. ⊛ Pop. 27,195.

North Ha·ven (hā′vən). A town of southern Connecticut north-northeast of New Haven. It was settled c.1650 and is mainly residential. ⊛ Pop. 22,249.

North Highlands. An unincorporated community of north-central California, a residential suburb of Sacramento. ⊛ Pop. 42,105.

North Island. An island of New Zealand separated from South Island by Cook Strait. It is the smaller but more populous of the country's two principal islands.

North Karroo. See **Karroo.**

North Kings·town (kĭng′stən). A town of south-central Rhode Island on Narragansett Bay south-southwest of Providence. The site was settled by the English cleric Roger Williams in 1641. ⊛ Pop. 23,786.

North Korea. A country of northeast Asia on the Korean Peninsula. Inhabited since ancient times, the region was occupied by Japan from 1910 until the end of World War II in 1945. After the war the peninsula was divided into a Soviet occupation zone in the north and an American zone in the south. A North Korean invasion of the south touched off the Korean War (June 1950–July 1953), in which Chinese Communist troops joined with North Korea against a U.S.-led United Nations force aiding South Korea. The truce left the border, roughly the 38th parallel, essentially unchanged. Under Kim Il Sung (ruled 1948–1994) North Korea became increasingly isolated, especially after the breakup of the Soviet Union in 1991. Suspicion that the government was developing nuclear weapons

led to calls for international inspection, which were initially refused but later (1995) allowed. After Kim's death in 1994 his son, Kim Jong Il, assumed power amid signs of severe economic problems. Pyongyang is the capital and the largest city. ◉ Pop. 23,904,124. **— North Ko·re'-an** *adj. & n.*

north·land also **North·land** (nôrth'lănd', -lənd). A region in the north of a country or an area. **— north'land·er** *n.*

North Las Vegas. A city of southeast Nevada, a residential suburb of Las Vegas. ◉ Pop. 47,707.

North Lau·der·dale (lô'dər-dāl'). A city of southeast Florida near the Everglades northwest of Fort Lauderdale. ◉ Pop. 26,506.

North Little Rock. A city of central Arkansas on the Arkansas River opposite Little Rock. Originally named Silver City after a small vein of ore discovered in the area, it is now a trade and manufacturing center. ◉ Pop. 61,741.

North Loup. A river, about 341 km (212 mi) long, of north-central Nebraska flowing southeast to unite with the Middle Loup and South Loup rivers and form the Loup River.

North·man (nôrth'mən). A Norseman.

North Massapequa. A community of southeast New York on Long Island near Massapequa. It is mainly residential. ◉ Pop. 23,100.

North Miami. A city of southeast Florida, a residential suburb of Miami on Biscayne Bay. ◉ Pop. 49,998.

North Miami Beach. A city of southeast Florida, a resort community on the Atlantic Ocean north of Miami Beach. ◉ Pop. 35,359.

North Minch. See **Minch.**

North New Hyde Park. An unincorporated community of southeast New York on western Long Island east of New York City. ◉ Pop. 16,100.

north-north·east (nôrth'nôrth-ēst', nôr'nôr-ēst'). *abbr.* **NNE. 1.** The direction or point on the mariner's compass halfway between due north and northeast, or 22°30' east of due north. **2.** To, toward, of, facing, or in the north-northeast.

north-north·west (nôrth'nôrth-wĕst', nôr'-nôr-wĕst'). *abbr.* **NNW. 1.** The direction or point on the mariner's compass halfway between due north and northwest, or 22°30' west of due north. **2.** To, toward, of, facing, or in the north-northwest.

North Olm·sted (ŭm'stĕd'). A city of northeast Ohio, a residential and industrial suburb of Cleveland. ◉ Pop. 34,204.

North Pacific Ocean. The northern part of the Pacific Ocean, extending northward from the equator to the Arctic Ocean.

North Park. A community of north-central Illinois, a suburb of Rockford near the Wisconsin border. ◉ Pop. 15,806.

North Plainfield. A borough of northeast-central New Jersey west-southwest of Elizabeth. It is mainly residential. ◉ Pop. 18,820.

North Platte. A city of west-central Nebraska at the confluence of the North Platte and South Platte rivers west of Grand Island. It is a processing and shipping center. ◉ Pop. 22,605.

North Platte River. A river rising in the Park Range of northern Colorado and flowing about 1,094 km (680 mi) north into southeast Wyoming then east and southeast through west-central Nebraska, where it joins the South Platte River to form the Platte River.

North Polar Region. See **Polar Regions.**

North Pole. 1. The northern end of Earth's axis of rotation, a point in the Arctic Ocean. **2. north pole.** The north-seeking magnetic pole of a straight magnet.

North Providence. A town of northeast Rhode Island, a mainly residential suburb of Providence. ◉ Pop. 32,090.

North Richland Hills. A city of northeast Texas, a residential suburb of Fort Worth. ◉ Pop. 45,895.

North Ridge·ville (rĭj'vĭl'). A city of northeast Ohio west-southwest of Cleveland. It is mainly residential. ◉ Pop. 21,564.

North River. An estuary of the Hudson River between New Jersey and New York City flowing into Upper New York Bay. The North River was so named by the Dutch to distinguish it from the "South River," which is known today as the Delaware River.

North Roy·al·ton (roi'əl-tən). A city of northeast Ohio, a residential suburb of Cleveland. ◉ Pop. 23,197.

North Saskatchewan. A river of south-central Canada flowing about 1,223 km (760 mi) generally eastward from the Rocky Mountains in western Alberta to central Saskatchewan where it joins the South Saskatchewan River to form the Saskatchewan River.

North Sea. An arm of the Atlantic Ocean between Great Britain and northwest Europe. It is connected with the English Channel by the Strait of Dover. Major reserves of oil and natural gas were discovered beneath its waters in the late 1960's.

North Slope. A region of northern Alaska between the Brooks Range and the Arctic Ocean. There are oil and natural gas reserves in the area around Prudhoe Bay.

North Temperate Zone. See **Temperate Zone.**

North Tonawanda. A city of western New

York on the Niagara River north of Buffalo. It is a port of entry and manufacturing center. ⊛ Pop. 34,989.

North Truchas Peak. See **Truchas Peaks.**

North·um·ber·land Strait (nôr-thŭm′bər-lənd). An arm of the Gulf of St. Lawrence separating Prince Edward Island from New Brunswick and Nova Scotia in southeastern Canada.

North·um·bri·a (nôr-thŭm′brē-ə). An Anglo-Saxon kingdom of northern England formed in the seventh century by the union of Bernicia and Deira, Angle kingdoms originally established c. A.D. 500. Much of Northumbria fell to invading Danes in the ninth century and was annexed to Wessex in 954.

North·um·bri·an (nôr-thŭm′brē-ən). **1.** Of or relating to Northumbria or its Old English dialect. **2.** Of or relating to the former or present-day county of Northumberland in northeast England. **3.** A native or inhabitant of Northumbria. **4.** A native or inhabitant of Northumberland. **5.** The Old English dialect spoken in Northumbria.

North Vancouver. A city of southwest British Columbia, Canada, on an inlet of the Strait of Georgia opposite Vancouver. It is a residential and industrial suburb. ⊛ Pop. 33,952.

North Vietnam. A former country of southeast Asia. It existed from 1954, after the fall of the French at Dien Bien Phu, to 1975, when the South Vietnamese government collapsed at the end of the Vietnam War. It is now part of the country of Vietnam. — **North Vi·et′nam·ese′** (-nə-mēz′, -mēs′) adj. & n.

North Waziristan. See **Waziristan.**

north·west (nôrth-wĕst′, nôr-wĕst′). abbr. **NW. 1.** The direction or point on the mariner's compass halfway between due north and due west, or 45° west of due north. **2.** An area or a region lying in the northwest. **3. Northwest. a.** A historical region of the north-central United States west of the Mississippi River and north of the Missouri River. **b.** A region of the northwest United States, generally including Washington, Oregon, and Idaho. **4.** To, toward, of, facing, or in the northwest. **5.** Originating in or coming from the northwest.

northwest by north. abbr. **NWbN. 1.** The direction or point on the mariner's compass halfway between northwest and north-northwest, or 33°45′ west of due north. **2.** Toward or from northwest by north.

northwest by west. abbr. **NWbW. 1.** The direction or point on the mariner's compass halfway between northwest and west-northwest, or 56°15′ west of due north. **2.** Toward or from northwest by west.

North-West Fron·tier Province (nôrth-wĕst′ frŭn-tîr′). A historical region of northwest Pakistan on the Afghanistan border. Long a strategic area because of its proximity to the Khyber Pass, it is the traditional home of the Pathans. The region was annexed by the British in 1849 and became part of Pakistan after independence was achieved in 1947.

Northwest Passage. A water route from the Atlantic to the Pacific through the Arctic Archipelago of northern Canada and along the northern coast of Alaska. Sought by navigators since the 16th century, the existence of such a route was proved in the early 19th century, but the passage was not traversed until the Norwegian explorer Roald Amundsen led an expedition across it in 1903 to 1906. The ice-breaking tanker *Manhattan* was the first commercial ship to cross the passage (1969), after the discovery of oil in northern Alaska.

Northwest Territories. abbr. **NT, NWT, N.W.T.** A territory of northern Canada including the Arctic Archipelago, islands in the northern Hudson Bay, and the mainland north of latitude 60° north. It joined the confederation in 1870. The English explorer Sir Martin Frobisher (1535?–1594) was the first European to reach the area, but major exploration of the region was spearheaded by the English navigator Henry Hudson in the 17th century, the Canadian explorer Alexander Mackenzie in the 18th century, and the British explorer Sir John Franklin in the 19th century. The Hudson's Bay Company transferred its holdings to Canada in 1869–1870, leading to the formation of the territory and the creation of the provinces of Manitoba (1870) and Alberta and Saskatchewan (1905). As of April 1, 1999, the eastern part will be governed and administered separately as a new territory, Nunavut. Yellowknife is the capital and the largest city. ⊛ Pop. 45,741.

Northwest Territory. Formerly **Old Northwest.** A historical region of the north-central United States extending from the Ohio and Mississippi rivers to the Great Lakes. The area was ceded to the United States by the Treaty of Paris in 1783. It was officially designated a territory in 1787 and later split up into the territories and present-day states of Ohio, Indiana, Illinois, Michigan, Wisconsin, and part of Minnesota. Control over the territory was a major issue in the War of 1812.

North Yemen. The former country of Yemen (1962–1990).

Nor·ton Shores (nôr′tn). A city of western Michigan on Lake Michigan south of Muskegon. ⊛ Pop. 21,755.

Norton Sound. An inlet of the Bering Sea in western Alaska south of Seward Peninsula.

Nor·walk (nôr′wôk′). **1.** A city of southern California north-northeast of Long Beach. It was settled in the 1850's. ◦ Pop. 94,279. **2.** A city of southwest Connecticut on Long Island Sound northeast of Stamford. Founded in the mid-1600's, it was burned by the British during the American Revolution (1775–1783). ◦ Pop. 78,331.

Nor·way (nôr′wā′). *abbr.* **Nor., Norw.** A country of northern Europe in the western part of the Scandinavian Peninsula. Beginning in the 9th century, Norway was ruled by numerous petty kingdoms, and raiding parties reached Normandy, Iceland, Greenland, islands off Scotland and Ireland, and the coast of the New World. Christianity was brought to Norway by English missionaries and became established under Olaf II (reigned 1015–1028). Norway was finally unified in the 12th century and reached the height of its medieval prosperity in the 13th century. After 1397 it was controlled at various times by Denmark and Sweden. Independence as a constitutional monarchy was achieved in 1905. Neutral during World War I, Norway was occupied (1940–1945) by the Germans during World War II, and broke from its tradition of neutrality in 1949 to join NATO. Oslo is the capital and the largest city. ◦ Pop. 4,325,000.

Nor·we·gian (nôr-wē′jən). *abbr.* **Norw., Nor.** **1.** Of or relating to Norway or its people, language, or culture. **2.** A native or inhabitant of Norway. **3. a.** Dano-Norwegian. **b.** New Norwegian.

Norwegian Sea. A section of the Atlantic Ocean off the coast of Norway north of the North Sea.

Nor·wich. 1. (nŏr′ĭch). A borough of eastern England northeast of London. The city was sacked by Danes in the 11th century and dev-

astated by the Black Death in 1348. ◦ Pop. 128,050. **2.** (nôr′wĭch′, nŏr′-). A city of southeast Connecticut north of New London. It is an industrial center and the birthplace of the Revolutionary general and traitor Benedict Arnold (1741–1801). ◦ Pop. 37,391.

Nor·wood (nôr′wŏŏd′). **1.** A town of eastern Massachusetts, a chiefly residential suburb of Boston. ◦ Pop. 28,700. **2.** A city of southwest Ohio surrounded by Cincinnati, of which it is a residential suburb with various light industries. ◦ Pop. 23,674.

notch (nŏch). A narrow pass or gap between mountains.

No·teć (nô′tĕch′). A river of northwest Poland flowing about 434 km (270 mi) generally westward. It is connected by canal with the Vistula River.

No·to·gae·a or **No·to·ge·a** (nō′tə-jē′ə). A zoogeographic region including Australia, New Zealand, and the islands of the southwest Pacific Ocean.

No·tre Dame Mountains (nō′trə dām′, däm′, nō′tər). A section of the Appalachian Mountains extending about 805 km (500 mi) from the Green Mountains of Vermont into the Gaspé Peninsula of southeast Quebec, Canada.

Not·ta·way (nŏt′ə-wā′). A river, about 644 km (400 mi) long, of southwest Quebec, Canada, flowing northwest into James Bay.

Not·ting·ham (nŏt′ĭng-əm). A borough of central England north of Leicester. Charles I raised his standard here in 1642, marking the beginning of the English Civil War. The city has long been a center for the manufacture of textiles, lace, and hosiery. According to tradition, it is the birthplace of the 12th-century outlaw Robin Hood. ◦ Pop. 282,590.

Not·to·way (nŏt′ə-wā′). A river of southern Virginia flowing about 282 km (175 mi) southeast to the North Carolina border.

Nouak·chott (nwäk-shŏt′). The capital and largest city of Mauritania, in the western part of the country on the Atlantic Ocean. It was chosen as capital in 1957. ◦ Pop. 150,000.

Nou·mé·a (nōō-mā′ə). The capital of New Caledonia, on the southwest coast of the island of New Caledonia in the southwest Pacific Ocean. It was an Allied air base in World War II. ◦ Pop. 65,110.

No·va I·gua·çu (nô′və ē′gwä-sōō′). A city of southeast Brazil, an industrial suburb of Rio de Janeiro. ◦ Pop. 1,293,611.

No·va·ra (nō-vär′ə, -vä′rä). A city of northwest Italy west of Milan. The Austrians defeated the Piedmontese here in 1849. ◦ Pop. 101,635.

No·va Sco·tia (nō′və skō′shə). *abbr.* **NS, N.S.** A province of eastern Canada comprising a mainland peninsula and the adjacent Cape Breton Island. It joined the confederation in 1867. The first successful settlement was made by the French at Port Royal (now Annapolis Royal) in 1610. France and Great Britain bitterly contested the area, part of Acadia, until 1763, when the Treaty of Paris awarded the French possessions in North America to the British. During the 18th century many Scots immigrated to the region, leading to its name, a Latinized version of "New Scotland." Halifax is the capital and the largest city. ⊛ Pop. 847,442. —**No′va Sco′-tian** *adj. & n.*

No·va·to (nə-vä′tō). A city of western California north of San Rafael. It is mainly residential. ⊛ Pop. 47,585.

No·va·ya Zem·lya (nō′və-yə zĕm′lē-ä′, zĭm-lyä′). An archipelago of north-central Russia in the Arctic Ocean between the Barents and Kara seas. Consisting of two main islands and many smaller ones, the archipelago has mineral deposits and an economy based on fishing, sealing, and trapping.

Nov·go·rod (nŏv′gə-rŏd′, nôv′gə-rət). A city of northwest Russia south-southeast of St. Petersburg. One of the oldest cities in Russia, it was strategically and economically important in the Middle Ages because of its location on the chief trade routes of eastern Europe. The city was overrun by Moscow in 1478 and lost its commercial dominance to St. Petersburg after 1703. ⊛ Pop. 232,534.

No·vi (nō′vī′). A village of southeast Michigan northwest of Detroit. Metal products are among its manufactures. ⊛ Pop. 32,998.

No·vi Sad (nō′vē säd′). A city of northern Yugoslavia on the Danube River northwest of Belgrade. It became a free city of Austria-Hungary in 1748 and was the center of a Serbian literary revival in the 18th and early 19th centuries. ⊛ Pop. 178,896.

No·vo·cher·kassk (nō′və-chər-käsk′, nə-və-chĭr-). A city of southwest Russia northeast of Rostov. Founded in 1805, it is a commercial and manufacturing center. ⊛ Pop. 187,283.

No·vo Ham·bur·go (nô′vŏŏ änm-bŏŏr′gŏŏ). A city of southern Brazil north of Pôrto Alegre. It was founded by German immigrants in the 19th century. ⊛ Pop. 205,479.

No·vo·kuz·netsk (nō′və-kŏŏz-nĕtsk′, nə-və-kŏŏz-nyĕtsk′). A city of south-central Russia southeast of Novosibirsk. Founded by Cossacks in 1617, it was developed as an iron and steel center in the 1930's. ⊛ Pop. 597,483.

No·vo·ros·siysk (nō′və-rə-sēsk′, nə-və-). A city of southwest Russia on the Black Sea south-southwest of Rostov. It is a naval base and shipbuilding center. ⊛ Pop. 193,387.

No·vo·si·birsk (nō′və-sə-bîrsk′, nə-və-sĭ-). A

city of south-central Russia on the Ob River east of Omsk. An important transportation hub on the Trans-Siberian Railroad, it prospered after the development of the Kuznetsk Basin. ⊛ Pop. 1,423,860.

Nu·ba (nŏŏ′bə, nyŏŏ′-). **1.** *pl.* **Nuba.** A member of any of several peoples inhabiting the hills of south-central Sudan. **2.** See **Nubian** (sense 2).

Nu·bi·a (nŏŏ′bē-ə, nyŏŏ′-). A desert region and ancient kingdom in the Nile River valley of southern Egypt and northern Sudan. After the 20th century B.C. it was controlled by the rulers of Egypt, although in the 8th and 7th centuries an independent kingdom arose that conquered Eygpt and ruled as the XXV Dynasty (712–663). Converted to Christianity in the 6th century A.D., Nubia united with Ethiopia but fell to the Muslims in the 14th century. Much of the region was flooded by the completion of the Aswan High Dam in the 1960's.

Nu·bi·an (nŏŏ′bē-ən, nyŏŏ′-). **1.** Of or relating to Nubia or its peoples, languages, or cultures. **2.** A native or inhabitant of Nubia. **3.** Any of a group of closely related Nilo-Saharan languages spoken in the Sudan. In this sense, also called *Nuba.*

Nubian Desert. A desert region of northeast Sudan extending east of the Nile River to the Red Sea.

Nu·e·ces (nŏŏ-ā′sĭs, nyŏŏ-). A river of southern Texas flowing about 507 km (315 mi) to **Nueces Bay,** an inlet of the Gulf of Mexico near Corpus Christi.

Nue·vo La·re·do (nŏŏ-ā′vō lə-rā′dō, nwĕ′vô lä-rĕ′thô). A city of northeast Mexico across the Rio Grande from Laredo, Texas. Founded in 1755, it was part of Laredo until the end of the Mexican War in 1848. ⊛ Pop. 201,731.

Nu·ku·‘a·lo·fa (nŏŏ′kŏŏ-ə-lô′fə). The capital of Tonga in the southwest Pacific Ocean. ⊛ Pop. 21,745.

nul·lah (nŭl′ə). A ravine or gully, especially in southern Asia.

Null·ar·bor Plain (nŭl′ə-bôr′, nŭl-är′bər). A region of south-central Australia south of the Great Victoria Desert and north of the Great Australian Bight. It is the site of a major rocket research center.

Nu·ma·zu (nŏŏ-mä′zŏŏ). A city of south-central Honshu, Japan, southwest of Yokohama. It is a popular resort. ⊛ Pop. 213,062.

Nu·mid·i·a (nŏŏ-mĭd′ē-ə, nyŏŏ-). An ancient country of northwest Africa corresponding roughly to present-day Algeria. It was part of the Carthaginian empire before the Punic Wars (third–second century B.C.) and became a separate kingdom after 201 B.C. Conquered by Rome in 46 B.C. and invaded by the Vandals in the fifth century A.D., Numidia was overrun by the Arabs in the eighth century. — **Nu·mid′i·an** *adj. & n.*

Nu·na·vut (nōō′nə-vōōt′). The eastern part of Northwest Territories, Canada, to be governed and administered as a new territory as of April 1, 1999. The designated capital is Iqualuit.

Nun·ea·ton (nŭ-nēt′n). A municipal borough of central England north of Coventry. It is a textile center in a coal-mining region. ⊛ Pop. 118,454.

Nu·ni·vak (nōō′nə-văk′). An island off western Alaska in the Bering Sea. It was first sighted by Russian explorers in 1821.

Nu·rem·berg (nōōr′əm-bûrg′, nyōōr′-) also **Nürn·berg** (nōōrn′bĕrk′, nürn′-). A city of southeast Germany north-northwest of Munich. First mentioned in 1050, it became a free imperial city in the 13th century and was a center of the German cultural renaissance in the 15th and 16th centuries. From 1933 to 1938 it was the site of annual Nazi party congresses. Largely destroyed in World War II, the city served as the venue for the Allied trials of war criminals (1945–1946). ⊛ Pop. 498,945.

Nu·ri·stan (nōōr′ĭ-stăn′, -stän′). A region of northeast Afghanistan on the southern slopes of the Hindu Kush.

Nu·ri·sta·ni (nōōr′ĭ-stä′nē), *pl.* **Nuristani** or **-nis.** A member of a Dardic-speaking people inhabiting parts of the Hindu Kush in northeast Afghanistan. Also called *Kafir.*

Nürn·berg (nōōrn′bĕrk′, nürn′-). See **Nuremberg.**

Nut·ley (nŭt′lē). A town of northeast New Jersey, a residential suburb of Newark. ⊛ Pop. 27,099.

Nuuk (nōōk). See **Godthåb.**

Nyan·ja (nyän′jə). A Bantu language closely related to Chewa and spoken in Malawi.

Ny·as·a (nī-ăs′ə, nyä′sä), **Lake** also **Lake Malawi.** A lake of southeast-central Africa between Tanzania, Mozambique, and Malawi. It was named by the Scottish missionary and explorer David Livingstone in 1899.

Ny·as·a·land (nī-ăs′ə-lănd′, nyä′sä-). See **Malawi.**

Nyí·regy·há·za (nē′rĕj-hä′zô, nyē′rĕd-yə-). A city of northeast Hungary north of Debrecen. Inhabited since the 13th century, it was destroyed by the Turks in the 16th century and rebuilt in the 18th century. ⊛ Pop. 115,462.

Ny·norsk (nōō-nôrsk′, nü′nôshk′). See **New Norwegian.**

O·a·hu (ō-ä′hōō). An island of central Hawaii between Molokai and Kauai. It is the chief island of the state, with major tourist areas, including Waikiki Beach and Diamond Head, and a U.S. naval base at Pearl Harbor.

Oak Creek (ōk). A city of southeast Wisconsin. It is an industrial suburb of Milwaukee on Lake Michigan. ⊛ Pop. 19,513.

Oak Forest. A city of northeast Illinois, a residential suburb of Chicago. ⊛ Pop. 26,203.

Oak·land (ōk′lənd). A city of western California on San Francisco Bay opposite San Francisco. Founded on a site settled by Spanish colonists in 1820, it is a port and rail terminus connected with other communities in the San Francisco Bay area by bridge, tunnel, and rapid transit. ⊛ Pop. 372,242.

Oakland Park. A city of southeast Florida on the Atlantic Ocean north of Fort Lauderdale. It is a resort center. ⊛ Pop. 27,596.

Oak Lawn. A village of northeast Illinois, a residential suburb of Chicago with some light industry. ⊛ Pop. 56,182.

Oak Park. 1. A village of northeast Illinois, a residential suburb of Chicago. The writer Ernest Hemingway (1899–1961) was born here. ⊛ Pop. 53,648. **2.** A city of southeast Michigan, a mainly residential suburb of Detroit. ⊛ Pop. 30,462.

Oak Ridge. A city of eastern Tennessee west of Knoxville. It was founded in 1942 as a research facility to produce materials needed for the first atomic bomb. ⊛ Pop. 27,310.

Oak·ville (ōk′vĭl′). A town of southeast Ontario, Canada, on Lake Ontario southwest of Toronto. It is a summer resort and manufacturing center. ⊛ Pop. 75,773.

o·a·sis (ō-ā′sĭs), *pl.* **-ses** (-sēz). A fertile or green spot in a desert or wasteland, made so by the presence of water.

Oa·xa·ca (wə-hä′kə). A city of southeast Mexico south of Orizaba. It was probably founded in 1486 as an Aztec garrison post and was conquered by the Spanish in 1521. ⊛ Pop. 154,223.

Ob (ŏb, ôb, ôp). A river, about 3,700 km (2,300 mi) long, of central Russia flowing generally northward to the **Gulf of Ob,** an arm of the Arctic Ocean.

O·ber·am·mer·gau (ō′bər-äm′ər-gou′). A town of southern Germany in the Bavarian Alps south-southwest of Munich. It is famed for its Passion plays, held every ten years since 1634 in thanksgiving for deliverance from the Black Death in 1633. ⊛ Pop. 4,980.

O·ber·hau·sen (ō'bər-hou'zən). A city of west-central Germany in the Ruhr Valley west-north-west of Essen. It is a port, rail junction, and industrial center. ◦ Pop. 226,254.

o·blast (ô'bləst, ô'bläst'). **1.** An administrative and territorial division within a constituent republic of the Soviet Union. **2.** An administrative and territorial division of the Russian Federation and Ukraine.

O·cal·a (ō-kăl'ə). A city of north-central Florida south-southeast of Gainesville. It is a trade, processing, and shipping center in a citrus-growing region. ◦ Pop. 42,045.

Oc·ci·dent (ŏk'sĭ-dənt, -dĕnt'). The countries of Europe and the Western Hemisphere.

Oc·ci·den·tal (ŏk'sĭ-dĕn'tl). **1.** Of or relating to the countries of the Occident or their peoples or cultures; western. **2.** A native or inhabitant of an Occidental country; a westerner.

o·cean (ō'shən). **1.** *abbr.* **oc.** The entire body of salt water that covers more than 70 percent of the earth's surface. **2.** often **Ocean.** *abbr.* **O, O., Oc.** Any of the principal divisions of the ocean, including the Atlantic, Pacific, and Indian oceans, their southern extensions in Antarctica, and the Arctic Ocean. **— o'ce·an'ic** (ō'shē-ăn'ĭk) *adj.*

O·ce·an·i·a (ō'shē-ăn'ē-ə, -ā'nē-ə, -ä'nē-ə). The islands of the southern, western, and central Pacific Ocean, including Melanesia, Micronesia, and Polynesia. The term is sometimes extended to encompass Australia, New Zealand, and the Malay Archipelago. **— O'ce·an'i·an** *adj. & n.*

O·cean·side (ō'shən-sīd'). **1.** A city of southern California north-northwest of San Diego. It is a seaside resort and trade center for nearby Camp Pendleton, a U.S. Marine Corps base. ◦ Pop. 128,398. **2.** An unincorporated community of southeast New York on the southern shore of Long Island. Oceanside is a residential and resort town. ◦ Pop. 32,423.

Oc·mul·gee (ōk-mŭl'gē). A river, about 410 km (255 mi) long, of Georgia rising near Atlanta and flowing southeast to join the Oconee River and form the Altamaha River.

O·co·nee (ə-kō'nē). A river rising in the Blue Ridge of northern Georgia and flowing about 454 km (282 mi) generally south to join the Ocmulgee River and form the Altamaha River.

O·den·se (ōd'n-sə, ōōd'-). A city of southern Denmark on Fyn Island near the **Odense Fjord,** an arm of the Kattegat. Founded in the tenth century, Odense is the birthplace of the writer Hans Christian Andersen (1805–1875). ◦ Pop. 180,799.

O·der (ō'dər). A river of central Europe flowing about 904 km (562 mi) from northeast Czech Republic through Poland and Germany to the Baltic Sea. It is a major waterway of Eastern Europe.

O·des·sa (ō-dĕs'ə). **1.** A city of southern Ukraine on **Odessa Bay,** an arm of the Black Sea. Said to occupy the site of an ancient Greek colony that disappeared between the 3rd and 4th centuries A.D., Odessa was established as a Tartar fortress in the 14th century, passed to Turkey in 1764, and was captured by Russia in the 1790's. It is a major port, naval base, and resort. ◦ Pop. 1,095,800. **2.** A city of western Texas south-southwest of Lubbock. It was a small ranching town until the discovery of oil in the area. ◦ Pop. 89,699.

Of·fen·bach (ôf'ən-bäk', -bäкн'). A city of central Germany north-northeast of Mannheim on the Main River. First mentioned in the tenth century, it is an industrial center noted for its leather goods. ◦ Pop. 116,870.

Of·fen·burg (ôf'ən-bûrg', -bōōrk', ŏf'ən-). A city of southwest Germany at the edge of the Black Forest north of Freiburg. It became a free imperial city in 1235. ◦ Pop. 50,048.

off·set (ôf'sĕt', ŏf'-). *Geology.* A spur of a mountain range or hills.

Og·bo·mo·sho (ŏg'bə-mō'shō). A city of southwest Nigeria north-northeast of Ibadan. It is a trade center in a farming region. ◦ Pop. 514,400.

Og·den (ŏg'dən, ŏg'-). A city of northern Utah north of Salt Lake City. Settled by Mormons in the 1840's, it is a railroad junction with aerospace and other industries. ◦ Pop. 63,909.

O·gee·chee (ō-gē'chē). A river, about 402 km (250 mi) long, of eastern Georgia flowing generally southeast to the Atlantic Ocean.

O·gla·la (ō-glä'lə). *pl.* **Oglala** or **-las.** A member of a Native American people constituting a subdivision of the Teton Sioux, formerly inhabiting the Black Hills region of western South Dakota, with a present-day population mainly in southwest South Dakota.

O·hi·o (ō-hī'ō). *abbr.* **OH, O.** A state of the north-central United States in the Great Lakes region. It was admitted as the 17th state in 1803. In prehistoric times Mound Builders inhabited the region, which was first visited by the French explorer La Salle in 1669. The French-British rivalry for control of the area led to the last of the French and Indian Wars (1754–1763), in which the French were defeated. Ohio was part of the vast area ceded to the United States by the Treaty of Paris in 1783 and became part of the Old Northwest by the Ordinance of 1787. It became a separate territory in 1799. Columbus is the capital and Cleveland the largest city. ◦ Pop. 10,887,325. **— O·hi'o·an** *adj.*

Ohio River. A river formed by the confluence of the Allegheny and Monongahela rivers in western Pennsylvania and flowing about 1,578 km (981 mi) to the Mississippi River at Cairo in southern Illinois. Control of the river was contested by the British and French until 1763. The region was ceded to the United States at the end of the Revolutionary War (1783).

Oil·dale (oil′dāl′). A community of south-central California, an oil-producing suburb of Bakersfield. ◉ Pop. 26,553.

oil patch (oil). *Informal.* The oil-producing region of the United States that includes Texas, Oklahoma, and Louisiana.

Oil Rivers (oil). A large delta region of the Niger River in southern Nigeria. The **Oil Rivers Protectorate** was administered by the British Royal Niger Company from 1885 to 1893.

Oise (wäz). A river rising in the Ardennes of southern Belgium and flowing about 299 km (186 mi) generally southwest to the Seine River in northern France. It is an important commercial waterway.

O·i·ta (ō′ĭ-tä′, ō-ē′tä). A city of northeast Kyushu, Japan, east-northeast of Nagasaki. It was a castle town in the 16th century and traded extensively with the Portuguese. It is now an industrial center and a transportation hub. ◉ Pop. 420,361.

O·jib·wa (ō-jĭb′wä′, -wə) also **O·jib·way** (-wā′). **1.** *pl.* **Ojibwa** or **-was** also **Ojibway** or **-ways.** A member of a Native American people originally located north of Lake Huron before moving westward in the 17th and 18th centuries into Michigan, Wisconsin, Minnesota, western Ontario, and Manitoba, with later migrations onto the northern Great Plains in North Dakota, Montana, and Saskatchewan. **2.** The Algonquian language of the Ojibwas. Also called *Chippewa*.

O·jos Del Sa·la·do (ō′hōz dĕl′ sə-lä′dō, ô′hôs dĕl sä-lä′thô). A peak, 6,874.3 m (22,539 ft) high, in the Andes on the border between Argentina and Chile.

O·ka (ō-kä′). **1.** A river, about 1,488 km (925 mi) long, of western Russia flowing north, east, and northeast to join the Volga River near Nizhny Novgorod. **2.** A river rising in the Sayan Mountains of south-central Russia and flowing about 965 km (600 mi) generally north to the Angara River.

O·ka·nog·an (ō′kə-nŏg′ən) also **O·ka·na·gan** (ō′kə-nŏg′ən). A river, about 483 km (300 mi) long, flowing southward from **Lake Okanagan** in southern British Columbia, Canada, to the Columbia River in north-central Washington.

O·ka·van·go (ō′kə-văng′gō) also **Cu·ban·go** or **Ku·ban·go** (kōō-bäng′gō). A river of southwest-central Africa flowing about 1,609 km (1,000 mi) from central Angola to the **Okavango Basin** or **Okavango Swamp,** a marshy region of northern Botswana.

O·ka·ya·ma (ō′kä-yä′mä). A city of western Honshu, Japan, on an inlet of the Inland Sea west of Kobe. It is an industrial center and a railroad hub. ◉ Pop. 604,513.

O·ka·za·ki (ō-kä′zä-kē, ō′kə-zä′kē). A city of southern Honshu, Japan, southeast of Nagoya. It is a textile center. ◉ Pop. 318,983.

O·kee·cho·bee (ō′kĭ-chō′bē), **Lake.** A lake of southeast Florida north of the Everglades. It is a link in the **Okeechobee Waterway,** or **Cross-Florida Waterway,** a water route from the Atlantic Ocean to the Gulf of Mexico. The waterway is used by small commercial and pleasure craft.

O·ke·fe·no·kee Swamp (ō′kə-fə-nō′kē). A large swampy area of southeast Georgia and northeast Florida. The region has small islands rising above the water and vegetation cover.

O·khotsk (ō-kŏtsk′, ə-ĸнôtsk′), **Sea of.** An arm of the northwest Pacific Ocean west of the Kamchatka Peninsula and Kuril Islands. It is connected with the Sea of Japan by narrow straits.

O·ki·na·wa (ō′kĭ-nä′wə, -nou′-). An island group of the central Ryukyu Islands in the western Pacific Ocean southwest of Japan. In World War II **Okinawa,** the largest island in the group, was the scene of fierce combat between the Japanese and U.S. Army and Marine forces (April 1–June 21, 1945). The islands were returned to the Japanese in 1972.

O·kla·ho·ma (ō′klə-hō′mə). *abbr.* **OK, Okla.** A state of the south-central United States. It was admitted as the 46th state in 1907. First explored by the Spanish, it was opened to settlement in 1889. The western part was organized in 1890 as the Oklahoma Territory, which was merged with the adjoining Indian Territory to form the present state boundaries. The Dust Bowl of the 1930's forced many farmers to move west as migrant laborers. Oklahoma City is the capital and the largest city. ◉ Pop. 3,157,604. —**O′kla·ho′man** *adj. & n.*

Oklahoma City. The capital and largest city of Oklahoma, in the central part of the state. It was settled during the land rush of April 1889 and became the capital in 1910. ◉ Pop. 444,719.

Ok·mul·gee (ōk-mŭl′gē). A city of east-central Oklahoma south of Tulsa. Oil was discovered in the area in 1907. ◉ Pop. 13,411.

O·ko·lo·na (ō′kə-lō′nə). A community of northwest Kentucky, a suburb of Louisville. ◉ Pop. 18,902.

Ö·land (œ′länd′). A narrow island of southeast Sweden in the Baltic Sea. It is a summer resort with an important fishing fleet. There are numerous Stone Age monuments on the island.

O·la·the (ō-lā′thə). A city of eastern Kansas southwest of Kansas City. It has varied manufacturing industries. ◉ Pop. 63,352.

Old Bulgarian (ōld). See **Old Church Slavonic.**

Old Castile. A historical region of north-central Spain that combined with New Castile to the south to form the kingdom of Castile. It was united with Aragon after the marriage of Ferdinand and Isabella (1469).

Old Church Slavonic. The language used by Saints Cyril and Methodius in their translation of the Bible and still used as a liturgical language by several churches of Eastern Orthodoxy in Slavic countries and elsewhere. This language was used in early literary manuscripts. Also called *Church Slavonic, Old Bulgarian.*

Old Danish. The Danish language from the beginning of the 12th century to the end of the 14th century.

Old Dutch. The Dutch language from the beginning of the 12th century to the middle of the 13th century.

Ol·den·burg (ōl′dən-bûrg′, -bŏŏrk′). A city of northwest Germany west of Bremen. First mentioned in 1108, it was chartered in 1345. It is now an industrial and transportation center. ◉ Pop. 138,469.

Old English. *abbr.* **OE, O.E.** The English language from the middle of the 5th century to the beginning of the 12th century. Also called *Anglo-Saxon.*

Old Faith·ful (fāth′fəl). A geyser in Yellowstone National Park in northwest Wyoming. Its eruptions, which last about 4 minutes, occur on the average of once every 65 minutes (the intervals can vary from 33 to 90 minutes). The geyser sends up a column of hot water and steam ranging from 35.4 to 53.4 m (116 to 175 ft) high.

Old Frisian. The Frisian language until about 1575.

Old·ham (ōl′dəm). A borough of northwest England northeast of Manchester. It is a manufacturing center with a textile industry. ◉ Pop. 220,520.

Old High German. High German from the middle of the 9th to the end of the 11th century.

Old Icelandic. Icelandic from the middle of the 12th to the middle of the 16th century.

Old Iranian. Any of the Iranian languages in use before the beginning of the Christian era.

Old Irish. The Irish language from 725 to about 950.

Old Italian. The Italian language until the middle of the 16th century.

Old Kingdom. Ancient Egypt during the III–VI Dynasties, from c. 2980 to 2475 B.C. The Old Kingdom was noted as "the Age of the Pyramids," with magnificent monuments built by rulers such as Cheops (2590–2567 B.C.).

Old Latin. The earliest recorded Latin, found in inscriptions from the beginning of the sixth century B.C. and in literature from the middle of the third century B.C. until the middle of the first century B.C.

Old Norse. *abbr.* **ON, O.N. 1.** The North Germanic languages until the middle of the 14th century. **2. a.** Old Icelandic. **b.** Old Norwegian.

Old North French. The dialects of Old French spoken in northern France, especially in Normandy and Picardy.

Old Northwest. See **Northwest Territory.**

Old Norwegian. The Norwegian language from the middle of the 12th to the end of the 14th century.

Old Persian. An Old Iranian language attested in cuneiform inscriptions dating from the sixth to the fifth century B.C.

Old Portuguese. The Portuguese language until the middle of the 16th century.

Old Provençal. The Provençal language before the middle of the 16th century.

Old Prussian. The Baltic language of eastern Prussia that became extinct in the 18th century.

Old Russian. The Russian language as used in documents from the middle of the 11th to the end of the 16th century.

Old Saxon. The Low German language of the continental Saxons until the 12th century.

Old Spanish. Spanish before the middle of the 16th century.

Old Stone Age. The Paleolithic Age.

Old Swedish. Swedish from the early 13th to the late 14th century.

Old Turkic. The language of the oldest texts of the Turkic dialects, written in a variety of scripts from the 7th to the 12th century.

Ol·du·vai Gorge (ōl′də-vī′, ôl′dŏŏ-). A ravine in northern Tanzania west of Mount Kilimanjaro. It contains archaeological sites rich in fossils and Paleolithic implements.

Old Welsh. The Welsh language before the 12th century.

Old World. The Eastern Hemisphere. The term is often used to refer specifically to Europe.

O·le·an (ō′lē-ăn′, ō′lē-ăn′). A city of western New York on the Allegheny River near the Pennsylvania border. It produces varied manufactures. ◉ Pop. 16,946.

O·lek·ma (ŏ-lĕk′mə). A river, about 1,319 km (820 mi) long, of eastern Russia flowing north to the Lena River.

O·le·nek (ŏl′ən-yôk′, ə-lə-nyôk′). A river of northeast Russia flowing about 2,172 km (1,350 mi) east then north to the Laptev Sea.

O·lin·da (ō-lĭn′də, ōō-lēɴ′dä). A city of northeastern Brazil, a suburb of Recife on the Atlantic Ocean. It was founded in 1537 as a colonial capital and held by the Dutch from 1630 to 1654. • Pop. 341,059.

Ol·ives (ŏl′ivz), **Mount of** also **Ol·i·vet** (ŏl′ə-vĕt′). A ridge of hills in the West Bank east of Jerusalem. At its western foot is the biblical site of the Garden of Gethsemane.

Ol·mec (ŏl′mĕk, ōl′-). **1.** An early Mesoamerican Indian civilization centered in the Veracruz region of southeast Mexico that flourished around 1300–400 B.C. and whose cultural influence was widespread throughout southern Mexico and Central America. **2.** pl. **Olmec** or **-mecs.** A member of any of various peoples who contributed to the Olmec civilization.

O·lo·mouc (ô′lô-mōts′). A city of northeast Czech Republic on the Morava River northeast of Brno. Possibly founded as a Roman fortress, it was ceded to Hungary in 1478 and was the capital of Moravia until c. 1640. It is now an industrial center. • Pop. 105,936.

Olsz·tyn (ōl′shtĭn). A city of northern Poland southeast of Gdańsk. Founded by the Teutonic Knights in 1348, it was ceded to Poland in 1466 and to Prussia in 1772. It reverted to Poland in 1945. • Pop. 163,905.

O·lym·pi·a¹ (ō-lĭm′pē-ə, ə-lĭm′-). A plain of southern Greece in the northwest Peloponnesus. It was a religious center devoted to the worship of Zeus, the principal god of the Greek pantheon, and the site of the ancient Olympic games. The statue of the Olympian Zeus by the fifth-century Athenian sculptor Phidias was one of the Seven Wonders of the World.

O·lym·pi·a² (ō-lĭm′pē-ə, ə-lĭm′-). The capital of Washington, in the western part of the state on the southern end of Puget Sound. Settled in 1845, it became the territorial capital in 1853. • Pop. 33,840.

Olympia Heights. A community of southeast Florida, a suburb of Miami. • Pop. 33,112.

O·lym·pi·an (ō-lĭm′pē-ən). **1.** Of or relating to the region of Olympia in Greece or its inhabitants. **2.** A native or inhabitant of the region of Olympia in Greece.

O·lym·pic Mountains (ō-lĭm′pĭk). A range of the Coast Ranges on the **Olympic Peninsula** of northwest Washington. The rugged peninsula is bounded by the Pacific Ocean, the Strait of Juan de Fuca, and Puget Sound. On the western slope of the mountains is a rain forest with an annual precipitation of more than 330 cm (130 in). Mount Olympus, in the center of the range, is the highest peak, rising to about 2,429.3 m (7,965 ft).

O·lym·pus (ə-lĭm′pəs, ō-lĭm′-). A mountain range of northern Greece near the Aegean coast. It rises to 2,918.9 m (9,570 ft) at **Mount Olympus,** the highest point in Greece and home of the mythical Greek gods.

O·lyn·thus (ō-lĭn′thəs). An ancient city of northeast Greece on the peninsula of Chalcidice. As head of a league of Chalcidian cities after the late fifth century B.C., it opposed the threats of Athens and Sparta but was captured briefly by Athens and subjugated by Sparta in 379. Philip of Macedon destroyed the city in 348.

Om (ôm). A river, about 724 km (450 mi) long, of south-central Russia flowing westward to join the Irtysh River at Omsk.

O·ma·ha¹ (ō′mə-hô′, -hä′). **1.** pl. **Omaha** or **-has.** A member of a Native American people inhabiting northeast Nebraska since the late 17th century. The Omahas are closely related to the Ponca in language and history. **2.** The Siouan language of the Omahas. **—O′ma·ha′** adj.

O·ma·ha² (ō′mə-hô′, -hä′). A city of eastern Nebraska on the Missouri River and the Iowa border. Founded in 1854 with the opening of the Nebraska Territory, it grew as a supply point for westward migration, especially after the coming of the railroad in 1869. It was territorial capital from 1855 to 1867. • Pop. 335,795.

O·man (ō-män′). Formerly **Mus·cat and Oman** (mŭs′kăt′, -kət, mŭs-kăt′). A sultanate of the southeast Arabian Peninsula on the **Gulf of Oman,** an arm of the Arabian Sea. Much of the area was controlled by the Portuguese from 1508 to 1659 and the Turks until 1741, when the present royal line was founded. British influence was established in the late 18th century and has remained strong despite a UN call in 1965 for Great Britain to sever its ties. In 1970 Sultan Said ibn Timur was deposed by his son Qabus bin Said, who promised to modernize the country. Although it did not become part of the OPEC oil cartel in the 1970's, Oman joined other Persian Gulf nations in founding the Gulf Cooperation Council in 1981. Muscat is the capital

and largest city. ⊕ Pop. 2,077,000. **— O·man'i** (ō-mä'nē) *adj. & n.*

Om·dur·man (ŏm'dŏor-män'). A city of northeast-central Sudan on the White Nile opposite Khartoum. Anglo-Egyptian troops defeated the Mahdists, followers of the Muslim religious leader Muhammad Ahmad, near here on September 2, 1898. ⊕ Pop. 526,287.

O·mi·ya (ō-mē'ə, ô'mē-yä'). A city of east-central Honshu, Japan, a commercial suburb of Tokyo. ⊕ Pop. 422,023.

Om·o·lon (ŏm'ə-lôn'). A river, about 965 km (600 mi) long, of northeast Russia flowing northward to the Kolyma River.

Omsk (ômsk). A city of south-central Russia at the confluence of the Irtysh and Om rivers. On the Trans-Siberian Railroad, it is a major river port and transportation hub. The city was founded in 1716. ⊕ Pop. 1,163,885.

O·ne·ga (ō-nē'gə, ə-nyĕ'-), **Lake**. A lake of northwest Russia northeast of St. Petersburg between Lake Ladoga and the White Sea. It remains frozen from November to May.

Onega Bay. An arm of the White Sea in northwest Russia. It receives the **Onega River,** about 418 km (260 mi) long.

O·nei·da¹ (ō-nī'də). **1.** *pl.* **Oneida** or **-das.** A member of a Native American people formerly inhabiting central New York south of Oneida Lake, with present-day populations in Wisconsin, New York, and Ontario. The Oneidas are one of the original members of the Iroquois confederacy. **2.** The Iroquoian language of the Oneidas.

O·nei·da² (ō-nī'də). A city of central New York east-northeast of Syracuse. The Oneida Community, a Utopian society established in 1848 by John Humphrey Noyes, was nearby. It prospered through its manufacture of silverware and was reorganized in 1881 as a joint stock company. ⊕ Pop. 10,850.

Oneida Lake. A lake of central New York northeast of Syracuse. It is part of the New York State Barge Canal system.

O·nit·sha (ō-nĭch'ə). A city of southeast Nigeria on the Niger River. It is a market town and manufacturing center. ⊕ Pop. 262,100.

On·on·da·ga (ŏn'ən-dô'gə, -dä'-, -dā'-). **1.** *pl.* **Onondaga** or **-gas.** A member of a Native American people formerly inhabiting the eastern Finger Lakes region of west-central New York, with present-day populations in this same area and in southeast Ontario. The Onondagas are one of the original members of the Iroquois confederacy. **2.** The Iroquoian language of the Onondagas. **— On'on·da'gan** *adj.*

On·tar·i·o (ŏn-târ'ē-ō'). **1.** *abbr.* **ON, Ont.** A province of east-central Canada. It joined the confederation in 1867. First visited by French explorers in the early 1600's, it passed to the British in 1763 and became part of the province of Quebec in 1774. It was called Upper Canada after its division from Quebec (then Lower Canada) in 1791. Reunited with Lower Canada in 1841, it became a separate province with the formation of the confederation. Toronto is the capital and the largest city. ⊕ Pop. 8,625,107. **2.** A city of southern California east of Los Angeles. It is a residential and industrial center in a citrus-growing region. ⊕ Pop. 133,179.

Ontario, Lake. The smallest of the Great Lakes, between southeast Ontario, Canada, and northwest New York. The St. Lawrence Seaway and Welland Ship Canal connect with the lake to afford passage by oceangoing vessels to the other Great Lakes.

O'o·dham (ō'ə-däm). See **Papago**.

Oost·en·de (ō-stĕn'də). See **Ostend**.

O·pe·li·ka (ō'pə-lī'kə). A city of eastern Alabama east-northeast of Montgomery. It is a commercial center. ⊕ Pop. 22,122.

Op·e·lou·sas (ŏp'ə-lōō'səs). A city of south-central Louisiana west-northwest of Baton Rouge. It was founded by French traders c. 1756 and served briefly as the state capital in 1862. ⊕ Pop. 18,151.

O·po·le (ô-pô'lə). A city of southern Poland on the Oder River southeast of Wroclaw. Originally a Slavic settlement, it passed to Prussia in 1742 and was assigned to Poland by the Potsdam Conference of 1945. ⊕ Pop. 128,873.

O·por·to (ō-pôr'tō, ō-pōr'-) also **Por·to** or **Pôr·to** (pôr'tōō). A city of northwest Portugal near the mouth of the Douro River north of Lisbon. Probably of pre-Roman origin, it was captured by the Moors in 716. Its wine trade was established in 1678. ⊕ Pop. 302,467.

Op·por·tu·ni·ty (ŏp'ər-tōō'nĭ-tē, -tyōō'-). An unincorporated community of eastern Washington, a residential suburb of Spokane. ⊕ Pop. 22,326.

O·ra·dea (ô-räd'yä). A city of northwest Romania near the Hungarian border. It was destroyed by the Tartars in 1241 and held by the Turks from 1660 to 1692. Hungary ceded it to Romania after World War I. ⊕ Pop. 221,559.

O·ran (ō-rän', ô-räɴ'). A city of northwest Algeria on the **Gulf of Oran,** an inlet of the Mediterranean Sea west-southwest of Algiers. Built on a site occupied since prehistoric times, Oran was captured by the Spanish in 1509 and by the Turks in 1708. It was occupied by the French in 1831 and held by Vichy France during World War II. Allied troops liberated the city in November 1942. ⊕ Pop. 490,788.

Or·ange (ôr'ĭnj, ŏr'-). **1.** A city of southern California north-northeast of Santa Ana. It is a manufacturing center in a citrus-growing area.

● Pop. 110,658. **2.** A city of northeast New Jersey, a chiefly residential suburb of Newark and New York City. ● Pop. 29,925. **3.** A city of southeast Texas east of Beaumont. It is a port and processing center. ● Pop. 19,381.

Orange Free State. A province and historical region of east-central South Africa. European settlement of the area began early in the 1800's and accelerated with an influx of Boer farmers after 1835. Great Britain annexed the region as the **Orange River Sovereignty** in 1848 and granted it independence as the Orange Free State in 1854. In 1900, during the Boer War, Great Britain once again annexed the territory, this time as the **Orange River Colony.** The renamed Orange Free State formed an independent government in 1907 and became a founding province of South Africa in 1910.

Orange River. A river, about 2,092 km (1,300 mi) long, of Lesotho, South Africa, and Namibia flowing southwest, northwest, and west to the Atlantic Ocean.

Or·ange·vale (ôr′ĭnj-vāl′, ŏr′-). A community of north-central California, a suburb of Sacramento. ● Pop. 20,585.

Or·dos (ôr′dŏs). A sandy desert plateau region of Nei Monggol (Inner Mongolia) in northern China bounded on the south and east by the Great Wall, a line of fortifications built in the third century B.C.

Or·dzho·ni·kid·ze (ôr′jŏn-ĭ-kĭd′zə, ər-jə-nyĭ-kyē′dzĭ). See **Vladikavkaz.**

Ör·e·bro (œ′rə-brōō′). A city of south-central Sweden west of Stockholm. Known since the 11th century, it has often been the site of national assemblies. ● Pop. 123,188.

Or·e·gon (ôr′ĭ-gən, -gŏn′, ŏr′-). **1.** *abbr.* **OR, Ore.** A state of the northwest United States in the Pacific Northwest. It was admitted as the 33rd state in 1859. Claimed by the United States after Capt. Robert Gray explored the mouth of the Columbia River in 1792, the area was further explored by Lewis and Clark in 1805 and was soon the site of fur-trading posts. The **Oregon Country,** a region encompassing all the land from the California border to Alaska and the Pacific Ocean to the Rocky Mountains, was held jointly by Great Britain and the United States from 1818 until 1846, when the international boundary was fixed at the 49th parallel. In 1848 the **Oregon Territory** was created, including all of present-day Washington and Idaho. The state's current boundaries were established in 1853. Salem is the capital and Portland the largest city. ● Pop. 2,853,733. **2.** A city of northwest Ohio, an industrial suburb of Toledo on Lake Erie. ● Pop. 18,334. —**Or′e·go′ni·an** (-gō′nē-ən) *adj.*

Oregon Trail. A historical overland route to the western United States extending from various cities on the Missouri River to the Oregon Country and later Oregon Territory. The trail was opened in 1842, and by 1845 more than 3,000 migrants had made the arduous journey. After the coming of the railroad, the trail fell into disuse and was finally abandoned in the 1870's.

O·re·kho·vo-Zu·ye·vo (ôr′ĭ-kôv′ə-zōō-yĕv′ō, ə-ryĕ′кнə-və-zōō′yĭ-və). A city of west-central Russia east of Moscow. Its textile industry dates from the 18th century. ● Pop. 134,538.

O·rel (ô-rĕl′, ō-rĕl′, ôr-yôl′). A city of western Russia on the Oka River south of Moscow. Founded in 1564 as a fortified settlement to protect the southern border of Muscovy against the Tartars, it is today an industrial center and a railroad junction. ● Pop. 342,846.

O·rem (ôr′əm, ōr′-). A city of north-central Utah north-northwest of Provo. It is a manufacturing center in an irrigated farming area. ● Pop. 67,561.

O·ren·burg (ôr′ən-bûrg′, ōr′-, ə-rĭn-bōōrk′). Formerly (1938–1957) **Chka·lov** (chə-kä′ləf, chkä′-). A city of western Russia on the Ural River. Founded as a fortress in 1735, it is a rail junction and processing center. ● Pop. 554,144.

O·ren·se (ô-rĕn′sĕ). A city of northwest Spain east of Vigo. Its hot sulfur springs have been known since Roman times. ● Pop. 103,042.

O·re·sund or **Ø·re·sund** (œ′rə-sŭn′, -sōōnd′). A narrow strait between southern Sweden and eastern Denmark connecting the Baltic Sea with the Kattegat.

O·ri·ent (ôr′ē-ənt, -ĕnt′, ōr′-). The countries of Asia, especially of eastern Asia.

O·ri·en·tal (ôr′ē-ĕn′tl, ōr′-). **1.** Of or relating to the countries of the Orient or their peoples or cultures; eastern; Asian. **2.** Of or designating the biogeographic region that includes Asia south of the Himalaya Mountains and the islands of the Malay Archipelago. **3.** *Sometimes offensive.* A native or inhabitant of an Oriental country; an Asian.

O·ril·lia (ô-rĭl′yə, ō-rĭl′-). A city of southeast Ontario, Canada, north of Toronto. It is a summer resort and has varied light industries. ● Pop. 23,955.

O·rin·da (ə-rĭn′də, ô-rĭn′-, ō-rĭn′-). An unincorporated community of western California, a residential suburb of the Oakland-Berkeley metropolitan area. ● Pop. 16,642.

O·ri·no·co (ôr′ə-nō′kō, ōr′-). A river of Venezuela flowing more than 2,414 km (1,500 mi), partly along the Colombia-Venezuela border, to the Atlantic Ocean. The mouth of the river was probably discovered by Columbus in 1498.

O·ri·ya (ô-rē′yə). The Indic language of Orissa, a state in eastern India.

O·ri·za·ba (ôr′ĭ-zä′bə, ōr′-, ô′rē-sä′vä). A city

of east-central Mexico west of Veracruz. It is a commercial and manufacturing center and a popular resort. ✹ Pop. 114,848.

Orizaba, Mount. See **Citlaltépetl.**

Ork·ney Islands (ôrk′nē). An archipelago comprising about 70 islands in the Atlantic Ocean and the North Sea off the northeast coast of Scotland. Originally settled by Picts, the islands were a Norse dependency after 875 and became part of Scotland in 1472.

Or·lan·do (ôr-lăn′dō). A city of central Florida east-northeast of Tampa. It is a trade and processing center with aerospace and electronics industries. Nearby Disney World has made the city a popular tourist area. ✹ Pop. 164,693.

Or·land Park (ôr′lənd). A village of northeast Illinois, a residential and manufacturing suburb of Chicago. ✹ Pop. 35,720.

Or·lé·a·nais (ôr′lē-ə-nā′, ôr-lā-ä-ně′). A historical region and former province of north-central France. Most of the area has been part of the royal domain since the tenth century.

Or·lé·ans (ôr-lā-äN′). A city of north-central France on the Loire River south-southwest of Paris. Founded by Celts and conquered by Julius Caesar in 52 B.C., the city was taken by Clovis I, king of the Franks, in A.D. 498 and became the center of the Frankish kingdom of **Orléans** in 511. It became a principal residence of the Capetian kings in the tenth century. The siege of Orléans by the English (1428–1429) was lifted by troops led by Joan of Arc, the Maid of Orléans. ✹ Pop. 105,099.

Or·ly (ôr′lē, ôr-lē′). A city of north-central France, a suburb of Paris. Orly Field is a major international airport serving the Paris region. ✹ Pop. 23,766.

Or·mond Beach (ôr′mənd). A city of northeast Florida on the Atlantic Ocean north of Daytona Beach. It was founded as a health resort in 1873. ✹ Pop. 29,721.

Or·muz (ôr′mŭz′, ôr-mōōz′), **Strait of.** See Strait of **Hormuz.**

O·ro·mo (ô-rō′mō). **1.** *pl.* **Oromo** or **-mos.** A member of a widely acculturated people of southern and central Ethiopia and northern Kenya. **2.** The Cushitic language of the Oromo. Also called *Galla.*

O·ron·tes (ô-rŏn′tēz). A river, about 402 km (250 mi) long, flowing through Lebanon, Syria, and southern Turkey to the Mediterranean Sea. It is used extensively for irrigation.

Orsk (ôrsk). A city of western Russia on the Ural River east-southeast of Orenburg. It is an industrial center in an area with rich mineral deposits. ✹ Pop. 274,601.

Ort·les (ôrt′läs) also **Ort·ler** (-lər). A range of

the Alps in northern Italy rising to 3,901.6 m (12,792 ft) at **Ortles** peak.

O·ru·ro (ô-rōō′rô). A city of western Bolivia southeast of La Paz. At an altitude of 3,708.5 m (12,159 ft), it depends on mineral deposits found in the area for its economy. ✹ Pop. 201,831.

os (ōs). See **esker.**

O·sage (ō′sāj′, ō-sāj′). **1.** *pl.* **Osage** or **O·sages.** A member of a Native American people formerly inhabiting western Missouri and later southeast Kansas, with a present-day population in north-central Oklahoma. Substantial oil reserves were discovered on Osage lands in the early 20th century. **2.** The Siouan language of the Osages.

Osage River. A river, about 579 km (360 mi) long, of central Missouri rising as the confluence of two smaller streams on the Kansas border and flowing east and northeast through the Lake of the Ozarks and on to the Missouri River near Jefferson City.

O·sa·ka (ō-sä′kə, ô′sä-kä′). A city of southern Honshu, Japan, on **Osaka Bay,** an inlet of the Pacific Ocean. Osaka was the leading commercial center of Japan during the feudal period and today is highly industrialized. ✹ Pop. 2,588,989.

O·sas·co (ōō-säs′kōō). A city of southeast Brazil, an industrial suburb of São Paulo. ✹ Pop. 566,949.

Os·can (ŏs′kən). **1.** A member of an ancient people of Campania. **2.** The Italic language of the Oscans. —**Os′can** *adj.*

Os·co-Um·bri·an (ŏs′kō-ŭm′brē-ən). A subdivision of the Italic languages that consists of Oscan and Umbrian.

Osh (ôsh). A city of southern Kyrgyzstan east-southeast of Tashkent, Uzbekistan. One of the oldest settlements of central Asia, it was long a major silk-producing center. ✹ Pop. 219,000.

Osh·a·wa (ŏsh′ə-wä′, -wə). A city of southeast Ontario, Canada, on Lake Ontario east-northeast of Toronto. Founded on the site of a French trading post, Oshawa is a manufacturing center. ✹ Pop. 129,344.

Osh·kosh (ŏsh′kŏsh). A city of eastern Wisconsin on Lake Winnebago north-northwest of Fond du Lac. It grew as a lumber town in the latter half of the 19th century and today is a resort center with varied industries. ✹ Pop. 55,006.

O·shog·bo (ō-shŏg′bō). A city of southwest Nigeria northeast of Ibadan. It is primarily a farm trade and commercial center. ✹ Pop. 336,000.

O·si·jek (ô′sē-ĕk, -yĕk′). A city of eastern Croatia on the Drava River east-southeast of Zagreb. The city grew on the site of a Roman colony and fortress and was under Turkish rule from 1526 to 1687. ✹ Pop. 129,792.

Os·lo (ŏz′lō, ŏs′-). Formerly (1624–1925) **Chris·**

ti·a·ni·a (krĭs'tē-ăn'ē-ə, -än'-, krĭs'chē-). The capital and largest city of Norway, in the southeast part of the country at the head of the **Oslo Fjord,** a deep inlet of the Skagerrak. Founded c. 1050, Oslo was rebuilt and renamed in 1624 by Christian IV (1577–1648; reigned 1588–1648). It has been the capital of the country since 1299. The Winter Olympics were held here in 1952. ◉ Pop. 473,454.

Os·man·li (ŏz-măn'lē, ŏs-). **1.** *pl.* **-lis.** An Ottoman Turk. **2.** Ottoman Turkish. **3.** Ottoman.

Os·na·brück (ŏz'nə-brŏŏk', ôs'nä-brük'). A city of northwest Germany northeast of Münster. On the site of an ancient Saxon settlement, it was a member of the Hanseatic League and an important center of the linen trade in the Middle Ages. ◉ Pop. 168,078.

Oss (ôs). A city of southern Netherlands southwest of Nijmegen. Chartered in 1399, it is an industrial and processing center. ◉ Pop. 50,086.

Os·sa (ŏs'ə), **Mount.** A peak, 1,979.1 m (6,489 ft) high, of the Olympus Mountains in northern Greece.

Os·set (ŏs'ĭt, ŏ-sĕt') also **Os·sete** (ŏs'ēt', ŏ-sĕt'). A member of a people of mixed Iranian and Caucasian origin inhabiting Ossetia.

Os·se·tia (ŏ-sē'shə, ə-syĕ'tĭ-yə). A region of the central Caucasus. The area was annexed by Russia between 1801 and 1806 and is now split into North Ossetia, an autonomous republic of the Russian Federation, and South Ossetia, a region of Georgia. South Ossetia became a part of Georgia in 1922, and following Georgian independence from the U.S.S.R. in 1991, Ossetian nationalists demanded either independence from Georgia or incorporation into the North Ossetian republic, touching off hostilities with the Georgian government. A peacekeeping force was installed in 1992, and in 1996 South Ossetia and Georgia agreed to begin talks on a full-scale political settlement. — **Os·se'tian** *adj. & n.*

Os·set·ic (ŏ-sĕt'ĭk). **1.** Of or relating to Ossetia, the Ossets, or their language or culture. **2.** The Iranian language of the Ossets.

Os·si·ning (ŏs'ə-nĭng'). A village of southeast New York on the Hudson River north of White Plains. Incorporated in 1813 as Sing Sing, it was renamed in 1901. Sing Sing state prison, established in 1824 and built from 1825 to 1828, is here. ◉ Pop. 22,582.

Ost·end (ŏs-tĕnd', ŏs'tĕnd') also **Oost·en·de** (ō-stĕn'də). A city of northwest Belgium on the North Sea west-southwest of Bruges. It was a German submarine base during World War I and was severely damaged by Allied bombing during World War II. ◉ Pop. 69,129.

Os·ti·a (ŏs'tē-ə, ô'styä). An ancient city of west-central Italy at the mouth of the Tiber River. According to legend, it was founded in

the seventh century B.C. Ostia developed as a port after the first century B.C. and declined after the third century A.D.

Os·ti·ak (ŏs'tē-ăk'). Variant of **Ostyak.**

Os·tra·va (ô'strä-vä). A city of northeast Czech Republic near the Oder River. It is a manufacturing center in a coal-mining area. ◉ Pop. 327,159.

Os·tro·goth (ŏs'trə-gŏth'). One of a tribe of eastern Goths that conquered and ruled Italy from A.D. 493 to 555. — **Os'tro·goth'ic** *adj.*

Os·ty·ak also **Os·ti·ak** (ŏs'tē-ăk'). **1.** *pl.* **Ostyak** or **-aks** also **Ostiak** or **-aks.** A member of a Finno-Ugric people inhabiting western Siberia. **2.** The Ugric language of this people.

Os·we·go (ŏs-wē'gō). A city of north-central New York at the mouth of the **Oswego River,** about 37 km (23 mi) long, on Lake Ontario northwest of Syracuse. A British trading post was founded in Oswego c. 1722. It is now a trade, shipping, and industrial center. ◉ Pop. 19,195.

Oś·wię·cim (ôsh-vyĕn'chēm, -tsĕm). Formerly **Ausch·witz** (oush'vĭts'). A city of southern Poland west of Cracow. During World War II it was the site of the largest Nazi concentration camp. ◉ Pop. 45,700.

O·to (ō'tō). **1.** *pl.* **Oto** or **-Otos.** A member of a Native American people formerly inhabiting eastern Nebraska along the Platte River, with present-day descendants living with the Missouri in north-central Oklahoma. **2.** The Siouan language of the Otos, which is dialectically related to Iowa.

O·tran·to (ō-trän'tō), **Strait of.** A passage between southeast Italy and western Albania connecting the Adriatic Sea with the Ionian Sea.

O·tsu (ō'tsōō). A city of southern Honshu, Japan, on the southern shore of Lake Biwa near Kyoto. It was an imperial seat in the second and seventh centuries A.D. ◉ Pop. 268,583.

Ot·ta·wa¹ (ŏt'ə-wə, -wä', -wô'). **1.** *pl.* **Ottawa** or **-was.** A member of a Native American people formerly inhabiting the northern shore of Lake Huron, with later settlements throughout the upper Great Lakes region. Present-day Ottawa populations are located mainly in southern Ontario, northern Michigan, and Oklahoma. **2.** The dialect of Ojibwa spoken by the Ottawas.

Ot·ta·wa² (ŏt'ə-wə). **1.** The capital of Canada, in southeast Ontario at the confluence of the Ottawa River and the Rideau Canal. It was founded as Bytown during the construction of the Rideau Canal and renamed Ottawa in 1854. Queen Victoria chose it as the capital of the United Provinces of Canada in 1858. In 1867 it became the capital of the newly formed confederation. ◉ Pop. 313,987. **2.** A city of north-central Illinois southwest of Chicago. It was the site of the first Lincoln-Douglas debate (1858). ⊙ Pop. 17,451.

Ottawa River. A river, about 1,126 km (700 mi) long, rising in the Laurentian Plateau of southwest Quebec, Canada, and flowing west and southeast to the St. Lawrence River near Montreal. It was an important waterway for early fur traders and missionaries.

Ot·to·man (ŏt′ə-mən). **1.** A Turk, especially a member of the family or tribe of Osman I (1258–1326?), founder of the Ottoman Empire. **2.** Of or relating to the Ottoman Empire or its people, language, or culture. **3.** Turkish.

Ottoman Empire also **Turk·ish Empire** (tûr′kĭsh). A vast Turkish sultanate of southwest Asia, northeast Africa, and southeast Europe. It was founded in the 13th century by Osman I and ruled by his descendents until its dissolution after World War I. Originally a small state controlled by Ottoman or Osmanli Turks, it spread rapidly, superseding the Byzantine Empire in the east.

Ottoman Turkish. The Turkic language spoken in Turkey, the Balkan Peninsula, Cyprus, central Asia, West Germany, and elsewhere.

Ot·tum·wa (ə-tŭm′wə, ō-tŭm′-). A city of southeast Iowa southeast of Des Moines. It is a commercial center in a farming and coal-mining area. ⊙ Pop. 24,488.

Ouach·i·ta Mountains (wŏsh′ĭ-tô′). A low mountain range between the Arkansas and Red rivers extending about 322 km (200 mi) from central Arkansas to southeast Oklahoma. Magazine Mountain, 839.7 m (2,753 ft), is the highest point in the range and the highest elevation in Arkansas.

Ouachita River. A river, about 965 km (600 mi) long, rising in the Ouachita Mountains of western Arkansas and flowing east, southeast, and south into eastern Louisiana.

Oua·ga·dou·gou (wä′gə-dōō′gōō). The capital and largest city of Burkina Faso, in the central part of the country. It was founded in the late 11th century and is today a trade and distribution center. ⊙ Pop. 634,479.

Oudh (oud). A historical region of north-central India. Dating from at least the 4th century A.D., it was ruled by the Moguls after the 16th century and annexed by Great Britain in 1856. The annexation was a major cause of the Indian Mutiny (1857–1858).

Ouj·da (ōōj-dä′). A city of northeast Morocco near the Algerian border. Founded in 944, it was occupied by the French in 1844, 1859, and 1907. ⊙ Pop. 331,000.

Ou·lu (ō′lōō, ou′-). A city of west-central Finland on the Gulf of Bothnia at the mouth of the

Oulu River, about 105 km (65 mi) long. Oulu grew around a castle built in 1590 and was chartered in 1610. ⊙ Pop. 96,525.

Ouse River (ōōz). **1.** also **Great Ouse River.** A river, about 249 km (155 mi) long, rising in south-central England and meandering east and northeast to the Wash, an inlet of the North Sea. **2.** A river, about 97 km (60 mi) long, of northeast England flowing southeast to join the Trent River and form the Humber River. It is an important commercial waterway.

out·back (out′băk′). The remote, rural part of a country, especially of Australia or New Zealand. —**out′back′er** n.

out·crop (out′krŏp′). A portion of bedrock or other stratum protruding through the soil level.

Out·er Hebrides (out′ər). See **Hebrides.**

Outer Mongolia. See **Mongolia** (sense 2).

out·fall (out′fôl′). The place where a sewer, drain, or stream discharges.

out·land (out′lănd′, -lənd). **1.** A foreign land. **2.** **outlands.** The outlying areas of a country; the provinces. —**out′land′** adj.

out·let (out′lĕt′, -lĭt). **1.** A stream that flows out of a lake or pond. **2.** The mouth of a river where it flows into a larger body of water.

Ou·tre·mont (ōō′trə-mŏnt′, ōō-trə-môn′). A city of southern Quebec, Canada, a residential section of greater Montreal on Montreal Island. ⊙ Pop. 24,338.

O·ver·land (ō′vər-lənd). A city of eastern Missouri, a suburb of St. Louis. ⊙ Pop. 17,987.

Overland Park. A city of northeast Kansas, a residential suburb of Kansas City. ⊙ Pop. 111,790.

Overland Trail. Any of several trails, such as the Oregon Trail or the Santa Fe Trail, of westward migration in the United States. The term is sometimes used to refer collectively to all the overland migration routes from the Missouri River to the Pacific Ocean.

O·vie·do (ō-vyā′dō, ô-vyĕ′thô). A city of northwest Spain near the Cantabrian Mountains. Founded c. 760, it flourished as the capital of Asturian kings until 910. The city was severely damaged during the Spanish Civil War (1936–1939). ⊙ Pop. 195,651.

O·vim·bun·du (ō′vĭm-bōōn′dōō). See **Mbundu** (sense 2).

O·wa·ton·na (ō′wə-tŏn′ə). A city of southeast Minnesota south of Minneapolis. It has diversified industries. ⊙ Pop. 19,386.

O·wens·bor·o (ō′ĭnz-bûr′ō, -bûr′ō). A city of northwest Kentucky on the Ohio River westsouthwest of Louisville. Settled c. 1800, it is a tobacco market and shipping point for a farm region. ⊙ Pop. 53,549.

Ow·en Sound (ō'ĭn). A city of southeast Ontario, Canada, on **Owen Sound,** an inlet of Georgian Bay. It is a port and railroad terminal with varied industries. ◉ Pop. 19,883.

Ow·ens River (ō'ĭnz). A river, about 193 km (120 mi) long, of eastern California rising in the Sierra Nevada and flowing generally southward, formerly to **Owens Lake,** now a dry lake bed near Mount Whitney, and currently via aqueduct to the reservoirs of Los Angeles.

Owen Stanley Range. A mountain range extending about 483 km (300 mi) southeast to northwest on New Guinea Island in Papua New Guinea. It rises to 4,075.7 m (13,363 ft).

O·wos·so (ō-wŏs'ō). A city of central Michigan west of Flint. It is a trade center in a farming region. ◉ Pop. 16,322.

O·wy·hee (ō-wī'ē, -hē). A river, about 483 km (300 mi) long, of southwest Idaho, northern Nevada, and southeast Oregon. It empties into the Snake River.

ox·bow (ŏks'bō'). **1.** A U-shaped bend in a river. **2.** The land within such a bend of a river.

oxbow lake. A crescent-shaped lake formed when a meander of a river or stream is cut off from the main channel.

Ox·ford (ŏks'fərd). **1.** A borough of south-central England on the Thames River west-northwest of London. First mentioned in 912, it was chartered in 1605. Oxford University was founded in the 12th century and still dominates the center of the city. ◉ Pop. 131,967. **2.** A city of northern Mississippi south-southeast of Memphis, Tennessee. It is the seat of the University of Mississippi ("Old Miss"), established in 1844, and was the writer William Faulkner's home town. ◉ Pop. 9,984. **3.** A village of southwest Ohio northwest of Hamilton near the Indiana border. Mainly residential, it is the seat of Miami University (founded 1809). ◉ Pop. 18,937.

Ox·nard (ŏks'närd'). A city of southern California west-northwest of Los Angeles on the Pacific coast. It is a commercial and industrial center. ◉ Pop. 142,216.

Ox·on Hill (ŏk'sŏn, -sən). A community of central Maryland, a suburb of Washington, D.C. ◉ Pop. 35,794.

Ox·o·ni·an (ŏk-sō'nē-ən). **1.** Of, relating to, or characteristic of Oxford or Oxford University. **2.** A native or inhabitant of Oxford. **3.** A person who studies or has studied at Oxford University.

Ox·us (ŏk'səs). See **Amu Darya.**

Oys·ter Bay (oi'stər). A village of southeast New York on northeast Long Island on an inlet of Long Island Sound. Nearby is Sagamore Hill, Theodore Roosevelt's estate, which is now a national historic site. ◉ Pop. 7,200.

O·zark Plateau or **O·zark Mountains** (ō'-zärk'). An upland region of the south-central United States extending from southwest Missouri across northwest Arkansas into eastern Oklahoma. Parts of the Ozarks are scenic tourist attractions.

O·zarks (ō'zärks'), **Lake of the.** A lake of central Missouri formed by Bagnell Dam (completed 1931) on the Osage River.

P

Pa·chu·ca (pə-chōō'kə, pä-chōō'kä) also **Pachuca de So·to** (dĭ sō'tō, dĕ). A city of central Mexico north-northeast of Mexico City. It was founded in 1534 as a silver-mining center on the site of an ancient Toltec city. ◉ Pop. 110,351.

Pa·cif·i·ca (pə-sĭf'ĭ-kə). A city of western California on the Pacific coast south of San Francisco. It is mainly residential. ◉ Pop. 37,670.

Pa·cif·ic Grove (pə-sĭf'ĭk). A city of western California at the southern end of Monterey Bay. It is a residential and resort community. ◉ Pop. 16,117.

Pacific Islands, Trust Territory of the. A group of more than 2,000 islands and islets of the northwest Pacific Ocean administered by the United States as a United Nations trust territory from 1947 to 1978. It originally included the Caroline, Marianas (excluding Guam), and Marshall islands. Most parts of the territory, including Palau, the Northern Mariana Islands, the Federated States of Micronesia, and the Marshall Islands, are now self-governing. **—Pacific Islander** *n.*

Pacific Northwest. A region of the northwest United States usually including the states of Washington and Oregon. The term is also used to refer to the southwest part of British Columbia, Canada.

Pacific Ocean. The largest of the world's oceans, divided into the **North Pacific** and the **South Pacific.** It extends from the western Americas to eastern Asia and Australia.

Pacific Rim. The countries and landmasses surrounding the Pacific Ocean, often considered as a socioeconomic region.

Pacific Standard Time. *abbr.* **PST, P.S.T.** Standard time in the eighth time zone west of Greenwich, England, reckoned at 120° west and used, for example, in the Pacific coastal states of the United States. Also called *Pacific Time.*

Pa·dang (pä'däng', pä-däng'). A city of western Indonesia on the Indian Ocean and the west-central coast of Sumatra. It is a major port, trading in tea, coffee, and spices. ◉ Pop. 631,543.

Pa·der·born (pä′dər-bôrn′). A city of west-central Germany northwest of Kassel. It joined the Hanseatic League in the 13th century and passed to Prussia in 1802. ⊛ Pop. 130,130.

Pa·dre Island (pä′drē). A low, sandy barrier island off the southern coast of Texas. First charted in 1519, it is famous as a graveyard for Spanish ships wrecked during a hurricane in 1553. Part of the island is a wildlife preserve.

Pad·u·a (păj′ōō-ə, păd′yōō-ə). A city of northeast Italy west of Venice. An important cultural center during the Middle Ages, it was known for its artistic and architectural works by Giotto, Mantegna, and Donatello. Galileo taught at its university from 1592 to 1610. ⊛ Pop. 215,025.

Pa·du·cah (pə-dōō′kə, -dyōō′-). A city of western Kentucky on the Ohio River and the Illinois border. It is a tobacco market and manufacturing center. ⊛ Pop. 27,256.

Paes·tum (pĕs′təm, pē′stəm). An ancient city of southern Italy on the Gulf of Salerno. Founded as a Greek colony before 600 B.C., it flourished as part of Magna Graecia and was taken by Rome in 273 B.C.

Pa·go Pa·go (päng′ō päng′ō, păng′gō päng′gō, päng′gō päng′gō, pä′gō pä′gō, pä′gō pä′gō) also **Pan·go Pan·go** (päng′ō päng′ō, păng′-gō păng′gō, päng′gō päng′gō). The capital of American Samoa, on the southern coast of Tutuila Island. It is a port and naval station. ⊛ Pop. 3,519.

Pah·la·vi (pä′lə-vē′) also **Peh·le·vi** (pā′-). An Iranian language used in Persia during the reign of the Sassanid dynasty (A.D. 224–651).

Paines·ville (pānz′vĭl′). A city of northeast Ohio northeast of Cleveland. It is a trade center in a farming area. ⊛ Pop. 15,699.

Paint·ed Desert (pān′tĭd). A plateau region of north-central Arizona east of the Colorado and Little Colorado rivers. Irregularly eroded layers of red and yellow sediment and clay have left striking bands of color.

Pais·ley (pāz′lē). A burgh of southwest Scotland west of Glasgow. It has been a textile center since the early 18th century and became famous in the 19th century for its colorful patterned shawls. ⊛ Pop. 86,100.

Pai·ute also **Pi·ute** (pī′yōōt′). *pl.* **Paiute** or **-utes** also **Piute** or **-utes.** A member of either of two distinct Native American peoples inhabiting parts of the Great Basin, specifically: **1.** A group occupying eastern Oregon, western Nevada, and adjacent areas of northeast California. Also called *Northern Paiute.* **2.** A group occupying southern Utah and Nevada, northern Arizona, and adjacent areas of southeast California. Also called *Southern Paiute.*

Pak·i·stan (păk′ĭ-stăn′, pä′kĭ-stän′). *abbr.* **Pak.** A country of southern Asia. Occupying land crisscrossed by ancient invasion paths, Pakistan was the home of the prehistoric Indus Valley civilization, which flourished until overrun by Aryans c. 1500 B.C. After being conquered by numerous rulers and powers, including Muslim Arabs and Turks, the region became part of the Mogul empire before passing to the British in the mid-19th century as part of India. Pressure from Muslim separatists finally led to the establishment of Pakistan as an independent state in 1947. The country originally included the Bengalese territory of East Pakistan, which achieved its separate independence in 1971 as Bangladesh. Pakistan became a republic in 1956, but military coups and periods of martial law dominated the country's political life for much of the post-independence era. The country has been involved in an ongoing dispute with India over the Kashmir region since the partition of British India in 1947. Islamabad is the capital and Karachi the largest city. ⊛ Pop. 126,610,000. **—Pak′i·stan′i** (-stăn′ē, -stä′nē) *adj. & n.*

Pa·lat·i·nate (pə-lăt′n-ĭt). Either of two historical districts and former states of southern Germany. The **Lower Palatinate** is in southwest Germany between Luxembourg and the Rhine River; the **Upper Palatinate** is to the east in eastern Bavaria. They were once under the jurisdiction of the counts palatine, who became electors of the Holy Roman Empire in 1356 and were then known as electors palatine.

Pal·a·tine¹ (păl′ə-tīn′). The most important of the seven hills of ancient Rome. Traditionally the location of the earliest Roman settlement, it was the site of many imperial palaces, including ones built by the emperors Tiberius, Nero, and Domitian. **—Pal′a·tine** *adj.*

Pal·a·tine² (păl′ə-tīn′). A village of northeast Illinois, a residential suburb of Chicago. ⊛ Pop. 39,253.

Pa·lau (pä-lou′, pə-) also **Be·lau** (bə-lou′). Formerly **Pe·lew** (pə-lōō′, pē-). A group of volcanic islands and islets in the Caroline Islands of the western Pacific Ocean. When the Carolines became part of the Federated States of Micronesia in 1978, Palau chose to form a republic in free association with the United States, which was responsible for its defense until 1996. The capital is Koror, but a new capital, Melekeok, is being built on the island of Babelthuap. ◉ Pop. 16,952.

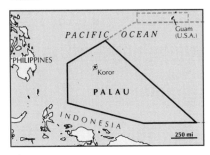

Pa·la·wan (pə-lä′wən, pä-lä′wän). A long, narrow island of the southwest Philippines north of Borneo. It lies between the Sulu Sea and the **Palawan Passage** of the South China Sea.

pale (pāl). **1.** The area enclosed by a fence or boundary. **2. Pale.** The medieval dominions of the English in Ireland. Used with *the.*

Pa·le·arc·tic (pā′lē-ärk′tĭk, -är′tĭk). Of or relating to the biogeographic region that includes Europe, the northwest coast of Africa, and Asia north of the Himalaya Mountains, especially with respect to distribution of animals.

Pa·lem·bang (pä′ləm-bäng′, -lĕm-). A city of Indonesia on southeast Sumatra Island. Center of a powerful Hindu kingdom in the seventh and eighth centuries, it became a Dutch trading post in 1617 and was later occupied intermittently by the British. ◉ Pop. 787,187.

Pa·len·cia (pə-lĕn′chə, pä-lĕn′syä). A city of northern Spain north-northeast of Valladolid. Site of an ancient Roman settlement, it was recovered from the Moors in the tenth century. Spain's first university was founded here in 1208 but was moved to Salamanca in 1238. ◉ Pop. 74,311.

Pa·len·que (pä-lĕng′kĕ). An ancient Mayan city of southern Mexico southeast of Villahermosa. The Temple of Inscriptions is noted for its hieroglyphic tablets.

Pa·le·o·In·di·an (pā′lē-ō-ĭn′dē-ən) *adj.* Of or relating to prehistoric human culture in the Western Hemisphere from the earliest habitation to around 5,000 B.C. Paleo-Indian cultures are distinguished especially by the various projectile points they produced. **— Pa′le·o·In′di·an** *n.*

Pa·le·o·lith·ic (pā′lē-ə-lĭth′ĭk) **1.** Of, belong-

ing to, or designating the cultural period of the Stone Age beginning with the earliest chipped stone tools, about 750,000 years ago, until the beginning of the Mesolithic Age, about 15,000 years ago. **2.** The Paleolithic Age.

Pa·ler·mo (pə-lûr′mō, -lâr′-, pä-lĕr′mô). A city of northwest Sicily, Italy, on the Tyrrhenian Sea. Founded by Phoenicians c. eighth century B.C., it later became a Carthaginian military base and was conquered by Rome in 254–253 B.C. The Arabs held the city from A.D. 831 until 1072, when it became capital of the independent kingdom of Sicily (until 1194). ◉ Pop. 697,162.

Pal·es·tine¹ (pălʹĭ-stīn′). Often called "the Holy Land." *abbr.* **Pal.** A historical region of southwest Asia between the eastern Mediterranean shore and the Jordan River roughly coextensive with modern Israel and the West Bank. Occupied since prehistoric times, it has been ruled by Hebrews, Egyptians, Romans, Byzantines, Arabs, and Turks. A British League of Nations mandate oversaw the affairs of the area from 1920 until 1948, when Israel declared itself a separate state and the West Bank territory was occupied by Jordan. The West Bank was subsequently annexed (1950) by Jordan and occupied (1967) by Israel. In 1988 the Palestine Liberation Organization under Yasir Arafat declared its intention of forming an Arab state of Palestine, probably including the West Bank, the Gaza Strip, and the Arab sector of Jerusalem. In 1993 and 1994 Israeli and Palestinian leaders succeeded in hammering out agreements for limited Palestinian self-rule and Israeli withdrawal from the Gaza Strip and the West Bank. **— Pal′es·tin′i·an** (-stĭn′ē-ən) *adj. & n.*

Pal·es·tine² (pălʹĭ-stīn′). A city of eastern Texas southeast of Dallas. It is a market and processing center. ◉ Pop. 18,042.

Pa·li (pä′lē). A Prakrit language that is a scriptural and liturgical language of Hinayana or Theravada Buddhism.

Pal·i·kir (pălʹĭ-kər, pä′lē-kîr′). The capital (since 1989) of the Federated States of Micronesia, on Pohnpei Island.

pal·i·sades (pălʹĭ-sādz′). A line of lofty, steep cliffs, usually along a river.

Pal·i·sades (pălʹĭ-sādz′). A row of cliffs in northeast New Jersey along the western bank of the Hudson River. Much of the area is parkland.

Palk Strait (pôk, pôlk). A waterway between southeast India and northern Sri Lanka. It is known for its reefs and treacherous waters.

Pall Mall (pălʹ mălʹ, pĕlʹ mĕlʹ). A fashionable street in London, England, noted as the site of St. James's Palace and many private clubs. It derives its name from the game pall-mall, which was played on the grounds in front of the palace in the 17th century.

Pal·ma (päl′mä) also **Palma de Mal·lor·ca** (də mä-yôr′kä, *thĕ* mä-lyôr′kä). A city of western Majorca Island, Spain, on the **Bay of Palma,** an inlet of the Mediterranean Sea. ⊕ Pop. 298,971.

Palm Bay (päm). A city of eastern Florida on the Indian River lagoon southeast of Orlando. It is a resort. ⊕ Pop. 62,632.

Palm Beach. A city of southeast Florida on a barrier beach of the Atlantic Ocean north of Fort Lauderdale. It was developed as a fashionable resort by the American capitalist Henry Flagler in the 1890's. ⊕ Pop. 9,814.

Pal·mer Archipelago (pä′mər, päl′-). Formerly **Ant·arc·tic Archipelago** (ănt-ärk′tĭk, -är′-tĭk). An island group between the southern tip of South America and the northwest coast of the Antarctic Peninsula. The islands are claimed by Great Britain.

Palmer Peninsula. See **Antarctic Peninsula.**

Pal·mi·ra (päl-mîr′ə, -mē′rä). A city of western Colombia southwest of Bogotá. Coffee and tobacco are grown in the area. ⊕ Pop. 181,157.

Palm Springs. A city of southeast California east-southeast of Riverside. It is a desert oasis and popular resort with hot springs known to the Spanish as early as 1774. ⊕ Pop. 40,181.

Pal·my·ra (păl-mī′rə). An ancient city of central Syria northeast of Damascus. Said to have been built by the biblical king Solomon, it prospered under the Romans because of its location on the trade route from Egypt to the Persian Gulf. The city was partially destroyed by the Roman emperor Aurelian after a people's revolt in A.D. 273.

Pal·o Al·to (päl′ō äl′tō). A city of western California northwest of San Jose. It is a residential community with an electronics industry. ⊕ Pop. 55,900.

Pal·o·mar (păl′ə-mär′), **Mount.** A peak, about 1,868.4 m (6,126 ft) high, of southern California northeast of San Diego. It is the site of an observatory with one of the world's largest reflecting telescopes.

Pa·los Hills (pä′ləs). A city of northeast Illinois, a suburb of Chicago. ⊕ Pop. 17,803.

Pa·louse (pə-lōōs′). *pl.* **Palouse** or **-louses.** A member of a Sahaptin-speaking Native American people formerly inhabiting an area of southeast Washington and northwest Idaho, with present-day descendants in northeast Washington.

Palouse River. A river, about 225 km (140 mi) long, rising in northwest Idaho and flowing west and south to the Snake River in southeast Washington.

Pa·mir (pə-mîr′, pä-). A mountainous region of south-central Asia mostly in Tajikistan with extensions in northern Afghanistan, northern Kashmir, and western China. The Pamirs rise to 7,500 m (24,590 ft) at Communism Peak.

Pam·li·co Sound (păm′lĭ-kō′). An inlet of the Atlantic Ocean between the eastern coast of North Carolina and a row of low, sandy barrier islands. Fish, oysters, and wildlife abound.

pam·pa (păm′pə). *pl.* **-pas** (-pəz, -pəs). In South America, a treeless, grassland area. — **pam′pe·an** (păm′pē-ən, păm-pē′ən) *adj.*

Pam·pa (păm′pə). A city of northwest Texas in the Panhandle east-northeast of Amarillo. It is an industrial and shipping center in a cattle and oil area. ⊕ Pop. 19,959.

Pam·pas (păm′pəz, -pəs, päm′päs). A vast plain of south-central South America. The Pampas extend for about 1,610 km (1,000 mi) from the lower Paraná River to south-central Argentina southwest of Buenos Aires. — **Pam′pe·an** (păm′pē-ən, păm-pē′ən) *adj.*

pam·pe·ro (păm-pâr′ō, päm-). A strong, cold southwest wind that blows across the Pampas.

Pam·plo·na (păm-plō′nə, päm-plô′nä). A city of northern Spain east-southeast of Bilbao. An ancient Basque city, it was captured by the Visigoths, Franks, and Moors and became the capital of the kingdom of Navarre (824–1512). The annual running of the bulls during the feast of San Fermin was celebrated in Ernest Hemingway's *The Sun Also Rises* (1926). ⊕ Pop. 181,349.

pan (păn). A basin or depression in the earth, often containing mud or water.

Pan·a·ma (păn′ə-mä′, -mô′). **1.** *abbr.* **Pan.** A country of southeast Central America. The region was inhabited by a variety of Indian peoples when Columbus landed on its Caribbean coast in 1502. In 1513 the Spanish explorer Vasco Núñez de Balboa first crossed the isthmus to discover the eastern Pacific Ocean. An important link in the shipment of gold from Peru to Spain, the area was controlled by the Spanish until 1821, when it became part of Colombia. Eager for a canal across the isthmus, the U.S. supported a revolution leading to Panamanian independence in 1903. The canal was completed

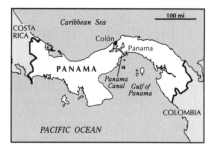

under U.S. direction in 1914, and a U.S.-administered Canal Zone was created to provide for its operation and defense. The Canal Zone was turned over to Panamanian control in 1977, with the canal itself scheduled to be returned in 1999. U.S. troops carried out a brief invasion of Panama in 1989 in order to capture Gen. Manuel Noriega, the de facto ruler of the country, who was subsequently tried in a U.S. court on charges of drug trafficking. Panama is the capital. ⊛ Pop. 2,583,000. **2.** also **Panama City.** The capital and largest city of Panama, in the central part of the country on the Gulf of Panama. The original city was founded in 1519, destroyed in 1671, and rebuilt a short distance away in 1673. ⊛ Pop. 445,902. — **Pan′a·ma′·ni·an** (-mā′nē-ən) *adj.*

Panama, Gulf of. A wide inlet of the Pacific Ocean on the southern coast of Panama.

Panama, Isthmus of. Formerly **Isthmus of Da·ri·én** (där′ē-ĕn′, där-yĕn′). An isthmus of Central America connecting North and South America and separating the Pacific Ocean from the Caribbean Sea.

Panama Canal. A ship canal, about 82 km (51 mi) long, crossing the Isthmus of Panama in the Canal Zone and connecting the Caribbean Sea with the Pacific Ocean. It was begun by the French in 1881, but the project was abandoned in 1889. The United States gained construction rights after Panama declared its independence in 1903, and the canal was opened to traffic on August 15, 1914, greatly reducing the travel time between the Atlantic and Pacific Oceans, though its strategic importance was lessened by the later development of commercial and naval vessels too large to fit its locks. A 1977 treaty stipulated that the Panamanians gain full rights of sovereignty over the canal on December 31, 1999.

Panama Canal Zone. See **Canal Zone.**

Panama City. **1.** A city of northwest Florida on the Gulf of Mexico east-southeast of Pensacola. It is a resort and fishing center and a port of entry. ⊛ Pop. 34,378. **2.** See **Panama** (sense 2).

Pan-A·mer·i·can (păn′ə-mĕr′ĭ-kən). Of or relating to North, South, and Central America.

Pan-American Highway. A system of roadways, about 25,744 km (16,000 mi) long, extending from Alaska to Chile and linking the nations of the Western Hemisphere.

Pan·a·mint Range (păn′ə-mĭnt′). A rugged range of mountains in eastern California between Death Valley and the **Panamint Valley.** Telescope Peak, 3,370 m (11,049 ft), is the highest elevation.

Pa·nay (pə-nī′, pä-). An island of the central Philippines in the Visayan Islands northwest of Negros. Corn and rice are among its crops.

Pan·gae·a also **Pan·ge·a** (păn-jē′ə). A hypothetical supercontinent that included all the landmasses of the earth before the Triassic Period, approximately 230 million years ago. When continental drift began, Pangaea broke up into Laurasia and Gondwanaland.

Pan·go Pan·go (päng′ō päng′ō, păng′gō păng′-gō, päng′gō päng′gō). See **Pago Pago.**

Pan·han·dle (păn′hăn′dl). A narrow strip of territory projecting from a larger, broader area, as in Alaska, Florida, Idaho, Oklahoma, Texas, and West Virginia.

Pan-Hel·len·ic also **Pan·hel·len·ic** (păn′hə-lĕn′ĭk). Of or relating to all Greek peoples or a movement to unify them.

Pan·ja·bi (pŭn-jä′bē, -jäb′ē). Variant of **Punjabi.**

Pan·mun·jom (pän′mōōn′jŭm′). A village of northwest South Korea just south of the 38th parallel. Truce negotiations for the Korean War were held here from October 1951 to July 27, 1953, when the truce was officially signed.

Pan·no·ni·a (pə-nō′nē-ə). An ancient Roman province of central Europe including present-day western Hungary and the northwest Balkan Peninsula. Its people were finally subjugated by Rome in A.D. 9, although the province was abandoned after 395. — **Pan·no′ni·an** *adj. & n.*

Pao·ki (bou′jē′). See **Baoji.**

Pao·ting (bou′dĭng′). See **Baoding.**

Pao·tow (bou′tō′). See **Baotou.**

Pa·pa·go (păp′ə-gō′, pä′pə-). **1.** *pl.* **Papago** or **-gos.** A member of a Native American people inhabiting desert regions of southern Arizona and northern Sonora, a state of northwest Mexico. **2.** The Uto-Aztecan language of this people, dialectically related to Pima. Also called *O'odham, Tohono O'odham.*

Pa·pal States (pā′pəl). A group of territories in central Italy ruled by the popes from 754 until 1870. They were originally given to the papacy by the Frankish king Pepin the Short and reached their greatest extent in 1859. The last papal state—the Vatican City—was formally established as a separate state by the Lateran Treaty of 1929.

Pa·pe·e·te (pä′pē-ā′tā, pə-pē′tē). The capital of the overseas territory of French Polynesia, a port on the northwest coast of Tahiti in the Society Islands of the southern Pacific Ocean. It is a commercial and tourist center. ⊛ Pop. 23,496.

Pa·pia·men·tu (pä′pyə-mĕn′tōō) also **Pa·pia·men·to** (-tō). A creole based on Portuguese and pidginized Spanish and spoken in the Netherlands Antilles.

Pap·u·a (păp′yōō-ə, pä′pōō-ä′), **Gulf of.** A

large inlet of the Coral Sea on the southeast coast of New Guinea.

Pap·u·an (păp′yōō-ən). **1.** Of or relating to the peoples, languages, or cultures of Papua New Guinea or New Guinea. **2.** Of or relating to the Papuan language. **3.** A native or inhabitant of Papua New Guinea or New Guinea. **4.** A member of any of the indigenous peoples of New Guinea and neighboring islands. **5.** Any of the indigenous languages of New Guinea, New Britain, and the Solomon Islands.

Papua New Guinea. An island country of the southwest Pacific Ocean comprising the eastern half of New Guinea, the Bismarck Archipelago, the western Solomons, and adjacent islands. Inhabited by a variety of Papuan and Melanesian peoples, the territory was visited by early Spanish and Portuguese explorers, though European settlement did not begin until the establishment of German and British protectorates in 1884. Australia assumed control of the British sector in 1905 and took over the German sector during World War I. The two territories were united as the Territory of Papua and New Guinea in 1949. The country, now named Papua New Guinea, became self-governing in 1973 and fully independent in 1975. Port Moresby, on New Guinea, is the capital and the largest city. ⊛ Pop. 3,997,000. — **Pap′u·a New Guin′e·an** adj. & n.

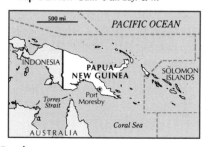

Pa·rá (pə-rä′). See **Belém.**

Par·a·dise (păr′ə-dīs′, -dīz′). An unincorporated community of north-central California in the foothills of the Sierra Nevada north of Sacramento. ⊛ Pop. 25,408.

Par·a·gould (păr′ə-gōōld′). A city of northeast Arkansas northeast of Jonesboro. It is a processing and trade center. ⊛ Pop. 18,540.

Par·a·guay (păr′ə-gwī′, -gwā′). abbr. **Par.** A landlocked country of south-central South America. Inhabited principally by the Guarani, the region was first explored by Europeans in 1516 and grew around the colony of Asunción, founded in the 1530′s. Jesuit missions established in the early 1600′s were important in the development of the country, which achieved de facto independence from Spain in 1811. Paraguay was ruled by a series of dictators in the 19th century and became involved in costly wars

with Argentina, Brazil, and Uruguay (1865–1870) and Bolivia (1932–1935). A coup in 1989 ended the authoritarian regime of Gen. Alfredo Stroessner (ruled 1954–1989), and the country's first democratic presidential elections were held in 1993. Asunción is the capital and the largest city. ⊛ Pop. 4,700,000. — **Par′a·guay′an** adj. & n.

Paraguay River. A river rising in southwest Brazil and flowing about 2,574 km (1,600 mi) southward to the Paraná River in southwest Paraguay. Part of its course forms the border between the two countries.

Pa·ra·í·ba (păr′ə-ē′bə, pä′rä-ē′bä) also **Paraíba do Sul** (dōō sōōl′). A river, about 1,046 km (650 mi) long, of southeast Brazil emptying into the Atlantic Ocean near Campos.

Par·a·mar·i·bo (păr′ə-măr′ə-bō′). The capital and largest city of Suriname, on the Suriname River near its mouth on the Atlantic Ocean. Settled by the British from Barbados in the 1630′s, Paramaribo came under Dutch rule in 1815. ⊛ Pop. 67,905.

Par·a·mount (păr′ə-mount′). A city of southern California southeast of Los Angeles. Originally a dairy center, it became industrialized after the 1950′s. ⊛ Pop. 47,669.

Pa·ram·us (pə-răm′əs). A borough of northeast New Jersey northeast of Paterson. It is mainly residential. ⊛ Pop. 25,067.

Pa·ra·ná (păr′ə-nä′, pä′rä-). A city of northeast Argentina on the Paraná River north of Rosario. It is a river port accessible for oceangoing vessels. ⊛ Pop. 206,848.

Pa·ra·na·í·ba (păr′ə-nə-ē′bə, pä′rä-nä-ē′bä). A river, about 805 km (500 mi) long, of south-central Brazil. It is one of the headstreams of the Paraná River.

Pa·ra·ña·que (pä′rä-nyä′kĕ). A city of southwest Luzon Island, Philippines, a residential suburb of Manila on southeast Manila Bay. ⊛ Pop. 252,791.

Paraná River. A river of central South America rising in east-central Brazil at the confluence of the Rio Grande and the Paranaíba and flowing about 2,896 km (1,800 mi) generally southwest to its junction with the Paraguay River then south and east to join the Uruguay River and form the Río de la Plata estuary in eastern Argentina. It was first ascended by Sebastian Cabot, the Italian-born explorer and cartographer, in 1526.

Par·du·bi·ce (pär′dōō-bǐ′tsə). A city of north-central Czech Republic on the Elbe River east of Prague. It is an industrial center. ◉ Pop. 93,822.

Par·i·an (pâr′ē-ən, păr′-). **1.** Of or relating to the island of Páros or its inhabitants. **2.** Of or being a type of white, semitranslucent marble quarried at Páros and highly valued in ancient times for making sculptures. **3.** A native or inhabitant of Páros.

Pa·ri·cu·tin (pä-rē′kōō-tēn′). A volcano, 2,272.3 m (7,450 ft) high, of west-central Mexico west of Mexico City. It erupted from a cornfield in February 1943 and grew more than 458 m (1,500 ft) in that year alone.

Par·is (păr′ĭs). **1.** The capital and largest city of France, in the north-central part of the country on the Seine River. Founded as a fishing village on the Île de la Cité, Paris (then called Lutetia) was captured and fortified by the Romans in 52 B.C. The Frankish king Clovis I made it his capital after A.D. 486, and Hugh Capet, successor to the Carolingian kings, established it as the capital of France after his accession to the throne in 987. Through the succeeding centuries, Paris grew rapidly as a commercial, cultural, and industrial center. The city was occupied by the Germans in World War II from June 14, 1940, to August 25, 1944. ◉ Pop. 2,152,329. **2.** A city of northeast Texas northeast of Dallas. It is a trade and processing center in the Red River valley. ◉ Pop. 24,699.

par·ish (păr′ĭsh). *abbr.* **par. 1.** A political subdivision of a British county, usually corresponding in boundaries to an original ecclesiastical parish. **2.** An administrative subdivision in Louisiana that corresponds to a county in other U.S. states.

park (pärk). *abbr.* **pk. 1.** An area of land set aside for public use, as: **a.** A piece of land with few or no buildings within or adjoining a town, maintained for recreational and ornamental purposes. **b.** A large tract of rural land kept in its natural state and usually reserved for the enjoyment and recreation of visitors. **2.** A broad, fairly level valley between mountain ranges.

Park Avenue (pärk). A wide thoroughfare extending north to south on the East Side of Man-

hattan Island. Traditionally associated with luxurious apartment houses, it is now the location of many high-rise commercial buildings.

Par·kers·burg (pär′kərz-bûrg′). A city of northwest West Virginia at the confluence of the Little Kanawha and Ohio rivers north of Charleston. It is an industrial and commercial center in a coal region. ◉ Pop. 33,862.

Park Forest. A village of northeast Illinois, a residential suburb of Chicago. ◉ Pop. 24,656.

park·land (pärk′lănd′). **1.** Land within or suitable for public parks. **2.** Grassland with scattered clusters of trees or shrubs.

Park·land (pärk′lənd). A community of west-central Washington. It is a residential suburb of Tacoma. ◉ Pop. 20,882.

Park Range. A range of the Rocky Mountains in north-central Colorado and southern Wyoming rising to 4,357.2 m (14,286 ft) at Mount Lincoln in Colorado.

Park Ridge. A city of northeast Illinois, a chiefly residential suburb of Chicago. ◉ Pop. 36,175.

Park·rose (pärk′rōz′). A community of northwest Oregon, a suburb of Portland. ◉ Pop. 21,103.

Park·ville (pärk′vĭl′). An unincorporated community of north-central Maryland, a chiefly residential suburb of Baltimore. ◉ Pop. 31,617.

Par·ma (pär′mə). **1.** A city of north-central Italy southeast of Milan. Founded by Romans in 183 B.C., it became a free city in the 12th century and was the center of the duchy of Parma and Piacenza after 1545. It became part of the kingdom of Sardinia in 1860 and of Italy in 1861. ◉ Pop. 168,905. **2.** A city of northeast Ohio, a chiefly residential suburb of Cleveland. ◉ Pop. 87,876.

Parma Heights. A city of northeast Ohio, a residential suburb of Cleveland. ◉ Pop. 21,448.

Par·na·í·ba (pär′nə-ē′bə, -nä-ē′bä). A river, about 1,287 km (800 mi) long, of northeast Brazil flowing generally northward to the Atlantic Ocean.

Par·nas·sus (pär-năs′əs) also **Par·nas·sós** (-näsôs′). A mountain, about 2,458 m (8,060 ft) high, of central Greece north of the Gulf of Corinth. In ancient times it was sacred to the gods Apollo and Dionysus and to the Muses. Delphi was at the foot of the mountain.

Pá·ros also **Par·os** (pâr′ŏs, pä′rôs). An island of southeast Greece in the Aegean Sea. One of the Cyclades, it was settled by Ionians and later founded colonies of its own in the seventh century B.C. The island was held by the Ottoman Turks from 1537 to 1832, when it became part of Greece. A fine white, semitranslucent marble quarried on the island was used by sculptors as early as the sixth century B.C.

Par·ra·mat·ta (păr′ə-măt′ə). A city of southeast Australia, a manufacturing suburb of Sydney. It was founded in 1788. ◉ Pop. 131,800.

Par·ris Island (păr′ĭs). An island of the Sea Islands off southern South Carolina. It has been a U.S. Marine Corps training installation since 1915.

Par·ry Channel (păr′ē). A water route of the central Arctic Archipelago of Northwest Territories, Canada, linking Baffin Bay on the east with the Beaufort Sea on the west.

Parry Islands. A group of islands of northern Northwest Territories, Canada, in the Arctic Ocean north of Victoria Island.

Par·see also **Par·si** (pär′sē, pär-sē′). **1.** pl. **-sees** also **-sis.** A member of a Zoroastrian religious sect in India, descended from Persians. **2.** The Iranian dialect used in the religious literature of the Parsees. — **Par′see′ism** n.

Par·thi·a (pär′thē-ə). An ancient country of southwest Asia corresponding to modern northeast Iran. It was included in the Assyrian and Persian empires, the Macedonian empire of Alexander the Great, and the Syrian empire. A Parthian kingdom lasted from c. 250 B.C. to A.D. 226, reaching the height of its influence and land holdings at the beginning of the first century B.C. Its people, of Scythian stock, were noted as horsemen and archers.

Par·thi·an (pär′thē-ən). **1.** Of or relating to Parthia or its people, language, or culture. **2.** A native or inhabitant of Parthia. **3.** The Iranian language of the Parthians.

Pas·a·de·na (păs′ə-dē′nə). **1.** A city of southern California northeast of Los Angeles. It is famous for its Rose Bowl and annual Tournament of Roses parade. ◉ Pop. 131,591. **2.** A city of southeast Texas, an industrial suburb of Houston. The Lyndon B. Johnson Manned Space Center is nearby. ◉ Pop. 119,363.

Pa·sar·ga·dae (pə-sär′gə-dē′). A ruined city of ancient Persia northeast of Persepolis. It was the Persian king Cyrus the Great's capital and is said to have been founded by him in 550 B.C.

Pa·say (pä′sī). A city of southwest Luzon, Philippines, a suburb of Manila on the eastern shore of Manila Bay. ◉ Pop. 388,129.

Pas·ca·gou·la (păs′kə-gōō′lə). A city of extreme southeast Mississippi east of Biloxi on Mississippi Sound. It is a port of entry, fishing center, and coastal resort. ◉ Pop. 25,899.

Pas·co (păs′kō). A city of southeast Washington on the Columbia River near its confluence with the Snake and Yakima rivers. It grew during World War II as a supply center for the nearby Hanford Atomic Works. ◉ Pop. 20,337.

Pas de Ca·lais (pä də kă-lā′, kăl′ā, kä-lĕ′). The Strait of Dover.

Pash·to (pŭsh′tō) also **Push·tu** (pŭsh̩′tōō). An Iranian language that is the principal vernacular language of Afghanistan and parts of western Pakistan. Also called *Afghan.*

Pa·sig (pä′sĭg). A city of southwest Luzon, Philippines, a suburb of Manila. It is an important market town. ◉ Pop. 318,853.

pass (păs). A way, such as a narrow gap between mountains, that affords passage around, over, or through a barrier.

Pas·sa·ic (pə-sā′ĭk). A city of northeast New Jersey south of Paterson on the **Passaic River,** about 129 km (80 mi) long. Settled by Dutch traders in 1678, the city is highly industrialized. ◉ Pop. 58,041.

Pas·sa·ma·quod·dy (păs′ə-mə-kwŏd′ē). **1.** pl. **Passamaquoddy** or **-dies.** A member of a Native American people formerly inhabiting parts of coastal Maine and New Brunswick, Canada, along the Bay of Fundy, with present-day descendants in eastern Maine. The Passamaquoddies helped form the Abenaki confederacy in the mid-18th century. **2.** The Algonquian language of the Passamaquoddies, dialectally related to Malecite.

Passamaquoddy Bay. An arm of the Bay of Fundy between southern New Brunswick, Canada, and eastern Maine. It is studded with islands, including Campobello.

Pas·sau (päs′ou′). A city of southeast Germany at the confluence of the Danube and Inn rivers near the Austrian border. Of ancient Celtic origin, it was a frontier outpost in Roman times. ◉ Pop. 52,356.

Pas·so Fun·do (pä′sōō fōōn′dōō). A city of southern Brazil northwest of Pôrto Alegre. Settled in the 1830's, it is a trade and processing center. ◉ Pop. 147,239.

Pas·to (päs′tō). A city of southwest Colombia near the Ecuadorian border. Founded in 1539, it was the site of an 1832 treaty by which Colombia and Ecuador became separate states. ◉ Pop. 203,742.

Pat·a·go·ni·a (păt′ə-gō′nē-ə, -gōn′yə). A tableland region of South America in southern Argentina and Chile extending from the Colorado River to the Straits of Magellan and from the Andes to the Atlantic Ocean. The study of its original inhabitants, the Tehuelche ("the Patagonian giants"), and its unusual wildlife have attracted many scientific expeditions, including that of the British naturalist Charles Darwin (1831–1836). — **Pat′a·go′ni·an** adj. & n.

Pat·er·son (păt′ər-sən). A city of northeast New Jersey on the Passaic River north of Newark. It was founded in 1791 as an industrial settlement of the Society for Establishing Useful Manufactures, chartered by Alexander Hamilton and others to promote independent American enterprise. ◉ Pop. 140,891.

Pa·than(pə-tän′). A member of a Pashto-speaking people of eastern Afghanistan and northwest Pakistan, constituting the majority population of Afghanistan.

Pa·ti·a·la(pŭt′ē-ä′lə). A city of northwest India north-northwest of Delhi. It was the center of a former princely state founded by a Sikh chieftain c. 1763. ◉ Pop. 238,368.

Pát·mos also **Pat·mos** (păt′mŏs, -məs, pät′-môs). An island of southeast Greece in the Dodecanese Islands of the Aegean Sea. Saint John was exiled to the island c. A.D. 95 and according to tradition wrote the Book of Revelation here.

Pat·na(pŭt′nə). A city of northeast India on the Ganges River northwest of Calcutta. It served as King Asoka's capital in the 3rd century B.C. and as a Mogul viceregal capital in the 16th century. ◉ Pop. 917,243.

Pa·tos(păt′əs, pä′tŏos), **Lagoa dos.** A shallow tidal lagoon of southeast Brazil. Separated from the Atlantic Ocean by a wide sandbar, it is an important fishing ground.

Pá·trai(pä′trĕ) also **Pa·tras** (pə-trăs′, păt′rəs). A city of southern Greece in the northwest Peloponnesus on the **Gulf of Pátrai,** or **Gulf of Patras,** an inlet of the Ionian Sea. The city was an important trade center by the fifth century B.C. but declined before the Roman conquest of Greece (146 B.C.). It is a commercial, industrial, and transportation center. ◉ Pop. 142,163.

Pau(pō). A city of southwest France in the foothills of the Pyrenees south of Bordeaux. It is a year-round tourist center noted for its scenery and winter sports. ◉ Pop. 83,790.

Pa·vi·a(pə-vē′ə, pä-vē′ä). A city of northwest Italy south of Milan. Originally a Roman stronghold known as Ticinum, it served as capital of the Lombard kings before 1359 and later became a leading Italian city-state. ◉ Pop. 85,056.

Pav·lo·dar (păv′lə-där′, pə-vlə-). A town of northeast Kazakstan on the Irtysh River southeast of Omsk, Russia. It is a processing and shipping center in a rich agricultural region. ◉ Pop. 349,000.

Paw·nee (pô-nē′). **1.** *pl.* **Pawnee** or **-nees.** A member of a Native American people formerly inhabiting the Platte River valley in south-central Nebraska and northern Kansas, with a present-day population in north-central Oklahoma. The Pawnees comprised a confederation of four relatively independent tribes living in permanent villages. **2.** The Caddoan language of the Pawnees.

Paw·tuck·et (pô-tŭk′ĭt, pə-). A city of northeast Rhode Island, an industrial suburb of Providence. The first successful water-powered cotton mill in the United States was built here

(1790–1793) by Samuel Slater, a British-born textile pioneer. ◉ Pop. 72,644.

Pea·bod·y(pē′bŏd′ē, -bə-dē). A city of northeast Massachusetts west of Salem. Settled c. 1633 and later called South Danvers, it was renamed after George Peabody, an American merchant and philanthropist, in 1868. ◉ Pop. 47,039.

Peace River (pēs). A river, about 1,521 km (945 mi) long, rising in central British Columbia, Canada, and flowing east to Alberta then northeast to the Slave River near Lake Athabasca. It was long an important waterway for fur traders.

peak(pēk). *abbr.* **pk. 1.** The pointed summit of a mountain. **2.** The mountain itself.

Pearl(pûrl). A city of central Mississippi, a suburb of Jackson. ◉ Pop. 19,588.

Pearl City. A village of Hawaii on Pearl Harbor in southern Oahu. It was severely damaged during the attack on Pearl Harbor (December 7, 1941). ◉ Pop. 30,993.

Pearl Harbor. An inlet of the Pacific Ocean on the southern coast of Oahu, Hawaii, west of Honolulu. It became the site of a naval base after the United States annexed Hawaii in 1900. On Sunday, December 7, 1941, Japanese planes attacked the base without warning, destroying or severely damaging 19 naval vessels and some 200 aircraft. The United States entered World War II the following day.

Pearl River[1]. A river, about 780 km (485 mi) long, of central and southern Mississippi flowing southwest then south to the Gulf of Mexico. Its lower course forms part of the Mississippi-Louisiana border.

Pearl River[2]. An unincorporated community of southeast New York, a residential suburb of New York City near the New Jersey border. ◉ Pop. 15,314.

Pea·ry Land (pîr′ē). A peninsula of northern Greenland extending into the Arctic Ocean. The American Arctic explorer Robert E. Peary first visited it on his 1891–1892 expedition.

Pe·cho·ra(pə-chôr′ə, -chōr′ə, pyĭ-). A river of northwest Russia flowing about 1,802 km (1,120 mi) northward into **Pechora Bay,** an arm of the Barents Sea.

Pe·cos(pā′kəs). A river of eastern New Mexico and western Texas flowing about 1,490 km (926 mi) south and southeast to the Rio Grande.

Pécs (pāch). A city of southwest Hungary near the Croatian border south-southwest of Budapest. It was a Celtic settlement and later the capital of a Roman province. ◉ Pop. 171,870.

ped·i·ment(pĕd′ə-mənt). *Geology.* A broad, gently sloping rock surface at the base of a steeper slope, often covered with alluvium, formed primarily by erosion.

Pee Dee (pē′ dē′) also **Great Pee Dee** (grāt). A

river, about 375 km (233 mi) long, of south-central North Carolina and northeast South Carolina.

Peeks·kill (pēk′skĭl′). A city of southeast New York on the Hudson River north of White Plains. Strategically important in the American Revolution, it was burned by the British in 1777. ● Pop. 19,536.

Peel River (pēl). A river, about 644 km (400 mi) long, of northern Yukon Territory and western Northwest Territories, Canada, flowing east and north to the Mackenzie River.

Pee·ne·mün·de (pā′nə-mo͞on′də, -mün′-). A village of northeast Germany on an offshore island in the Baltic Sea. It was a center for the development of guided missiles, especially the V-1 and V-2, prior to and during World War II (1937–1945).

Peh·le·vi (pā′lə-vē′). Variant of **Pahlavi.**

Pei·ping (pā′pĭng′). See **Beijing.**

Pei·pus (pī′pəs), **Lake.** A lake north-central Europe between eastern Estonia and northwest Russia. The Russian saint and national hero Alexander Nevski defeated the Teutonic Knights on the frozen lake in 1242.

Pe·kin (pē′kĭn). A city of central Illinois, an industrial suburb of Peoria on the Illinois River. ● Pop. 32,254.

Pe·king (pē′kĭng′, pā′-). See **Beijing.**

Pe·king·ese (pē′kĭng-ēz′, -ēs′) also **Pe·kin·ese** (pē′kə-nēz′, -nēs′). **1.** *pl.* **Pekingese** also **Pe·kinese.** A native or resident of Peking (Beijing). **2.** The Chinese dialect of Peking. — **Pe′king·ese′** *adj.*

Pe·las·gi·an (pə-lăz′jē-ən). A member of a people living in the region of the Aegean Sea before the coming of the Greeks. — **Pe·las′gi·an, Pe·las′gic** (-jĭk) *adj.*

Pe·lée (pə-lā′), **Mount.** A volcano, about 1,373 m (4,500 ft) high, on northern Martinique in the French West Indies. Its eruption on May 8, 1902, killed some 40,000 people.

Pe·lew (pə-lo͞o′, pē-). See **Palau.**

Pe·li·on (pē′lē-ən, -ŏn′), **Mount.** A peak, 1,602 m (5,252 ft) high, of northeast Greece in eastern Thessaly. According to Greek legend, it was the home of the centaurs.

Pel·la (pĕl′ə). An ancient city of Greek Macedonia. It was the capital of Macedonia from the fourth century to 168 B.C., when the territory was conquered by the Romans.

Pel·ly (pĕl′ē). A river, about 531 km (330 mi) long, of central Yukon Territory, Canada, flowing generally northwest to the Yukon River.

Pel·o·pon·ne·sus or **Pel·o·pon·ne·sos** (pĕl′ə-pə-nē′səs) also **Pel·o·pon·nese** (pĕl′ə-pə-nēz′, -nēs′). A peninsula forming the southern part of Greece south of the Gulf of Corinth. It was

dominated by Sparta until the fourth century B.C. — **Pel′o·pon·ne′sian** (-nē′zhən, -shən) *adj. & n.*

Pe·lo·tas (pə-lō′təs, pĭ-lô′täs). A city of southeast Brazil on a lagoon south-southwest of Pôrto Alegre. It is a major producer of dried beef. ● Pop. 290,660.

Pem·ba (pĕm′bə). An island of Tanzania in the Indian Ocean north of Zanzibar. In the 16th and 17th centuries the Portuguese occupied the island, which passed under British control in 1890.

Pem·broke Pines (pĕm′brŏok′, -brŏk′). A city of southeast Florida, a residential suburb of Fort Lauderdale. ● Pop. 65,452.

Pe·nang (pə-năng′, pē′näng′). See **George Town** (sense 1).

Pen·del·i·kón (pĕn-dĕl′ĭ-kŏn′, pĕn′dĕ-lē-kôn′). A mountain, about 1,119 m (3,670 ft) high, of east-central Greece northeast of Athens. White marble quarried here was used for many of the buildings of ancient Athens.

Pend O·reille (pŏn′də-rā′). A river, about 161 km (100 mi) long, rising in **Pend Oreille Lake** in northern Idaho and flowing generally northwest through northeast Washington to the Columbia River just north of the British Columbia, Canada, border.

pe·ne·plain also **pe·ne·plane** (pē′nə-plān′). *Geology.* A nearly flat land surface representing an advanced stage of erosion.

Peng·hu (pŭng′ho͞o′). See **Pescadores.**

Peng·pu (pŭng′po͞o′). See **Bengbu.**

pen·in·su·la (pə-nĭn′syə-lə, -sə-lə). A piece of land that projects into a body of water and is connected with the mainland by an isthmus. — **pen·in′su·lar** *adj.*

Pen·ki (bŭn′jē′). See **Benxi.**

Penn Hills (pĕn). A community of southwest Pennsylvania, a residential suburb of Philadelphia. ● Pop. 51,430.

Pen·nine Alps (pĕn′īn′). A range of the Alps extending southwest to northeast along the Swiss-Italian border from Great St. Bernard Pass to Simplon Pass. It rises to 4,636.9 m (15,203 ft) at Monte Rosa.

Pen·nines (pĕn′īnz′) also **Pennine Chain.** A range of hills extending about 257 km (160 mi) southward from the Cheviot Hills on the Scottish border to central England. Sometimes called "the backbone of England," it rises to 893.7 m (2,930 ft).

Penn·sau·ken (pĕn-sô′kĭn). A community of southwest New Jersey. It is an industrial and residential suburb of Camden and Philadelphia, Pennsylvania. ● Pop. 34,733.

Penn·syl·va·nia (pĕn′səl-vān′yə, -vā′nē-ə). *abbr.* **PA, Pa., Penn., Penna.** A state of the eastern United States. It was admitted as one of the original Thirteen Colonies in 1787. First explored in the early 1600's, the region was settled by Swedes in 1634 and granted by royal charter to William Penn in 1681. The Mason-Dixon Line (surveyed in 1763–1767) established the colony's southern boundary and was extended westward in 1784. Pennsylvania played a crucial role in the American Revolution and in the formation of the new republic. Harrisburg is the capital and Philadelphia the largest city. ⊛ Pop. 11,924,710. — **Penn′syl·va′nian** adj. & n.

Pennsylvania Dutch. 1. The descendants of German and Swiss immigrants who settled in Pennsylvania in the 17th and 18th centuries. **2.** The dialect of High German spoken by the Pennsylvania Dutch. Also called *Dutch, Pennsylvania German.*

Pe·nob·scot (pə-nŏb′skət, -skŏt′). **1.** pl. **Penobscot** or **-scots.** A member of a Native American people inhabiting Penobscot Bay and the Penobscot River valley in Maine. The Penobscots, who joined the Abenaki confederacy in the mid-18th century, are represented in the Maine legislature by a nonvoting delegate. **2.** The Algonquian language of the Penobscots, a dialect of Eastern Abenaki.

Penobscot River. A river rising in several lakes and tributaries in western and central Maine and flowing about 563 km (350 mi) to **Penobscot Bay,** an inlet of the Atlantic Ocean. The river is an important source of power for pulpwood and paper mills. The bay was first explored by English navigators in 1603.

Pen·sa·co·la (pĕn′sə-kō′lə). A city of extreme northwest Florida on **Pensacola Bay,** an inlet of the Gulf of Mexico. Originally settled by the Spanish in 1559, the city passed back and forth between the Spanish, French, and British until it was captured by Andrew Jackson in 1814 during the War of 1812. It formally became part of the United States in 1821. ⊛ Pop. 58,165.

Pen·tic·ton (pĕn-tĭk′tən). A city of southern British Columbia, Canada, east of Vancouver at the southern shore of Okanagan Lake. It is a trade center in a resort area. ⊛ Pop. 23,181.

Pent·land Firth (pĕnt′lənd). A narrow channel between northeast mainland Scotland and the Orkney Islands.

Pe·nu·ti·an (pə-nōō′tē-ən, -shən). A proposed stock of North American Indian languages spoken in Pacific coastal areas from California into British Columbia, Canada.

Pen·za (pĕn′zə, pyĕn′-). A city of west-central Russia south-southwest of Kazan. Founded as a fortress in 1666, it is a railroad junction and major industrial center. ⊛ Pop. 547,623.

Pen·zance (pĕn-zăns′). A municipal borough of southwest England west-southwest of Ply-

mouth. It is a port and summer resort and was frequently raided by pirates until the 18th century. ⊛ Pop. 19,521.

Pe·or·i·a¹ (pē-ôr′ē-ə, -ōr′-). pl. **Peoria** or **-as.** A member of a Native American people forming part of the Illinois confederacy.

Pe·or·i·a² (pē-ôr′ē-ə, -ōr′-). A city of northwest-central Illinois on the Illinois River north of Springfield. Founded on the site of a French fort established by the explorer La Salle in 1680, it is a transportation and industrial center. ⊛ Pop. 113,504.

Pe·quot (pē′kwŏt′). **1.** pl. **Pequot** or **-quots.** A member of a Native American people formerly inhabiting eastern Connecticut, with present-day descendants in the same area. The Pequots and the Mohegans were the same people until the Mohegan broke away under Uncas in the early 17th century. **2.** The Algonquian language of the Pequots, dialectally related to Mohegan and Montauk. — **Pe′quot** adj.

Pe·rei·ra (pə-rĕr′ə, pĕ-rā′rä). A city of west-central Colombia west of Bogotá. It is a distribution center for a coffee, livestock, and mineral region. ⊛ Pop. 241,927.

Per·ga·mum (pûr′gə-məm). An ancient Greek city and kingdom of western Asia Minor in modern-day western Turkey. It passed to Rome in the second century B.C. and was noted for its sculpture and its library, which Mark Antony gave to Cleopatra.

Per·i·bon·ca (pĕr′ə-bŏng′kə). A river, about 451 km (280 mi) long, of central Quebec, Canada, flowing southward through **Peribonca Lake** to Lake St. John.

Perm (pĕrm, pyĕrm). A city of west-central Russia on the Kama River in the foothills of the Ural Mountains. Settled since early times, it grew rapidly as an industrial center in the 19th century. ⊛ Pop. 1,091,056.

Per·pi·gnan (pĕr-pē-nyän′). A city of southern France near the Spanish border and the Mediterranean Sea. Probably founded in the 10th century, it was capital of the Spanish kingdom of Roussillon after the 12th century and became part of France in 1659. ⊛ Pop. 105,869.

Per·rine (pûr′īn′). An unincorporated community of southeast Florida southwest of Miami on Biscayne Bay. ⊛ Pop. 15,576.

Per·sep·o·lis (pər-sĕp′ə-lĭs). An ancient city of Persia northeast of modern Shiraz in southwest Iran. It was the ceremonial capital of the Persian king Darius I (550?–486 B.C.) and his successors. Its ruins include the palaces of Darius and his son Xerxes (519?–465) and a citadel that contained the treasury looted by Alexander the Great.

Per·sia (pûr′zhə, -shə). abbr. **Pers. 1.** also **Per·**

sian Empire (-zhən, -shən). A vast empire of southwest Asia founded by Cyrus II after 546 B.C. and brought to the height of its power and glory by his son Darius I (ruled 521–486) and his grandson Xerxes (ruled 486–465). Eventually the empire extended from the Indus River valley in present-day Pakistan to the Mediterranean Sea before Alexander the Great conquered it between 333 and 331 B.C. A later empire was established by the Sassanids (A.D. 226–637). **2.** See **Iran.**

Per·sian (pûr′zhən, -shən). *abbr.* **Pers. 1.** Of or relating to Persia or Iran, or to their peoples, languages, or cultures. **2.** A native or inhabitant of Persia or Iran. **3.** Any of the western Iranian dialects or languages of ancient or medieval Persia and modern Iran.

Persian Gulf also **A·ra·bi·an Gulf** (ə-rā′bē-ən). An arm of the Arabian Sea between the Arabian Peninsula and southwest Iran. It has been an important trade route since ancient times and gained added strategic significance after the discovery of oil in the Gulf States in the 1930's.

Perth (pûrth). **1.** A city of southwest Australia near the Indian Ocean. Founded in 1829, it grew rapidly after the discovery of gold in the region in the 1890's. ◉Pop. 1,018,702. **2.** A burgh of central Scotland north-northwest of Edinburgh on the Tay River. The capital of Scotland from the 11th to the mid-15th century, it was the site of a sermon against idolatry given by John Knox, the founder of Scottish Presbyterianism, in 1559. ◉Pop. 42,000.

Perth Am·boy (ăm′boi′). A city of east-central New Jersey on Raritan Bay opposite Staten Island. It was settled in the late 17th century and is today an industrial center and port of entry. The city was a summer resort during the first half of the 19th century. ◉Pop. 41,967.

Pe·ru (pə-rōō′). A country of western South America on the Pacific Ocean. Inhabited since at least the 9th millennium B.C., it was the center of an Incan empire established after the 12th century A.D. The Spanish under conquistador Francisco Pizarro conquered the empire in 1533 and set up in 1542 the viceroyalty of Peru, which at one time included Panama and all of Spanish South America except Venezuela. Independence from Spain was declared in 1821 and achieved militarily in 1824. Frequent revolutions and dictatorships dominated Peruvian political life thereafter, with brief periods of democratic rule in the 1940's and 1980's. Social disruption related to drug trafficking and the terrorist activities of the Communist Shining Path guerrillas prompted president Alberto Fujimori (elected 1990) to suspend the constitution in 1992, with a new constitution being approved in 1993.

Lima is the capital and the largest city. ◉Pop. 23,088,000. **— Pe·ru′vi·an** (-vē-ən) *adj. & n.*

Peru Current. See **Humboldt Current.**

Pe·ru·gia (pə-rōō′jə, -jē-ə, pĕ-rōō′jä). A city of central Italy on a hill overlooking the Tiber River north of Rome. An important Etruscan settlement, it fell to the Romans c. 310 B.C. and became a Lombard duchy in A.D. 592 and a free city in the 12th century. Perugia was later the artistic center of Umbria and is today a commercial, industrial, and tourist center. ◉Pop. 143,698. **— Pe·ru′gian** *adj. & n.*

Pe·sa·ro (pā′zə-rō′, pĕ′zä-rô). A city of north-central Italy on the Adriatic Sea west of Florence. On the site of a Roman colony, it became part of the Papal States in 1631. ◉Pop. 90,147.

Pes·ca·do·res (pĕs′kə-dôr′ēz, -ĭs, -dôr′-). In Pinyin **Peng·hu** (pŭng′hōō′). An island group of Taiwan in Taiwan Strait between the western coast of Taiwan and southwest China. The name, meaning "fishermen's islands," was given to the group by the Portuguese in the 16th century. Ceded to Japan in 1895 and returned to China after World War II, the islands have been administered by Taiwan since 1949.

Pes·ca·ra (pə-skär′ə, pĕ-skä′rä). A city of central Italy on the Adriatic Sea east-northeast of Rome. It is an industrial and commercial center. ◉Pop. 121,367.

Pe·sha·war (pə-shä′wər). A city of northwest Pakistan northwest of Lahore. It has long been strategically important for its proximity to the Khyber Pass. ◉Pop. 566,248.

Pes·sac (pĕ-săk′, pə-säk′). A city of southwest France, a suburb of Bordeaux. It is a distributing center of a wine-producing area. ◉Pop. 50,267.

Pest (pĕst, pĕsht). A former town of north-central Hungary on the left bank of the Danube River. Since 1873 it has been part of Budapest.

Pe·tah Tiq·wa (pĕt′ə tĭk′və, -vä, pĕ′täкн). A city of central Israel east of Tel Aviv–Jaffa. Founded in 1878, it is an industrial center in an agricultural region. ⊛ Pop. 151,000.

Pet·a·lu·ma (pĕt′l-ōō′mə). A city of western California north-northwest of San Rafael. It was founded in 1833 and is a trade and processing center. ⊛ Pop. 43,184.

Pe·ter·bor·ough (pē′tər-bûr′ə, -bər-ə, -bŭr′-ō). **1.** A city of southeast Ontario, Canada, northeast of Toronto. Settled in the 1820's as a lumbering town, it is now an industrial center and a railroad junction. ⊛ Pop. 60,620. **2.** A municipal borough of east-central England east of Leicester. Catherine of Aragon, first wife of King Henry VIII, is buried in the cathedral here. ⊛ Pop. 156,375.

Pe·ters·burg (pē′tərz-bûrg′). An independent city of southeast Virginia on the Appomattox River south of Richmond. A prolonged siege (June 15, 1864–April 3, 1865) during the Civil War led to the fall of Richmond and the subsequent surrender of the Confederate general Robert E. Lee. ⊛ Pop. 38,386.

Pe·tra (pē′trə, pĕt′rə). An ancient ruined city of Edom in present-day southwest Jordan. It flourished as a trade center from the 4th century B.C. until its capture by the Romans in A.D. 106. The city was taken by Muslims in the 7th century and by Crusaders in the 12th century. The ruins of the "rose-red city" were discovered in 1812.

Pet·ri·fied Forest (pĕt′rə-fīd′). A section of the Painted Desert in eastern Arizona reserved for its stonelike trees dating from the Triassic Period, 195 million to 230 million years ago.

Pet·ro·grad (pĕt′rə-grăd′, pyĭ-trə-grät′). See **Saint Petersburg.**

Pet·ro·pav·lovsk (pĕt′rə-păv′lôfsk′, pyĭ-trə-păv′ləfsk). **1.** A city of north-central Kazakstan west of Novosibirsk, Russia. It was founded as a fort in 1752. ⊛ Pop. 248,000. **2.** or **Pet·ro·pav·lovsk-Kam·chat·ski** (-kăm-chät′skē, -kə-chyät′-). A city of eastern Russia on the Pacific coast of the Kamchatka Peninsula. Ice-free seven months a year, it is a major port and naval base. ⊛ Pop. 265,254.

Pe·tróp·o·lis (pə-trŏp′ə-lĭs, pĭ-trô′pōō-). A city of southeast Brazil north of Rio de Janeiro. Mainly residential with some light industry, it was formerly the summer residence of the Brazilian emperor Dom Pedro II (ruled 1831–1889). ⊛ Pop. 255,261.

Pet·ro·za·vodsk (pĕt′rə-zə-vŏtsk′, pyĭ-trə-zə-vôtsk′). A city of northwest Russia on Lake Onega northeast of St. Petersburg. Peter the

Great built an ironworks here in 1703. ⊛ Pop. 278,986.

Pforz·heim (fôrts′hīm, fōrts′-, pfôrts′-). A city of southwest Germany west-northwest of Stuttgart. Chartered c. 1195, it has an important jewelry and watchmaking industry. ⊛ Pop. 117,450.

Pharr (fär). A city of extreme southern Texas west-northwest of Brownsville. It is a processing and distribution center. ⊛ Pop. 32,921.

Phar·sa·lus (fär-sā′ləs) or **Phar·sa·la** (fär′sä-lä). An ancient city of Thessaly in northeast Greece. Julius Caesar decisively defeated his political enemy Pompey nearby in 48 B.C.

Phe·nix City (fē′nĭks). A city of eastern Alabama on the Chattahoochee River across from Columbus, Georgia. It is a processing center in a cotton-growing area. ⊛ Pop. 25,312.

Phil·a·del·phi·a (fĭl′ə-dĕl′fē-ə). **1.** An ancient city of Asia Minor northeast of the Dead Sea in modern-day Jordan. The chief city of the Ammonites, it was enlarged and embellished by Ptolemy II Philadelphus (285–246 B.C.) and named in honor of him. Amman, the capital of Jordan, is now on the site. **2.** The largest city of Pennsylvania, in the southeast part of the state on the Delaware River. It was founded as a Quaker colony by William Penn in 1681 on the site of an earlier Swedish settlement. The First and Second Continental Congresses (1774 and 1775–1776) and the Constitutional Convention (1787) met in the city, which served as the capital of the United States from 1790 to 1800. ⊛ Pop. 1,585,577. — **Phil′a·del′phi·an** adj.

Phi·lae (fī′lē). A former island in the Nile River of southeast Egypt. Site of many ancient temples and monuments, it was particularly noted for its temple dedicated to Isis. The island is now covered by the waters of Lake Nasser.

Phi·lip·pi (fĭ-lĭp′ī). An ancient town of north-central Macedonia, Greece, near the Aegean Sea. It was the site of Octavian (later Augustus) and Mark Antony's decisive defeat of Brutus and Cassius, co-conspirators in the assassination of Julius Caesar, in 42 B.C. — **Phi·lip′pi·an** (-lĭp′-ē-ən) adj. & n.

Phil·ip·pines (fĭl′ə-pēnz′, fĭl′ə-pēnz′). abbr. **Phil.** A country of eastern Asia consisting of the **Philippine Islands,** an archipelago in the western Pacific Ocean southeast of China. Inhabited principally by Malays and various indigenous groups, the islands were first sighted by the Portuguese navigator Ferdinand Magellan in 1521 and were colonized by the Spanish after 1565. They came under U.S. control in 1898 as a result of Spain's defeat in the Spanish-American War. Growing nationalist sentiment prompted the creation of a self-governing commonwealth in 1934, with full independence following in 1946. The islands were occupied by Japan during much of World War II. Political turmoil led to the dictatorship of Ferdinand Marcos after 1965 and his exile in 1986 following the election of Corazon Aquino, widow of the assassinated (1983) opposition leader Benigno Aquino. A long U.S. military presence in the islands was ended in the early 1990's when Clark Air Base was abandoned and the Subic Bay naval base was turned over to the Philippine government. Manila is the capital and the largest city. ● Pop. 67,038,000. — **Phil′ip·pine** *adj.*

Philippine Sea. A section of the western Pacific Ocean east of the Philippines and west of the Marianas.

Phi·lis·ti·a (fĭ-lĭs′tē-ə). An ancient region of southwest Palestine. Strategically located on a trade route from Egypt to Syria, the cities of the region formed a loose confederacy important in biblical times.

Phil·is·tine (fĭl′ĭ-stēn′, fĭ-lĭs′tĭn, -tēn′). **1.** A member of an Aegean people who settled ancient Philistia around the 12th century B.C. **2.** Of or relating to ancient Philistia.

Phil·lips·burg (fĭl′ĭps-bûrg′). A town of northwest New Jersey on the Delaware River northwest of Trenton. Settled in the early 1700's, it is an industrial center. ● Pop. 15,757.

Phnom Penh (pə-nôm′ pĕn′, nŏm′). The capital and largest city of Cambodia, in the southwest part of the country on the Mekong River. It was founded in the 14th century and became the capital of the Khmer Empire after c. 1432 and the capital of Cambodia in 1867. The city suffered greatly during civil strife in the country beginning in 1970, when refugees from the war-torn countryside swelled the city's population. In 1975 Phnom Penh fell to the Khmer Rouge, who evacuated it as part of their extreme communist program. The city was revived in the 1980's after the overthrow of the Khmer Rouge (1979). ● Pop. 400,000.

Pho·cae·a (fō-sē′ə). An ancient Ionian Greek city of western Asia Minor on the Aegean Sea in present-day Turkey. It was an important maritime state c. 1000 to 600 B.C. but declined after a Persian siege in 540.

Pho·cis (fō′sĭs). A historical region of central Greece north of the Gulf of Corinth. In early times (before 590 B.C.) it controlled the oracle at Delphi. The region was ultimately conquered by Philip II of Macedon (346 B.C.).

Phoe·ni·cia (fĭ-nĭsh′ə, -nē′shə). An ancient maritime country of southwest Asia consisting of city-states along the eastern Mediterranean Sea in present-day Syria and Lebanon. Its people became the foremost navigators and traders of the Mediterranean by 1250 B.C. and established numerous colonies, including Carthage in northern Africa. The Phoenicians traveled to the edges of the known world at the time and introduced their alphabet, which was based on symbols for sounds rather than cuneiform or hieroglyphic representations, to the Greeks and other early peoples. Phoenicia's culture was gradually absorbed by Persian and later Hellenistic civilizations.

Phoe·ni·cian (fĭ-nĭsh′ən, -nē′shən). **1.** Of or relating to ancient Phoenicia or its people, language, or culture. **2.** A native or inhabitant of ancient Phoenicia. **3.** The Semitic language of ancient Phoenicia.

Phoe·nix (fē′nĭks). The capital and largest city of Arizona, in the south-central part of the state northwest of Tucson. Settled c. 1868, it became territorial capital in 1889 and state capital in 1912. The city is noted as a winter and health resort. ● Pop. 983,403.

Phoenix Islands. A group of eight small islands in the central Pacific Ocean north of Samoa. Discovered between 1823 and 1840 by British and American explorers, they were administered at various times by one or both of the countries and are now part of Kiribati.

pho·to·map (fō′tə-măp′). A map made by superimposing orienting data and markings on an aerial photograph.

Phryg·i·a (frĭj′ē-ə). An ancient region of central Asia Minor in modern-day central Turkey. It was settled c. 1200 B.C. and flourished from the eighth to the sixth century, after which it came under the influence of Lydia, Persia, Greece, Rome, and Byzantium.

Phryg·i·an (frĭj′ē-ən). **1.** Of or relating to Phrygia or its people, language, or culture. **2.** A native or inhabitant of Phrygia. **3.** The Indo-European language of the Phrygians.

phys·i·cal geography (fĭz′ĭ-kəl). The study of the natural features of the earth's surface, especially in its current aspects, including land formation, climate, currents, and distribution of flora and fauna.

Pia·cen·za (pyä-chĕn′zə, -tsä). A town of northern Italy on the Po River southeast of Milan. Founded by the Romans as Placentia in 218 B.C., it was occupied by Goths, Franks, and Lombards and became a free city and part of the Lombard League in the 12th century. ⊛ Pop. 102,252.

Pi·at·ra Ne·amt (pē-ä′trə nē-äms′, pyä′trä nyämts′). A city of northeast Romania in the foothills of the Carpathian Mountains. It is a processing and industrial center. ⊛ Pop. 125,157.

Pic·ar·dy (pĭk′ər-dē). A historical region of northern France bordering on the English Channel. The name was first used in the 13th century for a number of small feudal holdings. Picardy was contested by France and England during the Hundred Years' War (1337–1453) and became part of the French crown lands in 1477.

Pic·ca·dil·ly Cir·cus (pĭk′ə-dĭl′ē sûr′kəs). A traffic junction and popular meeting place in western London, England, noted for the statue known as *Eros*.

Pick·er·ing (pĭk′ər-ĭng). A town of southern Ontario, Canada, a suburb of Toronto on Lake Ontario. ⊛ Pop. 37,754.

Pi·co Ri·ve·ra (pē′kō rə-vîr′ə). A city of southern California, an industrial suburb of Los Angeles. ⊛ Pop. 59,177.

Pict (pĭkt). One of an ancient people of northern Britain. They remained undefeated by the Romans and in the mid-ninth century joined with the Scots to form a kingdom that later became Scotland.

Pict·ish (pĭk′tĭsh). **1.** Of or relating to the Picts or their language or culture. **2.** The language of the Picts, of uncertain affiliation, known chiefly from place names and extinct by the tenth century.

pidg·in (pĭj′ən). A simplified form of speech that is usually a mixture of two or more languages, has a rudimentary grammar and vocabulary, is used for communication between groups speaking different languages, and is not spoken as a first or native language. — **pidg′in·i·za′tion** *n.* — **pidg′in·ize′** *v.*

Pidg·in English also **pidg·in English** (pĭj′ən). Any of several pidgins based on English and now spoken mostly on the Pacific islands and in West Africa.

pied·mont (pēd′mŏnt′). **1.** An area of land formed or lying at the foot of a mountain or mountain range. **2.** Of, relating to, or constituting such an area of land.

Pied·mont (pēd′mŏnt′). **1.** A historical region of northwest Italy bordering on France and Switzerland. Occupied by Rome in the 1st century B.C., it passed to Savoy in the 11th century and was the center (after 1814) of the Italian Risorgimento, the nationalist movement that later led to the unification of Italy. **2.** A plateau region of the eastern United States extending from New York to Alabama between the Appalachian Mountains and the Atlantic coastal plain. — **Pied′mon·tese′** (-tēz′, -tēs′) *adj. & n.*

Pie·gan (pē-găn′). *pl.* **Piegan** or **-gans.** A member of the southernmost tribe of the Blackfoot confederacy, inhabiting northwest Montana and southern Alberta.

Pi·e·ri·a (pī-îr′ē-ə). A region of ancient Macedonia. It included Mount Olympus and Mount Pierus, seat of the worship of Orpheus, the legendary Thracian poet and musician, and the Muses, the daughters of Zeus who presided over the different arts and sciences.

Pierre (pîr). The capital of South Dakota, in the central part of the state on the Missouri River. Originally a small trading center, it thrived after the coming of the railroad and was chosen as state capital in 1889. ⊛ Pop. 12,906.

Pierre·fonds (pē-ĕr-fôn′, pyĕr-). A city of southern Quebec, Canada, on Montreal Island west of Montreal. ⊛ Pop. 38,390.

Pigs (pĭgz), **Bay of.** A small inlet of the Caribbean Sea on the southern coast of western Cuba. It was the site of an ill-fated invasion on April 17, 1961, when a force of 1,500 U.S.-trained guerrilla troops landed in an attempt to overthrow the government of Fidel Castro.

pike (pīk). *Chiefly British.* A hill with a pointed summit.

Pikes Peak (pīks). A mountain, 4,303.6 m (14,110 ft) high, in the Front Range of the Rocky Mountains in central Colorado. It was discovered in 1806 by the American explorer Zebulon M. Pike and is noted for the spectacular view from its summit.

Pikes·ville (pīks′vĭl′). An unincorporated community of north-central Maryland, a residential suburb of Baltimore. ⊛ Pop. 24,815.

Pi·la·tus (pĭ-lä′təs, pē-lä′tōōs). A peak, 2,121.3 m (6,955 ft) high, in the Alps of central Switzerland south-southwest of Lucerne. According to medieval folklore, the body of Pontius Pilate was thrown into a small lake on the mountain.

Pil·co·ma·yo (pĭl′kō-mä′yō, pēl′-). A river of central South America rising in central Bolivia and flowing about 1,609 km (1,000 mi) southeast along the Argentina-Paraguay border to the Paraguay River.

Pi·li·pi·no (pĭl′ə-pē′nō). The Filipino language.

Pil·lars of Her·cu·les (pĭl′ərz; hûr′kyə-lēz′). The ancient name for two promontories at the eastern end of the Strait of Gibraltar and the entrance to the Mediterranean Sea. They are usually identified as Gibraltar in Europe and Jebel Musa in North Africa.

Pi·ma (pē′mə). **1.** *pl.* **Pima** or **-mas.** A member of a Native American people inhabiting south-

central Arizona along the Gila and Salt rivers.
2. The Uto-Aztecan language of the Pimas, dialectally related to Papago. **—Pi′man** *adj.*

Pi·nang (pə-näng′, pē′näng′). See **George Town** (sense 1).

Pin·a·tu·bo (pĭn′ə-tōō′bō), **Mount.** An active volcano, 1,699 m (5,771 ft) high, of the Philippines, in the west-central part of Luzon Island northwest of Manila. It erupted catastrophically in June 1991 after 600 years of inactivity, killing hundreds of people and burying hundreds of square miles under volcanic ash.

Pin·dus Mountains (pĭn′dəs). A range of mountains extending about 161 km (100 mi) south from the southern border of Albania to northwest Greece and rising to 2,638.3 m (8,650 ft). They formed the border between ancient Thessaly and Epirus.

Pine Bar·rens (pīn băr′ənz). A coastal plain region of southeast-central and southern New Jersey. Its extensive forests of pine, cedar, and oak were all but exhausted by the 1860's as the result of indiscriminate cutting for shipbuilding and charcoal making.

Pine Bluff (blŭf′). A city of southeast-central Arkansas south-southeast of Little Rock. It was founded c. 1820 as Mount Marie and was renamed in 1832. Pine Bluff is an industrial and agricultural-marketing center. A branch of the University of Arkansas (established 1873) is located here. ⦿ Pop. 57,140.

Pine Hills A community of central Florida, a suburb of Orlando. ⦿ Pop. 35,322.

Pi·nel·las Park (pĭ-nĕl′əs). A city of west-central Florida, an industrial suburb of St. Petersburg. ⦿ Pop. 43,426.

Pines (pīnz), **Isle of.** See **Isle of Youth.**

Ping (pĭng). A river, about 563 km (350 mi) long, of western Thailand. It is a major tributary of the Chao Phraya.

pin·go (pĭng′gō). An Arctic mound or conical hill, consisting of an outer layer of soil covering a core of solid ice.

Pinsk (pĭnsk, pyēnsk). A city of southwest Belarus south-southwest of Minsk. First mentioned in chronicles in 1097, it was the capital of the Pinsk duchy in the 13th century. Pinsk passed to Lithuania in 1320, to Poland in 1569, to Russia in 1793, back to Poland in 1921, and then to the U.S.S.R. in 1945. ⦿ Pop. 128,300.

Pin·yin or **pin·yin** (pĭn′yĭn′, -yĭn). A system for transliterating Chinese ideograms into the Roman alphabet, officially adopted by the People's Republic of China in 1979 and replacing the older Wade-Giles system. Pinyin is not used in Taiwan.

Piq·ua (pĭk′wā′, -wə). A city of west-central Ohio north of Dayton. A supply base in the War of 1812, it is now an industrial center. ⦿ Pop. 20,612.

Pi·ra·ci·ca·ba (pĭr′ə-sĭ-kä′bə, pē′rä-sĭ-kä′bä). A city of southeast Brazil northwest of São Paulo. It is a trade and shipping center with a noted agricultural institute. ⦿ Pop. 283,634.

Pi·rae·us (pī-rē′əs, pī-rā′-). A city of east-central Greece on the Saronic Gulf southwest of Athens. Its port was built in the 5th century B.C. and after extensive development in the mid-19th century became the principal seaport of the country. In ancient times it was connected with Athens by the Long Walls, two parallel walls built approximately 183 m (600 ft) apart. ⦿ Pop. 196,389.

Pi·sa (pē′zə, -zä). A city of western Italy on the Arno River near the Tyrrhenian Sea. An important Etruscan town, it developed into a powerful maritime republic in the 9th to 11th centuries but was crushed by Genoa in 1284. Florence controlled the city from 1406 to 1509. The campanile of its cathedral, built 1174–c. 1350, is the famed Leaning Tower of Pisa. ⦿ Pop. 98,006. **—Pi′san** *adj. & n.*

Pis·cat·a·way (pĭs-kăt′ə-wā′). A community of north-central New Jersey north of New Brunswick. Founded before 1693, it is a manufacturing center. ⦿ Pop. 42,223.

Pis·to·ia (pĭ-stoi′ə, pē -stō′yä). A city of north-central Italy northwest of Florence. Settled by Romans in the 6th century B.C., it was an important banking center in the 13th century A.D. and came under the influence of Florence in the 14th century. ⦿ Pop. 83,600.

Pit·cairn Island (pĭt′kârn′). A volcanic island of the southern Pacific Ocean east-southeast of Tahiti. Discovered by a British navigator in 1767, it was settled in 1790 by mutineers from H.M.S. *Bounty* and has been administered by the British since 1839. Descendants of the original settlers still live on the island.

Pi·teş·ti (pĭ-tĕsh′tĭ). A city of south-central Romania west-northwest of Bucharest. It is a commercial center and an important rail junction. ⦿ Pop. 182,931.

Pit River¹ (pĭt). See **Achomawi** (sense 1).

Pit River² (pĭt). A river, about 322 km (200 mi) long, of northern California flowing south and west to the Sacramento River.

Pitts·burg (pĭts′bûrg′). **1.** A city of western California at the junction of the Sacramento and San Joaquin rivers northeast of Oakland. It is a manufacturing center in a fishing and farming region. ⦿ Pop. 47,564. **2.** A city of southeast Kansas near the Missouri border. Founded in 1876 as a mining town, it now has diversified industries. ⦿ Pop. 17,775.

Pitts·burgh (pĭts′bûrg′). A city of southwest

Pennsylvania at the point where the confluence of the Allegheny and Monongahela rivers forms the Ohio River. Fort Duquesne was built on the site by the French c. 1750 and fell to the British in 1758, when it was renamed Fort Pitt. The village surrounding the fort grew rapidly after the opening of the Northwest Territory. The city today is highly industrialized. ◉ Pop. 369,879.

Pitts·field (pĭts'fēld'). A city of western Massachusetts northwest of Springfield near the New York border. It is a center of the Berkshire Hills resort area. ◉ Pop. 48,622.

Piu·ra (pyo͞or'ə, pyo͞o'rä). A city of northwest Peru near the Pacific Ocean. Founded by the Spanish explorer Francisco Pizarro in 1532, it is the oldest Spanish settlement in Peru. ◉ Pop. 306,500.

Pi·ute (pī'yo͞ot'). Variant of **Paiute.**

Pla·cen·tia (plə-sĕn'chə, -shə). A city of southern California east-northeast of Long Beach. It is a residential community with light industries. ◉ Pop. 41,259.

Placentia Bay. An inlet of the Atlantic Ocean in southeast Newfoundland, Canada. On August 14, 1941, Franklin D. Roosevelt and Winston Churchill signed the Atlantic Charter, setting forth the Allied aims for a postwar settlement, while aboard the British battleship *Prince of Wales* anchored in the bay.

Plac·er·ville (plăs'ər-vĭl'). A city of east-central California east-northeast of Sacramento. It grew with the discovery of gold nearby in 1848 and is still a mining center. ◉ Pop. 8,355.

Plac·id (plăs'ĭd), **Lake.** A lake of northeast New York in the Adirondack Mountains. It is a noted winter sports center.

Plain·field (plān'fēld'). A city of northeast New Jersey southwest of Newark. Settled in 1684, it was formerly a residential town but has now become a trade and industrial center in a thickly populated area. ◉ Pop. 46,567.

Plains Indian (plānz). A member of any of the Native American peoples inhabiting the Great Plains of the United States and Canada. The Plains Indians spoke a variety of unrelated languages but shared certain cultural features such as nomadic buffalo hunting, the use of conical tepees, and a reliance on the horse in hunting and warfare.

Plain·view (plān'vyo͞o'). **1.** An unincorporated community of southeast New York on western Long Island. It is mainly residential. ◉ Pop. 26,207. **2.** A city of northwest Texas south of Amarillo. The city has large meat-packing and meat-processing industries. ◉ Pop. 21,700.

Plain·ville (plān'vĭl'). A town of central Connecticut southwest of Hartford. It is a manufacturing center in a farming area. ◉ Pop. 17,392.

Pla·no (plā'nō). A city of northeast Texas, a manufacturing suburb of Dallas. Settled in 1845, it grew rapidly after 1960. ◉ Pop. 128,713.

Plan·ta·tion (plăn-tā'shən). A city of southeast Florida, a residential suburb of Fort Lauderdale. ◉ Pop. 48,501.

Plant City (plănt). A city of west-central Florida east of Tampa. It is a processing and shipping center in a farming region. ◉ Pop. 22,754.

Pla·ta (plä'tə, -tä), **Río de la.** A wide estuary of southeast South America between Argentina and Uruguay formed by the Paraná and Uruguay rivers and opening on the Atlantic Ocean. It was explored by Ferdinand Magellan in 1520 and Sebastian Cabot from 1526 to 1529.

Pla·tae·a (plə-tē'ə). An ancient city of central Greece southwest of Thebes. It was the site of a major Greek victory over the Persians in 479 B.C. Between 431 and 373 B.C. it was attacked and destroyed by Thebes three times.

plate (plāt). *Geology.* In the theory of plate tectonics, one of the sections into which the earth's crust is divided, with each plate being in constant motion relative to other plates.

pla·teau (plă-tō'). *abbr.* **plat.** An elevated, comparatively level expanse of land; a tableland.

plate tectonics. A theory of global dynamics having to do with the movement of a small number of semirigid sections of the earth's crust, with seismic activity and volcanism occurring primarily at the margins of these sections. This movement has resulted in continental drift and changes in the shape and size of ocean basins and continents.

Platt·deutsch (plät'doich'). See **Low German** (sense 1).

Platte (plăt). A river, about 499 km (310 mi) long, of central Nebraska formed by the confluence of the North Platte and South Platte rivers and flowing eastward to the Missouri River at the Iowa border below Omaha.

Platts·burgh (plăts'bûrg'). A city of extreme northeast New York on Lake Champlain northwest of Burlington, Vermont. During the War of 1812 an American fleet decisively defeated the British in a naval battle here on September 11, 1814. ◉ Pop. 21,255.

Plau·en (plou'ən). A city of east-central Germany south-southwest of Leipzig. Founded by Slavs in the 12th century, it passed to Bohemia in 1327 and to Saxony in 1466 and was severely damaged in World War II. Its manufactures include textiles and machinery. ◉ Pop. 78,797.

pla·ya (plī'ə). A nearly level area at the bottom of an undrained desert basin, sometimes temporarily covered with water.

Pleas·ant Hill (plĕz'ənt). A city of western

California northeast of Berkeley. It is mainly residential. ◉ Pop. 31,585.

Pleasant Island. See **Nauru.**

Pleas·an·ton (plĕz′ən-tən). A city of western California southeast of Oakland. It is a residential and processing center in a grape-growing rè-gion. ◉ Pop. 50,553.

Pleas·ure Ridge Park (plĕzh′ər). An unincorporated community of north-central Kentucky, a residential suburb of Louisville. ◉ Pop. 25,131.

Plev·en (plĕv′ən, -ĕn) or **Plev·na** (-nə, -nä). A city of northern Bulgaria northeast of Sofia. Settled by Thracians, it was ruled by Turkey from the 15th to the 19th century. ◉ Pop. 130,747.

Plock (pwôtsk). A city of central Poland on the Vistula River west-southwest of Warsaw. Known since the tenth century, it passed to Prussia in 1793 and to Russia in 1815. It reverted to Poland after World War I and is a port and major oil-refining center. ◉ Pop. 124,456.

Plo·ieş·ti or **Plo·eş·ti** (plô-yĕsht′, -yĕsh′tē). A city of southeast-central Romania north of Bucharest. Founded in 1596, it is the center of a major oil-producing region. ◉ Pop. 254,304.

Plov·div (plôv′dĭf′). A city of south-central Bulgaria on the Maritsa River southeast of Sofia. Originally built by Thracians, it fell to Macedonia in 341 B.C. and to Rome in 46 B.C. The city changed hands frequently in the Middle Ages and was controlled by Russia from 1877 to 1885. It is the second largest city of Bulgaria and a railroad junction and market town in a fertile agricultural region. ◉ Pop. 341,374.

Plum (plŭm). A borough of southwest Pennsylvania, a suburb of Pittsburgh. ◉ Pop. 25,609.

Plym·outh (plĭm′əth). **1.** A borough of southwest England on **Plymouth Sound,** an inlet of the English Channel. A major port, it was the point of embarkation for the fleet that fought the Spanish Armada (1588) and for Sir Francis Drake, Sir Walter Raleigh, and several other early explorers. ◉ Pop. 259,040. **2.** A town of southeast Massachusetts on **Plymouth Bay,** an inlet of the Atlantic Ocean, southeast of Boston. Founded in 1620 by Pilgrims, who supposedly set foot on **Plymouth Rock** when disembarking from the *Mayflower,* it was the center of **Plymouth Colony.** The colony was governed under precepts laid down in the Mayflower Compact until 1691, when it was absorbed by the royal colony of Massachusetts. ◉ Pop. 45,608. **3.** A city of southeast Minnesota, a suburb of Minneapolis–St. Paul. ◉ Pop. 50,889.

Plzeň (pəl′zĕn′, -zĕn′yə). A city of western Czech Republic southwest of Prague. Founded in 1290, the city was an important trade center of Bohemia. It was part of the Austro-Hungarian Empire until its inclusion in the newly formed

country of Czechoslovakia in 1918. Plzeň is renowned for its beer (Pilsner) and its machine manufactures. ◉ Pop. 175,500.

Po (pō). A river of northern Italy flowing about 652 km (405 mi) generally eastward to the Adriatic Sea. The Po Valley is a major industrial and agricultural area.

Po·be·da Peak (pō-bĕd′ə, pə-byĕ′də). A mountain, 7,443.8 m (24,406 ft) high, of the Tien Shan on the border between eastern Kyrgyzstan and western China. It is the highest elevation in the range.

Po·ca·tel·lo (pō′kə-tĕl′ō, -tĕl′ə). A city of southeast Idaho south-southwest of Idaho Falls. It has been a railroad junction since 1882 and is the seat of Idaho State University (founded 1901). ◉ Pop. 46,080.

Po·co·no Mountains (pō′kə-nō′). A range of the Appalachian system in northeast Pennsylvania rising to about 488 m (1,600 ft). The Poconos are a popular year-round resort area.

po·co·sin (pə-kō′sĭn). *Chiefly South Atlantic U.S.* A swamp in an upland coastal region.

Pod·go·ri·ca (pŏd′gə-rēt′sə). Formerly **Ti·to·grad** (tē′tō-grăd′, -gräd′). A city of southern Yugoslavia. Known since ancient times, it is the capital of Montenegro and a commercial center with various industries. ◉ Pop. 118,059.

Po·dolsk (pə-dôlsk′). A city of west-central Russia south of Moscow. It was a frequent meeting place for Lenin and his followers prior to the Bolshevik Revolution (1917). Podolsk is an industrial center in a fertile agricultural region. ◉ Pop. 203,850.

Po Hai (bō′ hī′). See **Bo Hai.**

Po·hang (pō′häng′). A city of southeast South Korea on an inlet of the Sea of Japan northnortheast of Pusan. It is a processing center with heavy industries. ◉ Pop. 317,768.

Pohn·pei (pōn′pā′) or **Po·na·pe** (pō′nə-pā′). An island of the Federated States of Micronesia in the Caroline Islands of the western Pacific Ocean. Palikir, the capital of the Federated States of Micronesia, is located here.

Pointe aux Trem·bles (pwănt ō trăN′blə). A city of southern Quebec, Canada, a residential suburb of Montreal on northeast Montreal Island. ◉ Pop. 36,270.

Pointe Claire (point′ klâr′, pwănt). A city of southern Quebec, Canada, a suburb of Montreal on southwest Montreal Island. It is mainly residential. ◉ Pop. 24,571.

Point Pleasant (point). A borough of eastern New Jersey near the Atlantic Ocean south of Asbury Park. It is a residential and resort community. ◉ Pop. 18,177.

Point Suc·cess (sək-sĕs′). A peak, 4,318.2 m (14,158 ft) high, in the Cascade Range of west-central Washington near Mount Rainier.

Poi·tiers (pwä-tyā′). A city of west-central France east-southeast of Nantes. Settled by a Gallic people, it was an early Christian center with important monasteries. Nearby, Edward the Black Prince of England defeated and captured John II of France on September 19, 1356. ◉ Pop. 79,350.

Poi·tou (pwä-tōō′). A historical region of west-central France bordering on the Bay of Biscay. A part of the Roman province of Aquitania, it fell to the Visigoths (A.D. 418) and the Franks (507) and was frequently contested by France and England until the end of the Hundred Years' War, (1337–1453), when it was incorporated into the French crown lands.

Po·land (pō′lənd). *abbr.* **Pol.** A country of central Europe bordering on the Baltic Sea. Unified as a kingdom in the 10th century, it enjoyed a golden age under the Jagiello dynasty (1386–1572) and was a major power in the 15th and 16th centuries. National independence was lost in 1697, and it was carved up among Prussia, Austria, and Russia in three partitions (1772, 1793, and 1795) with Russia gaining the largest share. It then disappeared as a geographic entity until its reconstitution as a republic in 1918. In 1939 Poland was invaded by Germany, beginning World War II. Its present boundaries date from the end of the German occupation in 1945. In the years following the war several governments held power, including a Communist republic modeled after the Soviets. In 1980 strikes spread throughout the country, led by the independent trade union Solidarity under the leadership of Lech Walesa. Martial law was imposed (1981–1984), but in 1989 the government legalized Solidarity and granted it political-party status, and Walesa was elected president (1990–1995). Warsaw is the capital and the largest city. ◉ Pop. 38,544,000.

po·lar (pō′lər). Relating to, connected with, or located near the North Pole or South Pole.

polar cap. 1. Either of the regions around the poles of the earth that are permanently covered with ice. **2.** A high-altitude icecap.

polar circle. 1. The Arctic Circle. **2.** The Antarctic Circle.

Po·lar Regions (pō′lər). The various lands and waters surrounding the North Pole and the South Pole, known respectively as the **North Polar Region** and the **South Polar Region.**

pol·der (pōl′dər). An area of low-lying land, especially in the Netherlands, that has been reclaimed from a body of water and is protected by dikes.

pole (pōl). *abbr.* **p. 1.** Either extremity of an axis through a sphere. **2.** *Geography.* Either of the regions contiguous to the extremities of the earth's rotational axis, the North Pole or the South Pole. **3.** *Physics.* A magnetic pole.

Pole (pōl). **1.** A native or inhabitant of Poland. **2.** A person of Polish descent.

Po·lish (pō′lĭsh). *abbr.* **Pol. 1.** Of or relating to Poland or its people, their language, or culture. **2.** The Slavic language of the Poles.

Polish Corridor. A former strip of land between the German territories of Pomerania and East Prussia awarded to Poland by the Treaty of Versailles (1919) to afford access to the Baltic Sea. Friction over control of the area was an immediate cause of the German invasion of Poland (September 1, 1939) that marked the beginning of World War II.

Pol·ta·va (pəl-tä′və). A city of central Ukraine west-southwest of Kharkov. Probably settled by Slavic peoples in the 8th or 9th century, it was a Cossack stronghold in the 17th century. ◉ Pop. 323,600.

pol·y·con·ic projection (pŏl′ē-kŏn′ĭk). A conic map projection having distances between meridians along every parallel equal to those distances on a globe. The central geographic meridian is a straight line, whereas the others are curved and the parallels are arcs of circles.

Pol·y·ne·sia (pŏl′ə-nē′zhə, -shə). A division of Oceania including scattered islands of the central and southern Pacific Ocean roughly between New Zealand, Hawaii, and Easter Island. The larger islands are volcanic, the smaller ones generally coral formations.

Pol·y·ne·sian (pŏl′ə-nē′zhən, -shən). **1.** Of or relating to Polynesia or its peoples, languages, or cultures. **2.** A native or inhabitant of Polynesia. **3.** A subfamily of the Austronesian language family spoken in Polynesia.

po·lyn·ya (pŏl′ən-yä′, pə-lĭn′yə). An area of open water surrounded by sea ice.

Pom·er·a·ni·a (pŏm′ə-rā′nē-ə, -rān′yə). A historical region of north-central Europe bordering on the Baltic Sea in present-day northwest Poland and northeast Germany. It was inhabited by Slavic tribes in the 10th century and conquered by Poland in the 12th century. The territory was later split up and controlled by various powers, including the Holy Roman Empire, Prussia, Sweden, Denmark, and Germany.

Pom·er·a·ni·an (pŏm′ə-rā′nē-ən, -rān′yən). **1.** Of or relating to Pomerania or its people. **2.** A native or inhabitant of Pomerania.

Po·mo (pō′mō). **1.** *pl.* **Pomo** or **-mos.** A member of a group of Native American peoples inhabiting an area of the Coast Ranges of northern California. **2.** Any of the seven languages of the Pomos.

Po·mo·na[1] (pə-mō′nə). A city of southern California, a residential and industrial suburb of Los Angeles. ◉ Pop. 131,723.

Po·mo·na[2] (pə-mō′nə). See **Mainland Island.**

Pom·pa·no Beach (pŏm′pə-nō′). A city of southeast Florida on the Atlantic coast north of Miami. It is a resort community in a citrus and vegetable area. ◉ Pop. 72,411.

Pom·pe·ii (pŏm-pā′, -pā′ē). An ancient city of southern Italy southeast of Naples. Founded in the sixth or early fifth century B.C., it was a Roman colony by 80 B.C. and became a prosperous port and resort with many noted villas, temples, theaters, and baths. Pompeii was destroyed by an eruption of Mount Vesuvius in A.D. 79. The incredibly well-preserved ruins were rediscovered in 1748 and have been extensively excavated. — **Pom·pe′ian, Pom·pei′ian** *adj. & n.*

Po·na·pe (pō′nə-pā′). See **Pohnpei.**

Pon·ca (pŏng′kə). **1.** *pl.* **Ponca** or **-cas.** A member of a Native American people formerly inhabiting northeast Nebraska near the Niobrara River, with present-day populations in Oklahoma and Nebraska. The Poncas are closely related to the Omahas in language and history. **2.** The Siouan language of the Poncas, dialectally related to Omaha.

Ponca City. A city of northern Oklahoma on the Arkansas River north-northeast of Oklahoma City. It was founded in 1893 after the opening of the Cherokee Strip. ◉ Pop. 26,359.

Pon·ce (pôn′sā, -sĕ). A city of southern Puerto Rico southwest of San Juan. It is an agricultural trade and distribution center. ◉ Pop. 189,317.

pond (pŏnd). A still body of water smaller than a lake, often of artificial origin.

Pon·di·cher·ry (pŏn′dĭ-chĕr′ē, -shĕr′ē). A city of southeast India on the Bay of Bengal south-southwest of Madras. It consists of four former French coastal settlements whose administration was transferred to India in 1954. ◉ Pop. 203,065.

Pon·ta Del·ga·da (pŏn′tə dĕl-gä′də, pôN′-). A city of southwest São Miguel Island in the Azores. It is the chief commercial city of the island group. ◉ Pop. 21,187.

Ponta Gros·sa (grô′sä). A city of southern

Brazil west-northwest of Curitiba. It is a processing center in a farming and lumbering region. ◉ Pop. 233,857.

Pont·char·train (pŏn′chər-trān′), **Lake.** A lake of southeast Louisiana north of New Orleans. A causeway links New Orleans with the region north of the lake.

Pon·ti·ac (pŏn′tē-ăk′). A city of southeast Michigan northwest of Detroit. Its carriage-making industry of the 1880's was replaced by automobile manufacturing in the early 20th century. ◉ Pop. 71,166.

Pon·ti·a·nak (pŏn′tē-ä′näk). A city of western Borneo, Indonesia, at the northern edge of the Kapuas River delta. Capital of a sultanate founded in 1772, it later became a major gold-exporting center. ◉ Pop. 304,778.

Pon·tine Marshes (pŏn′tēn, -tīn). An area of central Italy between the Tyrrhenian Sea and the Apennine foothills. Once a malarial breeding ground, the land was drained during the 1930's to produce fertile farmland.

Pon·tus (pŏn′təs). An ancient country of northeast Asia Minor along the southern coast of the Black Sea. Established in the fourth century B.C., it flourished under Mithridates VI until his defeat by Pompey of Rome in 66 B.C. — **Pon′-tic** (-tĭk) *adj.*

Pon·ty·pool (pŏn′tə-pool′). An urban district of southeast Wales north-northeast of Cardiff. Its iron and tin industries began in the late 16th century. ◉ Pop. 90,300.

Poole (pool). A municipal borough of southern England west-southwest of Southampton on **Poole Bay,** an inlet of the English Channel. Chartered in 1248, Poole is a port and shipbuilding center with various other industries. ◉ Pop. 137,159.

Poo·na (poo′nə). A city of west-central India east-southeast of Bombay. It was a Maratha capital in the 17th and 18th centuries and passed to the British in 1818. ◉ Pop. 1,566,651.

Po·pa·yán (pō′pə-yän′, pô′pä-). A city of southwest Colombia south of Cali. Founded c. 1536, it was a prosperous trade center during the colonial era. ◉ Pop. 149,019.

Pop·lar Bluff (pŏp′lər). A city of southeast Missouri near the Arkansas border south of St. Louis. It is a trade, shipping, and manufacturing center in a farming area. ◉ Pop. 16,996.

Po·po·ca·té·petl (pō′pə-kăt′ə-pĕt′l, pô′pô-kä-tĕ′pĕt′l). A volcano, 5,455.5 m (17,887 ft) high, in central Mexico west of Puebla. It became active again in January 1994 after being dormant for decades.

Por·cu·pine River (pôr′kyə-pīn′). A river, about 721 km (448 mi) long, rising in northwest Yukon Territory, Canada, and flowing north then west to the Yukon River in northeast Alaska. It was explored by John Bell in 1842.

Por·de·no·ne (pôr′dn-ō′nē, -dĕ-nô′nĕ). A city of northeast Italy north-northeast of Venice. Controlled by Venice after 1508, it became part of Italy in 1866. ◉ Pop. 51,369.

Po·ri (pôr′ē). A city of southwest Finland on an inlet of the Gulf of Bothnia northwest of Helsinki. Chartered in 1564, it was initially dominated by the Hanseatic League. ◉ Pop. 78,933.

port (pôrt, pōrt). *abbr.* **pt. 1. a.** A place on a waterway with facilities for loading and unloading ships. **b.** A city or town on a waterway with such facilities. **2.** A place along a coast that gives ships and boats protection from storms and rough water; a harbor. **3.** A port of entry.

Por·tage (pôr′tĭj, pōr′-). **1.** A city of northwest Indiana, an industrial suburb of Gary on Lake Michigan. ◉ Pop. 29,060. **2.** A city of southwest Michigan south of Kalamazoo. It is a manufacturing center. ◉ Pop. 41,042.

Port Al·ber·ni (pôrt′ ăl-bûr′nē, pōrt′). A city of southwest British Columbia, Canada, on Vancouver Island in the southeast-central part. It is a fishing port with wood-products industries. ◉ Pop. 19,892.

Port An·ge·les (ăn′jə-lĭs). A city of northwest Washington on the Strait of Juan de Fuca south of Victoria, British Columbia, Canada. It is a port of entry, a boating and fishing center, and a resort. ◉ Pop. 17,710.

Port A·pra (ä′prə). See **Apra Harbor.**

Port Ar·thur (är′thər). **1.** A city of extreme southeast Texas on Sabine Lake near the Louisiana border. It is a major deep-water port connected by channel with the Gulf of Mexico. ◉ Pop. 58,724. **2.** See **Lüshun.**

Port-au-Prince (pôrt′ō-prĭns′, pōrt′-, pôr′tō-prăɴs′). The capital and largest city of Haiti, in the southwest part of the country on an arm of the Caribbean Sea. Founded by French sugar planters in 1749, it became the colonial capital in 1770 and the capital of independent Haiti in 1804. ◉ Pop. 690,168.

Port Charlotte. An unincorporated community of southwest Florida on an inlet of the Gulf of Mexico northwest of Fort Myers. It is a planned residential community. ◉ Pop. 41,535.

Port Chester. A village of southeast New York on Long Island Sound near the Connecticut border. It is an industrial and residential community. ◉ Pop. 24,728.

Port Col·borne (kōl′bûrn′). A city of southeast Ontario, Canada, on Lake Erie at the southern end of the Welland Ship Canal west of Buffalo, New York. It is a manufacturing and transshipment center. ◉ Pop. 19,225.

Port Co·quit·lam (kō-kwĭt′ləm). A city of southwest British Columbia, Canada, on the Fraser River east of Vancouver. It is a trade center in a stone-quarrying and farming region. ◉ Pop. 27,535.

Port Elizabeth. A city of southeast South Africa on an inlet of the Indian Ocean. It grew rapidly after the completion of the railroad to Kimberley in 1873. ◉ Pop. 303,353.

Por·ter·ville (pôr′tər-vĭl′, pōr′-). A city of south-central California north of Bakersfield in the San Joaquin Valley. Founded in 1859 on the Los Angeles–San Francisco stage route, it is chiefly residential. ◉ Pop. 29,563.

Port Har·court (här′kərt). A city of southern Nigeria in the Niger River delta southeast of Ibadan. Laid out by the British in 1912, it is a rail terminus and manufacturing center. ◉ Pop. 288,900.

Port Hue·ne·me (wī-nē′mē). A town of southern California west of Los Angeles. It was a naval training base during World War II. ◉ Pop. 20,319.

Port Huron. A city of southeast Michigan on Lake Huron at the mouth of the St. Clair River north-northeast of Detroit. First settled as a French fort in 1686, it grew as a lumbering town in the 19th century and is now a port of entry with diversified industries. ◉ Pop. 33,694.

Por·ti·ci (pôr′tē-chē′). A city of south-central Italy, a residential and resort suburb of Naples on the Bay of Naples. ◉ Pop. 79,259.

Port·land (pôrt′lənd, pōrt′-). **1.** A city of southwest Maine on an arm of the Gulf of Maine south of Lewiston. Settled c. 1632, it became a commercial center in the 17th century and was state capital from 1820 to 1832. It is the largest city in the state. ◉ Pop. 64,348. **2.** The largest city of Oregon, in the northwest part of the state on the Willamette River near its junction with the Columbia River. Founded in 1845, it grew as a lumber-exporting port and supply point for the California and Alaska goldfields. ◉ Pop. 437,319. —**Port′land·er** *n.*

Port Lou·is (lōō′ĭs, lōō′ē, lōō-ē′). The capital and largest city of Mauritius, in the northwest part of the island on the Indian Ocean. It was founded c. 1735. ◉ Pop. 143,509.

Port Mores·by (môrz′bē, mōrz′-). The capital and largest city of Papua New Guinea, on southeast New Guinea and the Gulf of Papua. It was named for the British explorer Capt. John Moresby (1830–1922), who landed here in 1873, and was occupied by the British after 1888. ◉ Pop. 173,500.

Por·to or **Pôr·to** (pôr′tōō). See **Oporto.**

Pôrto A·le·gre (ə-lĕ′grə). A city of southeast Brazil at the northern end of a large lagoon near the Atlantic Ocean. It was founded c. 1742 by emigrants from the Azores. ◉ Pop. 1,263,239.

port of entry. *pl.* **ports of entry.** *abbr.* **POE, P.O.E.** A place where travelers or goods may enter a country under official supervision.

Por·to·fi·no (pôr′tə-fē′nō, pōr′-, pôr′tô-fē′-nô). A town of northwest Italy on the coast of the Ligurian Sea east of Genoa. It is a popular tourist resort. ◉ Pop. 742.

Port of Spain or **Port-of-Spain** (pôrt′əv-spān′, pōrt′-). The capital of Trinidad and Tobago, on the northwest coast of Trinidad on an arm of the Atlantic Ocean. It is a commercial center and major port. ◉ Pop. 50,878.

Por·to-No·vo (pôr′tō-nō′vō, pōr′-). The capital of Benin, in the southeast part of the country on an inlet of the Gulf of Guinea. Probably founded in the 16th century, it was settled as a slave-trading center by the Portuguese in the 17th century. ◉ Pop. 179,138.

Port Orange. A city of northeast Florida on the Atlantic coast south-southeast of Daytona Beach. It is in a citrus-growing area. ◉ Pop. 35,317.

Pôrto Vel·ho (vĕl′yōō). A city of northwest Brazil on the Madeira River near the Bolivian border. Its economy is based on rubber and Brazil nuts. ◉ Pop. 286,471.

Por·to·vie·jo (pôr′tō-vyä′hō, -vyĕ′-). A city of western Ecuador north-northwest of Guayaquil. Founded c. 1535 near the Atlantic coast, it was moved to its present site in the 17th century. ◉ Pop. 132,937.

Port Phil·lip Bay (fĭl′əp). A large deep-water inlet of Bass Strait on the southeast coast of Australia. It was first entered and explored by Europeans in 1835.

Port Roy·al (roi′əl). See **Annapolis Royal.**

Port Sa·id (sä-ēd′). A city of northeast Egypt on the Mediterranean Sea at the northern entrance to the Suez Canal. It was founded in 1859 by the builders of the canal and was once an important coaling station. ◉ Pop. 460,000.

Ports·mouth (pôrt′sməth, pōrt′-). **1.** A borough of southern England on the English Channel opposite the Isle of Wight. Chartered in 1194, it is a major naval base. ◉ Pop. 189,073. **2.** A city of southeast New Hampshire on the Atlantic Ocean. The Treaty of Portsmouth, ending the Russo-Japanese War, was signed at the naval base here in 1905. ◉ Pop. 25,925. **3.** A city of southern Ohio on the Ohio River south of Columbus. An important industrial and rail center, it has prehistoric mounds and earthworks nearby. ◉ Pop. 22,676. **4.** A city of southeast Virginia on Hampton Roads opposite Norfolk. It has been a major naval base since pre-Revolutionary times. ◉ Pop. 103,907.

Port Stanley. See **Stanley.**

Port Sudan. A city of northeast Sudan on the Red Sea northeast of Khartoum. It was established after 1905 as a railroad terminus. ◉ Pop. 305,385.

Port Tal·bot (tôl′bət, tăl′-). A borough of southern Wales on an inlet of the Bristol Channel west-northwest of Cardiff. It is a port and has large iron and steel works. ◉ Pop. 54,600.

Por·tu·gal (pôr′chə-gəl, pōr′-). *abbr.* **Port.** A country of southwest Europe on the western Iberian Peninsula. It includes the Madeira Islands and the Azores in the northern Atlantic Ocean. Originally inhabited by the Lusitanians, a Celtiberian people, the mainland area was subjugated by the Romans in the 2nd century B.C. and was later conquered by the Visigoths, in the 5th century A.D., and after 711 by the Moors. Spain recognized Portugal as an independent kingdom in 1143, and it soon flourished as a maritime and colonial power. In 1249 the last of the Moors were driven out, and the kingdom became a consolidated entity. By the 15th century it had holdings that stretched from Africa to the Far East and across the Atlantic to Brazil. Spain seized the country in 1580 and ruled it until the mid-1600's, when a revolt established the last royal Portuguese line. Much of Portugal's empire was lost to the British and the Dutch in the 17th and 18th centuries. The mid-1800's saw the acceptance of a liberal constitution, and throughout the early 20th century numerous revolts and coups took place, with a moderate form of democracy established after a bloodless coup in 1974. The remaining colonies in Africa became independent at various times in the later 20th century. Lisbon is the capital and the largest city. ◉ Pop. 9,830,000.

Por·tu·ga·le·te (pôr′tə-gə-lä′tē, pōr′-, pôr′-
tōō-gä-lĕ′tĕ). A city of northern Spain, a suburb
of Bilbao on the Bay of Biscay. ● Pop. 59,307.

Por·tu·guese (pôr′chə-gēz′, -gēs′, pōr′-). *abbr.*
Pg., Port. 1. Of or relating to Portugal or its
people, language, or culture. **2.** *pl.* **Portuguese.
a.** A native or inhabitant of Portugal. **b.** A person of Portuguese descent. **3.** The Romance
language of Portugal and Brazil.

Port-Vi·la (pôrt′ vē′lə, pōrt′). See **Vila.**

Port Washington. An unincorporated community of southeast New York on the northern
shore of western Long Island. It is a residential
suburb and a resort. ● Pop. 15,387.

Po·sa·das (pə-sä′dəs, pô-sä′*th*äs). A city of
northeast Argentina on the Paraná River and the
Paraguayan border. It is a trade and processing
center. ● Pop. 201,943.

Po·ta·ro (pə-tär′ō, pô-tä′rô). A river, about 161
km (100 mi) long, of central Guyana. It has gold
deposits and is known for its Kaieteur Falls.

Pot·a·wat·o·mi (pŏt′ə-wŏt′ə-mē). **1.** *pl.* **Pot-
awatomi** or **-mis.** A member of a Native American people variously located in Michigan, Wisconsin, northern Illinois, and northern Indiana in
the 17th to the 19th century, with present-day
populations in Oklahoma, Kansas, Michigan, and
Ontario. **2.** The Algonquian language of the Pot-
awatomis.

Po·ten·za (pə-tĕn′zə, pô-tĕn′tsä). A city of
southern Italy in the Apennines east-southeast
of Naples. Founded by Romans in the second
century B.C., it was ruled by numerous feudal
overlords during the Middle Ages and is now a
railroad junction in an agricultural area. ● Pop.
65,388.

Pot·i·dae·a (pŏt′ĭ-dē′ə). An ancient city of
northeast Greece in Macedonia. Founded as a
Corinthian colony in 609 B.C., it revolted against
Athens in 432 but was reconquered in 429.
Philip of Macedon destroyed the city in 356 B.C.

Po·to·mac (pə-tō′mək). A community of central Maryland, a residential suburb of Washington, D.C. ● Pop. 22,800.

Potomac River. A river of the east-central
United States rising in northeast West Virginia
and flowing about 459 km (285 mi) along the
Virginia-Maryland border to Chesapeake Bay. It
is navigable for large ships to Washington, D.C.

Po·to·sí (pō-tə-sē′, pô-tô′-). A city of south-
central Bolivia southwest of Sucre in the Andes
at an altitude of about 4,203 m (13,780 ft). It
was founded after silver was discovered in 1545
and during its early days was a fabled source of
riches. ● Pop. 123,327.

Pots·dam (pŏts′dăm′). A city of northeast Germany on the Havel River near Berlin. First mentioned in the 10th century, it became in the 18th
century a favorite residence of Frederick the

Great, who built the rococo palace of Sans Souci
here (1745–1747). The city was the site of
the Potsdam Conference (July–August 1945), at
which American, British, and Soviet leaders
drew up preliminary plans for the postwar administration of Germany and assigned various
captured territories to Poland. ● Pop. 139,262.

Pot·ter·ies (pŏt′ə-rēz). A district of west-
central England in the Trent River valley. It
has been a center of the manufacture of china
and earthenware since the 16th century. Josiah
Wedgwood and Josiah Spode were among the
noted potters who worked in the area.

Potts·town (pŏts′toun′). A borough of southeast Pennsylvania on the Schuylkill River east-
southeast of Reading. Its first ironworks were
established in 1715. ● Pop. 21,831.

Potts·ville (pŏts′vĭl′). A city of east-central
Pennsylvania west-northwest of Allentown. It
was once a coal-mining town and is now a trade
and industrial center. ● Pop. 16,603.

Pough·keep·sie (pə-kĭp′sē, pō-). A city of
southeast New York on the Hudson River north
of New York City. Settled by the Dutch in 1687,
Poughkeepsie is the seat of Vassar College (chartered 1861). ● Pop. 28,844.

Pow·ay (pou′ā). A community of southern California north of San Diego. It is near a large naval
air base. ● Pop. 43,516.

Pow·der River (pou′dər). **1.** A river, about
241 km (150 mi) long, of northeast Oregon flowing generally north and southeast to the Snake
River on the Idaho border. **2.** A river rising in
several branches in the Bighorn Mountains of
central Wyoming and flowing about 782 km (486
mi) generally northeast into southern Montana.

Pow·ell (pou′əl), **Lake.** A reservoir of southern
Utah and north-central Arizona formed by the
Glen Canyon Dam on the Colorado River. It is
the second largest (after Lake Mead) artificial
lake in the United States. The dam, which was
built in 1964, is located in Arizona just south of
the Utah border.

Pow·ha·tan (pou′ə-tăn′, pou-hăt′n). **1.** *pl.*
Powhatan or **-tans.** A member of a confederacy
of Native American peoples of eastern Virginia
in the 16th and 17th centuries, with present-day
descendants in the same area. **2.** The Algonquian language of the Powhatans, a dialect of Virginia Algonquian.

Po·yang (pō′yäng′). A lake of eastern China
southeast of Wuhan. It is connected to the
Chang Jiang (Yangtze River) by canal.

Po·za Ri·ca de Hi·dal·go (pō′zə rē′kə dä hĭ-
däl′gō, pô′sä rē′kä *th*ĕ ē-*th*äl′gô). A city of
east-central Mexico south of Tampico near the
Bay of Campeche. ● Pop. 166,799.

Poz·nań (pōz′năn′, -nän′, pôz′nän′yə). A city
of west-central Poland west of Warsaw. Dating

from before the tenth century, it passed to Prussia in 1793 and reverted to Poland after World War I. ◦ Pop. 590,087.

Poz·zuo·li (pôt-swô′lē). A city of southern Italy west of Naples on the **Bay of Pozzuoli,** a section of the Bay of Naples. The city was founded by Greek exiles c. 529 B.C. and was an important commercial center during the Roman Empire. ◦ Pop. 61,300.

Prague (präg). The capital and largest city of Czech Republic, in the western part of the country on the Vltava River. Known since the 9th century, it was a leading cultural and commercial center by the 14th century and came under Hapsburg rule in 1526. The city became the capital of newly formed Czechoslovakia in 1918. Prague was occupied (1939–1945) by the Germans during World War II and was the center of Czech resistance to the Soviet invasion of 1968. After Czechoslovakia ceased to exist in 1993, it became the capital of Czech Republic. It is a port and a leading commercial, industrial, and cultural center of Europe. ◦ Pop. 1,216,513.

Prai·a (prī′ə). The capital of Cape Verde, on the southeast coast of São Tiago Island. ◦ Pop. 61,644.

prai·rie (prâr′ē). An extensive area of flat or rolling, predominantly treeless grassland, especially the large tract or plain of central North America.

Prai·rie Provinces (prâr′ē). The central Canadian provinces of Manitoba, Saskatchewan, and Alberta.

Prairie Village. A city of northeast Kansas, a suburb of Kansas City. ◦ Pop. 23,186.

Pra·krit (prä′krĭt). **1.** Any of the vernacular and literary Indic languages recorded from the third century B.C. to the fourth century A.D., as opposed to Sanskrit. **2.** Any of the modern Indic languages. **— Pra·krit′ic** adj.

Pra·to (prä′tō). A city of central Italy northwest of Florence. It has been a textile center since the 13th century. ◦ Pop. 165,364.

Pratt·ville (prăt′vĭl′, -vəl). A city of central Alabama, an industrial suburb of Montgomery. ◦ Pop. 19,587.

pre-Co·lum·bi·an (prē′kə-lŭm′bē-ən). Of, relating to, or originating in the Americas before the arrival of Columbus.

Pres·cott (prĕs′kət, -kŏt′). A city of central Arizona north-northwest of Phoenix. It was territorial capital from 1864 to 1867 and from 1877 to 1889 and is now a trade center and health resort. ◦ Pop. 26,455.

Pre·si·den·te Pru·den·te (prĕ′zĭ-dĕN′tĭ prōō-dĕN′tĭ). A city of south-central Brazil near the Paraná River west-northwest of São Paulo. It is a processing and shipping center for a coffee-growing region. ◦ Pop. 165,420.

Pres·ton (prĕs′tən). A borough of northwest England north-northeast of Liverpool. The Jacobites, supporters of the Stuart royal line, surrendered here after an uprising in 1715. ◦ Pop. 132,166.

Prest·wick (prĕst′wĭk). A burgh of southwest Scotland north of Ayr. It is a resort with a noted golf course and the site of an international airport. ◦ Pop. 13,174.

Pre·to·ri·a (prĭ-tôr′ē-ə, -tōr′-). The administrative capital of South Africa, in the northeast part of the country north of Johannesburg. Founded in 1855, it became the capital of Transvaal in 1860. ◦ Pop. 525,583.

Prib·i·lof Islands (prĭb′ə-lôf′). A group of islands off southwest Alaska in the Bering Sea. First visited and named by a Russian explorer in 1786, they are noted as a breeding ground for seals.

Prich·ard (prĭch′ərd). A city of southwest Alabama, an industrial suburb of Mobile. ◦ Pop. 34,311.

prime meridian (prīm). The zero meridian (0°), used as a reference line from which longitude east and west is measured. It passes through Greenwich, England.

Prince Albert (prĭns). A city of central Saskatchewan, Canada, on the North Saskatchewan River north-northeast of Saskatoon. It was founded as a Presbyterian mission in 1866. ◦ Pop. 31,380.

Prince Edward Island abbr. **PE, P.E.I.** A province of southeast Canada consisting of **Prince Edward Island** in the southern Gulf of St. Lawrence. It joined the confederacy in 1873. The island was discovered by the French explorer Jacques Cartier in 1534 and named Île St. Jean by the French explorer Samuel de Champlain in 1603. It was renamed in 1798 after Edward, Duke of Kent (1767–1820), the father of Queen Victoria. Charlottetown is the capital and the largest city. ◦ Pop. 122,506.

Prince George. A city of central British Columbia, Canada, at the confluence of the Fraser and Nechako rivers. Originally a fur-trading post called Fort George (established in 1807), it is now a distributing center for a lumbering region. ◦ Pop. 67,559.

Prince of Wales Island. 1. An island of northern Northwest Territories, Canada, in the Arctic Ocean northeast of Victoria Island. **2.** An island of extreme southeast Alaska in the Alexander Archipelago. It is the largest island in the group.

Prince Ru·pert (rōō′pərt). A city of western British Columbia, Canada, on the Pacific Ocean near the Alaska border. A railroad and highway terminus and ice-free port, it is a processing and shipping center. ◦ Pop. 16,197.

Prince·ton (prĭn′stən). A borough of central New Jersey north-northeast of Trenton. It was founded by Quakers in 1696 and is the seat of Princeton University (established in 1746 as the College of New Jersey and renamed in 1896). George Washington defeated the British here in January 1777. ⊛ Pop. 12,016.

Princeton, Mount. A mountain, about 4,330 m (14,197 ft) high, in the Sawatch Range of the Rocky Mountains in central Colorado.

Prince Wil·liam Sound (wĭl′yəm). An arm of the Gulf of Alaska east of the Kenai Peninsula. The worst oil spill in U.S. history occurred here in March 1989.

Prín·ci·pe (prĭn′sə-pə, prēɴ′sĭ-). An island of western Africa in the Gulf of Guinea, part of São Tomé and Príncipe.

Prip·et (prĭp′ĕt) or **Pri·pyat** (prē′pyət). A river, about 708 km (440 mi) long, of northern Ukraine and southern Belarus flowing generally eastward through the **Pripet Marshes,** a forested, swampy area, to the Dnieper River north of Kiev.

Priš·ti·na (prĭsh′tə-nä′). A city of southern Yugoslavia. It is the chief city of the Kosovo region and was the center of a separatist movement in the 1990's. ⊛ Pop. 155,000.

pro·jec·tion (prə-jĕk′shən). A system of intersecting lines, such as the grid of a map, on which part or all of the globe or another spherical surface is represented as a plane surface.

Pro·ko·pyevsk (prə-kôp′yəfsk). A city of south-central Russia east-southeast of Novosibirsk. It is a manufacturing and processing center in a major coal-mining region. ⊛ Pop. 264,959.

prom·on·to·ry (prŏm′ən-tôr′ē, -tōr′ē). *abbr.* **prom.** A high ridge of land or rock jutting out into a body of water; a headland.

pro·pri·e·tar·y colony (prə-prī′ĭ-tĕr′ē). Any of certain early North American colonies, such as Carolina and Pennsylvania, organized in the 17th century in territories granted by the English Crown to one or more proprietors who had full governing rights.

pro·tec·tor·ate (prə-tĕk′tər-ĭt). *abbr.* **protec.** **1.** A relationship of protection and partial control assumed by a superior power over a dependent country or region. **2.** The protected country or region.

pro·to·con·ti·nent (prō′tō-kŏn′tə-nənt). **1.** A landmass, actual or hypothetical, that could develop into a major continent. **2.** See **supercontinent.**

Pro·to-In·do-Eur·o·pe·an (prō′tō-ĭn′dō-yŏŏr′-ə-pē′ən). **1.** The reconstructed language that was the ancestor of the Indo-European languages. **2.** Of, relating to, or being Proto-Indo-European or one of its reconstructed linguistic features.

pro·to·lan·guage (prō′tō-lăng′gwĭj). A lan-

guage that is the recorded or hypothetical ancestor of another language or group of languages. Also called *Ursprache.*

Pro·ven·çal (prō′vən-säl′, -vän-, prŏv′ən-). *abbr.* **Prov. 1.** Of or relating to Provence or its people, language, or culture. **2.** The Romance language of Provence. **3.** A native or inhabitant of Provence.

Pro·vence (prə-väns′, prô-vaɴs′). A historical region and former province of southeast France bordering on the Mediterranean Sea. It was settled c. 600 B.C. by Greeks and later by Phoenician merchants and was colonized by Rome in the second century B.C. Provence became part of the kingdom of Arles in 933 A.D. and later passed to the Angevin dynasty (1246) and to France (1486).

Prov·i·dence (prŏv′ĭ-dəns). The capital and largest city of Rhode Island, in the northeast part of the state on Narragansett Bay. It was founded by Roger Williams in 1636 as a haven for religious dissenters and became prosperous as a port in the 18th century. Providence was joint capital with Newport until 1900. ⊛ Pop. 160,728.

Prov·ince·town (prŏv′ĭns-toun′). A town of southeast Massachusetts on the tip of Cape Cod. Pilgrims first landed on the site in 1620 before sailing on to Plymouth. The town is a popular resort famed for the Provincetown Players (1915–1929), a theater group that presented many new works by Eugene O'Neill. ⊛ Pop. 3,374.

pro·vin·cial (prə-vĭn′shəl). *abbr.* **prov. 1.** Of or relating to a province. **2.** A native or inhabitant of the provinces.

Pro·vo (prō′vō). A city of north-central Utah south-southeast of Salt Lake City. It was settled by Mormons in 1849 and is the seat of Brigham Young University (established 1875). ⊛ Pop. 86,835.

Prud·hoe Bay (prōōd′hō, prŭd′-). An inlet of the Arctic Ocean on the northern coast of Alaska east of the Colville River delta. Extensive oil reserves were discovered here in 1968.

Prus·sia (prŭsh′ə). A historical region and former kingdom of north-central Europe including present-day northern Germany and Poland. Its ancient inhabitants, of Baltic stock, were conquered by the Teutonic Knights in the 13th century. West Prussia was ceded to Poland in 1466, and East Prussia became a Polish fief that passed to Brandenburg in 1618. The kingdom of Prussia was proclaimed in 1701 and was greatly expanded and fortified by Emperor Frederick II (reigned 1740–1786). Prussia was instrumental in the unification of Germany, and in 1871 its king was declared Emperor William I of Germany. The state became a republic in 1918 and was formally abolished after World War II.

Prus·sian (prŭsh′ən). **1.** Of or relating to Prussia or its Baltic or German inhabitants. **2.** Any of the western Balts inhabiting the region between the Vistula and Neman rivers in ancient times. **3.** A Baltic inhabitant of Prussia. **4.** A German inhabitant of Prussia.

Prut (pro͞ot). A river rising in southwest Ukraine and flowing about 885 km (550 mi) generally southeast along the Romania-Moldova border to the Danube River.

Pskov (pə-skôf′, pskôf). A city of west-central Russia south-southwest of St. Petersburg. Dating from the eighth century, it became an important trade center and was annexed by Moscow in 1510. ◉ Pop. 207,560.

Pu·call·pa (po͞o-kī′pä). A city of east-central Peru on the Ucayali River northeast of Lima. It is an agricultural trade center. ◉ Pop. 161,200.

Pueb·la (pwĕb′lä). A city of east-central Mexico east-southeast of Mexico City. Founded by the Spanish in 1532, it is an agricultural, commercial, and manufacturing center. It is also known for its historic cathedral (built 1552–1649) and theater (built 1790). ◉ Pop. 1,007,170.

pueb·lo (pwĕb′lō). **1. Pueblo.** *pl.* **Pueblo** or **-los.** A member of any of some 25 Native American peoples, including the Hopi, Zuñi, and Taos, living in established villages in northern and western New Mexico and northeast Arizona. The Pueblo are descendants of the cliff-dwelling Anasazi peoples and are noted for their skilled craft in pottery, basketry, weaving, and metalworking. **2.** A permanent village or community of any of the Pueblo peoples, typically consisting of multilevel adobe or stone apartment dwellings of terraced design clustered around a central plaza.

Pueb·lo (pwĕb′lō). A city of southeast-central Colorado south-southeast of Colorado Springs. It is a shipping and industrial center for an irrigated agricultural region. ◉ Pop. 98,640.

Puer·to Ca·bel·lo (pwĕr′tō kä-bā′ō, -vĕ′yô). A city of northern Venezuela on the Caribbean Sea west of Caracas. It was frequently sacked by buccaneers during the colonial period. ◉ Pop. 143,765.

Puerto de San·ta Ma·rí·a (də săn′tə mə-rē′ə, *thĕ* sän′tä mä-rē′ä). A city of southwest Spain on the Gulf of Cádiz north of Cádiz. It is a commercial center known for its export of sherry. ◉ Pop. 59,844.

Puer·tol·la·no (pwĕr′tl-yä′nə, -tô-lyä′nô). A city of central Spain south-southwest of Madrid. It is an agricultural trade center in a mining region. ◉ Pop. 51,845.

Puer·to Ri·co (pwĕr′tə rē′kō, pôrt′ə, pōrt′ə, pwĕr′tō). *abbr.* **PR, P.R.** A self-governing island commonwealth of the United States in the Car-

ibbean Sea east of Hispaniola. Inhabited by Tainos when it was discovered by Columbus in 1493, it was colonized by the Spanish in the 16th century and ceded to the United States in 1898 after the Spanish-American War. Puerto Ricans were granted U.S. citizenship in 1917, although residents of the island do not vote in U.S. presidential elections. Commonwealth status was proclaimed in 1952 and has been upheld by various plebiscites since the 1960's. San Juan is the capital and the largest city. ◉ Pop. 3,646,000. **— Puer′-to Ri′can** *adj. & n.*

Puer·to Val·lar·ta (pwĕr′tō vä-yär′tə, -tä, pwĕr′tô). A city of west-central Mexico on the Pacific Ocean west of Guadalajara. It is a popular coastal resort. ◉ Pop. 38,645.

Pu·get Sound (pyo͞o′jĭt). A deep inlet of the Pacific Ocean in western Washington extending south from the Strait of Juan de Fuca through Admiralty Inlet. It was explored and named by the British navigator Capt. George Vancouver for his aide, Peter Puget, in 1792.

Pu·glia (po͞o′lyä). See **Apulia.**

Pu·la (po͞o′lä, -lä). A city of northwest Croatia on the Adriatic Sea. Captured by Rome in 178 B.C., it was a major naval station of the Hapsburg empire and passed to Italy in 1919 and to Yugoslavia in 1947. ◉ Pop. 77,278.

Pull·man (po͞ol′mən). A city of southeast Washington south of Spokane. An agricultural trade center, it is the seat of Washington State University (founded 1890). ◉ Pop. 23,478.

Pu·nic (pyo͞o′nĭk). **1.** Of or relating to ancient Carthage, its inhabitants, or their language. **2.** The dialect of Phoenician spoken in ancient Carthage.

Pun·jab (pŭn′jăb′, pŭn-jäb′). A historical region of the northwest Indian subcontinent bounded by the Indus and Jumna rivers. It was a center of the prehistoric Indus Valley civilization and after c. 1500 B.C. the site of early Aryan settlements. Muslims occupied the western part of the region by the 8th century introducing Islam, and although they later conquered the eastern part, Hinduism remained entrenched there. The Moguls brought the region to cultural eminence until their empire declined in the 18th century. The Punjab was controlled by Sikhs from 1799 to 1849, when it was annexed by Great Britain. It was partitioned between India and Pakistan in 1947.

Pun·ja·bi also **Pan·ja·bi** (pŭn-jä′bē, -jäb′ē). **1.** Of or relating to the Punjab or the Punjabi language. **2.** *pl.* **-bis.** A native or inhabitant of the Punjab. **3.** An Indic language of the Punjab.

Pun·ta A·re·nas (po͞on′tə ə-rĕn′əs, po͞on′tä ä-rĕ′näs). A city of southern Chile on the Strait of Magellan. Founded in the 1840's, it is the southernmost city in the world. ◉ Pop. 120,030.

Punx·su·taw·ney (pŭngk′sə-tô′nē). A city of west-central Pennsylvania northeast of Pittsburgh. It is an industrial center noted for its annual observance of Groundhog Day, February 2. ◉ Pop. 6,782.

Pu·ra·cé (pŏŏr′ə-sē′, pōō-rä-sĕ′). A volcano, 4,758 m (15,600 ft) high, in the Andes of southwest Colombia. It is an active volcano, having erupted a dozen times during the 20th century.

Pur·ga·toire (pûr′gə-twär′, -tôr′ē, -tōr′ē). A river, about 299 km (186 mi) long, of southeast Colorado flowing generally northeast to the Arkansas River.

Pu·rus (pə-rōōs′, pōō-). A river of east-central Peru and western Brazil flowing about 3,379 km (2,100 mi) generally northeast to the Amazon River.

Pu·san (pōō′sän′) also **Fu·san** (fōō′-). A city of extreme southeast South Korea on Korea Strait southeast of Seoul. It developed into a major port during the Japanese occupation of Korea (1910–1945). ◉ Pop. 3,814,000.

Push·tu (pŭsh′tōō). Variant of **Pashto.**

Put-in-Bay (pŏŏt′ĭn-bā′). A bay of western Lake Erie in an island off Ohio. The U.S. Navy under Oliver Hazard Perry defeated a British fleet here on September 10, 1813, in the War of 1812.

Pu·tong·hua also **Pu tong hua** (pōō′tông′-hwä′, -wä′, -tŏng′-). See **Mandarin** (sense 4).

Pu·tu·ma·yo (pōō′tə-mī′ō, pōō′tōō-mä′yô). A river of northwest South America rising in southwest Colombia and flowing about 1,609 km (1,000 mi) along the Colombia-Peru border to the Amazon River in northwest Brazil.

Puy·al·lup (pyōō-ăl′əp). A city of west-central Washington east-southeast of Tacoma. It is the site of an annual daffodil festival and fair. ◉ Pop. 23,875.

Pyg·my also **pyg·my** (pĭg′mē). A member of any of various peoples, especially of equatorial Africa and parts of southeast Asia, having an average height less than 5 feet (127 centimeters). —**pyg′moid′** (pĭg′moid′) *adj.* —**Pyg′my** *adj.*

Pyong·yang (pyŭng′yäng′, -yăng′, pyông′-). The capital and largest city of North Korea, in the southwest-central part of the country. It was an important cultural center and Chinese colony after 108 B.C., later fell to the Japanese, and became capital of North Korea in 1948. ◉ Pop. 2,355,000.

Pyr·a·mid Peak (pĭr′ə-mĭd). A mountain, 4,275.5 m (14,018 ft) high, in the Elk Mountains of west-central Colorado.

Pyr·e·nees (pĭr′ə-nēz′). A mountain range of southwest Europe extending along the French-Spanish border from the Bay of Biscay to the Mediterranean Sea. Pico de Aneto, its highest peak, rises to 3,406.2 m (11,168 ft). —**Pyr′e·ne′an** *adj.*

Q

Qan·da·har (kŭn′də-här′, kän′-). See **Kandahar.**

Qa·tar (kä′tär′, kə-tär′). A country of eastern Arabia on a peninsula in the southwest Persian Gulf. A traditional monarchy, it was under British protection from 1916 until 1971, when it became independent. Oil was first produced commercially in 1949, and its production still dominates Qatar's economy. Ethnic Qataris, Arabs of the Wahhabi sect, make up a quarter of the population, with the rest being immigrants and guest workers primarily from other Muslim countries. Qatar joined other Arab states in the formation of the Gulf Cooperation Council in 1981. Doha is the capital and the largest city. ◉ Pop. 540,000. —**Qa·tar′i** *adj. & n.*

Qat·ta·ra Depression (kə-tär′ə). A desert basin of northwest Egypt in the Libyan Desert. Its lowest point is about 134 m (440 ft) below sea level.

Qaz·vin also **Kaz·vin** (kăz-vēn′). A city of northwest Iran northwest of Tehran. Founded in the fourth century A.D., it was captured by the Arabs in 644 and was the capital of Persia from 1548 to 1598. ◉ Pop. 298,705.

Qi·lian Shan (chē′lyän′ shän′) also **Nan Shan** (nän′). A mountain range of north-central China extending northwest to southeast and having peaks rising from 5,490 m (18,000 ft) to more than 6,100 m (20,000 ft).

Qing·dao (chĭng′dou′) also **Tsing·tao** (tsĭng′-tou′). A city of eastern China on the Yellow Sea north-northwest of Shanghai. It is a leading industrial and tourist center. The city was leased

(1898–1919) to the Germans, who established a famed brewery. ⊛ Pop. 2,060,000.

Qing·hai also **Ching·hai** (chĭng'hī') or **Tsing·hai** (tsĭng'-). A province of northwest-central China. Its northern border is the Qilian Shan. Xining is the capital. ⊛ Pop. 4,070,000.

Qinghai Hu (hōō) also **Ko·ko Nor** (kō'kō' nôr', nōr'). A salt lake of north-central China south of the Qilian Shan. The largest lake in China, it is at an altitude of more than 3,050 m (10,000 ft).

Qin·huang·dao (chĭn'hwäng'dou') also **Chin·wang·tao** (chĭn'wäng'tou'). A city of northeast China on the Bo Hai east of Beijing. It was formerly a treaty port. ⊛ Pop. 518,912.

Qi·qi·har (chē'chē'här') also **Tsi·tsi·har** (tsē'-tsē'-). A city of northeast China in Manchuria northwest of Harbin. Founded as a fortress in 1691, it is a port and processing center. ⊛ Pop. 1,400,591.

Qom (kōm) also **Qum** (kōōm). A city of west-central Iran south-southwest of Tehran. It has been a Shiite Muslim center since early Islamic times and a pilgrimage site since the 17th century. ⊛ Pop. 780,453.

Quai d'Or·say (kā' dôr-sā', kē', kĕ dôr-sĕ'). A street paralleling the southern bank of the Seine River in Paris, France, notable for its governmental ministries. The name is used figuratively to refer to the French foreign office.

Quan·da·ry Peak (kwän'də-rē, -drē). A mountain, about 4,350.8 m (14,265 ft) high, in the Park Range of the Rocky Mountains in central Colorado.

Quan·ti·co (kwän'tĭ-kō'). A town of northeast Virginia on the Potomac River south-southwest of Alexandria. A U.S. Marine Corps base was established here in 1918. ⊛ Pop. 670.

Qua·paw (kwô'pô). **1.** pl. **Quapaw** or **-paws.** A member of a Native American people formerly inhabiting parts of Arkansas along the Arkansas River, with a present-day population in Oklahoma. **2.** The Siouan language of the Quapaws.

Qu'Ap·pelle (kwə-pĕl'). A river, about 434 km (270 mi) long, of southern Saskatchewan and southwest Manitoba, Canada, flowing east to the Assiniboine River.

Que·bec (kwĭ-bĕk') or **Qué·bec** (kā-). **1.** abbr. **PQ, P.Q., Que.** A province of eastern Canada. It joined the confederacy in 1867. The region was first explored and claimed for France by Jacques Cartier (1534) and Samuel de Champlain (1608) and was made a royal colony, known as New France, by Louis XIV in 1663. Conflict between the French and British for control of the territory ended in 1763 when Great Britain was given sovereignty, but the French influence has remained dominant. Quebec is the capital and Montreal the largest city. ⊛ Pop. 6,438,403. **2.** also **Quebec City** or **Québec City.** The capital of Quebec, Canada, in the southern part of the province on the St. Lawrence River. The French explorer Samuel de Champlain established a colony in its Lower Town in 1608. British forces under Gen. James Wolfe defeated the French forces led by Gen. Louis Montcalm at the Plains of Abraham here in 1759. The city is today a popular tourist center. ⊛ Pop. 167,517. —**Que·beck'er, Que·bec'er** n.

Qué·be·cois or **Que·be·cois** (kā'bĕ-kwä'). **1.** Of or relating to Quebec and especially to its French-speaking inhabitants or their culture. **2.** pl. **-cois.** A native or inhabitant of Quebec, especially a French-speaking one.

Que·chan (kĕch'ən). See **Yuma**[1].

Quech·ua also **Kech·ua** (kĕch'wə, -wä'). **1.** The Quechuan language of the Inca empire, now widely spoken throughout the Andes highlands from southern Colombia to Chile. **2.** pl. **Quech·ua** or **-uas** also **Kechua** or **-uas. a.** A member of a South American Indian people originally constituting the ruling class of the Inca empire. **b.** A speaker of the Quechua language.

Quech·uan (kĕch'wən). **1.** A subgroup of the Quechumaran languages, the most important language being Quechua. **2.** Of or relating to the Quechua or their language or culture.

Quech·u·mar·an (kĕch'ōō-mä-rän'). A group of languages found mostly in the Andes highlands from southern Colombia to northern Chile and Argentina, composed of the Quechuan and Aymaran languages.

Queen Charlotte Islands (kwēn). An archipelago off the western coast of British Columbia, Canada, separated from Vancouver Island to the southeast by **Queen Charlotte Sound,** an inlet of the Pacific Ocean.

Queen Elizabeth Islands. A group of islands of northern Northwest Territories, Canada, in the Arctic Archipelago north of Parry Channel. Oil deposits were first exploited here in the 1960's.

Queen Maud Land (môd). A region of Antarctica between the Weddell Sea and Enderby Land. It was claimed by Norway in 1939.

Queen Maud Mountains. A mountain range of Antarctica near the South Pole. It extends some 805 km (500 mi).

Queens (kwēnz). A borough of New York City in southeast New York on western Long Island. It was first settled by the Dutch in 1635 and became part of greater New York in 1898. ⊛ Pop. 1,951,598.

Que·moy (kĭ-moi'). In Pinyin **Jin·men** (jĭn'-mœn'). An island and group of 2 islands and 12 islets off southeast China in Taiwan Strait. The islands are heavily fortified and have been administered, along with Matsu, by Taiwan since the Chinese Revolution of 1949.

Que·ré·ta·ro (kə-rĕt′ə-rō′, kĕ-rĕ′tä-rō′). A city of central Mexico northwest of Mexico City. An ancient pre-Aztec settlement, it was conquered by the Spanish in 1531. Emperor Maximilian (ruled 1864–1867) was executed nearby by Mexican republicans in 1867. ● Pop. 215,976.

Quet·ta (kwĕt′ə). A city of west-central Pakistan west-southwest of Lahore. Ringed by mountains, Quetta commands the entrance through the strategic Bolan Pass into Afghanistan. It is also a trade center for much of central Asia. ● Pop. 285,719.

Que·zon City (kā′sôn′, -sŏn′). A city of central Luzon, Philippines, adjoining Manila. Chiefly residential with a textile industry, it was the official capital of the country from 1948 to 1976. ● Pop. 1,676,644.

Qui·ché (kē-chā′). **1.** *pl.* **Quiché** or **-chés.** A member of a Mayan people of Guatemala. **2.** The Mayan language of the Quiché.

Quil·mes (kēl′mĕs′). A city of eastern Argentina, an industrial suburb of Buenos Aires on the Río de la Plata. ● Pop. 509,445.

Quim·per (kăⁿ-pĕr′). A city of northwest France near the Bay of Biscay south-southeast of Brest. It is noted for its pottery, known as Quimper ware. ● Pop. 56,907.

Quin·cy. 1. (kwĭn′sē). A city of western Illinois on a bluff above the Mississippi River. It is a trade, industrial, and distributing center. ● Pop. 39,681. **2.** (kwĭn′zē). A city of eastern Massachusetts, an industrial suburb of Boston. Presidents John Adams (1735–1826) and John Quincy Adams (1767–1848) were born here; the Adams homestead is now a national historic site. ● Pop. 84,985.

Quir·i·nal (kwĭr′ə-nəl). One of the seven hills of ancient Rome, traditionally occupied by the Sabines. A papal palace was built here in the 16th century and served as the residence of Italian kings from 1870 to 1946. **— Quir′i·nal** *adj.*

Qui·to (kē′tō). The capital of Ecuador, in the north-central part of the country. Settled by the Quito people, it was captured by the Incas in 1487 and held by the Spanish from 1534 until 1822. The city has frequently been damaged by earthquakes. ● Pop. 890,355.

Qum (ko͞om). See **Qom.**

Qum·ran (ko͞om-rän′) also **Khir·bet Qumran** (kîr′bĕt). An ancient village of Palestine on the northwest shore of the Dead Sea in the West Bank east of Jerusalem. It is noted for the caves in which the Dead Sea Scrolls were found.

Qur·net es Sau·da (ko͞or′nĭt ĕs sou′də, -dä). A peak, 3,090 m (10,131 ft) high, of the Lebanon Mountains in northern Lebanon. It is the highest elevation in the country.

R

Ra·bat (rə-bät′, rä-). The capital of Morocco, on the Atlantic Ocean northeast of Casablanca. Settled in ancient times, it became a Muslim fortress c. 700. Rabat was the capital of the French protectorate of Morocco from 1912 until independence was achieved in 1956. It is a minor port and has textile industries. ● Pop. 1,220,000.

Rab·bin·ic Hebrew (rə-bĭn′ĭk). See **Mishnaic Hebrew.**

Rac·coon River (ră-ko͞on′). A river rising in northwest Iowa and flowing about 322 km (200 mi) southeast to the Des Moines River near the city of Des Moines.

Race (rās), **Cape.** A promontory of southeast-Newfoundland, Canada, on the coast of the Avalon Peninsula.

Ra·ci·bórz (rät-sē′bo͞osh′). A city of southern Poland on the Oder River near the Czech Republic border. First mentioned in the 12th century, it was later the capital of an independent principality and passed to Bohemia and Prussia before being incorporated into Poland in 1945. ● Pop. 59,800.

Ra·cine (rə-sēn′, rā-). A city of southeast Wisconsin on Lake Michigan south of Milwaukee. Founded in 1834, it is a port and manufacturing center. ● Pop. 84,298.

Ra·dom (rä′dôm). A city of east-central Poland south of Warsaw. Founded in the 14th century, it passed to Austria in 1795 and to Russia in 1815, reverting to Poland after World War I. ● Pop. 229,250.

Ra·gu·sa (rə-go͞o′zə, rä-go͞o′zä). **1.** A city of southeast Sicily, Italy, south-southwest of Messina. It is a manufacturing and food-processing center. ● Pop. 53,000. **2.** See **Dubrovnik.**

Rah·way (rô′wā′). A city of northeast New Jersey south-southwest of Elizabeth on the **Rahway River.** Rahway was settled c. 1720 and is a manufacturing center. ● Pop. 25,325.

Ra·ia·te·a (rī′ə-tā′ə). A volcanic island of the southern Pacific Ocean west-northwest of Tahiti. It is the largest of the Leeward group of the Society Islands in French Polynesia. Migration of its people to Hawaii, the Cook Islands, and New Zealand is believed to have begun some 600 years ago.

rain forest (rān). A dense evergreen forest occupying a tropical region with an annual rainfall of at least 2.5 meters (100 inches).

Rai·nier (rə-nîr′, rā-), **Mount.** A volcanic peak, 4,395.1 m (14,410 ft) high, of the Cascade Range in west-central Washington. It is the highest point in the range and the highest elevation in the state.

Rain·y Lake (rā′nē). A lake of northern Minnesota and southwest Ontario, Canada, drained by the **Rainy River,** which flows about 129 km (80 mi) generally westward along the U.S.-Canadian border to Lake of the Woods.

Rai·pur (rī′pōor). A city of east-central India east of Nagpur. It is a trade and processing center in an agricultural district. ⊛ Pop. 438,639.

Rai·sin River (rā′zĭn). A river, about 185 km (115 mi) long, of southeast Michigan flowing generally eastward to Lake Erie.

Ra·jah·mun·dry (rä′jə-mōōn′drē). A city of eastern India on the Godavari River east of Hyderabad. A pilgrimage center, it has timber and tobacco industries. ⊛ Pop. 324,851.

Raj·kot (räj′kōt′). A city of western India west-southwest of Ahmadabad. Formerly the capital of a princely state, it is now an educational center and a transportation hub. ⊛ Pop. 559,407.

Raj·put also **Raj·poot** (räj′pōot). A member of any of several powerful, predominantly Hindu landowning and military clans originating in the historical region of Rajputana in northwest India. In the 18th century the Rajputs expanded through central India, but they were pushed back in the early 19th century by the Marathas, Sikhs, and British. The Rajput princes gradually lost their power after Indian independence in 1947.

Ra·leigh (rô′lē, rä′-). The capital of North Carolina, in the east-central part of the state southeast of Durham. Selected as the capital in 1788, the city was laid out in 1792. It is the seat of a number of post-secondary schools, including North Carolina State University (established 1887). ⊛ Pop. 207,951.

Ra·lik Chain (rä′lĭk). The western group of the Marshall Islands in the western Pacific Ocean. It comprises 3 coral islands and 15 atolls, including Eniwetok.

Ra·ma's Bridge (rä′məz). See **Adam's Bridge.**

Ra·mat Gan (rə-mät′ gän′, rä′mät). A city of west-central Israel, a suburb of Tel Aviv–Jaffa. Its diamond exchange was founded in 1921. ⊛ Pop. 123,500.

Ram·pur (räm′pōor). A city of north-central India east of Delhi. Rampur is a processing and manufacturing center known for its library containing a fine collection of Mogul miniature paintings. ⊛ Pop. 243,742.

Ran·ca·gua (rän-kä′gwä, räng-). A city of central Chile south of Santiago. It is primarily an ag-

ricultural center in a copper-mining area. It was the site of a battle (1814), in which Chilean revolutionaries were defeated by superior Spanish forces. ⊛ Pop. 190,379.

Ran·chi (rän′chē). A city of northeast India west-northwest of Calcutta. It is a manufacturing center and health resort. ⊛ Pop. 599,306.

Ran·cho Cor·do·va (rän′chō kôr-dō′və, kôr′-də-). A community of north-central California, a suburb of Sacramento. ⊛ Pop. 48,731.

Rancho Cu·ca·mon·ga (kōō′kə-mŭng′gə, -mŏng′). An unincorporated community of southwest California west of San Bernadino. It is in a wine-producing area. ⊛ Pop. 101,409.

Rancho Pal·os Ver·des (păl′ōs vûr′dēz, păl′-əs). A city of southern California on the Pacific Ocean south-southwest of downtown Los Angeles. ⊛ Pop. 41,659.

Rand (rănd). See **Witwatersrand.**

Ran·dalls·town (răn′dlz-toun′). A community of north-central Maryland, a suburb of Baltimore. ⊛ Pop. 26,277.

Rand·ers (rä′nərs). A city of northern Denmark in the eastern part of the Jutland Peninsula north-northwest of Århus. It is a trade and manufacturing center in an agricultural and salmon-fishing area. ⊛ Pop. 61,410.

Ran·dolph (răn′dôlf). A town of eastern Massachusetts south-southwest of Quincy. It is mainly residential. ⊛ Pop. 30,093.

Rand·wick (rănd′wĭk). A city of southeast Australia, a suburb of Sydney on the Pacific Ocean and Botany Bay. ⊛ Pop. 116,600.

range (rānj). *abbr.* **Ra., r., R. 1.** A series of mountains forming part of system. **2.** An extensive area of open land on which livestock wander and graze.

Range·ley Lake (rānj′lē). A lake of west-central Maine near the New Hampshire border. It and other nearby lakes form a popular resort area.

Ran·goon (răn-gōōn′, răng-). See **Yangon.**

Rann of Kutch (rŭn; kŭch). An extensive salt marsh of western India and southeast Pakistan between the Gulf of Kutch and the Indus River delta. It was the scene of major border disputes in 1965 and 1971.

Ran·toul (răn-tōōl′). A village of east-central Illinois north of Champaign. A U.S. military air technical school was established here in 1917. ⊛ Pop. 17,212.

Ra·pa (rä′pə). An island of the southern Pacific Ocean in southern French Polynesia south-southeast of Tahiti. It was much visited by whalers in the early 19th century.

Ra·pal·lo (rə-pä′lō, rä-päl′-). A city of northwest Italy on the Ligurian Sea. It is a resort on the Italian Riviera. The treaty proclaiming

Fiume (now Rijeka) an independent city was signed here by Italy and Yugoslavia in November 1920. ⦿ Pop. 28,318.

Rapa Nu·i (nōō'ē). See **Easter Island.**

rap·id (răp'ĭd). An extremely fast-moving part of a river, caused by a steep descent in the riverbed. Often used in the plural.

Rap·id City (răp'ĭd). A city of southwest South Dakota west-southwest of Pierre in the eastern part of the Black Hills. It is a trade, transportation, and tourist center. ⦿ Pop. 54,523.

Rap·pa·han·nock (răp'ə-hăn'ək). A river of northeast Virginia rising in the Blue Ridge and flowing about 341 km (212 mi) generally southeast to form a long estuary that empties into Chesapeake Bay.

Rar·i·tan (răr'ĭ-tən). A river, about 129 km (80 mi) long, formed by the confluence of two tributaries in north-central New Jersey and flowing eastward to **Raritan Bay,** the western arm of Lower New York Bay, at Perth Amboy.

Rar·o·ton·ga (răr'ə-tŏng'gə). A volcanic island of the southern Pacific Ocean in the southwest Cook Islands. Discovered in the early 1820's by English missionaries, it is the largest and most important island in the group.

Ras Da·shan (räs də-shän'). A mountain, 4,623.2 m (15,158 ft) high, in northern Ethiopia south-southwest of Aksum. Of volcanic origin, it is the highest peak in the country.

Rasht (räsht) also **Resht** (rĕsht). A city of northwest Iran near the Caspian Sea east-southeast of Tabriz. It is a trade and silk-producing center. ⦿ Pop. 374,475.

Ra·tak Chain (rä'täk'). The eastern group of the Marshall Islands in the western Pacific Ocean. The chain comprises 2 coral islands and 14 atolls, including Bikini.

Ra·ting·en (rä'tĭng-ən). A city of west-central Germany north-northwest of Düsseldorf. Chartered in 1276, it is a manufacturing center. ⦿ Pop. 87,710.

Rat Islands (răt). A group of islands in the western Aleutian Islands of southwest Alaska. Kiska and **Rat Island** are included in the group.

Raur·ke·la or **Rour·ke·la** (rôr-kā'lə). A town of eastern India west of Calcutta. It has important iron and steel plants. ⦿ Pop. 140,408.

Ra·ven·na (rə-vĕn'ə, rä-vĕn'nä). A city of northeast Italy near the Adriatic Sea northeast of Florence. An important naval station in Roman times, it was an Ostrogoth capital in the fifth and sixth centuries A.D. and the center of Byzantine power in Italy from the late sixth century until c. 750, when it was conquered by the Lombards. Ravenna eventually became part of the papal dominions and was included in the kingdom of Italy in 1860. The city is famous for

its colorful mosaics of the fifth and sixth centuries and for its Roman and Byzantine buildings. ⦿ Pop. 135,435.

Ra·vi (rä'vē). A river, about 764 km (475 mi) long, of northwest India and northeast Pakistan. Rising in the Himalaya Mountains, it is one of the five rivers of the Punjab.

ra·vine (rə-vēn'). A deep, narrow valley or gorge worn by running water.

Ra·wal·pin·di (rä'wəl-pĭn'dē). A city of northeast Pakistan north-northwest of Lahore. Settled by Sikhs in 1765, it was interim capital of Pakistan from 1959 to 1970. ⦿ Pop. 794,843.

Ray (rā), **Cape.** A promontory of extreme southwest Newfoundland, Canada, on Cabot Strait.

Ray·side-Bal·four (rā'sīd-băl'fôr', -fər). A town of central Ontario, Canada. It is a suburb of Sudbury. ⦿ Pop. 15,017.

Ray·town (rā'toun'). A city of western Missouri, a residential suburb surrounded by Kansas City. ⦿ Pop. 30,601.

Read·ing (rĕd'ĭng). **1.** A borough of south-central England west of London. Occupied by the Danes in 871, it was chartered in 1253. ⦿ Pop. 137,749. **2.** A town of northeast Massachusetts, a primarily residential suburb of Boston. ⦿ Pop. 22,539. **3.** A city of southeast Pennsylvania on the Schuykill River northwest of Philadelphia. Settled in 1748, it is an important commercial, industrial, and transportation center. ⦿ Pop. 78,380.

Re·ci·fe (rə-sē'fə). A city of northeast Brazil on the Atlantic Ocean south of Natal. First settled in 1535, it was plundered by English privateers in 1595 and occupied by the Dutch from 1630 to 1654. It is the chief urban center of northeast Brazil and an important transportation hub. ⦿ Pop. 296,995.

Reck·ling·hau·sen (rĕk'lĭng-hou'zən). A city of west-central Germany southwest of Münster. Originally a Saxon settlement, it was held by the archbishop of Cologne after 1236 and passed to Prussia in 1815. ⦿ Pop. 127,150.

Red·car (rĕd'kär'). A municipal borough of northeast England on the North Sea northeast of Middlesbrough. It is a seaside resort and has iron and steel industries. ⦿ Pop. 85,600.

Red·cloud Peak (rĕd'kloud'). A mountain, 4,280.4 m (14,034 ft) high, in the San Juan Mountains of southwest Colorado.

Red Deer (rĕd' dîr'). A city of south-central Alberta, Canada, on the Red Deer River north of Calgary. It is a trade center in a farm and dairy region. ⦿ Pop. 46,393.

Red Deer River. A river rising in the Rocky Mountains of southwest Alberta, Canada, and flowing about 619 km (385 mi) northeast then southeast and east across the province and into the South Saskatchewan River just across the Saskatchewan border.

Red·ding (rĕd′ĭng). A city of northern California on the Sacramento River south of Shasta Lake. It is a resort and has lumbering and food-processing industries. ⊛ Pop. 66,462.

Red·ditch (rĕd′ĭch). An urban district of central England south of Birmingham. It was designated a new town in 1964 to alleviate overcrowding in Birmingham and the surrounding area. ⊛ Pop. 67,400.

Red·ford (rĕd′fərd). A community of southeast Michigan, a suburb of Detroit. ⊛ Pop. 58,441.

Red·lands (rĕd′ləndz). A city of southern California in the San Bernardino Valley. Redlands is primarily residential with varied light industries. ⊛ Pop. 60,394.

Red·mond (rĕd′mənd). A city of west-central Washington, a residential and industrial suburb of Seattle east of Lake Washington. Computers, computer software, and electronics are its main industries. ⊛ Pop. 35,800.

Re·don·do Beach (rĭ-dŏn′dō). A city of southern California, a residential suburb of Los Angeles on the Pacific Ocean. ⊛ Pop. 60,167.

Re·doubt (rē′dout′), **Mount.** A volcano, 3,111 m (10,200 ft) high, of southern Alaska. The highest peak of the Aleutian Range, it erupted in 1989 for the first time in 25 years.

Red River. 1. or in China **Yu·an Jiang** (yōo-än′ jyäng′, ywän′) and in Vietnam **Hong Ha** (hông′ hä′) or **Song Hong** (sông′ hông′). A river of southeast Asia rising in southern China and flowing about 1,175 km (730 mi) generally south through northern Vietnam to a fertile delta on the Gulf of Tonkin. 2. A river of the south-central United States rising in two branches in the Texas Panhandle and flowing about 1,638 km (1,018 mi) eastward along the Texas-Oklahoma border and into Arkansas, where it changes direction and flows southward into Louisiana and then southeast to the Mississippi River. 3. also **Red River of the North.** A river of the north-central United States and south-central Canada formed by the confluence of two tributaries in west-central Minnesota and flowing about 499 km (310 mi) north along the Minnesota–North Dakota border into southeast Manitoba, Canada, where it empties into Lake Winnipeg. The **Red River Valley** is a fertile region for growing wheat, flax, and barley.

Red Sea. A long, narrow sea between northeast Africa and the Arabian Peninsula. It is linked with the Mediterranean to the north through the Gulf of Suez and the Suez Canal and with the Gulf of Aden and the Arabian Sea to the south through the Bab el Mandeb.

Red Square. A large open area in central Moscow bordered by the Kremlin, Lenin's tomb, St. Basil's Cathedral, and the GUM department store. Major Soviet holidays, such as May Day and the commemoration of the Russian Revolution (November 7), were marked by elaborate parades in the square.

Red·wood City (rĕd′wŏod′). A city of western California northwest of Palo Alto. It is a chiefly residential community with an electronics industry. ⊛ Pop. 66,072.

reef (rēf). *abbr.* **rf.** A strip or ridge of rocks, sand, or coral that rises to or near the surface of a body of water.

Re·gens·burg (rā′gənz-bûrg′, -gəns-bŏork′). A city of southeast Germany on the Danube River north-northeast of Munich. An ancient Celtic settlement, it was an important Roman frontier station and later a free imperial city before passing to Bavaria in 1810. ⊛ Pop. 125,337.

Reg·gio di Ca·la·bri·a (rĕj′ē-ō dē kä-lä′brē-ä, rĕd′jō) also **Reggio** or **Reggio Calabria**. A city of extreme southern Italy on the Strait of Messina opposite Sicily. Founded by Greek colonists in the late eighth century B.C., it suffered frequent invasions because of its strategic location. Earthquakes have also caused extensive damage. ⊛ Pop. 169,709.

Reggio nell'E·mi·lia (nĕl′ĕ-mēl′yä) also **Reggio** or **Reggio Emilia**. A city of north-central Italy west-northwest of Bologna. Founded by Romans in the second century B.C., it was ruled by the Este family for many centuries. ⊛ Pop. 131,419.

Re·gi·na (rĭ-jī′nə). The capital and largest city of Saskatchewan, Canada, in the southern part of the province southeast of Saskatoon. It was the capital of the Northwest Territories until the province of Saskatchewan was created in 1905. ⊛ Pop. 179,178.

Rei·gate (rī′gĭt). A municipal borough of southern England, a residential suburb of London. ⊛ Pop. 53,000.

Reims (rēmz, ră̄ɴs). See **Rheims.**

Rein·deer Lake (rān′dîr′). A lake of northeast Saskatchewan and northwest Manitoba, Canada. It is drained by the **Reindeer River,** which flows about 230 km (143 mi) southward to the Churchill River.

Rei·sters·town (rī′stərz-toun′). A community of north-central Maryland, a residential suburb of Baltimore. ⊛ Pop. 19,314.

re·lief (rĭ-lēf′). *Geology.* The variations in elevation of an area of the earth's surface.

relief map. A map that depicts land configuration, usually with contour lines.

Rem·scheid (rĕm′shīt′). A city of west-central Germany northeast of Cologne. It is a center of the German tool and hardware industry. ⊛ Pop. 123,610.

Rennes (rĕn). A city of northwest France north

of Nantes. It was an important town in Roman times and became capital of Brittany in 1196. ◉ Pop. 197,497.

Re·no (rē′nō′). A city of western Nevada near the California border. Developed after the coming of the Union Pacific Railroad in 1868, it is a famous resort that was once noted primarily as a divorce center. ◉ Pop. 133,850.

Ren·ton (rĕn′tən). A city of west-central Washington, a suburb of Seattle. It has an extensive aircraft industry. ◉ Pop. 41,688.

Re·pen·ti·gny (rə-päN-tē-nyē′). A town of southern Quebec, Canada, a residential suburb of Montreal. ◉ Pop. 34,419.

re·pub·lic (rĭ-pŭb′lĭk). *abbr.* **rep., Rep., Repub. 1. a.** A political order whose head of state is not a monarch and in modern times is usually a president. **b.** A nation that has such a political order. **2. a.** A political order in which the supreme power lies in a body of citizens who are entitled to vote for officers and representatives responsible to them. **b.** A nation that has such a political order. **3.** often **Republic.** A specific republican government of a nation. **4.** An autonomous or partially autonomous political and territorial unit belonging to a sovereign federation. **—re·pub′li·can** *adj. & n.*

Re·pub·li·can River (rĭ-pŭb′lĭ-kən). A river, 676 km (420 mi) long, rising in eastern Colorado and flowing northeast and east across southern Nebraska then southeast through northeast-central Kansas, where it joins the Smoky Hill River to form the Kansas River.

res·er·voir (rĕz′ər-vwär′, -vwôr′, -vôr′). *abbr.* **res.** A natural or artificial pond or lake used for the storage and regulation of water.

Resht (rĕsht). See **Rasht.**

Re·sis·ten·cia (rĕs′ĭ-stĕn′sē-ə, rĕ′sĕs-tĕn′-syä). A city of northeast Argentina on the Paraná River opposite Corrientes. It is a major trade and shipping center. ◉ Pop. 228,199.

Re·și·ta (rĕ′shē-tsä′). A city of western Romania in the western Transylvanian Alps west-northwest of Bucharest. It has an important iron and steel industry. ◉ Pop. 110,300.

Res·ton (rĕs′tən). A community of northeast Virginia, a suburb of the Washington, D.C.–Alexandria, Virginia, area. ◉ Pop. 48,556.

Re·thondes (rə-tôNd′). A village of northern France west-northwest of Rheims. The armistice ending World War I was signed here on November 11, 1918.

Ré·un·ion (rē-yōōn′yən, rā-ü-nyôN′). An island of France in the western Indian Ocean southwest of Mauritius. Previously uninhabited, it was visited by the Portuguese in the early 16th century and first colonized by the French in the mid-1600's as the Isle de Bourbon. Renamed

Réunion in 1793, it became an overseas department in 1946.

Reus (rĕ′ōōs). A city of northeast Spain near the Mediterranean Sea west of Barcelona. Founded c. 13th century, it is a trade and industrial center. ◉ Pop. 82,354.

Reut·ling·en (roit′lĭng-ən). A city of southwest Germany south of Stuttgart. Reutlingen was a free imperial city from 1240 to 1802 and is now a manufacturing center with an important textile industry. ◉ Pop. 107,607.

Re·vere (rĭ-vîr′). A city of eastern Massachusetts, a mainly residential suburb of Boston on Massachusetts Bay. ◉ Pop. 42,786.

Re·vil·la·gi·ge·do Islands also **Re·vil·la Gi·ge·do Islands** (rĭ-vē′ə-hĭ-hā′dō, rĕ-vē′yä-hē-hĕ′thô). An island group of Mexico in the Pacific Ocean south of Baja California. The rocky islands are surrounded by good fishing grounds.

Reyes (rāz), **Point.** A promontory on the central California coast northwest of San Francisco. It is reported to be the windiest and foggiest place on the western coast of the continental United States, with an average of 137 foggy days a year.

Rey·kja·vík (rā′kyə-vēk′, -vĭk′). The capital and largest city of Iceland, in the southwest part of the island. Traditionally founded in 874, it became capital of the country in 1918 after Denmark recognized Iceland's sovereignty. ◉ Pop. 101,418.

Rey·nolds·burg (rĕn′əldz-bûrg′). A city of central Ohio, a suburb of Columbus in an agricultural area. ◉ Pop. 25,748.

Rey·no·sa (rā-nō′sə). A city of eastern Mexico on the Rio Grande east-northeast of Monterrey. It is a processing and shipping center in an agricultural region. ◉ Pop. 194,693.

Rhae·ti·a (rē′shē-ə, -shə). An ancient Roman province that included present-day eastern Switzerland and western Austria. It was added to the Roman Empire during the reign of Augustus. (27 B.C.–A.D. 14). **—Rhae′tian** *adj. & n.*

Rhaetian Alps. A range of the central Alps primarily in eastern Switzerland and along the Italian and Austrian borders. It rises to Piz Bernina, 4,051.6 m (13,284 ft) high, in the Bernina section of the range on the Italian border.

Rhae·to·Ro·mance (rē′tō-rō-mǎns′). A group of three Romance dialects, including Romansch, spoken in southern Switzerland, northern Italy, and the Tyrol.

Rha·gae (rā′jē). An ancient city of Media southeast of modern Tehran in north-central Iran. One of the greatest cities of ancient times, it was traditionally founded in 3000 B.C. and flourished until the Middle Ages. The city was finally destroyed by Tartars in the 12th century A.D.

Rheims or **Reims** (rēmz, rǎNs). A city of northeast France east-northeast of Paris. One of the most important cities of Roman Gaul, it was long the site of the coronation of French kings. In World War II the unconditional German surrender was signed at Allied headquarters here on May 7, 1945. ⊛ Pop. 180,611.

Rhei·ne (rī′nə). A city of northwest Germany on the Ems River north of Münster. It is a manufacturing center. ⊛ Pop. 70,685.

Rhen·ish (rĕn′ĭsh). Of or relating to the Rhine River or the lands bordering on it.

Rhine (rīn). A river of western Europe formed by the confluence of two tributaries in eastern Switzerland and flowing about 1,319 km (820 mi) north and northwest through Germany and the Netherlands to its two-pronged outlet on the North Sea. It is a major commercial shipping waterway linked by canals to other important European rivers and passes through a number of scenic valleys.

Rhine·land (rīn′lănd′, -lənd). A region along the Rhine River in western Germany. It includes noted vineyards and highly industrial sections north of Bonn and Cologne.

Rho (rō). A city of northern Italy, an industrial suburb of Milan. ⊛ Pop. 50,740.

Rhode Island[1] (rōd). An island of Rhode Island at the entrance to Narragansett Bay. Originally known as Aquidneck Island, it was renamed in 1644, probably after the isle of Rhodes.

Rhode Island[2] (rōd). *abbr.* **RI, R.I.** A state of the northeast United States on the Atlantic Ocean. It was admitted as one of the original Thirteen Colonies in 1790. Rhode Island was settled by religious exiles from Massachusetts, including Roger Williams, who founded Providence in 1636. It was granted a royal charter in 1663 and after the American Revolution (1775–1783) began the industrialization that is still a major part of the state's economy. Providence is the capital and the largest city. ⊛ Pop. 1,005,984. **—Rhode Is′land·er** *n.*

Rhodes (rōdz). An island of southeast Greece in the Aegean Sea off southwest Turkey. It is the largest of the Dodecanese Islands and was colonized by Dorians from Argos before 1000 B.C. and strongly influenced by the Minoan culture of Crete. The ancient city of **Rhodes,** on the northeast end of the island near the present-day city of **Rhodes,** was founded c. 408 B.C. Its harbor was the site of a bronze statue known as the Colossus of Rhodes, which was erected 292–280 B.C. and destroyed in 224 B.C. by an earthquake. It was one of the Seven Wonders of the World. The modern city has a population of 40,392.

Rho·de·sia (rō-dē′zhə). **1.** A region of south-central Africa south of Zaire and comprising modern-day Zambia and Zimbabwe. Probably in-

habited since ancient times, it was formerly administered by the British South Africa Company. **2.** See **Zimbabwe**[2]. **—Rho·de′sian** *adj. & n.*

Rhodesia and Nyasaland. A former British colonial federation (1953–1963) of south-central Africa that included the present-day countries of Zimbabwe, Zambia, and Malawi.

Rhod·o·pe Mountains (rŏd′ə-pē, rŏ-dō′-). A range in the Balkan Peninsula of southeast Europe extending southeast from southwest Bulgaria to northeast Greece and rising to 2,926.8 m (9,596 ft). In Roman times the range marked the boundary between Thrace and Macedonia.

Rhon·dda (rŏn′də, hrŏn′*th*ä). A municipal borough of southern Wales northwest of Cardiff. Coal mining was particularly important to its economy in the 1920's and 1930's and declined afterwards. ⊛ Pop. 81,700.

Rhone or **Rhône** (rōn). A river rising in the Alps of south-central Switzerland and flowing about 813 km (505 mi) west-southwest and northwest to Lake Geneva and then into eastern France, where it joins the Saône River at Lyon and continues southward to the Mediterranean Sea.

Ri·al·to (rē-ăl′tō). A city of southern California, a residential suburb of San Bernardino. ⊛ Pop. 72,388.

Ri·au Archipelago (rē′ou). An island group of western Indonesia off the southeast end of the Malay Peninsula. It is separated from Singapore by Singapore Strait.

Ri·bei·rão Prê·to (rē′bä-rouɴ′ prĕ′tōō). A city of southeast Brazil north-northwest of São Paulo. It is a processing center in an agricultural region. ⊛ Pop. 436,122.

Rich·ard·son (rĭch′ərd-sən). A city of northeast Texas, a residential and agricultural suburb of Dallas. ⊛ Pop. 74,840.

Ri·che·lieu (rĭsh′ə-lōō′). A river of southern Quebec, Canada, flowing about 121 km (75 mi) north from Lake Champlain to the St. Lawrence River. Discovered by the French explorer Samuel de Champlain in 1609, it was an important waterway for early explorers.

Rich·field (rĭch′fēld′). A city of southeast Minnesota, a residential suburb of Minneapolis. ⊛ Pop. 35,710.

Rich·land (rĭch′lənd). A city of southeast Washington on the Columbia River west-northwest of Walla Walla. It was developed in 1943–1945 to house employees of the nearby Hanford Atomic Works. Federal management of the city was relinquished in 1958. ⊛ Pop. 32,315.

Rich·mond (rĭch′mənd). **1.** A community of southwest British Columbia, Canada, a suburb of Vancouver on the Strait of Georgia. ⊛ Pop. 126,624. **2.** A city of western California on an inlet of San Francisco Bay north-northwest of Oakland. It is a port and industrial center.

 Pop. 87,425. **3.** A city of eastern Indiana east of Indianapolis. Settled in 1806 by Quakers, it is primarily an industrial center. Pop. 38,705. **4.** A city of east-central Kentucky south-southeast of Lexington. It is a tobacco and livestock market in the Bluegrass. Pop. 21,155. **5.** The capital of Virginia, in the east-central part of the state on the James River north of Petersburg. Settled in the 17th century, it became the capital of Virginia in 1779 and was strategically important in the American Revolution and the Civil War, during which it was the capital of the Confederacy. The evacuation of Richmond by Confederate troops on April 3, 1865, led to Gen. Robert E. Lee's surrender to Gen. Ulysses S. Grant on April 9. Pop. 203,056. **6.** See **Staten Island.**

Richmond Highlands. A community of west-central Washington, a residential suburb of Seattle. Pop. 26,037.

Richmond Hill. A city of southeast Ontario, Canada, north of Toronto. It is mainly residential. Pop. 37,778.

Ri·deau Canal (rĭ-dō′). A waterway, about 203 km (126 mi) long, of southeast Ontario, Canada, connecting the Ottawa River at Ottawa with Lake Ontario at Kingston. It follows the course of the **Rideau River** for much of its length and was constructed in 1826 to 1832.

ridge (rĭj). **1.** A long narrow chain of hills or mountains. Also called *ridgeline*. **2.** A long narrow elevation on the ocean floor.

Ridge·crest (rĭj′krĕst′). A city of south-central California east-northeast of Bakersfield. Pop. 27,725.

Ridge·field (rĭj′fēld′). A town of southwest Connecticut near the New York border north-northeast of Stamford. It is mainly residential. Pop. 20,919.

ridge·line (rĭj′līn′). See **ridge** (sense 2).

Ridge·wood (rĭj′wŏŏd′). A village of northeast New Jersey north-northeast of Paterson. Both British and American troops had encampments here during the Revolution. Pop. 24,152.

Rie·sa (rē′zə, -zä). A city of east-central Germany on the Elbe River east of Leipzig. Chartered in 1623, it is a port and an industrial center. Pop. 51,285.

Rif (rĭf). See **Er Rif.**

Riff or **Rif** (rĭf). **1.** *pl.* **Riff** or **Riffs** also **Rif·fi** (rĭf′ē) or **Rif** or **Rifs.** A member of any of several Berber peoples inhabiting Er Rif. **2.** The Berber language of this people. —**Rif′fi·an** *adj. & n.*

rift valley (rĭft). A deep fracture or break, about 25–50 km (15–30 mi) wide, in the earth's crust, creating an elongated valley bounded by two or more faults.

rift zone. A large area of the earth in which

plates of the earth's crust are moving away from each other, forming an extensive system of fractures and faults.

Ri·ga (rē′gə). The capital and largest city of Latvia on the **Gulf of Riga,** an inlet of the Baltic Sea bordering on Latvia and Estonia. Founded as a trading post on a site originally inhabited by Baltic tribes, the city became a member of the Hanseatic League in 1282 and later passed to Poland (1581), Sweden (1621), and Russia (1710). Pop. 865,227.

Right Bank (rīt). A district of Paris on the northern, or right, bank of the Seine River. The Arc de Triomphe, the Elysée Palace, the Louvre, fashionable shopping boulevards, and the picturesque area of Montmarte are on the Right Bank.

Ri·je·ka (rē-yĕk′ə). Formerly **Fi·u·me** (fyŏŏ′-mä, -mĕ). A city of western Croatia on the Adriatic Sea west-southwest of Zagreb. Held at various times by Austria, Croatia, France, and Hungary, it was seized by Italian irregulars in 1919. The Treaty of Rapallo between Italy and Yugoslavia (1920) guaranteed its status as an independent city, although it was formally annexed by Italy four years later. In 1947 the city was officially transferred to Yugoslavia. Pop. 167,964.

Rijs·wijk (rīs′vīk) also **Rys·wick** (rĭz′wĭk). A city of western Netherlands, a suburb of The Hague. The Treaty of Ryswick (1697) ended the War of the Grand Alliance between England and France and acknowledged William of Orange as William III of England. Pop. 49,790.

Ri·kers Island (rī′kərz). An island in the East River off the south coast of the Bronx, New York City. Part of the Bronx borough, it is the site of a large penitentiary.

Riks·mål (rĭks′môl′, rēks′-). See **Dano-Norwegian.**

rill also **rille** (rĭl). A small brook; a rivulet.

rill·et (rĭl′ĭt). A small rill.

Ri·mi·ni (rĭm′ə-nē). A city of northern Italy on the Adriatic Sea south-southeast of Ravenna. Founded by Umbrians, it became a strategic Roman military base after the third century B.C. Rimini was ruled as part of the Papal States from 1509 to 1860. Pop. 128,119.

Ri·mous·ki (rĭ-mŏŏ′skē). A city of southern Quebec, Canada, on the St. Lawrence River northeast of Quebec. It is a port and processing center. Pop. 29,120.

Ring of Fire (rĭng). An extensive zone of volcanic and seismic activity that coincides roughly with the borders of the Pacific Ocean.

Rí·o or **Ri·o** (rē′ō). For names of South American rivers, see the specific element; for example, **Plata, Río de la,** or **Roosevelt, Rio.**

Ri·o·bam·ba (rē′ō-bäm′bə, -väm′bä). A city of

central Ecuador in the Andes south of Quito. Ecuador's independence was proclaimed here in 1830. ⊛Pop. 75,455.

Rí·o Bra·vo (rē′ō brä′vō). See **Rio Grande¹**.

Ri·o Cla·ro (rē′ō klär′ō, rē′ōō). A city of southeast Brazil northwest of São Paulo. It is a trade and industrial center. ⊛Pop. 137,472.

Rí·o Cuar·to (rē′ō kwär′tō, rē′ô). A city of north-central Argentina south of Córdoba. It is a trade, processing, and industrial center. ⊛Pop. 110,254.

Ri·o de Ja·nei·ro (rē′ō dā zhə-nâr′ō, dē, rē′-ōō dĭ zhĭ-nā′rōō). Familiarly known as "Rio." A city of southeast Brazil on Guanabara Bay, an arm of the Atlantic Ocean. According to tradition, it was first visited in January 1502 by Portuguese explorers who believed Guanabara Bay to be the mouth of a river and therefore named the city Rio de Janeiro ("River of January"). It became capital of the colony of Brazil in 1763, of the Brazilian Empire in 1822, and of the independent country in 1889. In 1960 the capital was transferred to Brasília. ⊛Pop. 5,473,909.

Rí·o de O·ro (rē′ō dē ôr′ō, *th*ĕ). The southern part of Western Sahara in northwest Africa.

Ri·o Grande¹ (rē′ō gränd′, grän′dē). Or in Mexico **Rí·o Bra·vo** (rē′ō brä′vō). A river, about 3,033 km (1,885 mi) long, rising in southwest Colorado and flowing generally south through central New Mexico to southwest Texas, where it turns southeast and forms the U.S.-Mexican border for the rest of its course. It empties into the Gulf of Mexico near Brownsville, Texas, and Matamoros, Mexico.

Ri·o Gran·de² (rē′ō grän′də, rē′ōō grän′dĭ). A city of extreme southeast Brazil at the southern entrance of the Lagoa dos Patos. Founded in 1737, it is a major processing and shipping center. ⊛Pop. 172,408.

Rí·o Mu·ni (rē′ō mōō′nē). The mainland part of Equatorial Guinea, on the Bight of Biafra in western Africa.

ri·par·i·an (rĭ-pâr′ē-ən). Of, on, or relating to the banks of a natural course of water.

Rip·u·ar·i·an (rĭp′yōō-âr′ē-ən). **1.** Of, relating to, or being a group of Franks who settled along the Rhine, near Cologne, in the fourth century A.D. **2.** A Ripuarian Frank.

riv·er (rĭv′ər). *abbr.* **r., R., riv.** A large natural stream of water emptying into an ocean, a lake, or another body of water and usually fed along its course by converging tributaries.

river basin. The land area drained by a river and its tributaries.

riv·er·bed (rĭv′ər-bĕd′). The area between the banks of a river ordinarily covered by water.

riv·er·head (rĭv′ər-hĕd′). The source of a river.

riv·er·ine (rĭv′ə-rīn′, -rēn′). **1.** Relating to or resembling a river. **2.** Located on or inhabiting the banks of a river or waterway; riparian. **3.** An inland or coastal area constituting both land and water, characterized by limited landlines for communications, and extensive coastal waters and inland waterways providing natural routes for transport.

Riv·er·side (rĭv′ər-sīd′). A city of southern California northeast of Santa Ana. The navel orange was introduced here in 1873, and the city still has an important citrus industry. ⊛Pop. 226,505.

Riv·er·ton Heights (rĭv′ər-tən). A community of west-central Washington, a suburb of Seattle. ⊛Pop. 33,500.

Riv·i·er·a (rĭv′ē-ĕr′ə, rē-vyĕ′rä). A narrow coastal region between the Alps and the Mediterranean Sea extending from southeast France to northwest Italy. The Riviera, also known as the Côte d'Azur in France, is a popular resort area that is noted for its flowers grown for export and for use in perfumery.

Riviera Beach. A city of southeast Florida on the Atlantic Ocean north of West Palm Beach. Settled in 1920's, it is a popular winter resort with varied industries. ⊛Pop. 27,639.

Ri·yadh (rē-yäd′). The capital and largest city of Saudi Arabia, in the east-central part of the country east-northeast of Mecca. Situated in a desert oasis, it was formerly a walled city until the oil boom of the 1950's led to the demolition of older structures to make way for commercial expansion. ⊛Pop. 3,000,000.

Road Town (rōd). The capital of the British Virgin Islands, on Tortola Island in the West Indies east of Puerto Rico. It is a port of entry. ⊛Pop. 2,479.

Ro·a·noke (rō′ə-nōk′). An independent city of southwest Virginia west-southwest of Richmond. It grew with the coming of the railroad in 1882 and is today a tourist and industrial center. ⊛Pop. 96,397.

Roanoke Island. An island of northeast North Carolina off the Atlantic coast between Albemarle and Pamlico sounds. Colonists dispatched by Sir Walter Raleigh founded the first English settlement in North America in August 1585 but returned to England the following year. A second group of colonists organized by Raleigh landed on the island in July 1587 but vanished sometime before 1591.

Roanoke River. A river rising in southwest Virginia and flowing about 660 km (410 mi) generally east and southeast to Albemarle Sound in northeast North Carolina.

Rob·son (rŏb′sən), **Mount.** A mountain, 3,956.5 m (12,972 ft) high, of eastern British Columbia, Canada, on the border with Alberta. It is the highest elevation in the Canadian Rocky Mountains.

Ro·ca (rō′kə, rô′-), **Cape.** A cape of western Portugal on the Atlantic Ocean west-northwest of Lisbon. It is the westernmost extremity of continental Europe.

Roch·dale (rŏch′dāl′). A borough of northwest England north-northeast of Manchester. It is a manufacturing center with an important textile industry. ◉ Pop. 288,400.

Roch·es·ter (rŏch′ĭ-stər, -ĕs′tər). **1.** A municipal borough of southeast England southeast of London. Rochester was an important Roman and Saxon settlement. ◉ Pop. 56,030. **2.** A city of southeast Minnesota southeast of St. Paul. The Mayo Clinic (founded in 1889) is located here. ◉ Pop. 70,745. **3.** A city of southeast New Hampshire north-northwest of Dover. Settled in 1728, it has diverse industries. ◉ Pop. 25,630. **4.** A city of western New York east-northeast of Buffalo on the New York State Barge Canal near Lake Ontario. It was first settled c. 1812 and grew rapidly after the opening of the Erie Canal in 1825. ◉ Pop. 231,636.

Rock Creek Butte (rŏk). A mountain, 2,777 m (9,106 ft) high, in the Blue Mountains of northeast Oregon. It is the highest elevation in the range.

Rock·ford (rŏk′fərd). A city of northern Illinois west-northwest of Chicago. Founded in 1834, it is a trade, processing, and shipping center. ◉ Pop. 139,426.

Rock Hill. A city of northern South Carolina north of Columbia. It is a manufacturing and processing center with a textile industry. ◉ Pop. 41,643.

Rock·ies (rŏk′ēz). See **Rocky Mountains.**

Rock Island. A city of northwest Illinois on the Mississippi River adjacent to Moline. It was the site of a Union prison during the Civil War (1861–1865). ◉ Pop. 40,552.

Rock·land (rŏk′lənd). A town of eastern Massachusetts south-southeast of Boston. It is an industrial center. ◉ Pop. 16,123.

Rock River. A river rising in southeast Wisconsin and flowing about 459 km (285 mi) generally south and southwest to the Mississippi River in northwest Illinois.

Rock Springs. A city of southwest Wyoming north of the Utah border. It was a trading post and stagecoach station on the Oregon Trail in the 1860's. ◉ Pop. 19,050.

Rock·ville (rŏk′vĭl′, -vəl). A city of central Maryland north-northwest of Washington, D.C. It is the site of several research laboratories. ◉ Pop. 44,835.

Rockville Cen·tre (sĕn′tər). A village of southeast New York on southwest Long Island south-southwest of Hempstead. It is primarily residential. ◉ Pop. 24,727.

Rock·y Mount (rŏk′ē). A city of northeast North Carolina east-northeast of Raleigh. It is a manufacturing, processing, and shipping center in a rich agricultural region. ◉ Pop. 48,997.

Rocky Mountains also **Rock·ies** (rŏk′ēz). A major mountain system of western North America extending more than 4,827 km (3,000 mi) from northwest Alaska to the Mexican border. The system includes numerous ranges and forms the Continental Divide. Its highest elevation is Mount Elbert, 4,402.1 m (14,433 ft), in central Colorado. In Canada the Rockies rise to 3,956.5 m (12,972 ft) at Mount Robson in eastern British Columbia. Sections of the mountains were explored in early times by Francisco Vásquez de Coronado, Lewis and Clark, Zebulon Pike, Sir Alexander Mackenzie, and Simon Fraser.

Rocky Mountain States. A region of the western United States including Colorado, Idaho, Montana, Nevada, Utah, and Wyoming.

Rocky River. A city of northeast Ohio, a residential suburb of Cleveland. ◉ Pop. 20,410.

Roe·se·la·re (rōō′sə-lär′ə). A city of western Belgium west-northwest of Brussels. It is an industrial center. ◉ Pop. 51,649.

Rog·ers (rŏj′ərz). A city of northwest Arkansas north of Fayetteville. It is a processing center in a farming and tourist area. ◉ Pop. 24,692.

Rogue River (rōg). A river, about 322 km (200 mi) long, rising in the Cascade Range of southwest Oregon and flowing generally south and southwest to the Pacific Ocean.

Rohn·ert Park (rō′nərt). A city of west-central California, a residential suburb of Santa Rosa. ◉ Pop. 36,326.

Roll·ing Meadows (rō′lĭng). A city of northeast Illinois, a residential suburb of Chicago. ◉ Pop. 22,591.

Ro·ma·gna (rō-män′yə, rô-mä′nyä). A historical region of north-central Italy. It was the center of Byzantine influence in Italy and later came under papal rule. The region now forms part of Emilia-Romagna.

Ro·ma·ic (rō-mā′ĭk). Modern Greek. —**Ro·ma′ic** *adj.*

Ro·man (rō′mən). *abbr.* **Rom. 1. a.** Of or relating to ancient or modern Rome or its people or culture. **b.** Of or relating to the Roman Empire. **2. a.** Of, relating to, or composed in the Latin language. **b.** Of or using the Latin alphabet. **3.** A native, inhabitant, or citizen of ancient or modern Rome. **4.** The Italian language as spoken in Rome.

Roman Empire also **Rome** (rōm). An empire

that succeeded the Roman Republic during the time of Augustus, who ruled from 27 B.C. to A.D. 14. At its greatest extent it encompassed territories stretching from Britain and Germany to North Africa and the Persian Gulf. After 395 it was split into the Byzantine Empire and the Western Roman Empire, which rapidly sank into anarchy under the onslaught of barbarian invaders from the north and east. The last emperor of the West, Romulus Augustulus (born c. 461), was deposed by Goths in 476, the traditional date for the end of the empire.

Ro·ma·ni·a (rō-mā′nē-ə, -mān′yə) or **Ru·ma·ni·a** (rōō-). *abbr.* **Rom.** A country of southeast Europe with a short coastline on the Black Sea. Originally a Roman province, the area was conquered from the 3rd to the 12th century by a succession of invaders, including Goths, Huns, Magyars, and Mongols. In the 13th century two principalities, Moldavia and Walachia, emerged, becoming vassal states within the Turkish Empire and eventually Russian protectorates. They were united in 1861, became independent in 1878, and became a kingdom in 1881. Romania was on the side of the Allies in World War I and later fell into political disarray, with the rise of fascism in the 1930's leading to the overthrow of the monarchy and the establishment of a dictatorship in 1940. During World War II Romania was allied with the Germans against the U.S.S.R. and surrendered to the invading Soviet army in 1944. A communist republic was established, which from 1965 to 1989 was ruled by Nicolae Ceausescu. In 1989 army-supported countrywide revolts occurred, and Ceausescu was overthrown, tried, and executed. A new constitution established Romania as a presidential republic in 1991. Bucharest is the capital and the largest city. ◉ Pop. 22,736,000.

Ro·ma·ni·an (rō-mā′nē-ən, -mān′yən) also **Ru·ma·ni·an** (rōō-). *abbr.* **Rom. 1.** Of or relating to Romania or its people, language, or culture. **2.** A native or inhabitant of Romania. **3.** The Romance language of the Romanians.

Ro·man·ic (rō-măn′ĭk). **1.** Of or derived from the ancient Romans. **2.** Of or relating to the Romance languages. — **Ro·man′ic** *n.*

Ro·mansch also **Ro·mansh** (rō-mänsh′, -mănsh′). The Rhaeto-Romance dialect that is an official language of Switzerland. Also called *Ladin.*

Rom·a·ny (rŏm′ə-nē, rō′mə-). **1.** *pl.* **-nies.** A Gypsy. **2.** The Indic language of the Gypsies. Also called *Gypsy.* **3.** Of or relating to the Gypsies or their language or culture.

Rom·blon Islands (rŏm-blōn′). An island group of the central Philippines in the Sibuyan Sea. Part of the Visayan Islands, the group comprises 3 large islands, including **Romblon Island,** and about 30 smaller islands. They were visited by the Spanish at least as early as 1582.

Rome (rōm). **1.** The capital and largest city of Italy, in the west-central part of the country on the Tiber River. Traditionally founded by Romulus in 753 B.C., it was ruled first by Etruscans, who were overthrown c. 500 B.C. The Roman Republic gradually extended its territory and expanded its influence, giving way to the Roman Empire during the reign of Augustus (27 B.C.– A.D. 14). As capital of the empire, Rome was considered the center of the known world, but the city declined when Constantine transferred his capital to Byzantium (323). Alaric I, king of the Visigoths, conquered the city in 410, leading to a lengthy period of devastation by barbarian tribes. In the Middle Ages the city revived as the spiritual and temporal power of the papacy increased. During the 1800's Rome was held at various times by the French until it became the capital of Italy in 1871. Vatican City remains an independent enclave within the confines of Rome. ◉ Pop. 2,693,383. **2.** A city of northwest Georgia northwest of Atlanta. It was established in 1834 on the site of a Cherokee settlement. ◉ Pop. 30,326. **3.** A city of central New York on the Mohawk River westnorthwest of Utica. Because of its location as a portage point, the city was strategically important during the French and Indian Wars and the American Revolution. ◉ Pop. 44,350. **4.** See **Roman Empire.**

Ro·me·o·ville (rō′mē-ō-vĭl′). A village of northeast Illinois north of Joliet. It is a processing center. ◉ Pop. 14,074.

Rom·u·lus (rŏm′yə-ləs). A city of southeast Michigan, a suburb of Detroit. ◉ Pop. 22,897.

Ron·ces·valles (rŏn′sə-vălz′, rôn′thĕs-väl′-yĕs). A mountain pass, 1,057.7 m (3,468 ft) high, through the western Pyrenees in northern Spain. It is the traditional site of the death of the hero Roland during the defeat of Charlemagne's army by the Saracens (778).

Ron·kon·ko·ma (rŏng-kŏng′kə-mə, rŏn-kŏn′-).

A town of southeast New York on central Long Island. It is mainly residential. ⊙ Pop. 20,391.

Ron·ne Ice Shelf (rō′nə, rŏn′ə). An area of shelf ice in western Antarctica south of the Weddell Sea.

Roo·sen·daal (rō′sən-däl′). A city of southwest Netherlands near the Belgian border south of Rotterdam. Founded in 1268, it is a transportation and industrial center. ⊙ Pop. 56,519.

Roo·se·velt (rō′zə-vĕlt′, rōz′vĕlt′, rōō′-). An unincorporated community of southeast New York on western Long Island southeast of Hempstead. It is chiefly residential. ⊙ Pop. 15,030.

Roosevelt, Rio. A river, about 644 km (400 mi) long, of northwestern Brazil. Originally known as the River of Doubt, it was renamed in honor of Theodore Roosevelt, the 26th U.S. President (1901–1909), who explored it in 1913.

Roosevelt Island. 1. Formerly **Wel·fare Is·land** (wĕl′fâr′). An island in the East River off the coast of central Manhattan Island. It was long the site of a penal institution and municipal hospital, which earned it the name Welfare Island after 1921. Renamed Franklin D. Roosevelt in 1973, it is now largely residential. **2.** An island of Antartica in the eastern part of the Ross Ice Shelf. Richard E. Byrd discovered the ice-covered island in 1934.

Ro·sa (rō′zə, rô′zä), **Monte.** A mountain, 4,636.9 m (15,203 ft) high, in the Pennine Alps on the Swiss-Italian border. It is the highest elevation in the range.

Ro·sa·ri·o (rō-zär′ē-ō′, -sär′-). A city of east-central Argentina on the Paraná River northwest of Buenos Aires. It grew rapidly as a port after 1870 with the development of the surrounding region. ⊙ Pop. 894,645.

Ro·sar·i·o Strait (rō-zâr′ē-ō, -zär′-). A strait in the San Juan Islands of northwest Washington connecting Admiralty Inlet with the Strait of Georgia.

Rose (rōz), **Mount.** A mountain, 3,287 m (10,778 ft) high, of western Nevada. It is in a winter sports area near Reno and Lake Tahoe.

Ro·seau (rō-zō′). The capital of Dominica, in the Windward Islands of the West Indies. It is a port on the southwest coast of the island. ⊙ Pop. 16,243.

Rose·burg (rōz′bûrg′). A city of southwest Oregon south-southwest of Eugene. Lumbering is its chief industry. ⊙ Pop. 17,032.

Rose·dale (rōz′dāl′). A community of north-central Maryland, a residential suburb of Baltimore. ⊙ Pop. 18,703.

Ro·selle (rō-zĕl′). **1.** A city of northeast Illinois, a suburb of Chicago. ⊙ Pop. 20,819. **2.** A borough of northeast New Jersey, a residential

suburb in the Newark-Elizabeth area. The inventor Thomas A. Edison (1847–1931) had a laboratory here. ⊙ Pop. 20,314.

Rose·mead (rōz′mēd′). A city of southern California, a commercial and residential suburb of Los Angeles. ⊙ Pop. 51,638.

Ro·sen·berg (rō′zən-bûrg′). A city of southeast Texas on the Brazos River west-southwest of Houston. It was founded in 1883 with the coming of the railroad. ⊙ Pop. 20,183.

Ro·sen·heim (rō′zən-hīm′). A city of southeast Germany on the Inn River at the foot of the Alps southeast of Munich. It is an industrial and processing center. ⊙ Pop. 52,112.

Rose·ville (rōz′vĭl′). **1.** A city of north-central California northeast of Sacramento in the foothills of the Sierra Nevada. It is a processing center in an agricultural region. ⊙ Pop. 44,685. **2.** A city of southeast Michigan, a residential suburb of Detroit. ⊙ Pop. 51,412. **3.** A city of southeast Minnesota, an industrial suburb of St. Paul. ⊙ Pop. 33,485.

Ros·kil·de (rŭ′skē′lə). A city of eastern Denmark on Sjaelland Island west of Copenhagen. It was the capital of Denmark from the tenth century until 1443. ⊙ Pop. 49,110.

Ross Ice Shelf (rôs, rŏs). A vast area in Antarctica bordering on **Ross Sea,** an arm of the southern Pacific Ocean. In the western part of the sea is **Ross Island,** site of the active volcano Mount Erebus.

Ros·tock (rŏs′tŏk′, rôs′tôk′). A city of northeast Germany near the Baltic Sea north-northwest of Berlin. Originally a Slavic fortress, it was chartered in 1218 and was an important member of the Hanseatic League in the 14th century. ⊙ Pop. 237,307.

Ros·tov (rə-stôf′) also **Ros·tov-on-Don** (-ŏn-dŏn′, -dôn′, -ôn-). A city of southwest Russia on the Don River near its outlet on an arm of the Sea of Azov. The city grew around a fortress built in 1761 and was chartered in 1797. ⊙ Pop. 1,012,649.

Ros·well (rŏz′wĕl′, -wəl). **1.** A city of northwest Georgia, a residential suburb of Atlanta. ⊙ Pop. 47,923. **2.** A city of southeast New Mexico southeast of Albuquerque. It is a trade and processing center in an irrigated farming region. ⊙ Pop. 44,654.

Ro·ta (rō′tə, -tä). An island of the western Pacific Ocean in the southern Mariana Islands north of Guam. The Japanese used it as a base for their attack on Guam on December 11, 1941. Rota remained in Japanese hands until the end of the World War II.

Roth·er·ham (rŏth′ər-əm). A borough of northern England northeast of Sheffield. It is an industrial center. ⊙ Pop. 255,727.

Rot·ter·dam (rŏt′ər-däm′). **1.** A city of southwest Netherlands on the Rhine-Meuse delta south-southeast of The Hague. Chartered in 1328, it was a major commercial power during the 16th and 17th centuries and is today a thriving port accessible via canal to oceangoing vessels. The city was heavily bombed during World War II. ◦ Pop. 597,272. **2.** An unincorporated community of east-central New York northwest of Schenectady. It is primarily residential. ◦ Pop. 24,800.

Rou·baix (rōō-bě′). A city of northern France north-northeast of Lille near the Belgian border. It is one of the largest textile centers in France. ◦ Pop. 101,602.

Rou·en (rōō-än′, -äN′). A city of northern France on the Seine River west-northwest of Paris. Of pre-Roman origin, it was repeatedly raided by the Norse in the ninth century, became the capital of medieval Normandy in the tenth century, and was held by the English from 1418 to 1449. Joan of Arc was burned at the stake here in 1431. ◦ Pop. 102,722.

Rour·ke·la (rôr-kā′lə). See **Raurkela.**

Rous·sil·lon (rōō-sē-yôN′). A historical region of southern France bordering on Spain and the Mediterranean Sea. Originally inhabited by Iberians, it became part of Roman Gaul after c. 121 B.C. and later changed hands many times, eventually becoming a Spanish possession that was transferred to France by the Treaty of the Pyrenees (1659).

Rou·yn (rōō′ĭn, rwăN). A city of southwest Quebec, Canada, near the Ontario border west-northwest of Quebec City. It is a trade center in a mining region. ◦ Pop. 17,224.

Ro·vi·go (rō-vē′gō). A city of northeast Italy between the Adige and Po rivers southwest of Venice. It belonged to the Este family from 1194 until 1482, when it passed to Venice. ◦ Pop. 51,708.

Rov·no (rôv′nə). A city of southwest Ukraine west of Kiev. It was annexed by Russia in 1793 and by Poland in 1921. The city was occupied by Soviet troops in 1939. ◦ Pop. 244,000.

Ro·vu·ma (rō-vōō′mə). See **Ruvuma.**

Row·land Heights (rō′lənd). A community of southern California, a residential suburb of the Los Angeles–Long Beach metropolitan area. ◦ Pop. 28,252.

Roy (roi). A city of northern Utah, a suburb of Ogden. ◦ Pop. 24,603.

Roy·al Gorge (roi′əl). A long, narrow canyon formed by the Arkansas River in south-central Colorado. Its near-vertical walls are more than 305 m (1,000 ft) high. The gorge was discovered by American explorer Zebulon Pike's expedition in 1806.

Royal Leamington Spa . See **Leamington.**

Royal Oak (ōk). A city of southeast Michigan, a residential suburb of Detroit. ◦ Pop. 65,410.

Ru·an·da (rōō-än′də). See **Rwanda.**

Ru·an·da-U·run·di (rōō-än′də-ōō-rōōn′dē). A former colonial possession of central Africa. Once a part of German East Africa, the territory was occupied (1961) by Belgian troops during World War I and became (1919) a Belgian League of Nations Mandate under the name Ruanda-Urundi. When independence was achieved in 1962, the region split into the present-day countries of Rwanda and Burundi.

Rub al Kha·li (rōōb′ ăl kä′lē, äl KHä′lē). Sometimes called "the Empty Quarter." A desert region in the southeast interior of the Arabian Peninsula. Virtually without water and uninhabited, it was first visited by an English explorer in 1932 but has not yet been completely explored.

Ru·da Śląs·ka (rōō′də shlôN′skə). A city of south-central Poland, a suburb of Katowice in a mining area. ◦ Pop. 171,356.

Ru·dolf (rōō′dŏlf), **Lake.** See Lake **Turkana.**

Ru·eil-Mal·mai·son (rōō-ā′măl-mā-zōN′, rü-ĕ′yə-). A town of north-central France on the Seine River west of Paris. It is an industrial center and the site of a museum housed in the former estate of Malmaison, where Napoleon, emperor of the French (1804–1814), lived from 1800 to 1804. ◦ Pop. 63,412.

Rug·by (rŭg′bē). A municipal borough of central England east-southeast of Birmingham. It is noted primarily as the site of Rugby School, opened in 1574, where the game of Rugby was developed in the 19th century. ◦ Pop. 59,564.

Rü·gen (rōō′gən, rü′-). An island of northeast Germany in the Baltic Sea. Separated from the mainland by a narrow channel, it was seized by Denmark in 1168, passed to Pomerania in 1325 and to Sweden in 1648, and became part of Prussia in 1815.

Ruhr (rōōr). A region of northwest Germany along and north of the **Ruhr River,** which flows about 233 km (145 mi) westward to the Rhine River near Duisburg. The industrial development of the region began in the 19th century.

Ruk·wa (rŭk′wə), **Lake.** A lake of western Tanzania east of Lake Tanganyika.

Ru·ma·ni·a (rōō-mā′nē-ə, -mān′yə). See **Romania.**

Ru·ma·ni·an (rōō-mā′nē-ən, -mān′yən). Variant of **Romanian.**

Run·ny·mede (rŭn′ē-mēd′). A meadow in southeast England on the Thames River west of London. King John accepted the Magna Carta, the charter of English political and civil liberties, here or on a nearby island in 1215.

Ru·pert River (rōō′pərt). A river of west-central Quebec, Canada, rising in Lake Mistassini and flowing about 611 km (380 mi) westward to James Bay.

Ru·se (roo′sä). A city of northeast Bulgaria on the Danube River south of Bucharest, Romania. Founded as a Roman fortress in the second century A.D., it is today a major port and industrial center. ◉ Pop. 193,000.

Rush·more (rŭsh′môr′, -mōr′), **Mount.** A mountain, 1,708 m (5,600 ft) high, in the Black Hills of western South Dakota. Its monument with massive carved likenesses of the American Presidents Washington, Jefferson, Lincoln, and Theodore Roosevelt was carved under the direction of the American sculptor Gutzon Borglum (1867–1941).

Rus·sell (rŭs′əl), **Mount.** A peak, 4,296.8 m (14,088 ft) high, of the Sierra Nevada in eastern California.

Rüs·sels·heim (roos′əls-hīm′, rü′səls-). A city of west-central Germany, a manufacturing suburb of Mainz on the Main River. ◉ Pop. 58,167.

Rus·sia (rŭsh′ə). *abbr.* **Rus., Russ. 1.** A former empire of eastern Europe and northern Asia. Originally settled by Slavs from the 3rd to the 8th century, the region was long a conglomerate of independent principalities until Moscow gained ascendancy in the 14th, 15th, and 16th centuries. The empire achieved the height of its power and territorial influence under Peter the Great and Catherine the Great in the 17th and 18th centuries. The early 1800's were a period of reactionism, and although some liberal reforms were effected in the late 1800's, discontent remained and led directly to the Revolutions of 1905 and 1917, an internal power struggle, and the formation of the U.S.S.R. in 1922. **2.** Officially **Rus·sian Federation** (rŭsh′-ən). Formerly **Russian Soviet Federated Socialist Republic.** A country of eastern Europe and northern Asia stretching from the Baltic Sea to the Pacific Ocean. It was proclaimed a republic in 1917 after the Russian Revolution, and as a constituent republic of the U.S.S.R. (1922–1991), it constituted 75 percent of the country's total land area. In 1990 Boris Yeltsin became president of the Russian republic, and in June 1991 he was reelected to the position in the republic's first popular election. When the Soviet Union disintegrated later that year, Yeltsin took control of the central government, and with Belarus and Ukraine, Russia formed (December 1991) the Commonwealth of Independent States, which was then joined by most of the other breakaway Soviet republics. In March 1992 Russia signed a treaty with most of the remaining Soviet republics (except Chechnya and Tatarstan), establishing the Russian Federation. Boris Yeltsin was reelected to a second term in 1996. Moscow is the capital. ◉ Pop. 147,997,000. **3.** See **Union of Soviet Socialist Republics.**

Rus·sian (rŭsh′ən). *abbr.* **Rus., Russ. 1.** Of or relating to Russia or its people, language, or culture. **2.** Of or relating to the Soviet Union. **3. a.** A native or inhabitant of Russia. **b.** A person of Russian descent. **c.** A native or inhabitant of the Sovi et Union. **4.** The Slavic language of the Russians.

Russian Federation. See **Russia** (sense 2).

Russian Soviet Federated Socialist Republic. *abbr.* **RSFSR, R.S.F.S.R.** See **Russia** (sense 2).

Rus·ta·vi (roo-stä′vē, -vyĭ). A city of southern Georgia southeast of Tbilisi. An ancient town on the site was destroyed c. 1400 by the Mongol conqueror Tamerlane. ◉ Pop. 160,000.

Rus·ton (rŭs′tən). A city of northern Louisiana west of Monroe. It was settled in 1884 as a railroad town. ◉ Pop. 20,027.

Ru·the·nia (roo-thēn′yə, -thē′nē-ə). A region of eastern Europe in western Ukraine south of the Carpathian Mountains. Ruled for centuries by various powers, including Poland and Austria-Hungary, it was later a province of Czechoslovakia (1918–1939) and was annexed by the U.S.S.R. in 1945 and incorporated into the Soviet Ukraine.

Ru·the·ni·an (roo-thē′nē-ən, -thēn′yən). **1.** Of or relating to Ruthenia, the Ruthenians, or their language or culture. **2.** A native or inhabitant of Ruthenia. **3.** The variety of Ukrainian used by the Ruthenians.

Ruth·er·ford (rŭth′ər-fərd, rŭth′-). A borough of northeast New Jersey, a residential suburb of the New York City metropolitan area. ◉ Pop. 17,790.

Rut·land (rŭt′lənd). A city of central Vermont south-southwest of Montpelier. There are marble quarries in the area. ◉ Pop. 18,230.

Ru·vu·ma also **Ro·vu·ma** (roo-voo′mə). A river of southeast Africa flowing about 724 km (450 mi) eastward along the Mozambique-Tanzania border to the Indian Ocean.

Ru·wen·zo·ri (roo′wən-zôr′ē, -zōr′ē). A mountain range of east-central Africa on the Uganda-

Zaire border. The range was explored in 1889 by the British journalist Henry M. Stanley and has traditionally been associated with the Alexandrian geographer Ptolemy's Mountains of the Moon, which the ancients erroneously supposed was the source of the Nile River.

Rwan·da (rōō-än′də). Formerly **Ru·an·da** (rōō-än′də). A country of east-central Africa. By the late 18th century the region was the site of a Tutsi kingdom inhabited principally by Hutus. In 1890 it became part of German East Africa and later (1919) part of the Belgian League of Nations mandate of Ruanda-Urundi. In 1959 ethnic fighting broke out following the accession of a new Tutsi king, and large numbers of Tutsis fled to nearby countries. Rwanda achieved independence from Belgium in 1962. A military coup in 1973 abolished the only legal political party and dissolved the assembly. Civilian rule was restored by a new constitution (1978) that established a one-party state, but the military leader remained as president. In 1990 the country was invaded by the Rwandan Patriotic Front, a group largely composed of exiled Tutsis, which signed a peace agreement with the government in 1992. Ethnic fighting broke out again in 1994, however, with the Tutsis routing the Hutu government, causing over a million Hutus to flee to Zaire. Kigali is the capital and largest city. ● Pop. 7,750,000. — **Rwan′dan** *adj. & n.*

Rya·zan (ryĭ-zän′). A city of west-central Russia on the Oka River southeast of Moscow. Founded in 1095, it was the capital of an independent principality until it was annexed by Moscow in 1521. It is now a manufacturing and industrial center. ● Pop. 524,097.

Ryb·nik (rĭb′nĭk). A town of southern Poland west-southwest of Katowice. Chartered in the 14th century, it passed to Poland in 1921 and is today a manufacturing and industrial center. ● Pop. 144,627.

Rye (rī). A city of southeast New York on Long Island Sound northeast of New York City. It is primarily residential. ● Pop. 15,083.

Rys·wick (rĭz′wĭk). See **Rijswijk**.

Ryu·kyu Islands (rē-ōō′kyōō′, ryōō′kyōō). An island group of southwest Japan extending about 1,046 km (650 mi) between Kyushu and Taiwan. The archipelago was incorporated into Japan in 1879 and returned to Japanese sovereignty in 1972 after occupation by U.S. forces following World War II.

Rze·szów (zhĕ′shōōf′). A city of southeast Poland east of Cracow. Chartered in the 14th century, it passed to Austria in 1772 and reverted to Poland after World War I. ● Pop. 153,888.

S

Saa·le (zä′lə, sä′-). A river, about 426 km (265 mi) long, rising in central Germany east of Kassel and flowing north to the Elbe River.

Saar¹ (sär, zär). A river, about 241 km (150 mi) long, rising in northeast France and flowing north and north-northwest to the Moselle River in western Germany. The river's valley, also known as the **Saar Basin**, is a highly industrialized region.

Saar² (sär, zär). See **Saarland**.

Saar·brück·en (zär-brŏŏk′ən, sär-, zär-brük′-). A city of southwest Germany on the Saar River near the French border south of Bonn. Located on the site of earlier Celtic, Roman, and Frankish settlements, it was chartered in 1321. ● Pop. 190,902.

Saa·re·maa also **Sa·re·ma** (sär′ə-mä′). An island of western Estonia in the Baltic Sea at the mouth of the Gulf of Riga. Long strategically important, it has been controlled by the Teutonic Knights and by Denmark, Sweden, Livonia, and Russia.

Saar·land (sär′länd′, zär′-, -länt′) or **Saar** (sär, zär). A region of southwest Germany in the Saar River valley on the border with France. Because of its extensive coal deposits, it was long contested between Germany and France, especially after World War I, when the League of Nations assigned the administration of the newly formed **Saar Territory** to France. After a 1935 plebiscite Saarland became a German province, but it was again placed under French control in 1945. The notion of an autonomous Saarland was rejected by the populace in 1955, and the region officially became a state of West Germany in 1957. — **Saar′land′er** *n.*

Sa·ba (sä′bə, -bä). An island of the northern Netherlands Antilles in the West Indies between St. Martin and St. Eustatius. First occupied by the Dutch in 1632, the island is the cone of an extinct volcano.

Sa·ba·dell (sä′bə-dĕl′, sä′bä-*th*ĕl′). A city of northeast Spain, an industrial and manufacturing suburb of Barcelona. ◉ Pop. 189,904.

Sa·bah (sä′bä′). A region of Malaysia in northeast Borneo. Sabah was a British protectorate, originally controlled by the British North Borneo Company, from the early 1800's until it became part of Malaysia in 1963.

Sa·bel·li·an (sə-bĕl′ē-ən). **1.** A group of extinct Italic languages that includes Sabine. **2.** A speaker of one of these languages.

Sa·bine (sā′bīn′). **1.** A member of an ancient people of central Italy, conquered and assimilated by the Romans in 290 B.C. **2.** The Italic language of the Sabines. **3.** Of or relating to the Sabines or their language or culture.

Sa·bine River (sə-bēn′). A river of eastern Texas rising northeast of Dallas and flowing about 925 km (575 mi) generally southeast and south to the Gulf of Mexico. Its lower course forms the Texas-Louisiana border and crosses **Sabine Lake** before entering the Gulf.

Sa·ble (sā′bəl), **Cape. 1.** A promontory of extreme southern Nova Scotia, Canada. It is on an inlet south of **Sable Island,** a low, sandy island often called "the Graveyard of the Atlantic" because of its hazard to navigation. **2.** A cape at the southwest tip of Florida. Part of Everglades National Park, it is the southernmost extremity of the U.S. mainland.

Sac (săk, sôk). Variant of **Sauk.**

Sa·co (sô′kō). A river, about 169 km (105 mi) long, rising in the White Mountains of northeast-central New Hampshire and flowing southeast through Maine to the Atlantic Ocean.

Sac·ra·men·to (săk′rə-mĕn′tō). The capital of California, in the north-central part of the state on the Sacramento River northeast of Oakland. Discovery of gold nearby in 1848 led to the growth of the original settlement as a trade and shipping center. It became the state capital in 1854. ◉ Pop. 369,365.

Sacramento Mountains. A range of south-central New Mexico extending north and south to the Texas border and rising to 3,660.9 m (12,003 ft) at Sierra Blanca Peak.

Sacramento River. A river of northern California rising near Mount Shasta and flowing about 611 km (380 mi) generally southward to an extension of San Francisco Bay.

Sa·fi (săf′ē). A city of western Morocco on the Atlantic Ocean west-northwest of Marrakesh. A Portuguese base in the early 16th century, it is today a fishing, processing, and shipping center. ◉ Pop. 278,000.

Sa·ga·mi·ha·ra (sə-gä′mē-här′ə). A city of east-central Honshu, Japan, an industrial suburb of Tokyo. ◉ Pop. 560,366.

Sa·ga·mi Sea (sə-gä′mē, sä-). A bay of the western Pacific Ocean on the east-central coast of Honshu, Japan, south-southwest of Tokyo.

Sag Harbor (săg). A village of southeast New York on the eastern end of Long Island on an inlet of Long Island Sound. A major whaling port in the early 19th century, it is today primarily a resort. ◉ Pop. 2,581.

Sa·gi·naw (săg′ə-nô′). A city of east-central Michigan on the **Saginaw River,** which flows about 32 km (20 mi) northward into **Saginaw Bay,** an inlet of Lake Huron. The city is a port of entry and an industrial center. ◉ Pop. 69,572.

Sag·ue·nay (săg′ə-nā′). A river, about 201 km (125 mi) long, of southern Quebec, Canada, flowing from Lake St. John eastward to the St. Lawrence River. First visited by the French explorer Jacques Cartier in 1535, it was long an important route for explorers, missionaries, and fur traders.

Sa·gun·to (sə-gōōn′tō, sä-). A city of eastern Spain north-northeast of Valencia. Founded by Greek colonists and later allied with Rome, it was besieged and captured by Carthaginian forces led by Hannibal (219–218 B.C.), thus precipitating the Second Punic War. Sagunto was held by the Moors from A.D. 713 until 1238. ◉ Pop. 57,380.

Sa·hap·ti·an (sä-hăp′tē-ən) also **Sha·hap·ti·an** (shä-). **1.** A North American Indian language family spoken in Washington, Oregon, and Idaho and comprising the Sahaptin and Nez Perce languages. **2.** A speaker of a Sahaptian language.

Sa·hap·tin (sä-hăp′tĭn) also **Sha·hap·tin** (shä-). **1.** *pl.* **Sahaptin** or **-tins** also **Shahaptin** or **-tins.** A member of any of various Native American peoples of Idaho, Washington, and Oregon. **2.** The dialectally diverse Sahaptian language of the Sahaptin.

Sa·har·a (sə-hâr′ə, -hăr′ə, -hä′rə). A vast desert of northern Africa extending east from the Atlantic coast to the Nile Valley and south from the Atlas Mountains to the region of the Sudan. During the Ice Age (about 50,000 to 100,000 years ago), the Sahara was a region of extensive shallow lakes watering large areas of vegetation, most of which had disappeared by Roman times. Introduction of the camel (probably in the first century A.D.) led to occupation by nomadic tribes who moved from oasis to oasis in search of water. — **Sa·har′an** *adj.*

Sa·ha·ran·pur (sə-här′ən-pōōr′). A city of north-central India north-northeast of Delhi. It was once a summer resort for the Mogul court. ◉ Pop. 374,945.

Sa·hel (sə-hāl′, -hĕl′). A semiarid region of north-central Africa south of the Sahara Desert. Since the 1960's it has been afflicted by prolonged periods of extensive drought. — **Sa·hel′-i·an** *adj.*

Sai·gon (sī-gŏn'). See **Ho Chi Minh City.**

Sai·maa (sī'mä'), **Lake.** A lake of southeast Finland. It is the largest of the **Saimaa Lakes,** a group of more than 120 interconnected lakes in the south-central and southeast part of the country.

Saint Al·bans (sānt' ôl'bənz). A municipal borough of southeast England north-northwest of London. On the site of the Roman settlement of Verulamium, it was founded as an abbey town in 793 and was the home of numerous important early chroniclers, including the English monk Matthew Paris (1200?–1259). ⊛ Pop. 127,657.

Saint Albert. A city of central Alberta, Canada. It is an industrial suburb of Edmonton. ⊛ Pop. 31,996.

Saint An·drews (ăn'drōōz). **1.** A burgh of eastern Scotland southeast of Dundee on **Saint Andrews Bay,** an inlet of the North Sea. Chartered in 1160, it was an important ecclesiastical center during the Middle Ages. It is now primarily a resort known for its golf courses. ⊛ Pop. 10,358. **2.** A community of southeast South Carolina, a residential suburb of Charleston. ⊛ Pop. 26,692.

Saint Ann. A city of eastern Missouri, an industrial suburb of St. Louis. ⊛ Pop. 14,489.

Saint Au·gus·tine (ô'gə-stēn'). A city of northeast Florida on the Atlantic Ocean south-southeast of Jacksonville. Founded by the Spanish in 1565, it is the oldest permanent European settlement in the United States. The city was strategically important from 1586, when the English explorer Sir Francis Drake burned it, until the Civil War, when it was occupied (1862–1865) by Union troops. ⊛ Pop. 11,692.

Saint-Bar·thél·e·my (săn-bär-tāl-mē') or **Saint Bar·thol·o·mew** (sānt bär-thŏl'ə-myōō'). Familiarly known as **Saint Barts** (bärts). An island of the French overseas department of Guadeloupe in the Leeward Islands of the West Indies southeast of Saint Martin.

Saint Bru·no de Mon·tar·ville or **Saint-Bru·no-de-Mon·tar·ville** (sānt brōō'nō də mŏn'tər-vĭl', săN brü-nô' də môN-tär-vēl'). A town of southern Quebec, Canada, a suburb of Montreal on the eastern bank of the St. Lawrence River. ⊛ Pop. 22,880.

Saint Cath·a·rines (sānt kăth'ə-rĭnz', kăth'rĭnz). A city of southeast Ontario, Canada, on the Welland Ship Canal east-southeast of Hamilton. Founded in 1790, it is an industrial center. ⊛ Pop. 129,300.

Saint Charles (chärlz). **1.** A city of northeast Illinois west of Chicago. It is a manufacturing center in an agricultural area. ⊛ Pop. 22,501. **2.** A city of eastern Missouri on the Missouri River northwest of St. Louis. Settled by French

traders in 1769, it was the state capital from 1821 to 1826. ⊛ Pop. 54,555.

Saint Chris·to·pher-Ne·vis (krĭs'tə-fər-nē'-vĭs, -nĕv'ĭs). See **Saint Kitts and Nevis.**

Saint Clair (klâr), **Lake.** A lake between southwest Ontario, Canada, and southeast Michigan. It is connected with Lake Huron by the **Saint Clair River,** about 64 km (40 mi) long.

Saint Clair Shores. A city of southeast Michigan, a residential suburb of Detroit. ⊛ Pop. 68,107.

Saint Cloud (kloud). A city of central Minnesota on the Mississippi River northwest of Minneapolis. Granite has been quarried in the area since the 1860's. ⊛ Pop. 48,812.

Saint Croix (kroi). An island of the U.S. Virgin Islands in the West Indies east of Puerto Rico. Discovered by Columbus in 1493, it was controlled successively by Holland, England, Spain, France, and Denmark, which sold it to the United States in 1917.

Saint Croix River. 1. A river, about 264 km (164 mi) long, rising in northwest Wisconsin and flowing generally south along the Minnesota border to the Mississippi River southeast of St. Paul. **2.** A river, about 121 km (75 mi) long, forming part of the boundary between eastern Maine and southwest New Brunswick, Canada. It rises in a series of lakes and flows generally southeast to Passamaquoddy Bay. In 1604 the French explorer Samuel de Champlain established a colony on **Saint Croix Island** near the mouth of the river, but the settlement was abandoned in 1605.

Saint-Cyr-l'É·cole (săN-sîr-lā-kôl'). A town of north-central France west of Versailles. It was long noted as the site of a military academy founded by Napoleon I in 1808. ⊛ Pop. 14,996.

Saint-De·nis (săN-də-nē'). **1.** A city of north-central France, an industrial suburb of Paris. Dating from early Christian times as a place of pilgrimage, it is the site of a Benedictine abbey founded in 626. The city's 12th-century Gothic cathedral contains the tombs of numerous French monarchs, including those of Louis XVI and Marie Antoinette. ⊛ Pop. 121,974. **2.** The capital of Réunion, a port on the Indian Ocean. It was founded in the late 17th century as a way station on the route to the Far East. ⊛ Pop. 121,999.

Sainte Anne de Beau·pré or **Sainte-Anne-de-Beau·pré** (sānt ăn' də bō-prā', săn-tăn). A village of southern Quebec, Canada, on the St. Lawrence River northeast of Quebec City. Its famous shrine was established by shipwrecked sailors in 1620.

Sainte Foy or **Sainte-Foy** (sānt foi', săNt fwä'). A city of southern Quebec, Canada, a suburb of Quebec City. ⊛ Pop. 68,883.

Saint E·li·as (sānt ĭ-lī'əs), **Mount.** A peak,

5,492.4 m (18,008 ft) high, in the **Saint Elias Mountains,** a section of the Coast Ranges on the border between eastern Alaska and southwest Yukon Territory, Canada. Mount Logan, rising to 5,954.8 m (19,524 ft), is the highest peak in the range and the highest elevation in Canada.

Sainte Thé·rèse or **Sainte-Thé·rèse** (sānt′ tə-rēz′, săɴt tā-rĕz′). A city of southern Quebec, Canada, on the St. Lawrence River northwest of Montreal. It is a manufacturing center. ⊛ Pop. 18,750.

Saint-É·tienne (săɴ-tā-tyĕn′). A city of southeast-central France southwest of Lyon. It has been a textile-producing center since the 11th century. ⊛ Pop. 199,528.

Saint Eu·stache or **Saint-Eu·stache** (sānt′ ōō-stäsh′, săɴ-tœ-stäsh′). A town of southern Quebec, Canada, west of Montreal. It is a residential and resort community. ⊛ Pop. 29,716.

Saint Eu·sta·ti·us (sānt yōō-stā′shəs, -shē-əs). An island of the Netherlands Antilles in the Leeward Islands of the West Indies northwest of St. Kitts. Settled originally by the French, it passed to the Dutch in 1632. During the 18th century the island was a favorite haunt of pirates and smugglers.

Saint Fran·cis River (frăn′sĭs). A river, about 756 km (470 mi) long, rising in southeast Missouri and flowing generally southward in a meandering course to the Mississippi River in eastern Arkansas.

Saint Fran·çois or **Saint-Fran·çois** (sānt′ frănswä′, săɴ frän-swä′). A river, about 265 km (165 mi) long, of southern Quebec, Canada, flowing southwest and northwest to the Mississippi River.

Saint Gall (sānt gôl′, gäl′, săɴ gäl′). See **Sankt Gallen.**

Saint George's (sānt jôr′jəz). The capital of Grenada, a port on the southwest coast of the island in the Windward Islands of the West Indies. ⊛ Pop. 7,500.

Saint George's Channel. A strait between western Wales and southeast Ireland. It connects the Atlantic Ocean with the Irish Sea.

Saint Gott·hard (gŏt′ərd). A range of the Lepontine Alps in south-central Switzerland. It is crossed by **Saint Gotthard Pass,** 2,115.2 m (6,935 ft) high.

Saint He·le·na (hə-lē′nə). A volcanic island in the southern Atlantic Ocean west of Angola. Together with the islands of Ascension and Tristan da Cunha, it forms the British dependency of **Saint Helena** and has been occupied by the British since the mid-1600's. The island is best known as Napoleon's place of exile from 1815 until his death in 1821. Jamestown is the capital. ⊛ Pop. 7,000.

Saint Hel·ens (hĕl′ənz). A borough of northwest England east-northeast of Liverpool. It is an important center of glass manufacture. ⊛ Pop. 180,216.

Saint Helens, Mount. An active volcanic peak, 2,549 m (8,363 ft) high, of the Cascade Range in southwest Washington. Before its violent eruption on May 18, 1980, it was 2,949.7 m (9,671 ft) high. The eruption produced a smoke plume visible over much of western Washington and Oregon, set off fires and mud slides that killed at least 65 people, and covered a large area with a blanket of volcanic ash. Sporadic eruptions of lesser intensity have occurred since that time.

Saint Hel·ier (hĕl′yər). A town of Jersey, England, in the Channel Islands. Home to French writer Victor Hugo from 1852 to 1855, it is now a resort and residential center. ⊛ Pop. 24,941.

Saint Hu·bert or **Saint-Hu·bert** (sānt′ hyōō′-bərt, săɴ ü-bĕr′). A town of southern Quebec, Canada, a suburb of Montreal east of the St. Lawrence River. ⊛ Pop. 60,573.

Saint Hy·a·cinthe or **Saint-Hy·a·cinthe** (sānt′ hī′ə-sĭnth, săɴ-tyä-săɴt′). A city of southern Quebec, Canada, east-northeast of Montreal. It is an industrial center. ⊛ Pop. 38,246.

Saint Jean or **Saint-Jean** (săɴ zhäɴ′) or **Saint Johns** (sānt jōnz′). A city of southern Quebec, Canada, on the Richelieu River southeast of Montreal. Founded in 1666, it was an important British fortress in the 17th and 18th centuries. ⊛ Pop. 35,640.

Saint Jean or **Saint-Jean, Lake.** See Lake **Saint John.**

Saint Jé·rôme or **Saint-Jé·rôme** (sānt′ jə-rōm′, săɴ zhā-rōm′). A city of southern Quebec, Canada, northwest of Montreal. It is an industrial center with textile and paper mills. ⊛ Pop. 25,123.

Saint John[1] (sānt jŏn′). An island of the U.S. Virgin Islands in the West Indies east of Puerto Rico. Discovered by Columbus in 1493, it passed to various European powers before Denmark sold it to the United States in 1917.

Saint John[2] (sānt jŏn′). A city of southern New Brunswick, Canada, at the mouth of the St. John River on the Bay of Fundy. Settled as a French trading post in the 1630's, it was captured by the British in 1758 and was a refuge for Loyalists after the American Revolution. ⊛ Pop. 129,376.

Saint John (sānt jŏn) or **Saint Jean** or **Saint-Jean** (săɴ zhäɴ′), **Lake.** A lake of south-central Quebec, Canada, connected by the Saguenay River with the St. Lawrence River. The lake is a popular resort area.

Saint John River. A river, about 673 km (418 mi) long, rising in northern Maine and flowing northeast into New Brunswick, Canada, then generally southeast, south, east, and south into the Bay of Fundy. It was discovered in 1604 by the French explorer Samuel de Champlain.

Saint Johns (jŏnz). **1.** See **Saint Jean. 2.** See **Saint John's** (sense 1).

Saint John's (sānt jŏnz). **1.** also **Saint Johns.** The capital of Antigua and Barbuda, on the northern coast of Antigua in the Leeward Islands of the West Indies. Tourism is important to its economy. ◉ Pop. 22,342. **2.** The capital and largest city of Newfoundland, Canada, on the southeast coast of the island. One of the oldest settlements in North America, it was first colonized by the English in 1583 but did not come under permanent British control until 1762. ◉ Pop. 175,909.

Saint Johns River. A river, about 459 km (285 mi) long, of northeast Florida flowing generally north to Jacksonville then east to the Atlantic Ocean.

Saint Jo·seph (jō′zəf, -səf). A city of northwest Missouri on the Missouri River north-northwest of Kansas City. Laid out in 1843 on the site of a trading post founded in 1826, it became the eastern terminus of the Pony Express in 1860. ◉ Pop. 71,852.

Saint Joseph River. A river, about 338 km (210 mi) long, of southwest Michigan and northwest Indiana flowing generally west, south, west, and northwest into Lake Michigan.

Saint Kitts and Ne·vis (kĭts; nē′vĭs, něv′ĭs) also **Saint Chris·to·pher-Ne·vis** (krĭs′tə-fər-nē′vĭs, -něv′ĭs). An island country in the Leeward Islands of the West Indies east-southeast of Puerto Rico comprising **Saint Kitts,** the largest island of the group, and the islands of Nevis and Sombrero. The main islands were visited by Columbus in 1493 and settled by the English (1623) and French (1625), being officially awarded to Great Britain by the 1783 Treaty of Paris. They were part of the West Indies Federation from 1958 to 1962 and in 1967 joined in a short-lived association with Anguilla. St. Kitts and Nevis became independent in 1983. Basseterre, on St. Kitts, is the capital. ◉ Pop. 41,000.

Saint Lam·bert or **Saint-Lam·bert** (sānt lăm′-bərt, săn läm-běr′). A city of southern Quebec,

Canada, a residential suburb of Montreal on the St. Lawrence River. ◉ Pop. 20,557.

Saint Lau·rent or **Saint-Lau·rent** (sānt′ lô-rěnt′, săn lô-rän′). A city of southern Quebec, Canada, an industrial suburb of Montreal. ◉ Pop. 65,900.

Saint Law·rence (sānt lôr′əns, lŏr′-), **Gulf of.** An arm of the northwest Atlantic Ocean off southeast Canada bordered by New Brunswick, Nova Scotia, Newfoundland, and Quebec. It is connected with the Atlantic by Cabot Strait and the Straits of Canso and Belle Isle.

Saint Lawrence River. A river of southeast Canada flowing about 1,207 km (750 mi) northeast from Lake Ontario along the Ontario–New York border and through southern Quebec to the Gulf of St. Lawrence. The river was first sighted by the French explorer Jacques Cartier in 1534; in 1535 he ascended it as far as the modern-day city of Montreal. Long a water highway for explorers, missionaries, and fur traders, it is today a major shipping route.

Saint Lawrence Seaway. An international waterway, about 3,781 km (2,350 mi) long, consisting of a system of canals, dams, and locks in the St. Lawrence River and connecting channels through the Great Lakes. Jointly developed by the United States and Canada, the seaway opened in 1959 and provides passage for ocean-going ships as far west as Lake Superior.

Saint Lé·o·nard or **Saint-Lé·o·nard** (sānt′ lěn′-ərd, săn lā-ō-när′). A city of southern Quebec, Canada, a residential suburb of Montreal. ◉ Pop. 79,429.

Saint-Lô (sānt′lō′, săn-). A town of northwest France west of Caen. Its capture on July 18, 1944, played a pivotal role in the Allied invasion of Europe during World War II. ◉ Pop. 23,212.

Saint Lou·is (sānt lōō′ĭs). An independent city of eastern Missouri on the Mississippi River just south of its confluence with the Missouri River. Settled by the French as a trading post in 1763–1764, it passed to Spain (1770), to France again (1800), and to the United States as part of the Louisiana Purchase (1803). The city has long been a major river port, railroad hub, and industrial center. It is the largest city in the state. ◉ Pop. 396,685.

Saint-Lou·is (săn-lōō-ē′). A city of northwest Senegal at the mouth of the Senegal River. The oldest French colonial settlement in Africa, it was founded as a trading base c. 1658 and was the capital of French West Africa from 1895 to 1902. Dakar replaced it as the capital of Senegal in 1958. ◉ Pop. 132,499.

Saint Lou·is Park (sānt lōō′ĭs). A city of southeast Minnesota, an industrial suburb of Minneapolis. ◉ Pop. 43,787.

Saint Louis River. A river, about 257 km (160 mi) long, of northeast Minnesota flowing southwest then southeast to Lake Superior.

Saint Lu·cia (lŏŏ′shə, lŏŏ-sē′ə). An island country of the West Indies in the Windward Islands south of Martinique. The island was probably sighted by Columbus in 1502. Resistance from the Carib inhabitants defeated several attempts at colonization by the English in the early 17th century, although France succeeded in establishing a settlement in the mid-1600's. The island changed hands numerous times between the two powers until the end of the Napoleonic Wars (1814), when it passed definitively to Great Britain. St. Lucia joined the West Indies Federation (1958–1962), gaining self-government in 1967 and full independence in 1979. Castries is the capital. ⊛Pop. 141,000.

Saint Maar·ten (mär′tn). See **Saint Martin.**

Saint-Ma·lo (săN-mə-lō′). A town of northwest France north-northwest of Nantes on the **Gulf of Saint-Malo,** an inlet of the English Channel. Founded on the site of a 6th-century A.D. monastery, it was a base for French pirates in the 17th and 18th centuries. ⊛Pop. 46,347.

Saint Mar·tin or **Saint Maar·ten** (mär′tn). An island of the West Indies in the western Leeward Islands. Administration of the island is divided between the French overseas department of Guadeloupe and the Netherlands Antilles. The French and Dutch first assumed joint control in 1648.

Saint Mar·ys River (mâr′ēz). **1.** A river, about 282 km (175 mi) long, rising in southeast Georgia in the Okefenokee Swamp and flowing eastward along the Georgia-Florida border to the Atlantic Ocean. **2.** A river, about 101 km (63 mi) long, rising in the eastern Upper Peninsula of Michigan and flowing generally south and southeast to the northern end of Lake Huron. It forms part of the U.S.-Canadian border.

Saint-Maur-des-Fos·sés (săN-môr-dā-fô-sā′). A city of north-central France, a residential and industrial suburb of Paris. ⊛Pop. 80,811.

Saint Mau·rice or **Saint-Mau·rice** (sănt′ môr′-ĭs, -môr′-, săN mô-rēs′). A river, about 523 km (325 mi) long, of southern Quebec, Canada, flowing south and southeast to the St. Lawrence River at Trois Rivières.

Saint-Mi·hiel (sănt-mē-yĕl′, săN-). A village of northeast France on the Meuse River east of Paris. The World War I battle here (September 12–14, 1918) was the first major American offensive led by Gen. John J. Pershing and forced the Germans to relinquish a salient held since 1914.

Saint Mo·ritz (sănt′ mə-rĭts′, săN mô-rēts′). A city of southeast Switzerland on the Inn River in the Upper Engadine. It is noted as a skiing resort and was the site of the Winter Olympics in 1928 and 1948. ⊛Pop. 5,900.

Saint-Na·zaire (săN-nä-zĕr′). A city of westcentral France at the mouth of the Loire River west of Nantes. Once an ancient Roman town, it was an important naval base during both World Wars and was virtually destroyed by Allied bombing in World War II. It has since been rebuilt. ⊛Pop. 68,348.

Saint Paul (pôl). The capital of Minnesota, in the southeast part of the state on the Mississippi River adjacent to Minneapolis. Founded on the site of an early fur-trading post, it became territorial capital in 1849 and state capital in 1858. ⊛Pop. 272,235.

Saint Pe·ters (pē′tərz). A city of eastern Missouri west-northwest of St. Louis, of which it is a residential suburb. ⊛Pop. 45,779.

Saint Pe·ters·burg (pē′tərz-bûrg′). **1.** Formerly (1924–1991) **Len·in·grad** (lĕn′ĭn-grăd′, lyĭ-nĭn-grät′) and (1914–1924) **Pet·ro·grad** (pĕt′-rə-grăd′, pyĭ-trə-grät′). The second largest city of Russia, in the northwest part of the country on the Neva River at the head of the Gulf of Finland. Founded by Peter the Great in 1703, it was designed by French and Italian architects and soon flourished as his "window on Europe" after the capital was moved here from Moscow in 1712. By the mid 19th century it was Russia's leading seaport and a major center of commerce, industry, and culture. Discontent among workers, however, led to the formation of secret revolutionary societies, and St. Petersburg was the scene of the Decembrist revolt in 1825 and the original locus of the Russian Revolution (1917). The capital was moved back to Moscow in 1918. During World War II the city was besieged for more than two years by the Germans, and hundreds of thousands died from famine and disease. ⊛Pop. 4,328,851. **2.** A city of westcentral Florida on Tampa Bay south-southwest of Tampa. Settled in the mid-1800's, it is a port of entry and popular resort. ⊛Pop. 238,629.

Saint Pi·erre or **Saint-Pi·erre** (sānt′ pîr′, pē-âr′, săn pyĕr′). The capital of St. Pierre and Miquelon, on St. Pierre Island in the northern Atlantic Ocean. ◉ Pop. 5,371.

Saint Pierre and Mi·que·lon (mǐk′ə-lŏn′, mē-klôn′). A French island group and overseas department in the northern Atlantic Ocean south of Newfoundland, Canada. The group consists of nine small islands, including **Saint Pierre Island,** site of the capital, and Miquelon, the largest of the islands. Probably first visited by Breton and Basque fishermen, the islands were colonized by France in 1604, taken by the British three times, and finally awarded to France in 1814. They are the sole remnants of the once vast French territory in North America. St. Pierre is the capital. ◉ Pop. 6,041.

Saint-Quen·tin (sānt′kwĕn′tən, săn-kän-tăn′). A city of northern France on the Somme River north-northeast of Paris. Of Roman origin, the city was chartered in 1080 and was an important center of the woolen industry during the Middle Ages. ◉ Pop. 63,567.

Saint Tho·mas[1] (sānt tŏm′əs). An island of the U.S. Virgin Islands in the West Indies east of Puerto Rico. Discovered and named by Columbus in 1493, it was settled by the Dutch in 1657 and later passed to Denmark, which sold it to the United States in 1917.

Saint Tho·mas[2] (sānt tŏm′əs). A city of southern Ontario, Canada, near Lake Erie south of London. It is an industrial and manufacturing center. ◉ Pop. 28,165.

Saint-Tro·pez (săn-trô-pā′). A town of southeast France on the Mediterranean coast of the French Riviera. It is a noted seaside resort. ◉ Pop. 4,961.

Saint Vin·cent (sānt vǐn′sənt). An island of St. Vincent and the Grenadines in the central Windward Islands of the West Indies. Visited by Columbus in 1498, the island proved difficult to colonize due to strong resistance from its Carib inhabitants. The British established a settlement in the mid-1700's and held the island, except for a brief occupation by the French (1779–1783), thereafter, finally defeating the Caribs in 1797.

Saint Vincent, Cape. A promontory at the southwest extremity of Portugal. Prince Henry the Navigator established (c. 1420) an observatory and a school of navigation nearby.

Saint Vincent and the Gren·a·dines (grĕn′-ə-dēnz′). An island country in the central Windward Islands of the West Indies. It comprises St. Vincent Island and the northern islets of the Grenadines. Part of the West Indies Federation from 1958 to 1962, the country gained self-governing status in 1969 and full independence in 1979. Kingstown, on St. Vincent, is the capital. ◉ Pop. 111,000.

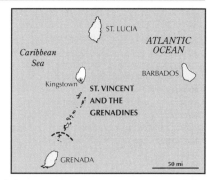

Sai·pan (sī-păn′, -pän′, sī′păn). The largest island of the Northern Mariana Islands in the western Pacific Ocean. It was held by Spain, Germany, and Japan before being captured by U.S. troops in July 1944 during World War II. It was part of the U.S. Trust Territory of the Pacific Islands from 1947 to 1978 and now serves as the capital of the Northern Marianas. — **Sai′-pa·nese′** (-nēz′, -nēs′) *adj. & n.*

Sa·ïs (sā′ĭs). A city of ancient Egypt in the west-central region of the Nile delta. It served as a royal residence during the XXVI Dynasty (663–525 B.C.).

Sa·ja·ma (sə-hä′mə). A mountain, 6,574.3 m (21,555 ft) high, in the Andes of western Bolivia near the Chilean border.

Sa·kai (sä′kī′). A city of southern Honshu, Japan, on Osaka Bay south of Osaka. It was a leading port from the 15th to the 17th century. ◉ Pop. 806,263.

Sak·a·ka·we·a (săk′ə-kə-wē′ə), **Lake.** A reservoir in west-central North Dakota. It is a widening of the Missouri River and was created in 1956 when the Garrison Dam was completed.

Sa·kha·lin (săk′ə-lēn′, -lən, să-кнä-lyēn′). An island of southeast Russia in the Sea of Okhotsk north of Hokkaido, Japan. Colonized by Russia and Japan in the 18th and 19th centuries, it passed under Russian control in 1875.

Sa·ki·shi·ma (sä′kē-shē′mä, sä-kē′shē-mä′). An island group of Japan in the southern Ryukyu Islands east of Taiwan. The islands were heavily bombed by the Allies in April–June 1945.

Sak·ka·ra (sə-kär′ə). See **Saqqara.**

Sa·la·do (sə-lä′dō, sä-lä′*th*ô). **1.** also **Salado del Nor·te** (dĕl nôr′tĕ). A river of northern Argentina rising in the Andes and flowing about 2,011 km (1,250 mi) southeast to the Paraná River. **2.** A river, about 1,368 km (850 mi) long, rising in western Argentina and flowing south-southeast to the Colorado River.

Sal·a·man·ca (săl′ə-măng′kə, sä′lä-mäng′kä). A city of west-central Spain west-northwest of Madrid. Conquered by Hannibal in 220 B.C., it was captured by Moors in the 8th century A.D.

and held by them until the late 11th century. ⊛ Pop. 163,400.

Sal·a·mis[1] (săl′ə-mĭs, sä′lä-mēs′). An island of Greece in the Saronic Gulf east of Athens. In an important naval battle off the island's northeast coast the Greeks, led by Themistocles, defeated the Persian fleet in 480 B.C.

Sal·a·mis[2] (săl′ə-mĭs, sä′lä-mēs′). An ancient city of eastern Cyprus. According to tradition, it was founded c. 1180 B.C. by Teucer, a hero of the Trojan War, and was visited by Saint Paul during his first missionary journey. The city was abandoned after A.D. 648.

Sal·can·tay (săl′kən-tī′, säl′kän-). A peak, 6,275.4 m (20,575 ft) high, of the Cordillera Oriental in southern Peru. It is the highest mountain in the range.

Sa·lé (sä-lā′) also **Sla** (slä). A city of northwest Morocco near Rabat on the Atlantic Ocean. It was a haven for Barbary pirates. ⊛ Pop. 521,000.

Sa·lem (sā′ləm). **1.** A city of southern India southwest of Madras. It is a trade center with an important textile industry. ⊛ Pop. 366,712. **2.** A city of northeast Massachusetts northeast of Boston. Founded in 1626, it is noted as the site of witchcraft trials (1692) and of the writer Nathaniel Hawthorne's House of the Seven Gables. ⊛ Pop. 38,091. **3.** A town of southeast New Hampshire east of Nashua. It was part of Haverhill, Massachusetts, until 1741. ⊛ Pop. 25,746. **4.** The capital of Oregon, in the northwest part of the state on the Willamette River south-southwest of Portland. Founded c. 1840, it became territorial capital in 1851 and state capital in 1859. ⊛ Pop. 107,786. **5.** An independent city of southwest Virginia, an industrial and residential suburb of Roanoke. ⊛ Pop. 23,756.

Sa·ler·no (sə-lûr′nō, sä-lĕr′-). A city of southern Italy on the **Gulf of Salerno,** an inlet of the Tyrrhenian Sea. Originally a Greek settlement and later a Roman colony (founded in 197 B.C.), Salerno was the site of a noted medical school during the Middle Ages. ⊛ Pop. 153,436.

Sal·ford (sôl′fərd). A borough of northwest England on the Manchester Ship Canal adjacent to Manchester. It was first chartered in 1230. ⊛ Pop. 229,260.

Sa·li·an (sā′lē-ən, sāl′yən). **1.** Of or relating to a tribe of Franks who settled in the Rhine region of the Netherlands in the fourth century A.D. **2.** A Salian Frank.

Sa·lic (sā′lĭk, săl′ĭk) also **Sa·lique** (sā′lĭk, săl′-ĭk, sə-lēk′). **1.** Of or relating to the Salian Franks. **2.** Of or being a law prohibiting a woman from succeeding to a throne.

sa·li·na (sə-lī′nə, -lē′-). **1.** A salt marsh, spring, pond, or lake. **2.** An area of land encrusted with salt.

Sa·li·na (sə-lī′nə). A city of central Kansas north-northwest of Wichita. It is a processing, trade, manufacturing, and shipping center in an oil-rich area. ⊛ Pop. 42,303.

Sa·li·nas (sə-lē′nəs). A city of western California east-northeast of Monterey on the **Salinas River,** about 241 km (150 mi) long, near its outlet on Monterey Bay. The city is a processing center and the birthplace of the writer John Steinbeck (1902–1968), who based many of his stories on the migratory farm workers of the Salinas Valley. ⊛ Pop. 108,777.

Salis·bur·y (sôlz′bĕr′ē, -brē). **1.** A municipal borough of southern England northwest of Southampton on the edge of **Salisbury Plain,** a chalky plateau that is the site of Stonehenge. The city was chartered in 1220 and developed around its noted cathedral. ⊛ Pop. 35,700. **2.** A city of southeast Maryland on the Eastern Shore south of Dover, Delaware. It is a processing and manufacturing center. ⊛ Pop. 20,592. **3.** A city of central North Carolina south-southwest of Winston-Salem. During the Civil War the city was the site of one of the largest Confederate prisons. ⊛ Pop. 23,087. **4.** See **Harare.**

Sa·lish (sā′lĭsh) also **Sa·lish·an** (-lĭ-shən). **1.** A family of Native American languages of the northwest United States and British Columbia. **2.** The group of Native American peoples speaking languages of this family. —**Sa′lish·an** adj.

Sal·mon River (săm′ən, săl′mən). A river of central Idaho rising in the **Salmon River Mountains** and flowing about 684 km (425 mi) to the Snake River. The mountain range rises to 3,153.7 m (10,340 ft) at Twin Peaks.

Sa·lo·ni·ka (sə-lŏn′ĭ-kə, săl′ə-nē′kə). See **Thessaloníki.**

Sal·ta (säl′tə, -tä). A city of northwest Argentina north-northeast of Córdoba. Founded in 1582, it is a processing and shipping center in an agricultural region. ⊛ Pop. 367,099.

Sal·til·lo (säl-tē′yō). A city of northeast Mexico southwest of Monterrey. It was founded in 1575 and occupied during the Mexican War by U.S. forces under Zachary Taylor, later the 12th President of the United States (1849–1850). ⊛ Pop. 284,937.

Salt Lake City (sôlt). The capital and largest city of Utah, in the north-central part of the state near Great Salt Lake. Brigham Young and his followers settled here in 1847 and established the community as the center of the Church of Jesus Christ of Latter-day Saints. ⊛ Pop. 159,936.

Sal·ton Sea (sôl′tən). A saline lake of southeast California in the Imperial Valley. It was a salt-covered depression known as the **Salton Sink**

until 1905, when flood waters of the Colorado River formed the lake.

Salt River. **1.** A river, about 322 km (200 mi) long, rising in eastern Arizona and flowing generally west to the Gila River near Phoenix. It has been used for irrigation for many centuries. **2.** A river rising in northeast Missouri and flowing about 322 km (200 mi) southeast to the Mississippi River.

Sa·lu·da (sə-lōō′də). A river, about 322 km (200 mi) long, of west-central South Carolina rising in the Blue Ridge and flowing southeast across the Piedmont to the Broad River.

Sal·va·dor (săl′və-dôr′, säl′və-dôr′). Formerly **Ba·hi·a** (bə-hē′ə, bä-ē′ə). A city of eastern Brazil on the Atlantic Ocean south-southwest of Recife. Founded in 1549, it was the capital of the Portuguese possessions in the New World until 1763. ◉ Pop. 2,072,058.

Sal·va·do·ran (săl′və-dôr′ən, -dôr′-) or **Sal·va·do·ri·an** (-dôr′ē-ən, -dôr′-). **1.** Of or relating to El Salvador or its people or culture. **2.** A native or inhabitant of El Salvador.

Sal·ween (săl′wēn′). A river of southeast Asia rising in eastern Xizang (Tibet) and flowing about 2,816 km (1,750 mi) generally east then south through Myanmar (Burma) into the Gulf of Martaban.

Salz·burg (sôlz′bûrg′, sälz′-, zälts′bŏŏrk′). A city of west-central Austria near the German border southwest of Linz. Originally a Celtic settlement and later a Roman colony, it was long the residence of powerful archbishops. The composer Mozart was born here in 1756, and the city now hosts an annual music festival in honor of him. ◉ Pop. 143,973.

Salz·git·ter (zälts′gĭt′ər). A city of central Germany southeast of Hanover. First mentioned c. 1000, it is an important metallurgical center in a rich iron ore region. ◉ Pop. 117,684.

Sa·ma (sä′mä). An Austronesian language spoken in the Sulu Archipelago. Also called *Samal.*

Sa·mal (sä-mäl′). See **Sama.**

Sa·mar (sä′mär′). An island of east-central Philippines in the Visayan Islands northeast of Leyte in the **Samar Sea,** an arm of the Pacific Ocean. The island was the first in the archipelago to be discovered by the Spaniards (1521).

Sa·ma·ra (sə-mä′rə). Formerly **Kuy·by·shev** or **Kui·by·shev** (kwē′bə-shef′, -shēv′, kŏŏ′ē-bə-shĭf′). A city of western Russia on the Volga River east-southeast of Moscow. Founded in 1586 as a stronghold to defend river trade and the eastern frontier, it was temporarily the capital (1941–1943) of the U.S.S.R. during World War II. It is now a major river port and rail center and has many industries. The city was named Kuybyshev from 1935 to 1991. ◉ Pop. 1,231,653.

Sa·mar·i·a (sə-măr′ē-ə, -mâr′-). An ancient city of central Palestine in present-day northwest Jordan. It was founded in the ninth century B.C. as the capital of the northern kingdom of Israel, also known as **Samaria.** Conquered by the Assyrian king Sargon II in 721 B.C., it was destroyed in the second century and rebuilt by Herod the Great (73?–4 B.C.). According to tradition, Saint John the Baptist is buried here. —**Sa·mar′i·tan** (-ĭ-tn) *adj. & n.*

Sam·ar·kand (săm′ər-kănd′, sə-mər-känt′). A city of southern Uzbekistan southwest of Tashkent. Dating from the third or fourth millennium B.C., the city was conquered by Alexander the Great in 329 B.C., taken by the Arabs in the eighth century A.D., and destroyed by Genghis Khan c. 1220. It was rebuilt as a fabled center of great splendor and opulence when it became (c. 1370) the capital of Tamerlane's empire. ◉ Pop. 370,000.

Sa·mar·ra (sə-mär′ə). A city of north-central Iraq on the Tigris River north-northwest of Baghdad. It was the capital of the Arabic Abbaside dynasty in the ninth century and is today a pilgrimage center for Shiite Muslims. ◉ Pop. 24,7406.

Sa·mi (sä′mē). *pl.* **Sami** or **-mis.** See **Lapp** (sense 1).

sam·iel (säm-yĕl′). See **simoom.**

Sam·ni·um (săm′nē-əm). An ancient country of central and southern Italy. The expansionist desires of its rulers led to the Samnite Wars (343–290 B.C.) and the ultimate defeat of Samnium by Rome. —**Sam′nite** (săm′nīt′) *adj. & n.*

Sa·mo·a (sə-mō′ə). An island group of the southern Pacific Ocean east-northeast of Fiji, divided between **American Samoa** and **Western Samoa.** The islands were originally populated by Polynesians perhaps as early as 1000 B.C. and were first sighted by European explorers in 1722. Dual administration of the archipelago was established by treaty in 1899.

Sa·mo·an (sə-mō′ən). **1.** Of or relating to Samoa or its people, language, or culture. **2.** A native or inhabitant of Samoa. **3.** The Polynesian language of Samoa.

Sa·mos (sā′mŏs, săm′ōs, sä′môs). An island of eastern Greece in the Aegean Sea off the western coast of Turkey. First inhabited in the Bronze Age, it was later colonized by Ionian Greeks and became an important commercial and maritime power in the sixth century B.C. Controlled in turn by Persia, Athens, Sparta, Rome, Byzantium, and the Ottoman Empire, it became part of modern-day Greece in 1913.

Sam·o·thrace (săm′ə-thrās′) or **Sam·o·thrá·ki** (sä′mô-thrä′kē). An island of northeast Greece in the northeast Aegean Sea off the coast of European Turkey. The *Winged Victory of Samo-*

thrace, now at the Louvre in Paris, was sculpted c. 200 B.C. and found on the island in 1863.

Sam·o·yed also **Sam·o·yede** (săm′ə-yĕd′, -oi-ĕd′, sə-moi′ĭd). See **Nenets.** —**Sam′o·yed′** *adj.* —**Sam′o·yed′ic** *adj.*

Sam·sun (säm-sōōn′). A city of northern Turkey northeast of Ankara on **Samsun Bay,** an inlet of the Black Sea. Ancient Samsun was an important Greek colony. ⊛ Pop. 326,900.

San (sän). **1.** *pl.* **San** or **Sans.** A member of a traditionally nomadic hunting people of southwest Africa. **2.** Any of the Khoisan languages of the San. Also called *Bushman.*

Sa·n'a or **Sa·na** or **Sa·naa** (sä-nä′). The capital of Yemen, in the western part of the country. Settled in ancient times, it became the capital of North Yemen in 1962 and the capital of united North Yemen and Southern Yemen in 1990. ⊛ Pop. 926,595.

San An·dre·as Fault (săn ăn-drā′əs). A major zone of fractures in the earth's crust extending along the coastline of California from the northwest part of the state to the Gulf of California. Movement of the tectonic plates along the fault has caused numerous tremors, including the devastating San Francisco earthquake of 1906.

San An·ge·lo (ăn′jə-lō′). A city of west-central Texas south-southwest of Abilene. A notorious frontier town in the 1870's, it grew after the coming of the railroad in 1888. ⊛ Pop. 84,474.

San An·to·ni·o (ăn-tō′nē-ō′). A city of south-central Texas southwest of Austin on the **San Antonio River,** flowing about 322 km (200 mi) southeast to **San Antonio Bay** on the Gulf of Mexico. The city was founded as a Franciscan mission in 1718 and is the site of the Alamo, which was besieged and captured by Mexican forces in February–March 1836. It has several military bases. ⊛ Pop. 935,933.

San Antonio Peak. A mountain, 3,074.4 m (10,080 ft) high, of the San Gabriel Mountains in southern California. It is the highest peak in the range.

San Be·ni·to (bə-nē′tō). A city of extreme southern Texas north of Brownsville. It is a processing and shipping center and a winter resort. ⊛ Pop. 20,125.

San Ber·nar·di·no (bûr′nə-dē′nō, -nər-). A city of southern California at the foot of the San Bernardino Mountains east of Los Angeles. First explored in 1772, it was the site of a mission (established 1810) and a city founded by Mormons (1850's). It is a trade and processing center. ⊛ Pop. 164,164.

San Bernardino Mountains. A mountain range of southern California in the Coast Ranges south of the Mojave Desert. It rises to 3,507.2 m (11,499 ft) at San Gorgonio Mountain.

San Bernardino Pass. A pass, about 2,065 m

(6,770 ft) high, through the Lepontine Alps in southeast Switzerland. It is thought to have been in use since prehistoric times.

San Ber·nar·do (săn bər-när′dō, sän bĕr-när′-thô). A city of central Chile, an industrial suburb of Santiago. ⊛ Pop. 188,156.

San Blas (săn bläs′, sän bläs′), **Gulf of.** An inlet of the Caribbean Sea on the northern coast of Panama east of the Panama Canal.

San Bru·no (săn brōō′nō). A city of western California, a residential suburb of San Francisco on San Francisco Bay. ⊛ Pop. 38,961.

San Car·los (kär′ləs). A city of western California southeast of San Francisco. It is mainly residential. ⊛ Pop. 26,167.

San Cle·men·te (klə-mĕn′tē). A city of southern California on the Pacific Ocean southeast of Long Beach. Founded in 1925, it is a popular resort center. ⊛ Pop. 41,100.

San Clemente Island. An island of southern California in the Santa Barbara Islands south of Santa Catalina Island.

San Cris·tó·bal (săn krĭs-tō′bəl, sän′ krē-stô′-väl). A city of extreme western Venezuela in a mountainous region near the Colombian border south-southwest of Maracaibo. Founded in 1561, it was severely damaged by an earthquake in 1875. ⊛ Pop. 238,670.

San·da·kan (săn-dä′kən, sän-dä′kän). A city of Malaysia in northern Borneo on **Sandakan Harbor,** an inlet of the Sulu Sea. It was the capital of British North Borneo (now Sabah) until 1947. ⊛ Pop. 73,144.

Sand·hurst (sănd′hûrst′). A village of south-central England southeast of Reading. Its famous Royal Military College (now Academy) was founded in the 1790's.

San·di·a Peak or **San·di·a Crest** (săn-dē′ə). A mountain, 3,256.2 m (10,676 ft) high, in the **Sandia Mountains** of north-central New Mexico northeast of Albuquerque.

San Di·e·go (săn dē-ā′gō). A city of southern California on **San Diego Bay,** an inlet of the Pacific Ocean near the Mexican border. First explored by the Spanish in 1542 the area was not settled until the 1700's. A noted zoological park is located in the city, which is a major port of entry and a commercial, industrial, and research center. ⊛ Pop. 1,110,549.

San Di·mas (dē′məs). A city of southern California east of Los Angeles. San Dimas is a residential community in a citrus-growing area. ⊛ Pop. 32,397.

San·dring·ham (săn′drĭng-əm). A village of eastern England near the Wash west-northwest of Norwich. Sandringham House, a private royal residence, was purchased in 1861 by Victoria for her son the Prince of Wales, later King Edward VII, and extensively rebuilt in the 1890's.

San·dus·ky (sən-dŭs′kē, săn-). A city of northern Ohio west of Cleveland on **Sandusky Bay,** an inlet of Lake Erie. The **Sandusky River,** about 241 km (150 mi) long, flows west and north into the bay. Sandusky was founded in the early 1800's and is a port of entry and manufacturing center. ⊛ Pop. 29,764.

Sand·wich (sănd′wĭch′, săn′-). A municipal borough of southeast England north of Dover. One of the original Cinque Ports, it is now a resort and market center. ⊛ Pop. 4,227.

Sandwich Islands. See **Hawaiian Islands.**

Sand·y or **Sand·y City** (săn′dē). A city of north-central Utah, a manufacturing suburb of Salt Lake City. ⊛ Pop. 75,058.

Sandy Hook. A low peninsula of eastern New Jersey at the entrance to Lower New York Bay. It separates **Sandy Hook Bay** from the Atlantic Ocean and was first explored in 1609.

Sandy Springs. An unincorporated community of northwest Georgia, a suburb of Atlanta. ⊛ Pop. 67,842.

San Fer·nan·do (săn fər-năn′dō). **1.** A city of eastern Argentina. It is an industrial suburb of Buenos Aires on the Río de la Plata. ⊛ Pop. 141,496. **2.** A city of southern Spain, a seaport and suburb of Cádiz on the Gulf of Cádiz. ⊛ Pop. 76,101. **3.** A city of southern California in the San Fernando Valley surrounded by Los Angeles. It is a residential community with varied light industries. ⊛ Pop. 22,580.

San Fernando Valley. A fertile valley of southern California northwest of central Los Angeles. First explored by the Spanish in 1769, it lies partly within the city limits of Los Angeles and includes many residential communities.

San·ford (săn′fərd). **1.** A city of central Florida north-northeast of Orlando. It is a manufacturing and shipping center in an agricultural region. ⊛ Pop. 32,387. **2.** A city of southwest Maine west of Biddeford. Formerly dependent on textile and clothing manufacturing, it now has diversified industries. ⊛ Pop. 10,296.

Sanford, Mount. A mountain, 4,952.3 m (16,237 ft) high, of southern Alaska in the Wrangell Mountains northeast of Anchorage.

San Fran·cis·co (frən-sĭs′kō). A city of western California on a peninsula between the Pacific Ocean and **San Francisco Bay,** an inlet of the Pacific. A Spanish presidio and mission were founded here in 1776. The first settlement was known as Yerba Buena, and the name was changed to San Francisco after control of the town passed to the United States in 1846. Discovery of gold nearby in 1848 changed the city into a thriving boom town known for its lawlessness and bawdy amusements. The city was all but destroyed by a devastating earthquake and

fire on April 18, 1906. ⊛ Pop. 723,959. **— San Fran·cis′can** (-kən) *n.*

San Francisco Peaks also **San Francisco Mountains.** A group of mountains in north-central Arizona north of Flagstaff. The range rises to 3,853.1 m (12,633 ft) at Humphreys Peak, the highest point in the state.

San Ga·bri·el (gā′brē-əl). A city of southern California, a residential suburb of Los Angeles. ⊛ Pop. 37,120.

San Gabriel Mountains. A mountain range of southern California east and northeast of Los Angeles. It rises to 3,074.4 m (10,080 ft) at San Antonio Peak.

San·ga·mon (săng′gə-mən). A river, about 402 km (250 mi) long, of central Illinois flowing southwest and west to the Illinois River.

San Gior·gio a Cre·ma·no (săn jôr′jō ä krī-mä′nō, krĕ-mä′nô, sän). A city of south-central Italy, a suburb of Naples on the Bay of Naples. ⊛ Pop. 61,721.

San Gor·go·ni·o Mountain (săn gôr-gō′nē-ō). A peak in the San Bernardino Mountains of southern California east of the city of San Bernardino. It rises to 3,507.2 m (11,499 ft) and is the highest elevation in the range.

San·gre de Cris·to Mountains (săng′grē dē krĭs′tō). A range of the southern Rocky Mountains extending about 354 km (220 mi) from south-central Colorado to north-central New Mexico. Blanca Peak, 4,375.2 m (14,345 ft), is the highest point.

San·i·bel Island (săn′ə-bəl). An island of southwest Florida in the Gulf of Mexico southwest of Fort Myers. The island's beaches are popular with seashell collectors.

San I·si·dro (săn′ ĭ-sē′drō, sän ē-sē′*th*rô). A city of eastern Argentina, a residential and industrial suburb of Buenos Aires. ⊛ Pop. 299,022.

San Ja·cin·to (săn jə-sĭn′tō). A river, about 209 km (130 mi) long, of southeast Texas flowing into Galveston Bay. The final battle of the Texas Revolution, in which insurgents under Sam Houston defeated the Mexican forces led by General Santa Anna, was fought on its banks on April 21, 1836.

San Joa·quin (wô-kēn′, wä-). A river of central California, rising in the Sierra Nevada and flowing about 515 km (320 mi) west and northwest to form a large delta with the Sacramento River. The **San Joaquin Valley** is a rich, irrigated agricultural region.

San Jo·se (hō-zā′). A city of western California southeast of San Francisco. Founded in 1777, it was the state capital from December 1849 to January 1852. ⊛ Pop. 782,248.

San Jo·sé (sän′ hô-sĕ′). The capital and largest city of Costa Rica, in the central part of the country. Settled c. 1736, it became the capital in 1823. ◉ Pop. 315,909.

San Juan (săn wän′, hwän′). **1.** A city of northwest Argentina west of Córdoba. Founded in 1562, it was moved to its present site in the 1590's. ◉ Pop. 119,492. **2.** The capital and largest city of Puerto Rico, in the northeast part of the island on the Atlantic Ocean. First settled by the Spanish explorer Ponce de León in 1508–1509, it was attacked by English buccaneers in the 1590's and sacked by the Dutch in 1625. American forces took control of the city during the Spanish-American War (1898). ◉ Pop. 441,401.

San Juan Cap·is·tra·no (kăp′ĭ-strä′nō). A city of southern California southeast of Santa Ana. Founded as a mission in 1776, it is famous for the swallows that supposedly return to the area every year on March 19 and depart on October 23, the date on which Saint John of Capistrano died in 1456. ◉ Pop. 26,183.

San Juan Hill. An elevation in eastern Cuba near Santiago de Cuba. It was captured by Cuban and American forces on July 1, 1898, during the Spanish-American War. Theodore Roosevelt and his Rough Riders became famous for a charge up the hill during the battle.

San Juan Islands. An archipelago of northwest Washington off the southeast coast of Vancouver Island north of Puget Sound. The islands were discovered and named c. 1790 by Spanish explorers and were later claimed by both Great Britain and the United States. The boundary dispute was finally settled in 1872.

San Juan Mountains. A range of the Rocky Mountains in southwest Colorado extending northwest to southeast and rising to 4,364.2 m (14,309 ft) at Uncompahgre Peak.

San Juan River. A river rising in southern Colorado and flowing about 579 km (360 mi) into northwest New Mexico and southeast Utah, where it joins the Colorado River.

Sankt Gal·len (zängkt gä′lən) also **Saint Gall** (sānt gôl′, gäl′, sän gäl′). A city of northeast Switzerland east of Zurich. Developed around a Benedictine abbey founded by an Irish missionary in the seventh century, it joined the Swiss Confederation in 1454. ◉ Pop. 73,500.

Sankt Pöl·ten (pœl′tən). A city of northern Austria west of Vienna. It was chartered in 1159. ◉ Pop. 50,419.

San-ku-ru (säng-kōr′ōō). A river, about 1,207 km (750 mi) long, of southern and central Zaire flowing west-northwest to the Kasai River.

San Le·an·dro (săn lē-ăn′drō). A city of western California southeast of Oakland. It is a residential community with varied light industries. ◉ Pop. 68,223.

San Lo·ren·zo (lə-rĕn′zō). An unincorporated community of western California, a residential suburb of Oakland. ◉ Pop. 19,987.

San Lu·cas (săn lōō′kəs, sän lōō′käs), **Cape.** A cape of western Mexico at the southern tip of Baja California extending into the Pacific Ocean.

San Lu·is O·bis·po (săn lōō′ĭs ə-bĭs′pō). A city of southwest California northwest of Santa Barbara. A Franciscan mission was founded on the site in 1772. ◉ Pop. 41,958.

San Luis Peak. A mountain, 4,274.3 m (14,014 ft) high, in the San Juan Mountains of southwest Colorado.

San Lu·is Po·to·sí (sän lōō-ēs′ pô′tô-sē′). A city of central Mexico northeast of León. It was founded in the late 1500's and is a mining, transportation, and industrial center. ◉ Pop. 362,371.

San Mar·cos (săn mär′kəs). **1.** A city of southern California north-northwest of San Diego. It is a manufacturing center in an agricultural region. ◉ Pop. 38,974. **2.** A city of south-central Texas northeast of San Antonio. Food processing is important to its economy. ◉ Pop. 28,743.

San Ma·ri·no (mə-rē′nō). A country in the Apennines near the Adriatic Sea. It is surrounded by Italy and is the world's smallest republic. Traditionally founded in the fourth century A.D., San Marino was recognized by the papacy in 1631 and has maintained its independence, with a few brief interruptions, ever since. It signed a treaty of friendship with Italy in 1862, was allied with Italy in World Wars I and II, and was bombed by the Allied forces in 1944. The city of **San Marino** is its capital. The country's population is 25,000; the city's, 2,792.

San Ma·te·o (săn mə-tā′ō). A city of western California south-southeast of San Francisco. Named by a Spanish expedition in 1776, it was the center of a Mexican colony from 1822 to 1846. ◉ Pop. 85,486.

San Mi·guel de Tu·cu·mán (săn′ mĭ-gĕl′ də tōō′kə-män′, sän′ mē-gĕl′ dĕ tōō′kōō-män′) or **Tucumán.** A city of northern Argentina at the foot of an eastern range of the Andes northnorthwest of Córdoba. The country's independence was proclaimed here in July 1816. ◉ Pop. 470,604.

San Ni·co·lás de los Gar·zas (sän nē′kô-läs' dĕ lôs gär'säs). A city of northern Mexico, a suburb of Monterrey in a citrus-growing area. ⊛ Pop. 280,696.

San Pab·lo (păb'lō). A city of western California north-northwest of Oakland near **San Pablo Bay,** a northern arm of San Francisco Bay. It is one of the oldest Spanish settlements in the region. ⊛ Pop. 25,158.

San Pe·dro Channel (pē'drō). A strait of southern California between the mainland and Santa Catalina Island. **San Pedro Bay** is an inlet of the channel.

San Pe·dro Su·la (săn pē'drō sōō'lə, sän pĕ'-thrô sōō'lä). A city of northwest Honduras northwest of Tegucigalpa. It is a commercial center. ⊛ Pop. 397,201.

San Ra·fael (săn rə-fĕl'). A city of western California north-northwest of San Francisco. It is a residential community with varied light industries. ⊛ Pop. 48,404.

San Re·mo (rā'mō, rĕ'-). A city of northwest Italy on the Ligurian Sea east of Monaco. It is a fashionable resort on the Italian Riviera. ⊛ Pop. 50,200.

San River (sän). A river, about 451 km (280 mi) long, of southeast Poland flowing generally north-northwest from the Carpathian Mountains to the Vistula River.

San Sal·va·dor[1] (săn săl'və-dôr', sän săl'və-dôr'). Formerly **Wat·lings Island** (wät'lĭngz). An island of the central Bahamas in the West Indies. It is generally identified as the first landfall of Christopher Columbus (October 12, 1492).

San Sal·va·dor[2] (săn săl'və-dôr', sän säl'vä-thôr'). The capital and largest city of El Salvador, in the west-central part of the country. Founded in the 16th century, it became the national capital in 1841. ⊛ Pop. 422,570.

San Se·bas·tián (săn sə-băs'chĭn, sän' sĕ-väs-tyän'). A city of northern Spain on the Bay of Biscay near the French border east of Bilbao. It is a fashionable seaside resort and has fishing and chemical industries. ⊛ Pop. 171,540.

San Se·ve·ro (săn sə-vĕr'ō, sĕ-). A city of southeast Italy north-northwest of Foggia. It is an agricultural trade center. ⊛ Pop. 54,273.

San·skrit (săn'skrĭt'). *abbr.* **Skr., Skt.** An ancient Indic language that is the language of Hinduism and the Vedas and is the classical literary language of India. —**San'skrit'ist** *n.*

San·skrit·ic (săn-skrĭt'ĭk). See **Indic.**

San·ta An·a (săn'tə ăn'ə). **1.** (*also* sän'tä ä'-nä). A city of western El Salvador northwest of San Salvador. It is an important commercial, industrial, and processing center. ⊛ Pop. 202,337. **2.** A city of southern California east of Long Beach in the fertile valley of the **Santa Ana River,** about 145 km (90 mi) long. Santa

Ana is a manufacturing and trade center for a large metropolitan area. ⊛ Pop. 293,742.

Santa Bar·ba·ra (bär'bər-ə, bär'brə). A city of southern California on the Santa Barbara Channel west-northwest of Los Angeles. Site of an early Spanish presidio and mission, it is a residential and resort community with aerospace and electronics research and development industries. ⊛ Pop. 85,571.

Santa Barbara Islands. A chain of islands and islets off southern California in the Pacific Ocean. The islands are separated from the mainland by **Santa Barbara Channel** in the north and San Pedro Channel in the south.

Santa Cat·a·li·na Island (kăt'l-ē'nə) or **Catalina Island.** An island off southern California in the southern Santa Barbara Islands. Discovered in 1542, it has been a resort since the 1920's.

Santa Cla·ra (klăr'ə, klâr'ə). **1.** (*also* sän'tä klä'rä). A city of central Cuba east-southeast of Havana. Founded in 1689, it is a processing center and rail junction. ⊛ Pop. 204,775. **2.** A city of western California northwest of San Jose. It is mainly a residential community. ⊛ Pop. 93,613.

San·ta Co·lo·ma de Gra·ma·net (săn'tə kə-lō'mə də grä'mə-nĕt', sän'tä kô-lô'mä thĕ grä'mä-nĕt'). A city of northeast Spain, an industrial suburb of Barcelona. ⊛ Pop. 133,138.

San·ta Cruz (săn'tə krōōz'). **1.** (*also* sän'tä krōōs'). A city of central Bolivia northeast of Sucre. Founded c. 1560, it is a trade and processing center. ⊛ Pop. 767,260. **2.** A city of western California on Monterey Bay south-southwest of San Jose. It is a tourist center with varied processing and manufacturing industries. ⊛ Pop. 49,040.

San·ta Cruz de Te·ne·ri·fe (săn'tə krōōz' də tĕn'ə-rē'fä, -rēf', -rĭf', sän'tä krōōth' thĕ tĕn'-ĕ-rē'fĕ). A city of the Canary Islands on the northeast coast of Tenerife Island. It is a popular resort. ⊛ Pop. 202,112.

San·ta Cruz Island (săn'tə krōōz'). An island off southern California in the northern Santa Barbara Islands.

Santa Cruz Islands. An island group in the southwest Pacific Ocean in the southeast Solomon Islands. They were discovered in 1595.

Santa Fe (fā'). **1.** (*also* sän'tä fĕ'). A city of northeast Argentina on the Salado River northwest of Buenos Aires. Founded in 1573, it is a port with various light industries. ⊛ Pop. 342,796. **2.** The capital of New Mexico, in the north-central part of the state northeast of Albuquerque. The Spanish established a settlement here c. 1609 on the site of ancient Native American ruins and developed it as a trade center over the next 200 years. Occupied by U.S. forces in 1846, it became territorial capital in 1851 and state capital in 1912. ⊛ Pop. 55,859.

Santa Fe Trail. A trade route to the southwest United States extending about 1,287 km (800 mi) westward from Independence, Missouri, to Santa Fe, New Mexico. Opened in 1821, it was the primary wagon and stage route to the Southwest until the coming of the railroad in 1880.

San·ta Is·a·bel (săn′tə ĭz′ə-bĕl′, sän′tä ē-sä-bĕl′). See **Malabo.**

San·ta Ma·ri·a (săn′tə mə-rē′ə). **1.** (also säN′tä mä-rē′ä). A city of southern Brazil west of Pôrto Alegre. It is a rail junction and processing center. ◉Pop. 217,604. **2.** A city of southern California northwest of Santa Barbara. It is a trade, processing, and shipping center in an agricultural region. Nearby Vandenberg Air Force Base is also important to its economy. ◉Pop. 61,284.

San·ta Mar·ta (săn′tə mär′tə, sän′tä mär′tä). A city of northern Colombia on the Caribbean Sea east-northeast of Barranquilla. Founded in 1525, it is the oldest city in the country and an important processing and shipping center. It is also a resort. ◉Pop. 193,160.

San·ta Mon·i·ca (săn′tə mŏn′ĭ-kə). A city of southern California on the Pacific Ocean west of Los Angeles. Laid out in 1875, it is a resort and residential community with varied light industries. ◉Pop. 86,905.

San·tan·der (sän′tän-dĕr′). A city of northern Spain on the Bay of Biscay west-northwest of Bilbao. It was a major port after the discovery of America and is now a resort and industrial center. ◉Pop. 191,155.

Santa Pau·la (pô′lə). A city of southern California east of Santa Barbara. Food processing is important to its economy. ◉Pop. 25,062.

San·ta·rém (săn′tə-rĕm′, säN′tä-rāN′). A city of northern Brazil on the Amazon River east of Manaus. Founded in 1661, it is a major river port. ◉Pop. 264,779.

Santa Ro·sa (rō′zə). A city of western California north-northwest of San Francisco. The American horticulturist Luther Burbank lived here, and his experimental gardens are preserved as a memorial. ◉Pop. 113,313.

Santa Rosa Island. 1. An island of southern California in the northwest Santa Barbara Islands separated from the mainland by the Santa Barbara Channel. **2.** A barrier island of northwest Florida extending about 80 km (50 mi) eastward from Pensacola Bay along the coast of the Gulf of Mexico.

San·tee¹ (săn-tē′). pl. **Santee** or **-tees.** A member of the eastern branch of the Sioux, comprising the Mdewakanton, Sisseton, Wahpekute, and Wahpeton peoples, with present-day populations in Nebraska, Minnesota, the Dakotas, and Canada. Also called *Eastern Sioux, Santee Dakota, Santee Sioux.*

San·tee² (săn-tē′). A community of southern California, a suburb of San Diego. ◉Pop. 52,902.

Santee Dakota. See **Santee¹.**

Santee River. A river, about 230 km (143 mi) long, of central South Carolina flowing southeast to the Atlantic Ocean.

Santee Sioux. See **Santee¹.**

San·ti·a·go (săn′tē-ä′gō, sän′-). **1.** The capital and largest city of Chile, in the central part of the country east-southeast of Valparaiso. On a plain in the foothills of the Andes, it was founded in 1541. ◉Pop. 4,385,481. **2.** also **Santiago de los Ca·bal·le·ros** (dä′ lôs kä′bəl-yĕr′ōz, thĕ lôs kä′vä-yĕ′rôs). A city of northern Dominican Republic northwest of Santo Domingo. Settled c. 1500, it is a transportation hub in a fertile agricultural region. ◉Pop. 690,000. **3.** also **Santiago de Com·pos·te·la** (də kŏm′pə-stĕl′ə, thĕ kôm′pôs-tĕ′lä). A city of northwest Spain south-southwest of La Coruña. The city grew around a shrine housing the reputed tomb of Saint James the Great (discovered in the ninth century) and has long been a pilgrimage center. ◉Pop. 62,300.

Santiago de Cu·ba (də kyōō′bə, thĕ kōō′vä). A city of southeast Cuba on an inlet of the Caribbean Sea. Founded in 1514, it was a haven for buccaneers and smugglers during its early history. ◉Pop. 432,898.

Santiago del Es·te·ro (dĕl ə-stĕr′ō, thĕl ĕ-stĕ′rô). A city of north-central Argentina north of Córdoba. Founded in 1553, it is one of the oldest cities in the country. ◉Pop. 148,758.

San·to An·dré (säN′tōō äN-drā′). A city of southern Brazil, an industrial suburb of São Paulo. ◉Pop. 615,112.

San·to Do·min·go (săn′tō də-mĭng′gō, sän′tô dô-). Formerly (1936–1961) **Ci·u·dad Tru·jil·lo** (sē′ōō-däd′ trōō-hē′yō, syōō-thäth′). The capital and largest city of the Dominican Republic, in the southeast part of the island of Hispaniola on the Caribbean Sea. Founded in 1496 by Christopher Columbus's brother Bartholomew, it is the oldest continuously inhabited European settlement in the Americas. The name has also been used for a Spanish colony on Hispaniola and for the Dominican Republic. ◉Pop. 2,100,000.

San·to·rin (săn′tə-rēn′). See **Thíra.**

San·tos (săn′təs, säN′tōōs). A city of southeast Brazil on an offshore island in the Atlantic Ocean southeast of São Paulo. Settled in the 1540's, it is a major port, especially for coffee. ◉Pop. 428,512.

São Ber·nar·do do Cam·po (souN bĕr-när′-dōō dōō kän′pōō). A city of southeast Brazil. It is an industrial suburb of São Paulo. ◉Pop. 566,330.

São Cae·ta·no do Sul (kī-tä′nōō dōō sōōl′).

A city of southeast Brazil, an industrial suburb of
São Paulo. ⊛ Pop. 149,203.

São Car·los (kär′ləs, -lōōs). A city of southeast
Brazil northwest of São Paulo. It is a commercial
and processing center. ⊛ Pop. 158,186.

São Fran·cis·co (frən-sĭs′kō, frän-sēs′kōō). A
river of eastern Brazil flowing about 2,896 km
(1,800 mi) generally north-northeast and east to
the Atlantic Ocean.

São Gon·ça·lo (gōn-säl′ōō). A city of southeast Brazil, an industrial suburb on Guanabara
Bay opposite Rio de Janeiro. ⊛ Pop. 778,831.

São João de Me·ri·ti (zhwouN′ də mə-rē′tē,
dĭ mĭ-rĭ-tē′). A city of southeast Brazil. It is
a residential suburb of Rio de Janeiro. ⊛ Pop.
424,689.

São Jo·sé do Ri·o Prêt·o (zhōō-zā′ dōō rē′ōō
prĕt′ōō). A city of southeast Brazil, an industrial
suburb of São Paulo. ⊛ Pop. 283,345.

São José dos Cam·pos (dōōs kăN′pōōs). A
city of southeast Brazil east-northeast of São
Paulo. It is a major center of Brazil's aircraft industry. ⊛ Pop. 442,009.

São Lu·ís (lōō-ēs′). A city of northeast Brazil on
an offshore island in the Atlantic Ocean east-
southeast of Belém. It was founded by the
French in 1612 and named in honor of Louis
XIII. ⊛ Pop. 695,199.

São Mi·guel (mē-gĕl′). An island of the eastern
Azores in the Atlantic Ocean. It is the largest island in the group and a popular tourist center.

Saône (sōn). A river, about 431 km (268 mi)
long, rising in the Vosges Mountains of northeast France and flowing generally south-southwest to the Rhone River at Lyon.

São Pau·lo (pou′lō, -lōō). A city of southeast
Brazil west-southwest of Rio de Janeiro. It was
founded by Jesuits in 1554 and developed rapidly
as an industrial and commercial center after the
1880's and is now the largest city in South
America. ⊛ Pop. 9,626,894.

São Tia·go (tē-ä′gōō, tyä′gōō). An island of
southern Cape Verde in the northern Atlantic
Ocean. It is the largest island in the group and
the site of the capital, Praia.

São To·mé (tə-mā′, tōō-mĕ′). An island of São
Tomé and Príncipe in the Gulf of Guinea off
western Africa. The city of **São Tomé,** the capital of the country, is on the southeast coast. Its
(the city's) population is 43,420.

São Tomé and Prín·ci·pe (prĭn′sə-pə, prēN′-
sē-pə). An island country in the Gulf of Guinea
off western Africa. Probably uninhabited at the
time of European discovery in 1471, the islands
were settled (1483) by the Portuguese, who
held them, except for a period of Dutch rule in
the 17th century, until they gained full independence in 1975. São Tomé is the capital. ⊛ Pop.
144,128.

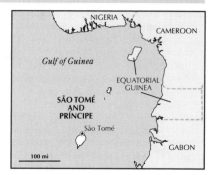

São Vi·cen·te (vē-sĕN′tə). A city of southeast
Brazil on an offshore island in the Atlantic Ocean
west of Santos. Founded in 1532, it was sacked
by English pirates in 1591. ⊛ Pop. 268,732.

Sap·po·ro (sə-pôr′ō, -pōr′ō). A city of southwest Hokkaido, Japan, near the head of Ishikari
Bay. A processing and commercial center, it was
the site of the 1972 Winter Olympics. ⊛ Pop.
1,731,670.

Sa·pul·pa (sə-pŭl′pə). A city of east-central
Oklahoma south-southwest of Tulsa. It is a trade
center in a farming region. ⊛ Pop. 18,074.

Saq·qa·ra also **Sak·ka·ra** (sə-kär′ə). A village of
northern Egypt near Cairo. It is the site of the
oldest Egyptian pyramids, including the Step
Pyramid built by Zoser during the III Dynasty
(c. 2980–2900 B.C.).

Sar·a·cen (săr′ə-sən). **1.** A member of a pre-
Islamic nomadic people of the Syrian-Arabian
deserts. **2.** An Arab. **3.** A Muslim, especially
of the time of the Crusades. — **Sar′a·cen′ic**
(-sĕn′ĭk) adj.

Sar·a·gos·sa (săr′ə-gŏs′ə) also **Za·ra·go·za**
(zăr′ə-gō′zə, thä′rä-gô′thä). A city of northeast
Spain on the Ebro River northeast of Madrid.
An important city under Roman rule, it was held
by the Moors from 713 until 1118. ⊛ Pop.
598,078.

Sa·ra·je·vo (săr′ə-yā′vō, sär′ə-yĕ-vô′). The
capital of Bosnia and Herzegovina, in the south-
central part of the country southwest of Belgrade, Yugoslavia. Built on the site of an ancient
settlement, it fell to the Turks in 1429 and
passed to Austria-Hungary in 1878. The city became a center of Serbian nationalism, and the
assassination (June 28, 1914) of Archduke Francis Ferdinand and his wife here triggered the
outbreak of World War I. After the war Sarajevo
was incorporated into Yugoslavia, and it became
the capital of independent Bosnia and Herzegovina in 1992. The city, known for its Muslim
architecture and an important industrial and
educational center, was severely damaged by
Serbian shelling (1992–1994) during the war
that followed independence. ⊛ Pop. 415,631.

Sar·a·nac Lakes (săr′ə-năk′). A group of three

lakes in the Adirondack Mountains of northeast New York. They are linked by the **Saranac River,** which flows about 161 km (100 mi) generally northeast to Lake Champlain. The lakes are in a popular year-round resort area.

Sa·ransk (sə-ränsk′). A city of western Russia west of Ulyanovsk. Founded as a fort in the 1600's, it is a manufacturing and processing center. ⊛ Pop. 321,221.

Sar·a·so·ta (săr′ə-sō′tə). A city of west-central Florida south of Tampa Bay on **Sarasota Bay,** an inlet of the Gulf of Mexico. A yachting and fishing resort with varied industries, Sarasota is the site of the Circus Hall of Fame. ⊛ Pop. 50,961.

Sar·a·to·ga (săr′ə-tō′gə). **1.** A city of west-central California southwest of San Jose. It is a residential community in a wine-producing region. ⊛ Pop. 28,061. **2.** A former village of eastern New York on the west bank of the Hudson River east of Saratoga Springs. The surrender of Gen. John Burgoyne's British army on October 17, 1777, ended the hard-fought Saratoga Campaign (June–October) and was a major turning point in the American Revolution.

Saratoga Springs. A city of eastern New York in the foothills of the Adirondack Mountains north of Albany. The city's mineral springs led to its development as a health resort in the late 18th century. It has also been an important horseracing, sporting, and arts center since the 1860's. ⊛ Pop. 25,001.

Sa·ra·tov (sə-rä′təf). A city of southwest Russia on the Volga River north-northeast of Volgograd. Founded on a nearby site in 1590, it is a major industrial center. ⊛ Pop. 899,173.

Sa·ra·wak (sə-rä′wäk, -wăk, -wä). A region of Malaysia on northwest Borneo. A British protectorate after 1888 and a crown colony after 1946, it joined Malaysia in 1963.

Sar·celles (sär-sĕl′). A city of north-central France. It is a residential suburb of Paris with some light industry. ⊛ Pop. 53,630.

Sar·din·i·a (sär-dĭn′ē-ə, -dĭn′yə). An island of Italy in the Mediterranean Sea south of Corsica. Settled by Phoenicians, Greeks, and Carthaginians before the sixth century B.C., the island was taken by Rome in 238 B.C. and later fell to the Vandals (fifth century A.D.) and the Byzantines (early sixth century). Numerous European powers controlled the island before 1720, when it passed to the House of Savoy and became the nucleus of the Kingdom of Sardinia. Victor Emmanuel II of Sardinia became the first king of Italy in 1861. — **Sar·din·i·an** (sär-dĭn′ē-ən, -yən). **1.** Of or relating to Sardinia or its people, language, or culture. **2.** A native or inhabitant of Sardinia. **3.** The Romance language of the Sardinians.

Sar·dis (sär′dĭs). An ancient city of western Asia Minor northeast of modern-day Izmir, Turkey. As the capital of Lydia it was the political and cultural center of Asia Minor from 650 to c. 550 B.C. and remained an important city during Roman and Byzantine times. It was destroyed by the Mongol conqueror Tamerlane in 1402.

Sa·re·ma (sär′ə-mä′). See **Saaremaa.**

Sar·gas·so Sea (sär-găs′ō). A part of the northern Atlantic Ocean between the West Indies and the Azores. The relatively calm sea is noted for the dense gulfweed floating on its surface.

Sar·go·dha (sər-gō′də). A city of northeast Pakistan west-northwest of Lahore. It is an agricultural trade center with varied manufactures. ⊛ Pop. 235,000.

Sark (särk). One of the Channel Islands in the English Channel east of Guernsey. It comprises **Great Sark** and **Little Sark,** which are joined by a natural causeway. — **Sark·ese′** (-ēz′, -ēs′) adj. & n.

Sar·ma·tia (sär-mā′shə, -shē-ə). An ancient region of eastern Europe northeast of the Black Sea. The Sarmatian people occupied the area after the fourth century B.C. and fled across the Carpathian Mountains and along the Danube River after the onslaught of the Huns (third century A.D.). The term is also applied to the territory between the Vistula and Volga rivers during the time of the Roman Empire. — **Sar·ma′tian** adj. & n.

Sar·ni·a (sär′nē-ə). A city of southeast Ontario, Canada, at the southern end of Lake Huron west of London. Settled by the French in 1807 and the British in 1833, it is a port and manufacturing center. ⊛ Pop. 50,892.

Sa·ron·ic Gulf (sə-rŏn′ĭk). An arm of the Aegean Sea in southern Greece between Attica and the Peloponnesus east of Corinth. A canal links it with the Gulf of Corinth.

Sa·ros (sâr′ŏs′, sä′rôs), **Gulf of.** An inlet of the northeast Aegean Sea indenting northwest European Turkey north of Gallipoli.

Sarthe (särt). A river, about 285 km (177 mi) long, of northwest France flowing generally south to Angers.

Sa·se·bo (sä′sĕ-bō′). A city of northwest Kyushu, Japan, on the East China Sea north-northwest of Nagasaki. A naval base was established here in 1886. ⊛ Pop. 245,108.

Sas·katch·e·wan (să-skăch′ə-wän′, -wən). abbr. **SK, Sask.** A province of south-central Canada. It joined the Confederation in 1905. The French established trading posts in the area c. 1750, but the first permanent settlement was made by the Hudson's Bay Company in 1774. The region became part of the Northwest Territories in 1870. Regina is the capital and the largest city. ⊛ Pop. 968,313.

Saskatchewan River. A river, about 547 km

(340 mi) long, of south-central Canada formed by the confluence of the North and South Saskatchewan rivers in central Saskatchewan and flowing generally eastward to Lake Winnipeg in Manitoba.

Sas·ka·toon (săs′kə-tōōn′). A city of south-central Saskatchewan, Canada, on the South Saskatchewan River northwest of Regina. Settled in 1883, it is a trade and processing center. ● Pop. 186,058.

Sas·sa·ri (sä′sə-rē′). A city of northwest Sardinia, Italy, north-northwest of Cagliari. An important trading center in the Middle Ages, it was held by the Genoese and Aragonese before passing to Piedmont in 1718. ● Pop. 116,989.

sas·tru·ga (să-strōō′gə, săs′trə-, sä′strə-) also **zas·tru·ga** (ză-strōō′gə, ză-). A long wavelike ridge of snow, formed by the wind and found on the polar plains.

Sa·til·la (sə-tĭl′ə). A river, about 354 km (220 mi) long, of southeast Georgia flowing generally east and south to an inlet of the Atlantic Ocean.

Sa·tu-Ma·re also **Sa·tu Ma·re** (sä′tōō-mär′ĕ). A city of northwest Romania near the Hungarian border northwest of Bucharest. It is a commercial, cultural, and industrial center in an agricultural region. ● Pop. 131,386.

Sa·u·di Arabia (sou′dē, sô′dē, sä-ōō′dē). A country occupying most of the Arabian Peninsula. Inhabited since ancient times by nomadic Semitic tribes, the region is the site of Islam's holiest cities, Mecca and Medina. After the caliphate was moved from Medina to Damascus in 661, the region remained fragmented until most of the peninsula was united in the 18th century under the Saud family and its Bedouin followers, who adopted the Wahhabi form of Islam. Wahhabi power was crushed by Egyptian and Ottoman opposition in the 19th century, but Saudi forces reconquered the peninsula in the early 20th century under King Ibn Saud (1882–1953). The unified kingdom of Saudi Arabia was created in 1932 as an absolute monarchy under Wahhabi law. Oil was discovered in 1932 and soon became the mainstay of the Saudi economy. Saudi Arabia remained neutral during most of World War II, joined in the 1948–1949 war

against Israel, and supported Iraqi war efforts against Iran in the 1980's. Alarmed by Iraq's 1990 invasion of Kuwait, the Saudis joined the U.S.-led coalition against Iraq and served as the main base for coalition forces in the Gulf War (1991). Saudi Arabia declared a new constitution in 1992, but the royal family's power remained fundamentally undiminished. Riyadh is the capital and the largest city. ● Pop. 17,451,000. —**Sa·u′di, Sa·u′di A·ra′bi·an** *adj. & n.*

Sau·gus (sô′gəs). A town of northeast Massachusetts, a residential and manufacturing suburb of Boston. ● Pop. 25,549.

Sauk (sôk) also **Sac** (săk, sôk). **1.** *pl.* **Sauk** or **Sauks** also **Sac** or **Sacs.** A member of a Native American people formerly inhabiting parts of Wisconsin, Illinois, and Iowa, with a present-day population mainly in Oklahoma. Sauk resistance to removal from their Illinois lands ended in 1832 with the Black Hawk War. **2.** The Algonquian language of the Sauks, dialectally related to Fox.

Sauk Cen·tre (sôk sĕn′tər). A city of central Minnesota west-northwest of Minneapolis. Sinclair Lewis was born here and used the community as the setting for a number of novels, including *Main Street* (1920). ● Pop. 3,581.

Sault Sainte Ma·rie (sōō′ sānt′ mə-rē′). A city of southern Ontario, Canada, at the falls of the St. Marys River opposite Upper Michigan. It is an industrial center in a resort area. ● Pop. 82,698.

Sault Sainte Marie Canals. Popularly called **Soo Canals** (sōō). Three ship canals bypassing the rapids on the St. Marys River between Lakes Superior and Huron. The Canadian canal, opened in 1895, follows the route of the canal built around the rapids by a fur company in 1797–1798. The first American canal was completed in 1855 and was enlarged and split into two canals, opened in 1896 and 1919. Though often icebound in winter, the canals are vital links in the Great Lakes waterway system.

Sau·sa·li·to (sô′sə-lē′tō). A city of western California on San Francisco Bay at the northern terminus of the Golden Gate Bridge. It is a residential community, an artists' colony, and a popular boating resort. ● Pop. 7,152.

Sa·va (sä′və, -vä). A river, about 933 km (580 mi) long, rising in two headstreams in the Julian Alps of Slovenia and flowing generally eastward to the Danube River at Belgrade, Yugoslavia.

Sa·vai′i or **Sa·vai·i** (sä-vī′ē). An island of Western Samoa in the southwest Pacific Ocean. It is the largest of the Samoa Islands.

sa·van·na also **sa·van·nah** (sə-văn′ə). A flat grassland of tropical or subtropical regions.

Sa·van·nah (sə-văn′ə). A city of southeast

Georgia near the mouth of the Savannah River. Founded by James Oglethorpe in 1733, it is the oldest city in Georgia and has been a major port since the early 19th century. ⊛ Pop. 137,560.

Savannah River. A river, about 505 km (314 mi) long, rising in northwest South Carolina and flowing southeast along the South Carolina–Georgia border to the Atlantic Ocean.

Sa·vo·na (sə-vō′nə, sä-vô′nä). A city of northwest Italy on an arm of the Ligurian Sea westsouthwest of Genoa. Known since early Roman times, it was an important commercial center in the Middle Ages. ⊛ Pop. 75,069.

Sa·voy (sə-voi′). A historical region and former duchy of southeast France, western Switzerland, and northwest Italy. The region changed hands many times after its conquest by Julius Caesar and became a duchy in the early 15th century. In 1720 the duke of Savoy gained the title king of Sardinia, and in 1861 the Savoyard Victor Emmanuel II ascended the throne of the newly formed kingdom of Italy. Much of the original territory was ceded to France at the same time. — **Sa·voy′ard** (sə-voi′ärd′, säv′oi-yärd′) *adj. & n.*

Savoy Alps. A range of the western Alps in southeast France rising to 4,810.2 m (15,771 ft) at Mont Blanc, the highest elevation in Europe.

Sa·watch Range (sə-wŏch′). A range of the Rocky Mountains in central Colorado rising to 4,402.1 m (14,433 ft) at Mount Elbert.

Sax·on (săk′sən). *abbr.* **Sax., S. 1.** A member of a West Germanic tribal group that inhabited northern Germany and invaded Britain in the fifth and sixth centuries A.D. with the Angles and Jutes. **2.** A person of English or Lowland Scots birth or descent as distinguished from one of Irish, Welsh, or Highland Scots birth or descent. **3.** A native or inhabitant of Saxony. **4.** The West Germanic language of any of the ancient Saxon peoples. — **Sax′on** *adj.*

Sax·o·ny (săk′sə-nē). A historical region of northern Germany. The original home of the Saxons, it was conquered by Charlemagne in the eighth century and became a duchy after his death (814). Its borders were eventually extended southeastward as the region was subdivided and redivided. The dukes of Saxony became electors of the Holy Roman Empire in 1356, and in 1806 the elector was elevated to kingship but lost half his territory to Prussia in 1815. A later kingdom of Saxony was part of the German Empire (1871–1918).

Sa·yan Mountains (sä-yän′). A range of mountains in south-central Russia west of Lake Baikal. The mountains have important mineral deposits.

Say·re·ville (sā′ər-vĭl′, sâr′-). A borough of east-central New Jersey southeast of New

Brunswick. It is a manufacturing and residential center. ⊛ Pop. 34,986.

Say·ville (sā′vĭl). An unincorporated community of southeast New York on south-central Long Island. Mainly residential, it is also a resort with light industries. ⊛ Pop. 16,550.

scab·land (skăb′lănd′). An elevated area of barren, rocky land with little or no soil cover, often crossed by dry stream channels.

Sca·fell Pike (skô′fĕl′). A mountain in the Cumbrian Mountains of northwest England. At 979.1 m (3,210 ft), it is the highest peak in the range and the highest elevation in England.

Scan·di·a (skăn′dē-ə). An ancient and poetic name for Scandinavia or the Scandinavian Peninsula. — **Scan′di·an** *adj. & n.*

Scan·di·na·vi·a (skăn′də-nā′vē-ə, -nāv′yə). *abbr.* **Scand.** A region of northern Europe consisting of Norway, Sweden, and Denmark. Finland, Iceland, and the Faeroe Islands are often included in the region.

Scan·di·na·vi·an (skăn′də-nā′vē-ən, -nāv′yən). *abbr.* **Scand. 1.** Of or relating to Scandinavia or to its peoples, languages, or cultures. **2.** A native or inhabitant of Scandinavia. **3.** See **North Germanic.**

Scandinavian Peninsula. A peninsula of northern Europe comprising the countries of Norway and Sweden.

Scap·a Flow (skăp′ə). A sheltered area of water in the Orkney Islands off northern Scotland. It was the site of the chief British naval base in both World Wars. The German fleet was scuttled here in June 1919 at the end of World War I.

Scar·bor·ough (skär′bûr′ō, -bŭr′ō, -bər-ə). A municipal borough of northeast England on the North Sea north of Hull. Site of a Bronze Age village and a fourth-century A.D. Roman signaling tower, it is a noted seaside resort. ⊛ Pop. 43,300.

Scars·dale (skärz′dāl′). A city of southeast New York, a residential suburb of New York City. ⊛ Pop. 16,987.

Schaer·beek (skär′bāk′, sκHär′-). A city of central Belgium, an industrial suburb of Brussels. ⊛ Pop. 105,672.

Schaum·burg (shäm′bûrg′). A village of northeast Illinois, a mainly residential suburb of Chicago. ⊛ Pop. 68,586.

Scheldt (skĕlt). A river rising in northern France and flowing about 434 km (270 mi) generally northeast across western Belgium and southwest Netherlands. It empties into the North Sea through two estuaries.

Sche·nec·ta·dy (skə-nĕk′tə-dē). A city of eastern New York on the Mohawk River northwest of Albany. First settled in 1661, it prospered after the opening of the Erie Canal and the coming of the railroad in the early 19th century. Its electrical industry dates to the 1880's. ⊛ Pop. 65,566.

Schie·dam (skē-däm′, sкнē-). A city of southwest Netherlands, an industrial suburb of Rotterdam. Chartered in 1275, it is noted for its gin distilleries. ⊛ Pop. 69,849.

Schles·wig (shlĕs′wĭg, -wĭk, shläs′vĭk). A historical region and former duchy of northern Germany and southern Denmark in southern Jutland. The duchy was created in 1115 and passed, along with the duchy of Holstein, to Christian I of Denmark in 1460. After subdivisions caused by complex hereditary holdings, the duchies were once more reunited under the Danish crown in 1773. Denmark, Prussia, and Austria contended for the region until 1866, when it was annexed by Prussia. In 1920 the northern part of Schleswig was returned to Denmark by plebiscite. The southern portion became (1946) part of the West German state of Schleswig-Holstein, which became a state of northern Germany after German reunification (1990).

Schou·ten Islands (skout′n). An island group of eastern Indonesia in the southern Pacific Ocean off the northern coast of New Guinea.

Schuyl·kill (skōōl′kĭl′, skōō′kəl). A river, about 209 km (130 mi) long, of southeast Pennsylvania flowing generally southeast to the Delaware River at Philadelphia.

Schwä·bisch Gmünd (shvä′bĭsh gə-mōont′, -münt′). A city of southwest Germany east of Stuttgart. Chartered in 1162, it was a free imperial city from 1268 to 1803. ⊛ Pop. 56,073.

Schwedt (shvāt). A city of northeast Germany on the Oder River northeast of Berlin. A processing center, it was heavily damaged during World War II. ⊛ Pop. 51,881.

Schwein·furt (shvīn′fōort′). A city of central Germany on the Main River east of Frankfurt. First mentioned c. 791, it became a free imperial city in 1282 and passed to Bavaria in 1803. ⊛ Pop. 51,079.

Schwe·rin (shvä-rēn′). A city of north-central Germany on **Schwerin Lake** southwest of Rostock. Originally a Wendish settlement, it was chartered c. 1160 and is today a commercial, industrial, and transportation center in an agricultural region. ⊛ Pop. 122,189.

Scil·ly Islands (sĭl′ē) or **Isles of Scilly.** An archipelago comprising more than 140 small islands and rocky islets off southwest England at the entrance of the English Channel west-southwest of Land's End. The islands were formerly a haven for pirates and smugglers.

Sci·o·to (sī-ō′tə). A river, about 381 km (237 mi) long, rising in western Ohio and flowing east then south to the Ohio River in south-central Ohio.

sci·roc·co (shə-rŏk′ō, sə-). Variant of **sirocco.**

Scit·u·ate (sĭch′ōō-āt′, -ĭt). A town of eastern Massachusetts on Massachusetts Bay southeast of Boston. It is a residential community and summer resort. ⊛ Pop. 16,786.

Scone (skōōn). A village of central Scotland northeast of Perth. The old part of the village was the coronation site of Scottish kings until 1651. The Stone of Scone, or Stone of Destiny, which served as a throne during the coronation rites, was taken to England by Edward I in 1296 and kept in Westminster Abbey beneath the chair used during the crowning of British monarchs. The Stone of Scone was returned to Scotland in November 1996.

Scores·by Sound (skôrz′bē, skōrz′-). An arm of the Norwegian Sea indenting eastern Greenland. It has numerous fjords branching generally westward toward the icecap.

Scot (skŏt). **1.** A native or inhabitant of Scotland. **2.** A member of the ancient Gaelic tribe that migrated to the northern part of Britain from Ireland in about the sixth century A.D.

Scotch (skŏch). *abbr.* **Sc., Scot. 1.** The people of Scotland. **2.** Scots English. **3.** Scottish.

Scotch-I·rish (skŏch′ī′rĭsh). **1.** The people of Scotland who settled in northern Ireland or their descendants, especially those who emigrated to America. **2.** Of or relating to the Scotch-Irish.

Scotch·man (skŏch′mən). A Scotsman.

Scotch Plains. A community of northeast New Jersey west of Elizabeth. It is primarily residential. ⊛ Pop. 21,160.

Scotch·wom·an (skŏch′wōom′ən). A Scotswoman.

Sco·tia (skō′shə). A medieval and poetic name for Scotland.

Scot·land (skŏt′lənd). *abbr.* **Scot.** A constituent country of the United Kingdom comprising the northern part of the island of Great Britain and the Hebrides, Shetland Islands, and Orkney Islands. Inhabited by Picts in prehistoric times, the region was invaded but never conquered by the Romans and split into a variety of small kingdoms after the fifth century A.D. In the ninth century most of Scotland was unified into one kingdom, but conflicts with the English to the south soon erupted, leading to a series of bloody wars. When Mary Queen of Scots's son James VI succeeded to the English throne in 1603, the two kingdoms were united. Scotland became a part of the kingdom of Great Britain by a parliamentary act of 1707. Edinburgh is the capital and Glasgow the largest city. ⊛ Pop. 5,149,500.

Scot·land·ville (skŏt′lənd-vĭl′). An unincorporated community of southeast Louisiana, a residential suburb of Baton Rouge. ⊛ Pop. 15,113.

Scots (skŏts). *abbr.* **Sc. 1.** Scottish. **2.** The dialect of English used in the Lowlands of Scotland.

Scots·man (skŏts′mən). A man who is a native or inhabitant of Scotland.

Scots·wom·an (skŏts′wŏŏm′ən). A woman who is a native or inhabitant of Scotland.

Scot·tish (skŏt′ĭsh). *abbr.* **Sc., Scot. 1.** Of or relating to Scotland or its people, language, or culture. **2.** Scots English. **3.** The people of Scotland.

Scottish Gaelic. The Goidelic language of Scotland. Also called *Erse.*

Scott Peak (skŏt). A mountain, 3,474.9 m (11,393 ft) high, in the Bitterroot Range of eastern Idaho. It is the highest elevation in the range.

Scotts·dale (skŏts′dāl′). A city of south-central Arizona, a suburb of Phoenix. Settled in 1895, it is a noted resort area and retirement community. ⊛ Pop. 130,069.

Scran·ton (skrăn′tən). A city of northeast Pennsylvania northeast of Wilkes-Barre. Settled in the late 1700's, it is a commercial and industrial center in an anthracite coal region. ⊛ Pop. 81,805.

Scun·thorpe (skŭn′thôrp′). A municipal borough of eastern England southwest of Hull. It has an important iron and steel industry. ⊛ Pop. 65,900.

Scu·ta·ri (skŏŏ′tə-rē), **Lake.** A lake of southeast Europe on the border between southwest Yugoslavia and northwest Albania. It was once an inlet of the Adriatic but is now separated from the sea by an alluvial isthmus.

Scy·ros (skī′rŏs, skē′rôs). See **Skíros.**

Scyth·i·a (sĭth′ē-ə, sĭth′-). An ancient region of Eurasia extending from the mouth of the Danube River on the Black Sea to the territory east of the Aral Sea. The nomadic people of the region flourished from the eighth to the fourth century B.C. but were conquered by the Sarmatians in the second century and were soon subsumed into other cultures.

Scyth·i·an (sĭth′ē-ən, sĭth′-). **1.** Of or relating to Scythia. **2.** A member of the ancient nomadic people inhabiting Scythia. **3.** The Iranian language of the Scythians.

Scyth·o-Dra·vid·i·an (sĭth′ō-drə-vĭd′ē-ən, sĭth′). Of or relating to an ethnic group of northwest India having mixed Iranian and Dravidian characteristics.

sea (sē). *abbr.* **s., S. 1.** The continuous body of salt water covering most of the earth's surface, especially this body regarded as a geophysical entity distinct from earth and sky. **2.** A tract of water within an ocean. **3.** A relatively large body of salt water completely or partially enclosed by land. **4.** A relatively large landlocked body of fresh water.

Sea·ford (sē′fərd). An unincorporated community of southeast New York on the southern shore of Long Island south of Bethpage. It is mainly residential. ⊛ Pop. 15,597.

Sea Islands (sē). A chain of islands in the Atlantic Ocean off South Carolina, Georgia, and northern Florida. The Spanish discovered and first inhabited the islands in the 16th century but were displaced by English colonists after the 17th century.

Seal Beach (sēl). A city of southern California on the Pacific Ocean south-southeast of Los Angeles. It is a resort community with various light industries. ⊛ Pop. 25,098.

sea level. *abbr.* **SL.** The level of the ocean's surface, especially the level halfway between mean high and low tide, used as a standard in reckoning land elevation or sea depths.

sea·mount (sē′mount′). An underwater mountain rising from the ocean floor and having a summit below the surface of the sea.

Sea·side (sē′sīd′). A city of western California on Monterey Bay west-southwest of Salinas. It is a resort and commercial and residential center adjoining the nearby U.S. military installation Fort Ord. ⊛ Pop. 38,901.

Se·at·tle (sē-ăt′l). A city of west-central Washington bounded by Puget Sound and Lake Washington. First settled in the 1850's, it prospered after the coming of the railroad in 1884 and became a boom town during the Alaskan gold rush of 1897. It is now an important commercial, transportation, and industrial hub and a major port of entry. ⊛ Pop. 516,259.

Se·bas·to·pol (sə-băs′tə-pōl′). See **Sevastopol.**

Sech·ua·na (sĕch-wä′nə). Variant of **Setswana.**

sec·ond (sĕk′ənd). *abbr.* **s.** A unit of angular measure equal to one sixtieth of a minute.

Sec·ond World (sĕk′ənd). During the Cold War, the industrialized Communist nations of the world.

sec·tion (sĕk′shən). *abbr.* **sec., sect. 1.** A distinct area of a town, county, or country. **2.** A land unit equal to one square mile (2.59 square kilometers), 640 acres, or 1/36 of a township.

Se·da·lia (sĭ-dāl′yə). A city of central Missouri east-southeast of Kansas City. It is a processing and manufacturing center. ⊛ Pop. 19,800.

Se·dan (sĭ-dăn′, sə-däN′). A town of northeast France on the Meuse River near the Belgian border. It was the site of the decisive defeat and surrender of Napoleon III (September 2, 1870) in the Franco-Prussian War. ⊛ Pop. 23,477.

Sedge·moor (sĕj′mŏŏr′, -môr′, -mōr′). A marshy tract in southwest England where the forces of James II defeated (June 6, 1685) the Duke of Monmouth, pretender to the English throne.

Se·ges·ta (sĭ-jĕs'tə, sĕ-jĕs'tä). An ancient city of northwest Sicily near modern-day Alcamo. Traditionally a Trojan colony, it was a Carthaginian dependency after c. 400 B.C. but declined during the first century.

Se·go·vi·a (sĭ-gō'vē-ə, sĕ-gô'vyä). A city of central Spain north-northwest of Madrid. An important Roman town, it was held sporadically by the Moors from 714 to 1079. Its Roman aqueduct (first or second century A.D.) is still in use. ◉ Pop. 53,005.

Se·guin (sĭ-gēn'). A city of south-central Texas east-northeast of San Antonio. Founded in 1838, it is an agricultural processing center in an oil- and livestock-producing region. ◉ Pop. 18,853.

Se·gu·ra (sā-gōor'ə, sĕ-gōo'rä). A river, about 322 km (200 mi) long, of southeast Spain flowing generally eastward to the Mediterranean Sea.

Seine (sān, sĕn). A river of northern France flowing about 772 km (480 mi) generally northwest to the **Bay of the Seine,** an inlet of the English Channel, near Le Havre. It has been an important commercial waterway since Roman times and has figured significantly in the histories of Paris, Rouen, and Le Havre.

Sek·on·di-Ta·ko·ra·di (sĕk'ən-dē'tä-kə-rä'-dē). A city of southwest Ghana on the Gulf of Guinea west-southwest of Accra. The two parts of the city developed around Dutch and English forts built in the 17th century. ◉ Pop. 93,882.

Sel·den (sĕl'dən). An unincorporated community of southeast New York on north-central Long Island. It is mainly residential. ◉ Pop. 24,100.

Se·len·ga (sĕl'ĕng-gä'). A river of northern Mongolia and southeast Russia flowing about 1,207 km (750 mi) east and north to Lake Baikal.

Se·leu·ci·a (sĭ-lōo'shē-ə, -shə). An ancient city of Mesopotamia on the Tigris River southsoutheast of modern Baghdad. Founded c. 300 B.C., it was an important commercial center and the chief city of the empire founded by Seleucus I (ruled 312–281 B.C.).

Sel·kirk Mountains (sĕl'kûrk'). A range of the Rocky Mountains in southeast British Columbia, Canada. It rises to 3,524.3 m (11,555 ft) at Mount Sir Sandford.

Sel·ma (sĕl'mə). A city of south-central Alabama west of Montgomery. In 1965 it was the site of a voter registration drive led by Martin Luther King, Jr. ◉ Pop. 23,755.

Se·ma·rang (sə-mär'äng). A city of northern Java, Indonesia, on the Java Sea east of Jakarta. It is a major port and industrial center. ◉ Pop. 1,026,671.

sem·i·ar·id (sĕm'ē-ăr'ĭd). Characterized by relatively low annual rainfall of 25 to 50 centimeters (10 to 20 inches) and having scrubby vegetation with short, coarse grasses; not completely arid. —**sem'i·a·rid'i·ty** (-ə-rĭd'ĭ-tē, -ă-rĭd'-) n.

sem·i·des·ert (sĕm'ē-dĕz'ərt, sĕm'ĭ-). A semi-arid area often located between a desert and a grassland or woodland.

Sem·i·nole (sĕm'ə-nōl'). pl. **Seminole** or **-noles. 1.** A member of a Native American people made up of various primarily Creek groups who moved into northern Florida during the 18th and 19th centuries, later inhabiting the Everglades region as well, with present-day populations in Oklahoma and southern Florida. The Seminole Wars ended in the removal of the majority of the Seminoles to Indian Territory. **2.** Either of the Muskogean languages spoken by the Seminoles.

Sem·i·pa·la·tinsk (sĕm'ē-pə-lä'tĭnsk, syĭ-myĭ-). A city of northeast Kazakstan on the Irtysh River north-northeast of Almaty. Founded as a fortress in 1718, it is a port and processing center. ◉ Pop. 342,000.

Sem·ite (sĕm'īt'). **1.** A member of a group of Semitic-speaking peoples of the Near East and northern Africa, including the Arabs, Arameans, Babylonians, Carthaginians, Ethiopians, Hebrews, and Phoenicians. **2.** A Jew.

Se·mit·ic (sə-mĭt'ĭk). abbr. **Sem. 1.** Of or relating to the Semites or their languages or cultures. **2.** Of or constituting a subgroup of the Afro-Asiatic language group that includes Arabic, Hebrew, Amharic, and Aramaic. **3.** The Semitic languages. **4.** Any one of the Semitic languages.

sem·i·trop·i·cal (sĕm'ē-trŏp'ĭ-kəl, sĕm'ī-). Partly tropical; subtropical.

Sen·dai (sĕn-dī'). A city of northeast Honshu, Japan, on an inlet of the Pacific Ocean north of Tokyo. It is an important cultural and educational center. ◉ Pop. 950,893.

Sen·e·ca (sĕn'ĭ-kə). **1.** pl. **Seneca** or **-cas.** A member of a Native American people formerly inhabiting western New York from Seneca Lake to Lake Erie, with present-day populations in this same area and in southeast Ontario. The Senecas are the westernmost member of the original Iroquois confederacy. **2.** The Iroquoian language of the Senecas.

Seneca Falls. A village of west-central New York on the Seneca River east-southeast of Rochester. The first U.S. women's rights convention was held here in 1848. ◉ Pop. 7,370.

Seneca Lake. A lake of west-central New York connected with Cayuga Lake by the **Seneca River,** about 105 km (65 mi) long. Seneca Lake is the largest of the Finger Lakes.

Sen·e·gal (sĕn'ĭ-gôl', -gäl'). A country of western Africa on the Atlantic Ocean. The coast was settled by Wolof and other West Atlantic peoples, while the interior formed part of the medieval empires of Ghana, Mali, and Songhai. Coastal trading posts were established by the Portuguese in the mid-15th century and by the Dutch and French in the 17th century. Control of the coast alternated between the French and British until 1815, when the Treaty of Paris awarded the region to France. The French expanded their control into the interior, and Senegal became a French colony in 1895 as part of French West Africa, with full independence being won in 1960 under the leadership of Léopold Senghor (president 1960–1980). Senegal joined with Gambia in the short-lived confederation of Senegambia (1981–1989). Dakar is the capital and the largest city. ◉ Pop. 8,102,000. —**Sen′-e·ga·lese′** (-gô-lēz′, -lēs′, -gə-) *adj. & n.*

Senegal River. A river of western Africa rising in western Mali and flowing about 1,609 km (1,000 mi) generally northwest and west along the Mauritania-Senegal border to the Atlantic.

Sen·e·gam·bi·a (sĕn′ĭ-găm′bē-ə). **1.** A region of western Africa watered by the Senegal and Gambia rivers. **2.** A confederation of Senegal and Gambia (1981–1989) intended to promote cooperation between the two countries in matters of foreign policy, security, and economic affairs. Senegal dissolved the confederation when Gambia refused to move closer toward union.

Sen·lac (sĕn′lăk′). A hill in southern England near Hastings. The battle fought here in 1066, in which William the Conqueror defeated Harold II, is known as the Battle of Hastings.

Seoul (sōl). The capital and largest city of South Korea, in the northwest part of the country east of Inchon. Founded in the 14th century, it became the country's capital in 1948 and was twice occupied by Communist forces during the Korean War (1950–1953). ◉ Pop. 10,726,862.

Se·phar·di (sə-fär′dē). *pl.* **-dim** (-dĭm). A descendent of the Jews who lived in Spain and Portugal during the Middle Ages until persecution culminating in expulsion in 1492 forced them to leave. —**Se·phar′dic** (-dĭk) *adj.*

Se·pik (sā′pĭk). A river, about 1,126 km (700 mi) long, of northern Papua New Guinea.

Sept Îles or **Sept-Îles** (sĕt-ēl′) also **Sev·en Isles** (sĕv′ən). A city of eastern Quebec, Canada, on the St. Lawrence River near its mouth. The French explorer Jacques Cartier sailed into the harbor in 1535. ◉ Pop. 29,262.

Se·raing (sə-răN′). A city of eastern Belgium on the Meuse River south-southwest of Liège. It is a glassmaking and metallurgical center. ◉ Pop. 63,001.

Serb (sûrb). A member of a southern Slavic people that is the principal ethnic group of Serbia and adjacent regions.

Ser·bi·a (sûr′bē-ə). A republic comprising most of Yugoslavia. Serbs settled in the region in the 6th–7th century, were Christianized in the 9th century, and formed an independent kingdom in the 13th century. Defeated (1389) at Kosovo Field, the Serbs fell under Turkish domination, which ended when Serbia was granted full independence in 1878. The new kingdom of Serbia gained territory and power during the Balkan wars (1912–1913). Austria-Hungary declared war on Serbia after the assassination (1914) of Archduke Francis Ferdinand by a Serbian nationalist, sparking World War I. In 1918 Serbia became a major constituent of the Kingdom of Serbs, Croats, and Slovenes, which was later (1929) renamed Yugoslavia. Croatia, Slovenia, and Bosnia and Herzegovina declared independence from Yugoslavia in 1991, leading to war with Serbia, which, with the help of the largely Serbian Yugoslav army, sought first to preserve a Serbian dominated federation and then to create a "Greater Serbia" with Serbian enclaves in the other republics. In April 1992 Serbia and Montenegro formed a new Yugoslav state.

Ser·bi·an (sûr′bē-ən). **1.** A native or inhabitant of Serbia; a Serb. **2.** Serbo-Croatian as spoken in Serbia and adjacent region, written in a Cyrillic alphabet. **3.** Of or relating to Serbia or its people, language, or culture.

Ser·bo-Cro·a·tian (sûr′bō-krō-ā′shən). **1.** The Slavic language of the Serbs and the Croats. **2.** A native speaker of Serbo-Croatian. **3.** Of or relating to Serbo-Croatian or its speakers.

Ser·en·get·i Plain (sĕr′ən-gĕt′ē). An area of northern Tanzania bordering on Kenya and Lake Victoria. It is internationally well-known for its extensive wildlife preserve.

Ser·gi·yev Po·sad (sĕr′gē-yĭf pō-säd′). Formerly **Za·gorsk** (zə-gôrsk′). A city of west-central Russia northeast of Moscow. It developed around a monastery founded in 1340. ◉ Pop. 114,586.

Ser·pu·khov (sĕr-pōō′kəf, syĕr′pōō-кнəf). A city of west-central Russia on the Oka River south of Moscow. Founded as a fortified outpost, it is now an important textile and manufacturing center. ◉ Pop. 139,944.

Ser·ra da Es·tre·la (sĕr′ə dä ĕs-trĕl′ə, ĕsh-, sĕ′rä). A mountain range of central Portugal including the highest elevation, 1,994.4 m (6,539 ft), in the country.

Ses·tos (sĕs′təs, -tŏs). An ancient town of European Turkey at the narrowest point of the Dardanelles. In 481 B.C. the Persian king Xerxes I built a bridge of boats here to cross the Hellespont and invade Greece. Sestos is also the site of the legendary tale of Hero and Leander.

Ses·to San Gio·van·ni (sĕs′tō sän′ jô-vä′nē, sän′). A city of northern Italy, an industrial suburb of Milan. ● Pop. 94,738.

Sets·wa·na (sĕt-swä′nə) also **Sech·ua·na** (sĕchwä′-). See **Tswana** (sense 2).

Se·tú·bal (sə-tōō′bəl). A city of southwest Portugal southeast of Lisbon on the **Bay of Setúbal,** an inlet of the Atlantic Ocean. Setúbal is a port and processing center with a shipbuilding industry. ● Pop. 103,634.

Se·vas·to·pol (sə-văs′tə-pōl′, sĕv′ə-stō′pəl, syĭvə-). Formerly **Se·bas·to·pol** (sə-băs′tə-pōl′). A city of southern Ukraine in the Crimea on the Black Sea west of Yalta. Founded on the site of an ancient Greek colony, it became Russia's principal Black Sea naval base after the late 18th century. The city resisted lengthy sieges during the Crimean War and World War II. ● Pop. 371,400.

Sev·en Hills of Rome (sĕv′ən). The hills upon which the ancient city of Rome was built, including the Palatine (traditional site of the founding of the city), Aventine, Caelian, Capitoline, Esquiline, Quirinal, and Viminal hills.

Seven Isles. See **Sept Îles.**

seven seas also **Seven Seas.** All the oceans of the world.

Sev·enth Avenue (sĕv′ənth). Called "Fashion Avenue." A thoroughfare in New York City on Manhattan Island. It has long been considered the center of the garment and fashion industry in the United States.

Seven Wonders of the World. In ancient times, the pyramids of Egypt; the Hanging Gardens of Babylon; Phidias's statue of Zeus at Olympia; the temple of Artemis at Ephesus; the tomb, or mausoleum, of King Mausolus at Halicarnassus; the Colossus of Rhodes; and either the Pharos, or lighthouse, at Alexandria or the walls of Babylon. The list of manmade wonders was first compiled by a Hellenistic traveler in the second century B.C.

Sev·ern (sĕv′ərn). A community of north-central Maryland, a residential suburb of Baltimore. ● Pop. 24,499.

Se·ver·na Park (sə-vûr′nə). An unincorporated community of central Maryland on the **Severn River,** an inlet of Chesapeake Bay. The city is mainly residential. ● Pop. 25,879.

Se·ver·na·ya Zem·lya (sĕv′ər-nə-yä′ zĕm′lē-ä′, -lyä′, syĭ-vyĭr-). An archipelago of north-central Russia in the Arctic Ocean north of the Taimyr Peninsula. Discovered in 1913, the group comprises three major islands and several smaller ones.

Severn River. **1.** A river of northwest Ontario, Canada, flowing about 676 km (420 mi) northeast to Hudson Bay. **2.** A river of southwest Great Britain rising in central Wales and flowing about 338 km (210 mi) in a curve through western England. It empties into Bristol Channel through a long estuary.

Se·ve·rod·vinsk (sĕv′ər-əd-vĭnsk′, syĭ-vyĭ-rəd-). A city of northwest Russia on an arm of the White Sea west of Arkhangelsk. It is a timbershipping port. ● Pop. 249,071.

Se·vier River (sə-vîr′). A river, about 451 km (280 mi) long, of west-central Utah flowing generally north then southwest through the **Sevier Desert.** It empties into **Sevier Lake,** a shrinking salt lake that is usually dry.

Se·ville (sə-vĭl′). A city of southwest Spain on the Guadalquivir River north-northeast of Cádiz. An important settlement under the Romans, Vandals, and Visigoths, it was conquered by the Moors in A.D. 712 and later taken by Ferdinand III of Castile, who made it his royal residence in 1248. The city especially prospered after the discovery of the New World and served as the chief port of colonial trade until the early 18th century, when it was supplanted by Cádiz. ● Pop. 678,902.

Sew·ard Peninsula (sōō′ərd). A peninsula of western Alaska projecting into the Bering Sea just below the Arctic Circle.

Sey·chelles (sā-shĕl′, -shĕlz′). An island country in the western Indian Ocean north of Madagascar. Previously uninhabited, the islands were explored by the Portuguese navigator Vasco da Gama in the early 1500's and colonized by the French in the mid-1700's. They were taken by the British in 1794, and Britain gained permanent control of them by the Treaty of Paris in 1814. The Seychelles were a crown colony from

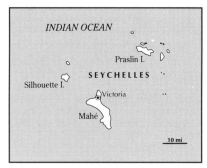

1903 until 1975 when they became self-governing. Independence as a Commonwealth nation was achieved in 1976. Victoria, on Mahé Island, is the capital. ⊚ Pop. 74,000.

Sey·mour (sē′môr′, -mōr′). A city of southeast Indiana south-southeast of Indianapolis. It is a manufacturing and shipping center in an agricultural region. ⊚ Pop. 15,576.

's Gra·ven·ha·ge (skrä′vən-hä′gə, sкнrä′vən-hä′кнə). See The **Hague.**

Shaan·xi (shän′shē′) also **Shen·si** (shĕn′sē′). A province of east-central China crossed by the Wei He. One of the earliest cultural and political centers of China, the province is densely populated and highly industrialized. Xi'an is the capital. ⊚ Pop. 30,020,000.

Sha·ba (shä′bə). Formerly **Ka·tan·ga** (kə-täng′-gə, -täng′-). A region of southeast Zaire bordering on Zambia. It proclaimed itself the republic of Katanga in 1960 and seceded from Congo (now Zaire). The insurrection was put down in 1963 with the aid of UN troops. Shaba was captured by rebel troops in 1997 in a drive to oust Zairian president Mobutu Sese Seko.

Sha·hap·ti·an (shä-hăp′tē-ən). Variant of **Sahaptian.**

Sha·hap·tin (shä-hăp′tĭn). Variant of **Sahaptin.**

Shak·er Heights (shā′kər). A city of northeast Ohio, a residential suburb of Cleveland. It is named after a Shaker community that existed here from 1822 to 1889. ⊚ Pop. 30,831.

Shakh·ty (shäk′tē, shäкн′-). A city of southwest Russia northeast of Rostov. Founded in 1829, it is an industrial city in an anthracite-mining region. ⊚ Pop. 226,595.

Shan (shän, shăn). **1.** A member of any of a group of tribes inhabiting the hills and plateaus of northeast Myanmar (Burma) and adjacent regions of China, Laos, and Thailand. **2.** The Tai language of the Shan. **3.** Of or relating to the Shan or their language or culture.

Shan·dong (shän′dông′) also **Shan·tung** (shän′-tŭng′, shän′tŏong′). A province of eastern China bordered by the Bo Hai and the Yellow Sea. The eastern part of the province forms the **Shandong Peninsula.** Settled since very early times, it became a province under the Ming dynasty. Jinan is the capital. ⊚ Pop. 76,950,000.

Shang·hai (shăng-hī′, shäng′-). A city of eastern China at the mouth of the Chang Jiang (Yangtze River) southeast of Nanjing. The largest city in the country, Shanghai was opened to foreign trade by the Treaty of Nanking (1842) and quickly prospered. France, Great Britain, and the United States all held large concessions in the city until the early 20th century. Shanghai is located in Jiangsu province but is administered as a separate governmental unit. ⊚ Pop. 8,205,598.

Shan·non (shăn′ən). A river, about 386 km (240 mi) long, rising in north-central Ireland and flowing generally south and west to the Atlantic Ocean through a long, deep estuary.

Shan·si (shän′sē′). See **Shanxi.**

Shan·tou (shän′tou′) also **Swa·tow** (swä′tou′). A city of southeast China on the South China Sea east-northeast of Hong Kong. It is a trade and industrial center with shipbuilding facilities. ⊚ Pop. 884,543.

Shan·tung (shǎn′tŭng′, shän′tŏong′). See **Shandong.**

Shan·xi (shän′shē′) also **Shan·si** (-sē′). A province of northeast China bordered on the north by a section of the Great Wall. In the Chinese-Japanese War (1937–1945) it was a center of guerrilla warfare. Taiyuan is the capital. ⊚ Pop. 26,270,000.

Sha·ri (shä′rē) also **Cha·ri** (shä′rē, shä-rē′). A river rising in the Central African Republic and flowing about 2,253 km (1,400 mi) northwest through southern Chad to Lake Chad.

Shar·on (shär′ən). A city of western Pennsylvania on the Ohio border north-northwest of Pittsburgh. It is an industrial center. ⊚ Pop. 17,493.

Sharon, Plain of. A fertile plain of western Israel extending along the Mediterranean coast south of Haifa.

Sharps·burg (shärps′bûrg′). A town of northern Maryland west of Frederick. It is the site of the Civil War Battle of Antietam (September 16–17, 1862), in which Union forces repulsed Gen. Robert E. Lee's troops. The engagement, also known as the Battle of Sharpsburg, was one of the bloodiest of the war, with heavy losses on both sides.

Shas·ta (shăs′tə), **Lake.** A reservoir of north-central California formed by **Shasta Dam** on the Sacramento River. It is the largest artificial lake in California and a popular water resort. The dam was completed in 1945.

Shasta, Mount. A volcanic peak, 4,319.4 m (14,162 ft) high, of the Cascade Range in northern California. Discovered in 1827, it has hot sulfurous springs near the summit.

Shatt al Ar·ab or **Shatt-al-Ar·ab** (shăt′ ăl är′-əb, shät′). A river channel, about 193 km (120 mi) long, of southeast Iraq formed by the confluence of the Tigris and Euphrates rivers and flowing southeast to the Persian Gulf. The Shatt al Arab forms part of the Iraq-Iran border, and navigation rights to the channel have long been disputed by the two countries.

Sha·win·i·gan (shə-wĭn′ĭ-gən). A city of southern Quebec, Canada, on the St. Maurice River northwest of Trois Rivières. Its hydroelectric station supplies power for the city's pulp and paper mills and other processing plants. ⊚ Pop. 23,011.

Shaw·nee¹ (shô-nē′). **1.** *pl.* **Shawnee** or **-nees.** A member of a Native American people formerly inhabiting parts of the Cumberland and central Ohio valleys, with present-day populations in Oklahoma. The Shawnees figured prominently in the resistance to white settlement of the Ohio Valley in the late 18th and early 19th centuries. **2.** The Algonquian language of the Shawnees.

Shaw·nee² (shô-nē′, shô′nē). **1.** A city of northeast Kansas, a residential suburb of Kansas City. ◉ Pop. 29,653. **2.** A city of central Oklahoma on the North Canadian River east-southeast of Oklahoma City. The city boomed after the discovery of oil in the 1920's and is now a trade and shipping center for an agricultural region. ◉ Pop. 26,017.

She·ba (shē′bə). An ancient country of southern Arabia comprising present-day Yemen. Its people colonized Ethiopia in the tenth century B.C. and were known for their wealth and commercial prosperity. In the Bible, the queen of Sheba made a celebrated visit to King Solomon.

She·bel·le or **She·be·li** (shə-bā′lē). A river, about 1,609 km (1,000 mi) long, of northeast Africa rising in central Ethiopia and flowing southeast into Somalia then southwest in a course parallel to the Indian Ocean coastline. It disappears in a swampland in southern Somalia.

She·boy·gan (shə-boi′gən). A city of eastern Wisconsin on Lake Michigan north of Milwaukee. Founded c. 1835 on the site of a fur-trading post established in 1795, it is a shipping and manufacturing center. ◉ Pop. 49,676.

shed (shĕd). An elevation in the earth's surface or a divide from which water flows in two directions; a watershed.

Shef·field (shĕf′ēld′). A borough of north-central England east of Manchester. One of the leading industrialized cities of England, it has long specialized in the production of cutlery and steel. ◉ Pop. 531,928.

Shel·by (shĕl′bē). A city of southwest North Carolina in the Piedmont west of Charlotte. It is a textile and processing center in an agricultural region. ◉ Pop. 14,669.

shelf ice (shĕlf). An extension of glacial ice into coastal waters that is in contact with the bottom near the shore but not toward the outer edge of the shelf.

Shel·i·kof Strait (shĕl′ĭ-kôf′). A strait of southern Alaska between the Alaska Peninsula and Kodiak and Afognak islands. Cook Inlet is at its northern end.

Shel·ton (shĕl′tən). A city of southwest Connecticut north-northeast of Bridgeport on the Housatonic River. Settled in 1697, it is a manufacturing center. ◉ Pop. 35,418.

Shen·an·do·ah Valley (shĕn′ən-dō′ə). A valley of northern Virginia between the Allegheny Mountains and the Blue Ridge. Drained by the **Shenandoah River,** about 241 km (150 mi) long, the valley was first explored in the early 1700's and was an important gateway to the frontier.

Shen·si (shĕn′sē′). See **Shaanxi.**

Shen·yang (shŭn′yäng′). Formerly **Muk·den** (mŏŏk′dən, -dĕn′, mŏŏk′-). A city of northeast China east-northeast of Beijing. The capital of Liaoning province, it was the site of the so-called Mukden, or Manchurian, Incident (1931), in which the Japanese army used an explosion on the railroad north of the city as a pretext to occupy Manchuria. ◉ Pop. 4,655,280.

Sher·brooke (shûr′brŏŏk′). A city of southern Quebec, Canada, on the St. François River east of Montreal. It is a trade and manufacturing center. ◉ Pop. 74,075.

Sher·i·dan (shĕr′ĭ-dn). A city of north-central Wyoming near the Montana border north-northwest of Casper. It is a trade center and transportation hub. ◉ Pop. 13,900.

Sher·man (shûr′mən). A city of northeast Texas near the Oklahoma border north of Dallas. Settled as a way station on a stagecoach route, it is now a highway and rail junction with varied industries. ◉ Pop. 31,601.

Sherman, Mount. A peak, 4,281 m (14,036 ft) high, in the Park Range of the Rocky Mountains in central Colorado.

Sher·pa (shûr′pə). *pl.* **Sherpa** or **-pas.** A member of a people of Tibetan descent living on the southern side of the Himalaya Mountains in Nepal and Sikkim, noted especially for their ability at mountaineering.

's Her·to·gen·bosch (sĕr′tō-gən-bôs′, -кнən-). A city of south-central Netherlands north-northwest of Eindhoven. Chartered c. 1185, it was a fortress city until 1874. ◉ Pop. 94,893.

Sher·wood Forest (shûr′wŏŏd′). A former royal forest of central England famed as the site of the legendary exploits of the 12th-century outlaw Robin Hood and his followers.

Sherwood Park. A city of central Alberta, Canada, a suburb of Edmonton. ◉ Pop. 29,285.

Shet·land Islands (shĕt′lənd). An archipelago of northern Scotland in the Atlantic Ocean northeast of the Orkney Islands. The islands were occupied by Norse invaders and colonists after the late ninth century and were annexed by Scotland in 1472.

Shey·enne (shī-ĕn′, -ăn′). A river, about 523 km (325 mi) long, rising in central North Dakota and flowing east, south, and northeast to the Red River of the North above Fargo.

shield (shēld). *Geology.* A large lowland area, the geologic nucleus of a continent, whose bedrock consists of igneous and metamorphic rocks that usually date to the Precambrian era, more than 600 million years ago.

shift (shĭft). *Geology.* See **fault.**

Shi·jia·zhuang (shœ′jyä′jwäng′) also **Shih·kia·chwang** (-kyä′chwäng′). A city of northeast China southwest of Beijing. An industrial and transportation center, it is the capital of Hebei province. ◉ Pop. 1,372,109.

Shi·ko·ku (shē-kô′kōō, shē′kô-kōō′). An island of southern Japan between southwest Honshu and eastern Kyushu. It was held by various feudal families from early times until c. 1600.

Shil·luk (shĭ-lŏŏk′). **1.** *pl.* **Shilluk** or **-luks.** A member of a people inhabiting the western bank of the Nile River in southern Sudan. **2.** The Nilotic language of the Shilluk.

Shi·loh (shī′lō). **1.** An ancient village of central Palestine northwest of the Dead Sea. In the Bible, it was a meeting place and sanctuary for the Israelites and the site of a tabernacle where the Ark of the Covenant was kept until its capture by the Philistines. **2.** A locality in southwest Tennessee east of Memphis. The Civil War Battle of Shiloh (April 6–7, 1862) ended in the withdrawal of Confederate troops but claimed more than 10,000 casualties on both the Union and Confederate sides.

Shi·mi·zu (shē-mē′zōō, shē′mē-zōō′). A city of east-central Honshu, Japan, southwest of Yokohama on Suruga Bay. It is a port and processing center. ◉ Pop. 241,152.

Shi·mo·no·se·ki (shĭm′ə-nō-sĕk′ē, shē′mô-nô-). A city of extreme southwest Honshu, Japan, on Korea Strait. The treaty ending the Sino-Japanese War was signed here on April 17, 1895. ◉ Pop. 259,898.

Shi·nar (shī′nər, -när′). In the Bible, a country on the lower courses of the Tigris and Euphrates rivers.

Shi·raz (shē-räz′). A city of southwest-central Iran south-southeast of Tehran. It has long been an important commercial center noted for its carpets and metalworks. The ruins of ancient Persepolis are nearby. ◉ Pop. 1,042,801.

shire (shīr). A former administrative division of Great Britain, equivalent to a county.

shire town. *Chiefly British.* See **county town.**

Shive·ly (shīv′lē). A city of northern Kentucky, a suburb of Louisville. ◉ Pop. 15,535.

Shi·zu·o·ka (shē′zōō-ô′kä). A city of east-central Honshu, Japan, on Suruga Bay southwest of Yokohama. It is a port and processing center. ◉ Pop. 474,219.

Shko·dër (shkō′dər). A city of northwest Albania on Lake Scutari. It was under Turkish rule from 1479 to 1913. ◉ Pop. 71,200.

shoal (shōl). **1.** A shallow place in a body of water. **2.** A sandy elevation of the bottom of a

body of water, constituting a hazard to navigation; a sandbank or sandbar.

Sho·la·pur (shō′lə-pŏŏr′). A city of west-central India on the Deccan Plateau east-southeast of Bombay. It is a trade and textile-manufacturing center. ◉ Pop. 604,215.

shore (shôr, shōr). **1.** The land along the edge of an ocean, a sea, a lake, or a river; a coast. **2.** often **shores.** Land; country.

Shore·view (shôr′vyōō′, shōr′-). A city of eastern Minnesota, a residential suburb of St. Paul. ◉ Pop. 24,587.

Sho·sho·ne also **Sho·sho·ni** (shō-shō′nē). **1.** *pl.* **Shoshone** or **-nes** also **Shoshoni** or **-nis.** A member of a Native American people comprising three divisions, specifically: **a.** A group inhabiting parts of Idaho, northern Utah, eastern Oregon, and western Montana, now mostly in southeast Idaho. Also called *Northern Shoshone, Snake.* **b.** A group inhabiting the Great Basin area of Idaho, Utah, and Nevada south to Death Valley, California, now mostly in Nevada. Also called *Western Shoshone.* **c.** A group inhabiting the Wind River valley of western Wyoming. Also called *Eastern Shoshone, Wind River Shoshone.* **2.** Any of the languages of the Shoshone people. —**Sho·sho′ne·an** *adj.*

Shoshone Falls. A waterfall, 64.7 m (212 ft) high, in the Snake River of southern Idaho.

Shoshone River. A river, about 193 km (120 mi) long, of northwest Wyoming flowing northeast to the Bighorn River.

shott (shŏt). Variant of **chott.**

Shreve·port (shrēv′pôrt′, -pōrt′). A city of northwest Louisiana on the Red River near the Texas border. Founded in the 1830's, it grew rapidly after the discovery of oil in the region (1906). ◉ Pop. 198,525.

Shrews·bur·y (shrōōz′bĕr′ē, -bə-rē). **1.** A municipal borough of western England on the Severn River west-northwest of Birmingham. An ancient Saxon and Norman stronghold, it is now a transportation hub with varied industries. ◉ Pop. 60,400. **2.** A town of central Massachusetts, a chiefly residential suburb of Worcester. ◉ Pop. 24,146.

Shrop·shire (shrŏp′shîr′, -shər). A historical region of western England on the Welsh border. It was part of the kingdom of Mercia during Anglo-Saxon times.

Shu·bra al Khay·mah (shōō-brä′ äl kī-mä′, -mäкн′). A city of northeast Egypt, an industrial suburb of Cairo. ◉ Pop. 834,000.

Shu·men (shōō′mĕn′). A city of northeast Bulgaria west of Varna. Founded in 927, the city was strategically important during the Russo-Turkish Wars of the 18th and 19th centuries. ◉ Pop. 109,800.

Si·al·kot (sē-äl'kōt'). A city of northeast Pakistan north of Lahore. It is a trade and processing center. ◉ Pop. 302,009.

Si·am (sī-ăm'). See **Thailand.**

Si·a·mese (sī'ə-mēz', -mēs'). **1.** Of or relating to Siam; Thai. **2.** pl. **Siamese.** A native or inhabitant of Siam; a Thai. **3.** The Thai language.

Si·an (sē'än', shē'-). See **Xi'an.**

Siang Kiang (syäng' kyäng', shyäng'). See **Xiang Jiang.**

Siang·tan (syäng'tän', shyäng'-). See **Xiangtan.**

Šiau·liai (shyou'lyī'). A city of northern Lithuania northwest of Vilnius. Under the control of the Polish crown from 1589 until 1772, it passed to Russia in 1795 and to independent Lithuania in 1920. ◉ Pop. 147,900.

Si·be·ri·a (sī-bîr'ē-ə). abbr. **Sib.** A region of central and eastern Russia stretching from the Ural Mountains to the Pacific Ocean. Inhabited by a variety of peoples including the Ostyak, Chukchi, Evenki, and Yakut, the extensive area was annexed by Russia in stages during the 16th and 17th centuries. Used as a place of exile for political prisoners since the early 17th century, it was settled by Russians after the construction of the Trans-Siberian Railroad (completed in 1905) and developed for its mineral resources after World War II. — **Si·be'ri·an** adj. & n.

Si·biu (sē-byōō'). A city of central Romania northwest of Bucharest. Settled in the 12th century by German colonists from Saxony, it was destroyed by Tartars in 1241. The rebuilt city came under Austrian control in 1699. ◉ Pop. 168,619.

Si·bu·yan Sea (sē'bōō-yän'). A sea in the central Philippines bordered by southern Luzon, Mindoro, and the Visayan Islands.

Si·chuan also **Sze·chwan** or **Sze·chuan** (sĕch'-wän'). A province of south-central China. Settled by non-Chinese peoples including Tibetans, the Miao, and the Hui, it was incorporated into the empire (c. third century A.D.) by the Qin dynasty. Chengdu is the capital. ◉ Pop. 101,800,000.

Si·ci·ly (sĭs'ə-lē). abbr. **Sic.** An island of southern Italy in the Mediterranean Sea west of the southern end of the Italian peninsula. It was colonized from the 8th century B.C. by Greeks, who displaced the earlier Phoenician settlers. The next conquerors were Carthaginians, who in turn were conquered by Romans in the 3rd century B.C. After a succession of other rulers the island came under the control of the Normans in the 11th century A.D. and formed the nucleus of the Kingdom of the Two Sicilies, consisting of Sicily and southern Italy. The island continued to change hands until a later kingdom

was conquered by the Italian general Giuseppe Garibaldi in 1860 and became part of unified Italy. — **Si·cil'ian** (sĭ-sĭl'yən) adj. & n.

Si·cy·on (sĭsh'ē-ŏn', sĭs'-). An ancient city of southern Greece in the northeast Peloponnesus near the Gulf of Corinth. It reached the height of its power under the tyrant Cleisthenes in the sixth century B.C.

Si·di-bel-Ab·bès (sē'dē-bĕl-ə-bĕs'). A city of northwest Algeria south of Oran. It was the headquarters of the French Foreign Legion until 1962. ◉ Pop. 112,988.

Sid·ley (sĭd'lē), **Mount.** A mountain, 4,183.7 m (13,717 ft) high, of Marie Byrd Land in Antarctica. It was discovered by Richard E. Byrd in 1934.

Sid·ney (sĭd'nē). A city of west-central Ohio west-northwest of Columbus. It is a manufacturing center. ◉ Pop. 18,710.

Si·don (sīd'n). An ancient city of Phoenicia on the Mediterranean Sea in present-day southwest Lebanon. Founded in the third millennium B.C., it was an important trade center known for its glassware and purple dyes.

Sid·ra (sĭd'rə), **Gulf of.** An inlet of the Mediterranean Sea off northern Libya west of Benghazi.

Sie·gen (zē'gən). A city of west-central Germany east of Cologne. The birthplace of the Flemish painter Peter Paul Rubens (1577–1640), it is today heavily industrialized. ◉ Pop. 111,845.

Si·en·a (sē-ĕn'ə, syĕ'nä). A city of west-central Italy south of Florence. Founded by Etruscans, it became independent in the 12th century and gradually evolved into a wealthy city known especially for its leadership of the Sienese school of art (13th–14th centuries). ◉ Pop. 61,888. — **Si'e·nese'** (-nēz', -nēs') adj. & n.

Si·er·ra Blan·ca Peak (sē-ĕr'ə blăng'kə). A mountain, 3,660.9 m (12,003 ft) high, in the Sacramento Mountains of south-central New Mexico. It is the highest elevation in the range.

Sierra Le·one (lē-ōn', -ō'nē). A country of western Africa on the Atlantic coast. Inhabited by the Temne when the Portuguese first visited

the coast in 1460, the region was later settled by Mande-speaking peoples from present-day Liberia. In 1792 freed slaves were brought from Nova Scotia to found the colony of Freetown, which was transferred to British administration in 1808 and continued to attract further settlement by liberated slaves. The region became a British protectorate in 1896 and achieved independence in 1961. Sierra Leone became a republic in 1971, although one-party rule and military coups dominated the country's political life in the following decades. Freetown is the capital and the largest city. ◉ Pop. 4,402,000.

Si·er·ra Ma·dre del Sur (sē-ĕr′ə mä′drä dĕl sŏōr′, syĕr′ä mä′thrĕ). A mountain range of southern Mexico along the Pacific coast.

Sierra Madre Oc·ci·den·tal (ŏk′sĭ-dĕn′təl, ôk′sē-thĕn-täl′). A mountain range of northwest Mexico running parallel to the Pacific coastline and adjoining the Mexican plateau. It extends for about 1,609 km (1,000 mi) southward from the border of Arizona.

Sierra Madre Or·ien·tal (ôr′ē-ĕn-täl′, ô-ryĕn-). A mountain range of northeast Mexico rising as barren hills south of the Rio Grande and roughly paralleling the coast of the Gulf of Mexico.

Si·er·ra Ne·va·da (sē-ĕr′ə nə-văd′ə, -vä′də). **1.** (syĕr′ä nĕ-vä′thä). A mountain range of southern Spain along the Mediterranean coast east of Granada. It rises to 3,480.4 m (11,411 ft) at Mulhacén. **2.** A mountain range of southern California extending about 644 km (400 mi) between the Sacramento and San Joaquin valleys and the Nevada border. Mount Whitney, 4,420.7 m (14,494 ft), is the highest elevation.

Sierra Vis·ta (vĭs′tə). A city of southeast Arizona southeast of Tucson near the Mexican border. It is in a cattle-raising and mining region. ◉ Pop. 32,983.

Si·ha·sa·pa (sə-hä′sə-pə). *pl.* **Sihasapa** or **-pas.** A member of a Native American people constituting a subdivision of the Teton Sioux. Also called *Blackfoot, Blackfoot Sioux.*

Sikes·ton (sīk′stən). A city of southeast Missouri west-southwest of Cairo, Illinois. It is a trade and processing center. ◉ Pop. 17,641.

Si Kiang (sē′ kyäng′, shē′). See **Xi Jiang.**

Sik·kim (sĭk′ĭm). A region and former kingdom of northeast India in the eastern Himalaya Mountains between Nepal and Bhutan. Long isolated from the outside world, Sikkim was settled by Tibetans in the 16th century and became a British protectorate in 1890. Sikkim passed to India in 1949 and became a state of that country in 1975.

Si·le·sia (sī-lē′zhə, -shə, sĭ-). A region of central Europe primarily in southwest Poland and northern Czech Republic. Settled by Slavic peoples c. A.D. 500, the region was long contested by various states and principalities. After World War I Silesia was partitioned among Germany, Poland, and Czechoslovakia. Much of the Czechoslovakian section passed to Germany and Poland after the signing of the Munich Pact in 1938. Germany occupied Polish Silesia from 1939 to 1945, and after World War II Poland annexed most of German Silesia. **Upper Silesia,** in southern Poland, is a highly industrialized area. **—Si·le′sian** *adj. & n.*

Sil·i·con Valley (sĭl′ĭ-kən, -kŏn′). A region of western California southeast of San Francisco known for its high-technology design and manufacturing industries.

Silk Road (sĭlk). An ancient trade route between China and the Mediterranean Sea extending some 6,440 km (4,000 mi) and linking China with the Roman Empire. The Venetian traveler Marco Polo (1254–1324) followed the route on his journey to Cathay.

Sill (sĭl), **Mount.** A peak, 4,316.7 m (14,153 ft) high, in the Sierra Nevada range of east-central California.

Sil·u·res (sĭl′yə-rēz′). A people described by the Roman historian Tacitus (A.D. 55?–120?) as occupying southeast Wales at the time of the Roman invasion. **—Si·lu′ri·an** (sĭ-lŏŏr′ē-ən, sī-) *adj.*

Sil·ver Spring (sĭl′vər). An unincorporated community of west-central Maryland, a residential suburb of Washington, D.C. ◉ Pop. 76,046.

Sim·coe (sĭm′kō), **Lake.** A lake of southeast Ontario, Canada, between Georgian Bay and Lake Ontario. It is a popular resort area.

Sim·fer·o·pol (sĭm′fə-rō′pəl, syĭm-fyə-rô′-). A city of southern Ukraine in the southern Crimea northeast of Sevastopol. Originally settled by Scythians, it was under Tatar rule from the 15th to the 18th century and was annexed by Russia in 1784. It became part of the Ukrainian S.S.R. in 1954. ◉ Pop. 357,000.

Si·mi Valley (sē′mē, sĭm′ē). A city of southern California, a manufacturing suburb of Los Angeles. ◉ Pop. 100,217.

si·moom (sĭ-mŏŏm′) also **si·moon** (-mŏŏn′). A strong, hot, sand-laden wind of the Sahara and Arabian deserts. Also called *samiel.*

Sim·plon Pass (sĭm′plŏn′, săN-plôN′). A pass, 2,010 m (6,590 ft) high, between the Lepontine and Pennine Alps in southern Switzerland. A nearby railroad tunnel system, 19.8 km (12.3 mi) long, extends southeastward into Italy.

Simp·son Desert (sĭmp′sən). A desert region of central Australia. The barren, uninhabited area was first crossed in 1939.

Sims·bur·y (sĭmz′bĕr′ē, -bə-rē). A town of

northern Connecticut northwest of Hartford. Incorporated in 1670, it is a manufacturing center. ⦿ Pop. 22,023.

Si·nai (sī′nī′), **Mount.** A mountain, about 2,288 m (7,500 ft) high, of the south-central Sinai Peninsula. It is thought to be the peak on which Moses received the Ten Commandments.

Sinai Peninsula. A peninsula linking southwest Asia with northeast Africa at the northern end of the Red Sea between the Gulf of Suez to the west and the Gulf of Aqaba to the east. Long held by the Egyptian kings, Israel occupied the peninsula in 1956 and from 1967 to 1982, when it was returned to Egypt under the terms of the Camp David Accords (1978) and an Egyptian-Israeli treaty (1979).

Sin·ce·le·jo (sĭn′sə-lĕ′hō, -sĕ′-). A town of northwest Colombia south of Cartagena. It is a trade and processing center. ⦿ Pop. 122,484.

Sind (sĭnd). A historical region of southern Pakistan along the lower Indus River. Inhabited since prehistoric times, it was held by Muslim dynasties from the 11th century until 1843, when it was annexed to British India. Sind became part of Pakistan in 1947.

Sin·del·fin·gen (zĭn′dl-fĭng′ən). A city of southwest Germany. It is an industrial suburb of Stuttgart. ⦿ Pop. 55,362.

Sin·dhi (sĭn′dē). **1.** *pl.* **Sindhi** or **-dhis.** A member of a predominantly Muslim people of Sind. **2.** The Indic language of Sind. **3.** Of or relating to Sind or its people, language, or culture.

Sin·ga·pore (sĭng′gə-pôr′, -pōr′, sĭng′ə-). A country of southeast Asia comprising **Singapore Island** and adjacent smaller islands. A trading center as early as the 14th century, Singapore was later part of Johor, a region of the southern Malay Peninsula, under the Malacca Sultanate. The sparsely populated island of Singapore was ceded to the British East India Company in 1819, and the city was founded the same year by Sir Thomas Raffles. The British took complete control in 1824 and added Singapore to the newly formed Straits Settlements in 1826. It became one of the leading ports in the world in the late 19th and early 20th centuries. During World War II it was held by the Japanese (1942–1945)

before being retaken by the British. Singapore became a crown colony in 1946, a self-governing state in 1959, part of the Federation of Malaysia in 1963, and a fully independent republic in 1965. The city of **Singapore** is the capital. ⦿ Pop. 2,930,000. — **Sin′ga·por′e·an** *adj. & n.*

Singapore Strait. A strait off the southern end of the Malay Peninsula between Singapore Island and the Riau Archipelago. It connects the Strait of Malacca with the South China Sea.

Sin·gha·lese (sĭng′gə-lēz′, -lēs′) or **Sin·ha·lese** (sĭn′hə-). **1.** *pl.* **Singhalese** or **Sinhalese.** A member of a people constituting the majority of the population of Sri Lanka. **2.** The Indic language spoken by the Singhalese that is the chief language of Sri Lanka. **3.** Of or relating to Sri Lanka, the Singhalese, or their language or culture.

Si·nit·ic (sī-nĭt′ĭk, sĭ-). The branch of Sino-Tibetan comprising Chinese. — **Si·nit′ic** *adj.*

sink·hole (sĭngk′hōl′). A natural depression in a land surface communicating with a subterranean passage, generally occurring in limestone regions and formed by solution or by collapse of a cavern roof.

Sin·kiang Ui·ghur or **Sin·kiang Ui·gur** (sĭn′-kyäng′ wē′gər, shĭn′jyäng′). See **Xinjiang Uygur.**

Si·no-Ti·bet·an (sī′nō-tĭ-bĕt′n, sĭn′ō-). A language family that includes the Sinitic and Tibeto-Burman branches. — **Si′no-Ti·bet′an** *adj.*

Sint-Ni·klaas (sĭnt-nē′kläs). A city of northwest Belgium west-southwest of Antwerp. It is a commercial, industrial, and transportation center. ⦿ Pop. 68,157.

Sin·ui·ju (shĭn′wē-jōō′). A city of western North Korea on Korea Bay at the mouth of the Yalu Jiang. It is a port and railroad terminus connected by bridge with Dandong, China. ⦿ Pop. 300,000.

si·nu·soi·dal projection (sī′nə-soid′l, -nyə-). A map projection in which areas are equal to corresponding areas on a globe, the parallels and the prime meridian being straight lines and the other meridians being increasingly curved outward from the prime meridian.

Siou·an (sōō′ən). **1.** A large North American Indian language family spoken from Lake Michigan to the Rocky Mountains and southward to Arkansas. **2.** A member of a Siouan-speaking people. — **Siou′an** *adj.*

Sioux (sōō). **1.** *pl.* **Sioux.** A member of a group of Native American peoples, also known as the Dakota, inhabiting the northern Great Plains from Minnesota to eastern Montana and from southern Saskatchewan to Nebraska. Present-day Sioux populations are located mainly in

North and South Dakota. **2.** Any of the Siouan languages of the Sioux peoples.

Sioux City. A city of northwest Iowa on the Missouri River near the Nebraska–South Dakota border. It is a shipping and processing center for an agricultural and livestock area. ⊛ Pop. 80,505.

Sioux Falls. A city of southeast South Dakota near the Minnesota border. First settled c. 1856, it was abandoned in 1862 and reestablished as a military post in 1865. It is now the largest city in the state. ⊛ Pop. 100,814.

Sip·par (sĭ-pär′). An ancient city of northern Babylonia on the Euphrates River south-southwest of present-day Baghdad. In early times it was a religious center devoted to the worship of the sun god Shamash.

si·roc·co (sə-rŏk′ō) also **sci·roc·co** (shə-, sə-). A hot, humid south or southeast wind of southern Italy, Sicily, and the Mediterranean islands, originating in the Sahara Desert as a dry, dusty wind but becoming moist as it passes over the Mediterranean.

Sí·ros (sē′rôs′). See **Syros.**

Sir Sand·ford (sər sănd′fərd), **Mount.** A peak, 3,524.3 m (11,555 ft) high, in the Selkirk Mountains of southeast British Columbia, Canada. It is the highest elevation in the range.

Sir Wil·fred Lau·ri·er (wĭl′frĭd lôr′ē-ā′, lôr′-), **Mount.** A peak, 3,583.8 m (11,750 ft) high, in the Cariboo Mountains of southeast British Columbia, Canada. It is the highest elevation in the range.

Sis·se·ton (sĭs′ĭ-tən). *pl.* **Sisseton** or **-tons.** A member of a Native American people of the Santee branch of the Sioux.

Sit·ka (sĭt′kə). A town of southeast Alaska on the western coast of Baranof Island. Founded in 1799 by Aleksandr Baranov, the first governor of the Russian colony of Alaska, it was the capital of Russian America and later the capital of Alaska from 1867 to 1906. ⊛ Pop. 8,588.

Si·vas (sĭ-väs′, sē-). A city of central Turkey east of Ankara. An important city of Asia Minor under the Romans, Byzantines, and Seljuk Turks, it was sacked by the Mongol conqueror Tamerlane in 1400 and fell to the Ottoman Turks in the 15th century. ⊛ Pop. 240,100.

Si·vash Sea (sĭ-väsh′). A salt lagoon of southern Ukraine along the northeast coast of the Crimea.

Si·wa·lik Hills (sĭ-wä′lĭk). A range of the southern Himalaya Mountains extending about 1,689 km (1,050 mi) from southwest Kashmir through northern India into southern Nepal. The hills are noted for their extensive fossil remains.

Six Nations (sĭks). The Iroquois confederacy after it was joined by the Tuscarora in 1722.

Sjael·land (shĕl′än′) also **Zea·land** (zē′lənd). An island of eastern Denmark bounded by the Kattegat and the Baltic Sea. Separated from Sweden by the Oresund, it is the largest island of Denmark and the site of Copenhagen, the country's capital.

Skag·er·rak also **Skag·er·ak** (skăg′ə-răk′, skä′gə-räk′). A broad strait between southeast Norway and northwest Denmark linking the North Sea and the Kattegat.

Skag·it (skăj′ĭt). A river, about 241 km (150 mi) long, of southwest British Columbia, Canada, and northwest Washington flowing into **Skagit Bay,** an inlet of Puget Sound.

Skag·way (skăg′wā′). A town of southeast Alaska at the head of the Lynn Canal north-northwest of Juneau. It was a boom town and the gateway to the Klondike during the Alaskan gold rush (1897–1898). ⊛ Pop. 692.

Skan·e·at·e·les Lake (skăn′ē-ăt′ləs, skĭn′-). A lake of central New York. It is one of the Finger Lakes.

Skaw (skô). A cape on the northern extremity of Jutland, Denmark, bordered by the Skagerrak and the Kattegat.

Skee·na (skē′nə). A river rising in western British Columbia, Canada, and flowing about 579 km (360 mi) generally south and west to the Pacific Ocean near Prince Rupert.

sker·ry (skĕr′ē). A small rocky reef or island.

Skí·ros also **Sky·ros** or **Scy·ros** (skī′rəs, skē′rôs). An island of eastern Greece in the Aegean Sea northeast of Euboea. Occupied by Athenians in the fifth century B.C., it is the largest of the Northern Sporades Islands.

Sko·kie (skō′kē). A village of northeast Illinois, an industrial suburb of Chicago. ⊛ Pop. 59,432.

Skop·je (skôp′yä′, -yĕ) or **Skop·lje** (-lä′, -lyĕ). The capital of Macedonia, in the north-central part of the country on the Vardar River. Dating from Roman times, it fell to Serbia in 1282 and was under Turkish control from 1392 until 1913. The city was incorporated into Yugoslavia after World War I and became (1946) the capital of the constituent republic of Macedonia, which declared its independence in January of 1992. ⊛ Pop. 448,229.

Skunk River (skŭngk). A river, about 425 km (264 mi) long, rising in central Iowa and flowing generally southeast to the Mississippi River.

Skye (skī), **Isle of.** An island of northwest Scotland in the Inner Hebrides. It is known for its rugged mountainous scenery.

Sky·ros (skī′rəs, skē′rôs). See **Skíros.**

Sla (slä). See **Salé.**

slack (slăk). *Chiefly British.* **1.** A small dell or hollow. **2.** A bog; a morass.

Slav (släv). A member of one of the Slavic-speaking peoples of eastern Europe.

Slave Coast (släv). A region of western Africa bordering the Bight of Benin on the Gulf of Guinea. It was notorious as the exportation base for slaves from the 16th century to the early 19th century.

Slave River. A river, about 499 km (310 mi) long, of west-central Canada flowing between Lake Athabasca in northeast Alberta and Great Slave Lake in the southern Northwest Territories. It forms the central section of the Mackenzie River system.

Slav·ic (slä′vĭk). *abbr.* **Slav. 1.** Of or relating to the Slavs or their languages. **2.** A branch of the Indo-European language family that includes Bulgarian, Belorussian, Czech, Macedonian, Polish, Russian, Serbo-Croatian, Slovak, Slovene, Ukrainian, and Wendish.

Sla·vo·ni·a (slə-vō′nē-ə, -vōn′yə). A historical region of Croatia between the Drava and Sava rivers. Originally part of the Roman province of Pannonia, it became a Slavic state in the seventh century and, with Croatia, was united with Hungary in 1102. Following the collapse of Austria-Hungary in 1918, Slavonia became a part of Yugoslavia. The region, which was inhabited by a large number of Serbs, was invaded by Serbia in 1991 following Croatia's declaration of independence from Yugoslavia. Croatia retook western Slavonia in 1995, and by the Dayton Peace Accord signed later that year, Serbia agreed to return control of eastern Slavonia to Croatia. — **Sla·vo′ni·an** *adj. & n.*

Sla·von·ic (slə-vŏn′ĭk). The Slavic language branch; Slavic. — **Sla·von′ic** *adj.*

Slav·yansk (slə-vyänsk′). A city of eastern Ukraine southeast of Kharkov. Founded in 1676, it is a railroad junction and health resort. ⊚ Pop. 137,600.

slew (slo͞o). Variant of **slough.**

Sli·dell (slī-dĕl′). A city of southeast Louisiana northeast of New Orleans. It is primarily residential. ⊚ Pop. 24,124.

Sli·go (slī′gō). A municipal borough of northern Ireland on **Sligo Bay,** an inlet of the Atlantic Ocean. There are megalithic ruins in the area. ⊚ Pop. 17,232.

slip (slĭp). *Geology.* **1.** A small fault. **2.** The relative displacement of formerly adjacent points on opposite sides of a fault.

Sli·ven (slĭv′ən). A city of east-central Bulgaria east of Sofia. Contested by Bulgaria and the Byzantine Empire in medieval times and by Russia and Turkey in the 19th century, it is now a textile center with varied industries. ⊚ Pop. 106,225.

slough (slo͞o, slou) also **slew** (slo͞o). **1.** A depression or hollow, usually filled with deep mud

or mire. **2.** also **slue** (slo͞o). A stagnant swamp, marsh, bog, or pond, especially as part of a bayou, an inlet, or a backwater.

Slough (slou). A municipal borough of southeast England, a residential and industrial suburb of London. ⊚ Pop. 103,454.

Slo·vak (slō′väk′, -văk′) also **Slo·va·ki·an** (slō-vä′kē-ən, -văk′ē-ən). **1.** A member of a Slavic people living in Slovakia. **2.** The Slavic language of the Slovaks. **3.** Of or relating to Slovakia or its people, language, or culture.

Slo·vak·i·a (slō-vä′kē-ə, -văk′ē-ə). A country of central Europe east of Czech Republic. Settled by Slavic peoples c. sixth century A.D., the region was conquered by Magyars in the early 10th century and was generally under Hungarian rule until 1918, when it joined the Czech lands of Bohemia, Moravia, and part of Silesia to become the new state of Czechoslovakia. Slovakia became a German puppet state during World War II and was liberated by the Soviets in 1945. After the war Slovakia rejoined Czechoslovakia. In 1948 a Communist government assumed power, and Slovakia was again subject to a Czech-dominated central government. Demands for greater autonomy led to the establishment of the Slovak Socialist Republic of Czechoslovakia in 1968. After the end of Communist rule in 1989, the rivalry between the Czech and Slovak republics was renewed, and government leaders reached an agreement to separate the country into two fully independent republics. The Republic of Slovakia came into existence on January 1, 1993. Bratislava is the capital and largest city. ⊚ Pop. 5,347,000.

Slo·vene (slō′vēn′) also **Slo·ve·ni·an** (slō-vē′-nē-ən, -vēn′yən). **1.** A member of a Slavic people living in Slovenia. **2.** The Slavic language of the Slovenes. **3.** Of or relating to Slovenia or its people, language, or culture.

Slo·ve·ni·a (slō-vē′nē-ə, -vēn′yə). A country of the northwest Balkan Peninsula. In ancient times Illyrian and Celtic peoples inhabited the area, which was ruled by Rome after the first century B.C. and settled by Slavs in the sixth century A.D. Slovenia came under Austrian control after 1335 and joined the Kingdom of Serbs, Croats, and Slovenes (later Yugoslavia) in 1918 after the collapse of Austria-Hungary. During World War II Slovenia was divided among Germany, Italy, and Hungary, but returned to Yugoslavia after the war. Slovenia declared its independence from Yugoslavia in June 1991. War broke out as Serbia, with the help of the Serbian-dominated Yugoslav army, tried to keep Slovenia from seceding. After some brief fighting, the Yugoslav army withdrew. Ljubljana is the capital and largest city. ⊛ Pop. 1,942,000.

slue (slōō). Variant of **slough** (sense 2).

Smith·town (smĭth′toun′). A community of southeast New York on northern Long Island north of Bay Shore. It is mainly residential. ⊛ Pop. 25,638.

Smok·y Hill River (smō′kē). A river rising in eastern Colorado and flowing about 901 km (560 mi) eastward across central Kansas to join the Republican River and form the Kansas River.

Smoky Mountains. See **Great Smoky Mountains.**

Smoky River. A river, about 402 km (250 mi) long, of west-central Alberta, Canada, flowing generally northward to the Peace River.

Smo·lensk (smō-lĕnsk′, smə-). A city of western Russia on the Dnieper River west-southwest of Moscow. First mentioned in the 9th century, Smolensk became an important port situated on various medieval trade routes. It was sacked by Mongols in the 13th century and captured by Lithuania (1408), Russia (1514), Poland (1611), and Russia again (1654) before being seized by Napoleon I in 1812. The city was also the scene of heavy fighting in World War II and was occupied by German forces from 1941 to 1943. A shipping point for the surrounding agricultural region, it is also an industrial, cultural, and educational center. ⊛ Pop. 349,326.

Smyr·na (smûr′nə). **1.** A city of northwest Georgia, a residential suburb of Atlanta. ⊛ Pop. 30,981. **2.** See **Izmir.**

Snake (snāk). *pl.* **Snake** or **Snakes.** See **Shoshone** (sense 1a).

Snake River. A river of the northwest United States rising in northwest Wyoming and flowing about 1,670 km (1,038 mi) through southern Idaho, along the Oregon-Idaho and Idaho-Wash-

ington borders, and through southeast Washington to the Columbia River. Discovered in 1805 by the Lewis and Clark expedition, the river has spectacular deep gorges and is an important source of hydroelectric power.

Snef·fels (snĕf′əlz), **Mount.** A peak, 4,315.8 m (14,150 ft) high, in the San Juan Mountains of southwest Colorado.

Sno·qual·mie Falls (snō-kwŏl′mē). A waterfall, 82.4 m (270 ft) high, in the **Snoqualmie River,** about 113 km (70 mi) long, of west-central Washington.

Snow·belt also **Snow Belt** (snō′bĕlt′). The northern and northeast United States.

snow·cap (snō′kăp′). Snow covering a mountain peak, especially such snow existing year-round. **—snow′capped′** *adj.*

Snow·don (snōd′n). A massif of northwest Wales. Rising to 1,085.8 m (3,560 ft), it is the highest elevation in Wales.

snow line (snō). **1.** The lower altitudinal boundary of a snow-covered area, especially of one that is perennially covered. **2.** The fluctuating latitudinal boundaries around the polar regions marking the extent of snow cover.

Snow·mass Mountain (snō′măs). A peak, 4,298.1 m (14,092 ft) high, in the Elk Mountains of west-central Colorado.

So·chi (sō′chē, sô′chĭ). A city of southwest Russia on the northeast shore of the Black Sea. It is a popular health resort. ⊛ Pop. 327,739.

So·ci·e·ty Islands (sə-sī′ĭ-tē). An island group of French Polynesia in the southern Pacific Ocean east of Samoa. The group is made up of the Windward Islands, which include Tahiti, and the Leeward Islands, which include Raiatea and Bora Bora. First visited by a Portuguese navigator in the 17th century, the islands were claimed for France by the French explorer Louis Antoine de Bougainville in 1768 and named by the English explorer Capt. James Cook in 1769. They became a French protectorate in 1843 and a part of the overseas territory of French Polynesia in 1946.

So·co·tra (sə-kō′trə). An island of Yemen in the Indian Ocean at the mouth of the Gulf of Aden. Known to the ancient Greeks, it came under British protection in 1886 and joined Southern Yemen (now Yemen) in 1967.

Sö·der·täl·je (sœ′dər-tĕl′yə). A city of southeast Sweden, an industrial suburb of Stockholm. ⊛ Pop. 79,429.

Sod·om (sŏd′əm). A city of ancient Palestine possibly located south of the Dead Sea. In the Bible, it was destroyed along with Gomorrah because of its wickedness and depravity.

So·fi·a (sō′fē-ə, sō-fē′ə). The capital and largest city of Bulgaria, in the west-central part of the country. Originally a Thracian settlement, it passed over the centuries to Rome, Byzantium, two Bulgarian kingdoms, Ottoman Turkey, and Russia. In 1879 it became the capital of independent Bulgaria. During World War II the city was occupied by German forces and suffered much damage from Allied bombing. It was liberated (1944) by the Soviets, who installed a Communist government. Sofia is the leading commercial, industrial, and transportation center of Bulgaria. ⊛ Pop. 1,114,476.

Sog·na·fjord or **Sog·ne Fjord** (sông′nə-fyôr′). An inlet of the Norwegian Sea in southwest Norway extending inland about 193 km (120 mi). It is the longest and deepest fjord in the country.

So·ho (sō′hō′). **1.** A district of central London, England. Inhabited in the 17th century mainly by immigrants, it is known today for its restaurants, theaters, and nightclubs. **2.** also **SoHo.** A district of New York City on southwest Manhattan Island noted for its galleries, shops, restaurants, and artists' lofts. The area is *so*uth of *Ho*uston Street, hence the name.

Sois·sons (swä-sŏN′). A city of northern France northwest of Paris. An ancient Roman town, Soissons was long the scene of conflict, including the Frankish king Clovis I's defeat of the Roman legions (A.D. 486) and heavy bombardment during World Wars I and II. ⊛ Pop. 30,213.

So·le·dad (sō′lə-dăd′, sô′lĕ-*thäth*′). A city of northern Colombia, a suburb of Barranquilla. ⊛ Pop. 168,291.

So·lent (sō′lənt). A narrow channel between the Isle of Wight and the southern mainland of England. The Solent provides access to the port of Southampton.

So·li·hull (sō′lĭ-hŭl′). A borough of central England, a chiefly residential suburb of Birmingham. ⊛ Pop. 200,393.

So·ling·en (zō′lĭng-ən). A city of west-central Germany east-southeast of Düsseldorf. Chartered in 1374, it is noted for its cutlery. ⊛ Pop. 166,064.

Sol·o·mon Islands[1] (sŏl′ə-mən). An island group of the western Pacific Ocean east of New Guinea. Inhabited primarily by Melanesian peoples since at least 2000 B.C., the volcanic islands were first visited by European explorers in the 1560's and were divided between Germany and Great Britain in the late 19th century. Australia assumed control of the northern islands in 1920. Today the northern Solomons are part of Papua New Guinea. The southern islands are an independent country.

Sol·o·mon Islands[2] (sŏl′ə-mən). A country comprising the Solomon Islands southeast of Bougainville. First visited by Spain in 1568, the islands attracted little European attention until planters and missionaries began arriving in the 18th and 19th centuries. In 1885 Germany took

over the Solomons but relinquished all claims except to Bougainville and Buka (now part of Papua New Guinea) by 1900. The southern islands became a British protectorate (1893) which later extended to the northern group. Some of the islands were occupied by the Japanese during World War II, but were liberated by U.S. troops (1943–1944), with some of the heaviest fighting in the Pacific theater taking place on Guadalcanal. The islands became self-governing in 1976 and achieved independence in 1978. Honiara, on Guadalcanal Island, is the capital. ⊛ Pop. 366,000.

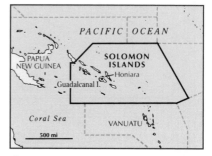

Solomon Sea. The northern part of the Coral Sea between Papua New Guinea to the north and west and the Solomon Islands to the west.

Sol·way Firth (sŏl′wā′). An arm of the Irish Sea separating northwest England from southwest Scotland.

So·ma·li (sō-mä′lē). **1.** *pl.* **Somali** or **-lis.** A member of a Muslim people of Somalia and adjacent parts of Ethiopia, Kenya, and Djibouti. **2.** The Cushitic language of the Somali and an official language of Somalia.

So·ma·li·a (sō-mä′lē-ə, -mäl′yə). *abbr.* **Som.** A country of extreme eastern Africa on the Gulf of Aden and the Indian Ocean. Arab and Persian traders first established outposts in the region between the 7th and 10th centuries. European colonization began in the 19th century, with the protectorate of British Somaliland established in the north in 1887 and the much smaller French Somaliland (later Djibouti) established in 1896. The southern territory eventually came under Italian control and in 1936 was combined with newly conquered Ethiopian territory to form Italian East Africa. Britain ruled the entire region after World War II, with Italy returning in 1950 to administer its former protectorate under a UN mandate. The independent republic of Somalia was created in 1960 out of the British and Italian territories. The country adopted socialism in 1969 but later broke with the Soviet Union. Defeated in a border clash with Ethiopia (1979), Somalia fell into increasing disarray, culminating in internal warfare in the early 1990's and the threat of famine throughout the region. A U.S. force intervened in 1992, with control of the relief effort passing to the UN in 1993, but continued fighting forced the withdrawal of all outside troops by 1995. Mogadishu is the capital and the largest city. ⊛ Pop. 9,077,000. — **So·ma'li·an** *adj. & n.*

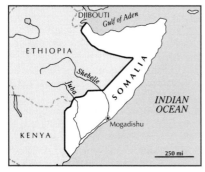

So·ma·li·land (sō-mä'lē-lănd', sə-). A region of eastern Africa comprising present-day Somalia, Djibouti, and southeast Ethiopia. The area was a target of European colonization after the opening of the Suez Canal in 1869.

Som·bre·ro (sŏm-brâr'ō, səm-). An island of St. Kitts and Nevis in the Leeward Islands of the West Indies.

Som·er·set (sŭm'ər-sĕt', -sĭt). **1.** A town of southeast Massachusetts, a residential suburb of Fall River. ⊛ Pop. 17,655. **2.** A community of central New Jersey, a suburb of New Brunswick. ⊛ Pop. 21,731.

Somerset Island. An island of Northwest Territories, Canada, separated from Boothia Peninsula by a narrow strait.

Som·er·ville (sŭm'ər-vĭl'). A city of eastern Massachusetts, a residential and industrial suburb of Boston. ⊛ Pop. 76,210.

Somme (sŏm, sôm). A river, about 241 km (150 mi) long, of northern France flowing west and northwest to the English Channel. Tanks were first used in warfare during the devastating Battle of the Somme (1916).

Song Da (sông' dä'). See **Black River** (sense 1).

Song·hai also **Song·hay** (sông'hī', sŏng-gī'). An ancient empire of western Africa in present-day Mali. It was founded c. 700 by Berbers and reached the height of its power around 1500.

Song Hong (sông' hông'). See **Red River** (sense 1).

Song·hua (sōong'hwä') also **Sun·ga·ri** (sōong'-gə-rē'). A river of northeast China rising near the North Korean border and flowing about 1,850 km (1,150 mi) northwest, east, and northeast to the Amur River.

Soo Canals (sōo). See **Sault Sainte Marie Canals.**

Soo·chow (sōo'chou', -jō'). See **Suzhou.**

Sop·ron (shō'prōn'). A city of northwest Hungary near the Austrian border. Originally a Celtic settlement, it was a military outpost during Roman times and is one of the oldest cultural centers in Hungary. ⊛ Pop. 56,421.

Sorb (sôrb). See **Wend.**

Sor·bi·an (sôr'bē-ən). **1.** See **Wend. 2.** See **Wendish.** — **Sor'bi·an** *adj.*

So·rel (sə-rĕl', sô-). A city of southern Quebec, Canada, at the confluence of the St. Lawrence and Richelieu rivers. It was founded in 1672 on the site of Fort Richelieu, established in 1665. ⊛ Pop. 20,347.

So·ro·ca·ba (sôr'ōo-kä'bä). A city of southern Brazil west of São Paulo. It is a commercial and industrial center. ⊛ Pop. 378,366.

Sor·ren·to (sə-rĕn'tō, sôr-rĕn'tô). A town of southern Italy on the **Sorrento Peninsula,** separating the Bay of Naples from the Gulf of Salerno. The city is a popular tourist center and summer resort. ⊛ Pop. 17,301.

So·sno·wiec (sŏs-nô'vyĕts). A city of southern Poland, an industrial suburb of Katowice. ⊛ Pop. 259,481.

So·tho (sō'tō). **1.** A group of closely related Bantu languages, including Tswana, spoken in southern Africa. **2.** Any of these languages.

Sou·fri·ère (sōo'frē-ĕr'). A volcano, 1,234.6 m (4,048 ft) high, on St. Vincent Island in the Windward Islands of the West Indies. A violent eruption in 1902 killed more than 1,000 people. There were also eruptions in 1971–1972 and 1979.

Sou·ris (sōor'ĭs). A river, about 724 km (450 mi) long, rising in southern Saskatchewan, Canada, and flowing southeast in a great loop into northern North Dakota then north and northeast to the Assiniboine River in southwest Manitoba.

Sousse (sōos) also **Su·sah** or **Su·sa** (sōo'sə, -zə). A city of northeast Tunisia on an inlet of the Mediterranean Sea. Founded in ancient times by the Phoenicians, it was an important city under the Romans and Carthaginians and later under the Arabs (9th–11th centuries) and the French (19th–20th centuries). ⊛ Pop. 69,530.

south (south). *abbr.* **S, S., s, s., so., So., sou., Sou. 1. a.** The direction along a meridian 90° clockwise from east; the direction to the right of sunrise. **b.** The cardinal point on the mariner's compass 180° clockwise from due north and directly opposite north. **2.** An area or a region lying in the south. **3.** often **South. a.** The southern part of the earth. **b.** The southern part of a region or country. **4. South.** The southern part of the United States, especially the states that fought for the Confederacy in the Civil War. **5.** To, toward, of, facing, or in the south. **6.** Originating in or coming from the south. **—south'-ern, South'ern** *adj.*

South Africa. *abbr.* **S.Afr., S.A.** A country of southern Africa on the Atlantic and Indian oceans. Originally inhabited by the San and Khoikhoin, the region was settled by various Bantu peoples c. 1500. European settlement began with the Dutch, who founded Cape Town on the Cape of Good Hope in 1652. The British occupied the Cape Colony in 1795 and were granted official possession of the territory at the conclusion of the Napoleonic Wars in 1814, further extending their control to Natal in 1843. To escape British rule many Dutch-descended Boers migrated inland (1835–1843), where they clashed with the Xhosa and Zulu and founded the republics of Orange Free State and Transvaal. Tension between the British and Afrikaners, fanned by the discovery of gold and diamonds in the interior, led to the Boer War (1899–1902) in which Britain took possession of the entire territory, creating the Union of South Africa in 1910. South Africa declared itself a republic in 1961, severed ties with the British Commonwealth, and further consolidated the apartheid system of racial segregation begun earlier in the century. Internal dissent, guerrilla resistance from the African National Congress, and international condemnation created pressures for political reform, and in 1989 President F.W. de Klerk began the process of repealing apartheid. An interim constitution ending white rule was adopted in 1993, and the first multiracial elections were held in 1994, with Nelson Mandela, an ANC leader (imprisoned 1964–1990), becoming the first nonwhite president. Pretoria is the administrative capital; Cape Town, the legislative capital; and Bloemfontein, the judicial capital. Johannesburg is the largest city. ⊛ Pop. 40,436,000. **—South African** *adj. & n.*

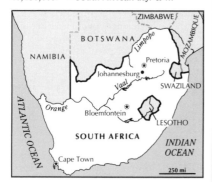

South America. *abbr.* **S.A.** A continent of the southern Western Hemisphere southeast of North America between the Atlantic and Pacific oceans. It extends from the Caribbean Sea southward to Cape Horn. **—South American** *adj. & n.*

South·amp·ton (south-hămp'tən, sou-thămp'-). **1.** A borough of south-central England on an inlet of the English Channel opposite the Isle of Wight. Founded on the site of Roman and Saxon settlements, it has long been a major port, especially for passenger ships. ⊛ Pop. 209,192. **2.** A village of southeast New York on the southeast coast of Long Island. It is primarily a summer resort. ⊛ Pop. 4,000.

Southampton Island. An island of eastern Northwest Territories, Canada, at the entrance to Hudson Bay.

South Atlantic Ocean. The southern part of the Atlantic Ocean, extending southward from the equator to Antarctica.

South·a·ven (south'ā'vən). A community of extreme northwest Mississippi, a suburb of Memphis, Tennessee. ⊛ Pop. 16,071.

South Bend. A city of northern Indiana near the Michigan border northwest of Fort Wayne. A fur-trading post was established here in 1820. ⊛ Pop. 105,511.

South·bridge (south'brĭj'). A town of south-central Massachusetts southwest of Worcester. Incorporated in 1816, it is a manufacturing center. ⊛ Pop. 17,816.

south by east. *abbr.* **SbE. 1.** The direction or point on the mariner's compass halfway between due south and south-southeast, or 168°45' east of due north. **2.** Toward or from south by east.

south by west. *abbr.* **SbW. 1.** The direction or point on the mariner's compass halfway between due south and south-southwest, or 168°45' west of due north. **2.** Toward or from south by west.

South Carolina. *abbr.* **SC, S.C.** A state of the southeast United States bordering on the Atlantic Ocean. It was admitted as one of the original Thirteen Colonies in 1788. First visited by Spanish explorers in the early 1500's, the region was granted by Charles II of England to eight of his principal supporters in 1663. The territory was divided into the colonies of North Carolina and South Carolina in 1729. South Carolina was a leader in the movement for independence from Great Britain and was the first state to secede from the Union (1860), thus precipitating the Civil War. Columbia is the capital and the largest city. ⊛ Pop. 3,505,707. **—South Carolinian** *adj. & n.*

South Central Niger-Congo. A branch of the Niger-Congo language family.

South Charleston. A city of west-central West Virginia, an industrial suburb of Charleston. ⊛ Pop. 13,645.

South China Sea. An arm of the western Pacific Ocean bounded by southeast China, Taiwan, the Philippines, Borneo, and Vietnam.

South Dakota. *abbr.* **SD, S.D., S.Dak.** A state of the north-central United States. It was admitted as the 40th state in 1889. Acquired in the Louisiana Purchase, the region became part of the Dakota Territory in 1861 and was split off from North Dakota at the time it achieved statehood. Pierre is the capital and Sioux Falls the largest city. ◉ Pop. 699,999. — **South Dakotan** *adj. & n.*

South Decatur. A community of northwest Georgia, a suburb of Atlanta. ◉ Pop. 28,100.

South Downs. See **Downs.**

South Dum Dum (dŭm′ dŭm′). A city of eastern India, a suburb of Calcutta. ◉ Pop. 232,811.

south·east (south-ēst′, sou-ēst′). *abbr.* **SE. 1.** The direction or point on the mariner's compass halfway between due south and due east, or 135° east of due north. **2.** An area or a region lying in the southeast. **3. Southeast.** A region of the southeast United States generally including Alabama, Georgia, South Carolina, and Florida. **4.** To, toward, of, facing, or in the southeast. **5.** Originating in or coming from the southeast. — **south·east′ern** *adj.*

Southeast Asia. A region of Asia bounded roughly by the Indian subcontinent on the west, China on the north, and the Pacific Ocean on the east. It includes Indochina, the Malay Peninsula, and the Malay Archipelago. — **Southeast Asian** *adj. & n.*

southeast by east. *abbr.* **SEbE. 1.** The direction or point on the mariner's compass halfway between southeast and east-southeast, or 123°45′ east of due north. **2.** Toward or from southeast by east.

southeast by south. *abbr.* **SEbS. 1.** The direction or point on the mariner's compass halfway between southeast and south-southeast, or 146°15′ east of due north. **2.** Toward or from southeast by south.

South El Mon·te (ĕl mŏn′tē). A city of southern California, a residential and industrial suburb of Los Angeles. ◉ Pop. 20,850.

South·end-on-Sea (sou′th-ĕnd-ŏn-sē′, -ôn-). A borough of southeast England at the mouth of the Thames River estuary. It is a manufacturing center and also a popular seaside resort. ◉ Pop. 167,523.

Southern Alps. A mountain range of South Island, New Zealand, paralleling the western coast and rising to 3,766.4 m (12,349 ft).

Southern Bug. See **Bug** (sense 2).

Southern Hemisphere. The half of the earth south of the equator.

Southern Paiute. 1. See **Paiute** (sense 2). **2.** The Uto-Aztecan language of the Southern Paiute.

Southern Sporades. See **Sporades.**

Southern Yemen. A former country of southwest Asia on the Arabian Peninsula. A British protectorate from 1882 to 1914, it became fully independent in 1967 and united with North Yemen in 1990 to form the new country of Yemen.

South Euclid. A city of northeast Ohio, a residential suburb of Cleveland. ◉ Pop. 23,866.

South Farm·ing·dale (fär′mĭng-dāl′). An unincorporated community of southeast New York on Long Island east of New York City. It is mainly residential. ◉ Pop. 20,500.

South·field (south′fēld′). A city of southeast Michigan, an industrial suburb of Detroit on the Rouge River. ◉ Pop. 75,728.

South Frigid Zone. See **Frigid Zone.**

South·gate (south′gāt′). A city of southeast Michigan, a primarily residential suburb of Detroit. ◉ Pop. 30,771.

South Gate. A city of southern California, an industrial suburb of Los Angeles. ◉ Pop. 86,284.

South Georgia. A British-administered island in the southern Atlantic Ocean east of Cape Horn. A dependency of the Falkland Islands, it was claimed by the British navigator and explorer Capt. James Cook in 1775.

South Had·ley (hăd′lē). A town of western Massachusetts on the Connecticut River north of Springfield. Mainly residential, it is the site of Mount Holyoke College (established 1837). ◉ Pop. 16,685.

South Holland. A village of northeast Illinois, a residential and industrial suburb of Chicago. ◉ Pop. 22,105.

South·ing·ton (sŭth′ĭng-tən). A town of central Connecticut northeast of Waterbury. It has been a manufacturing center since the 1770's. ◉ Pop. 38,518.

South Island. An island of New Zealand southwest of North Island, from which it is separated by Cook Strait. It is the larger but less populous of the country's two principal islands.

South Kingstown. A town of southern Rhode Island south-southwest of Providence. It was a stronghold of the Narragansett during King Philip's War (1675–1676). ◉ Pop. 20,414.

South Korea. A country of eastern Asia at the southern end of the Korean peninsula. A united kingdom since the 7th century A.D., Korea was occupied by Japan (1910–1945) and divided into a northern Soviet zone and a southern American zone after World War II. Soviet resistance to reunification led to the establishment in 1948 of two separate countries, with the Korean

War (1950–1953) leaving the peninsula divided along much the same line as before. Ruled by a series of authoritarian military leaders, South Korea developed a prosperous economy on the strength of trade ties with Japan and the United States. President Roh Tae Woo (served 1988–1992) attempted to improve relations with North Korea and established diplomatic ties with the U.S.S.R. (1990) and China (1992). In 1992 Kim Young Sam became the first civilian to win the presidency since the Korean War. Seoul is the capital and the largest city. ⊕ Pop. 44,453,000. — **South Korean** *adj. & n.*

South Lake Tahoe. A city of eastern California on Lake Tahoe near the Nevada border. It is a year-round resort. ⊕ Pop. 21,586.

South Loup. A river, about 245 km (152 mi) long, of central Nebraska flowing east and southeast to unite with the North Loup and Middle Loup rivers and form the Loup River.

South Miami Heights. A city of southeast Florida, a suburb of Miami. ⊕ Pop. 30,030.

South Milwaukee. A city of southeast Wisconsin, a manufacturing suburb of Milwaukee. ⊕ Pop. 20,958.

South Na·han·ni (nə-hăn′ē). A river, about 563 km (350 mi) long, of southwest Northwest Territories, Canada, flowing to the Liard River.

South Orange. A village of northeast New Jersey west of Newark. Mainly residential, it is the site of Seton Hall University (established 1856). ⊕ Pop. 16,390.

South Orkney Islands. A group of British-administered islands in the southern Atlantic Ocean southeast of Cape Horn. First visited by sealers in 1821, the island group was formerly part of the Falkland Islands Dependency and is now included (since 1962) in the British Antarctic Territory.

South Pacific Ocean. The southern part of the Pacific Ocean, extending southward from the equator to Antarctica.

South Pasadena. A city of southern California, a mainly residential suburb of Los Angeles. ⊕ Pop. 23,936.

South Pass. A broad valley in southwest Wyoming at the southern end of the Wind River Range. It was a gateway for immigration to the Far West along the Oregon Trail.

South Plainfield. A borough of northeast-central New Jersey southwest of Elizabeth. It is an industrial center. ⊕ Pop. 20,489.

South Platte River. A river of central and northeast Colorado and west-central Nebraska flowing about 724 km (450 mi) generally eastward to the North Platte River to form the Platte River.

South Polar Region. See **Polar Regions.**

South Pole. 1. The southern end of Earth's axis of rotation, a point in Antarctica. 2. **south pole.** The south-seeking magnetic pole of a straight magnet.

South·port (south′pôrt′, -pōrt′). A borough of northwest England on Liverpool Bay north of Liverpool. It is a seaside resort with varied light industries. ⊕ Pop. 90,000.

South Portland. A city of southwest Maine, a residential and commercial suburb of Portland. ⊕ Pop. 23,163.

South River. The Delaware River. It was so named by Dutch explorers to distinguish it from the North River, an estuary of the Hudson River.

South Saint Paul. A city of southeast Minnesota, an industrial suburb of St. Paul on the Mississippi River. ⊕ Pop. 20,197.

South Sandwich Islands. A group of British-administered volcanic islands in the southern Atlantic Ocean east-southeast of Cape Horn. Part of the Falkland Islands Dependency, the islands were discovered in 1775.

South San Francisco. A city of western California, an industrial suburb of San Francisco on San Francisco Bay. ⊕ Pop. 54,312.

South Saskatchewan. A river of Canada flowing about 885 km (550 mi) from southern Alberta to central Saskatchewan to join the North Saskatchewan River and form the Saskatchewan River.

South Sea Islands. The islands of the southern Pacific Ocean, roughly coextensive with Oceania. — **South Sea Islander** *n.*

South Seas. The oceans south of the equator, especially the southern Pacific Ocean. The name **South Sea,** or *El Mar del Sur,* was originally used for the entire Pacific Ocean by the Spanish explorer Vasco Núñez de Balboa, who in 1513 became the first European to discover it.

South Shetland Islands. An archipelago in

the southern Atlantic Ocean off Antarctica. Formerly used as land bases by sealers and whalers, the islands are part of the British Antarctic Territory although they have also been claimed by Argentina and Chile.

South Shields (shēldz). A borough of northeast England at the mouth of the Tyne River east of Newcastle. Founded in the 13th century, it is a major port and shipbuilding center. ⊛ Pop. 86,488.

south-south·east (south′south-ēst′, sou′sou-ēst′). *abbr.* **SSE. 1.** The direction or point on the mariner's compass halfway between south and southeast, or 157°30′ east of due north. **2.** To, toward, of, facing, or in the south-southeast.

south-south·west (south′south-wĕst′, sou′-sou-wĕst′). *abbr.* **SSW. 1.** The direction or point on the mariner's compass halfway between due south and southwest, or 157°30′ west of due north. **2.** To, toward, of, facing, or in the south-southwest.

South Temperate Zone. See **Temperate Zone.**

South Vietnam. A former country of southeast Asia. It existed from 1954, after the fall of the French at Dien Bien Phu, to 1975, when the South Vietnamese government collapsed at the end of the Vietnam War. It is now part of the country of Vietnam. —**South Vietnamese** *adj. & n.*

South Waziristan. See **Waziristan.**

south·west (south-wĕst′, sou-wĕst′). *abbr.* **SW. 1.** The direction or point on the mariner's compass halfway between due south and due west, or 135° west of due north. **2.** An area or a region lying in the southwest. **3. Southwest.** A region of the southwest United States generally including New Mexico, Arizona, Texas, California, and Nevada and sometimes Utah and Colorado.

South-West Africa (south′wĕst′). See **Namibia.**

southwest by south. *abbr.* **SWbS. 1.** The direction or point on the mariner's compass halfway between southwest and south-southwest, or 146°15′ west of due north. **2.** Toward or from southwest by south.

southwest by west. *abbr.* **SWbW. 1.** The direction or point on the mariner's compass halfway between southwest and west-southwest, or 123°45′ west of due north. **2.** Toward or from southwest by west.

South Whittier. A community of southern California, a residential suburb of Los Angeles. ⊛ Pop. 43,815.

South Windsor. A town of north-central Con-

necticut north-northeast of Hartford. It was set off from Windsor in 1845. ⊛ Pop. 22,090.

sov·er·eign·ty (sŏv′ər-ĭn-tē, sŏv′rĭn-). **1.** Complete independence and self-government. **2.** A territory existing as an independent state.

So·vi·et Union (sō′vē-ĕt′, -ĭt, sŏv′ē-, sō′vē-ĕt′). See **Union of Soviet Socialist Republics.**

So·we·to (sə-wē′tō, -wā′-). A city of northeast South Africa southwest of Johannesburg. Comprised of a number of townships inhabited by Black South Africans, it was the scene of violent rioting in 1976, when a student protest led to clashes with police in which hundreds of people were killed. ⊛ Pop. 596,632.

Spain (spān). A country of southwest Europe comprising most of the Iberian Peninsula and the Balearic and Canary Islands. Inhabited since the Stone Age, the region was colonized by Phoenicians and Greeks and later ruled by Carthage and Rome (after 201 B.C.). Barbarians first invaded Spain in A.D. 409 but were supplanted by Moors from North Africa (711–719), who organized a kingdom known for its learning and splendor. The Moors were gradually displaced by small Christian states and were ousted from their last stronghold, Granada, in 1492. Ferdinand of Aragon and Isabella of Castile then became rulers of a united Spain, which became a world power through exploration and conquest. With the discovery of America in 1492 by Columbus, the beginnings of Spain's colonial empire were established. In 1588 the Spanish Armada was defeated by Britain, and a series of wars followed throughout the next several centuries that greatly weakened the country. The last of Spain's American holdings was lost in 1898 during the Spanish-American War. The loss of empire and the occupation by French troops during the Napoleonic Wars initiated a period of political and social instability that culminated in the military dictatorship of Primo de Rivera (1923–1930), the Spanish Civil War (1936–1939), and the subsequent dictatorship of Gen. Francisco Franco. Although Spain did not enter World War II, it aided the Axis powers throughout the war. After Franco's death in 1975 the

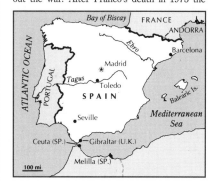

monarchy was restored under King Juan Carlos, who oversaw the creation of a parliamentary democracy. Madrid is the capital and the largest city. ◉ Pop. 39,143,000.

Span·dau (spän'dou', shpän'-). A district of Berlin, Germany. Chartered in 1232, it is the site of a fortress used for Nazi war criminals after the Nuremburg trials of 1945 to 1946. Spandau was incorporated into Berlin in 1920.

Span·iard (spăn'yərd). A native or inhabitant of Spain.

Span·ish (spăn'ĭsh). *abbr.* **Sp., Span. 1.** Of or relating to Spain or its people or culture. **2.** Of or relating to the Spanish language. **3.** The Romance language of the largest part of Spain and most of Central and South America. **4.** The people of Spain.

Spanish America. The former Spanish possessions in the New World, including most of South and Central America, Mexico, Cuba, Puerto Rico, the Dominican Republic, and other small islands in the Caribbean Sea.

Spanish American. 1. A native or inhabitant of Spanish America. **2.** A U.S. citizen or resident of Hispanic descent. **—Span'ish-A·mer'- i·can** *adj.*

Spanish Lake. A community of east-central Missouri, a suburb of St. Louis. ◉ Pop. 20,322.

Spanish Main (mān). **1.** The coastal region of mainland Spanish America in the 16th and 17th centuries, extending from the Isthmus of Panama to the mouth of the Orinoco River. **2.** The section of the Caribbean Sea crossed by Spanish ships in colonial times. The treasure-laden ships were often raided by English buccaneers.

Spanish Peaks. Adjacent mountains, 3,868.3 m (12,683 ft) and 4,155 m (13,623 ft) high, in the Sangre de Cristo Mountains of southern Colorado. They were landmarks for early explorers and traders.

Spanish River. A river, about 241 km (150 mi) long, of southern Ontario, Canada, flowing generally south to Lake Huron.

Spanish Sahara. See **Western Sahara.**

Sparks (spärks). A city of western Nevada east of Reno. It is a tourist center with varied light industries. ◉ Pop. 53,367.

Spar·ta (spär'tə) also **Lac·e·dae·mon** (lăs'ĭ-dē'mən). A city-state of ancient Greece in the southeast Peloponnesus. Settled by Dorian Greeks, it was noted for its militarism and reached the height of its power in the sixth century B.C. A protracted rivalry with Athens led to the Peloponnesian Wars (460–404) and Sparta's hegemony over all of Greece. Its ascendancy was broken by the Thebans in 371 B.C. **—Spar'- tan** *adj. & n.*

Spar·tan·burg (spär'tn-bûrg'). A city of north-

west South Carolina northwest of Columbia at the foot of the Blue Ridge. It is a processing and manufacturing center. ◉ Pop. 43,467.

Speed·way (spēd'wā'). A town of central Indiana west of Indianapolis. It is the site of the annual Indianapolis 500 auto race. ◉ Pop. 12,641.

Spen·cer Gulf. (spĕn'sər). An inlet of the Indian Ocean off south-central Australia between the Eyre and Yorke peninsulas. It was discovered in 1802.

Spey·er (spīr, spī'ər, shpī'ər) also **Spires** (spīrz). A city of southwest Germany on the Rhine River. Settled by the Celts, colonized by the Romans, and destroyed (c. A.D. 450) by the Huns, it was later rebuilt and made a free imperial city in the 13th century. Speyer was ceded to France in 1797 and to Bavaria in 1815. It is an important river port and an industrial and manufacturing center. ◉ Pop. 43,748.

Spice Islands (spīs). See **Moluccas.**

Spires (spīrz). See **Speyer.**

spit (spĭt). A narrow point of land extending into a body of water.

Spit·head (spĭt'hĕd'). A channel off southern England between Portsmouth and the Isle of Wight. It connects with the Solent on the west and was formerly used as a rendezvous for the British fleet.

Spits·ber·gen (spĭts'bûr'gən). An island of Norway in Svalbard in the Arctic Ocean east of northern Greenland. Discovered by the Dutch explorer Willem Barents in 1596, the island became part of Norway in 1925.

Split (splĭt). A city of southwest Croatia on the Dalmatian coast of the Adriatic Sea. Founded as a Roman colony, it later grew around a palace built in the early fourth century A.D. by the Roman emperor Diocletian. ◉ Pop. 200,459.

Spo·kane (spō-kăn'). A city of eastern Washington near the Idaho border on the falls of the **Spokane River,** about 193 km (120 mi) long. Settled on the site of a trading fort established in 1810, Spokane is a trade and processing center in an agricultural, lumbering, and mining region. ◉ Pop. 177,196.

Spor·a·des (spôr'ə-dēz', spô-rä'thēs). Two island groups of Greece in the Aegean Sea, consisting of the **Northern Sporades** off the central mainland and the **Southern Sporades** off the coast of Turkey.

Spot·syl·va·nia (spŏt'səl-văn'yə). A village of northeast Virginia southwest of Fredericksburg. It was the site of a major but inconclusive Civil War battle (May 8–21, 1864).

Spree (sprā, shprā). A river, about 402 km (250 mi) long, of eastern Germany rising near the Czech border and flowing generally north to the Havel River at Berlin.

spring (sprĭng). A small stream of water flowing naturally from the earth.

Spring·dale (sprĭng'dāl'). A city of northwest Arkansas north of Fayetteville. It is a trade, processing, and shipping center. ⊛ Pop. 29,941.

Spring·field (sprĭng'fēld'). **1.** The capital of Illinois, in the central part of the state. It became the state capital in 1837 and is the site of Abraham Lincoln's grave. ⊛ Pop. 105,227. **2.** A city of southwest Massachusetts on the Connecticut River near the Connecticut border. Settled in 1636, it is an important manufacturing center. ⊛ Pop. 156,983. **3.** A city of southwest Missouri south-southwest of Kansas City. In a resort area of the Ozark Plateau, it is a trade, shipping, and manufacturing center. ⊛ Pop. 140,494. **4.** A township of northeast New Jersey, a mainly residential suburb of Newark. ⊛ Pop. 13,420. **5.** A city of west-central Ohio west of Columbus. It grew as a trade and manufacturing center after the completion (1833) of the National Road, a highway extending from Maryland to Missouri, and the coming of the railroad (mid-1800's). ⊛ Pop. 70,487. **6.** A city of west-central Oregon east of Eugene. Near the foothills of the Cascade Range, it is a processing center. ⊛ Pop. 44,683. **7.** A community of southeast Pennsylvania, a suburb of Philadelphia. ⊛ Pop. 24,160.

Spring Valley (sprĭng). **1.** An unincorporated community of southwest California, a residential suburb within the confines of San Diego. ⊛ Pop. 40,191. **2.** A village of southeast New York near the New Jersey border west-northwest of White Plains. Mainly residential, it is also a summer resort. ⊛ Pop. 21,802.

Spuy·ten Duy·vil Creek (spīt'n dī'vəl). A narrow channel in southeast New York separating northern Manhattan Island from the mainland and linking the Harlem and Hudson rivers.

Squaw Valley (skwô). A valley of northeast California in the Sierra Nevada west of Lake Tahoe. A popular ski resort, it was the site of the 1960 Winter Olympics.

Sra·nan (srä'nən). See **Sranantongo.**

Sra·nan·ton·go (srä'nən-tŏng'gō). A creole based on English, spoken in coastal Suriname and widely used as a lingua franca. Also called *Sranan, taki-taki.*

Sri Lan·ka (srē läng'kə). Formerly **Cey·lon** (sĭ-lŏn', sā-). An island country in the Indian Ocean off southeast India. Singhalese migrants from northern India arrived on the island in the 6th century B.C., conquering and absorbing its original inhabitants, the Vedda. The Tamil arrived from southern India in the 11th and 12th centuries, establishing a kingdom in the north in the 14th century. Control over the lucrative spice trade passed from the Arabs (12th century) and Portuguese (16th century) to the Dutch (17th century). In 1798 the British took control and made the island the crown colony of Ceylon, retaining power well into the 20th centruy. During World War I a nationalist movement for independence arose, and autonomy was granted by Britain in 1948. In 1972 the island was declared a republic with the adoption of a new constitution and the Sinhalese name of Sri Lanka. Fighting between separatist Tamil guerrillas and government forces kept the country in a state of civil war throughout much of the 1980's and into the 1990's. Colombo is the capital and largest city. ⊛ Pop. 17,865,000. — **Sri Lan'kan** *adj. & n.*

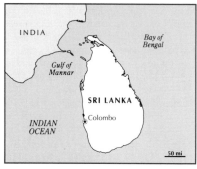

Sri·na·gar (srē-nŭg'ər). A city of northern India on the Jhelum River north of Amritsar. Founded in the sixth century A.D., it has long been a noted resort. ⊛ Pop. 586,038.

Staf·fa (stăf'ə). An island of western Scotland in the Inner Hebrides west of Mull.

Staf·ford (stăf'ərd). A municipal borough of west-central England north-northwest of Birmingham. The birthplace of the English writer Izaak Walton (1593–1683), it is a manufacturing center. ⊛ Pop. 121,483.

Sta·gi·ra (stə-jī'rə) or **Sta·gi·rus** (-rəs). An ancient city of Macedonia in northeast Greece, the birthplace of the philosopher Aristotle (384–322 B.C.).

Staines (stānz). An urban district of southeast England on the Thames River west-southwest of London. It is mainly residential with some varied industries. ⊛ Pop. 92,800.

Sta·lin·grad (stä'lĭn-grăd', stə-lyĭn-grät'). See **Volgograd.**

Stam·ford (stăm'fərd). A city of southwest Connecticut on Long Island Sound and the New York border. Settled in 1641, it is primarily residential. ⊛ Pop. 108,056.

stan·dard time. (stăn'dərd). *abbr.* **ST.** The time in any of 24 time zones, usually the mean solar time at the central meridian of each zone. In the continental United States, there are four standard time zones: Eastern, using the 75th meridian; Central, using the 90th meridian; Mountain, using the 105th meridian; and Pacific, using the 120th meridian.

Stan·ley or **Port Stan·ley** (stăn′lē). A town of the eastern Falkland Islands on the Atlantic Ocean. It is the administrative capital of the British dependency. ◉ Pop. 1,557.

Stanley Pool. A lakelike expansion of the Congo River in west-central Africa on the Congo-Zaire border between Kinshasa and Brazzaville.

Stan·ley·ville (stăn′lē-vĭl′). See **Kisangani.**

Stan·o·voy Range or **Stan·o·voi Range** (stăn′-ə-voi′, stə-nə-voi′). A mountain range, about 724 km (450 mi) long, of southeast Russia north of the Amur River.

Stan·ton (stăn′tən). A city of southern California, a residential suburb in the Los Angeles–Long Beach metropolitan area. ◉ Pop. 30,491.

Sta·ra Za·go·ra (stä′rə zə-gôr′ə, stä′rä zä-gô′rä). A city of central Bulgaria east-northeast of Plovdiv. It is an industrial center and railroad hub. ◉ Pop. 150,451.

Stark·ville (stärk′vĭl′, -vəl). A city of eastern Mississippi west of Columbus. It is a trade and processing center. ◉ Pop. 15,169.

state (stāt). *abbr.* **st. 1.** A body politic, especially one constituting a nation. **2.** One of the more or less internally autonomous territorial and political units composing a federation under a sovereign government.

State Col·lege (stāt kŏl′ĭj). A borough of central Pennsylvania northwest of Harrisburg. Mainly residential, it is the seat of Pennsylvania State University (established 1855). ◉ Pop. 38,923.

Stat·en Island (stăt′n). Formerly **Rich·mond** (rĭch′mənd). A borough of New York City coextensive with **Staten Island** in New York Bay in southeast New York southwest of Manhattan Island. First visited by the English navigator Henry Hudson in 1609, the island was permanently settled in the mid-1600's and became part of New York City in 1898. The borough name was officially changed in April 1975, although the island still constitutes the county of Richmond. ◉ Pop. 378,977.

States·ville (stāts′vĭl′, -vəl). A city of west-central North Carolina north of Charlotte. Founded in 1789, it is a trade and processing center. ◉ Pop. 17,567.

Staun·ton (stăn′tən). An independent city of north-central Virginia west-northwest of Charlottesville. The birthplace of President Woodrow Wilson (1856–1924), it is a trade and processing center. ◉ Pop. 24,461.

Sta·vang·er (stə-väng′ər). A city of southwest Norway south of Bergen on an inlet of the North Sea. Probably founded in the eighth century, it is a processing center with a shipbuilding industry. ◉ Pop. 101,403.

Stav·ro·pol (stăv-rō′pəl, stäv′rə-pəl). A city of southwest Russia southeast of Rostov. It was founded as a fortress town in 1777. ◉ Pop. 333,347.

Steele (stēl), **Mount.** A mountain, 5,076.4 m (16,644 ft) high, in the St. Elias Mountains of southwest Yukon Territory, Canada.

steppe (stĕp). A vast semiarid grass-covered plain, as found in southeast Europe, Siberia, and central North America.

Ster·ling (stûr′lĭng). A city of northwest Illinois southwest of Rockford. It is an industrial center. ◉ Pop. 15,132.

Sterling Heights. A city of southeast Michigan, a residential and industrial suburb of Detroit. ◉ Pop. 117,810.

Ster·li·ta·mak (stĕr′lĭ-tə-măk′, stĭr′lyĭ-tə-mäk′). A city of eastern Russia west of Magnitogorsk. Center of a chemical complex, it has varied heavy industries. ◉ Pop. 255,344.

Stet·tin (stə-tēn′, shtĕ-). See **Szczecin.**

Steu·ben·ville (stōō′bĭn-vĭl′, styōō′-). A city of eastern Ohio on the Ohio River south of Youngstown. Permanent settlement began here in 1797 on the site of Fort Steuben (built 1786–1787). ◉ Pop. 22,125.

Ste·ven·age (stē′və-nĭj). An urban district of southeast England north of London. It was the first new town to be designated under a parliamentary act of 1946 to decentralize population and industry. ◉ Pop. 74,500.

Ste·vens Point (stē′vənz). A city of central Wisconsin south of Wausau. Paper and furniture are among its manufactures. ◉ Pop. 23,006.

Stew·art Island (stōō′ərt, styōō′-). A volcanic island of southern New Zealand off the southern coast of South Island. It was discovered in 1808 by the British, who bought it from the Maoris in 1864.

Stewart River. A river, about 533 km (331 mi) long, of central Yukon Territory, Canada, flowing generally west to the Yukon River.

Sti·kine (stĭ-kēn′). A river rising in the **Stikine Mountains** of northwest British Columbia, Canada, and flowing about 539 km (335 mi) generally west and southwest through southeast Alaska to the Pacific Ocean.

Still·wa·ter (stĭl′wô′tər, -wŏt′ər). A city of north-central Oklahoma north-northeast of Oklahoma City. Founded in 1889, it is the seat of Oklahoma State University (established 1890). ◉ Pop. 36,676.

Stir·ling (stûr′lĭng). A borough of central Scotland on the Forth River west-northwest of Edinburgh. Its medieval castle was the birthplace of James II of Scotland (1633–1701). ◉ Pop. 38,400.

Stock·bridge (stŏk′brĭj′). A subtribe of the Mahican confederacy formerly inhabiting southwest Massachusetts, with a present-day population in central Wisconsin.

Stock·holm (stŏk′hōlm′, -hōm′). The capital and largest city of Sweden, in the eastern part of the country on the Baltic Sea. Founded in the mid-13th century, it grew as a trade center allied with the Hanseatic League. Stockholm was the leading city of the kingdom of Sweden after 1523 but did not become the official capital until 1634. The Nobel Institute is here. ◉ Pop. 684,576.

Stock·port (stŏk′pôrt′, -pōrt′). A borough of northwest England on the Mersey River south of Manchester. Chartered in 1220, it produces textiles and machinery. ◉ Pop. 291,447.

Stock·ton (stŏk′tən). A city of central California on the San Joaquin River south of Sacramento. Settled in 1848 just prior to the gold rush, it is an inland port and a trade and processing center. ◉ Pop. 210,943.

Stock·ton-on-Tees (stŏk′tən-ŏn-tēz′, -ôn-). A borough of northeast England west-northwest of Middlesbrough. It is a shipbuilding center. ◉ Pop. 177,794.

Stoke-on-Trent (stōk′ŏn-trĕnt′, -ôn-). A borough of west-central England south of Manchester. Center of an important pottery-making industry, it also has iron and steel mills. The British potters Josiah Wedgwood and Josiah Spode lived here. ◉ Pop. 252,914.

Stoke Po·ges (stōk pō′jĭs). A village of southeast-central England west of London. It is generally considered to be the setting for the poet Thomas Gray's *Elegy Written in a Country Churchyard* (published 1751).

Stol·berg (stôl′bûrg′, shtôl′bĕrk′). A city of west-central Germany west-southwest of Cologne. It has been a brassmaking center since c. 1600. ◉ Pop. 56,550.

Stone Age (stōn). The earliest known period of human culture, characterized by the use of stone tools. The Stone Age is divided into the Paleolithic, Mesolithic, and Neolithic periods.

Stone·ham (stō′nəm). A town of northeast Massachusetts, a residential suburb of Boston. ◉ Pop. 22,203.

Stone·henge (stōn′hĕnj′). A group of standing stones on Salisbury Plain in southern England. Dating to c. 2000–1800 B.C., the megaliths are enclosed by a circular ditch and embankment that may date to c. 2800. The arrangement of the stones suggests that Stonehenge was used as a religious center and also as an astronomical observatory.

Stone Mountain. A massive granite monadnock, 514.2 m (1,686 ft) high, in northwest-

central Georgia east of Atlanta. Its northeast wall contains a huge Confederate memorial (carved 1917–1967).

Ston·ey Creek (stō′nē). A town of southeast Ontario, Canada, at the west end of Lake Ontario south of Hamilton. The British defeated the Americans here on June 6, 1813, during the War of 1812. ◉ Pop. 36,762.

Ston·ing·ton (stō′nĭng-tən). A town of southeast Connecticut on Long Island Sound east of New London. Settled in 1649, it was once a major shipbuilding and whaling center. ◉ Pop. 16,919.

Ston·y Point (stō′nē). A village of southeast New York on the Hudson River north of New City. Its blockhouse, captured during the American Revolution by British troops in May 1779, was retaken in July by Gen. Anthony Wayne's forces. ◉ Pop. 10,587.

Stony Tunguska. See **Tunguska.**

Stough·ton (stōt′n). A town of eastern Massachusetts northwest of Brockton. It is a manufacturing center. ◉ Pop. 26,777.

Stour (stour, stŏŏr, stōr). A river, about 64 km (40 mi) long, of southeast England emptying into the North Sea in two channels enclosing the Isle of Thanet.

Stow (stō). A city of northeast Ohio, a chiefly residential suburb of Akron. ◉ Pop. 27,702.

strait (strāt) also **straits** (strāts). *abbr.* **str., Str., st., St.** A narrow channel joining two larger bodies of water.

Straits Settlements (strāts). A former British crown colony comprising parts of the southern and western Malay Peninsula and adjacent islands, including Singapore. Formed in 1826, it was under Indian control until 1867, when the British assumed direct authority. Singapore became a separate colony in 1946; the remaining portions of the Straits Settlements were granted to Australia and the Federation of Malaya (later Malaysia) in the 1950's.

Stral·sund (sträl′sŏŏnt′, shträl′zŏŏnt′). A city of northeast Germany on an inlet of the Baltic Sea opposite Rügen Island. Chartered in 1234, it was a leading member of the Hanseatic League and changed hands many times before it passed to Prussia in 1815. ◉ Pop. 75,335.

Strand (stränd). A thoroughfare in west-central London, England, running parallel to the northern bank of the Thames River and eastward from Trafalgar Square in the West End to the City of London. Among its well-known fixtures is the Savoy Hotel.

Stras·bourg (sträs′bŏŏrg′, sträz′-, sträz-bŏŏr′). A city of northeast France near the German border east of Nancy. Strategically important since ancient times, it became a free imperial city in 1262, was occupied by France in 1681, and passed to Germany in 1871. The city was recovered by France in 1919. ⊛ Pop. 252,274.

Strat·ford (străt′fərd). **1.** A city of southeast Ontario, Canada, west-southwest of Toronto. It is an industrial center and the home of the Stratford Shakespearean Festival (founded 1953). ⊛ Pop. 26,262. **2.** A town of southwest Connecticut on Long Island Sound northeast of Bridgeport. Settled in 1639, it is a manufacturing center. ⊛ Pop. 49,389.

Strat·ford-on-Av·on (străt′fərd-ŏn-ā′vən, -ŏn-) also **Strat·ford-up·on-Av·on** (-ə-pŏn-, -ə-pôn-). A municipal borough of central England south-southeast of Birmingham. William Shakespeare (1564–1616) was born and died in the borough, which has long been a popular tourist center. An annual festival includes performances by the Royal Shakespeare Company. ⊛ Pop. 108,600.

strath (străth). *Scots.* A wide, flat river valley.

stream (strēm). A flow of water in a channel or bed, as a brook, rivulet, or small river.

Stream·wood (strēm′wŏod′). A village of northeast Illinois, a residential suburb of Chicago. ⊛ Pop. 30,987.

Strom·bo·li (strŏm′bə-lē, strôm′bô-). An island of southern Italy in the Lipari Islands off northeast Sicily in the Tyrrhenian Sea. Its active volcano, 926.6 m (3,038 ft) high, erupted violently in 1930 and 1966.

Strongs·ville (strôngz′vĭl′). A city of northeast Ohio, a residential suburb of Cleveland. ⊛ Pop. 35,308.

Stru·ma (strŏo′mə). A river, about 348 km (216 mi) long, of western Bulgaria and northeast Greece flowing southward to an inlet of the Aegean Sea.

Stutt·gart (stŭt′gärt′, stŏot′-, shtŏot′-). A city of southwest Germany on the Neckar River south-southeast of Heidelberg. Chartered in the 13th century, it developed as an industrial center in the 19th and early 20th centuries and was heavily bombed during World War II. ⊛ Pop. 594,406.

Styr (stîr). A river, about 436 km (271 mi) long, of northwest Ukraine flowing northward to the Pripet River.

sub·ant·arc·tic (sŭb′ănt-ärk′tĭk, -är′tĭk). Of or resembling regions just north of the Antarctic Circle.

sub·arc·tic (sŭb-ärk′tĭk, -är′tĭk). Of or resembling regions just south of the Arctic Circle.

sub·ar·id (sŭb-ăr′ĭd). Somewhat arid; moderately dry.

sub·con·ti·nent (sŭb′kŏn′tə-nənt, sŭb-kŏn′-). **1.** A large landmass, such as India, that is part of a continent but is considered either geographi-

cally or politically as an independent entity. **2.** A large landmass, such as Greenland, that is smaller than a continent. **— sub′con·ti·nen′tal** (-něn′tl) *adj.*

sub·e·qua·to·ri·al (sŭb′ē-kwə-tôr′ē-əl, -tōr′-, -ěk-wə-). Belonging to a region adjacent to an equatorial area.

Su·bic Bay (sŏo′bĭk). An inlet of the South China Sea off west-central Luzon, Philippines, west of Manila Bay. A U.S. naval base established here in 1901 was held by the Japanese from 1942 to 1945. It was turned over to the Philippine government in 1992.

sub·lit·to·ral (sŭb-lĭt′ər-əl). **1.** Of or situated near the seashore. **2.** Lying between the low tide line and the edge of the continental shelf or ranging in depth to about 100 fathoms or 200 meters (660 feet).

Su·bo·ti·ca also **Su·bo·ti·tsa** (sŏo′bə-tē′tsə, -bô-). A city of northern Yugoslavia near the Hungarian border. It is a railroad junction and an industrial center. ⊛ Pop. 100,219.

sub·re·gion (sŭb′rē′jən). A subdivision of a region, especially an ecological region. **— sub′-re′gion·al** *adj.*

sub·Sa·har·an (sŭb′sə-hâr′ən, -hăr′-, -här′-). Of, relating to, or situated in the region of Africa south of the Sahara.

sub·tem·per·ate (sŭb-tĕm′pər-ĭt, -tĕm′prĭt). Of, relating to, or occurring within the colder regions of the Temperate Zones.

sub·tor·rid (sŭb-tôr′ĭd, -tŏr′-). Subtropical.

sub·trop·i·cal (sŭb-trŏp′ĭ-kəl). Of or being the geographic areas adjacent to the Tropics.

sub·trop·ics (sŭb-trŏp′ĭks). Subtropical regions.

sub·urb (sŭb′ûrb′). *abbr.* **sub. 1.** A usually residential area or community outlying a city. **2. suburbs.** The usually residential region around a major city; the environs. **— sub·ur′ban** *adj.*

Sü·chow (sŏo′chou′, sü′jō′). See **Xuzhou.**

Su·cre (sŏo′krā, -krě). The constitutional capital of Bolivia, in the south-central part of the country southeast of La Paz. Founded in 1538 as Chuquisaca, it was renamed in 1840 to honor Antonio José de Sucre (1795–1830), the South American revolutionary leader and first president of Bolivia. ⊛ Pop. 144,994.

Su·dan (sŏo-dăn′). **1.** A region of northern Africa south of the Sahara and north of the equator. It extends across the continent from the Atlantic coast to the mountains of Ethiopia. **2.** A country of northeast Africa south of Egypt. Northern Sudan formed part of the ancient kingdoms of Nubia and Cush, undergoing conversion to Coptic Christianity in the 6th century and to Islam in the 14th century. The region was conquered by Egypt in 1820–1822 and jointly administered by Great Britain and Egypt after the defeat of the Mahdist revolt (1881–1898) by an Anglo-Egyptian force led by the British soldier H.H. Kitchener. Sudan achieved independence in 1956. Tensions between the Muslim north and the animist south led to an intermittent civil war which intensified in the early 1990's following government efforts to impose strict Islamic law throughout the country. Khartoum is the capital and the largest city. ● Pop. 28,947,000. —**Su'da·nese'** (sōōd'n-ēz', -ēs') *adj. & n.*

Sud·bur·y (sŭd'bĕr'ē, -bə-rē). A city of southeast Ontario, Canada, north of Georgian Bay. It is the center of a rich mining region. ● Pop. 165,720.

Su·de·ten (sōō-dā'tn, zōō-) also **Su·de·tes** (sōō-dē'tēz). A series of mountain ranges along the Czech-Polish border between the Elbe and Oder rivers. The mountains extend for about 298 km (185 mi) and rise to 1,603 m (5,256 ft).

Su·de·ten·land (sōō-dāt'n-lănd', -länt', zōō-). A historical region of northern Czech Republic along the Polish border. Long inhabited by ethnic Germans, it was seized by the Nazis in September 1938 and was restored to Czechoslovakia in 1945, after which the German population was expelled.

Su·de·tes (sōō-dē'tēz). See **Sudeten.**

Su·ez (sōō-ĕz', sōō'ĕz'). A city of northeast Egypt at the head of the Gulf of Suez and the southern terminus of the Suez Canal. It became a major port after the opening of the canal. ● Pop. 388,000.

Suez, Gulf of. An arm of the Red Sea off northeast Egypt west of the Sinai Peninsula.

Suez, Isthmus of. An isthmus of northeast Egypt connecting Africa and Asia. It is bordered by the Mediterranean Sea on the north and the Gulf of Suez on the south.

Suez Canal. A ship canal, about 166 km (103

mi) long, traversing the Isthmus of Suez and linking the Red Sea and the Gulf of Suez with the Mediterranean Sea. Built under the supervision of the French diplomat and engineer Ferdinand de Lesseps, it was opened in November 1869 and after 1875 came under British control. The British withdrew in June 1956, and in July President Gamal Abdel Nasser of Egypt nationalized the canal, precipitating a crisis in which Israel invaded Egypt and Great Britain and France sent armed forces to retake the canal. United Nations intervention forced an armistice, and the canal was reopened in April 1957. The canal was again closed in July 1967 during the Arab-Israeli War and remained closed until June 1975.

Suf·folk (sŭf'ək). **1.** A historical region of eastern England bordering on the North Sea. Settled in prehistoric times, it was part of the Anglo-Saxon kingdom of East Anglia. Its name means the "southern people," as opposed to the "northern people" of Norfolk. **2.** An independent city of southeast Virginia southeast of Portsmouth. It was burned by the British in 1779 and occupied by Union forces in 1862. ● Pop. 52,141.

Sug·ar·loaf Mountain (shōog'ər-lōf'). A rocky peak in Rio de Janeiro, Brazil, at the entrance to Guanabara Bay. An aerial railroad leads to the summit, 395.3 m (1,296 ft) high.

Suhl (zōōl). A city of central Germany southsouthwest of Erfurt. It had a noted arms industry during the Thirty Years' War (1618–1648). It is an industrial and manufacturing center. ● Pop. 51,731.

Su·i·ta (sōō-ē'tə, -tä). A city of southern Honshu, Japan, an industrial suburb of Osaka. ● Pop. 339,970.

Suit·land (sōōt'lənd). An unincorporated community of central Maryland, a suburb of Washington, D.C. ● Pop. 35,111.

Su·khu·mi (sōōk'ə-mē, sōō-кнōō'myĭ). A city of western Georgia on the Black Sea westnorthwest of Tbilisi. It is a popular resort. ● Pop. 122,000.

Su·la·we·si (sōō'lä-wā'sē). See **Celebes.**

Sul·phur (sŭl'fər). A city of southwest Louisiana west of Lake Charles. It is a trade center in an oil and natural gas region. ● Pop. 20,125.

sul·tan·ate (sŭl'tə-nāt'). **1.** The office, power, or reign of a sultan. **2.** A country or state ruled by a sultan.

Su·lu (sōō'lōō). *pl.* **Sulu** or **-lus.** A member of a Muslim people inhabiting the Sulu Archipelago.

Sulu Sea. An arm of the western Pacific Ocean between the Philippines and Borneo. The **Sulu Archipelago,** a chain of small islands belonging to the Philippines, separates the Sulu Sea from the Celebes Sea southwest of Mindanao.

Su·ma·tra (sōō-mä'trə). An island of western

Indonesia in the Indian Ocean south of the Malay Peninsula. Visited by the Venetian traveler Marco Polo c. 1292, the island came under Dutch control in the 17th century although the English continued to press territorial claims. Sumatra joined newly independent Indonesia in 1949. — **Su·ma′tran** *adj. & n.*

Sum·ba (sŏŏm′bə, -bä). An island of south-central Indonesia in the Lesser Sunda Islands south of Flores. First visited by Europeans in 1522, it passed to the Dutch in 1866.

Sum·ba·wa (sŏŏm-bä′wə, -wä). A volcanic island of south-central Indonesia in the Lesser Sunda Islands west of Flores. The Dutch gained control in 1905 after signing treaties with the local chieftains.

Su·mer (sŏŏ′mər). An ancient country of southern Mesopotamia in present-day southern Iraq. Archaeological evidence dates the beginnings of Sumer to the fifth millennium B.C. By 3000 a flourishing civilization existed, which gradually exerted power over the surrounding area and culminated in the Akkadian dynasty founded (c. 2340) by Sargon I. Sumer declined after 2000 and was later absorbed by Babylonia and Assyria. The Sumerians are believed to have invented the cuneiform system of writing.

Su·me·ri·an (sŏŏ-mîr′ē-ən, -mêr′-). **1.** Of or relating to ancient Sumer or its people, language, or culture. **2.** A member of an ancient people, probably of non-Semitic origin, who established a nation of city-states in Sumer in the fourth millennium B.C. that is one of the earliest known historic civilizations. **3.** The language of the Sumerians, of no known linguistic affiliation.

Sum·ga·it (sŏŏm′gä-ēt′). A city of eastern Azerbaijan on the Caspian Sea northwest of Baku. It is an industrial center. ⊕ Pop. 235,000.

Sum·mit (sŭm′ĭt). A city of northeast New Jersey west of Newark. It is mainly residential. ⊕ Pop. 19,757.

Sum·ter (sŭm′tər). A city of central South Carolina east of Columbia. Founded in 1799, it is a trade and processing center. ⊕ Pop. 41,943.

Su·my (sŏŏ′mē). A city of northern Ukraine northwest of Kharkov. Its manufactures include mining equipment and heavy machinery. ⊕ Pop. 305,000.

Sun·belt also **Sun Belt** (sŭn′bĕlt′). The southern and southwest United States.

Sun City (sŭn). A community of south-central Arizona, a suburb of Phoenix. Founded in 1960, it is a planned retirement community. ⊕ Pop. 40,505.

Sun·da Islands (sŭn′də, sŏŏn′-). A group of islands of the western Malay Archipelago between the South China Sea and the Indian Ocean. The **Greater Sunda Islands** include Sumatra, Borneo, Java, and Celebes; the **Lesser**

Sunda Islands lie east of Java and extend from Bali to Timor. Sumatra and Java are separated by the **Sunda Strait,** a narrow channel linking the Indian Ocean with the Java Sea.

Sun·der·land (sŭn′dər-lənd). A borough of northeast England on the North Sea east-southeast of Newcastle. It was established as a shipbuilding center in the 14th century on the site of a Saxon community. ⊕ Pop. 297,806.

Sunds·vall (sŭnts′väl′). A city of east-central Sweden on an inlet of the Gulf of Bothnia. Chartered in 1621, it is a major shipping center. ⊕ Pop. 50,600.

Sun·ga·ri (sŏŏng′gə-rē). See **Songhua.**

Sun·light Peak (sŭn′līt′). A mountain, 4,288 m (14,059 ft) high, in the San Juan Mountains of southwest Colorado.

Sun·ny·vale (sŭn′ē-vāl′). A city of western California west-northwest of San Jose. Its manufactures include electronic equipment and pharmaceuticals. ⊕ Pop. 117,229.

Sun·rise (sŭn′rīz′). A city of southeast Florida west-northwest of Fort Lauderdale. It is a commercial hub and retirement community. ⊕ Pop. 64,407.

Sunrise Manor. A community of southeast Nevada, a suburb of Las Vegas. ⊕ Pop. 95,362.

Sun River. A river, about 209 km (130 mi) long, of northwest Montana flowing south and east to the Missouri River.

Sun Valley. A resort town of south-central Idaho east of Boise. Its lodge, opened in 1936, was built by the Union Pacific Railroad to attract passenger traffic to the West. ⊕ Pop. 545.

su·per·con·ti·nent (sŏŏ′pər-kŏn′tə-nənt). A large hypothetical continent, especially Pangaea, that is thought to have split into smaller ones in the geologic past. Also called *protocontinent.*

Su·pe·ri·or (sŏŏ-pîr′ē-ər). A city of northwest Wisconsin on Lake Superior opposite Duluth, Minnesota. The city grew after the discovery of iron ore nearby in the 1880's. ⊕ Pop. 27,134.

Superior, Lake. The largest and westernmost of the Great Lakes, between the north-central United States and southern Ontario, Canada. Probably first sighted by French explorers in the early 1600's, it is an important link in the Great Lakes–St. Lawrence Seaway system.

Su·qua·mish (sə-kwä′mĭsh). **1.** *pl.* **Suquamish** or **-mish·es.** A member of a Native American people inhabiting an area of the eastern shore of Puget Sound. **2.** The Salish language of the Suquamish.

Su·ra·ba·ya also **Su·ra·ba·ja** (sŏŏr′ə-bä′yə). A city of northeast Java, Indonesia, on the Java Sea. It is an important naval base. ⊕ Pop. 2,027,913.

Su·ra·kar·ta (sŏŏr′ə-kär′tə). A city of south-central Java, Indonesia, east of Bandung. It is a market and processing center noted for its vast, walled palace built by the former sultans of the region. ⊛ Pop. 469,888.

Su·rat (so͝or′ət, sə-răt′). A city of west-central India on the Gulf of Cambay north of Bombay. Once the chief port of India, it is now a railroad and manufacturing hub. ⊛ Pop. 1,498,817.

Sur·gut (sər-go͞ot′). A city of north-central Russia on the Ob River north of Omsk. It is in an oil-producing region. ⊛ Pop. 261,197.

Su·ri·ba·chi (so͝or′ə-bä′chē), **Mount.** A volcanic hill on Iwo Jima in the western Pacific Ocean. It is famous for the dramatic photograph of U.S. Marines raising the American flag on its summit on February 23, 1945, after the island was captured from the Japanese.

Su·ri·na·me (sü′rē-nä′mə) also **Su·ri·nam** (so͝or′-ə-năm′, -näm′). Formerly **Dutch Gui·a·na** (dŭch gē-ăn′ə, -ä′nə, gī-). *abbr.* **Sur.** A country of northeast South America on the Atlantic Ocean. The region was first colonized by the British in 1650 but was ceded to the Dutch, along with the rest of Guiana, by the Treaty of Breda (1667). In 1815 the Congress of Vienna awarded the area of present-day Guyana to the British, leaving Suriname as a Dutch possession. The Dutch granted the colony a parliament in 1866, and in 1954 it became an autonomous territory of the Netherlands. Full independence was achieved in 1975. Paramaribo is the capital and the largest city. ⊛ Pop. 418,000. **—Su′ri·na·mese′** (-nä-mēz′, -mēs′) *adj. & n.*

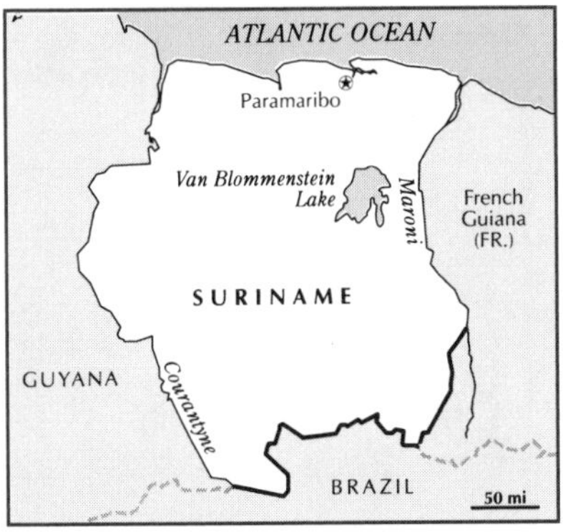

Suriname River also **Surinam River.** A river of Suriname flowing about 644 km (400 mi) northward to the Atlantic Ocean.

Sur·rey (sûr′ē, sŭr′ē). A historical region of southeast England. Dominated by Mercia and Wessex in Anglo-Saxon times, it was overrun by the Danes in the ninth century.

Su·ru·ga Bay (so͞o′ro͞o-gä′). An inlet of the Pacific Ocean on the southeast coast of Honshu, Japan, southwest of Tokyo.

Su·sa (so͞o′sə, -zə). A ruined city of southwest Iran south of Hamadan. It was the capital of the kingdom of Elam and a capital of the Persian Empire under Cyrus the Great (ruled 550–529 B.C.).

Su·sah or **Su·sa** (so͞o′sə, -zə). See **Sousse.**

Su·si·a·na (so͞o′zē-ä′nə, -ăn′ə). See **Elam.**

Sus·que·han·na (sŭs′kwə-hăn′ə). *pl.* **Susquehanna** or **-nas.** See **Susquehannock** (sense 1).

Susquehanna River. A river of the northeast United States rising in central New York and flowing about 714 km (444 mi) south through eastern Pennsylvania and northeast Maryland to Chesapeake Bay.

Sus·que·han·nock (sŭs′kwə-hăn′ək). **1.** *pl.* **Susquehannock** or **-nocks.** A member of a Native American people formerly located along the Susquehanna River in New York, Pennsylvania, and Maryland. The Susquehannocks were extinct by 1763. Also called *Conestoga, Susquehanna.* **2.** The Iroquoian language of the Susquehannocks.

Sus·sex (sŭs′ĭks). An Anglo-Saxon kingdom of southern England bordering on the English Channel. Founded in the fifth century A.D., it was captured by the kingdom of Wessex in 825.

Su·su (so͞o′so͞o). **1.** *pl.* **Susu** or **-sus.** A member of a West African people inhabiting parts of Guinea and Sierra Leone. **2.** The Mande language of the Susu.

Suth·er·land Falls (sŭth′ər-lənd). A waterfall, 581 m (1,904 ft) high, of southwest South Island, New Zealand.

Sut·lej (sŭt′lĕj′). A river, about 1,448 km (900 mi) long, flowing from southwest Xizang (Tibet) through northern India and eastern Pakistan, where it is joined by the Chenab River. It is one of the five rivers of the Punjab.

Su·va (so͞o′və, -vä). The capital of Fiji, on the southeast coast of Viti Levu. It is a commercial and shipping center. ⊛ Pop. 74,000.

Su·wan·nee (sə-wä′nē). A river, about 386 km (240 mi) long, flowing from southeast Georgia across northern Florida to the Gulf of Mexico.

Su·won (so͞o′wŭn′). A city of northwest South Korea south of Seoul. Suwon is a textile-manufacturing center. ⊛ Pop. 644,805.

Su·zhou (so͞o′jō′) also **Soo·chow** (-chou′, -jō′). A city of eastern China west-northwest of Shanghai. The capital (6th–5th century B.C.) of an ancient feudal kingdom, the city was almost destroyed (1853) in the Taiping Rebellion against the Manchu dynasty but was rebuilt. It became a treaty port in 1896, was occupied by the Japanese during World War II, and fell to Chinese Communists in 1949. Suzhou is famous for its beautiful bridges and pagodas and for its silk industry, which dates back to the Song dynasty (960–1279). ⊛ Pop. 3,273,010.

Sval·bard (sväl′bär′). A Norwegian archipelago

comprising Spitsbergen and other islands in the Arctic Ocean north of the mainland. The islands are rich in mineral resources.

Sverd·lovsk (sfĕrd-lôfsk′, svyĭrd-). See **Yekaterinburg.**

Sver·drup Islands (sfĕr′drəp, svĕr′-). A group of islands of the northern Northwest Territories, Canada, in the Arctic Ocean west of Ellesmere Island.

Swa·bi·a (swā′bē-ə). A historical region of southwest Germany that originally included parts of present-day France and Switzerland. It was divided into small principalities and fiefdoms after 1268, but its prosperous towns often banded together in defensive leagues, most notably the **Swabian League** of 1488 to 1534. — **Swa′bi·an** *adj. & n.*

Swa·hi·li (swä-hē′lē). **1.** *pl.* **Swahili** or **-lis.** A member of a predominantly Muslim people inhabiting the coast and islands of eastern Africa from Somalia to Mozambique. **2.** The Bantu language of the Swahili that is the official language of Tanzania and is widely used as a lingua franca in eastern and east-central Africa. In this sense, also called *Kiswahili.* — **Swa·hi′li·an** *adj.*

swamp (swŏmp, swômp). **1.** A seasonally flooded bottomland with more woody plants than a marsh and better drainage than a bog. **2.** A lowland region saturated with water. — **swamp′i·ness** *n.* — **swamp′y** *adj.*

Swan·sea (swän′zē, -sē). **1.** A town of southeast Massachusetts, an industrial suburb of Fall River. ◉ Pop. 15,411. **2.** A borough of southern Wales west-northwest of Cardiff. It is an industrial port on **Swansea Bay,** an inlet of the Bristol Channel. ◉ Pop. 189,329.

Swa·tow (swä′tou′). See **Shantou.**

Swa·zi (swä′zē). **1.** *pl.* **Swazi** or **-zis.** A member of a southeast African people of Swaziland and adjacent parts of South Africa. **2.** The Nguni language of this people, closely related to Xhosa and Zulu.

Swa·zi·land (swä′zē-lănd′). *abbr.* **Swaz.** A country of southeast Africa between South Africa and Mozambique. Settled in the early 19th century by Swazi groups fleeing Zulu attacks,

the region became a South African protectorate (1894–1899) and was subsequently transferred to British administration in 1903. Swaziland was granted limited autonomy in 1963 and achieved full independence as a kingdom in 1968. The country's first democratic elections were held in 1993. Mbabane is the capital and the largest city. ◉ Pop. 832,000.

Swede (swēd). A native or inhabitant of Sweden.

Swe·den (swēd′n). *abbr.* **Swe., Swed.** A country of northern Europe on the eastern Scandinavian Peninsula. The region was settled by Germanic tribes probably in Neolithic times, and by the 10th century A.D. the Swedes had extended their influence as far as the Black Sea. Christianity was introduced in the 9th century and became fully established in the 12th. During the 14th century Sweden and Norway, and for a while Denmark, formed a union, but in the 16th century the Swedes revolted and established a separate state. By the 17th century Sweden was a major European power, controlling most of the Baltic coast. It lost much of its territory to Russia and its allies in the Great Northern War (1700–1721), but acquired Norway (1814) in the Napoleonic Wars, ruling it until 1905. Remaining neutral in both World Wars, Sweden later embarked on a program of economic expansion and social reform that made it one of the most progressive nations in the world. Stockholm is the capital and the largest city. ◉ Pop. 8,780,000.

Swed·ish (swē′dĭsh). *abbr.* **Sw. 1.** Of or relating to Sweden, the Swedes, or their culture or language. **2.** The North Germanic language of Sweden and Finland.

Swin·don (swĭn′dən). A municipal borough of south-central England east-northeast of Bristol. It has an important locomotive industry. ◉ Pop. 151,600.

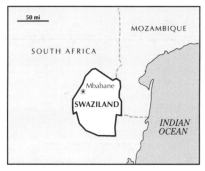

Swiss (swĭs). **1.** Of or relating to Switzerland or its people or culture. **2.** A native or inhabitant of Switzerland.

Swit·zer (swĭt′sər). A Swiss.

Swit·zer·land (swĭt′sər-lənd). *abbr.* **Switz.** A country of west-central Europe. The region was conquered by Germanic tribes in the 5th century and by Swabia and Burgundy in the 9th, becoming part of the Holy Roman Empire in 1033. Protesting Hapsburg control in the 13th century, the Swiss formed a defense league made up of cantons that became the basis of their confederation, and by 1499 they had achieved independence. The Reformation in the 16th century led to religious civil wars that lasted through the next two centuries. The French took brief control of Switzerland during the French Revolution, but the confederacy was restored in 1815, with the Congress of Vienna guaranteeing Swiss neutrality. Switzerland adopted a federal constitution (1848) and maintained a policy of neutrality through both World Wars. Bern is the capital and Zurich the largest city. ⊕ Pop. 6,995,000.

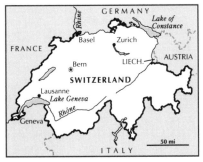

Syb·a·ris (sĭb′ər-ĭs). An ancient Greek city of southern Italy on the Gulf of Taranto. Noted for its wealth and luxury, it was destroyed in warfare with Crotona in 510 B.C. —**Syb′a·rite** *n.*

Syd·ney (sĭd′nē). **1.** A city of southeast Australia on an inlet of the Tasman Sea. The largest city in Australia, it is the country's chief port and main cultural and financial center. ⊕ Pop. 3,713,500. **2.** A city of Nova Scotia, Canada, on eastern Cape Breton Island. It is a commercial and industrial center. ⊕ Pop. 29,444.

Syk·tyv·kar (sĭk-tĭf-kär′). A city of northwest Russia southeast of Arkhangelsk. It is a major supplier of lumber. ⊕ Pop. 226,304.

Syl·va·nia (sĭl-vān′yə). A city of northern Ohio on the Michigan border northwest of Toledo. It is a manufacturing center. ⊕ Pop. 17,301.

Syr·a·cuse (sĭr′ə-kyōōs′, -kyōōz′). **1.** A city of southeast Sicily, Italy, on the Ionian Sea south-southeast of Catania. Founded by colonists from Corinth in the eighth century B.C., it reached the height of its power in the fifth century but

fell to the Romans in 212 B.C. ⊕ Pop. 126,136. **2.** A city of central New York east-southeast of Rochester. Originally a trading post and salt-works, it is now a manufacturing and educational center. ⊕ Pop. 163,860.

Syr Dar·ya (sîr där′yə, dər-yä′). A river of central Asia rising in two headstreams in the Tien Shan and flowing about 2,220 km (1,380 mi) generally southwest through eastern Uzbekistan and northern Tajikistan, then flowing generally northwest back through Uzbekistan and south-central Kazakstan to the Aral Sea.

Syr·i·a (sîr′ē-ə). *abbr.* **Syr.** A country of southwest Asia on the eastern Mediterranean coast. Ancient Syria also included Lebanon, most of present-day Israel and Jordan, and part of Iraq and Saudi Arabia. Settled c. 2100 B.C. by Amorites, the region was later conquered by Hittites, Assyrians, Babylonians, Persians, Greeks, and Romans. Islam was introduced in the seventh century by Muslim Arab conquerers. Syria was a province of the Ottoman Empire from 1516 until 1918, and the part comprising present-day Syria and Lebanon became a French League of Nations mandate in 1920. Separated from Lebanon by the French, Syria achieved full independence in 1946. In 1958 it merged with Egypt to form the United Arab Republic, which disintegrated in 1961. During the Six-Day War with Israel in 1967, Syria lost the Golan Heights, which Israel annexed in 1981. Hafez al-Assad became president in 1971 following a bloodless coup. Syria sent troops to Lebanon in 1976 as part of a peacekeeping force at the outbreak of the Lebanese civil war. As other peacekeepers withdrew, Syria came to dominate Lebanon politically as well as militarily. During the late 1980's Syria worked to improve its relations with the West and agreed to initial peace talks with Israel in 1991. Damascus is the capital and the largest city. ⊕ Pop. 13,844,000. —**Syr′i·an** *adj. & n.*

Syr·i·ac (sîr′ē-ăk′). An ancient Aramaic language spoken in Syria from the 3rd to the 13th century that survives as the liturgical language of several Eastern Christian churches.

Syrian Desert. A desert region of northern Arabia occupying northern Saudi Arabia, western Iraq, southeast Syria, and eastern Jordan. It is crossed by a number of oil pipelines.

Sy·ros (sī′rŏs′) also **Sí·ros** (sē′rôs′). An island of Greece in the north-central Cyclades. It is the richest and most populous of the Cyclades.

Syz·ran (sĭz′rən). A city of western Russia on the Volga River west of Samara. It is a major river port and rail center. ◉ Pop. 174,947.

Szcze·cin (shchĕt′sēn′) also **Stet·tin** (stə-tēn′, shtĕ-). A city of northwest Poland near the mouth of the Oder River. It was ruled by Sweden from 1648 to 1720, when it was ceded to Prussia. After World War II the city became part of Poland. ◉ Pop. 413,561.

Sze·chuan (sĕch′wän′). See **Sichuan.**

Sze·chwan (sĕch′wän′). See **Sichuan.**

Sze·ged (sĕg′ĕd′). A city of southern Hungary on the Tisza River near the Yugoslavian border. It is a major river port and an agricultural center. ◉ Pop. 178,690.

Szé·kes·fe·hér·vár (sā′kĕsh-fĕ′hâr-vär′). A city of central Hungary on the Danube River south-southwest of Budapest. It was the coronation and burial place of Hungary's kings from 1027 to 1527. ◉ Pop. 109,714.

Szol·nok (sōl′nōk′). A city of central Hungary east-southeast of Budapest. It is an industrial and commercial center. ◉ Pop. 79,619.

Szom·bat·hely (sōm′bôt-hā′). A city of western Hungary near the Austrian border. Founded in Roman times, it is an industrial center and an important railroad junction. ◉ Pop. 85,830.

T

Taal¹ (tä-äl′). A lake of southwest Luzon, Philippines, south of Manila. It contains Volcano Island, the site of the active volcano **Mount Taal.**

Taal² (täl). See **Afrikaans.**

Tab·las (tä′bläs). An island of the central Philippines east of Mindoro. It is the largest of the Romblon Islands.

Ta·ble Bay (tā′bəl). An inlet of the Atlantic Ocean off southwest South Africa that forms the harbor of Cape Town.

ta·ble·land (tā′bəl-lănd′). A flat, elevated region; a plateau or mesa.

Ta·briz (tə-brēz′, tä-). A city of northwest Iran east of Lake Urmia. A commercial and industrial center, Tabriz has been subject to devastating earthquakes since 858. ◉ Pop. 1,166,203.

Tä·by (tĕ′bü). A city of southeast Sweden, an industrial suburb of Stockholm. ◉ Pop. 52,771.

Tac·na (tăk′nə, täk′nä). A town of southern Peru north of Arica, Chile. The object of a long-standing dispute between Peru and Chile, it became part of Peru in 1929. ◉ Pop. 152,200.

Ta·co·ma (tə-kō′mə). A city of west-central Washington on an arm of Puget Sound south of Seattle. A major seaport and railroad center, it is one of the chief industrial cities in the Northwest. ◉ Pop. 176,664.

Ta·con·ic Mountains (tə-kŏn′ĭk). A range of the Appalachian Mountains in southeast New York, western Massachusetts, and southwest Vermont rising to 1,163.9 m (3,816 ft).

Ta·dzhik (tä-jĭk′, tə-). Variant of **Tajik.**

Ta·dzhik·i (tä-jĭk′ē, tə-). Variant of **Tajiki.**

Ta·dzhik·i·stan (tä-jĭk′ĭ-stăn′, -stän′, tə-jĭ-kyĭ-stän′). See **Tajikistan.**

Tae·gu (tī-gōō′). A city of southeast South Korea north-northwest of Pusan. It is an industrial and commercial center. ◉ Pop. 2,031,000.

Tae·jon (tī-jôn′, -jŏn′). A city of central South Korea south-southeast of Seoul. It is an agricultural center and a railroad hub. ◉ Pop. 866,148.

Ta·ga·log (tə-gä′lôg, -läg). **1.** *pl.* **Tagalog** or **-logs.** A member of a people native to the Philippines and inhabiting Manila and its adjacent provinces. **2.** The Austronesian language of the Tagalog on which Filipino is based.

Tag·an·rog (tăg′ən-rŏg′, tə-gən-rôk′). A city of southwest Russia on the **Gulf of Taganrog,** an arm of the Sea of Azov. Originally a colony of Pisa, it was destroyed by Mongols in the 13th century and later (1698) established by Peter the Great as a fortress and naval base. In the early 18th century it was captured by Turks but was annexed by Russia in 1769. Taganrog is the birthplace of the writer Anton Chekhov (1860–1904). ◉ Pop. 290,457.

Ta·gus (tā′gəs) also **Ta·jo** (tä′hō). A river of the Iberian Peninsula rising in east-central Spain and flowing generally westward about 941 km (585 mi) through central Portugal to the Atlantic Ocean.

Ta·hi·ti (tə-hē′tē). An island of the southern Pacific Ocean in the Windward group of the Society Islands in French Polynesia. It was first settled by Polynesians in the 14th century. The French artist Paul Gauguin (1848–1903) painted his best-known works here.

Ta·hi·tian (tə-hē′shən). **1.** Of or relating to Tahiti or its people, language, or culture. **2.** A native or inhabitant of Tahiti. **3.** The Polynesian language of Tahiti.

Ta·hoe (tä′hō), **Lake.** A lake on the California-Nevada border west of Carson City, Nevada. It is a popular resort area.

Tai (tī) also **Dai** (dī). **1.** A family of languages spoken in southeast Asia and southern China that includes Thai, Lao, and Shan. **2.** A member of any of the Tai-speaking peoples of Thailand, Myanmar (Burma), Laos, China, and Vietnam. **3.** Of or relating to Tai, its speakers, or their culture. **4.** Relating to Thailand; Thai.

Tai·chung (tī′chŏŏng′, -jŏŏng′) also **Tai·zhong** (-jông′). A city of west-central Taiwan southwest of Taipei. It is a food-processing and distribution center. ◉ Pop. 621,566.

Tai Hu (tī′ hŏō′). A lake of east-central China west of Shanghai. Its basin is one of China's richest agricultural areas.

Tai·myr Peninsula also **Tai·mir Peninsula** or **Tay·myr Peninsula** (tī-mîr′). A peninsula of north-central Russia extending northward between the Laptev and Kara seas.

Tai·nan (tī′nän′). A city of southwest Taiwan on the South China Sea. Settled in 1590, it is Taiwan's oldest city. ◉ Pop. 609,934.

Taí·na·ron (tä′nə-rôn′, tĕ′nä-), **Cape.** Formerly **Cape Mat·a·pan** (măt′ə-păn′). A cape at the southernmost point of mainland Greece. The British won an important naval battle against the Italians off Cape Taínaron in 1941.

Tai·no (tī′nō). **1.** *pl.* **Taino** or **-nos.** A member of an Arawak people of the Greater Antilles and the Bahamas who became extinct as a people under Spanish colonization during the 16th century. **2.** The language of this people.

Tai·pei also **Tai·peh** (tī′pā′, -bā′). The capital and largest city of Taiwan, in the northern part of the country. Founded in the 18th century, it was developed under Japanese rule (1895–1945) and later became the headquarters of Chiang Kai-shek and the Chinese Nationalists when they fled mainland China (1949). ◉ Pop. 2,327,641.

Tai·wan (tī′wän′). Officially **Republic of China.** Formerly **For·mo·sa** (fôr-mō′sə). A country off the southeast coast of China comprising the island of **Taiwan,** the Pescadores, and other smaller islands. Chinese began settling Taiwan in the 7th century, largely replacing the original Malay inhabitants. Explored by the Portuguese in 1590, the island was held by the Dutch in the mid-1600's before being seized (1683) by Qing-dynasty Chinese, who controlled it for the next three centuries. Taiwan was ceded to Japan in 1895 after the First Sino-Japanese War, remaining in Japanese hands until 1945, when it was regained by China. Taiwan broke off from mainland China in 1949 when the Nationalists (Kuomintang) under Gen. Chiang Kai-Shek (1887–1975) fled from Mao Zedong's forces and established their government on the island. Though enjoying active U.S. support, Nationalist hopes of conquering the mainland eventually faded. In 1971 Taiwan lost its seat in the UN to the People's Republic of China, and in 1979 the United States ended diplomatic relations with the Taiwanese

government in favor of the mainland, though strong commercial ties remained. Taipei is the capital and the largest city. ◉ Pop. 20,546,500.

Tai·wan·ese (tī′wä-nēz′, -nēs′). **1.** Of or relating to Taiwan or its peoples, languages, or cultures. **2.** *pl.* **-nese.** A native or inhabitant of Taiwan. **3.** The Minnan dialect of Chinese spoken on Taiwan.

Taiwan Strait. See **Formosa Strait.**

Tai·yu·an also **Tai·yü·an** (tī′yŏō-än′, -ywän′). A city of northeast China southwest of Beijing. It is a coal-mining and steel-manufacturing center. ◉ Pop. 2,224,580.

Tai·zhong (tī′jông′). See **Taichung.**

Ta·jik also **Ta·dzhik** (tä-jĭk′, tə-). **1.** *pl.* **Tajik** or **-jiks** also **Tadzhik** or **-dzhiks.** A member of a people inhabiting Tajikistan and neighboring areas including Uzbekistan, Afghanistan, and China. **2.** Tajiki.

Ta·jik·i also **Ta·dzhik·i** (tä-jĭk′ē, tə-). **1.** The Iranian language of the Tajik people, closely related to Persian. **2.** Of or relating to the Tajik people or their language or culture.

Ta·jik·i·stan (tä-jĭk′ĭ-stăn′, -stän′, tə-jĭ-kyĭ-stän′). Formerly **Ta·dzhik Soviet Socialist Republic** (tä-jĭk′, tə-) or **Ta·dzhik·i·stan** (tä-jĭk′ĭ-

stăn', -stän', tə-jĭ-kyĭ-stän'). A country of south-central Asia. The region was settled by the Tajik by the 10th century and conquered by Mongols in the 13th century. By the mid-19th century it was divided among several weak khanates. The region was acquired by Russia in 1895 and was a constituent republic of the U.S.S.R. from 1929 to 1991. Civil war involving the country's Communist former leaders and Islamic and pro-democracy factions erupted in 1992. Dushanbe is the capital and largest city. ⊛ Pop. 5,933,000.

Ta·jo (tä'hō). See **Tagus.**

Ta·ka·mat·su (tä'kä-mät'soo). A city of northeast Shikoku, Japan, on the Inland Sea. It is a major seaport. ⊛ Pop. 331,031.

Ta·ka·sa·ki (tä'kä-sä'kē). A city of central Honshu, Japan. A silk-manufacturing center, the city is best known for its statue of Kannon, goddess of mercy. ⊛ Pop. 238,055.

Ta·ka·tsu·ki (tə-kät'soo-kē, tä'kä-tsoo'kē). A city of southwest Honshu, Japan. It is a commercial center roughly halfway between Osaka and Kyoto. ⊛ Pop. 361,283.

Tak·ka·kaw (tăk'ə-kô'). A waterfall, 503.3 m (1,650 ft) high, in southeast British Columbia, Canada. It is the highest waterfall in Canada.

Ta·kli·ma·kan also **Ta·kla·ma·kan** (tä'klə-mə-kän'). A desert of western China between the Tien Shan and the Kunlun Mountains.

Ta·ko·ma Park (tə-kō'mə). A city of central Maryland, a residential suburb of Washington, D.C. ⊛ Pop. 16,700.

Ta·la·ud Islands (tə-lout', tä-lä'ood) or **Ta·laur Islands** (-lour', -lä'oor). A group of islands of northeast Indonesia northeast of Celebes. The islands came under Dutch rule in 1677.

Ta·la·ve·ra de la Rei·na (tä'lə-vâr'ə də lä rā'nə, tä'lä-vĕ'rä thĕ lä rā'nä). A town of central Spain west-southwest of Madrid. The British and Spanish defeated the French here in 1809. ⊛ Pop. 67,216.

Tal·ca (täl'kä). A city of central Chile between Santiago and Concepción. Chile's independence was proclaimed here in 1818. ⊛ Pop. 164,492.

Tal·ca·hua·no (tăl'kə-wä'nō, -hwä'-, täl'kä-). A city of central Chile on the Pacific Ocean near Concepción. It is an important naval base. ⊛ Pop. 246,853.

Ta·lien (tä'lyĕn'). See **Dalian.**

Tal·la·de·ga (tăl'ə-dē'gə). A city of east-central Alabama east of Birmingham. Incorporated in 1835, it is an agricultural, quarrying, and mining center. ⊛ Pop. 18,175.

Tal·la·has·see (tăl'ə-hăs'ē). The capital of Florida, in the northwest part of the state. Originally a Native American village, it was settled by the Spanish after 1539 and founded as the capital of the Florida Territory in 1824. ⊛ Pop. 124,773.

Tal·la·hatch·ie (tăl'ə-hăch'ē). A river, about 371 km (230 mi) long, rising in northern Mississippi and flowing southwest to the Yazoo River.

Tal·la·poo·sa (tăl'ə-poo'sə). A river rising in northwest Georgia and flowing about 431 km (268 mi) generally southwest to central Alabama, where it joins the Coosa River to form the Alabama River.

Tal·linn also **Tal·lin** (tăl'ĭn, tä'lĭn). The capital and largest city of Estonia, in the northwest part of the country on the Gulf of Finland opposite Helsinki, Finland. A major port, it was a member of the Hanseatic League from 1285 and later passed to the Livonian Knights (1346–1561) and Sweden (1561–1710) before being formally ceded to Russia (1721). The city became the capital of independent Estonia in 1919 and was the capital of the Estonian Soviet Socialist Republic (1940–1991). ⊛ Pop. 447,672.

Tall·madge (tăl'mĭj). A city of northeast Ohio, an industrial suburb of Akron. ⊛ Pop. 14,870.

Ta·man (tə-män'). A peninsula of southwest Russia projecting westward between the Sea of Azov and the Black Sea. It is rich in petroleum deposits.

Tam·a·rac (tăm'ə-răk'). A city of southeast Florida northwest of Fort Lauderdale. It is a retirement community. ⊛ Pop. 44,822.

Tam·bov (täm-bôf', -bôv'). A city of western Russia southeast of Moscow. Founded as a fortress in 1636, it is a manufacturing center and railroad junction. ⊛ Pop. 311,303.

Tam·il (tăm'əl, tŭm'-, tä'məl). **1.** pl. **Tamil** or **-ils.** A member of a Dravidian people of southern India and northern Sri Lanka. **2.** The Dravidian language of the Tamil. **3.** Of or relating to the Tamil or their language or culture.

Tam·pa (tăm'pə). A city of west-central Florida on **Tampa Bay,** an inlet of the Gulf of Mexico. First visited by Spanish explorers in 1528, Tampa is a port of entry, a processing and shipping hub, and a tourist center. ⊛ Pop. 280,015.

Tam·pe·re (tăm'pə-rä', täm'-). A city of southwest Finland north-northwest of Helsinki. An important trade center since the 11th century, it is noted for its textile industry. ⊛ Pop. 175,504.

Tam·pi·co (tăm-pē'kō, täm-). A city of east-central Mexico near the Gulf of Mexico north-northeast of Mexico City. Settled by the Spanish in the 1530's, it is a major port, manufacturing center, and tourist resort. ⊛ Pop. 267,957.

Tam·worth (tăm'wûrth'). A municipal borough of central England northeast of Birmingham. It is an industrial center. ⊛ Pop. 65,100.

Tan (tăn). See **Tanka.**

Ta·na (tä'nə, -nä), **Lake** also **Lake Tsa·na** (tsä'-). A lake of northwest Ethiopia. The largest lake in the country, it is the source of the Blue Nile.

Tan·a·gra (tăn'ə-grə, tə-năg'rə). An ancient

city of east-central Greece in eastern Boeotia. The Spartans defeated Athenian forces here in 457 B.C.

Tan·a·na (tăn′ə-nô′). A river of eastern and southern Alaska flowing about 764 km (475 mi) from the Wrangell Mountains northwest to the Yukon River.

Ta·nan·a·rive (tə-năn′ə-rēv′, tä-nä-nä-rēv′). See **Antananarivo**.

Tana River. 1. A river, about 805 km (500 mi) long, of central Kenya flowing in an arc northeast and south to the Indian Ocean. **2.** A river, about 322 km (200 mi) long, of northeast Norway forming part of the Norway-Finland border and emptying into an inlet of the Arctic Ocean.

Tan·gan·yi·ka (tăn′gən-yē′kə, tăng′-). A former country of east-central Africa. A British mandate after 1920, it became independent in 1961 and joined with Zanzibar to form Tanzania in 1964. —**Tan′gan·yi′kan** adj. & n.

Tanganyika, Lake. A lake of east-central Africa between Zaire and Tanzania. The British explorers John Speke and Sir Richard Burton first sighted the lake in 1858.

Tan·gier (tăn-jîr′) also **Tan·giers** (-jîrz′). A city of northern Morocco at the west end of the Strait of Gibraltar. Founded in Roman times and later controlled by a variety of powers, including Portugal and Great Britain, it was administered as part of an international zone from 1923–1924 until 1956. ◉ Pop. 307,000.

Tang·shan (täng′shän′, däng′-). A city of northeast China east-southeast of Beijing. It was devastated in 1976 by a massive earthquake in which an estimated 242,000 people were killed. ◉ Pop. 1,484,515.

Ta·nim·bar Islands (tə-nĭm′bär′, tä-). An island group of southeast Indonesia in the southern Moluccas east-northeast of Timor. The islands were discovered by the Dutch in 1629.

Ta·nis (tā′nĭs). An ancient city of Egypt in the eastern delta of the Nile River. Important during the XIX and XXI Dynasties (c. 1342–1200 and 1085–945 B.C.), it was abandoned after the sixth century A.D.

Tan·ka (täng′kä). pl. **Tanka** or **-kas**. A member of a people in southern China and Hong Kong who live on small boats clustered in colonies. Also called *Tan*.

Ta·no·an (tä′nō-ən). An American Indian language family of New Mexico and northeast Arizona. —**Ta′no·an** adj.

Tan·ta (tän′tä). A city of northern Egypt in the Nile River delta north of Cairo. It is a processing center and railroad hub. ◉ Pop. 380,000.

Tan·tung (tän′tŏong′). See **Dandong**.

Tan·za·ni·a (tăn′zə-nē′ə). abbr. **Tanz.** A country of east-central Africa on the Indian Ocean. Site of numerous early hominid fossils, the region has been inhabited since Paleolithic times. Arab and Indian traders visited the coast from the eighth century on, and Bantu peoples had settled in the interior by the tenth century. The coast was controlled by Portugal from 1503 to 1698 and by Omani Arabs until 1861. In 1891 most of the region became a German protectorate and in 1920 passed as Tanganyika to the British, who had already established a protectorate (1890) in the coastal islands of Zanzibar. Tanganyika achieved independence in 1961 and joined with Zanzibar in 1964 to form Tanzania. A socialist country under president Julius Nyerere (governed 1962–1985), Tanzania went to war with Uganda in 1979, contributing to the ouster of Ugandan president Idi Amin. Dar es Salaam is the de facto capital and the largest city; Dodoma is the new official capital. ◉ Pop. 28,846,000. —**Tan·za′ni·an** adj. & n.

Ta·or·mi·na (tä′ôr-mē′nä). A town of eastern Sicily, Italy, at the foot of Mount Etna overlooking the Ionian Sea. First founded in the eighth century B.C., it is a famous winter resort. ◉ Pop. 10,085.

Taos¹ (tous, tä′ōs). **1.** pl. **Taos.** A member of a Pueblo people located north-northeast of Santa Fe, New Mexico. **2.** The Tanoan language of the Taos people.

Taos² (tous, tä′ōs). **1.** A town of northern New Mexico north-northeast of Santa Fe. It developed as an art colony after 1898 and has attracted many artists and writers, including John Marin (1870–1953) and D.H. Lawrence (1885–1930). ◉ Pop. 4,065. **2.** A pueblo of northern New Mexico northeast of the town of Taos. ◉ Pop. 1,187.

Ta·pa·jós also **Ta·pa·joz** (tăp′ə-zhôs′, tä′pä-). A river, about 965 km (600 mi) long, of northern Brazil flowing northeast to the Amazon River.

Tap·pan Zee (tăp′ən zē′). A widening of the

Hudson River in southeast New York. The British army officer Maj. John André was hanged for treason in 1780 at the nearby village of **Tappan.**

Tar·a (tăr′ə). A village of eastern Ireland northwest of Dublin. It was the seat of Irish kings from ancient times until the sixth century A.D.

Ta·ra·hu·ma·ra (tär′ə-hōō-mär′ə, tăr′-, tä′rä-ōō-mä′rä). **1.** *pl.* **Tarahumara** or **-ras.** A member of a Native American people of north-central Mexico. **2.** The Uto-Aztecan language of the Tarahumara.

Ta·ran·to (tär′ən-tō′, tə-rän′tō, tä′rän-tô′). A city of southeast Italy east-southeast of Naples on the **Gulf of Taranto,** an arm of the Ionian Sea. Founded by Greeks from Sparta in the eighth century B.C., it was known as Tarentum in Roman times. Ruled by varied powers over the centuries, it became part of Italy in 1860. ⊛ Pop. 232,200.

Ta·ra·wa (tə-rä′wə, tär′ə-wä′, tä′rä-). An atoll of Kiribati in the northern Gilbert Islands of the western Pacific Ocean. It was occupied by the Japanese in 1942 and retaken by U.S. Marines after a hard-fought battle in November 1943.

Tarbes (tärb). A city of southwest France near the Pyrenees west-southwest of Toulouse. It is an industrial, commercial, and tourist center. ⊛ Pop. 51,422.

Ta·rim He (tä′rēm′ hə′). A river of western China flowing about 2,092 km (1,300 mi) eastward to Lop Nur.

Tarim Pen·di (pŭn′dē′). An arid basin of western China south of the Tien Shan and traversed by the Tarim He. The ancient Silk Road passed through the region.

tarn (tärn). A small mountain lake, especially one formed by glaciers.

Tarn (tärn). A river, about 378 km (235 mi) long, of southern France flowing generally west and southwest to the Garonne River.

Tar·nów (tär′nōōf′). A city of southeast Poland east of Cracow. It was a religious and cultural center in the 15th and 16th centuries. ⊛ Pop. 121,582.

Tar·quin·i·i (tär-kwĭn′ē-ī′). An ancient city of central Italy northwest of Rome. Head of the Etruscan League, it was defeated by Roman forces in the fourth century B.C. and lost its independence in the third century. The modern village of Tarquinia has a museum displaying notable Etruscan antiquities.

Tar·ra·go·na (tăr′ə-gō′nə, tä′rä-gô′nä). A city of northeast Spain on the Mediterranean Sea west-southwest of Barcelona. A leading town of Roman Spain after the third century B.C., it fell to the Moors in A.D. 714. ⊛ Pop. 110,837.

Tar·ra·sa (tə-rä′sə, tä-rä′sä). A city of northeast Spain north-northwest of Barcelona. It was

founded in Roman times, and is an industrial center noted for its textiles. ⊛ Pop. 158,063.

Tar River (tär). A river, about 346 km (215 mi) long, of northeast North Carolina flowing southeast to an estuary of Pamlico Sound.

Tar·ry·town (tăr′ē-toun′). A village of southeast New York on the Hudson River north of New York City. Founded by the Dutch in the 17th century, it was the home of the writer Washington Irving (1783–1859) and the setting for many of his short stories. ⊛ Pop. 10,739.

Tar·sus (tär′səs). A city of southern Turkey near the Mediterranean Sea west of Adana. Settled in the Neolithic Period, it was one of the most important cities of Asia Minor under Roman rule (after 67 B.C.). Saint Paul (A.D. 5?–67?) was born in Tarsus. ⊛ Pop. 225,000.

Tar·tar (tär′tər). **1.** also **Ta·tar** (tä′tər). A member of any of the Turkic and Mongolian peoples of central Asia who invaded western Asia and eastern Europe in the Middle Ages. **2.** Variant of **Tatar** (senses 1, 2).

Tar·ta·ry (tär′tə-rē) or **Ta·ta·ry** (tä′-). A vast region of eastern Europe and northern Asia controlled by the Mongols in the 13th and 14th centuries. It extended as far east as the Pacific Ocean under the rule of Genghis Khan.

Tar·tu (tär′tōō). A city of southeast Estonia southeast of Tallinn. Founded in 1030, it was a member of the Hanseatic League and became part of Russia in 1704. ⊛ Pop. 107,303.

Tash·kent (täsh-kĕnt′, täsh-). The capital and largest city of Uzbekistan in the foothills of the Tien Shan. One of the oldest cities of central Asia, it was ruled by Arabs and then Turks until 1865, when it was annexed by Russia. In 1930 it replaced Samarkand as the capital of the Uzbek Soviet Socialist Republic. ⊛ Pop. 2,094,000.

Tas·ma·ni·a (tăz-mā′nē-ə, -mān′yə). Formerly **Van Die·men's Land** (văn dē′mənz, vän). *abbr.* **Tas.** An island of southeast Australia separated from the mainland by Bass Strait. It was discovered by the Dutch explorer Abel Tasman in 1642 and renamed in his honor in 1853. Tasmania joined Australia in 1901. **—Tas·ma′ni·an** *adj. & n.*

Tas·man Sea (tăz′mən). An arm of the southern Pacific Ocean between southwest Australia and western New Zealand.

Ta·ta·bán·ya (tŏ′tŏ-bän′yə). A city of northwest Hungary west of Budapest. It is an industrial center. ⊛ Pop. 76,823.

Ta·tar (tä′tər). **1.** also **Tar·tar** (tär′tər). A member of a group of Turkic peoples inhabiting Russia and parts of central Asia. **2.** also **Tartar.** Any of the Turkic languages of the Tatars. **3.** Variant of **Tartar** (sense 1).

Ta·tar·stan (tä′tər-stän′, -stän′). Formerly **Tatar Autonomous Soviet Socialist Republic.** An autonomous republic of west-central Russia. The site of a powerful state after the 8th century, the region was conquered by Mongols in the 13th century and by Moscow in 1552. The Tatar A.S.S.R. was established in 1920, and in 1991 it declared its independence. Along with Chechnya, the republic was not a signatory to the 1992 treaty that created the Russian Federation but did join later in 1994.

Tatar Strait. A channel of southeast Russia between Sakhalin Island and the mainland. It connects the Sea of Japan on the south with the Sea of Okhotsk on the north.

Ta·ta·ry (tä′tə-rē). See **Tartary.**

Ta·tra Mountains (tä′trə). A range of the Carpathian Mountains in east-central Europe along the Slovakia-Poland border. The Tatras are a popular resort area.

Ta·tung (tä′tŏong′). See **Datong.**

Tau·ba·té (tou′bä-tĕ′). A city of southeast Brazil northeast of São Paulo. Founded in 1645, it is a commercial center with an important textile industry. ⊛ Pop. 206,416.

Taun·ton (tôn′tən, tŏn′-). A city of southeast Massachusetts on the **Taunton River** north of Fall River. Settled in the 1630's, it is a manufacturing center. ⊛ Pop. 49,832.

Tau·nus Mountains (tou′nəs, -nŏŏs′). A range of western Germany extending northeast from the Rhine River. The range includes notable vineyards and popular resort areas.

Tau·rus Mountains (tôr′əs). A range of southern Turkey extending about 563 km (350 mi) parallel to the Mediterranean coast. It rises to 3,736.6 m (12,251 ft) and has important mineral deposits.

Tau·sug (tô′sŏog′). An Austronesian language spoken in the Sulu Archipelago.

Tax·co (täs′kō). A town of southern Mexico south-southwest of Mexico City. An important mining town founded in 1529, it is a popular resort center. ⊛ Pop. 36,315.

Tay (tā). A river of central Scotland rising in the Grampian Mountains and flowing about 190 km (118 mi) through **Loch Tay** to the **Firth of Tay,** an inlet of the North Sea.

Tay·lor (tā′lər). A city of southeast Michigan, a suburb of Detroit. ⊛ Pop. 70,811.

Tay·lors·ville (tā′lərz-vĭl′). A community of north-central Utah, a suburb of Salt Lake City. ⊛ Pop. 52,351.

Tay·myr Peninsula (tī-mîr′). See **Taimyr Peninsula.**

Tbi·li·si (tə-bə-lē′sē, -byĭ-lē′syĭ) also **Tif·lis** (tĭf′lĭs, tyə-flēs′). The capital and largest city of Georgia, in the southeast part of the country on the Kura River. An ancient city astride trade and migration routes between Europe and Asia Minor,

it was the capital of an independent Georgian state from 1096 to 1225 and was held by Mongols, Iranians, and Turks before coming under Russian control in 1801. Tbilisi was a center of revolutionary activity in 1905 and was the capital of independent Georgia (1918–1920), the Transcaucasian Soviet Federated Socialist Republic (1922–1936), and the Georgian Soviet Socialist Republic (1936–1991). ⊛ Pop. 1,268,000.

Tea·neck (tē′nĕk′). A township of northeast New Jersey east-southeast of Paterson. It is mainly residential. ⊛ Pop. 37,825.

Tea·pot Dome (tē′pŏt′). A former U.S. Navy oil reserve in east-central Wyoming north of Casper. Secretly leased to Harry F. Sinclair's oil company by Secretary of the Interior Albert B. Fall in 1921, it became a symbol of the governmental scandals of the Harding administration.

tec·ton·ic (tĕk-tŏn′ĭk). *Geology.* Relating to, causing, or resulting from structural deformation of the earth's crust.

tec·ton·ics (tĕk-tŏn′ĭks). The study of the earth's structural features.

Tees (tēz). A river, about 113 km (70 mi) long, of northeast England flowing generally east to the North Sea.

Te·gu·ci·gal·pa (tĕ-gōō′sē-gäl′pə, -gäl′pä). The capital and largest city of Honduras, in the south-central part of the country. Founded in the late 16th century as a mining center, it became capital of the country in 1880. ⊛ Pop. 597,512.

Te·hach·a·pi Mountains (tə-hăch′ə-pē). A range of southern California extending from east to west between the Sierra Nevada and the Coast Ranges north of Los Angeles.

Teh·ran or **Te·he·ran** (tĕ′ə-răn′, -rän′, tĕ-răn′, -rän′). The capital and largest city of Iran, in the north-central part of the country south of the Caspian Sea. A commercial and industrial center, it became capital of Persia (Iran) in 1788 and was modernized under Shah Muhammed Reza Pahlavi (ruled 1941–1979). In November 1979 revolutionary militants invaded the U.S. embassy here and held staff members as hostages until January 1981. ⊛ Pop. 6,750,043.

Te·huan·te·pec (tə-wän′tə-pĕk′, tĕ-wän′tĕ-), **Isthmus of.** An isthmus of southern Mexico between the Bay of Campeche and the **Gulf of Tehuantepec,** a wide inlet of the Pacific Ocean.

Te·huel·che (tə-wĕl′chē, tä-wĕl′chä). **1.** *pl.* **Tehuelche** or **-ches.** A member of a South American Indian people of Patagonia, virtually exterminated by the European settlers. **2.** The language of the Tehuelche. —**Te·huel′che·an** (-chē-ən) *adj.*

Tel A·viv–Jaf·fa (tĕl′ ə-vēv′-jäf′ə, -yäf′ə, ä-vēv′-). A city of west-central Israel on the Mediterranean Sea west-northwest of Jerusalem. Tel Aviv was founded in 1909 by settlers from the ancient city of Jaffa. The communities merged in 1950, forming what is now the largest city in Israel. ⊛ Pop. 357,100.

Tel·e·gu (tĕl′ə-gōō′). Variant of **Telugu.**

Tel·e·scope Peak (tĕl′ĭ-skōp′). A mountain, 3,370 m (11,049 ft) high, in the Panamint Range of the Sierra Nevada in southeast California near the Nevada border. It is the highest elevation in the range.

Te·les Pi·res (tĕl′ĭs pîr′ĭs). A river, about 965 km (600 mi) long, of central Brazil flowing northwest as a tributary of the Tapajós River.

Tel·u·gu also **Tel·e·gu** (tĕl′ə-gōō′). **1.** A Dravidian language spoken in central India. **2.** *pl.* **Telugu** or **-gus** also **Telegu** or **-gus.** A member of the Dravidian people who speak Telugu. **3.** Of or relating to Telugu or its speakers.

Te·mir·tau (tā′mîr-tou′, tyĭ-mĭr-tä′ōō). A city of central Kazakstan northwest of Karaganda. It is a center for heavy industry. ⊛ Pop. 213,000.

Tem·ne (tĕm′nē). **1.** *pl.* **Temne** or **-nes.** A member of a people living in Sierra Leone. **2.** The West Atlantic language of this people.

Tem·pe (tĕm′pē′). A city of south-central Arizona east of Phoenix. It is a resort and the seat of Arizona State University (established 1885). ⊛ Pop. 141,865.

Tempe, Vale of. A valley of northeast Greece between Mount Olympus and Mount Ossa. Strategically important in ancient times, it is noted for its rugged scenery.

Tem·per·ate Zone (tĕm′pər-ĭt, tĕm′prĭt). Either of two intermediate latitude zones of the earth, the **North Temperate Zone,** between the Arctic Circle and the Tropic of Cancer, or the **South Temperate Zone,** between the Antarctic Circle and the Tropic of Capricorn.

Tem·ple (tĕm′pəl). A city of central Texas south of Fort Worth. It is a processing and manufacturing center. ⊛ Pop. 46,109.

Temple City. A city of southern California, a suburb of Los Angeles. ⊛ Pop. 31,100.

Te·mu·co (tě-mōō′kō). A city of central Chile south-southwest of Concepción. Founded in 1881, it is a trade center. ⊛ Pop. 211,693.

Ten·er·ife (tĕn′ə-rĭf′, -rēf′, tĕ′nĕ-rē′fĕ). An island in the Canary Islands of Spain in the Atlantic Ocean. It is the largest island in the group.

Ten·nes·see (tĕn′ĭ-sē′, tĕn′ĭ-sē′). *abbr.* **TN, Tenn.** A state of the southeast United States. It was admitted as the 16th state in 1796. First visited by the Spanish in 1540, the region was explored by the American frontiersman Daniel Boone in 1769 and became part of the United States in 1783. The state of Franklin (1784–1788) formed the basis for the Territory of the United States South of the River Ohio (1790)

and the later state of Tennessee. Nashville is the capital and Memphis the largest city. ⊛ Pop. 4,896,641. — **Ten′nes·se′an** *adj. & n.*

Tennessee River. A river of the southeast United States rising in eastern Tennessee and flowing about 1,049 km (652 mi) through northern Alabama, western Tennessee, and western Kentucky to the Ohio River.

Te·noch·ti·tlán (tě-nôch′tē-tlän′). An ancient Aztec capital on the site of present-day Mexico City. Founded c. 1325, it was destroyed by the Spanish in 1521.

Te·nos (tē′nŏs′, -nôs′). See **Tínos.**

Ten·sas (tĕn′sô′). A river, about 402 km (250 mi) long, of northeast Louisiana flowing south to the Ouachita River.

Te·o·ti·hua·cán (tā′ə-tē′wä-kän′, tě′ô-). An ancient city of central Mexico northeast of present-day Mexico City. It flourished c. A.D. 300–900 and its ruins include the Pyramid of the Sun and the Temple of Quetzalcoatl.

Te·pic (tě-pēk′). A city of western Mexico northwest of Guadalajara. It is a commercial and transportation center. ⊛ Pop. 145,741.

Te·pli·ce (tĕp′lĭ-tsě). A city of northwest Czech Republic in the Erzgebirge near the German border. In the heart of a coal-mining region it is a health resort with mineral springs known since Roman times. ⊛ Pop. 53,928.

Te·quen·da·ma Falls (tā′kən-dä′mə, tě′kĕn-*th*ä′mä). A waterfall, 129.6 m (425 ft) high, in central Colombia south of Bogotá.

Ter·cei·ra (tər-sîr′ə, tĕr-sā′rə). A Portuguese island of the central Azores in the northern Atlantic Ocean.

Te·re·si·na (tĕr′ĭ-zē′nə). A city of northeast Brazil on the Parnaíba River east-southeast of Belém. Founded in 1852, it is a trade and distribution center. ⊛ Pop. 598,411.

Ter·na·te (tər-nä′tā, tĕr-nä′tĕ). An island of eastern Indonesia in the northern Moluccas east of northeast Celebes. Settled by the Portuguese (1521–1574), it was subjugated by the Dutch in 1683.

Ter·ni (tĕr′nē). A city of central Italy north of Rome. It was part of the Papal States in the 14th century. ⊛ Pop. 107,333.

Ter·no·pol (tĕr-nō′pəl, tĭr-nô′-). A city of western Ukraine west-southwest of Kiev. It was founded in 1540, passed to Austria in 1772, and was later held by Poland (until 1939). ⊛ Pop. 224,900.

ter·ra in·cog·ni·ta (tĕr′ə ĭn′kŏg-nē′tə, -kŏg′-nĭ-tə). An unknown land; an unexplored region.

Ter·re Haute (tĕr′ə hōt′, hŭt′, hôt′). A city of western Indiana on the Wabash River west-southwest of Indianapolis. Founded as Fort Harrison in 1811, it is a commercial and industrial center and the seat of Indiana State University (established 1865). ⊛ Pop. 57,483.

ter·ri·to·ry (tĕr′ĭ-tôr′ē, -tōr′ē). *pl.* **-ries.** *abbr.* **ter., terr., t., T.** **1.** An area of land; a region. **2.** The land and waters under the jurisdiction of a government. **3. a.** A political subdivision of a country. **b.** A geographic region, such as a colonial possession, that is dependent on an external government. **4.** often **Territory. a.** A subdivision of the United States that is not a state and is administered by an appointed or elected governor and elected legislature. **b.** A similar political subdivision of Canada or Australia.

Te·ton (tē′tŏn′). *pl.* **Teton** or **-tons.** A member of the largest and westernmost of the Sioux peoples, made up of seven groups including the Oglala, Hunkpapa, Brulé, and Miniconjou. The Tetons became nomadic buffalo hunters after migrating westward in the 18th century and figured prominently in the resistance to white encroachment on the northern Great Plains. Also called *Lakota, Teton Dakota, Teton Sioux.*

Teton Range. A range of the Rocky Mountains in northwest Wyoming and southeast Idaho. The Tetons rise to 4,198.6 m (13,766 ft) at Grand Teton.

Teton River. A river, about 230 km (143 mi) long, of northwest-central Montana flowing eastward to the Missouri River.

Teton Sioux. See **Teton.**

Teu·to·bur·ger Wald (tōō′tə-bûr′gər wôld′, toi′tō-bōōr′gər vält′). A range of hills in northwest Germany between the upper Ems and the Weser rivers. A monument near Detmold commemorates the victory of the German hero Arminius over Roman legions in A.D. 9.

Teu·ton (tōōt′n, tyōōt′n). *abbr.* **Teut.** **1.** A member of an ancient people, probably of Germanic or Celtic origin, who lived in Jutland until about 100 B.C. **2.** A member of any of the Germanic peoples, especially a German.

Teu·ton·ic (tōō-tŏn′ĭk, tyōō-). *abbr.* **Teut.** **1.** Of or relating to the ancient Teutons. **2.** Of or relating to the Germanic languages or their speakers. **3.** Germanic.

Te·wa (tā′wə, tē′wə). **1.** *pl.* **Tewa** or **-was.** A member of a group of Pueblo peoples of northern New Mexico. **2.** The group of Tanoan languages spoken by the Tewa.

Tewkes·bur·y (tōōks′bĕr′ē, -bə-rē, -brē, tyōōks′-). A municipal borough of west-central England on the Severn River north-northeast of Gloucester. Edward IV's Yorkist forces defeated the Lancastrians here (1471) in the final battle of the Wars of the Roses. ⊛ Pop. 9,554.

Tewks·bur·y (tōōks′bĕr′ē, -bə-rē, tyōōks′-). A town of northeast Massachusetts south of Lowell. It is mainly residential. ⊛ Pop. 27,266.

Tex·ar·kan·a (tĕk′sär-kăn′ə). A city of southwest Arkansas on the Texas border southwest of Little Rock. ⊛ Pop. 22,631. It is adjacent to **Texarkana,** Texas, in the northeast part of that state. ⊛ Pop. 31,656. The twin cities form a trade and transportation center for the surrounding region.

Tex·as (tĕk′səs). *abbr.* **TX, Tex.** A state of the south-central United States. It was admitted as the 28th state in 1845. Explored by the Spanish in the 16th and 17th centuries, the region became a province of Mexico in the early 19th century. Texans won their independence in 1836 after a gallant but losing stand at the Alamo in February and a defeat of Santa Anna's forces at the Battle of San Jacinto (April 21). Denied admission as a state by antislavery forces in the U.S. Congress, the leaders of Texas formed an independent republic that lasted until 1845. Austin is the capital and Houston the largest city. ⊛ Pop. 17,059,805. — **Tex′an** *adj. & n.*

Texas City. A city of southeast Texas, an industrial suburb of Galveston on Galveston Bay. ⊛ Pop. 40,822.

Tex·el (tĕk′səl, tĕs′əl). An island of northwest Netherlands in the North Sea in the southwest Frisian Islands. It is the largest of the West Frisian Islands and a popular resort area.

Thai (tī). **1.** *pl.* **Thai** or **Thais. a.** A native or inhabitant of Thailand. **b.** A member of a Tai-speaking people who constitute the predominant ethnic group of Thailand. **2.** The language of the Tai family that is the official language of Thailand. **3.** Of or relating to Thailand or its peoples, languages, or cultures.

Thai·land (tī′lănd′, -lənd). Formerly **Si·am** (sī-ăm′). *abbr.* **Thai.** A country of southeast Asia on the **Gulf of Thailand** (formerly the Gulf of Siam), an arm of the South China Sea. Occupied since prehistoric times, the area was settled by Thai peoples moving southward from China after the 10th century. Various Thai kingdoms were founded from the 13th century on, frequently coming into conflict with neighboring Burmese and Cambodian powers. European influence began with Portuguese traders and missionaries in the early 16th century, but Siam managed to avoid European colonization even while relinquishing its claims in Cambodia and Laos to France in the 19th century. Siam remained an absolute monarchy until 1932, when the king was compelled to accept a constitution, and the country was renamed Thailand in 1939. Thailand was occupied by the Japanese in World War II. Most of its numerous postwar governments were controlled by the military, and the country became a strong supporter of the United States in the Vietnam War (1954–1975), allowing U.S. bombers to operate from its territory. Large numbers of refugees from Cambodia, Vietnam, and Laos fled to camps in Thailand in the late 1970's and early 1980's, creating economic and social problems for the rest of the decade. Bangkok is the capital and the largest city. ⊛ Pop. 59,396,000.

Thames (tĕmz). **1.** A river, about 257 km (160 mi) long, of southeast Ontario, Canada, flowing southwest to Lake St. Clair. In the War of 1812 Gen. William Henry Harrison defeated British and Native American forces in the Battle of the Thames (October 5, 1813). **2.** A river of southern England flowing about 338 km (210 mi) eastward to a wide estuary on the North Sea. Navigable for large ships as far as London, it is the principal commercial waterway of the country. In its upper course above Oxford it is often called Isis. **3.** A tidal estuary of southeastern Connecticut flowing about 24 km (15 mi) southward to Long Island Sound.

Tha·na (tä′nə). A city of west-central India, a suburb of Bombay. ⊛ Pop. 803,389.

Than·et (thăn′ĭt), **Isle of.** A peninsula of southeast England on the North Sea separated from the mainland by arms of the Stour River.

Thap·sus (thăp′səs). An ancient city of northern Africa on the Mediterranean Sea in present-day Tunisia. Julius Caesar defeated Pompey's forces here in 46 B.C.

Thar Desert (tär) also **Great In·di·an Desert** (grāt′ ĭn′dē-ən). A sandy region of northwest India and southeast Pakistan between the Indus and Sutlej river valleys.

Thá·sos (thā′sŏs′, thä′sôs). An island of northeast Greece in the northern Aegean Sea. It was colonized by Phoenicians and later ruled by Athens, Rome, Byzantium, and Turkey. The island was ceded to Greece in 1913.

Thebes (thēbz). **1.** An ancient city of Upper Egypt on the Nile River in present-day central Egypt. It flourished from the mid-22nd to the 18th century B.C. as a royal residence and a religious center for the worship of Amen, the god of life and reproduction. Its archaeological remains include many splendid temples and the tomb of Tutankhamen in the nearby Valley of the Kings. **2.** An ancient city of Boeotia in east-central Greece northwest of Athens. Originally a Mycenaen city, it reached the height of its power in the fourth century B.C. but was largely destroyed by Alexander in 336 B.C. — **The′-ban** (thē′bən) *adj. & n.*

The Dalles (*th*ə dălz′). See **The Dalles.**

The·lon (thē′lŏn′). A river, about 885 km (550 mi) long, of south-central Northwest Territories, Canada, east of Great Slave Lake.

Ther·mop·y·lae (thər-mŏp′ə-lē). A narrow pass of east-central Greece. It was the site of an unsuccessful Spartan stand against the Persians in 480 B.C.

Thes·sa·lo·ní·ki (thĕ′sä-lô-nē′kē) also **Thes·sa·lo·ni·ca** (-lô-nī′kə, -lŏn′ĭ-kə) or **Sa·lo·ni·ka** (sə-lŏn′ĭ-kə, săl′ə-nē′kə). A city of northeast Greece on an inlet of the Aegean Sea. Founded c. 315 B.C., it flourished after c. 146 as the capital of the Roman province of Macedon. Today it is a major port and the second-largest city in Greece. ⊛ Pop. 406,413.

Thes·sa·ly (thĕs′ə-lē). A region of east-central Greece between the Pindus Mountains and the Aegean Sea. Settled before 1000 B.C., it reached the height of its power in the sixth century B.C. but soon declined because of internal conflicts. — **Thes·sa′lian** (thĕ-sā′lē-ən, -săl′yən), **Thes′-sa·lo′ni·an** (-lō′nē-ən) *adj. & n.*

Thet·ford Mines (thĕt′fərd). A city of southern Quebec, Canada, south of Quebec City. It developed as a mining center after the discovery of extensive asbestos deposits in 1876. ⊛ Pop. 19,965.

Thi·bo·daux (tĭb′ə-dō′). A city of southeast Louisiana west-southwest of New Orleans. It is a commercial, industrial, and processing center. ⊛ Pop. 14,035.

Thim·phu (thĭm′pōō′, tĭm′-) also **Thim·bu** (-bōō′). The capital of Bhutan, in the western part of the country in the eastern Himalaya Mountains. ⊛ Pop. 30,340.

Thí·ra (thîr′ə, thē′rä). Formerly **San·to·rin** (săn′tə-rēn′). An island of southeast Greece in the southern Cyclades Islands north of Crete. The volcanic island has remains of important Minoan settlements.

Third World also **third world** (thûrd). The underdeveloped or developing countries of Africa, Asia, and Latin America, especially those that were not allied with either the Communist or non-Communist bloc during the cold war.

Thir·teen Colonies (thûr'tēn'). The thirteen British colonies in North America that joined together to form the original states of the United States, including New Hampshire, Massachusetts, Rhode Island, Connecticut, New York, New Jersey, Pennsylvania, Delaware, Maryland, Virginia, North Carolina, South Carolina, and Georgia.

Thom·as·ville (tŏm'əs-vĭl'). A city of southern Georgia south-southwest of Moultrie. It is a farm trade center and winter resort. ⊛ Pop. 17,457.

Thomp·son River (tŏmp'sən, tŏm'-). A river, about 489 km (304 mi) long, of southern British Columbia, Canada, formed by the confluence of northern and southern branches and flowing west and southwest to the Fraser River. It was discovered by Simon Fraser, an American-born Canadian explorer, in 1808.

Thorn·ton (thôrn'tən). A city of north-central Colorado, a suburb of Denver. ⊛ Pop. 55,031.

Tho·rold (thôr'əld, thŏr'-). A city of southeast Ontario, Canada, on the Welland Ship Canal southeast of St. Catharines. It is an industrial center. ⊛ Pop. 15,412.

Thou·sand Islands (thou'zənd). A group of more than 1,800 islands of northern New York and southeast Ontario, Canada, in the St. Lawrence River at the outlet of Lake Ontario. The islands, some of which are privately owned, are a popular resort area.

Thousand Oaks. A city of southern California west of Los Angeles. Mainly residential, it has some light industry. ⊛ Pop. 104,352.

Thrace (thrās). A region and ancient country of the southeast Balkan Peninsula north of the Aegean Sea. In ancient times it extended as far north as the Danube River. The region was colonized by Greeks in the seventh century B.C. and later passed under the control of Rome, Byzantium, and Ottoman Turkey. Northern Thrace was annexed by Bulgaria in 1885, and eastern Thrace passed to Turkey in 1923.

Thra·cian (thrā'shən). **1.** Of or relating to Thrace or its people. **2.** A native or inhabitant of Thrace. **3.** The Indo-European language of the ancient Thracians.

Three Mile Island (thrē). An island in the Susquehanna River in southeast Pennsylvania southeast of Harrisburg. It was the site of a major nuclear accident on March 28, 1979, when a partial meltdown released radioactive material and forced the evacuation of thousands of nearby residents.

Thu·le¹ (thoo'lē). The most northerly region of the habitable world to ancient Greek geographers. Posited as an island north of Britain, it has been variously identified with Iceland, Norway, and the Shetland Islands.

Thu·le² (too'lē). A town of northwest Greenland northwest of Cape York. A U.S. naval base was built here during World War II. ⊛ Pop. 449.

Thun (toon), **Lake of.** A lake of central Switzerland southeast of Bern in the foothills of the Bernese Alps.

Thun·der Bay (thŭn'dər). A city of southwest Ontario, Canada, on **Thunder Bay,** an inlet on the northwest shore of Lake Superior. A major port and industrial center, it was created in 1970 by the amalgamation of the twin cities of Port Arthur and Fort William. ⊛ Pop. 129,775.

Thu·rin·gi·a (thoo-rĭn'jē-ə, -jə). A historical region of central Germany south of the Harz Mountains and crossed by the **Thuringian Forest,** a range of low, wooded mountains. The region fell to the Franks in the 6th century A.D. and became a principality of the Holy Roman Empire in the 11th century.

Thu·rin·gi·an (thoo-rĭn'jē-ən, -jən). **1.** Of or relating to Thuringia or its people or culture. **2.** A member of an ancient tribe inhabiting central Germany until the sixth century A.D. **3.** A native or inhabitant of Thuringia.

Thur·rock (thûr'ək, thŭr'-). An urban district of southeast England on the Thames River east of London. It is a port and an industrial center. ⊛ Pop. 131,226.

Thurs·day Island (thûrz'dē, -dā'). An island of northeast Australia in Torres Strait northwest of Cape York. It is noted for its pearl fishing beds.

Thurs·ton Island (thûr'stən). An island off Antarctica between the Bellingshausen and Amundsen seas. Before 1961 it was thought to be a peninsula of the mainland.

Ti·a·hua·na·co (tē'ə-wə-nä'kō). A site of pre-Incan ruins in western Bolivia near the southern end of Lake Titicaca. The ruins, including statues, monoliths, and a temple of the sun, are evidence of a civilization that flourished here from c. 1000 to 1300.

Tian·an·men Square (tyän'än'mĕn'). An extensive open area in central Beijing, China, adjacent to the Forbidden City. It has long been the site of festivals, government rallies, parades, and demonstrations, particularly in 1989, when student demonstrations were crushed by military force.

Tian·jin (tyän'jĭn') also **Tien·tsin** (tyĕn'tsĭn'). A city of northeast China near the Bo Hai southeast of Beijing. It developed rapidly after becoming a treaty port in 1860 but was badly damaged (1900) during the Boxer Rebellion. Today it is a major industrial center. ⊛ Pop. 5,804,023.

Tian Shan (tyän′ shän′). See **Tien Shan.**

Ti·ber (tī′bər). A river of central Italy flowing about 406 km (252 mi) south and southwest through Rome to the Tyrrhenian Sea at Ostia.

Ti·be·ri·as (tī-bîr′ē-əs), Lake. See Sea of **Galilee.**

Ti·bet (tə-bĕt′). **1.** A historical region of central Asia between the Himalaya and Kunlun mountains. A center of Lamaist Buddhism, Tibet first flourished as an independent kingdom in the seventh century. It fell under Mongol influence from the 13th to the 18th century and later came under Chinese control (1720). Tibet regained its independence in 1911 but was invaded by the Chinese in 1950 and made an autonomous region of China in 1951. **2.** See **Xizang.**

Ti·bet·an (tĭ-bĕt′n). **1.** Of or relating to Tibet, the Tibetans, or their language or culture. **2. a.** A native or inhabitant of Tibet. **b.** A member of a Buddhist people constituting the predominant ethnic population of Tibet and neighboring regions in China, Bhutan, and Nepal, with large displaced populations in India.

Ti·bet·o-Bur·man (tĭ-bĕt′ō-bûr′mən). A branch of the Sino-Tibetan language family that includes Tibetan and Burmese.

Ti·bur (tī′bər). See **Tivoli.**

Ti·ci·no (tĭ-chē′nō). A river, about 248 km (154 mi) long, of southern Switzerland and northern Italy flowing generally southward to the Po River. The Carthaginian general Hannibal defeated the Romans along the banks of the river in 218 B.C.

Ti·con·der·o·ga (tī′kŏn-də-rō′gə). A resort village of northeast New York between Lake George and Lake Champlain. Fort Carillon, built by the French in 1755, was taken in 1759 by the British, who renamed it Fort Ticonderoga. American Revolutionary troops captured the fort in May 1775, but it was later abandoned without a struggle to British forces in July 1777 during the Saratoga Campaign.

tide·land (tīd′lănd′). Coastal land submerged during high tide.

tide·wa·ter (tīd′wô′tər, -wŏt′ər). Low coastal land drained by tidal streams.

Tien Shan (tyĕn′ shän′) also **Tian Shan** (tyän′). A mountain range of central Asia extending about 2,414 km (1,500 mi) east-northeast through western Kyrgyzstan, southwest Kazakstan, and northwest China. It rises to 7,443.8 m (24,406 ft) at Pobeda Peak.

Tien·tsin (tyĕn′tsĭn′). See **Tianjin.**

Ti·er·ra del Fue·go (tē-ĕr′ə dĕl fwä′gō, tyĕr′-rä thĕl fwĕ′gô). An archipelago off southern South America separated from the mainland by the Strait of Magellan. The main island, also called **Tierra del Fuego,** is divided between Chile and Argentina. Smaller islands of the archipelago are administered individually by the two countries. The Portuguese navigator Ferdinand Magellan first sighted Tierra del Fuego in 1520.

Tie·tê (tyə-tā′, tyĭ-tĕ′). A river, about 805 km (500 mi) long, of southeast Brazil flowing generally northwest to the Paraná River.

Tif·fin (tĭf′ĭn). A city of north-central Ohio south-southwest of Toledo. It is an industrial center. ⊛ Pop. 18,604.

Tif·lis (tĭf′lĭs, tyə-flēs′). See **Tbilisi.**

Ti·gre (tē′grä, -grĕ). A city of eastern Argentina, a suburb of Buenos Aires in a fruit-growing area. ⊛ Pop. 199,366.

Ti·gré (tē-grā′). A Semitic language of Eritrea.

Ti·gri·nya (tə-grēn′yə). A Semitic language of northern Ethiopia.

Ti·gris (tī′grĭs). A river of southwest Asia rising in eastern Turkey and flowing about 1,850 km (1,150 mi) generally southeast through Iraq to the Euphrates River. It was a major transportation route in ancient times.

Ti·jua·na (tē′ə-wä′nə, tē-hwä′nä). A city of extreme northwest Mexico on the U.S. border south of San Diego. It is a popular tourist center. ⊛ Pop. 429,500.

Ti·kal (tē-käl′). A ruined Mayan city of northern Guatemala. It was the largest of the Mayan cities and may also be the oldest. Excavation and restoration of the ruins began in 1956.

Til·burg (tĭl′bûrg′, -bœrкн′). A city of southern Netherlands near the Belgian border southeast of Rotterdam. It has a major textile industry. ⊛ Pop. 162,891.

Til·la·mook Bay (tĭl′ə-mŏŏk′). An inlet of the Pacific Ocean in northwest Oregon. The surrounding area is noted for its cheese.

tim·ber·line (tĭm′bər-līn′). **1.** The elevation in a mountainous region above which trees do not grow. **2.** The northern or southern latitude beyond which trees do not grow.

Tim·buk·tu (tĭm′bŭk-tŏŏ′, tĭm-bŭk′tŏŏ). A city of central Mali near the Niger River northeast of Bamako. Founded in the 11th century by the Tuareg, it became a major trading center (primarily for gold and salt) by the 14th century. Timbuktu was sacked by invaders from Morocco in 1593 and fell to the French in 1894. ⊛ Pop. 19,166.

Times Square (tīmz). An intersection in New York City formed by the juncture of Broadway, Seventh Avenue, and 42nd Street in midtown Manhattan. Long noted as a center of the city's entertainment district, it is the site of annual New Year's Eve celebrations.

time zone (tīm). Any of the 24 longitudinal divisions of Earth's surface in which a standard time is kept, the primary division being that bisected by the Greenwich meridian. Each zone is 15° of longitude in width, with local variations, and observes a clock time one hour earlier than the zone immediately to the east.

Tim·gad (tĭm′găd′). An ancient Roman city in northeast Algeria. Founded by the emperor Trajan in A.D. 100, it is sometimes called "the Pompeii of North Africa" because of its extensive, well-preserved ruins.

Ti·mi·şoa·ra (tē′mē-shwär′ə). A city of western Romania near the Yugoslavian border west-northwest of Bucharest. First mentioned in 1247, it is a railroad hub and an industrial center. ◉ Pop. 325,359.

Tim·mins (tĭm′ĭnz). A city of central Ontario, Canada, northeast of Sault Sainte Marie. It is a gold-mining center. ◉ Pop. 46,114.

Ti·mor (tē′môr, tē-môr′). An island of southeast Indonesia, the easternmost of the Lesser Sundas. The western half of the island, formerly Netherlands Timor, became part of Indonesia in 1949. The eastern half was an overseas province of Portugal from 1914 until 1975, when it declared its independence as East Timor. Indonesia invaded East Timor the same year and forcibly annexed it in 1976, resulting in tens of thousands of deaths from famine, disease, and fighting.

Timor Sea. An arm of the Indian Ocean between Timor and Australia.

Tim·pa·no·gos (tĭm′pə-nō′gəs), **Mount.** The highest of the Wasatch Mountains in north-central Utah, rising to 3,662 m (12,008 ft).

Tim·u·cu·a (tĭm′ə-kōō′ə). **1.** *pl.* Timicua or -cu·as. A member of a Native American people formerly inhabiting much of northern Florida, extinct since the early 18th century. **2.** The extinct language of the Timucuas.

Ti·ni·an (tĭn′ē-ăn′, tē′nē-än′). An island of the Northern Marianas in the western Pacific Ocean. The planes that dropped atomic bombs on Hiroshima (August 6, 1945) and Nagasaki (August 9, 1945) were flown from Tinian.

Tin·ley Park (tĭn′lē). A city of northeast Illinois, a suburb of Chicago. ◉ Pop. 37,121.

Tí·nos (tē′nôs′) also **Te·nos** (tē′nŏs′, -nôs′). An island of southeast Greece in the Cyclades Islands east-southeast of Athens. It is a major producer of wine.

Tin·tag·el Head (tĭn-tăj′əl). A promontory in southwest England northeast of Plymouth. The site of the ruins of a 12th century castle, it is said to be the birthplace of King Arthur.

Tip·pe·ca·noe (tĭp′ē-kə-nōō′). A river, about 274 km (170 mi) long, rising in northeast Indiana and flowing generally southwest to the Wabash River. Gen. William Henry Harrison defeated the Shawnee in the Battle of Tippecanoe (1811).

Tip·per·ar·y (tĭp′ə-rär′ē). A town of south-central Ireland southwest of Dublin. The song "It's a Long Way to Tipperary" was used as marching music by the British Expeditionary Force in World War I. ◉ Pop. 4,984.

Ti·ran (tə-rän′). A strait off the southern tip of the Sinai Peninsula in northeast Egypt connecting the Red Sea with the Gulf of Aqaba.

Ti·ra·në also **Ti·ra·na** (tə-rä′nə, tē-). The capital and largest city of Albania, in the west-central part of the country. Founded in the early 17th century by the Turks, it became the capital of Albania in 1920. The city was held by Italy from 1939 to 1943 and was the scene in the early 1990's of strikes and demonstrations which forced the Communist government to resign. ◉ Pop. 244,153.

Ti·ras·pol (tə-räs′pəl). A city of southwest Moldova on the Dniester River east of Kishinev. Founded c. 1792 as a Russian fortress on the site of a Moldavian settlement, it is an agricultural processing center. ◉ Pop. 186,200.

Tîr·gu-Mu·reş (tîr′gōō-mōōr′ĕsh). A city of north-central Romania east-southeast of Cluj-Napoca. It was ceded to Romania by Hungary in 1918. ◉ Pop. 165,502.

Ti·rich Mir (tîr′ĭch mîr′). A mountain, 7,695.2 m (25,230 ft) high, of the Hindu Kush in northern Pakistan. It is the highest elevation in the range.

Ti·rol (tə-rōl′, tī-, tī′rōl′). See **Tyrol.**

Ti·ruch·chi·rap·pal·li (tîr′ə-chə-rä′pə-lē). A city of southeast India south-southwest of the Madras River. It is the site of a famous shrine to the Hindu god Shiva. ◉ Pop. 387,223.

Tir·yns (tîr′ĭnz, tī′rĭnz). An ancient city of southern Greece in the eastern Peloponnesus. It contains the ruins of pre-Homeric palaces as well as prehistoric structures.

Ti·sza (tĭs′ô) also **Ti·sa** (tē′sə). A river of central Europe rising in the Carpathian Mountains in western Ukraine and flowing about 965 km (600 mi) southward across eastern Hungary and northern Yugoslavia to the Danube River.

Ti·ti·ca·ca (tĭt′ĭ-kä′kə, tē′tē-kä′kä), **Lake.** A freshwater lake of South America in the Andes on the Bolivia-Peru border.

Ti·to·grad (tē′tō-grăd′, -gräd′). See **Podgorica.**

Ti·tus·ville (tī′təs-vĭl′). **1.** A city of eastern Florida east of Orlando. Incorporated in 1886, it is a commercial and residential center. ◉ Pop. 39,394. **2.** A city of northwest Pennsylvania north-northeast of Pittsburgh. The first oil well in the United States was drilled here in April 1859. ◉ Pop. 6,434.

Ti·vo·li (tĭv′ə-lē, tē′vô-lē) also **Ti·bur** (tī′bər). A city of central Italy east-northeast of Rome. Tivoli contains the ruins of several ancient Roman villas and is also noted for its waterfalls. ◈ Pop. 50,969.

Ti·wa (tē′wə). **1.** *pl.* **Tiwa** or **-was.** A member of a group of Pueblo peoples of northern New Mexico. **2.** The group of Tanoan languages spoken by the Tiwa.

Tlal·ne·pan·tla (tläl′nə-pänt′lä, -nĕ-). A city of south-central Mexico north of Mexico City. It is a communications and industrial center. ◈ Pop. 778,173.

Tla·que·pa·que (tlä′kĕ-pä′kĕ). A city of west-central Mexico southeast of Guadalajara. Tlaquepaque is noted for its folklore and crafts. ◈ Pop. 133,500.

Tlin·git (tlĭng′gĭt, tlĭng′ĭt). **1.** *pl.* **Tlingit** or **-gits.** A member of a Native American people inhabiting the coastal and island areas of southeast Alaska. **2.** The language of the Tlingits.

To·ba·go (tə-bā′gō). An island of Trinidad and Tobago in the southeast West Indies northeast of Trinidad. Inhabited by Caribs when Columbus discovered it in 1498, the island was captured by the French in 1781 and ceded to the British in 1892. Tobago was united with Trinidad to form the colony of Trinidad and Tobago in 1898.

To·bol (tə-bôl′). A river of north-central Kazakstan and west-central Russia rising in the southeast foothills of the Ural Mountains and flowing about 1,690 km (1,050 mi) northeastward to the Irtysh River.

To·can·tins (tō′kän-tēns′). A river, about 2,639 km (1,640 mi) long, flowing from central Brazil near Brasília northward to the Pará River southwest of Belém.

To·char·i·an also **To·khar·i·an** (tō-kâr′ē-ən, -kär′-, -kär′-). **1.** A member of a people of possible European origin, living in Chinese Turkistan until about the tenth century. **2.** The language of this people, recorded in two dialects dating from the seventh century and forming its own branch within Indo-European.

toft (tôft, tŏft). *Chiefly British.* A hillock.

To·gliat·ti also **Tol·yat·ti** (tōl-yä′tē, tô-lyät′tē). A city of western Russia on the Volga River northwest of Samara. It is a manufacturing center. ◈ Pop. 682,256.

To·go (tō′gō′). A country of western Africa on the Gulf of Guinea. Situated between the Dahomey and Ashanti kingdoms, the region was held by Denmark in the 18th century and became the German protectorate of Togoland in 1884. The territory forming the present-day country was administered as French Togoland from 1922 to 1960, when it achieved independence as the republic of Togo. It has been ruled as a one-party state during most of its post-

independence history. Lomé is the capital and the largest city. ◈ Pop. 3,928,000. —**To′go·lese′** *adj. & n.*

To·go·land (tō′gō-lănd′). A historical region of western Africa including modern Togo and parts of Ghana. A German protectorate after 1884, the area was divided between Britain and France under a League of Nations mandate (1922), later administered as separate UN trust territories. British Togoland became part of independent Ghana in 1957, with French Togoland gaining independence as Togo in 1960.

To·ho·no O′o·dham (tə-hō′nō ō′ə-däm). *pl.* **Tohono O′odham** or **-dhams.** See **Papago.**

To·ka·ra Islands (tō-kär′ə, -kä′rä). A group of islands of Japan in the northern Ryukyu group south of Kyushu.

To·ke·lau Islands (tō′kə-lou′). An island group of the central Pacific Ocean in the northern Ryukyu Islands north of Samoa. They became part of New Zealand in 1948.

To·khar·i·an (tō-kâr′ē-ən, -kär′-, -kär′-). Variant of **Tocharian.**

To·ko·ro·za·wa (tō′kō-rō′zä-wä). A city of central Honshu, Japan, a commercial suburb of Tokyo. ◈ Pop. 315,517.

Tok Pis·in (tŏk′ pĭs′ĭn). A pidgin based on English and spoken in Papua New Guinea.

To·ku·shi·ma (tō′kə-shē′mä). A city of eastern Shikoku, Japan, on the Inland Sea. It is a major port and manufacturing center. ◈ Pop. 265,243.

To·ky·o (tō′kē-ō′, -kyō). Formerly **E·do** (ĕd′ō). The capital and largest city of Japan, in east-central Honshu on **Tokyo Bay,** an inlet of the Pacific Ocean. Founded in the 12th century as Edo, Tokyo became the imperial capital in 1868. Much of the city was destroyed by an earthquake in 1923 and by bombing raids during World War II. ⊛ Pop. 8,080,286.

Tol·bu·khin (tôl-bōō′kĭn, -кнĭn). A city of northeast Bulgaria north of Varna. It is a commercial and cultural center. ⊛ Pop. 105,000.

To·le·do (tə-lē′dō). **1.** A city of central Spain near the Tagus River south-southwest of Madrid. It fell to the Romans in 193 B.C. and was later the capital of the Visigoth kingdom (534–712). As a Moorish capital (712–1031) it was a center of Arab and Hebrew learning. ⊛ Pop. 57,778. **2.** A city of northwest Ohio on Lake Erie. Incorporated in 1837, it has oil and natural gas reserves and is a major shipping center. ⊛ Pop. 332,943.

Tol·tec (tŏl′tĕk′, tŏl′-). **1.** *pl.* **Toltec** or **-tecs.** A member of a Nahuatl-speaking people of central and southern Mexico whose empire flourished from the 10th century until it collapsed under invasion by the Aztecs in the 12th century. **2.** also **Tol·tec·an** (-tĕk′ən, tŏl-). Of or relating to the Toltec or their culture.

To·lu·ca (tə-lōō′kə, tô-lōō′kä). A city of south-central Mexico west of Mexico City. Established as a settlement by the Spanish conquistador Hernando Cortés in 1530, it is a commercial center. ⊛ Pop. 487,612.

Tol·yat·ti (tōl-yä′tē, tô-lyät′tē). See **Togliatti.**

To·ma·szów Ma·zo·wiec·ki (tô-mä′shōōf mä′-zô-vyĕt′skē). A city of east-central Poland southeast of Lódź. It is a manufacturing center. ⊛ Pop. 66,100.

Tom·big·bee (tŏm-bĭg′bē). A river, about 644 km (400 mi) long, rising in northeast Mississippi and flowing generally southward through western Alabama to join the Alabama River and form the Mobile River.

Tomb·stone (tōōm′stōn′). A city of southeast Arizona southeast of Tucson. After silver was discovered here in 1877, Tombstone became one of the richest and most lawless frontier mining towns. ⊛ Pop. 1,220.

Tomsk (tŏmsk, tômsk). A city of central Russia northeast of Novosibirsk. It is a major river port and an industrial center. ⊛ Pop. 497,662.

Ton·a·wan·da (tŏn′ə-wŏn′də). A city of western New York, an industrial suburb of Buffalo. ⊛ Pop. 17,284.

Ton·ga (tŏng′gə) also **Friend·ly Islands** (frĕnd′-lē). A country in the southwest Pacific Ocean east of Fiji comprising about 150 islands, some 36 of which are inhabited. Long inhabited by Polynesians, the islands were first sighted by the Dutch in 1616 and visited by the British navigator Capt. James Cook in the late 1700's. The arrival of English missionaries in 1797 solidified Britain's political influence, and the islands became a British protectorate in 1900. British control was reduced in 1968, with Tonga gaining

complete independence as a constitutional monarchy in 1970. Efforts in the 1980's to make the government more democratic were blocked by the king. Nuku'alofa is the capital and the largest city. ⊛ Pop. 98,000.

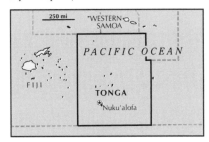

Ton·gan (tŏng′gən, tŏng′ən). **1.** Of or relating to Tonga or its people, language, or culture. **2.** A native or inhabitant of Tonga. **3.** The Polynesian language of Tonga.

Tongue River (tŭng). A river, about 396 km (246 mi) long, rising in northern Wyoming and flowing generally northeast to the Yellowstone River in southeast Montana.

Ton·kin (tŏn′kĭn′, tŏng′-). A historical region of southeast Asia on the **Gulf of Tonkin,** an arm of the South China Sea, now forming most of northern Vietnam. Tonkin was part of French Indochina from 1887 to 1946. **— Ton′kin·ese′** (-ēz′, -ēs′) *adj. & n.*

Ton·le Sap (tŏn′lä săp′, säp′). A lake of central Cambodia, the largest lake in southeast Asia.

To·pe·ka (tə-pē′kə). The capital of Kansas, in the northeast part of the state west of Kansas City. Founded in 1854, it became capital when Kansas was admitted to the Union in 1861. ⊛ Pop. 119,883.

to·pog·ra·phy (tə-pŏg′rə-fē). *abbr.* **topog. 1.** Graphic representation of the surface features of a place or region on a map, indicating their relative positions and elevations. **2.** The surface features of a place or region. **3.** The surveying of the features of a place or region. **— top′o·graph′** (tŏp′ə-grăf′) *n.* **— to·pog′ra·pher** *n.* **— top′o·graph′ic** (-grăf′ĭk), **top′o·graph′i·cal** (-ĭ-kəl) *adj.*

to·pol·o·gy (tə-pŏl′ə-jē). Topographic study of a given place, especially the history of a region as indicated by its topography. **— top′o·log′ic** (tŏp′ə-lŏj′ĭk), **top′o·log′i·cal** (-ĭ-kəl) *adj.* **— to·pol′o·gist** *n.*

top·o·nym (tŏp′ə-nĭm′). **1.** A place name. **2.** A name derived from a place or region. **— top′-o·nym′ic, top′o·nym′i·cal** *adj.*

tor (tôr). **1.** A high rock or pile of rocks on the top of a hill. **2.** A rocky peak or hill.

Tor·bay (tôr-bā′, tôr′bā′). A borough of southwest England east-northeast of Plymouth. It is in a resort area. ⊛ Pop. 121,113.

To·ri·no (tô-rē′nô). See **Turin.**

Tor·ne (tôr′nə) also **Tor·ni·o** (tôr′nē-ō′). A river of northern Sweden rising near the Norwegian border in **Lake Torne** and flowing about 402 km (250 mi) generally southeast to the Gulf of Bothnia. It forms the Swedish-Finnish border in its lower course.

To·ron·to (tə-rŏn′tō). The capital and largest city of Ontario, Canada, in the southern part of the province on Lake Ontario. Originally a French trading post, it was founded as York by the British in 1793 and renamed as Toronto in 1834. Toronto is an important Great Lakes port and an industrial center. ◉ Pop. 4,084,134.

Tor·rance (tôr′əns, tŏr′-). A city of southern California south of Los Angeles. Founded in 1911, it is a commercial, financial, and industrial center. ◉ Pop. 133,107.

Tor·re An·nun·zi·a·ta (tôr′ä ə-nōōn′sē-ä′tə, tôr′rĕ ä-nōōn′tsē-ä′tä). A city of southern Italy on the Bay of Naples. Founded in the 14th century, the city was destroyed by an eruption of Mount Vesuvius in 1631. It is now a port and seaside resort. ◉ Pop. 57,097.

Torre de Cer·re·do (də sə-rā′dō, *thĕ* sĕ-rĕ′-*thô*). A mountain, 2,649.8 m (8,688 ft) high, of the Cantabrian Mountains in northwest Spain. It is the highest elevation in the range.

Torre del Gre·co (dĕl grĕk′ō). A city of southern Italy on the Bay of Naples near Mount Vesuvius. It is a fishing port and tourist resort. ◉ Pop. 101,456.

Tor·rens (tôr′ənz, tŏr′-). A salt lake of south-central Australia north-northwest of Adelaide.

Tor·ren·te (tô-rĕn′tĕ). A city of eastern Spain southwest of Valencia. It is a truck-farming center. ◉ Pop. 55,028.

Tor·re·ón (tôr′ē-ōn′, -rĕ-ôn′). A city of northern Mexico west of Monterrey. Founded in 1893, it is a commercial and railcenter in an agricultural area. ◉ Pop. 328,086.

Tor·res Strait (tôr′ĭs). A strait between New Guinea and Cape York Peninsula of northeast Australia. It connects the Arafura Sea with the Coral Sea.

Tor·reys Peak (tôr′ēz, tŏr′-). A mountain, 4,351.4 m (14,267 ft) high, in the Front Range of the Rocky Mountains in central Colorado.

Tor·rid Zone (tôr′ĭd, tŏr′-). The central latitude zone of the earth, between the Tropic of Cancer and the Tropic of Capricorn.

Tor·ring·ton (tôr′ĭng-tən, tŏr′-). A city of northwest Connecticut west of Hartford. The process of milk homogenization was invented here. ◉ Pop. 33,687.

Tór·shavn (tôr′shouN′). The capital of the Faeroe Islands, on southeast Straymoy Island. It is a major port and shipping center. ◉ Pop. 14,671.

Tor·to·la (tôr-tō′lə). An island of the West Indies east of Puerto Rico. It is the largest of the British Virgin Islands.

Tor·tu·ga (tôr-tōō′gə). An island in the West Indies off northern Haiti. It was a pirate refuge in the 17th century.

To·ruń (tôr′ōōn′, -ōōn′yə). A city of north-central Poland on the Vistula River northwest of Warsaw. Founded by the Teutonic Knights in 1231, it became part of the kingdom of Poland in 1454. Toruń was taken by Sweden (1703) and Prussia (1793 and 1815) before being returned to Poland in 1919. ◉ Pop. 202,360.

Tou·lon (tōō-lôN′). A city of southeast France on the Mediterranean Sea east-southeast of Marseille. First mentioned in the third century A.D. as a Roman naval station, it became part of France in 1481. ◉ Pop. 167,788.

Tou·louse (tōō-lōōz′). A city of southern France on the Garonne River southeast of Bordeaux. Originally part of Roman Gaul, it was the capital of the Visigoths (419–507) and the Carolingian kingdom of Aquitaine (781–843). Toulouse was a cultural center of medieval Europe. ◉ Pop. 358,598.

Tou·raine (tōō-rān′, -rĕn′). A historical region and former province of west-central France. Taken by the English in 1152, it was recaptured by Philip II of France in 1204 and incorporated into the royal domain by Henry III.

Tou·rane (tōō-rän′). See **Da Nang.**

Tour·coing (tōōr-kwăN′). A city of northern France northeast of Lille near the Belgian border. It is an important textile center. ◉ Pop. 96,908.

Tours (tōōr). A city of west-central France on the Loire River. Dating to pre-Roman times, it was a prosperous silk-manufacturing town from the 15th century to the 17th century and a Huguenot stronghold until the revocation of the Edict of Nantes in 1685. Today it is a tourist center with varied industries. ◉ Pop. 129,506.

town (toun). **1.** *abbr.* **t., T., tn.** A population center, often incorporated, larger than a village and usually smaller than a city. **2.** A township. **3.** *Informal.* A city. **4.** *Chiefly British.* A rural village that has a market or fair periodically. **5.** The commercial district or center of an area.

town·ship (toun′shĭp′). *abbr.* **t., T., twp., tp. 1.** A subdivision of a county in most northeast and Midwest U.S. states, having the status of a unit of local government with varying governmental powers; a town. **2.** A public land surveying unit of 36 sections or 36 square miles. **3.** An ancient administrative division of a large parish in England. **4.** A racially segregated area in South Africa established under the apartheid system as a residence for people of color.

Tow·son (tou′sən). A city of northern Maryland, a residential and industrial suburb of Baltimore. ⊛ Pop. 49,445.

To·ya·ma (tō-yä′mä). A city of west-central Honshu, Japan, on **Toyama Bay,** an inlet of the Sea of Japan. Toyama is noted for its patent medicine industry. ⊛ Pop. 324,073.

To·yo·ha·shi (tô′yô-hä′shē). A city of south-central Honshu, Japan, southeast of Nagoya on the Pacific Ocean. It is a textile-manufacturing center. ⊛ Pop. 349,590.

To·yo·na·ka (tô′yô-nä′kä). A city of southern Honshu, Japan, a mainly residential suburb of Osaka. ⊛ Pop. 403,224.

To·yo·ta (toi-ō′tə, tô-yô′tä). A city of south-central Honshu, Japan, east-southeast of Nagoya. It is an industrial center. ⊛ Pop. 341,453.

Trab·zon (träb-zŏn′, träb-zôn′) or **Treb·i·zond** (trĕb′ĭ-zŏnd′). A city of northeast Turkey on the Black Sea. Founded by Greek colonists in the eighth century B.C., the city was part of the Roman, Byzantine, Trebizond, and Ottoman empires. ⊛ Pop. 145,400.

Tra·cy (trā′sē). A city of west-central California south-southwest of Stockton. It is a food-processing center. ⊛ Pop. 33,558.

trade language (trād). A language, especially a pidgin, used by speakers of different native languages for commercial trade.

trade wind. Any of a consistent system of prevailing winds occupying most of the tropics, constituting the major component of the general circulation of the atmosphere, and blowing northeasterly in the Northern Hemisphere and southeasterly in the Southern Hemisphere. Often used in the plural.

Tra·fal·gar (trə-făl′gər), **Cape.** A cape on the southwest coast of Spain northwest of the Strait of Gibraltar. The British navy under Adm. Horatio Nelson defeated the French and Spanish fleets off Cape Trafalgar in 1805.

Tra·lee (trə-lē′). An urban district of southwest Ireland at the head of **Tralee Bay,** an inlet of the Atlantic Ocean. Tralee is a seaport and manufacturing center. ⊛ Pop. 16,495.

tra·mon·tane (trə-mŏn′tān′, trăm′ən-tān′). **1.** Dwelling beyond or coming from the far side of the mountains, especially the Alps as viewed from Italy. **2.** A cold north wind in Italy.

Trans A·lai (trăns′ ə-lī′, trănz′). A range of the Pamir Mountains in eastern Tajikistan and southern Krygyzstan rising to 7,138.5 m (23,405 ft) at Lenin Peak.

trans·al·pine (trăns-ăl′pīn′, trănz-). Relating to, living on, or coming from the other side of the Alps, especially as viewed from Italy.

Trans·al·pine Gaul (trăns-ăl′pīn′, trănz-). The part of ancient Gaul northwest of the Alps, including modern France and Belgium.

trans·at·lan·tic (trăns′ət-lăn′tĭk, trănz′-). **1.** Situated on or coming from the other side of the Atlantic Ocean. **2.** Spanning the Atlantic.

Trans·cau·ca·sia (trăns′kô-kā′zhə, -zhē-ə, trănz′-). A region comprising present-day Georgia, Armenia, and Azerbaijan between the Caucasus Mountains and the borders of Turkey and Iran. — **Trans′cau·ca′sian** adj. & n.

trans·con·ti·nen·tal (trăns′kŏn-tə-nĕn′tl). Spanning or crossing a continent.

Trans·jor·dan (trăns′jôr′dn, trănz′-). See **Jordan.** — **Trans′jor·da′ni·an** (-jôr-dā′nē-ən) adj. & n.

Trans·kei (trăns-kā′, -kī′). A former internally self-governing Black African homeland in southeast South Africa on the Indian Ocean coast. It was designated a semiautonomous territory in 1963, granted nominal independence in 1976, and dissolved and reintegrated into South Africa by the 1993 interim constitution. — **Trans·kei′an** adj. & n.

trans·mon·tane (trăns-mŏn′tān′, trănz-, trăns′-mŏn-tān′, trănz′-). Tramontane.

trans·o·ce·an·ic (trăns′ō-shē-ăn′ĭk, trănz′-). **1.** Situated beyond or on the other side of the ocean. **2.** Spanning or crossing the ocean.

trans·pa·cif·ic (trăns′pə-sĭf′ĭk, trănz′-). **1.** Situated on or coming from the other side of the Pacific Ocean. **2.** Spanning the Pacific.

trans·po·lar (trăns-pō′lər). Extending across or crossing either of the Polar Regions.

Trans·vaal (trăns-väl′, trănz-). A region of northeast South Africa. Inhabited by Bantu-speaking Black Africans, the area was settled by Boer farmers who formed an independent state, called the South African Republic, in the 1850's. Great Britain annexed the territory in 1877, but the discovery of gold in 1886 led to an influx of settlers, further tensions between the British and the Boers, and the eventual formation of the Transvaal as a crown colony (1900) after the Boer War. Transvaal became a part of South Africa in 1910.

Tran·syl·va·nia (trăn′sĭl-vān′yə, -vā′nē-ə). A historical region of western Romania bounded by the Transylvanian Alps and the Carpathian Mountains. Part of the Roman province of Dacia after A.D. 107, it was later overrun by Germanic peoples and came under Hungarian rule in 1003. Transylvania passed to various powers over the following centuries and finally became part of modern-day Romania after World War II. — **Tran′syl·va′ni·an** adj. & n.

Transylvanian Alps. A range of the southern Carpathian Mountains extending across central Romania and rising to 2,544.6 m (8,343 ft).

Tra·pa·ni (trä′pə-nē, -pä-). A city of northwest Sicily, Italy, on the Mediterranean Sea west-southwest of Palermo. An important Carthaginian naval base, it fell to Rome in 241 B.C. ⊙Pop. 61,900.

Tra·si·me·no (trä′zə-mā′nō, -zē-mě′-), **Lake.** A lake in central Italy west of Perugia. Hannibal defeated a Roman force here in 217 B.C.

Trav·erse City (trăv′ərs). A city of northwest Michigan on Grand Traverse Bay north of Grand Rapids. It is a trade center in a resort area. ⊙Pop. 15,155.

Treas·ure Island (trězh′ər). An artificial island of San Francisco Bay in western California. Built for the Golden Gate International Exposition in 1939, it became a U.S. Navy base in 1941.

trea·ty port (trē′tē). A port kept open for foreign trade according to the terms of a treaty, especially formerly in China, Korea, and Japan.

Treb·bia (trěb′yä). A river, about 113 km (70 mi) long, of northwest Italy flowing northward to the Po River. Hannibal defeated the Romans on the banks of the river in 218 B.C.

Treb·i·zond (trěb′ĭ-zŏnd′). **1.** A former Greek empire occupying much of the land along the southern coast of the Black Sea. It was founded as an offshoot of the Byzantine Empire by Alexius I Comnenus in 1204 and retained its autonomy until it was conquered by Ottoman Turks in 1461. **2.** See **Trabzon.**

Trent (trěnt) also **Tren·to** (trěn′tō). A city of northern Italy northwest of Venice. Probably founded in the fourth century B.C., it was the site of the Council of Trent (1545–1563), which established the foundations of the Counter Reformation. ⊙Pop. 98,833.

Tren·ti·no-Al·to-A·di·ge (trěn-tē′nō-äl′tō-ä′-dē-jě′). A region of northeast Italy bordering on Switzerland and Austria. Annexed by Austria in 1814, it was ceded to Italy in sections between 1866 and 1919.

Tren·to (trěn′tō). See **Trent.**

Tren·ton (trěn′tən). **1.** A town of southeast Ontario, Canada, on an inlet of Lake Ontario east-northeast of Toronto. It is a processing and industrial center. ⊙Pop. 15,085. **2.** A city of southeast Michigan, an industrial suburb of Detroit. ⊙Pop. 20,586. **3.** The capital of New Jersey, in the west-central part of the state on the Delaware River northeast of Philadelphia. Settled c. 1679 by Quakers, it was the site of a pivotal battle in the American Revolution in which George Washington's troops captured a Hessian encampment in a surprise attack (December 26, 1776). ⊙Pop. 88,675.

Trent River. **1.** A river, about 241 km (150 mi) long, of southeast Ontario, Canada. It is part of the **Trent Canal** system, about 386 km (240 mi) long, that connects Lake Ontario with Georgian Bay. **2.** A river, about 274 km (170 mi) long, of

central England flowing northeast to join the Ouse River and form the Humber estuary.

Trèves (trěv). See **Trier.**

Tre·vi·so (trə-vē′zō, trě-). A city of northeast Italy north-northwest of Venice. An ancient Roman town, it was later the seat of a Lombard duchy and passed to Venice in the 14th century. ⊙Pop. 101,340.

trib·u·tar·y (trĭb′yə-tĕr′ē). A stream that flows into a larger stream or other body of water.

Trier (trîr) also **Trèves** (trěv). A city of southwest Germany on the Moselle River near the Luxembourg border. Settled by the Treveri, an eastern Gaulish people, it was an important commercial center under the Romans and later as part of the Holy Roman Empire. The city was under French control from 1797 until 1815. ⊙Pop. 94,190.

Tri·este (trē-ěst′, -ěs′tě). A city of extreme northeast Italy on the **Gulf of Trieste,** an inlet of the Gulf of Venice at the head of the Adriatic Sea. Held by Austria from 1382 until 1919, Trieste became in 1947 the center of the **Free Territory of Trieste** administered by the United Nations. In 1954 the city and the northern zone of the territory were returned to Italy; the remainder of the area became part of Yugoslavia (in present-day Slovenia and Croatia). ⊙Pop. 229,216.

Trin·i·dad (trĭn′ĭ-dăd′). An island of Trinidad and Tobago in the Atlantic Ocean off northeast Venezuela. The island was inhabited by Arawaks when discovered by Columbus in 1498. A Spanish possession for the next three centuries, it was largely neglected by Spain and was a frequent target for Dutch, French, and British buccaneers. Britain seized the island in 1797, joining it with Tobago to form the colony of Trinidad and Tobago in 1898. Trinidad's population is mainly divided between a Black majority descended from African slaves and a large minority of Asian Indians descended from indentured servants imported in the 19th century. **—Trin′i·dad′i·an** adj. & n.

Trinidad and Tobago. A country of the southeast West Indies in the Atlantic Ocean off

Caribbean Sea • Tobago • TRINIDAD AND TOBAGO • Port of Spain • Trinidad • Gulf of Paria • ATLANTIC OCEAN • VENEZUELA • 50 mi

northeast Venezuela. The two islands were united as a British colony in 1898 and achieved limited self-government in 1923. Part of the West Indies Federation from 1958 to 1962, the country was granted independence in 1962 and became a republic in 1976. Port of Spain, on Trinidad, is the capital. ⊛ Pop. 1,257,000.

Trin·i·ty River (trĭn′ĭ-tē). A river, about 821 km (510 mi) long, of eastern Texas formed near Dallas by the juncture of three forks and flowing generally southeast to **Trinity Bay,** an arm of Galveston Bay.

Trip·o·li (trĭp′ə-lē). **1.** A historical region of northern Africa roughly coextensive with the ancient region of Tripolitania. It became part of the Barbary States in the 16th century and later passed to Turkey and Italy. **2.** A city of northwest Lebanon on the Mediterranean Sea northeast of Beirut. Probably founded after the seventh century B.C., it was capital of a Phoenician federation and later flourished under the Seleucid and Roman empires. Tripoli was captured by the Arabs in A.D. 638 and taken by the Crusaders in 1109 after a long siege. ⊛ Pop. 198,000. **3.** The capital and largest city of Libya, in the northwest part of the country on the Mediterranean Sea. Settled by Phoenicians from Tyre, it has Roman and Byzantine remains. ⊛ Pop. 858,500. — **Tri·pol′i·tan** (trĭ-pŏl′ĭ-tn) *adj. & n.*

Tri·pol·i·ta·ni·a (trĭ-pŏl′ĭ-tā′nē-ə, -tān′yə, trĭp′-ə-lĭ-). A historical region of northern Africa bordering on the Mediterranean Sea. Originally a Phoenician colony, it was later held by Carthage, Numidia, and Rome (after 46 B.C.). Tripolitania fell to the Vandals in A.D. 435, to the Arabs in the seventh century, and finally to the Ottoman Turks in 1553. — **Tri·pol′i·ta′ni·an** *adj. & n.*

Tris·tan da Cun·ha (trĭs′tən də kōō′nə). An island and volcanic island group of the southern Atlantic Ocean between southern Africa and southern South America. Discovered by the Portuguese in 1506, the islands were annexed by Great Britain in 1816 and are now administered as a dependency of St. Helena.

Tri·van·drum (trə-văn′drəm). A city of southwest India on the Arabian Sea south-southwest of Bangalore. It is a port and manufacturing center. ⊛ Pop. 524,000.

Tro·as (trō′ăs′) also **Tro·ad** (-ăd′). An ancient region of northwest Asia Minor surrounding the city of Troy. It formed the setting for the events recounted in the *Iliad.*

Tro·bri·and Islands (trō′brē-ănd′, -änd′). An island group of Papua New Guinea in the Solomon Sea off eastern New Guinea. The islands were occupied by Allied forces in June 1943.

Trois·dorf (trōs′dôrf′). A city of west-central Germany north-northeast of Bonn. It is a manufacturing center. ⊛ Pop. 60,267.

Trois Ri·vières or **Trois-Rivières** (trwä rē-vyěr′). A city of southern Quebec, Canada, at the confluence of the St. Lawrence and St. Maurice rivers. Founded in 1634, it is a river port and manufacturing center with a pulp and paper industry. ⊛ Pop. 140,891.

Tro·jan (trō′jən). A native or inhabitant of ancient Troy. — **Tro′jan** *adj.*

Trom·sø (trŏm′sō′, trōōm′sœ). A city of northern Norway on an offshore island in the Arctic Ocean. Founded as a center for herring fisheries, it is the chief city of northern Norway. ⊛ Pop. 47,322.

Trond·heim (trŏn′hām′, trôn′-). A city of central Norway on **Trondheim Fjord,** an inlet of the Norwegian Sea. Founded in 997, it was the capital of Norway until 1380. ⊛ Pop. 140,656.

trop·ic (trŏp′ĭk). *abbr.* **trop. 1. a.** Either of two parallels of latitude on the earth, one 23°27′ north of the equator and the other 23°27′ south of the equator, representing the points farthest north and south at which the sun can shine directly overhead and constituting the boundaries of the Torrid Zone. **b. Tropics** or **tropics.** The region of the earth's surface lying between these latitudes. **2.** Of or relating to the Tropics; tropical.

tropic of Cancer. The parallel of latitude 23°27′ north of the equator, the northern boundary of the Torrid Zone, and the most northerly latitude at which the sun can shine directly overhead.

tropic of Capricorn. The parallel of latitude 23°27′ south of the equator, the southern boundary of the Torrid Zone, and the most southerly latitude at which the sun can shine directly overhead.

Trou·ville (trōō-vēl′) or **Trou·ville-sur-Mer** (-sōōr-měr′, -sür-). A town of northwest France on the English Channel south of Le Havre. It is a popular resort. ⊛ Pop. 6,008.

Troy (troi). **1.** also **Il·i·on** (ĭl′ē-ən, -ŏn′) or **Il·i·um** (-ē-əm). An ancient city of northwest Asia Minor near the Dardanelles. Originally a Phrygian city dating from the Bronze Age, it is the legendary site of the Trojan War and was captured and destroyed by Greek forces c. 1200 B.C. The ruins of Troy were discovered by the German archaeologist Heinrich Schliemann in 1871. **2.** A city of southeast Michigan, a residential and industrial suburb of Detroit. ⊛ Pop. 72,884. **3.** A city of eastern New York on the Hudson River northeast of Albany. Settled in the 1780's, it is a manufacturing center with a clothing industry. ⊛ Pop. 54,269. **4.** A city of west-central Ohio north of Dayton. Founded in 1807, it is a manufacturing center. ⊛ Pop. 19,478.

Troyes (trwä). A city of northeast France on the Seine River east-southeast of Paris. A pre-Roman town, it was a prosperous commercial center in the Middle Ages and was noted for its annual fairs, which set standards of weights and measures for all of Europe. ⊛ Pop. 125,000.

Tru·chas Peaks (trōō′chəs). Three mountains in northern New Mexico northeast of Santa Fe, rising to 3,998.6 m (13,110 ft) at **North Truchas Peak.**

Tru·cial Oman (trōō′shəl). See **United Arab Emirates.**

Truck·ee (trŭk′ē). A river, about 193 km (120 mi) long, rising in eastern California and flowing east and northeast into northwest Nevada.

Tru·ji·llo (trōō-hē′ō, -yō). A city of northwest Peru northwest of Lima. Founded in 1534, it was provisional capital of Peru in 1825 and is now a processing center. ⊛ Pop. 521,200.

Truk (trŭk, trōōk). An island group and state of the Federated States of Micronesia in the Caroline Islands of the western Pacific Ocean. Site of a major Japanese naval base during World War II, the islands were part of the U.S. Trust Territory of the Pacific Islands from 1947–1978.

Trum·bull (trŭm′bəl). A town of southwest Connecticut north of Bridgeport. It is a residential community with varied industries. ⊛ Pop. 32,016.

Tru·ro (trōōr′ō). A town of central Nova Scotia, Canada, north-northeast of Halifax. A major Acadian settlement, it was destroyed in 1755 when the Acadians were expelled by the British but was resettled by New Englanders a few years later. ⊛ Pop. 12,552.

trus·tee·ship (trŭ-stē′shĭp′). **1.** Administration of a territory by a country or countries so commissioned by the United Nations. **2.** See **trust territory.**

trust territory (trŭst). *abbr.* **TT.** A colony or territory placed under the administration of a country or countries by commission of the United Nations. Also called *trusteeship.*

Tsa·na (tsä′nə, -nä), **Lake.** See Lake **Tana.**

Tse·lin·o·grad (tsə-lĭn′ə-grād′, tsĭ-lyĭ-nə-grät′). A city of north-central Kazakstan north-northwest of Karaganda. It is a railroad junction in a mining region. ⊛ Pop. 287,000.

Tshi·lu·ba (chĭ-lōō′bə). *pl.* **Tshiluba** or **-bas.** See **Luba** (sense 2).

Tsiao·tso (jyou′jō′). See **Jiaozuo.**

Tsim·shi·an (chĭm′shē-ən, tsĭm′-). **1.** *pl.* **Tsimshian** or **-ans.** A member of a Native American people inhabiting a coastal area of western British Columbia and extreme southeast Alaska. **2.** The family of languages spoken by the Tsimshian and related peoples.

Tsi·nan (jē′nän′). See **Jinan.**

Tsing·hai (tsĭng′hī′). See **Qinghai.**

Tsing·tao (tsĭng′dou′). See **Qingdao.**

Tsi·tsi·har (tsē′tsē′här′). See **Qiqihar.**

Tsu·ga·ru Strait (tsōō-gä′rōō). A channel between Honshu and Hokkaido in northern Japan.

Tsu·shi·ma (tsōō-shē′mə, tsōō′shē-mä′). Two islands of southwest Japan in Korea Strait between Kyushu and southeast South Korea. They are separated from Kyushu by **Tsushima Strait,** the site of a major naval battle (May 1905) in the Russo-Japanese War in which the Russian fleet was largely destroyed.

Tswa·na (tswä′nə, swä′-). **1.** *pl.* **Tswana** or **-nas.** A member of a Bantu people inhabiting Botswana and western South Africa. Also called *Batswana, Bechuana.* **2.** The Sotho language of the Tswana. Also called *Setswana.*

Tu·a·mo·tu Archipelago (tōō′ə-mō′tōō). An island group of French Polynesia in the southern Pacific Ocean east of Tahiti. Discovered by the Spanish in 1606, the islands were annexed by France in 1881.

Tua·reg (twä′rĕg′). *pl.* **Tuareg** or **-regs.** A member of a Muslim, Berber-speaking people inhabiting the western and central Sahara and western Sahel of northwest Africa.

Tü·bing·en (tōō′bĭng-ən, tü′-). A city of southwest Germany on the Neckar River south of Stuttgart. Its university was founded in 1477. ⊛ Pop. 75,333.

Tu·bu·a·i Islands (tōōb-wä′ē, tōō′bōō-ī′). An island group of southern French Polynesia in the southern Pacific Ocean south of Tahiti. Visited by the British navigator and explorer Capt. James Cook in 1769 and 1777, the islands were annexed by France between 1850 and 1889.

Tuc·son (tōō′sŏn′). A city of southeast Arizona south-southeast of Phoenix. A Spanish mission was founded nearby in 1700, and the present city was first settled in 1775 as a walled presidio. It became part of the United States after the Gadsden Purchase (1853) and served as territorial capital from 1867 until 1877. ⊛ Pop. 405,390.

Tu·cu·mán (tōō′kə-män′, -kōō-). See **San Miguel de Tucumán.**

Tu·ge·la Falls (tōō-gā′lə). A series of five waterfalls in the **Tugela River,** about 483 km (300 mi) long, of eastern South Africa. The falls have a total drop of 915 m (3,000 ft).

Tu·la (tōō′lə). **1.** A town of central Mexico north of Mexico City. Impressive Toltec ruins have been discovered on the site. ⊛ Pop. 10,720. **2.** A city of western Russia south of Moscow. First mentioned in 1146, it was an important fortress in the 16th century and became an armament-manufacturing center in 1712. ⊛ Pop. 533,640.

Tu·lare (tōō-lâr′ē, -lâr′). A city of south-central California southeast of Fresno in the San Joaquin Valley. It is a processing center. ⊛ Pop. 33,249.

Tul·la·ho·ma (tŭl'ə-hō'mə). A city of south-central Tennessee northwest of Chattanooga. It is a resort and processing center. ◉ Pop. 16,761.

Tul·sa (tŭl'sə). A city of northeast Oklahoma on the Arkansas River northeast of Oklahoma City. A port and manufacturing center, it grew rapidly after the discovery of oil nearby in the early 20th century. ◉ Pop. 367,302.

tu·mu·lus (tōō'myə-ləs, tyōō'-). *pl.* **-li** (-lī'). An ancient grave mound; a barrow.

tun·dra (tŭn'drə). A treeless area between the icecap and the tree line of Arctic regions, having a permanently frozen subsoil and supporting low-growing vegetation such as lichens, mosses, and stunted shrubs.

Tun·gus (tōōng-gōōz', tŭn-). See **Evenki**.

Tun·gus·ic (tōōng-gōō'zĭk, tŭn-). **1.** A subfamily of the Altaic language family spoken in eastern Siberia and northern Manchuria that includes Evenki and Manchu. Also called *Manchu-Tungus.* **2.** Of or relating to the Tungusic language or its speakers.

Tun·gus·ka (tōōng-gōō'skə, tōōn-). The name of three rivers of central Russia. The **Upper Tunguska** is the lower course of the Angara River. The **Lower Tunguska** flows about 3,218 km (2,000 mi) north and west to the Yenisey River. The **Stony Tunguska,** about 1,609 km (1,000 mi) long, flows generally west-northwest to the Yenisey.

Tu·nis (tōō'nĭs, tyōō'-). **1.** A former Barbary state on the northern coast of Africa south and west of the ancient city of Carthage. It was conquered by the Turks in 1575 and later became a French protectorate (1881). **2.** The capital and largest city of Tunisia, in the northern part of the country on the **Gulf of Tunis,** an inlet of the Mediterranean Sea. It occupies a site near the ruins of ancient Carthage. ◉ Pop. 596,654.

Tu·ni·sia (tōō-nē'zhə, -shə, -nĭzh'ə, -nĭsh'ə, tyōō-). *abbr.* **Tun.** A country of northern Africa bordering on the Mediterranean Sea. Settled in ancient times by the Phoenicians, Tunisia was dominated after the 6th century B.C. by the Carthaginians, whose influence spread from the city-state of Carthage to many parts of the Mediterranean. After the destruction of Carthaginian power by the Romans, the area fell to the Vandals (5th century A.D.) and Byzantines (6th century) before being conquered by the Arabs in the 7th century, at which time the Berber population was converted to Islam. Tunisia was taken over by the Ottoman Turks in the late 16th century and, as one of the Barbary States, was used as a base by pirates raiding ships in the Mediterranean. France invaded Tunisia in 1881 and made it a French protectorate. After World War I a nationalist movement gained strength, and by the end of World War II France had

granted Tunisia a large degree of autonomy. Full independence was achieved in 1956, with the country becoming a republic in 1957. Tunis is the capital and the largest city. ◉ Pop. 8,733,000.

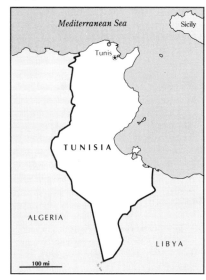

Tu·ni·sian (tōō-nē'zhən, -shən, -nĭzh'ən, -nĭsh'-, tyōō-). *abbr.* **Tun. 1.** Of or relating to Tunisia or Tunis or their inhabitants. **2.** A native or inhabitant of Tunisia or Tunis.

Tu·ol·um·ne (tōō-ŏl'ə-mē). A river, about 249 km (155 mi) long, of central California flowing generally westward to the San Joaquin River.

Tu·pe·lo (tōō'pə-lō', tyōō'-). A city of northeast Mississippi north-northwest of Columbus. It was the site of a Civil War battle (July 14, 1864) in which Union forces defeated the Confederate troops led by Gen. Nathan B. Forrest. ◉ Pop. 30,685.

Tu·pi (tōō'pē, tōō-pē'). **1.** *pl.* **Tupi** or **-pis.** A member a group of South American Indian peoples living along the coast of Brazil, in the Amazon River valley, and in Paraguay. **2.** The Tupian language of the Tupi.

Tu·pi·an (tōō'pē-ən, tōō-pē'-). **1.** A subdivision of Tupi-Guarani that includes Tupi. **2.** A member of a Tupian-speaking people. **3.** Relating to Tupian or a Tupian-speaking people.

Tu·pi-Gua·ra·ni (tōō-pē'gwär-ə-nē', tōō'pē-). A language family widely spread throughout the Amazon River valley, coastal Brazil, and northeast South America. — **Tu·pi'-Gua·ra·ni', Tu·pi'-Gua·ra·ni'an** *adj.*

Tu·pun·ga·to (tōō'pōōng-gä'tō). A mountain, 6,804.6 m (22,310 ft) high, in the Andes on the Chile-Argentina border east of Santiago, Chile.

Tu·ra·ni·an (tōō-rä'nē-ən, -rä'-, tyōō-). **1.** Of or relating to the Ural-Altaic languages or to the peoples who speak them. **2.** See **Ural-Altaic.** **3.** A member of any of the peoples who speak languages of the Ural-Altaic group.

Tur·co·man (tûr′kə-mən). Variant of **Turkmen.**

Tu·rin (to͝or′ĭn, tyo͝or′-) also **To·ri·no** (tô-rē′-nô). A city of northwest Italy on the Po River west-southwest of Milan. An important Roman town, it was later a Lombard duchy and the capital of the kingdom of Sardinia (1720–1861). It was also the first capital of the new kingdom of Italy. ◉ Pop. 961,916.

Turk (tûrk). **1.** A native or inhabitant of Turkey. **2.** A member of the principal ethnic group of modern-day Turkey or, formerly, of the Ottoman Empire. **3.** A member of any of the Turkic-speaking peoples.

Tur·ka·na (tər-kăn′ə, to͝or-kä′nə), **Lake** also **Lake Ru·dolf** (ro͞o′dŏlf′). A lake of northwest Kenya in the Great Rift Valley bordering on Ethiopia.

Tur·ke·stan (tûr′kĭ-stăn′, -stän′). See **Turkistan.**

Tur·key (tûr′kē). *abbr.* **Tur., Turk.** A country of southwest Asia and southeast Europe between the Mediterranean and the Black seas. The region was dominated by many ancient civilizations and peoples, among them the Hittites (1800 B.C.), the Greeks (8th century B.C.), and the Persians (6th century B.C.). In A.D. 395 it became part of the Byzantine Empire, centered around the newly rebuilt city of Constantinople. The area was conquered by the Ottoman Turks between the 13th and 15th centuries and remained the core of the Ottoman Empire for more than 600 years. Turkey's modern history dates to the rise of the Young Turks (after 1908) and the collapse of the Ottoman Empire in 1918. The Treaty of Lausanne (1923) established the present boundaries of Turkey, and it was proclaimed a republic in 1923 under the leadership of Kemal Atatürk. Neutral during most of World War II, Turkey joined the Allies in 1945. A second Turkish republic was established in 1961 after a military coup; the first woman prime minister was appointed in 1993. Ankara is the capital and Istanbul the largest city. ◉ Pop. 61,183,000.

Tur·ki (tûr′kē). **1.** Of or relating to the Turkic language subfamily, especially the eastern Turkic languages, or their speakers. **2.** The Turkic language subfamily, especially the eastern Turkic languages. **3.** *pl.* **Turki** or **-kis.** A member of a Turki-speaking people.

Turk·ic (tûr′kĭk). **1.** A subfamily of the Altaic language family that includes Turkish. **2.** Of or relating to Turkic or the peoples who speak Turkic. **3.** Relating to Turkey; Turkish.

Turk·ish (tûr′kĭsh). *abbr.* **Tur., Turk.** **1.** Of or relating to Turkey or its peoples, languages, or cultures. **2.** Ottoman Turkish.

Turkish Empire. See **Ottoman Empire.**

Tur·ki·stan also **Tur·ke·stan** (tûr′kĭ-stăn′, -stän′). A historical region of west-central Asia extending east from the Caspian Sea into western China and south from the Aral Sea into Afghanistan. It was long a crossroads for trade and conquest between East and West.

Turk·men (tûrk′mĕn, -mən) also **Tur·ko·man** or **Tur·co·man** (tûr′kə-mən). **1.** *pl.* **Turkmen** or **-mens** also **-ko·mans** or **-co·mans.** A member of a traditionally nomadic Turkic people inhabiting Turkmenistan and neighboring areas in Iran and Afghanistan. **2.** The Turkic language of the Turkmen. **3.** Of or relating to the Turkmen or their language or culture.

Turk·men·i·stan (tûrk′mĕn-ĭ-stăn′, -stän′). Formerly also **Turk·men Soviet Socialist Republic** (tûrk′mən). A country of west-central Asia east of the Caspian Sea. Once part of ancient Persia and later ruled by Arabs (8th century), Turks (11th century), Mongols (13–14th century), and Uzbeks (late 15th century), it was annexed by Russia in 1881 and became a constituent republic of the U.S.S.R. in 1925. Turkmenistan declared its independence in 1991 following the collapse of the Soviet Union. A new constitution was adopted in 1992, but the former Communist party remains in control and formal opposition parties are outlawed. With rich reserves of natural gas and oil, the country experienced less economic disruption than other former soviet republics after independence. Ashkhabad is the capital. ◉ Pop. 4,010,000.

Turks and Cai·cos Islands (tûrks; kā′kəs, kī′kōs). Two island groups of the British West

Indies in the Atlantic Ocean in the southeast part of the Bahama Islands. The islands were a dependency of Jamaica after 1848 and became a crown colony in 1962.

Tur·ku (tōōr′kōō′). A city of southwest Finland on the Baltic Sea west of Helsinki. Settled in the early 13th century, it was the capital of Finland until 1812. ⊛ Pop. 160,153.

Tur·lock (tûr′lŏk′). A city of central California southeast of Modesto. It is the center of an irrigated farming region. ⊛ Pop. 42,198.

Tus·ca·loo·sa (tŭs′kə-lōō′sə). A city of west-central Alabama southwest of Birmingham. Established in 1819 on the site of a Creek village, it was the state capital from 1826 to 1846. ⊛ Pop. 77,759.

Tus·can (tŭs′kən). **1.** Of or relating to Tuscany, its people, or their language. **2.** A native or inhabitant of Tuscany. **3. a.** Any of the dialects of Italian spoken in Tuscany. **b.** The standard literary form of Italian.

Tus·ca·ny (tŭs′kə-nē′). A region of northwest Italy between the northern Apennines and the Ligurian and Tyrrhenian seas. Inhabited in ancient times by the Etruscans, it fell to Rome in the mid-fourth century B.C. Tuscany was a grand duchy under the Medicis (1569–1860) and subsequently became united with the kingdom of Sardinia.

Tus·ca·ro·ra (tŭs′kə-rôr′ə, -rōr′ə). **1.** *pl.* **Tuscarora** or **-ras.** A member of a Native American people formerly inhabiting parts of North Carolina, with present-day populations in western New York and southeast Ontario, Canada. The Tuscaroras migrated northward in the 18th century, joining the Iroquois confederacy in 1722 and adopting aspects of the Iroquois culture. **2.** The Iroquoian language of the Tuscaroras.

Tus·cu·lum (tŭs′kə-ləm, -kyə-). A city of ancient Latium southeast of modern-day Rome, Italy. Pliny the Younger, Cicero, and the emperors Nero and Titus were among the prominent Romans who built villas here.

Tus·ke·gee (tŭs-kē′gē). A city of eastern Alabama east of Montgomery. It is the seat of the Tuskegee Institute, founded by the educator Booker T. Washington in 1881. ⊛ Pop. 12,257.

Tus·tin (tŭs′tĭn). A city of southern California, a residential and manufacturing suburb of the Greater Los Angeles area. ⊛ Pop. 50,689.

Tu·tu·i·la (tōō′tōō-ē′lə). An island of American Samoa in the southwest-central Pacific Ocean. It is the largest island in the group.

Tu·va·lu (tōō-vä′lōō, tōō′və-lōō′). Formerly **Ellice Islands** (ĕl′ĭs). An island country of the western Pacific Ocean north of Fiji. Organized as a British protectorate in 1892, the islands became part of the Gilbert and Ellice Islands Colony in 1915 and achieved independence in

1978. Fongafale, on Funafuti Island, is the capital. ⊛ Pop. 9,000.

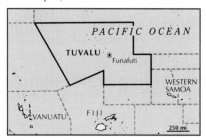

Tux·tla Gu·tié·rez (tōōs′tlə gōō-tyĕr′ĕs). A city of southeast Mexico near the Isthmus of Tehuantepec. It is a distribution point in an agricultural area. ⊛ Pop. 131,096.

Tuz·la (tōōz′lä). A city of northeast Bosnia and Herzegovina north-northeast of Sarajevo. It is an industrial center with salt springs known since Roman times. In 1995 the city was shelled by Bosnian Serbs and became a command post for UN peacekeeping troops. ⊛ Pop. 61,100.

Tver (tə-ver′). Formerly **Ka·li·nin** (kə-lē′nĭn, kəl-yē′-). A city of west-central Russia on the Volga River northwest of Moscow. It was settled around a fort established in the 12th century and was a powerful principality in the 13th and 14th centuries. Today it is an industrial center and a major port. Tver was named Kalinin from 1931 to 1992 in honor of M.I. Kalinin, a Soviet president. ⊛ Pop. 449,461.

Tweed (twēd). A river, 156 km (97 mi) long, of southeast Scotland forming part of the Scottish-English border. It flows eastward to the North Sea and has rich salmon fisheries.

Twi (chwē, chē). A variety of the Akan language spoken in Ghana.

Twin Falls (twĭn). A city of south-central Idaho west of Pocatello near the **Twin Falls** of the Snake River. The southern falls are a source of hydroelectric power. The city is a processing and trade center. ⊛ Pop. 27,591.

Twin Peaks. A mountain, 3,153.7 m (10,340 ft) high, in the Salmon River Mountains of central Idaho. It is the highest elevation in the range.

Two Sic·i·lies (tōō sĭs′ə-lēz). A former kingdom comprising Sicily and Naples. The two territories were ruled jointly at various times and were united in 1816. The Italian general Giuseppe Garibaldi conquered the kingdom in 1860 and annexed it to Italy.

Ty·chy (tĭk′ē). A town of south-central Poland south of Katowice. It was largely developed as a resettlement community after World War II. ⊛ Pop. 139,562.

Ty·gart (tī′gərt). A river, about 257 km (160 mi) long, of northern West Virginia flowing northward as a tributary of the Monongahela River.

Ty·ler (tī′lər). A city of northeast Texas east-southeast of Dallas. It is a refining, shipping, and manufacturing center noted for its rose-growing industry. ◉ Pop. 75,450.

Tyn·dall (tĭn′dl), **Mount**. A mountain, 4,275.8 m (14,019 ft) high, in the Sierra Nevada of south-central California.

Tyne (tīn). A river, about 129 km (80 mi) long, of northern England flowing eastward to the North Sea.

Tyne·mouth (tīn′mouth′, -məth). A borough of northeast England on the North Sea at the mouth of the Tyne River. It is a port, shipbuilding center, and seaside resort. ◉ Pop. 60,022.

Tyre (tīr). An ancient Phoenician city on the Mediterranean Sea in present-day southern Lebanon. The capital of Phoenicia after the 11th century B.C., it was a flourishing commercial center noted for its purple dyestuffs and rich, silken clothing. Tyre was besieged and captured by Alexander the Great in 332 B.C. and was finally destroyed by Muslims in A.D. 1291.

Ty·rol or **Ti·rol** (tə-rōl′, tī-, tī′rōl′). A region of the eastern Alps in western Austria and northern Italy. Inhabited in ancient times by Celtic peoples, the Tyrol constantly passed back and forth, in whole or in part, between Austria and Italy in the 1800's. Its present division dates from the Treaty of St. Germain in 1919. The Tyrolean Alps are a popular tourist area. **—Ty·rol′le·an**, **Tyr′o·lese′** (tĭr′ə-lēz′, -lēs′, tī′rə-) *adj. & n.*

Tyr·rhe·ni·an Sea (tə-rē′nē-ən). An arm of the Mediterranean Sea between the Italian peninsula and the islands of Corsica, Sardinia, and Sicily. The Strait of Messina connects it with the Ionian Sea.

Tyu·men (tyŏŏ-mĕn′). A city of west-central Russia east of Yekaterinburg. Founded in 1585, it is the oldest Russian settlement east of the Ural Mountains. ◉ Pop. 490,857.

Tze·kung (tsŭ′kŏŏng′, dzŭ′gŏŏng′). See **Zigong.**

Tze·po (tsŭ′pō′, dzŭ′bō′). See **Zibo.**

U

Uau·pés (wou-pĕs′). In its upper course called **Vau·pés** (vou-pās′, -pĕs′). A river of northwest South America rising in south-central Colombia and flowing about 805 km (500 mi) east-southeast through northwest Brazil to the Río Negro.

U·ban·gi (yŏŏ-băng′gē, ōō-bäng′-). A river of central Africa flowing about 1,126 km (700 mi) along the northwest border of Zaire to the Congo River.

U·be·ra·ba (ōō′bĭ-rä′bə, -bä). A city of eastern Brazil west of Belo Horizonte. It is located in a cattle-raising area. ◉ Pop. 211,356.

U·ber·lân·di·a (ōō′bĭr-läɴ′dē-ə, -dyä). A city of eastern Brazil west-northwest of Belo Horizonte. It is a shipping and trade center. ◉ Pop. 366,729.

U·ca·ya·li (ōō′kä-yä′lē). A river of eastern Peru flowing about 1,609 km (1,000 mi) northward to join the Marañón River and form the Amazon River.

Uc·cle (ōōk′lə, ü′klə). A city of central Belgium, a suburb of Brussels. ◉ Pop. 75,675.

U·dai·pur (ōō-dī′pŏŏr, ōō′dī-pŏŏr′). A city of northwest India north-northeast of Ahmadabad. Center of a former princely state, it is noted for its 16th-century palace. ◉ Pop. 308,571.

U·di·ne (ōō′dē-nā′). A city of northeast Italy northeast of Venice. It was the headquarters (1915–1917) of the Italian army in World War I. ◉ Pop. 101,264.

Ue·le (wĕl′ē, wĕl′ā). A river, about 1,126 km (700 mi) long, of northern Zaire flowing westward as a tributary of the Ubangi River.

U·fa (ōō-fä′). A city of west-central Russia in the southern Ural Mountains at the confluence of the Belaya and **Ufa** rivers. The Ufa flows about 965 km (600 mi) northwest and southwest. The city was founded as a fortress (1586) and is now a major industrial center. ◉ Pop. 1,064,000.

U·gan·da (yōō-găn′də, ōō-gän′dä). A country of east-central Africa. Inhabited since Paleolithic times, the region was settled by migrating Bantu people around A.D. 1100 and by Nilotic peoples from the north in the late 17th century. Various kingdoms and states were established beginning in the 14th century, including the Bantu kingdom of Buganda, which was crossed

by the British explorer J.H. Speke in 1862 and became a British protectorate in 1894. The protectorate was later extended to the entire region, which became independent as Uganda in 1962. President Milton Obote (governed 1966–1971 and 1980–1985) was deposed by Col. Idi Amin Dada, who created a dictatorial reign of terror until forced into exile in 1979 by an invading army from Tanzania. The rapid spread of AIDS along with political unrest in neighboring Rwanda and Zaire created ongoing problems in the 1980's and 1990's. Kampala is the capital and the largest city. ⊛ Pop. 20,621,000. — U·gan′dan *adj. & n.*

U·ga·rit (ōō′gə-rēt′). An ancient city of western Syria on the Mediterranean Sea. It flourished as a trade center from c. 1450 to 1195 B.C. but was destroyed soon after by an earthquake. Excavation of the ruins (beginning in 1929) have unearthed important cuneiform tablets.

U·ga·rit·ic (ōō′gə-rĭt′ĭk, yōō′-). The Semitic language of Ugarit. — U′ga·rit′ic *adj.*

U·gri·an (ōō′grē-ən, yōō′-). **1.** A member of a group of Finno-Ugric peoples of western Siberia and Hungary, including the Magyars. **2.** Ugric. — U′gri·an *adj.*

U·gric (ōō′grĭk, yōō′-). The branch of the Finno-Ugric subfamily of languages that includes Hungarian. — U′gric *adj.*

Ui·gur also **Ui·ghur** (wē′gŏŏr). **1.** *pl.* **Uigur** or **-gurs** also **Uighur** or **-ghurs.** A member of a mainly agricultural Turkic people inhabiting the Xinjiang region in China. **2.** The Turkic language of the Uigurs. — Ui·gu′ri·an (-gŏŏr′ē-ən), Ui·gu′ric (-gŏŏr′ĭk) *adj.*

U·in·ta Mountains (yōō-ĭn′tə). A range of the Rocky Mountains extending about 193 km (120 mi) eastward from northeast Utah to southwest Wyoming. It rises to 4,116.9 m (13,498 ft) at King's Peak in Utah.

Uj·jain (ōō′jīn′). A city of west-central India east of Ahmadabad. A Hindu pilgrimage site, it is one of the oldest cities in India and was a center of Sanskrit learning. ⊛ Pop. 362,266.

U·jung Pan·dang (ōō-jŏŏng′ pän-däng′). Formerly **Ma·kas·sar** or **Ma·ka·sar** (mə-kăs′ər). A city of central Indonesia on southwest Celebes Island. First visited by the Portuguese in 1512, it was settled by the Dutch in 1607. ⊛ Pop. 709,038.

U·kraine (yōō-krān′). Formerly also **U·krain·i·an Soviet Socialist Republic** (yōō-krā′nē-ən). A country of eastern Europe bordering on the Black Sea. Inhabited in early times by Scythians and Sarmatians, it was overrun by a number of conquerors, including Goths and Huns, until the rise of Kiev in the 9th century. Mongols invaded in the 13th century, and the region came under the control of Lithuania in the mid-14th century.

It later passed to Poland and then to Russia (between 1680 and 1793). After the Russia Revolution a short-lived independent republic was proclaimed (1918), but Soviet troops regained control of Ukraine, and in 1922 it became one of the original constituent republics of the U.S.S.R. During World War II the republic suffered severe devastation under German occupation (1941–1944) and underwent many territorial changes. The world's worst nuclear accident occured in April 1986 at the Chernobyl nuclear power plant. In 1991 Ukraine declared its independence from the U.S.S.R. and, with Russia and Belarus, formed the Commonwealth of Independent States. Kiev is the capital and largest city. ⊛ Pop. 51,910,000.

U·krain·i·an (yōō-krā′nē-ən). **1.** A native or inhabitant of the Ukraine. **2.** The Slavic language of the Ukrainians, which is closely related to Russian. — U·krain′i·an *adj.*

Ukrainian Soviet Socialist Republic. See **Ukraine.**

U·lan Ba·tor or **U·laan·baa·tar** (ōō′län-bä′tôr′). The capital and largest city of Mongolia, in the north-central part of the country. It was founded as a monastery town in 1649 and was long a trading center on various caravan routes between Russia and China. ⊛ Pop. 515,100.

U·lan-U·de (ōō′län-ōō-dā′, ōō-län′ōō-dĕ′). A city of southern Russia near Lake Baikal north of the Mongolian border. Founded in 1649 as a Cossack fortress in 1649, it is a transportation hub and a processing and manufacturing center. ⊛ Pop. 363,967.

Ul·has·na·gar (ōōl′häs-nŭg′ər). A city of west-central India, a residential and industrial suburb of Bombay. ⊛ Pop. 369,077.

Ulm (ōōlm). A city of southern Germany on the Danube River southeast of Stuttgart. First mentioned in 854, it was later a free imperial city and reached the height of its influence in the 15th century. The French emperor Napoleon defeated Austrian troops here in October 1805. ⊛ Pop. 114,839.

Ul·san (ool'sän'). A city of southwest South Korea on Korea Strait north-northeast of Pusan. It is an industrial center. ☉ Pop. 682,411.

Ul·ster (ŭl'stər). A historical region and ancient kingdom of northern Ireland. Largely annexed by the English Crown during the reign of James I (1603–1625), it is now divided between Ireland and Northern Ireland, which is often called Ulster.

ul·ti·ma Thu·le (ŭl'tə-mə thoo'lē). The northernmost region of the habitable world as thought of by ancient geographers.

ul·tra·mon·tane (ŭl'trə-mŏn'tān', -mŏn-tān'). **1.** Of or relating to peoples or regions lying beyond the mountains, especially the Alps. **2.** One who lives beyond the mountains, especially south of the Alps.

U·lugh Muz·tagh (oo'lə məz-tä', -täg'). A mountain, 7,729 m (25,341 ft) high, of the Kunlun Mountains in western China.

Ul·ya·novsk (ool-yä'nəfsk). A city of western Russia on the Volga River east-southeast of Moscow. Founded in 1648 on the site of an earlier fort, it was the birthplace of V.I. Lenin, the first head of the U.S.S.R. (1922–1924). ☉ Pop. 664,025.

U·ma·til·la (yoo'mə-tĭl'ə). **1.** *pl.* **Umatilla** or **-las.** A member of a Native American people of northeast Oregon. **2.** The dialect of Sahaptin spoken by the Umatillas.

Um·bri·a (ŭm'brē-ə, oom'brē-ä). A region of central Italy in the Apennines. Occupied by the Umbrians in ancient times, it later fell to the Etruscans and then the Romans (c. 300 B.C.). After passing to various powers, Umbria came under the control of the papacy in the 16th century and joined the kingdom of Sardinia in 1860.

Um·bri·an (ŭm'brē-ən). **1.** Of or relating to Umbria. **2.** The Italic language of ancient Umbria. **3.** A native or inhabitant of Umbria.

Um·bun·du (oom-boon'doo, əm-). *pl.* **Umbundu** or **-dus.** See **Mbundu** (sense 2).

U·me (oo'mə, ü'mə). A river, about 459 km (285 mi) long, of northern Sweden flowing southeast into the Gulf of Bothnia.

U·me·å (oo'mə-ô', ü'mə-ô'). A city of northeast Sweden on an inlet of the Gulf of Bothnia at the mouth of the Ume River. Founded in 1622, it is a manufacturing center. ☉ Pop. 54,900.

Um·nak Island (oom'năk'). An island of southwest Alaska in the east-central Aleutian Islands. It is separated from Unalaska Island by **Umnak Pass.**

Ump·qua (ŭmp'kwô'). A river, about 322 km (200 mi) long, of southwest Oregon rising in two branches and flowing north and west to the Pacific Ocean.

Un·a·las·ka Island (ŭn'ə-lăs'kə). An island of southwest Alaska in the eastern Aleutian Islands southwest of Unimak Island. It was discovered c. 1759 by Russian explorers and used as a fur-trading center.

U·na·mi (oo-nä'mē, yoo-năm'ē). **1.** One of the two Algonquian languages of the Delaware peoples, originally spoken in central and southern New Jersey, eastern Pennsylvania, and northern Delaware. **2.** *pl.* **Unami** or **-mis.** A speaker of this language.

Un·com·pah·gre Peak (ŭn'kəm-pä'grē). A mountain, 4,364.2 m (14,309 ft) high, in the San Juan Mountains of southwest Colorado. It is the highest elevation in the range.

Un·ga·va Bay (ŭn-gä'və, -gä'-). An inlet of Hudson Strait in northeast Quebec, Canada, between northern Labrador and **Ungava Peninsula,** which is bordered on the west by Hudson Bay. The peninsula has vast mineral resources.

U·ni·mak Island (yoo'nə-măk'). An island of southwest Alaska in the eastern Aleutian Islands separated from the Alaska Peninsula by a narrow strait. It is the largest island of the group.

Un·ion (yoon'yən). A community of northeast New Jersey west-northwest of Elizabeth. Settled c. 1749 by colonists from Connecticut, it is a manufacturing center. ☉ Pop. 50,024.

Union City. 1. A city of western California southeast of Oakland. It is a mainly residential community. ☉ Pop. 53,762. **2.** A city of northeast New Jersey on the Hudson River adjoining Jersey City. Its varied manufactures include embroidery and perfumes. ☉ Pop. 58,012.

Un·ion·dale (yoon'yən-dāl'). An unincorporated community of southeast New York on southwest Long Island. It is mainly residential. ☉ Pop. 20,328.

Union of So·vi·et Socialist Republics (sō'vē-ĕt', -ĭt, sŏv'ē-, sō'vē-ĕt'). Commonly called **Soviet Union** or **Rus·sia** (rŭsh'ə). *abbr.* **U.S.S.R., USSR.** A former country of eastern Europe and northern Asia with coastlines on the Baltic and Black seas and the Arctic and Pacific oceans. It was established in December 1922 with the union of the Russian S.F.S.R. (proclaimed after the Russian Revolution of 1917) and various other soviet republics, including Belorussia and the Ukraine. After a strife-torn beginning, marked by internal power struggles and disastrous economic plans, it became a major industrial and manufacturing nation, with influence far beyond its borders. Under Mikhail S. Gorbachev, who was chosen as Soviet leader in 1985, important changes were made in the country's leadership, and the government loosened some of its control on the economy and approved changes in the structure of the Soviet system. The new openness led to the fall in 1989 of the Soviet-dominated Communist governments of eastern Europe, and disagreements over the pace of reform led to the fragmentation of the Communist party in the Soviet Union. In 1991 a number of constituent republics, including Estonia, Latvia, Lithuania, Belorussia (now Belarus), Ukraine, Moldavia (now Moldova), Georgia, Azerbaijan, Armenia, Turkmenistan, Uzbekistan, Kazakhstan, Kyrgyzstan, and Tajikistan, declared their independence, and the U.S.S.R. was officially dissolved on December 31, 1991. Moscow was the capital.

U·nit·ed Arab E·mir·ates (yōo-nī′tĭd; ĭ-mîr′-ĭts, ĕm′ər-). Formerly **Tru·cial Oman** (trōo′-shəl). *abbr.* **U.A.E.** A country of eastern Arabia, a federation of seven sheikdoms on the Persian Gulf and the Gulf of Oman. The area was converted to Islam in the 7th century. A powerful sect formed in the late 9th century whose armies sacked Mecca in 930 before being defeated by Bedouins. The area later became a base for pirates in the Persian Gulf and was known as the Pirate Coast into the 19th century. The British intervened by signing a series of truces with the ruling sheiks between 1820 and 1892, and the area became known as the Trucial States or Trucial Oman. After World War II Britain granted internal autonomy to the sheikdoms or emirates, with the United Arab Emirates being formed in 1971 after Britain withdrew from the area completely. The United Arab Emirates joined the Gulf Cooperation Council in 1981. Abu Dhabi is the capital. ⊛Pop. 1,861,000.

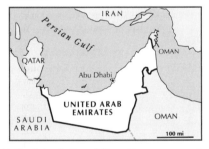

United Arab Republic. *abbr.* **U.A.R. 1.** A former union of Egypt and Syria that lasted from 1958 until 1961. Yemen also joined the union in 1958, thus creating the **United Arab States. 2.** See **Egypt.**

United Kingdom or **United Kingdom of Great Britain and Northern Ireland.** Commonly called **Great Britain** or **Britain.** *abbr.* **U.K., UK.** A country of western Europe comprising England, Scotland, Wales, and Northern Ireland. Beginning with the kingdom of England, it was created by three acts of union: with Wales (1536), Scotland (1707), and Northern Ireland (1800). War abroad with France in the 18th century left Great Britain the world's chief colonial

power, especially in North America and India, and the empire reached its commercial, economic, and political height under Queen Victoria (ruled 1837–1901). Also in the 19th century the country experienced the Industrial Revolution, which dramatically changed social and economic life. Growing rivalry with Germany led Great Britain, with France and Russia, to enter World War I in 1914, and following Germany's invasion of Poland in 1939, Great Britain entered World War II, during which the country was heavily bombarded. After the war many of the colonies gained their independence, and Great Britain's status as a world power declined. Economic problems plagued the country in the 1970's, and in 1979 Conservative Margaret Thatcher became Great Britain's first woman prime minister. Under Thatcher social programs were cut and many state-owned businesses were privatized, undoing many of the changes made by the postwar governments. Mrs. Thatcher was succeeded as prime minister in 1990 by John Major, who was succeeded in 1997 by Tony Blair in an election that restored the Labor Party to power after 18 years. London is the capital and the largest city. ⊛Pop. 58,091,000.

United Nations. *abbr.* **UN, U.N.** An international organization composed of most of the countries of the world. It was founded in 1945 to promote international peace, security, and economic development.

United States or **United States of America.** *abbr.* **U.S., US, U.S.A., USA.** A country of central and northwest North America with coastlines on the Atlantic and Pacific oceans. It includes the noncontiguous states of Alaska and Hawaii and various island territories in the Caribbean Sea and Pacific Ocean. The area now occupied by the contiguous 48 states was originally inhabited by numerous Native American peoples and was colonized beginning in the 16th century by Spain, France, the Netherlands, and England. Great Britain eventually controlled most of the Atlantic coast and, after the French and Indian Wars (1754–1763), the Northwest Territory and Canada. The original Thirteen Colonies declared their independence from Great Britain in 1776 and formed a government under the Articles of Confederation in 1781, adopting (1787) a new constitution that went into effect after 1789. The nation soon began to expand westward as various territories were purchased, annexed, or acquired by treaty. Growing tensions over the issue of Black slavery, an important source of labor for southern plantations, divided the country along geographic lines, and after the election of Abraham Lincoln (1860) to the Presidency, the South seceded and formed the Confederacy, sparking the Civil War (1861–1865). The remainder of the 19th century was marked by increased westward expansion, industrialization, and the influx of millions of immigrants, mainly from Europe. The nation entered World War I on the side of the Allies in 1917. The Great Depression began in 1929, prompting President Franklin Roosevelt to launch the domestic reform program known as the New Deal. The United States entered World War II after the Japanese attack (1941) on Pearl Harbor and emerged after the war as a world power and a major adversary of the Soviet Union in the cold war. During the 1960's the country was the scene of social turmoil and violence connected with the civil rights movement and demonstrations against U.S. involvement in the Vietnam War. In 1974, under pressure following the Watergate scandal, Richard Nixon be-

came the first U.S. President to resign his office. The terms of Ronald Reagan (1981–1989) and George Bush (1989–1993) were marked by conservative policies, especially in the areas of social spending and decreased government regulation. In 1991 the United States led the coalition that defeated Iraq in the Persian Gulf War. Bill Clinton (elected 1992) became the first Democratic President in 12 years, winning reelection to a second term in 1996. Washington, D.C., is the capital and New York the largest city. ◉ Pop. 260,651,000.

u·ni·ver·sal time (yo͞o′nə-vûr′səl). *abbr.* **UT.** The mean solar time for the meridian at Greenwich, England, used as a basis for calculating time throughout most of the world. Also called *Greenwich time.*

U·ni·ver·si·ty City (yo͞o′nə-vûr′sĭ-tē). A city of eastern Missouri, a residential suburb of St. Louis. Washington University (established 1853) is located here. ◉ Pop. 40,087.

University Heights. A city of northeast Ohio, a suburb of Cleveland. ◉ Pop. 14,790.

University Park. A city of northeast Texas, a residential suburb entirely surrounded by Dallas. ◉ Pop. 22,259.

Un·na (o͝on′ə). A city of west-central Germany, an industrial suburb of Essen. ◉ Pop. 57,569.

Up·land (ŭp′lənd). A city of southern California east of Los Angeles. It is a manufacturing and processing center in a citrus-growing region. ◉ Pop. 63,374.

U·po·lu (o͞o-pō′lo͞o). A volcanic island of Western Samoa in the southern Pacific Ocean. It is the site of Apia, the country's capital.

Up·per Arlington (ŭp′ər). A city of central Ohio, a residential suburb of Columbus. ◉ Pop. 34,128.

Upper Avon. See **Avon.**

Upper California. See **Alta California.**

Upper Canada. A historical region and province of British North America. Roughly coextensive with southern Ontario, Canada, it was formed in 1791 and joined Lower Canada in 1841.

Upper Dar·by (där′bē). An unincorporated community of southeast Pennsylvania, a residential and manufacturing suburb of Philadelphia. ◉ Pop. 84,054.

Upper East Side. See **East Side.**

Upper Egypt. A region of ancient Egypt in the valley of the Nile River south of the delta area, which was known as Lower Egypt. The two regions were united c. 3100 B.C.

Upper Engadine. See **Engadine.**

Upper Klamath Lake. A lake of south-central Oregon east of Medford. It is in a popular resort area.

Upper New York Bay. See **New York Bay.**

Upper Palatinate. See **Palatinate.**

Upper Peninsula. The northern part of Michigan between Lakes Superior and Michigan. It is separated from the Lower Peninsula by the Straits of Mackinac.

Upper Saint Clair (sānt clâr′). A community of southwest Pennsylvania, a suburb of Pittsburgh. ◦ Pop. 19,023.

Upper Silesia. See **Silesia.**

Upper Tunguska. See **Tunguska.**

Upper Volta. See **Burkina Faso.** — **Upper Voltan** adj. & n.

Upp·sa·la (ŭp′sə-lə, -sä′-, ōōp′sä′lä). A city of eastern Sweden north-northwest of Stockholm. Capital of a pre-Christian kingdom in the early Middle Ages, it became an episcopal see in 1164 and the coronation place of Swedish kings. The University of Uppsala was founded in 1477. ◦ Pop. 174,554.

Ur (ûr, ōōr). Known in biblical times as **Ur of the Chal·dees** (kăl′dēz′, kăl-dēz′). A city of ancient Sumer in southern Mesopotamia on a site in present-day southeast Iraq. One of the oldest cities in Mesopotamia, it was an important center of Sumerian culture after c. 3000 B.C. and the birthplace of the biblical patriarch Abraham. The city declined after the sixth century B.C.

U·ral-Al·ta·ic (yōōr′əl-ăl-tā′ĭk). A hypothetical language group that comprises the Uralic and Altaic language families. Also called *Turanian.*

U·ral·ic (yōō-răl′ĭk) also **U·ra·li·an** (yōō-rā′lē-ən). A language family that comprises the Finno-Ugric and Samoyedic subfamilies.

U·ral Mountains (yōōr′əl). A range of western Russia forming the traditional boundary between Europe and Asia and extending about 2,414 km (1,500 mi) from the Arctic Ocean southward to Kazakstan.

Ural River. A river of western Russia and western Kazakstan rising in the southern Ural Mountains and flowing about 2,533 km (1,574 mi) south, west, and south to the Caspian Sea.

U·ralsk (yōō-rălsk′, ōō-rălsk′). A city of northwest Kazakstan on the Ural River west-northwest of Aktyubinsk. Founded by Cossacks c. 1622, it is a processing and manufacturing center. ◦ Pop. 220,000.

U·ra·wa (ōō-rä′wə, -wä). A city of east-central Honshu, Japan, a commercial suburb of Tokyo. ◦ Pop. 442,381.

Ur·ban·a (ûr-băn′ə). A city of east-central Illinois adjoining Champaign. It is a trade, medical, and educational center. ◦ Pop. 36,344.

Ur·ban·dale (ûr′bən-dāl′). A city of south-central Iowa, a residential and industrial suburb of Des Moines. ◦ Pop. 23,500.

ur·ban district (ûr′bən). An administrative district of England, Wales, and Northern Ireland, usually composed of several densely populated communities, resembling a borough but lacking a borough charter.

Ur·du (ōōr′dōō, ûr′-). An Indic language that is the official literary language of Pakistan. It is written in an Arabic alphabet and is also widely used in India, chiefly by Muslims.

Ur·fa (ōōr-fä′). A city of southeast Turkey near the Syrian border. Founded as Edessa in ancient times, it was incorporated into the Ottoman Empire in 1637 and renamed Urfa. It is a trade center in a rich agricultural region. ◦ Pop. 357,900.

Ur·mi·a (ōōr′mē-ə), **Lake.** A shallow saline lake of northwest Iran between Tabriz and the Turkish border. The city of **Urmia,** on the western side of the lake, is reputed to be the birthplace of Zoroaster, the sixth-century Persian prophet. ◦ Pop. 300,746.

Ur·spra·che (ōōr′shprä′ĸнə). See **protolanguage.**

U·rua·pan (ōōr-wä′pən, -pän). A city of southwest-central Mexico west of Mexico City. It was founded in 1540 and is noted for its lacquerware. ◦ Pop. 122,828.

U·ru·bam·ba (ōō′rōō-bäm′bə). A river of Peru rising in the Andes and flowing about 724 km (450 miles) north-northwest to join the Apurímac River and form the Ucayali River.

U·ru·guay (yōōr′ə-gwī′, -gwā′, ōō′rōō-gwī′). *abbr.* **Urug.** A country of southeast South America on the Atlantic Ocean and the Río de la Plata. Known from explorations of the Río de la Plata in the early 16th century, the area was settled by the Spanish (1624) and Portuguese (1680), with Spain establishing sole dominance after 1724. Uruguay declared independence from Spain in 1810 and from Argentina in 1814, struggling against Brazilian occupation (1820–

1827) to finally achieve independent nationhood in 1828. After a period of internal and external warfare in the 19th century, Uruguay became a stable and prosperous country until social and economic problems led to a military dictatorship (1973–1985) marked by repressive measures against the Marxist Tupamaro guerrilla movement. Subsequent civilian governments were only partially successful in solving the country's economic problems. Montevideo is the capital and the largest city. ⊛ Pop. 3,167,000. —U'ru·guay'an *adj. & n.*

Uruguay River. A river of southeast South America rising in southern Brazil and flowing about 1,609 km (1,000 mi) west and south along the Brazil-Argentina border and the Argentina-Uruguay border to the Río de la Plata.

Ü·rüm·qi also **U·rum·chi** (ŏŏ-rŏŏm'chē, ü'-rüm'chē'). A city of northwest China in the Tien Shan. Its agricultural college was founded in 1952. ⊛ Pop. 1,160,775.

Ush·ant (ŭsh'ənt). An island of northwest France in the Atlantic Ocean off western Brittany. Naval battles between the French and the British occurred off the island in 1778 and 1794.

Us·pal·la·ta Pass (ŏŏ'spä-yä'tə, -tä). A pass, about 3,813 m (12,500 ft) high, through the Andes between Mendoza, Argentina, and Santiago, Chile. A monumental sculpture of Christ stands in the pass.

U·sti nad La·bem (ŏŏ'stē näd lä-běm'). A city of northwest Czech Republic on the Elbe River near the German border. Founded before the 13th century, it was ceded to Germany by the Munich Pact of 1938 and reverted to Czechoslovakia in 1945. ⊛ Pop. 106,500.

U·sti·nov (ŏŏ-stĭn'ôf). See **Izhevsk.**

Ust-Ka·me·no·gorsk (ŏŏst'kə-měn'ə-gôrsk', -myĭ-nə-). A city of northeast Kazakstan on the Irtysh River southeast of Novosibirsk, Russia. Founded as a military outpost in 1720, it is now a metallurgical center. ⊛ Pop. 334,000.

U·su·ma·cin·ta (ŏŏ'sə-mə-sĭn'tə, -sŏŏ-mä-sēn'-tä). A river, about 965 km (600 mi) long, of southeast Mexico. It forms part of the Guatemala-Mexico border.

U·tah (yŏŏ'tô', -tä'). *abbr.* **UT, Ut.** A state of the western United States. It was admitted as the 45th state in 1896. First explored by the Spanish in 1540, the region was settled in 1847 by Mormons led by Brigham Young. Salt Lake City is the capital and the largest city. ⊛ Pop. 1,727,784. —U'tah·an, U'tahn *adj. & n.*

Ute (yŏŏt). **1.** *pl.* **Ute** or **Utes.** A member of a Native American people formerly inhabiting a large area of Colorado, Utah, and northern New Mexico, with present-day populations in north-

east Utah and along the Colorado–New Mexico border. **2.** The Uto-Aztecan language of the Utes.

U·ti·ca (yŏŏ'tĭ-kə). **1.** An ancient city of northern Africa on the Mediterranean Sea northwest of Carthage. According to tradition, it was founded c. 1100 B.C. by Phoenicians from Tyre. The city declined in the first century B.C. and was finally destroyed by the Arabs c. A.D. 700. **2.** A city of central New York east-northeast of Syracuse. Settled in 1773 on the site of Fort Schuyler (established in 1758), it developed as an industrial center after the opening of the Erie Canal in 1825. ⊛ Pop. 68,637.

U·to-Az·tec·an (yŏŏ'tō-ăz'těk'ən). **1.** A language phylum of North and Central America that includes Ute, Hopi, Nahuatl, and Shoshone. **2.** A member of a tribe speaking a Uto-Aztecan language. **3.** Of or relating to the Uto-Aztecans or to the languages spoken by them.

U·trecht (yŏŏ'trěkt', ü'trěкнt). A city of central Netherlands south-southeast of Amsterdam. Dating to pre-Roman times, it was an important textile and commercial center during the Middle Ages. The Treaty of Utrecht ended the War of the Spanish Succession (1701–1713). ⊛ Pop. 234,139.

U·tsu·no·mi·ya (ŏŏt'sə-nō'mē-ə, ŏŏ-tsŏŏ'nô-mē'yä). A city of central Honshu, Japan, north of Tokyo. It is a resort and tobacco-processing center. ⊛ Pop. 434,029.

Ux·mal (ŏŏs-mäl'). An ancient ruined Mayan city of Yucatán in southeast Mexico. It flourished from 600 to 900. The ruins include many impressive structures, such as the Pyramid of the Magician.

Uz·bek (ŏŏz'běk', ŭz'-). **1.** *pl.* **Uzbek** or **-beks.** A member of a Turkic people inhabiting Uzbekistan and neighboring areas. **2.** The Turkic language of the Uzbeks.

Uz·bek·i·stan (ŏŏz-běk'ĭ-stän', -stän', ŭz-). Formerly also **Uz·bek Soviet Socialist Republic** (ŏŏz'běk', ŭz'-). A country of west-central Asia. Settled in ancient times, it was conquered by Alexander the Great, Genghis Khan, and Tamerlane and finally overrun by Uzbek peoples in

the early 16th century. Russia conquered the area in the 19th century. Split into various administrative territories after 1917, it was consolidated as a constituent republic of the U.S.S.R. in 1924. Uzbekistan declared its independence in 1991 after the collapse of the Soviet Union. Following independence the former Communist party retained its hold on power, and opposition groups were suppressed. Tashkent is the capital. ⊛ Pop. 22,349,000.

V

Vaal (väl). A river rising in eastern South Africa and flowing about 1,207 km (750 mi) southwest to the Orange River.

Vaa·sa (vä′sə, -sä). A city of western Finland on the Gulf of Bothnia northwest of Helsinki. Chartered in 1606, it was rebuilt after a devastating fire in 1852. Vaasa is a port and agricultural market. ⊛ Pop. 54,497.

Vac·a·ville (văk′ə-vĭl′). A city of central California west-southwest of Sacramento. It is a processing center. ⊛ Pop. 71,479.

Va·duz (vä-do͞ots′, fä-). The capital of Liechtenstein, in the western part of the country on the Rhine River. Destroyed during a conflict between Switzerland and the Holy Roman Empire (1499), it was rebuilt in the 1520's and is now a tourist center. ⊛ Pop. 4,927.

Váh (vä, väкн). A river, about 394 km (245 mi) long, of western Slovakia flowing west and south to the Danube River.

Val·dai Hills also **Val·day Hills** (väl-dī′). An upland region of northwest Russia between St. Petersburg and Moscow. It forms the watershed for numerous rivers, including the Volga, the Western Dvina, and the Dnieper.

Val·dez (văl-dĕz′). A city of southern Alaska on an inlet of Prince William Sound. A military base during World War II, it is the southern terminus of the oil pipeline from Prudhoe Bay. An oil spill in the waters of the sound caused extensive environmental damage in 1989. ⊛ Pop. 4,068.

Val·di·via (väl-dē′vē-ə, bäl-dē′vyä). A city of south-central Chile near the Pacific Ocean south of Concepción. Founded in 1552, it grew rapidly after the arrival of German immigrants in the mid-19th century. ⊛ Pop. 113,512.

Val d'Or (văl′ dôr′, väl dôr′). A town of southwest Quebec, Canada, near the Ontario border. It is a mining center. ⊛ Pop. 21,321.

Val·dos·ta (văl-dŏs′tə). A city of southern Georgia near the Florida border east-northeast

of Tallahassee. Settled in 1859, it is a processing and trade center. ⊛ Pop. 39,806.

vale (väl). A valley, often coursed by a stream.

Va·lence (və-läns′, vă-). A city of southeast France on the Rhone River south of Lyon. Settled in Roman times, it was captured by the Visigoths in A.D. 413 and by the Arabs c. 730. ⊛ Pop. 104,000.

Va·len·ci·a (və-lĕn′shē-ə, -chə, -sē-ə). **1.** A region and former kingdom of eastern Spain on the Mediterranean coast south of Catalonia. Inhabited by Iberian peoples in early times, it was colonized by Greek and Carthaginian traders and fell to the Moors in the eighth century. The Spanish soldier and hero the Cid ruled the region and the city of Valencia from 1094 until his death in 1099. **2.** A city of eastern Spain on the **Gulf of Valencia,** a wide inlet of the Mediterranean Sea. First mentioned as a Roman colony in 138 B.C., Valencia was taken by the Visigoths in A.D. 413, the Moors in 714, and James I of Aragon in 1238, after which it flowered commercially and culturally. The city was the seat (1936–1937) of the Loyalist government during the Spanish Civil War. Spain's third-largest city, it is a popular resort and a commercial and industrial center. ⊛ Pop. 749,361. **3.** A city of northern Venezuela west-southwest of Caracas on the western shore of **Lake Valencia.** Founded in 1555, it is a major industrial center. ⊛ Pop. 1,034,033.

Va·len·ci·ennes (və-lĕn′sē-ĕnz′, vă-län-syĕn′). A city of northern France near the Belgian border southeast of Lille. An important medieval town, it became noted for its lace industry in the 15th century. ⊛ Pop. 40,275.

Va·le·ra (və-lâr′ə, bä-lĕ′rä). A city of northwest Venezuela southwest of Barquisimento. It is a commercial center in an agricultural region. ⊛ Pop. 107,236.

Val·la·do·lid (văl′ə-də-lĭd′, bä′lyä-thô-lēth′). A city of northwest-central Spain north-northwest of Madrid. It became the chief residence of the Castilian court in the mid-15th century and was the site of the marriage of Ferdinand and Isabella in 1469. ⊛ Pop. 331,885.

Val·le d'A·os·ta (vä′lā dä-ō′stə, -ô′stä). A region of northwest Italy bordering on France and Switzerland. Separated from Piedmont in the 1940's, it has a predominantly French linguistic and cultural heritage.

Val·le·du·par (vä′yä-do͞o-pär′, bä′yĕ-). A town of northern Colombia east-southeast of Barranquilla. It is an agricultural trade center. ⊛ Pop. 150,838.

Val·le·jo (və-lā′ō, -hō). A city of western California on San Pablo Bay north of Oakland. It is a trade and processing center and has a large naval shipyard, founded by Adm. David Farragut in 1854. ⊛ Pop. 109,199.

Val·let·ta (və-lĕt′ə). The capital of Malta, on the northeast coast of the main island. Dating to the 16th century, it contains many relics of the Knights of Malta. Tourism is an important industry. ⊛ Pop. 9,149.

val·ley (văl′ē). *abbr.* **val. 1.** An elongated lowland between ranges of mountains, hills, or other uplands, often having a river or stream running along the bottom. **2.** An extensive area of land drained or irrigated by a river system.

Val·ley East (văl′ē). A town of central Ontario, Canada, a suburb of Sudbury. ⊛ Pop. 20,433.

Val·ley·field (văl′ē-fēld′). A city of southern Quebec, Canada, on the St. Lawrence River southwest of Montreal. It is a port of entry and an industrial center. ⊛ Pop. 29,574.

Valley Forge (fôrj, fōrj). A village of southeast Pennsylvania on the Schuylkill River northwest of Philadelphia. It was the site of the Continental Army headquarters from December 1777 to June 1778. The encampment was subjected to severe winter weather that caused extensive illness and suffering.

Valley of Ten Thousand Smokes. A volcanic region of southwest Alaska at the upper end of the Alaska Peninsula. It was formed by the eruption of Mount Katmai in 1912 and continues to emit hot gases through some of the countless cracks in the surface.

Valley of the Kings. A narrow valley of east-central Egypt surrounding the site of ancient Thebes between Karnak and Luxor. The valley contains the tombs of numerous pharaohs of the XVIII, XIX, and XX Dynasties, including that of Tutankhamen (flourished c. 1358 B.C.).

Valley Sta·tion (stā′shən). An unincorporated community of north-central Kentucky, a suburb of Louisville. ⊛ Pop. 22,840.

Valley Stream. A village of southeast New York on southwest Long Island. It is mainly residential. ⊛ Pop. 33,946.

Va·lois (văl′wä′, väl-wä′). A historical region and former duchy of northern France. A county from the 10th to the 12th century, it was an appanage of the royal house of Valois after 1285.

Val·pa·rai·so (văl′pə-rī′zō). **1.** also **Val·pa·ra·í·so** (bäl′pä-rä-ē′sô). A city of central Chile on the Pacific Ocean west-northwest of Santiago. Founded in 1536, it has frequently been subject to severe earthquakes. The modern city developed as an industrial center and the chief port of Chile in the early 20th century. ⊛ Pop. 276,756. **2.** A city of northwest Indiana southeast of Gary. It is a manufacturing and educational center. ⊛ Pop. 24,414.

Van (văn, vän), **Lake.** A salt lake of eastern Turkey. It is the largest lake in the country.

Van·cou·ver (văn-kōō′vər). **1.** A city of southwest British Columbia, Canada, on the Strait of Georgia opposite Vancouver Island. The largest city in the province, it is a major port, commercial and industrial center, and railroad hub. ⊛ Pop. 471,844. **2.** A city of southwest Washington on the Columbia River opposite Portland, Oregon. Founded as Fort Vancouver by the Hudson's Bay Company in the 1820's, it is a deep-water port with shipyards, lumber mills, and other processing facilities. ⊛ Pop. 46,380.

Vancouver, Mount. A peak, 4,873.6 m (15,979 ft) high, in the St. Elias Mountains of southwest Yukon Territory, Canada, near the Alaskan border.

Vancouver Island. An island of southwest British Columbia, Canada, in the Pacific Ocean separated from the mainland by the Strait of Georgia and Queen Charlotte Sound. The Strait of Juan de Fuca flows between the southern end of the island and the coastline of northwest Washington. First sighted by Spanish explorers in 1774 and visited by the British explorer Capt. James Cook in 1778, it was named in honor of the British navigator Capt. George Vancouver, who circumnavigated the island in 1792.

Van·dal (văn′dl). **1.** A member of a Germanic people that overran Gaul, Spain, and northern Africa in the fourth and fifth centuries A.D. and sacked Rome in 455. — **Van·dal·ic** (văn-dăl′ĭk) *adj.*

Van Die·men's Land (văn dē′mənz, vän). See **Tasmania.**

Vä·nern (vā′nərn, vĕ′-). A lake of southwest Sweden. It is the largest lake in the country and navigable for small oceangoing ships via the Göta Canal.

Va·nier (văn-yā′). A city of southeast Ontario, Canada, an industrial suburb of Ottawa on the Ottawa River. ⊛ Pop. 18,792.

Van·taa (vän′tä). A city of southern Finland, a suburb of Helsinki. ⊛ Pop. 160,158.

Va·nu·a Le·vu (və-nōō′ə lĕv′ōō). A volcanic island of Fiji in the southern Pacific Ocean northeast of Viti Levu. Sugar cane is important to the island's economy.

Va·nu·a·tu (vä′nōō-ä′tōō). Formerly **New Heb·ri·des** (nōō hĕb′rĭ-dēz′, nyōō). An island country of the southern Pacific Ocean east of northern Australia. Inhabited primarily by Melanesian peoples, the islands were first sighted by the Portuguese in 1606 and charted by the British navigator Capt. James Cook in 1774. In 1887 they came under a joint British-French naval commission, and in 1906 a condominium government was established. The area avoided Japanese occupation in World War II, becoming the site of U.S. military bases after 1942. In 1980 New Hebrides achieved independence as Vanuatu. Vila, on Efate Island, is the capital. ◉ Pop. 165,000. — **Va'nu·a'tu·an** *adj. & n.*

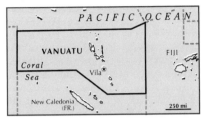

Va·ra·na·si (və-rä'nə-sē) also **Be·na·res** or **Ba·na·ras** (bə-när'əs, -ēz). A city of northeast-central India on the Ganges River southeast of Lucknow. One of India's oldest cities, it is a sacred Hindu pilgrimage site with some 1,500 temples, palaces, and shrines. ◉ Pop. 929,270.

Var·dar (vär'där'). A river, about 386 km (240 mi) long, rising in northwest Macedonia and flowing southward to an arm of the Aegean Sea in northeast Greece.

Va·re·se (və-rä'sē, vä-rě'zě). A city of northern Italy northwest of Milan. It is the center of a popular resort area. ◉ Pop. 90,285.

Var·na (vär'nə). A city of eastern Bulgaria on the Black Sea north-northeast of Burgas. Founded in the sixth century B.C. as a Greek colony, it came under Turkish control in 1391 and was ceded to newly independent Bulgaria in 1878. It is a port and an industrial center. ◉ Pop. 308,601.

Vash·on Island (văsh'ŏn). An island of west-central Washington in Puget Sound between Seattle and Tacoma.

Väs·ter·ås (věs'tə-rōs'). A city of eastern Sweden west-northwest of Stockholm. Founded before 1000, it was an important medieval city and a center of the Swedish Reformation. ◉ Pop. 120,889.

Va·ti·can City (văt'ĭ-kən). An independent papal state on the Tiber River within Rome, Italy. Created by the Lateran Treaty signed by Pope Pius XI and Victor Emmanuel III of Italy in

1929, it issues its own currency and postage stamps and has its own newspaper and broadcasting facilities. The government is run by a lay governor and council, all responsible to the pope. ◉ Pop. 766.

Vät·tern (vět'ərn). A lake of south-central Sweden southeast of Lake Vänern. It is connected with the Baltic Sea by the Göta Canal.

Vaughan (vôn, vän). A town of southeast Ontario, Canada, a residential suburb of Toronto. ◉ Pop. 111,359.

Vau·pés (vou-pās', -pěs'). See **Uaupés.**

Ved·da also **Ved·dah** (věd'ə). *pl.* **Vedda** or **-das** also **Veddah** or **-dahs.** A member of the earliest people of Sri Lanka, originally forest-dwelling hunters but now almost completely assimilated into the modern Singhalese population.

Ve·ii (vē'ī). An ancient city of Etruria north of modern-day Rome, Italy. A powerful member of the Etruscan League, it was almost constantly at war with Rome and finally succumbed in 396 B.C. after a ten-year siege.

Vel·bert (fěl'bərt). A city of west-central Germany in the Ruhr Valley northeast of Düsseldorf. It is a manufacturing center specializing in iron goods. ◉ Pop. 89,261.

veldt also **veld** (vělt, fělt). Any of the open grazing areas of southern Africa.

Ve·li·a (vē'lē-ə). See **Elea.**

Ve·li·ki·ye Lu·ki (və-lē'kē-ə lōō'kē, vyĭ-lē'kē-yə lōō'kyĭ). A city of west-central Russia west of Moscow. First mentioned in the 12th century, it is a railroad junction and processing center. ◉ Pop. 115,822.

Vel·lore (və-lôr', -lōr'). A town of southeast India west-southwest of Madras. The Sepoy Mutiny began here in 1806. ◉ Pop. 174,247.

Ven·da (věn'də). A former internally self-governing Black African homeland in northeast South Africa near the Zimbabwe border. It was granted limited self-government in 1962, nominal independence in 1979, and was dissolved and reintegrated into South Africa by the 1993 interim constitution.

Ve·ne·ti·a (və-nē'shē-ə, -shə). A historical region of northeast Italy between the Po River and the Alps. Named after the Veneti, a people who settled the area in c. 1000 B.C., it was joined with Istria by the Roman emperor Augustus to form a separate province. The area was devastated by the Huns in the 5th century, but its towns later became powerful communes, with Venice becoming dominant by the 15th century. It passed to Austria in 1797 and to Italy in 1866.

Ve·ne·tian (və-nē'shən). **1.** Of or relating to Venice, Italy, or its people, language, or culture. **2.** A native or inhabitant of Venice, Italy. **3.** The variety of Italian spoken in Venice.

Ve·ne·to (věn′ĕ-tō′). A region of northeast Italy bordering on the Adriatic Sea. It is roughly coextensive with the historical region of Venetia.

Ven·e·zue·la (věn′ə-zwä′lə, -zwē′-). *abbr.* **Ven., Venez.** A country of northern South America on the Caribbean Sea. Inhabited by a variety of Arawakan and other peoples, the region was discovered by Columbus in 1498 and settled beginning in the 1520's, becoming part of the Spanish colony (later viceroyalty) of New Granada. Venezuela won independence in 1821 in federation with Colombia and Ecuador and broke away to form a separate country in 1830. It developed economically and industrially under the dictatorial regime of Gen. Juan Vicente Gómez (governed 1908–1935) and enjoyed democratic rule under Rómulo Betancourt (governed 1945–1948 and 1959–1964) and succeeding presidents. Venezuela's oil industry was nationalized in 1976. Caracas is the capital and the largest city. ◉ Pop. 21,177,000. — **Ven′e·zue′lan** *adj. & n.*

Venezuela, Gulf of. An inlet of the Caribbean Sea between northwest Venezuela and northern Colombia. It extends southward as Lake Maracaibo.

Ven·ice (věn′ĭs). A city of northeast Italy on islets within a lagoon in the **Gulf of Venice,** a wide inlet of the northern Adriatic Sea. Founded in the 5th century A.D. by refugees fleeing the Lombard invaders who had gained control of the mainland, it became a major maritime power by the 13th century and spread its influence over northern Italy and the eastern Mediterranean by the 15th century. Its territories were gradually lost to the Turks, and in 1797 it passed to Austria. Venice was ceded to Italy in 1866. It is a tourist and commercial center known for its canals. ◉ Pop. 308,717.

Vé·nis·sieux (vā-nē-syœ′). A city of east-central France, an industrial suburb of Lyon. ◉ Pop. 64,804.

Ven·lo (věn′lō). A town of southeast Netherlands near the German border. Formerly a fortress city, it is now an agricultural trade center. ◉ Pop. 62,935.

vent (věnt). *Geology.* **1.** The opening of a volcano in the earth's crust. **2.** An opening on the ocean floor that emits hot water and dissolved minerals.

Ven·tu·ra (věn-chŏor′ə, -tŏor′ə). A city of southern California on the Pacific Ocean west of Los Angeles. It was founded as the mission of San Buenaventura (still the official name of the city) in 1782. ◉ Pop. 92,575.

Ve·ra·cruz (věr′ə-krōōz′, bě′rä-krōōs′). A city of east-central Mexico on the Gulf of Mexico east of Puebla. Founded in 1599 on a site visited earlier (1519) by the Spanish explorer Hernando Cortés, it was frequently sacked by buccaneers in the 17th and 18th centuries. U.S. troops led by Gen. Winfield Scott captured the city in 1847 during the Mexican-American War. It is a large port and a tourist resort. ◉ Pop. 284,822.

Ver·cel·li (věr-chěl′ē). A city of northwest Italy west-southwest of Milan. Founded in Roman times, it was ruled by the Visconti family of Milan from 1335 to 1427 and thereafter by the house of Savoy. ◉ Pop. 51,975.

Verde (vûrd), **Cape.** A peninsula of western Senegal projecting into the Atlantic Ocean. First sighted by the Portuguese in 1445, it is the westernmost point of Africa.

Ver·de River (vûr′dē, věr′-). A river, about 306 km (190 mi) long, of central Arizona flowing generally southeast to the Salt River.

Ver·di·gris (vûr′dĭ-grĭs). A river, about 451 km (280 mi) long, of southeast Kansas and northeast Oklahoma flowing generally southward to the Arkansas River.

Ver·dun (vər-dŭn′, věr-dœn′). **1.** A city of southern Quebec, Canada, a residential suburb of Montreal on Montreal Island. ◉ Pop. 61,287. **2.** A city of northeast France on the Meuse River west of Metz. Dating to Roman times and an important Carolingian commercial center, it was the site of a prolonged World War I battle (February–December 1916) in which French forces repelled a massive German offensive. The total casualties have been estimated at more than 700,000. The city was rebuilt after the war. ◉ Pop. 21,516.

Ver·kho·yansk Range (věr′kə-yänsk′, vĭr-KHÔ-). A mountain chain of northeast Russia parallel to and east of the lower Lena River. The lowest temperature for an inhabited area, −68°C (−90°F), was recorded here on February 6, 1933.

Ver·mont (vər-mŏnt′). *abbr.* **VT, Vt.** A state of the northeast United States bordering on Canada. It was admitted as the 14th state in 1791. Explored by Samuel de Champlain in 1609, the region was first permanently settled by the

British in 1724. Claims to the area were relinquished by Massachusetts in 1781, New Hampshire in 1782, and New York in 1790. Montpelier is the capital and Burlington the largest city. ⊛Pop. 564,964. — Ver·mont′er *n.*

Ver·non (vûr′nən). **1.** A city of southern British Columbia, Canada, near the northern end of Okanagan Lake. It is a processing center in a lumbering region. ⊛Pop. 19,987. **2.** A town of northern Connecticut northeast of Hartford. Settled c. 1726, it is a manufacturing center. ⊛Pop. 29,841.

Ve·ro Beach (vîr′ō). A city of eastern Florida on the Indian River lagoon north-northwest of West Palm Beach. It is a fishing resort in a citrus-growing area. ⊛Pop. 17,350.

Ve·ro·na (və-rō′nə). A city of northern Italy on the Adige River west of Venice. The original settlement on the site was conquered by Rome in 89 B.C. and later fell to barbarian invaders. Verona became an independent republic in A.D. 1107 and formed the powerful Veronese League in 1164. It became part of Italy in 1866. ⊛Pop. 252,689. — Ve′ro·nese′ (vĕr′ə-nēz′, -nēs′) *adj. & n.*

Ver·sailles (vər-sī′, vĕr-). A city of north-central France west-southwest of Paris. It is best known for its magnificent palace, built by Louis XIV in the mid-17th century, where the treaty ending World War I was signed in 1919. ⊛Pop. 91,494.

Ver·viers (vĕr-vyā′). A city of eastern Belgium east of Liège. It is a manufacturing center with a textile industry. ⊛Pop. 54,294.

Ves·ta·vi·a Hills (vĕ-stā′vē-ə). A city of north-central Alabama, a residential suburb of Birmingham. ⊛Pop. 19,749.

Ve·su·vi·us (vĭ-sōō′vē-əs), **Mount.** A volcano, 1,281 m (4,200 ft) high, of southern Italy on the eastern shore of the Bay of Naples. A violent eruption in A.D. 79 destroyed the nearby cities of Pompeii and Herculaneum. Since that time it has erupted about three dozen times, most recently in the period from 1913 to 1944. — Ve·su′vi·an *adj.*

Vesz·prém (vĕs′prām). A city of western Hungary north of Lake Balaton. It is a commercial and processing center. ⊛Pop. 63,058.

Vet·lu·ga (vĕt-lōō′gə). A river, about 850 km (528 mi) long, of central Russia flowing generally southward to the Volga River.

Vi·a·reg·gio (vē′ə-rĕj′ō, vyä-rĕd′jô). A city of northwest Italy on the Ligurian Sea southeast of Genoa. It is a fishing center and fashionable resort. ⊛Pop. 58,136.

Vi·cen·te Ló·pez (və-sĕn′tē lō′pĕz′, vē-sĕn′-tĕ lô′pĕs). A city of east-central Argentina, a suburb of Buenos Aires. ⊛Pop. 289,142.

Vi·cen·za (vĭ-chĕn′sə, vē-chĕn′dzä). A city of

northeast Italy west of Venice. Founded by Ligurians c. first century B.C., it became a free city in A.D. 1164, passed to Austria in 1797, and to the kingdom of Italy in 1866. ⊛Pop. 107,076.

Vi·chu·ga (vĭ-chōō′gə). A city of west-central Russia on the Volga River northeast of Moscow. It is a textile-processing center. ⊛Pop. 51,000.

Vi·chy (vĭsh′ē, vē′shē). A city of central France south-southeast of Paris. A noted spa with hot mineral springs, it was the capital of unoccupied France (under the regime organized by Henri Pétain) from July 1940 until November 1942 during World War II. The Vichy government was widely considered a tool of the Nazis and was never recognized by the Allies. ⊛Pop. 30,527.

Vicks·burg (vĭks′bûrg′). A city of western Mississippi on bluffs above the Mississippi River west of Jackson. During the Civil War it was besieged from 1862 to 1863 and finally captured by troops led by the Union general Ulysses S. Grant on July 4, 1863. It is an important port. ⊛Pop. 20,908.

Vic·to·ri·a (vĭk-tôr′ē-ə, -tōr′-). **1.** The capital of British Columbia, Canada, on southeast Vancouver Island at the eastern end of the Strait of Juan de Fuca. Founded in 1843 as a Hudson's Bay Company outpost, it became provincial capital in the late 1860's. ⊛Pop. 299,290. **2.** The capital of Hong Kong, on the northwest coast of Hong Kong Island. It has extensive shipping facilities and is the seat of the University of Hong Kong (established 1911). ⊛Pop. 1,183,621. **3.** The capital of Seychelles, on the northeast coast of Mahé Island on the Indian Ocean. ⊛Pop. 23,000. **4.** A city of southeast Texas southeast of San Antonio. It is connected with the Intracoastal Waterway by the Victoria Barge Canal. ⊛Pop. 55,076.

Victoria, Lake also **Victoria Ny·an·za** (nī-ăn′-zə, nyän′-). A lake of east-central Africa bordered by Uganda, Kenya, and Tanzania. It was sighted in 1858 by the British explorer John Speke, who was searching for the source of the Nile River.

Victoria Falls. A waterfall, 108.3 m (355 ft) high, of south-central Africa in the Zambezi River between southwest Zambia and northwest Zimbabwe. The falls were discovered by the Scottish explorer David Livingstone in November 1855.

Victoria Island. An island of north-central Northwest Territories, Canada, in the Arctic Archipelago east of Banks Island. It was discovered in the late 1830's and explored by the Englishman John Rae in 1851.

Victoria Land. A mountainous region of Antarctica bounded by Ross Sea and Wilkes Land. It was discovered by the British explorer Sir James Clark Ross during his 1839–1843 expedition.

Victoria Nile. A section of the Nile River, about 418 km (260 mi) long, between Lake Victoria and Lake Albert in central Uganda.

Victoria Ny·an·za (nī-ăn′zə, nyän′-). See Lake Victoria.

Vic·to·ri·a·ville (vĭk-tôr′ē-ə-vĭl′, -tôr′-). A town of southern Quebec, Canada, southeast of Trois Rivières. It is a manufacturing and processing center. ⊛ Pop. 21,838.

Vi·din (vē′dĭn). A city of extreme northwest Bulgaria on the Danube River near the Yugoslav border. Founded in the first century A.D. as a Roman fortress, it was under Turkish rule from 1396 to 1807. ⊛ Pop. 64,000.

Vi·en·na (vē-ĕn′ə). **1.** The capital and largest city of Austria, in the northeast part of the country on the Danube River. Originally a Celtic settlement, it became the official residence of the house of Hapsburg in 1278 and a leading cultural center in the 18th century, particularly under the reign (1740–1780) of Maria Theresa. Vienna was designated the capital of Austria in 1918 and remains one of the great historic cities of Europe. ⊛ Pop. 1,560,471. **2.** A town of northeast Virginia, a residential suburb of Washington, D.C. ⊛ Pop. 14,852.

Vienne (vyĕn). A river, about 349 km (217 mi) long, of southwest-central France flowing generally northwest to the Loire River.

Vi·en·nese (vē′ə-nēz′, -nēs′). **1.** Relating to or characteristic of Vienna, Austria. **2.** *pl.* **-nese.** A native or inhabitant of Vienna. **3.** The variety of German spoken in Vienna.

Vien·tiane (vyĕn-tyän′). The capital and largest city of Laos, in the north-central part of the country on the Mekong River and the Thailand border. It became the capital of the French protectorate of Laos in 1899 and later the capital of independent Laos. ⊛ Pop. 210,000.

Vier·sen (fîr′zən). A city of west-central Germany west of Düsseldorf. It is a textile-manufacturing center. ⊛ Pop. 78,784.

Viet·nam (vē-ĕt′näm′, -năm′, vē′ĭt-, vyĕt′-). *abbr.* **Viet.** A country of southeast Asia in eastern Indochina on the South China Sea. Modern Vietnam is made up of the historical regions of Tonkin, Annam, and Cochin China, much of which was under Chinese control from the 3rd century B.C. to the 15th century A.D. The first Europeans to arrive were Portuguese traders in 1535. The area came under French influence in the mid-19th century as part of French Indochina. Japanese occupation during World War II was resisted by a coalition of nationalist and Communist forces known as the Vietminh, led by Ho Chi Minh, which continued to oppose

French control after the Japanese were defeated. With the fall of Dien Bien Phu in 1954 the area was partitioned into **North Vietnam** and **South Vietnam.** The Vietnam War (1954–1975) grew out of the attempt by Communist Vietcong guerrillas backed by North Vietnam to overthrow the U.S.-supported regime of Ngo Dinh Diem (governed 1955–1963) in the south. The war eventually broadened to include large numbers of U.S. troops and massive bombing of North Vietnam and parts of Cambodia. After 1970 the United States began turning over conduct of the war to the South Vietnamese government, which collapsed in 1975. Unified under Communist rule, Vietnam invaded Cambodia in 1978 to drive out the Pol Pot government. During the 1990's the Vietnamese government relaxed many of its economic restrictions, and the United States lifted its trade embargo in 1994. Hanoi is the capital and Ho Chi Minh City the largest city. ⊛ Pop. 72,510,000.

Viet·nam·ese (vē-ĕt′nə-mēz′, -mēs′, vē′ĭt-, vyĕt′-). *abbr.* **Viet. 1.** Of or relating to Vietnam or its people, language, or culture. **2.** *pl.* **-ese.** A native or inhabitant of Vietnam. **3.** The language of the largest ethnic group in Vietnam and the official language of the nation.

Vi·ge·va·no (vē-jĕv′ə-nō′, -jĕ′vä-). A city of northwest Italy southwest of Milan. It is a manufacturing center. ⊛ Pop. 65,228.

Vi·go (vē′gō, bē′gô). A city of northwest Spain on the **Bay of Vigo,** an inlet of the Atlantic Ocean. Vigo is a naval base and major shipping and fishing center. ⊛ Pop. 276,109.

Vi·ja·ya·wa·da (vĭj′ə-yə-wä′də, vē′jə-). Formerly **Bez·wa·da** (bĕz-wä′də). A city of southeast India east-southeast of Hyderabad. It is a trade center and an administrative and transportation hub. ◉ Pop. 454,577.

Vi·king (vī′kĭng). **1.** One of a seafaring Scandinavian people who plundered the coasts of northern and western Europe from the eighth through the tenth century. **2.** A Scandinavian.

Vi·la (vē′lə) or **Port-Vi·la** (pôrt′vē′lə, pōrt′-). The capital of Vanuatu, on Efate Island in the southwest Pacific Ocean. It was a Japanese base during World War II. ◉ Pop. 13,067.

Vila No·va de Gai·a (nō′və də gī′ə). A city of northwest Portugal, a manufacturing suburb of Oporto. ◉ Pop. 62,469.

Vil·lach (fĭl′äk′, -äкн′). A city of southern Austria on the Drava River southwest of Vienna. Originally a Roman settlement, it is an industrial and transportation center with thermal mineral springs. ◉ Pop. 52,692.

Vil·la·her·mo·sa (vē′ə-ĕr-mō′sə, bē′yä-). A city of southeast Mexico east of the Isthmus of Tehuantepec. It was founded in the 16th century near the site of an Olmec settlement. ◉ Pop. 158,216.

Vil·la Park (vĭl′ə). A village of northeast Illinois, a suburb of Chicago. ◉ Pop. 22,253.

Vil·la·vi·cen·ci·o (vē′ə-vĭ-sĕn′sē-ō′, bē′yä-vē-sĕn′syô). A city of central Colombia southeast of Bogotá. It is an urban trade and processing center in an agricultural region. ◉ Pop. 162,556.

Ville·juif (vēl-zhwēf′). A city of north-central France, a suburb of Paris. ◉ Pop. 52,448.

Ville·ur·banne (vē′lər-băn′, vēl-ür-bän′). A city of southeast France, an industrial suburb of Lyon. ◉ Pop. 116,851.

Vil·ling·en-Schwen·ning·en (fĭl′ĭng-ən-shvĕn′-ĭng-ən). A city of southwest Germany south-southwest of Stuttgart. Founded in 999, it is a manufacturing center. ◉ Pop. 76,600.

Vil·ni·us (vĭl′nē-əs) or **Vil·na** (-nə). The capital and largest city of Lithuania, in the southeast part of the country. Founded in the 10th century, it was frequently devastated by plagues, fires, and invasions from the 15th to the 18th century. Vilnius passed to Russia in 1795 and became a provincial capital (1801–1815). A center of Jewish learning in the 18th and 19th centuries, the city was occupied by Soviet troops in 1939 and by German troops from 1941 to 1944, during which time the city was heavily damaged and the Jewish population exterminated. It became the capital of the Lithuanian Soviet Socialist Republic in 1944 and of independent Lithuania in 1991. ◉ Pop. 581,500.

Vil·yu·i (vĭl-yōō′ē). A river of eastern Russia

flowing about 2,446 km (1,520 mi) eastward to the Lena River.

Vim·i·nal (vĭm′ə-nəl). One of the seven hills of ancient Rome. The baths of the emperor Diocletian (ruled 284–305) were built at the foot of the hill. — **Vim′i·nal** adj.

Vi·ña del Mar (vēn′yə dĕl mär′, bē′nyä thĕl). A city of central Chile, a resort and residential suburb east of Valparaiso on the Pacific Ocean. ◉ Pop. 281,063.

Vin·cennes. 1. (văN-sĕn′) A city of north-central France east of Paris. Its 14th-century castle was once a royal residence and later a state prison. ◉ Pop. 42,870. **2.** (vĭn-sĕnz′) A city of southwest Indiana on the Wabash River south of Terre Haute. The oldest city in the state, it was founded as a mission and fur-trading post by the French in the early 18th century. ◉ Pop. 19,859.

Vin·dhya Range (vĭn′dyə). A chain of hills in central India extending east-northeast for about 965 km (600 mi) and rising to approximately 915 m (3,000 ft).

Vine·land (vīn′lənd). A city of southern New Jersey south-southwest of Camden. It is a trade, manufacturing, and processing center. ◉ Pop. 54,780.

Vin·land (vĭn′lənd). An unidentified coastal region of northeast North America visited by Norse voyagers as early as c. 1000. The region, variously located from Labrador to New Jersey, was named for the grapes growing plentifully in the area.

Vin·ni·tsa (vĭn′ĭ-tsə, vyē′nĭ-). A city of west-central Ukraine southwest of Kiev. Founded in the 14th century, it passed to Russia in 1793 and is now a processing center and railroad junction. ◉ Pop. 384,400.

Vin·son Mas·sif (vĭn′sən mă-sēf′). A peak, 5,142.3 m (16,860 ft) high, in the Ellsworth Mountains of western Antarctica. It is the highest elevation in the range.

Vir·gin·ia (vər-jĭn′yə). abbr. **VA, Va.** A state of the eastern United States on Chesapeake Bay and the Atlantic Ocean. It was admitted as one of the original Thirteen Colonies in 1788. Early colonizing attempts (1584–1587) by Sir Walter Raleigh failed, but in 1607 colonists dispatched by the London Company established the first permanent settlement at Jamestown (May 13). Virginia was a prime force in the move for independence and was the site of British military leader Lord Cornwallis's surrender in 1781. Virginia seceded in April 1861 and was the scene of many major battles during the Civil War, including the final campaigns that led to the surrender of Confederate general Robert E. Lee. Richmond is the capital and Norfolk the largest city. ◉ Pop. 6,216,568. — **Vir·gin′ian** adj. & n.

Virginia Algonquian. The extinct Eastern Algonquian language of eastern Virginia.

Virginia Beach. An independent city of southeast Virginia on the Atlantic Ocean east of Norfolk. Mainly residential, it is a popular resort. ◉ Pop. 393,069.

Virginia City. A town of southwest Montana south of Helena. It was founded in 1863 after the discovery of gold and soon became notorious as a rowdy mining town. Virginia City is now a tourist center, with many restored structures. ◉ Pop. 142.

Vir·gin Islands (vûr′jĭn). **1.** *abbr.* **V.I.** A group of islands of the northeast West Indies east of Puerto Rico. They are divided politically into the **British Virgin Islands** to the northeast and the Virgin Islands of the United States to the southwest. The islands were first sighted and named by Christopher Columbus in 1493. **2.** *abbr.* **VI, V.I.** Officially **Virgin Islands of the United States.** A United States territory constituting the southwest group of the Virgin Islands. The islands were purchased from Denmark in 1917 because of their strategic location at the approach to the Panama Canal. Charlotte Amalie, on St. Thomas Island, is the capital. ◉ Pop. 104,000.

Virgin River. A river, about 322 km (200 mi) long, of southwest Utah and southeast Nevada flowing southwest and south to Lake Mead.

Vis (vēs). An island of western Croatia off the Dalmatian coast south-southwest of Split. Major naval battles occurred off the island in 1811 and 1866. In the first, the British defeated the French; in the second, the Austrians were victorious over the Italians. It is a popular resort.

Vi·sa·kha·pat·nam (vĭ-sä′kə-pŭt′nəm) or **Vi·sha·kha·pat·nam** (-shä′-) also **Vi·za·ga·pa·tam** (vĭ-zä′gə-pŭt′əm). A city of eastern India on the Bay of Bengal northeast of Madras. Established by the English as a trading post in 1683, it is a health resort and processing center with a protected harbor and shipping facilities. ◉ Pop. 752,037.

Vi·sa·lia (vī-sāl′yə). A city of south-central California southeast of Fresno. Agricultural products of the San Joaquin Valley are important to its economy. ◉ Pop. 75,636.

Vi·sa·yan (vĭ-sī′ən). **1.** A member of the largest ethnic group indigenous to the Philippines, found in the Visayan Islands. **2.** The Austronesian language of the Visayans.

Visayan Islands. An island group of the central Philippines in and around the **Visayan Sea** between Luzon and Mindanao.

Vis·by (vĭz′bē, vēs′bü). A city of southeast Sweden on western Gotland Island on the Baltic Sea. It was a member of the Hanseatic League and a commercial center from the 10th to the 14th century but declined after its capture by the Danes in 1362. Visby was a pirate stronghold for the next two centuries and passed to Sweden in 1645. It is a resort and an industrial center. ◉ Pop. 20,100.

Vis·count Mel·ville Sound (vī′kount mĕl′-vĭl′, -vəl). An arm of the Arctic Ocean between Victoria and Melville islands in northern Northwest Territories, Canada. It is a section of the Northwest Passage but is navigable only under favorable weather conditions.

Vi·sha·kha·pat·nam (vĭ-shä′kə-pŭt′nəm). See **Visakhapatnam.**

Vis·i·goth (vĭz′ĭ-gŏth′). A member of the western Goths that invaded the Roman Empire in the fourth century A.D. and settled in France and Spain, establishing a monarchy that lasted until the early eighth century. — **Vis′i·goth′ic** *adj.*

Vi·so (vē′zō), **Mount.** A peak, 3,843.6 m (12,602 ft) high, of northwest Italy in the Cottian Alps near the French border. It is the highest elevation in the range.

Vis·ta (vĭs′tə). An unincorporated community of southern California north of San Diego. It is a resort and agricultural area. ◉ Pop. 71,872.

Vis·tu·la (vĭs′chə-lə, -chōō-). A river of Poland, about 1,091 km (678 mi) long, rising near the Czech Republic border and flowing northeast, northwest, and north to the Gulf of Gdańsk.

Vi·tebsk (vē′tĕpsk′, vye′tyĭpsk′). A city of northeast Belarus on the Western Dvina River northeast of Minsk. First mentioned in 1021, it passed to Russia in 1772 and is now a port, railroad junction, and processing center. ◉ Pop. 365,100.

Vi·ti Le·vu (vē′tē lĕv′ōō). The largest of the Fiji Islands, in the southwest Pacific Ocean. Suva, the capital of Fiji, is on the southeast coast of the island.

Vi·tim (vĭ-tēm′). A river of southeast Russia flowing about 1,834 km (1,140 mi) generally northeast and north to the Lena River.

Vi·to·ri·a (vĭ-tôr′ē-ə, -tōr′-, bē-tô′ryä). A city of north-central Spain south-southeast of Bilbao. Probably founded by the Visigoths in the sixth century A.D., it is a manufacturing and processing center. ◉ Pop. 208,755.

Vi·tó·ri·a (vĭ-tôr′ē-ə, -tōr′-, vē-tôr′yä). A city of eastern Brazil on the Atlantic Ocean northeast of Rio de Janeiro. It was founded in 1535 and is now a major shipping and processing center. ◉ Pop. 258,243.

Vitória de Con·quis·ta (dä kôN-kēs′tä). A city of east-central Brazil north-northeast of Rio de Janeiro. It is a trade center in a mining and cattle-raising area. ◉ Pop. 224,896.

Vi·try-sur-Seine (vē-trē′sōōr-sĕn′, -sür-). A city of north-central France, an industrial suburb of Paris. ◉ Pop. 85,263.

Vit·to·ri·a (vĭ-tôr'ē-ə, -tōr'-, vēt-tô'ryä). A city of southeast Sicily, Italy, west of Ragusa. Wine and olive oil are produced and exported here. ⊛ Pop. 50,220.

Vi·za·ga·pa·tam (vĭ-zä'gə-pŭt'əm). See **Visakhapatnam.**

Vlaar·ding·en (vlär'dĭng-ən). A city of southwest Netherlands, a port and industrial suburb of Rotterdam. ⊛ Pop. 76,466.

Vla·di·kav·kaz (vlăd'ĭ-kăf'kăz', vlə-dyē'käf-kăz). Formerly **Or·dzho·ni·kid·ze** (ôr'jŏn-ĭ-kĭd'zə, ər-jə-nyĭ-kyē'dzĭ). A city of southwest Russia at the foot of the Caucasus Mountains north-northwest of Tbilisi, Georgia. Founded in 1784 as a fortress during the Russian conquest of the Caucasus, it is a metallurgical and industrial center. ⊛ Pop. 307,575.

Vla·di·mir (vlăd'ə-mîr', vlə-dyē'mĭr). A city of west-central Russia east of Moscow. Probably founded in the 10th century, it came under the control of Moscow during the 15th century. ⊛ Pop. 335,352.

Vlad·i·vos·tok (vlăd'ə-və-stŏk', -vŏs'tŏk', vlə-dyə-və-stôk'). A city of extreme southeast Russia on an arm of the Sea of Japan. It has been a naval base since 1872 and grew rapidly after the completion of the Trans-Siberian Railroad in the early 1900's. ⊛ Pop. 637,351.

Vlis·sing·en (vlĭs'ĭng-ən) also **Flush·ing** (flŭsh'-ĭng). A city of southwest Netherlands on an island in the Schelde estuary and the North Sea. Chartered in 1247, it was one of the first Dutch towns to rebel against Spain (1572). It is a port and an industrial center. ⊛ Pop. 26,500.

Vlo·rë (vlôr'ə, vlōr'ə) also **Vlo·ne** (vlō'nə). A city of southwest Albania on **Vlorë Bay,** an inlet of the Adriatic Sea. Albania's independence was proclaimed here on November 28, 1912. In February–March 1997 the city became a center of a rebellion set off by the collapse of fraudulent pyramid schemes that had caused many Albanians to lose their life savings. ⊛ Pop. 61,100.

Vl·ta·va (vŭl'tə-və, vəl'tä-vä). A river, about 434 km (270 mi) long, of western Czech Republic flowing southeast then north to the Elbe River.

Vo·gul (vō'gōōl). **1.** *pl.* **Vogul** or **-guls.** A member of a people inhabiting the region of the Ob River in western Siberia, closely related to the Ostyak. **2.** The Ugric language of this people.

Voj·vo·di·na (voi'və-dē'nə). A region of northern Yugoslavia in the Serbian republic. An agricultural area long a part of Hungary, it became an autonomous region of the former Yugoslavia in 1946. Its autonomy was revoked by Serbia in 1990 as Yugoslavia disintegrated, and in 1995 many ethnic Hungarians and Croats inhabiting the region were forced out by incoming Serbian refugees.

vol·ca·no (vŏl-kā'nō). *pl.* **-noes** or **-nos.** *abbr.* **vol. 1.** An opening in the earth's crust through which molten lava, ash, and gases are ejected. **2.** A mountain formed by the materials ejected from a volcano. — **vol·can'ic** (-kăn'ĭk) *adj.*

Vol·ca·no Islands (vŏl-kā'nō). A group of Japanese islands in the northwest Pacific Ocean north of the Mariana Islands. Annexed by Japan in the late 19th century, the islands were under U.S. administration from 1945 until 1968.

Vol·ga (vŏl'gə, vôl'-, vōl'-). A river of western Russia rising in the Valdai Hills northwest of Moscow and flowing about 3,701 km (2,300 mi) generally east and south to the Caspian Sea. It is the longest river of Europe and the main commercial waterway of Russia. The Volga is linked by canals and other rivers to the Baltic Sea.

Vol·go·grad (vŏl'gə-grăd', vôl'-, vŭl-gə-grät'). Formerly **Sta·lin·grad** (stä'lĭn-grăd', stə-lyĭn-grät'). A city of southwest Russia on the Volga River northeast of Rostov. Founded in 1589 as a defensive stronghold named Tsaritsyn, it was renamed Stalingrad in 1925 and Volgograd in 1961. The city was besieged and severely damaged during a prolonged battle in World War II, with extensive casualties of both German and Soviet troops. It is a port and major rail center. ⊛ Pop. 996,992.

Vo·log·da (vô'ləg-də). A city of western Russia north-northeast of Moscow. It was founded in the mid-12th century by merchants from Novgorod and passed to Moscow in 1478. ⊛ Pop. 289,537.

Vó·los (vō'lŏs', vô'lôs). A city of eastern Greece in Thessaly on the **Gulf of Vólos,** an inlet of the Aegean Sea. Vólos is a major port and an industrial, commercial, and transportation center. ⊛ Pop. 71,378.

Vol·sci (vôl'skē, vŏl'sī, -sē, -shē). An Italic people of ancient Italy whose territory was conquered by the Romans in the fourth century B.C. — **Vol'scian** (-shən, -skē-ən) *adj. & n.*

Vol·ta (vŏl'tə, vōl'-, vôl'-). A river formed in central Ghana by the confluence of the White Volta and the Black Volta and flowing about 467 km (290 mi) southward through artificial **Lake Volta** to the Bight of Benin in the Gulf of Guinea.

Vol·ta Re·don·da (vôl'tä rĭ-dŏn'də, -dôɴ'dä). A city of eastern Brazil on the Paraíba River west-northwest of Rio de Janeiro. Founded in 1941, it is the center of a major steel industry. ⊛ Pop. 220,189.

Volzh·skiy (vôlzh'skē, vôlsh'-). A city of southwest Russia on the Volga River, a manufacturing suburb of Volgograd. ⊛ Pop. 281,947.

Vor·ku·ta (vôr-kōō'tə, vôr'kōō-tä). A city of extreme northeast Russia above the Arctic Circle. It was founded in 1932 to accommodate extensive penal-labor camps. The camps were reportedly closed after the death of the Soviet premier Joseph Stalin in 1953. ⊕Pop. 111,277.

Vo·ro·nezh (və-rô′nĭsh). A city of southwest Russia on the Don River south of Lipetsk. Founded as a frontier fortress in 1586, it was a shipbuilding center during the reign of Peter the Great. ⊕Pop. 898,854.

Vo·ro·shi·lov·grad (vôr′ə-shē′ləf-grăd′, və-rə-shē-ləf-grät′). See **Lugansk.**

Vorst (vôrst) also **Fo·rest** (fô-rĕ′). A city of central Belgium, a manufacturing suburb of Brussels. ⊕Pop. 50,260.

Vosges (vōzh). A mountain range of northeast France extending about 193 km (120 mi) parallel to the Rhine River. The mountains have rounded or nearly flat summits.

Vra·tsa (vrät′sə, vrä′tsä). A city of northwest Bulgaria north-northeast of Sofia. It is a commercial center and railroad junction. ⊕Pop. 77,000.

Vul·gar Latin (vŭl′gər). *abbr.* **VL.** The common speech of the ancient Romans, which is distinguished from standard literary Latin and is the ancestor of the Romance languages.

Vyat·ka (vyät′kə). A river, about 1,368 km (850 mi) long, of west-central Russia rising in the foothills of the Ural Mountains and flowing west, south, and southeast to the Kama River.

Vy·borg (vē′bôrg′, -bərk). A city of northwest Russia northwest of St. Petersburg on the Gulf of Finland near the Finnish border. A Swedish castle was built here in 1293 and captured by Russian forces in 1710. ⊕Pop. 80,000.

Vy·cheg·da (vĭch′ĭg-də). A river, about 1,126 km (700 mi) long, of northwest Russia flowing generally westward to the Northern Dvina River.

W

Waal (väl). The southern branch of the Lower Rhine River in southern Netherlands, rising near the German border and flowing about 84 km (52 mi) westward to join the Maas River.

Wa·ba·na·ki (wä′bə-nä′kē). *pl.* **Wabanaki** or **-kis.** See **Abenaki.**

Wa·bash (wô′băsh′). A river of the east-central United States rising in western Ohio and flowing about 764 km (475 mi) generally southwest across Indiana and southward on the Indiana-Illinois border to the Ohio River.

Wa·co (wā′kō). A city of east-central Texas south of Dallas–Fort Worth. A shipping and industrial center, it is also the seat of Baylor University (established 1845). A prolonged standoff between the government and an armed religious compound here drew international attention in early 1993. ⊕Pop. 103,590.

Wad·den·zee (väd′n-zā′). An inlet of the North Sea off northern Netherlands between the Ijsselmeer and the West Frisian Islands.

Wad·ding·ton (wŏd′ĭng-tən), **Mount.** A peak, 3,996.7 m (13,104 ft) high, in southwest British Columbia, Canada. It is the highest elevation in the Coast Mountains.

wa·di also **wa·dy** (wä′dē). *pl.* **-dis** or **-dies. 1. a.** A valley, gully, or streambed in northern Africa and southwest Asia that remains dry except during the rainy season. **b.** A stream that flows through such a channel. **2.** An oasis.

Wads·worth (wŏdz′wûrth′). A city of northeast Ohio, a suburb of Akron. ⊕Pop. 15,718.

wa·dy (wä′dē). Variant of **wadi.**

Wa·gram (vä′gräm′). A town of northeast Austria northeast of Vienna. Napoleon defeated the Austrians here in July 1809.

Wah·ha·bi or **Wa·ha·bi** (wä-hä′bē). *pl.* **-bis.** A member of a Muslim sect founded by Abdul Wahhab (1703–1792), known for its strict observance of the Koran and flourishing mainly in Arabia. — **Wah·ha′bism** *n.*

Wa·hi·a·wa (wä′hē-ə-wä′). A city of central Oahu, Hawaii, northwest of Honolulu. The surrounding area is noted for its pineapple plantations. ⊕Pop. 17,386.

Wah·pe·ku·te (wä′pə-kōō′tē). *pl.* **Wahpekute** or **-tes.** A member of a Native American people of the Santee branch of the Sioux.

Wah·pe·ton (wô′pĭ-tn). *pl.* **Wahpeton** or **-tons.** A member of a Native American people of the Santee branch of the Sioux.

Wai·a·na·e Mountains (wī′ə-nä′ā). A mountain range of western Oahu, Hawaii, rising to 1,227.6 m (4,025 ft) at Mount Kaala.

Wai·ka·to (wī-kä′tō). A river of New Zealand rising in central North Island and flowing about 434 km (270 mi) northwest to the Tasman Sea. It is the longest river in the country.

Wai·ki·ki (wī′kĭ-kē′). A famous beach and resort district of Oahu Island, Hawaii, southeast of Honolulu. It is known for its fine surfing.

Wai·pa·hu (wī-pä′hōō). A city of southern Oahu, Hawaii, on the northwest shore of Pearl Harbor. It was damaged by the Japanese attack on Pearl Harbor (December 7, 1941). ⊕Pop. 31,435.

Wa·kash·an (wä-kăsh′ən, wô′kə-shăn′). A family of North American Indian languages spoken by the Nootkas and other peoples of Washington and British Columbia.

Wa·ka·ya·ma (wä′kə-yä′mə). A city of southern Honshu, Japan, south-southwest of Osaka on the Inland Sea. It is a railroad hub and a manufacturing center. ⊕Pop. 395,496.

Wake·field (wāk′fēld′). **1.** A borough of north-central England east-northeast of Manchester. In the Battle of Wakefield (1460) Richard Plantagenet, the third duke of York (1411–1460), was slain by Lancastrian forces in the Wars of the Roses. **2.** A town of eastern Massachusetts, a residential and industrial suburb of Boston. ◉ Pop. 24,825.

Wake Island (wāk). An island of the western Pacific Ocean between Hawaii and Guam. Annexed by the United States in 1898, it was a commercial air base and later a military base. Wake Island was held by the Japanese from 1941 to 1945.

Wa·la·chi·a (wə-lā′kē-ə, wŏ-). See **Wallachia**.

Wal·brzych (välb′zhĭk′, -zhĭкн′). A city of southwest Poland southwest of Wroclaw. A coal-mining center, it passed from Germany to Poland after the Potsdam Conference of 1945. ◉ Pop. 141,067.

Wal·che·ren (wäl′kə-rən, wôl′кнə-). A region, formerly an island, of southwest Netherlands in the Scheldt estuary.

Wal·den Pond (wôl′dən). A pond of northeast Massachusetts near Concord. The American writer Henry David Thoreau lived in a cabin near the pond from 1845 to 1847.

Wales (wālz). A principality of the United Kingdom on the western peninsula of the island of Great Britain. Incorporated with England since the Act of Union (1536), Wales has maintained its own distinct culture and a strong nationalist sentiment. Cardiff is the capital and the largest city. ◉ Pop. 2,790,462.

Wal·ker (wô′kər). A city of west-central Michigan, a suburb of Grand Rapids. ◉ Pop. 17,279.

Walker Lake. A salt lake of western Nevada southeast of Carson City.

Wal·la·chi·a also **Wa·la·chi·a** (wə-lā′kē-ə, wŏ-). A historical region of southeast Romania between the Transylvanian Alps and the Danube River. Founded as a principality c. 1290, it was ruled by Turkey from 1387 until it was united with Moldavia to form Romania (1861). —**Wal·la′chi·an** adj. & n.

Wal·la Wal·la (wŏl′ə wŏl′ə). A city of southeast Washington near the Oregon border south-southwest of Spokane. Founded in 1856 near the site of an army fort, it is a manufacturing center in an agricultural region. ◉ Pop. 26,478.

Wal·ling·ford (wŏl′ĭng-fərd). A town of southern Connecticut north-northeast of New Haven. It is a manufacturing center. ◉ Pop. 40,822.

Wal·lis and Futuna Islands (wŏl′ĭs). A French overseas territory consisting of two groups of islands in the southwest Pacific Ocean west of Samoa and northeast of Fiji. Controlled by the French from 1842, the islands became an overseas territory in 1961.

Wal·lo·ni·a (wä-lō′nē-ə). A French-speaking region of southern Belgium. It was granted limited autonomy in 1980.

Wal·loon (wŏ-lōōn′). **1.** One of a French-speaking people of Celtic descent inhabiting southern and southeast Belgium and adjacent regions of France. **2.** The dialect of French spoken by this people.

Wal·low·a Mountains (wä-lou′ə). A range of mountains in northeast Oregon rising to 3,013.4 m (9,880 ft) at Sacajawea Peak.

Wal·nut Creek (wôl′nŭt′, -nət). A city of western California northeast of Oakland. It is an industrial center. ◉ Pop. 60,569.

Wal·pole (wôl′pōl′, wŏl′-). A town of eastern Massachusetts southwest of Boston. Settled in 1659, it is a manufacturing center and the site of a large state prison. ◉ Pop. 20,212.

Wal·sall (wôl′sôl′, -səl). A borough of west-central England northwest of Birmingham. It is a mining and manufacturing center. ◉ Pop. 264,716.

Wal·tham (wôl′thăm′, -thəm). A city of eastern Massachusetts west of Boston. It is a manufacturing center and the seat of Brandeis University (established 1947). ◉ Pop. 57,878.

Wal·ton and Wey·bridge (wôl′tən; wā′brĭj). A district of southeast England, a residential suburb of London. ◉ Pop. 50,031.

Wal·vis Bay (wôl′vĭs). An inlet of the Atlantic Ocean on the western coast of Namibia. The town of **Walvis Bay** (population 11,600) and the surrounding area constituted an exclave of South Africa until passing to Namibia in 1994.

Wam·pa·no·ag (wäm′pə-nō′ăg). **1.** pl. **Wampanoag** or **-ags.** A member of a Native American people formerly inhabiting eastern Rhode Island and southeast Massachusetts, including Martha's Vineyard and Nantucket, with present-day descendants in this same area. **2.** The Algonquian language of the Wampanoag, a variety of Massachusett.

Wands·worth (wŏndz′wûrth′). A borough of greater London in southeast England on the Thames River. It is a railroad junction and an industrial center. ◉ Pop. 265,686.

Wan·tagh (wŏn′tô′). A town of southeast New York on the southern shore of Long Island. It is mainly residential. ◉ Pop. 18,567.

Wap·pin·ger (wä′pĭn-jər). pl. **Wappinger** or **-gers.** A member of a Native American people formerly inhabiting the east bank of the Hudson River from Poughkeepsie to Manhattan and closely related to the Munsee-speaking peoples. The Wappingers dispersed to other Native American groups after warfare with the Dutch in the mid-17th century.

Wap·si·pin·i·con (wŏp′sə-pĭn′ĭ-kən). A river

rising in southern Minnesota and flowing about 410 km (255 mi) generally southeast through eastern Iowa to the Mississippi River.

Wa·ran·gal (wə-rŭng′gəl, wôr′əng-). A city of southeast India northeast of Hyderabad. It was the capital of the Telugu Kingdom in the 12th century and is now a market town known for its textile production. ⊛ Pop. 447,657.

Ware·ham (wâr′əm, -hăm′). A town of southeast Massachusetts on Buzzards Bay northeast of New Bedford. It is a resort town in a cranberry-growing region. ⊛ Pop. 19,232.

War·ner Rob·ins (wôr′nər rŏb′ĭnz). A city of central Georgia south of Macon. Incorporated in 1943, it includes one of the largest Air Force bases in the South. ⊛ Pop. 43,726.

War·ren (wôr′ən, wŏr′-). **1.** A city of southeast Michigan, an industrial suburb of Detroit. ⊛ Pop. 144,864. **2.** A city of northeast Ohio northwest of Youngstown. It is a manufacturing center. ⊛ Pop. 50,793.

War·rens·ville Heights (wôr′ĭnz-vĭl′, wŏr′-). A city of northeast Ohio, a residential suburb of Cleveland. ⊛ Pop. 15,745.

War·ring·ton (wôr′ĭng-tən, wŏr′-). **1.** A borough of west-central England east of Liverpool on the Mersey River. It is a manufacturing center. ⊛ Pop. 185,005. **2.** A town of northwest Florida, a residential suburb of Pensacola. ⊛ Pop. 16,040.

War·saw (wôr′sô′). The capital of Poland, in the east-central part of the country on the Vistula River. Founded in the 13th century, it replaced Cracow as Poland's capital in 1596. Warsaw was ruled by Russia as an independent kingdom (1815–1917) and became capital of Poland again in 1918. Most of the city's Jewish residents were executed during the German occupation in World War II. Rebuilt after 1945, Warsaw is a major cultural, commercial, and industrial center. ⊛ Pop. 1,654,491.

War·ta (vär′tə, -tä). A river, about 764 km (475 mi) long, rising in south-central Poland northwest of Cracow and flowing generally north and west to the Oder River.

War·wick (wôr′wĭk). A city of east-central Rhode Island on Narragansett Bay south of Providence. Settled in 1643, it is a popular summer resort. ⊛ Pop. 85,427.

Wa·satch Range (wô′săch′). A range of the Rocky Mountains extending about 402 km (250 mi) from southeast Idaho to central Utah and rising to 3,662.4 m (12,008 ft) at its highest peak, Mount Timpanogos.

wash (wŏsh, wôsh). **1. a.** Low or marshy ground washed by tidal waters. **b.** A stretch of shallow water. **2.** *Western U.S.* The dry bed of a stream.

Wash (wŏsh, wôsh). An inlet of the North Sea off east-central England. The Wash has a dredged ship channel that leads to King's Lynn.

Wash·ing·ton (wŏsh′ĭng-tən, wô′shĭng-). **1.** *abbr.* **WA, Wash.** A state of the northwest United States on the Pacific Ocean. It was admitted as the 42nd state in 1889. Originally explored by the British navigator and explorer Capt. James Cook (1778), Washington was the object of a dispute between England and the United States until 1846, when its northern border was set at the 49th parallel. Washington is noted for its lumber and defense industries. Olympia is the capital and Seattle the largest city. ⊛ Pop. 4,887,941. **2.** The capital of the United States, on the Potomac River between Virginia and Maryland and coextensive with the District of Columbia. It was designed by the French-born architect Pierre L'Enfant and became the capital in 1800. In the War of 1812 the British captured and sacked (1814) Washington, burning most of the public buildings, including the Capitol and the White House. ⊛ Pop. 609,909. **3.** A city of southwest Pennsylvania southwest of Pittsburgh. Settled in 1769, it is a manufacturing center and the seat of Washington and Jefferson College (first chartered 1787). ⊛ Pop. 15,864. —**Wash′ing·to′ni·an** (wŏsh′-ĭng-tō′nē-ən, wô′shĭng-) *adj. & n.*

Washington, Lake. A lake in west-central Washington on the eastern boundary of Seattle.

Washington, Mount. A mountain, 1,917.8 m (6,288 ft) high, of eastern New Hampshire. It is the highest elevation in the White Mountains.

Washington Island. An island of northeast Wisconsin in northwest Lake Michigan off the northern tip of the Door Peninsula.

Wash·i·ta (wŏsh′ĭ-tô′, wô′shĭ-). A river rising in northwest Texas and flowing about 724 km (450 mi) generally east-southeast across Oklahoma to the Red River.

Wa·ter·bur·y (wô′tər-bĕr′ē, wŏt′ər-). A city of west-central Connecticut north-northwest of New Haven. Incorporated as a town in 1686 and as a city in 1853, it is today a manufacturing center. ⊛ Pop. 108,961.

wa·ter·course (wô′tər-kôrs′, -kōrs′, wŏt′ər-). **1.** A natural or artificial channel through which water flows. **2.** A stream or river.

Wa·ter·ee (wô′tə-rē, wŏt′ə-). A river, about 233 km (145 mi) long, of central South Carolina flowing southward to form the Santee River. Its upper course, in North Carolina, is called the Catawba River.

wa·ter·fall (wô′tər-fôl′, wŏt′ər-). A steep descent of water from a height; a cascade.

Wa·ter·ford (wô′tər-fərd, wŏt′ər-). **1.** A borough of southeast Ireland south-southwest of Dublin. A major port, Waterford is famous for its glass-manufacturing industry. ⊕ Pop. 38,473. **2.** A town of southeast Connecticut on Long Island Sound. Settled c. 1653, it is a residential community. ⊕ Pop. 17,930.

wa·ter gap (wô′tər, wŏt′ər). A transverse cleft in a mountain ridge through which a stream flows.

water hole. A small natural depression in which water collects, especially a pool where animals come to drink.

water level. 1. The level of the surface of a body of water. **2.** *Geology.* See **water table.**

Wa·ter·loo (wô′tər-lōō′, wŏt′ər-, wô′tər-lōō′, wŏt′ər-). **1.** A town of central Belgium near Brussels. Napoleon met his final defeat in the Battle of Waterloo (June 18, 1815). **2.** A city of southeast Ontario, Canada, a manufacturing suburb of Kitchener. ⊕ Pop. 24,933. **3.** A city of northeast Iowa northwest of Cedar Rapids. First settled in 1845, it is a trade center in an agricultural region. ⊕ Pop. 66,467.

wa·ter·shed (wô′tər-shĕd′, wŏt′ər-). **1.** A ridge of high land dividing two areas that are drained by different river systems. Also called *water parting.* **2.** The region draining into a river, river system, or other body of water.

water table. The level below which the ground is completely saturated with water. Also called *water level.*

Wa·ter·town (wô′tər-toun′, wŏt′ər-). **1.** A town of western Connecticut near Waterbury. Set off from Waterbury in 1780, it is a manufacturing center. ⊕ Pop. 20,456. **2.** A town of eastern Massachusetts, a residential suburb of Boston. ⊕ Pop. 33,284. **3.** A city of northern New York north of Syracuse. Settled c. 1800, it is a manufacturing center. ⊕ Pop. 29,429. **4.** A city of northeast South Dakota north-northwest of Sioux Falls. It is a commercial center in an agricultural region. ⊕ Pop. 17,592. **5.** A city of southeast Wisconsin east-northeast of Madison. It is thought to be the site of the first kindergarten in the United States (established 1856). ⊕ Pop. 19,142.

Wa·ter·ville (wô′tər-vĭl′, wŏt′ər-). A city of southern Maine north of Augusta. Settled in 1754, it is a trade and manufacturing center and the seat of Colby College (founded 1813). ⊕ Pop. 17,173.

wa·ter·way (wô′tər-wā′, wŏt′ər-). A navigable body of water, such as a river or canal.

Wat·ford (wŏt′fərd). A municipal borough of southeast England northwest of London. Mainly residential, it is also a commercial and publishing center. ⊕ Pop. 74,700.

Wat·lings Island (wät′lĭngz). See **San Salvador**[1].

Wat·son·ville (wŏt′sən-vĭl′). A city of western

California east-southeast of Santa Cruz near Monterey Bay. Founded in 1852, it is an agricultural processing center. ⊕ Pop. 31,099.

Watts (wŏts). A district of Los Angeles, California. It was the scene of severe racial tensions and violence in 1965 and again in 1992.

Wau·ke·gan (wô-kē′gən). A city of northeast Illinois on Lake Michigan north of Chicago. A major lake port, Waukegan is also an industrial center. ⊕ Pop. 69,392.

Wau·ke·sha (wô′kə-shô′). A city of southeast Wisconsin west of Milwaukee. It was a health resort after the Civil War and is now a manufacturing center. ⊕ Pop. 56,958.

Wau·sau (wô′sô′). A city of north-central Wisconsin west-northwest of Green Bay. Settled in 1839, it grew as a lumber town and now has diversified industries. ⊕ Pop. 37,060.

Wau·wa·to·sa (wô′wə-tō′sə). A city of southeast Wisconsin, an industrial suburb of Milwaukee. ⊕ Pop. 49,366.

Wa·ver·ley (wā′vər-lē). A city of southeast Australia, an industrial suburb of Melbourne. ⊕ Pop. 122,471.

Way·cross (wā′krôs′, -krŏs′). A city of southeast Georgia southwest of Savannah. It is a railroad center in a timber and farming region. ⊕ Pop. 16,410.

Wayne (wān). **1.** A city of southeast Michigan, a residential and manufacturing suburb of Detroit. ⊕ Pop. 19,899. **2.** A town of northern New Jersey west of Paterson. It is a manufacturing center. ⊕ Pop. 47,025.

Waynes·bor·o (wānz′bûr′ō, -bŭr′ō). An independent city of central Virginia west of Charlottesville. Settled in the early 18th century, it is a manufacturing center in an agricultural region. ⊕ Pop. 18,549.

Wa·zir·i·stan (wə-zîr′ĭ-stăn′, -stän′). A mountainous region of northwest Pakistan on the Afghanistan border, divided into **North Waziristan** and **South Waziristan.** The region became part of Pakistan in 1947. It absorbed thousands of refugees during the Soviet occupation of Afghanistan (1979–1989).

We·ber River (wē′bər). A river rising in northern Utah and flowing about 201 km (125 mi) generally northwest to join the Ogden River and empty into the Great Salt Lake.

Web·ster Groves. (wĕb′stər). A city of eastern Missouri, a mainly residential suburb of St. Louis. ⊕ Pop. 22,987.

Wed·dell Sea (wĭ-dĕl′, wĕd′l). A sea of the southern Atlantic Ocean off western Antarctica east of the Antarctic Peninsula. It is named for James Weddell (1787–1834), a British navigator.

Wee·haw·ken (wē-hô′kən). A township of northeast New Jersey on the Hudson River opposite New York City. It is mostly residential. The duel in which Aaron Burr mortally wounded Alexander Hamilton took place here on July 11, 1804. ◉ Pop. 12,385.

Wei He (wā' hə'). A river of central China flowing about 724 km (450 mi) generally eastward to the Huang He (Yellow River).

Wei·mar (wī'mär', vī'-). A city of central Germany southwest of Leipzig. First mentioned in 975, it became the capital of the duchy of Saxe-Weimar in 1547 and developed as the most important cultural center in Germany after the arrival of Goethe, the German writer and scientist, in 1775. In 1919 the German National Assembly met here and established the **Weimar Republic,** which lasted until 1933. ◉ Pop. 64,007.

Weir·ton (wîr'tn). A city of northern West Virginia in the Panhandle on the Ohio River northeast of Wheeling. Its first steel mills were built in 1909. ◉ Pop. 22,124.

Wel·fare Island (wĕl'fâr'). See **Roosevelt Island** (sense 1).

Wel·land (wĕl'ənd). A city of southeast Ontario, Canada, on the **Welland Ship Canal,** 44.4 km (27.6 mi) long, which connects Lake Erie with Lake Ontario and bypasses Niagara Falls. The current canal, completed in 1932, replaced a canal originally built between 1824 and 1833. The city is a port and a market and industrial center. ◉ Pop. 45,448.

Welles·ley (wĕlz'lē). A town of eastern Massachusetts west-southwest of Boston. It is a residential community and the seat of Wellesley College (established 1870). ◉ Pop. 26,615.

Wel·ling·ton (wĕl'ĭng-tən). The capital of New Zealand, on an inlet of Cook Strait in extreme southern North Island. It was founded in 1840 and supplanted Auckland as capital in 1865. ◉ Pop. 150,100.

Wels (vĕls). A city of northern Austria southwest of Linz. On a site occupied since ancient times, it is an agricultural market and a manufacturing center. ◉ Pop. 51,060.

Welsh (wĕlsh, wĕlch). *abbr.* **W. 1.** Of or relating to Wales or its people, language, or culture. **2.** The people of Wales. **3.** The Celtic language of Wales. In this sense, also called *Cymric.*

Welsh·man (wĕlsh'mən, wĕlch'-). A man who is a native or inhabitant of Wales.

Welsh·wom·an (wĕlsh'wŏŏm'ən, wĕlch'-). A woman who is a native or inhabitant of Wales.

We·natch·ee (wə-năch'ē). A city of central Washington on the Columbia River north-northeast of Yakima. It is a trade and processing center in a fertile fruit-growing valley noted for apples. ◉ Pop. 21,756.

Wen·chow (wĕn'chou', wŭn'jō'). See **Wenzhou.**

Wend (wĕnd). One of a Slavic people inhabiting Saxony and Brandenburg. Also called *Sorb, Sorbian.* — **Wend** *adj.*

Wend·ish (wĕn'dĭsh). **1.** Of or relating to the Wends or their language. **2.** The Slavic language of the Wends. Also called *Sorbian.*

Wen·zhou (wŭn'jō') also **Wen·chow** (wĕn'-chou', wŭn'jō'). A city of eastern China near the East China Sea south of Shanghai. Founded in the fourth century A.D., it was opened to foreign trade in 1876. ◉ Pop. 1,650,419.

Wer·ra (vĕr'ə). A river rising in central Germany and flowing about 291 km (181 mi) generally northward to join the Fulda River and form the Weser.

We·sel (vā'zəl). A city of west-central Germany on the Rhine River northwest of Essen. First mentioned in the eighth century, it joined the Hanseatic League in 1407 and passed to Brandenburg in the mid-1600's. Wesel was almost totally destroyed by air raids during World War II. ◉ Pop. 54,895.

We·ser (vā'zər). A river, about 483 km (300 mi) long, of central and northwest Germany, flowing generally northward to the North Sea through a long estuary.

Wes·la·co (wĕs'lə-kō'). A city of extreme southern Texas northwest of Brownsville. It is a processing and shipping center. ◉ Pop. 21,877.

Wes·sex (wĕs'ĭks). A region and ancient Anglo-Saxon kingdom of southern England. According to tradition, the kingdom was founded by the Saxon conquerors of Britain and at its greatest extent occupied the territory between the English Channel and the Thames River.

west (wĕst). *abbr.* **W, W., w, w. 1. a.** The cardinal point on the mariner's compass 270° clockwise from due north and directly opposite east. **b.** The direction opposite to the direction of the earth's axial rotation. **2.** An area or a region lying in the west. **3.** often **West. a.** The western part of the earth, especially Europe and the Western Hemisphere. **b.** The western part of a region or country. **4.** often **West. a.** A former region of the United States west of the Allegheny Mountains. **b.** The region of the United States west of the Mississippi River. **c.** The non-Communist countries of Europe and the Americas during the cold war. **5.** To, toward, of, facing, or in the west. **6.** Originating in or coming from the west. — **west'ern, West'ern** *adj.*

West Africa. A region of western Africa between the Sahara Desert and the Gulf of Guinea. It was largely controlled by colonial powers until the 20th century. — **West African** *adj. & n.*

West Al·lis (ăl'ĭs). A city of southeast Wisconsin, a residential and industrial suburb of Milwaukee. ◉ Pop. 63,221.

West Atlantic. The westernmost branch of the Niger-Congo language family.

West Babylon. A community of southeast New York on southern Long Island west of Bay Shore. It is mainly residential. ⊛ Pop. 32,500.

West Bank. A disputed territory of southwest Asia between Israel and Jordan west of the Jordan River. Part of Jordan after 1949, it was occupied by Israel in the 1967 Arab-Israeli War. In 1994 an accord between Israel and the PLO was signed, giving Palestinians limited self-rule and requiring measured withdrawal of Israeli troops from the West Bank.

West Bend (bĕnd). A city of southeast Wisconsin north-northwest of Milwaukee. It is an industrial center in a dairy region. ⊛ Pop. 23,916.

West Berlin. See **Berlin.** —**West Berliner** *n.*

West Beskids. See **Beskids.**

west by north. *abbr.* **WbN. 1.** The direction or point on the mariner's compass halfway between due west and west-northwest, or 78°45′ west of due north. **2.** Toward or from west by north.

west by south. *abbr.* **WbS. 1.** The direction or point on the mariner's compass halfway between due west and west-southwest, or 101°15′ west of due north. **2.** Toward or from west by south.

West·ches·ter (wĕst′chĕs′tər). A village of northeast Illinois, an inner suburb of Chicago. ⊛ Pop. 17,301.

West Ches·ter (chĕs′tər). A borough of southeast Pennsylvania west of Philadelphia. It is primarily residential with some light industry. ⊛ Pop. 18,041.

West Coast. A region of the western United States bordering on the Pacific Ocean and including Washington, Oregon, and California.

West Covina. A city of southern California east of Los Angeles. It is mainly residential. ⊛ Pop. 96,086.

West Des Moines. A city of south-central Iowa, a manufacturing suburb of Des Moines. ⊛ Pop. 31,702.

West End. The western section of central London, England, noted for its fashionable districts and its shops and theaters. It includes Mayfair and Hyde Park.

Wes·ter·ly (wĕs′tər-lē). A town of extreme southwest Rhode Island on the border of Connecticut east of New London. It was first settled in 1648 and has a textile industry dating to 1814. ⊛ Pop. 21,605.

Western Bug. See **Bug** (sense 1).

Western Dvina. See **Dvina** (sense 2).

Western Empire or **Western Roman Empire.** The western section of the Roman Empire, first set apart in A.D. 286 by Emperor Diocletian and later (395) formalized after the death of Theodosius I. It comprised Italy, Spain, Gaul, Britain, Illyricum, and northern Africa and lasted until 476.

Western Europe. The countries of western Europe, especially those that are allied with the United States and Canada in the North Atlantic Treaty Organization (established 1949 and usually known as NATO).

Western Ghats. See **Ghats.**

Western Hemisphere. The half of the earth comprising North America, Mexico, Central America, and South America.

Western Islands. See **Hebrides.**

Western Reserve. A region of northeast Ohio bordering on Lake Erie. It was retained by Connecticut after other western claims were ceded to the U.S. Congress in 1786. Much of the area was given or sold to immigrants from Connecticut (1786–1800), and the remainder of the territory was ceded to Ohio in 1800 and became part of the Northwest Territory.

Western Roman Empire. See **Western Empire.**

Western Sahara also **Span·ish Sahara** (spăn′-ĭsh). A region of northwest Africa on the Atlantic coast. Sparsely settled primarily by Berbers, the region was first visited by Portuguese navigators in 1434. Spain claimed it as a protectorate in 1884, establishing the province of Spanish Sahara in 1958, but transferred the territory to Morocco and Mauritania in 1976. Mauritania renounced all claims in 1979, with Morocco occupying its portion, but guerrilla resistance from the nationalist Polisario Front forced the Moroccans in 1991 to agree to a UN-monitored referendum on the region's status. Though the cease-fire held, disagreements between the two parties continued to postpone the voting.

Western Samoa. An island country of the southern Pacific Ocean comprising the western Samoa Islands. The islands were discovered and visited by the Dutch and the French in the 18th century. The eastern islands were annexed by the United States in 1899 as American Samoa, with the western islands going to Germany. Oc-

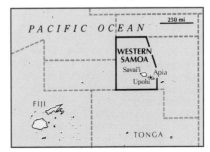

Western Shoshone

426

cupied by New Zealand during World War I, the western islands were later administered as a League of Nations mandate and a UN trust territory. Western Samoa achieved independence as a constitutional monarchy in 1962. Apia, on Upolu Island, is the capital. ◉ Pop. 209,360.

Western Shoshone. See **Shoshone** (sense 1b).

Wes·ter·ville (wĕs′tər-vĭl′). A city of central Ohio, an industrial suburb of Columbus. ◉ Pop. 30,269.

West·field (wĕst′fēld′). **1.** A city of southwest Massachusetts, a residential and industrial suburb of Springfield. ◉ Pop. 38,372. **2.** A town of northeast-central New Jersey southwest of Newark. It is a residential community. ◉ Pop. 28,870.

West Frisian Islands. See **Frisian Islands.**

West Germanic. A subdivision of the Germanic languages that includes High German, Low German, Yiddish, Dutch, Afrikaans, Flemish, Frisian, and English.

West Germany. Officially **Federal Republic of Germany.** A former country of central Europe bordering on the North Sea. It was part of Germany until 1945, when the country was divided into U.S., French, British, and Soviet zones of occupation. In 1949 the three western zones were reconstituted as West Germany; the Soviet zone became East Germany. West Germany was reunified with East Germany in October 1990. — **West German** *adj. & n.*

West Hartford. A town of central Connecticut, a residential suburb of Hartford. ◉ Pop. 60,110.

West Ha·ven (hā′vən). A city of southern Connecticut, a residential suburb of New Haven. ◉ Pop. 54,021.

West Hempstead. An unincorporated community of southeast New York on western Long Island. It is mainly residential. ◉ Pop. 26,500.

West Hollywood. A community of southern California northeast of Beverly Hills. It is mainly residential. ◉ Pop. 36,118.

West Indies. *abbr.* **W.I.** An archipelago between southeast North America and northern South America, separating the Caribbean Sea from the Atlantic Ocean and including the Greater Antilles, the Lesser Antilles, and the Bahama Islands. The original inhabitants were Caribs and Arawaks. Several of the islands were originally sighted and explored by Columbus during his voyages of 1492–1504. The first permanent European settlement was made by the Spanish on Hispaniola in 1496. During the colonial period the English, French, and Dutch also laid claim to various islands, and the United States acquired Puerto Rico and part of the Virgin Islands in the late 19th and early 20th centuries. — **West Indian** *adj. & n.*

West Indies Federation. A group of ten former British colonies in the West Indies, including Jamaica, Trinidad and Tobago, and Barbados. It was established in 1958 and slated for independence in 1962 but broke up in May 1962 because of economic disagreements among the members. Some of the islands later formed the British-sponsored **West Indies Associated States,** which was gradually disbanded as the islands achieved independence in the 1970's and early 1980's.

West Jordan. A city of northern Utah, a suburb of Salt Lake City. ◉ Pop. 42,892.

West Lafayette. A city of western Indiana on the Wabash River opposite Lafayette. It is the seat of Purdue University (established 1869). ◉ Pop. 25,907.

West·lake (wĕst′lāk′). A city of northeast Ohio, a commuter and manufacturing suburb of Cleveland. ◉ Pop. 27,018.

West·land (wĕst′lənd). A city of southeast Michigan, a residential suburb west of Detroit. ◉ Pop. 84,724.

West Memphis. A city of eastern Arkansas near the Mississippi River west of Memphis, Tennessee. It is a shipping and processing center. ◉ Pop. 28,259.

West Mif·flin (mĭf′lĭn). A borough of southwest Pennsylvania, an industrial suburb of Pittsburgh on the south bank of the Monongahela River. ◉ Pop. 23,644.

West·min·ster (wĕst′mĭn′stər). **1.** Officially **City of Westminster.** A borough of Greater London in southeast England on the Thames River. It includes the principal offices of the British government, especially along Whitehall and Downing streets, and such famous structures as Westminster Abbey and Buckingham Palace. ◉ Pop. 188,600. **2.** A city of southern California, a residential suburb of Long Beach. ◉ Pop. 78,118. **3.** A city of north-central Colorado, a residential and industrial suburb of Denver. ◉ Pop. 74,625.

West·mont (wĕst′mŏnt′). **1.** A community of southern California, a residential suburb between Los Angeles and Long Beach. ◉ Pop. 31,044. **2.** A village of northeast Illinois, a residential suburb of Chicago. ◉ Pop. 21,228.

West·mount (wĕst′mount′). A city of southern Quebec, Canada, a residential suburb of Montreal on Montreal Island. ◉ Pop. 20,480.

West New York. A town of northeast New Jersey on the Hudson River opposite Manhattan. It is a residential community with varied light industries. ◉ Pop. 38,125.

west-north·west (wĕst′nôrth′wĕst′, -nôr-wĕst′). *abbr.* **WNW. 1.** The direction or point on the mariner's compass halfway between due west and northwest, or 67°30′ west of due north. **2.** To, toward, of, facing, or in the west-northwest.

Wes·ton-su·per-Mare (wĕs′tən-sōō′pər-mâr′). A municipal borough of southwest England on the Bristol Channel west-southwest of Bristol. It is a popular seaside resort. ◉ Pop. 57,900.

West Orange. A town of northeast New Jersey, a residential suburb of Newark. ◉ Pop. 39,103.

West Pakistan. A former region of Pakistan (after 1947) separated by about 1,609 km (1,000 mi) from East Pakistan, formerly part of Bengal. In 1971 East Pakistan declared its independence as Bangladesh, and West Pakistan became the sole territory governed by Pakistan.

West Palm Beach. A city of southeast Florida opposite Palm Beach. It is a winter resort and research center. The American capitalist Henry M. Flagler developed the city as a commercial center for Palm Beach in 1893. ◉ Pop. 67,643.

West Pensacola. A community of northwest Florida, a suburb of Pensacola in the Florida Panhandle. ◉ Pop. 22,107.

West·pha·lia (wĕst-fāl′yə, -fā′lē-ə). A historical region and former duchy of west-central Germany east of the Rhine River. The duchy was created in the 12th century and was administered for many centuries by ecclesiastical princes, especially the archbishop of Cologne. The Peace of Westphalia (1648) marked the end of the Thirty Years' War. Napoleon seized the area in 1807 and designated a portion of it as the kingdom of Westphalia, to be ruled by his brother Jérôme. The region became part of Prussia after 1815. — **West·pha′lian** adj. & n.

West Point. A U.S. military installation in southeast New York on the western bank of the Hudson River north of New York City. It has been a military post since 1778 and the seat of the U.S. Military Academy since 1802.

West·port (wĕst′pôrt, -pōrt′). A town of southwest Connecticut on Long Island Sound. First settled in 1645, it is a residential community and summer resort. ◉ Pop. 24,410.

West Prussia. A historical region of northeast Germany between Pomerania and East Prussia south of the Baltic Sea. Most of the territory was awarded to Poland in 1919 but reannexed by Germany in 1939. In 1945 West Prussia again became part of Poland.

West Saint Paul. A city of southeast Minnesota, a residential and industrial suburb of St. Paul. ◉ Pop. 19,248.

West Saxon. 1. The dialect of Old English used in southern England that was the chief literary dialect of England before the Norman Conquest. **2.** One of the Saxons inhabiting Wessex during the centuries before the Norman Conquest.

West Seneca. An unincorporated community of northwest New York, a suburb of Buffalo. ◉ Pop. 47,866.

West Side. The western part of Manhattan Island in New York City bordering on the Hudson River. It includes a theater and entertainment district and many residential areas.

west-south·west (wĕst′south′wĕst′, -sou-wĕst′). abbr. **WSW. 1.** The direction or point on the mariner's compass halfway between due west and southwest, or 112°30′ west of due north. **2.** To, toward, of, facing, or in the west-southwest.

West Springfield. 1. A town of southwest Massachusetts, a manufacturing suburb of Springfield. ◉ Pop. 27,537. **2.** A community of northeast Virginia, a residential suburb of Alexandria. ◉ Pop. 28,126.

West Vancouver. A city of southwest British Columbia, Canada, a suburb of Vancouver. ◉ Pop. 35,728.

West Virginia. abbr. **WV, W.Va.** A state of the east-central United States. It was admitted as the 35th state in 1863. West Virginia was part of Virginia until the area refused to endorse the ordinance of secession in 1861. Charleston is the capital and the largest city. ◉ Pop. 1,801,625. — **West Virginian** adj. & n.

West Warwick. A town of east-central Rhode Island south-southwest of Providence. Textile manufacturing is important to its economy. ◉ Pop. 29,268.

Weth·ers·field (wĕth′ərz-fēld′). A town of central Connecticut, a suburb of Hartford on the Connecticut River. It was first settled by English colonists in 1634. ◉ Pop. 25,651.

wet·land (wĕt′lănd′). A lowland area, such as a marsh or swamp, that is saturated with moisture, especially when regarded as the natural habitat of wildlife.

Wet·ter·horn Peak (vĕt′ər-hôrn′). A mountain, 4,274.6 m (14,015 ft) high, in the San Juan Mountains of southwest Colorado.

Wey·mouth (wā′məth). A town of eastern Massachusetts, a manufacturing suburb of Boston. ◉ Pop. 54,063.

Whales (hwālz, wālz), **Bay of.** An inlet of the Ross Sea in the Ross Ice Shelf of Antarctica. It has been used as a base for Antarctic expeditions since 1911.

Whea·ton (hwēt′n, wēt′n). **1.** A city of northeast Illinois west of Chicago. Settled in the 1830's, it is mainly residential. ◉ Pop. 51,464. **2.** An unincorporated community of central Maryland, a residential suburb of Washington, D.C. ◉ Pop. 53,720.

Wheat Ridge (hwēt′, wēt′). A city of north-central Colorado, a residential suburb of Denver. ⊛ Pop. 29,419.

Whee·ler Peak (hwē′lər, wē′-). A mountain, 4,014.1 m (13,161 ft) high, in north-central New Mexico. It is the highest point in the state.

Wheel·ing (hwē′lĭng, wē′-). **1.** A village of northeast Illinois, a suburb of Chicago. ⊛ Pop. 29,911. **2.** A city of northwest West Virginia in the Panhandle on the Ohio River southwest of Pittsburgh, Pennsylvania. Settled in 1769, it was an important trading post on the Cumberland Road until the 1850's. Wheeling was the state capital from 1863 to 1870 and from 1875 to 1885. ⊛ Pop. 34,882.

Whid·bey Island (hwĭd′bē, wĭd′-). An island of northwest Washington in Puget Sound northwest of Everett and east of Admiralty Inlet.

Whit·by (hwĭt′bē, wĭt′-). A town of southeast Ontario, Canada, on Lake Ontario northeast of Toronto. It is a port of entry and manufacturing center. ⊛ Pop. 36,698.

White Bear Lake (hwīt, wīt). A city of eastern Minnesota, a residential suburb of St. Paul. ⊛ Pop. 24,704.

White Center. A community of west-central Washington, a residential suburb of Seattle. ⊛ Pop. 20,531.

White·hall[1] (hwīt′hôl′, wīt′-). A wide thoroughfare in London, England, running north and south between Trafalgar Square and the Houses of Parliament. Named after Whitehall Palace (1529–1698), the chief residence of the Court of London, it is noted for its government offices.

White·hall[2] (hwīt′hôl′, wīt′-). **1.** A city of central Ohio, an industrial suburb of Columbus. ⊛ Pop. 20,572. **2.** A borough of southwest Pennsylvania, a residential suburb of Pittsburgh. ⊛ Pop. 14,451.

White·horse (hwīt′hôrs′, wīt′-). The capital and largest city of Yukon Territory, Canada, in the southern part of the territory on the Yukon River. It was an important supply and trading center during the Klondike gold rush (1897–1898) and has been the territorial capital since 1952. ⊛ Pop. 14,814.

White Mountain. A peak, 4,345 m (14,246 ft) high, in the Sierra Nevada range of east-central California.

White Mountains. A section of the Appalachian Mountains in northern New Hampshire rising to 1,917.8 m (6,288 ft) at Mount Washington. They are a popular resort area.

White Nile. A section of the Nile River in eastern Africa flowing generally northward to Khartoum, where it joins the Blue Nile to form the Nile River proper.

White Pass. A pass, 880.8 m (2,888 ft) high, in the Coast Mountains between southeast Alaska and northwest British Columbia, Canada, north of Skagway.

White Plains. A city of southeast New York, a suburb of New York City. ⊛ Pop. 48,718.

White River. **1.** A river of northern Arkansas and southern Missouri flowing about 1,110 km (690 mi) generally southeast to the Mississippi River. **2.** A river, about 257 km (160 mi) long, of northwest Colorado and eastern Utah flowing westward to the Green River. **3.** A river of northwest Nebraska and southern South Dakota flowing about 523 km (325 mi) northeast and east to the Missouri River.

White Russia. See Belarus.

White Sea. A sea of northwest Russia, an inlet of the Barents Sea. It was the principal outlet for Muscovite seagoing trade during the 16th century.

White Volta. A river of Burkina Faso and northern Ghana flowing about 885 km (550 mi) southward to join the Black Volta and form the Volta River.

Whit·ney (hwĭt′nē, wĭt′-), **Mount.** A peak, 4,420.7 m (14,494 ft) high, in the Sierra Nevada of east-central California. It is the highest elevation in the continental United States.

Whit·ti·er (hwĭt′ē-ər, wĭt′-). A city of southern California east-southeast of Los Angeles. Founded by Quakers in 1887, it is chiefly a residential community. ⊛ Pop. 77,671.

Wich·i·ta[1] (wĭch′ĭ-tô′). **1.** pl. **Wichita** or **-tas.** A member of a Native American confederacy formerly inhabiting south-central Kansas and later moving southward into Oklahoma and Texas, with a present-day population in southwest Oklahoma. **2.** The Caddoan language of the Wichita.

Wich·i·ta[2] (wĭch′ĭ-tô′). A city of south-central Kansas on the Arkansas River southwest of Kansas City. It was founded in the 1860's on the site of an earlier Wichita Village and boomed as a cow town after the coming of the railroad in 1872. ⊛ Pop. 304,011.

Wichita Falls. A city of north-central Texas near the Oklahoma border northwest of Fort Worth. It prospered after the discovery of oil in the early 20th century. ⊛ Pop. 96,259.

Wick·liffe (wĭk′lĭf). A city of northeast Ohio, an industrial suburb of Cleveland on Lake Erie. ⊛ Pop. 14,558.

Wid·nes (wĭd′nĭs). A municipal borough of northwest England on the Mersey River east-southeast of Liverpool. It is a processing and manufacturing center. ⊛ Pop. 55,973.

Wie·ner·wald (vē′nər-vält′). A forested range of northeast Austria west and northwest of Vienna. It is a popular resort area.

Wies·ba·den (vēs′bäd′n). A city of west-central Germany on the Rhine River west of Frankfurt. Founded as a Celtic settlement in the third century B.C., it has been a noted spa since Roman times. Wiesbaden became a free imperial city c. A.D. 1242 and passed to Prussia in 1866. ⊛ Pop. 270,873.

Wig·an (wĭg′ən). A borough of northwest England northeast of Liverpool. An important market town in the Middle Ages, it is an industrial city in a coal-mining region. ⊛ Pop. 313,196.

Wight (wīt), **Isle of.** An island in the English Channel off south-central England. It is a popular resort area and yachting center. Queen Victoria often stayed at the Osborne House near Cowes.

Wil·der·ness Road (wĭl′dər-nĭs). The principal route for westward migration in the United States from c. 1790 to 1840. Blazed largely by American frontiersman Daniel Boone in 1775, it stretched from Virginia and across the Appalachian Mountains to the Cumberland Gap and the Ohio River.

Wil·helms·ha·ven (vĭl′hĕlmz-hä′fən). A city of northwest Germany on an inlet of the North Sea. It was a major naval base during World Wars I and II and is now a port, an industrial center, and a resort with a new naval base rebuilt after 1956. ⊛ Pop. 97,495.

Wilkes-Bar·re (wĭlks′băr′ē, -băr′ə). A city of northeast Pennsylvania on the Susquehanna River southwest of Scranton. It was settled in 1769 and was twice burned (1778 and 1784) by the British and their allies during the American Revolution. ⊛ Pop. 47,523.

Wilkes Land (wĭlks). A coastal region of Antarctica south of Australia. Most of the area has been included in Australia's Antarctic claims since 1936.

Wil·kins·burg (wĭl′kĭnz-bûrg′). A borough of southwest Pennsylvania, a mainly residential suburb of Pittsburgh. ⊛ Pop. 21,080.

Wil·lam·ette (wə-lăm′ĭt). A river, about 473 km (294 mi) long, of northwest Oregon flowing generally northward to the Columbia River near Portland. The **Willamette Valley,** a fertile agricultural region, was first settled in the 1830's by pioneers traveling west along the Oregon Trail.

Wil·lem·stad (vĭl′əm-stät′). The capital of the Netherlands Antilles, on the southern coast of Curaçao. Founded in 1634, it is a free port, a tourist resort, and a commercial and industrial center. ⊛ Pop. 43,547.

Wil·liams·burg (wĭl′yəmz-bûrg′). A city of southeast Virginia northwest of Newport News. Settled c. 1632, it was the capital of Virginia from 1699 to 1779 but declined after the capital was moved to Richmond. In 1926 a large-scale restoration project, financed mainly by John D. Rockefeller, Jr., was begun, in which some 700

modern buildings were removed, 83 colonial buildings were renovated, and more than 400 buildings were reconstructed on their original sites. The city is now a popular tourist center and the seat of William and Mary College (established 1693). ⊛ Pop. 11,530.

Wil·liam·son (wĭl′yəm-sən), **Mount.** A peak, 4,382.9 m (14,370 ft) high, in the Sierra Nevada of east-central California.

Wil·liams·port (wĭl′yəmz-pôrt′, -pōrt′). A city of central Pennsylvania north of Harrisburg. It developed as a lumbering center in the 19th century. ⊛ Pop. 31,933.

Wil·ling·bo·ro (wĭl′ĭng-bûr′ō, -bûr′ō). A community of south-central New Jersey northeast of Camden. It is a residential and industrial town. ⊛ Pop. 36,291.

wil·li·waw (wĭl′ē-wô′). A violent gust of cold wind blowing seaward from a mountainous coast, especially in the Straits of Magellan.

Will·mar (wĭl′mär′, -mər). A city of southwest-central Minnesota west-northwest of Minneapolis. It is an industrial, processing, and medical center. ⊛ Pop. 17,531.

Wil·lough·by (wĭl′ə-bē). A city of northeast Ohio on Lake Erie northeast of Cleveland. Its manufactures include electronic components and auto parts. ⊛ Pop. 20,510.

Wil·low (wĭl′ō). A town of southern Alaska north of Anchorage. It was once proposed as a new state capital because of its central location.

Willow Grove. A community of southeast Pennsylvania, an industrial suburb of Philadelphia. ⊛ Pop. 16,325.

Wil·lo·wick (wĭl′ə-wĭk′). A city of northeast Ohio, a residential suburb of Cleveland on Lake Erie. ⊛ Pop. 15,269.

Wil·mette (wĭl-mĕt′). A village of northeast Illinois, a residential suburb of Chicago on Lake Michigan. ⊛ Pop. 26,690.

Wil·ming·ton (wĭl′mĭng-tən). **1.** A city of northeast Delaware on the Delaware River southwest of Philadelphia, Pennsylvania. It was founded as Fort Christina by Swedish settlers in 1638 and held by the Dutch from 1655 until 1664, when it was taken by the English. The name Wilmington dates from 1739. E.I. Du Pont established a powder mill nearby in 1802. The city is now a port of entry and manufacturing center with an extensive chemical industry. It is also the largest city in the state. ⊛ Pop. 71,529. **2.** A town of northeast Massachusetts, an industrial suburb of Boston. ⊛ Pop. 17,654. **3.** A city of southeast North Carolina on the Cape Fear River south-southeast of Raleigh. Settled c. 1730, it was used as a port by blockade runners during the Civil War and is now a manufacturing and resort center and the state's largest port. ⊛ Pop. 55,530.

Wil·son (wĭl'sən). A city of east-central North Carolina east of Raleigh. It is a trade and processing center. ⊚ Pop. 36,930.

Wilson, Mount. 1. A mountain, 1,741.6 m (5,710 ft) high, in the San Gabriel Mountains of southwest California northeast of Pasadena. Its observatory was established in 1904. **2.** A peak, 4,345 m (14,246 ft) high, in the San Juan Mountains of southwest Colorado.

Wil·ton (wĭl'tən). A town of southwest Connecticut north of Norwalk. It is mainly residential. ⊚ Pop. 15,989.

Wim·ble·don (wĭm'bəl-dən). A district of southern Greater London, England. It is the site of a major annual tennis tournament.

Win·ches·ter (wĭn'chĕs'tər, -chĭ-stər). **1.** A municipal borough of south-central England southwest of London. The capital of the Anglo-Saxon kingdom of Wessex, it was an important center of learning that attracted many religious scholars after the Norman Conquest (1066). ⊚ Pop. 32,100. **2.** A city of east-central Kentucky east-southeast of Lexington. It is a manufacturing and processing center in a tobacco and livestock area. ⊚ Pop. 15,799. **3.** A town of northeast Massachusetts, a residential suburb of Boston. ⊚ Pop. 20,267. **4.** A community of southeast Nevada, a suburb of Las Vegas. ⊚ Pop. 23,365. **5.** An independent city of northern Virginia west-northwest of Washington, D.C. Settled c. 1744, it was an important military base during the French and Indian War and the Civil War, in which it changed hands a number of times. George Washington began his career as a surveyor here in 1748. ⊚ Pop. 21,947.

Win·der·mere (wĭn'dər-mîr'), **Lake.** A lake of northwest England in the Cumbrian Mountains. It is the largest lake in England and a popular tourist area in the Lake District.

wind gap (wĭnd). A shallow notch in the crest of a mountain ridge.

Wind·ham (wĭn'dəm). A town of east-central Connecticut north-northwest of Norwich. It is an industrial center. ⊚ Pop. 22,039.

Wind·hoek (vĭnt'hook'). The capital and largest city of Namibia, in the central part of the country. Originally the headquarters of a Nama leader, it was occupied by German forces in 1885 and made the capital of the German colony of South-West Africa in 1892. ⊚ Pop. 88,700.

Win·dom Peak (wĭn'dəm). A mountain, 4,295 m (14,082 ft) high, in the San Juan Mountains of southwest Colorado.

Wind River (wĭnd). A river, about 193 km (120 mi) long, of west-central Wyoming flowing generally southeast as a tributary of the Bighorn River.

Wind River Range. A section of the Rocky Mountains in west-central Wyoming rising to 4,210.2 m (13,804 ft) at Gannett Peak.

Wind River Shoshone. See **Shoshone** (sense 1c).

Wind·sor (wĭn'zər). **1.** A city of southeast Ontario, Canada, on the Detroit River opposite Detroit, Michigan. Settled by the French after 1701, it is a port of entry and an industrial center. ⊚ Pop. 191,435. **2.** A municipal borough of south-central England on the Thames River southwest of London. Windsor Castle has been a royal residence since the time of William the Conqueror. ⊚ Pop. 28,700. **3.** A town of northern Connecticut north of Hartford. Settled c. 1635, it is the site of the first English settlement in the state. ⊚ Pop. 27,817.

Wind·ward Islands (wĭnd'wərd). An island group of the southeast West Indies, including the southern group of the Lesser Antilles from Martinique south to Grenada.

Windward Passage. A channel between eastern Cuba and northwest Haiti connecting the Atlantic Ocean with the Caribbean Sea.

Win·ne·ba·go (wĭn'ə-bā'gō). **1.** *pl.* **Winnebago** or **-gos.** A member of a Native American people formerly inhabiting the Green Bay area of Wisconsin, with present-day populations in Wisconsin and Nebraska. **2.** The Siouan language of the Winnebagos.

Winnebago, Lake. A lake of eastern Wisconsin traversed by the Fox River. It is a popular recreation area.

Win·ni·peg (wĭn'ə-pĕg'). The capital and largest city of Manitoba, Canada, in the southeast part of the province at the confluence of the Red and Assiniboine rivers. Founded as a fur-trading post, it developed rapidly after the coming of the railroad in 1881. It is a commercial center and one of the world's largest wheat markets. ⊚ Pop. 616,790.

Winnipeg, Lake. A lake of south-central Manitoba, Canada. A remnant of the glacial Lake Agassiz, it is now a popular resort area surrounded by valuable timberlands.

Win·ni·pe·go·sis (wĭn'ə-pĭ-gō'sĭs), **Lake.** A lake of southwest Manitoba, Canada, west of Lake Winnipeg. It drains southward into Lake Manitoba and has important fisheries.

Winnipeg River. A river, about 322 km (200 mi) long, of southwest Ontario and southeast Manitoba, Canada, flowing northwest to Lake Winnipeg.

Win·ni·pe·sau·kee (wĭn'ə-pĭ-sô'kē), **Lake.** A lake of east-central New Hampshire. It is in a popular resort area.

Wi·no·na (wĭ-nō'nə). A city of southeast Minnesota on the Mississippi River southeast of St.

Paul. It is a manufacturing and trade center. ⊛ Pop. 25,399.

Win·ston-Sa·lem (wĭn'stən-sā'ləm). A city of north-central North Carolina north-northeast of Charlotte. Salem was founded by Moravians in 1766, and Winston was established in 1849; the cities were consolidated in 1913. Winston-Salem is chiefly known for tobacco production but also has a wide variety of manufacturing industries. ⊛ Pop. 143,485.

Win·ter Ha·ven (wĭn'tər hā'vən). A city of central Florida east of Lakeland. It is a winter resort and processing center. ⊛ Pop. 24,725.

Winter Park. A city of central Florida north of Orlando. It is a tourist center in a citrus-growing area. ⊛ Pop. 22,242.

Win·ter·thur (vĭn'tər-tŏŏr'). A city of northern Switzerland northeast of Zurich. It passed to the Hapsburgs in 1264 and became a free imperial city in 1415. It is an industrial and cultural center. ⊛ Pop. 86,779.

Win·throp (wĭn'thrəp). A town of eastern Massachusetts, a resort and residential suburb of Boston. ⊛ Pop. 18,127.

Wis·con·sin (wĭs-kŏn'sĭn). *abbr.* **WI, Wis.** A state of the north-central United States. It was admitted as the 30th state in 1848. First settled by the French, the region was ceded to Great Britain in 1763 and became part of the Northwest Territory in 1787. Madison is the capital and Milwaukee is the largest city. ⊛ Pop. 4,906,745. — **Wis·con'sin·ite'** *n.*

Wisconsin Rapids. A city of central Wisconsin south of Wausau on the Wisconsin River. It is a processing center. ⊛ Pop. 18,245.

Wisconsin River. A river of central and southwest Wisconsin flowing about 692 km (430 mi) south and west to the Mississippi River.

Wis·mar (vĭz'mär', vĭs'-). A city of north-central Germany on an inlet of the Baltic Sea. It was an important member of the Hanseatic League after 1266 and later passed to Sweden (1648). The city was heavily damaged during World War II. ⊛ Pop. 57,874.

With·la·coo·chee (wĭth'lə-kŏŏ'chē). **1.** A river, about 257 km (160 mi) long, of central Florida flowing into the Gulf of Mexico. **2.** A river, about 185 km (115 mi) long, of southern Georgia and northwest Florida, where it empties into the Suwannee River.

Wit·ten (vĭt'n). A city of west-central Germany on the Ruhr River east-southeast of Essen. Chartered in 1825, it is an industrial center. ⊛ Pop. 105,807.

Wit·ten·berg (wĭt'n-bûrg', vĭt'n-běrk'). A city of east-central Germany on the Elbe River east of Dessau. Martin Luther made the city the center of the Protestant Reformation when he

nailed his 95 theses to the door of the Schlosskirche in 1517. ⊛ Pop. 54,306.

Wit·wa·ters·rand (wĭt-wô'tərz-rănd', -ränd', -wŏt'ərz-). Often called **Rand** (rănd). A region of northeast South Africa between the Vaal River and Johannesburg. It has been one of the richest gold-mining areas in the world since the discovery of gold in 1886.

Wlo·cla·wek (vlôt-slä'věk). A city of central Poland on the Vistula River west-northwest of Warsaw. It was founded in the 12th century, passed to Russia in 1815, and reverted to Poland after World War I. ⊛ Pop. 122,329.

Wo·burn (wŏŏ'bərn, wō'-). A city of northeast Massachusetts, an industrial suburb of Boston. ⊛ Pop. 35,943.

Wod·zi·slaw Slą·ski (vô-jē'swäf shlôɴ'skē). A city of southern Poland southwest of Katowice. It is a rail junction and manufacturing center. ⊛ Pop. 111,955.

Wo·king (wō'kĭng). An urban district of southeast England, a residential suburb of London. ⊛ Pop. 81,800.

wold (wōld). An unforested plain; a moor.

Wolds (wōldz). A range of chalk hills in northeast England along both banks of the Humber River.

Wolfs·burg (wŏŏlfs'bûrg', vôlfs'bŏŏrk'). A city of north-central Germany northeast of Brunswick. Wolfsburg grew after the establishment of a Volkswagen automobile factory in the late 1930's. ⊛ Pop. 128,032.

Wol·las·ton Lake (wŏŏl'ə-stən, wŏl'-). A lake of northeast Saskatchewan, Canada, draining into the Churchill and Mackenzie river systems.

Wol·lon·gong (wŏŏl'ən-gŏng', -gông'). A city of southeast Australia on the Tasman Sea southsouthwest of Sydney. It is an iron and steel center. ⊛ Pop. 176,500.

Wo·lof (wō'lŏf'). **1.** *pl.* **Wolof** or **-lofs.** A member of a West African people primarily inhabiting coastal Senegal. **2.** The West Atlantic language of this people, widely used as a lingua franca in Senegal.

Wol·ver·hamp·ton (wŏŏl'vər-hămp'tən, -hăm'-). A borough of west-central England northwest of Birmingham. It is a highly industrialized city. ⊛ Pop. 246,439.

Won·san (wŭn'sän'). A city of southeast North Korea on the Sea of Japan east of Pyongyang. Opened to foreign trade in 1883, it is a major port and naval base. ⊛ Pop. 350,000.

Wood·bridge (wŏŏd'brĭj'). **1.** A city of northeast New Jersey south-southwest of Elizabeth. Settled in 1665, it is an industrial center. ⊛ Pop. 90,074. **2.** A community of northwest Virginia, a suburb of Alexandria and Washington, D.C. ⊛ Pop. 26,401.

Wood·land (wŏŏd′lənd). A city of north-central California west-northwest of Sacramento. It is a manufacturing center in an agricultural area. ⊛ Pop. 39,802.

Wood·mere (wŏŏd′mîr). A town of southeast New York on western Long Island. It is mainly residential. ⊛ Pop. 19,700.

Wood·ridge (wŏŏd′rĭj′). A village of northeast Illinois west of Chicago. It is a residential community in a farm area. ⊛ Pop. 26,256.

Woods (wŏŏdz), **Lake of the.** A lake of southwest Ontario and southeast Manitoba, Canada, and northern Minnesota. It is a popular fishing and resort area.

Wood·stock (wŏŏd′stŏk′). **1.** A city of southern Ontario, Canada, on the Thames River west-southwest of Toronto. It is a manufacturing center. ⊛ Pop. 26,603. **2.** A village of southeast New York south-southwest of Albany. In 1969 a large rock music festival named after the village was held at another small town in the Catskill Mountains. ⊛ Pop. 1,870.

Woon·sock·et (wŏŏn-sŏk′ĭt, wŏŏn′sŏk′-). A city of northern Rhode Island north-northwest of Providence near the Massachusetts border. Settled c. 1666, it has long been a manufacturing center. ⊛ Pop. 43,877.

Woo·ster (wŏŏs′tər). A city of north-central Ohio southwest of Akron. It is a manufacturing center in a farming region. ⊛ Pop. 22,191.

Worces·ter (wŏŏs′tər). **1.** A borough of west-central England on the Severn River south-southwest of Birmingham. Oliver Cromwell and the Parliamentarian army gained their final victory over Charles II and the Scottish army here on September 3, 1651. ⊛ Pop. 73,900. **2.** A city of central Massachusetts west of Boston. It is a commercial, industrial, and educational center. ⊛ Pop. 169,759.

Worms (wûrmz, vôrms). A city of southwest Germany on the Rhine River north-northwest of Mannheim. Originally a Celtic settlement, it was the site of the Diet of Worms (1521) in which Martin Luther refused to recant his beliefs and was outlawed by the Roman Catholic Church. It is an industrial city. ⊛ Pop. 72,610.

Wor·thing (wûr′thĭng). A borough of southeast England on the English Channel south-southwest of London. It is a seaside resort. ⊛ Pop. 92,600.

Wor·thing·ton (wûr′thĭng-tən). A city of central Ohio, a mainly residential suburb of Columbus. ⊛ Pop. 14,869.

Wound·ed Knee (wŏŏn′dĭd nē′). A creek of southwest South Dakota. Some 200 Native Americans were massacred here by U.S. troops on December 29, 1890. In 1973 a standoff between Indian activists and U.S. law officers resulted in deaths on both sides.

Wran·gel Island (răng′gəl, vrăn′gyĭl). An island of northeast Russia in the Arctic Ocean northwest of the Bering Strait. Discovered in 1867, it is named in honor of Ferdinand Petrovich von Wrangel (1796–1870), a Russian explorer who made an unsuccessful attempt to locate the island (1820–1824).

Wran·gell (răng′gəl), **Mount.** A peak, 4,319.7 m (14,163 ft) high, of the central Wrangell Mountains in southern Alaska.

Wrangell Mountains. A mountain range of southern Alaska extending about 161 km (100 mi) from the Copper River to the Canadian border. Mount Bona, at 5,032.5 m (16,500 ft), is the highest peak.

Wrath (răth), **Cape.** A promontory at the northwest extremity of the Scottish mainland.

Wro·claw (vrôt′släf′) also **Bres·lau** (brĕs′lou). A city of southwest Poland on the Oder River. It was a member of the Hanseatic League (1368–1474) before passing to the Hapsburgs (1526) and Prussia (1742). Wroclaw was assigned to Poland by the Potsdam Conference (1945). ⊛ Pop. 643,071.

Wu·han (wŏŏ′hän′). A city of east-central China on the Chang Jiang (Yangtze River). It is the industrial, commercial, and transportation center of central China and the capital of Hubei province. ⊛ Pop. 3,832,536.

Wu·hu (wŏŏ′hŏŏ′). A city of east-central China on the Chang Jiang (Yangtze River) south-southwest of Nanjing. It is a commercial center and a deep-water port. ⊛ Pop. 552,932.

Wu Jiang (wŏŏ′ jyäng′). A river rising in south-central China and flowing about 805 km (500 mi) east and north to the Chang Jiang (Yangtze River).

Wup·per·tal (vŏŏp′ər-täl′). A city of west-central Germany north-northeast of Düsseldorf. It is an industrial center. ⊛ Pop. 386,625.

Würt·tem·berg (wûr′təm-bûrg′, vür′təm-bĕrk′). A historical region and former kingdom of southwest Germany. A duchy after 1495, it was a kingdom from 1806 to 1918 and came under German sovereignty in 1934.

Würz·burg (wûrts′bûrg′, vürts′bŏŏrk′). A city of south-central Germany on the Main River. Originally a Celtic settlement, it is an industrial city in a winemaking region. ⊛ Pop. 128,875.

Wu·sih (wŏŏ′shē′). See **Wuxi.**

Wu·tai Shan (wŏŏ′tī′ shän′). A range of mountains in northeast China between Taiyuan and Beijing, rising to 3,507.5 m (11,500 ft).

Wu·xi also **Wu·sih** (wŏŏ′shē′). A city of eastern China between Shanghai and Nanjing. It is a shipping center. ⊛ Pop. 3,181,985.

Wy·an·dot also **Wy·an·dotte** (wī′ən-dŏt′). **1.** *pl.* **Wyandot** or **-dots** also **Wyandotte** or

-dottes. A member of a Native American people formed of groups displaced by the destruction of the Huron confederacy in the mid-17th century, formerly located in Ohio and the upper Midwest and now living in northeast Oklahoma. **2.** The Iroquoian language of the Wyandots.

Wyandotte. A city of southeast Michigan, an industrial suburb of Detroit. ◉ Pop. 30,938.

Wyandotte Cave. A cave of southern Indiana west of New Albany. Discovered in 1898, it is one of the largest caverns in the United States.

Wyck·off. (wī′kôf, -kŏf). A town of northeast New Jersey north of Paterson. It is mainly residential. ◉ Pop. 15,372.

Wy·o·ming (wī-ō′mǐng). **1.** *abbr.* **WY, Wyo.** A state of the western United States. It was admitted as the 44th state in 1890. Acquired by the United States as part of the Louisiana Purchase (1803), Wyoming became a ranching center after the Union Pacific Railroad was established (1868). Cheyenne is the capital and the largest city. ◉ Pop. 455,975. **2.** A city of west-central Michigan, a manufacturing suburb of Grand Rapids. ◉ Pop. 63,891.

X

Xan·thus (zăn′thəs). An ancient city of Lycia in present-day southwest Turkey. It was besieged and taken by the Persians (c. 546 B.C.) and the Romans (c. 42 B.C.). Both times the residents destroyed the city before surrendering.

Xen·ia (zēn′yə, zē′nē-ə). A city of southwest-central Ohio east-southeast of Dayton. It is a manufacturing center. ◉ Pop. 24,664.

Xho·sa also **Xo·sa** (kō′sä, -zə). **1.** *pl.* **Xhosa** or **-sas** also **Xosa** or **-sas.** A member of a Bantu people inhabiting the eastern part of Cape Province, South Africa. **2.** The Nguni language of this people, closely related to Zulu.

Xia·men (shyä′mən) also **A·moy** (ä-moi′). A city of eastern China east-northeast of Guangzhou. One of the earliest seats of European commerce in China, it is a major harbor and a manufacturing center. ◉ Pop. 639,436.

Xi'an (shē′än′, shyän) also **Si·an** (sē′än′, shē′-) or **Hsian** (shyän). A city of central China southwest of Beijing. The capital (221–206 B.C.) of the Qin dynasty, it is a major commercial center and the capital of Shaanxi province. ◉ Pop. 2,872,539.

Xiang Jiang (shyäng′ jyäng′) also **Siang Kiang** (syäng′ kyäng′, shyäng′) or **Hsiang Kiang** (shyäng′). A river, about 1,150 km (715 mi) long, flowing generally northward from south-

east China. Its valley has important mineral resources.

Xiang·tan (shyäng′tän′) also **Siang·tan** (syäng′-, shyäng′-). A city of south-central China on the Xiang Jiang south-southwest of Changsha. It is an industrial center. ◉ Pop. 1,531,117.

Xi Jiang (shē′ jyäng′) also **Si Kiang** (sē′ kyäng′, shē′). A river, about 2,011 km (1,250 mi) long, rising in southeast China and flowing eastward to the South China Sea near Guangzhou.

Xin·gu (shēng-gōō′). A river of central and northern Brazil rising in several streams and flowing about 1,979 km (1,230 mi) generally northward to the Amazon River at the head of the Amazon delta.

Xi·ning (shē′nǐng′). A city of central China north-northeast of Chengdu. The capital of Qinghai province, it has long been a commercial center on the caravan route to Xizang (Tibet). ◉ Pop. 697,780.

Xin·jiang Uy·gur (shǐn′jyäng′ wē′gər) also **Sin·kiang Ui·ghur** or **Sin·kiang Ui·gur** (sǐn′-kyäng′ wē′gər, shǐn′jyäng′). An autonomous region of extreme western China. It came under Chinese control in the 16th century and was the site of a conflict between China and the Soviet Union in 1969. Ürümqi is the capital. ◉ Pop. 13,610,000.

Xin·xiang (shǐn′shyäng′). A city of eastern China south-southeast of Taiyuan. It is a rail center. ◉ Pop. 1,770,370.

Xi·zang (shē′dzäng′) or **Ti·bet** (tə-bĕt′). An autonomous region of China in the southwest part of the country north and east of the Himalaya Mountains. Controlled by China since 1720, it became an autonomous province in 1951 and was formally proclaimed an autonomous region in 1965. Xizang is a center of Buddhism, but many Buddhists have fled since the 1950's to escape religious persecution. Lhasa is the capital. ◉ Pop. 1,990,000.

Xo·sa (kō′sä, -zə). Variant of **Xhosa.**

Xu·zhou (shōō′jō′) also **Sü·chow** (sōō′chou′, sü′jō′). A city of eastern China north-northwest of Nanjing. It is a rail and manufacturing center. ◉ Pop. 841,000.

Y

Ya·blo·no·vy Range (yä′blə-nə-vē′). A mountain chain of southeast Russia extending northeast from near the Mongolian border. It forms part of the watershed for rivers flowing to the Arctic and Pacific oceans.

Ya·ki·ma¹ (yăk′ə-mô, -mə). **1.** *pl.* **Yakima** or

-mas. A member of a Native American people inhabiting south-central Washington. **2.** The dialect of Sahaptin spoken by the Yakima.

Ya·ki·ma² (yăk′ə-mô′, -mə). A city of south-central Washington southeast of Seattle. It is a trade, processing, and shipping center for an irrigated agricultural region. ◉ Pop. 54,827.

Yakima River. A river, about 327 km (203 mi) long, of central and southeast Washington rising in the Cascade Range and flowing generally southeast to the Columbia River.

Ya·kut (yä-ko͞ot′). **1.** *pl.* **Yakut** or **-kuts.** A member of a people inhabiting the region of the Lena River in eastern Siberia. **2.** The Turkic language of the Yakut.

Ya·kutsk (yə-ko͞otsk′). A city of east-central Russia on the Lena River. Founded as a fort in 1632, it is a port and processing center. ◉ Pop. 196,341.

Yale (yāl), **Mount.** A peak, 4,329.8 m (14,196 ft) high, in the Sawatch Range of the Rocky Mountains in central Colorado.

Ya·long Jiang (yä′lo͞ong′ jyäng′). A river of south-central China flowing about 1,287 km (800 mi) generally southward to the Chang Jiang (Yangtze River).

Yal·ta (yôl′tə). A city of southeast Ukraine in the southern Crimea on the Black Sea. A popular resort, it was the site of an Allied conference (attended by Franklin D. Roosevelt, Winston Churchill, and Joseph Stalin) in February 1945. ◉ Pop. 86,000.

Ya·lu Jiang (yä′lo͞o′ jyäng′). A river, about 805 km (500 mi) long, forming part of the North Korea–China border.

Ya·ma·ga·ta (yä′mə-gä′tə, yä′mä-gä′tä, yä-mä′gä-tä). A city of northern Honshu, Japan, west of Sendai. It is a processing center, especially for silk. ◉ Pop. 251,354.

Ya·ma·see (yä′mə-sē′). *pl.* **Yamasee** or **-sees.** A member of a Native American people formerly inhabiting parts of coastal Georgia and South Carolina. The Yamasee dispersed to other Native American groups after conflict with English colonists in the early 18th century.

Yam·bol (yäm′bôl). A city of southeast Bulgaria east of Stara Zagora. Under Turkish rule from the 15th to the 19th century, it is a commercial center. ◉ Pop. 91,000.

Yam·pa (yăm′pə). A river, about 402 km (250 mi) long, of northwest Colorado flowing north then west to the Green River near the Utah border.

Ya·na (yä′nə). A river, about 1,207 km (750 mi) long, of northeast Russia flowing northward to the Laptev Sea.

Yang·chow (yäng′jō′). See **Yangzhou.**

Yang·chü·an (yäng′chwän′, -chü′än′). See **Yangquan.**

Yan·gon (yän′gôn′). Formerly **Ran·goon** (răn-go͞on′, răng-). The capital and largest city of Myanmar (Burma), in the southern part of the country in the Irrawaddy River delta. It was a small fishing village until it became the capital of Burmese kings after the 1750's. Further growth was spurred by the British occupation of the city in 1852. ◉ Pop. 513,023.

Yang·quan (yäng′chwän′) also **Yang·chü·an** (-chwän′, -chü′än′). A city of eastern China southwest of Beijing. It is an industrial center in a coal and iron area. ◉ Pop. 574,832.

Yang·tze River (yăng′sē′, -tsē′, yäng′dzə′). See **Chang Jiang.**

Yang·zhou also **Yang·chow** (yäng′jō′). A city of east-central China on the Grand Canal. It was a capital of China in the sixth century A.D. and an important literary and cultural center. The Venetian traveler Marco Polo was governor of the city from 1282 to 1285. ◉ Pop. 2,769,300.

Yan·kee (yăng′kē). **1.** A native or inhabitant of New England. **2.** A native or inhabitant of a northern U.S. state, especially a Union soldier during the Civil War. **3.** A native or inhabitant of the United States.

Yank·ton (yăngk′tən). *pl.* **Yankton** or **-tons.** A member of a division of the Sioux people formerly inhabiting northern Minnesota, now located mainly in the eastern Dakotas. The Yanktons and Yanktonais occupy a middle position between the Santee and Teton divisions of the Sioux.

Yank·to·nai (yăngk′tə-nī′). *pl.* **Yanktonai** or **-nais.** A member of a division of the Sioux people formerly inhabiting northern Minnesota, now located mainly in North and South Dakota and eastern Montana.

Yao¹ (you). **1.** *pl.* **Yao** or **Yaos.** A member of a people related to the Hmong and inhabiting southern China, northern Laos, Thailand, and Vietnam. **2.** The Miao-Yao language of the Yao.

Yao² (you). A city of southern Honshu, Japan, a suburb of Osaka. ◉ Pop. 276,324.

Ya·oun·dé (yä-o͞on-dā′). The capital of Cameroon, in the south-central part of the country. It was founded in 1888 as an ivory-trading post. ◉ Pop. 653,670.

Yap (yăp, yäp). An island group and state of the Federated States of Micronesia in the western Caroline Islands of the western Pacific Ocean. Discovered by the Spanish in 1791, it became part of a Japanese mandate after 1920 and fell to U.S. forces in 1945.

Ya·qui (yä′kē). **1.** *pl.* **Yaqui** or **-quis.** A member of a Native American people of Sonora, a state of northwest Mexico, now also located in southern Arizona. Many Yaquis sought asylum in the United States in the early 19th century because of conflict with the Mexican government. **2.** The Uto-Aztecan language of the Yaquis.

Yar·kant He (yär-kănt′ hə′, -känt′) also **Yar·kand River** (-kănd′, -känd′). A river, about 805 km (500 mi) long, of northwest China rising in the Karakoram Range and flowing generally northeast to the Tarim He.

Yar·mouth (yär′məth). A town of southeast Massachusetts on south-central Cape Cod east of Barnstable. It is a resort and processing center. ⊕ Pop. 21,174.

Ya·ro·slavl (yär′ə-slä′vəl, yə-rə-). A city of west-central Russia on the Volga River northeast of Moscow. Traditionally founded in 1010, it was annexed by Moscow in 1463. It is a transportation hub and a center for tourism and industry. ⊕ Pop. 628,302.

Ya·va·pai (yăv′ə-pī′, yä′və-). **1.** pl. **Yavapai** or **-pais.** A member of a Native American people inhabiting western Arizona. **2.** The Yuman language of the Yavapais.

Yazd (yăzd). A city of central Iran south-southeast of Tehran. Dating from the fifth century B.C., it is a textile and carpet-weaving center. ⊕ Pop. 306,268.

Ya·zoo (yə-zōō′, yăz′ōō). A river, 302.5 km (188 mi) long, of west-central Mississippi flowing generally southwest to the Mississippi River above Vicksburg.

Ye·ka·te·rin·burg (yĭ-kăt′ə-rən-bûrg′) also **E·ka·te·rin·burg** (ĭ-kăt′ə-rən-bûrg′). Formerly **Sverdlovsk** (sfĕrd-lôfsk′). A city of west-central Russia in the eastern foothills of the Ural Mountains. Founded in 1721 and named for Catherine the Great, it was the site of the execution (1918) of Nicholas II and his family after the Russian Revolution. The city was named Sverdlovsk from 1924 to 1991. ⊕ Pop. 1,350,861.

Ye·lets (yə-lĕts′, yĭ-lyĕts′). A city of west-central Russia east-southeast of Orel. It is a manufacturing center and rail junction. ⊕ Pop. 116,000.

Yel·low·knife (yĕl′ō-nīf′). The capital of Northwest Territories, Canada, on the northern shore of Great Slave Lake. It was founded in 1935 after the discovery of gold and silver deposits in the area and became the provincial capital in 1967. ⊕ Pop. 9,483.

Yel·low River (yĕl′ō). See **Huang He.**

Yellow Sea. An arm of the Pacific Ocean between the Chinese mainland and the Korean Peninsula. It connects with the East China Sea to the south.

Yel·low·stone (yĕl′ō-stōn′). A river, about 1,080 km (671 mi) long, of northwest Wyoming and southern and eastern Montana. It flows northward through **Yellowstone Lake** and **Yel-**

lowstone National Park then east and northeast to the Missouri River. The park includes numerous geysers, including Old Faithful.

Yem·en (yĕm′ən, yä′mən). A country of southwest Asia at the southern tip of the Arabian peninsula. It was ruled by various peoples in ancient times, such as the Sabaeans, Himyarites, Romans, Ethiopians, and Persians; it was conquered in the 7th century A.D. by Muslim Arabs, became part of the Ottoman Empire in the 16th century, and remained so until the end of World War I. The northern part (known as Yemen or North Yemen) was established as an independent kingdom in 1918 and made a republic in 1962. The southern part consisted of several British protectorates in the late 19th and early 20th centuries. Britain withdrew from the area in 1967, and Southern Yemen became independent soon after. The two united in May 1990. San'a is the capital and Aden the largest city. ⊕ Pop. 12,672,000. **—Yem′en·ite′, Yem′e·ni** (ə-nē) adj. & n.

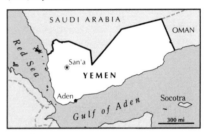

Yen·a·ki·ye·vo (yĕn-ə-kē′yə-və). A city of eastern Ukraine east of Donetsk, of which it is an industrial suburb. ⊕ Pop. 119,900.

Ye·ni·sey also **Ye·ni·sei** (yĕn′ĭ-sā′, yĭ-nĭ-syā′). A river of central Russia flowing about 4,023 km (2,500 mi) westward and generally north to the Kara Sea through **Yenisey Bay,** a long estuary.

Ye·re·van also **E·re·van** or **E·ri·van** (yĕ′rĭ-vän′). The capital and largest city of Armenia south of Tbilisi, Georgia. An ancient city founded on the site of a fortress established in the eighth century B.C., it was strategically important as a trade center on caravan routes linking Transcaucasia and India after the seventh century A.D. It was the capital of the Armenian Soviet Socialist Republic, which gained its independence from the U.S.S.R. in 1991. ⊕ Pop. 1,254,000.

Yid·dish (yĭd′ĭsh). The language historically of Ashkenazic Jews of Central and Eastern Europe, resulting from a fusion of elements derived principally from medieval German dialects and secondarily from Hebrew and Aramaic, various Slavic languages, and Old French and Old Italian. **—Yid′dish** adj. **—Yid′dish·ism** n.

Yin·chuan also **Yin·chwan** (yĭn′chwän′). A city of north-central China west-southwest of Beijing. In the 13th century the Venetian traveler Marco Polo visited the city, which is now the capital of Ningxia Huizu province. ● Pop. 502,080.

Yog·ya·kar·ta (yŏg′yə-kär′tə, jôk′jä-, jŏk′yə-). See **Jogjakarta.**

Yok·kai·chi (yō-kī′chē, yô′kä-ē′chē). A city of southern Honshu, Japan, on Ise Bay southwest of Nagoya. It is a manufacturing and shipping center. ● Pop. 282,197.

Yo·ko·ha·ma (yō′kə-hä′mə, yô′kô-hä′mä). A city of southeast Honshu, Japan, on the western shore of Tokyo Bay. It was a small fishing village when the American naval officer Matthew Perry visited it in 1854 but was chosen as a site for foreign settlement in 1859 and grew rapidly thereafter. Almost entirely destroyed by an earthquake and fire in 1923, it was quickly rebuilt and modernized. The city is now a leading port and an industrial center. ● Pop. 3,288,464.

Yo·ko·su·ka (yō′kə-soō′kə, yô′kô-soō′kä). A city of southeast Honshu, Japan, on Tokyo Bay. It is a naval base with shipyards and ironworks. ● Pop. 435,383.

Yo·kuts (yō′kŭts). **1.** *pl.* **Yokuts.** A member of a group of Native American peoples formerly inhabiting the southern San Joaquin Valley and adjacent foothills of the Sierra Nevada, with present-day descendants in the same area. **2.** Any or all of the languages of the Yokuts.

Yon·kers (yŏng′kərz). A city of southeast New York north of New York City. First inhabited by the Dutch in the mid-1600's, it is a residential and manufacturing center. ● Pop. 188,082.

Yor·ba Lin·da (yôr′bə lĭn′də). A city of southern California southeast of Los Angeles. It is the site of the presidential library of Richard M. Nixon (dedicated 1990). ● Pop. 52,422.

York (yôrk). **1.** A borough of northern England on the Ouse River east-northeast of Leeds. Originally a Celtic settlement, it was later held by Romans, Angles, Danes, and Normans. During the Middle Ages the city was a prosperous wool market and an educational center. Its archbishopric is second only to Canterbury. ● Pop. 103,968. **2.** A city of southern Pennsylvania south-southeast of Harrisburg. Settled in 1735, it was the meeting place of the Continental Congress in 1777–1778 during the British occupation of Philadelphia. ● Pop. 42,192.

York, Cape. 1. The northernmost point of Australia, on Torres Strait at the tip of Cape York Peninsula. **2.** A cape of northwest Greenland in northern Baffin Bay. It was used as a base by the American explorer Robert E. Peary, who discovered its famous iron meteorites.

Yorke Peninsula (yôrk). A narrow peninsula of southern Australia bounded by Spencer Gulf.

York River. An estuary, about 64 km (40 mi) long, of eastern Virginia flowing southeast into Chesapeake Bay.

York·shire (yôrk′shîr, -shər). A historical region and former county of northern England. It was part of Northumbria in Anglo-Saxon times.

York·ton (yôrk′tən). A city of southeast Saskatchewan, Canada, northeast of Regina. It is a railroad junction and processing center in a farming region. ● Pop. 15,339.

York·town (yôrk′toun′). A village of southeast Virginia on the York River north of Newport News. It was the site of Cornwallis's surrender of the British forces (1781) in the American Revolution. During the Civil War Union troops occupied the town after a siege lasting from April to May 1862.

Yo·ru·ba (yôr′ə-bə, yō′roō-bä). **1.** *pl.* **Yoruba** or **-bas.** A member of a West African people living chiefly in southwest Nigeria. **2.** The South Central Niger-Congo language of this people. — **Yo′ru·ban** *adj.*

Yo·sem·i·te Valley (yō-sĕm′ĭ-tē). A valley of east-central California along the Merced River. It is surrounded by **Yosemite National Park** and has many waterfalls, including **Yosemite Falls,** with a total drop of 739.6 m (2,425 ft).

Yosh·kar-O·la (yəsh-kär′ə-lä′). A city of west-central Russia northwest of Kazan. Founded in 1578 as a frontier outpost, it is a manufacturing center. ● Pop. 231,000.

Youngs·town (yŭngz′toun′). A city of northeast Ohio east of Akron. It is a major center of iron and steel production with extensive manufacturing facilities. ● Pop. 95,732.

Youth (yoōth), **Isle of.** Formerly **Isle of Pines.** An island off southwest Cuba. Discovered by Columbus in 1494, it was claimed by both the United States and Cuba until a 1925 treaty confirmed Cuba's sovereignty.

Y·pres (ē′prə). See **Ieper.**

Yp·si·lan·ti (ĭp′sə-lăn′tē). A city of southeast Michigan west-southwest of Detroit. Founded on the site of a Native American village and French trading post, it is a residential, commercial, and industrial center. ● Pop. 24,846.

Yu·an Jiang (yoō′än′ jyäng′, ywän′). See **Red River** (sense 1).

Yu·ba City (yoō′bə). A city of north-central California north of Sacramento. It is a processing hub in an agricultural area. ● Pop. 27,437.

Yu·cai·pa (yoō-kī′pə). A community of southern California in the foothills of the San Bernardino Mountains east of Los Angeles. It is a processing center. ● Pop. 32,824.

Yu·ca·tán (yoō′kə-tăn′, -tän′). A peninsula mostly in southeast Mexico between the Caribbean Sea and the Gulf of Mexico. It includes many Mayan and Toltec sites and is separated from Cuba by the **Yucatán Channel.**

Yuc·a·tec (yōō'kə-tĕk'). **1.** *pl.* **Yucatec** or **-tecs.** A member of a Mayan people inhabiting the Yucatán Peninsula. **2.** The Mayan language of the Yucatec.

Yu·chi (yōō'chē). **1.** *pl.* **Yuchi** or **-chis.** A member of a Native American people formerly inhabiting northern Georgia and eastern Tennessee, politically included in the Creek confederacy since the 19th century. **2.** The language of the Yuchis.

Yu·go·sla·vi·a (yōō'gō-slä'vē-ə). **1.** A former country of southeast Europe bordering on the Adriatic Sea. It was formed in 1918 after the collapse of the Austro-Hungarian Empire as the Kingdom of Serbs, Croats, and Slovenes and was renamed Yugoslavia in 1929. Occupied by German forces (1941–1944), the country became a Communist state under Marshal Tito after World War II. Tito broke with the U.S.S.R. in 1948, and Yugoslavia became the most liberal of the eastern European countries, although intellectual freedom was still restricted. After Tito's death in 1980, a collective presidency assumed power, but economic problems and ethnic tensions grew. Communist party control ended in 1990, and four of the six constituent republics, namely Slovenia, Croatia, Bosnia and Herzegovina, and Macedonia, declared independence in 1991. Belgrade was the capital. **2.** A country of southeast Europe formed in April 1992 by the two remaining Yugoslav republics of Serbia and Montenegro. As the original Yugoslav federation disintegrated in 1991 and 1992, the region became the scene of intense fighting among ethnic groups, and the Serbian-led Yugoslav army succeeded in capturing a large portion of Bosnia and Herzegovina and Croatia. In May 1992 the United Nations imposed economic sanctions, which were lifted in December 1995

after the signing of the Dayton Peace Accords by Balkan leaders. Opposition victories in the November 1996 municipal elections were nullified by the government of Serbian president Slobodan Milosevic, touching off weeks of street demonstrations. Belgrade is the capital and largest city. ◉ Pop. 10,515,000. — **Yu'go·slav'**, **Yu'go·sla'vi·an** *adj. & n.*

Yu·kon (yōō'kŏn'). A city of central Oklahoma west of Oklahoma City. It is a processing center. ◉ Pop. 20,935.

Yukon River. A river flowing about 3,218 km (2,000 mi) from southern Yukon Territory, Canada, through Alaska to the Bering Sea. It was a major route to the Klondike during the gold rush of 1897–1898.

Yukon Territory. *abbr.* **Y.T.** A territory of northwest Canada east of Alaska. It joined the Confederacy in 1898. The region was first explored by fur traders in the 1840's and was acquired by Canada from the Hudson's Bay Company in 1870. A land claim made by the Yukon tribe of Native Americans was approved by the federal government in 1991. Whitehorse is the capital and the largest city. ◉ Pop. 23,153.

Yu·ma¹ (yōō'mə). **1.** *pl.* **Yuma** or **-mas.** A member of a Native American people inhabiting an area along the lower Colorado River, formerly on both banks but now mainly on the California side. **2.** The Yuman language of the Yumas. Also called *Quechan.*

Yu·ma² (yōō'mə). A city of southwest Arizona on the Colorado River and the California border. It is a resort and processing center in a gold-mining region. ◉ Pop. 54,923.

Yu·man (yōō'mən). A language family constituting the languages of the Yuma and Mohave peoples and other Native American languages of western Arizona and adjacent parts of California and Mexico. — **Yu'man** *adj.*

Yun·nan (yōō'nän'). A province of south-central China bordering on Vietnam, Laos, and Myanmar (Burma). The region was overrun by Mongols in 1253 and became part of China in the 17th century. The area is known for its vast mineral resources. Kunming is the capital. ◉ Pop. 34,060,000.

Yu·pik (yōō'pĭk). **1.** *pl.* **Yupik** or **-piks.** A member of a group of Eskimoan peoples inhabiting coastal areas of western Alaska and extreme northeast Russia. **2.** The group of Eskimoan languages spoken by the Yupik.

Yu·rok (yŏŏr'ŏk). **1.** *pl.* **Yurok** or **-roks.** A member of a Native American people inhabiting northwest California along the Pacific coast and lower Klamath River. **2.** The language of this people, distantly related to Algonquian.

Z

Zaan·dam (zän-dăm′, -däm′). A city of western Netherlands west-northwest of Amsterdam. Peter the Great of Russia lived here in 1697 while studying shipbuilding. ◉ Pop. 132,146.

Zab·rze (zäb′zhĕ). A city of south-central Poland west of Katowice. Founded in the 13th century, it passed to Prussia in 1742 and was ceded to Poland in 1945. ◉ Pop. 205,544.

Za·gorsk (zə-gôrsk′). See **Sergiyef Posad**.

Za·greb (zä′grĕb). The capital and largest city of Croatia on the Sava River in the north-central part of the country. Originally a Roman town, it came under the control of Hungary in the 13th century. During the 19th century the city was a center of Croatian nationalism, and it became the capital of an autonomous Croatia within the kingdom of Hungary in 1868. Zagreb was a part of Yugoslavia from after World War I until 1991. ◉ Pop. 867,717.

Zag·ros Mountains (zăg′rəs). A range of western Iran forming the western and southern borders of the central Iranian plateau and rising to 4,550.6 m (14,920 ft).

Zaire (zī′îr, zä-îr′). Formerly (1885–1908) **Congo Free State** (kŏng′gō) and (1908–1960) **Belgian Congo** (bĕl′jən) and (1960–1971) **Congo**. A country of central Africa astride the equator. First inhabited by Pygmy peoples, the region was settled by Bantu and Nilotic groups migrating from the north during the first millenium A.D. Portuguese influence was established after 1482, but colonization took place mainly under King Leopold II of Belgium (reigned 1865–1909), whose privately founded Congo Free State was later (1908) annexed by Belgium as the colony of Belgian Congo. Nationalist sentiment forced Belgium to grant the colony independence as the republic of Congo in 1960, but the country was immediately plunged into civil war by the secession of Katanga (now Shaba) province. Patrice Lumumba, the first prime minister, was murdered in 1961 following a coup staged by president Joseph Kasavubu. Belgian and UN peacekeeping forces helped end the Katanga rebellion in 1963, and a second rebellion in the northeast was put down later that year. In 1965 army general Mobutu Sese Seko took control of the country, which was renamed Zaire in 1971. Mobutu's regime brought political stability but became increasingly corrupt and repressive. In 1996 rebel forces took advantage of the refugee crisis along the Rwanda border to capture a large portion of the country and succeeded (1997) in ousting Mobutu, renaming the country

Congo. Kinshasa is the capital and the largest city. ◉ Pop. 42,552,000. — **Za·ir′e·an, Za·ir′i·an** adj. & n.

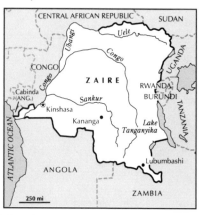

Zaire River. See **Congo River**.

Za·ma (zā′mə, zä′mä). An ancient town of northern Africa southwest of Carthage in present-day northern Tunisia. The Romans decisively defeated Hannibal here in the final battle of the Second Punic War (202 B.C.).

Zam·be·zi (zăm-bē′zē). A river, about 2,735 km (1,700 mi) long, of central and southern Africa rising in northwest Zambia and flowing south and west to the Mozambique Channel.

Zam·bi·a (zăm′bē-ə). A country of south-central Africa. The original San inhabitants were pushed out by migrating Bantu peoples, most of whom settled between the 16th and 18th century, and the area was explored by the Scottish missionary David Livingstone in the 1850's. It was administered after 1889 by the British South Africa Company, founded by British financier Cecil Rhodes, becoming the protectorate of Northern Rhodesia in 1911 and passing to British administration in 1924. From 1953 to 1963 it became part of the colonial federation of Rhodesia and Nyasaland, gaining independence in 1964 as the republic of Zambia under President Kenneth Kaunda. Kaunda's active opposition to

the minority-white government of neighboring Southern Rhodesia (now Zimbabwe) created severe economic problems for the country, and his one-party rule became increasingly unpopular. Kaunda was defeated in the country's first multiparty elections in 1991. Lusaka is the capital and the largest city. ⊛ Pop. 9,169,000. — **Zam'·bi·an** *adj. & n.*

Za·mo·ra (zə-môr'ə, -mōr'ə, thä-mô'rä). A city of northwest Spain on the Douro River northwest of Madrid. Because of its strategic location, it was frequently contested during the Middle Ages. ⊛ Pop. 61,151.

Zanes·ville (zānz'vĭl'). A city of east-central Ohio east of Columbus. Incorporated in 1800, it was state capital from 1810 to 1812. It is a trade and industrial center. ⊛ Pop. 26,778.

Zan·zi·bar (zăn'zə-bär'). **1.** A region of eastern Africa, comprising **Zanzibar Island** and several adjacent islands off the northeast coast of Tanzania. Arab and Portuguese traders visited the region in early times, and it was controlled by the Omanis in the 18th and 19th centuries. Britain established a protectorate (1890) that became an independent sultanate in December 1963 and a republic after an uprising in January 1964. In April 1964 it joined Tanganyika to form a new republic that was renamed Tanzania in October 1964. **2.** A city of Tanzania on the western coast of Zanzibar Island. Founded in the 16th century as a Portuguese trading post, it was a major center of the East African ivory trade in the 19th century. ⊛ Pop. 133,000.

Za·po·pan (zä'pō-pän', sä'pô-). A city of southwest Mexico west of Guadalajara. It is a commercial center. ⊛ Pop. 345,390.

Za·po·ro·zhe (zä'pə-rô'zhə, zə-pə-rô'zhyĕ). Formerly **A·lek·san·drovsk** (ăl'ĭk-săn'drəfsk, ə-lĭk-sän'-). A city of southern Ukraine west of Donetsk. It was founded in 1770 on the site of a Cossack camp. ⊛ Pop. 897,600.

Za·po·tec (zä'pə-tĕk', sä'pô-). **1.** *pl.* **Zapotec** or **-tecs. a.** A member of a Mesoamerican Indian people centered at Monte Albán in southern Mexico, whose civilization reached its height around A.D. 300–900. **b.** A modern-day descendant of this people. **2.** Any of a group of related languages spoken in southern Mexico.

Za·ra·go·za (zăr'ə-gō'zə, thä'rä-gô'thä). See **Saragossa**.

Za·ri·a (zä'rē-ə). A city of north-central Nigeria south-southwest of Kano. It is a processing center in a cotton-growing region. ⊛ Pop. 267,300.

zas·tru·ga (ză-strōō'gə, zä-). Variant of **sastruga**.

Za·wier·ci (zäv-yĕr'chē). A city of southern Poland northwest of Cracow. It passed to Prussia in 1795, to Russia in 1815, and to Poland after World War I. ⊛ Pop. 55,700.

Zea·land (zē'lənd). See **Sjaelland**.

Zee·land (zē'lənd, zā'länt). A historical region of southwest Netherlands bordering on Belgium and the North Sea. It has been a part of Holland since the tenth century.

Zeist (zīst). A city of central Netherlands east of Utrecht. It is largely residential. ⊛ Pop. 60,478.

Zer·matt (tsĕr-mät'). A village of southern Switzerland in the Pennine Alps northwest of the Matterhorn. It is a noted tourist resort. ⊛ Pop. 3,548.

Ze·ya (zā'yə, zyĕ'-). A river of southeast Russia flowing about 1,287 km (800 mi) south and southeast to the Amur River.

Zgierz (zgyĕzh). A city of central Poland north of Lódź. Chartered c. 1300, it grew as a textile center after 1818. ⊛ Pop. 54,900.

Zhang·jia·kou (jäng'jyä'kō') also **Kal·gan** (käl'gän'). A city of northeast China near the Great Wall northwest of Beijing. It was a commercial and military center under the Ming and Manchu dynasties. ⊛ Pop. 719,672.

Zhan·jiang also **Chan·chiang** (jän'jyäng') or **Chan·kiang** (chän'kyäng'). A city of southeast China southwest of Guangzhou on an inlet of the South China Sea. It is a seaport and trade center with varied industries. ⊛ Pop. 1,048,720.

Zhda·nov (zhdä'nəf). See **Mariupol**.

Zhe·jiang (jœ'jyäng') also **Che·kiang** (chŭ'-kyäng', jə'gyäng'). A province of eastern China on the East China Sea. It was a cultural center of early China and now is one of the most densely populated regions in the country. Hangzhou is the capital. ⊛ Pop. 40,300,000.

Zheng·zhou also **Cheng·chow** (jŭng'jō', jœng'-). A city of east-central China south-southwest of Beijing. An important railroad junction and industrial center, it is the capital of Henan province. ⊛ Pop. 1,752,374.

Zhen·jiang (jŭn'jyäng', jœn'-) also **Chin·kiang** (chĭn'kyäng', jĭn'gyäng'). A city of eastern China on the Grand Canal east of Nanjing. It was an important trade center during the Ming and Manchu dynasties. ⊛ Pop. 1,280,027.

Zhi·to·mir (zhĭ-tô'mîr). A city of west-central Ukraine west of Kiev. First mentioned in 1240, it was a way station on the trade route between Scandinavia and Constantinople, passed to Lithuania (1320) and Poland (1569), and was incorporated into Russia in the late 1770's. ⊛ Pop. 299,400.

Zhu Jiang (jōō' jyäng') also **Can·ton River** (kăn'tŏn', kăn'tŏn') or **Chu Kiang** (chōō' kyäng', jōō' gyäng'). A river, about 177 km (110 mi) long, of southeast China flowing into the South China Sea.

Zi·bo (dzē'bō') also **Tze·po** (tsŭ'pō', dzŭ'bō'). A city of eastern China east of Jinan. ⊛ Pop. 2,484,206.

Zie·lo·no Gó·ra (zhĕ-lô′nə gŏŏr′ə). A city of western Poland west of Lódź. Founded in the 13th century, it was assigned to Poland by the Postdam Conference in 1945. ⊚ Pop. 114,302.

Zi·gong (dzē′gŏŏng′) also **Tze·kung** (tsŭ′-kŏŏng′, dzŭ′gŏŏng′). A city of south-central China west of Chongqing. It is an oil and natural gas center. ⊚ Pop. 977,147.

Zim·bab·we¹ (zĭm-bäb′wē, -wä). A ruined city of southeast Zimbabwe south of Harare. First occupied by Iron Age peoples in the third century A.D., it was rediscovered c. 1870 and is believed by some to be the site of King Solomon's mines.

Zim·bab·we² (zĭm-bäb′wē, -wä). Formerly **Rho·de·sia** (rō-dē′zhə). A country of southern Africa. Various Bantu peoples migrated into the area during the first millenium, displacing the earlier San inhabitants. European colonization began in 1889 under the British South Africa Company founded by British financier Cecil Rhodes. In 1923 the region became the self-governing British colony of Southern Rhodesia (often just Rhodesia), which formed part of the colonial federation of Rhodesia and Nyasaland from 1953 to 1963. In 1965 Rhodesia's white-minority government declared its independence from Britain under Prime Minister Ian Smith, who maintained white rule in the face of international criticism, UN sanctions, and attacks by guerrilla forces under Robert Mugabe and Joshua Nkomo. Economic deterioration and political isolation eventually caused Smith to propose a biracial government, and open elections were held in 1980, with Mugabe's Patriotic Front gaining a large majority. Britain recognized Zimbabwe as an independent country later that year. Mugabe retained the presidency in succeeding elections, modifying his Marxist-Leninist positions and reaching accommodations with rival leader Nkomo as well as with the remaining white farmers whose lands were scheduled to be taken over by the government. Ha-

rare is the capital and the largest city. ⊚ Pop. 11,150,000. — **Zim·bab′we·an** adj. & n.

Zi·on¹ (zī′ən). A city of northeast Illinois on Lake Michigan north of Waukegan. Mainly residential, it was founded in 1901 as a communal settlement with a theocratic government, which ended in 1935. ⊚ Pop. 19,775.

Zi·on² (zī′ən) also **Si·on** (sī′ən). **1.** The historic land of Israel as a symbol of the Jewish people. **2.** The Jewish people; Israel.

Zla·to·ust (zlä′tə-ōōst′, zlə-). A city of western Russia in the southern Ural Mountains west of Chelyabinsk. It is a rail junction and metallurgical center. ⊚ Pop. 206,779.

Zlin (zə-lēn′). Formerly **Gott·wald·ov** (gôt′väl-dôf′). A city of eastern Czech Republic east of Brno. The center of an important shoemaking industry, it was named Gottwaldov from 1949 to 1989 in honor of Klement Gottwald, the first Communist president of Czechoslovakia. ⊚ Pop. 87,082.

zone (zōn). abbr. **z. 1.** An area or a region distinguished from adjacent parts by a distinctive feature or characteristic. **2.** Any of the five regions of the surface of the earth that are loosely divided according to prevailing climate and latitude, including the Torrid Zone, the North and South Temperate zones, and the North and South Frigid zones.

Zon·gul·dak (zông′gŏŏl däk′). A city of northern Turkey on the Black Sea. It is in the center of a coal-mining region. ⊚ Pop. 115,900.

Zug·spit·ze (zŏŏg′spĭt-sə, tsŏŏk′shpĭt-). A mountain, 2,964.9 m (9,721 ft) high, in the Bavarian Alps of south-central Germany. It is the highest peak in the range.

Zui·der Zee (zī′dər zē′, zä′, zoi′dər zä′). A former shallow inlet of the North Sea in northeast Netherlands. Originally a lake, it was joined with the North Sea by heavy flooding. A dike, completed in 1932, turned the southern section into the Ijsselmeer, which has largely been reclaimed for agriculture.

Zu·lu (zōō′lōō). **1.** pl. **Zulu** or **-lus.** A member of a Bantu people of southeast Africa, primarily inhabiting northeast Natal province in South Africa. **2.** The Nguni language of this people, closely related to Xhosa.

Zu·lu·land (zōō′lōō-lănd′). A historical region of northeast Natal province in South Africa. Settled by Zulus, it was annexed by the British in 1887.

Zu·ni (zōō′nē) also **Zu·ñi** (-nyē, -nē). **1.** pl. **Zuni** or **-nis** also **Zuñi** or **-ñis.** A member of a Pueblo people located in western New Mexico. **2.** The language of the Zunis.

Zu·ni·an (zōō′nē-ən) or **Zu·ñi·an** (zōōn′yē-). A language family consisting only of Zuni.

Zu·rich (zŏŏr′ik). A city of northeast Switzerland at the northern tip of the **Lake of Zurich.**

Founded before Roman times, Zurich became a free imperial city after 1218 and joined the Swiss Confederation in 1351. In the 16th century it was a center of the Swiss Reformation under the leadership of Ulrich Zwingli. Today it is the largest city in the country. Zurich is known for its international banking and financial institutions. ⊛ Pop. 343,981.

Zwick·au (zwĭk′ou, tsvĭk′-). A city of east-central Germany south of Leipzig. Chartered in the early 13th century, it was a free imperial city from 1290 to 1323. ⊛ Pop. 107,988.

Zwol·le (zwôl′ə, zvôl′ə). A city of the northern Netherlands on the Ijssel River. The German ecclesiastic and writer Thomas à Kempis (1380?–1471) lived at a monastery nearby for more than 60 years. It is a transportation and industrial center. ⊛ Pop. 87,340.

Abbreviations

Geographic Feature Lists

Currency Table

Measurement Table

Abbreviations

A

a also **a.** are (measurement).
A 1. also **a.** or **A.** acre. **2.** area.
a. 1. acreage. **2.** *Lat.* anno (in the year). **3.** *Lat.* annus (year). **4.** *Lat.* ante (before).
A. America; American.
AB Alberta.
ac acre.
A.C.T. Australian Capital Territory.
A.D. *Lat.* anno Domini (in the year of the Lord). —Usu. used in small capitals (A.D.).
AFB air force base.
Afg. Afghanistan; Afghani.
Afr. Africa; African.
A.H. *Lat.* **1.** anno Hebraico (in the Hebrew year). **2.** anno Hegirae (in the year of the Hegira). —Often used in small capitals (A.H.).
AK Alaska.
AL or **Ala.** Alabama.
Alas. Alaska.
Alb. Albania; Albanian.
Alg. Algeria; Algerian.
alt. altitude.
Alta. Alberta.
Am. America; American.
A.M. *Lat.* anno mundi (in the year of the world). —Usu. used in small capitals (A.M.).
Amer. America; American.
AN also **A.N.** Anglo-Norman.
an. *Lat.* **1.** anno (in the year). **2.** ante (before).
anc. ancient.
And. Andorra; Andorran.
Ang. Angola; Angolan.
Ant. Antarctica.
ANZUS Australia-New Zealand-United States Treaty.
APO or **A.P.O.** Army Post Office.
approx. approximate; approximately.
AR Arkansas.
Ar. 1. Arabia; Arabian. **2.** Arabic.
A.R. also **AR** Autonomous Region.
Arab. 1. Arabia; Arabian. **2.** Arabic.
arch. archipelago.
Arg. Argentina; Argentine.
Ariz. Arizona.
Ark. Arkansas.

Arm. Armenia; Armenian.
AS 1. American Samoa. **2.** also **A.S.** Anglo-Saxon.
As. Asia; Asian.
ASEAN Association of South East Asian Nations.
ASSR or **A.S.S.R.** Autonomous Soviet Socialist Republic.
Assyr. Assyrian.
Atl. Atlantic.
atm. or **atmos.** atmosphere; atmospheric.
Aus. or **Aust. 1.** Australia; Australian. **2.** Austria; Austrian.
Austl. Australia; Australian.
ave. or **Ave.** avenue.
AZ Arizona.
Azer. or **Azerb.** Azerbaijan; Azerbaijani.
Azo. Azores.

B

b. or **B. 1.** bolivar (currency). **2.** born.
B. 1. Baumé scale. **2.** British.
Ba. Bahamas.
Bab. Babylonia; Babylonian.
bar. barometer; barometric.
Barb. Barbados; Barbadian.
Bav. Bavaria; Bavarian.
B.C. 1. before Christ. —Usu. used in small capitals (B.C.). **2.** or **BC** British Columbia.
B.C.E. before the Common Era. —Often used in small capitals (B.C.E.).
Bel. or **Belg.** Belgian; Belgium.
Bhu. Bhutan; Bhutanese.
blvd. boulevard.
B.N.A. British North America.
Bngl. Bangladesh; Bangladeshi.
Boh. Bohemia; Bohemian.
Bol. Bolivia; Bolivian.
bor. borough.
Bots. Botswana.
bpl. birthplace.
Br. 1. Breton. **2.** Britain; British.
Braz. Brazil; Brazilian.
Br. Gu. British Guiana.
Br. Hond. British Honduras.
Br. I. British India.
Brit. Britain; British.
Bru. Brunei.
Bul. or **Bulg.** Bulgaria; Bulgarian.
Bur. Burma; Burmese.
B.W.A. British West Africa.
B.W.I. British West Indies.

C

C 1. Celsius. **2.** centigrade.
c. or **C. 1.** cape. **2.** cent. **3.** centime. **4.** century. **5.** circa.
C. 1. Celtic. **2.** city.
ca 1. centare. **2.** circa.
CA California.
C.A. Central America.
Cal. California.
Calif. California.
Cam. Cameroon; Cameroonian.
Camb. Cambodia; Cambodian.
Can. also **Canad.** Canada; Canadian.
Can. Is. Canary Islands.
Cant. Cantonese.
cap. capital (city).
cc cubic centimeter.
CDT or **C.D.T.** Central Daylight Time.
C.E. Common Era.
cen. 1. central. **2.** century.
Cen. Afr. Rep. Central African Republic.
cent. 1. centime. **2.** central. **3.** *Lat.* centum (hundred). **4.** century.
CENTO Central Treaty Organizations.
cg centigram.
ch chain (measurement).
Ch. China; Chinese.
chan. channel.
Chin. Chinese.
CIS Commonwealth of Independent States.
cl centiliter.
cm centimeter.
cmm cubic millimeter.
CO Colorado.
co. county.
col. colonial; colony.
Col. 1. Colombia; Colombian. **2.** Colorado.
Colo. Colorado.
comm. commonwealth.
Con. Congo; Congolese.
Conn. Connecticut.
cont. continent.
CONUS Continental United States.
C.P. Cape Province.
cr. creek.
C.R. Costa Rica; Costa Rican.
C.S.A. Confederate States of America.
CST or **C.S.T.** Central Standard Time.

CT 1. or **C.T.** Central Time. **2.** or **Ct.** Connecticut.
ct. cent.
cu. or **cu** cubic.
cu ft cubic foot.
cu in cubic inch.
cu m cubic meter.
cur. 1. currency. **2.** current.
C.V. Cape Verde; Cape Verdean.
CVA Columbia Valley Authority.
CZ or **C.Z.** Canal Zone.
Czech. Czechoslovakia; Czechoslovakian.

D

d. 1. *Lat.* denarius (penny). **2.** died. **3.** or **D.** drachma.
D. Dutch.
Da. Danish.
dag decagram.
dam decameter.
Dan. Danish.
das dekastere.
DC or **D.C.** District of Columbia.
DE Delaware.
deg or **deg.** degree.
Del. Delaware.
Den. Denmark.
dep. department.
Dep. dependency.
dept. department.
Des. desert.
dg decigram.
dial. dialect; dialectal.
din. dinar (currency).
dist. district.
dkg dekagram.
dkl dekaliter.
dkm dekameter.
dks dekastere.
dl deciliter.
dm decimeter.
DM Deutsche mark.
dol. dollar.
dom. dominion.
Dom. Dominican.
Dom. Rep. Dominican Republic.
dr dram.
Dr. drive (in street names).
dr ap apothecaries' dram.
dr avdp avoirdupois dram.
dr t troy dram.
ds decistere.
DST or **D.S.T.** daylight-saving time.
DT or **D.T.** daylight time.
Du. Dutch.

E

E 1. also **E.** or **e** or **e.** east; eastern. **2.** or **E.** English.

EbN east by north.
EbS east by south.
EC European Community (Common Market).
Ec. Ecuador; Ecuadorian.
ECM European Common Market.
EDT or **E.D.T.** Eastern Daylight Time.
EEC European Economic Community.
EFTA European Free Trade Association.
Eg. Egypt; Egyptian.
E.I. East Indian; East Indies.
elev. elevation.
ENE east-northeast.
Eng. England; English.
Equat. Gui. Equatorial Guinea.
ESE east-southeast.
Esk. Eskimo.
EST or or **E.S.T.** Eastern Standard Time.
est. or **estab.** established.
Est. Estonia; Estonian.
ET or **E.T.** Eastern Time.
Eth. Ethiopia; Ethiopian.
EU European Union.
Eur. Europe; European.
EURATOM European Atomic Energy Community.

F

F Fahrenheit.
f. 1. farthing. **2.** founded. **3.** franc.
F. French.
Fahr. Fahrenheit.
Falk. Is. Falkland Islands.
fath or **fath.** fathom.
fd. fjord.
fed. federal; federated; federation.
Fin. Finland; Finnish.
FL Florida.
fl. 1. florin. **2.** *Lat.* floruit (flourished).
Fla. Florida.
Flem. Flemish.
Flor. Florida.
fm. fathom.
fort. fortification.
fr. franc.
Fr. France; French.
F.R.G. Federal Republic of Germany (West Germany).
Fr. Gu. French Guiana.
Fri. Friday.
Fris. or **Frs.** Frisian.
ft foot.
ft. fort; fortification.
fth. fathom.
fur. furlong.

G

g gram.
g. 1. or **G.** gourde (currency). **2.** or **G.** guilder (currency). **3.** or **G.** guinea (currency). **4.** or **G.** gulf.
GA or **Ga.** Georgia.
gal. gallon.
Gam. Gambia; Gambian.
GATT General Agreement on Tariffs and Trade.
gaz. gazette; gazetteer.
G.B. Great Britain.
GCT or **G.c.t.** Greenwich civil time.
gde. gourde (currency).
G.D.R. German Democratic Republic (East Germany).
geog. geographer; geographic; geography.
geol. geologic; geologist; geology.
Ger. German; Germany.
gi gill (liquid measure).
Gib. Gibraltar.
Gk. Greek.
gld. guilder (currency).
gm gram.
GMT or **G.m.t.** Greenwich mean time.
Goth. Gothic.
Gr. Greece; Greek.
Grc. Greece.
Grnld. Greenland.
GST or **G.s.t.** Greenwich sidereal time.
Gt. Brit. Great Britain.
GU Guam.
Guad. Guadaloupe.
Guat. Guatemala; Guatemalan.
Guin. Guinea; Guinean.
Guy. Guyana; Guyanese.

H

h. or **H.** harbor.
ha hectare.
Hai. Haiti; Haitian.
Heb. Hebrew.
hg hectogram.
HG also **H.G.** High German.
hgwy. highway.
HI Hawaii.
H.I. Hawaiian Islands.
Hind. Hindustani.
hl hectoliter.
hm hectometer.
Hond. Honduras; Honduran.
H.R.E. Holy Roman Emperor; Holy Roman Empire.
HST or **H.S.T.** Hawaiian Standard Time.
HT or **H.T.** Hawaiian Time.

Hts. Heights.
Hun. or **Hung.** Hungarian; Hungary.
HWM high-water mark.
hwy. highway.

I

i or **I.** island; isle.
IA or **Ia.** Iowa.
Ice. or **Icel.** Iceland; Icelandic.
ID or **Id.** Idaho.
IL Illinois.
Ill. Illinois.
IMF International Monetary Fund.
in or **in.** inch.
IN Indiana.
Ind. 1. India. **2.** Indian. **3.** Indiana. **4.** Indies.
Indon. Indonesia; Indonesian.
Ion. Ionic.
IPA International Phonetic Alphabet.
Ir. Irish.
Ire. Ireland.
is. or **Is.** island.
isl. island.
Isr. Israel; Israeli.
isth. isthmus.
It. Italian; Italy.
Ital. Italian; Italy.

J

J. Japanese.
Jam. Jamaica; Jamaican.
Jav. Javanese.
junc. junction.

K

K 1. kelvin (temperature unit). **2.** Kelvin (temperature scale).
k. or **K. 1.** kopeck. **2.** koruna. **3.** krona. **4.** krone.
Kans. Kansas.
Ken. Kentucky.
kg kilogram.
km kilometer.
kn. 1. krona. **2.** krone.
Kor. Korea; Korean.
kr. 1. krona. **2.** krone.
KS Kansas.
Kuw. Kuwait; Kuwaiti.
KY or **Ky.** Kentucky.

L

l liter.
l. 1. also **L.** lake. **2.** land. **3.** lira.
L. Latin.
LA or **La.** Louisiana.
L.A. also **LA** Los Angeles.

Lab. Labrador.
lang. language.
lat. latitude.
Lat. 1. Latin. **2.** Latvia; Latvian.
LB Labrador.
lb. *Lat.* libra (pound).
Leb. Lebanese; Lebanon.
Leso. Lesotho.
LG also **L.G.** Low German.
L.I. Long Island.
Lib. Liberia; Liberian.
Liech. Liechtenstein.
lit. liter.
Lith. Lithuania; Lithuanian.
LMT local mean time.
long. longitude.
l.t. or **LT** local time.
Lux. Luxembourg.
LW low water.
LWM low-water mark.
LZ landing zone.

M

m meter.
m. 1. or **M.** meridian. **2.** mile.
M. 1. mark (currency). **2.** medieval. **3.** mill (currency).
MA Massachusetts.
Maced. Macedonia; Macedonian.
Mad. or **Madag.** Madagascar; Madagascan.
Mala. Malaysia; Malaysian.
Man. Manitoba.
Mart. Martinique.
Mass. Massachusetts.
MB Manitoba.
MD or **Md.** Maryland.
MDT or **M.D.T.** Mountain Daylight Time.
ME 1. or **Me.** Maine. **2.** also **M.E.** Middle English.
Medit. Mediterranean.
Med. Lat. Medieval Latin.
met. metropolitan.
METO Middle East Treaty Organization.
Mex. Mexican; Mexico.
mg milligram.
MHW mean high water.
mi mile.
MI Michigan.
mi. 1. mile. **2.** mill (currency).
Mich. Michigan.
Minn. Minnesota.
Miss. Mississippi.
mk. markka (currency).
ml milliliter.
MLW mean low water.
mm millimeter.
MN 1. magnetic north. **2.** Minnesota.
MO or **Mo.** Missouri.

Mong. Mongolia; Mongolian.
Mont. Montana.
Mor. Moroccan; Morocco.
Moz. Mozambique; Mozambican.
MS Mississippi.
m.s.l. or **M.S.L.** mean sea level.
MST or **M.S.T.** Mountain Standard Time.
MT 1. Montana. **2.** or **M.T.** Mountain Time.
mt. or **Mt.** mount; mountain.
mtn. mountain.
mts. or **Mts.** mountains.
mun. or **munic.** municipal; municipality.

N

N also **N.** or **n** or **n.** north; northern.
n. *Lat.* natus (born).
N. Norse.
N.A. North America.
nat. 1. or **natl.** national. **2.** native.
NATO North Atlantic Treaty Organization.
naut. nautical.
nav. 1. naval. **2.** navigable. **3.** navigation.
NB or **N.B.** New Brunswick.
NbE north by east.
NbW north by west.
NC or **N.C.** North Carolina.
N.Cal. New Caledonia.
ND or **N.D.** North Dakota.
N.Dak. North Dakota.
NE 1. Nebraska. **2.** or **N.E.** New England. **3.** northeast.
NEATO Northeast Asian Treaty Organization.
NEbE northeast by east.
NEbN northeast by north.
Nebr. Nebraska.
Nep. Nepal; Nepalese.
Neth. Netherlands.
Nev. Nevada.
Newf. Newfoundland.
New Hebr. New Hebrides.
NF Newfoundland.
Nfld. Newfoundland.
NGr or **NGr.** New Greek.
NH or **N.H.** New Hampshire.
N.Heb. New Hebrides.
Nic. Nicaragua; Nicaraguan.
Nig. Nigeria; Nigerian.
N.Ire. Northern Ireland.
NIS Newly Independent States.
NJ or **N.J.** New Jersey.
NL also **N.L.** New Latin.
NM or **N.M.** New Mexico.
N.Mex. New Mexico.

NNE north-northeast.
NNW north-northwest.
no. or **No.** north; northern.
Nor. 1. Norman. **2.** north.
   3. Norway; Norwegian.
Norm. Norman.
Norw. Norway; Norwegian.
NS or **N.S.** Nova Scotia.
N.S.W. New South Wales.
NT Northwest Territories.
NV Nevada.
NW northwest.
NWbN northwest by north.
NWbW northwest by west.
N.W.T. Northwest Territories.
NY or **N.Y.** New York.
NYC or **N.Y.C.** New York City.
N.Z. New Zealand.

O

O or **O.** ocean.
O. Ohio.
OAS Organization of American
   States.
OAU Organization for African
   Unity.
oc. or **Oc.** ocean.
OCAS Organization of Central
   American States.
occ. occident; occidental.
OE also **O.E.** Old English.
O.F.S. Orange Free State.
OH Ohio.
OK Oklahoma.
Okla. Oklahoma.
Om. Oman; Omani.
OM. ostmark (currency).
ON 1. also **O.N.** Old Norse.
   2. Ontario.
Ont. Ontario.
OPEC Organization of Petroleum
   Exporting Countries.
OR or **Or.** Oregon.
Ore. Oregon.
orig. original; originally.
Ox. or **Oxf.** Oxford.
Oxon. *Lat.* Oxoniensis (of Ox-
   ford).
oz also **oz.** ounce.
oz ap apothecaries' ounce.
oz av or **oz avdp** avoirdupois
   ounce.
oz t troy ounce.

P

p. 1. penny. **2.** peseta. **3.** peso.
   4. pint. **5.** population.
PA or **Pa.** Pennsylvania.
Pac. or **Pacif.** Pacific.
Pak. Pakistan; Pakistani.

Pal. Palestine.
Pan. Panama; Panamanian.
par. parish.
Par. or **Para.** Paraguay; Para-
   guayan.
PATO Pacific-Asian Treaty Orga-
   nization.
PAU or **P.A.U.** Pan American
   Union.
PDT or **P.D.T.** Pacific Daylight
   Time.
PE Prince Edward Island.
P.E.I. Prince Edward Island.
pen. or **Pen.** peninsula.
Penn. or **Penna.** Pennsylvania.
Pers. Persia; Persian.
pf. pfennig.
pfg. pfennig.
Pg. Portugal; Portuguese.
Phil. Philippines; Philippine.
Phil. I. or **Phil. Is.** Philippine Is-
   lands.
P.I. Philippine Islands.
pkwy. parkway.
POE or **P.O.E. 1.** port of embar-
   kation. **2.** port of entry.
Pol. Poland; Polish.
pop. 1. popular. **2.** population.
Port. Portugal; Portuguese.
P.Q. or **PQ** Province of Quebec.
PR or **P.R.** Puerto Rico.
Pr. Provençal.
protec. protectorate.
prov. province; provincial.
Prov. Provençal.
PST or **P.S.T.** Pacific Standard
   Time.
pt. point.
P.T. also **PT** Pacific Time.
pta. peseta.

Q

Q quetzal (currency).
q. 1. quart. **2.** quintal (measurement).
ql. quintal (measurement).
Qld. Queensland.
qt or **qt.** quart.
Que. Quebec.

R

R or **R.** Réaumur (scale).
r. 1. or **R.** railroad; railway. **2.** or
   R. river. **3.** or **R.** road. **4.** rod
   (unit of length). **5.** rouble.
   6. or **R.** rupee.
Ra. Range.
rd rod (unit of length).
rd. or **Rd.** road.
Re. rupee.

reg. region.
rep. or **Rep.** republic.
Repub. republic.
Res. 1. Reservation. **2.** Reservoir.
rf. reef.
RFD also **R.F.D.** rural free deliv-
   ery.
RI or **R.I.** Rhode Island.
riv. river.
RJ road junction.
RM also **Rm.** reichsmark.
ro. rood (measurement).
Rom. 1. Roman. **2.** Romance (language). **3.** Romania; Romanian.
RR also **R.R. 1.** railroad. **2.** rural
   route.
rte. route.
Rus. or **Russ.** Russia; Russian.
Rw. Rwanda; Rwandan.
rwy. or **ry.** railway.

S

S also **S.** or s or **s.** south; south-
   ern.
s. 1. or **S.** sea. **2.** shilling. **3.** sou.
S. 1. saint. **2.** Saxon.
S.A. 1. South Africa. **2.** South
   America.
S.Afr. South Africa.
Sal. El Salvador; Salvadoran.
Sask. Saskatchewan.
Sau. Ar. Saudi Arabia.
Sax. Saxon; Saxony.
SbE south by east.
SbW south by west.
SC or **S.C.** South Carolina.
Sc. Scotch; Scottish.
Scand. Scandinavia; Scandina-
   vian.
Scot. Scotch; Scotland; Scottish.
SD or **S.D.** South Dakota.
sd. sound.
S.Dak. South Dakota.
SE southeast; southeastern.
SEATO Southeast Asia Treaty
   Organization.
SEbE southeast by east.
SEbS southeast by south.
Sem. Semitic.
Serb. Serbia; Serbian.
S.F.S.R. Soviet Federated Social-
   ist Republic.
SI *French.* Système Internation-
   ale d'Unités (International Sys-
   tem of Units).
Sib. Siberia; Siberian.
Sic. Sicilian; Sicily.
SK Saskatchewan.
Skr. or **Skt.** Sanskrit.
SL **1.** sea level **2.** south latitude.

S.L. Sierra Leone.
Slav. Slavic.
so. or **So.** south; southern.
Sol. Is. Solomon Islands.
Som. Somalia; Somali.
sou. or **Sou.** south; southern.
Sov. Un. Soviet Union.
Sp. Spain; Spanish.
Span. Spanish.
spt. seaport.
sq. square.
SSE south-southeast.
SSR or **S.S.R.** Soviet Socialist Republic.
SSW south-southwest.
ST standard time.
st. 1. or **St.** strait. **2.** or **St.** street.
St. saint.
sta. station.
Ste. *French.* sainte (feminine form of saint).
str. or **Str.** strait.
sub. suburb; suburban.
Sud. Sudan; Sudanese.
Sur. Surinam; Surinamese.
SW southwest.
Sw. Sweden; Swedish.
Swaz. Swaziland.
SWbS southwest by south.
SWbW southwest by west.
Swe. or **Swed.** Sweden; Swedish.
Switz. Switzerland.
Syr. 1. Syria; Syrian. **2.** Syriac.

T _____

t 1. ton. **2.** troy (system of weights).
T temperature.
t. 1. *Lat.* tempore (in the time of). **2.** or **T.** territory. **3.** or **T.** time. **4.** or **T.** town; township.
Tan. Tanzania; Tanzanian.
Tas. or **Tasm.** Tasmania; Tasmanian.
temp. 1. temperature. **2.** *Lat.* tempore (in the time of).

Tenn. Tennessee.
ter. 1. terrace. **2.** territorial; territory.
terr. 1. terrace. **2.** territorial; territory.
Teut. Teuton; Teutonic.
Tex. Texas.
Thai. Thailand.
TN Tennessee.
tn. 1. ton. **2.** town.
tnpk. turnpike.
topog. topographic; topography.
tp. township.
tpk. turnpike.
trib. tributary.
Tun. Tunisia; Tunisian.
Tur. or **Turk.** Turkey; Turkish.
TVA Tennessee Valley Authority.
twp. township.
TX Texas.

U _____

U.A.E. United Arab Emirates.
U.A.R. United Arab Republic.
Ug. Uganda; Ugandan.
U.K. United Kingdom.
Ukr. or **Ukrain.** Ukraine; Ukrainian.
UN or **U.N.** United Nations.
UNESCO United Nations Educational, Scientific, and Cultural Organization.
UNICEF United Nations International Children's Emergency Fund.
UNRRA United Nations Relief and Rehabilitation Administration.
UNRWA United Nations Relief and Works Agency.
Ur. Uruguay; Uruguayan.
US or **U.S.** United States.
USA or **U.S.A.** United States of America.
USSR or **U.S.S.R.** Union of Soviet Socialist Republics.
UT 1. Universal time. **2.** Utah.

Ut. Utah.

V _____

v. or **V.** village.
VA or **Va.** Virginia.
Ven. or **Venez.** Venezuela; Venezuelan.
VI or **V.I.** Virgin Islands.
Viet. Vietnam; Vietnamese.
vil. village.
vol. volcano.
VT or **Vt.** Vermont.

W _____

W also **W.** or **w** or **w.** west; western.
W. Welsh.
WA Washington.
W.A. Western Australia.
Wash. Washington.
WbN west by north.
WbS west by south.
whf. wharf.
WI Wisconsin.
W.I. West Indian; West Indies.
Wis. Wisconsin.
WL or **w.l.** water line.
WNW west-northwest.
WSW west-southwest.
wt. weight.
WV or **W.Va.** West Virginia.
WW I or **W.W.I** World War I.
WW II or **W.W.II** World War II.
WY or **Wyo.** Wyoming.

XYZ _____

X —Used to indicate location, as on a map.
Y yen (currency).
yd yard (measurement).
Yem. Yemen; Yemeni.
YT or **Y.T.** Yukon Territory.
Yug. or **Yugo.** Yugoslavia; Yugoslavian.
Zl zloty (currency).

Geographic Feature Lists

Longest Rivers of the World

1. **Nile,** Africa
   6,677 km (4,150 mi)
2. **Amazon,** S. America
   6,275 km (3,900 mi)
3. **Mississippi-Missouri,** U.S.A.
   6,020 km (3,740 mi)
4. **Ob-Irtysh,** Asia
   5,570 km (3,460 mi)
5. **Chang Jiang (Yangtze River),** China
   5,551 km (3,450 mi)
6. **Huang He (Yellow River),** China
   4,827 km (3000 mi)
7. **Murray-Darling,** Australia
   4,684 km (2,911 mi)
8. **Congo (Zaire),** Africa
   4,666 km (2,900 mi)
9. **Lena,** Russia
   4,296 km (2,670 mi)
10. **Irtysh,** Asia
    4,264 km (2,650 mi)
11. **Mackenzie-Peace-Finlay,** Canada
    4,183 km (2,600 mi)
11. **Mekong,** Asia
    4,183 km (2,600 mi)
11. **Niger,** Africa
    4,183 km (2,600 mi)
12. **Missouri,** U.S.A.
    4,127 km (2,565 mi)
13. **Yenisey,** Russia
    4,023 km (2,500 mi)
14. **Mississippi,** U.S.A.
    3,781 km (2,350 mi)
15. **Volga,** Russia
    3,701 km (2,300 mi)
15. **Ob,** Russia
    3,700 km (2,300 mi)
16. **Purus,** S. America
    3,379 km (2,100 mi)
17. **Madeira,** S. America
    3,315 km (2,060 mi)
18. **Yukon,** Canada-Alaska
    3,218 km (2,000 mi)
19. **Rio Grande,** U.S.A.-Mexico
    3,033 km (1,885 mi)
20. **Paraná,** S. America
    2,896 km (1,800 mi)
20. **Amur River,** Asia
    2,896 km (1,800 mi)

Highest Mountains of the World

1. **Everest,** Nepal-Tibet	8,853.5 m (29,028 ft)
2. **K2/Godwin-Austen,** Kashmir	8,616.3 m (28,250 ft)
3. **Kanchenjunga,** Nepal-Sikkim	8,603.4 m (28,208 ft)
4. **Lhotse,** Nepal-Tibet	8,506.5 m (27,890 ft)
5. **Makalu,** Nepal	8,476 m (27,790 ft)
6. **Dhaulagiri,** Nepal	8,177.1 m (26,810 ft)
7. **Cho Oyu,** Nepal-China	8,158.8 m (26,750 ft)
8. **Nanga Parbat,** Kashmir	8,131.3 m (26,660 ft)
9. **Annapurna I,** Nepal	8,083.7 m (26,504 ft)
10. **Gasherbrum I,** Kashmir	8,073.4 m (26,470 ft)
11. **Gasherbrum II,** Kashmir	8,033 m (26,360 ft)
12. **Gasherbrum III,** Kashmir	7,952 m (26,090 ft)
13. **Annapurna II,** Nepal	7,942.5 m (26,041 ft)
14. **Gasherbrum IV,** Kashmir	7,930 m (26,000 ft)
15. **Masherbrum,** Kashmir	7,826.3 m (25,660 ft)
16. **Nanda Devi,** India	7,821.7 m (25,645 ft)
17. **Kamet,** India	7,761.3 m (25,447 ft)
18. **Ulugh Muztagh,** China	7,729 m (25,341 ft)
19. **Muztagata,** China	7,550.9 m (24,757 ft)
20. **Communism Peak,** Tajikistan	7,500 m (24,590 ft)

Highest Mountains of the United States

1. **Mount McKinley,** Alaska	6,197.6 m (20,320 ft)
2. **Mount St. Elias,** Alaska	5,492.4 m (18,008 ft)
3. **Mount Foraker,** Alaska	5,307 m (17,400 ft)
4. **Mount Blackburn,** Alaska	5,039.5 m (16,523 ft)
5. **Mount Bona,** Alaska	5,032.5 m (16,500 ft)
6. **Mount Sanford,** Alaska	4,952.3 m (16,237 ft)
7. **Mount Vancouver,** Alaska	4,873.6 m (15,979 ft)
8. **Mount Churchill,** Alaska	4,769.6 m (15,638 ft)
9. **Mount Fairweather,** Alaska	4,666.5 m (15,300 ft)
10. **Mount Hubbard,** Alaska	4,559.8 m (14,950 ft)
11. **Mount Bear,** Alaska	4,523.5 m (14,831 ft)
12. **Mount Whitney,** California	4,420.7 m (14,494 ft)
13. **Mount Elbert,** Colorado	4,402.1 m (14,433 ft)
14. **Mount Massive,** Colorado	4,398.4 m (14,421 ft)
15. **Mount Harvard,** Colorado	4,398.1 m (14,420 ft)
16. **Mount Rainier,** Washington	4,395.1 m (14,410 ft)
17. **Mount Williamson,** California	4,382.9 m (14,370 ft)
18. **La Plata Peak,** Colorado	4,380.1 m (14,361 ft)
19. **Blanca Peak,** Colorado	4,375.2 m (14,345 ft)
20. **Uncompahgre Peak,** Colorado	4,364.2 m (14,309 ft)

Largest Countries (by area)

1. Russia	17,075,200 sq km	(6,659,328 sq mi)
2. Canada	9,976,140 sq km	(3,890,695 sq mi)
3. China	9,596,960 sq km	(3,742,814 sq mi)
4. United States	9,372,610 sq km	(3,655,318 sq mi)
5. Brazil	8,511,965 sq km	(3,319,666 sq mi)
6. Australia	7,686,850 sq km	(2,997,872 sq mi)
7. India	3,287,590 sq km	(1,282,160 sq mi)
8. Argentina	2,766,890 sq km	(1,079,087 sq mi)
9. Kazakstan	2,717,300 sq km	(1,059,747 sq mi)
10. Sudan	2,505,810 sq km	(977,266 sq mi)

Largest Countries (by population)

1. China	1,208,841,000
2. India	918,570,000
3. United States	260,651,000
4. Indonesia	192,217,000
5. Brazil	153,725,000
6. Russia	147,997,000
7. Pakistan	126,610,000
8. Japan	124,961,000
9. Bangladesh	117,787,000
10. Nigeria	108,467,000

Most Populous Cities of the World

1. Seoul, S. Korea	10,726,862
2. Bombay, India	9,925,891
3. São Paulo, Brazil	9,626,894
4. Moscow, Russia	8,526,750
5. Jakarta, Indonesia	8,259,266
6. Mexico City, Mexico	8,235,744
7. Shanghai, China	8,205,598
8. Tokyo, Japan	8,080,286
9. Istanbul, Turkey	7,615,500
10. Beijing, China	7,362,426
11. New York City, U.S.A.	7,322,564
12. Delhi, India	7,206,704
13. London, U.K.	6,904,600
14. Tehran, Iran	6,750,043
15. Lima, Peru	6,414,500
16. Bangkok, Thailand	5,876,000
17. Tianjin, China	5,804,023
18. Rio de Janeiro, Brazil	5,473,909
19. Karachi, Pakistan	5,180,562
20. Bogotá, Colombia	5,025,989

Most Populous Cities of the United States

1. New York City	7,322,564
2. Los Angeles	3,485,398
3. Chicago	2,783,726
4. Houston	1,630,553
5. Philadelphia	1,585,577
6. San Diego	1,110,549
7. Detroit	1,027,974
8. Dallas	1,006,877
9. Phoenix	983,403
10. San Antonio	935,933
11. San Jose	782,248
12. Baltimore	736,014
13. Indianapolis	731,327
14. San Francisco	723,959
15. Jacksonville (FL)	672,971
16. Columbus (OH)	632,910
17. Milwaukee	628,088
18. Memphis	610,337
19. Washington, D.C.	609,909
20. Boston	574,283

Currency Table   Listed By Country

Country	Basic Unit	Subunit
Afghanistan	afghani	100 puls
Albania	lek	100 qindarka
Algeria	dinar	100 centimes
Andorra	peseta	100 centimos
Angola	kwanza	100 lwei
Antigua and Barbuda	dollar	100 cents
Argentina	peso	100 centavos
Armenia	dram	100 lumma
Australia	dollar	100 cents
Austria	schilling	100 groschen
Azerbaijan	manat	100 qepiq
Bahamas	dollar	100 cents
Bahrain	dinar	1000 fils
Bangladesh	taka	100 paisa
Barbados	dollar	100 cents
Belarus	rubel	100 kapeik
Belgium	franc	100 centimes
Belize	dollar	100 cents
Benin	franc	100 centimes
Bhutan	ngultrum	100 chetrum
Bolivia	boliviano	100 centavos
Bosnia and Herzegovina	dinar	100 para
Botswana	pula	100 thebe
Brazil	real	100 centavos
Brunei	dollar	100 cents
Bulgaria	lev	100 stotinki
Burkina Faso	franc	100 centimes
Burundi	franc	100 centimes
Cambodia	riel	100 sen
Cameroon	franc	100 centimes
Canada	dollar	100 cents
Cape Verde	escudo	100 centavos
Central African Republic	franc	100 centimes
Chad	franc	100 centimes
Chile	peso	100 centavos
China	yuan	10 jiao
Colombia	peso	100 centavos
Comoros	franc	100 centimes
Congo	franc	100 centimes
Costa Rica	colon	100 centimos
Croatia	kuna	100 lipa
Cuba	peso	100 centavos
Cyprus	pound	100 cents
Czech Republic	koruna	100 haleru
Denmark	krone	100 öre
Djibouti	franc	100 centimes
Dominica	dollar	100 cents
Dominican Republic	peso	100 centavos

Country	Basic Unit	Subunit
Ecuador	sucre	100 centavos
Egypt	pound	100 piasters
El Salvador	colon	100 centavos
Equatorial Guinea	franc	100 centimes
Eritrea	birr	100 cents
Estonia	kroon	100 senti
Ethiopia	birr	100 cents
Fiji	dollar	100 cents
Finland	markka	100 pennia
France	franc	100 centimes
Gabon	franc	100 centimes
Gambia	dalasi	100 butut
Georgia	lari	100 tetri
Germany	deutsche mark	100 pfennigs
Ghana	cedi	100 pesewas
Greece	drachma	100 lepta
Grenada	dollar	100 cents
Guatemala	quetzal	100 centavos
Guinea	franc	100 centimes
Guinea-Bissau	peso	100 centavos
Guyana	dollar	100 cents
Haiti	gourde	100 centimes
Honduras	lempira	100 centavos
Hong Kong	dollar	100 cents
Hungary	forint	100 filler
Iceland	krona	100 aurar
India	rupee	100 paise
Indonesia	rupiah	100 sen
Iran	rial	100 dinars
Iraq	dinar	1000 fils
Ireland	pound	100 pence
Israel	shekel	100 agorot
Italy	lira	100 centesimi
Ivory Coast	franc	100 centimes
Jamaica	dollar	100 cents
Japan	yen	100 sen
Jordan	dinar	1000 fils
Kazakstan	tenge	100 tiyin
Kenya	shilling	100 cents
Kiribati	dollar	100 cents
Kuwait	dinar	1000 fils
Kyrgyzstan	som	100 tyyn
Laos	kip	100 at
Latvia	lats	100 santimi
Lebanon	pound	100 piasters
Lesotho	loti	100 lisente
Liberia	dollar	100 cents
Libya	dinar	1000 dirhams
Liechtenstein	franc	100 centimes

Country	Basic Unit	Subunit	Country	Basic Unit	Subunit
Lithuania	litas	100 centų	São Tomé and		
Luxembourg	franc	100 centimes	Príncipe	dobra	100 centimos
			Saudi Arabia	riyal	100 halalah
Macao	pataca	100 avos	Senegal	franc	100 centimes
Macedonia	denar	100 deni	Seychelles	rupee	100 cents
Madagascar	franc	100 centimes	Sierra Leone	leone	100 cents
Malawi	kwacha	100 tambala	Singapore	dollar	100 cents
Malaysia	ringgit	100 sen	Slovakia	koruna	100 halier
Maldives	rufiyaa	100 laari	Slovenia	tolar	100 stotins
Mali	franc	100 centimes	Solomon		
Malta	lira	100 cents	Islands	dollar	100 cents
Marshall			Somalia	shilling	100 cents
Islands	dollar	100 cents	South Africa	rand	100 cents
Mauritania	ouguiya	5 khoums	South Korea	won	100 chon
Mauritius	rupee	100 cents	Spain	peseta	100 centimos
Mexico	peso	100 centavos	Sri Lanka	rupee	100 cents
Micronesia	dollar	100 cents	Sudan	dinar	10 pounds
Moldova	leu	100 bani	Suriname	guilder	100 cents
Monaco	franc	100 centimes	Swaziland	lilangeni	100 cents
Mongolia	tugrik	100 mongos	Sweden	krona	100 öre
Morocco	dirham	100 centimes	Switzerland	franc	100 centimes
Mozambique	metical	100 centavos	Syria	pound	100 piasters
Myanmar	kyat	100 pyas	Taiwan	dollar	100 cents
Namibia	rand	100 cents	Tajikistan	ruble	100 tanga
Nauru	dollar	100 cents	Tanzania	shilling	100 cents
Nepal	rupee	100 paisa	Thailand	baht	100 satang
Netherlands	guilder	100 cents	Togo	franc	100 centimes
New Zealand	dollar	100 cents	Tonga	pa'anga	100 seniti
Nicaragua	cordoba	100 centavos	Trinidad and		
Niger	franc	100 centimes	Tobago	dollar	100 cents
Nigeria	naira	100 kobo	Tunisia	dinar	1000 millimes
North Korea	won	100 chon	Turkey	lira	100 kuruş
Norway	krone	100 öre	Turkmenistan	manat	100 tenge
Oman	rial	1000 baiza	Tuvalu	dollar	100 cents
Pakistan	rupee	100 paisa	Uganda	shilling	100 cents
Palau	dollar	100 cents	Ukraine	hryvnia	100 kopiyka
Panama	balboa	100 centesimos	United Arab		
Papua New			Emirates	dirham	100 fils
Guinea	kina	100 toea	United		
Paraguay	guarani	100 centimos	Kingdom	pound	100 pence
Peru	sol	100 centimos	United States	dollar	100 cents
Philippines	peso	100 centavos	Uruguay	peso	100 centesimos
Poland	zloty	100 groszy	Uzbekistan	sum	100 tyyn
Portugal	escudo	100 centavos	Vanuatu	vatu	
Qatar	riyal	100 dirhams	Vatican City	lira	100 centesimi
Romania	leu	100 bani	Venezuela	bolivar	100 centimos
Russia	ruble	100 kopeks	Vietnam	dong	10 hao
Rwanda	franc	100 centimes	Western		
Saint Kitts			Samoa	tala	100 sene
and Nevis	dollar	100 cents	Yemen	rial	100 fils
Saint Lucia	dollar	100 cents	Yugoslavia	dinar	100 para
Saint Vincent			Zaire	zaire	100 makuta
and the			Zambia	kwacha	100 ngwee
Grenadines	dollar	100 cents	Zimbabwe	dollar	100 cents
San Marino	lira	100 centesimi			

Currency Table Listed By Basic Unit (Bold) and Subunit

Unit	Country	Unit	Country	Unit	Country
afghani	Afghanistan		Solomon		Guinea
agora	Israel		Islands		Haiti
at	Laos		Somalia		Ivory Coast
aurar	(pl. of *eyrir*)		South Africa		Liechtenstein
avo	Macao		Sri Lanka		Luxembourg
			Suriname		Madagascar
baht	Thailand		Swaziland		Mali
baiza	Oman		Taiwan		Monaco
balboa	Panama		Tanzania		Morocco
ban	Moldova		Trinidad and		Niger
	Romania		Tobago		Rwanda
birr	Eritrea		Tuvalu		Senegal
	Ethiopia		Uganda		Switzerland
bolivar	Venezuela		United States		Togo
boliviano	Bolivia		Zimbabwe	centimo	Andorra
butut	Gambia	centas	Lithuania		Costa Rica
		centavo	Argentina		Paraguay
cedi	Ghana		Bolivia		Peru
cent	Antigua and		Brazil		São Tomé and
	Barbuda		Cape Verde		Príncipe
	Australia		Chile		Spain
	Bahamas		Colombia		Venezuela
	Barbados		Cuba	chetrum	Bhutan
	Belize		Dominican	chon	North Korea
	Brunei		Republic		South Korea
	Canada		Ecuador	**colon**	Costa Rica
	Cyprus		El Salvador		El Salvador
	Dominica		Guatemala	**cordoba**	Nicaragua
	Eritrea		Guinea-Bissau		
	Ethiopia		Honduras	**dalasi**	Gambia
	Fiji		Mexico	**denar**	Macedonia
	Grenada		Mozambique	deni	Macedonia
	Guyana		Nicaragua	**deutsche mark**	Germany
	Hong Kong		Philippines	**dinar**	Algeria
	Jamaica		Portugal		Bahrain
	Kenya	centesimo	Italy		Bosnia and
	Kiribati		Panama		Herzegovina
	Liberia		San Marino		Iraq
	Malta		Uruguay		Jordan
	Marshall Islands		Vatican City		Kuwait
	Mauritius	centime	Algeria		Libya
	Micronesia		Belgium		Sudan
	Namibia		Benin		Tunisia
	Nauru		Burkina Faso		Yugoslavia
	Netherlands		Burundi	dinar	Iran
	New Zealand		Cameroon	**dirham**	Morocco
	Palau		Central African		United Arab
	Saint Kitts and		Republic		Emirates
	Nevis		Chad	dirham	Libya
	Saint Lucia		Comoros		Qatar
	Saint Vincent		Congo	**dobra**	São Tomé and
	and the		Djibouti		Príncipe
	Grenadines		Equatorial	**dollar**	Antigua and
	Seychelles		Guinea		Barbuda
	Sierra Leone		France		Australia
	Singapore		Gabon		Bahamas

Unit	Country
dollar	Barbados
	Belize
	Brunei
	Canada
	Dominica
	Fiji
	Grenada
	Guyana
	Hong Kong
	Jamaica
	Kiribati
	Liberia
	Marshall Islands
	Micronesia
	Nauru
	New Zealand
	Palau
	Saint Kitts and Nevis
	Saint Lucia
	Saint Vincent and the Grenadines
	Singapore
	Solomon Islands
	Taiwan
	Trinidad and Tobago
	Tuvalu
	United States
	Zimbabwe
dong	Vietnam
drachma	Greece
dram	Armenia
escudo	Cape Verde
	Portugal
eyrir	Iceland
filler	Hungary
fils	Bahrain
	Iraq
	Jordan
	Kuwait
	United Arab Emirates
	Yemen
forint	Hungary
franc	Belgium
	Benin
	Burkina Faso
	Burundi
	Cameroon
	Central African Republic
	Chad
	Comoros
	Congo
	Djibouti
	Equatorial Guinea
	France
	Gabon
	Guinea
	Ivory Coast
	Liechtenstein
	Luxembourg
	Madagascar
	Mali
	Monaco
	Niger
	Rwanda
	Senegal
	Switzerland
	Togo
gourde	Haiti
groschen	Austria
grosz	Poland
guarani	Paraguay
guilder	Netherlands
	Suriname
halalah	Saudi Arabia
haler	Czech Republic
halier	Slovakia
hao	Vietnam
hryvnia	Ukraine
jiao	China
kapeik	Belarus
khoum	Mauritania
kina	Papua New Guinea
kip	Laos
kobo	Nigeria
kopek	Russia
kopiyka	Ukraine
koruna	Czech Republic
	Slovakia
krona	Iceland
	Sweden
krone	Denmark
	Norway
kroon	Estonia
kuna	Croatia
kuruş	Turkey
kwacha	Malawi
	Zambia
kwanza	Angola
kyat	Myanmar
laari	Maldives
lari	Georgia
lats	Latvia
lek	Albania
lempira	Honduras
leone	Sierra Leone
lepton	Greece
leu	Moldova
	Romania
lev	Bulgaria
likuta	Zaire
lilangeni	Swaziland
lipa	Croatia
lira	Italy
	Malta
	San Marino
	Turkey
	Vatican City
lisente	(pl. of *sente*)
litas	Lithuania
loti	Lesotho
lumma	Armenia
lwei	Angola
makuta	(pl. of *likuta*)
manat	Azerbaijan
	Turkmenistan
markka	Finland
metical	Mozambique
millime	Tunisia
mongo	Mongolia
naira	Nigeria
ngultrum	Bhutan
ngwee	Zambia
öre	Denmark
	Norway
	Sweden
ouguiya	Mauritania
pa'anga	Tonga
paisa	Bangladesh
	India
	Nepal
	Pakistan
para	Bosnia and Herzegovina
	Yugoslavia
pataca	Macao
penni	Finland
penny	Ireland
	United Kingdom
peseta	Andorra
	Spain
pesewa	Ghana
peso	Argentina
	Chile
	Colombia
	Cuba
	Dominican Republic
	Guinea-Bissau
	Mexico
	Philippines
	Uruguay
pfennig	Germany
piaster	Egypt
	Lebanon
	Syria
pound	Cyprus
	Egypt
	Ireland
	Lebanon
	Syria

Unit	Country	Unit	Country	Unit	Country
pound	United Kingdom		Nepal	**sum**	Uzbekistan
pound	Sudan		Pakistan	**taka**	Bangladesh
pul	Afghanistan		Seychelles	**tala**	Western Samoa
pula	Botswana		Sri Lanka	tambala	Malawi
pya	Myanmar	**rupiah**	Indonesia	tanga	Tajikistan
		santims	Latvia	**tenge**	Kazakstan
qepiq	Azerbaijan	satang	Thailand	tenge	Turkmenistan
qindarka	Albania	**schilling**	Austria	tetri	Georgia
quetzal	Guatemala	sen	Cambodia	thebe	Botswana
			Indonesia	tiyin	Kazakstan
rand	Namibia		Japan	toea	Papua New Guinea
	South Africa		Malaysia		
real	Brazil	sene	Western Samoa	**tolar**	Slovenia
rial	Iran	seniti	Tonga	**tugrik**	Mongolia
	Oman	sent	Estonia	tyyn	Kyrgyzstan
	Yemen	sente	Lesotho		Uzbekistan
riel	Cambodia	**shekel**	Israel		
ringgit	Malaysia	**shilling**	Kenya	**vatu**	Vanuatu
riyal	Qatar		Somalia	**won**	North Korea
	Saudi Arabia		Tanzania		South Korea
rubel	Belarus		Uganda		
ruble	Russia	**sol**	Peru	**yen**	Japan
	Tajikistan	**som**	Kyrgyzstan	**yuan**	China
rufiyaa	Maldives	stotinka	Bulgaria		
rupee	India	stotins	Slovenia	**zaire**	Zaire
	Mauritius	**sucre**	Ecuador	**zloty**	Poland

Measurement

Length

U.S. Customary Unit	U.S. Equivalents	Metric Equivalents
inch	1/12 foot	2.540 centimeters
foot	1/3 yard, 12 inches	0.305 meter
yard	3 feet, 36 inches	0.914 meter
rod	5 1/2 yards, 16 1/2 feet	5.029 meters
mile (statute, land)	1,760 yards, 5,280 feet	1.609 kilometers
mile (nautical, international)	1.151 statute miles	1.852 kilometers

Metric Unit	Number of Meters	U.S. Equivalent
kilometer	1,000	0.621 mile
hectometer	100	109.361 yards
decameter	10	32.808 feet
meter	1	39.370 inches
decimeter	0.1	3.937 inches
centimeter	0.01	0.394 inch
millimeter	0.001	0.039 inch

Area

U.S. Customary Unit	U.S. Equivalents	Metric Equivalents
square inch	0.007 square foot	6.452 square centimeters
square foot	144 square inches	929.030 square centimeters
square yard	1,296 square inches, 9 square feet	0.836 square meters
acre	43,560 square feet, 4,840 square yards	4,047 square meters
square mile	640 acres	2.590 square kilometers

Metric Unit	Square Meters	U.S. Equivalent
square kilometer	1,000,000	0.386 square mile
hectare	10,000	2.471 acres
are	100	119.599 square yards
deciare	10	11.960 square yards
centare	1	10.764 square feet
square centimeter	0.0001	0.155 square inch

Volume and Capacity

U.S. Customary Unit	U.S. Equivalent	Metric Equivalents
cubic inch	0.00058 cubic foot	16.387 cubic centimeters
cubic foot	1,728 cubic inches	0.028 cubic meter
cubic yard	27 cubic feet	0.765 cubic meter

U.S. Customary Liquid Measure	U.S. Equivalent	Metric Equivalents
fluid ounce	8 fluid drams, 1.805 cubic inches	29.574 milliliters
pint	16 fluid ounces, 28.875 cubic inches	0.473 liter
quart	2 pints, 57.75 cubic inches	0.946 liter
gallon	4 quarts, 231 cubic inches	3.785 liters
barrel	varies from 31 to 42 gallons, established by law or usage	

U.S. Customary Dry Measure	U.S. Equivalents	Metric Equivalents
pint	1/2 quart, 33.6 cubic inches	0.551 liter
quart	2 pints, 67.2 cubic inches	1.101 liters
peck	8 quarts, 537.605 cubic inches	8.810 liters
bushel	4 pecks, 2,150.421 cubic inches	35.239 liters

Metric Unit of Volume	Cubic Meters	U.S. Equivalent
decastere	10	13.079 cubic yards
stere	1	1.308 cubic yards
decistere	0.1	3.531 cubic feet
cubic centimeter	0.000001	0.061 cubic inch

Metric Unit of Capacity	Liters	U.S. Equivalent
hectoliter	100	2.838 bushels (dry), 26.42 gallons (liquid)
decaliter	10	1.135 pecks (dry), 2.642 gallons (liquid)
liter	1	.908 quart (dry), 1.057 quarts (liquid)
deciliter	0.10	.182 pint (dry), .211 pint (liquid)
centiliter	0.01	.338 fluid ounce
milliliter	0.001	.271 fluid dram

Weight and Mass

U.S. Customary Unit (Avoirdupois)	U.S. Equivalents	Metric Equivalents
grain	0.037 dram, 0.002285 ounce	64.799 milligrams
dram	27.344 grains	1.772 grams
ounce	16 drams, 437.5 grains	28.350 grams
pound	16 ounces, 7,000 grains	453.592 grams
ton (short)	2,000 pounds	0.907 metric ton (1,000 kilograms)
ton (long)	1.12 short tons, 2,240 pounds	1.016 metric tons

Metric Unit	Number of Grams	U.S. Equivalent
metric ton	1,000,000	1.102 tons
quintal	100,000	220.462 pounds
kilogram	1,000	2.205 pounds
hectogram	100	3.527 ounces
decagram	10	0.353 ounce
gram	1	0.035 ounce
decigram	0.1	1.543 grains
centigram	0.01	0.154 grain
milligram	0.001	0.015 grain

METRIC CONVERSION CHART

Length

When You Know	Multiply By	To Find
millimeters	0.04	inches
centimeters	0.39	inches
meters	3.28	feet
meters	1.09	yards
kilometers	0.62	miles
inches	25.40	millimeters
inches	2.54	centimeters
feet	30.48	centimeters
yards	0.91	meters
miles	1.61	kilometers

Mass and Weight

When You Know	Multiply By	To Find
grams	0.035	ounce
kilograms	2.20	pounds
tons (1,000 kg)	1.10	short tons
ounces	28.35	grams
pounds	0.45	kilograms
short tons (2,000 lb)	0.91	metric tons

METRIC CONVERSION CHART (continued)

Area

When You Know	Multiply By	To Find
square centimeters	0.16	square inches
square meters	1.20	square yards
square kilometers	0.39	square miles
hectares (10,000m²)	2.47	acres
square inches	6.45	square centimeters
square feet	0.09	square meters
square yards	0.84	square meters
square miles	2.59	square kilometers
acres	0.40	hectares

Volume

When You Know	Multiply By	To Find
milliliters	0.20	teaspoons
milliliters	0.07	tablespoons
milliliters	0.03	fluid ounces
liters	4.23	cups
liters	2.11	pints
liters	1.06	quarts
liters	0.26	gallons
cubic meters	35.31	cubic feet
cubic meters	1.31	cubic yards
teaspoons	4.93	milliliters
tablespoons	14.79	milliliters
fluid ounces	29.57	milliliters
cups	0.24	liters
pints	0.47	liters
quarts	0.95	liters
gallons	3.79	liters
cubic feet	0.03	cubic meters
cubic yards	0.76	cubic meters

Speed

When You Know	Multiply By	To Find
miles per hour	1.61	kilometers per hour
kilometers per hour	0.62	miles per hour

Temperature

When You Know	Use This Formula	To Find
degrees Fahrenheit	$(°F - 32) \div 1.8$	degrees Celsius
degrees Celsius	$(°C \times 1.8) + 32$	degrees Fahrenheit

AB